University Casebook Series

May, 1989

ACCOUNTING AND THE LAW, Fourth Edition (1978), with Problems Pamphlet (Successor to Dohr, Phillips, Thompson & Warren)

George C. Thompson, Professor, Columbia University Graduate School of Business.
Robert Whitman, Professor of Law, University of Connecticut.
Ellis L. Phillips, Jr., Member of the New York Bar.
William C. Warren, Professor of Law Emeritus, Columbia University.

ACCOUNTING FOR LAWYERS, MATERIALS ON (1980)

David R. Herwitz, Professor of Law, Harvard University.

ADMINISTRATIVE LAW, Eighth Edition (1987), with 1983 Problems Supplement (Supplement edited in association with Paul R. Verkuil, Dean and Professor of Law, Tulane University)

Walter Gellhorn, University Professor Emeritus, Columbia University.
Clark Byse, Professor of Law, Harvard University.
Peter L. Strauss, Professor of Law, Columbia University.
Todd D. Rakoff, Professor of Law, Harvard University.
Roy A. Schotland, Professor of Law, Georgetown University.

ADMIRALTY, Third Edition (1987), with Statute and Rule Supplement

Jo Desha Lucas, Professor of Law, University of Chicago.

ADVOCACY, see also Lawyering Process

AGENCY, see also Enterprise Organization

AGENCY—PARTNERSHIPS, Fourth Edition (1987)

Abridgement from Conard, Knauss & Siegel's Enterprise Organization, Fourth Edition.

AGENCY AND PARTNERSHIPS (1987)

Melvin A. Eisenberg, Professor of Law, University of California, Berkeley.

ANTITRUST: FREE ENTERPRISE AND ECONOMIC ORGANIZATION, Sixth Edition (1983), with 1983 Problems in Antitrust Supplement and 1988 Case Supplement

Louis B. Schwartz, Professor of Law, University of Pennsylvania.
John J. Flynn, Professor of Law, University of Utah.
Harry First, Professor of Law, New York University.

BANKRUPTCY, Second Edition (1989)

Robert L. Jordan, Professor of Law, University of California, Los Angeles.
William D. Warren, Professor of Law, University of California, Los Angeles.

BANKRUPTCY AND DEBTOR-CREDITOR LAW, Second Edition (1988)

Theodore Eisenberg, Professor of Law, Cornell University.

BUSINESS ORGANIZATION, see also Enterprise Organization

UNIVERSITY CASEBOOK SERIES—Continued

BUSINESS PLANNING, Temporary Second Edition (1984)

David R. Herwitz, Professor of Law, Harvard University.

BUSINESS TORTS (1972)

Milton Handler, Professor of Law Emeritus, Columbia University.

CHILDREN IN THE LEGAL SYSTEM (1983) with 1988 Supplement

Walter Wadlington, Professor of Law, University of Virginia.
Charles H. Whitebread, Professor of Law, University of Southern California.
Samuel Davis, Professor of Law, University of Georgia.

CIVIL PROCEDURE, see Procedure

CIVIL RIGHTS ACTIONS (1988), with 1988 Supplement

Peter W. Low, Professor of Law, University of Virginia.
John C. Jeffries, Jr., Professor of Law, University of Virginia.

CLINIC, see also Lawyering Process

COMMERCIAL AND DEBTOR-CREDITOR LAW: SELECTED STATUTES, 1988 EDITION

COMMERCIAL LAW, Second Edition (1987)

Robert L. Jordan, Professor of Law, University of California, Los Angeles.
William D. Warren, Professor of Law, University of California, Los Angeles.

COMMERCIAL LAW, Fourth Edition (1985)

E. Allan Farnsworth, Professor of Law, Columbia University.
John Honnold, Professor of Law, University of Pennsylvania.

COMMERCIAL PAPER, Third Edition (1984)

E. Allan Farnsworth, Professor of Law, Columbia University.

COMMERCIAL PAPER, Second Edition (1987) (Reprinted from COMMERCIAL LAW, Second Edition (1987))

Robert L. Jordan, Professor of Law, University of California, Los Angeles.
William D. Warren, Professor of Law, University of California, Los Angeles.

COMMERCIAL PAPER AND BANK DEPOSITS AND COLLECTIONS (1967), with Statutory Supplement

William D. Hawkland, Professor of Law, University of Illinois.

COMMERCIAL TRANSACTIONS—Principles and Policies (1982)

Alan Schwartz, Professor of Law, University of Southern California.
Robert E. Scott, Professor of Law, University of Virginia.

COMPARATIVE LAW, Fifth Edition (1988)

Rudolf B. Schlesinger, Professor of Law, Hastings College of Law.
Hans W. Baade, Professor of Law, University of Texas.
Mirjan P. Damaska, Professor of Law, Yale Law School.
Peter E. Herzog, Professor of Law, Syracuse University.

COMPETITIVE PROCESS, LEGAL REGULATION OF THE, Third Edition (1986), with 1987 Selected Statutes Supplement

Edmund W. Kitch, Professor of Law, University of Virginia.
Harvey S. Perlman, Dean of the Law School, University of Nebraska.

UNIVERSITY CASEBOOK SERIES—Continued

CONFLICT OF LAWS, Eighth Edition (1984), with 1987 Case Supplement

Willis L. M. Reese, Professor of Law, Columbia University.
Maurice Rosenberg, Professor of Law, Columbia University.

CONSTITUTIONAL LAW, Eighth Edition (1989)

Edward L. Barrett, Jr., Professor of Law, University of California, Davis.
William Cohen, Professor of Law, Stanford University.
Jonathan D. Varat, Professor of Law, University of California, Los Angeles.

CONSTITUTIONAL LAW, CIVIL LIBERTY AND INDIVIDUAL RIGHTS, Second Edition (1982), with 1987 Supplement

William Cohen, Professor of Law, Stanford University.
John Kaplan, Professor of Law, Stanford University.

CONSTITUTIONAL LAW, Eleventh Edition (1985), with 1988 Supplement (Supplement edited in association with Frederick F. Schauer, Professor of Law, University of Michigan)

Gerald Gunther, Professor of Law, Stanford University.

CONSTITUTIONAL LAW, INDIVIDUAL RIGHTS IN, Fourth Edition (1986), (Reprinted from CONSTITUTIONAL LAW, Eleventh Edition), with 1988 Supplement (Supplement edited in association with Frederick F. Schauer, Professor of Law, University of Michigan)

Gerald Gunther, Professor of Law, Stanford University.

CONSUMER TRANSACTIONS (1983), with Selected Statutes and Regulations Supplement and 1987 Case Supplement

Michael M. Greenfield, Professor of Law, Washington University.

CONTRACT LAW AND ITS APPLICATION, Fourth Edition (1988)

Arthur Rosett, Professor of Law, University of California, Los Angeles.

CONTRACT LAW, STUDIES IN, Third Edition (1984)

Edward J. Murphy, Professor of Law, University of Notre Dame.
Richard E. Speidel, Professor of Law, Northwestern University.

CONTRACTS, Fifth Edition (1987)

John P. Dawson, late Professor of Law, Harvard University.
William Burnett Harvey, Professor of Law and Political Science, Boston University.
Stanley D. Henderson, Professor of Law, University of Virginia.

CONTRACTS, Fourth Edition (1988)

E. Allan Farnsworth, Professor of Law, Columbia University.
William F. Young, Professor of Law, Columbia University.

CONTRACTS, Selections on (statutory materials) (1988)

CONTRACTS, Second Edition (1978), with Statutory and Administrative Law Supplement (1978)

Ian R. Macneil, Professor of Law, Cornell University.

COPYRIGHT, PATENTS AND TRADEMARKS, see also Competitive Process; see also Selected Statutes and International Agreements

COPYRIGHT, PATENT, TRADEMARK AND RELATED STATE DOCTRINES, Second Edition (1981), with 1988 Case Supplement, 1987 Selected Statutes Supplement and 1981 Problem Supplement

Paul Goldstein, Professor of Law, Stanford University.

COPYRIGHT, Unfair Competition, and Other Topics Bearing on the Protection of Literary, Musical, and Artistic Works, Fourth Edition (1985), with 1985 Statutory Supplement

Ralph S. Brown, Jr., Professor of Law, Yale University.
Robert C. Denicola, Professor of Law, University of Nebraska.

CORPORATE ACQUISITIONS, The Law and Finance of (1986), with 1988 Supplement

Ronald J. Gilson, Professor of Law, Stanford University.

CORPORATE FINANCE, Third Edition (1987)

Victor Brudney, Professor of Law, Harvard University.
Marvin A. Chirelstein, Professor of Law, Columbia University.

CORPORATE READJUSTMENTS AND REORGANIZATIONS (1976)

Walter J. Blum, Professor of Law, University of Chicago.
Stanley A. Kaplan, Professor of Law, University of Chicago.

CORPORATION LAW, BASIC, Third Edition (1989), with Documentary Supplement

Detlev F. Vagts, Professor of Law, Harvard University.

CORPORATIONS, see also Enterprise Organization

CORPORATIONS, Sixth Edition—Concise (1988), with Statutory Supplement (1988)

William L. Cary, late Professor of Law, Columbia University.
Melvin Aron Eisenberg, Professor of Law, University of California, Berkeley.

CORPORATIONS, Sixth Edition—Unabridged (1988), with Statutory Supplement (1988)

William L. Cary, late Professor of Law, Columbia University.
Melvin Aron Eisenberg, Professor of Law, University of California, Berkeley.

CORPORATIONS AND BUSINESS ASSOCIATIONS—STATUTES, RULES AND FORMS (1988)

CORPORATIONS COURSE GAME PLAN (1975)

David R. Herwitz, Professor of Law, Harvard University.

CORRECTIONS, SEE SENTENCING

CREDITORS' RIGHTS, see also Debtor-Creditor Law

CRIMINAL JUSTICE ADMINISTRATION, Third Edition (1986), with 1988 Case Supplement

Frank W. Miller, Professor of Law, Washington University.
Robert O. Dawson, Professor of Law, University of Texas.
George E. Dix, Professor of Law, University of Texas.
Raymond I. Parnas, Professor of Law, University of California, Davis.

CRIMINAL LAW, Fourth Edition (1987)

Fred E. Inbau, Professor of Law Emeritus, Northwestern University.
Andre A. Moenssens, Professor of Law, University of Richmond.
James R. Thompson, Professor of Law Emeritus, Northwestern University.

CRIMINAL LAW AND APPROACHES TO THE STUDY OF LAW (1986)

John M. Brumbaugh, Professor of Law, University of Maryland.

UNIVERSITY CASEBOOK SERIES—Continued

CRIMINAL LAW, Second Edition (1986)

Peter W. Low, Professor of Law, University of Virginia.
John C. Jeffries, Jr., Professor of Law, University of Virginia.
Richard C. Bonnie, Professor of Law, University of Virginia.

CRIMINAL LAW, Fourth Edition (1986)

Lloyd L. Weinreb, Professor of Law, Harvard University.

CRIMINAL LAW AND PROCEDURE, Seventh Edition (1989)

Ronald N. Boyce, Professor of Law, University of Utah.
Rollin M. Perkins, Professor of Law Emeritus, University of California, Hastings College of the Law.

CRIMINAL PROCEDURE, Third Edition (1987), with 1988 Supplement

James B. Haddad, Professor of Law, Northwestern University.
James B. Zagel, Chief, Criminal Justice Division, Office of Attorney General of Illinois.
Gary L. Starkman, Assistant U. S. Attorney, Northern District of Illinois.
William J. Bauer, Chief Judge of the U.S. Court of Appeals, Seventh Circuit.

CRIMINAL PROCESS, Fourth Edition (1987), with 1988 Supplement

Lloyd L. Weinreb, Professor of Law, Harvard University.

DAMAGES, Second Edition (1952)

Charles T. McCormick, late Professor of Law, University of Texas.
William F. Fritz, late Professor of Law, University of Texas.

DECEDENTS' ESTATES AND TRUSTS, Seventh Edition (1988)

John Ritchie, late Professor of Law, University of Virginia.
Neill H. Alford, Jr., Professor of Law, University of Virginia.
Richard W. Effland, late Professor of Law, Arizona State University.

DISPUTE RESOLUTION, Processes of (1989)

John S. Murray, President and Executive Director of The Conflict Clinic, Inc., George Mason University.
Alan Scott Rau, Professor of Law, University of Texas.
Edward F. Sherman, Professor of Law, University of Texas.

DOMESTIC RELATIONS, see also Family Law

DOMESTIC RELATIONS, Successor Edition (1984) with 1988 Supplement

Walter Wadlington, Professor of Law, University of Virginia.

EMPLOYMENT DISCRIMINATION, Second Edition (1987), with 1988 Supplement

Joel W. Friedman, Professor of Law, Tulane University.
George M. Strickler, Professor of Law, Tulane University.

EMPLOYMENT LAW (1987), with 1987 Statutory Supplement and 1988 Case Supplement

Mark A. Rothstein, Professor of Law, University of Houston.
Andria S. Knapp, Adjunct Professor of Law, University of California, Hastings College of Law.
Lance Liebman, Professor of Law, Harvard University.

ENERGY LAW (1983) with 1986 Case Supplement

Donald N. Zillman, Professor of Law, University of Utah.
Laurence Lattman, Dean of Mines and Engineering, University of Utah.

ENTERPRISE ORGANIZATION, Fourth Edition (1987), with 1987 Corporation and Partnership Statutes, Rules and Forms Supplement

Alfred F. Conard, Professor of Law, University of Michigan.
Robert L. Knauss, Dean of the Law School, University of Houston.
Stanley Siegel, Professor of Law, University of California, Los Angeles.

ENVIRONMENTAL POLICY LAW 1985 Edition, with 1985 Problems Supplement (Supplement in association with Ronald H. Rosenberg, Professor of Law, College of William and Mary)

Thomas J. Schoenbaum, Professor of Law, University of Georgia.

EQUITY, see also Remedies

EQUITY, RESTITUTION AND DAMAGES, Second Edition (1974)

Robert Childres, late Professor of Law, Northwestern University.
William F. Johnson, Jr., Professor of Law, New York University.

ESTATE PLANNING, Second Edition (1982), with 1985 Case, Text and Documentary Supplement

David Westfall, Professor of Law, Harvard University.

ETHICS, see Legal Profession, Professional Responsibility, and Social Responsibilities

ETHICS AND PROFESSIONAL RESPONSIBILITY (1981) (Reprinted from THE LAWYERING PROCESS)

Gary Bellow, Professor of Law, Harvard University.
Bea Moulton, Legal Services Corporation.

EVIDENCE, Sixth Edition (1988 Reprint)

John Kaplan, Professor of Law, Stanford University.
Jon R. Waltz, Professor of Law, Northwestern University.

EVIDENCE, Eighth Edition (1988), with Rules, Statute and Case Supplement (1988)

Jack B. Weinstein, Chief Judge, United States District Court.
John H. Mansfield, Professor of Law, Harvard University.
Norman Abrams, Professor of Law, University of California, Los Angeles.
Margaret Berger, Professor of Law, Brooklyn Law School.

FAMILY LAW, see also Domestic Relations

FAMILY LAW Second Edition (1985), with 1988 Supplement

Judith C. Areen, Professor of Law, Georgetown University.

FAMILY LAW AND CHILDREN IN THE LEGAL SYSTEM, STATUTORY MATERIALS (1981)

Walter Wadlington, Professor of Law, University of Virginia.

FEDERAL COURTS, Eighth Edition (1988)

Charles T. McCormick, late Professor of Law, University of Texas.
James H. Chadbourn, late Professor of Law, Harvard University.
Charles Alan Wright, Professor of Law, University of Texas, Austin.

UNIVERSITY CASEBOOK SERIES—Continued

FEDERAL COURTS AND THE FEDERAL SYSTEM, Hart and Wechsler's Third Edition (1988), with the Judicial Code and Rules of Procedure in the Federal Courts (1988)

Paul M. Bator, Professor of Law, University of Chicago.
Daniel J. Meltzer, Professor of Law, Harvard University.
Paul J. Mishkin, Professor of Law, University of California, Berkeley.
David L. Shapiro, Professor of Law, Harvard University.

FEDERAL COURTS AND THE LAW OF FEDERAL-STATE RELATIONS, Second Edition (1989)

Peter W. Low, Professor of Law, University of Virginia.
John C. Jeffries, Jr., Professor of Law, University of Virginia.

FEDERAL PUBLIC LAND AND RESOURCES LAW, Second Edition (1987), with 1984 Statutory Supplement

George C. Coggins, Professor of Law, University of Kansas.
Charles F. Wilkinson, Professor of Law, University of Oregon.

FEDERAL RULES OF CIVIL PROCEDURE and Selected Other Procedural Provisions, 1988 Edition

FEDERAL TAXATION, see Taxation

FOOD AND DRUG LAW (1980), with Statutory Supplement

Richard A. Merrill, Dean of the School of Law, University of Virginia.
Peter Barton Hutt, Esq.

FUTURE INTERESTS (1958)

Philip Mechem, late Professor of Law Emeritus, University of Pennsylvania.

FUTURE INTERESTS (1970)

Howard R. Williams, Professor of Law, Stanford University.

FUTURE INTERESTS AND ESTATE PLANNING (1961), with 1962 Supplement

W. Barton Leach, late Professor of Law, Harvard University.
James K. Logan, formerly Dean of the Law School, University of Kansas.

GOVERNMENT CONTRACTS, FEDERAL, Successor Edition (1985)

John W. Whelan, Professor of Law, Hastings College of the Law.

GOVERNMENT REGULATION: FREE ENTERPRISE AND ECONOMIC ORGANIZATION, Sixth Edition (1985)

Louis B. Schwartz, Professor of Law, Hastings College of the Law.
John J. Flynn, Professor of Law, University of Utah.
Harry First, Professor of Law, New York University.

HEALTH CARE LAW AND POLICY (1988)

Clark C. Havighurst, Professor of Law, Duke University.

HINCKLEY, JOHN W., JR., TRIAL OF: A Case Study of the Insanity Defense (1986)

Peter W. Low, Professor of Law, University of Virginia.
John C. Jeffries, Jr., Professor of Law, University of Virginia.
Richard C. Bonnie, Professor of Law, University of Virginia.

INJUNCTIONS, Second Edition (1984)

Owen M. Fiss, Professor of Law, Yale University.
Doug Rendleman, Professor of Law, College of William and Mary.

INSTITUTIONAL INVESTORS, (1978)

David L. Ratner, Professor of Law, Cornell University.

INSURANCE, Second Edition (1985)

William F. Young, Professor of Law, Columbia University.
Eric M. Holmes, Professor of Law, University of Georgia.

INTERNATIONAL LAW, see also Transnational Legal Problems, Transnational Business Problems, and United Nations Law

INTERNATIONAL LAW IN CONTEMPORARY PERSPECTIVE (1981), with Essay Supplement

Myres S. McDougal, Professor of Law, Yale University.
W. Michael Reisman, Professor of Law, Yale University.

INTERNATIONAL LEGAL SYSTEM, Third Edition (1988), with Documentary Supplement

Joseph Modeste Sweeney, Professor of Law, University of California, Hastings.
Covey T. Oliver, Professor of Law, University of Pennsylvania.
Noyes E. Leech, Professor of Law Emeritus, University of Pennsylvania.

INTRODUCTION TO LAW, see also Legal Method, On Law in Courts, and Dynamics of American Law

INTRODUCTION TO THE STUDY OF LAW (1970)

E. Wayne Thode, late Professor of Law, University of Utah.
Leon Lebowitz, Professor of Law, University of Texas.
Lester J. Mazor, Professor of Law, University of Utah.

JUDICIAL CODE and Rules of Procedure in the Federal Courts, Students' Edition, 1988 Revision

Daniel J. Meltzer, Professor of Law, Harvard University.
David L. Shapiro, Professor of Law, Harvard University.

JURISPRUDENCE (Temporary Edition Hardbound) (1949)

Lon L. Fuller, late Professor of Law, Harvard University.

JUVENILE, see also Children

JUVENILE JUSTICE PROCESS, Third Edition (1985)

Frank W. Miller, Professor of Law, Washington University.
Robert O. Dawson, Professor of Law, University of Texas.
George E. Dix, Professor of Law, University of Texas.
Raymond I. Parnas, Professor of Law, University of California, Davis.

LABOR LAW, Tenth Edition (1986), with 1986 Statutory Supplement

Archibald Cox, Professor of Law, Harvard University.
Derek C. Bok, President, Harvard University.
Robert A. Gorman, Professor of Law, University of Pennsylvania.

LABOR LAW, Second Edition (1982), with Statutory Supplement

Clyde W. Summers, Professor of Law, University of Pennsylvania.
Harry H. Wellington, Dean of the Law School, Yale University.
Alan Hyde, Professor of Law, Rutgers University.

LAND FINANCING, Third Edition (1985)

The late Norman Penney, Professor of Law, Cornell University.
Richard F. Broude, Member of the California Bar.
Roger Cunningham, Professor of Law, University of Michigan.

LAW AND MEDICINE (1980)

Walter Wadlington, Professor of Law and Professor of Legal Medicine, University of Virginia.
Jon R. Waltz, Professor of Law, Northwestern University.
Roger B. Dworkin, Professor of Law, Indiana University, and Professor of Biomedical History, University of Washington.

LAW, LANGUAGE AND ETHICS (1972)

William R. Bishin, Professor of Law, University of Southern California.
Christopher D. Stone, Professor of Law, University of Southern California.

LAW, SCIENCE AND MEDICINE (1984), with 1989 Supplement

Judith C. Areen, Professor of Law, Georgetown University.
Patricia A. King, Professor of Law, Georgetown University.
Steven P. Goldberg, Professor of Law, Georgetown University.
Alexander M. Capron, Professor of Law, University of Southern California.

LAWYERING PROCESS (1978), with Civil Problem Supplement and Criminal Problem Supplement

Gary Bellow, Professor of Law, Harvard University.
Bea Moulton, Professor of Law, Arizona State University.

LEGAL METHOD (1980)

Harry W. Jones, Professor of Law Emeritus, Columbia University.
John M. Kernochan, Professor of Law, Columbia University.
Arthur W. Murphy, Professor of Law, Columbia University.

LEGAL METHODS (1969)

Robert N. Covington, Professor of Law, Vanderbilt University.
E. Blythe Stason, late Professor of Law, Vanderbilt University.
John W. Wade, Professor of Law, Vanderbilt University.
Elliott E. Cheatham, late Professor of Law, Vanderbilt University.
Theodore A. Smedley, Professor of Law, Vanderbilt University.

LEGAL PROFESSION, THE, Responsibility and Regulation, Second Edition (1988)

Geoffrey C. Hazard, Jr., Professor of Law, Yale University.
Deborah L. Rhode, Professor of Law, Stanford University.

LEGISLATION, Fourth Edition (1982) (by Fordham)

Horace E. Read, late Vice President, Dalhousie University.
John W. MacDonald, Professor of Law Emeritus, Cornell Law School.
Jefferson B. Fordham, Professor of Law, University of Utah.
William J. Pierce, Professor of Law, University of Michigan.

LEGISLATIVE AND ADMINISTRATIVE PROCESSES, Second Edition (1981)

Hans A. Linde, Judge, Supreme Court of Oregon.
George Bunn, Professor of Law, University of Wisconsin.
Fredericka Paff, Professor of Law, University of Wisconsin.
W. Lawrence Church, Professor of Law, University of Wisconsin.

LOCAL GOVERNMENT LAW, Second Revised Edition (1986)

Jefferson B. Fordham, Professor of Law, University of Utah.

MASS MEDIA LAW, Third Edition (1987)

Marc A. Franklin, Professor of Law, Stanford University.

MENTAL HEALTH PROCESS, Second Edition (1976), with 1981 Supplement

Frank W. Miller, Professor of Law, Washington University.
Robert O. Dawson, Professor of Law, University of Texas.
George E. Dix, Professor of Law, University of Texas.
Raymond I. Parnas, Professor of Law, University of California, Davis.

MUNICIPAL CORPORATIONS, see Local Government Law

NEGOTIABLE INSTRUMENTS, see Commercial Paper

NEGOTIATION (1981) (Reprinted from THE LAWYERING PROCESS)

Gary Bellow, Professor of Law, Harvard Law School.
Bea Moulton, Legal Services Corporation.

NEW YORK PRACTICE, Fourth Edition (1978)

Herbert Peterfreund, Professor of Law, New York University.
Joseph M. McLaughlin, Dean of the Law School, Fordham University.

OIL AND GAS, Fifth Edition (1987)

Howard R. Williams, Professor of Law, Stanford University.
Richard C. Maxwell, Professor of Law, University of California, Los Angeles.
Charles J. Meyers, late Dean of the Law School, Stanford University.
Stephen F. Williams, Judge of the United States Court of Appeals.

ON LAW IN COURTS (1965)

Paul J. Mishkin, Professor of Law, University of California, Berkeley.
Clarence Morris, Professor of Law Emeritus, University of Pennsylvania.

PATENTS AND ANTITRUST (Pamphlet) (1983)

Milton Handler, Professor of Law Emeritus, Columbia University.
Harlan M. Blake, Professor of Law, Columbia University.
Robert Pitofsky, Professor of Law, Georgetown University.
Harvey J. Goldschmid, Professor of Law, Columbia University.

PLEADING AND PROCEDURE, see Procedure, Civil

POLICE FUNCTION, Fourth Edition (1986), with 1988 Case Supplement

Reprint of Chapters 1–10 of Miller, Dawson, Dix and Parnas's CRIMINAL JUSTICE ADMINISTRATION, Third Edition.

PREPARING AND PRESENTING THE CASE (1981) (Reprinted from THE LAWYERING PROCESS)

Gary Bellow, Professor of Law, Harvard Law School.
Bea Moulton, Legal Services Corporation.

PROCEDURE (1988), with Procedure Supplement (1988)

Robert M. Cover, late Professor of Law, Yale Law School.
Owen M. Fiss, Professor of Law, Yale Law School.
Judith Resnik, Professor of Law, University of Southern California Law Center.

PROCEDURE—CIVIL PROCEDURE, Second Edition (1974), with 1979 Supplement

The late James H. Chadbourn, Professor of Law, Harvard University.
A. Leo Levin, Professor of Law, University of Pennsylvania.
Philip Shuchman, Professor of Law, Cornell University.

PROCEDURE—CIVIL PROCEDURE, Fifth Edition (1984), with 1988 Supplement

Richard H. Field, late Professor of Law, Harvard University.
Benjamin Kaplan, Professor of Law Emeritus, Harvard University.
Kevin M. Clermont, Professor of Law, Cornell University.

PROCEDURE—CIVIL PROCEDURE, Fourth Edition (1985), with 1988 Supplement

Maurice Rosenberg, Professor of Law, Columbia University.
Hans Smit, Professor of Law, Columbia University.
Harold L. Korn, Professor of Law, Columbia University.

PROCEDURE—PLEADING AND PROCEDURE: State and Federal, Fifth Edition (1983), with 1988 Supplement

David W. Louisell, late Professor of Law, University of California, Berkeley.
Geoffrey C. Hazard, Jr., Professor of Law, Yale University.
Colin C. Tait, Professor of Law, University of Connecticut.

PROCEDURE—FEDERAL RULES OF CIVIL PROCEDURE, 1988 Edition

PRODUCTS LIABILITY (1980)

Marshall S. Shapo, Professor of Law, Northwestern University.

PRODUCTS LIABILITY AND SAFETY, Second Edition, (1989)

W. Page Keeton, Professor of Law, University of Texas.
David G. Owen, Professor of Law, University of South Carolina.
John E. Montgomery, Professor of Law, University of South Carolina.
Michael D. Green, Professor of Law, University of Iowa

PROFESSIONAL RESPONSIBILITY, Fourth Edition (1987), with 1989 Selected National Standards Supplement

Thomas D. Morgan, Dean of the Law School, Emory University.
Ronald D. Rotunda, Professor of Law, University of Illinois.

PROPERTY, Fifth Edition (1984)

John E. Cribbet, Professor of Law, University of Illinois.
Corwin W. Johnson, Professor of Law, University of Texas.

PROPERTY—PERSONAL (1953)

S. Kenneth Skolfield, late Professor of Law Emeritus, Boston University.

PROPERTY—PERSONAL, Third Edition (1954)

Everett Fraser, late Dean of the Law School Emeritus, University of Minnesota.
Third Edition by Charles W. Taintor, late Professor of Law, University of Pittsburgh.

PROPERTY—INTRODUCTION, TO REAL PROPERTY, Third Edition (1954)

Everett Fraser, late Dean of the Law School Emeritus, University of Minnesota.

PROPERTY—REAL AND PERSONAL, Combined Edition (1954)

Everett Fraser, late Dean of the Law School Emeritus, University of Minnesota.
Third Edition of Personal Property by Charles W. Taintor, late Professor of Law, University of Pittsburgh.

PROPERTY—FUNDAMENTALS OF MODERN REAL PROPERTY, Second Edition (1982), with 1985 Supplement

Edward H. Rabin, Professor of Law, University of California, Davis.

PROPERTY—PROBLEMS IN REAL PROPERTY (Pamphlet) (1969)

Edward H. Rabin, Professor of Law, University of California, Davis.

PROPERTY, REAL (1984), with 1988 Supplement

Paul Goldstein, Professor of Law, Stanford University.

PROSECUTION AND ADJUDICATION, Third Edition (1986), with 1988 Case Supplement

Reprint of Chapters 11–26 of Miller, Dawson, Dix and Parnas's CRIMINAL JUSTICE ADMINISTRATION, Third Edition.

PSYCHIATRY AND LAW, see Mental Health, see also Hinckley, Trial of

PUBLIC REGULATION OF DANGEROUS PRODUCTS (paperback) (1980)

Marshall S. Shapo, Professor of Law, Northwestern University.

PUBLIC UTILITY LAW, see Free Enterprise, also Regulated Industries

REAL ESTATE PLANNING, Third Edition (1989), with Problem and Statutory Supplement

Norton L. Steuben, Professor of Law, University of Colorado.

REAL ESTATE TRANSACTIONS, Revised Second Edition (1988), with Statute, Form and Problem Supplement (1988)

Paul Goldstein, Professor of Law, Stanford University.

RECEIVERSHIP AND CORPORATE REORGANIZATION, see Creditors' Rights

REGULATED INDUSTRIES, Second Edition, (1976)

William K. Jones, Professor of Law, Columbia University.

REMEDIES, Second Edition (1987)

Edward D. Re, Chief Judge, U. S. Court of International Trade.

REMEDIES, (1989)

Elaine W. Shoben, Professor of Law, University of Illinois.
Wm. Murray Tabb, Professor of Law, Baylor University.

RESTITUTION, Second Edition (1966)

John W. Wade, Professor of Law, Vanderbilt University.

SALES, Second Edition (1986)

Marion W. Benfield, Jr., Professor of Law, University of Illinois.
William D. Hawkland, Chancellor, Louisiana State Law Center.

SALES AND SALES FINANCING, Fifth Edition (1984)

John Honnold, Professor of Law, University of Pennsylvania.

SALES LAW AND THE CONTRACTING PROCESS (1982)

Reprint of Chapters 1–10 of Schwartz and Scott's Commercial Transactions.

SECURED TRANSACTIONS IN PERSONAL PROPERTY, Second Edition (1987) (Reprinted from COMMERCIAL LAW, Second Edition (1987))

Robert L. Jordan, Professor of Law, University of California, Los Angeles.
William D. Warren, Professor of Law, University of California, Los Angeles.

SECURITIES REGULATION, Sixth Edition (1987), with 1988 Selected Statutes, Rules and Forms Supplement and 1988 Cases and Releases Supplement

Richard W. Jennings, Professor of Law, University of California, Berkeley.
Harold Marsh, Jr., Member of California Bar.

SECURITIES REGULATION, Second Edition (1988), with Statute, Rule and Form Supplement (1988)

Larry D. Soderquist, Professor of Law, Vanderbilt University.

SECURITY INTERESTS IN PERSONAL PROPERTY, Second Edition (1987)

Douglas G. Baird, Professor of Law, University of Chicago.
Thomas H. Jackson, Professor of Law, Harvard University.

SECURITY INTERESTS IN PERSONAL PROPERTY (1985) (Reprinted from Sales and Sales Financing, Fifth Edition)

John Honnold, Professor of Law, University of Pennsylvania.

SENTENCING AND THE CORRECTIONAL PROCESS, Second Edition (1976)

Frank W. Miller, Professor of Law, Washington University.
Robert O. Dawson, Professor of Law, University of Texas.
George E. Dix, Professor of Law, University of Texas.
Raymond I. Parnas, Professor of Law, University of California, Davis.

SOCIAL RESPONSIBILITIES OF LAWYERS, Case Studies (1988)

Philip B. Heymann, Professor of Law, Harvard University.
Lance Liebman, Professor of Law, Harvard University.

SOCIAL SCIENCE IN LAW, Cases and Materials (1985)

John Monahan, Professor of Law, University of Virginia.
Laurens Walker, Professor of Law, University of Virginia.

TAX, POLICY ANALYSIS OF THE FEDERAL INCOME (1976)

William A. Klein, Professor of Law, University of California, Los Angeles.

TAXATION, FEDERAL INCOME (1989)

Stephen B. Cohen, Professor of Law, Georgetown University

TAXATION, FEDERAL INCOME, Second Edition (1988)

Michael J. Graetz, Professor of Law, Yale University.

TAXATION, FEDERAL INCOME, Sixth Edition (1987)

James J. Freeland, Professor of Law, University of Florida.
Stephen A. Lind, Professor of Law, University of Florida and University of California, Hastings.
Richard B. Stephens, late Professor of Law Emeritus, University of Florida.

TAXATION, FEDERAL INCOME, Successor Edition (1986), with 1988 Legislative Supplement

Stanley S. Surrey, late Professor of Law, Harvard University.
Paul R. McDaniel, Professor of Law, Boston College.
Hugh J. Ault, Professor of Law, Boston College.
Stanley A. Koppelman, Professor of Law, Boston University.

TAXATION, FEDERAL INCOME, VOLUME II, Taxation of Partnerships and Corporations, Second Edition (1980), with 1988 Legislative Supplement

Stanley S. Surrey, late Professor of Law, Harvard University.
William C. Warren, Professor of Law Emeritus, Columbia University.
Paul R. McDaniel, Professor of Law, Boston College.
Hugh J. Ault, Professor of Law, Boston College.

TAXATION, FEDERAL WEALTH TRANSFER, Successor Edition (1987)

Stanley S. Surrey, late Professor of Law, Harvard University.
Paul R. McDaniel, Professor of Law, Boston College.
Harry L. Gutman, Professor of Law, University of Pennsylvania.

TAXATION, FUNDAMENTALS OF CORPORATE, Second Edition (1987)

Stephen A. Lind, Professor of Law, University of Florida and University of California, Hastings.
Stephen Schwarz, Professor of Law, University of California, Hastings.
Daniel J. Lathrope, Professor of Law, University of California, Hastings.
Joshua Rosenberg, Professor of Law, University of San Francisco.

TAXATION, FUNDAMENTALS OF PARTNERSHIP, Second Edition (1988)

Stephen A. Lind, Professor of Law, University of Florida and University of California, Hastings.
Stephen Schwarz, Professor of Law, University of California, Hastings.
Daniel J. Lathrope, Professor of Law, University of California, Hastings.
Joshua Rosenberg, Professor of Law, University of San Francisco.

TAXATION, PROBLEMS IN THE FEDERAL INCOME TAXATION OF PARTNERSHIPS AND CORPORATIONS, Second Edition (1986)

Norton L. Steuben, Professor of Law, University of Colorado.
William J. Turnier, Professor of Law, University of North Carolina.

TAXATION, PROBLEMS IN THE FUNDAMENTALS OF FEDERAL INCOME, Second Edition (1985)

Norton L. Steuben, Professor of Law, University of Colorado.
William J. Turnier, Professor of Law, University of North Carolina.

TAXES AND FINANCE—STATE AND LOCAL (1974)

Oliver Oldman, Professor of Law, Harvard University.
Ferdinand P. Schoettle, Professor of Law, University of Minnesota.

TORT LAW AND ALTERNATIVES, Fourth Edition (1987)

Marc A. Franklin, Professor of Law, Stanford University.
Robert L. Rabin, Professor of Law, Stanford University.

TORTS, Eighth Edition (1988)

William L. Prosser, late Professor of Law, University of California, Hastings.
John W. Wade, Professor of Law, Vanderbilt University.
Victor E. Schwartz, Adjunct Professor of Law, Georgetown University.

TORTS, Third Edition (1976)

Harry Shulman, late Dean of the Law School, Yale University.
Fleming James, Jr., Professor of Law Emeritus, Yale University.
Oscar S. Gray, Professor of Law, University of Maryland.

TRADE REGULATION, Second Edition (1983), with 1987 Supplement

Milton Handler, Professor of Law Emeritus, Columbia University.
Harlan M. Blake, Professor of Law, Columbia University.
Robert Pitofsky, Professor of Law, Georgetown University.
Harvey J. Goldschmid, Professor of Law, Columbia University.

TRADE REGULATION, see Antitrust

TRANSNATIONAL BUSINESS PROBLEMS (1986)

Detlev F. Vagts, Professor of Law, Harvard University.

TRANSNATIONAL LEGAL PROBLEMS, Third Edition (1986) with Documentary Supplement

Henry J. Steiner, Professor of Law, Harvard University.
Detlev F. Vagts, Professor of Law, Harvard University.

TRIAL, see also Evidence, Making the Record, Lawyering Process and Preparing and Presenting the Case

TRUSTS, Fifth Edition (1978)

George G. Bogert, late Professor of Law Emeritus, University of Chicago.
Dallin H. Oaks, President, Brigham Young University.

TRUSTS AND SUCCESSION (Palmer's), Fourth Edition (1983)

Richard V. Wellman, Professor of Law, University of Georgia.
Lawrence W. Waggoner, Professor of Law, University of Michigan.
Olin L. Browder, Jr., Professor of Law, University of Michigan.

UNFAIR COMPETITION, see Competitive Process and Business Torts

UNITED NATIONS LAW, Second Edition (1967), with Documentary Supplement (1968)

Louis B. Sohn, Professor of Law, Harvard University.

WATER RESOURCE MANAGEMENT, Third Edition (1988)

The late Charles J. Meyers, formerly Dean, Stanford University Law School.
A. Dan Tarlock, Professor of Law, II Chicago-Kent College of Law.
James N. Corbridge, Jr., Chancellor, University of Colorado at Boulder, and Professor of Law, University of Colorado School of Law.
David H. Getches, Professor of Law, University of Colorado School of Law.

WILLS AND ADMINISTRATION, Fifth Edition (1961)

Philip Mechem, late Professor of Law, University of Pennsylvania.
Thomas E. Atkinson, late Professor of Law, New York University.

WORLD LAW, see United Nations Law

WRITING AND ANALYSIS IN THE LAW (1989)

Helene S. Shapo, Professor of Law, Northwestern University
Marilyn R. Walter, Professor of Law, Brooklyn Law School
Elizabeth Fajans, Writing Specialist, Brooklyn Law School

University Casebook Series

PRODUCTS LIABILITY

AND

SAFETY

CASES AND MATERIALS

By

W. PAGE KEETON
W. Page Keeton Professor of Law of Torts
University of Texas

DAVID G. OWEN
Roy Webster Professor of Tort Law
University of South Carolina

JOHN E. MONTGOMERY
Dean and Professor of Law
University of South Carolina

MICHAEL D. GREEN
Professor of Law
University of Iowa

SECOND EDITION

Westbury, New York
THE FOUNDATION PRESS, INC.
1989

615 Merrick Ave.
Westbury, N.Y. 11590

Printed in the United States of America
96 95 94 93 92 91 90 89 8 7 6 5 4 3 2 1 0

Library of Congress Cataloging-in-Publication Data

Products liability and safety: cases and materials / by W. Page
Keeton . . . [et al.].
p. cm. — (University casebook series)
Includes index.
ISBN 0-88277-648-7
1. Products liability—United States—Cases. 2. Product safety—
Law and legislation—United States—Cases. I. Keeton, Page.
II. Series.
KF1296.A7P765 1989
346.7303'82—dc19
[347.306382] 89-1375
CIP

K., O., M. & G. Prod.Liab. & Safety 2nd Ed. UCB

W.P.K.
To Madge Keeton

*

D.G.O.
To Nathan and Janet Owen

*

J.E.M.
To Euclid and Mona Montgomery

*

M.D.G.
To Carol Green

*

PREFACE TO THE SECOND EDITION

This second edition appears one decade after the publication of the first edition. Although the 1980s saw much less doctrinal change than the 1960s and 1970s, a variety of significant judicial developments in products liability law did occur. In addition, many states enacted tort or products liability "reform" legislation, altering some of the established principles in this area of the law.

In addition to adding important new cases and legislative developments, we have made certain structural changes in an effort to streamline the book and to reflect developments in the law over the last decade. Certain sections have been condensed, and others have been added. Problems of proof have been integrated throughout the book, rather than being segregated in a separate chapter. New sections have been added on federal government liability, the government contractor defense, product disposal and destruction, intergenerational harm, and the second wave of "crisis" and "reform" developments. Finally, two new chapters have been added on the special problems of automotive and toxic substance litigation, to allow in-depth exploration of these expanding areas of products liability litigation.

Most footnotes are omitted from the materials presented, but the original numbering is used for those footnotes that are retained. Asterisks are used to designate footnotes of the editors. All omissions from cases and from the interior of excerpts from articles and books are indicated by asterisks or brackets.

In the process of revision, we have undoubtedly dropped certain materials which various users wish we had retained. To them, we express our regrets and extend our permission to reproduce selected materials from the first edition for classroom use. Many of the improvements in this edition are attributable to comments received from users of the first edition. We appreciate all such suggestions and hope that users of the second edition will continue to pass along their ideas on how the book may be improved.

W. PAGE KEETON
DAVID G. OWEN
JOHN E. MONTGOMERY
MICHAEL D. GREEN

Columbia, South Carolina
March 1989

*

ACKNOWLEDGMENTS

We are grateful to the following law students who assisted in the preparation of this edition: John Buckley, Lee Coggiola, Rosemary Coreley, Dirk Derrick, Brian Foster, David Frohlich, Janet Hess, Robert Hill, Gary Hill, Tim Moore, Joan Owen, Robert Persse, Aida Saracevic, Mark Schroeder, and Kristy Smith. Numerous law professors provided us with many valuable suggestions, for which we express our gratitude. Those who devoted substantial time and effort were Richard Daynard, Susanah Mead, Michael Saks, and Roderick Surratt. Ginger Butler provided dedicated secretarial assistance, and Laura Long provided important administrative support.

Our largest debt is to our families, Madge Keeton, Joan, Wendy and Ethan Owen, Megan Dantzler, Bonnie and John B. Montgomery, and Carol, Abby and Brett Green, whose sacrifices were the greatest and whose support fueled the enterprise.

Finally, we acknowledge the cooperation of the following publishers and authors who granted us permission to use various materials included herein.

American Law Institute, 1961 ALI Proceedings. Copyright 1962 by The American Law Institute. Reprinted with the permission of The American Law Institute.

American Law Institute, Restatement of the Law, Torts, Second. Copyright 1965 by The American Law Institute. Reprinted with the permission of The American Law Institute.

Associated Press, Company Stops Making Morning Sickness Drug, June 10, 1983. Reprinted with the permission of the Associated Press.

Associated Press, Heinz Co. Recalling All Instant Dry Baby Cereals, reprinted in The State, Columbia, S.C., p. 14–B (Jan. 13, 1975). Reprinted with the permission of the Associated Press.

Black and Lilienfield, Epidemiologic Proof in Toxic Tort Litigation, 52 Fordham L.Rev. 732 (1984). Reprinted by permission of the authors.

Broude, The Consumer and the Parol Evidence Rule: Section 2–202 of the Uniform Commercial Code. Copyright © 1970 by Duke Law Journal. Reprinted with permission. Originally published at 1970 Duke L.J. 881.

Bureau of National Affairs, Cipollone Jury, reprinted by permission from Product Safety and Liability Reporter, Vol. 16, No. 25, p. 565 (June 17, 1988). Copyright 1988 by the Bureau of National Affairs, Inc.

Bureau of National Affairs, Free Choice Question Emphasized By Attorneys In Cipollone Trial, reprinted by permission from Product Safety and Liability Reporter, Vol. 16, No. 24, p. 532 (June 10, 1988). Copyright 1988 by the Bureau of National Affairs, Inc.

Bureau of National Affairs, State Tort Reform, reprinted by permission from Product Safety and Liability Reporter, Vol. 16, No. 4, p. 108 (January 22, 1988). Copyright 1988 by the Bureau of National Affairs, Inc.

Charlotte Observer, "Ford: Faulty Capri Wipers Safer Than Recall Hazards," p. 2A, col. 4 (June 3, 1978). Reprinted with permission of the newspaper.

"Coke on Littleton" (drawing), 43 Cal.L.Rev. 374 (1955). Copyright © 1970, California Law Review, Inc. Reprinted with permission of the California Law Review and Fred B. Rothman & Co.

Comment, Bell v. Industrial Vangas: The Employer-Manufacturer and the Dilemma of Dual Capacity, 34 Hastings L.J. 461 (1982). Copyright 1982 Hastings Law Journal. Reprinted from 34 Hastings L.J. 461–490 with permission.

A. Corbin, Contracts (1963). Copyright 1952 by West Publishing Co. Reprinted with the permission of the West Publishing Company.

Cowan, Some Policy Bases of Products Liability, 17 Stan.L.Rev. 1077 (1965). Copyright 1965 by the Board of Trustees of the Leland Stanford Junior University. Reprinted with permission of the Stanford Law Review.

Danforth, A Need for Uniform Laws, Faster Trials. Copyright © 1985 by The New York Times Company. Reprinted by permission.

Dickerson, Products Liability: How Good Does A Product Have to Be?, 42 Ind.L.J. 301 (1967). Reprinted with the permission of the Indiana Law Journal and Fred B. Rothman & Co.

Donaher, Piehler, Twerski & Weinstein, The Technological Expert in Products Liability Litigation, 52 Tex.L.Rev. 1303 (1974). Reprinted with permission of the Texas Law Review.

Employers Insurance of Wausau, "The Product Liability Menace." Advertisement printed in The Wall Street Journal, p. 15 (Dec. 9, 1976). Reprinted with the permission of the advertiser.

Epstein, Products Liability: The Gathering Storm, 1 Regulation: AEI J. on Gov't & Soc. 15 (Sept./Oct. 1977). Reprinted with the permission of the American Enterprise Institute.

Epstein, Products Liability: The Search for the Middle Ground, 56 N.C.L.Rev. 643 (1978). Reprinted with the permission of the author.

Feezer, Manufacturer's Liability for Injuries Caused by His Products: Defective Automobiles, 37 Mich.L.Rev. 1 (1938). Reprinted with the permission of the Michigan Law Review.

Fischer, Products Liability—The Meaning of Defect, 39 Mo.L.Rev. 339 (1974). Copyright 1976 by The Curators of the University of Missouri. Reprinted with the permission of the Missouri Law Review.

Franklin, When Worlds Collide: Liability Theories and Disclaimers in Defective-Product Cases, 18 Stan.L.Rev. 974 (1966). Copyright 1966 by the Board of Trustees of the Leland Stanford Junior University. Reprinted with the permission of the Stanford Law Review.

Gillam, Products Liability in a Nutshell, 37 Or.L.Rev. 119 (1958). Reprinted with the permission of the Oregon Law Review.

Goldberg, Manufacturers Take Cover. Reprinted with permission from the July 1986 issue of ABA Journal, The Lawyer's Magazine, published by the American Bar Association.

Hamilton, The Ancient Maxim Caveat Emptor. Reprinted by permission of The Yale Law Journal Company and Fred B. Rothman & Co. from The Yale Law Journal, Vol. 40, pp. 1133–65 (1931).

F. Harper & F. James, The Law of Torts. Boston: Little, Brown and Co., 1956. Reprinted with the permission of the publisher.

Henderson, Coping With The Time Dimension In Products Liability. © 1981 California Law Review, Inc. Reprinted from the California Law Review, Vol. 69, No. 4, July 1981, pp. 919–949, by permission.

Henderson, Manufacturers' Liability for Defective Product Design: A Proposed Statutory Reform, 56 N.C.L.Rev. 625 (1978). Reprinted with the permission of the author.

James, Products Liability (pt. 2), 34 Tex.L.Rev. 227 (1955). Reprinted with the permission of the Texas Law Review.

Keeton, Torts, Annual Survey of Texas Law, 32 Sw.L.J. 1 (1978). Reprinted with permission of the copyright holder. Copyright 1978 by Southern Methodist University.

Klemme, The Enterprise Liability Theory of Torts, 47 Colo.L.Rev. 153 (1976). Reprinted with the permission of the Colorado Law Review.

Larson, Workmen's Compensation: Third Party's Action Over Against Employer, 65 Nw.U.L.Rev. 351 (1970). Reprinted with the permission of the Northwestern Law Review.

Leidy, Another New Tort?, 38 Mich.L.Rev. 964 (1940). Reprinted with the permission of the Michigan Law Review.

Merrill, Risk-Benefit Decisionmaking by the Food and Drug Administration, 45 Geo.Wash.L.Rev. 994 (1977). Reprinted with the permission of The George Washington Law Review.

Mitchell, Products Liability, Workmen's Compensation and the Industrial Accident, 14 Duq.L.Rev. 349 (1976). Reprinted with the permission of the Duquesne Law Review.

Montgomery & Owen, Reflections on the Theory and Administration of Strict Tort Liability for Defective Products, 27 S.C.L.Rev. 803 (1976). Copyright 1976 by the South Carolina Law Review. Reprinted by permission.

The New York Times, Agent Orange—Let it Lie. Copyright © 1986 by The New York Times Company. Reprinted by permission.

The New York Times, Art by Niculae Asciu. Copyright © 1985 by The New York Times Company. Reprinted by permission.

R. Nordstrom, Law of Sales (1970). Copyright 1970 by West Publishing Co. Reprinted with permission of the West Publishing Company.

Owen, The Highly Blameworthy Manufacturer: Implications on Rules of Liability and Defense in Products Liability Actions, 10 Ind.L.Rev. 769 (1977). Reprinted with the permission of the Indiana Law Review and Fred B. Rothman & Co.

D. Peck, Decision At Law (1961). Reprinted by permission of Dodd, Mead and Company, Inc. from DECISION AT LAW by David W. Peck. Copyright 1961 by David W. Peck.

Phillips, Contribution and Indemnity in Products Liability. Reprinted with permission of the author and the Tennessee Law Review Association, Inc. from 42 Tennessee Law Review 85 (1974).

Posner, A Theory of Negligence, 1 J.Leg.Stud. 29 (1972). Reprinted with the permission of the Journal of Legal Studies.

Posner, Strict Liability: A Comment, 2 J.Leg.Stud. 205 (1973). Reprinted with the permission of the Journal of Legal Studies.

R. Pound, Social Control Through Law (1942). Copyright 1942 by Yale University Press from Social Control Through Law by Roscoe Pound. Reprinted in 1968 by Archon Books, Hamden, Connecticut. Reprinted with the permission of the publisher.

Prosser, The Assault Upon the Citadel (Strict Liability to the Consumer). Reprinted by permission of The Yale Law Journal Company and Fred B. Rothman & Co. from The Yale Law Journal, Vol. 69, pp. 1099, 1120–21 (1960).

Prosser, The Fall of the Citadel (Strict Liability to the Consumer), 50 Minn.L.Rev. 791 (1966). Reprinted with the permission of the Minnesota Law Review.

Prosser, The Implied Warranty of Merchantable Quality, 27 Minn.L.Rev. 117 (1943). Reprinted with the permission of the Minnesota Law Review.

Rheingold, The Expanding Liability of the Product Supplier: A Primer, 2 Hofstra L.Rev. 521 (1974). Reprinted with the permission of the Hofstra Law Review.

Roberts, Circular Saw Design: A Hazard Analysis, 1 J. of Prod.Liab. 127 (1977). Reprinted with the permission of the author and the Institute of Product Safety.

Rothschild, The Magnuson-Moss Warranty Act: Does It Balance Warrantor and Consumer Interests?, 44 Geo.Wash.L.Rev. 335 (1976).

Reprinted with the permission of The George Washington Law Review.

Russell, Manufacturers Liability to the Ultimate Consumer, 21 Ky.L.J. 388 (1933). Reprinted with the permission of the Kentucky Law Journal.

Schwartz, Products Liability, Corporate Structure and Bankruptcy: Toxic Substances and the Remote Risk Relationship, 14 J.Leg.Stud. 689 (1985). Reprinted with permission of the Journal of Legal Studies.

Shapo, A Representational Theory of Consumer Protection: Doctrine, Function and Legal Liability for Product Disappointment, 60 Va.L. Rev. 1109 (1974). Reprinted with the permission of the Virginia Law Review Association and Fred B. Rothman & Co.

Speidel, The Virginia "Anti-Privity" Statute: Strict Products Liability Under the Uniform Commercial Code, 51 Va.L.Rev. 804 (1965). Reprinted with the permission of the Virginia Law Review Association and Fred B. Rothman & Co.

"The Toxic Avenger," reprinted by permission. © 1984, Troma, Inc./ The HCH Co. from the motion picture "The Toxic Avenger," a Lloyd Kaufman/Michael Hesz Production. The producer conditioned use of the picture on the inclusion of the following additional credit: "The Toxic Avenger," a horror/comedy motion picture dealing with the consequences of toxic waste, was a tremendous box-office hit for TROMA, INC. in 1985 that enjoyed a successful six-month run in New York City.

J. Thomas, Textbook of Roman Law (1976). Reprinted with the permission of the author and Elsevier-North Holland Publishing Co.

Time Magazine, The Copper-7's Costly Legacy, September 26, 1988. Copyright 1988 Time, Inc. Reprinted by permission.

Titus, Restatement (Second) of Torts Section 402A and the Uniform Commercial Code, 22 Stan.L.Rev. 713 (1970). Copyright 1970 by the Board of Trustees of the Leland Stanford Junior University. Reprinted with the permission of the Stanford Law Review.

Trial Lawyer's Guide, photographs of defective screws, p. 327 (1971). Reprinted with permission from Trial Lawyer's Guide, 1971 Annual, published by Callaghan & Company, 3201 Old Glenview Road, Wilmette, Illinois 60091.

Twerski, The Many Faces of Misuse, 29 Mercer L.Rev. 403 (1978). Reprinted with the permission of the author and the Mercer Law Review.

Twerski, Weinstein, Donaher & Piehler, The Use and Abuse of Warnings in Products Liability—Design Defect Litigation Comes of Age, 61 Cornell L.Rev. 495 (1976). Copyright 1976 by Cornell University.

Reprinted with the permission of the authors, the Cornell Law Review and Fred B. Rothman & Co.

Uniform Commercial Code, Official Text and Comments. Copyright 1987 by the American Law Institute and the National Conference of Commissioners on Uniform State Laws. Reprinted with permission of the Permanent Editorial Board for the Uniform Commercial Code.

Wade, On the Nature of Strict Tort Liability for Products, 44 Miss.L.J. 825 (1973). Reprinted with the permission of the Mississippi Law Journal.

The Wall Street Journal, Ford Cuts '86 Coverage for Product Liability. Reproduced by permission of the Wall Street Journal. © Dow Jones & Company, Inc. 1986. All rights reserved worldwide.

The Wall Street Journal, Litigation Load. Reproduced by permission of the Wall Street Journal. © Dow Jones & Company, Inc. 1976. All rights reserved worldwide.

Weintraub, Disclaimers and Limitation of Damages for Breach of Warranty Under the UCC, 53 Tex.L.Rev. 60 (1974). Reprinted with the permission of the Texas Law Review.

Weisgall, Workers' Compensation and Third Party Rights, 1977 Wis.L. Rev. 1035. Reprinted with the permission of the author and the Wisconsin Law Review.

White, Infante & Walker, "Occupational Exposure to Benzene," 1 Am.J. Indus.Med. 233. © 1980 by the American Journal of Industrial Medicine. Reprinted with permission.

J. White & R. Summers, Uniform Commercial Code, Third Edition. Copyright 1988 by West Publishing Co. Reprinted with the permission of the West Publishing Company.

SUMMARY OF CONTENTS

CHAPTER 7. SPECIAL TYPES OF DEFENDANTS

CHAPTER 8. SPECIAL TYPES OF PRODUCTS AND TRANSACTIONS

CHAPTER 9. SPECIAL ISSUES IN AUTOMOTIVE LITIGATION

CHAPTER 10. SPECIAL ISSUES IN TOXIC SUBSTANCE LITIGATION

CHAPTER 11. "CRISIS" AND "REFORM"

TABLE OF CONTENTS

CHAPTER 3. THE CONCEPT OF DEFECTIVENESS

CHAPTER 4. CAUSATION

CHAPTER 5. DEFENSES BASED ON PLAINTIFF'S CONDUCT

CHAPTER 6. DAMAGES

CHAPTER 7. SPECIAL TYPES OF DEFENDANTS

CHAPTER 11. "CRISIS" AND "REFORM"

TABLE OF CASES

Principal cases are in italic type. Non-principal cases are in roman type. References are to Pages.

PRODUCTS LIABILITY

AND

SAFETY

CASES AND MATERIALS

*

Chapter 1

INTRODUCTION

SECTION 1. THE SOCIAL PROBLEM OF DANGEROUS PRODUCTS

> [T]oday we face an unparalleled profusion of new products spawned by space-age technology. A somber by-product of this proliferation of new products in the home has been the growth of new categories and dimensions of home injuries.

So said Senator Warren G. Magnuson of Washington in urging the Senate in June 1967 to establish a national commission to survey product safety. See Final Report, National Commission on Product Safety 123 (June 1970) [Final Report]. Congress responded. Asserting that "the American Consumer has a right to be protected against unreasonable risk of bodily harm from products purchased on the open market for the use of himself and his family," the United States Congress by Joint Resolution in November 1967 established the National Commission on Product Safety. Public Law 90–146, 90th Cong., S.J. Res. 33, Nov. 20, 1967. The Commission was directed to perform various tasks: (1) to study the nature and magnitude of the problem of accidental injuries associated with the use of consumer products; (2) to determine the extent to which such injuries were attributable to product hazards reasonably avoidable by manufacturers and hence "unnecessary"; (3) to examine the effectiveness of the then-existing structure of regulatory and common-law rules governing products liability and safety; and (4) to propose any appropriate remedial legislation. In particular, the Commission was instructed to "conduct a comprehensive study and investigation of the scope and adequacy of measures now employed to protect consumers against unreasonable risk of injuries which may be caused by hazardous household products" and to identify "categories of household products * * * which may present an unreasonable hazard to the health and safety of the consuming public." Id., § 2(a)(1).

In June of 1970, the Commission presented its findings:

> Americans—20 million of them—are injured each year in the home as a result of incidents connected with consumer products. Of the total, 110,000 are permanently disabled and 30,000 are killed. A significant number could have been spared if more attention had been paid to hazard reduction. The annual cost to the Nation of product-related injuries may exceed $5.5 billion.

> The exposure of consumers to unreasonable consumer product hazards is excessive by any standard of measurement.

Final Report 1 (June 1970).

Because these findings excluded data on product accidents outside the Commission's jurisdiction—accidents occurring in the workplace, and those involving motor vehicles, food, drugs, cosmetics, insecticides, firearms, cigarettes, radiological hazards, and certain flammable fabrics—the total number and cost of product accidents in this nation is considerably higher. As of the late 1980s, the number of product accidents (including injuries from toxic substances) may be roughly estimated at 50 million per year, at an annual cost to the nation of $50 billion.*

FINAL REPORT
NATIONAL COMMISSION ON PRODUCT SAFETY

Chapter 2, pp. 9–34 (1970).

PRODUCT RISKS TO CONSUMERS: HOUSEHOLD HAZARDS IDENTIFIED

The primary charge to the National Commission on Product Safety was to "consider the identity of categories of household products * * * which may present an unreasonable hazard to the health and safety of the consuming public."

* * *

The role of specific products is, however, difficult to define. The estimate of 6,200 killed by home fires and 1,300,000 injured by burns received at home leaves open the question of cause: matches, stoves, wiring, fabrics, or cigarettes?

Home falls kill about 12,000 a year and injure 6,900,000, but again the precise causes are uncertain: high heels, loose treads, rough floors, flimsy ladders, worn stairs, slippery floors, torn carpets, alcohol?

STATISTICAL SUMMARY OF INJURIES FROM CONSUMER PRODUCTS BASED ON DEPARTMENT OF HEALTH, EDUCATION AND WELFARE ESTIMATES

APPLIANCES	
burns from gas and electric ranges	100,000
burns from coffeepots	40,000
burns from vaporizers	15,000
burns from irons	20,000
burns from sun and heat lamps	20,000
burns from other sources	30,000
injuries from wringer washing machines	100,000
other injuries from appliances	175,000
TOTAL	500,000

COOKING DEVICES	
burns from skillets	80,000
burns from pressure cookers	10,000
other injuries from cooking devices	60,000
TOTAL	150,000

KITCHEN GADGETS AND SERVING UTENSILS	
injuries from knives	190,000
other injuries from gadgets and utensils	310,000
TOTAL	500,000

* See the CPSC's Annual Reports and the National Safety Council's annual editions of Accident Facts.—Eds.

STATISTICAL SUMMARY OF INJURIES FROM CONSUMER PRODUCTS BASED ON DEPARTMENT OF HEALTH, EDUCATION AND WELFARE ESTIMATES

HOME FURNISHINGS

injuries involving beds	150,000
injuries involving chairs	100,000
injuries involving tables	60,000
injuries involving stools	50,000
injuries involving sofas	45,000
injuries involving venetian blinds	40,000
other injuries from home furnishings	55,000
TOTAL	500,000

HOME FIXTURES

injuries from windows	100,000
injuries from stairs	1,800,000
injuries from tubs and showers	125,000
injuries from glass doors (patio, bath, etc.)	100,000
burns from hot water in bathroom	25,000
injuries from doors other than glass	150,000
other injuries from home fixtures	200,000
TOTAL	2,500,000

HEATING DEVICES

burns from furnaces		30,000
gas explosions	20,000	
burns from hot water heaters		10,000
burns from room heaters		35,000
burns from floor furnaces		25,000
burns from other heating devices		35,000
other injuries from heating devices		40,000
TOTAL		175,000

HOME WORKSHOP

injuries from power saws	75,000
injuries from power drills	15,000
other injuries from home workshop	35,000
TOTAL	125,000

HOME TOOLS

injuries involving ladders	180,000
injuries involving saws	100,000
injuries involving hammers	150,000
other injuries from home tools	320,000
TOTAL	750,000

LAUNDERING, CLEANING, POLISHING PRODUCTS

poisonings from soaps, detergents, cleaners	40,000
poisonings from bleach	35,000
poisonings from disinfectants, deodorizers	20,000
poisonings from furniture polish	20,000
poisonings from lye, corrosives	15,000
other poisonings from laundering, cleaning and polishing products	20,000
other injuries from laundering, cleaning and polishing products	100,000
TOTAL	250,000

YARD AND GARDEN EQUIPMENT

injuries from power mowers	140,000
other injuries from yard and garden equipment	360,000
TOTAL	500,000

RECREATIONAL EQUIPMENT

injuries involving swings	500,000
injuries involving slides	200,000
injuries involving seesaws	50,000
other injuries from stationary equipment	250,000
injuries involving bicycles	1,000,000

RECREATIONAL EQUIPMENT

injuries involving tricycles	100,000
other injuries from mobile equipment	200,000
injuries involving skates	200,000
injuries involving winter sports	400,000
injuries involving baseballs	500,000
injuries involving footballs	1,000,000
injuries involving basketballs	800,000
other injuries involving balls	700,000
injuries involving camping	200,000
injuries involving fishing	300,000
other and unknown injuries from sports eqpmt	500,000
poisoning from airplane glue	25,000
other injuries from hobby equipment	375,000
injuries involving toys	700,000
TOTAL	8,000,000

INCINERATORS

TOTAL	50,000

FLAMMABLE LIQUIDS

burns from gasoline	40,000
burns from lighter fluid	10,000
other burns from flammable liquids	10,000
poisonings from lighter fluid	15,000
poisonings from kerosene	15,000
poisonings from turpentine	25,000
other poisonings from flammable liquids	10,000
TOTAL	125,000

FLAME PRODUCING DEVICES

burns from flame producing devices	75,000
TOTAL	75,000

CLOTHING INJURIES OTHER THAN BURNS

TOTAL	200,000

FIREARMS AND EXPLOSIVES

injuries from firearms	120,000
injuries from fireworks	10,000
other injuries from firearms and explosives	20,000
TOTAL	150,000

COSMETICS

injuries from perfume, toilet water	20,000
injuries from lotions and creams	10,000
other injuries from cosmetics	30,000
TOTAL	60,000

PERSONAL USE ITEMS

injuries from shaving equipment	30,000
other injuries from personal use items	20,000
TOTAL	50,000

PESTICIDES

poisonings from insecticides	35,000
poisonings from rodenticides	20,000
other poisonings from pesticides	20,000
TOTAL	75,000

CONTAINERS

injuries involving cans and jars	160,000
injuries involving bottles	40,000
other injuries involving containers	50,000
TOTAL	250,000

ESTIMATED TOTAL INJURIES FROM LISTED CONSUMER PRODUCTS 14,960,000

Every hour of the day, on the average, household hazards in America kill three victims. For every one they kill, more than 1,000 suffer injuries. The injuries restrict activities of about half of the victims and force a third of these to take to bed to recover. A tenth of the bedridden require hospital care.

* * *

EVALUATING HAZARDS

In assessing individual hazards, we studied data relating frequency, severity, duration, and sequelae of injury to the frequency and degree of exposure to the product. Other variables we looked at were the degree of inherent risk, the essentiality of the product, and the feasibility and approximate cost of safety improvements.

We also considered whether there were acceptable alternatives for a hazardous product; effects on the product of aging and wear; the contribution to hazards of defective maintenance and repair; exposure to instructions or warnings; influence of product advertising on behavior; the extent and forms of abnormal uses of the product; effects of storage, distribution, and disposal; and characteristics of the persons injured, including age, sex, skills, training, and experience.

UNREASONABLE HAZARDS

Beyond the foregoing guidelines for defining "unreasonable hazards," we believe that no completely satisfactory definition is possible. Prof. Corwin D. Edwards of the University of Oregon has presented an excellent statement which supplements our guidelines:

> "Risks of bodily harm to users are not unreasonable when consumers understand that risks exist, can appraise their probability and severity, know how to cope with them, and voluntarily accept them to get benefits that could not be obtained in less risky ways. When there is a risk of this character, consumers have reasonable opportunity to protect themselves; and public authorities should hesitate to substitute their value judgments about the desirability of the risk for those of the consumers who choose to incur it.
>
> "But preventable risk is not reasonable (*a*) when consumers do not know that it exists; or (*b*) when, though aware of it, consumers are unable to estimate its frequency and severity; or (*c*) when consumers do not know how to cope with it, and hence are likely to incur harm unnecessarily; or (*d*) when risk is unnecessary in * * * that it could be reduced or eliminated at a cost in money or in the performance of the product that consumers would willingly incur if they knew the facts and were given the choice.
>
> "Risks that are unreasonable by this definition of unreasonableness seem * * * to be common".

* * *

While we prefer to emphasize positive recommendations for the future protection of consumers, we find that within each of the categories discussed in the pages immediately following, there are makes, models, and types of products which constitute "an unreasonable hazard to the health and safety of the consuming public" within the meaning of our mandate.

[The following data on particular products was collected by the Commission during 1968–70 from physicians, the insurance industry, and various hospitals.]

ARCHITECTURAL GLASS

Every year, about 150,000 victims of broken windows, doors, or glass walls discover that what they can't see can hurt them. About 100,000 walked through glass doors last year, probably believing the space to be open. If the doors had been safety glazed, most of the serious injuries would not have occurred. But the fragile, brittle panels of ordinary glass shatter even under a light blow from a child. The crystal knives and daggers slice through the hand or wrist, cut vital organs, and cause permanent disfigurement, paralysis, or death. Victims may bleed to death before medical aid can arrive.

A pilot survey by Florida's Dade County Health Department, expanded to 16 communities by the Public Health Service, the National Safety Council, and industry representatives, identified characteristic glass-door injuries. Of 110 injuries studied, all could have been prevented or limited by the use of safety glass. One-third of the victims were between 5 and 14 years old. One of seven required hospitalization.

* * *

COLOR TELEVISION SETS

* * *

Among the 85 million TV sets in the United States in 1969, including about 20 million color sets, about 10,000 sets caught fire. Most of the fires were in color sets: the incident rate for color versus monochrome was found to be on the order of 40 to 1.

* * *

The reason for the higher rate of fires in color sets is that they require up to and sometimes more than 25,000 volts. If conductors in the set are not well insulated, the high voltage forces a short circuit. Resistance to this flow of current builds up temperatures to the flaming point.

Operating temperatures of color sets are in the 110°–115° F. range. Heat generated in normal circuits in some sets changed the properties of a wax insulating coating around the high-voltage transformer, so that it broke down. This form of insulation has since, for the most part, been replaced by a more durable, less combustible silicone rubber.

Improperly dressed wire, another weakness in insulation, can be avoided either by 100 percent inspection and correction or a method of assuring full dressing and insulation of component connections.

The spread of fire is enhanced by the present use of flammable paper or cardboard to enclose capacitors; flammable lubricants; accumulation of dust around components; frayed leads; and closely packed circuitry. Other components considered to be potential fire sources are the deflection yoke around the cathode-ray tube, automatic tuning devices, printed circuit parts in the chassis, the AC switch, and ceramic resistors.

HOT-WATER VAPORIZERS

The McCormack family bought a Hankscraft vaporizer advertised as tipproof, foolproof, and safe. It bore the seals of *Good Housekeeping* and *Parents'* magazines, and the mark of Underwriters' Laboratories. They placed it on a stool in their home, plugged in the house circuit, and waited for the steam to rise. While it was steaming, their 3–year–old daughter caught herself in its electric cord. The vaporizer tipped and spilled scalding water onto the child. Andrea McCormack spent 5 months in the hospital enduring a series of painful operations. She will bear the scars all her life. In 1960 a court awarded damages of $150,000.

As of 1968, there were more than 100 claims open and pending against the Hankscraft Co. in the Travelers Insurance Co. office in Milwaukee. The insurer recommended that Hankscraft recall the model and replace it with a safer design. When the manufacturer did not respond, the insurer reduced the coverage and eventually canceled.

In the 10 reports we studied in depth of burns and scalds related to hot water vaporizers, nine were children under 5. Evidence indicated the product to be at least partially at fault in every instance.

The Underwriters' Laboratories voluntary standard applicable to vaporizers (UL 499) provides that: "The stability of a heating appliance shall be such that it will not be overturned readily in normal use". The standard does not further define stability requirements. A model listed by UL could be tipped over with a force of 2 pounds.

Even if unstable, a vaporizer does not need to heat water to scalding temperatures. "Cool mist" vaporizers do not rely on hot water. Physicians say for most purposes they are quite as effective as the hot ones.

Hot vaporizers, after 4 minutes, bring the water to 212° F. At 145°, water will scald; at 180°, it produces a third-degree burn. In almost every hot vaporizer, of whatever manufacture, water temperatures exceed human tolerance.

* * *

The Denver Injury Study Unit of the U.S. Public Health Service * * * informed UL that a vaporizer could be designed to keep water in the storage tank below 115 degrees. One such vaporizer has been on the market for several years. Following studies of water temperatures of saturated clothing, UL revised its standard in November 1968 to 130° F., to become effective July 1, 1972, though it is expected that most companies will comply earlier.

HOUSEHOLD CHEMICALS

* * *

Because young children are so curious, household chemicals pose a major hazard: every liquid or chewable substance is something for them to sample.

* * *

Furniture polish may produce chemical pneumonia if even a small quantity gets into the lungs.

Dr. Charles C. Edwards, Commissioner of the Food and Drug Administration, estimated that ingestions of potentially harmful household substances range from 500,000 to 1 million a year. * * *

* * *

Parents often are aware that a household chemical may be hazardous but unfamiliar with the degree of hazard.

Manufacturers do not inform consumer users of the degree of potential injury. Warning labels which conform to the legal requirements of the Hazardous Substances Act fail to list relative alkalinity or toxicity levels. Names of hazardous ingredients and antidotes, as well as instructions for treatment, frequently are missing.

The Food and Drug Administration has the power to ban a product which it deems so hazardous that labeling will not protect the public, but this procedure has not been used for caustics or petroleum distillates.

Many household chemicals look like food, are attractively packaged, and pleasantly scented. Types of liquid furniture polish resemble milk, strawberry soda, or lemon soda.

Since almost anything within reach of tiny hands frequently will go into an infant's mouth, repackaging with child-resistant spouts might reduce the hazard. Single-use packets or a substitution of solids for liquid or powdered forms might also help.

Most important, many products can use less hazardous ingredients without loss of function. According to testimony from Cornell Aeronautical Laboratory, all brands of dishwasher detergent, regardless of causticity, are of approximately equal effectiveness. Yet alkalinity (pH value of solutions) ranges from that of lye to that of milk of magnesia. Highly caustic soda ash can be replaced by sodium tri-polyphosphate. Although the phosphate costs slightly more, less caustic brands using phosphates sell for the same price as alkaline detergents. Phosphates, however, constitute a growing source of water pollution. If there can be no salutary tradeoff between these factors, a substitute may have to be found.

The unreasonable hazards presented by household chemicals, particularly strong alkaline dishwasher detergents and petroleum-based furniture polishes, can be substantially reduced by standards requiring reformulation and protective packaging as well as by more effective warnings.

* * *

ROTARY LAWN MOWERS

On the first warm Saturday in spring, hospital emergency room crews expect a parade of patients holding a bloody towel around a lacerated or amputated hand or foot. On opening day of the grass-grooming season, the rotary power mower begins its work of trimming lawns, fingers, and toes. About 70 percent of the injuries from power mowers are lacerations, amputations, and fractures that result from the cutting and crushing action of the fast whirling blade.

In addition, there are high-velocity ejections of wire, glass, stones, and debris that can puncture vital body parts.

* * *

Missiles thrown by the rotary blades strike bystanders as well as operators. The blades hurl such debris as pebbles, nails, glass, and wires like shrapnel 50 feet or more, no matter how carefully a lawn is policed before mowing.

NOTES

1. After reviewing these and other product categories, the Commission observed: "It has been our purpose to identify these hazards, but we cannot forbear mention of ways of moderating undue risks," noting that improvements could often be made "in the original concept, in the design, in systems of assuring quality throughout production, storage, and distribution, in information for the consumer and repairman, and in methods of disposal or recycling of the product." Id. at 36.

2. The Commission noted a "dearth of factors motivating producers toward safety" and further observed that "[o]nly a few of the largest manufacturers have coherent, articulated safety engineering programs." Id. at 2.* The Commission concluded that government intervention was necessary to reduce the incidence of unreasonably hazardous products facing the consumer. Its reasoning in the following excerpts from its Final Report sheds light upon a variety of products liability and safety issues.

* This had changed materially by the late 1980s. Although products liability and safety had still not become a "central focus of most corporate decision makers in the conduct of their business," most major manufacturers by then had integrated these considerations into the corporate structure in some manner or another. N. Weber, Product Liability: The Corporate Response 15 (Conference Board Report No. 893, 1987).—Eds.

FINAL REPORT
NATIONAL COMMISSION ON PRODUCT SAFETY

Chapters 1 & 6, pp. 3–4, 69–72 (1970).

PATHS TO SAFETY

* * *

Injury Factors

There are those who believe that safety, like charity, begins at home in the behavior of the family—steadying ladders, storing knives, supervising children. Others believe that safety begins with the home itself, the environment where hazardous products find their uses—good lighting, well-insulated wiring, slipproof bathtubs and rugs, latched cabinets for medicine and household chemicals. A third view is that safety begins in the factory and involves design, construction, hazard analysis, and quality control.

None of these views is wholly right or wrong. The classical concept of epidemiology counts all three factors: host, environment, and agent. Close examination of the three uncovers many subsidiary factors: hosts of different capacities and habits; differing social, political, and psychological as well as physical environments; and agents acting in combination, additively, or serially.

With due regard for the multiple factors affecting household safety, sound strategy for a safety program is to seek the weak link in a chain of events leading to injury and to break the chain at that point.

After considering the many forces contributing to the toll of injuries in and around the American home, we have concluded that the greatest promise for reducing risks resides in energizing the manufacturer's ingenuity.

We do not mean that manufacturers by themselves can do all that is needed to achieve an optimal safety record. We mean that with Government stimulation they can accomplish more for safety with less effort and expense than any other body—more than educators, the courts, regulatory agencies, or individual consumers.

Manufacturers have it in their power to design, build, and market products in ways that will reduce if not eliminate most unreasonable and unnecessary hazards. Manufacturers are best able to take the longest strides to safety in the least time. The capacity of individual manufacturers to devise safety programs, without undue extra cost, has been demonstrated repeatedly in the course of our short history: in safety glass, double-insulated power tools, baffles on rotary mowers, noncombustible TV transformers, and releases on wringer washers.

* * *

Behavioral Factors

Danger is a regrettable but unavoidable facet of life. Many persons who like to fly, surf, dive, or speed are proud of their ability to cope with it. Usually, they are keenly conscious of the hazards and take pains to control them.

But everyone, at one time or another, suffers from complacency, a certainty that everything is under control, that injuries happen only to the other fellow. Then in that moment of carefree confidence, disaster strikes. The mower goes over a grade, slips out of control, and the blades chop at the feet. Many, with utmost care, commit themselves to handling dangerous instruments which, for lack of experience, knowledge, or skill, they cannot manage. An ineradicable minority is careless; they will wear a flammable garment near an open fire; use a power saw without a guard; work a lathe without safety glasses.

* * *

Manufacturers' Responsibility

Prospects for measurable reform of human behavior are distant. Similarly, there is little hope for an early improvement of the home environment. The limited power of conventional educational methods has been described by our witnesses.

Consequently, while continuing to educate and seeking even better ways, there seems little choice but to concentrate on reducing unreasonable hazards by encouraging additional care in the design and manufacture of products.

The law has tended in recent years to place full responsibility for injuries attributable to defective products upon the manufacturer.

But beyond his liability for damages, a producer owes society-at-large the duty to assure that unnecessary risks of injury are eliminated. He is in the best position to know what are the safest designs, materials, construction methods, and modes of use. Before anyone else, he must explore the boundaries of potential danger from the use of his product. He must be in a position to advise the buyer competently how to use and how to maintain and repair the product.

* * *

TRADE-OFFS

Every transaction implies a decision about safety costs and benefits. But to the consumer, the benefits of a product seem less related to safety than to performance, appearance, ease of operation, durability, freedom from maintenance or repair, price, availability of credit, and low down payment.

To the manufacturer, the chief benefits of a product may be marketability, ease of manufacture, economies of materials or labor, assurance of a continuing or expanding demand, and profit.

For such benefits, both manufacturer and consumer trade off certain costs. But each figures his personal costs and benefits, if he figures at all. Thus, the existing mechanism of the competitive market requires decisions on social costs and benefits by people who customarily calculate personal costs and benefits.

MARKET FORCES

The theoretical function of the market is to arrive at mutually satisfactory cost/benefit ratios for buyers and sellers. As applied to product safety, the market in theory asks, given limited resources, what goods and performance should be traded off at what cost for the removal of specific hazards?

Because absolute safety is unattainable and because every product presents some risks, the seller and buyer are compelled to decide what level of hazard is acceptable.

Increasingly, however, complex technology has diminished the consumer's ability to exercise a rational choice among risks in the market. The forces of supply and demand are distorted by unequal bargaining powers, lack of information, and other intervening factors.

The theory that a free market can reduce undue risks in consumer products is based on the assumption that the consumer has a freedom of choice in the market and, by trial and error if not by rational inquiry, is able to select or reject hazardous products.

Role of Consumer

Hendrik S. Houthakker, a member of the President's Council of Economic Advisers, testified that a buyer can decide how much safety is worth, if he understands the risks in a product and provided the transaction does not endanger others. But, Houthakker added, a buyer seldom is sufficiently informed, and most transactions with unreasonably hazardous products do endanger parties innocent of any share in the sale or purchase.

Consumers generally have no way of knowing how much more they would have to pay to obtain a comparable product as serviceable and less hazardous. Even when aware of a risk in a product, consumers cannot predict the frequency, severity, or probability of injury.

Lacking specialized technical knowledge, the consumer relies on the seller or manufacturer for guidance and information about products, their use, the inherent risks, the potential injury, and what to do about the risks. As Professor of Economics Corwin Edwards of the University of Oregon observed, "Only people trained to meet risks that they understand can cope with them reliably".

Role of Manufacturer

What can the manufacturer in a free market do to reduce unreasonable hazards? With or without effective methods of informing the consumer, a change in the product's design would seem to be the most effective solution.

When safety is enhanced at small cost, the manufacturer can scarcely excuse a failure to change. The difficulty arises when a change in design for safety sends the cost of the product up or its performance, and thus marketability, down. * * *

* * *

How High the Risk

One perplexing question * * * is, What level of risk is acceptable? * * *

Presumably, the acceptable risk will vary with the product, its utility, necessity, and inherent dangers.

* * *

CONCLUSIONS

As the Council on Trends and Perspectives of the Chamber of Commerce of the United States has recently observed:

> "The time has long since passed when the seller can successfully fall back on the argument that 'rational consumer choice' will protect the buyer * * * ".

The competitive market currently fails to reduce unreasonable hazards because, as a consequence of modern technology, consumers cannot evaluate the risks to themselves or others, and the judgments of buyers and sellers reflect a personal rather than a social interest. Product redesign, whether voluntary or enforced, appears to be the most economical method of protecting consumers from unacceptable product hazards.

Although there remains ample room for private enterprise to reduce undue risks, even in a competitive market, only a Government presence can require prompt compliance with responsible manufacturing practices in the interest of safety. * * *

NOTES

1. The Commission concluded: "Because of the inadequacy of existing controls on product hazards, we find a need for a major Federal role in the development and execution of methods to protect the American consumer." Final Report, supra, at 3. It thus proposed the creation of a federal product safety regulatory agency. Congress thereupon enacted the Consumer Product Safety Act, establishing the Consumer Product Safety Commission (CPSC). P.L. 92–573, 92nd Cong., S. 3419, Oct. 27, 1972, 15 U.S.C.A. §§ 2051–2081. Among other duties, the CPSC is directed by the Act (1) to study possible causes and cures for product accidents (§ 5), (2) to establish minimum product safety standards for products containing unreasonable hazards (§ 7), and (3) to ban products containing hazards incapable of being reduced to a reasonable level (§ 8).

2. From its inception, the CPSC has been a controversial agency. It has been criticized for being poorly organized, poorly managed, and ineffective in accomplishing its charge of reducing product accidents. President Carter considered abolishing it in 1978, and there was substantial sentiment in the House of Representatives in the late 1980s to restructure the Commission significantly. See BNA Prod.Saf. & Liab.Rep. 673 (Sept. 25, 1987). Upon his resignation from the CPSC in 1986, Commissioner Stuart Statler warned of a "cloud on the horizon" for the agency due to the reduction of funding and staff. In the previous six years, funding had declined by 34% and the staff by 41%. Such cuts "mean that, for the future, the agency will be unable to assess emerging risks from new products, or even identify them in the first place. * * * As a result, more Americans will be maimed and charred and killed before we can even begin to seek solutions." BNA Prod.Saf. & Liab.Rep. 673 (March 28, 1986).

3. The budgets of the regulatory agencies give some idea of their clout. For fiscal 1988, their budgets were as follows: CPSC—$33 million; NHTSA—$221 million; OSHA—$235 million; FDA—$477 million.

SECTION 2. THE NATURE OF PRODUCTS LIABILITY AND SAFETY LAW

"Products liability" and "product safety" are phrases used to describe the law concerning product-related accidents and illnesses. A central issue in both products liability law and product safety law is the determination of when products are fairly classifiable as "excessively" or "unreasonably" hazardous. Both areas of law are concerned with reducing the toll of accidents from such hazards. But there the parallels stop.

Product Safety Law. The law of product safety is regulatory law—the systems of rules established by legislatures and administrative agencies of federal, state, and occasionally even municipal governments to regulate the safety of products sold to the public. Its purpose is *ex ante,* to prevent unnecessary product-caused accidents and diseases before they happen.

Municipal authorities regulate the safety of certain building products through building codes and sometimes prohibit the sale of miscellaneous other products. At the state level, departments of health, employment safety, fire boards, consumer protection and other agencies administer safety laws on a variety of diverse products, such as glue, architectural glass, industrial tools and machinery, fireworks, mattresses, refrigerators, household chemicals, life preservers, power tools, toys, elevators, BB guns, sling shots, unvented gas heaters, food and drugs, blood, plastic bags and, until recently in Connecticut, used hats.* These state and local laws have aptly been described as "a hodgepodge of tragedy-inspired responses" to the product safety problem and are

* Conn.Gen.Stat.Ann. § 19–425, repealed in 1981.

generally characterized by "narrow scope, diffuse jurisdiction, miniscule budgets, absence of enforcement, mild sanctions, and casual administration." The primary administration of such laws is often through education rather than enforcement. See Final Report, National Commission on Product Safety 2, 81–88 (1970). Because of the diversity and relatively minimal impact of such laws on either product safety or liability, there is little further reference to them in this book.

Product safety law at the federal level is much more significant, although regulation even at this level has so far proved to be of questionable effectiveness in many areas. Nevertheless, various federal agencies do exert considerable control over product safety on a national scale. The CPSC, already briefly discussed above, has broad jurisdiction to regulate consumer product safety under (1) the Consumer Product Safety Act (15 U.S.C.A. § 2051 et seq.), (2) the Federal Hazardous Substances Act (15 U.S.C.A. § 1261 et seq.), (3) the Poison Prevention Packaging Act (15 U.S.C.A. § 1471 et seq.), (4) the Flammable Fabrics Act (15 U.S.C.A. § 1191 et seq.), and (5) the Refrigerator Safety Act (15 U.S.C.A. § 1211 et seq.).

Other product safety regulatory jurisdiction of major importance is vested in (1) the National Highway Traffic Safety Administration (NHTSA) of the Department of Transportation (administering the National Traffic and Motor Vehicle Safety Act of 1966, 15 U.S.C.A. § 1381 et seq.), (2) the Food and Drug Administration (FDA) of the Department of Health, Education and Welfare (administering the Federal Food, Drug, and Cosmetic Act, 21 U.S.C.A. § 301 et seq.), (3) the Occupational Safety and Health Administration (OSHA) of the Department of Labor (administering the Occupational Safety and Health Act of 1970, 29 U.S.C.A. § 651 et seq.), (4) the Federal Aviation Administration (FAA) of the Department of Transportation (administering the safety provisions of the Federal Aviation Act of 1958, 49 U.S.C.A. § 1301 et seq.), and (5) the Environmental Protection Agency (EPA) (administering the Toxic Substances Control Act, 15 U.S.C.A. § 2601 et seq., the Federal Insecticide, Fungicide, and Rodenticide Act, 7 U.S.C.A. § 135 et seq., and the Clean Air Act (including regulation of asbestos removal) 42 U.S.C.A. § 7412).

These and other federal agencies also regulate the safety of pesticides, fungicides, meat, poultry, eggs, perishable agricultural commodities, railroad safety appliances, firearms, firearm carriage, cigarette labeling, and boat safety. Federal regulation of product safety is considered at various points in the book.

For general information on federal regulation of product safety, see BNA Product Safety & Liability Reporter; BNA Occupational Safety & Health Reporter, CCH Consumer Product Safety Guide, and CCH Food Drug Cosmetic Law Reports.

Products Liability Law. The law of products liability governs the private litigation of product accidents. Its rules define the legal responsibility of the seller or other transferor of a product for damages caused by that product.

Products liability law is full of mixtures. It is a mixture of tort law—negligence, strict tort, and deceit—and of the contract law of sales—mostly warranty. It is a mixture of common law, especially on its tort side, and statutory law, generally on its contract side—today notably the Uniform Commercial Code. In addition, state legislatures are increasingly enacting products liability "reform" acts which may cover actions in both tort and contract. Because of these hybrid characteristics of products liability law, plaintiffs in such actions often have a variety of bases of recovery to allege. Negligence, strict liability in tort, and the contract law claim for breach of implied warranty are based on the notion that something was wrong with the product, that it was "defective" or excessively dangerous. Remedies for breach of express warranty and tortious misrepresentation are available where the product turns out to have been more dangerous than it was stated to be, even though it may not have been defective or unfit when tested by standards of negligence or implied warranty.

As will be seen throughout the book, many of the most difficult products liability issues facing courts today spring from the doctrinal mixture of contract and tort. This blending of doctrines has generated perplexing questions involving, for example, the standard of liability, defenses, statutes of limitation, and the type of damages recoverable.

A typical products liability case will involve a claim for damages against the manufacturer or retailer of a product by a person injured while using the product. The plaintiff will seek to prove that his injury was caused by some deficiency in the way the product was made or marketed—that the product was in some manner "defective." He will also seek to demonstrate that he was using the product properly or at least in a predictable manner. His damages sought will typically include medical expenses, disability and disfigurement, pain and suffering, lost earnings and earning capacity, perhaps some kind of property damage, and possibly damage to the product itself. The defendant usually will attempt to show that the product was *not* defective—that it was in fact reasonably made and reasonably marketed. Further, the defendant will often seek to establish that the accident was largely the result of the plaintiff's (or some other person's) improper use of the product. These are the central issues in a typical case.

In some cases, however, the transaction may not involve a sale. The product may have been leased or merely loaned by the owner. Or the injury-producing "product" may not be a typical, mass-produced chattel but instead a house, a toxic substance, a recipe, electricity, or a poisonous spider in a pair of pants. Or the defendant may be a wholesaler, component part manufacturer, employer, publisher, hospital, trademark owner, or the federal government.

All of these examples raise questions about the outer boundaries of products liability law. What really is a "product"? To what kinds of transactions should products liability principles apply? Where should the line be drawn between products liability and professional malpractice? Landlord-tenant law? Workers' compensation?

These are some of the issues of products liability law—the primary topic of this book.

SECTION 3. EARLY PRODUCTS LIABILITY LAW

Products liability law, as we know it today, is of recent origin. As late as 1955, for example, one writer remarked, "Products liability does not yet rank as a term of art in the courts of law." Wilson, Products Liability (pt. 1), 43 Calif.L.Rev. 614 (1955). With the exception of a few cases involving fraud and the sale of defective medicines and food, the appearance of products liability cases in the law reports coincides with the rise of the industrial revolution in the late 1800s. By 1900, such cases begin to appear with some frequency. The birth of modern products liability law may safely be dated at 1916 with the case of MacPherson v. Buick Motor Co., 217 N.Y. 382, 111 N.E. 1050, decided by Judge Cardozo of the New York Court of Appeals. And while modern products liability law was "born" in 1916, it was "revolutionized" in the late 1950s and early 1960s with the development of generalized theories of strict manufacturer liability in both warranty and tort.

Though products liability cases prior to the last quarter of the 19th century are few in number, the roots of products liability law reach deep into history. Most of its early beginnings are found in the tort-contract hybrid warranties of quality, express and implied.

Roman Law. In ancient Rome, the law of tort (*delict*) was quite undeveloped and apparently afforded little if any protection to a person injured by a defective product. Nor did the law of sales (*emptio venditio*) aid the disappointed purchaser much under the early classical law as set forth in the Twelve Tables of 450 B.C. "The original principle [although not the maxim] of the civil law was *caveat emptor* ["let the buyer beware"]. The seller was not liable for any defects in the thing unless he had by *stipulatio* expressly undertaken such liability." B. Nicholas, An Introduction to Roman Law 181 (1962).

Under the rule of the curules aediles, who were magistrates charged (from 367 B.C.) with policing activities in the public market, limited implied warranty protection was extended to the purchase of slaves and cattle. By the time of Justinian (553 A.D.), a basic warranty of quality against latent defects was apparently being implied in the sale of goods in general. The extent of damages recoverable for breach, however, apparently still depended upon whether the seller knew of the defect and failed to disclose it.

Early English Law. As we move from the laws of Justinian to the early English law of the Middle Ages, we observe a shift from a moderately sophisticated system of sales law to one that was crude at best. Indeed, private law, under which an aggrieved purchaser might sue his seller for damages caused by defective goods, was largely unknown in early England. Instead, there developed a rustic and localized criminal law that was designed to protect the public more from being cheated than injured. The Roman law's insistence on the fair quality of goods sold found its way into medieval English law through the dominant role in society of the church, whose scholars were trained in the civil law.

HAMILTON, THE ANCIENT MAXIM CAVEAT EMPTOR

40 Yale L.J. 1133, 1136–64 (1931).

Caveat emptor is not to be found among the reputable ideas of the Middle Ages. As custom of trade or rule of law it is not to be met with upon the highways of mediaeval culture. To priest and lord, to yeoman and villain, and even to burgl[a]r and lawyer, it would have fallen strangely upon the ear. They did not talk that language.

* * *

The church manuals, even as late as the seventeenth century, laid down standards of mercantile conduct for Christians. [Thomas] Aquinas [1225?–1274 A.D.], theologian or lawyer as you will, discusses with his usual common sense and his usual display of neat distinctions, the delicate problems which traffic in wares brings. In his didactic fashion he asks, "Is a sale rendered unlawful by a defect in the thing sold?" He answers that a defect in kind, in quantity, or in quality, if known to the vendor and unrevealed, is sin and fraud, and the sale is void. If the defect be unknown it is no sin. Yet the seller must make good to the buyer his loss, and likewise the buyer must recompense the seller if he discovers that he has received more than he paid for. He next inquires, "Is the seller bound to mention any flaw in the thing sold?" By an argument that moves straight to its appointed result, he concludes that the seller is bound to reveal secret flaws that may occasion loss through a decrease in the value of the article or danger through the ware becoming harmful in use. But if the flaw is manifest, he is not bound to reveal it "by any duty of justice," though to do so would exhibit "the more exuberant virtue." His judgment accords with an ancient adage that "a buyer's eye is his merchant where the defect is obvious." * * *

* * *

It was in the courts of custom, of manor and baron, of leet and tolsey, that secular justice made its most immediate contact with the activities of the people. At the beginning life was lived very close to the soil, a standard hardly up to subsistence prevailed, the list of necessities which demanded protection was short, the wares which came to an intermittent market and fell under control were few. As the crafts increased in number and claimed more followers, the scrutiny of the community was progressively extended. The intent of the folkways, which were just passing into law, was to insure an open market, a fair price, an honest measure, and a quality good after the fashion of the day. * * *

[A system of regulation of quality slowly developed that was more criminal than civil in nature.]

As trade lost its adventitious character, the fair was succeeded by the market town. The b[o]rough * * * claimed over manufacture and sale the control which the manor had exercised over agriculture; upon the ancient foundations, in the spirit of the authoritarian ideal, it erected a detailed and elaborate system of regulation. The gilds, decked out in the trappings of religious orders and dedicated to the worship of God, Our Lady the Virgin, and all the Saints, held themselves out to serve as roundly as any Rotary Club. The conduct of the several handicrafts were regulated by their own statutes, which became rather generally ordinances of the town. Their enforcement rested with the officers of the gild, under the oversight of officials of the city. The Mayor and Alderman constituted an authority which was alike an administrative body and a court. Away from the marts of organized trade were to be found the wayfaring palmer with his relics and trinkets, the peripatetic peddlar with gew-gaws and ornaments, strangers here today and there tomorrow, wayfaring men of no place and without the law. In such wares one had to trade at his peril; there was no authentic test for holy water and bones of the saints, for Venetian glass and spices of Araby. Nor could a standard have been used; before the latent became the obvious fault, the itinerant was far on his unknown way. * * * There, too, was the horse-trader, the erratic properties of whose merchandise could not be reduced to a standard model; he was not expected to cry the uncertain defects of his steed or nag from the house-tops. Among such persons without rank or of mean estate a redress of wrongs was practically not to be had. It took time and the bitterness of experience to subdue the idea into compact language; but here it came to be understood that one's unconsidered bargain was his own tough luck.

How the trick of phrase was turned, and *caveat emptor* came into being we do not know. The wisdom seems to be the afterthought of the good man who has bargained, perhaps in a horse trade, once too often; the manner suggests the lawyer regretfully stating that the grievance seems to be without redress. * * *

* * *

The expression *caveat emptor,* in its upward climb, appears in print for the first time well along in the sixteenth century. * * * An ordinance of Lancaster, relating to the purchase of malt, ignored the distinction between obvious and latent defects and restated an old proverb, "let their eye be their chapman." [208] At the beginning of the

208. [Citation.] The date is 1562. "It was proverbial in France, '*qui n'ouvre pas yeux doit ouvrir la bourse.*'" [Citation.]

seventeenth century the expression appears to be quite well known. * * * [A much-quoted passage from Coke on Littleton (1633), provided:] "Note that by the civil law every man is bound to warrant the thing he selleth or conveyeth, albeit there be no express warranty, either in deed or in law; but the common law bindeth him not, for *caveat emptor.*"

Coke on Littleton

NOTE

The maxim of *caveat emptor* first appears in the law reports in 1601. Moore v. Hussey, 80 Eng.Rep. 243. Two years later, the judges and barons of the Exchequer-Chamber decided the famous case of the bezoar stone, Chandler v. Lopus, 79 Eng.Rep. 3 (1603). Plaintiff alleged that the defendant goldsmith sold him a stone "which he affirmed to Lopus to be a bezar-stone * * * for one hundred pounds; *ubi revera* it was not a bezar-stone: the defendant pleaded not guilty, and verdict was given and judgment entered for the plaintiff in the King's Bench." Holding the declaration deficient, the Exchequer–Chamber reversed. "[T]he bare affirmation that it was a bezar-stone, without warranting it to be so, is no cause of action: and although he knew it to be no bezar-stone, it is not material; for every one in selling his wares will affirm that his wares are good, or the horse which he sells is sound; yet if he does not warrant them to be so, it is no cause of action * * *."

As Chandler v. Lopus came to be interpreted, it announced a simple rule governing the rights of the buyer of inferior goods: "He had a cause of action if he had exacted an express warranty at the time of the sale from a seller who knew his representations to be false. An affirmation, no matter how many holy saints were invoked, fell short of a warranty; latent defects, however impervious to ordinary vision, were the purchaser's own lookout. When in time writs were accommodated more sharply to specific complaints, * * * the buyer had the alternative of a suit in assumpsit on express warranty or in deceit by proving a *scienter.* The exactions of a ceremonial were set down as an injunction to the buyer to look to himself for protection." Hamilton, *supra,* at 1168–69. For the next two centuries, except for cases of fraud, or breach of express warranty, *caveat emptor* ruled supreme.

Early American Law. The courts in early nineteenth-century America adopted the notion of *caveat emptor* with a gusto reflecting the country's devotion to individualism and free enterprise.* And while

* That the doctrine of *caveat emptor* was the prevailing legal ethic during the seventeenth and eighteenth centuries is the conventional historical wisdom. See, e.g., Prosser, The Implied Warranty of Merchantable Quality, 27 Minn.L.Rev. 117 (1943), infra p. 117. At least in the eighteenth and early nineteenth centuries, how-

some courts began to impose an implied warranty of quality on manufacturers (and growers) toward the end of the century, the *caveat emptor* principle persisted in most states in retailer cases through the end of the century. See, e.g., National Oil Co. v. Rankin, 68 Kan. 679, 75 P. 1013 (1904). The following remarks of the Supreme Court in Barnard v. Kellogg, 77 U.S. (10 Wall.) 383, 388–89, 19 L.Ed. 987 (1870), are illustrative:

> No principle of the common law has been better established, or more often affirmed, both in this country and in England, than that in sales of personal property, in the absence of express warranty, where the buyer has a opportunity to inspect the commodity, and the seller is guilty of no fraud, and is neither the manufacturer nor grower of the article he sells, the maxim of *caveat emptor* applies. Such a rule, requiring the purchaser to take care of his own interests, has been found best adapted to the wants of trade in the business transactions of life. And there is no hardship in it, because if the purchaser distrusts his judgment he can require of the seller a warranty that the quality or condition of the goods he desires to buy corresponds with the sample exhibited. * * * Of such universal acceptance is the doctrine of *caveat emptor* in this country, that the courts of all the States in the Union where the common law prevails, with one exception (South Carolina), sanction it.

As the functions of manufacturing and retailing increasingly separated with the industrialization of the nation in the nineteenth century, the law developed another obstacle to consumer recovery. Winterbottom v. Wright, 10 M. & W. 109, 152 Eng.Rep. 402 (Ex.1842), and its progeny made clear that an action would not lie against a "remote" manufacturer with whom the plaintiff had no "privity of contract." See, e.g., Lebourdais v. Vitrified Wheel Co., 194 Mass. 341, 80 N.E. 482 (1907); Loop v. Litchfield, 42 N.Y. 351 (1870).

The privity requirement was an effective instrument of social policy for a nation bent on promoting the development of its infant industry. One court explained: "If a contractor who erects a house, who builds a bridge, or performs any other work; a manufacturer who constructs a boiler, a piece of machinery, or a steamship, owes a duty to the whole world, that his work or his machine or his steamship, shall contain no hidden defect, it is difficult to measure the extent of his responsibility, and no prudent man would engage in such occupations

ever, there is evidence of some pockets of resistance to the doctrine in the form of support for an implied warranty of quality, in a few American jurisdictions and possibly in England, perhaps reflecting aberrational mercantile customs in certain areas. Yet once the nineteenth century was well under way, apparently all American jurisdictions except South Carolina adhered to the principle of *caveat emptor*. See generally M. Horwitz, The Transformation of American Law, 1780–1860, at 167, 180, 330 n. 13 (1977). Horwitz argues, however, that a "sound price" rule *generally* prevailed during the seventeenth and eighteenth century and that the *caveat emptor* notion did not take hold until about 1800.

upon such conditions. It is safer and wiser to confine such liabilities to the parties immediately concerned." Curtin v. Somerset, 140 Pa. 70, 80, 21 A. 244, 245 (1891). At least one early scholar disagreed: "To encourage commerce and industry by removing all duty and incentive to protect the public is to invite wholesale sacrifice of individual rights on the altar of commercial greed. * * * While it is undoubtedly to the interests of society, especially in a country the natural resources of which are still comparatively undeveloped, to encourage trade and manufacture, it cannot be to the interest of any community to encourage carelessness and disregard of human life and property therein." Bohlen, The Basis of Affirmative Obligations in the Law of Tort (pt. 3), 53 U.Pa.L.Rev. 337, 355 (1905).

"Modern" products liability law, and Chapter 2, begin with the fall of the privity defense in negligence cases occasioned by MacPherson v. Buick Motor Company in 1916.

On the Roman law origins of products liability, see W. Buckland, A Text–Book of Roman Law from Augustus to Justinian 491–94 (3d ed. Stein rev. 1966); R. Lee, The Elements of Roman Law 13, 15, 314–16 (4th ed. 1956); J. Thomas, Textbook of Roman Law 15, 16, 286–88 (1976); F. de Zulueta, The Roman Law of Sale 46–51, 124 (corr. ed. 1945). On the common-law background, see Bohlen, The Basis of Affirmative Obligations in the Law of Tort (pts. 2 & 3), 53 U.Pa.L.Rev. 273, 337 (1905); Hamilton, The Ancient Maxim Caveat Emptor, 40 Yale L.J. 1133 (1931); Llewellyn, On Warranty of Quality, and Society (pts. 1 & 2), 36 Colum.L.Rev. 699 (1936), 37 Colum.L.Rev. 341 (1937); Prosser, The Implied Warranty of Merchantable Quality, 27 Minn.L.Rev. 117, 118–22 (1943).

SECTION 4. MODERN PRODUCTS LIABILITY LAW

A. AN ANATOMY OF MODERN PRODUCTS LIABILITY LITIGATION

As a prelude to examining the rules of products liability law as presently applied by the courts, it is helpful to acquire an overview of the nature of such litigation. A comprehensive study of products liability litigation was conducted under the auspices of the Interagency Task Force on Product Liability, formed in 1976 to study the increase in products liability litigation and resulting insurance premiums. Under the direction of Professor Victor Schwartz, working out of The Department of Commerce, the Task Force analyzed 655 decisions in eight state and ten federal courts over the period 1965–76. The Task Force report, released in 1977, revealed the following information:

The Forum

Seventy-eight per cent of the cases were tried in state court, 22% in federal court. (Only in Pennsylvania were more cases tried in federal court.)

Suit was usually brought in the state where the injury occurred, usually *not* where the product was manufactured, and almost always in the plaintiff's home state.

Juries heard 86% of the cases tried.

Increase in Cases

The number of products liability cases reported in the eight states doubled from 1965–70 to 1971–76.

Type of Product

About one-third of all the cases involved the automobile, followed in frequency by industrial-type machinery and construction and loading equipment.

Parties

The injured party (rather than another party seeking to recoup losses already paid to the injured party) was plaintiff in 96% of the cases. Manufacturers were defendants in 79% of the cases, retailers in 33%, wholesalers 5%, manufacturers' suppliers 5%, employers 4%, lessors 3%, and installers 5%.

Manufacturers were third-party plaintiffs in 15% of the cases in which they were original defendants; retailers in 16%. Manufacturers were third-party defendants in about 10% of the cases; employers in 8%.

Age of Product

About 10% of the products were over 20 years old, 4% were over 25. However, when automobiles are excluded, 21% of the products were over 20 years and 10% exceeded 25 years of age.

Work-Related Injuries

In 1965–70, 46% of the cases involved work-related injuries (as from machinery and tools) increasing to 50% in 1971–76.

Type of Defect

The bases of liability asserted were manufacturing (and inadequate inspection) defects in 42% of the cases, design defects in 39%, and warning defects in 21%. The product was purportedly unavoidably unsafe in about 2% of the cases. (By comparison, a 1973 survey indicated the following breakdown for 222 cases brought in strict tort: manufacturing defects—28%; design defects—46%; warning defects—25%; and misrepresentation—1%.) Of the automotive cases, 54% involved claims of defective manufacture, 39% defective design, and

7% inadequate warnings. Of the machinery cases, 57% involved claims of defective design, 27% defective manufacture, and 15% inadequate warnings. Most of the container cases alleged defective manufacture, most of the recreation product cases alleged defective design, and most of the chemical cases alleged inadequate warnings. Allegations of unavoidably unsafe products were largely in the chemical cases.

Prevailing Party

Plaintiffs prevailed in 50% of all the cases, defendants in 50% . Of cases decided on the merits, plaintiffs prevailed 41% of the time in Arizona, 44% in Illinois, 58% in California, and 63% in Texas. Plaintiffs won 60% of the jury trials but only 44% of the non-jury trials. (The latter figure may be misleading, however, since plaintiffs in non-jury trials are frequently not the injured party.)

Plaintiffs won 50% of the manufacturing defect (and inadequate inspection) cases, 49% of the warnings cases, 46% of the design defect cases, and 31% of the unavoidably unsafe cases.

From the 1965–70 period to 1971–76, the rate of successful plaintiff cases rose 4%.

Damages

The average damage award in cases in which the plaintiff ultimately prevailed rose from $104,000 in 1965–70 to $222,000 in 1971–76, for an average over the entire period of $181,000. By state, average damage awards for the entire period were as follows: California ($272,000), Texas ($221,000), New York ($170,000), Pennsylvania ($137,000), and Illinois ($119,000). Much of the increase in awards between the two periods was attributable to inflation, especially the cost of medical care which is often the largest component of products liability claims.

NOTE

The above information is collected in Product Liability: Final Report of the Legal Study, vol. 3 (Interagency Task Force on Product Liability: U.S. Dept. of Comm., 1977), and summarized in id., vol. 1, at 17–18.

A comprehensive insurance industry survey completed in 1977 found that less than 4% of all products liability claims went all the way to verdict and, in contrast to the findings of the Task Force, fewer than 25% of the defendants in these cases were found liable. See Highlights, Insurance Services Office Product Liability Closed Claim Survey: A Technical Analysis of Survey Results 6 (1977).

An insurance industry study of large products liability claims closed in 1985 reveals the following data on claims in excess of $100,000. Although such claims represent only 1–2% of all products liability claims, they account for 50–60% of payments by insurers.

Payments at Various Stages of Litigation

In the 4% of large claims where no suit was filed, the average payment was $232,000. In the 71% of claims where suit was filed, but where settlement was reached before trial, payments averaged $441,000. Where settlement was reached during trial (14% of the cases), payments averaged $649,000. In cases that went to verdict (11%), payments averaged $532,000.

Theory of Liability

Strict liability was the only theory alleged in 22% of the claims; negligence the only theory in 15%; and breach of warranty the only theory in 3%. All three theories of liability were alleged in 30% of the claims; strict liability and negligence were alleged in 14%; negligence and breach of warranty in 8%; and strict liability and breach of warranty in 7%.

Strict liability was the main theory relied upon in settlement in 60% of the cases, negligence in 31%, and warranty in 8%.

Type of Defect

Where strict liability was the main theory of liability, defective design was the applicable theory in 75% of the claims, and warning defects in 18%.

Punitive Damages

Punitive damages were demanded in 18% of the incidents; separate payments for such damages were awarded by a jury or paid for in settlement in 1% of the cases. Yet the threat of such damages probably increased the size of other settlements.

Number of Defendants

There was only one defendant in 56% of the cases. There were two defendants in 22%, three defendants in 9%, four defendants in 6%, and more than four in 7%.

Miscellaneous Issues

In the opinion of the claim reviewers, the question of product defect was too technical for the jury to understand and decide in 17% of the incidents; damage, alteration, modification, or misuse was a cause of the accident in 34% of the incidents; and 12% of the products failed to comply with governmental safety standards.

NOTES

1. The above data is from A Study of Large Product Liability Claims Closed in 1985, a joint study of the Alliance of American Insurers (L. Soular, Research Department) and the American Insurance Association (1986).

2. A recent study, based upon cases from the late 1970s, found that 19% of the products liability claims filed were dropped, and 95% of the remainder

were settled. Of the 5% that went to verdict, plaintiffs won 37% and lost 63%. Viscusi, The Determinants of the Disposition of Product Liability Claims and Compensation for Bodily Injury, 15 J.Leg.Stud. 321 (1986). By contrast, a Rand Corporation study indicated that plaintiffs won about 50% of the products liability trials in San Francisco and Cook County, Illinois in the early 1980s. D. Hensler, Summary of Research Results on Products Liability (Institute for Civil Justice, Oct. 1986).

3. The plaintiff success rate and size of products liability verdicts varied considerably among regions in the early 1980s. The success rates and median awards in various locations were as follows: Maricopa County, Arizona: 44%—$135,000; Los Angeles: 44%—$428,000; San Diego: 30%—$255,000; Cook County, Illinois: 35%—$279,000; New York, N.Y.: 61% —$1,132,000. Six cases were tried in Westchester, N.Y. The plaintiff won only one (17%), and recovered $16,710. Daniels & Martin, Jury Verdicts and the "Crisis" in Civil Justice: Some Findings from an Empirical Study (American Bar Foundation, unpublished paper, 1987) (tables 2 and 4).

B. A CASE EXAMPLE

---

1. THE PROBLEM

ROBERTS, CIRCULAR SAW DESIGN: A HAZARD ANALYSIS

1 J.Prod.Liab 127 (1977).

The portable electric circular power saw has grown in popularity to the point that there are over 30 million currently in use in the United States alone. With their increasing use and availability at a low price has come an associated trend toward home use and a paralleled use by the untrained or novice user.

[The CPSC's Bureau of Epidemiology studied in depth seventy-four of the 5,000 accidents that involved portable circular saws in 1975.]

* * *

The greatest value provided by the in-depth reports is to be found in the narrative discussion of the accident circumstances. Three types of circumstances predominate in studying circular saw accidents. They are:

(1) *Human Error:* For thirty-three of the seventy-four cases, operator error is the only appropriate description of the accident process. * * * A truly incredible number of individuals saw directly into their hands or legs which frequently are beneath the piece they are sawing. It is difficult to conceive of a mechanical solution to this type of accident.

Another significant group covered under operator error involved guards which were tied back or removed. While there may be circumstances under which guard tieback or removal will improve operability, the inherent danger of kickback, binding, or blade free wheeling has apparently not been stressed sufficiently to adequately warn the users (Philo and Rine, 1977). Turning a portable saw upside down and trying to use it as a table saw also falls into the same category. [Other operator errors reported were, "hand slipped into saw," "put hand in saw," "walked into saw," "changing blades while saw plugged in," and electrocution from cutting cord or using improper extension cord.]

* * *

(2) *Guards Which Failed to Operate:* Circular saws are commonly equipped with a retractable lower guard which slides up into the housing over the top of the blade while cutting. The guard is pulled by a spring or falls due to gravity over the lower part of the blade after the cut is completed. There were seventeen occasions when the guards failed to operate properly and prevent the accident. * * *

These accidents consistently involve the leg of the victim. The usual set of circumstances involves an operator, who when finished with a cut, will lower his hand to his side. The guard fails to return to its position over the bottom of the blade and the still-turning blade cuts deeply into the upper or lower leg.

This injury is interesting because it is so correctable. In a subsequent section the actual circumstances involving a specific saw will be developed and the simple design measure which could have yielded a solution is described.

There were also accidents which implied guard failure wherein the guard apparently operated by gravity. There is an indication from the reports that the saw kickback which caused the injury could have been prevented had a spring with significant retarding force been present to restore the guard before the blade came in contact with the operator. In either event the accidents could not be attributed to the user but rather to the design specifications and manufacturing procedures of the manufacturer. * * *

(3) *Saw Kickback:* [The third predominant cause of circular saw injuries is from "saw kickback." This phenomenon sometimes occurs when the blade binds, or hits a knot or defect in the wood. It is usually preventable by the addition of a safety device, a "riving knife," which "acts as a wedge behind the blade to prevent the wood from closing around the blade and binding."]

Injury Data—Detailed Investigation

The mass data regarding portable circular saw accidents as well as the results acquired through the mechanism of the in-depth accident investigations have yielded a great deal of information regarding the nature, pattern and causal factors associated with saw design and injury. This section concerns an analysis of a saw involved in an

Figure 4: Circular Saw with Lower Guard in Down Position

accident during its first day of use. Figure 4 shows the saw with the blade guard in the down position.

The saw involved was a Skilsaw Model 537 manufactured by the Skil Corporation, Chicago, Illinois. It is powered by a $1^7/_8$ horsepower motor and operates at 5200 r.p.m. At this angular velocity with a $7^1/_4$ inch blade, the blade edge velocity is 164.5 feet per second or 112 mph.

At the time of the accident the victim who is regularly employed as a carpentry contractor was using his new saw while working on a ladder to cut rafters over his head. He completed a cut, released the trigger and lowered his arm to his side. The blade guard failed to return to the closed position and as a result the still rotating blade produced a deep and extensive laceration in the victim's right thigh.

* * * Figure 4 illustrates the saw as it was received for analysis. Note that the blade guard can be pushed to the full open position and that it will remain open and not snap back to protect the blade.

Physical examination revealed that the action of the blade guard is controlled either manually by the plastic lever at the top of the saw or

Figure 5: Circular Saw with Lower Guard in Up Position Held in Place by Friction

by stock being cut physically pushing the lower guard up into the housing. As the guard is pushed up a small coil spring attached at one end to the fixed upper guard and at the other to the movable lower guard is stretched around the motor shaft-mandrel.

The stretching of the spring produces a restoring force and associated torque which tends to cause the lower housing to automatically return to the closed position. When the lower guard is fully pushed into the upper position exposing the blade as shown in Figure 5, the spring is stretched a total of two and one half inches. The spring was removed from the saw and found to have a spring constant of one pound of developed force per inch of extension. Thus the maximum force which the spring could develop to return the guard to the down position is two and one half pounds.

While the spring was removed, the saw blade was removed as well and the force required to return the guard to the down position measured as shown in Figure 6. The restoring force was measured with a Pelouze tension scale model 10–T modified to record the maximum force exerted. Ten trials produced force values which ranged

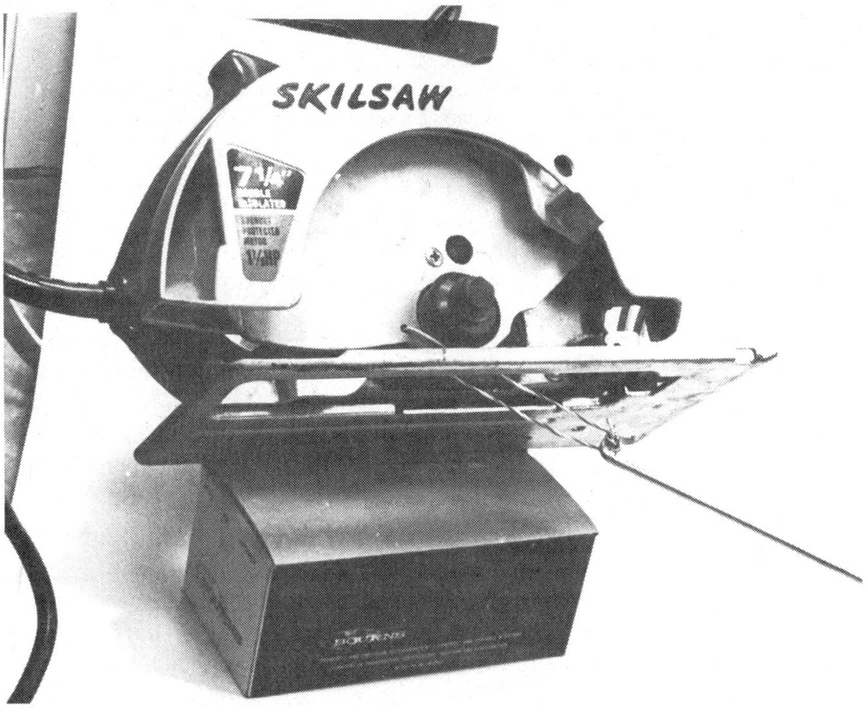

Figure 6: Procedure Used to Measure Force Necessary to Restore Lower Guard to Down Position

from three to four and one half pounds. The average force required was three and three quarter pounds.

As was indicated earlier, the maximum force which the spring—designed and installed by the manufacturer—could produce was two and one half pounds. Given the physical evidence above, it is easy to see why the guard did not return to the closed position, thus exposing the victim's leg to the still-turning blade.

This particular saw involves both problems of design and manufacturing liability. The blade guard tends to stay in the upper position because of friction and binding between the upper and lower guards. This is usually the result of poor quality control over the dimensional tolerances of the finished parts. Dimensional interference which produce friction and binding can be overcome by the spring. However, the spring must be stiff enough to develop sufficient force when it is extended. If the saw in question had had a spring of proper design or parts of proper dimension, the accident described above could [not] have occurred.

* * *

* * * Safe design is not an accident. The circular power saw proves the point.

NOTE

The Roberts article illustrates the type of failure analysis engineers are capable of providing to lawyers handling products liability cases. This type of assistance is invaluable to the lawyer throughout the case, from the initial investigatory stages through trial.

---

2. THE REGULATORY RESPONSE

Two federal agencies have jurisdiction over the safety of portable power circular saws: the Consumer Product Safety Commission and the Occupational Safety and Health Administration. In 1976, the CPSC issued a "Product Profile" on consumer power saws, including portable power circular saws, describing the nature and frequency of accidents from such saws. In 1977 the CPSC accorded power saws a "medium" priority for the issuance of safety standards. See 42 Fed.Reg. 47,859 (1977). As of 1988, the agency still had not issued such standards.

The Occupational Safety and Health Administration has jurisdiction over the safety of portable power circular saws used in the workplace. It has issued the following general industry job safety and health standard:

GUARDING OF PORTABLE POWERED TOOLS

29 CFR § 1910.243 (1988).

(a) Portable Powered Tools.

(1) *Portable Circular Saws.* (i) All portable, power-driven circular saws having a blade diameter greater than 2 in. shall be equipped with guards above and below the base plate or shoe. The upper guard shall cover the saw to the depth of the teeth, except for the minimum arc required to permit the base to be tilted for bevel cuts. The lower guard shall cover the saw to the depth of the teeth, except for the minimum arc required to allow proper retraction and contact with the work. When the tool is withdrawn from the work, the lower guard shall automatically and instantly return to covering position.

NOTES

1. An identical standard covers the construction industry. See 29 CFR 1926.304(d) (1988). These are apparently the only OSHA regulations specifically governing the safety of portable power circular saws. Cf. 29 CFR 1910.213(d)–(h) (1988).

2. Do you think the OSHA regulations adequately address the safety hazards in portable power circular saws? Why do you suppose the CPSC

accorded such tools only a "medium" priority for regulation? Why do you suppose they have never issued safety standards?

---

3. THE JUDICIAL RESPONSE

AGOSTINO v. ROCKWELL MANUFACTURING COMPANY

Superior Court of Pennsylvania, 1975.
236 Pa.Super. 434, 345 A.2d 735.

Spaeth, Judge.

* * *

* * * During the month of November, 1969, appellant purchased from appellee Greensburg Lumber & Mill Company a power saw manufactured by appellee Rockwell Manufacturing Company. At the time, appellant was employed as a manager of the Modern Tea Room in Greensburg, Pennsylvania, and his duties included remodeling the restaurant building. Appellant was familiar with power saws since he had used them for approximately twenty-five years in various carpentry jobs. The Rockwell saw that appellant had purchased was constructed so that after the completion of a cut, a telescopic guard would be automatically released from the housing, covering the blade and thereby preventing the user from being cut. On December 16, 1969, appellant went to the restaurant to finish the work he had begun on a second floor wall. He had owned the saw for approximately one month and had used it approximately ten times; no one else had used it. On this specific day, he was going to use the saw to cut 2″ by 8″ boards. He plugged in the saw, checked the telescopic guard to make sure it was operating properly, and cut two boards. After each cut he put the saw on a bench behind him. On the third cut, appellant finished severing the board, but as he attempted to put the saw on the rear bench the blade grabbed his trousers and cut deeply into his thigh. He dropped the saw on the floor. As he moved away to keep the saw (which was still running) from cutting his feet, he noticed that the telescopic guard was not covering the blade but was "jammed" in the housing.

[Plaintiff-appellant sued appellees in strict tort and, at the conclusion of his case, was nonsuited by the trial court. Plaintiff-appellant's motion to remove the nonsuit was denied, and this appeal followed.]

In Webb v. Zern, 422 Pa. 424, 220 A.2d 853 (1966), our Supreme Court expressly adopted Section 402A of the Restatement (Second) of Torts, which provides:

> (1) One who sells any product in a defective condition unreasonably dangerous to the user or to his property is subject to liability for physical harm thereby caused to the ultimate user or consumer, or to his property, if

(a) the seller is engaged in the business of selling such a product, and

(b) it is expected to and does reach the user or consumer without substantial change in the condition in which it is sold.

(2) The rule stated in Subsection (1) applies although

(a) The seller has exercised all possible care in the preparation and sale of his product, and

(b) The user or consumer has not bought the product from or entered into any contractual relation with the seller.

Here, as has been mentioned, appellant stated that he bought the saw from appellee Greensburg Lumber & Mill Company and that appellee Rockwell Manufacturing Company made the saw. There was therefore sufficient evidence to establish that appellees were "engaged in the business of selling" the saw. To maintain his action under § 402A, however, appellant also had to show that the saw had a defect that was unreasonably dangerous to the user, that the defect existed when the saw left Rockwell's plant, and that there was a causal connection between the defect and appellant's injury. [Citations.]

I

Appellees argue that there was insufficient evidence to allow the jury to infer that a defect existed because the record does not contain any evidence establishing a specific defect. If this were a negligence suit, that absence would be fatal to appellant's case, for in a negligence suit the plaintiff must connect his injury with a specific defect in the manufacture or design of a product. MacDougall v. Ford Motor Co., 214 Pa.Super. 384, 387, 257 A.2d 676, 678 (1969), allocatur refused, 215 Pa.Super. xxxviii. Mere proof that an accident happened as alleged is not sufficient proof that the defendant was negligent. Radio v. Reading L.G.S. & Soc., 197 Pa.Super. 509, 513, 178 A.2d 789, 791 (1962). However, in Greco v. Bucciconi Engineering Co., 283 F.Supp. 978 (W.D.Pa. 1967), aff'd, 407 F.2d 87 (3d Cir.1969), the district court in construing Pennsylvania law held that § 402A actions are governed by the evidentiary standards of warranty law, not by the evidentiary standards of negligence law. There, a steel company employee was injured because a magnetic sheet piler malfunctioned. At trial he did not attempt to trace this malfunction to any particular part of the piler, nor did he try by expert testimony otherwise to offer a theory for the malfunction. The issue was simply whether "the mere occurrence of a malfunction by machinery evidence[s] a 'defective condition' within the meaning of Section 402A of the Restatement." Id. at 981. The district court held that the plaintiff's evidence was sufficient to maintain his action because under warranty law proof that the product functioned improperly in the absence of abnormal use and reasonable secondary causes establishes circumstantially that there was a defective condition.

* * *

In the present case, it will be recalled, appellant testified that the telescopic guard on the saw would be automatically released, covering the blade and thereby preventing the user from being cut, that the saw functioned properly on the first two cuts, but that on the third it did not.

A. * * * On the third piece I was cutting, when [I] was setting the guard, it didn't come back and got a hold of my trouser and cut through to my leg and I let it drop on the floor.

Q. Let's go through this with some detail. What do you mean the telescopic guard did not come back? Where was it?

A. In that position (indicating). It was jammed.

Later, on cross-examination, appellant stated that he did not actually notice where the guard was at the very moment his leg was injured, but that he assumed it was still in the housing because his leg was cut and the guard was "jammed" in the housing immediately after the accident.

The lower court in its opinion and appellees in their briefs state that it cannot be inferred from this testimony that there was a malfunction at all. * * * Because a malfunction did not occur on the first or second cut does not mean it did not occur on the third; and it would be most unreasonable to bar recovery because appellant did not observe the location of the guard at the moment his leg was being lacerated. The jury could have properly inferred from appellant's testimony that the guard did not function properly. Since there was no evidence of abnormal use or secondary causes, this evidence was sufficient, under *Greco, MacDougall,* and their progeny, to establish a "defective condition unreasonably dangerous to the user."

II

The next question is whether the evidence was such that the jury could have found that the defective condition existed at the time of the sale. The lower court held the jury could not have so found and cited Stein v. General Motors Corporation, 58 Pa.D. & C.2d 193 (1972), aff'd, 222 Pa.Super. 751, 295 A.2d 111 (1972).

In *Stein* the plaintiff claimed that his automobile accident was caused by a defective steering mechanism. However, the trial judge granted the defendant's motion for a compulsory nonsuit, and this court affirmed *per curiam.* Throughout its opinion the lower court emphasized that the car was twenty-six months old, had been driven 17,700 miles, and had passed through at least one repair shop before the accident. The court reasoned from these facts that if there were a defect in the automobile, "the likelihood that such defect grew out of mishandling * * * is much more compelling than that it grew out of any original defect at the time of manufacture or, behind that, of design." Id. 58 Pa.D. & C.2d at 209. The court therefore held that the plaintiff had not met "his burden to prove that the vehicle was in a defective condition at the time it left the hands of the seller." Id.

In the present case, it will be recalled, appellant testified that the saw was only a month old, had been used approximately ten times, and by no one else. He also testified that the saw was completely assembled when he bought it, and that he had not tampered with the guard nor had he sent the saw out to a repair shop. This case, therefore, is not like *Stein,* where ordinary wear and tear or faulty repair could have caused the defect. * * *

III

The last question is whether there was sufficient evidence for a jury to find that the defect caused appellant's injury. According to appellant's testimony, the saw was designed so that the telescopic guard would cover the blade of the saw when the cut was complete. He stated:

> Q. If the telescopic guard is working properly—
>
> A. It is impossible for you to get cut.
>
> * * *
>
> Q. If the telescopic blade guard is covering the blade, can you cut your leg?
>
> A. No way.

It is clear that the jury could have found from this testimony and from its own examination of the saw that appellant's injury would not have occurred if the saw had not been defective.

In sum, we conclude that there was sufficient evidence for the jury to find that appellees were engaged in the business of selling the power saw, that there was a defect in the saw which made it unreasonably dangerous to the user, that the defect existed at the time of its sale, and that there was a causal connection between the defect and appellant's injury. The compulsory nonsuit should, therefore, not have been entered.

[Reversed and remanded.]

NOTES

1. Why do you suppose the plaintiff was nonsuited by the trial court? Why do you suppose the trial court refused to let the plaintiff's expert testify?

2. Is the result in Agostino socially and morally appropriate? Did the saw hurt Mr. Agostino, or did Mr. Agostino hurt himself with the saw? Might Mr. Agostino have "forgotten" some "relevant" facts about how the accident occurred? If Mr. Agostino were to have prevailed on remand, who ultimately would have paid for his injuries? Is such a result on balance good or bad?

3. In Skil Corp. v. Lugsdin, 168 Ga.App. 754, 309 S.E.2d 921 (1983), plaintiff cut his hand when the lower blade guard of defendant's circular saw

failed to close. The trial court ordered a retrial after the jury returned a verdict for the defendant, and the case was retried. Evidence that the manufacturer had received at least 48 complaints and lawsuits involving the failure of the blade guard was admitted on the issue of the defendant's knowledge of a dangerous condition, and hence as relevant to the issues of negligence, the strict liability duty to warn, and punitive damages.

> After the incident in which appellee was injured, the saw was sent as a matter of routine to be repaired, and was then returned to the construction site. Thus, both parties were prevented from examining the saw to determine whether any defect was present at the time of appellee's injury. However, evidence established that immediately after appellee was injured, the lower blade guard, which should have closed automatically and instantaneously after appellee completed his cut in the wood, was still in the open position, leaving the blade exposed. Appellee's expert witness testified that the cause of the open guard was failure of the spring that should have closed the guard, and that such failure was a defect in the saw. Appellant's expert testified that any failure of the guard to close would have been caused by damage to the saw by banging or dropping and that spring failure was very unlikely.

Id. at 923. *Held,* the circumstantial evidence of defect and cause was sufficient; verdict for plaintiff affirmed. See also Roth v. Black & Decker, U.S., Inc. 737 F.2d 779 (8th Cir.1984) (Mo. law) (failure of guard to retract may have been caused by sawdust clogging spring; verdict for compensatory damages affirmed, punitive damages reversed).

Compare McKinnon v. Skil Corp., 638 F.2d 270 (1st Cir.1981) (Mass. law), in which the plaintiff's foot was cut when he either dropped his circular saw or placed it on the ground near his foot. Although he had known for some time that the guard was not retracting properly, and that he could return it to the retailer, he chose to continue to use it until his accident. *Held,* verdict for defendant affirmed: the OSHA regulation, dealing with workplace safety, was properly excluded in a consumer products liability case; the Underwriter's Laboratory (UL) standard, requiring that the guard close in less then three-tenths of a second, was properly admitted; the plaintiff's evidence of prior accidents was properly excluded since there was no showing that any had involved problems with the lower blade guard; and the CPSC reports were properly excluded as (often double) hearsay and irrelevant.

4. "Plaintiffs' lawyers often avoid product cases involving portable circular saws. This is because these tools have been in use for many years, are very similar in design from manufacturer to manufacturer, and there is a public perception that people injured by a power tool simply were careless." Kalin, Portable Circular Saws, Useful—but Dangerous—Tools, Trial 60 (Nov. 1986).

5. Having learned of 18 injuries, two fatal, to users of Skil circular saws, the CPSC sought to inspect Skil documents at its premises. The Commission obtained a warrant, from a federal magistrate, which was upheld by the district court and the court of appeals. In re Establishment Inspection of Skil Corporation, 846 F.2d 1127 (7th Cir.1988).

6. Who is doing a better job, the safety regulators or the courts? Should society spend more money on regulating the safety of portable power circular saws so that it may spend less on litigating injuries caused by such saws?

7. For an extensive bibliography of products liability and safety source materials, see Beaird, Products Liability Bibliography, 73 L.Lib.J. 968 (1980). For a recent scholarly overview, see M. Shapo, The Law of Products Liability (1987).

Chapter 2

THEORIES OF MANUFACTURER LIABILITY

This chapter examines the various theories of recovery that may support a products liability action against a manufacturer. The theories of liability may be divided into three basic groups: (1) negligence; (2) misrepresentation, both tortious and by breach of warranty; and (3) strict liability in tort for defective products. While the principles of these liability theories are often applicable to suppliers generally, they are developed in this chapter primarily with respect to the manufacturer, the usual defendant. Issues of liability theory more germane to actions against retailers and other defendants are treated in Chapters 7 and 8. A recurring issue in this chapter, pertinent to the development of each of the theories examined, is the threshold question of whether the manufacturer owes a duty to persons who may be affected by its products but with whom it did not directly deal—the issue of "privity" of contract. Finally, the manufacturer's ability to limit by contract the scope of its legal responsibility for harm caused by its products, through disclaimers of liability and limitations on remedies, is considered in the context of the separate theories of liability.

In examining the various theories of recovery in this chapter, it should be kept in mind that a manufacturer or other supplier may be subject to liability in a single case on two, three, or even more separate theories of recovery. As each new theory is studied, its similarities with and variations from the other theories of liability should be given careful consideration.

SHAPO, A REPRESENTATIONAL THEORY OF CONSUMER PROTECTION: DOCTRINE, FUNCTION AND LEGAL LIABILITY FOR PRODUCT DISAPPOINTMENT

60 Va.L.Rev. 1109, 1153–55 (1974).

IV. THEORIES OF LIABILITY AND THEIR IMPLICATIONS

A. *Basic Analytical Classifications*

1. Theoretical Architectonics

There are many conceptual shelves, primarily though not exclusively in the "torts" library, from which judges may select answers to product frustration cases. Some theorists emphasize distributional effects and speak the language of "fairness"; others deal primarily with allocational consequences and risk assumption and stress "reasonableness" and utility. Some find answers in philosophical frameworks overlaid on tort history; some may superimpose an economic model on traditional doctrines of personal injury law; others focus on the nature of the transaction as a commercial event, placing varying emphases on the historical and policy bases of common law remedies and of the UCC.

It would be folly to suggest that any of these models, or indeed the one advanced in this study, will cabin neatly the products area under discussion. One can visualize the problem as one of overlapping geometric figures, in which the central concern is the rectangle labeled "product disappointment cases." * * *

2. Specific Theories

Judges have painted product frustration cases in a rainbow of classifications. "Tort" categories have supplied the primary ground of analysis, although there have been frequent excursions into "contract" territory. Conventional tort theory describes a continuum that runs from situations in which the defendant acts deliberately in a way that he knows will cause consequences that society condemns, reaching through "negligent" conduct, and extending to actions that cannot be called "unreasonable" but for which the law imposes compensatory obligations on policy grounds when injury results. In the consumer product area the continuum may be viewed as starting with fraud, in which the defendant makes untrue representations knowingly or reckless of their falsity and with the intent that the plaintiff will rely on them. It continues through negligence to classifications that are technically denominated non-fault. "Strict liability in tort" has received the most attention in the terrain beyond negligence but there are important sibling theories of liability. One of these concepts is "innocent misrepresentation," a specific recent version of which is embodied in the non-fault misrepresentation theory of section 402B of the *Restatement (Second) of Torts.* Closely related contract doctrines are the "implied warranty" theories, both of merchantability and of fitness for a particular purpose. Another contract based doctrine which does not require a showing of fault is the theory of "express warranty." Superimposed upon these theories is a classification of the cases which distinguishes between those that primarily involve hazards to physical safety and those concerned principally with economic injury.

[Each of these theories is separately examined below.—Eds.]

SECTION 1. NEGLIGENCE

Most lawyers consider negligence to be the "classic" theory of products liability. And while its importance in products liability litigation has waned of late because of the development of the strict theories of manufacturer liability, negligence is still a most important theory of recovery. Some states, for example, have not yet adopted the theory of strict liability in tort. In states that have, there may be good tactical reasons for a plaintiff to base recovery at least in part on negligence. Moreover, many judges have stated that the basis of strict liability in design and warnings cases is similar—if not identical—to negligence liability. Indeed, many of the recent "reform" proposals have called for such a return, on a formal basis, to the principles of negligence. So negligence remains a vital theory of recovery.

Following an introductory section on privity, the negligence cases are presented in the three contexts in which the manufacturer may fail in its duties toward consumers: (1) manufacture; (2) the supplying of warnings and instructions; and (3) design. Since these are also the three categories of "defectiveness," discussion of the many recurring issues concerning defectiveness in general (such as problems concerning obvious dangers) is delayed until Chapter 3. Note also that while the various negligence principles are generally applicable to all three contexts, for brevity they usually are developed in one subsection only.

A. THE PRIVITY OBSTACLE

"When the consumer deals with the retailer rather than directly with the manufacturer, he establishes a contractual relation with the retailer to which the manufacturer is not, legally speaking, a party. The manufacturer sells (directly or indirectly) to the retailer; the retailer sells to the consumer. The marketing process is a series of sales—a series of contracts. The parties to these contracts overlap in the middle of the marketing process but not at the ends: there is an ultimate supplier and an ultimate consumer. The retailer has contractual relations with both his supplier and his customer, and so is the connecting link between them. The customer, however, makes no contract with the supplier—the manufacturer. These two do not deal with one another; typically they are strangers. In legal phraseology, there is no 'privity of contract' between them." Gillam, Products Liability in a Nutshell, 37 Or.L.Rev. 119, 131 (1958).

Whether the plaintiff was in privity with the defendant became a crucial issue in products liability litigation with the decision in Winterbottom v. Wright, 10 M. & W. 109, 152 Eng.Rep. 402 (Ex.1842). The defendant, Wright, a manufacturer and repairer of stagecoaches, supplied a stagecoach to the Postmaster General under a contract to keep it in good repair. The coach subsequently broke down and overturned, injuring the driver, Winterbottom, who sued for damages. In a decision that was to exert enormous influence over products liability litigation for the next century or so, Lord Abinger, C.B., delivered an opinion that reflected the views of the other judges as well:

> I am clearly of the opinion that the defendant is entitled to our judgment. We ought not to permit a doubt to rest upon this subject, for our doing so might be the means of letting in

> upon us an infinity of actions. * * * There is no privity of contract between these parties; and if the plaintiff can sue, every passenger, or even any person passing along the road, who was injured by the upsetting of the coach, might bring a similar action. Unless we confine the operation of such contracts as this to the parties who entered into them, the most absurd and outrageous consequences, to which I can see no limit, would ensue. * * * By permitting this action, we should be working this injustice, that after the defendant had done everything to the satisfaction of his employer, and after all matters between them had been adjusted, and all accounts settled on the footing of their contract, we should subject them to be ripped open by this action of tort brought against him.

Judgment was given for the defendant. The rule of *Winterbottom,* that no action could be maintained against a remote seller, continued as the law of the land well into the twentieth century. This was so even in negligence actions, despite the fact that Mr. Winterbottom had based his right to relief in his declaration solely upon the contract between his employer, the Postmaster General, and the defendant.*

By the turn of the twentieth century, dissatisfaction with the privity bar rule had generated certain exceptions, perhaps best summarized in Judge Sanborn's lucid opinion in Huset v. J.I. Case Threshing Mach. Co., 120 F. 865 (8th Cir.1903):

> The first is that an act of negligence of a manufacturer or vendor which is imminently dangerous to the life or health of mankind, and which is committed in the preparation or sale of an article intended to preserve, destroy, or affect human life, is actionable by third parties who suffer from the negligence. * * *
>
> The second exception is that an owner's act of negligence which causes injury to one who is invited by him to use his defective appliance upon the owner's premises may form the basis of an action against the owner. * * *
>
> The third exception to the rule is that one who sells or delivers an article which he knows to be imminently dangerous to life or limb to another without notice of its qualities is liable to any person who suffers an injury therefrom which might have been reasonably anticipated, whether there were any contractual relations between the parties or not. * * *

Although there were minor variations in the formulation of the exceptions among the cases, the three *Huset* exceptions were widely

* That the principle of the case may thus have been improperly extended to the nascent action in negligence has been argued by some scholars. See Bohlen, The Basis of Affirmative Obligations in the Law of Tort (pt. 2), 53 U.Pa.L.Rev. 273, 281–84 (1905); Feezer, Tort Liability of Manufacturers and Vendors, 10 Minn.L.Rev. 1, 3 (1925) (calling *Winterbottom*'s progeny in negligence cases "bastard offspring"). But see C.J. Miller & P. Lovell, Product Liability 7 (1977), a leading English authority on products liability law.

accepted at the time. To recover against a negligent manufacturer or other remote vendor, a plaintiff was required to squeeze his case into one of the three exceptions. This was usually quite hard to do, since most courts at the time interpreted the exceptions narrowly. Thus, there were not many cases involving defective appliances on the owner's premises (Judge Sanborn's exception no. 2). Cases falling within this exception most often involved defective scaffolding; others involved, for example, a chain furnished to unload a vessel, a ladder on a vessel, and defective machinery.

Nor was it very easy for a plaintiff to qualify under Judge Sanborn's exception no. 3, which involved a knowing failure to warn of an imminent and latent danger in the product. Often, perhaps usually, the manufacturer would not know that its product was dangerously defective; when it did have such knowledge, obtaining proof of it was difficult. Even in *Huset,* where a nonsuit was denied on the basis of this exception, Judge Sanborn made the following observation in remanding the case for trial: "It is perhaps improbable that the defendant was possessed of the knowledge of the imminently dangerous character of this threshing machine when it delivered it, and * * * upon the trial of the case it [may] be found to fall under the general rule [of nonliability]." 120 F. at 873.

Clearly the most important exception (Judge Sanborn's exception no. 1) involved the sale of products that could be classified as "imminently" or "inherently" dangerous. When *Huset* was decided in 1903, however, the exception was still quite narrowly confined to products like poisons, drugs, guns, explosives and foodstuffs. Seven years later, a Scottish-American gravestone maker from upstate New York purchased quite a different kind of product—a marvelous new machine called a "car."

D. PECK, DECISION AT LAW

40–64 (1961).

It was the year 1911, probably the single most significant year in automobile history. The industry had not yet concentrated into a few giant organizations, but it had definitely emerged from the machine shops and Henry Ford had already made the assembly line famous. Packard, Pierce-Arrow and Peerless were the great names of fine cars, but there were a dozen other notable names, now mostly forgotten, adorning hoods of distinctive design.

* * *

It was [in 1910] that Donald MacPherson, a stone cutter and dealer in monuments and gravestones, of Galway Village near Saratoga Springs in the state of New York, purchased a new Buick automobile from Close Brothers, local automobile dealers. The car had a front seat for two, a rumble seat for one, and was called a runabout. It had four cylinders of twenty-two horsepower.

Late in July of [1911] Mr. MacPherson drove his car on an errand of mercy—to take a neighbor to the hospital. Mr. MacPherson was accompanied on the ride by the sick man and his brother. The car did not reach the hospital. But Mr. MacPherson did, as a patient, by means of another conveyance. His new Buick automobile ended up in a ditch, with the owner pinioned under the axle.

As he and his two companions described the accident, in their testimony eighteen months later at the trial of MacPherson v. Buick Motor Company, they were driving along at about fifteen miles an hour when the rear of the machine started to skid. The road was dry and there was no apparent reason for the skid. As they looked back, they heard a crash, like the breaking of wood, and saw the left rear of the car swerve and go down. Mr. MacPherson tried to straighten the car out and bring it to a halt, but it would not respond to his steering; it headed into a telephone pole and overturned.

An inspection at the scene of the accident immediately afterward revealed the left rear wheel detached from the car and lying on the ground, the spokes broken and scattered around.

* * *

When MacPherson, a wiry little Scotsman, sufficiently recovered from his injuries to get around again, called upon Senator Brackett and asked him to take the case, he was somewhat more cordially received as a constituent than as a client. Edgar T. Brackett was the leading lawyer in Saratoga County. He was also the political leader of the county and the state senator from the district. * * * He resembled a minister both in appearance and adeptness in quoting scripture and Shakespeare. He was thorough in the preparation and persuasive in the presentation of both facts and law, and enjoyed a reputation throughout the state as a master both in the trial of cases and argument of appeals.

Mr. MacPherson thought that he had a simple case of an automobile with a rotten wheel, which had collapsed and fallen apart under normal driving conditions. He felt that he had a claim in simple justice against the manufacturer of the car. Brackett knew better. The claim was novel, not simple. He knew that a long, hard and uncertain legal road lay ahead and that every inch of the way would be closely contested. During the next five years, while the case was in litigation in three courts, MacPherson learned this too. He learned that he was a guinea pig for testing out a proposition of law of much larger significance than the amount of any verdict he would receive at the hands of a country jury.

The problem and difficulty, as Brackett explained, was to persuade the court that the Buick Company should be held responsible to MacPherson for any defect in the machine, when he had not bought the car from or had any dealings with the Buick Company. He had bought the car from an independent dealer. The dealer might be liable for selling a bad car, although his liability was more academic than real as it was doubtful that he would be good for any judgment that might be taken against him. But if the Buick Company was to be held responsible directly to MacPherson, with whom it had no contact, a new theory of law would have to be propounded and established—for no court had as yet recognized any responsibility on the part of a manufacturer in favor of a purchaser who did not buy from the manufacturer.

* * *

What would be the consequences if MacPherson won his lawsuit? Investors the country over asked the question and pondered the answer. An automobile might break down for a number of reasons—a cracked axle, blown tire, steering gear out of alignment, faulty brakes, careless operation. It was difficult to tell after a little wear and tear whether the cause was some mechanical failure or human failure or neglect in care of the car. If every breakdown could be made the basis of a claim against the manufacturer, the industry would be subject to risks and hazards beyond calculation. The possible liabilities would be a threat to solvency. The hopes and fears of Detroit, Indianapolis and every other city that boasted of an automobile plant were thus gathered in Saratoga.

No country lawyer was to be trusted with the defense of this case. Disadvantageous as it might be to have a stranger appear against the local idol in the local forum, that was a handicap which had to be accepted. This case could not be won for the defendant on the basis of personality or sympathy. It could be won only on the strength of compelling reason—an overwhelming demonstration that practically nothing more could have been done to assure the production of a safe and sound machine than Buick had done—and a convincing revelation of the dire consequences that would follow the imposition of responsibility upon the manufacturers of automobiles.

Not unnaturally the lawyer selected by the defendant came from the automobile capital. William Van Dyke of Detroit was chosen for his knowledge of the automobile industry and his forensic skill. * * * Both in presence and manner he was a commanding figure, and courts always listened respectfully to his legal learning and cogent argument.

[At trial, plaintiff was nonsuited at the close of his case because of the absence of privity. The nonsuit was reversed on appeal, 153 App. Div. 474, 138 N.Y.S. 224 (1912), on the ground that one of the exceptions to the privity requirement may have applied, and the case was remanded for a new trial. The following summary of the case presumably is from the second trial.]

Brackett was fairly well satisfied from the start of the case that the jury would accept MacPherson's account of how the accident happened. He was not so sure that he could show the jury what was wrong with the wheel or convince them that the Buick Company was to blame. But that was his immediate task. The trial, therefore, became an inquiry into wheels, the wood from which they were made, and the available means for testing their soundness and strength.

Wheel making was a trade in which many were engaged in those days. The makers of carriage and wagon wheels—a numerous body of artisans—had turned to making automobile wheels. Wheels were made not only in factories, but also in small shops by individual wheelwrights. In fact, wheel making was such a specialty that it had not been integrated into the manufacturing process of any of the automobile companies except Peerless, the only company which manufactured its own wheels. All other companies bought their wheels from specialists in wheel making. Buick bought its wheels from the Imperial Wheel Company, a well-known and reliable old company.

As every community had at least one wheelwright among its established and essential occupations, Brackett did not have to go far from home for his expert witnesses.

George A. Palmer from Saratoga Springs had been a carriage maker for thirty years and for the past several years his occupation had been making and repairing automobile wheels. The wheel from MacPherson's Buick, that is, its collected parts, had been brought * * * to Mr. Palmer's shop for examination.

Mr. Palmer pointed out to the judge and jury that the spokes had broken off square, which indicated that the wood was poor. "Apparently the wood was brittle," he said, "coarse grained such as you find in old trees. I never saw a spoke broke off as square as they were. Good quality of sound hickory, when it breaks, brooms up, slivers up. The fact that they are broken square across indicates that they were brittle, of poor quality, trash."

* * *

Adelbert Payne came from the nearby town of Amsterdam, where he had built carriages and made wheels for twenty years. "A good class of carriage requires the best hickory," he said.

"Are you able to tell the quality of a wood from an examination of the surface of the sides of a hickory spoke?" Brackett asked.

"Yes, sir. The integrity of hickory can be determined from an examination of the surface by an experienced eye. A sound, good quality of hickory has a very firm grain that shows distinctly through the outer surface."

The witness conceded that if a wheel came painted one could not tell anything about the grain. "That is why," he explained, "I never let a wheel come painted—so I can see the quality of hickory used." If the wood came painted, the test would be to scrape off sufficient paint to see the grain and fiber of the wood—it was "a perfectly feasible and easy test to determine the character of a spoke that way, and make sure."

Mr. Payne agreed with Mr. Palmer that the hickory in the spokes of the MacPherson wheel was of poor quality—"light and poor, no heft, broken off too squarely for good hickory."

[The plaintiff's next expert, another wheelwright, the local carriage maker, who had examined each of the spokes on the car's wheels, agreed: "There is not a single one of these pieces that I would style as good as second-class hickory."]

[Anticipating Buick's argument that it could not inspect the grain of the spokes since it received the wheels from the supplier already painted with a prime coat, Brackett went to the Thomas Motor Car Company of Buffalo for his last expert—a wheel tester.] This man testified that the Thomas Company bought its wheels in the natural wood. They were first inspected in the Receiving Department. They then went to the Wheel Department where each wheel was tried out separately under pressure—by hydraulic pressure applied on the hub. Buick made no such test.

Van Dyke, for the defense, approached the problem of proof from a different angle and on a different level. He sought to give the jury a more scientific understanding of wood and the means of determining its suitability for spokes, and to show the virtual impossibility, as a practical matter, of examining or testing the wood after a wheel was made. The automobile companies had to rely on the wheel makers, he said, and he argued that if the companies selected wheel makers who had demonstrated their dependability over the years, that should be regarded as a discharge of their responsibility.

Van Dyke began the defense with the director of the laboratory for testing materials at Purdue University. This man had a long background in the testing of woods for the Forestry Service of the United States. He gave the jury a briefing on the tests to determine the weight, grain and strength of wood. He rejected as unfounded prejudice the notion that wood from young trees was better than that from old trees or that coarseness or fineness of grain affected the strength. The studies of the Forestry Service established, he said, that the fast growing hickories have the greater shock resisting capacity; growth was measured by the count of rings on the stem; good hickory was produced at a rate of growth of from five to twenty-five rings per inch. Shown the spokes from the wheel of MacPherson's Buick, he said that they were first-class, running about fifteen rings per inch.

It would be impossible, he explained, to determine the strength and suitability of a spoke by an examination of the side surface because the rings did not show in that way. It would be necessary to look at the ends to observe the rings, which was impossible in a finished wheel.

The attorney for Buick also called representatives of the leading automobile makers and wheel makers of the day. All uniformly testified that no test was made or could be made by the motor companies to determine the quality or strength of the spokes in wheels supplied by the wheel makers. Any pressure test was ridiculed as worthless—it would tell only that a wheel could carry so much weight, without revealing how it would bear up under the stress and strain of the actual operation of a car. No automobile company employed wood experts to pass on the wood in wheels. None was known to remove any portion of the priming coat for the purpose of examining the grain of the wood.

* * *

After the experts were called and all the other evidence was in, the defense called witnesses from the Buick Company and the Imperial Wheel Company to testify to their experience with wheels over the years. Up to that time Buick had turned out 125,000 cars, with 500,000 wheels, all obtained from the Imperial Company. Never before had a complaint been made of a wheel breaking down, the witnesses testified. Imperial had never received a complaint of a single wheel failing because of the quality of the wheel.

The Buick representative acknowledged that Buick attempted no test of the wheels it received other than the road test given all finished cars. This test consisted of driving the car over a ten-mile course of an ordinary country road as fast as the car could go and taking the turns at ten to twenty-five miles an hour.

So the issues were drawn as to the cause of the accident, the worth of the wheel, and the responsibility of the Buick Company.

[The judge instructed the jury that it should find for the plaintiff if it found (1) that the accident was caused by the crumbling of the spokes of the wheel, and (2) that Buick had failed to employ such tests "that a person skilled in the manufacture of cars * * * ought to have used to discover a defect."]

The jury brought in a verdict for MacPherson for five thousand dollars.

The verdict of the jury was, however, only an opening gambit in the contest. It determined the facts—that the wheel was bad and the Buick Company was at fault. It remained for an appellate court to decide finally the legal consequence of that finding by the jury. From the jury's verdict and trial court's judgment, Brackett and Van Dyke went on to argue, with great learning and skill, the most important and far-reaching commercial-legal issue of the day.

[The intermediate appellate court affirmed the judgment for MacPherson, 160 App.Div. 55, 145 N.Y.S. 462 (1914), and Buick took the case to the New York Court of Appeals.]

The issue was whether the manufacturer of an article should be held liable to a person injured by reason of a defect in the article—when that person was not one to whom the manufacturer sold the article or with whom the manufacturer had any contact. Or, to put it another way, the question was whether the New York Court of Appeals, in the year 1916, should follow the decision and law established by the Court of [Exchequer of Pleas] in Winterbottom v. Wright in the year

1842, or turn the law about and place a higher responsibility on the manufacturer for the better protection of the ultimate user.

* * *

Van Dyke for the defense stressed the proposition that "an automobile is not an inherently dangerous article." And from that premise he reached the corollary conclusion in law—"An automobile not being an article inherently dangerous, defendant was not liable in simple negligence to a third party not in contractual relation with it."

* * *

Van Dyke * * * summed up the philosophy and practicality of the law in favor of the Buick Company in his own words:

> "We believe that the limitation of the liability of the manufacturer of an innocuous article is based upon sound reasoning. The maker of an innocuous article, such as a chair, table or buggy, cannot follow it through every hand for all time. He cannot know as to whether it goes into prudent or imprudent hands, or whether it has had minor accidents, or undue exposure, which have weakened it. He cannot trace the history of his article through every subsequent and remote user for all time and in all places. Therefore, the law recognizes this inability and holds him liable only where it is definitely shown that he created or had knowledge of the defect and was wilfully careless or practiced a fraud."

Senator Brackett, fully sensitive to the legal force of the argument against him, made no attempt to reduce the reach of his own. Sympathy for his client and countryman was a moving force in his argument, and he played upon it, but he never lost sight of the scope and sweep of the argument he was advancing. He need hardly have called the court's attention to the importance of the case and the wide effect the decision would have, but he did not neglect at the outset to put the case in its broad perspective. "The decision of this question," he noted, "is of the utmost interest, not simply to this little tombstone dealer in the remote hamlet of Galway in Saratoga County, but to every person, everywhere, who shall hereafter use this modern means of locomotion."

* * *

"What substantial difference, what difference in morals, should be made" he pleaded, "in testing this defendant's liability for this maiming of the plaintiff, whether, having first manufactured, it sells this machine directly to MacPherson or sells it to Close Brothers, with the expectation and intention that Close Brothers will sell it to some MacPherson? The defendant was equally culpable in either case. The plaintiff has suffered equal damage; and it is close to, if not quite, immoral and wicked to allow the recovery in one case and deny it in the other."

* * *

With this closing analysis * * * Brackett delivered his client and his case into the hands of the court.

MacPHERSON v. BUICK MOTOR CO.

Court of Appeals of New York, 1916.
217 N.Y. 382, 111 N.E. 1050.

CARDOZO, J. The defendant is a manufacturer of automobiles. It sold an automobile to a retail dealer. The retail dealer resold to the plaintiff. While the plaintiff was in the car, it suddenly collapsed. He was thrown out and injured. One of the wheels was made of defective wood, and its spokes crumbled into fragments. The wheel was not made by the defendant; it was bought from another manufacturer. There is evidence, however, that its defects could have been discovered by reasonable inspection, and that inspection was omitted. There is no claim that the defendant knew of the defect and willfully concealed it. * * * The charge is one, not of fraud, but of negligence. The question to be determined is whether the defendant owed a duty of care and vigilance to any one but the immediate purchaser.

The foundations of this branch of the law, at least in this state, were laid in Thomas v. Winchester (6 N.Y. 397) [1852]. A poison was falsely labeled. The sale was made to a druggist, who in turn sold to a customer. The customer recovered damages from the seller who affixed the label. "The defendant's negligence," it was said, "put human life in imminent danger." A poison falsely labeled is likely to injure any one who gets it. Because the danger is to be foreseen, there is a duty to avoid the injury. * * *

Thomas v. Winchester became quickly a landmark of the law. In the application of its principle there may at times have been uncertainty or even error. There has never in this state been doubt or disavowal of the principle itself. The chief cases are well known, yet to recall some of them will be helpful. Loop v. Litchfield (42 N.Y. 351)[1870] is the earliest. It was the case of a defect in a small balance wheel used on a circular saw. The manufacturer pointed out the defect to the buyer, who wished a cheap article and was ready to assume the risk. The risk can hardly have been an imminent one, for the wheel lasted five years before it broke. In the meanwhile the buyer had made a lease of the machinery. It was held that the manufacturer was not answerable to the lessee. Loop v. Litchfield was followed in Losee v. Clute (51 N.Y. 494)[1873], the case of the explosion of a steam boiler. That decision has been criticised (Thompson on Negligence, 233; Shearman & Redfield on Negligence [6th ed.], § 117); but it must be confined to its special facts. It was put upon the ground that the risk of injury was too remote. The buyer in that case had not only accepted the boiler, but had tested it. The manufacturer knew that his own test was not the final one. The finality of the test has a bearing on the measure of diligence owing to persons other than the purchaser (Beven, Negligence [3d ed.], pp. 50, 51, 54; Wharton, Negligence [2d ed.], § 134).

These early cases suggest a narrow construction of the rule. Later cases, however, evince a more liberal spirit. First in importance is Devlin v. Smith (89 N.Y. 470)[1882]. The defendant, a contractor, built a scaffold for a painter. The painter's servants were injured. The contractor was held liable. He knew that the scaffold, if improperly constructed, was a most dangerous trap. He knew that it was to be used by the workmen. He was building it for that very purpose. Building it for their use, he owed them a duty, irrespective of his contract with their master, to build it with care.

From Devlin v. Smith we pass over intermediate cases and turn to the latest case in this court in which Thomas v. Winchester was followed. That case is Statler v. Ray Mfg. Co. (195 N.Y. 478, 480)[1909]. The defendant manufactured a large coffee urn. It was installed in a restaurant. When heated, the urn exploded and injured the plaintiff. We held that the manufacturer was liable. We said that the urn "was of such a character inherently that, when applied to the purposes for which it was designed, it was liable to become a source of great danger to many people if not carefully and properly constructed."

* * * The defendant argues that things imminently dangerous to life are poisons, explosives, deadly weapons—things whose normal function it is to injure or destroy. But whatever the rule in Thomas v. Winchester may once have been, it has no longer that restricted meaning. A scaffold (Devlin v. Smith, supra) is not inherently a destructive instrument. It becomes destructive only if imperfectly constructed. A large coffee urn (Statler v. Ray Mfg. Co., supra) may have within itself, if negligently made, the potency of danger, yet no one thinks of it as an implement whose normal function is destruction. * * *

Devlin v. Smith was decided in 1882. A year later a very similar case came before the Court of Appeal in England (Heaven v. Pender, L.R. [11 Q.B.D.] 503). We find in the opinion of Brett, M.R., afterwards Lord Esher (p. 510), the same conception of a duty, irrespective of contract, imposed upon the manufacturer by the law itself: "Whenever one person supplies goods, or machinery, or the like, for the purpose of their being used by another person under such circumstances that every one of ordinary sense would, if he thought, recognize at once that unless he used ordinary care and skill with regard to the condition of the thing supplied or the mode of supplying it, there will be danger of injury to the person or property of him for whose use the thing is supplied, and who is to use it, a duty arises to use ordinary care and skill as to the condition or manner of supplying such thing." He then points out that for a neglect of such ordinary care or skill whereby injury happens, the appropriate remedy is an action for negligence. The right to enforce this liability is not to be confined to the immediate buyer. The right, he says, extends to the persons or class of persons for whose use the thing is supplied. * * * What was said by Lord Esher in that case did not command the full assent of his associates. His opinion has been criticised "as requiring every man to take affirmative precautions to protect his neighbors as well as to refrain from injuring them" (Bohlen, Affirmative Obligations in the Law of Torts, 44 Am.Law Reg. [N.S.] 341). It may not be an accurate exposition of the law of England. Perhaps it may need some qualification even in our own state. Like most attempts at comprehensive definition, it may involve errors of inclusion and of exclusion. But its tests and standards, at least in their underlying principles, with whatever qualification may be called for as they are applied to varying conditions, are the tests and standards of our law.

We hold, then, that the principle of Thomas v. Winchester is not limited to poisons, explosives, and things of like nature, to things which in their normal operation are implements of destruction. If the nature of a thing is such that it is reasonably certain to place life and limb in peril when negligently made, it is then a thing of danger. Its nature gives warning of the consequences to be expected. If to the element of danger there is added knowledge that the thing will be used by persons other than the purchaser, and used without new tests, then, irrespective of contract, the manufacturer of this thing of danger is under a duty to make it carefully. * * * We have put aside the notion that the duty to safeguard life and limb, when the consequences of negligence may be foreseen, grows out of contract and nothing else. We have put the source of the obligation where it ought to be. We have put its source in the law.

From this survey of the decisions, there thus emerges a definition of the duty of a manufacturer which enables us to measure this defendant's liability. Beyond all question, the nature of an automobile gives warning of probable danger if its construction is defective. This automobile was designed to go fifty miles an hour. Unless its wheels were sound and strong, injury was almost certain. It was as much a thing of danger as a defective engine for a railroad. The defendant knew the danger. It knew also that the car would be used by persons other than the buyer. This was apparent from its size; there were seats for three persons. It was apparent also from the fact that the buyer was a dealer in cars, who bought to resell. The maker of this car supplied it for the use of purchasers from the dealer just as plainly as the contractor in Devlin v. Smith supplied the scaffold for use by the servants of the owner. The dealer was indeed the one person of whom it might be said with some approach to certainty that by him the car would not be used. Yet the defendant would have us say that he was the one person whom it was under a legal duty to protect. The law does not lead us to so inconsequent a conclusion. Precedents drawn from the days of travel by stage coach do not fit the conditions of travel to-day. The principle that the danger must be imminent does not change, but the things subject to the principle do change. They are whatever the needs of life in a developing civilization require them to be.

In reaching this conclusion, we do not ignore the decisions to the contrary in other jurisdictions. * * * The earlier cases are summarized by Judge Sanborn in Huset v. J.I. Case Threshing Machine Co. (120 Fed.Rep. 865). Some of them, at first sight inconsistent with our conclusion, may be reconciled upon the ground that the negligence was too remote, and that another cause had intervened. But even when they cannot be reconciled, the difference is rather in the application of the principle than in the principle itself. Judge Sanborn says, for example, that the contractor who builds a bridge, or the manufacturer who builds a car, cannot ordinarily foresee injury to other persons than the owner as the probable result (120 Fed.Rep. 865, at p. 867). We take a different view. We think that injury to others is to be foreseen not merely as a possible, but as an almost inevitable result. (See the trenchant criticism in Bohlen, supra, at p. 351). Indeed, Judge Sanborn concedes that his view is not to be reconciled with our decision in Devlin v. Smith (supra). The doctrine of that decision has now become the settled law of this state, and we have no desire to depart from it.

* * *

There is nothing anomalous in a rule which imposes upon A, who has contracted with B, a duty to C and D and others according as he knows or does not know that the subject-matter of the contract is intended for their use. * * *

* * * Subtle distinctions are drawn by the defendant between things inherently dangerous and things imminently dangerous, but the case does not turn upon these verbal niceties. If danger was to be expected as reasonably certain, there was a duty of vigilance, and this whether you call the danger inherent or imminent. In varying forms that thought was put before the jury. * * *

We think the defendant was not absolved from a duty of inspection because it bought the wheels from a reputable manufacturer. It was not merely a dealer in automobiles. It was a manufacturer of automobiles. It was responsible for the finished product. It was not at liberty to put the finished product on the market without subjecting the component parts to ordinary and simple tests (Richmond & Danville R.R. Co. v. Elliott, 149 U.S. 266, 272). Under the charge of the trial judge nothing more was required of it. The obligation to inspect must vary with the nature of the thing to be inspected. The more probable the danger, the greater the need of caution.

* * *

The judgment should be affirmed with costs.

[Dissenting opinion of BARTLETT, C.J., omitted.]

NOTES

1. What interpretation of the imminently dangerous product exception, that would have precluded recovery in *MacPherson,* did defense counsel argue

to the court? Was this particularly creative lawyering on the part of Buick's counsel, or was it an argument that he naturally should have been expected to make?

2. While many courts followed *MacPherson* quite quickly, others did not, and by 1933 the case law on the scope of the "imminently dangerous" exception was in a state of utter confusion. See Russell, Manufacturers' Liability to the Ultimate Consumer, 21 Ky.L.J. 388, 397–99 (1933). One by one, however, the courts swung over to *MacPherson.* Among the later but more important of such cases was Carter v. Yardley & Co., 319 Mass. 92, 103, 64 N.E.2d 693, 700 (1946), where the court stated: "The doctrine of the MacPherson case is now generally accepted. * * * [It] caused the exception to swallow the asserted general rule of nonliability, leaving nothing upon which that rule could operate." See Peairs, The God in the Machine, 29 B.U.L.Rev. 37 (1949). By 1955, Professor James could write that "[t]he citadel of privity has crumbled, and today the ordinary tests of duty, negligence and liability are applied widely to the man who supplies a chattel for the use of another." James, Products Liability (pt. 1), 34 Tex.L.Rev. 44 (1955). Lingering on in some states longer than others, the privity requirement in negligence actions was finally abolished in Maine in 1982. Adams v. Buffalo Forge Co., 443 A.2d 932 (Me.1982). The *MacPherson* rule has been extended to property damage, to non-purchasers including mere bystanders, to non-manufacturer suppliers, and even to repairmen and building contractors. "It has become, in short, a general rule imposing negligence liability upon any supplier, for remuneration, of any chattel." Prosser, The Assault Upon the Citadel (Strict Liability to the Consumer), 69 Yale L.J. 1099, 1102 (1960). "Probably no other case has been as frequently cited in following decisions or has made as great an impact on industry." D. Peck, Decision at Law 69 (1961).

3. How can the rise and dogmatic adherence to the privity rule in the 1800's be explained? What accounts for its fall from 1916 to 1982? "This trend was responsive to ever-growing pressure for protection of the consumer coupled with a realization that liability would not unduly inhibit the enterprise of manufacturers and that they were well placed both to profit from its lessons and to distribute its burdens." James, Products Liability (pt. 1), 34 Tex.L.Rev. 44 (1955). Do you think the fall of the privity bar to negligence actions is to be explained on the basis of changes in the nature of manufacturing enterprises? On changes in attitudes toward manufacturing enterprises? On the basis of "the historically late development of the idea of negligence and the * * * full appreciation of its 'reach and power' "? See Feezer, Tort Liability of Manufacturers and Vendors, 10 Minn.L.Rev. 1, 9 (1925).

4. *MacPherson* was noted in 29 Harv.L.Rev. 866 (1916) and 25 Yale L.J. 679 (1916). England's *MacPherson* came in 1932 in Donoghue v. Stevenson, [1932] A.C. 562, (H.L.). See C.J. Miller & P. Lovell, Product Liability 171–75 (1977).

B. THE MANUFACTURING PROCESS: FABRICATION AND QUALITY CONTROL

The manufacture of products requires the performance of many individual tasks, from the selection or fabrication of component parts to the assembly of those parts into the final product. While the manufacture of even simple products involves many such tasks, the manufacture of complex products, such as cars and airplanes, involves many thousands. It should therefore be expected that the performance of an occasional manufacturing task, such as the tightening of a nut on a bolt as in the *Jenkins* case that follows, will be done inadequately. Nor will the manufacturer's quality control procedures usually be capable of catching all such products that contain production defects. When the manufacturing process goes awry in this manner, and a "flawed" product that deviates from the manufacturer's specifications is thereby produced and sold, persons are sometimes injured as a result. Whether the manufacturer will be liable in negligence to such persons will depend upon a determination of whether the manufacturer's production and quality control procedures were conducted with "reasonable" care.

JENKINS v. GENERAL MOTORS CORP.

United States Court of Appeals, Fifth Circuit, 1971.
446 F.2d 377.

INGRAHAM, CIRCUIT JUDGE. Ione Jenkins was severely injured when the Corvair automobile in which she was a passenger suddenly veered off the road and landed in a ditch on April 15, 1962. She predicated her action against General Motors Corporation on the grounds of negligent failure to properly tighten and inspect a nut on a bolt in the left rear suspension system. A jury returned a verdict for plaintiff and awarded damages in the sum of $425,000 and judgment was entered thereon. On this appeal appellant raises (1) the insufficiency of evidence to submit to the jury, (2) the alleged error of the district court in excluding certain evidence regarding one of appellee's expert witnesses, and (3) the alleged error in denying appellant's motion to exclude certain testimony of Ione Jenkins.

The evidence in the case indicates that appellee and her date, Billy Mixon, each sixteen years of age, left a drivein theater near Swainsboro, Georgia on the night of April 15, 1962, and headed toward Swainsboro on a straight and level gravel-top asphalt road. Mixon was driving the two months' old 1962 Corvair which registered about 2200 miles on its odometer. Having traveled approximately 1800 feet, the car suddenly veered and pulled to the left, became "uncontrollable", slammed into a concrete culvert off the left shoulder of the road and turned over into a ditch. As a result appellee Jenkins was permanently paralyzed in a major portion of her body.

Testimony of appellee's witnesses, including the trooper who investigated the accident scene, established that there was no evidence of excessive speed, of use of alcoholic beverages, or of improper driving. Appellee Jenkins and Billy Mixon, the only eyewitnesses to the occurrence, testified that they were driving along when the automobile suddenly veered to the left and became uncontrollable. Mixon tried to counteract this by turning the wheel fully to the right. In response to

Miss Jenkins' inquiry, Mixon cried out "I have lost my steering." Mixon testified that he tried to apply his brakes, but that when he hit them, the pedal went to the floor board and he got no braking action.

Appellee's theory of the cause of the accident was that a nut on a bolt in the left rear suspension system was inadequately torqued during assembly at the appellant's factory and that under normal operation conditions this nut worked loose and dropped off, allowing the bolt to drop out. The absence of this bolt and the concomitant additional stresses and strains on the remaining adjacent bolt caused this second bolt to "wallow out" the hole in which it was placed during normal operation of the car. Consequently, at the time of the accident, this second bolt pulled through leaving the components unsecured and causing the left rear suspension assembly to sweep back, canting the wheel outward and to the rear. Appellee contends that this not only created the sudden pull to the left, but also resulted in a loss of a portion of the brake assembly and the subsequent brake failure.

The principal question in this case is presented by appellant's contention that the district court erred in denying its motions for a directed verdict and for judgment notwithstanding the verdict. Appellant vigorously asserts that the damage to the rear suspension system was the result, not the cause, of the accident, and that the theory developed by appellee is so speculative that the jury should not have been permitted to draw the series of inferences required to establish the ultimate fact of appellant's negligence.

* * *

Appellant asserts that the facts are "equiponderant" as to what caused the automobile to strike the culvert. In support of its position at trial, appellant introduced numerous films, exhibits and expert opinion testimony concerning the degree of tightening of the bolt, the shape of the pull-through hole, and of tests conducted on Corvair automobiles. A witness testified that he found the "missing" bolt forty-one feet away from the scene of the accident, and according to appellant's experts the bolt was sheared at impact. This was contrasted with the expert testimony utilized by appellee supporting her theory of the case, including evidence of the condition of the brakes, of rotational marks on the left rear axle indicating it was out of position before impact, and of the condition of the left rear wheel, found "canted out" after the accident but with evidence of only minimal damage from impact.

It all boils down to a battle of experts and, as such, the trial court did not err in submitting the case to the jury. The jury was allowed to inspect and even handle the various components of the rear suspension assembly involved, including the "wallowed out" hole and the "missing" bolt. In addition, they viewed the hundreds of photographs, exhibits and the movies that were shown. The jury was not bound by the appellant's evidence, nor forced to accept the testimony of its experts, even if uncontradicted. [Citations.] The jury was authorized to make reasonable inferences even if some speculation and conjecture was required. [Citations.] We reject appellant's contention that there was an absence of probative facts to support the conclusion reached by the jury.

[I]n Nevels v. Ford Motor Co., 439 F.2d 251 (5th Cir., 1971), this court was faced with an automobile accident case involving a 1967 Mustang in which plaintiff claimed that Ford Motor Company was negligent in the manufacturing or assembling of the steering mechanism because a retaining nut was not properly torqued or secured with a sealing compound:

> "The experts were diametrically opposed concerning the condition of the splines and the retaining nut, as well as the cause of the conditions found. On the one hand, it was unequivocally stated that so long as the retaining nut was on the shaft, even in a loose condition, there could be no slippage of the shaft and no wear on the splines—that the splines showed no evidence of wear but showed only damage undoubtedly caused by the impact of the accident. On the other hand, it was stated, equally explicitly, that the splines showed considerable wear caused by the shaft slipping because the retaining nut was loose. This condition, it was said, made the steering virtually inoperable." 439 F.2d at 254.

Nevertheless, the court held:

> "The jury could have fairly concluded from all of the evidence, though disputed, that Ford was negligent in not having tightened the wheel retaining nut by applying a proper torque on it, and in failing to properly secure the nut to the shaft by a sealer or on an epoxy material. No error was committed in submitting the case to the jury. Indeed, it would have been error to do otherwise." 439 F.2d at 256.

The trial court in the instant case likewise correctly overruled appellant's motions for directed verdict, J.N.O.V., and for new trial.

* * *

The judgment of the district court is affirmed.

NOTES

1. Products liability cases often are like detective stories. In many cases after a product accident has occurred, neither the injured party nor the manufacturer will have any idea what went wrong. And if the person using the product is killed in the accident, no one may know whether the product was being misused at the time of the accident. It is a principal responsibility of the lawyers for the parties, and their experts, to piece together the facts surrounding the accident—to "reconstruct" it—to develop theories of how and why the accident happened.

In *Jenkins,* what was plaintiff's theory of why the car crashed? What was defendant's theory? Which theory appears more plausible from the facts as stated in the reported opinion? By what process was this conflict in theories of causation resolved at trial? Might the jury reasonably have believed the defendant's version of how the accident happened?

2. Note the complexity—and commensurate expense—of litigating the relatively simple issues in this typical products liability case, where hundreds of photographs, exhibits, and films were shown to the jury. Most products liability cases cannot be tried, as illustrated by the *Jenkins* case, without the assistance of at least one expert. Since the "battle of experts" thus may largely determine the outcome of the case, the selection and effective use of skilled—and credible—expert witnesses is one of the most important tasks facing the products liability lawyer. In an omitted portion of the *Jenkins* opinion, the court held that the trial judge had properly excluded evidence that one of plaintiff's expert witnesses was under indictment for perjury. Beware of the expert who is a "professional" witness!

3. Note the absence of any discussion of whether the defendant's failure to tighten the nut properly was a "negligent" act or omission. This, it would seem, apart from the causation issue, should have been the principal issue in the case. Yet the court seemed almost casually to assume that, if in fact the accident were caused by a defect in the car, the defendant had been negligent in its manufacture, or so the jury properly could have found. Other courts have generally agreed. See, e.g., Pouncey v. Ford Motor Co., 464 F.2d 957 (5th Cir. 1972).

What if plaintiff's expert cannot identify the specific problem or defect that caused the accident, as for example where the product is severely damaged in the accident? "Where there is no evidence of a specific defect, dangerous and unusual performance by an article subjected to ordinary use is sometimes held to warrant an inference of the maker's negligence as well as of a defect, if other likely explanations of the mishap are ruled out by a preponderance of the evidence." 5 F. Harper, F. James & O. Gray, The Law of Torts 442 (2d ed. 1986). Matters of proof are treated more extensively in Chapter 3.

4. **The Negligence Standard of Liability.** Most courts use ordinary negligence parlance in defining the standard of care applicable to products liability cases. When courts attempt any definition at all of the standard, which often they do not, they generally go no further than to state that the duty is one of "reasonable," "ordinary," or "due" care. E.g., Atkins v. American Motors Corp., 335 So.2d 134 (Ala.1976) (automobile manufacturer; "due care"); Ulrich v. Kasco Abrasives Co., 532 S.W.2d 197 (Ky.1976) (grinding machine manufacturer; "ordinary care"). Sometimes a court will be a little more explicit: "[N]egligence is the doing of something that a person of ordinary prudence would not have done in the same or similar circumstances or a failure to do something that a person of ordinary prudence would have done in the same or similar circumstances." Rhoads v. Service Machine Co., 329 F.Supp. 367, 373 (E.D.Ark.1971). And some courts tailor these principles to the products liability context by measuring the defendant's conduct against that of a mythical "manufacturer of ordinary prudence in the exercise of ordinary care." Id. at 376. Finally, courts sometimes focus on the particular industry of the defendant, and apply the standard prevailing in his own business, e.g., "a press manufacturer of ordinary prudence." See id. at 377.

Note, however, that while industry practice or custom is important evidence of the reasonableness of the defendant's conduct, it is generally not conclusive, since the industry as a whole may have been derelict in failing to adopt precautionary procedures dictated by ordinary prudence. See The T.J.

Hooper, 60 F.2d 737 (2d Cir.) (Hand, C.J.,), cert. denied 287 U.S. 662, 53 S.Ct. 220, 77 L.Ed. 571 (1932); W.P. Keeton, D. Dobbs, R. Keeton & D. Owen, Prosser and Keeton on Torts 193–95 (5th ed. 1984). Moreover, the manufacturer "will be held to the skill of an expert in that business and to an expert's knowledge of the arts, materials, and processes. Thus manufacturers must keep reasonably abreast of scientific knowledge and discoveries touching their products and of techniques and devices used by practical people in their trade." 5 F. Harper, F. James & O. Gray, The Law of Torts 350–51 (2d ed. 1986).

5. Liability for negligent manufacture is set forth in § 395 of the Restatement (Second) of Torts (1965):

§ 395. Negligent Manufacture of Chattel Dangerous Unless Carefully Made

A manufacturer who fails to exercise reasonable care in the manufacture of a chattel which, unless carefully made, he should recognize as involving an unreasonable risk of causing physical harm * * * is subject to liability for physical harm caused * * * by its lawful use in a manner and for a purpose for which it is supplied.

Comment:

* * *

* * * [T]he amount of care which the manufacturer must exercise is proportionate to the extent of the risk involved in using the article if manufactured without the exercise of these precautions. Where, as in the case of an automobile or high speed machinery or high voltage electrical devices, there is danger of serious bodily harm or death unless the article is substantially perfect, it is reasonable to require the manufacturer to exercise almost meticulous precautions * * * in order to secure substantial perfection. On the other hand, it would be ridiculous to demand equal care of the manufacturer of an article which, no matter how imperfect, is unlikely to do more than some comparatively trivial harm to those who use it.

6. Comment *d* to § 395 provides that the "unreasonableness" of a risk is to be determined in accordance with the principles set forth in § 291 (as supplemented by §§ 292 and 293) which provides as follows:

§ 291. Unreasonableness; How Determined; Magnitude of Risk and Utility of Conduct

Where an act is one which a reasonable man would recognize as involving a risk of harm to another, the risk is unreasonable and the act is negligent if the risk is of such magnitude as to outweigh what the law regards as the utility of the act or of the particular manner in which it is done.

7. In determining negligence liability, therefore, a manufacturer's conduct is to be judged on the basis of whether the risks involved were greater or less than the utility of the conduct. This method of "risk-benefit" or "utility" analysis for examining a defendant's conduct in the negligence context was well articulated by Judge Learned Hand in two cases decided in the 1940's:

The degree of care demanded of a person by an occasion is the resultant of three factors: [1] the likelihood that his conduct will injure others, taken with [2] the seriousness of the injury if it happens, and

> balanced against [3] the interest which he must sacrifice to avoid the risk. All these are practically not susceptible of any quantitative estimate, and the second two are generally not so, even theoretically. For this reason a solution always involves some preference, or choice between incommensurables, and it is consigned to a jury because their decision is thought most likely to accord with commonly accepted standards, real or fancied.

Conway v. O'Brien, 111 F.2d 611, 612 (2d Cir.1940), rev'd on other grounds 312 U.S. 492, 61 S.Ct. 634, 85 L.Ed. 969 (1941).

> Possibly it serves to bring this notion into relief to state it in algebraic terms: if the probability be called P; the injury, L [for "Loss"]; and the burden [or, the cost of precautions to avoid the risk], B; liability depends upon whether B is less than L multiplied by P: i.e., whether $B < PL$.

United States v. Carroll Towing Co., 159 F.2d 169, 173 (2d Cir.1947).

Learned Hand's negligence "formula" thus may be described in full as:

$$\mathbf{B < PL \rightarrow N.}$$

POSNER, A THEORY OF NEGLIGENCE

1 J.Leg.Stud. 29, 32–34 (1972).

It is time to take a fresh look at the social function of liability for negligent acts. The essential clue, I believe, is provided by Judge Learned Hand's famous formulation of the negligence standard—one of the few attempts to give content to the deceptively simple concept of ordinary care. * * * In a negligence case, Hand said, the judge (or jury) should attempt to measure three things: the magnitude of the loss if an accident occurs; the probability of the accident's occurring; and the burden of taking precautions that would avert it. If the product of the first two terms exceeds the burden of precautions, the failure to take those precautions is negligence. Hand was adumbrating, perhaps unwittingly, an economic meaning of negligence. Discounting (multiplying) the cost of an accident if it occurs by the probability of occurrence yields a measure of the economic benefit to be anticipated from incurring the costs necessary to prevent the accident. The cost of prevention is what Hand meant by the burden of taking precautions against the accident. It may be the cost of installing safety equipment or otherwise making the activity safer, or the benefit for[e]gone by curtailing or eliminating the activity. If the cost of safety measures or of curtailment—whichever cost is lower—exceeds the benefit in accident avoidance to be gained by incurring that cost, society would be better off, in economic terms, to for[e]go accident prevention. A rule making the enterprise liable for the accidents that occur in such cases cannot be justified on the ground that it will induce the enterprise to increase the safety of its operations. When the cost of accidents is less than the cost of prevention, a rational profit-maximizing enterprise will pay tort judgments to the accident victims rather than incur the larger cost of avoiding liability. Furthermore, overall economic value or welfare would be diminished rather than increased by incurring a higher accident-prevention cost in order to avoid a lower accident cost. If, on the other hand, the benefits in accident avoidance exceed the costs of prevention, society is better off if those costs are incurred and the accident averted, and so in this case the enterprise is made liable, in the expectation that self-interest will lead it to adopt the precautions in order to avoid a greater cost in tort judgments.

* * *

Perhaps, then, the dominant function of the fault system is to generate rules of liability that if followed will bring about, at least approximately, the efficient—the cost-justified—level of accidents and safety. Under this view, damages are assessed against the defendant as a way of measuring the costs of accidents, and the damages so assessed are paid over to the plaintiff (to be divided with his lawyer) as the price of enlisting their participation in the operation of the system. Because we do not like to see resources squandered, a judgment of negligence has inescapable overtones of moral disapproval, for it implies that there was a cheaper alternative to the accident. Conversely, there is no moral indignation in the case in which the cost of prevention would have exceeded the cost of the accident. Where the measures necessary to avert the accident would have consumed excessive resources, there is no occasion to condemn the defendant for not having taken them.

If indignation has its roots in inefficiency, we do not have to decide whether regulation, or compensation, or retribution, or some mixture of these best describes the dominant purpose of negligence law. In any case, the judgment of liability depends ultimately on a weighing of costs and benefits.

NOTES

1. Assume that a punch press manufacturer knows that over a one year period the cost of adding guards to each press (B) will be $1 million and that the cost of injuries thereby averted (PL) will be $2 million. Assuming with Posner that the manufacturer is a "rational profit-maximizing enterprise," will it necessarily add the guards? Why or why not?

2. Not all scholars agree with Judge Posner's economic analysis of negligence law. Compare, for example, Calabresi & Hirschoff, Toward a Test for Strict Liability in Torts, 81 Yale L.J. 1055 (1972). What weaknesses do you see in his model? Consider the observations of Professor Vandall in his article, Judge Posner's Negligence—Efficiency Theory: A Critique, 35 Emory L.J. 383, 401 (1986): "One of the most disturbing aspects of Posner's efficiency theory is that it enables users of the theory to give pop answers to serious issues that have troubled society and the legal profession for hundreds of years by plugging numbers into formulas."

3. Whatever its weaknesses, the risk-benefit model of negligence responsibility is a helpful analytical tool. It probably explains, even if only in rough terms, a principal characteristic of the negligence litigation process, from the type of proof and argument offered by counsel to the decision-making mechanism of juries and courts. As you examine the negligence cases that follow,

evaluate the conduct of the defendants from a risk-benefit perspective. In the process, try to discern the strengths and weaknesses of this form of analysis.

FORD MOTOR CO. v. ZAHN

United States Court of Appeals, Eighth Circuit, 1959.
265 F.2d 729.

MATTHES, CIRCUIT JUDGE. This is a Minnesota negligence action, in which appellee-plaintiff received a judgment for $26,350 following jury verdict, as damages for loss of his eye occasioned by a defective ash tray in a Ford automobile manufactured by appellant-defendant. Jurisdiction rests on diversity and amount in controversy. At the conclusion of all of the evidence, defendant moved unsuccessfully for a directed verdict; and after trial, moved for judgment notwithstanding the verdict. Following denial of the latter, defendant appealed.

* * *

* * * On April 28, 1956, plaintiff was riding as a passenger in the front seat of a 1956 model Ford automobile that was owned and being driven by Clarence Dailey. The automobile was proceeding * * * at 45 to 50 miles per hour. As the automobile approached a crossroad, plaintiff dropped a lighted cigarette. While plaintiff was attempting to retrieve the same from the floor of the vehicle, with his head down, the brakes of the automobile were applied suddenly and with great force, throwing plaintiff forward and causing his face to come in contact with the dashboard. Dailey, the driver, applied the brakes suddenly in order to avoid a collision with an unidentified automobile which was apparently driven suddenly from the crossroad, directly in the path of the Dailey automobile. Immediately following plaintiff's contact with the dashboard, he realized that his right eye had been injured, as it was paining him and blood and liquid was emerging therefrom. * * *

The Ford automobile was equipped with an ash tray which was located in the center of the dashboard. This tray was found on the floor of the vehicle after plaintiff was injured. * * * [T]he upper right-hand corner of the front portion of this accessory is not only sharp, but a small protrusion, described by witnesses as a ["jagged"] burr, extends therefrom. Testimony indicated that such a defect would be occasioned by a dull cutting die. This sharp edge and burr is the defect upon which plaintiff predicates his case.

* * *

* * * Was the defendant negligent? * * * We do not understand that defendant seeks to escape [liability] on the theory that the sharp edge of the ash tray with the projecting burr did not constitute a defect—rather, its position is that the inspection made by it, particularly in view of the nature, position, and size of the defect, and the for[e]seeability of injury resulting therefrom, constituted the exercise of reasonable care on its part.

[T]here is imposed upon the manufacturer of an article for sale or use the duty to exercise reasonable care to prevent defective conditions caused by a miscarriage in the manufacturing process. This duty requires reasonable skill and care in the process of manufacture and for *reasonable inspection or tests* to discover defects. [Citations.]

Applying this general rule to our facts, it appears that the evidence leaves doubt as to whether the subject ash tray was actually inspected. From the testimony of Mr. Van Scoy, the quality control manager for defendant, who was stationed at the Twin City Assembly Plant in St. Paul, where Dailey's automobile was assembled, we find that defendant followed certain practices designed to insure inspection of automobiles. Ash trays were inspected at various stages—in his words they passed "through roughly seven inspectors," but the same witness also testified that insofar as the face of the ash tray was concerned (the portion containing the instant defect) the inspection was a sampling operation. "We don't look over each one individually." This witness stated that the exposed faces of the ash trays are supposed to have rounded corners, and that they were so constructed to prevent injuries. Regardless of the procedure followed and practiced by defendant, the fact of the matter is the defect was not discovered, although, according to Mr. Van Scoy it was readily discoverable. Referring to the defect, he testified: "I can feel it very easily with my finger. I have done so, both out in the corridor yesterday and here on the witness stand today. * * * Apparently every one of our inspectors missed that. * * * If each ash tray had been inspected, this defect that we are concerned with here could possibly have been discovered."

[T]he defendant insists that a reasonably prudent person was not required to anticipate or foresee the unusual occurrence and resulting injury to plaintiff; that the harm to be anticipated from the defect was perhaps a "cut finger" or "snagged clothing," and that since the extent of the foreseeable risk was minimal, the argument follows that the inspection as made, fully complied with the standard of reasonable care so as to completely insulate defendant from liability.

We do not subscribe to the view that the foreseeable risk attending the defective ash tray was minimal and necessarily limited to a lacerated finger or comparable injury. While the risk of danger was perhaps not as great as that which might inhere in a defective wheel or a defective steering mechanism, nevertheless, the fact remains that plaintiff *did* suffer a serious injury, and the jury could properly consider as a circumstance that in this era of fast moving automobiles, emergencies arise frequently which require the sudden application of brakes which in turn throw the occupants of the automobile forward and against the dashboard. The record reveals that defendant was fully conscious of the necessity of guarding against injuries resulting from such occurrences. Mr. Van Scoy testified: " * * * I would imagine there would be occasions when the brakes are applied suddenly and children and other persons are thrown forward in cars. * * * "

[The negligence question was properly for the jury. Judgment for plaintiff affirmed.]

NOTES

1. "Pernicious products should be scrapped in the factory rather than dodged in the home." Morris, Negligence in Tort Law—With Emphasis on Automobile Accidents and Unsound Products, 53 Va.L.Rev. 899, 909 (1967).

2. **Production Errors.** Plaintiffs sometimes seek to prove the defendant's negligence in performing a particular assembly line skill, or in improperly adjusting, operating or maintaining an assembly line machine. See, e.g., Jenkins v. General Motors Corp., supra; Mitchell v. Four States Machinery Co., 74 Ill.App.2d 59, 220 N.E.2d 109 (1966) (miswired punch press control switch).

What failure in Ford's production process was responsible for the flawed ash tray? How might the plaintiff have argued that this failure was negligent? What proofs would have been helpful? How might defendant have responded?

3. **Quality Control Failures.** As in *Zahn,* many negligent manufacture cases are fought, not on negligence in the production process, but on the adequacy of the defendant's quality control program—the sufficiency of its testing and inspection procedures for *screening out* mistakes made on the assembly line. Why do you suppose the battles are often fought at this secondary stage of the manufacturing process?

4. Might a risk-benefit analysis of the facts in *Zahn* have been helpful in determining the reasonableness of Ford's inspection procedures? On which component(s) of the Hand "formula" did the defendant largely rest its argument that it had not been negligent? Do you agree with the court's treatment of the defendant's argument?

5. Assume that Ford was negligent in its production of the ash tray, but not negligent in its inspection of the trays. Should it be liable? Compare Nicklaus v. Hughes Tool Co., 417 F.2d 983, 986 (8th Cir.1969), citing *Zahn* ("To permit recovery for negligent manufacture, ordinarily plaintiff must show, in addition to lack of reasonable skill and care in the process of manufacture, that the manufacturer failed to make a reasonable inspection or test to discover defects."), with Rest. (2d) Torts § 437 ("If the actor's negligent conduct is a substantial factor in bringing about harm to another, the fact that after the risk has been created by his negligence the actor has exercised reasonable care to prevent it from taking effect in harm does not prevent him from being liable for the harm.").

6. Recall Judge Cardozo's words in *MacPherson:* "The obligation to test must vary with the nature of the thing to be inspected. The more probable the danger the greater the need of caution." 217 N.Y. at 395, 111 N.E. at 1055. This is still good law. See Rest. (2d) Torts § 395, Comment *e*: "A garment maker is not required to subject the finished garment to anything like so minute an inspection for the purpose of discovering whether a basting needle has not been left in a seam as is required of the maker of an automobile or of high speed machinery or of electrical devices, in which the slightest inaccuracy may involve danger of death."

7. **Degrees of Care.** A legacy from the privity days are cases holding that the standard of care is higher than ordinary in the manufacture of "inherently" dangerous products. For example, *food and drink:* Eisenbeiss v. Payne, 42 Ariz. 262, 25 P.2d 162 (1933) ("highest duty known to the law");

drugs: Henderson v. National Drug Co., 343 Pa. 601, 23 A.2d 743 (1942) ("high degree of responsibility"); *explosives:* Hopkins v. E.I. Du Pont de Nemours & Co., 212 F.2d 623 (3d Cir.), cert. denied 348 U.S. 872, 75 S.Ct. 108, 99 L.Ed. 686 (1954) ("high degree of care"). Most modern courts, however, take the position that the magnitude of the danger posed by the product is but one aspect of the negligence calculus for determining how much care is "due" or "reasonable" under the circumstances. See Dimeo v. Minster Mach. Co., 388 F.2d 18 (2d Cir. 1968); Restatement, Second, Torts § 395, Comment *d* (1965).

8. **Manufacturer Responsibility for Defective Materials and Components.** Even prior to the production process, a manufacturer may be negligent in the selection, inspection or testing of materials and component parts. "The exercise of reasonable care in selecting raw material and parts to be incorporated in the finished article usually requires something more than a mere inspection of the material and parts. A manufacturer should have sufficient technical knowledge to select such a type of material that its use will secure a safe finished product. So, too, a manufacturer who incorporates a part made by another manufacturer into his finished product should exercise reasonable care to ascertain not only the material out of which the part is made but also the plan under which it is made." Restatement, Second, Torts § 395, Comment *g* (1965). The fact that the assembler purchased the part from a reputable supplier does not relieve it of its responsibility to make its own tests and inspections. E.g., MacPherson v. Buick Motor Co., 217 N.Y. 382, 394, 111 N.E. 1050, 1055 (1916) (defective wheel for car).

What if the component part is permanently sealed or otherwise must be destroyed to test or inspect it? Can the manufacturer-assembler in such circumstances ever be liable in negligence for injuries caused by defective components? See, e.g., Pabon v. Hackensack Auto Sales, Inc., 63 N.J.Super. 476, 164 A.2d 773 (1960) (ball bearings that to be tested had to be crushed).

9. **Product Sponsorship.** Some courts have held the manufacturer-assembler vicariously liable for defects in components attributable to the negligence of the component part manufacturer. E.g., Ford Motor Co. v. Mathis, 322 F.2d 267, 273–74 (5th Cir.1963) (defective headlight dimmer switch in car). See Rest. (2d) Torts § 400. Compare Brandimarti v. Caterpillar Tractor Co., 527 A.2d 134 (Pa.Super.1987) (§ 400 applied to strict tort design case). See ch. 7, § 5, infra.

10. **Sampling.** In *Zahn,* Ford tested or inspected for defects by "sampling" only a fraction of the total number of ash trays. "Through statistical theory it has been calculated that, *if proper samples of a certain size are taken for testing,* the average of the results for these tests will differ by no more than a measurable amount at an acceptable probability level from the average of the results that would be obtained if all the items were to be tested. * * * In most cases sufficient information concerning the items can be obtained without going through the time and expense of testing all items." Gaffney & Bein, Sampling in Legal Cases, in 1 L. Frumer & M. Friedman, Products Liability § 2.10[6][d] (1987) (emphasis in original). When a defendant's inspection or testing process is conducted by sampling, should plaintiff's attorney be more interested in the absolute size of the sample or in its proportion to the total population? In the standard error of the sample? Sampling is apt to catch at least one of a run of bad products resulting, for example, from the maladjustment of an assembly line machine. What type of flaws is sampling not likely to catch? Do you consider it a "reasonable" quality control technique? How should the risk-benefit calculus be applied to a sampling case such as *Dimeo?*

See generally 1 L. Frumer & M. Friedman, Products Liability §§ 2.09, 2.10 (1987); Cowan, Some Policy Bases of Products Liability, 17 Stan.L.Rev. 1077, 1090 (1965); Annot., 6 A.L.R.3d 91, 114 (1966).

11. Keller v. Coca Cola Bottling Co., 214 Or. 654, 662, 330 P.2d 346, 350 (1958), was a cigar-stub-in-a-Coke case. "Following the filling process the bottles were exposed to strong artificial light while moving along a conveyor chain. Two employees, sometimes only one, had the responsibility to examine the bottles and their contents and at the same time remove the bottles from the conveyor and place them in cases. The employees were so engaged six to eight hours per day. Occasionally, foreign substance was detected. The ability of a person to carefully inspect under these conditions was clearly for the jury to determine." Compare Haynes v. Coca Cola Bottling Co., 39 Ill.App.3d 39, 42, 350 N.E.2d 20, 23 (1976) (1200 cans per minute passed by one employee primarily responsible for preventing cans from jamming). In both cases, plaintiff's judgments were affirmed.

C. THE DESIGN PROCESS: THE PRODUCT CONCEPT

It is only in recent years that courts in any number have begun to examine the reasonableness of the design of products involved in accidents. Yet the formulation of the product concept is the first and in many ways most important safety function of manufacturers. For it is at this step that decisions are made that will affect the safety of the entire product line: decisions concerning the types and strengths of raw materials and component parts, the manner in which they will be combined into the finished product, whether safety devices are to be built in, and the overall product concept. The determination of whether the design of any particular product was "adequately" safe—or was, instead, "unreasonably" hazardous—is often a difficult task, particularly since the process may well involve second-guessing (with the benefit of hindsight) the defendant's professional design engineers. Yet "mistakes" of this type sometimes are made, and resulting injuries are sometimes traceable to the manufacturer's failure to exercise reasonable care in designing the product.

EXUM v. GENERAL ELECTRIC COMPANY

United States Court of Appeals, District of Columbia Circuit, 1987.
819 F.2d 1158.

MIKVA, CIRCUIT JUDGE:

Appellant Reginald Exum suffered first- and second-degree burns while using a french fryer designed and marketed by General Electric ("GE"). He sued the company under several theories, the most important of which for purposes of this appeal is negligent design. At the close of Exum's case, the trial court directed a verdict for General Electric. Exum contends in this appeal that the trial court erroneously excluded expert testimony and evidence of similar accidents. He also argues that the evidence he did adduce at trial was sufficient to send the case to the jury. * * *

Mr. Exum was 19 years old and a new employee at a Wendy's franchise on June 10, 1983, the date of the accident giving rise to this suit. One of Exum's duties was filtering the hot grease used in his employer's GE Model 811 french fryer (the "Model 811"). This task required Exum to lift a six-pound pan containing 15 pounds of grease at a temperature of 350 degrees and pour the grease through a paper cone filter into a second pan placed on the floor.

Exum is asthmatic and carries with him a pressurized asthma inhaler. As he poured the grease through the filter, the inhaler dropped from his shirt pocket into the scalding liquid. An explosion occurred, and Exum was burned and scarred on his face, neck, and chest.

* * *

The premise of Exum's negligent design theory was that the Model 811 is an obviously and unreasonably dangerous machine. At trial, Exum hoped to show that the company was unreasonable to market an industrial french fryer requiring the use of two open pans when a safer fryer with a closed filtration system could have been created by installing an inexpensive manual siphon. In support of this theory, Exum sought to introduce evidence of other cases in which young employees of Wendy's had been burned seriously while filtering grease with the Model 811. The trial court first made a tentative decision to admit evidence of these other incidents, but ultimately it excluded the evidence. The court reasoned that all but one of the other cases were not sufficiently similar to Mr. Exum's to be relevant, because they did not involve an employee's accidentally dropping an object into the grease. The court excluded the remaining case on the rationale that because it occurred after Exum's accident, it could not be used to show either notice or dangerousness.

Exum also sought to introduce the expert testimony of a Mr. Stanley Kalin, a registered professional engineer who had experience with occupational injuries and issues of safety and health. Exum intended to use Mr. Kalin to demonstrate that there were feasible and economical alternatives to GE's open-pan system. This testimony would have tended to show that the Model 811 is unreasonably dangerous. The court, however, decided that Kalin was not qualified to testify because he had no experience with kitchen equipment, including french fryers, found in fast food restaurants such as Wendy's.

* * *

The D.C. Court of Appeals elaborated District law on negligent design in Westinghouse Electric Corp. v. Nutt, 407 A.2d 606 (D.C.App. 1979). The court endorsed a "danger-utility test" for determining whether a particular product poses unreasonable danger in light of available alternatives. *See* W. Keeton, D. Dobbs, R. Keeton & D. Owen,

Prosser & Keeton on the Law of Torts 699 (5th ed. 1984). The court explained, "[w]hat constitutes 'reasonable care' will vary with the circumstances, and involves 'a balancing of the likelihood of harm, and the gravity of harm if it happens, against the burden of precaution which would be effective to avoid the harm.'" * * *

Applying these established principles to this case, we conclude that Mr. Exum presented a jury question as to whether GE failed to exercise reasonable care in its design and marketing of the Model 811. Although Exum was stymied in his efforts to introduce expert testimony and evidence of other accidents with the Model 811, he was able to bring certain key bits of evidence to the jury's attention. First, the court permitted Exum to introduce a blueprint of a siphon that could have converted the Model 811 into a closed, and therefore safer, system. Second, the court permitted plaintiff's counsel to read into the record GE's answers to interrogatories in which the company admitted it designed and marketed the siphon and indicated it believed the siphon sold for under $100.

Armed with this knowledge, and aware of the circumstances of Exum's injury, a reasonable jury could have found GE negligent. First, the jury would have had to inquire whether it was unreasonable for the company not to spend the extra money to install a manual siphon, given the gravity and apparent likelihood of harm arising from an open system. GE argues on appeal that evidence of available design alternatives is irrelevant to the question of dangerousness. GE's position appears to be that the possibility of an accident such as Exum's was too remote to have figured in the company's calculations. This argument misconstrues the law that applies in negligent design cases. To find GE had acted unreasonably, the jury would not have to determine that Exum's injury was foreseeable in all its particulars; rather, it would have to find that a reasonable manufacturer, seeking to minimize many classes of harms including injuries like that to Exum, would have opted to install the siphon. As Exum's counsel pointed out in resisting GE's motion for a directed verdict, "It doesn't matter whether General Electric had any knowledge that Reginald Exum, or anybody, was going to drop an asthma inhaler. What we are talking about is a dangerous system, a dangerous design. * * * [A] reasonable manufacturer * * * wouldn't manufacture something like that. They would provide an alternative system that is readily available." Tr. 165. The court apparently rejected this argument, but we find it is an accurate account of the law. * * * Under this standard, a reasonable jury certainly could have found that it was unreasonable of GE to market the Model 811 as an open system.

* * *

Our analysis of District of Columbia law also leads us to disagree with the trial court's evidentiary rulings. Exum offered about 15 case files detailing incidents in which young employees were burned while filtering grease with the Model 811. In one of the cases, the victim, like Exum, had dropped an object in the grease; the other incidents involved slightly different and sundry fact patterns—for example, spillages.

* * *

In appraising the relevancy of similar incidents in product liability cases, courts have required the other incidents to be "substantially similar" to the case at bar. * * *

There is without doubt a high degree of similarity between Exum's case and the incident in which a Wendy's employee was injured by dropping an object into the hot grease in the Model 811. In fact, the court excluded that case not on substantial similarity grounds but because it occurred after June 10, 1983, the date of Exum's accident. However, although subsequent incidents cannot be introduced to prove the manufacturer had notice, they are relevant to show dangerousness. * * *

The other incidents appear relevant to show both dangerousness and notice. In order to determine whether the Model 811 was negligently designed and marketed, a jury would have to balance " 'the likelihood of harm, and the gravity of harm if it happens, against the burden of precaution which would be effective to avoid the harm.' " *Westinghouse Electric,* supra, 407 A.2d at 610 (quoting 2 Harper & James, *The Law of Torts* § 28.4, at 1542 (1956)). The similar incidents could have aided the jury in its calculations of one side of the balance—the likelihood and the gravity of harm arising from the use of the Model 811. [Citations.] Since the incidents are admissible on a dangerousness theory, they are, *a fortiori,* also admissible under a theory of notice, which imposes a less rigorous requirement of similarity. Certainly these other accidents were "of a kind which should have served to warn" GE of the risks of an open system fryer. * * *

The district court also erred in excluding the expert testimony of Mr. Kalin. Admission of experts is governed by Federal Rule of Evidence 702, which prescribes a two-part test. First, the witness must be qualified; i.e., he must have "knowledge, skill, experience, training, or education" in the field. Second, the witness's testimony must be able to assist the trier of fact. In this case, the court relied on the first prong of the Rule 702 test. It found Kalin unqualified to testify, because Kalin had no specific expertise in kitchen design and had never examined a kitchen of a fast food restaurant.

* * *

In this case, Kalin is amply qualified as an expert witness. He is a registered engineer who has worked at OSHA and the Institute of Safety Analysis. He has considerable experience with issues of industrial safety and product design and has testified as an expert in several other defective design cases. Kalin's engineering background and special expertise in the area of safe industrial design are more than adequate credentials under Rule 702.

Moreover, Kalin's training enables him to provide testimony that would aid the jury. See Jenkins v. U.S., 307 F.2d 637 (D.C.Cir.1962) (en banc). His testimony thus passes the second prong of the Rule 702 test. Since Exum's allegations of defective design focus on the open filtration system (and alternatives to it), Mr. Kalin's expertise could be helpful whether or not he knows precisely how the Model 811 performs in frying potatoes of Wendy's. Mr. Kalin stands ready to describe the probable expense and effectiveness of installing a manual siphon on the Model 811. These are matters which a reasonable manufacturer would have weighed in deciding whether to market the Model 811 without a siphon. They therefore are highly relevant considerations for a jury attempting to determine whether GE discharged its duty of reasonable care. See *Westinghouse Electric,* supra, 407 A.2d at 611. ("To show lack of due care, expert testimony is admissible regarding the nature and feasibility of safeguards and precautions which could have been taken.")

* * *

[Reversed and remanded.]

NOTES

1. Explain the risk-benefit analysis applied by the court. Was its analysis correct?

2. Compare Pike v. Frank G. Hough Co., 2 Cal.3d 465, 85 Cal.Rptr. 629, 467 P.2d 229 (1970). The plaintiff's decedent was a construction worker run over by a large, earth-moving machine (a "paydozer") which was being backed up by the operator whose view to the rear was blocked by the body of the machine. *Held,* the jury could properly have found that the manufacturer's failure to include rear-view mirrors was negligence in design.

3. How, if at all, does *dangerousness* figure into the calculus of risk? How about *notice? Foreseeability?*

4. What if there simply is no feasible way to improve the safety of a hazardous product? Can its design still be negligent? How does the "feasibility" of safer alternative designs bear on the calculus of risk? *Compare* Maxted v. Pacific Car & Foundry Co., 527 P.2d 832 (Wyo.1974) (failure to provide means to jettison trailer portion of tractor-trailer to prevent "jack-knife" when no evidence of feasibility: not negligent), and Garst v. General Motors Corp., 207 Kan. 2, 484 P.2d 47 (1971) (design of 40–ton earthmover that could neither be turned nor braked quickly: not negligent), *with* South Austin Drive–In Theatre v. Thomison, 421 S.W.2d 933 (Tex.Civ.App.1967) (failure to provide $3 shield for drive chain and rear sprocket of power mower: negligent), and Calkins v. Sandven, 256 Iowa 682, 129 N.W.2d 1 (1964) (absence of simple, inexpensive shield over exposed conveyor mechanism on power farm wagon, where shield would not interfere with operation: negligent).

5. **Product Testing.** Just as there is a duty to test and inspect products for manufacturing flaws, so also is there a duty on the manufacturer to test the product prototype for hidden dangers in design. Consider the remarks of Justice Jackson, dissenting in Dalehite v. United States, 346 U.S. 15, 52, 73 S.Ct. 956, 976, 97 L.Ed. 1427, 1449 (1953):

> This is a day of synthetic living, when to an ever-increasing extent our population is dependent upon mass producers for its food and drink, its cures and complexions, its apparel and gadgets. These no longer are natural or simple products but complex ones whose compositions and qualities are often secret. Such a dependent society must exact greater care than in more simple days and must require from manufacturers or producers increased integrity and caution as the only protection of its safety and well-being. Purchasers cannot try out drugs to determine whether they kill or cure. Consumers cannot test the youngster's cowboy suit or the wife's sweater to see if they are apt to burst into fatal flames. Carriers, by land or by sea, cannot experiment with the combustibility of goods in transit. Where experiment or research is necessary to determine the presence or the degree of danger, the product must not be tried out on the public, nor must the public be expected to possess the facilities or the technical knowledge to learn for itself of inherent but latent dangers.

Compare Banks v. Koehring Co., 538 F.2d 176, 179 (8th Cir.1976), where plaintiff was injured while dislodging sorghum stalks from his new harvester machine that clogged every ten feet. "When a manufacturer offers a machine or equipment to the public for use in harvesting, the user is entitled to presume that the manufacturer has fully tested the mechanism * * *."

D. THE MARKETING PROCESS: WARNINGS AND INSTRUCTIONS

A product may be designed and produced exactly as intended by the manufacturer yet still be unduly hazardous to consumers who do not appreciate its dangerous characteristics. This is increasingly true as consumers are faced with a burgeoning variety of products of ever-increasing complexity, spawned by modern technology. Consumers are often dependent upon the expert manufacturer to supply them with information on product dangers and how to avoid them. Reasonable care may thus obligate the manufacturer "to speak out if the product is capable of harm and does not itself carry a message of danger." Dillard & Hart, Product Liability: Directions for Use and the Duty to Warn, 41 Va.L.Rev. 145, 147 (1955). In most instances, of course, "[t]he purpose of a warning is to apprise a party of a danger of which he is not aware, and thus enable him to protect himself against it." Jonescue v. Jewel Home Shopping Service, 16 Ill.App.3d 339, 345, 306 N.E.2d 312, 316 (1973). In passing along the finished product to the ultimate consumer, the prudent manufacturer must therefore attach whatever information reasonably appears to be necessary to permit the consumer to use the product with reasonable safety. Thus, a manufacturer may be negligent if it fails adequately to warn of dangers in its product or to instruct on methods for its safe use. "It is not necessary that the product be negligently designed or manufactured; the failure to warn of hazards associated with foreseeable uses of a product is itself negligence, and if that negligence proximately results in a plaintiff's injuries, the plaintiff may recover." Laaperi v. Sears, Roebuck & Co., Inc., 787 F.2d 726, 729 (1st Cir.1986).

As was seen in Chapter 1, the maker's obligation to warn of hidden dangers in its products is an ancient one. Its roots reach back into early Roman sales law and both the ecclesiastical and secular law of medieval England. It will be recalled that one of the three privity exceptions articulated in *Huset v. J.I. Case Threshing Machine Co.,* supra, was for "one who sells or delivers an article which he knows to be imminently dangerous to life or limb of another without notice of its qualities." Negligence in the failure to supply adequate warnings or instructions continues today to be a central issue in many products liability cases. Since the various issues of warning "defectiveness" receive full consideration in Chapter 3, the focus here is on the nature of the negligence principles at work in the warnings context.

BOYL v. CALIFORNIA CHEMICAL CO.

United States District Court, District of Oregon, 1963.
221 F.Supp. 669.

EAST, DISTRICT JUDGE.

[The case was tried to the court, which found as follows: Defendant, a chemical manufacturer, makes and sells a liquid weed killer called "Triox." A major market for Triox is the "do-it-yourself garden-type consumer."]

Substantially 50% of the Triox solution is a chemical compound referred to as sodium arsenite, which compound is compared as being four to six times as toxic to humans as arsenide trioxide (rat poison); the minimum human lethal dosage of sodium arsenite is 20 to 30 milligrams and it is a very stable compound with long-lasting toxic contamination propensities, and a disabling dosage of the compound, varying in degrees to fatal, can be taken into the human bloodstream by way of absorption through the skin or by inhalation as readily as by ingestion.

* * *

PLAINTIFF'S USE OF TRIOX

During the latter part of May, 1960, plaintiff purchased from a third party retail outlet a quart-sized can of the Triox product for the intended ultimate use on weed growth in and about the driveway of her residence, and the container so purchased exhibited the following pertinent labels and warnings:

[FRONT OF CAN]
ORTHO
TRIOX
KILLS VEGETATION
An Arsenical Weed Killer!

Prevents Plant Growth for 1 to 2 years

Use on driveways, brick walks, paths, tile patios, tennis courts, parking areas; along fence lines, curbs and gutters; around garages, house foundations and other structures, where soil can be poisoned and no plant growth is wanted.

POISON
[Skull and crossbones]

Active Ingredient	by Wt.
Sodium Arsenite ($NaAsO_2$)	55%
Inert Ingredients	45%

Equivalent to 41.9% of arsenic trioxide.
Arsenic expressed as metallic, all in water-soluble form 31.7%
Pounds Arsenic Trioxide per gallon at 68° F 6

DO NOT USE ON LAWNS

[RIGHT SIDE OF CAN]

TRIOX
KILLS WEEDS IN
[picture]
Tile Patios
[picture]
Curbs and Gutters
[picture]
Brick Walks
Driveways
Paths
Tennis Courts
Parking Areas
Along Fence Lines

USE WHERE SOIL CAN BE POISONED AND NO PLANT GROWTH IS WANTED

[LEFT SIDE OF CAN] Manufactured by [manufacturer's name and address omitted.]

[BACK OF CAN]

DILUTION TABLE
[omitted]

READ ENTIRE LABEL. USE STRICTLY IN ACCORDANCE WITH LABEL CAUTIONS, WARNINGS AND DIRECTIONS.

TO POISON SOIL AND PREVENT PLANT GROWTH: [Dilution and instruction of preparation of ground—omitted]

TO KILL ANNUAL WEEDS AND TOP GROWTH OF PERENNIAL WEEDS: [Dilution and instruction of application—omitted]

NOTE: INSTRUCTIONS AS TO FREEZING TEMPERATURES [omitted]

WARNING: TRIOX is a strong poison. It should be kept away from children and animals. Avoid breathing spray mist. Avoid contact with skin, eyes, or clothing. Wash thoroughly after using. Avoid getting TRIOX into cuts, sores, etc. Should this occur, wash off at once. Livestock and poultry will be poisoned if allowed to feed on treated areas.[2] Avoid getting TRIOX on painted surfaces as peeling of paint will occur. Rinse spray hoses thoroughly after use as TRIOX will deteriorate hose materials. *When container is empty, immediately wash thoroughly and destroy.* Never re-use.[3]

[poison skull & crossbones]

ANTIDOTE FOR ARSENIC: Give a tablespoonful of salt in a glass of warm water and repeat until vomit fluid is clear. Then give two tablespoonfuls of Epsom Salts or Milk of Magnesia in water and plenty of milk and water. Have victim lie down and keep quiet. CALL A PHYSICIAN IMMEDIATELY.

* * *

On May 27, 1960 (a Friday), plaintiff proceeded to apply the Triox, and after perusing the labels and warnings on the container she put on protective clothing such as gloves and a scarf, and then proceeded, while standing windward, to apply the Triox to the driveway area with the use of a backpack air-pressure spray pump;

That after applying the bulk of the Triox solution in the spray tank, she thereupon rinsed the spray tank with garden hose water and poured out the rinse water containing the tank residue of Triox upon a "waste area" (rough grass area) of the back yard immediately adjoining a clear patio space;

That afternoon plaintiff and her family motored to the Oregon beach area for the Memorial Day weekend, and plaintiff recalls no physical malfunctioning effects or discomforts from her spraying activities except for a bad headache during the same evening.

2. Indicative of defendant's knowledge of long-lasting earth-contaminating potentials of sodium arsenite.

3. Italicized to indicate defendant's knowledge of the stability of sodium arsenite.

INJURY

On the following Wednesday early afternoon the weather was sunny and warm and plaintiff, while dressed in a "bra and shorts" type sunsuit, had just finished hanging a clothes washing on the dryer rack in the patio area when she unwittingly lay stomach down for a sunning in the rough grass area where she had poured out the Triox rinse;

Very shortly thereafter she noticed a "heat rash" and severe itching about her thighs, and within half an hour she broke out with red spots followed by hives; thereafter, her condition worsened in that her body became generally swollen, and by 6:00 P.M. she was dizzy and confused and had developed muscle tremors and twitching, and by 7:00 to 8:00 P.M. she had been and was hospitalized for the following three days, during the first 24–hour period of which hospitalization her worsened physical condition was listed as critical. No useful purpose will be here served by further describing plaintiff's symptoms, physical malfunctioning and disabilities nor the medical treatment therefor extended over some 18 months, as I am satisfied from the medical expert testimony that plaintiff's acute physical malfunctioning immediately following the exposure, with resulting disability during the slow recovery, was due to the introduction into her blood supply through skin absorption and inhalation of an intolerable quantity of toxic sodium arsenite during the time she lay upon the ground which had been contaminated with the Triox rinse.

DUTY TO WARN

I conclude that with its experience and expertise the defendant knew or should have known of the stable quality (see n. 3) and long-lasting contamination propensities of the sodium arsenite contained in the Triox solution upon the earth (see n. 2) and of the hazard or danger to humans coming in contact with such contaminated earth;

Further, that a prudent producer of such a potential danger to humans would reasonably foresee an injury such as that sustained by plaintiff in the absence of, or but for some reasonable notice or warning concerning a safe disposal of the rinse residue after the use of the product for the intended purpose for which it was produced and sold. * * *

* * *

[A] manufacturer who undertakes to produce and sell to the general public a product with high risk of human harm must provide specification, instruction, and warning, so that it is reasonably safe for ordinary persons to use it, *not only* for the purposes for which it is produced and intended to be used *but also* all other necessarily incidental and attendant uses (such as storage or disposal) and to give reasonable notice and warning of after or delayed effect or latent or lingering dangers not known or reasonably to be expected by the ordinary user, but which are "foreseeably probable" to the manufacturer with his expertise.[5]

* * *

DEFENDANT'S FAILURE TO WARN AND LIABILITY

A perusal of the warnings and instructions on the can of Triox here tells us in no uncertain words that Triox is "an arsenical * * *" compound and that it contains a large quantity of "sodium arsenite" and that such solution is "poison," as I am sure everyone knows. The warning gives an antidote for *internal* ingestion. Also, directions for prevention of personal injury *while using and applying the liquid;* however, no warning or protective advice whatsoever as to disposal of the fluid or of any risk to unadvised persons from the stability or long-lasting qualities or propensities and lingering risks of the liquid after returning to a dry or solid form is given, or even reasonably inferable. In fact, the directions as to use and advice as to avoiding skin or other personal contact with the liquid or breathing the spray mist of Triox and the washing of the person after using, and total lack of advice as to disposal of the rinse, could mislead a user to concluding that there was no lingering risk after immediate use and airwashing.

From the foregoing, I conclude that the defendant was negligent towards plaintiff in failing to give any reasonable notice or warning of a risk or danger to her personal safety from contact with earth lately contaminated with the Triox solution, and that such negligence on the part of the defendant was the proximate cause of plaintiff's resulting physical malfunctioning and disabilities.

* * *

[Judgment for plaintiff in the amount of $7,910.60.]

NOTES

1. Did defendant warn users that contact of the weed killer with the skin could be dangerous? What language on the label do you suppose defendant relied upon? If defendant did warn users of the danger, why was it held negligent?

2. Do you agree with the court that no warning was given of the long-lasting nature of the danger?

3. Was it really foreseeable that a person informed of the danger of contact with Triox would dump out the chemical residue and then lie down, partially unclothed, on top of it?

4. Was the decision correct? Did the court use a calculus of risk approach in finding the defendant negligent? Can you?

5. Some courts expressly apply risk-benefit analysis to warnings cases. See, e.g., Holladay v. Chicago, Burlington & Quincy R. Co., 255 F.Supp. 879, 884 (S.D.Iowa 1966) (failure to warn of skin irritation from herbicide) ("In determin-

5. * * * The likelihood of an accident taking place and the seriousness of the consequences are always pertinent matters to be considered with respect to the duty to provide a sufficient label. See Rest., Torts, §§ 291, 388, Comment 1, pp. 1051–1052; § 397, Comments b–d. * * *

ing the duty of care required of defendant in the case at hand, the likelihood of harm, and the gravity of the harm if it happens, must be weighed against the burden of precaution which would be effective to avoid the harm."); Wright v. Carter Products, Inc., 244 F.2d 53, 59 (2d Cir.1957) (failure to warn of very slight risk of possibly serious skin disorder from use of deodorant); Dougherty v. Hooker Chemical Corp., 540 F.2d 174 (3d Cir.1976); Jonescue v. Jewel Home Shopping Service, 16 Ill.App.3d 339, 306 N.E.2d 312 (1973) (no warning of danger to child from drinking all-purpose cleaner). Perhaps the clearest statement of the principle is in Moran v. Faberge, Inc., 273 Md. 538, 543, 332 A.2d 11, 15 (1975), where the defendant failed to warn that its perfume was flammable:

> To begin with we note that a manufacturer's duty to produce a safe product, with appropriate warnings and instructions when necessary, is no different from the responsibility each of us bears to exercise due care to avoid unreasonable risks of harm to others. 2 Harper & James, The Law of Torts, § 28.3 (1956); Prosser, The Law of Torts, § 31 (4th ed. 1971). Whether any such unreasonable risk exists in a given situation depends on balancing the probability and seriousness of harm, if care is not exercised, against the costs of taking appropriate precautions. 2 Harper & James, supra, §§ 16.9, 28.4; Restatement, Second, Torts §§ 291–93, 298 (1965). However, we observe that in cases such as this the cost of giving an adequate warning is usually so minimal, amounting only to the expense of adding some more printing to a label, that this balancing process will almost always weigh in favor of an obligation to warn of latent dangers, if the manufacturer is otherwise required to do so.

6. **Foreseeability of Danger.** A failure to warn may be negligent, of course, only if the danger is reasonably foreseeable to the manufacturer. See generally Note, Foreseeability in Product Design and Duty to Warn Cases—Distinctions and Misconceptions, 1968 Wis.L.Rev. 228. But foreseeability is often viewed from the perspective of an expert in the business who is held to know the characteristics of its products and the uses to which they possibly may be put. See, e.g., Thornhill v. Carpenter–Morton Co., 220 Mass. 593, 108 N.E. 474 (1915) (duty to warn of explosive character of walnut oil stain, although it had never previously ignited, where the ingredients were largely petroleum derivatives that generated flammable gases). Put another way, a manufacturer is deemed to possess the knowledge of an expert in the field: See, e.g., Stahlheber v. American Cyanamid Co., 451 S.W.2d 48, 61 (Mo.1970) (manufacturer of polio vaccine "knew or, by using the skill of an expert in defendant's business, could have known of the dangerous potentiality of said product" when administered to adults). This is sometimes put in terms of constructive knowledge: "Negligence based on the failure to warn requires actual or constructive knowledge of the danger on the part of the manufacturer, and the lack of a warning notice." Smith v. United States, 155 F.Supp. 605, 609 (E.D.Va.1957). " 'Constructive knowledge' refers to knowledge that one has the opportunity to possess by the exercise of ordinary care." First Nat. Bank v. Nor–Am Agricultural Products, 88 N.M. 74, 537 P.2d 682, 690 (1975).

7. Defendant sent plaintiff science teacher on request a free display of oil products showing various forms of oil ranging from crude petroleum to the most highly refined products. Water had been placed in the bottle labeled "kerosene" to increase safety in mailing. No warning was given that the labels

were incorrect. It happens that kerosene acts to preserve a certain substance, sodium metal, whereas water causes it to explode. Was it foreseeable that a teacher would use the liquid in the bottle marked "kerosene" to illustrate the preservative characteristics of kerosene on metallic sodium? See Pease v. Sinclair Refining Co., 104 F.2d 183 (2d Cir.1939).

8. Is it foreseeable that cleaning fluid may be splashed in the eye? See Sawyer v. Pine Oil Sales Co., 155 F.2d 855 (5th Cir.1946) (no). Paint? Haberly v. Reardon Co., 319 S.W.2d 859 (Mo.1958) (yes).

9. For a considered analysis of the duty to warn under § 388 of the Restatement (Second) of Torts, see Lockett v. General Electric Co., 376 F.Supp. 1201 (E.D.Pa.1974).

SECTION 2. TORTIOUS MISREPRESENTATION

There are three primary theories of tortious misrepresentation recognized today by the common law, differing largely in the culpability of the defendant's state of mind in making the representation. Fraud and deceit requires a showing that the defendant intended to mislead the plaintiff, or some similar state of mind. Negligent misrepresentation requires proof only that the defendant was negligent in not knowing the falsity of his representations, or that he communicated them in a negligent manner. A defendant may be strictly liable in tort for certain public misrepresentations about its products, regardless of its good faith or its exercise of reasonable care. Other differences between these three theories of recovery will be considered below.

A. FRAUD

ST. JOSEPH HOSPITAL v. CORBETTA CONSTRUCTION CO., INC.

Illinois Appellate Court, 1974.
21 Ill.App.3d 925, 316 N.E.2d 51.

* * *

The St. Joseph Hospital (the Hospital) in 1958 entered into a contract with architect Belli & Belli of Missouri (Belli) for the erection of a hospital on a new site in Chicago to replace one erected before the Great Chicago Fire of 1871, and the general construction of the hospital was undertaken by the Corbetta Construction Company (Corbetta). In April of 1965, when the building had been substantially completed, the Hospital was advised by the city collector that its application for a license to operate the Hospital had been disapproved because the wall paneling (General Electric's "Textolite") which covered its rooms and corridors, and had been manufactured and furnished by the General Electric Company (General Electric), did not comply with a Chicago code requirement that such paneling have a "flame spread" rating of not to exceed 15. Actually it had a rating of 255, 17 times the maximum. The city also threatened criminal action against the Hospital for operating without said license.

* * *

[The Hospital thereupon filed a complaint for a declaratory judgment against Corbetta, Belli, and General Electric to determine liability for the loss. The jury rendered a verdict for the Hospital on liability, and a subsequent jury awarded damages to the Hospital for the cost of replacing the Textolite paneling with other paneling that complied with the Chicago Building Code. The following portion of the court's opinion pertains only to the liability of General Electric, the manufacturer of Textolite. Throughout the case, G.E. argued that it had warned the parties, over and over, that Textolite was "not rated."]

On August 28, 1962, a series of flame spread tests were made at the Underwriters Laboratories in Northbrook. Herbert Day, an employee of General Electric, was there. The tests were performed by Walter Haas of Underwriters and seven different products were tested. General Electric's product Textolite (the same as was here installed) was placed in one of the tunnels and the fire turned on. The test lasted only 2 minutes and 16 seconds because by then the flames had traversed the entire (25 feet) length of the tunnel and the sample of Textolite was removed with its surface completely charred. That concluded the test and the flame spread was calculated at 254.6 or 255. The Textolite had the highest flame-spread rating of any of the products tested that day.

On August 31, 1962, Day reported to General Electric by a letter addressed to Mr. Thomas, with copies to Mr. Derbyshire of General Electric, and others. Haas, of Underwriters, explained the nature of the test and the result of the test on Textolite and said that the product was not given a flame-spread rating because they felt that no product testing out over 200 should be given a rating because it would be highly inflammable and dangerous.

On October 26, 1962, 2 months after said test, General Electric entered into its subcontract with Corbetta for the installation of this highly inflammable material on the walls of the plaintiff's hospital in Chicago. No one other than General Electric knew at that time of the disastrous results of this test.

In December of 1962, representatives of General Electric, including Derbyshire, and of Corbetta met and discussed further the installation of Textolite in the plaintiff's hospital. Again, Derbyshire said nothing of the results of said test to Corbetta's representatives, or even to Warner, his own salesman.

On January 3, 1963, Derbyshire wrote Mr. Egidi, of Corbetta, as follows:

> "Further at this time I wish to point out that our Batten Panel System does not carry a flame spread rating of any kind.

> I have brought up the need of a fire rating of this System in several of our initial discussions and again on December 12, 1962. I have been told [by the architect Belli] that it was none of our concern and that everything was taken care of in this respect. Nowhere is a rating mentioned in the specification. If we now find that our System must have a flame spread rating, then our contracted price no longer can apply. We must at this point reevaluate the requirements and reengineer the paneling and pricing accordingly.
>
> "We can supply a U–L flame spread rated panel but not under the terms and drawings submitted in conjunction with the contract."

It should be noted that, again, the fact that the Textolite paneling had actually been flame tested and had tested out a disastrous 17 times the maximum permitted under the Code is masked and concealed. Rather, it was a "coverup." Furthermore, General Electric did not then have (nor has it had since) a wall paneling meeting the flame-spread test fixed in the Chicago Code.

* * *

In view of these facts, we agree, as it said in plaintiff's (and Corbetta's) brief, that:

> "Regardless of how many times General Electric might say, either orally or in writing, that 'Our material is not flame rated,' the statement is still a 'gross deception' covering up the real truth namely that General Electric was proposing for installation in this hospital a material which it actually knew was utterly unfit for use in such an institution."

Under these facts, we are of the considered opinion that General Electric is liable to the Hospital on the basis of fraud and deceit in not disclosing that its said paneling had actually been tested by Underwriters Laboratory and had been found to have a flame spread 17 times the maximum under the Chicago Building Code; which theory does not require privity in the traditional sense.

(i)

It is well established that a statement which is technically true as far as it goes may nevertheless be fraudulent, where it is misleading because it does not state matters which materially qualify the statement as made. In other words, a half-truth is sometimes more misleading than an outright lie.

* * *

(ii)

It is also well established that where one has made a statement which at that time is true but subsequently acquires new information which makes it untrue or misleading, he must disclose such information to anyone whom he knows to be acting on the basis of the original statement—or be guilty of fraud or deceit.

* * *

(iii)

It is also well established that in fraud cases based on misrepresentation it is not a prerequisite to recovery that there be privity, at least in the traditional sense. It is enough that the statements by the defendant be made with the intention that it reach the plaintiff and influence his action and that it does reach him and that he does rely upon it, to his damage.

[Verdict for Hospital against G.E. affirmed.]

NOTES

1. One of the earliest reported products liability opinions was based on fraud and deceit. See Langridge v. Levy, 2 M. & W. 519, 150 Eng.Rep. 863 (1836), aff'd 4 M. & W. 337, 150 Eng.Rep. 1458 (1838).

2. Consider Dobbin v. Pacific Coast Coal Co., 25 Wash.2d 190, 201–02, 170 P.2d 642, 648 (1946) (distributor of defective furnace not liable in fraud):

> Of all civil liabilities, fraud is the most difficult to establish. In the comparatively recent case of Andrews v. Standard Lbr. Co., 2 Wash.2d 294, 300, 97 P.2d 1062, 1065, the court said:
>
> "The first question presented is whether the evidence established facts showing the commission of fraud.
>
> "In Webster v. L. Romano Engineering Corp., 178 Wash. 118, 34 P.2d 428, 430, we set out the essential elements of fraud in the following language:
>
> " 'But what is fraud? This court has been reluctant to circumscribe it by definition. [Citations.] We have, however, along with all other courts, recognized certain essential elements that enter into its composition. These are: (1) A representation of an existing fact; (2) its materiality; (3) its falsity; (4) the speaker's knowledge of its falsity or ignorance of its truth; (5) his intent that it should be acted on by the person to whom it is made; (6) ignorance of its falsity on the part of the person to whom it is made; (7) the latter's reliance on the truth of the representation; (8) his right to rely upon it; (9) his consequent damage.' "

In the principal case, did the complaint make out a case of fraud on each of the *Dobbin* elements? Some courts combine the nine *Dobbin* elements into five or six for purposes of defining the tort, but even in such jurisdictions a fraud case will fail if plaintiff does not establish each of the requirements set forth in *Dobbin.*

3. A misrepresentation may be accomplished by conduct as well as by words, and manufacturers and other sellers have been held liable for fraudulent concealment of a dangerous defect. See Kuelling v. Roderick Lean Mfg. Co., 183 N.Y. 78, 75 N.E. 1098 (1905) (beam on farm machine made of unfit, cross-grained wood with knothole): "[D]efendant concealed this knothole with a plug of soft wood nailed in, and then the knot, the plug, the hole, the cross-grain of the wood, and the kind of wood used were covered up and concealed by

the defendant with putty and paint * * *." This amounted to "an affirmative representation that the [beam] was sound * * *." See also Woodward v. Miller & Karwisch, 119 Ga. 618, 46 S.E. 847 (1904) (large crack in axel of buggy covered over with grease). See generally P. Keeton, Fraud—Concealment and Nondisclosure, 15 Texas L.Rev. 1 (1936).

4. Most courts hold that the misrepresentation must be of an *existing* fact rather than being a prediction of future facts. However, a promise of future performance made with no present intention of keeping it may satisfy the rule. See Willard v. Chrysler Corp., 248 S.C. 42, 148 S.E.2d 867 (1966).

5. Opinions, including "sales talk" that extol the quality of a product in general terms, will not ordinarily support an action of deceit. See, e.g., Lambert v. Sistrunk, 58 So.2d 434 (Fla.1952) (step-ladder would "last a lifetime" and customer would "never break it"); Holley v. Central Auto Parts, 347 S.W.2d 341 (Tex.Civ.App.1961) (tire rim was "a good one").

However, "[w]here the party making the representations has superior knowledge regarding the subject matter of his representations, and the other party is so situated that he may reasonably rely on such supposed superior knowledge or special information, the representations may be construed as fact and not opinion." Toole v. Richardson-Merrell, Inc., 251 Cal.App.2d 689, 60 Cal.Rptr. 398, 411 (1967) (drug that produced serious eye damage to defendant's test animals, and later to humans, advertised as "virtually non-toxic," "safe," and free of "significant side effects"). See generally Keeton, Fraud: Misrepresentations of Opinion, 21 Minn.L.Rev. 643 (1937).

6. Plaintiffs in fraud cases often have difficulty establishing the defendant's "scienter"—the defendant's knowledge of the falsity and/or his intent to deceive. See, e.g., Limited Flying Club, Inc. v. Wood, 632 F.2d 51 (8th Cir.1980).

In recent years, however, some courts have begun to liberalize the scienter requirement, holding for example that "deliberate deception or scienter is not a necessary element of the cause of action for fraud * * *. It is sufficient if the speaker makes the statement as of his own knowledge without knowing whether it is true or false." Clements Auto Co. v. Service Bureau Corp., 298 F.Supp. 115, 126 (D.Minn.1969). Thus, while such a defendant may not know that what he says is false, he actually does know that he does not know whether it in fact be true. " '[F]raud' includes pretense of knowledge, where there is no knowledge." Sgarlata v. Carioto, 23 Misc.2d 263, 201 N.Y.S.2d 384, 385 (Albany City Ct.1960). See Aaron v. Hampton Motors, Inc., 240 S.C. 26, 33, 124 S.E.2d 585, 588 (1962) (actual knowledge of falsity not necessary if defendant makes statement as of his personal knowledge "with reckless disregard of his lack of information as to its truth"). Cf. Cooper v. R.J. Reynolds Tobacco Co., 234 F.2d 170, 174–75 (1st Cir.1956) (Magruder, J., concurring), on reappeal 256 F.2d 464 (1st Cir.1958) (lung cancer from Camel cigarettes allegedly advertised as "healthful" and "harmless to the respiratory system"). See generally Keeton, Fraud: The Necessity for an Intent to Deceive, 5 U.C.L.A.L. Rev. 583 (1958).

7. The misrepresentation must of course be the cause of the plaintiff's harm, and so the element of reliance. Thus, the representative of a person who dies of lung cancer may have difficulty convincing a court that the malady was attributable to cigarette advertisements first seen by the decedent two or three years before his death. Cf. Cooper v. R.J. Reynolds Tobacco Co., 256 F.2d 464, 466 (1st Cir.1958). Of course a plaintiff who did not hear or see the misrepresentation at all will usually have considerable difficulty with this element.

The reliance need not be by the plaintiff personally, however, so long as it is by someone who is acting on his behalf. See Wechsler v. Hoffman–La Roche, Inc., 198 Misc. 540, 99 N.Y.S.2d 588, 590 (Sup.Ct.1950) (prescription drug alleged to have been fraudulently marketed to doctors); Toole v. Richardson–Merrell, Inc., 251 Cal.App.2d 689, 60 Cal.Rptr. 398 (1967) (misrepresentations of drug's safety made to Food and Drug Administration to obtain approval to market new drug). "Where a patient relies on a physician for treatment or advice as to an ethical or prescription device, justifiable reliance by the physician * * * constitutes justifiable reliance by the patient." Tetuan v. A.H. Robins Co., 241 Kan. 441, 738 P.2d 1210, 1228 (1987) (upholding awards of $1.7 million compensatory and $7.5 million punitive damages for fraudulently marketing dangerous Dalkon Shield IUD). See generally Owen, The Highly Blameworthy Manufacturer: Implications on Rules of Liability and Defense in Products Liability Actions, 10 Ind.L.Rev. 769, 781–84 (1977); Phillips, Product Misrepresentation and the Doctrine of Causation, 2 Hofstra L.Rev. 561 (1974).

8. Many of the more recent cases of fraud and deceit are against retailers, often used—car dealers, for loss of bargain rather than for personal injury. For example, the dealer may be charged with falsely having said that the car had only been used as a demonstrator, or that it had never been involved in a crash. The recurring problem of used car dealers misrepresenting the mileage by turning back the odometer was addressed by Congress in 1972 in the Motor Vehicle Information and Cost Savings Act, 15 U.S.C.A. § 1981 et seq. Section 1984 provides: "It is unlawful for any person or his agent to disconnect, reset, or alter the odometer of any motor vehicle with the intent to change the number of miles indicated thereon." Purchasers of such vehicles are entitled to (1) the greater of treble damages or $1,500, and (2) costs of suit and reasonable attorneys fees. 15 U.S.C.A. § 1989.

9. Some states have statutes that broadly prohibit false, misleading or deceptive trade practices. Similar to the federal odometer statute, such laws often provide for treble damages and attorneys fees. Such statutes were generally not enacted, however, to provide remedies to persons suffering physical injuries from defective products, and so their remedies may not be available in such cases. See generally Boswell, Stagg & Myers, Deceptive Trade Practice—Consumer Protection Acts and Their Effect on Product Liability Litigation, 15 Forum 716 (Spring 1980).

10. **Treble Damages Under RICO.** In 1970, Congress enacted the Racketeer Influenced and Corrupt Organizations Act, 18 U.S.C.A. § 1961 et seq. ("RICO"). Had the facts in the principal case arisen thereafter, the St. Joseph Hospital might have had a RICO civil action for treble damages and attorneys' fees against G.E. had it been able to prove G.E. guilty of a "pattern of racketeering activity," defined in part in the statute as engaging in mail fraud twice within ten years. Derbyshire's January 3 letter might have been so classified, so that G.E. might have been subject to RICO liability had it mailed one additional fraudulent letter in its efforts to sell the Textolite paneling. Recent decisions have interpreted the statute restrictively, however, holding that a "pattern of racketeering activity" requires more than "a single, nonrecurring scheme to defraud a single entity." Instead, a plaintiff may be required to prove a "continuous engagement in criminal conduct" that "embodies a threat of continued like activity in the future." Eastern Publishing and Advertising, Inc. v. Chesapeake Publishing and Advertising, Inc., 831 F.2d 488, 492 (4th Cir.1987).

RICO treble damages actions are unavailable in ordinary products liability actions for *personal injuries*, in any event, since the statute provides only that civil damages are available for injuries to a person's "business or property." See § 1964(c); Bast v. A.H. Robins Co., Inc., 616 F.Supp. 333 (E.D.Wis.1985). On RICO civil damages actions, see generally Annot., 70 A.L.R.Fed. 538 (1984).

11. The U.C.C. remedies for breach of warranty are available for fraudulent breach. U.C.C. § 2–721.

12. Today, products liability actions involving personal injuries are only infrequently brought in fraud and deceit. Why do you suppose this is so?

Depending on the jurisdiction, however, proof of fraud may advantage a plaintiff's case with respect to privity, the statute of limitations, the effect of a disclaimer, contributory negligence, and perhaps the availability of punitive damages.

13. On fraud and deceit in products liability litigation, see generally Phillips, Product Misrepresentation and the Doctrine of Causation, 2 Hofstra L.Rev. 561 (1974); Shapo, A Representational Theory of Consumer Protection: Doctrine, Function and Legal Liability for Product Disappointment, 60 Va.L. Rev. 1109, 1155–68 (1974); Annot., 75 A.L.R.2d 112, 140 (1961); Restatement (Second) of Torts §§ 557A (1977) and 310 (1965).

B. NEGLIGENT MISREPRESENTATION

Although a person injured as the result of a misrepresentation is unable to make out a fraud case, as from lack of evidence on the defendant's scienter, he nevertheless may be able to prove a claim of negligent misrepresentation. In Pabon v. Hackensack Auto Sales, Inc., 63 N.J.Super. 476, 164 A.2d 773, 784 (1960), the plaintiff was injured when the steering on his new automobile locked, causing the car to crash. He had noticed a "clicking" and "chopping" sensation in the steering and had brought it to the attention of the defendant's service manager on three occasions prior to the accident. Each time, the service manager without checking the problem said something like, "It's a new car. Don't worry about it. It'll wear out." Holding that a jury could find the defendant liable for negligent misrepresentation on these facts, the court stated:

> Negligence may be inferred not only from Hackensack's failure or refusal to repair or even to examine the reported defect, but also from its representation to Alphonse that the steering deficiency was normal and should cause him no concern. A false statement negligently made, and on which justifiable reliance is placed, may be the basis for the recovery of damages for injury sustained as a consequence of such reliance. [Citations.] The statement need not be a factual report, but may consist of an expert opinion. Justification for the imposition of a duty of care upon the speaker is found in the respective positions of the one making the representation and the relying party, the former purporting to exercise the

skill and competency compatible with his profession or calling, the latter openly placing his faith on such reputed skill. There must be knowledge, or reason to know, on the part of the speaker that the information is desired for a serious purpose, that the seeker of the information intends to rely upon it, and that if the information or opinion is false or erroneous, the relying party will be injured in person or property. [Citation.] While privity of contract is generally thought to be a prerequisite to the right to recover for financial loss caused by a negligent statement, Kahl v. Love, 37 N.J.L. 5, 8 (Sup.Ct.1874), where the resulting damage is physical in nature the test becomes one of foreseeability rather than contractual privity.

NOTES

1. Most of the cases of negligent misrepresentation involve retailers. The defendant's negligence usually consists of its failure to exercise reasonable care to ascertain the accuracy of its representation. Typical are the used car cases. E.g., Boos v. Claude, 69 S.D. 254, 9 N.W.2d 262 (1943) (car with defective steering said to be in "perfect mechanical condition," yet "defendants had not used reasonable care in making tests for the purpose of ascertaining defects"); Flies v. Fox Bros. Buick Co., 196 Wis. 196, 218 N.W. 855 (1928) (Owen, J.) (dealer representing car, restored after wreck, to be "in perfect operating condition" negligent in not discovering defective brakes).

2. Manufacturers on occasion have been held responsible for negligent misrepresentation, usually in connection with representations on a product's label or in advertising. Typically the product is labeled or advertised to be "harmless" or "safe" when it in fact contains a hidden danger. The manufacturer's failure to warn of the danger in these cases often appears to be as important as its affirmative misrepresentation of safety. See, e.g., Henry v. Crook, 202 App.Div. 19, 195 N.Y.S. 642 (1922) (sparklers advertised as "A harmless and delightful amusement for children" ignited seven-year-old plaintiff's dress); Crist v. Art Metal Works, 230 App.Div. 114, 243 N.Y.S. 496 (1930), aff'd 225 N.Y. 624, 175 N.E. 341 (1931) (toy revolver, advertised as "absolutely harmless," ignited plaintiff's Santa Claus beard and costume during demonstration of product in department store window); LaPlant v. E.I. DuPont de Nemours & Co., 346 S.W.2d 231 (Mo.App.1961) (plaintiff's cattle died from eating willows sprayed with defendant's weed killer labeled "not hazardous to livestock").

3. False labeling or advertising concerning a product's safety may contravene a misbranding or false advertising statute and thus support a claim for negligence per se. Although defendant received over 373 complaints of skin irritation over a four year period, it continued to advertise its deodorant, "Arrid," as "safe" and "harmless," and that it "does not irritate the skin." Plaintiff, who suffered a skin disorder from using Arrid, alleged that defendant had misrepresented and falsely advertised its product:

> [T]here is some authority in other jurisdictions for grounding recovery upon a claim of negligent advertising. Although our attention has not been directed to any Massachusetts cases espousing this particular theory of recovery, the plaintiffs, as possible bases for granting them relief, do rely upon two Massachusetts statutes, which prohibit false

advertising and misbranding. They contend that the defendant violated those statutes by advertising and labeling its product as "safe," "harmless," and "does not irritate the skin."

> It is well established that a statutory violation may be the basis for civil liability if the injured person is a member of the class for whose express benefit the statute was enacted and the harm resulting from the violation is of the type that the statute was designed to prevent.

Wright v. Carter Products, Inc., 244 F.2d 53, 61 (2d Cir.1957). See also Tetuan v. A.H. Robins Co., 241 Kan. 441, 738 P.2d 1210 (1987) (false advertising of dangerous Dalkon Shield IUD).

4. The negligent misrepresentation theory of liability has been used infrequently in products liability litigation, especially against manufacturers. Why? For a modern, if limited, role for the theory in the case of certifiers of product safety, see Chapter 7, § 6, infra.

C. STRICT LIABILITY FOR MISREPRESENTATION

BAXTER v. FORD MOTOR CO.

Supreme Court of Washington, 1932.
168 Wash. 456, 12 P.2d 409.

HERMAN, J.

[While plaintiff was driving his Model A Ford, a pebble from a passing car struck his windshield, causing small pieces of glass to fly into his eye which he lost as a result. In a suit against Ford for misrepresenting the windshield's characteristics in its advertising catalogues, the trial court rendered judgment for the defendant, and plaintiff appealed. The catalogues stated:]

"TRIPLEX SHATTER-PROOF GLASS WINDSHIELD. All of the new Ford cars have a Triplex shatter-proof glass windshield—so made that it will not fly or shatter under the hardest impact. This is an important safety factor because it eliminates the dangers of flying glass—the cause of most of the injuries in automobile accidents. In these days of crowded, heavy traffic, the use of this Triplex glass is an absolute necessity. Its extra margin of safety is something that every motorist should look for in the purchase of a car—especially where there are women and children."

Respondent Ford Motor Company contends that there can be no implied or express warranty without privity of contract, and warranties as to personal property do not attach themselves to, and run with, the article sold.

* * *

In the case at bar, the automobile was represented by the manufacturer as having a windshield of non-shatterable glass "so made that it will not fly or shatter under the hardest impact." An ordinary person would be unable to discover by the usual and customary examination of the automobile whether glass which would not fly or shatter was used in the windshield. In that respect, the purchaser was in a position similar to that of the consumer of a wrongly labeled drug, who has bought the same from a retailer, and who has relied upon the manufacturer's representation that the label correctly set forth the contents of the container. For many years, it has been held that, under such circumstances, the manufacturer is liable to the consumer, even though the consumer purchased from a third person the commodity causing the damage. Thomas v. Winchester, 6 N.Y. 397, 57 Am.Dec. 455.

The rule in such cases does not rest upon contractual obligations, but rather on the principle that the original act of delivering an article is wrong, when, because of the lack of those qualities which the manufacturer represented it as having, the absence of which could not be readily detected by the consumer, the article is not safe for the purposes for which the consumer would ordinarily use it.

* * *

Since the rule of *caveat emptor* was first formulated, vast changes have taken place in the economic structures of the English speaking peoples. Methods of doing business have undergone a great transition. Radio, bill boards and the products of the printing press have become the means of creating a large part of the demand that causes goods to depart from factories to the ultimate consumer. It would be unjust to recognize a rule that would permit manufacturers of goods to create a demand for their products by representing that they possess qualities which they, in fact, do not possess; and then, because there is no privity of contract existing between the consumer and the manufacturer, deny the consumer the right to recover if damages result from the absence of those qualities, when such absence is not readily noticeable.

* * *

[Reversed and remanded.]

NOTE

The case was retried, and plaintiff prevailed. The Supreme Court affirmed, ruling that Ford's belief in the truth of its representations was irrelevant, as was its evidence that the windshield was as good as any made. 179 Wash. 123, 35 P.2d 1090 (1934). "As to this general field—negligence, deceit, warranty, or whatever the *Baxter* case may really involve—I take it we are feeling our way. * * * Perhaps we are actually witnessing the birth of a new type of tort liability." Leidy, Another New Tort?, 38 Mich.L.Rev. 964, 986 (1940). See also Feezer, Manufacturer's Liability for Injuries Caused by His Products: Defective Automobiles, 37 Mich.L.Rev. 1, 26 (1938).

Compare Worley v. Proctor & Gamble Mfg. Co., 241 Mo.App. 1114, 253 S.W. 2d 532 (1952), defendant manufacturer represented that "Tide is kind to your hands." *Held,* representation could support non-contractual warranty action imposing strict liability for its breach on manufacturer despite absence of privity. Cf. Rogers v. Toni Home Permanent Co., 167 Ohio St. 244, 147 N.E.2d 612 (1958).

RESTATEMENT (SECOND) OF TORTS (1965)

§ 402B. Misrepresentation by Seller of Chattels to Consumer

One engaged in the business of selling chattels who, by advertising, labels, or otherwise, makes to the public a misrepresentation of a material fact concerning the character or quality of a chattel sold by him is subject to liability for physical harm to a consumer of the chattel caused by justifiable reliance upon the misrepresentation, even though

(a) it is not made fraudulently or negligently, and

(b) the consumer has not bought the chattel from or entered into any contractual relation with the seller.

HAUTER v. ZOGARTS

Supreme Court of California, 1975.
14 Cal.3d 104, 120 Cal.Rptr. 681, 534 P.2d 377.

TOBRINER, JUSTICE. After the jury found for defendants in this products liability case, the trial court granted plaintiffs' motion for judgment notwithstanding the verdict. (Code Civ.Proc. § 629.) Defendants appeal, claiming that substantial evidence supports the jury's verdict.

We discuss below each theory of liability: plaintiffs' first cause of action for misrepresentation, their second cause of action for breach of express and implied warranties, and their third cause of action for strict liability in tort based on the defective design of defendants' product. We have concluded that plaintiffs are entitled to recover as a matter of law under each theory and, therefore, we affirm the trial court's order of judgment notwithstanding the verdict.

1. *The facts.*

Defendants [1] manufacture and sell the "Golfing Gizmo" (hereinafter Gizmo), a training device designed to aid unskilled golfers improve their games. Defendants' catalogue states that the Gizmo is a "completely equipped backyard driving range." In 1966, Louise Hauter purchased a Gizmo from the catalogue and gave it to Fred Hauter, her 13½-year-old son, as a Christmas present.

The Gizmo is a simple device consisting of two metal pegs, two cords—one elastic, one cotton—and a regulation golf ball. After the pegs are driven into the ground approximately 25 inches apart, the elastic cord is looped over them. The cotton cord, measuring 21 feet in length, ties to the middle of the elastic cord. The ball is attached to the end of the cotton cord. When the cords are extended, the Gizmo

1. Defendants are Rudy C. Zogarts, who does business as House of Zog [manufacturer] and Miles Kimball Company [seller].

resembles the shape of a large letter "T," with the ball resting at the base.

The user stands by the ball in order to hit his practice shots. The instructions state that when hit correctly, the ball will fly out and spring back near the point of impact; if the ball returns to the left, it indicates a right-hander's "slice"; a shot returning to the right indicates a right-hander's "hook." If the ball is "topped," it does not return and must be retrieved by the player. The label on the shipping carton and the cover of the instruction booklet urge players to "drive the ball with full power" and further state: "COMPLETELY SAFE BALL WILL NOT HIT PLAYER."

On July 14, 1967, Fred Hauter was seriously injured while using defendants' product. Thereafter, plaintiffs filed the instant suit on his behalf, claiming false representation, breach of express and implied warranties and strict liability in tort.

Fred Hauter testified at trial that prior to his injury, he had practiced golf 10 to 20 times at driving ranges and had played several rounds of golf. His father instructed him in the correct use of the Gizmo. Fred had read the printed instructions that accompany the product and had used the Gizmo about a dozen times. Before the accident, Fred set up the Gizmo in his front yard according to the printed instructions. The area was free of objects that might have caused the ball to ricochet, and no other persons were nearby. Fred then took his normal swing with a seven-iron. The last thing he remembers was extreme pain and dizziness. After a period of unconsciousness, he staggered into the house and told his mother that he had been hit on the head by the ball. He suffered brain damage and, in one doctor's opinion, is currently an epileptic.

George Peters, a safety engineer and an expert on the analysis and reconstruction of accidents, testified for plaintiffs. In Peters' opinion, Fred Hauter had hit underneath the ball and had caught the cord with his golf club, thus drawing the cord upwards and toward him on his follow-through. The ball looped over the club producing a "bolo" effect and struck Fred on the left temple. Peters, an expert on the cause of accidents, concluded that the Gizmo is a "major hazard."

Ray Catan, a professional golfer, also testified for plaintiffs. He added that even if the club had hit the lower part of the ball, the same result probably would have occurred. He personally tested the Gizmo, intentionally hitting low shots, and found that his club became entangled in the cord, bringing the ball back toward him as he completed his swing. Describing Fred Hauter as a beginner, Catan stated that since such a golfer's swing usually is very erratic, he rarely hits the ball solidly.

Defendants did not dispute plaintiffs' version of the accident. The manufacturer merely stated that he bought the rights to manufacture and distribute the Gizmo from a former professional golfer in 1962 and that the product had been on the market since that time.

Following a unanimous jury verdict for defendants on each cause of action, the trial judge granted plaintiffs' motion for judgment notwithstanding the verdict and plaintiffs' alternative motion for a new trial. Defendants have limited their appeal to the order granting judgment notwithstanding the verdict.

* * *

3. *As a matter of law, plaintiffs should recover on their cause of action for false representation.*

Plaintiffs' claim of false representation relies on common law tort principles reflected in section 402B of the Restatement Second of Torts. For plaintiffs to recover under this section, defendants' statement "COMPLETELY SAFE BALL WILL NOT HIT PLAYER" must be a misrepresentation of material fact upon which plaintiffs justifiably relied. (Rest. 2d Torts, § 402B, coms. f, g, and j.) [4]

If defendants' assertion of safety is merely a statement of opinion—mere "puffing"—they cannot be held liable for its falsity. (Cf. Willson v. Municipal Bond Co. (1936) 7 Cal.2d 144, 150, 59 P.2d 974; Pacesetter Homes, Inc. v. Brodkin (1970) 5 Cal.App.3d 206, 211–212, 85 Cal.Rptr. 39.) [5] Defendants' statement is so broad, however, that it properly falls within the ambit of section 402B. The assertion that the Gizmo is completely safe, that the ball will not hit the player, does not indicate the seller's subjective opinion about the merits of his product but rather factually describes an important characteristic of the product. Courts have consistently held similar promises of safety to be representations of fact. (See, e.g., McCormack v. Hankscraft Co. (1967) 278 Minn. 322, 154 N.W.2d 488 [vaporizer called "safe" and "practically foolproof"]; Spiegel v. Saks 34th St. (N.Y.S.Ct.1964) 43 Misc.2d 1065, 1070, 252 N.Y.S.2d 852 [representation that cosmetic was "safe"]; Pritchard v. Liggett & Myers Tobacco Co. (3d Cir.1961) 295 F.2d 292, 301 (concurring opinion) [representation that cigarettes "can cause no ills"]; Hansen v. Firestone Tire & Rubber Co. (6th Cir.1960) 276 F.2d 254, 259 [tires

4. The fact that Fred Hauter did not purchase the Gizmo and hence is not in "privity" with defendants does not bar his claim of false representation. Section 402B eliminates the privity requirement and affords protection to all injured consumers. (Rest. 2d Torts, 402B, com. i.)

5. California case law is replete with examples of sellers who have "puffed" their wares. (See Williams v. Lowenthal (1932) 124 Cal.App. 179, 12 P.2d 75 [jukebox a "good machine" and "would probably not get out of order"]; Steen v. Southern Cal. Supply Co. (1925) 74 Cal.App. 265, 239 P. 1098 [caramel coloring matter "just as good or perhaps better than any"]; Blumer v. Rauer (1924) 69 Cal.App. 195, 230 P. 964 [fertilizer would increase productivity of vineyard]; W.J. Bush & Co. v. Van Camp Sea Food Co. (1921) 55 Cal.App. 672, 203 P. 1026 [peach kernel oil was "equal to the best grades of imported olive oil"]; Alexander v. Stone (1916) 29 Cal.App. 488, 156 P. 998 [goods "first class"]; see also, Performance Motors, Inc. v. Allen (1972) 280 N.C. 385, 186 S.E.2d 161 [mobile home would "last a lifetime"]; Jacquot v. Wm. Filene's Sons Co. (1958) 337 Mass. 312, 149 N.E.2d 635 [artificial fingernail kit described as "wonderful"]; Silverman v. Samuel Mallinger Co. (1954) 375 Pa. 422, 100 A.2d 715 [glassware "as good [as] anyone else's"].)

In the instant case, for example, defendant seller appears to "puff" when he says in his catalogue, "[y]ou may be a duffer and divot digger but just give yourself a few hours with this and you'll be challenging Jack Nicklaus! * * * Practice with [the Gizmo] and you'll have even your golf pro watching admiringly."

described as "safe" within stated limits]; Hamon v. Digliani (1961) 148 Conn. 710, 718, 174 A.2d 294 [representation implying that detergent was safe for all household tasks]; Rogers v. Toni Home Permanent Co. (1958) 167 Ohio St. 244, 249, 147 N.E.2d 612 [permanent wave solution represented as safe and harmless].)

These decisions evidence the trend toward narrowing the scope of "puffing" and expanding the liability that flows from broad statements of manufacturers as to the quality of their products. Courts have come to construe unqualified statements such as the instant one liberally in favor of injured consumers. Furthermore, the illustrations in the Restatement indicate that the assertion "COMPLETELY SAFE BALL WILL NOT HIT PLAYER" constitutes a factual representation. Defendants' statement parallels that of an automobile dealer who asserts that the windshield of a car is "shatterproof." (Rest. 2d Torts, § 402B, illus. 1, based on Baxter v. Ford Motor Co. (1932) 168 Wash. 456, 461–463, 12 P.2d 409), or that of a manufacturer who guarantees his product is "safe" if used as directed (Rest. 2d Torts, § 402B, illus. 3, based on Rogers v. Toni Home Permanent Co. (1958) 167 Ohio St. 244, 259, 147 N.E.2d 612, and Markovich v. McKesson & Robbins, Inc. (1958) 106 Ohio App. 265, 149 N.E.2d 181, 186).

Moreover, the materiality of defendants' representation can hardly be questioned; anyone learning to play golf naturally searches for a product that enables him to learn safely. Fred Hauter's testimony that he was impressed with the safety of the item demonstrates the importance of defendants' statement. That Fred's injury occurred while he used the Gizmo as instructed proves the inaccuracy of the assertion on the carton.

Defendants, however, maintain that plaintiffs' reliance upon the assurance of safety is not justifiable. (See Rest. 2d Torts, § 402B, com. j.) Alluding to the danger inherent to the sport, defendants argue that the Gizmo is a "completely safe" training device only when the ball is hit squarely. Defendants repeatedly state that an improperly hit golf shot exposes the player, as well as others nearby, to a serious risk of harm; they point to testimony recounting how an experienced player once hit a shot so poorly that the ball flew between his legs. As a result, contend defendants, plaintiffs cannot reasonably expect the Gizmo to be "completely safe" under all circumstances, particularly those in which the player hits beneath the ball.

Defendants' argument does not withstand analysis. Fred Hauter was not "playing golf." He was home on his front lawn *learning* to play the game with the aid of defendants' supposedly danger-free training device. By practicing in an open, isolated area apart from other golfers and free of objects off which a poorly hit shot could ricochet, Fred Hauter *eliminated* most of the dangers present during a normal round of play. Moreover, even though certain dangers are inherent in playing golf, the risk that the golfer's own ball will wrap itself around his club and strike the golfer on the follow-through is not among those dangers. Fred Hauter's injury stemmed from a risk inherent in defendants' product, not a risk inherent in the game of golf.

Additionally, defendants' analysis would render their representation of safety illusory. Were we to adopt their analysis, the words "COMPLETELY SAFE BALL WILL NOT HIT PLAYER" would afford protection to consumers only in *relatively infrequent instances* in which the "duffers" using the Gizmo managed to hit the ball solidly. Yet defendants' instructions supplied with the Gizmo clearly indicate that defendants anticipated the users of their product would "hook," "slice" and "top" the ball. They expected their customers to commit the errors that normally plague beginning golfers. Thus, when they declared their product "completely safe," the only reasonable inference is that the Gizmo was a safe training device for all golfers regardless of ability and regardless of how squarely they hit the ball.

Although defendants claim they did not intend their statement to cover situations such as the one at bar, subjective intent is irrelevant. The question is not what a seller intended, but what the consumer reasonably believed. The rule "is one of strict liability for physical harm to the consumer, resulting from a misrepresentation of the character or quality of the chattel sold, even though the misrepresentation is an innocent one, and not made fraudulently or negligently." (Rest. 2d Torts, § 402B, com. a.)

We conclude that Fred Hauter reasonably believed he could use the Gizmo with safety and agree with the trial court that plaintiffs established all the elements of a cause of action for misrepresentation.

* * *

[Affirmed and remanded for trial to determine damages.]

[The concurring opinion of Clark, J., is set forth below at p. 101.]

NOTES

1. Consider the following variations:

A. Fred hit the ball squarely, but was injured when the ball bounced off a tree—ten feet away, at a 45° angle from where he was standing—and hit him in the temple.

B. Fred's father injured his back when he hit underneath the ball, tangling his club in the cord in a way that caused his back to twist.

C. Fred was injured exactly as in the case, but the only relevant representation was that the Gizmo was "safe."

D. Fred was hit in the temple and injured when he missed a plastic frisbee that had been advertised as "the best form of safe and wholesome fun."

2. **Interpretation: Truth or Falsity.** Whether a representation should be interpreted as true or false on the facts of a particular case is sometimes a matter of contention. Plaintiff truck driver sustained injuries to head and chest when another truck hit the side of his vehicle thrusting him against the steering wheel. Plaintiff claimed that the steering column, advertised as "telescopic," failed to telescope adequately, contrary to the representation. Noting that the column would have telescoped more had the collision been

head-on, and that it had telescoped somewhat even though plaintiff had been hit at an angle, the court concluded that the representation was not false: "The statement of appellant * * * never asserted that the steering column would telescope under any and all circumstances and conditions." General Motors Corp. v. Howard, 244 So.2d 726, 728 (Miss.1971).

3. Consider Klages v. General Ordnance Equip. Corp., 240 Pa.Super. 356, 367 A.2d 304 (1976). After once being held up by armed robbers, plaintiff, the night clerk at a motel, purchased the defendant's mace weapon for protection. The promotional literature for the weapon stated in part: "Rapidly vaporizes on face of assailant effecting *instantaneous incapacitation* * * * an attacker is *subdued—instantly* * * *. Time Magazine stated the Chemical Mace is '* * * a weapon that *disables as effectively* as a gun and yet does no permanent injury' * * *." When plaintiff was again held up soon thereafter, he removed the mace from the cash register where it was stored. "Using the cash register as a shield, Klages squirted the mace, hitting the intruder 'right beside the nose.' Klages immediately ducked below the register, but the intruder followed him down and shot him in the head." Rejecting the manufacturer's argument that plaintiff had assumed the risk, a defense subsumed in misrepresentation cases under the umbrella of justifiable reliance, the court affirmed a judgment for the plaintiff on the principles of § 402B.

Is this decision tantamount to holding that the defendant's promotional statements effectively (and inadvertently) extended to users of the mace an insurance policy against criminally inflicted harm when the mace was used, no matter how dangerous the situation?

Compare Harlacher v. Anti Crime Industries, No. 466698, Maricopa Cty. Super.Ct., Ariz., Sept. 6, 1984, where a young real estate saleswoman on duty in a model home was approached by a man who was exposing himself. When he was about two feet away, the plaintiff sprayed him with mace, but he attacked and beat her. In an action against the manufacturer, the plaintiff claimed that the label on the mace falsely stated that it would render an assailant helpless. The defendant claimed that the product had performed as represented, and hence was true: it had blinded him temporarily, thus rendering him helpless. He was only able to continue the attack because he was so close that he could feel the direction from which the spray was coming. The defendants further contended that the purpose of the mace was to allow the victim to escape, not to drop the assailant in his tracks.

Plaintiff proved medical expenses of $2,500, and claimed lost earnings for one year and lost earning capacity of $400,000. Prior to trial, plaintiff demanded $185,000; defendant offered $35,000. *Held,* jury verdict for defendant. See Verdicts and Settlements 495–96 (Dec. 1984).

4. **Justifiable Reliance.** The plaintiff, an off-duty, general duty policeman riding his personal motorcycle, received head injuries when he collided with a truck and his helmet popped off before he hit the ground. The helmet he was wearing was a general duty model 1601, designed with a special snap harness for quick release to permit an officer to remove the helmet easily in a riot if someone grabbed his head. The police department issued a different helmet (model 1602) to the motorcycle police, as plaintiff knew. Both models were packaged in the same type box, with illustrations on both sides of the box depicting a motorcyclist wearing a helmet. In an action against the manufacturer under § 402B, the plaintiff claimed that he relied upon the illustrations on the box in deciding to use his model 1601 helmet for personal motorcycle

riding. In American Safety Equip. Corp. v. Winkler, 640 P.2d 216, 223 (Colo. 1982) (4–3), a bare majority of the court rejected his claim, concluding that he had not justifiably relied upon the representations because he knew that the motorcycle officers were issued the model 1602, not the 1601: "Justifiable reliance contemplates the reasonable exercise of knowledge and intelligence in assessing the represented facts. Unsupportable subjective reliance is inadequate."

The dissenting judges thought that a jury question on the issue had been made out, since the plaintiff's knowledge that the motorcycle officers used the model 1602 was "not the equivalent of actual knowledge of the unsuitability of helmet model 1601 for motorcycling purposes." Id. at 225. Moreover, two of the dissenters thought that the majority's definition of justifiable reliance incorrectly imposed on the plaintiff an independent duty to investigate the truth of the representation.

5. **"Puffing."** In Berkebile v. Brantly Helicopter Corp., 462 Pa. 83, 337 A.2d 893 (1975), plaintiff was killed in a helicopter crash when his engine failed. Advertising brochures touted that the craft was "a safe, dependable helicopter" and was "easy to fly" for beginning as well as professional pilots. One of plaintiff's contentions was that the average pilot could not react quickly enough in case of engine failure to activate the helicopter's "auto-rotation" system—an emergency safety system, operated by a "collective pitch stick," that changed the angle of the rotor blades so that the disabled craft could be glided to a safe landing. *Held,* the representations were "mere puffs." Compare Hoffman v. A.B. Chance Co., 339 F.Supp. 1385 (M.D.Pa.1972) (representation that brake on hydraulic aerial platform offered "unprecedented safety"—puffing).

In addition to undermining the materiality and factual character of a representation, how else does the "puffy" nature of a statement weaken a plaintiff's case? See § 402B, comment *j.*

6. What if Fred Hauter had not seen the affirmations of safety on the shipping carton or on the cover of the instruction booklet for the Gizmo, but his mother had? Would it matter whether she saw the representations before or after buying the product? What if neither had noticed the affirmations until after the accident? See § 402B, comment *j.*

7. Vehicle manufacturer tells dealer that new model truck's cooling system can support addition of air conditioner without overheating. Dealer installs air conditioner on truck and passes along the representation to buyer who purchases truck on strength of this information. Engine subsequently overheats and sprays buyer with scalding water when radiator hose bursts. Buyer sues dealer, and dealer seeks indemnification from manufacturer. Can dealer recover over against the manufacturer under § 402B? See Ford Motor Co. v. Russell & Smith Ford Co., 474 S.W.2d 549 (Tex.Civ.App.1971); § 402B, comments *a, h* and *i.*

Should a car dealer be liable under § 402B for the manufacturer's misrepresentations in the owner's manual? See Jack Roach–Bissonnet, Inc. v. Puskar, 417 S.W.2d 262, 275 (Tex.1967) (Smith, J., dissenting); § 402B, comment *e.*

8. In *Hauter,* was the testimony of either of plaintiffs' expert witnesses necessary to the § 402B claim?

9. Note that the *Hauter* jury found *unanimously* for the defendants. Assuming that the case was handled competently at trial by plaintiffs' attorney, and considering that the appellate court found for the plaintiffs on *each* of

their four theories of recovery *as a matter of law,* what can account for a legal result so at variance with the community's sense of justice?

10. See generally Sales, The Innocent Misrepresentation Doctrine: Strict Tort Liability Under Section 402B, 16 Hous.L.Rev. 239 (1979).

SECTION 3. WARRANTY

This section first examines the three Code warranties: express warranty, the implied warranty of merchantability, and the implied warranty of fitness for a particular purpose. The privity of contract problem will be seen to be a threshold issue for the injured purchaser seeking to reach a remote seller through the law of warranty, just as it was in negligence law until recent years. The scope of warranty protection beyond the purchaser to family members and other potential injury victims is also examined. Last to be considered is the system of rules defining the method and extent to which a seller may limit its potential liability by disclaimers of responsibility and limitations of remedies.

A. EXPRESS WARRANTY

LANE v. C.A. SWANSON & SONS

District Court of Appeals of California, 1955.
130 Cal.App.2d 210, 278 P.2d 723.

SHINN, PRESIDING JUSTICE.

[Plaintiff bought a can of the defendants' canned chicken and was injured while eating the chicken when a bone lodged in his throat. He sued for breach of an express warranty that the chicken was free from bones. The trial court found no evidence of an express warranty and entered judgment for the defendants. Plaintiff appeals.]

The can purchased by plaintiff contained six ounces of chicken, salted. Upon the label were the words "Swanson," then in still larger letters "Boned Chicken" and in small letters "Ever Fresh" and beneath that in still smaller letters the word "Brand". The words "Boned Chicken" are in bold type, the word "Brand" in type so small as to be unnoticeable except on close inspection. In addition there was the following evidence: The Los Angeles Times of June 18, 1953, carried a full-page illustrated advertisement by defendant Swanson of its "Boned Chicken," "Boned Turkey," "Boneless Chicken Fricassee," "Chicken Fricassee," and other products. The ad pictures a can of "Swanson Boned Chicken," and beside the can this description of what is in the can: "Swanson Boned Chicken All luscious white and dark meat. *No bones.* No waste. Swanson chicken—finest in the land. Chosen by poultry experts. Specially bred and fed. Swanson-cooked to juicy perfection. Wonderful for salads and casseroles. Quick! Thrifty, too!" (Italics added.) * * *

Plaintiff testified that prior to the purchase of the can of "Boned Chicken" he had read advertising of defendant Swanson's products similar in form and content to that in the ad of June 18, 1953. Defendants did not introduce any evidence.

It is apparent that the court adopted the theory of the defendants that the term "Boned Chicken" was merely descriptive of the manner in which the product was prepared and packaged and that it did not constitute a warranty that the contents of the can were wholly free from bones. This, they contend, would be the understanding the general public would receive from the description.

* * *

There are a great many such descriptive terms in common use such as "Fireproof," "Stainless," "Rustproof," "Nonskid," "Punctureproof," "Nonbreakable," "Waterproof," "Shelled," "Boneless," etc. Such a list could be extended to great lengths. Descriptive names constitute a warranty as to the general characteristics of the article and that it is substantially what the name represents it to be. They do not, as a rule, amount to a representation of perfection.

* * *

Defendants say "The manufacturer's express warranty is merely to the extent that the chicken has been boned and that all bones such as the leg, thigh, wing and other bones which carry identifiable structural names, instead of parts or fragments of such identifiable names, have been removed. * * * While it is true every manufacturer uses every possible precaution to see that no slivers or fragments of bone of any kind become a part of this product, nevertheless it is humanly impossible to be one hundred percent positive that all such bone fragments have been removed. * * * Furthermore, defendants did not expressly warrant that the product was free from chicken bones in any event. Merely because the word 'boned' appears on the label does not imply that the product is entirely free from bone fragments which are normal to the product." etc.

"Any affirmation of fact or any promise by the seller relating to the goods is an express warranty if the natural tendency of such affirmation or promise is to induce the buyer to purchase the goods, and if the buyer purchases the goods relying thereon. * * * " [Uniform Sales Act § 12, predecessor of U.C.C. § 2–313] * * *

* * *

The tendency of the modern cases is to construe liberally in favor of the buyer language used by the seller in making affirmations respecting the quality of his goods and to enlarge the responsibility of the seller to construe every affirmation by him to be a warranty when such construction is at all reasonable. [Citation.]

The representation in the newspaper advertisements may be considered a part of the contract of sale. [Citations.]

Defendants' argument is centered upon the use of the word "boned" on the label of the can. Little is said of the use of the statement "no bones" in the advertising. The question is whether the statement that "boned chicken" contained "no bones" would reasonably be understood by the buying public to mean that the principal bones had been removed but there might be fragments of bone remaining or that all bones, large and small, and all pieces of bone had been removed. From a strictly anatomical standpoint it may be said that if a leg bone of a chicken has been removed with the exception of small fragments the leg bone has been removed; but the fragments of bone that remained would be "bone" to anyone who might attempt to swallow them. "No bones," no doubt, means to the manufacturer that great care has been used to remove all bones and all pieces of bone, but we think it would mean to a buyer that no bones whatever would be found in the product. Unless it can be said that a small piece of bone is no bone at all when it sticks in one's throat it cannot be said that a product which contains one or more bone fragments contains no bones. And with respect to the theories of the defendants it may be asked how many bone fragments would be permissible without contradicting the representation that there were no bones. Defendants argue that it is impossible to extract the bones of a defunct chicken without leaving in the remains small slivers or pieces of bone and that if they are held to liability under such facts as were in evidence here it will be impossible for them to continue the processing and sale of boned or boneless poultry and that they and many processors of similar products would be forced out of that business. We do not believe this dark outlook is justified, but even if Swanson and other manufacturers they mention may find it necessary or wise to change their methods of doing business this would be no reason for abrogating the principles of law under which they must operate.

Plaintiff testified that his understanding at the time he purchased the "Boned Chicken" was "just what the reading on the label implied, chicken without bones." On motion of defendants this testimony was stricken, although there was no objection to the question as to what his understanding was. In our opinion, the ruling was erroneous. The evidence was admissible for the purpose of showing that plaintiff, the buyer, relied on the affirmation on the label that the can contained chicken from which the bones had been removed. [Citations.]

Our conclusion is that the label on the can, coupled with the representation in the newspaper ads that the contents contained no bones, constituted an express warranty and that the same was breached. If there could be a doubt as to the meaning of "boned chicken," it was removed by the statement that it contained no bones.

The judgment is reversed.

UNIFORM COMMERCIAL CODE

§ 2–313. Express Warranties by Affirmation, Promise, Description, Sample

(1) Express warranties by the seller are created as follows:

(a) Any affirmation of fact or promise made by the seller to the buyer which relates to the goods and becomes part of the basis of the bargain creates an express warranty that the goods shall conform to the affirmation or promise.

(b) Any description of the goods which is made part of the basis of the bargain creates an express warranty that the goods shall conform to the description.

(c) Any sample or model which is made part of the basis of the bargain creates an express warranty that the whole of the goods shall conform to the sample or model.

(2) It is not necessary to the creation of an express warranty that the seller use formal words such as "warrant" or "guarantee" or that he have a specific intention to make a warranty, but an affirmation merely of the value of the goods or a statement purporting to be merely the seller's opinion or commendation of the goods does not create a warranty.

NOTES

1. Although not discussed by the *Lane* court, the issue of privity of contract presented a stumbling block for plaintiffs relying on express warranty in many jurisdictions at the time. Rogers v. Toni Home Permanent Co., 167 Ohio St. 244, 147 N.E.2d 612, 4 O.O.2d 291 (1958), is the landmark case abolishing the privity bar in express warranty cases. Noting that the express warranty action derived originally from tort (deceit) rather than contract, the court relied upon Baxter v. Ford Motor Co. in extending the privity exception recognized in food cases to products generally, observing as follows:

> What sensible or sound reason * * * exists as to why, when the goods purchased by the ultimate consumer on the strength of the advertisements aimed squarely at him do not possess their described qualities and goodness and cause him harm, he should not be permitted to move against the manufacturer to recoup his loss[?] * * * The warranties made by the manufacturer in his advertisements and by the labels on his products are inducements to the ultimate consumers, and the manufacturer ought to be held to strict accountability to any consumer who buys the product in reliance on such representations and later suffers injury because the product proves to be defective or deleterious.

It is now widely accepted that express warranties run directly to the purchaser, despite the absence of privity of contract. See, e.g., Reid v. Volkswagen of America, Inc., 512 F.2d 1294 (6th Cir.1975); Hauter v. Zogarts, 14 Cal. 3d 104, 120 Cal.Rptr. 681, 534 P.2d 377 (1975); Hamon v. Digliani, 148 Conn. 710, 174 A.2d 294 (1961); Kinlaw v. Long Mfg. N.C., Inc., 298 N.C. 494, 259 S.E. 2d 552 (1979). *Rogers* is noted in 58 Colum.L.Rev. 1092 (1958); 19 Ohio St.L.J.

733 (1958); 44 Iowa L.Rev. 229 (1958); 11 Vand.L.Rev. 1459 (1958); 44 Va.L. Rev. 1002 (1958); 75 A.L.R.2d 112 (1961).

2. It is axiomatic that breach of express warranty requires no showing of fault and thus is truly "strict" liability. Moreover, "no 'defect' other than a failure to conform to the warrantor's representations need be shown in order to establish a breach of an express warranty." McCarty v. E.J. Korvette, Inc., 28 Md.App. 421, 347 A.2d 253, 264 (1975) (tire guaranteed against blowouts); Collins v. Uniroyal, Inc., 64 N.J. 260, 315 A.2d 16 (1974) (ditto).

3. Do you suppose the *Lane* decision forced C.A. Swanson & Sons out of the business of processing and selling boned and boneless poultry, as predicted by counsel? As Swanson's attorney, what advice would you have given after the rendering of this opinion?

4. Plaintiff's teeth were injured when he bit down on an unshelled nut in a selection of shelled "PLANTERS Dry Roasted MIXED NUTS." Plaintiff argued that "the container, a clear glass jar, which allegedly failed to disclose the unshelled filbert, was a representation" within the purview of U.C.C. § 2–313. The court did not agree: "[T]he jar, while revealing shelled nuts, was a mere passive marketing tool. It was not an affirmative representation and as such was insufficient to give rise to an express warranty." Coffer v. Standard Brands, Inc., 30 N.C.App. 134, 226 S.E.2d 534 (1976). Do you agree?

5. Certain recipients of defendant manufacturer's Type I Sabin oral polio vaccine contract polio from the vaccine. Should defendant be liable in express warranty for publicity that had been placed in the media by the local medical society, but with defendant's knowledge, stating that the vaccine was "safe"? See Grinnell v. Charles Pfizer & Co., 274 Cal.App.2d 424, 79 Cal.Rptr. 369 (1969) (no, where no agency relationship found, despite fact that defendant had supplied medical society with news clippings from similar publicity campaign in another community).

The defendant's package insert that accompanied the oral polio vaccine advised: "The Surgeon General's Advisory Committee on Poliomyelitis Control [has found that] 'There are no known contraindications to oral polio virus vaccines.'" Studies released several months earlier had in fact revealed that on rare occasions the vaccine did induce polio in recipients. Should the manufacturer be liable on the basis of this representation?

6. **Interpretation.** Perhaps the most prevalent issue in express warranty litigation involves the interpretation of the representation. Information may be communicated through pictures as well as words. In Sylvestri v. Warner & Swasey Co., 398 F.2d 598 (2d Cir.1968), plaintiff was thrown from the operator's seat of a backhoe manufactured by defendant. The vehicle tipped when its stabilizing outriggers shifted while it was being used to lift boulders and swing them around to different locations. An advertising brochure showed the backhoe lifting a length of pipe and stated that "Hydraulic system provides powerful lift force for material handling." Upholding plaintiff's verdict, the court remarked: "While Sylvestri apparently did not attach the rock to the backhoe in exactly the same manner that the pipe was attached in the brochure picture, and while lifting rock may in some way be different from lifting pipe, we conclude that the jury was properly left to determine * * * whether the brochure picture and statements as a whole represented an affirmation of fact or promise that the machine could be used as Sylvestri used it. It is the 'essential idea' conveyed by the advertising representations which is relevant * * *."

7. Plaintiff fell while skiing and suffered a broken leg when his ski bindings failed to release. In Salk v. Alpine Ski Shop, Inc., 115 R.I. 309, 342 A.2d 622 (1975), he sued the manufacturer of the bindings in express warranty on the basis of the following advertisements: "Cubco is the precise binding that releases when it's supposed to. * * * Both heel and toe release at the exact tension you set. And release whichever way you fall." *Held,* no recovery for breach of warranty:

> For the facts of this case to make out a breach of express warranty, plaintiff must first establish that Cubco warranted its bindings would release in every situation presenting a danger to the user's limbs. It is our judgment that Cubco's advertising falls short of this blanket guarantee. During the course of the trial, [it was shown that] no binding could be set at a tension sufficiently low to release during a slow fall and still keep the skier on his skis during normal skiing, [and that] Cubco bindings had a multi-directional release which could be adjusted to operate at a variety of tensions * * *. The advertisements brought to our attention do no more than affirm these uncontroverted facts.

8. General representations of safety may support an express warranty action, as may generalized guarantees. See Drayton v. Jiffee Chemical Corp., 395 F.Supp. 1081 (N.D.Ohio 1975) (advertising claims that particularly caustic drain cleaner was safe for household use); Jones v. Cranman's Sporting Goods, 142 Ga.App. 838, 237 S.E.2d 402 (1977) (explosion of rifle sold as "fully guaranteed").

9. Consider also Whitmer v. Schneble, 29 Ill.App.3d 659, 331 N.E.2d 115 (1975) (no recovery on breach of warranty where female Doberman Pinscher, represented by sellers to be "docile," bit child viewing dog's new puppies two and a half years after sale: "Even a docile dog is known and expected to bite under some circumstances"; moreover, statement pertained to dog's personality at the time of sale and did not mean that its personality could not change); Whittington v. Eli Lilly & Co., 333 F.Supp. 98 (S.D.W.Va.1971) (no promise of *absolute* protection where birth control pills, said to "offer virtually 100% protection," in fact offered 98.1% protection); Beyette v. Ortho Pharmaceutical Corp., 823 F.2d 990 (6th Cir.1987) (no warranty recovery for pelvic inflammatory disease, based upon IUD manufacturer's representations (1) estimating PID rate, and (2) stating that more than a million women had used IUDs successfully; first representation was merely a future prediction, and second was true, not a warranty of risk-free use); Huebert v. Federal Pac. Elec. Co., 208 Kan. 720, 494 P.2d 1210 (1972) (current passed through electrical panel injuring plaintiff electrician although handle had been switched to "off" position; *held,* express warranty made and breached by panel manufacturer).

10. Plaintiff's General Electric Smoke Detector alarm fails to go off in a fire, and her house is burned to the ground. Breach of express warranty?

STANG v. HERTZ CORPORATION

Court of Appeals of New Mexico, 1971.
83 N.M. 217, 490 P.2d 475.*

WOOD, CHIEF JUDGE. The automobile accident involved in this case occurred when a tire blew out. The tire, manufactured by Firestone Tire & Rubber Company, was mounted on a car belonging to Hertz Corporation. The car had been rented by a nun, and Catherine Lavan, also a nun, was a passenger in the car when the blowout occurred. Catherine Lavan suffered injuries in the accident resulting in her death. * * * The verdict was in favor of Firestone. There is no appeal from this verdict. The trial court directed a verdict in favor of Hertz. The dispositive issues in this appeal concern the liability of Hertz. Plaintiffs contend there were issues for the jury concerning: (1) an express warranty and (2) strict liability in tort.

Express warranty.

Plaintiffs assert the rental agreement contains an express warranty. They rely on a statement that the "vehicle" was in good mechanical condition. Defendant contends that "vehicle" does not include tires because twice in the rental agreement "tires" were referred to in a sense separate from "vehicle."

Apart from the rental agreement, a Hertz representative, in a conversation with one of the nuns, stated: "you have got good tires." Plaintiffs contend this statement was also an express warranty as to the tires. Defendant asserts this statement was no more than "puffing." See § 50A–2–313(2), N.M.S.A.1953 (Repl.Vol. 8, pt. 1).

It is not necessary to answer these contentions. * * *

* * * Under § 50A–2–313(1), supra, the affirmation of fact (the rental agreement) creates an express warranty if it "becomes part of the basis of the bargain." Similarly, the description of the goods (the reference to good tires) creates an express warranty if the description "is made part of the basis of the bargain." * * *

There is no evidence that any of the nuns relied on, or in any way considered, the terms of the rental agreement before agreeing to the rental. See Speed Fastners, Inc. v. Newsom, 382 F.2d 395 (10th Cir. 1967). The comment concerning "good tires" was made after the car had been rented. See Terry v. Moore, 448 P.2d 601 (Wyo.1968). There is no evidence that either the terms of the rental agreement or the reference to "good tires" were part of the basis of the bargain. There was insufficient evidence for the question of express warranty to be submitted to the jury.

* * *

[Affirmed.]

---

* Reversed on other grounds, 83 N.M. 730, 497 P.2d 732 (1972).

HAUTER v. ZOGARTS

Supreme Court of California, 1975.
14 Cal.3d 104, 120 Cal.Rptr. 681, 534 P.2d 377.

[This is the "Golfing Gizmo" case. For the statement of facts and a discussion of defendant's "puffing" defense, see supra, p. 86.]

* * * [T]he claim for breach of express warranty * * * is governed by California Commercial Code section 2313. The key under this section is that the seller's statements—whether fact or opinion—must become "part of the basis of the bargain." [10] (See Cal.U.Com. Code, § 2313, com. 8; Ezer, supra, at p. 287, fn. 39). The basis of the bargain requirement represents a significant change in the law of warranties. Whereas plaintiffs in the past have had to prove their reliance upon specific promises made by the seller (Grinnell v. Charles Pfizer & Co. (1969) 274 Cal.App.2d 424, 440 [79 Cal.Rptr. 369]), the Uniform Commercial Code requires no such proof. According to official comment 3 to the Uniform Commercial Code following section 2313, "no particular reliance * * * need be shown in order to weave [the seller's affirmations of fact] into the fabric of the agreement. Rather, any fact which is to take such affirmations, once made, out of the agreement requires clear affirmative proof."

The commentators have disagreed as to the impact of this new development. (See generally, Note, "Basis of the Bargain"—What Role Reliance? (1972) 34 U.Pitt.L.Rev. 145, 149–150). Some have said that the basis of the bargain requirement merely shifts the burden of proving non-reliance to the seller. (See 1 Carroll, Cal.Commercial Law, supra, § 6.7, p. 210; Boyd, Representing Consumers—The Uniform Commercial Code and Beyond (1968) 9 Ariz.L.Rev. 372, 385.) Indeed, the comments to section 2313 seem to bear out this analysis; they declare that "all of the statements of the seller [become part of the basis of the bargain] *unless good reason is shown to the contrary.*" (Cal. U.Com.Code, § 2313, com. 8 (italics added).) [11]

Other writers, however, find that the code eliminates the concept of reliance altogether. (See Note, supra, 34 U.Pitt.L.Rev. at p. 150;

10. As we explained above, defendants' statement is one of fact and is subject to construction as an express warranty. It is important to note, however, that even statements of opinion can become warranties under the code if they become part of the basis of the bargain. (Cal.U.Com.Code, § 2313, com. 8; Ezer, supra, at p. 287, fn. 39.) Thus the California Uniform Commercial Code expands sellers' liability beyond the former Uniform Sales Act (former Civ.Code, §§ 1732–1736) and provides greater coverage than Restatement Second of Torts, section 402B, discussed earlier.

11. The code relegates "the metaphysical 'buyer's reliance' requirement to secondary status, where it properly belongs." (Ezer, The Impact of the Uniform Commercial Code on the California Law of Sales Warranties (1961) 8 U.C.L.A.L.Rev. 281, 285.) Ezer also notes: "The Code's implicit premise is that buyer's reliance is prima facie established from the fact that he made the purchase. If the seller can establish that the buyer in fact did not rely on the seller, that the affirmation or promise was not the 'basis of the bargain,' to use the Code language, then there is no express warranty." (Id. at p. 285, fn. 30.)

Nordstrom, Sales (1970) §§ 66–68.) Support can be found in the comments to the code for this view also; they declare that "[i]n view of the principle that the whole purpose of the law of warranty is to determine what it is that the seller *has in essence agreed to sell,* the policy is adopted of those cases which refuse except in unusual circumstances to recognize a material deletion of the seller's obligation. Thus, a contract is normally a contract for a sale of something describable and described." (Cal.U.Com.Code, § 2313, com. 4 (italics added).) To these observers, the focus of the warranty shifts from the buyer, who formerly had to rely upon specific statements in order to recover, to the seller, who now must stand behind his words if he has failed adequately to disclaim them. "[T]he seller must show by clear affirmative proof either that the statement was retracted by him before the deal was closed or that the parties understood that the goods would not conform to the affirmation or description. Under such an interpretation, the affirmation, once made, is a part of the agreement, and lack of reliance by the buyer is not a fact which would take the affirmation out of the agreement." (Note, supra, 34 U.Pitt.L.Rev. at p. 151.) [12]

We are not called upon in this case to resolve the reliance issue.[13] The parties do not discuss the changes wrought by the Uniform Commercial Code, and plaintiffs are fully able to meet their burden regardless of which test we employ. Fred Hauter's testimony shows that he read and relied upon defendants' representation; he was impressed by "something on the cover dealing with the safety of the item." More importantly, defendants presented no evidence which could remove their assurance of safety from the basis of the bargain. The trial court properly concluded, therefore, that defendants expressly warranted the safety of their product and are liable for Fred Hauter's injuries which resulted from a breach of that warranty.

* * *

[Trial court's judgment for the plaintiff notwithstanding the verdict affirmed; case remanded to determine damages.]

CLARK, JUSTICE (concurring).

I concur with the majority that the record here establishes breach of express warranty as a matter of law—requiring affirmance of the judgment and disposing of this appeal. However, beyond this first issue, the majority's discussion [on the Restatement, Second, Torts § 402B] is both unnecessary and unpersuasive.

12. Thus if a seller agrees to sell a certain quality of product, he cannot avoid liability for selling lower grade goods. No longer can he find solace in the fact that the injured consumer never saw his warranty. [Citations.]

13. Although the code has been the law in California since 1965, we know of no California case which analyzes the basis of the bargain requirement. The scattered cases from other jurisdictions generally have ignored the significance of the new standard and have held that consumer reliance still is a vital ingredient for recovery based on express warranty. (See, e.g., Stang v. Hertz Corp. (1971) 83 N.M. 217, 219 [490 P.2d 475], revd. on other grounds, 83 N.M. 730 [497 P.2d 732, 52 A.L.R.3d 112]; [citations]).

NOTES

1. Compare, with Justice Clark's concurring opinion in *Hauter,* the following observations of the court in Klages v. General Ordnance Equip. Corp., supra p. 91 n. 3, in support of its adoption of § 402B of the Restatement, Second, Torts:

> In so doing, we note the extensive similarity between § 2–313 of the Uniform Commercial Code, supra, and § 402B. Specifically, § 2–313 provides that a seller creates express warranties by "[a]ny affirmation of fact or promise" or by "[a]ny description of the goods." Section 402B provides that the misrepresentation must be of a "material fact concerning the character or quality" of the product which is contained in an advertisement, label, or otherwise conveyed. Both provisions, therefore, are concerned with the manufacturer's express statement about his product and whether the product in fact conforms to that representation. Once noncompliance is demonstrated, both sections, in effect, impose liability without fault on the manufacturer. Because the elimination of the privity requirement allows the buyer to sue the manufacturer directly in assumpsit for noncompliance with his express statements, we see no sound reason for not recognizing a similar cause of action in trespass.

2. **Reliance.** The requirement of reliance has proved a major stumbling block for plaintiffs in express warranty cases over the years. It was an explicit requirement under § 12 of the Uniform Sales Act. See, e.g., McCully v. Fuller Brush Co., 68 Wash.2d 675, 415 P.2d 7 (1966) (insufficient proof that plaintiff, who suffered dermatitis on the hands, had relied on label statement, "It's Kind To Your Hands"). *Stang* is illustrative of the modern decisions that still appear to require reliance in express warranty cases, although U.C.C. § 2–313(1) provides only that the representation be "part of the basis of the bargain."

Comment 3 to § 2–313 specifically addresses the issue:

> In actual practice affirmations of fact made by the seller about the goods during a bargain are regarded as part of the description of those goods; hence no particular reliance on such statements need be shown in order to weave them into the fabric of the agreement. Rather, any fact, which is to take such affirmations, once made, out of the agreement requires clear affirmative proof. The issue normally is one of fact.

3. **Post-sale Statements.** With the *Stang* court's treatment of the salesman's "good tires" statement, compare comment 7 to § 2–313:

> The precise time when words of description or affirmation are made or samples are shown is not material. The sole question is whether the language or samples or models are fairly to be regarded as part of the contract. If language is used after the closing of the deal (as when the buyer when taking delivery asks and receives an additional assurance), the warranty becomes a modification, and need not be supported by consideration if it is otherwise reasonable and in order (Section 2–209).

For how long after the sale should the seller's affirmations be construed as modifications of the contract? Until buyer has passed over seller's threshold? So long as sale is still "hot"? As long as seller would permit the product to be returned? See Nordstrom, supra, at 205–07; J. White & R. Summers, Handbook of the Law under the Uniform Commercial Code § 9.5 (3d ed.1988).

Should the seller's public advertisements made shortly after plaintiff purchases a product be held to modify the plaintiff's contract of sale under the principle of comment 7? Consider White & Summers, supra, at 402–03, noting that "section 2–209 contemplates an 'agreement modifying a contract * * *.' It is far from self-evident that a seller's post-sale words uttered during delivery are an 'agreement of modification,' and one can hardly attribute that bilateral connotation to an advertisement that is not published until after the sale. Indeed, Comment 7 seems to contemplate only the cases of face-to-face dealings that occur while the deal is still warm."

Should representations in brochures sealed in a package and thus not read until the package is opened several hours after sale be deemed express warranties under the principles of comment 7? See Nordstrom, supra, at 207.

4. What if the affirmations are made before the purchase, but not learned about by plaintiff until after the *accident*? Plaintiff is injured when her new automobile tire is punctured by a nail and blows out. If the manufacturer had advertised the tire on national television as "blowout-proof" prior to purchase, how might plaintiff who did not see or learn about the commercial until after her accident argue that it was nevertheless part of the basis of *her* bargain? Does comment 3 help or hurt her case? See R. Nordstrom, Handbook of the Law of Sales 209 (1970):

> The court's task is to determine whether the injury was caused by a defect in the product, and any statements made by the seller designed to induce the public to buy his product are relevant in making this determination. The "basis of the bargain" includes the dickered terms, but is not limited to them. The "basis of the bargain" is also the item purchased, and a part of that bargain includes the statements which the seller made about what he sold.

Compare *Hauter* footnote 12, supra. Might some sort of estoppel argument be in order?

5. Should a patient injured by defendant's drug, falsely warranted to be safe for certain uses, have an express warranty action against the manufacturer where the doctor who read the false information in the package insert already had formed an independent belief in the drug's safety for such uses from medical journals or from his own research? Compare Putensen v. Clay Adams, Inc., 12 Cal.App.3d 1062, 91 Cal.Rptr. 319 (1970) (whether representation was "part of the basis of the bargain" was jury question), with McDaniel v. McNeil Labs., Inc., 196 Neb. 190, 241 N.W.2d 822 (1976), and Ball v. Mallinkrodt Chemical Works, 53 Tenn.App. 218, 381 S.W.2d 563 (1964) (no reliance if independent knowledge).

6. **Obvious Defects and Inspections.** What effect, if any, should the obviousness of a condition contrary to seller's representation have on the existence of an express warranty? Used car dealer sells plaintiff a car with bald tires, representing that "the car is practically new and in excellent shape."

What if prior to purchase buyer submits the product to an inspection that should or does reveal that a latent defect makes the representation false? See Werner v. Montana, 117 N.H. 721, 378 A.2d 1130 (1977); Nordstrom, supra, at 209–12.

7. **Perennial, Perplexing and Persnickety Problems of "Puffs."** Note that § 2–313(2) provides in pertinent part that "a statement purporting to be merely the seller's opinion or commendation of the goods does not create a warranty." Was the salesman's "good tires" statement in *Stang* an affirmation of fact or did it purport to be merely the lessor's (possibly prejudiced) personal opinion? Should the fact that the statement was made to a nun affect the result?

As noted in *Lane* and in the portion of *Hauter* previously excerpted in the section on misrepresentation, the area of allowable puffing has been increasingly narrowed. But predicting whether a particular statement will be construed as fact or opinion is risky business. "Only a foolish lawyer will be quick to label a seller's statement as puffs or not puffs, and only a reckless one will label a seller's statement at all without carefully examining such factors as the nature of the defect (was it obvious or not) and the buyer's and seller's relative knowledge." White & Summers, supra, at 395–96. Or, as put by another: "In one sense, every statement made by a seller is nothing more than his opinion as to the goods or how the goods will operate; yet at some point he makes his statement in a manner and under such conditions that the buyer does not understand that *only* this seller's opinion is involved." Nordstrom, supra, at 219. Compare Carney v. Sears, Roebuck & Co., 309 F.2d 300 (4th Cir.1962) ("good quality ladder"; *held,* opinion), with Turner v. Central Hardware Co., 353 Mo. 1182, 186 S.W.2d 603 (1945) (ladder "mighty strong and durable"; *held,* fact: "the seller's protection lies in the fact that his is the choice of language and action"). Compare also Guess v. Lorenz, 612 S.W.2d 831 (Mo.App.1981) (used car "in good shape": puff), with Jones v. Kellner, 5 Ohio App.3d 242, 451 N.E.2d 548, 550 (1982) (used car "mechanically A–1": warranty) ("although it was unclear how long this warranty would have lasted, it should have lasted at least long enough for the appellee to get the car home").

Carpenter v. Alberto Culver Co., 28 Mich.App. 399, 184 N.W.2d 547 (1970), was an express warranty action against a drug store for an adverse skin reaction from a hair dye plaintiff bought at the store. "[T]he clerk indicated that several of her friends had used the hair-dyeing product in question, and that her own hair came out 'very nice' and 'very natural' [and that] she 'would get very fine results.'" Both the box and bottle carried warnings of the risk of skin irritation and of the need to make a preliminary patch test. The court remarked in part as follows:

> In determining whether a statement of the seller is to be deemed a warranty, it is important to consider whether in the statement the seller assumes to assert a fact of which the buyer is ignorant, or merely states an opinion or judgment upon a matter of which the seller has no special knowledge and on which the buyer may be expected also to have an opinion and to exercise his judgment. Representations which merely express the seller's opinion, belief, judgment, or estimate do not constitute a warranty. 67 A.L.R.2d 619, § 2, p. 625.
>
> In the instant case, from all the factual evidence, we cannot agree that such statements made by the retail seller can be considered that of express warranty for use by this plaintiff. From the context in which such statements were made, coupled with the cautionary instructions printed on both the bottle and the box, warning against possible adverse reaction, nothing more existed than an implied warranty that the product was reasonably fit for use as a hair dye.

Should it make any difference how specific is the information represented? How specific is "safe"? Do you agree that "safe" should be considered to be a statement of fact rather than opinion? What if a statement is in writing?

Will the Code's statute of frauds present the purchaser relying on oral warranties with additional problems? See U.C.C. § 2–201; Nordstrom, supra, at 213.

8. **Federal Warranty Act.** The Magnuson–Moss Warranty Act, 15 U.S.C.A. §§ 2301–12, enacted by Congress in 1975, has had little substantive impact on express warranty litigation in products liability cases. Basically a consumer protection statute, the Act requires that written warranties given in connection with consumer products be complete, comprehensible, and available for review prior to purchase. Certain minimum standards are prescribed if a warranty is designated as a "Full Warranty"; other warranties are to be designated as "Limited." A seller offering a full warranty may not require the return of a warranty registration card as a condition precedent to warranty coverage. See 15 U.S.C.A. § 104(b)(i); 16 CFR § 700.7 (1988).

Two procedural aspects of the Act would seem to have interesting implications for express warranty products liability actions: (1) Consumers are given a federal cause of action, for breach of a written (or implied) warranty; and (2) Consumers who "finally prevail" in such actions may be allowed litigation costs and expenses, including attorney's fees. See § 110(d) of the Act, 15 U.S.C.A. § 2310(d). However, "[c]ourts have uniformly held that the act does not create a federal cause of action for personal injury claims which are otherwise state law claims for breach of warranty." Washington v. Otasco, Inc., 603 F.Supp. 1295, 1296 (N.D.Miss.1985).

The major substantive changes wrought by the Act affecting personal injury litigation concern certain restrictions on disclaimers, discussed infra at pp. 156–57.

9. On express warranties, see generally R. Nordstrom, Handbook of the Law of Sales §§ 63–73 (1970); J. White & R. Summers, Handbook of the Law under the Uniform Commercial Code §§ 9.3–9.6 (3d ed. 1988).

B. IMPLIED WARRANTY OF MERCHANTABILITY

"It has been said that the concept of implied warranty rests upon the foundation of business ethics and constitutes an exception to the maxim 'let the buyer beware,' itself encompassing the idea that there is no warranty implied with respect to the quality of the goods being sold." Lambert v. Sistrunk, 58 So.2d 434–35 (Fla.1952). "Under the rule of *caveat venditor,* a sale 'raises an implied warranty (against latent defects) from the fairness and fullness of the price paid, upon this clear and reasonable ground, that in the contract of sale, the purchaser is not supposed to part with his money, but in expectation of an adequate advantage, or recompense.' Champneys v. Johnson, [2 Brevard 268, 272 (1809)]. 'Selling for a sound price raises an implied warranty that the thing sold is free from defects, known and unknown (to the seller).' Southern Iron & Equipment Co. v. Railway Co., [151

S.C. 506, 525, 149 S.E. 271, 278 (1929)]." Lane v. Trenholm Bldg. Co., 267 S.C. 497, 503, 229 S.E.2d 728, 730 (1976).

PROSSER, THE IMPLIED WARRANTY OF MERCHANTABLE QUALITY

27 Minn.L.Rev. 117–22 (1943).

Is there such a thing as a standard warranty of quality presumptively to be implied in every sale of goods made by a dealer? Otherwise stated, are there certain minimum requirements of quality in the thing sold which every purchaser from such a dealer is entitled to demand unless there is express agreement to the contrary, or circumstances are shown which indicate a contrary understanding?

Section 15(2) of the Uniform Sales Act reads as follows:

Where the goods are bought by description from a seller who deals in goods of that description (whether he be the grower or manufacturer or not), there is an implied warranty that the goods shall be of merchantable quality.

This section, which has been enacted thus far in thirty-four states, as well as the District of Columbia, Alaska and Hawaii, was copied almost verbatim from the first part of Section 14(2) of the English Sale of Goods Act of 1894, which was itself a restatement and codification of the common law of England as it existed at that date. As it is stated in the American act, * * * it has been recognized as merely declaratory of established common law rules. * * *

HISTORY

In its inception, breach of warranty was a tort. The action was upon the case, for breach of an assumed duty, and the wrong was conceived to be a form of misrepresentation, in the nature of deceit and not at all clearly distinguished from deceit. Warranty has never entirely lost this tort character which it had in the beginning; and this may have important consequences at the present day. * * * [The tort perspective] has continued to color the substantive law of warranty itself, by introducing some idea of misrepresentation of fact, however innocent, and of reliance on the part of the buyer upon the seller's knowledge, skill or judgment, or some implied assertion concerning the character of the goods sold.

* * *

The leading case is Gardiner v. Gray,[19] at nisi prius in 1815. * * * Lord Ellenborough stated the fundamental principle of the implied warranty of merchantable quality:

19. (1815) 4 Camp. 144, 171 Eng.Rep. 46. The decision was repeated in substance the same year, in Laing v. Fidgeon, (1815) 6 Taunt. 108, 4 Camp. 169, 128 Eng. Rep. 974.

"[T]he purchaser has a right to expect a saleable article answering the description in the contract. Without any particular warranty, this is an implied term in every such contract. Where there is no opportunity to inspect the commodity, the maxim of *caveat emptor* does not apply. He cannot without a warranty insist that it shall be of any particular quality or fineness, but the intention of both parties must be taken to be, that it shall be saleable in the market under the denomination mentioned in the contract between them. The purchaser cannot be supposed to buy goods to lay them on a dunghill. * * *" * * *

A long line of later cases rounded out the picture. The seller's warranty, as a matter of contract, was held to mean not only that the goods delivered must be genuine according to the name, kind or description specified, but that they must be of a quality to pass in the market under that description, and this in turn to mean that they must be reasonably fit for the ordinary uses to which such goods are put. * * *

At about the same time, if not earlier, the idea began to make its appearance that warranties arose by implication "of law" from what had been said and done, and were independent of any intent on the part of the seller to contract with regard to them, or to be bound by them. This idea, now generally accepted as to express warranties, was carried over all the more readily into those "implied," where it became involved with the development of modern notions of policy, based upon the increasing practice of reputable sellers to assume responsibility for defective goods sold, together with the feeling that such responsibility is best placed upon the seller as a cost of his business, which he may distribute to the public at large as a part of the price. As a result, it is often said that implied warranties of quality arise by operation of law and are independent of any intention to agree upon their terms as a matter of fact; and there are many cases, at least, in which to hold that the warranty is a term of the contract is "to speak the language of pure fiction." [32]

THE RISE AND (SUBSTANTIAL) FALL OF THE VERTICAL PRIVITY DEFENSE IN IMPLIED WARRANTY ACTIONS

"In earlier times the one who made the article generally sold it directly to the ultimate user, and thus the consumer, being in privity of contract with the manufacturer, was allowed to recover on the usual warranties for losses caused by defective workmanship." Jeanblanc, Manufacturers' Liability to Persons Other Than Their Immediate Vendees, 24 Va.L.Rev. 134 (1937). Yet, just as the courts began imposing warranties of quality on manufacturers in the latter part of the nineteenth century, manufacturers increasingly were spinning off

32. Williston, Liability for Honest Misrepresentation, (1911) 24 Harv.L.Rev. 415, 420; Smith, Surviving Fictions, (1917) 27 Yale L.J. 147, 317, 326.

the retail function to third party dealers. This meant, of course, that the typical consumer began to deal contractually only with the retailer. Thus, manufacturers sued in warranty by consumers of defective products in the late 1800's had available the ready-made defense of no privity of contract, a defense that had just begun to prove its effectiveness in actions brought in negligence. But the harshness of the rule in cases of consumer injury was readily apparent, and the courts began to riddle it with exceptions at an early date. See Gillam, Products Liability in a Nutshell, 37 Or.L.Rev. 119, 152–55 (1958) (listing 29 such exceptions).

The first decisions to abolish outright the manufacturer's privity defense in implied warranty case were decided at the turn of the century and involved defective foodstuffs. See Mazetti v. Armour & Co., 75 Wash. 622, 135 P. 633 (1913); Parks v. G.C. Yost Pie Co., 93 Kan. 334, 144 P. 202 (1914). See also Jackson Coca–Cola Bottling Co. v. Chapman, 106 Miss. 864, 869, 64 So. 791, 791 (1914):

> A "sma' mousie" caused the trouble in this case. The "wee, sleekit, cow'rin', tim'rous beastie" drowned in a bottle of coca-cola * * *. [The consumer] did not get joy from the anticipated refreshing drink. He was in the frame of mind to approve the poet's [Robert Burns'] words:
>
> "The best-laid schemes o' mice an' men
> Gang aft aglay
> An' lea'e us nought but grief an' pain
> For promis'd joy!"

The rationale for abolishing the defense in food cases was lucidly explained in Jacob E. Decker & Sons, Inc. v. Capps, 139 Tex. 609, 612, 164 S.W.2d 828, 829 (1942):

> Liability in such case is not based on negligence, nor on a breach of the usual implied contractual warranty, but on the broad principle of the public policy to protect human health and life. It is a well-known fact that articles of food are manufactured and placed in the channels of commerce, with the intention that they shall pass from hand to hand until they are finally used by some remote customer. It is usually impracticable, if not impossible, for the ultimate customer to analyze the food and ascertain whether or not it is suitable for human consumption. Since it has been packed and placed on the market as a food for human consumption, and marked as such, the purchaser usually eats it or causes it to be served to his family without the precaution of having it analyzed by a technician to ascertain whether or not it is suitable for human consumption. In fact, in most instances the only satisfactory examination that could be made would be only at the time and place of the processing of the food. It seems to be the rule that where food products sold for human consumption are unfit for

> that purpose, there is such an utter failure of the purpose for which the food is sold, and the consequences of eating unsound food are so disastrous to human health and life, that the law imposes a warranty of purity in favor of the ultimate consumer as a matter of public policy.

The breakdown of the remote seller's privity defense in implied warranty cases began to spread in the 1950s to animal food and products for intimate bodily use, such as soap, hair dye, and permanent wave solution. Then, in the late 1950s and early 1960s, several courts in rapid succession extended the idea to durable goods. It was in 1960, in Henningsen v. Bloomfield Motors, Inc., 32 N.J. 358, 161 A.2d 69 (1960), that the privity bar was forcefully repudiated in a landmark implied warranty case involving injuries from a defective automobile. In the words of Dean Prosser, *Henningsen* marked the "fall of the citadel of privity." Prosser, The Fall of the Citadel (Strict Liability to the Consumer), 50 Minn.L.Rev. 791 (1966). Writing for the court, Judge Francis reasoned with compelling logic: "We see no rational doctrinal basis for differentiating between a fly in a bottle of beverage and a defective automobile. The unwholesome beverage may bring illness to one person, the defective car, with its great potentiality for harm to the driver, occupants, and others, demands even less adherence to the narrow barrier of privity." 32 N.J. at 383, 161 A.2d at 83. Courts quickly fell into line after *Henningsen,* and a majority of jurisdictions have now abolished the manufacturer's privity defense in implied warranty actions involving durable goods.

Some of the states that still retain the manufacturer's privity defense as a general rule make an exception if the manufacturer has provided the consumer with an express warranty. Of course if the retailer is found to be an agent of the manufacturer the buyer can satisfy the privity requirement. Finally, some jurisdictions have abolished the defense in personal injury and property damage cases but have retained it where the plaintiff seeks recovery for economic loss. See generally Annot., 16 A.L.R.3d 683 (1967).

The privity defense has been abolished by statute in several states. Virginia's "anti-privity" statute is illustrative:

> Lack of privity between plaintiff and defendant shall be no defense in any action against the manufacturer or seller of goods to recover damages for breach of warranty, express or implied, or for negligence, although the plaintiff did not purchase the goods from the defendant, if the plaintiff was a person whom the manufacturer or seller might reasonably have expected to use, consume or be affected by the goods * * *.

Va.Code § 8.2–318 (1965). A few states have interpreted U.C.C. § 2–318 as abolishing the remote seller's vertical privity defense. This issue is discussed further below, at pp. 121–28.

UNIFORM COMMERCIAL CODE

§ 2–314. Implied Warranty: Merchantability; Usage of Trade

(1) Unless excluded or modified (Section 2–316), a warranty that the goods shall be merchantable is implied in a contract for their sale if the seller is a merchant with respect to goods of that kind. Under this section the serving for value of food or drink to be consumed either on the premises or elsewhere is a sale.

(2) Goods to be merchantable must be at least such as

(a) pass without objection in the trade under the contract description; and

(b) in the case of fungible goods, are of fair average quality within the description; and

(c) are fit for the ordinary purposes for which such goods are used; and

(d) run, within the variations permitted by the agreement, of even kind, quality and quantity within each unit and among all units involved; and

(e) are adequately contained, packaged, and labeled as the agreement may require; and

(f) conform to the promises or affirmations of fact made on the container or label if any.

(3) Unless excluded or modified (Section 2–316) other implied warranties may arise from course of dealing or usage of trade.

NOTE

Is subsection (2)(f) misplaced? See comment 10.

J. WHITE & R. SUMMERS, HANDBOOK OF THE LAW UNDER THE UNIFORM COMMERCIAL CODE *

408–18 (3d ed. 1988).

The implied warranty of merchantability in 2–314 is by far the most important warranty in the Code. It is a first cousin to strict tort liability, and "products liability" cases are often tried under the merchantability banner. Section 2–314 is not revolutionary; it is simply a modernized version of the comparable Uniform Sales Act provision.

Although section 2–314 offers a form of "strict liability," the plaintiff is not assured of winning with ease. Except that he need not prove negligence on the part of the defendant, the wise plaintiff's lawyer will regard a 2–314 case as highly similar to a negligence suit.

A plaintiff in a merchantability lawsuit must prove that the defendant deviated from the standard of merchantability and that this deviation caused the plaintiff's injury both proximately and in fact. These necessities of proof make the merchantability case a first cousin to a negligence lawsuit. Under 2–314, a plaintiff must prove that (1) a merchant sold goods, (2) which were not "merchantable" at the time of sale, and (3) injury and damages to the plaintiff or his property (4) caused proximately and in fact by the defective nature of the goods, and (5) notice to seller of injury. The plaintiff can fail on any of the points listed; he can also succumb to any of the affirmative defenses that the defendant may raise, for instance, warranty disclaimed, notice of breach not timely, or statute of limitations expired. Recall that a merchantability case is likely to be somewhat more difficult for the plaintiff than an express warranty case, for implied warranties are more easily disclaimed than are express warranties, and proof of breach of an explicit express warranty is likely to be easier than is proof of breach of the standard of merchantability.

* * *

The most widely quoted of the synonyms in subsection (2) is paragraph (c), which provides that goods must be "fit for the ordinary purposes for which such goods are used." However, in most cases, to say that goods are fit for the ordinary purposes does little to advance the analysis; it simply substitutes one synonym for another and does nothing to tell a lawyer whether the protective guards around the sides of a rotary lawn mower are sufficient to make it fit for the ordinary purposes or whether the design is fatally defective and the mower, therefore, unmerchantable. * * * [W]e cannot hope to summarize the thousands of cases that deal with the question of merchantability; we can only suggest where a frustrated lawyer might look for help in determining whether the goods in his particular case ought to be classified as merchantable or nonmerchantable.

Certainly the first place one should look is to the usage in the trade. * * *

Comment 7 to 2–314 suggests another source of information about the parties' intention: [price]. If, for example, there is a dispute on the question whether an airplane that is the subject of a sale must be flyable to be merchantable, it would be revealing to find that the agreed price fell precisely within the price range charged for flyable airplanes and twenty to thirty per cent above the price normally charged for nonflyable airplanes. In such a case, the price is an objective manifestation of the intention of the parties to deal over a flyable aircraft.

Obviously, one will also wish to look at the characteristics exhibited by goods of the same class that are manufactured by persons other than the seller in question.

Finally, one should get some idea about merchantability in cases from government standards and regulations which are now published by an increasing number of federal and state agencies. If, for example, a used car lacks shoulder harnesses, which are required under federal law for a car made in that year, that fact is powerful evidence that the car is not merchantable.

A concluding question * * * is how the merchantability standard differs from the comparable strict tort standard "defective condition, unreasonably dangerous. * * * " [Apart from a couple minor points,] we would find the terms nearly synonymous and would expect a court to hold that any automobile which was not merchantable was also in a defective condition unreasonably dangerous. * * *

The student and lawyer should understand that "merchantable" is not a synonym for perfect. Fish chowder containing bones that stick in the buyer's craw may nevertheless be merchantable as may a cigarette that kills or a car that maims. It is the lawyer's challenging job to define the term "merchantability" in his case in some objective way so that the court or jury can make a determination whether that standard has been breached.

NOTE

Compare the observations of R. Nordstrom, Handbook of the Law of Sales 235–36 (1970): *

> [Whether a product is "fit for the purposes for which such goods are used" under U.C.C. § 2–314(2)(c)] is the key thought—the heart—of the merchantability warranty. When a merchant sells goods of the kind in which he deals, there is a warranty that the goods purchased will be fit for their ordinary purpose. Shoes must have their heels attached so that they will not break off under normal use, but if those shoes are used for mountain climbing, there is no implied warranty that the heels will be fit for this extraordinary purpose—unless, of course, the elements of a warranty of fitness for purpose are present. Likewise, shoes are warranted against producing dermatitis, shotgun shells against premature explosion, marine engines against excessive smoking, machinery against defective operation, rivet studs against splitting, and hair lotion against scalp burns.
>
> * * *
>
> The warranty of merchantability is broader than that the goods will do the ordinary job for which they were made. They must also, unless the further warranty is disclaimed, do the job safely. The hair lotion might do an excellent job of putting a wave in a woman's hair but, if it also causes dermatitis in a substantial number of users, the lotion is not *fit* for its ordinary purpose. * * * Thus, fitness for ordinary purpose is a broader concept than just that of doing a single job; it contains ideas of doing that job safely. However, the law does not require that the goods sold be accident-proof. A hammer is fit for its ordinary purpose even though it is capable of mashing thumbs, and shoes may be merchantable even though they slip on wet asphalt.

There is no escape from the proposition that the issue is one of fact for the jury: were the goods fit for their ordinary purposes?

MAYBANK v. S.S. KRESGE

Court of Appeals of North Carolina, 1980.
46 N.C.App. 687, 266 S.E.2d 409.*

[Plaintiff sued K–Mart, the retailer of a G.T.E. Sylvania Blue Dot flashcube that exploded in her face, injuring her eye. The carton had warned of the risk that damaged cubes might shatter. There was no evidence that the cube had been damaged prior to use. The trial court severed K–Mart's third party action against Sylvania for trial at a later date, and, after the plaintiff's evidence, directed a verdict for defendant. Plaintiff appealed.]

VAUGHN, JUDGE.

* * *

Plaintiff purchased the package of flashcubes for $.88 from defendant's K–Mart store. Defendant was a merchant within the definition of that term in the Uniform Commercial Code as provided in the first clause of G.S. 25–2–104(1). Defendant sold the flashcube to plaintiff and "is a merchant with respect to goods of that kind." G.S. 25–2–314(1).

Whether the flashcube was merchantable can be resolved in part by examining G.S. 25–2–314(2) [(a)–(f)]. These are the minimum standards which a good must have in order to be merchantable. A flashcube which does not work properly and which causes the unexpected harm this flashcube caused is not merchantable. A flashcube can "pass without objection," be "of fair average quality" and "fit for ordinary purposes" and be far short of perfect. But these minimum requirements embodied in G.S. 25–2–314(2)(a), (b), (c) are not met by a flashcube which explodes. Contrast Coffer v. Standard Brands, 30 N.C. App. 134, 226 S.E.2d 534 (1976). Such a flashcube is not "within the variations permitted by the agreement." The package contained a warning of possible shattering of a flashcube. The warning of possible shattering or static electricity does not mean that an exploding flashcube has been "adequately contained, packaged and labeled" or that it "conform[ed] to the promises or affirmations of fact made on the container." This was not an adequate warning of the consequences of this case. A flashcube which shatters might be merchantable. An exploding flashcube is not, however, merchantable. The attributes listed in G.S. 25–2–314(2) are not exclusive nor exhaustive. The evidence of this case is to the effect that the attributes of merchantability found in subsection (2) of G.S. 25–2–314 were not present in the flashcube. This is sufficient proof that the flashcube was not merchantable to reach the jury.

* Modified on other grounds, and affirmed, 302 N.C. 129, 273 S.E.2d 681 (1981).

* * *

Reversed and remanded.

NOTES

1. Which subsection(s) of § 2–314(2) might fairly be applicable to the facts in *Maybank*? What do the words "as the agreement may require" mean in subsection (e)? See comment 10 to § 2–314; Nordstrom, Law of Sales 236–37 (1970).

Does it matter whether the container itself is sold? What if a Coke bottle that explodes was "returnable" at which time a deposit was to be returned? Cf. Petella v. Corp Bros., Inc., 107 R.I. 599, 268 A.2d 699 (1970).

2. Certain preliminary issues may arise concerning the coverage of a case under § 2–314. For example, the defendant must be a "merchant." See, e.g., Samson v. Riesing, 62 Wis.2d 698, 215 N.W.2d 662 (1974) (no recovery under § 2–314 for salmonella food poisoning from turkey salad prepared by Wauwatosa High School Band Mothers, since mothers were not "merchants"); Ballou v. Trahan, 133 Vt. 185, 334 A.2d 409 (1975) (private person who sold used Porsche to plaintiff not "merchant"). Further, the defendant must be a merchant *with respect to the type of goods sold to the plaintiff.* A bank, for example, which sells a repossessed boat to the plaintiff in an isolated transaction, may not be a "merchant" for purposes of § 2–314. Donald v. City Nat. Bank, 295 Ala. 320, 329 So.2d 92 (1976). See also Siemen v. Alden, 34 Ill.App.3d 961, 341 N.E.2d 713 (1975) (sawmill operator, who sold his used power saw to plaintiff after replacing it with new one, not a merchant with respect to goods of that kind). Compare McHugh v. Carlton, 369 F.Supp. 1271 (D.C.S.C.1974) (service station operator who kept stock of new and used tires held to be merchant with respect to recapped tires, although he did not keep stock of recapped tires and ordered them only on specific request). See comment 3 to § 2–314: "A person making an isolated sale of goods is not a 'merchant' within the meaning of the full scope of this section * * *." See also U.C.C. § 2–104 ("merchant" defined). See generally Annot., 91 A.L.R.3d 876 (1979).

There must be a contract for the "sale" of "goods." The lease of realty, therefore, is not covered by § 2–314. See infra, Chapter 8.

Comment 1 to § 2–314 provides in part: "The seller's obligation applies to present sales as well as to contracts to sell * * *." A recurring issue in exploding pop bottle cases is whether the requisite contract exists prior to payment by the purchaser at the check-out counter. In Fender v. Colonial Stores, Inc., 138 Ga.App. 31, 225 S.E.2d 691 (1976), plaintiff was injured when a bottle of Coca–Cola exploded as she was placing it on the defendant grocer's check-out counter. Defendant argued that U.C.C. § 2–314 did not apply since a "contract for sale" had not yet been formed at the time of injury. *Held,* that defendant had offered the beverage for sale by placing it on the shelf; that plaintiff had accepted the offer by taking physical possession of the item; and that § 2–314 was thereafter applicable. See U.C.C. § 2–106(1). See also Giant Food, Inc. v. Washington Coca–Cola Bottling Co., 273 Md. 592, 332 A.2d 1 (1975).

3. **Standard of Liability.** The meaning of "merchantability," its essential nature, and how it differs from the standards underlying the other theories of liability are issues of central importance in § 2–314 litigation. Three wrongful death actions arising out of the crash of a helicopter were consolidated in Krause v. Sud–Aviation, Soc. Nat. de Constr. Aero., 301 F.Supp. 513 (S.D.

N.Y.1968), aff'd 413 F.2d 428 (2d Cir.1969). Holding inter alia that an implied warranty action may be brought in admiralty under the Death on the High Seas Act, 46 U.S.C.A. § 761 et seq., the court remarked:

> Although breach of implied warranty is in one sense a form of absolute liability, or liability without fault, in another sense it is not. The "fault" involved is breach of the warranty, but this is in a way tautological because the warranty is always "implied" ex post to fit the facts. Nevertheless, we cannot and do not assign liability at random or on a "deep pocket" basis; a true "deep pocket" theory would simply make all injury, whatever the source, compensable by some giant central insurer. Until that nirvana is achieved, we are faced with the task of rationalizing who warrants what to whom and why.
>
> A warranty is in essence a promise. We think it is reasonable for a passenger in an aircraft to proceed on the assumption that the manufacturer has made the plane, if not perfectly, at least in such a way that its ordinary use will not prove harmful. The very fact of manufacturing and offering the airplane for sale implies a promise to this effect made to all persons who might reasonably be expected to ride in it. Accordingly, we hold that respondent SUD impliedly warranted that its helicopter would not prove dangerous or harmful in ordinary use. We further hold that by virtue of the crash on November 30, 1959 that warranty was breached.

Logan v. Montgomery Ward & Co., 216 Va. 425, 427–428, 219 S.E.2d 685, 687 (1975), was a suit for injuries caused by the explosion of a stove. Discussing the nature of the warranty of merchantability implied by the sale, the court stated as follows:

> Mrs. Logan's cause of action depends upon the existence of a defect in the stove at the time it left the control of Montgomery Ward. The standard of safety of goods imposed on the seller or manufacturer of a product is essentially the same whether the theory of liability is labeled warranty or negligence. The product must be fit for the ordinary purposes for which it is to be used. There was an implied warranty of merchantability that the stove was reasonably safe for its intended use. Under either the warranty theory or the negligence theory the plaintiff must show, (1) that the goods were unreasonably dangerous either for the use to which they would ordinarily be put or for some other reasonably foreseeable purpose, and (2) that the unreasonably dangerous condition existed when the goods left the defendant's hands.

Some courts equate failure of the warranty of merchantability with "defectiveness." See, e.g., Lariviere v. Dayton Safety Ladder Co., ___ R.I. ___, 525 A.2d 892 (1987) (ladder that collapsed).

If plaintiff can show a malfunction of the product, for example that the brakes or steering on his new car suddenly failed, but is unable to show the specific cause of the failure, has plaintiff established a breach of the implied warranty of merchantability? "When machinery 'malfunctions', it obviously lacks fitness regardless of the cause of the malfunction. Under the theory of warranty, the 'sin' is the lack of fitness as evidenced by the malfunction itself rather than some specific dereliction by the manufacturer in constructing or designing the machinery." Greco v. Bucciconi Eng'g Co., 283 F.Supp. 978, 982 (W.D.Pa.1967), aff'd, 407 F.2d 87 (3d Cir.1969).

4. An inadequate warning of danger may render a product unmerchantable under § 2–314(2)(c), (e) and (f). Reid v. Eckerds Drugs, Inc., 40 N.C.App. 476, 253 S.E.2d 344 (1979) (plaintiff liberally applied deodorant, lit a cigarette, and burst into blue flame).

5. What if the use to which the product was put was not intended by the manufacturer? See Hardman v. Helene Curtis Indus., Inc., 48 Ill.App.2d 42, 198 N.E.2d 681, 691 (1964): "The essential question presented by a claim of breach of implied warranty of merchantability is whether the product failed to safely and adequately satisfy the uses to which such products are ordinarily put." *Held,* jury question whether small child's spraying of defendant's flammable hair spray on her dress and hair, because of pleasant fragrance, was "ordinary" use.

6. **Reliance.** "It has never been contended, to our knowledge, that a buyer must prove reliance on the skill or judgment of the manufacturer in order that he may recover for the breach of an implied warranty of merchantability. The warranty is implied because the manufacturer holds himself out as being skilled in the construction of his products and as being able to manufacture them without latent defects in materials or workmanship." Vitro Corp. of America v. Texas Vitrified Supply Co., 71 N.M. 95, 106, 376 P.2d 41, 49 (1962). Indeed, this is perhaps the central notion that supported the shift from *caveat emptor* to the basic implied warranty of quality (merchantability) in the nineteenth century.

The warranty of merchantability will thus accompany the sale of a product even though the buyer asks for it by trade name. E.g., Dougall v. Brown Bay Boat Works & Sales, Inc., 287 Minn. 290, 178 N.W.2d 217 (1970). Similarly, the fact that the buyer specifically identifies the product in some other manner, as by selecting it himself from among the seller's stock, will not exclude the implied warranty of merchantability. See comment 3. However, "when the buyer before entering into the contract has examined the goods or the sample or model as fully as he desired or has refused to examine the goods there is no implied warranty with regard to defects which an examination ought in the circumstances to have revealed to him * * *." U.C.C. § 2–316(3)(b). "Of course if the buyer discovers the defect and uses the goods anyway, or if he unreasonably fails to examine the goods before he uses them, resulting injuries may be found to result from his own action rather than proximately from a breach of warranty." Id., comment 8. See also § 2–314, comment 13.

7. Plaintiff is injured when the blade of a power saw, which was very wobbly at the time of purchase, flies off during initial use. Warranty of merchantability made and breached?

8. Prior to or in lieu of adopting the doctrine of strict liability in tort, some states—such as Delaware, Massachusetts, Michigan, North Carolina, and Virginia—have used an implied warranty of quality to fill the void. Thus, some such courts speak of a common law "implied warranty" in tort. For most purposes such "implied warranties" are nearly identical to strict liability in tort.

9. See generally Annot., 83 A.L.R.3d 694 (1978).

C. IMPLIED WARRANTY OF FITNESS FOR A PARTICULAR PURPOSE

UNIFORM COMMERCIAL CODE

§ 2–315. Implied Warranty: Fitness for Particular Purpose

Where the seller at the time of contracting has reason to know any particular purpose for which the goods are required and that the buyer is relying on the seller's skill or judgment to select or furnish suitable goods, there is unless excluded or modified under the next section an implied warranty that the goods shall be fit for such purpose.

Official Comment

* * *

2. A "particular purpose" differs from the ordinary purpose for which the goods are used in that it envisages a specific use by the buyer which is peculiar to the nature of his business whereas the ordinary purposes for which goods are used are those envisaged in the concept of merchantability and go to uses which are customarily made of the goods in question. For example, shoes are generally used for the purpose of walking upon ordinary ground, but a seller may know that a particular pair was selected to be used for climbing mountains.

A contract may of course include both a warranty of merchantability and one of fitness for a particular purpose.

* * *

BARB v. WALLACE

Court of Special Appeals of Maryland, 1980.
45 Md.App. 271, 412 A.2d 1314.

COUCH, JUDGE.

At the age of sixteen, George William Barb purchased a small, used gasoline powered engine for five dollars from Robert Wallace for use in a go-cart. A short while after George returned home he attempted to start the engine, which was mounted on a sturdy base at the time of purchase. Almost immediately upon starting, the engine exploded and caused severe injuries to George's head. George and his father, appellants here, sued appellee, Robert Wallace, [on various grounds, including breach of implied warranty of fitness for a particular purpose under U.C.C. § 2–315. The trial court granted defendant's motion for summary judgment, and plaintiffs appealed.]

George's deposition discloses that George informed appellee that he intended to use the engine in a "go-cart". The appellee responded, according to George, that the engine could be used in a "go-cart" because the "shaft was out the side of the engine" and that the engine "ran good". Appellee admits in his brief that he was apprised of the purpose for which George was purchasing the engine. The issue, then, in our review of the trial court's granting of the motion for summary judgment, is whether there is a genuine dispute as to George's reliance on the appellee's skill or judgment. See Shay v. Joseph, 219 Md. 273, 275, 149 A.2d 3 (1959).

Appellee, in his brief, relies upon George's statement that at the time he purchased the engine he was taking a course in auto mechanics where he had worked on small engines for the proposition that George's judgment and skill was at least as good as appellee's. We believe this evidence presents a factual dispute as to whether George relied upon himself or actually relied upon appellee's skill and judgment to select or furnish suitable goods. * * * Moreover, Comment 1 to § 2–315 states that the question of whether an implied warranty of fitness for a particular purpose exists in any particular case is basically a question of fact to be determined by the circumstances of the contracting. [Citations.] The fact that George may have had some experience with engines does not necessarily preclude the possibility that he was relying upon appellee's knowledge of the capabilities of this particular engine. We believe this raises a factual dispute which should not have been resolved on a motion for summary judgment.

We note that § 2–315 does not limit the application of an implied warranty of fitness for a particular purpose to merchants only. The official comment to that section states that, "Although normally the warranty will arise only where the seller is a merchant with the appropriate 'skill or judgment', it can arise as to nonmerchants where this is justified by the particular circumstances." *Md.Com.Law Code Ann.* § 2–315, Comment 4 (1975). The burden of proof carried by the buyer where a nonmerchant seller is involved poses greater difficulties, particularly on the issue of appellee's possession of appropriate skill and judgment, but it does not warrant the granting of a motion for summary judgment. * * *

* * *

[Reversed and remanded.]

NOTES

1. The distinction between the implied warranties of merchantability and fitness for a particular purpose is well described in comment 2 to § 2–315 set forth above. The courts are split on whether a § 2–315 action will lie if the buyer's particular purpose for the product was also an ordinary one. Compare Fred's Excavating & Crane Service, Inc. v. Continental Ins. Co., 340 So.2d 1220 (Fla.App.1976) (claim for breach of implied warranty of fitness for a particular purpose dismissed for failure to allege "a particular or unusual use different from the purpose for which the item sold is ordinarily used"), with Nelson v. Wilkins Dodge, Inc., 256 N.W.2d 472, 476 n. 2 (Minn.1977) (particular as well as ordinary use of pickup truck was to be driven at sustained high rates of speed). Many courts remain confused. See, e.g., Lariviere v. Dayton Safety Ladder Co.,

___ R.I. ___, 525 A.2d 892, 897 (1987). "Such confusion under the Code is inexcusable. Sections 2–314 and 2–315 make plain that the warranty of fitness for a particular purpose is narrower, more specific, and more precise." J. White & R. Summers, Handbook of the Law under the Uniform Commercial Code 418–19 (3d ed. 1988).

One problem arising out of the overlap between the two implied warranties is one of terminology. Especially in earlier years some courts referred to the implied warranty of merchantability as an "implied warranty of fitness." This confusion of labels is contrary to the usage of the Uniform Commercial Code and is only occasionally seen in modern decisions.

The implied warranty of fitness for a particular purpose may also overlap with a seller's express warranties. See Filler v. Rayex Corp., 435 F.2d 336, 338 (7th Cir.1970) (sunglasses advertised as "Baseball Sunglasses," that splintered when hit by baseball, "not fit for baseball playing, the particular purpose for which they were sold").

On the overlap between the warranties, see Ezer, The Impact of the Uniform Commercial Code on the California Law of Sales Warranties, 8 U.C. L.A.L.Rev. 281, 299 (1961); Annot., 83 A.L.R.3d 656 (1978). Compare U.C.C. § 2–317.

2. Plaintiffs bought a particular model riding mower upon the recommendation of the defendant's salesman for use on their hilly property, subject to the salesman's inspection of the property to confirm that the mower was appropriate. When the salesman delivered the mower, he inspected the property and pronounced the mower suitable, provided it was driven vertically up the steepest hills. Plaintiff husband was injured when the mower tipped over backwards while he was mowing vertically up a 19° slope. The owner's manual warned against using on slopes in excess of 15°. *Held,* jury verdict for plaintiff, for breach of implied warranty of fitness for a particular purpose, affirmed. Klein v. Sears Roebuck and Co., 773 F.2d 1421 (4th Cir.1985).

3. Note that the seller need not be a "merchant" under § 2–315, as in § 2–313, but unlike § 2–314. Why the distinction?

4. **Reliance.** A fundamental difference between §§ 2–314 and 2–315 is the requirement in § 2–315 that plaintiff establish reliance (and, additionally, the seller's reason to know of it). At common law, there were certain specific rules designed to assure plaintiff's reliance. For example, plaintiff's inspection of the product, or in some jurisdictions even his opportunity to inspect, negated both the fitness and merchantability implied warranties. Section 15(3) of the Uniform Sales Act restricted this exclusion to actual examinations and defects which ought to have been revealed thereby. A plaintiff's reliance was also assured by the rule that precluded implied warranties of fitness for a particular purpose in the case of articles that were "known, described and definite." Nor could such warranties arise "[i]n the case of a contract to sell or a sale of a specified article under its patent or other trade name. * * * " Uniform Sales Act § 15(4). See generally 1 Williston on Sales §§ 234–36a (rev. ed. 1948). Compare comment 5 to § 2–315:

> The elimination of the "patent or other trade name" exception constitutes the major extension of the warranty of fitness which has been made by the cases and continued in this Article. Under the present section the existence of a patent or other trade name and the designation of the article by that name, or indeed in any other definite manner, is only one of the facts to be considered on the question of

whether the buyer actually relied on the seller, but it is not of itself decisive of the issue. If the buyer himself is insisting on a particular brand he is not relying on the seller's skill and judgment and so no warranty results. But the mere fact that the article purchased has a particular patent or trade name is not sufficient to indicate nonreliance if the article has been recommended by the seller as adequate for the buyer's purposes.

5. Plaintiff's reliance on the seller's skill and judgment is sometimes very clear. See, e.g., Newmark v. Gimbel's, Inc., 102 N.J.Super. 279, 246 A.2d 11 (1968), aff'd, 54 N.J. 585, 258 A.2d 697 (1969) (beauty shop customer, who suffered injuries to scalp and loss of hair from permanent wave solution, relied on beauty shop operator to select appropriate lotion); Caldwell v. Brown Serv. Funeral Home, 345 So.2d 1341 (Ala.1977) (purchasers of casket and vault relied on defendant funeral home to select casket that would fit in vault).

However, a buyer who inspects the product, or otherwise participates in its selection, may have some difficulty in establishing his reliance on the seller's judgment in selecting the product. In Carney v. Sears, Roebuck & Co., 309 F.2d 300 (4th Cir.1962), plaintiff told defendant's salesman that he needed to replace his five foot Sears step-ladder with one tall enough to reach the lights in his ten foot ceiling. Plaintiff looked over the various ladders on display, and the salesman "recommended" a six foot ladder of the same type and design plaintiff already had. The ladder was defectively constructed and plaintiff was injured. The court stated: "We find no basis for an implied warranty of fitness for a particular purpose because it is not shown in the evidence that the selection of a ladder suitable for plaintiff's purpose was exclusively within the control of the defendant's salesman. * * * Here the evidence shows that the plaintiff in fact selected the ladder; at the very least, that he did not rely solely upon the salesman's judgment in selecting the ladder. His discretion and judgment played a major part in the selection of the ladder which he ultimately purchased."

But compare Peters v. Lyons, 168 N.W.2d 759, 764 (Iowa 1969). Buyer asked for a dog chain strong enough to restrain his 100–120 pound German shepherd. The saleswoman selected the strongest chain, which she and buyer both inspected, and both agreed that it would be sufficient. It was not, and plaintiff was attacked and injured by the dog. *Held,* since the defect was not discoverable by inspection, reliance on the seller's skill and judgment had been established: " 'The buyer's reliance on the seller need not be total reliance. The buyer may rely on his own judgment as to some matters and on the seller's skill and judgment as to others.' "

6. **Miscellaneous Applications.** As the number of indemnity and contribution actions brought by assemblers against their suppliers of component parts increases, so also may the use of § 2–315 in this context. See, e.g., Gellenbeck v. Sears, Roebuck & Co., 59 Mich.App. 339, 229 N.W.2d 443 (1975) (supplier of chains for use in swing sets had reason to know of assembler's reliance on its skill and judgment in selecting chains that could withstand stresses of twisting as well as load-carrying).

An employee may be able to recover under § 2–315 against the supplier of a product sold to his employer that was not fit for the employer's particular purpose. See, e.g., Ploof v. B.I.M. Truck Serv., Inc., 53 A.D.2d 750, 384 N.Y.S.2d

521 (1976) (worker killed when cable too large for pulley system in unloading device snapped).

7. On the implied warranty of fitness for a particular purpose, see generally Annot., 83 A.L.R.3d 669 (1978).

D. PERSONS PROTECTED BY WARRANTIES: THIRD PARTY BENEFICIARIES

Privity of contract is once again the topic of discussion. The specific aspect of the problem treated here, however, concerns the issue of "horizontal" privity, rather than the "vertical" privity issue principally considered in the preceding materials.

"Vertical privity" refers to the contractual relationship between the parties up and down the chain of distribution, from suppliers of raw materials and component parts, at the top, through the manufacturer, wholesaler, retailer and, at the bottom of the chain, the purchaser. The important issue of vertical privity is: *Who can be sued?*

The separate issue of "horizontal privity" involves the rights of nonpurchasing parties who may be affected by the product and who seek to stand in the purchaser's shoes to obtain the benefits of whatever warranties flowed to him by virtue of his contract of purchase. Such parties, extending horizontally away from the purchaser in decreasing order of affinity, include family, members of the household, guests in the home, employees, and bystanders. The important issue of horizontal privity is: *Who can sue?*

Early cases denied warranty recovery to users injured by products which they had not bought themselves. E.g., Chysky v. Drake Bros. Co., 235 N.Y. 468, 139 N.E. 576 (1923) (waitress bit into nail baked into cake purchased by her employer from defendant). Especially in the context of food purchases for other family members, some courts employed agency principles to avoid the problem. See, e.g., Greenberg v. Lorenz, 9 N.Y.2d 195, 213 N.Y.S.2d 39, 173 N.E.2d 773 (1961) (presumption that food purchase by father was made for all members of household).

This issue is now addressed in § 2–318 of the Uniform Commercial Code.

UNIFORM COMMERCIAL CODE

§ 2–318. Third Party Beneficiaries of Warranties Express or Implied

Note: *If this Act is introduced in the Congress of the United States this section should be omitted. (States to select one alternative.)*

Alternative A

A seller's warranty whether express or implied extends to any natural person who is in the family or household of his buyer or who is a guest in his home if it is reasonable to expect that such person may use, consume or be affected by the goods and who is injured in person by breach of the warranty. A seller may not exclude or limit the operation of this section.

Alternative B

A seller's warranty whether express or implied extends to any natural person who may reasonably be expected to use, consume or be affected by the goods and who is injured in person by breach of the warranty. A seller may not exclude or limit the operation of this section.

Alternative C

A seller's warranty whether express or implied extends to any person who may reasonably be expected to use, consume or be affected by the goods and who is injured by breach of the warranty. A seller may not exclude or limit the operation of this section with respect to injury to the person of an individual to whom the warranty extends. As amended 1966.

Amendments

The 1966 Amendment added alternatives B and C.

Editorial Board Note on 1966 Amendment

Source:

Colorado, Delaware, South Carolina, South Dakota, Vermont, Wyoming. Compare Proposed Final Draft, Spring 1950, and non-uniform versions enacted in Alabama, Arkansas, Texas, Virginia. The section was omitted in California and Utah.

Reason for Change:

This section as drawn in 1950 was substantially in the form of the new Alternative B. The form shown as Alternative A was substituted in 1951, limiting beneficiaries to the family, household and guests of the buyer. Beyond this, according to Comment 3, the section was neutral and was not intended to enlarge or restrict "the developing case law." The section was criticized in California as "a step backward," and was omitted from the Code as enacted in California and in Utah. Nonuniform versions were enacted in ten states, and proposals for amendment have been made elsewhere. There appears to be no national consensus as to the scope of warranty protection which is proper, but the promulgation of alternatives may prevent further proliferation of separate variations in state after state. Alternative B is therefore promulgated in substantially the 1950 form, and Alternative C is drawn to reflect the trend of more recent decisions as indicated by Restatement of Torts 2d § 402A (Tentative Draft No. 10, 1965) extending the rule beyond personal injuries.

[Conforming changes were made in pars. 2 and 3 of the Official Comment, infra, in 1966].

Official Comment

2. The purpose of this section is to give certain beneficiaries the benefit of the same warranty which the buyer received in the contract of sale, thereby freeing any such beneficiaries from any technical rules as to "privity." It seeks to accomplish this purpose without any derogation of any right or remedy resting on negligence. It rests primarily upon the merchant-seller's warranty under this Article that the goods sold are merchantable and fit for the ordinary purposes for which such goods are used rather than the warranty of fitness for a particular purpose. Implicit in the section is that any beneficiary of a warranty may bring a direct action for breach of warranty against the seller whose warranty extends to him [As amended in 1966].

WHITAKER v. LIAN FENG MACHINE CO.

Appellate Court of Illinois, 1987.
156 Ill.App.3d 316, 108 Ill.Dec. 895, 509 N.E.2d 591.

JUSTICE WHITE delivered the opinion of the court.

[Plaintiff cut his hand while using a bandsaw manufactured by defendant 1, Lian, which sold it to defendant 2, an importer, which sold it to defendant 3, a distributor, which sold it to plaintiff's employer, DuPage. The trial court granted the motions of defendants 2 and 3 to dismiss plaintiff's breach of implied warranties counts on grounds of lack of privity, and plaintiff appealed.]

Plaintiff asks us to resolve a single question in this appeal: can the employee of the ultimate purchaser of a product recover from the seller for breach of warranty? Our research indicates that this question has not been squarely decided by the state courts of Illinois. * * *

Federal courts in Illinois have addressed this question in three published decisions which have been brought to our attention. In In the Matter of Johns–Manville Asbestosis Cases (N.D.Ill.1981), 511 F.Supp. 1235, the court held that the right to recover for breach of warranty is limited in Illinois to purchasers and the narrow class of persons listed in section 2–318 of the UCC. (Ill.Rev.Stat.1985, ch. 26, par. 2–318.) Since that section does not mention employees of purchasers, the court dismissed suits brought by employees of ultimate purchasers for the seller's breach of implied warranties. (511 F.Supp. 1235, 1239–40.) Similarly in Hemphill v. Sayers (S.D.Ill.1982), 552 F.Supp. 685, the district court held that the purchaser's employees could not sue the seller for breach of warranty. (552 F.Supp. 685, 692.) In Eisenmann v. Cantor Bros., Inc. (N.D.Ill.1983), 567 F.Supp. 1347, on the other hand, the court indicated that it would allow employees of purchasers to sue for breach of warranty as third-party beneficiaries of the contract * * *. * * *

Defendants, relying on *Johns–Manville* and *Hemphill,* contend that plaintiff has no right to recover for breach of warranty because he does not fall within the class of persons listed in [U.C.C. § 318, Alternative A, as adopted in Illinois.] Section 2–318 does not, on its face, state any limitation on the rights of persons to recover for breach of warranty. Our supreme court has held that section 2–318 does not list the only exceptions to the requirement of privity in breach of warranty cases: "It is clear from the language of section 2–318 * * * and the commentary thereon, that the requirement of privity between the purchaser and remote manufacturer is not established." Berry v. G.D. Searle & Co. (1974), 56 Ill.2d 548, 558, 309 N.E.2d 550.

The courts in *Hemphill* and *Johns–Manville* distinguished *Berry* on the grounds that plaintiffs in *Berry* were purchasers, in "vertical privity" with defendant manufacturer, whereas plaintiffs in *Hemphill* and *Johns–Manville,* like plaintiffs in the instant case, were non-purchasing users, in "horizontal privity" with those defendants. Defendants in this case argue that section 2–318 establishes a limitation on the right of persons in "horizontal privity" to recover for breach of warranty, although it does not act as a bar for persons in "vertical privity." Defendants point to the three alternative versions of section 2–318 written by the drafters of the UCC. Alternatives B and C require courts to extend the right to recover for breach of warranty to a larger class of non-purchasing users than that class named in alternative A. [Citation.] Plaintiff, as an employee of a purchaser, would clearly be allowed to recover for breach of warranty under alternatives B and C. Illinois adopted alternative A. Defendants argue that the Illinois legislature has by implication decided not to extend the right to recover to persons like plaintiff, who are expressly embraced only under the alternative versions of section 2–318 which the Illinois legislature decided not to adopt.

The Illinois legislature enacted section 2–318 of the UCC in 1961. (Ill.Rev.Stat.1963, ch. 26, par. 2–318.) At that time there were no alternative versions of the section. However, several states refused to enact this section in the form suggested by the drafters of the UCC, so alternatives B and C were added in 1966 as recommended alternative forms of section 2–318. ([1 Current Materials] U.C.C.Rep.Serv. (Callaghan) par. 2–318, p. 22–24.) Illinois, like most states, retained the original version of the section. (1 Anderson, Uniform Commercial Code par. 2–318:3.) Following the addition of alternatives B and C to the UCC, the drafters revised the UCC Comment [in 1966] to clarify the import of each alternative. The revised UCC Comment states in subsection 3:

> The first alternative [the version adopted in Illinois] expressly includes as beneficiaries within its provisions the family, household and guests of the purchaser. Beyond this, the section in this form is neutral and is not intended to enlarge or restrict the developing case law on whether the seller's warranties, given to his buyer who resells, extend to other persons in the distributive chain. The second alternative is designed for states where the case law has already developed further and for those that desire to expand the class of beneficiaries. The third alternative goes further, following the trend of modern decisions as indicated by Restatement of Torts 2d § 402A (Tentative Draft No. 10, 1965) in extending the rule beyond injuries to the person.

S.H.A. (Supp.1986), ch. 26, sec. 2–318, p. 101.

Thus, the Illinois version of the statute does not "restrict the developing case law * * *." The questions left for developing case law are clearly indicated by its subsequent sentences: "The second alternative is designed for states where the case law has already developed further * * *. The third alternative goes further, following the trend of modern decisions * * *." (S.H.A. (Supp.1986), ch. 26, sec. 2–318, p. 101.) Thus it is apparent that where the comment speaks of "developing case law" it includes developing case law regarding persons in horizontal privity with sellers. The Wisconsin Supreme Court, interpreting a statute and comments identical to section 2–318 in Illinois, found that the statute did not limit the seller's liability to non-purchasing users for breach of warranty to those persons specified in the statute. (Dippel v. Sciano (1967), 37 Wis.2d 443, 155 N.W.2d 55, 62.) We agree. The Illinois legislature expressly stated that warranty coverage must extend to the family or household of the purchaser, if the members of the household would reasonably be expected to use the product; the legislature left it for the courts to decide, in accord with common law principles and with the guidance of the UCC, whether warranty coverage should further extend to any other non-purchasing users of a product. * * *

* * *

Certain parties are allowed to sue for breach of warranty as third-party beneficiaries under section 2–318, which establishes, in essence, a conclusive presumption that the purchaser who bargained for a warranty of safety sought the warranty on behalf of himself and "any natural person who is in [his] family or household * * * or who is a guest in his home if it is reasonable to expect that such person may use, consume or be affected by the goods * * *." (Ill.Rev.Stat.1985, ch. 26, par. 2–318.) We hold that the warranty extends to any employee of a purchaser who is injured in the use of the goods, as long as the safety of that employee in the use of the goods was either explicitly or implicitly part of the basis of the bargain when the employer purchased the goods.

In the instant case, plaintiff alleged that DuPage bought a bandsaw from defendants which did not comply with the implied warranty of merchantability, nor was it fit for the particular purpose for which it was purchased. Insofar as DuPage bargained for a bandsaw that was as safe to use as any merchantable bandsaw, it sought the safety on behalf of its employees who were to use the saw. A corporation cannot use the bandsaw at all unless its employees operate it. If, as plaintiff alleged, DuPage bargained for a bandsaw which was sufficiently safe for the particular purpose for which DuPage sought to use the saw, DuPage sought the safety features on behalf of its employees who were to use the saw. We find that plaintiff has alleged facts which, if proved, would show that defendants either implicitly or explicitly promised to provide a bandsaw which was safe enough for plaintiff to use. Therefore, we find that the causes of action for breach of warranties are not barred by plaintiff's lack of privity with defendants.

[Reversed and remanded.]

JUSTICE RIZZI specially concurring:

I agree with the result reached by the majority. However, I do not agree that this case should be decided on the basis of privity or a lack thereof. In my opinion, it is a mistake to decide this case, or any other personal injury case, by exhuming concepts of privity in Illinois. * * *

* * *

NOTES

1. Is it apparent that the phrase "the developing case law" in comment 3 refers to horizontal—as opposed to vertical—privity? Do the court's partial quotations from comment 3 accurately portray its meaning?

More fundamentally, in construing a state statute enacted in 1961, of what relevance is "Official Comment" rewritten by national law revision entities (the ALI and the NCCUSL) in 1966? To the extent that the actual intent of the state legislators is relevant, what do you suppose it was?

2. Some courts have agreed with *Whitaker.* See, e.g., Salvador v. Atlantic Steel Boiler Co., 457 Pa. 24, 319 A.2d 903 (1974). Others have disagreed. See, e.g., Hester v. Purex Corp., 534 P.2d 1306 (Okla.1975) (legislature's adoption of Alternative A language in 1961, and its subsequent failure to substitute either Alternative B or C, precluded suit by an employee against the manufacturer in warranty; however, injured employees were not left without a remedy since they could still sue in negligence and strict tort).

3. McNally v. Nicholson Mfg. Co., 313 A.2d 913, 920 (Me.1973), held that employees are in the "business family" of their employers for purposes of Alternative A. With a clarity of expression rarely to be seen, the *McNally* court explained why employees are proper beneficiaries of the Code warranties although they do not fall within any of the categories specifically described in Alternative A: "The literal specifications of Section 2–318 are the guideposts of a fundamental course of policy flow adaptable to encompass other relationships which, policy-wise, may be fairly regarded as functionally equivalent to those textually designated." Webber, J., sat at argument but retired before the decision was rendered.

By analogy to the "business family" principle of *McNally*, should a soldier injured by defective equipment sold to the military be considered for purposes of Alternative A to be part of the military's "warrior family"? Cf. Miles v. Bell Helicopter Co., 385 F.Supp. 1029, 1031 (N.D.Ga.1974) (no).

Florida has expanded its version of Alternative A to include any person "who is an employee, servant or agent of his buyer." 19A Fla.Stat.Ann. § 672.2–318 (1977 Cum.Supp.).

4. Family members who do not live in the purchaser's household have presented a problem for some courts. See, e.g., Wolfe v. Ford Motor Co., 6 Mass.App. 346, 376 N.E.2d 143, 149 (1978) (niece, not in household, within Alternative A). Is a mother in the "family" of her married daughter? See Lane v. Barringer, 407 N.E.2d 1173 (Ind.App.1980).

5. Compare Thompson v. Reedman, 199 F.Supp. 120, 121 (E.D.Pa.1961) ("It is too much of a leap, it seems, to classify a guest passenger in an automobile as a guest in the *home;*" warranty nevertheless ran to plaintiff under "the developing case law" of Pennsylvania). Guests *outside* the home are guests "*in* the home." Handrigan v. Apex Warwick, Inc., 108 R.I. 319, 275 A.2d 262 (1971) (plaintiff, friend of purchaser of ladder, fell while helping paint friend's house). Cf. Tomczuk v. Town of Cheshire, 26 Conn.Sup. 219, 217 A.2d 71 (Conn.Super.Ct.1965) (friend fell from purchaser's bike—no mention of problem of inclusion under § 2–318; moreover, third party beneficiary "guest" is not "buyer" for purposes of § 2–607(3)(a) and so need not "notify the seller of breach or be barred from any remedy"); Miller v. Sears, Roebuck and Co., 148 Ill.App.3d 1022, 102 Ill.Dec. 664, 500 N.E.2d 557 (1986) (patron in shop not "guest in home") (partially overruled in *Whitaker*).

6. Verddier v. Neal Blun Co., 128 Ga.App. 321, 196 S.E.2d 469, 470 (1973), held that a maid whose finger was amputated on her employer's garage door could not maintain a warranty action against a seller of the door because she "simply does not fall into the category of persons benefiting from" Alternative A. Right result?

7. Other classes of plaintiffs have had poor fortune with Alternative A. See, e.g., Stovall & Co. v. Tate, 124 Ga.App. 605, 184 S.E.2d 834 (1971) (no warranty action for school girl struck in eye by rock thrown by rotary lawnmower through open classroom window); Barry v. Ivarson Inc., 249 So.2d 44 (Fla.Dist.Ct.App.1971) (no warranty action for tenant injured by defective table purchased by landlord).

8. Should a spouse be able to recover for loss of consortium under § 2–318? See Phipps v. General Motors Corp., 278 Md. 337, 363 A.2d 955 (1976) (Alternative A: yes). What specifically is the issue?

9. Should a divorced wife, who acquires a defective trailer from her ex-husband under the terms of the divorce decree, be entitled to maintain a warranty action against the seller under Alternative A? Cf. Chandler v. Hunter, 340 So.2d 818 (Ala.Ct.Cir.App.1976) (case decided under Alternative B). What is the issue?

10. **Vertical Privity.** At least a couple of states have held that Alternative B by its terms eliminates vertical as well as horizontal privity. See Bishop v. Sales, 336 So.2d 1340 (Ala.1976). See also Gasque v. Eagle Mach. Co., 270 S.C. 499, 243 S.E.2d 831 (1978). Do you agree?

11. Will any of the three alternatives to § 2–318 help a retailer, held liable to an injured consumer, reach over a wholesaler for indemnity against a remote manufacturer?

12. Alternative A is presently law in about half the states. The other states have adopted either Alternative B or C, some variation thereon, or some other type of "anti-privity" statute such as that of Virginia, set forth above with citations to other states' provisions, at p. 121. Texas leaves the matter entirely to the courts, Garcia v. Texas Instruments, Inc., 610 S.W.2d 456 (Tex. 1980), and California has no provision on point at all.

13. On horizontal privity, see generally Murray, Pennsylvania Products Liability: A Clarification of the Search for a Clear and Understandable Rule, 33 U.Pitt.L.Rev. 391 (1972); Reitz and Seabolt, Warranties and Products Liability: Who Can Sue and Where?, 46 Temp.L.Q. 527 (1973); Comment, 38 U.Chi.L. Rev. 625 (1971); Comment, 19 Kan.L.Rev. 251 (1971).

E. CONTRACTUAL LIMITATIONS ON RESPONSIBILITY

1. THE PROBLEM AND JUDICIAL SOLUTION: HENNINGSEN v. BLOOMFIELD MOTORS

HENNINGSEN v. BLOOMFIELD MOTORS, INC.

Supreme Court of New Jersey, 1960.
32 N.J. 358, 161 A.2d 69.

FRANCIS, J. Plaintiff Claus H. Henningsen purchased a Plymouth automobile, manufactured by defendant Chrysler Corporation, from defendant Bloomfield Motors, Inc. His wife, plaintiff Helen Henningsen, was injured while driving it and instituted suit against both defendants to recover damages on account of her injuries. * * * At the trial the negligence counts were dismissed by the court and the cause was submitted to the jury for determination solely on the issues of implied warranty of merchantability. Verdicts were returned against both defendants and in favor of the plaintiffs. Defendants appealed * * *.

* * *

The purchase order was a printed form of one page. On the front it contained blanks to be filled in with a description of the automobile to be sold, the various accessories to be included, and the details of the financing. The particular car selected was described as a 1955 Plymouth, Plaza "6," Club Sedan. The type used in the printed parts of the form became smaller in size, different in style, and less readable toward the bottom where the line for the purchaser's signature was placed. The smallest type on the page appears in the two paragraphs, one of two and one-quarter lines and the second of one and one-half lines, on which great stress is laid by the defense in the case. * * *

The two paragraphs are:

> "The front and back of this Order comprise the entire agreement affecting this purchase and no other agreement or understanding of any nature concerning same has been made or entered into, or will be recognized. I hereby certify that no credit has been extended to me for the purchase of this motor vehicle except as appears in writing on the face of this agreement.
>
> "I have read the matter printed on the back hereof and agree to it as a part of this order the same as if it were printed above my signature. I certify that I am 21 years of age, or older, and hereby acknowledge receipt of a copy of this order."

* * *

[Claus Henningsen testified that he did not read these two fine print paragraphs, nor the matter referred to on the back, nor did anyone direct his attention to them.]

The reverse side of the contract contains 8½ inches of fine print. It is not as small, however, as the two critical paragraphs described above. The page is headed "Conditions" and contains ten separate paragraphs consisting of 65 lines in all. The paragraphs do not have headnotes or margin notes denoting their particular subject * * *. In the seventh paragraph, about two-thirds of the way down the page, the warranty, which is the focal point of the case, is set forth. It is as follows:

> "7. It is expressly agreed that there are no warranties, express or implied, *made* by either the dealer or the manufacturer on the motor vehicle, chassis, or parts furnished hereunder except as follows:
>
> " 'The manufacturer warrants each new motor vehicle (including original equipment placed thereon by the manufacturer except tires), chassis or parts manufactured by it to be free from defects in material or workmanship under normal use and service. Its obligation under this warranty being limited to making good at its factory any part or parts thereof which shall, within ninety (90) days after delivery of such vehicle *to the original purchaser* or before such vehicle has been driven 4,000 miles, whichever event shall first occur, be returned to it with transportation charges prepaid and which its examination shall disclose to its satisfaction to have been thus defective; *this warranty being expressly in lieu of all other warranties expressed or implied, and all other obligations or liabilities on its part,* and it neither assumes nor authorizes any other person to assume for it any other liability in connection with the sale of its vehicles. * * *.' " (Emphasis ours)

* * *

[The Henningsens took delivery of the car on May 9 and drove it 468 miles without incident until May 19. On that day, Mrs. Henningsen was driving alone when the car suddenly veered sharply off the highway and into a brick wall, injuring Mrs. Henningsen and destroying the car. The insurance company's appraiser concluded that a mechanical defect in the steering mechanism had caused the failure.]

[The court proceeded to address the defendants' argument that the disclaimer of liability and limitation of remedy clauses in the warranty shielded them from liability for breach of warranty. Noting that such attempts at avoiding "the obligations that normally attend a sale * * * are not favored, and * * * are strictly construed against the seller," the court proceeded with its analysis.]

The terms of the warranty are a sad commentary upon the automobile manufacturers' marketing practices. Warranties developed in the law in the interest of and to protect the ordinary consumer who cannot be expected to have the knowledge or capacity or even the opportunity to make adequate inspection of mechanical instrumentalities, like automobiles, and to decide for himself whether they are reasonably fit for the designed purpose. [Citations.] But the ingenuity of the Automobile Manufacturers Association, by means of its standardized form, has metamorphosed the warranty into a device to limit the maker's liability. * * *

* * *

* * * The language gave little and withdrew much. In return for the delusive remedy of replacement of defective parts at the factory, the buyer is said to have accepted the exclusion of the maker's liability for personal injuries arising from the breach of the warranty, and to have agreed to the elimination of any other express or implied warranty. An instinctively felt sense of justice cries out against such a sharp bargain. But does the doctrine that a person is bound by his signed agreement, in the absence of fraud, stand in the way of any relief?

In the modern consideration of problems such as this, Corbin suggests that practically all judges are "chancellors" and cannot fail to be influenced by any equitable doctrines that are available. And he opines that "there is sufficient flexibility in the concepts of fraud, duress, misrepresentation and undue influence, not to mention differences in economic bargaining power" to enable the courts to avoid enforcement of unconscionable provisions in long printed standardized contracts. 1 Corbin on Contracts (1950) § 128, p. 188. Freedom of contract is not such an immutable doctrine as to admit of no qualification in the area in which we are concerned. * * *

The traditional contract is the result of free bargaining of parties who are brought together by the play of the market, and who meet each other on a footing of approximate economic equality. In such a society there is no danger that freedom of contract will be a threat to the social order as a whole. But in present-day commercial life the standardized mass contract has appeared. * * *

* * *

The warranty before us is a standardized form designed for mass use. It is imposed upon the automobile consumer. He takes it or leaves it, and he must take it to buy an automobile. No bargaining is engaged in with respect to it. In fact, the dealer through whom it comes to the buyer is without authority to alter it; his function is ministerial—simply to deliver it. The form warranty is not only standard with Chrysler but, as mentioned above, it is the uniform warranty of the Automobile Manufacturers Association. * * *

The gross inequality of bargaining position occupied by the consumer in the automobile industry is thus apparent. There is no competition among the car makers in the area of the express warranty. Where can the buyer go to negotiate for better protection? Such control and limitation of his remedies are inimical to the public welfare and, at the very least, call for great care by the courts to avoid injustice through application of strict common-law principles of freedom of contract. * * *

Although the courts, with few exceptions, have been most sensitive to problems presented by contracts resulting from gross disparity in buyer-seller bargaining positions, they have not articulated a general principle condemning, as opposed to public policy, the imposition on the buyer of a skeleton warranty as a means of limiting the responsibility of the manufacturer. They have endeavored thus far to avoid a drastic departure from age-old tenets of freedom of contract by adopting doctrines of strict construction, and notice and knowledgeable assent by the buyer to the attempted exculpation of the seller. 1 Corbin, supra, 337; 2 Harper & James, [The Law of Torts], 1590; Prosser, "Warranty of Merchantable Quality," 27 Minn.L.Rev. 117, 159 [1943]. Accordingly to be found in the cases are statements that disclaimers and the consequent limitation of liability will not be given effect if "unfairly procured," [citations]; if not brought to the buyer's attention and he was not made understandingly aware of it, [citations]; or if not clear and explicit, [citation].

* * *

It is undisputed that the president of the dealer with whom Henningsen dealt did not specifically call attention to the warranty on the back of the purchase order. The form and the arrangement of its face, as described above, certainly would cause the minds of reasonable men to differ as to whether notice of a yielding of basic rights stemming from the relationship with the manufacturer was adequately given. * * *

But there is more than this. Assuming that a jury might find that the fine print referred to reasonably served the objective of directing a buyer's attention to the warranty on the reverse side, and, therefore, that he should be charged with awareness of its language, can it be said that an ordinary layman would realize what he was relinquishing in return for what he was being granted? Under the law, breach of warranty against defective parts or workmanship which caused personal injuries would entitle a buyer to damages even if due care were used in the manufacturing process. Because of the great potential for harm if the vehicle was defective, that right is the most important and fundamental one arising from the relationship. Difficulties so frequently encountered in establishing negligence in manufacture in the ordinary case make this manifest. [Citations.] Any ordinary layman of reasonable intelligence, looking at the phraseology, might well conclude that Chrysler was agreeing to replace defective parts and perhaps replace anything that went wrong because of defective workmanship during the first 90 days or 4,000 miles of operation, but that he would not be entitled to a new car. It is not unreasonable to believe that the entire scheme being conveyed was a proposed remedy for physical deficiencies in the car. *In the context* of this warranty, only the abandonment of all sense of justice would permit us to hold that, as a matter of law, the phrase "its obligation under this warranty being limited to making good at its factory any part or parts thereof" signifies to an ordinary reasonable person that he is relinquishing any personal injury claim that might flow from the use of a defective automobile. Such claims are nowhere mentioned. The draftsmanship is reflective of the care and skill of the Automobile Manufacturers Association in undertaking to avoid warranty obligations without drawing too much attention to its effort in that regard. No one can doubt that if the will to do so were present, the ability to inform the buying public of the intention to disclaim liability for injury claims arising from breach of warranty would present no problem.

* * *

Public policy at a given time finds expression in the Constitution, the statutory law and in judicial decisions. In the area of sale of goods, the legislative will has imposed an implied warranty of merchantability as a general incident of sale of an automobile by description. The warranty does not depend upon the affirmative intention of the parties. It is a child of the law; it annexes itself to the contract because of the very nature of the transaction. [Citation.] The judicial process has recognized a right to recover damages for personal injuries arising from a breach of that warranty. The disclaimer of the implied warranty and exclusion of all obligations except those specifically assumed by the express warranty signify a studied effort to frustrate that protection.

* * *

[W]e conclude that the disclaimer of an implied warranty of merchantability by the dealer, as well as the attempted elimination of all obligations other than replacement of defective parts, are violative of public policy and void.

* * *

[Affirmed.]

NOTE

Compare Marshall v. Murray Oldsmobile Co., 207 Va. 972, 154 S.E.2d 140 (1967), where the court explicitly rejected the *Henningsen* approach. Pointing to the legislative approval of disclaimers in § 2–316 of the Uniform Commercial Code, adopted in Virginia in 1966 after the case sub judice had arisen, the court reaffirmed its commitment to the principles of freedom of contract.

---

2. DISCLAIMERS UNDER THE UCC

UNIFORM COMMERCIAL CODE

§ 2–316. Exclusion or Modification of Warranties

(1) Words or conduct relevant to the creation of an express warranty and words or conduct tending to negate or limit warranty shall be construed wherever reasonable as consistent with each other; but subject to the provisions of this Article on parol or extrinsic evidence (Section 2–202) negation or limitation is inoperative to the extent that such construction is unreasonable.

(2) Subject to subsection (3), to exclude or modify the implied warranty of merchantability or any part of it the language must mention merchantability and in case of a writing must be conspicuous, and to exclude or modify any implied warranty of fitness the exclusion must be by a writing and conspicuous. Language to exclude all implied warranties of fitness is sufficient if it states, for example, that "There are no warranties which extend beyond the description on the face hereof."

(3) Notwithstanding subsection (2)

(a) unless the circumstances indicate otherwise, all implied warranties are excluded by expressions like "as is", "with all faults" or other language which in common understanding calls the buyer's attention to the exclusion of warranties and makes plain that there is no implied warranty; and

(b) when the buyer before entering into the contract has examined the goods or the sample or model as fully as he desired or has refused to examine the goods there is no implied warranty with regard to defects which an examination ought in the circumstances to have revealed to him; and

(c) an implied warranty can also be excluded or modified by course of dealing or course of performance or usage of trade.

(4) Remedies for breach of warranty can be limited in accordance with the provisions of this Article on liquidation or limitation of damages and on contractual modification of remedy (Sections 2–718 and 2–719).

NOTES

1. Comment 1 to § 2–316 provides:

> This section is designed principally to deal with those frequent clauses in sales contracts which seek to exclude "all warranties, express or implied." It seeks to protect a buyer from unexpected and unbargained language of disclaimer by denying effect to such language when inconsistent with language of express warranty and permitting the exclusion of implied warranties only by conspicuous language or other circumstances which protect the buyer from surprise.

2. Plaintiff was injured when the accelerator-carburetor linkage malfunctioned on the used car that he had purchased six days earlier from defendant dealer. The salesman had written "30 day warranty" on the face of the purchase agreement. A printed clause on the back provided in part: "It is expressly agreed that there are no warranties, express or implied, made by either the selling dealer or the manufacturer * * *." Citing § 2–316(1), the court ruled: "This attempted disclaimer of any express warranties is inoperative since to give effect to the disclaimer would be unreasonable in view of the writing on the face." Realmuto v. Straub Motors, Inc., 65 N.J. 336, 322 A.2d 440, 442 n. 2 (1974). See also Woodruff v. Clark Cty. Farm Bureau Coop. Ass'n, 153 Ind.App. 31, 286 N.E.2d 188, 200 (1972) (noting the "judicial aversion to negation of express warranties").

How can an express warranty and words disclaiming it *ever* be "consistent"? See Neville Construction Co. v. Cook Paint & Varnish Co., 671 F.2d 1107 (8th Cir.1982).

3. Comment 2 to § 2–316 provides: "The seller is protected under this Article against false allegations of oral warranties by its provisions on parol and extrinsic evidence and against unauthorized representations by the customary 'lack of authority' clauses. * * *" The parol evidence rule of § 2–202 provides in part that written agreements "intended by the parties as a final expression of their agreement" may not be contradicted by evidence of "inconsistent" oral agreements. Evidence of even "consistent" additional terms is excluded if the parties by merger or integration clause intended the writing to be a "complete and exclusive statement" of the agreement. § 2–202(b). See, e.g., Avery v. Aladdin Products Div., 128 Ga.App. 266, 196 S.E.2d 357 (1973).

But how does this Article protect the *buyer* in cases of *true* allegations of oral warranties? Will a seller giving a false oral warranty be shielded by boilerplate "no express warranty" and "exclusive agreement" clauses? Consider § 2–313, comment 4 and § 2–316, comment 1. See Broude, The Consumer and the Parol Evidence Rule: Section 2–202 of the Uniform Commercial Code, 1970 Duke L.J. 881, 912–18:

> [B]y limiting the function of section 2–202 to protecting sellers against "false allegations of oral warranties," the draftsmen implicitly recognize that section 2–202 will not protect sellers from "true" allegations of oral warranties. If the disclaimer was not "intended" by both parties, the allegation of oral warranty may be true, and section 2–202 will not protect the seller. This conclusion is in all respects consistent with the draftsmen's belief that express warranties often form an integral part of the bargain of the parties. Realism will prevail over boilerplate.

4. Comment 8 to § 2–316 provides in part:

> In order to bring the transaction within the scope of "refused to examine" in paragraph (b), it is not sufficient that the goods are available for inspection. There must in addition be a demand by the seller that the buyer examine the goods fully. The seller by the demand puts the buyer on notice that he is assuming the risk of defects which the examination ought to reveal.

Could this section have any effect on the sale of new goods? What if the retailer tells the buyer to be sure to read the instruction book carefully, which he fails to do, and the buyer is injured because he fails to take precautions inconspicuously set forth in the instruction book?

DORMAN v. INTERNATIONAL HARVESTER CO.

Court of Appeals of California, 1975.
46 Cal.App.3d 11, 120 Cal.Rptr. 516.

STEPHENS, ASSOCIATE JUSTICE.

* * *

Facts

Dorman entered into a "Retail Installment Conditional Sales Contract" with I.H. purportedly on October 31, 1968 (he testified that he executed a second contract on November 3) to purchase a new tractor and backhoe for $12,912.26, including finance charges, and had paid a total of $7,233.68 on the contract. Dorman purchased this equipment for use in his earthgrading business and took delivery on November 4, 1968. The evidence adduced at trial shows that Dorman experienced problems with the tractor from the day he took delivery. The tractor broke down on numerous other occasions during the period of November 7, 1968 to August 21, 1969 and it had to be returned to I.H. [International Harvester] for repairs.

[Dorman filed suit against International Harvester in December, 1969, alleging breach of warranty, and I.H. cross-claimed for the return of the equipment. The jury returned verdicts for the plaintiff on both claims but the trial judge granted defendant's motion for judgment notwithstanding the verdicts and reduced plaintiff's verdict to the amount paid on the contract. Both parties appealed.

Reversed, for erroneous rulings on validity of disclaimer and on damages.]

Disclaimer

At the outset of the trial, the court considered the issue of whether the Retail Installment Conditional Sales Contract contained a valid disclaimer of implied warranties. The disclaimer in question is shown in its context in the facsimile below (appearing after paragraph "9. Terms of Payment"):

RETAIL INSTALMENT CONDITIONAL SALE CONTRACT FOR FARM AND INDUSTRIAL EQUIPMENT

DATE 10/31/68 — CONTRACT NO. D 198 A19

PURCHASER (LAST NAME FIRST): Bill Dorman 899 4500 — SELLER: IH Select Service

ADDRESS / CITY / COUNTY / STATE / ZIP CODE: 12470 Osborne · Pacoima Calif — ADDRESS: Van Nuys Calif

Purchaser hereby purchases, and seller hereby sells, subject to all terms, conditions and agreements contained herein including the ADDITIONAL PROVISIONS printed on the reverse side hereof, the following described property, delivery, inspection and acceptance of which are hereby acknowledged by purchaser:

QU.	N/U	DESCRIPTION (SHOW ALL SERIAL AND MOTOR NUMBERS)	CASH SALE PRICE
1	N	International 3616 Diesel w/3141 Backhoe with Hydrashuttle Transmission 12"·18"·24" Bucket 16.9 x 28 Tires Front weights 900 x 16 Truck front S/N 1695	$

TRADE-IN			
1	2606 Diesel w/wain roy 12-18-24 bucket	$	TOTAL $ 14796 00
			ADD SALES OR USE TAX 887 80
			1. TOTAL CASH SALE PRICE $ 15684 40
			2. DOWN PAYMENT: CASH $
			TRADE-IN ALLOWANCE 4500 00
			TOTAL DOWN PAYMENT $ 4500 00
	ALLOWANCE	$ 4500 00	3. UNPAID CASH BALANCE (1 LESS 2) $ 11184 40

SCHEDULE OF INSTALMENTS

	AMOUNT	DUE DATE		AMOUNT	DUE DATE
1	500 00	12/1/68	9	WAIVER OF	
2	500 00	1/1/69	10	FINANCE ON	
3	500 00	2/1/69	11		
4	500 00	3/1/69	12	2000 —	
5			13		
6			14		
7			15		
8			16		

4. OTHER CHARGES (DESCRIBE): UCC-1	5 00
5. PRINCIPAL BALANCE (TOTAL OF 3 AND 4)	$ 11189 40
6. FINANCE CHARGE (TIME PRICE DIFFERENTIAL)	1722 80
7. TIME BALANCE (TOTAL OF 5 AND 6)	$ 12912 20
8. TIME SALE PRICE (TOTAL OF 2 AND 7)	$

9. TERMS OF PAYMENT: Purchaser agrees to pay the Time Balance in 4 instalments of $500.00 each and 30 instalments of 363.74 each, and — instalments of $— payable on the same day of each successive month commencing 12/1/, 1968 or as indicated in the Schedule of Instalments printed hereon, at office of the seller, or if this contract is assigned, assignee of seller. Purchaser agrees to pay all expenses including reasonable attorney's fees, court costs and out-of-pocket expenses incurred in the collection, by suit or otherwise, of any amount payable under this contract. After maturity each instalment shall draw interest at the rate of 10 percent per annum. (In South Dakota purchaser agrees to pay a delinquency charge on each instalment in default for a period of 10 days or more in an amount of 5% of each instalment or $5.00, whichever is less.)

The equipment covered hereby is sold subject only to the applicable manufacturer's standard printed warranty, if any, in effect at the date hereof, receipt of a copy of which is hereby acknowledged, and no other warranties, express or implied, including without limitation, the implied warranties of *merchantability and fitness for a particular purpose shall apply.*

Purchaser agrees that this contract, including the ADDITIONAL PROVISIONS printed on the reverse side hereof, which he has read and to which he agrees, contains the entire agreement relating to the instalment sale of said property and supersedes all previous contracts and agreements between purchaser and seller relating to the order or sale of said property.

THIS CONTRACT IS NOT BINDING UPON SELLER, UNLESS SIGNED BY THE STORE MANAGER OF SELLER OR OWNER.

Purchaser acknowledges receipt of an exact completed copy of this contract.

APPROVED FOR SELLER — PRINT OR TYPE NAMES BENEATH SIGNATURE. ALL SIGNATURES MUST BE WITNESSED.

SIGNATURE: Jim L Baker — SELLER BY Bill Hickey TITLE — WITNESS — PURCHASER BY William A Dorman

OFFICIAL TITLE: STORE MANAGER — PURCHASER BY — TITLE

FH-1203-D (PAGE 2) — FORM APPROVED 11-1-68

The court concluded that the disclaimer provision was sufficiently conspicuous to constitute a valid disclaimer of the implied warranties of merchantability and fitness for particular purpose pursuant to California Commercial Code section 2316 [U.C.C. § 2–316]. The court thus limited the issues to be determined at trial to whether I.H. had fulfilled its standard printed warranty.

Contentions

Dorman contends that the trial court erred in its ruling on the validity of the disclaimer provision for the following reasons: (1) the disclaimer provision is not "conspicuous"; (2) the disclaimer provision as interpreted by the court is unconscionable; and (3) the court did not allow the introduction of parol evidence of warranties consistent with the contract provision as well as the parties' interpretation of the provision by their subsequent actions.

(1) *Conspicuousness*

It was well settled in California under pre-Commercial Code law that a provision disclaiming implied warranties was to be strictly construed (Burr v. Sherwin Williams Co., 42 Cal.2d 682, 694, 268 P.2d 1041) and was ineffectual unless the buyer assented to the provision or was charged with notice of the disclaimer before the bargain was completed. [Citations.] At trial, Dorman testified that he did not sign the contract dated October 31, 1968 but that he did read it on that date; that on November 3, 1968, he signed but did not read a contract represented to him to be the same as the one he had read on October 31; and that he did not receive a copy of the standard manufacturer's warranty at the time he signed the contract even though the contract contained a clause stating that he acknowledged receipt of the warranty. Although Dorman did not assent to the disclaimer provision and did not read the contract at the time he signed it, the court concluded that the provision was conspicuous and that he should be charged with notice of the disclaimer.

Commercial Code section 2316, subdivision (2) provides that an exclusion of the implied warranty of merchantability "in case of a writing must be conspicuous," and that an exclusion of the implied warranty of fitness for particular purpose "must be by a writing and conspicuous." The code defines "conspicuous" as "so written that a reasonable person against whom it is to operate ought to have noticed it. A printed heading in capital letters (as: NONNEGOTIABLE BILL OF LADING) is conspicuous. Language in the body of a form is 'conspicuous' if it is in larger or other contrasting type or color. * * * Whether a term or clause is 'conspicuous' or not is for decision by the court." (§ 1201, subd. (10).) [U.C.C. § 1–201]

There is no statutory counterpart of section 1201, subdivision (10) in pre-code law; nor have we found any California cases under the code which have dealt with this section. Therefore, we must rely predominantly on the official comments to sections 2316 and 1201, subdivision (10), and to foreign law. The official comment to subdivision (10) of section 1201 states that the "test [of conspicuousness] is whether attention can reasonably be expected to be called to [the disclaimer provision]." (Cf. Gray v. Zurich Insurance Co., 65 Cal.2d 263, 271, 54 Cal.Rptr. 104, 419 P.2d 168.) We must examine this comment in the light of the official comment to section 2316, which states: "This section is designed principally to deal with those frequent clauses in sales contracts which seek to exclude 'all warranties, express or implied.' It seeks to protect a buyer from *unexpected* and unbargained language of disclaimer by denying effect to such language when inconsistent with language of express warranty and permitting the exclusion of implied warranties only by conspicuous language or other circumstances which protect the buyer from surprise." (Emphasis added.) In other words, section 2316 seeks to protect the buyer from the situation where the salesman's "pitch," advertising brochures, or large print in the contract, giveth, and the disclaimer clause—in fine print—taketh away.

Here, the disclaimer provision appears in close proximity to where Dorman signed the contract, but emphasized (italicized) the implied-warranties wording "*merchantability and fitness for particular purpose shall apply.*" Although the disclaimer provision was printed in a slightly larger type face than was the preceding paragraph of the contract, it was not in bold face type, and we are of the opinion that it was not sufficiently conspicuous to have negated the implied warranties, particularly where no "standard printed warranty" was in fact given to Dorman at the time of execution of the contract.[9] The slightly larger type face and location of the disclaimer paragraph are not conclusive. As stated by the court in Woodruff v. Clark County Farm Bureau Coop. Assn. (Ind.App.1972) 286 N.E.2d 188, 198 (quoting from Greenspun v. American Adhesives, Inc. (E.D.Pa.1970) 320 F.Supp. 442), "[w]hile there is some slight contrasting set-off, this is not sufficient. *A provision is not conspicuous when there is only a slight contrast* with the balance of the instrument." The instant disclaimer does not reach that level of conspicuousness so as to exclude the right of the buyer to implied warranties which are an integral part of the transaction. (Henningsen v. Bloomfield Motors, Inc. (1960), 32 N.J. 358, 161 A.2d 69, 76.) It thus violated the underlying rationale of section 2316 as set forth in the official comment of protecting the buyer from an unbargained for limitation in the purchase of a product. In order to have a valid disclaimer provision, it must be in clear and distinct language and prominently set forth in large, bold print in such position as to compel notice. (§ 1201, subd. (10).) In the instant contract, the only large size type (in relation to other type on the page) that may satisfy these criteria is that used for the words "ADDITIONAL PROVISIONS" on the signature page (in a reference to matters on the reverse side of the contract which are extraneous to the warranties disclaimer). Though the size of the type in those words may be large enough, the remainder of the provision is insufficiently "conspicuous." The contract here also failed to have an adequate heading at the beginning of the disclaimer provision, such as "DISCLAIMER OF WARRANTIES," to call the buyer's attention to the disclaimer clause.

The attempted disclaimer of implied warranties in the instant case is ineffective for another reason. Construing the language of the provision strictly [citation], the construction of the wording is ambiguous and could easily be misleading. A purchaser glancing at the provision would reasonably observe the *italicized* language, which

9. There is no indication that a copy of a "Retail Order Form" containing the standard manufacturer's warranty was ever given to Dorman.

reads: "*merchantability and fitness for the particular purpose shall apply,*" and would be lulled into a sense of security. This is directly contrary to the actual intent of the provision. "An implied warranty * * * must be disclaimed by the most precise terms; in other words, so clear, definite and specific as to leave no doubt as to the intent of the contracting parties." (Boeing Airplane Co. v. O'Malley (8th Cir.1964) 329 F.2d 585, 593.)

Moreover, the manufacturer's standard printed warranty (which also endeavored to limit the warranties and the introduction of consequential damages) was not included in the contract which Dorman signed on November 3, 1968. It was on the reverse side of the purchase order, a separate document not shown to have been signed by Dorman or delivered to him at any time. A disclaimer of warranties must be specifically bargained for so that a disclaimer in a warranty given to the buyer *after* he signs the contract is *not* binding. * * *

We conclude that the disclaimer was insufficiently conspicuous to inform a reasonable buyer that he was waiving his right to have a quality product. As the Supreme Court of the State of Washington succinctly stated in Berg v. Stromme (1971) 79 Wash.2d 184, 484 P.2d 380, 385: "The purported disclaimers of warranty in the conditional sale contract form and the waiver of warranty in the purchase order form highlight the absurdity of a rule of law which elevates these bland and substantially meaningless terms and conditions above the individually and expressly negotiated terms and conditions, and gives them controlling effect over specifically agreed upon items and conditions of the contract. To adhere to such a rule means that the law presumes that the buyer of a brand new automobile intends to nullify in general all of the things for which he has specifically bargained and will pay. We would presume the buyer does just the opposite."

(2) *Unconscionability*

Accordingly, we need not reach the issue of whether the disclaimer provision of implied warranties is unconscionable under California common law.[11] * * *

* * *

[Reversed.]

NOTES

1. What broadly does § 2–316 allow, and what broadly does it prohibit?

2. What would have been the effect in Dorman of a clause in boldface type providing: "NO IMPLIED WARRANTIES ACCOMPANY THE SALE OF THIS PRODUCT"? Compare § 2–316(2) and comment 1.

3. Compare and contrast the methods of disclaiming responsibility for defective products in subsections (2) and (3)(a). Seller asks you to draft a clause for its purchase contract to shield it from potential implied warranty liability

11. California did not adopt Uniform Commercial Code section 2302 * * *.

for injuries caused by defects in its power lawnmowers. Would you select the approach of subsection (2) or of subsection (3)? Why? Does your answer make you question whether the policies expressed in comment 1, supra p. 151, above are in fact achieved by operation of the section? See Weintraub, Disclaimer of Warranties and Limitation of Damages for Breach of Warranty Under the UCC, 53 Tex.L.Rev. 60, 65–66 (1974).

4. **Conspicuousness.** In Koellmer v. Chrysler Motors Corp., 6 Conn.Sup. 478, 276 A.2d 807 (1970), the buyer of a new Dodge truck sued the dealer and manufacturer for breach of the implied warranty of merchantability. The defense was the plaintiff's execution of a purchase order form on the back of which was a disclaimer in the 7th of 10 separate paragraphs, printed in the same size and style type, in the same color, totalling over 800 words, and with nothing characteristic about the disclaimer clause to distinguish it from the other paragraphs. *Held,* the disclaimer clause did not satisfy the conspicuousness requirement of § 2–316(2). See also Christopher v. Larson Ford Sales, Inc., 557 P.2d 1009 (Utah 1976) (ditto, "unless it is shown that the provision [on the back of the form] was actually called to his attention"). "The reason for this provision is that it is the policy of the law to look with disfavor upon semi-concealed or obscured self-protective provisions of a contract prepared by one party, which the other is not likely to notice." Id. at 1012.

Compare Houck v. DeBonis, 38 Md.App. 85, 379 A.2d 765 (1977), where a reverse-side disclaimer was held "conspicuous." The court reasoned as follows: "The face of the contract mentions in two separate places that additional terms and conditions are contained on its reverse side. Furthermore, the disclaimer language is separately underscored in Item No. 7, and a heading in capital letters ['DISCLAIMER OF IMPLIED WARRANTY'] demarcates the section." 379 A.2d at 773. Would it have made any difference if half of the reverse side had been underscored and all 12 paragraphs had been preceded by headings in capital letters? Cf. Jones v. Abriani, 169 Ind.App. 556, 350 N.E.2d 635 (1976).

Suppose the buyer in fact does read an inconspicuous but otherwise effective disclaimer of implied warranty of merchantability. Should the disclaimer be enforced against him? Compare §§ 2–316(2) and 1–201(10) with comment 1 to § 2–316. See White and Summers, supra, at 361.

5. **"As is."** May an "as is" clause alone be effective to disclaim the implied warranty of merchantability? Need it be conspicuous? Consider Fairchild Ind. v. Maritime Air Service, Ltd., 274 Md. 181, 333 A.2d 313 (1975), where the court split 4 to 3 on the conspicuousness issue. Holding that the conspicuousness requirement of subsection (2) should be read into subsection (3), the majority quoted from Gindy Mfg. Corp. v. Cardinale Trucking Corp., 111 N.J.Super. 383, 268 A.2d 345, 352–54 (1970): " 'It serves no intelligible design to protect buyers by conspicuous language when the term "merchantability" is used, but to allow an effective disclaimer when the term "as is" is buried in fine print. * * * The expectations of the buyer need as much protection in one case as in another.' " 333 A.2d at 317. Relying upon Lord Mildew's dictum in Bluff v. Father Gray to the effect that "If Parliament does not mean what it says, it must say so" [A.P. Herbert, Uncommon Law 192 (1936)], the position of the dissent was simple: "[I]f this is what the draftsmen meant, they could easily have said so." Id. at 319. Compare Pearson v. Franklin Labs., Inc., 254 N.W.2d 133, 142 (S.D.1977) ("The phrase ' * * * we accept no responsibility for the results following its use,' buried in the middle of the purported disclaimer is ambiguous at best" and thus ineffective to disclaim liability under subsection (3)(a)).

6. **Timeliness.** In accord with Rehurek v. Chrysler Credit Corp., cited in the principal case, is Taterka v. Ford Motor Co., 86 Wis.2d 140, 271 N.W.2d 653 (1978), where the court similarly ruled that a purchaser is not bound by a disclaimer in the owner's manual delivered with the car subsequent to the signing of the contract of sale.

7. Should the seller be deemed to have impliedly warranted the absence of defects that are discovered by the buyer prior to purchase? Subsection (3)(b) addresses this point. See also Harison–Gulley Chevrolet, Inc. v. Carr, 134 Ga. App. 449, 214 S.E.2d 712 (1975) (no recovery in implied warranty for death of purchaser of car, where accident may have been caused by oversized steering wheel and tires, since purchaser had inspected and test-driven car prior to purchase). What result if plaintiff's inspection had not in fact revealed these "defects"? What result if plaintiff had not examined the car at all prior to purchase despite the salesman's suggestion that she "look it over to see just what she was getting"? See comment 8, indicating that the seller's demand to examine "puts the buyer on notice that he is assuming the risk of defects which the examination ought to reveal." Compare Rose v. Epley Motor Sales, 288 N.C. 53, 215 S.E.2d 573, 578 (1975), where the court held that the implied warranty of merchantability was not defeated by the buyer's examination and test drive prior to sale. "[N]othing in the evidence would compel, or even support, a finding that the defect, if any, which caused the fire should have been discovered by him through such test driving and inspection, he not being a mechanic." Consider comment 13 to § 2–314, comment 8 to § 2–316, and comment 5 to § 2–715 which suggest that an injured buyer will be barred from recovery on grounds of proximate cause if the defect is discovered or should have been from a reasonable inspection.

8. Suppose a fork lift operator is injured when the load he is carrying slips off the raised forks and falls on his head. Further assume that the manufacturer has a nondelegable duty to attach overhead roof guards to all of its lifts, but omitted the guard in this case since the operator's employer needed a lift with low overall height and so specified in its order that the guards be left off. Can the employee maintain a defective design action under § 2–314? "[W]here the buyer gives detailed specifications as to the goods, neither of the implied warranties as to quality will normally apply to the transaction unless consistent with the specifications." Comment 9 to § 2–316. See also § 2–317(c) which provides that "Express warranties displace inconsistent implied warranties [of merchantability]."

9. If the seller markets a product knowing it to be defective, should an otherwise effective disclaimer be denied effect on some ground of public policy? See Owen, The Highly Blameworthy Manufacturer: Implications on Rules of Liability and Defense in Products Liability Actions, 10 Ind.L.Rev. 769, 796 n. 130 (1977).

10. Should a third party beneficiary of a warranty be bound by a disclaimer of which he was not aware? See U.C.C. § 2–318, supra, and comment 1 thereto; Comment, 27 Okla.L.Rev. 284 (1974). Cf. Matthews v. Ford Motor Co., 479 F.2d 399, 403 (4th Cir.1973) ("Generally, express warranties and disclaimers do not run with personal property.").

What is the meaning of the last sentence of each alternative to § 2–318? See Comment 1 thereto.

11. As an affirmative defense, a disclaimer must be pleaded affirmatively in the defendant's answer. Skeen v. C & G Corp., 155 W.Va. 547, 185 S.E.2d

493 (1971). And "the burden is upon the party asserting the disclaimer to establish that [it] was delivered at the time of sale and constituted an integral part of the transaction." Noel Transfer & Pack. Delivery Service, Inc. v. General Motors Corp., 341 F.Supp. 968, 970 (D.C.Minn.1972).

12. On disclaimers generally, see Weintraub, Disclaimer of Warranties and Limitation of Damages for Breach of Warranty Under the UCC, 53 Tex.L. Rev. 60 (1974); Franklin, When Worlds Collide: Liability Theories and Disclaimers in Defective–Product Cases, 18 Stan.L.Rev. 974, 1004–16 (1966); Note, 63 Va.L.Rev. 791 (1977).

---

3. LIMITATIONS UNDER THE U.C.C.

UNIFORM COMMERCIAL CODE

§ 2–719. Contractual Modification or Limitation of Remedy

(1) Subject to the provisions of subsections (2) and (3) of this section and of the preceding section on liquidation and limitation of damages,

(a) the agreement may provide for remedies in addition to or in substitution for those provided in this Article and may limit or alter the measure of damages recoverable under this Article, as by limiting the buyer's remedies to return of the goods and repayment of the price or to repair and replacement of non-conforming goods or parts; and

(b) resort to a remedy as provided is optional unless the remedy is expressly agreed to be exclusive, in which case it is the sole remedy.

(2) Where circumstances cause an exclusive or limited remedy to fail of its essential purpose, remedy may be had as provided in this Act.

(3) Consequential damages may be limited or excluded unless the limitation or exclusion is unconscionable. Limitation of consequential damages for injury to the person in the case of consumer goods is prima facie unconscionable but limitation of damages where the loss is commercial is not.

NOTE

Comment 1 provides:

Under this section parties are left free to shape their remedies to their particular requirements and reasonable agreements limiting or modifying remedies are to be given effect.

* * *

McCARTY v. E.J. KORVETTE, INC.

Court of Special Appeals of Maryland, 1975.
28 Md.App. 421, 347 A.2d 253.

[Action for breach of express tire warranty. Plaintiffs were injured, and their car damaged, in an accident caused by the blowout of a tire under warranty. Defendants' motions for directed verdicts were granted at the conclusion of plaintiffs' case. Reversed and remanded. Excerpts from the opinion pertaining to attempted warranty limitations on plaintiffs' remedies follow.]

[The "Korvette Tire Centers All–Road–Hazards Tire Guarantee" provided:

> "*The tires identified hereon are guaranteed for* the number of months (or miles) designated [*36,000 miles*] *against all road hazards* including stone bruises, impact bruises, *blow out,* tread separation, glass cuts and fabric breaks, only when used in normal, non-commercial passenger car service. *If a tire fails to give satisfactory service under the terms of this guarantee,* return it to the nearest Korvette Tire Center. *We will replace the tire* charging only the proportionate part of the sale price for each month elapsed (or mileage used) from date of purchase, plus the full federal tax.
>
> "The above guarantee does not cover tires run flat, or simply worn out; tires injured by a fire, collision, vandalism, misalignment or mechanical defects of the vehicle. Radial or surface fissures, discoloration or ordinary repairable punctures, do not render tires unfit for service. Punctures will be repaired free.
>
> "*Neither the manufacturer nor Korvette Tire Centers shall be liable for any consequential damage and our liability is limited solely to replacement of the product.*"]
>
> [Emphasis added by court.]

[After holding that the first sentence in the "tire guarantee" warranted against blowouts, the court addressed the limitation of remedy issue.]

Questions remain as to what impact the additional language appearing on the invoice has upon the scope and extent of the express warranty. Comm.L.Art., § 2–316 [4] specifically recognizes a right on the part of the warrantor to negate, modify or limit an express or implied warranty under certain circumstances. It also implicitly recognizes that warranties may be limited in two different ways—one by "disclaiming" the warranty or a part of the warranty itself in the manner prescribed by subsections (1)–(3), and the other by "limiting the reme-

4. "§ 2–316. Exclusion or modification of warranties.

* * *

"(4) Remedies for breach of warranty can be limited in accordance with the provisions of this subtitle on liquidation or limitation of damages and on contractual modification of remedy (§§ 2–718 and 2–719)." [Emphasis omitted.]

dy" available upon breach (subsection (4)) in the manner prescribed by Comm.L.Art., §§ 2–718 and 2–719.[5]

Here the language which says that the guarantee applies only when the tires are used in normal non-commercial passenger car service, and does not apply to tires that are run flat, or simply worn out, injured by a fire, collision, vandalism, misalignment or mechanical defects of the vehicle, constitutes a disclaimer under Comm.L.Art., § 2–316(1). The language which not only promises to replace the tire if a blowout occurs, but also attempts to avoid consequential damages and restrict the remedies of the buyer solely to replacement, constitutes a limitation of remedies under Comm.L.Art., § 2–316(4), governed by the provisions of Comm.L.Art., § 2–719.[6] Comm.L.Art., § 2–316.1 is inapplicable.[7]

Comm.L.Art., § 2–719 gives the parties considerable latitude in which to fashion their remedies to their particular requirements.[8] It expressly recognizes that parties may limit their remedies to repair and replacement. The parties, however, must accept the legal consequence that there be some fair remedy for breach of the obligations or duties outlined in the contract. Reasonable agreements which limit or modify remedies will be given effect, but the parties are not free to shape their

5. The difference between the two modes of negating or modifying a warranty has been clearly expressed in J. White & R. Summers, Handbook of the Law Under the Uniform Commercial Code § 12–11, at 383–84 (1972):

"A disclaimer clause is a device used to exclude or limit the seller's warranties; it attempts to control the seller's liability, by reducing the number of situations in which the seller can be in breach. An exclusionary clause [limitation of remedies], on the other hand, restricts the remedies available to one or both parties once a breach is established. Assume, for example, that a new-car buyer sues for breach of warranty, and the seller raises defenses based on disclaimer and exclusionary clauses. The disclaimer defense denies the existence of any cause of action. The exclusionary-clause defense, on the other hand, denies that the buyer is entitled to the remedy he demands—for example, consequential damages * * *."

6. Comm.L.Art., § 2–316, Official Comment 2, provides, in pertinent part:

"This Title treats the limitation or avoidance of consequential damages as a matter of limiting remedies for breach, separate from the matter of creation of liability under a warranty. If no warranty exists, there is of course no problem of limiting remedies for breach of warranty. Under subsection (4) the question of limitation of remedy is governed by the sections referred to rather than by this section."

7. Comm.L.Art., § 2–316.1, Limitation of exclusion or modification of warranties to consumers, provides, in pertinent part:

"(1) The provisions of § 2–316 [including subsection (4)] do not apply to sales of consumer goods, as defined by § 9–109, services, or both."

The fact that the instant warranty was made on 25 February 1971 precludes the applicability of § 2–316.1 which did not become effective until 1 July 1971. See Blankenship v. Morrison Machine Co., 255 Md. 241, 247, 257 A.2d 430, 433 (1969).

8. Comm.L.Art., § 2–719, Contractual modification or limitation of remedy [is set out by the court].

Comm.L.Art., § 2–714(3) provides that "[i]n a proper case any incidental and consequential damages under the next section may also be recovered." See Fred J. Miller, Inc. v. Raymond Metal Products Co., 265 Md. 523, 528, 290 A.2d 527, 530 (1972).

Comm.L.Art., § 2–715(2)(b) defines consequential damages as "injury to person or property proximately resulting from any breach of warranty."

Comm.L.Art., § 9–109(1) defines consumer goods as goods "used or bought for use primarily for personal, family or household purposes."

remedies in an unreasonable or unconscionable way. Comm.L.Art., § 2–719(3) recognizes the validity of clauses limiting or excluding consequential damages, otherwise available under Comm.L.Art., § 2–714(3), but expressly states that they may not operate in an unconscionable manner. That subsection also establishes that limitation of consequential damages for injury to the person in the case of consumer goods is *prima facie* unconscionable.[10]

Comm.L.Art., § 2–302(1) sets forth the alternatives available to a court when it finds a limitation of remedy to be unconscionable.[11] That section permits the court in its discretion, after a finding of unconscionability, to refuse to enforce the contract as a whole, if it is permeated by the unconscionability, or *to strike any single clause or group of clauses which are so tainted* or which are contrary to the essential purpose of the agreement, or to simply limit unconscionable clauses so as to avoid unconscionable results.[12] Thus, any clause purporting to modify or limit remedies in an unconscionable manner is subject to deletion and will not be given effect.[13]

Here the executory promise to replace the tire in the event of a blowout, found in the first paragraph of the warranty, is, in and of itself, nothing more than an express statement that the remedy of replacement is available in addition to all of the other remedies provided by law.[14] But that executory promise, coupled with the clause purporting to exclude liability for consequential damages and to limit liability solely to replacement, clearly expresses an intent that replacement be the sole remedy under the contract.

The record shows, however, that the warranted tires which Mrs. McCarty purchased were bought for "her" stationwagon, which was ordinarily driven about 150 miles per week; that she did not seek damages for loss of employment; and that her husband was employed as a "locomotive engineer" and did not, therefore, use an automobile for business purposes. This evidence supports a rational inference that the warranted tires here constitute consumer goods as defined by Comm.L. Art., § 9–109,[15] so that the provisions of Comm.L.Art., § 2–719(3) are applicable.

The clause purporting to limit the consumers' remedy solely to replacement of the tire purports to exclude liability for both personal

10. Comm.L.Art., § 2–719, Official Comment 3.

11. Comm.L.Art., § 2–302(1) provides:

"If the court as a matter of law finds the contract or any clause of the contract to have been unconscionable at the time it was made the court may refuse to enforce the contract, or *it may enforce the remainder of the contract without the unconscionable clause,* or it may so limit the application of any unconscionable clause as to avoid any unconscionable result." (Emphasis added.)

12. Comm.L.Art., § 2–302, Official Comment 2.

13. Comm.L.Art., § 2–719, Official Comment 1.

14. Comm.L.Art., § 2–719(1)(b) creates a presumption that clauses prescribing remedies are cumulative rather than exclusive. If the parties intend such a clause to describe the sole remedy under the contract, such intent must be clearly expressed. Comm.L.Art., § 2–719, Official Comment 2.

15. See note 8 above.

injury and property damage. At trial, the appellees presented no evidence to show that the purported exclusion of consequential damages for personal injury was not unconscionable. Accordingly, to the extent that the clause purports to limit consequential damages for personal injury, it is unconscionable as a matter of law.

In Collins v. Uniroyal Inc., 64 N.J. 260, 315 A.2d 16 (1974), [a case on similar facts, the] Court cogently expressed the reasons for regarding a provision limiting the remedy to replacement of the tire to be "patently" unconscionable, and, therefore, invalid by stating:

> "A tire manufacturer warrants against blowouts in order to increase tire sales. Public advertising by defendant relative to these tires stated: 'If it only saves your life once, it's a bargain.' The seller should be held to realize that the purchaser of a tire buying it because so warranted is far more likely to have made the purchase decision in order to protect himself and the passengers in his car from death or personal injury in a blowout accident than to assure himself of a refund of the price of the tire in such an event. That being the natural reliance and the reasonable expectation of the purchaser flowing from the warranty, it appears to us patently unconscionable for the manufacturer to be permitted to limit his damages for a breach of warranty proximately resulting in the purchaser's death to a price refund or a replacement of the tire. We consequently agree with the determination of the Appellate Division that the statutory presumption of unconscionability was not here overcome and that the trial court ruled correctly on the issue." Id., 315 A.2d at 18.

While there is no statutory presumption of unconscionability with respect to a limitation of consequential damages for injury to property in the case of consumer goods, the rationale in *Collins* persuades us that the clause here, which attempts to exclude liability for both personal injury and property damage is so tainted by unconscionability as to warrant deletion in its entirety. If the appellees do not want to be liable for consequential damages, they should not expressly warrant the tires against blowouts.[17]

Under the present circumstances, the clause purporting to restrict remedies solely to replacement is ineffective. It cannot serve to convert the express warranty against blowouts into a guarantee that if a tire blew out, "the tire would be replaced."

* * *

NOTES

1. "[I]t is virtually impossible to imagine what the disclaiming party can do or show to overcome the 'prima facie' language. In effect we probably have

17. Comm.L.Art., § 2–719, Official Comment 3, provides: "The seller in all cases is free to disclaim warranties in the manner provided in Section 2–316."

an absolute bar in section 2–719." Franklin, When Worlds Collide: Liability Theories and Disclaimers in Defective–Product Cases, 18 Stan.L.Rev. 974, 1013 (1966). Compare the dissenting opinion of Judge Clifford in Collins v. Uniroyal, Inc., 64 N.J. 260, 315 A.2d 16, 18 (1974), where the purchaser of a tire manufactured by the defendant and guaranteed against blowouts was killed when the tire blew out. Since the warranty guaranteed against blowouts from external causes as well as from defects in the tires, and since no defect was shown in this case, the dissent argued that the manufacturer's limitation of remedy to repair or replacement should be enforced:

> The drafters presumably had something in mind when they chose the expression "prima facie unconscionable" instead of "per se unconscionable" or simply "unconscionable" * * *.
>
> * * * I think it not unreasonable * * * to conclude that where the express warranty goes beyond what is required by the Code and the common law of this state, and where the product is found to be free from defect, the prima facie unconscionability contemplated by the Code has been overcome. I would so hold. I emphasize that I would limit this holding to the "extra" guarantee case * * *.

See also Note, 50 N.Y.U.L.Rev. 148, 174–75 (1975): "[P]erhaps the strongest argument against calling limitation of remedies in the cases of nondefective failures prima facie unconscionable is that such limitations simply do not seem to be unfair if the consumer is given an understanding of their operation and effect."

2. In accord with *McCarty,* on similar facts, is Tuttle v. Kelly–Springfield Tire Co., 585 P.2d 1116 (Okl.1978). The court noted: "One author suggests somewhat skeptically it could be possible for a seller to rebut the presumption [of § 2–719(3)] by showing the [remedy limitation] clause was conspicuously printed, that it was explained to the buyer, that the parties bargained over it, and that the buyer knew the products had a tendency to be dangerous. See White & Summers, Uniform Commercial Code, p. 385 n. 48 (1972)." Id. at n. 11.

FORD MOTOR CO. v. MOULTON

Supreme Court of Tennessee, 1974.

511 S.W.2d 690, cert. denied 419 U.S. 870, 95 S.Ct. 129, 42 L.Ed.2d 109.

CHATTIN, JUSTICE. This is a personal injury suit brought by Moulton and his wife, Pauline, [respondents], against Ford Motor Company and a retail Ford dealer, Hull–Dobbs [petitioners].

Moulton seeks $1,000,000.00 in damages and charges the defendants with: negligence; breach of express and implied warranties; tortious misrepresentation based on public advertisement; and strict liability in tort.

[Moulton and his wife filed a complaint on May 13, 1971, alleging that Mr. Moulton purchased a Ford LTD from Hull–Dobbs and took delivery on April 30, 1969; that he was seriously injured while driving on July 5, 1970 when the car "suddenly veered to the right, jumped the guard rail, and fell twenty-six feet to a street below"; and that the loss of control was due to a defect in the steering mechanism of the car. The trial judge dismissed plaintiffs' tort claims as barred by the statute of limitations and their warranty claims for failure to state a cause of action. The Court of Appeals reinstated the tort claims but upheld the dismissal of the warranty counts, and both parties petitioned for review. [T]he Supreme Court reinstated the trial court's dismissal of the entire action. Excerpts from the Supreme Court opinion concerning the validity of the time and mileage limitations on the defendants' warranties follow.]

The Court of Appeals concluded that Hull–Dobbs had not given Moulton an express warranty. This conclusion is supported by the evidence. That Court found that Ford had given Moulton a one-year or twelve thousand mile express warranty. However, the Court of Appeals held that this warranty had expired, thereby precluding an action for its breach.

Both Hull–Dobbs and Ford had disclaimer clauses in their contracts with Moulton, which purportedly disclaimed all implied warranties. The Court of Appeals found these disclaimer clauses to be valid; and, therefore, sufficient to prevent respondents from having a cause of action for breach of implied warranty.

Respondents make three arguments: First, they insist the disclaimer clauses were not properly drawn in that they failed to comply with the provisions of the Uniform Commercial Code; and are, therefore, invalid. Second, if the disclaimer clauses are properly drawn, they are prima facie unconscionable * * *. Finally, respondents insist that the one-year or twelve thousand mile limitation on the express warranty is prima facie unconscionable under T.C.A. 47–2–719.

T.C.A. 47–2–316(2) provides that implied warranties of merchantability and fitness may be disclaimed if the disclaimer is conspicuous and mentions merchantability, and if it is in writing with reference to the fitness warranty. The Court of Appeals concluded that the requirement of T.C.A. 47–2–316(2) had been complied with; and, consequently, the disclaimers were validly drawn. We agree with this conclusion.

Respondents insist that even if the disclaimers were drawn in accordance with the provisions of T.C.A. 47–2–316 they are, nevertheless, invalid because they violate T.C.A. 47–2–719.

T.C.A. 47–2–719(3) provides:

> "Consequential damages may be limited or excluded unless the limitation or exclusion is unconscionable. Limitation of consequential damages for injury to the person in the case of consumer goods is prima facie unconscionable but limitation of damages where the loss is commercial is not."

Respondents' argument is that as a result of the accident Moulton sustained personal injuries; that because of the valid disclaimer of warranties, he is unable to bring an action for consequential damages resulting from the accident; and that such an exclusion is violative of T.C.A. 47–2–719(3) since that section "expressly prohibits exclusion of personal injuries by warranty."

In answer to this argument, the Court of Appeals said:

> "* * * Plaintiffs misconstrues the scope of this Section. (2–719(3)). Subsection (3) thereof provides the limitation of consequential damages for injury to the person in case of consumer goods is prima facie unconscionable, but that Section does not control disclaimer of implied warranties. Official comment 3 to T.C.A. 47–2–719 states that the seller 'in all cases is free to disclaim warranties in the manner provided in Section 2–316.'
>
> "The latter Section, which is T.C.A. 47–2–316, provides in subsection (2) that implied warranties of merchantability and fitness may be disclaimed if the disclaimer is conspic[u]ous and mentions merchantability, and if it is in writing with reference to the fitness warranty. The disclaimer here is in writing, and merchantability is explicitly mentioned in the disclaimer of the motor vehicle sales contract."

Most Uniform Commercial Code commentaries agree with the conclusion of the Court of Appeals that disclaimers drawn in accordance with 47–2–316 cannot be considered to violate the provisions of 47–2–719. The following analysis is offered in the one volume treatise of the U.C.C. by White and Summers:

> "* * * The proposition enunciated by * * * (a few courts) * * * that a disclaimer that has the effect of modifying or excluding consequential damages may be unconscionable under 2–719(3) * * * is out of line with the scheme of the Code. Comment 3 to 2–719(3) provides: * * * 'Subsection (3) recognizes the validity to clauses limiting or excluding consequential damages but makes it clear that they may not operate in an unconscionable manner. Actually such terms are merely an allocation of unknown or undeterminable risks. The seller in all cases is free to disclaim warranties in a manner provided in Section 2–316.'
>
> "The last sentence seems to be telling the seller, 'if you really want to limit your liability why don't you disclaim all warranties? Then you won't have to worry about limiting damages.' * * *
>
> "This implication is buttressed by comment [2] to 2–316 * * *: '* * * If no warranty exists, there is of course no problem of limiting remedies for breach of warranty.'
>
> "The comment's reasoning is elementary: there can be no consequential damages if there is no breach; there can be no breach of warranty if there is no warranty; there can be no warranty if the seller has disclaimed them pursuant to 2–316.

> Although a particular disclaimer may be unconscionable under 2–302, it seems clear that the scheme of the Code does not permit a court to disregard that disclaimer on the basis that it operates to exclude the consequential damages that could not be excluded under 2–719(3)."

We think the Court of Appeals correctly determined that the disclaimer clauses did not violate the provisions of 2–719(3).

Respondents did not argue that the Court of Appeals did not consider the question as to whether a warranty disclaimer which meets the provisions of 2–316 can be considered unconscionable within the meaning of the term as used in 2–302. Most commentaries answer this question in the negative. See Leff, Unconscionability and the Code, the Emperor's New Clause, 115 U.Pa.L.Rev. 485 (1967).

Finally, respondents contend that the one-year or twelve thousand mile limitation on the express warranty is prima facie unconscionable under T.C.A. 47–2–719(3). This is essentially the same argument made above. Again, the Court of Appeals rejected respondents' reasoning stating:

> "This provision has to do with limitation of remedies, and not with a limitation on the time within which a claim may be asserted. T.C.A. 47–2–607(3)(a) provides for the time within which a claim must be asserted. It states that where goods have been accepted, 'the buyer must within a reasonable time after he discovers or should have discovered a breach notify the seller of the breach or be barred from any remedy.' T.C.A. 47–1–204(1) provides that whenever any provision in the Sales Act requires an action to be taken within a reasonable time 'any time which is not manifestly unreasonable may be fixed by agreement.'
>
> "Limitation of the period of the express warranty is in effect a limitation of the time within which a claim must be asserted under that warranty. The warranty actually provides for repair or replacement of such parts 'found to be defective' within the limited period, and if such discovery were made presumably a further reasonable period of time would be allowed for giving notice. Here, however, no such discovery within the limited period was made. Thus, plaintiff has no valid claim of breach of express or implied warranty.
>
> "There is no assignment of error that the limited period of express warranty is 'manifestly unreasonable' within the meaning of T.C.A. 47–1–204(1). In the absence of any such assignment, we deem the issue waived by the plaintiffs."

The Court of Appeals, also, rejected Mrs. Moulton's contention that she had a breach of warranty action stating: " * * * her action being derivative, she is entitled to no greater warranty rights under this

Section than the buyer himself. Since Mr. Moulton has no warranty rights * * * neither does Mrs. Moulton."

We agree with the foregoing conclusions of the Court of Appeals.

* * *

[The Court of Appeals' decision upholding the dismissal of the warranty counts affirmed; action dismissed.]

[Dissenting opinion of Fones, J., omitted.]

NOTES

1. U.C.C. § 2–725(1) provides: "An action for breach of any contract for sale must be commenced within four years after the cause of action has accrued. By the original agreement the parties may reduce the period of limitation to not less than one year but may not extend it." Subsection (2) provides that a cause of action for breach of warranty accrues upon tender of delivery, unless the warranty "explicitly extends to future performance of the goods * * *."

2. A few courts have held that disclaimers valid under § 2–316 may be invalidated for being unconscionable under § 2–719(3). See Walsh v. Ford Motor Co., 59 Misc.2d 241, 298 N.Y.S.2d 538 (1969); Ford Motor Co. v. Tritt, 244 Ark. 883, 890A, 430 S.W.2d 778 (1968). There is in fact some academic support for this approach. E.g., Note, 63 Va.L.Rev. 791 (1977). See generally White & Summers, supra, at §§ 12–11 & 12–12.

3. Might the disclaimer have been held invalid under § 2–302, the general section on unconscionability? As indicated in *Moulton,* there has been very little support for such an approach. Consider, however, the following analysis.

WEINTRAUB, DISCLAIMERS AND LIMITATION OF DAMAGES FOR BREACH OF WARRANTY UNDER THE UCC

53 Texas L.Rev. 60, 80–83 (1974).

One of the most difficult questions in the unconscionability area is whether section 2–302, the general unconscionability section, applies to disclaimers of warranties. Both courts [107] and commentators [108] have indicated that something the Code specifically permits (disclaimer of warranties under 2–316) cannot be "unconscionable" under another

107. See Avery v. Aladdin Prod. Div., 128 Ga.App. 266, 196 S.E.2d 357 (1973); Ford Motor Co. v. Moulton, 511 S.W.2d 690 (Tenn.1974) (dictum); Marshall v. Murray Oldsmobile Co., 207 Va. 972, 154 S.E.2d 140 (1967). But see Matthews v. Ford Motor Co., 479 F.2d 399 (4th Cir.1973) (pointing out that *Murray Oldsmobile* involved a transaction that occurred before Virginia adopted the UCC and that the suit was for rescission not for personal injuries).

108. See N.Y.Law Revision Comm'n, supra note 63, at 586:

[T]he question remains whether a disclaimer which is effective under the rigid requirements of Section 2–316 can be "unconscionable" under Section 2–302 when the goods cause consequential damages. The text of the Code provides little support for such a far-reaching application of Section 2–302 or of Section 2–719(3).

See also Leff, Unconscionability and the Code, 115 U.Pa.L.Rev. 485, 524–25 (1967).

section of the same statute. Section 2–316 provides its own policing against improper exclusion or modification of warranties and, unlike section 2–719, contains no internal reference to unconscionability. Comment 3 to section 2–719, after pointing out that damages limitation clauses "may not operate in an unconscionable manner," declares that "[t]he seller in all cases is free to disclaim warranties in the manner provided in Section 2–316." [109]

This argument has a certain surface logic based on the Code's internal structure. Nevertheless, section 2–302 is a general policing provision designed to protect against unconscionability of "the contract or any clause of the contract." It would be anomalous to declare in section 2–719 that "[l]imitation of consequential damages for injury to the person in the case of consumer goods is prima facie unconscionable," and at the same time to allow complete exclusion of the warranty from whose breach those "consequential damages" must flow. Little light is shed on this argument by the cryptic text of the official comment following section 2–302. Comment 1 states:

> The basic test is whether, in the light of the general commercial background and the commercial needs of the particular trade or case, the clauses involved are so one-sided as to be unconscionable under the circumstances existing at the time of the making of the contract. * * * The principle is one of the prevention of oppression and unfair surprise * * * and not of disturbance of allocation of risks because of superior bargaining power.

A number of the cases cited in comment 1 to illustrate "[t]he underlying basis of this section" do, however, indicate that the unconscionability concept was intended to apply to the disclaimer of warranties. * * *

It therefore seems consistent with Code policy that section 2–302 be used to police against unconscionable warranty disclaimers, even those that have meticulously adhered to the formal requirements of section 2–316. When and how warranty disclaimers will be declared unconscionable will probably depend on the interplay of such factors as the following: First, what remedy is the buyer seeking? The chances that a warranty disclaimer will be upheld increase as we move from suits for personal injuries, to attempts to revoke acceptance and recover the purchase price, to suits for lost profits far in excess of the purchase price. Second, how clearly and completely was the buyer, considering his skill and experience, apprised of the meaning and practical consequences of the warranty disclaimer? Third, to what extent was the buyer able to bargain for terms more favorable to him? These three factors—type of remedy excluded, advertence, and adhesion—are probably close to the core of any viable concept of "unconscionability."

109. U.C.C. § 2–719, Comment 3.

NOTES

1. "The issue of unconscionability presents a question of law for the court; not an issue of fact for the jury." Schroeder v. Fageol Motors, Inc., 86 Wash.2d 256, 544 P.2d 20, 24 (1975).

2. Consideration of issues arising from the purchase of products with multiple and repeated problems, "lemons," and the role in such cases of § 2–719(2), are deferred to Chapter 6.

3. In addition to the authorities cited at note 12, supra p. 142, see Fahlgren, Unconscionability: Warranty Disclaimers and Consequential Damage Limitations, 20 St. Louis U.L.J. 435 (1976); Mueller, Contracts of Frustration, 78 Yale L.J. 576 (1969); Note, 50 N.Y.U.L.Rev. 148 (1975).

---

4. STATUTORY REFORM

STATE

Discontent with the disclaimer and limitations provisions of the Uniform Commercial Code within the consumer context has been voiced for some time. See, e.g., Peters, Remedies for Breach of Contracts Relating to the Sale of Goods Under the Uniform Commercial Code: A Roadmap for Article Two, 73 Yale L.J. 199, 282–83 (1963). As interest in consumer rights increased during the late 1960s and early 1970s, so too did criticisms of the Code's treatment of this problem:

> The disclaimer section of the UCC is the most controversial and ambiguous warranty section. Although its principal purpose is to protect the buyer from unexpected and unbargained-for language of disclaimer, its requirement that any disclaimer must mention "merchantability" almost ensures failure of this purpose because the term conveys so little information to the average consumer. This provision has enabled merchants to continue shifting the risk of loss back to consumers while camouflaging their action with legal jargon.
> * * *
>
> The Code purports to set the permissible boundaries for contractual terms limiting remedies or liquidating damages with its concepts of reasonableness and unconscionability. These terms, however, are vague, and to the extent that they are vague, they do not sufficiently protect the consumer.

Rothschild, The Magnuson–Moss Warranty Act: Does It Balance Warrantor and Consumer Interests?, 44 Geo.Wash.L.Rev. 335, 343–44 (1976).

In an attempt to tip the scales more in favor of the consumer, several states have enacted legislation restricting in consumer transactions the ability of sellers to disclaim warranty liability or to limit the remedies therefor. These statutes vary considerably, from simple amendments to the UCC, the typical approach illustrated by the statutes set forth below, to rather complex consumer protection statutes, as in Kansas, Rhode Island and California.

VT.STAT.ANN. tit. 9A, § 2–316(5) (Supp.1987):

> The provisions of subdivisions (2), (3) and (4) of this subsection shall not apply to sales of new or unused consumer goods or services. Any language, oral or written, used by a seller or manufacturer of consumer goods and services, which attempts to exclude or modify any implied warranties of merchantability and fitness for a particular purpose or to exclude or modify the consumer's remedies for breach of those warranties, shall be unenforceable. * * *

ALA.CODE § 7–2–316(5) (1975):

> Nothing in subsection (2) or subsection (3)(a) or in section 7–2–317 shall be construed so as to limit or exclude the seller's liability for damages for injury to the person in the case of consumer goods.

ALA.CODE § 7–2–719(4) (1975):

> Nothing in this section or in section 7–2–718 shall be construed so as to limit the seller's liability for damages for injury to the person in the case of consumer goods. (Acts 1965, No. 549, p. 811.)

See Cal.Civ.Code § 1790 et seq. (1985 & Supp.1987). See generally Clark & Davis, Beefing Up Product Warranties: A New Dimension in Consumer Protection, 23 U.Kan.L.Rev. 567 (1975).

FEDERAL

ROTHSCHILD, THE MAGNUSON–MOSS WARRANTY ACT: DOES IT BALANCE WARRANTOR AND CONSUMER INTERESTS?

44 Geo.Wash.L.Rev. 335, 353–56 (1976).

On January 4, 1975, President Ford signed the Magnuson–Moss Act into law to take effect July 4, 1975. The Act is the culmination of a long line of warranty legislation introduced in both Houses of Congress.

Structure of the Act

The Act[152] provides that any written warranty given for consumer products actually costing the consumer more than $5 must contain the terms and conditions of the written warranty in readily understood language according to standards set by the Federal Trade Commission.[153] Nothing in the Act commands that a consumer product be warranted or that a product be warranted for any specific length of time. If, however, a written warranty is offered, full disclosure is required, and the warranty information must be made available to consumers before the product is sold. * * *

If the product actually costs the consumer more than $10, any written warranty must be labeled either "full warranty", indicating that it meets federal standards, or "limited warranty", indicating that it does not meet federal standards. * * *

A "full warranty" designation obligates the warrantor to correct defects, malfunctions, or nonconforming quality defects without charge and within a reasonable time, to disclose clearly on the face of the warranty the exclusions or limitations of consequential damages, and to permit refund or replacement after reasonable but unsuccessful attempts to repair. Further, the warrantor may not limit the duration of implied warranties or impose any duties on the consumer, other than notice, as a condition of remedying defective quality. These duties extend from the "full warranty" warrantor to each person who is a consumer of the warranted product.

* * * Where a written warranty is given or a service contract is entered into, the warrantor may not disclaim or modify any implied warranties, except to limit them to the duration of the written warranty, if that limitation is reasonable, conscionable, and prominently displayed on the face of the warranty in clear, unmistakable language.

Violation of the Warranty Act or a Commission rule is a violation of the Federal Trade Commission Act. The Attorney General or FTC attorneys may sue to restrain deceptive warranties or noncompliance with the Act in the United States district courts. In addition, a consumer who is damaged by a breach of warranty or noncompliance with the Act or with Commission rules promulgated thereunder may sue for injunctive relief, damages, or other legal relief in any state or appropriate United States district court. The court may award costs and expenses, including attorneys' fees, to the consumer if he/she prevails. Nothing in the Act invalidates any right or remedy of a

152. The Act's 12 sections are: section 101, definitions; section 102, warranty provisions; section 103, description of warranties; section 104, federal minimum standards for warranties; section 105, full and limited warranty of a consumer product; section 106, service contracts; section 107, designation of representatives; section 108, limitation on disclaimer of implied warranties; section 109, Commission rules; section 110, remedies; section 111, effect on other laws; and section 112, effective date.

153. Magnuson–Moss Warranty Act § 102(a), (e), 15 U.S.C.A. § 2302(a), (e). The FTC has set $15 as the minimum price for consumer products that will trigger warrantors' and sellers' duties under the Act. * * *

consumer under state law or under any other federal law. At the same time, state laws covering warranty provisions are governed by the Act unless the Commission specifically exempts them.

NOTES

1. The key substantive provision of the Act relevant to products liability litigation, § 108, pertains to disclaimers. As codified at 15 U.S.C.A., it provides as follows:

> **§ 2308. Implied warranties—Restrictions on disclaimers or modifications**
>
> (a) No supplier may disclaim or modify (except as provided in subsection (b) of this section) any implied warranty to a consumer with respect to such consumer product if (1) such supplier makes any written warranty to the consumer with respect to such consumer product, or (2) at the time of sale, or within 90 days thereafter, such supplier enters into a service contract with the consumer which applies to such consumer product.
>
> **Limitation on duration**
>
> (b) For purposes of this chapter (other than section 2304(a)(2) of this title), implied warranties may be limited in duration to the duration of a written warranty of reasonable duration, if such limitation is conscionable and is set forth in clear and unmistakable language and prominently displayed on the face of the warranty.
>
> **Effectiveness of disclaimers, modifications, or limitations**
>
> (c) A disclaimer, modification, or limitation made in violation of this section shall be ineffective for purposes of this chapter and State law.

Section 2304(a)(2) provides that the duration of implied warranties may not be limited in the case of "full" warranties.

2. Note that limitations on consequential damages are not prohibited by § 108. Indeed, they are specifically permitted by § 104(a)(3), 15 U.S.C.A. § 2304(a)(3), so long as the "exclusion or limitation conspicuously appears on the face of the warranty." In the case of personal injuries, however, the draftsmen quite clearly intended to leave U.C.C. § 2–719(3) intact. See § 111(b) of the Act, 15 U.S.C.A. § 2311(b).

3. **Jurisdiction and Attorney's Fees.** Section 2310(d) provides that a consumer damaged by a supplier's failure "to comply with any obligation under this chapter, or under a written warranty, implied warranty, or service contract," may (1) sue for damages in state court or, if the amount in controversy is at least $50,000, federal court, and (2) recover attorney's fees, if he finally prevails. Commentators have read this section to open up important new opportunities for injured persons: "[C]onsumers suddenly have a federal forum, as well as the prospect of recovering their attorney's fees, for a violation of UCC section 2–314! In many respects, this 'muscling up' of the UCC could be one of the most important aspects of the Federal Act." Clark & Davis, Beefing Up Product Warranties: A New Dimension in Consumer Protection, 23 Kan.L.Rev. 567, 616 (1975). With respect to personal injury actions, however, the courts have disagreed:

We agree with the conclusion of the district court in *Saf–T–Mate:*

> * * * Congress was content to let the question of personal injury products liability remain a matter of state-law causes of action, except to the extent that certain substantive provisions in the Magnuson–Moss Act overrule contrary state laws relating to the warrantor's ability to disclaim personal injury liability.

Gorman v. Saf–T–Mate, Inc., N.D.Ind.1981, 513 F.Supp. 1028, 1035. We hold that § 2311(b)(2) of the MMWA prohibits claims arising from personal injury based solely on a breach of warranty, express or implied. One may, however, recover personal injury damages under the MMWA where there has been a violation of the substantive provisions of § 2308 (prohibiting disclaimer of implied warranties), § 2304(a)(2) (prohibiting full warrantors from limiting the duration of implied warranty coverage) or § 2304(a)(3) [17] (prohibiting full warrantors from excluding or limiting consequential damages unless such exclusion or limitation conspicuously appears on the face of the warranty).[18]

Boelens v. Redman Homes, Inc., 748 F.2d 1058, 1068 (5th Cir.1984), denying petition for rehearing 759 F.2d 504 (5th Cir.1985). Accord, Hughes v. Segal Enterprises, Inc., 627 F.Supp. 1231 (W.D.Ark.1986); Washington v. Otasco, Inc., 603 F.Supp. 1295 (N.D.Miss.1984), supra, p. 105 n. 8.

4. Would a case like Ford Motor Co. v. Moulton, supra p. 147, be any stronger if it were brought under the Federal Warranty Act rather than under state warranty law alone?

5. Articles on the federal warranty act include Roberts & Mann, The Magnuson–Moss Federal Warranty Act and Uniform Commercial Code Section 2–719: Further Reflections and Recent Developments, 1979 Ariz.St.L.J. 765; Schroeder, Private Actions under the Magnuson–Moss Warranty Act, 66 Calif. L.Rev. 1 (1978); Eddy, Effects of the Magnuson–Moss Act Upon Consumer Product Warranties, 55 N.C.L.Rev. 835 (1977); Denicola, The Magnuson–Moss Warranty Act: Making Consumer Product Warranty a Federal Case, 44 Fordham L.Rev. 273 (1975); Note, 62 Corn.L.Rev. 738 (1977); Annot., 59 A.L.R.Fed. 461 (1982).

---

17. [The statutory reference to § 2304(a)(4) in § 2311(b)(2) was "evidently" an error in draftspersonship.]

18. Section 2310(e), which applies to both state and federal court actions, provides that no action for breach of warranty may be instituted under § 2310(d) unless the warrantor has first been afforded a "reasonable opportunity to cure" the pertinent "failure to comply" with the warranty. Actions for breach of the substantive obligations of the MMWA, however, are not reached by § 2310(e). Claims for personal injury based on a breach of the provisions of §§ 2308, 2304(a)(2), or 2304(a)(3) are therefore not subject to the opportunity-to-cure limitation.

SECTION 4. STRICT LIABILITY IN TORT

JAMES, PRODUCTS LIABILITY (PT. 2)

34 Tex.L.Rev. 227–28 (1955).

As the accident toll of modern life has increased, the urge towards strict liability has grown. Many older forms of liability were vehicles for such a principle but none of them is well adapted to solving our present accident problem. Warranty is a case in point. This was fashioned to serve commercial needs in a commercial context, and however well or ill adapted it is to that end today, its technicalities and limitations reflect those needs. If it occasionally happens to fit the needs of accident law, that is pure coincidence. As a general proposition it does not. If strict liability should be imposed in these cases as a matter of policy, there is no more reason than there is in connection with the negligence doctrine to confine the scope of liability to those in privity of agreement. The need for protection is as wide as the likelihood of this kind of harm, and all such harm may fairly be regarded as a casualty of the supplier's enterprise. Not only the rule of privity, but also many other limitations on warranty liability which we have treated here, are out of place in the context of accident law. They would all be abandoned in a rational scheme of strict liability for injurious products. In some cases this may require legislation. Yet the concept of the warranty implied in law on grounds of policy was devised by courts in the past to meet commercial needs. Why should not the courts of today—entirely within the tradition of a dynamic common law—develop a warranty theory in products liability cases which is tailored to meet modern needs in that field—at least where existing legislation does not positively and clearly forbid such a development? To some extent this has taken place. The process should and no doubt will continue.

NOTE

Other early writings suggesting the need for strict manufacturer responsibility and pointing out the inability of traditional warranty law to meet the need include James, General Products—Should Manufacturers Be Liable Without Negligence?, 24 Tenn.L.Rev. 923 (1957); Noel, Manufacturers of Products—The Drift Toward Strict Liability, 24 Tenn.L.Rev. 963 (1957). See generally Priest, The Invention of Enterprise Liability: A Critical History of the Intellectual Foundations of Modern Tort Law, 14 J.Leg.Stud. 461 (1985) (excellent review of early theoretical development).

ESCOLA v. COCA COLA BOTTLING CO. OF FRESNO

Supreme Court of California, 1944.
24 Cal.2d 453, 150 P.2d 436.

GIBSON, CHIEF JUSTICE. Plaintiff, a waitress in a restaurant, was injured when a bottle of Coca Cola broke in her hand. She alleged that defendant company, which had bottled and delivered the alleged defective bottle to her employer, was negligent in selling "bottles containing said beverage which on account of excessive pressure of gas or by reason of some defect in the bottle was dangerous * * * and likely to explode." This appeal is from a judgment upon a jury verdict in favor of plaintiff.

[Plaintiff testified that the bottle exploded in her hand as she was transferring it from its case to the refrigerator. A fellow employee who saw the accident testified that plaintiff did not knock the bottle against any other object. Unable to prove any specific act of negligence, plaintiff relied entirely upon the doctrine of res ipsa loquitur. Defendant contended that the doctrine did not apply and that the evidence was insufficient to support the judgment.]

Upon an examination of the record, the evidence appears sufficient to support a reasonable inference that the bottle here involved was not damaged by any extraneous force after delivery to the restaurant by defendant. It follows, therefore, that the bottle was in some manner defective at the time defendant relinquished control, because sound and properly prepared bottles of carbonated liquids do not ordinarily explode when carefully handled.

* * *

Although it is not clear in this case whether the explosion was caused by an excessive charge or a defect in the glass there is a sufficient showing that neither cause would ordinarily have been present if due care had been used. Further, defendant had exclusive control over both the charging and inspection of the bottles. Accordingly, all the requirements necessary to entitle plaintiff to rely on the doctrine of res ipsa loquitur to supply an inference of negligence are present.

* * *

The judgment is affirmed.

SHENK, CURTIS, CARTER, and SCHAUER, JJ., concurred.

TRAYNOR, JUSTICE. I concur in the judgment, but I believe the manufacturer's negligence should no longer be singled out as the basis of a plaintiff's right to recover in cases like the present one. In my opinion it should now be recognized that a manufacturer incurs an absolute liability when an article that he has placed on the market, knowing that it is to be used without inspection, proves to have a defect that causes injury to human beings. MacPherson v. Buick Motor Co., 217 N.Y. 382, 111 N.E. 1050, L.R.A.1916F, 696, Ann.Cas.1916C, 440 established the principle, recognized by this court, that irrespective of privity of contract, the manufacturer is responsible for an injury caused by such an article to any person who comes in lawful contact with it. Sheward v. Virtue, 20 Cal.2d 410, 126 P.2d 345; Kalash v. Los Angeles Ladder Co., 1 Cal.2d 229, 34 P.2d 481. In these cases the source of the manufacturer's liability was his negligence in the manufacturing process or in the inspection of component parts supplied by others. Even if there is no negligence, however, public policy demands that responsibility be fixed wherever it will most effectively reduce the hazards to life and health inherent in defective products that reach the market. It is evident that the manufacturer can anticipate some hazards and guard against the recurrence of others, as the public cannot. Those who suffer injury from defective products are unprepared to meet its consequences. The cost of an injury and the loss of time or health may be an overwhelming misfortune to the person injured, and a needless one, for the risk of injury can be insured by the manufacturer and distributed among the public as a cost of doing business. It is to the public interest to discourage the marketing of products having defects that are a menace to the public. If such products nevertheless find their way into the market it is to the public interest to place the responsibility for whatever injury they may cause upon the manufacturer, who, even if he is not negligent in the manufacture of the product, is responsible for its reaching the market. However, intermittently such injuries may occur and however haphazardly they may strike, the risk of their occurrence is a constant risk and a general one. Against such a risk there should be general and constant protection and the manufacturer is best situated to afford such protection.

The injury from a defective product does not become a matter of indifference because the defect arises from causes other than the negligence of the manufacturer, such as negligence of a submanufacturer, of a component part whose defects could not be revealed by inspection [citations], or unknown causes that even by the device of res ipsa loquitur cannot be classified as negligence of the manufacturer. The inference of negligence may be dispelled by an affirmative showing of proper care. * * * An injured person, however, is not ordinarily in a position to refute such evidence or identify the cause of the defect, for he can hardly be familiar with the manufacturing process as the manufacturer himself is. In leaving it to the jury to decide whether the inference has been dispelled, regardless of the evidence against it, the negligence rule approaches the rule of strict liability. It is needlessly circuitous to make negligence the basis of recovery and impose what is in reality liability without negligence. If public policy demands that a manufacturer of goods be responsible for their quality regardless of negligence there is no reason not to fix that responsibility openly.

In the case of foodstuffs, the public policy of the state is formulated in a criminal statute. [Pure food acts] of this kind result in a strict liability of the manufacturer in tort to the member of the public injured. See cases cited in Prosser, Torts, p. 693, note 69.

The statute may well be applicable to a bottle whose defects cause it to explode. In any event it is significant that the statute imposes criminal liability without fault, reflecting the public policy of protecting the public from dangerous products placed on the market, irrespective of negligence in their manufacture. While the Legislature imposes criminal liability only with regard to food products and their containers, there are many other sources of danger. It is to the public interest to prevent injury to the public from any defective goods by the imposition of civil liability generally.

The retailer, even though not equipped to test a product, is under an absolute liability to his customer, for the implied warranties of fitness for proposed use and merchantable quality include a warranty of safety of the product. [Citations.] This warranty is not necessarily a contractual one (Chamberlain Co. v. Allis–Chalmers, etc., Co., 51 Cal. App.2d 521, 524, 125 P.2d 113; see 1 Williston on Sales, 2d ed., §§ 197–201), for public policy requires that the buyer be insured at the seller's expense against injury. [Citations.] The courts recognize, however, that the retailer cannot bear the burden of this warranty, and allow him to recoup any losses by means of the warranty of safety attending the wholesaler's or manufacturer's sale to him. Ward v. Great Atlantic & Pacific Tea Co., supra; see Waite, Retail Responsibility and Judicial Law Making, 34 Mich.L.Rev. 494, 509. Such a procedure, however, is needlessly circuitous and engenders wasteful litigation. Much would be gained if the injured person could base his action directly on the manufacturer's warranty.

The liability of the manufacturer to an immediate buyer injured by a defective product follows without proof of negligence from the implied warranty of safety attending the sale. * * *

This court and many others have extended protection according to such a standard to consumers of food products, taking the view that the right of a consumer injured by unwholesome food does not depend "upon the intricacies of the law of sales" and that the warranty of the manufacturer to the consumer in absence of privity of contract rests on public policy. [Citations.] Dangers to life and health inhere in other consumers' goods that are defective and there is no reason to differentiate them from the dangers of defective food products. [Citations.]

In the food products cases the courts have resorted to various fictions to rationalize the extension of the manufacturer's warranty to the consumer: that a warranty runs with the chattel; that the cause of action of the dealer is assigned to the consumer; that the consumer is a third party beneficiary of the manufacturer's contract with the dealer. * * * Such fictions are not necessary to fix the manufacturer's liability under a warranty if the warranty is severed from the contract of sale between the dealer and the consumer and based on the law of torts (Decker & Sons v. Capps, supra; Prosser, Torts, p. 689) as a strict liability. * * *

As handicrafts have been replaced by mass production with its great markets and transportation facilities, the close relationship between the producer and consumer of a product has been altered. Manufacturing processes, frequently valuable secrets, are ordinarily either inaccessible to or beyond the ken of the general public. The consumer no longer has means or skill enough to investigate for himself the soundness of a product, even when it is not contained in a sealed package, and his erstwhile vigilance has been lulled by the steady efforts of manufacturers to build up confidence by advertising and marketing devices such as trademarks. [Citations.] Consumers no longer approach products warily but accept them on faith, relying on the reputation of the manufacturer or the trademark. [Citations.] Manufacturers have sought to justify that faith by increasingly high standards of inspection and a readiness to make good on defective products by way of replacements and refunds. See Bogert and Fink, Business Practices Regarding Warranties In The Sale Of Goods, 25 Ill. L.Rev. 400. The manufacturer's obligation to the consumer must keep pace with the changing relationship between them; it cannot be escaped because the marketing of a product has become so complicated as to require one or more intermediaries. Certainly there is greater reason to impose liability on the manufacturer than on the retailer who is but a conduit of a product that he is not himself able to test. [Citations.]

* * *

NOTE

> Dean Pound once denounced [Traynor's opinion in *Escola*] as a piece of "authoritarian law," and a major step in the direction of socialism [in New Paths of the Law 39–47 (1950), and Law in the Service State: Freedom versus Equality, 36 A.B.A.J. 977, 981 (1950)]. Assuming that we are not nowadays disposed to flee shrieking in terror from the prospect of a spot of socialism in our law when the public interest demands it, the question remains whether our courts, our legislators, and public sentiment in general, are yet ready to adopt so sweeping a legal philosophy, and to impose so heavy a burden abruptly and all at once upon all producers. Thus far there has been relatively little indication that the time is yet ripe for what may very possibly be the law of fifty years ahead. As in the case of the related agitation for strict liability on the part of all automobile drivers, there are too many vested interests in the way, and the sudden change is likely to be regarded as too radical and disruptive; and progress in the direction of any such broad general rule cannot be expected to be rapid.

Prosser, The Assault Upon the Citadel (Strict Liability to the Consumer), 69 Yale L.J. 1099, 1120–21 (1960).

HENNINGSEN v. BLOOMFIELD MOTORS, INC.

Supreme Court of New Jersey, 1960.
32 N.J. 358, 161 A.2d 69.

FRANCIS, J. [Mr. and Mrs. Henningsen sued Chrysler Corporation (the manufacturer) and Bloomfield Motors (the dealer) for losses suffered in an accident caused by a steering defect in their Plymouth Plaza 6 Club Sedan ten days after they took delivery from the dealer. *Held,* plaintiffs could recover for breach of an implied warranty of merchantability, despite the absence of privity of contract with Chrysler, and despite the presence of a disclaimer of implied warranties in the purchase contract. The aspect of the opinion addressing the privity issue is discussed above at p. 109, and the portion discussing the disclaimer issue is set forth above at p. 128.]

GREENMAN v. YUBA POWER PRODUCTS, INC.

Supreme Court of California, 1963.
59 Cal.2d 57, 27 Cal.Rptr. 697, 377 P.2d 897.

TRAYNOR, JUSTICE. Plaintiff brought this action for damages against the retailer and the manufacturer of a Shopsmith, a combination power tool that could be used as a saw, drill, and wood lathe. He saw a Shopsmith demonstrated by the retailer and studied a brochure prepared by the manufacturer. He decided he wanted a Shopsmith for his home workshop, and his wife bought and gave him one for Christmas in 1955. In 1957 he bought the necessary attachments to use the Shopsmith as a lathe for turning a large piece of wood he wished to make into a chalice. After he had worked on the piece of wood several times without difficulty, it suddenly flew out of the machine and struck him on the forehead, inflicting serious injuries. About ten and a half months later, he gave the retailer and the manufacturer written notice of claimed breaches of warranties and filed a complaint against them alleging such breaches and negligence.

After a trial before a jury, the court ruled that there was no evidence that the retailer was negligent or had breached any express warranty and that the manufacturer was not liable for the breach of any implied warranty. Accordingly, it submitted to the jury only the cause of action alleging breach of implied warranties against the retailer and the causes of action alleging negligence and breach of express warranties against the manufacturer. The jury returned a verdict for the retailer against plaintiff and for plaintiff against the manufacturer in the amount of $65,000. The trial court denied the manufacturer's motion for a new trial and entered judgment on the verdict. The manufacturer and plaintiff appeal. Plaintiff seeks a reversal of the part of the judgment in favor of the retailer, however, only in the event that the part of the judgment against the manufacturer is reversed.

Plaintiff introduced substantial evidence that his injuries were caused by defective design and construction of the Shopsmith. His expert witnesses testified that inadequate set screws were used to hold parts of the machine together so that normal vibration caused the tailstock of the lathe to move away from the piece of wood being turned permitting it to fly out of the lathe. They also testified that there were other more positive ways of fastening the parts of the machine together, the use of which would have prevented the accident. The jury could therefore reasonably have concluded that the manufacturer negligently constructed the Shopsmith. The jury could also reasonably have concluded that statements in the manufacturer's brochure were untrue, that they constituted express warranties,[1] and that plaintiff's injuries were caused by their breach.

The manufacturer contends, however, that plaintiff did not give it notice of breach of warranty within a reasonable time and that therefore his cause of action for breach of warranty is barred by section 1769 of the Civil Code. * * *

* * *

Like other provisions of the uniform sales act (Civ.Code, §§ 1721–1800), section 1769 deals with the rights of the parties to a contract of sale or a sale. It does not provide that notice must be given of the breach of a warranty that arises independently of a contract of sale between the parties. Such warranties are not imposed by the sales act, but are the product of common-law decisions that have recognized them in a variety of situations. * * *

The notice requirement of section 1769 * * * is not an appropriate one for the court to adopt in actions by injured consumers against manufacturers with whom they have not dealt. (La Hue v. Coca-Cola Bottling, 50 Wash.2d 645, 314 P.2d 421, 422; Chapman v. Brown, D.C., 198 F.Supp. 78, 85, affd. Brown v. Chapman, 9 Cir., 304 F.2d 149.) "As between the immediate parties to the sale [the notice requirement] is a sound commercial rule, designed to protect the seller against unduly delayed claims for damages. As applied to personal injuries, and notice to a remote seller, it becomes a booby-trap for the unwary. The injured consumer is seldom 'steeped in the business practice which justifies the rule,' [James, Product Liability, 34 Texas L.Rev. 44, 192, 197] and at least until he has had legal advice it will not occur to him to give notice to one with whom he has had no dealings." (Prosser, Strict Liability to the Consumer, 69 Yale L.J. 1099, 1130, footnotes omitted.) * * * We conclude, therefore, that even if plaintiff did not give timely notice of breach of warranty to the manufacturer, his cause of action based on the representations contained in the brochure was not barred.

1. In this respect the trial court limited the jury to a consideration of two statements in the manufacturer's brochure. (1) "WHEN SHOPSMITH IS IN HORIZONTAL POSITION—Rugged construction of frame provides rigid support from end to end. Heavy centerless ground steel tubing insures perfect alignment of components." (2) "SHOPSMITH maintains its accuracy because every component has positive locks that hold adjustments through rough or precision work."

Moreover, to impose strict liability on the manufacturer under the circumstances of this case, it was not necessary for plaintiff to establish an express warranty as defined in section 1732 of the Civil Code. A manufacturer is strictly liable in tort when an article he places on the market, knowing that it is to be used without inspection for defects, proves to have a defect that causes injury to a human being. Recognized first in the case of unwholesome food products, such liability has now been extended to a variety of other products that create as great or greater hazards if defective. [Citations of cases involving a grinding wheel, bottles, a vaccine, an insect spray, a surgical pin, a skirt, a tire, a home permanent, a hair dye, and automobiles, including the *Henningsen* decision.]

Although in these cases strict liability has usually been based on the theory of an express or implied warranty running from the manufacturer to the plaintiff, the abandonment of the requirement of a contract between them, the recognition that the liability is not assumed by agreement but imposed by law [citations], and the refusal to permit the manufacturer to define the scope of its own responsibility for defective products [citations] make clear that the liability is not one governed by the law of contract warranties but by the law of strict liability in tort. Accordingly, rules defining and governing warranties that were developed to meet the needs of commercial transactions cannot properly be invoked to govern the manufacturer's liability to those injured by their defective products unless those rules also serve the purposes for which such liability is imposed.

We need not recanvass the reasons for imposing strict liability on the manufacturer. They have been fully articulated in the cases cited above. (See also 2 Harper and James, Torts, §§ 28.15–28.16, pp. 1569–1574; Prosser, Strict Liability to the Consumer, 69 Yale L.J. 1099; Escola v. Coca Cola Bottling Co., 24 Cal.2d 453, 461, 150 P.2d 436, concurring opinion.) The purpose of such liability is to insure that the costs of injuries resulting from defective products are borne by the manufacturers that put such products on the market rather than by the injured persons who are powerless to protect themselves. Sales warranties serve this purpose fitfully at best. (See Prosser, Strict Liability to the Consumer, 69 Yale L.J. 1099, 1124–1134.) In the present case, for example, plaintiff was able to plead and prove an express warranty only because he read and relied on the representations of the Shopsmith's ruggedness contained in the manufacturer's brochure. Implicit in the machine's presence on the market, however, was a representation that it would safely do the jobs for which it was built. Under these circumstances, it should not be controlling whether plaintiff selected the machine because of the statements in the brochure, or because of the machine's own appearance of excellence that belied the defect lurking beneath the surface, or because he merely assumed that it would safely do the jobs it was built to do. It should not be controlling whether the details of the sales from manufacturer to retailer and from retailer to plaintiff's wife were such that one or more of the implied warranties of the sales act arose. (Civ.Code, § 1735.) "The remedies of injured consumers ought not to be made to depend upon the intricacies of the law of sales." (Ketterer v. Armour & Co., D.C., 200 F. 322, 323; Klein v. Duchess Sandwich Co., 14 Cal.2d 272, 282, 93 P.2d 799.) To establish the manufacturer's liability it was sufficient that plaintiff proved that he was injured while using the Shopsmith in a way it was intended to be used as a result of a defect in design and manufacture of which plaintiff was not aware that made the Shopsmith unsafe for its intended use.

* * *

The judgment is affirmed.

NOTE

Two years prior to *Greenman* an important development had begun with the American Law Institute's reconsideration of the rules governing the liability of suppliers of products. This development was summarized by Judge Wisdom in Putnam v. Erie City Mfg. Co., 338 F.2d 911, 918–19 (5th Cir.1964):

> The original Restatement of Torts had no provision for strict liability based on a seller's implied warranty. In April 1961, Tentative Draft No. 6 of the Restatement, Second, recommended adoption of a new section, Section 402A. This section recognized the seller's strict liability but limited liability to claims for "food for human consumption". By April 1962 it had become apparent that "food for human consumption" was too narrow a category. Tentative Draft No. 7 expanded the coverage of the section to include "products intended for intimate bodily use", "whether or not [they] ha[ve] any nutritional value." A comment explained that "intimate bodily use" also included "products intended for external application or contact" where it was "of an intimate character" [such as chewing gum, chewing tobacco, snuff, cigarettes, drugs, clothing, soap, cosmetics, liniments, hair dye, and permanent wave solutions, 338 F.2d at 918–19, n. 16]. In two years even this greatly broadened version was obsolete. In May 1964, the Institute approved the final draft of Section 402A making the rule applicable to all products.

Section 402A was published the next year in volume 2 of the Second Restatement of Torts.

RESTATEMENT (SECOND) OF TORTS (1965)

§ 402A. Special Liability of Seller of Product for Physical Harm to User or Consumer

(1) One who sells any product in a defective condition unreasonably dangerous to the user or consumer or to his property is subject to liability for physical harm thereby caused to the ultimate user or consumer, or to his property, if

(a) the seller is engaged in the business of selling such a product, and

(b) it is expected to and does reach the user or consumer without substantial change in the condition in which it is sold.

(2) The rule stated in Subsection (1) applies although

(a) the seller has exercised all possible care in the preparation and sale of his product, and

(b) the user or consumer has not bought the product from or entered into any contractual relation with the seller.

Caveat:

The Institute expresses no opinion as to whether the rules stated in this Section may not apply

(1) to harm to persons other than users or consumers;

(2) to the seller of a product expected to be processed or otherwise substantially changed before it reaches the user or consumer; or

(3) to the seller of a component part of a product to be assembled.

Comment:

a. This Section states a special rule applicable to sellers of products. The rule is one of strict liability, making the seller subject to liability to the user or consumer even though he has exercised all possible care in the preparation and sale of the product. * * * The rule stated here is not exclusive, and does not preclude liability based upon the alternative ground of negligence of the seller, where such negligence can be proved.

* * *

m. *"Warranty."* The liability stated in this Section does not rest upon negligence. It is strict liability, similar in its nature to that covered by Chapters 20 and 21. The basis of liability is purely one of tort.

A number of courts, seeking a theoretical basis for the liability, have resorted to a "warranty," either running with the goods sold, by analogy to covenants running with the land, or made directly to the consumer without contract. In some instances this theory has proved to be an unfortunate one. Although warranty was in its origin a matter of tort liability, and it is generally agreed that a tort action will still lie for its breach, it has become so identified in practice with a contract of sale between the plaintiff and the defendant that the warranty theory has become something of an obstacle to the recognition of the strict liability where there is no such contract. There is nothing in this Section which would prevent any court from treating the rule stated as a matter of "warranty" to the user or consumer. But if this is done, it should be recognized and understood that the "warranty" is a very different kind of warranty from those usually found in the sale of goods, and that it is not subject to the various contract rules which have grown up to surround such sales.

The rule stated in this Section does not require any reliance on the part of the consumer upon the reputation, skill, or judgment of the seller who is to be held liable, nor any representation or undertaking on the part of that seller. The seller is strictly liable although, as is frequently the case, the consumer does not even know who he is at the time of consumption. The rule stated in this Section is not governed by the provisions of the Uniform Sales Act, or those of the Uniform Commercial Code, as to warranties; and it is not affected by limitations on the scope and content of warranties, or by limitation to "buyer" and "seller" in those statutes. Nor is the consumer required to give notice to the seller of his injury within a reasonable time after it occurs, as is provided by the Uniform Act. The consumer's cause of action does not depend upon the validity of his contract with the person from whom he acquires the product, and it is not affected by any disclaimer or other agreement, whether it be between the seller and his immediate buyer, or attached to and accompanying the product into the consumer's hands. In short, "warranty" must be given a new and different meaning if it is used in connection with this Section. It is much simpler to regard the liability here stated as merely one of strict liability in tort.

NOTES

1. "Although the writer was perhaps the first to voice it, the suggestion was sufficiently obvious that all of the trouble lay with the one word 'warranty,' which had been from the outset only a rather transparent device to accomplish the desired result of strict liability. No one disputed that the 'warranty' was a matter of strict liability. No one denied that where there was no privity, liability to the consumer could not sound in contract and must be a matter of tort. Why not, then, talk of the strict liability in tort, a thing familiar enough in the law of animals, abnormally dangerous activities, nuisance, workmen's compensation, libel, misrepresentation, and respondeat superior, and discard the word 'warranty' with all its contract implications?" Prosser, The Fall of the Citadel (Strict Liability to the Consumer), 50 Minn.L.Rev. 791, 802 (1966).

2. "The modern synthesis of the theory of enterprise liability was achieved during the period 1960–64. The synthesis represents the convergence of once independent streams of contracts and torts scholarship. Contracts scholarship established that warranty law was insufficient to protect relatively powerless consumers from the efforts of powerful manufacturers to avoid liability for product-related injuries. Torts scholarship established that society would benefit from internalizing injury costs to manufacturing enterprises to encourage such enterprises either to prevent injuries or to insure for them. The convergence of these streams of thought constitutes the mature theory of enterprise liability that dominates modern tort law today." Priest, The Invention of Enterprise Liability: A Critical History of the Intellectual Foundations of Modern Tort Law, 14 J.Leg.Stud. 461, 505 (1985).

PHIPPS v. GENERAL MOTORS CORP.

Court of Appeals of Maryland, 1976.
278 Md. 337, 363 A.2d 955.

ELDRIDGE, JUDGE.

[Plaintiff was injured while driving a car manufactured by the defendant when without warning the accelerator suddenly stuck. The car accelerated out of control and crashed into a tree. Plaintiff brought suit against General Motors in federal district court on grounds of negligence, warranty and strict liability in tort. G.M. moved to dismiss the strict tort count, arguing that the doctrine had not been adopted by the Maryland courts. The federal court certified this question to the Maryland Court of Appeals.]

The theory of strict liability is set forth in the Restatement (Second) of Torts § 402A (1965) * * *.

* * *

Various justifications for imposing strict liability in tort on manufacturers have been advanced by the courts. It has been said that the cost of injuries caused by defective products should in equity be "borne by the manufacturers that put such products on the market rather than by the injured persons who are powerless to protect themselves" and that "warranties serve this purpose fitfully at best." Greenman v. Yuba Power Products, Inc., supra, 377 P.2d at 901. It has also been suggested that imposing strict liability on manufacturers for defective products is equitable because it shifts the risk of loss to those better able financially to bear the loss. Seely v. White Motor Company, 63 Cal.2d 9, 45 Cal.Rptr. 17, 403 P.2d 145, 151 (1965). Another reason advanced is that a consumer relies upon the seller in expecting that a product is safe for the uses for which it has been marketed, and that this expectation is better fulfilled by the theory of strict liability than traditional negligence or warranty theories. Markle v. Mulholland's, Inc., 265 Or. 259, 509 P.2d 529, 532–534 (1973). And still another reason advanced is that the requirement of proof of a defect rendering a product unreasonably dangerous is a sufficient showing of fault on the part of the seller to impose liability without placing an often impossible burden on the plaintiff of proving specific acts of negligence. McCormack v. Hankscraft Company, 278 Minn. 322, 154 N.W.2d 488, 500 (1967); Dippel v. Sciano, 37 Wis.2d 443, 155 N.W.2d 55, 63 (1967).[3]

The essential elements of an action in strict liability are set forth in § 402A. For recovery, it must be established that (1) the product was in a defective condition at the time that it left the possession or control of the seller, (2) that it was unreasonably dangerous to the user or consumer, (3) that the defect was a cause of the injuries, and (4) that

3. For a discussion of these reasons see Calabresi, Some Thoughts on Risk Distribution and the Law of Torts, 70 Yale L.J. 499 (1961); Keeton, Products Liability—Liability Without Fault and the Requirement of a Defect, 41 Tex.L.Rev. 855 (1963); Shapo, A Representational Theory of Consumer Protection: Doctrine, Function, and Legal Liability for Product Disappointment, 60 Va.L.Rev. 1109 (1974).

the product was expected to and did reach the consumer without substantial change in its condition. However, in an action founded on strict liability in tort, as opposed to a traditional negligence action, the plaintiff need not prove any specific act of negligence on the part of the seller. The relevant inquiry in a strict liability action focuses not on the conduct of the manufacturer but rather on the product itself. See Weinstein, Twerski, Piehler, Donaher, Product Liability: An Interaction of Law and Technology, 12 Duquesne L.Rev. 425, 429 (1974). Thus the standard to be applied in determining whether a product is defective becomes critical.

* * *

In those cases where the defect is a result of an error in the manufacturing process, that is where the product is in a condition not intended by the seller, there is less difficulty in applying the defectiveness test of § 402A. See Frumer and Friedman, Products Liability § 16A[4] at pp. 3–318–3–320 (1976). Where, however, the alleged defect is the result of the design process so that the product causing injury was in a condition intended by the manufacturer, the test has proved more difficult to apply. This difficulty has caused some courts and commentators to suggest that the theory of strict liability in tort is not really applicable in cases involving design defects as opposed to construction or manufacturing defects but rather that, analytically, traditional negligence standards still apply. See Dorsey v. Yoder Company, 331 F.Supp. 753, 759–760 (E.D.Pa.1971), aff'd 474 F.2d 1339 (3d Cir. 1973); Balido v. Improved Machinery, Inc., 29 Cal.App.3d 633, 105 Cal. Rptr. 890, 895 (1973); Wade, On the Nature of Strict Tort Liability for Products, 44 Miss.L.J. 825, 836–838 (1973). The reasoning of these authorities is that in a design defect case the standard of defectiveness under § 402A, involving as it does the element of unreasonable danger, still requires a weighing of the utility of risk inherent in the design against the magnitude of the risk. Cf. Volkswagen of America v. Young, 272 Md. 201, 321 A.2d 737 (1974). However, there are those kinds of conditions which, whether caused by design or manufacture, can never be said to involve a reasonable risk. For example, the steering mechanism of a new automobile should not cause the car to swerve off the road, Henningsen v. Bloomfield Motors, Inc., supra; the drive shaft of a new automobile should not separate from the vehicle when it is driven in a normal manner, Elmore v. American Motors Corporation, 70 Cal.2d 578, 75 Cal.Rptr. 652, 451 P.2d 84, 33 A.L.R.3d 406 (1969); the brakes of a new automobile should not suddenly fail, Sharp v. Chrysler Corporation, 432 S.W.2d 131 (Tex.Civ.App.1968); and the accelerator of a new automobile should not stick without warning, causing the vehicle suddenly to accelerate. Conditions like these, even if resulting from the design of the products, are defective and unreasonably dangerous without the necessity of weighing and balancing the various factors involved.

Under § 402A, various defenses are still available to the seller in an action based on strict liability in tort. These defenses are set forth and explained in the official comments following § 402A. For example, the seller is not liable where injury results from abnormal handling or use of the product (Comment h), where mishandling or alteration after delivery of the product renders it unsafe (Comment g), or if warnings or instructions supplied with the product are disregarded by the consumer where, if used in accordance with these warnings, the product would be safe (Comment j). Additionally, where the plaintiff unreasonably proceeds to use a product despite a known risk or danger, the defense of assumption of the risk is still available (Comment n). As to defenses in strict liability actions generally, see Noel, Defective Products: Abnormal Use, Contributory Negligence, and Assumption of Risk, 25 Vand.L. Rev. 93 (1972).

This Court has in prior cases, where the question was raised, declined to adopt the strict liability principles of § 402A, finding that under the facts of those cases § 402A was not applicable and would have afforded no additional basis of liability. * * *

* * *

General Motors argues that we should not adopt the doctrine of strict liability for several reasons. It contends that the warranty provisions of the Maryland Uniform Commercial Code and the doctrine of strict liability in tort are substantially the same in protecting the interests of both consumers and sellers, and thus, in its view, there is no need to adopt the theory of strict liability. General Motors further contends that, even if we were to conclude that the differences between the two theories of liability were significant enough to adopt § 402A of the Restatement, the Legislature in enacting the warranty provisions of the Uniform Commercial Code has "preempted the field of products liability law." Finally, General Motors claims that the adoption of strict liability would substantially alter the rights of consumers and sellers as presently defined by the law of negligence and contract, and that the policy reasons advanced by the courts for altering those traditional rights are more properly a matter of legislative rather than judicial determination.

We do not agree with any of General Motors' contentions. With respect to the differences between strict liability in tort and warranty actions, it is true that the requirement of privity, once an obstacle to recovery under a contract action, and a major reason for the adoption of § 402A of the Restatement (Second), has been eliminated by the General Assembly of Maryland in actions where personal injuries result from a breach of warranty. Sections 2–318 and 2–314 of the Maryland Uniform Commercial Code. See Frericks v. General Motors Corp., Md., 363 A.2d 460 (1976). But there still remain various other requirements and limitations imposed by contract law which may be encountered when pursuing an action for breach of warranty but not when seeking damages for injury caused by a defective product under the theory of strict liability in tort.

One of the more significant differences between the two theories is the right of the seller to disclaim or limit remedies for breach of warranty. Although the Maryland Legislature has eliminated the right of sellers to disclaim or limit warranties arising from the sale of *consumer* goods, §§ 2–316.1, 2–719(3) of the Maryland Uniform Commercial Code, there is no similar limitation on the right to exclude warranties where the goods involved are not consumer goods as defined in § 9–109 [see § 2–103(3)]. Under § 402A of the Restatement, a limitation or exclusion of warranties is irrelevant to the question of the seller's liability for injury caused by defective goods regardless of the classification of the goods (Comment m). The notice requirement of § 2–607 of the Uniform Commercial Code may also prove to be an obstacle to recovery. Although we have recently held that a third party beneficiary of a seller's warranties is not required to give notice of breach as a precondition to maintaining a breach of warranty action, Frericks v. General Motors, supra, Md., at ___, an actual buyer is still required by § 2–607(3) to give notice or be barred from any recovery for breach of warranty. There is no similar notice requirement for bringing an action based on strict liability in tort. Also, an action for breach of warranty is governed by the limitations period contained in § 2–725 of the Uniform Commercial Code, which provides that an action must be brought within four years of the time it accrues. A cause of action in a warranty case accrues "when tender of delivery is made." An action under the theory of strict liability in tort, however, would be governed by the general tort limitations period, Maryland Code (1974), § 5–101 of the Courts and Judicial Proceedings Article, which is three years but may begin to run at a later time. These are examples of significant differences between actions based upon contract and strict liability in tort.

Additionally, we cannot agree with General Motors that the Legislature has preempted the field of product liability law, precluding our adoption of Restatement § 402A. The only authority cited by General Motors in support of this contention is the concurring opinion in Markle v. Mulholland's, Inc., supra, 509 P.2d at 536–539. As the majority in that case noted in rejecting a similar contention and adopting strict liability, there is no indication that the Legislature, in enacting the Uniform Commercial Code, intended to prevent the further development of product liability law by the courts. In the absence of any expression of intent by the Legislature to limit the remedies available to those injured by defective goods exclusively to those provided by the Maryland Uniform Commercial Code, we believe that General Motors' preemption contention is without merit.

Finally, we disagree with General Motors' argument that adoption of strict liability would result in such a radical change of the rights of sellers and consumers that the matter should be left to the Legislature. As we have previously discussed, the major distinction between an action in strict liability in tort and one founded on traditional negligence theory relates to the proof which must be presented by the plaintiff. Although the plaintiff need not prove any specific act of negligence on the part of the seller, as in other product liability cases, proof of a defect existing in the product at the time it leaves the seller's control must still be presented. As one commentator has observed, the doctrine of strict liability is really but another form of negligence per se, in that it is a judicial determination that placing a defective product on the market which is unreasonably dangerous to a user or consumer is itself a negligent act sufficient to impose liability on the seller (Wade, Strict Tort Liability of Manufacturers, 19 Sw.L.J. 5, 14 (1965)):

> "In essence, strict liability in this sense is not different from negligence per se. Selling a dangerously unsafe product is the equivalent of negligence regardless of the defendant's conduct in letting it become unsafe. * * * Thus, a court which appears to be taking the radical step of changing from negligence to strict liability for products is really doing nothing more than adopting a rule that selling a dangerously unsafe chattel is negligence within itself."

Thus, the theory of strict liability is not a radical departure from traditional tort concepts. Despite the use of the term "strict liability" the seller is not an insurer, as absolute liability is not imposed on the seller for any injury resulting from the use of his product. Dippel v. Sciano, supra, 155 N.W.2d at 63; Wade, supra, 19 Sw.L.J. at 13. Proof of a defect in the product at the time it leaves the control of the seller implies fault on the part of the seller sufficient to justify imposing liability for injuries caused by the product. Where the seller supplies a defective and unreasonably dangerous product, the seller or someone employed by him has been at fault in designing or constructing the product.

Almost all of the courts of our sister states have adopted the strict liability principles set forth in § 402A of the Restatement (Second) of Torts. Several reasons for adopting strict liability are summarized in Comment c to § 402A as follows:

> "* * * the justification for the strict liability has been said to be that the seller, by marketing his product for use and consumption, has undertaken and assumed a special responsibility toward any member of the consuming public who may be injured by it; that the public has the right to and does expect, in the case of products which it needs and for which it is forced to rely upon the seller, that reputable sellers will stand behind their goods; that public policy demands that the burden of accidental injuries caused by products intended for consumption be placed upon those who market them, and be treated as a cost of production against which liability insurance can be obtained; and that the consumer of such products is entitled to the maximum of protection at the hands of someone, and the proper persons to afford it are those who market the products."

We find the above reasons persuasive. In our view, there is no reason why a party injured by a defective and unreasonably dangerous product, which when placed on the market is impliedly represented as safe, should bear the loss of that injury when the seller of that product is in a better position to take precautions and protect against the defect. Yet this may be the result where injured parties are forced to comply with the proof requirements of negligence actions or are confronted with the procedural requirements and limitations of warranty actions. Therefore, we adopt the theory of strict liability as expressed in § 402A of the Restatement (Second) of Torts.

For these reasons, we conclude that the third and sixth counts of the complaint state a cause of action under Maryland law. The certified question is answered "Yes."

* * *

NOTES

1. By the time *Phipps* was decided in 1976, the doctrine of strict manufacturer liability in tort had already been adopted by a substantial majority of American jurisdictions. Indeed, the general adoption of the doctrine in this country from 1963 to the mid-1970s is one of the most rapid and dramatic doctrinal developments ever to occur in the law of torts. As of 1988, all states except Delaware, Massachusetts, Michigan, North Carolina, Virginia and the District of Columbia had adopted strict products liability in tort. The most recent adoption was Wyoming, in Ogle v. Caterpillar Tractor Co., 716 P.2d 334 (Wyo.1986). For citations to adopting cases and statutes, see 2 American Law of Products Liability §§ 16:8–16:27 (3d ed. 1987); Annot., 13 A.L.R.3d 1057, § 4 (1967); Prod.Liab.Rep. (CCH) ¶¶ 4060–70; West v. Caterpillar Tractor Co., Inc., 336 So.2d 80, 87 n. 1 (Fla.1976).

2. From the start, however, critics complained that (1) the American Law Institute had improperly "restated" a *new* rule of tort law, and (2) the new tort doctrine blatantly intruded into an area that was at the time being expressly addressed by the state legislatures through the warranty provisions of the Uniform Commercial Code. See, e.g., Titus, Restatement (Second) of Torts Section 402A and The Uniform Commercial Code, 22 Stan.L.Rev. 713 (1970).

3. **Comparison with Other Theories of Liability.** Is strict liability in tort in fact any different from warranty, or even from negligence? Consider the answer given by the court in Chestnut v. Ford Motor Co., 445 F.2d 967, 968 (4th Cir.1971): "The standard of safety of goods imposed on the seller or manufacturer of a product is essentially the same whether the theory of liability is labeled warranty or negligence or strict tort liability: the product must not be unreasonably dangerous at the time that it leaves the defendant's possession * * *." Many other courts have agreed. Do you? Has all of the effort to distinguish between the different doctrines been nothing but a tempest in a teapot?

A. **Warranty.** It is often said that strict liability in tort "is essentially the liability of implied warranty divested of the contract doctrines of privity, disclaimer, and notice." E.g., Nave v. Rainbo Tire Service, Inc., 123 Ill.App.3d 585, 592–93, 78 Ill.Dec. 501, 506, 462 N.E.2d 620, 625 (1984). "To recover on either theory—implied warranty or strict liability—the plaintiff in a products liability case must satisfy three basics from an evidentiary standpoint: (1) the existence of a defect, (2) the attribution of the defect to the seller, and (3) a causal relation between the defect and the injury." Virgil v. "Kash N' Karry" Service Corp., 61 Md.App. 23, 484 A.2d 652, 656 (1984).

Some courts have thus held that conflicting jury verdicts on the two theories are irreconcilable and, hence, the basis for reversal. E.g., Gumbs v. International Harvester, Inc., 718 F.2d 88 (3d Cir.1983). Contra Malawy v. Richards Mfg. Co., 150 Ill.App.3d 549, 103 Ill.Dec. 355, 501 N.E.2d 376 (1986) (distinguishing the two theories). Similarly, if the two claims are redundant, a court may not be in error for refusing to instruct on both doctrines. See, e.g., Goblirsch v. Western Land Roller Co., 310 Minn. 471, 246 N.W.2d 687, 690 (1976).

Do you agree with these cases? If so, is the case for preemption by the U.C.C. strengthened?

Which system of strict liability is better for dealing with the product accident problem, tort or warranty? Consider the remarks of a teacher of commercial law, Speidel, The Virginia "Anti-Privity" Statute: Strict Products Liability Under The Uniform Commercial Code, 51 Va.L.Rev. 804, 851 (1965):

> On balance, nagging doubts about the propriety of a judicial imposition of strict products liability, recurring attacks upon the bases of liability itself, the complexity of the underlying problems of cost allocation among the various enterprises and individuals involved, and a suspicion that in a zealous attempt to protect the consumer interest the courts may have created more problems than they can solve all dictate against the type of "unrealistic absolutism" displayed in Section 402A of the *Restatement of Torts, Second.* The value of some contractual risk allocation is that the alternatives for private decision-making are both strengthened and expanded under controlled conditions. The small enterprise which does not conform to the paradigm upon which strict liability is based may attempt to shift its risk to the consumer rather than simply absorb the loss or go out of business. The informed consumer can choose to accept the risk or not. Whatever the outcome of this choice, the result is more attuned to the needs and capabilities of the particular parties. Until an ultimate legislative solution to the problem is formulated and enacted into law, the treacherous uncertainties of strict products liability imposed by courts can be reduced by at least one firm anchor to the traditional values of freedom of contract.

Compare the thoughts of a teacher of tort law, Franklin, When Worlds Collide: Liability Theories and Disclaimers in Defective-Product Cases, 18 Stan.L.Rev. 974, 1019–20 (1966):

> [O]ne is left with regret that the Code, devoted so extensively to dealings within the business community, decided to try its hand at the products liability problem. That it did so is clear. That it should have is much less clear. The considerations involved in the products cases are so different from traditional commercial dealings that the Code's insistence on covering all of an abstract "commercial" area may unfortunately lead to similar treatment for dissimilar problems.

Most courts have been little concerned with the argument that strict tort might impermissibly invade a field preempted by the U.C.C. The most notable exception is the thorough analysis in Cline v. Prowler Indus. of Maryland, Inc., 418 A.2d 968, 980 (Del.1980) ("the General Assembly did not intend to permit the adoption of a competing theory of liability in cases involving the sales of goods and, thus, preempted the field"). The last word in a decade-long debate on the issue between Professor Dickerson and Dean Wade was had by the latter in Wade, Tort Liability for Products Causing Physical Injury and Article 2 of the U.C.C., 48 Mo.L.Rev. 1 (1983).

B. **Negligence.** Are you at all uncomfortable with the assertion that the basis of liability in strict tort is essentially the same as that in negligence? Why or why not? While most courts have valiantly attempted over the years to distinguish between negligence and strict liability in tort, many have recognized their similarity, if not identity, in design and perhaps warnings cases. See, e.g., Jones v. Hutchinson Mfg., Inc., 502 S.W.2d 66, 69–70 (Ky.1973) (In a design case "the distinction between the so-called strict liability principle and negligence is of no practical significance so far as the standard of conduct required of the defendant is concerned. In either event the standard required is reasonable care."); Prentis v. Yale Mfg. Co., 421 Mich. 670, 365 N.W.2d 176 (1984) (ditto: implied warranty). See generally Powers, The Persistence of Fault in Products Liability, 61 Tex.L.Rev. 777, 815 (1983) ("fault is analytically implicit in current products liability law and cannot be purged"); Birnbaum, Unmasking the Test for Design Defect: From Negligence [to Warranty] to Strict Liability to Negligence, 33 Vand.L.Rev. 593, 649 (1980) ("Calling a theory of liability based on a duty of due care and a standard of reasonable conduct anything other than negligence is pure sophistry.").

The similarity of strict tort and negligence in certain contexts has given rise to a thorny problem involving inconsistent jury verdicts. Suppose a case is submitted to the jury on both negligence and strict liability in tort and the jury decides for the plaintiff on negligence but for the defendant on strict liability. What is the problem? What should be done? See Greiten v. LaDow, 70 Wis.2d 589, 603, 235 N.W.2d 677, 685–86 (1975) (concurring opinion of Hefferson, J., subsequently elevated to "majority" status) ("there may be recovery for the negligent design of a product even though it is not unreasonably dangerous in the 402A sense"). Accord, Hasson v. Ford Motor Co., 19 Cal.3d 530, 138 Cal. Rptr. 705, 564 P.2d 857 (1977). Fortunately, this kind of nonsense is rejected by most courts. Compare Halvorson v. American Hoist & Derrick Co., 307 Minn. 48, 240 N.W.2d 303, 307 (1976) ("If a product is not * * * defective * * *, it is not negligence to manufacture it that way."). See also Sprankle v. Bower Ammonia & Chemical Co., 824 F.2d 409, 413 (5th Cir.1987) (any "theoretical error" in failing to instruct jury on negligent failure to warn theory was harmless in view of jury's rejection of strict tort failure to warn theory); Garrett v. Hamilton Standard Controls, Inc., 850 F.2d 253, 257 (5th Cir. 1988).

Why *might* a jury find a manufacturer negligent for selling a product *not* in a "defective condition unreasonably dangerous" to users? Because of a feeling that even an inadequately designed product, or one carrying inadequate warnings, cannot fairly be considered "defective" in the ordinary sense of the word? Cf. Rinker v. Ford Motor Co., 567 S.W.2d 655, 659–60 (Mo.Ct.App.1978). Because the phrase "unreasonably dangerous" may sound to the jury "as if the requisite proof for a product defect is some form of 'extraordinary' danger."? Twerski, From Defect to Cause to Comparative Fault—Rethinking Some Product Liability Concepts, 60 Marq.L.Rev. 297, 334 (1977), relied upon in Hansen v. Cessna Aircraft Co., 578 F.2d 679 (7th Cir.1978).

One solution to all this would be to require the plaintiff to elect a single theory upon which to submit the case to the jury. Is this a good idea? Most courts do not require the plaintiff to elect between negligence and strict tort.

Hansen v. Cessna Aircraft Co., supra; Howes v. Deere & Co., 71 Wis.2d 268, 238 N.W.2d 76 (1976). Compare comment *a* to § 402A, supra. A few courts, on the other hand, withdraw the negligence count from the jury on grounds that it would be "superfluous and would tend to confuse the jurors" if included with a count for strict liability in tort. Mather v. Caterpillar Tractor Corp., 23 Ariz. App. 409, 533 P.2d 717, 719 (Ct.App.1975). The cases are collected in Annot., 52 A.L.R.3d 101 (1973). See generally Slattery, Terschan & Griffin, Product Liability Verdict Formulation in Wisconsin, 61 Marq.L.Rev. 381 (1978).

The Model Uniform Product Liability Law provides in § 102(D) for a single "product liability claim" in lieu of claims in negligence, warranty and strict tort.

C. **Abnormally dangerous activities.** Distinguish the doctrine of strict tort liability for selling defective products (Restatement, Second, Torts § 402A) from the doctrine of strict tort liability for conducting abnormally dangerous activities (§§ 519–24A). Section 520 provides as follows:

> **§ 520. Abnormally Dangerous Activities**
>
> In determining whether an activity is abnormally dangerous, the following factors are to be considered:
>
> (a) existence of a high degree of risk of some harm to the person, land or chattels of others;
>
> (b) likelihood that the harm that results from it will be great;
>
> (c) inability to eliminate the risk by the exercise of reasonable care;
>
> (d) extent to which the activity is not a matter of common usage;
>
> (e) inappropriateness of the activity to the place where it is carried on; and
>
> (f) extent to which its value to the community is outweighed by its dangerous attributes.

Comment *f* states in part: "The essential question is whether the risk created is so unusual, either because of its magnitude or because of the circumstances surrounding it, as to justify the imposition of strict liability for the harm that results from it, even though it is carried on with all reasonable care. In other words, are its dangers and inappropriateness for the locality so great that, despite any usefulness it may have for the community, it should be required as a matter of law to pay for any harm it causes, without the need of a finding of negligence."

The courts have steadfastly kept these two theories of strict tort liability separate and distinct. See Cavan v. General Motors Corp., 280 Or. 455, 571 P.2d 1249, 1252 (1977) ("The fact that a product may create an 'ultrahazardous' condition by virtue of defective design or manufacture is thus of no moment under our present law."); Morningstar v. Black and Decker Mfg. Co., 162 W.Va. 857, 253 S.E.2d 666 (1979); Sprankle v. Bower Ammonia & Chemical Co., 824 F.2d 409 (5th Cir.1987). Why do you suppose this is so? Shouldn't "strict liability in tort," like negligence, be a single theory? Are the policies underlying the two strict tort doctrines the same? See generally Montgomery & Owen, Reflections on the Theory and Administration of Strict Tort Liability for Defective Products, 27 S.C.L.Rev. 803, 825–28 (1976).

D. **Strategy.** Many plaintiffs' lawyers generally plead and try a case on *all* theories of liability that may be available—typically negligence, breach of implied warranty of merchantability and strict liability in tort—in order to avoid the risk of omitting the one theory that the court or jury may find appropriate. Other lawyers prefer pleading and trying a case on a single theory—such as negligence or strict liability in tort—in order to keep the issues simpler for a jury which may be confused by the multiple theory approach. Indeed, there is a risk under the "shotgun" approach that the jury will mistakenly believe that the plaintiff can recover only if he makes his case on *each* of his separate claims.

Assuming that a plaintiff's lawyer is compelled to take his case to the jury on a single claim, or for simplicity so chooses, will he always select a strict liability theory over negligence? Consider the observations of a leading plaintiffs' advocate, Rheingold, The Expanding Liability of the Product Supplier: A Primer, 2 Hofstra L.Rev. 521, 531–32 (1974):

> *What Difference Does Strict Liability Really Make to the Practitioner?*
>
> The advent of strict liability a decade ago was then hailed and still tends to be hailed today as a major change in product liability law. Without question, the "enterprise system" philosophy behind it is a major step forward in the social consciousness of the courts. What strict liability has done in fact for the consumer-plaintiff and his lawyer is another question. In my view, it has accomplished little for the consumer and it has had little impact upon practice.
>
> More plaintiffs would prefer to present their respective cases to a jury on a negligence, rather than on a strict liability, basis. In McLuenesque terms negligence is "hot" and strict liability is "cold." It is easier to prevail by showing that the defendant did something wrong than that there is something technically defective about the product. It is easier to win (and collect substantial damages) by showing that a drug company concealed information about side effects than to show that in fact there was no warning on the labeling about the risks.
>
> If strict liability makes a difference it is in the "impure" defect case. Here it makes counsel's life much easier if he can have the judge instruct the jury that the mere presence of glass in a can of spinach creates liability, than if he has to prove how the defendant carelessly put it in or failed to detect it. But those cases had traditionally been won by plaintiffs—in the rare instance when they weren't settled.
>
> It is sometimes argued that the plaintiff in every type of strict liability case gains a direct benefit by having the defendant barred from proving due care. The trouble with this argument is that the defendant, directly or indirectly, does get this sort of defense before the jury. Not only are many such defenses allowed * * * but also § 402A does not really divorce itself from "negligence talk." * * *

4. **Privity; Bystanders.** One key reason for the development of strict liability in tort was the inability of warranty law to deal adequately with the product accident problem for the person not in privity of contract with the seller of a defective product.

While the existence of any contractual relationship between the parties is irrelevant to liability under subsection (2)(b) of § 402A, and while "users" and "consumers" are defined broadly in comment *l*, the question of whether liability under § 402A extends to "bystanders" (persons who are *not* "users" or "consumers") is expressly left open in caveat (1). See comment *o*. Nevertheless, the courts have almost unanimously allowed recovery for bystanders where injury to them is reasonably foreseeable, reasoning that the policies arguing for user or consumer recovery in strict tort generally apply with equal force to the innocent bystander. Indeed, since the bystander has no choice in the selection of the product (and hence has no control over whether safety or price should be preferred in choosing between products), nor has any control over the product's inspection (no ability to "kick the tires") nor the manner of its use, it has been argued that he deserves if anything even greater protection than the user himself. See Elmore v. American Motors Corp., 70 Cal.2d 578, 75 Cal.Rptr. 652, 451 P.2d 84 (1969). Nor does the extension of strict tort liability to bystanders place any additional burden upon the manufacturer "for the reason that the same precautions required to protect the buyer or user would generally do the same for the bystander." Giberson v. Ford Motor Co., 504 S.W.2d 8 (Mo.1974) (court permitted strict tort suit by occupants of car involved in pile-up that occurred when engine in police car manufactured by defendant exploded in traffic, creating dense smoke that obscured vision). "Innocent victims should not be required to bear the burden of injuries caused by defective products." Osborne v. International Harvester Co., 69 Or.App. 629, 688 P.2d 390, 397 (1984) (plaintiff's car struck by defective truck). But the *Palsgraf* doctrine lives on, and the risk to the plaintiff must be reasonably foreseeable. See Kirk v. Michael Reese Hosp. & Med. Center, 117 Ill.2d 507, 111 Ill.Dec. 944, 513 N.E.2d 387, 394 (1987) (passenger injured when driver, who consumed alcohol after taking prescription drugs, lost control of car; *held,* on inadequate warnings claim, that manufacturers "[could not] have reasonably foreseen that their drugs would be dispensed without warnings by the physicians, that the patient would be discharged from the hospital, drink alcohol, drive a car, lose control of his car, hit a tree, and injure the passenger [all] on the same day").

On the extension of strict tort protection to bystanders, see generally Note, 38 U.Chi.L.Rev. 625 (1971); Annot., 33 A.L.R.3d 415 (1970). One particularly well reasoned decision is Howes v. Hansen, 56 Wis.2d 247, 201 N.W.2d 825 (1972).

5. **Disclaimers.** Another key aspect of warranty law that led to the development of strict liability in tort was the seller's ability to relieve himself of responsibility by a disclaimer. The effect of disclaimers in strict tort cases will be examined after their effect under the law of negligence is first considered.

A. **Negligence.** The rule applied in most negligence cases is quite simple: A disclaimer is effective only if it clearly and unequivocally relieves the seller of responsibility for harm caused by his negligence. To most courts this has meant that the word "negligence" or "fault" must appear in the disclaimer provision. See, e.g., Willard Van Dyke Productions, Inc. v. Eastman Kodak Co., 12 N.Y.2d 301, 239 N.Y.S.2d 337, 189 N.E.2d 693 (1963), and a case against the same defendant on nearly identical facts, where the disclaimer redrafted in an attempt to comply with *Willard's* requirements was found still inadequate, Posttape Assoc. v. Eastman Kodak Co., 387 F.Supp. 184 (E.D.Pa.1974), rev'd on other grounds 537 F.2d 751 (3d Cir.1976).

The negligence disclaimer cases have usually involved commercial parties suffering commercial losses. Very few of the cases have involved the garden variety consumer action against a manufacturer for injuries caused by a defective product. Even if a disclaimer is effective between the parties, it will not bar a negligence action by an injured third party against the manufacturer or other seller. Blanchard v. Monical Mach. Co., 84 Mich.App. 279, 269 N.W.2d 564 (1978) ("as is" sale of used machine from defendant to plaintiff's employer). Several courts have held that a disclaimer is void if the defendant's negligence resulted in a violation of a duty imposed by statute for the benefit of the public. See, e.g., Dessert Seed Co. v. Drew Farmers Supply, Inc., 248 Ark. 858, 454 S.W.2d 307, 311 (1970). As under warranty principles, the plaintiff must be made aware of the disclaimer at the time of sale, and it will be ineffective if it is buried in fine print in an owner's manual not given to plaintiff until after sale. See Omni Flying Club, Inc. v. Cessna Aircraft Co., 366 Mass. 154, 315 N.E.2d 885 (1974).

B. **Strict tort.** Even simpler than the negligence rule is the one applied to strict liability in tort: Manufacturers and other sellers of new products may not disclaim strict tort liability for personal injuries caused by defects in their products. See Restatement (2d) of Torts § 402A, comment *m:* "The consumer's cause of action * * * is not affected by any disclaimer * * *." Most of the difficult problems with disclaimers in strict tort involve their effectiveness in commercial contexts involving economic losses. On this point, see Chapter 6, § 3, below, and McNichols, Who Says that Strict Tort Disclaimers Can Never Be Effective? The Courts Cannot Agree, 28 Okla.L.Rev. 494 (1975); Note, 10 Tulsa L.J. 612 (1975).

6. **Variations on a Common Theme.** Most courts, like the Maryland court in *Phipps,* have embraced the theory of strict liability in tort by "adopting" § 402A. A few states have been more independent and, while adhering generally to the principles of § 402A and the surrounding jurisprudence, have developed their own strict tort doctrines under other names. One such state is Oklahoma where, in Kirkland v. General Motors Corp., 521 P.2d 1353 (Okl. 1974), the state supreme court adopted an extensively described theory of strict liability in tort, called "Manufacturers' Products Liability." See generally McNichols, The Kirkland v. General Motors Manufacturers' Products Liability Doctrine—What's In a Name?, 27 Okla.L.Rev. 347 (1974). See also Casrell v. Altec Indus., Inc., 335 So.2d 128 (Ala.1976), and Atkins v. American Motors Corp., 335 So.2d 134 (Ala.1976) ("extended manufacturer's liability," likened to negligence per se).

The California Supreme Court, which gave birth to strict liability in tort in *Greenman* in 1963, seemed to adopt § 402A in Pike v. Hough, 2 Cal.3d 465, 85 Cal.Rptr. 629, 467 P.2d 229 (1970), but then repudiated the Restatement formulation of the rule and returned to the *Greenman* approach in Cronin v. J.B.E. Olson Corp., 8 Cal.3d 121, 104 Cal.Rptr. 433, 501 P.2d 1153 (1972). This development is discussed further in Section 1 of Chapter 3 below.

Several states have adopted the doctrine by statute. The statutes in Maine, 14 Me.Rev.Stat.Ann. § 221, Oregon, 1979 Or.Laws Ch. 866, and South Carolina, S.C.Code Ann. §§ 15–73–10 to –30, are nearly verbatim restatements of § 402A. Statutes in Arkansas, Ark.Stat.Ann. § 85–2–318.2 to .3, Georgia, Ga.Code Ann. § 105–106 (prescribing action in tort for injuries from unmerchantable products), and Indiana, Ind.Code §§ 33–1–1.5–1 et seq., all provide variations on the same theme.

7. The literature is replete with discussions of the development and nature of strict liability in tort. Among the classic articles are two by Prosser, The Assault Upon the Citadel (Strict Liability to the Consumer), 69 Yale L.J. 1099 (1960), and The Fall of the Citadel (Strict Liability to the Consumer), 50 Minn.L.Rev. 791 (1966). For Judge Traynor's reflections on the topic, see The

Ways and Meanings of Defective Products and Strict Liability, 32 Tenn.L.Rev. 363 (1965). Perhaps the "modern" classic is Dean Wade's article, On the Nature of Strict Tort Liability for Products, 44 Miss.L.J. 825 (1973). See also Priest, The Invention of Enterprise Liability: A Critical History of the Intellectual Foundations of Modern Tort Law, 14 J.Leg.Stud. 461 (1985); Montgomery & Owen, Reflections on the Theory and Administration of Strict Tort Liability for Defective Products, 27 S.C.L.Rev. 803, 807–08 (citing articles).

POLICY CONSIDERATIONS

An understanding of the strengths and weaknesses of the common arguments for strict manufacturer liability is necessary to a reasoned consideration of whether the strict liability principles should be applied in particular contexts. Indeed, the proper resolution of many of the complex issues of modern products liability law depends upon a clear articulation and evaluation of the competing social policies involved. Space constraints preclude consideration here of the different models of products liability theory developed in recent years that purport to optimize "justice," "fairness" or economic efficiency. Yet the lawyer should bear in mind that the principles of products liability law are rooted in social policy and, ultimately, in political theory.

1. The conventional policy arguments advanced by courts and commentators in the 1960s and 1970s for strict manufacturer liability are summarized in Montgomery & Owen, Reflections on the Theory and Administration of Strict Tort Liability for Defective Products, 27 S.C.L.Rev. 803, 809–10 (1976):

> (1) Manufacturers convey to the public a general sense of product quality through the use of mass advertising and merchandising practices, causing consumers to rely for their protection upon the skill and expertise of the manufacturing community.
>
> (2) Consumers no longer have the ability to protect themselves adequately from defective products due to the vast number and complexity of products which must be "consumed" in order to function in modern society.
>
> (3) Sellers are often in a better position than consumers to identify the potential product risks, to determine the acceptable levels of such risks, and to confine the risks within those levels.
>
> (4) A majority of product accidents not caused by product abuse are probably attributable to the negligent acts or omissions of manufacturers at some stage of the manufacturing or marketing process, yet the difficulties of discovering and proving this negligence are often practicably insurmountable.
>
> (5) Negligence liability is generally insufficient to induce manufacturers to market adequately safe products.
>
> (6) Sellers almost invariably are in a better position than consumers to absorb or spread the costs of product accidents.
>
> (7) The costs of injuries flowing from typical risks inherent in products can fairly be put upon the enterprises marketing the products as a cost of their doing business, thus assuring that these enterprises will fully "pay their way" in the society from which they derive their profits.

Do you agree with all of the rationales for strict liability expressed above? Do they in combination make a good case for imposing strict liability on all manufacturers of defective products of all kinds?

On some types of manufacturers? On retailers? On sellers of used products? Do the rationales apply with equal force to cases involving inadequate warnings and designs as well as to cases of manufacturing flaws? To cases where the consumer has abused the product?

For a critical review of the traditional policy arguments, see Owen, Rethinking the Policies of Strict Products Liability, 33 Vand.L.Rev. 681 (1980). See also Klemme, The Enterprise Liability Theory of Torts, 47 Colo.L.Rev. 153 (1976); A. Schwartz, Products Liability and Judicial Wealth Redistributions, 51 Ind.L.J. 558 (1976); Birnbaum, Unmasking the Test for Design Defect: From Negligence [to Warranty] to Strict Liability to Negligence, 33 Vand.L.Rev. 593 (1980); R. Epstein, Modern Products Liability Law, ch. 4 (1980); Priest, The Invention of Enterprise Liability: A Critical History of the Intellectual Foundations of Modern Tort Law, 14 J.Leg.Stud. 461 (1985).

2. Consider the observations of Cowan, Some Policy Bases of Products Liability, 17 Stan.L.Rev. 1077, 1086–92 (1965):

III. *The Policy of Consumer Perspective*

The third policy operating in this change of law is a clear recognition of the effect upon consumers of mass production and distribution of goods and services, aided by the mass media of advertising. The policy which the decisions exemplify can be stated as an attempt to tilt the balance more favorably toward the single or individual consumer injured by a vast impersonal merchandising juggernaut. The tendency is the age-old practice by which courts yield to the temptation to slip David a more lethal slingshot, even though, as events turn out, it is Goliath that needs protection.

This policy tries to equalize the position of injured consumers vis-a-vis the mass producers and advertisers. To put the matter bluntly, a large proportion of mass products are consciously made as inferior as the traffic will bear and are advertised by conscious misrepresentation as far superior to their known quality. The combination of low quality production and high quality lying makes it impossible for those using the products of mass manufacture to distinguish good merchandise from bad without the services of a general testing laboratory.

* * *

IV. *The Policy of Recognizing Deliberately Created Risk as Expropriation*

This brings us to a fundamental division in the law of torts, namely, the distinction between the rule of reasonable care that governs liability in negligence and the rule of strict liability for consciously appropriating or expropriating the valuable interests of another. Its applicability to the products field requires a brief examination of actual manufacturing and marketing practices. We deal here with a question of risk distribution but one which involves not the rules of tort law by which the burdens of injuries caused by risky conduct may be shifted. It goes beyond this species of legal risk distribution to the actual practices by which modern mass producers allocate risks of injury from defective products among themselves and their consumers. This allocation is deliberate. Where the consumer participates in the allocation we have contract law, presumably, to govern the event. Where the consumer does not participate in the allocation, but has it imposed upon him by the producer, we are in the shadowland between tort and contract, with tort intervening here as elsewhere to substitute general rules of behavior for the uncontrolled forces of the market. The medium is some form of strict liability. This is especially true where the risky product is apt to cause personal injury.

Where the producer one-sidedly shifts to the consumer a calculated risk of injury from a defective product, we may look upon this process as a conscious expropriation of a certain valuable interest of the consumer, namely, his interest in freedom from bodily harm.

It may be, then, that the law of torts which is now shifting more of the risks onto producers is doing so in conformity with the ancient practice of tort law of making those who deliberately throw loss, or risk of loss that eventuates in loss, on others pay for the loss incurred. * * *

* * *

Naturally, the question arises as to who sets the level of the risk. If the manufacturer is producing for another manufacturer or for the government, the level of consumer's risk is set by negotiation. If, however, the manufacturer is producing for the general public, he sets the level of consumer's risk himself and is restrained, if at all, only by market conditions and by the law. * * * Now the question arises, why should the manufacturer be allowed to pass the so-called consumer's risk on to the consumer at all? Especially the risk of property loss or serious bodily injury resulting from a defective product? The answer of the manufacturer that he must pass *some* risk on to the consumer is now met with the reply: then pay for the damages. This is not absolute liability. It has nothing to do with insurance. It has nothing to do with subjective fault. It has to do with compensation for a loss resulting from a deliberately assigned risk—assigned, that is, to the other fellow.

It is apparent that this analysis of shifted risk gives no hint of a solution to the perplexing problem of whether the risk *should* fall on the consumer or be returned to the manufacturer, or be shifted to anyone else, for that matter. That is a question of legal policy. As such, the trend toward shifting the risk away from the consumer is but another manifestation of what Edmond Cahn called "the consumer perspective." All contemporary governments whatever their political form or economic base purport to advance what I have elsewhere called "social security interests." The trend toward greater consumer protection is simply a manifestation, appropriate to a mass-producing, mass-marketing, and mass-advertising culture, of a purpose to lighten the burden of the plaintiff injured by defective products * * *.

3. **Risk Spreading.** One of the principal justifications said to support the rule of strict manufacturer liability is to "spread the risk of loss." Thus, products liability law has been viewed by some as an instrument of social engineering to bridge the gap until social welfare programs take care of the

accident compensation problem. "Until Americans have a comprehensive scheme of social insurance, courts must resolve by a balancing process the head-on collision between the need for adequate recovery and viable enterprises. This balancing task should be approached with a realization that the basic consideration involves a determination of the most just allocation of the risk of loss between the members of the marketing chain." Helene Curtis Ind., Inc. v. Pruitt, 385 F.2d 841, 862 (5th Cir.1967), citing Wilson, Products Liability, 43 Calif.L.Rev. 809 (1955). Compare Plant, Strict Liability of Manufacturers for Injuries Caused by Defects in Products—An Opposing View, 24 Tenn.L.Rev. 938, 946 (1957), arguing that "what is sometimes euphemistically called 'social engineering' * * * frequently turns out to be crass expediency seeking its ends without any particular regard for basic principles." Compare also Markle v. Mulholland's Inc., 265 Or. 259, 509 P.2d 529, 546 (1973) (Bryson, J., dissenting) (" * * * I am not willing to place the court in a position of adopting a law based on a socialistic theory.").

Apart from the political soundness of the risk spreading rationale, are its underlying assumptions correct? Consider the following analysis by Klemme, The Enterprise Liability Theory of Torts, 47 Colo.L.Rev. 153, 191–92 n. 107 (1976):

> [A]t least today and probably for some time, the courts and legislatures have implicitly recognized that whether a loss was shifted to the defendant or left on the plaintiff, the loss (or a major portion of it) could and would be shifted by the plaintiff or the defendant to other members of the community. Hence the basic "fairness" question is: which group in society ought ultimately to bear the loss—the persons to whom the plaintiff would shift it through his casualty insurance (Blue Cross, employer's sick leave, social security benefits, veteran's benefits, unemployment compensation, welfare programs and the like) or the persons to whom the defendant would shift it through his liability insurance, the market place, or, in some cases, a government subsidy program.
>
> * * *
>
> [T]ext writers have suggested that it is "better" or "fairer" for a loss (tort-like, or otherwise) to be distributed among many people rather than leaving it entirely on the person who sustains it.
>
> * * *
>
> [M]y position as to what is the basic question of fairness in distributing losses * * * diverges from those of many text writers and some courts * * * on the further assumption that, generally, defendants (actors) are more likely to be carrying liability insurance through which tort losses can be distributed than are accident victims likely to be carrying casualty insurance through which the loss could also be distributed. When Justice Traynor, for example, wrote in *Greenman* * * * that it is better to have a loss caused by a defective product distributed via the manufacturer's liability insurance to the members of the public than to leave it on the victim who is "powerless" to protect himself, he could have been thinking either that Mr. Greenman was "powerless" to prevent such losses or that he was "powerless" to provide adequate insurance protection against such losses. My impression of what many text writers and courts have been thinking is the latter, namely, that in most cases involving tort losses, the accident victim is less likely to be covered by casualty or welfare benefits, and

> therefore it is generally "fairer" to impose liability on actors (who are more likely to be insured) than leave it on victims (who are more likely to be uninsured).
>
> If this is what is considered to be the basic "fairness" justification for distribution of losses under the enterprise liability theory, then a major determinant in establishing liability rules should be: which participants in an enterprise are most likely to be carrying adequate insurance to cover the kind of loss involved, the actors (e. g., manufacturers, wholesalers, and retailers) or victims (e. g., consumers, users, or bystanders)? In short, who is most likely to be able to distribute the loss most widely as well as most efficiently? Probably today in many, if not most, cases the answer to this question, with the exception of losses for pain and suffering, will be that the victim is, through his casualty insurance, employment benefits, and various welfare programs.

For further, similar analyses, see Epstein, Products Liability: The Gathering Storm, 1 Regulation 15, 19–20 (Sept./Oct. 1977); Epstein, Products Liability: The Search for the Middle Ground, 56 N.C.L.Rev. 643 (1978); Owen, Rethinking the Policies of Strict Products Liability, 33 Vand.L.Rev. 681, 703–07 (1980), infra p. 427.

Compare Kalven, Torts: The Quest for Appropriate Standards, 53 Calif.L. Rev. 189, 205–06 (1965) ("The economist would tell us that if we put liability strictly on the manufacturer we are in effect compelling the consumer through increased prices to buy accident insurance for himself."), with Lange, Compensation of Victims—A Pious and Misleading Platitude, 54 Calif.L.Rev. 1559, 1562–63 (1966) ("Whenever it is open to men to decide for themselves upon whom losses should fall, there will be a tendency for them to impose the loss upon the person or persons who can most conveniently insure.").

Beginning about 1975, rapidly increasing premiums for products liability insurance made the use of such insurance impossible as a practical matter for many small manufacturers and retailers. Is this fact relevant to whether the strict tort principle should be applied to these kinds of defendants? Can manufacturers in fact pass on to consumers the entire cost of products liability insurance? Of products liability judgments?

Who really is paying for what? And who is making the decision?

Is the doctrine of strict manufacturer liability subject to attack on grounds of moral principle or natural law? What might be some of the arguments that it is? See Coleman, The Morality of Strict Tort Liability, 18 Wm. & Mary L.Rev. 259 (1976); Epstein, A Theory of Strict Liability, 2 J.Leg.Stud. 151 (1973); Fletcher, Fairness and Utility in Tort Theory, 85 Harv.L.Rev. 537 (1972); Lucey, Liability Without Fault and the Natural Law, 24 Tenn.L.Rev. 952 (1957).

4. **Deterrence.** Mr. Huckleby fed his hogs grain that unknown to him had been treated with Panogen–15, a seed disinfectant manufactured by the defendant. The disinfectant contained mercury. The Huckleby family ate one of the hogs that had eaten the treated grain, and the children suffered blindness and paralysis from mercury poisoning. In an action against the manufacturer for failure adequately to warn of the danger, the court considered whether the manufacturer could appropriately be held to a standard of strict liability in tort. Holding that the defendant was not entitled to summary judgment, the court remarked in part as follows:

> (1) Public interest in human life, health and safety requires that the law give consumers maximum protection against dangerous product defects.
>
> * * *
>
> (3) The marketing of dangerously defective products can have tragic consequences. Allowing injured plaintiffs to proceed on a theory of a manufacturer's liability, without the necessity of proving negligence, will cause manufacturers to take cautionary steps to prevent the marketing of dangerously defective products. Such preventive measures may avert tragedies such as befell the Huckleby family, and thereby save our system the cost of lawsuits such as this one.
>
>> Where a defendant's product is adjudged by a jury to be dangerously defective, imposition of liability on the manufacturer will cause him to take some steps (or at least make calculations) to improve his product. * * * We suspect that, in the final analysis, the imposition of liability has a beneficial effect on manufacturers of defective products both in the care they take and in the warning they give.
>
> Phillips v. Kimwood Machine [Co., 269 Or. 485, 525 P.2d 1033, 1041–42 (1974)].

First Nat. Bank v. Nor–Am Agricultural Prod., Inc., 88 N.M. 74, 537 P.2d 682, 695 (1975).

Will raising the level of a manufacturer's legal responsibility from "reasonable" care to "strict" accountability in fact increase the manufacturer's care in making and selling its products? Is there any practical distinction between "reasonable" care and "super" care? Some economists argue that the level of safety will not be increased by a strict liability rule: "It is tempting to conclude that strict liability encourages higher, and in the long run more efficient, levels of safety, but this is incorrect. Rather than creating an incentive to engage in research on safety, a rule of strict liability merely shifts that incentive [to consumers]." Posner, Strict Liability: A Comment, 2 J.Leg.Stud. 205, 209 (1973). He concludes: "The question whether a general substitution of strict for negligence liability would improve efficiency seems at this stage hopelessly conjectural; the question is at bottom empirical and the empirical work has not been done." Id. at 211–12. See also Sachs, Negligence or Strict Product Liability: Is There Really a Difference in Law or Economics?, 8 Ga.J.Int'l & Comp.L. 259 (1978).

Defense lawyers argue that the standard of legal "defectiveness" (at least in design cases) is too *vague* to be a meaningful deterrent and so instead is often simply ignored. See Raleigh, The "State of the Art" in Product Liability: A New Look at an Old "Defense," 4 Ohio N.L.Rev. 249, 250–52 (1977), for a valuable perspective on the dissatisfaction of General Motors' chief products liability lawyer with the prevailing rules of products liability. Others have argued that manufacturers are generally as careful as reasonably possible anyway, regardless of the theory of liability, in order to safeguard their valuable reputations. See Plant, Strict Liability of Manufacturers for Injuries Caused by Defects in Products—An Opposing View, 24 Tenn.L.Rev. 938 (1957). Cf. Sugarman, Doing Away with Tort Law, 73 Calif.L.Rev. 555, 566 (1985) (citing 1983 Rand study by Eads & Reuter which found that some manufacturers treat specific case outcomes as "random noise").

Reconsider the remarks of the court in *Nor–Am,* supra. The court's reliance on the *Phillips* case was somewhat disingenuous since the *Phillips* court was addressing the argument of the manufacturer of an industrial machine that it should be relieved of *all* responsibility, since the *employer* could absorb the risk of loss (through workers' compensation insurance) and thus was "just as capable of spreading [it] by the sale of its product as is the defendant." The sentence omitted in the *Nor-Am* court's quotation from *Phillips* reads as follows: "Although such inducement may not be any greater under a system of strict liability than under a system of negligence recovery, it is certainly greater than if the liability was imposed on another party simply because that other party was a better risk distributor." 525 P.2d at 1041–42.

It appears quite clear that the increasing impact of products liability has caused many manufacturers to devote more attention, personnel and money to product safety, and that products today are in general safer as a result. See Final Report, Interagency Task Force on Product Liability VI–47 (1977); N. Weber, Product Liability: The Corporate Response (Conf.Bd.1987); The Benefits of the Modernization of the Tort Law in the Context of the Social Movement for Improved Safety and Quality in the National Economy (Cons.Fed. of Amer. Sept. 1987).

What of the problem of *overdeterrence*—discouraging manufacturers from developing and selling inherently dangerous but socially beneficial products, such as football helmets, IUDs, and many prescription drugs. See generally Huber, Safety and the Second Best: The Hazards of Public Risk Management in the Courts, 85 Colum.L.Rev. 277 (1985).

5. One concluding point should be considered. This chapter has examined the array of different theories of liability that may be separately applicable to the problem of a consumer suffering a single injury caused by a single product defect. "The resulting complexity of litigation strongly suggests that development of a single theory of recovery for a particular kind of loss would promote a more efficient and just administration of products liability claims." Werdner P. Keeton, Annual Survey of Texas Law: Torts, 32 Sw.L.J. 1, 2 (1977). The Model Uniform Product Liability Act adopted this position in §§ 102(D) and 103(A). Do you agree with this approach? Do you suppose that in, say, 20 years there will be a single, unified theory of recovery?

6. A somewhat converse problem, which should be kept in mind while studying the next chapter, is whether "defectiveness," which is now generally treated as a single issue under whatever theory of liability, should be pulled apart into its three separate components—defects in manufacture, warnings and design. Should different standards (or theories) of liability be applied to different types of defects? Specifically, should truly "strict" liability be applied only to manufacturing defects, and only negligence liability to defective warnings and designs? This basic approach has the support of some commentators, see, e.g., Henderson, Manufacturers' Liability for Defective Product Design: A Proposed Statutory Reform, 56 N.C.L.Rev. 625 (1978), and of the Interagency Task Force on Product Liability, which concluded:

> When the product is not made in accord with the manufacturer's own specifications (a defect in construction) and this causes an injury, manufacturers should be strictly liable. On the other hand, when the defect is one of design or failure to warn, it may not be sound to subject a manufacturer to liability unless considerations such as the foreseeability of harm and the seriousness of harm are balanced against the

> utility of the product and the burden on the manufacturers to avoid the risk. In sum, open-ended "strict liability" under the *tort system* in these areas does not appear to be sound long-range policy.

Final Report at VII–19 to 20 (1977). See also "The Basic Standard of Responsibility in Product Liability Cases: A Crisis of Confusion," Interagency Task Force on Product Liability, 4 Legal Study Final Report 86–94 (1977) (calling for a "return to negligence" in design and warnings cases).

7. Were Judge Traynor and Dean Prosser simply wrong?

Chapter 3

THE CONCEPT OF DEFECTIVENESS

The previous chapter considered the nature of the various causes of action that may be available to a plaintiff injured by a defective product. This chapter examines the principles used to determine whether particular injury-producing products should be classified as "defective." A central principle pervading many of the cases is the idea that perfect safety is generally not technologically possible and that, when it is, it often costs too much in any event. See generally G. Calabresi, The Costs of Accidents 17–18 (1970). Thus, many courts begin their opinions with a statement that the manufacturer is not to be held as an insurer of its products' safety. Since absolute safety thus is not to be the rule, at least not in design and warnings cases, the question resolves into one of degree—of judging the soundness of the trade-offs between safety and cost. In short, the question of "defectiveness" becomes one of: How safe is safe enough?

SECTION 1. THEORIES AND TESTS OF DEFECTIVENESS

In the last section of Chapter 2 we examined some of the fundamental theoretical bases of products liability generally and of strict manufacturer liability in particular. This section explores the search for appropriate yardsticks or tests to be used in determining whether the level of safety of particular products is adequate.

This search gives rise to two distinct levels of inquiry. The first and more fundamental inquiry, an outgrowth of the preceding section, concerns the development of theoretical models of defectiveness. To date the courts have propounded two principal theories of defectiveness, (1) consumer expectancy and (2) risk-benefit, both of which are considered below. The second level of the inquiry involves the problem of semantics—most particularly, how this creature called "strict" liability can best be described to the jury which is charged with the difficult task of deciding whether a particular product on trial should be deemed "defective." The second problem is thus one of administration of the theory—of making it workable in judging real products in the real world. The last subsection thus examines the continuing search for appropriate verbal tests for use in translating the theory into practice.

As the reader progresses through this section, two important perspectives should be borne in mind. The first is a recognition of the significance of the overlap and interrelationships between the various theories and tests of liability, theories and tests that are separately treated here for clarity of analysis. Second, the reader should appreciate that a theory or test that operates well in one context, say in a manufacturing flaw case, may work poorly in a different context, such as in a design or warnings case. Although this point has received little judicial consideration so far, it probably accounts for much of the confusion that presently surrounds the defectiveness concept and is one issue on which further judicial development may be expected in the years ahead.

A. CONSUMER EXPECTATIONS

R. POUND, SOCIAL CONTROL THROUGH LAW

114 (1942, 1968 reprint).

In civilized society men must be able to assume that those with whom they deal in the general intercourse of society will act in good faith and hence

(a) will make good reasonable expectations which their promises or other conduct reasonably create; [and]

(b) will carry out their undertakings according to the expectations which the moral sentiment of the community attaches thereto; * * *.

CORBIN ON CONTRACTS *

Vol. 1, at 1–2 (1963).

§ 1. The Main Purpose of Contract Law is the Realization of Reasonable Expectations Induced by Promises

The underlying purpose of law and government is human happiness and contentment, to be brought about by the satisfaction of human desires in the highest practicable degree. * * *

That portion of the field of law that is classified and described as the law of contracts attempts the realization of reasonable expectations that have been induced by the making of a promise. Doubtless, this is not the only purpose by which men have been motivated in creating the law of contracts; but it is believed to be the main underlying purpose, and it is believed that an understanding of many of the existing rules and a determination of their effectiveness require a lively consciousness of this underlying purpose.

The law does not attempt the realization of every expectation that has been induced by a promise; the expectation must be a reasonable one. Under no system of law that has ever existed are all promises enforceable. The expectation must be one that most people would have; and the promise must be one that most people would perform. This necessarily leads to a complexity in the law, to the construction of the various rules determining the circumstances under which a promise is said to be enforceable and those under which its performance will be excused.

It must not be supposed that contract problems have been solved by the dictum that expectations must be "reasonable." Reasonableness is no more absolute in character than is justice or morality. Like them it is an expression of the customs and mores of men—the customs and mores that are themselves complex, variable with time and place, inconsistent and contradictory. Nevertheless, the term is useful, giving direction to judicial research, and producing workable results. The reasonably prudent man, reasonable care and diligence, reasonable expectations, are terms that are not to be abandoned, at least until we can demonstrate that others will work better.

NOTE

"Many courts have used consumer expectations as a criteria for defining defect. If a consumer reasonably expects a product to be safe to use for a purpose, the product is defective if it does not meet those expectations. The consumer expectations test is natural since strict liability in tort developed from the law of warranty. The law of implied warranty is vitally concerned with protecting justified expectations since this is a fundamental policy of the law of contracts." Fischer, Products Liability—The Meaning of Defect, 39 Mo. L.Rev. 339, 348 (1974).

VINCER v. ESTHER WILLIAMS ALL-ALUMINUM SWIMMING POOL COMPANY

Supreme Court of Wisconsin, 1975.
69 Wis.2d 326, 230 N.W.2d 794.

This is a products liability case. The second amended complaint alleges that Curt Vincer, the injured plaintiff-appellant, who was two years old at the time of the July 13, 1970, incident, fell into a swimming pool in the backyard of the home of his grandparents, whom he was visiting. The complaint alleges that a retractable ladder to the above-ground pool had been left in the down position, that the pool was unsupervised, and that Curt climbed the ladder, fell into the water and remained there for an extended period of time, resulting in severe brain damage causing permanent and total disablement. [An action in negligence and strict tort was brought against the manufacturer and the retailer-installer of the pool. The strict tort count alleged in part,] "That the swimming pool was defective and unreasonably dangerous because [defendants] failed to take the reasonable and low-cost precaution of building the swimming pool so that the fencing extended across the deck at the top of the ladder opening, with a self-closing, self-latching gate on the deck of the swimming pool so as to prevent access to the swimming pool area by children of the age of Curt Vincer, even when the ladder from the deck to the ground was in the down position."

[The manufacturer demurred, and the trial court sustained the demurrer and dismissed the complaint. Plaintiff appealed.]

CONNOR T. HANSEN, JUSTICE.

* * *

In *Dippel v. Sciano,* this court adopted sec. 402A of Restatement, 2 Torts 2d, pertaining to strict liability in tort. Under this section, where the plaintiff proves he was injured by a product "in a defective condition unreasonably dangerous to the user" and establishes the other requisite elements listed in the section, he is relieved of the burden of proving specific acts of negligence by the manufacturer who is then deemed negligent per se. * * *

Comment *g* to sec. 402A of Restatement, 2 Torts 2d, defines "defective condition" in part as follows:

> "*g. Defective condition.* The rule stated in this Section applies only where the product is, at the time it leaves the seller's hands, in a condition not contemplated by the ultimate consumer, which will be unreasonably dangerous to him."

The particular defect in the design of the swimming pool, as alleged in the complaint, is the absence of a self-latching and closing gate to prevent entry to the pool. We are satisfied that the swimming pool is not defective in this respect because, as a matter of law, the swimming pool was as safe as it reasonably could be since it did contain a retractable ladder, which unfortunately was allegedly left down and led to the injury of the small child.

Even if a product is defective, it must be shown to be unreasonably dangerous to the user or consumer. Comment *i* to sec. 402A of the Restatement defines "unreasonably dangerous" in part as follows:

> "*i. Unreasonably dangerous.* The rule stated in this Section applies only where the defective condition of the product makes it unreasonably dangerous to the user or consumer. Many products cannot possibly be made entirely safe for all consumption, and any food or drug necessarily involves some risk of harm, if only from over-consumption. Ordinary sugar is a deadly poison to diabetics, and castor oil found use under Mussolini as an instrument of torture. That is not what is meant by 'unreasonably dangerous' in this Section. *The article sold must be dangerous to an extent beyond that which would be contemplated by the ordinary consumer who purchases it, with the ordinary knowledge common to the community as to its characteristics.*" (Emphasis supplied.)

* * *

Thus, the test in Wisconsin of whether a product contains an unreasonably dangerous defect depends upon the reasonable expectations of the ordinary consumer concerning the characteristics of this type of product. If the average consumer would reasonably anticipate the dangerous condition of the product and fully appreciate the attendant risk of injury, it would not be unreasonably dangerous and defective. This is an objective test and is not dependent upon the knowledge of the particular injured consumer, although his knowledge may be evidence of contributory negligence under the circumstances.

* * *

Based upon the principles discussed above, we conclude that the swimming pool described in plaintiff's complaint does not contain an unreasonably dangerous defect. The lack of a self-latching gate certainly falls within the category of an obvious rather than a latent condition. Equally important, the average consumer would be completely aware of the risk of harm to small children due to this condition, when the retractable ladder is left in a down position and the children are left unsupervised. We conclude, therefore, that plaintiffs' second amended complaint fails to state a cause of action.

Judgment and order affirmed.

[Dissenting opinion of Wilkie, C.J., omitted.]

NOTES

1. **Obvious Dangers.** When a consumer is injured by an obvious hazard will his expectations ever be frustrated? The expectancy test plainly precludes liability in most such cases. Consider for example Hartman v. Miller Hydro Co., 499 F.2d 191, 194 (10th Cir.1974). Defendant manufactured and sold a bottle washing machine with an unguarded drive shaft to plaintiff's employer, The Pepsi Cola Bottling Company. Plaintiff leaned over the revolving shaft to set up some fallen bottles and was injured when his trousers were pulled into the machine. Applying the expectancy test of comment *i* the court reasoned as follows:

> Hartman testified he was never warned that a guard should be placed over the shaft, and that he did not know leaning against the exposed shaft was dangerous. As assistant production manager responsible for plant safety, however, he must be accredited with sufficient intelligence to realize that an exposed revolving shaft is dangerous. This conclusion is supported by the fact that another employee had previously become caught in the same shaft. Thus, it cannot be said that a danger existed which was beyond contemplation of an ordinary user. The danger was obvious.

See also Menard v. Newhall, 135 Vt. 53, 373 A.2d 505, 507 (1977) (plaintiff's eye put out in BB gun fight: "A BB gun which is neither defectively designed nor manufactured is not dangerous beyond that which would be contemplated by the ordinary consumer * * *. A warning by the defendant Daisy that a BB gun, if fired at a person, could injure an eye, is nothing that even a seven-year-old child does not already know."); Vineyard v. Empire Machinery Co., Inc., 119 Ariz. 502, 581 P.2d 1152 (1978) (absence of roll-over bar on large earth-moving scraper, which rolled over and crushed operator's leg, not a danger beyond consumer's expectations since its absence was "immediately evident").

2. **Children.** Why did the *Vincer* court test the adequacy of the pool's design against the expectations of the ordinary *adult* consumer? Were not the expectations of the injured child deserving of protection? Were they not quite plainly disappointed?

In Bellotte v. Zayre Corp., 116 N.H. 52, 352 A.2d 723 (1976), a five-year old child was burned when his cotton pajama top ignited while he was playing with matches. In deciding whether the pajamas were "unreasonably dangerous to the user or consumer" because the fabric had not been treated with an effective fire-retardant substance, the court addressed the question of whether the safety characteristics of the pajamas should be measured according to the expectations of the "consuming" child or the "purchasing" parent. Plaintiffs contended that "the test should be whether they were dangerous to an extent beyond that which would be contemplated by the ordinary five-year old child." The court did not agree: "Children of that age do not contemplate even the unavoidable dangers of cotton pajamas and their flammable characteristics. There would therefore be no base from which to determine unreasonableness and the seller would become an insurer." Id. at 725. See also Novak v. Piggly Wiggly Puget Sound Co., 591 P.2d 791 (Wash.Ct.App.1979).

Do *Vincer* and *Bellotte* deny young children the reasonable protection of the law? Do they represent a subtle reversion to the now-discredited doctrine of imputed contributory negligence which barred an injured child's action against a third party tortfeasor if the child's parent was guilty of negligent supervision? What if the child in *Bellotte* had been ten years old? Eighteen? What if Mr. Bellotte had bought his *wife* an excessively flammable nightgown that ignited as she leaned over the stove? Whose expectations should control, those of the "ultimate consumer," under comment *g*, or those of the "ordinary consumer who purchases" the product, under comment *i?*

3. **Patients.** Whose expectations should control concerning an injury-producing prescription drug or medical device, those of the patient or of the physician? Mueller & Co. v. Corley, 570 S.W.2d 140, 145 (Tex.Civ.App.1978), was an action against the manufacturer and distributor of a silicone breast prosthesis that broke open inside the plaintiff. Verdict was for the plaintiff, and defendant appealed, arguing that the jury should have been instructed to measure the adequacy of the product against the expectations of the surgeon who had selected the device rather than those of the patient into whom it had been implanted. *Held,* plaintiff's judgment affirmed:

> The defendants argue that a prosthesis is a specialized medical product, requiring the exercise of a physician's skill and judgment in the determination of its use, and that the physician, rather than the user, would be required to determine whether the product exposed the user to an unreasonable risk of harm.
>
> The defective condition in the prosthesis in question rendered it unreasonably dangerous to Mrs. Corley, not to her physician, Dr. Leeves. The appropriate question for the jury, therefore, was whether the defective condition was one which was not contemplated by the user, the "ultimate consumer." Restatement (2d) of Torts § 402A (1965). The trial court properly keyed its instructions to the mind of the person who would be injured by the dangerous condition of the product.

See also Ethicon, Inc. v. Parten, 520 S.W.2d 527, 533 (Tex.Civ.App.1975) (surgical needle broke in patient's body).

Is *Corley* consistent with *Vincer* and *Bellotte?*

4. **Employees.** In Jackson v. Coast Paint & Lacquer Co., 499 F.2d 809, 812 (9th Cir.1974), plaintiff was injured while spray-painting the inside of a tank car when the accumulated paint fumes ignited unexpectedly. Plaintiff sued the paint manufacturer for failing to warn of this risk. The defendant contended that no warning was necessary since plaintiff's employer knew of the risk, even if plaintiff did not. *Held,* for plaintiff. Since warnings could have been placed effectively upon the paint container labels, the "community" whose expectations were relevant consisted of the painters who would be exposed to the danger, not the employers who bought the paint.

5. **Bystanders.** Suppose plaintiff is walking along a sidewalk when without warning he is hit from the rear by an automobile with an unusual steering characteristic known to the purchaser but not to the operator. Whose expectations should control? Cf. Cornelius v. Bay Motors, Inc., 258 Or. 564, 484 P.2d 299 (1971); Ewen v. McLean Truck Co., 300 Or. 24, 706 P.2d 929 (1985) (pedestrian, struck by truck with poor visibility, not "consumer" under comment *i*); Trespalacios v. Valor Corp. of Fla., 486 So.2d 649 (Fla.App.1986) (defendant manufacturer's "riot and combat" shotgun, used by mad gunman to kill plaintiff and seven others, not defective under comment *g*).

How does the bystander issue here differ from the liability to bystander in strict tort issue discussed at p. 178 n. 4, above?

6. What characteristic do the children, patients, employees and bystanders in these situations all share in common? Should identical expectancy principles accordingly be applied to all four types of plaintiffs? Why or why not?

7. How about the *expert* consumer, the one who knows *more* about a product's dangers, and thus has lower expectations as to its safety than the average person in the community? "[A] consumer with less than ordinary expectations, based upon particular expertise, should not gain from having *ordinary* expectations credited to him." Rheingold, What Are the Consumer's "Reasonable Expectations"?, 22 Bus.Law. 589, 593 n. 16 (1967).

Compare Utah Code Ann.1953, § 78–15–6(2) (Act of 1977): " '[U]nreasonably dangerous' means that the product was dangerous to an extent beyond which would be contemplated by the ordinary and prudent buyer, consumer or user of that product in that community considering the product's characteristics * * * together with any actual knowledge, training, or experience possessed by that particular buyer, user or consumer."

Consider, however, the objective nature of the test prescribed in comment *i*; cf. comment *g*. It is sometimes said that the injured consumer's special knowledge of the danger is not relevant to the defectiveness issue but goes instead to his contributory negligence or assumption of risk.

Which approach do you prefer? Should the test allow a product to be deemed defective when used by one type of person but not when used by another? What do you think of this type of "shifting defectiveness"?

8. Consider the broader issue: Why an *objective* basis to the test? "[Are] not the expectations of the specific injured consumer enough? He must be given credit for expecting a product that was reasonably safe. He certainly did not expect an unreasonably dangerous product." Green, Strict Liability Under

Sections 402A and 402B: A Decade of Litigation, 54 Tex.L.Rev. 1185, 1211 (1976).

9. Suppose the plaintiff in *Vincer* had been able to establish that dozens of young children are similarly injured or killed each year and that the addition of a self-closing and latching gate would have raised the cost of the $1,000 pool by only $3. Same result?

Consider Seattle–First Nat. Bank v. Tabert, 86 Wash.2d 145, 542 P.2d 774, 779 (1975): "In considering the reasonable expectations of the ordinary consumer, a number of factors must be considered including [t]he relative cost of the product, the gravity of the potential harm from the claimed defect and the cost and feasibility of eliminating or minimizing the risk * * *."

Does the *Tabert* approach shift the inquiry into something quite different from consumer expectations?

DICKERSON, PRODUCTS LIABILITY: HOW GOOD DOES A PRODUCT HAVE TO BE?

42 Ind.L.J. 301, 306–14 (1967).

The reasonable expectations of consumers provide a helpful guide, but a slippery one. If defectiveness depends on the reasonable expectations of particular classes of consumers, how can we measure those expectations? How, for instance, can we measure the expectations of the normal housewife as to whether and how fully particular pork products need to be cooked? Consumer expectations are as subtle as perceived meanings; both depend on the particular environments in which they operate. Fortunately, problems of this kind are common grist for the courts, and a judgment as to the reasonable expectations for a particular product is no harder to make than the lexicographical judgment as to what a particular phrase normally means in a particular speech community. It is a familiar exercise in judicial empathy.

The most troublesome situations are those in which consumer attitudes have not sufficiently crystallized to define an expected standard of performance. What, for instance, should the law do about tractors that overturn, surgical implants that break, and rear-engined automobiles that tend to swerve at high speeds? These are products that tend to involve allegedly faulty design. If it is not feasible to improve the product's performance or to provide a safety device for situations in which the consumer appears to be undesirably vulnerable, the answer may lie in requiring appropriate warnings or instructions for use.

Although there is a tendency in such cases to refer to a "duty to warn" or "duty to provide a safety device" as if they were independent duties, it seems preferable to approach these "duties" as alternative means of discharging a single, broader duty to provide, under prescribed conditions, a product that does not violate the consumer's normal expectations by exposing him to an unreasonable and concealed danger. * * *

HEATON v. FORD MOTOR CO.

Supreme Court of Oregon, 1967.
248 Or. 467, 435 P.2d 806.

GOODWIN, JUSTICE. The plaintiff appeals a judgment entered after an involuntary nonsuit in a products-liability case involving a wheel on a Ford 4–wheel–drive pickup truck. The principal question is whether the plaintiff produced sufficient evidence to support his allegation that the wheel was dangerously defective.

Plaintiff purchased the truck new in July 1963 to use for hunting and other cross-country purposes as well as for driving upon paved highways. He drove the truck some 7,000 miles without noticing anything unusual about its performance. Prior to the day of the accident the truck had rarely been off the pavement, and plaintiff swore that it had never been subjected to unusual stress of any kind.

On the day of the accident, however, the truck, while moving on a "black-top" highway at normal speed, hit a rock which plaintiff described as about five or six inches in diameter. The truck continued uneventfully for about 35 miles, when [the wheel came apart and the truck] left the road and tipped over.

* * *

An article is dangerously defective when it is in a condition unreasonably dangerous to the user. Restatement (Second) of Torts § 402A. Unreasonable, in this context, means dangerous to an extent beyond that which would be contemplated by the ordinary purchaser. Restatement (Second) of Torts § 402A, comment g. Such a definition is conceptually related to the traditional warranty of merchantable quality in the law of sales.

In some cases the plaintiff can produce direct evidence of a mistake in fabrication or of a design which is unreasonably dangerous. The user has the right to expect a reasonably safe design and reasonable quality controls in fabrication according to that design. Restatement (Second) of Torts § 402A; § 395, Comment f.

In the type of case in which there is no evidence, direct or circumstantial, available to prove exactly what sort of manufacturing flaw existed, or exactly how the design was deficient, the plaintiff may nonetheless be able to establish his right to recover, by proving that the product did not perform in keeping with the reasonable expectations of the user.[4] When it is shown that a product failed to meet the reasonable expectations of the user the inference is that there was some sort of

4. "The article sold must be dangerous to an extent beyond that which would be contemplated by the ordinary consumer who purchases it, with the ordinary knowledge common to the community as to its characteristics." Restatement (Second) of Torts § 402A, Comment i.

defect, a precise definition of which is unnecessary. If the product failed under conditions [5] concerning which an average consumer of that product could have fairly definite expectations, then the jury would have a basis for making an informed judgment upon the existence of a defect. The case at bar, however, is not such a case.

In this case plaintiff failed to introduce evidence of flawed manufacture or dangerous design. His own expert witness expressed an opinion that the wheel was not defective. He now urges that this court should declare the wheel unreasonably dangerous as a matter of law for the reason that it failed to perform as an ordinary consumer would have expected it to perform. While the Restatement indicates that such a failure would permit a finding that a product is generally defective, it is for the jury rather than the court to say in the ordinary case whether a given product failed to meet the standard. [Citations.]

The court's function is to decide whether the evidence furnishes a sufficient basis for the jury to make an informed decision. If the record permits, the jury determines whether the product performed as an ordinary consumer would have expected. In the case at bar the record furnishes no basis for a jury to do anything but speculate.

Where the performance failure occurs under conditions with which the average person has experience, the facts of the accident alone may constitute a sufficient basis for the jury to decide whether the expectations of an ordinary consumer of the product were met. High-speed collisions with large rocks are not so common, however, that the average person would know from personal experience what to expect under the circumstances. Nor does anything in the record cast any light upon this issue. The jury would therefore be unequipped, either by general background or by facts supplied in the record to decide whether this wheel failed to perform as safely as an ordinary consumer would have expected. To allow the jury to decide purely on its own intuition how strong a truck wheel should be would convert the concept of strict liability into the absolute liability of an insurer.

The argument has been made that the question of the ordinary consumer's expectations should be treated for jury purposes in the same way that the question of reasonable conduct in a negligence case is treated. But in deciding in a negligence case what is reasonable conduct, the jury is deciding in a context of "right and wrong" how someone *should* have behaved. In making this decision they are presumed to know the relevant factors. If not, such information is provided, as in a medical malpractice case where there is expert testimony as to the proper standards.

In the defective-product area, courts have already decided how strong products *should* be: they should be strong enough to perform as the ordinary consumer expects. In deciding what the reasonable consumer expects, the jury is not permitted to decide how strong products

5. "A product is not in a defective condition when it is safe for normal handling and consumption * * *." Restatement (Second) of Torts § 402A, Comment h.

should be, nor even what consumers should expect, for this would in effect be the same thing. The jury is supposed to determine the basically factual question of what reasonable consumers do expect from the product. Where the jury has no experiential basis for knowing this, the record must supply such a basis. In the absence of either common experience or evidence, any verdict would, in effect, be the jury's opinion of how strong the product *should* be. Such an opinion by the jury would be formed without the benefit of data concerning the cost or feasibility of designing and building stronger products. Without reference to relevant factual data, the jury has no special qualifications for deciding what is reasonable.

* * *

While the matter was never presented to the trial court, and thus requires no extended discussion in this appeal, the plaintiff has referred in this court to certain advertising published by the defendant, to reinforce the plaintiff's claim that a consumer would have expected the wheel in question to be engineered and manufactured in such a manner as to withstand the kind of force applied to it in this case. The plaintiff does not contend that the advertising constituted misrepresentation under Restatement (Second) of Torts § 402B, but rather that the advertising in general tends to create expectations of strength and durability under Section 402A. A general impression of durability, however, does not help a customer to form an expectation about the breaking point of a wheel. A "rugged" Ford truck could be expected to negotiate rough terrain, including five-or-six-inch rocks, at appropriate off-the-road speeds, but it does not follow that a user could expect the same thing at highway speeds. If such expectations do exist, the record should contain evidence to support the inference that they do.

Affirmed.

O'CONNELL, JUSTICE (dissenting).

* * *

* * * The gist of plaintiff's argument is summed up as follows:

> "* * * It is not unreasonable to suggest that the driver of a vehicle promoted as 'solid,' 'rugged' and 'built like a truck' will subject that vehicle and its passengers to hazards to which he would not subject a vehicle otherwise promoted. With specific reference to this case, it is not unreasonable to surmise that a driver of a vehicle so promoted who runs over a rock on the highway will not even consciously consider the possibility of stopping to check for damage because he takes it for granted that such an impact will not harm a vehicle which he has been conditioned to think of as 'solid,' 'rugged,' and 'like a truck.' "

Plaintiff, then, is asking us to "take judicial notice of facts which form part of the common knowledge of people who possess average intelligence, * * * as, for example, the capabilities of a 'jeep,' Olson v. Riverview Cemetery, 220 Or. 220, 349 P.2d 279 (1960)."

Apparently the majority opinion would hold that there was a failure of proof, irrespective of whether the question of strict liability is for the court or jury in a case of this kind. I disagree. If we had been presented with the same facts with the modification that plaintiff had struck a rock one inch in diameter rather than a five-inch rock, I am sure that the majority would have held that at least a jury question was made out. The beginning point of our reasoning would be that a manufacturer of automobiles must construct wheels of sufficient durability to withstand the impact of one-inch rocks, because one-inch rocks are not an uncommon obstacle on highways. A buyer could reasonably expect to have the wheel withstand such an impact and it would not be unreasonable for him to proceed on his journey after the impact. However, the buyer could not reasonably expect a wheel to remain safe after striking a rock two feet in diameter at seventy miles an hour. Somewhere along the continuum between one inch and two feet it will be necessary to draw a line. The line is drawn by deciding whether a manufacturer should be required to construct a wheel of such durability as to withstand the impact of a rock of the size in question. Whether the manufacturer has that duty in a particular case should depend, it seems to me, upon whether the manufacturer could reasonably foresee the likelihood that the hazard would be encountered by those using the product, and this would, of course, depend to some extent upon the representations made by the manufacturer with respect to the durability of the product.

The manufacturer's conduct must be measured against a standard of reasonableness, a standard similar to that employed in determining whether a defendant is negligent. Here, however, we do not measure defendant's conduct in terms of fault but simply upon the basis of its foreseeability. A jury is just as well equipped to judge the reasonableness of defendant's conduct on this score as it is when the inquiry is made as to defendant's negligence. The members of the jury draw upon their experiences and observations and set up some kind of a standard as a measure against which to appraise the defendant's conduct in the particular case. They would be justified in concluding that the wheel in this case was unreasonably dangerous according to the test stated in Restatement (Second) of Torts § 402A, p. 352 (1965), requiring a finding that "[t]he article sold must be dangerous to an extent beyond that which would be contemplated by the ordinary consumer who purchases it, with the ordinary knowledge common to the community as to its characteristics."

The majority apparently would require some evidence of what this community standard is. How is this to be done? Certainly this is not the type of question which calls for the testimony of an expert witness. Are we to call lay witnesses to testify what "would be contemplated by the ordinary consumer"? If that is required in the present case, it would be equally necessary in an ordinary negligence case to inform the jury of the community standard on such questions as the reasonableness of conduct in driving a car with respect to speed, lookout and control.

But we submit these questions of the reasonableness of defendant's conduct to the jury and, subject to the right of the court to decide as a matter of law that the standard was or was not met, we are willing to trust the jury's judgment as to the community standard and to appraise the defendant's conduct in light of it.

I believe that the question of defendant's liability is kept from the jury in the present case not because there is a lack of evidence upon which to sustain a verdict for plaintiff, but because the majority of the court, finding the imposition of strict liability a severe burden upon the seller, attempts to limit that burden by distorting the concept of the jury's function.

NOTES

1. Just what would be the expectations of a typical owner of such a truck concerning the ability of its wheels to withstand the stresses of hitting five-inch rocks at normal highway speeds? "[A]n attempt to determine the consumer's reasonable expectations of safety concerning a technologically complex product may well be an exercise in futility, for the consumer may have at most only a generalized expectancy—perhaps more accurately only an unconscious hope—that the product will not harm him if he treats it with a reasonable amount of care." Montgomery & Owen, Reflections on the Theory and Administration of Strict Tort Liability for Defective Products, 27 S.C.L.Rev. 803, 823 (1976).

2. What "relevant factual data" missing from the record did the majority suggest might have supported a jury verdict for the plaintiff? Would the use of this type of evidence have converted the inquiry from consumer expectancy into something basically different?

3. How else might plaintiff have reached the jury? Consider the appropriateness of the following types of evidence:

A. Testimony by the plaintiff as to his own expectations;

B. Testimony by the truck dealer as to the expectations of owners generally under similar circumstances;

C. The results of an expectations poll taken in the relevant community.

See Turner v. General Motors Corp., 514 S.W.2d 497, 500 (Tex.Civ.App. 1974) ("Raymond Kliesing, the defendant dealer, testified that, based upon his forty-five years of sales experience, the average consumer believes that a sedan vehicle will be a reasonably safe product in a roll-over.").

4. **Judge and Jury.** Contrast the positions of the majority and dissent concerning the proper roles of the court and jury. Which was right? The majority's position as to the special role of the court in this type of case reflects the same court's reliance in an earlier products case, Wights v. Staff Jennings, 241 Or. 301, 405 P.2d 624 (1965), on the doctrine of strict liability for ultrahazardous activities, a context in which courts generally have accepted more responsibility for decision-making than in other areas of tort law. With certain notable exceptions treated in the following sections of this chapter, the courts have generally left "defectiveness," like negligence, to the jury. The Oregon

court itself subsequently swung over to this approach. See Roach v. Kononen, 269 Or. 457, 525 P.2d 125 (1974).

5. In Lamke v. Futorian Corp., 709 P.2d 684 (Okl.1985), plaintiff fell asleep on a sofa manufactured by defendant Futorian while smoking a cigarette manufactured by defendant Phillip Morris. The sofa ignited and the plaintiff was burned. The petition claimed that the cigarette was defective because it was designed to burn longer and hotter than other cigarettes, and because no warnings were given of these characteristics. The sofa was alleged to be defective because it had not been flame retarded, nor had warnings of this fact been provided to consumers. Plaintiff's third amended petition was dismissed, and plaintiff appealed. *Held* (6–3), affirmed: For the majority, Justice Hodges reasoned as follows:

> The plaintiff * * * alleged that the cigarettes were defective because they had additional chemicals and special paper which prolonged burning, increased the intensity of the fire of the cigarettes and caused the cigarette to ignite the couch. She also alleged that the cigarette should have been self-extinguishing.
>
> None of the plaintiff's allegations, if deemed true, establish that these cigarettes were more likely to cause the fire in question than might be *anticipated by the ordinary* consumer. In her brief, plaintiff argues that she established this fact since she says this cigarette was not an "ordinary" cigarette, but had been chemically treated to increase its intensity and prolong its fire between puffs. That argument is not supported by the allegations of the petition.
>
> Plaintiff did not allege that "ordinary" cigarettes had not been so treated, nor that the defendant's cigarettes were different from the cigarettes with which the ordinary consumer is familiar. The plaintiff alleges only that at the time of the manufacture of these cigarettes there were other cigarettes which had not been treated chemically as had the defendant's cigarettes. Apparently, the plaintiff would hold the manufacturer responsible if his product is not as safe as some other product on the market. That is not the test in these cases. Only when a defect in the product renders it less safe than expected by the ordinary consumer will the manufacturer be held responsible.
>
> This is particularly true in cases such as the instant case where the "defect" alleged is the failure to minimize an obvious danger which is inherent in the product itself. In order for a cigarette to be used, it must burn. The simple allegation that the cigarette should have been self-extinguishing or that some other cigarettes would not have burned as long, nor as intensely, does not establish that the cigarettes involved in this case were more likely to cause the fire than might be expected by the consumer. * * *.
>
> By the same analysis, the plaintiff's petition is insufficient with regard to * * * the sofa manufacturer. Plaintiff alleges only that the sofa was "unreasonably dangerous" because it was not sufficiently flame retardant, and because Futorian Corporation issued no warning as to this defect. No allegations are made which would support a conclusion that the ordinary consumer expects a sofa to be flame retardant to the degree suggested by the plaintiff, and the petition, if deemed true, does not establish that the sofa in question was any more likely to be ignited than is expected by the ordinary consumer.

VICE CHIEF JUSTICE DOOLIN dissented:

The majority of this Court has today blunted the development of strict liability under Products Liability cases in this state particularly as to chemical additives and the like.

* * *

The cigarette manufactured by Phillip Morris is alleged to have been dangerous to an extent beyond that which would be contemplated by an ordinary consumer with the ordinary knowledge common to the community as to its characteristics. Plaintiff alleges that Phillip Morris adulterated the cigarette with chemicals designed to make the cigarette burn longer and hotter than an ordinary cigarette would. She also alleges that the paper which formed the outer shell of the cigarette was "highly porous," which is said to make the cigarette burn longer and hotter. Assuming these facts to be true, we cannot say as a matter of law that the cigarette was not unreasonably dangerous.

* * *

* * * It is not a matter of common knowledge that some cigarettes are designed to burn longer and hotter than others.

* * *

A product which is unreasonably dangerous without warnings may not be unreasonably dangerous if proper warnings are provided. * * * By giving a proper warning, the manufacturer is increasing the knowledge of the community as to that product's characteristics. The plaintiff alleges that Phillip Morris failed to provide adequate warnings about the excessive flammability of its cigarette. If indeed the cigarette manufactured by Phillip Morris were designed in a manner which made it dangerous to an extent beyond that which is contemplated by the ordinary consumer, then Phillip Morris had a duty to warn consumers of the dangerous characteristics of its product.

The sofa manufactured by Futorian is also alleged to have been unreasonably dangerous. Plaintiff alleged that Futorian designed the sofa to be sold without flame-resistant fabric. At first blush, it would appear that an ordinary consumer with ordinary knowledge common to the community would expect a sofa to ignite if a cigarette were dropped on the surface of its fabric. If most sofas were made with flame-resistant fabric, however, an ordinary consumer might very well expect a sofa to merely scorch. The point is, we should not say as a matter of law that ordinary consumers expect sofas to have or not to have flame-resistant fabrics. Ordinary knowledge common to the community changes as technology and science changes the community's environment. Whereas a couch manufactured in 1950 might be expected to ignite easily, a couch made in 1970 or 1980 or 1990 might be expected to have different characteristics. The very existence of safer fabrics might cause the community to expect sofas in general to be safer than they once were. We should not say as a matter of law that an ordinary consumer expects a sofa to ignite when confronted with the glowing ember of a cigarette. The jury can supply that answer.

* * * I would hold that the general acceptance by an industry of a new standard of safety, and a corresponding rise in the expectation of consumers as to the safety of that industry's products, may cause the product of a particular manufacturer who does not accept the indus-

try's standard of safety to fall below the community's expectations. Since the reasonableness of a product's dangerousness is defined by consumer expectations, a design once safe may become a defective design over time. Of course a product made when the design was considered safe does not become defective when the design later improves. Thus an automobile manufactured in 1920 does not become defective merely because cars made in 1980 are designed more safely. But a car made in 1980 from a 1920 design would be unreasonably dangerous.

* * *

How has the majority blunted the development of Manufacturers' Products Liability in Oklahoma?

I believe the majority opinion has not considered the role and effect chemical additives, polymers, fire inhibiting fabrics and manufacturers' techniques play in assembling or manufacturing products of today. A plaintiff is entitled to prove, if he can, the dangers of such items. A myriad of products and processes are available and used or incorporated into such ordinary items as food, clothing, materials, fabrics, hardware, etc. The use of face masks, inhalers, goggles, protective clothing, and many other devices by firemen, police or servicing personnel gives abundant evidence actionable dangers, unknown to former generations, exist in our homes, buildings, automobiles, aircraft and our every surroundings.

5. What is it that lies behind consumer expectations that justifies imposing liability on the basis of their frustration? See Markle v. Mulholland's Inc., 265 Or. 259, 509 P.2d 529, 532 & 534 (1973), where the majority remarked that consumer expectations are "the result of the manufacturer's or seller's placing the article in the stream of commerce with the intention that it be purchased. This expectation is given legal sanction by the law through an assumption that the seller, by so placing the article in the stream of commerce, has represented that the article is not unreasonably dangerous if put to its intended use. * * * One can only determine what a purchaser has a right to expect by the implications express or inherent in the sale to him. These implications are analogous to those underlying a representation of merchantable quality."

In a masterful piece of scholarship, Professor Shapo constructed a comprehensive representational model of products liability law. See Shapo, A Representational Theory of Consumer Protection: Doctrine, Function and Legal Liability for Product Disappointment, 60 Va.L.Rev. 1109, 1370 (1974), where his thesis is partially set forth as follows:

> Judgments of liability for consumer product disappointment should center initially and principally on the portrayal of the product which is made, caused to be made or permitted by the seller. This portrayal should be viewed in the context of the impression reasonably received by the consumer from representations or other communications made to him about the product by various means: through advertising, by the appearance of the product, and by the other ways in which the product projects an image on the mind of the consumer, including impressions created by widespread social agreement about the product's function. This judgment should take into consideration the result objectively determinable to have been sought by the seller, and the seller's apparent motivation in making or permitting the representation or communication.

6. A helpful perspective on the expectancy idea was provided by Judge Traynor who perceived the test to be principally directed to the "surprise element of danger." Traynor, The Ways and Meanings of Defective Products and Strict Liability, 32 Tenn.L.Rev. 363, 370 (1965).

7. Is it not true that most consumers are sophisticated enough to know that some percentage of cars leaving the assembly line (perhaps largely those put together on Mondays) are dangerously defective? That some pop bottles and "hamburgers" do contain foreign matter? How should such expectations of a cynically realistic society be dealt with under the expectancy model when a consumer is in fact injured by one of the many "lemons" spewed out by an imperfect industrial system? See Dickerson, Products Liability: How Good Does a Product Have to Be?, 42 Ind.L.J. 301, 315–16 (1967).

8. If occasional "lemons" are indeed an unavoidable element of our industrial system, given today's resources and technology, should consumers have a "right" to expect anything more? Stated otherwise, is it logical for the legal system to demand more perfection from the industrial system than it is in fact capable of achieving? Or are these the right questions at all?

9. What is your view as to whether any of the following "flaws" in the expectancy model diminish its usefulness as a decision-making tool: "(1) humans lack the data necessary to form expectations; (2) humans are psychologically unable to contemplate injury to themselves and thus underestimate the importance of such injury in making decisions; and (3) people overvalue short-term gains and losses and undervalue long-range considerations." See Hubbard, Reasonable *Human* Expectations: A Normative Model for Imposing Strict Liability for Defective Products, 29 Mercer L.Rev. 465, 475 (1978).

10. After nine years of intense debate, the 12–nation European Economic Community (E.E.C.) in 1985 adopted a Directive "Concerning Liability for Defective Products," providing in Article 6 as follows:

> 1. A product is defective when it does not provide the safety which a person is entitled to expect, taking all circumstances into account, including:
>
> (a) the presentation of the product;
>
> (b) the use to which it could reasonably be expected that the product would be put; and
>
> (c) the time when the product was put into circulation.
>
> 2. A product shall not be considered defective for the sole reason that a better product is subsequently put into circulation.

See Albanese & Del Duca, Developments in European Product Liability, 5 Dick. J.Int.L. 193 (1987).

11. See generally Bernacchi, A Behavioral Model for Imposing Strict Liability in Tort: The Importance of Analyzing Product Performance in Relation to Consumer Expectation and Frustration, 47 U.Cinn.L.Rev. 43 (1978); Hubbard, Reasonable *Human* Expectations: A Normative Model For Imposing Strict Liability for Defective Products, 29 Mercer L.Rev. 465 (1978); Fischer, Products Liability—The Meaning of Defect, 39 Mo.L.Rev. 339, 348–52 (1974); Shapo, A Representational Theory of Consumer Protection: Doctrine, Function and Legal Liability for Product Disappointment, 60 Va.L.Rev. 1109 (1974); Dickerson, Products Liability: How Good Does a Product Have to Be?, 42 Ind. L.J. 301 (1967); Rheingold, What Are the Consumer's "Reasonable Expectations"?, 22 Bus.Law. 589 (1967).

B. RISK–BENEFIT ANALYSIS

Discontent with some of the shortcomings of the consumer expectations test, and hesitant to abandon the familiar calculus of risk principles of negligence law, many courts have used a "risk-benefit" approach for determining "defectiveness" under strict liability in tort. Consider the observations of Donaher, Piehler, Twerski & Weinstein, in The Technological Expert in Products Liability Litigation, 52 Tex.L.Rev. 1303, 1307 (1974):

> It is time to abandon the perspective of the reasonable consumer and the reasonable seller and formulate the strict liability question for what it is. The issue in every products case is whether the product qua product meets society's standards of acceptability. The unreasonable danger question, then, is posed in terms of whether, given the risks and benefits of and possible alternatives to the product, we as a society will live with it in its existing state or will require an altered, less dangerous form. Stated succinctly, the question is whether the product is a reasonable one given the reality of its use in contemporary society.

The basic "risk-benefit," "risk-utility," or "calculus of risk" approach to products liability decision-making was initially explored in the negligence section of Chapter 2, above. Yet the fundamentals are worth restating. "The basic notion of cost-benefit analysis is not new. Any individual decision is usually the consequence of the actor's assessment of the advantages (benefits) and disadvantages (costs) of the action. Government, no less than individuals, has always made such assessments." Green, Cost–Risk Benefit Assessment and the Law: Introduction and Perspective, 45 Geo.Wash.L.Rev. 901, 903–04 (1977). Consider also Merrill, Risk–Benefit Decision–Making by the Food and Drug Administration, 45 Geo.Wash.L.Rev. 994, 996 (1977): "'Risk-benefit' * * * includes any technique for making choices that explicitly or implicitly attempts to measure the potential adverse consequences of an activity and to predict its benefits. In its most refined form, such an analysis may make use of refined mathematical methods for calculating risks and benefits, attempting to assign uniform values, usually in dollars, to all factors, including human lives."

The principles of risk-benefit analysis were applied to the products liability context in Raney v. Honeywell, Inc., 540 F.2d 932, 935 (8th Cir. 1976), where the court observed that the determination of whether a design risk is "unreasonable" involves "a balancing of the probability and seriousness of harm against the costs of taking precautions. [Citations.] Factors to be considered include the availability of alternative designs, the cost and feasibility of adopting alternative designs, and the frequency or infrequency of injury resulting from the design." In sum, under a risk-benefit test, a product is considered "defective" if the costs of improving its safety are less than the benefits resulting from the improvement.

While one purpose of the risk-benefit approach is to provide manufacturers with an incentive to improve the safety of excessively hazardous products, for various reasons the rule in practice may not operate to reduce product accidents to their "optimal" level—the point at which the sum of accident costs and accident avoidance costs is minimized. See, e.g., Calabresi, Optimal Deterrence and Accidents, 84 Yale L.J. 656 (1975); Calabresi & Hirschoff, Toward a Test for Strict Liability in Torts, 81 Yale L.J. 1055 (1972). Nevertheless, many courts have found risk (or "cost")-benefit analysis to be a helpful tool in deciding how to allocate losses from product accidents. While economic efficiency may not be precisely optimized through liability determinations based upon risk-benefit analysis, the test may help achieve a roughly efficient allocation of resources by discouraging manufacturers from marketing products in conditions which generate more accident costs than social utility. Moreover, higher prices from liability judgments and settlements should discourage "excessive" consumption of such products by consumers. Finally, judicial use of an efficiency-based standard of liability may have important symbolic value in punishing the wasteful (unjustified) sacrifice of human life and limb.

As you consider the strengths and weaknesses of risk-benefit analysis in making product "defectiveness" determinations, bear in mind that the courts have found it most useful in design cases and only marginally helpful in warnings cases. In manufacturing flaw cases decided in strict tort, this method of analysis has been virtually ignored. As you proceed through this section and the remainder of this chapter, try to determine the reasons for the varying usefulness of this method of analysis in these three different contexts.

NICHOLS v. UNION UNDERWEAR COMPANY, INC.

Supreme Court of Kentucky, 1980.
602 S.W.2d 429.

STEPHENS, JUSTICE.

This is a products liability case. Four-year-old Richard Nichols was badly burned while playing with matches when his T-shirt caught fire. Through his father, as next friend, he sued Union Underwear Company, Inc., the manufacturer and seller of the shirt. The basis of the suit was strict liability for design defect. Following a jury trial in the Franklin Circuit Court, a verdict was returned for Union Underwear and judgment was entered on the verdict.

Nichols appealed to the Court of Appeals, which affirmed the judgment. Because of the importance of the question presented, we granted discretionary review. The sole issue to be determined is whether the trial court erred in instructing the jury on the definition of "unreasonably dangerous" which appears in comment i of section 402A of the second Restatement of Torts.

Because we are concerned with the instruction given, we need not burden this opinion with an extensive description of the evidence presented to the jury. Nichols concedes that the evidence was of such a nature that the jury had a right to believe that presented by Union Underwear. However, it is relevant here that the proof presented concerned itself with the following major areas: (1) the flammability of the fabric of the shirt; (2) the risk of clothing-inflicted burns to children; (3) the availability of commercially feasible, alternative designs and fabrics for this particular article of clothing; (4) the extent of consumer awareness of the danger inherent in flammable children's clothing; (5) the alleged lack of such awareness of danger by this child and his mother; and (6) the significance of the fact that the fabric complies with applicable federal statutory standards for flammability. It is clear that the jury was given ample evidence on which to base its decision.

* * *

No objection was raised by Nichols to [the] instructions which simply set out the doctrine of strict liability provided in section 402A as applied to the facts developed in the present case. Then, over the strenuous and continuing objection of Nichols, the court gave an instruction defining "unreasonably dangerous."

Instruction #4

> A product is "unreasonably dangerous" only if it is dangerous to an extent beyond that which would be contemplated by an ordinary adult purchaser thereof, with ordinary knowledge as to its inherent characteristics.

Nichols contends that this instruction was erroneous and prejudicial. He claims that danger beyond an ordinary purchaser's contemplation is only one of several factors to be considered in determining if a product is, in fact, unreasonably dangerous. Further, he argues that a product's danger does not become reasonable simply because it is within the contemplation or actual awareness of the average consumer. Finally, he contends that no definition of the term "unreasonably dangerous" should have been given, but, as one was given, it should not have singled out one factor (consumer awareness) but, instead, should have brought *all* factors relevant to that determination to the attention of the jury.

* * *

The effect of this instruction is to insulate a product from liability simply because it is patently dangerous, or because it is no more dangerous than would be anticipated by the ordinary person. Some seventeen jurisdictions adhere to this rule, eighteen have repudiated it, and sixteen, including Kentucky, have not addressed the issue. [Citation.] We now join those which have considered and rejected "patent danger" or "consumer expectation" as an absolute defense to strict liability for defective design. * * *

We are immediately met with the difficult problem [1] of describing the standard to which the fact finder should compare the product to decide whether it was in a "defective condition unreasonably dangerous" when sold * * *

* * *

We believe that consumer knowledge, the factor considered below, is only one of the factors that should be before the jury in determining whether a product is unreasonably dangerous. We will not set out an exclusive list of the factors which lead to this determination. * * * Noted commentators have suggested many factors. But the facts of the individual case will determine what is relevant to each action.

In the event of another trial, the jury should be instructed as follows:

> You will find for the plaintiff only if you are satisfied from the evidence that the material of which the T-shirt was made created such a risk of its being accidentally set on fire by a child wearing it that an ordinarily prudent company engaged in the manufacture of clothing, being fully aware of the risk, would not have put it on the market; otherwise, you will find for the defendant.

[Reversed and remanded.]

LUKOWSKY, JUSTICE, concurring.

I agree with the opinion of the majority as far as it goes. However, the opinion leaves the law in products liability design defect cases amorphous. It fails to identify the gut issue.

I believe that whether a design is unreasonably dangerous must be determined by a social utility standard—risk versus benefit. If the benefits to be gained by the consuming public outweigh the risks of danger inherent in a particular design, such a product cannot be "unreasonably dangerous." [Citations.] The bottom line is that the trier of fact is required to balance two pairs of factors existing at the time of manufacture: (1) the likelihood that the product would cause the claimants harm or similar harms, and the seriousness of those harms; against (2) the manufacturer's burden of designing a product that would have prevented those harms, and the adverse effect that

1. It seems to us that the entire field of product liability law is especially fertile for comprehensive legislative review and action. Its rows need to be stably defined by legislative survey of the socioeconomic policies which determine its contours. Additionally, uniformity of law among all the states may be desirable because product liability insurance rates are set on a countrywide basis. Thus, the current system of having individual state courts develop product liability law on a case-to-case basis is not consistent with commercial necessity. Uniformity and stability in this area are desirable if product liability insurance rates are to be stabilized at reasonable levels. Under the sponsorship of the U.S. Department of Commerce, the Task Force on Product Liability and Accident Compensation, chaired by Professor Victor E. Schwartz, has published its Model Uniform Product Liability Act at 44 Fed.Reg. 62714 (1979). We respectfully call these matters to the attention of the General Assembly.

alternative design would have on the usefulness of the product. That is to say that the manufacturer is not liable unless at the time of manufacture the magnitude of the danger to the claimant outweighed the utility of the product to the public. [Citations.] The ultimate inquiry is risk versus benefit.

In the event of another trial, I believe the jury should be instructed as follows:

> You will find for the Plaintiff if you are satisfied from the evidence that at the time of the manufacture of the cotton and polyester T-shirt the risk of harm from its being accidentally set on fire while being worn by a child outweighed the benefit to the public from its availability in the marketplace. Otherwise, you will find for the defendant.

STEPHENSON, JUSTICE, dissenting.

In my opinion the only error on the part of the trial court was the failure to give a directed verdict to the respondent here.

Ordinarily in "products liability" cases, I think of design defects as failure to provide proper safety measures in design. For example: lawn mowers, farm machinery, etc. In the machinery cases it is the product itself that has the propensity to cause harm to the user.

Here the T-shirt was manufactured in conformity with applicable federal standards for flammability. In the circumstances of this case, it is absurd to have a jury decide whether the T-shirt is "unreasonably dangerous." Had the manufacturer used highly flammable materials in the garment, I could understand submission of the case to the jury, but not in this situation.

PHILLIPS v. KIMWOOD MACHINE CO.

Supreme Court of Oregon, 1974.
269 Or. 485, 525 P.2d 1033.

HOLMAN, J. Plaintiff was injured while feeding fiberboard into a sanding machine during his employment with Pope and Talbot, a wood products manufacturer. The sanding machine had been purchased by Pope and Talbot from defendant. Plaintiff brought this action on a products liability theory, contending the sanding machine was unreasonably dangerous by virtue of defective design. At the completion of the testimony, defendant's motion for a directed verdict was granted and plaintiff appealed.

As is required in such a situation, the evidence is recounted in a manner most favorable to the plaintiff. The machine in question was a six-headed sander. Each sanding head was a rapidly moving belt which revolved in the direction opposite to that which the pieces of fiberboard moved through the machine. Three of the heads sanded the top of the fiberboard sheet and three sanded the bottom. The top half of the machine could be raised or lowered depending upon the thickness of the fiberboard to be sanded. The bottom half of the machine had powered rollers which moved the fiberboard through the machine as the fiberboard was being sanded. The top half of the machine had pinch rolls, not powered, which, when pressed down on the fiberboard by use of springs, kept the sanding heads from forcefully rejecting it from the machine.

On the day of the accident plaintiff was engaged in feeding the sheets of fiberboard into the sander. Because of the defective operation of a press, a large group of sheets of extra thickness was received for sanding. These sheets could not be inserted into the machine as it was set, so the top half of the sander was adjusted upwards to leave a greater space between the top and bottom halves to accommodate the extra thick fiberboard sheets. During the sanding of the extra thick sheets, a thin sheet of fiberboard, which had become mixed with the lot, was inserted into the machine. The pressure exerted by the pinch rolls in the top half of the machine was insufficient to counteract the pressure which the sanding belts were exerting upon the thin sheet of fiberboard and, as a result, the machine regurgitated the piece of fiberboard back at plaintiff, hitting him in the abdomen and causing him the injuries for which he now seeks compensation.

Plaintiff asserts in his complaint that the * * * machine was defective and was unreasonably dangerous because there were no safety devices to protect the person feeding the machine from the regurgitation of sheets of fiberboard.

While we do not here attempt to recount all of the testimony presented by plaintiff concerning the defective design of the machine, there was evidence from which the jury could find that at a relatively small expense there could have been built into, or subsequently installed on, the machine a line of metal teeth which would point in the direction that the fiberboard progresses through the machine and which would press lightly against the sheet but which, in case of attempted regurgitation, would be jammed into it, thus stopping its backward motion. The evidence also showed that after the accident such teeth were installed upon the machine for that purpose by Pope and Talbot, whereupon subsequent regurgitations of thin fiberboard sheets were prevented while the efficiency of the machine was maintained. There was also evidence that defendant makes smaller sanders which usually are manually fed and on which there is such a safety device.

* * *

In defense of its judgment based upon a directed verdict, defendant contends there was no proof of a defect in the product, and therefore strict liability should not apply. This court and other courts continue to flounder while attempting to determine how one decides whether a product is "in a defective condition unreasonably dangerous to the user." It has been recognized that unreasonably dangerous defects in products come from two principal sources: (1) mismanufacture and (2) faulty design.[2] * * *

The problem with strict liability of products has been one of limitation. No one wants absolute liability where all the article has to do is to cause injury. To impose liability there has to be something about the article which makes it dangerously defective without regard to whether the manufacturer was or was not at fault for such condition. A test for unreasonable danger is therefore vital. A dangerously defective article would be one which a reasonable person would not put into the stream of commerce *if he had knowledge of its harmful character.*[5] The test, therefore, is whether the seller would be negligent if he sold the article *knowing of the risk involved.*[6] Strict liability imposes what amounts to constructive knowledge of the condition of the product.

On the surface such a test would seem to be different than the test of 2 Restatement (Second) of Torts § 402A, Comment *i.*, of "dangerous to an extent beyond that which would be contemplated by the ordinary consumer who purchases it." This court has used this test in the past. These are not necessarily different standards, however. As stated in Welch v. Outboard Marine Corp.,[8] where the court affirmed an instruction containing both standards:

> "We see no necessary inconsistency between a seller-oriented standard and a user-oriented standard when, as here, each turns on foreseeable risks. They are two sides of the same standard. A product is defective and unreasonably dangerous when a reasonable seller would not sell the product if he knew of the risks involved or if the risks are greater than a reasonable buyer would expect."

To elucidate this point further, we feel that the two standards are the same because a seller acting reasonably would be selling the same product which a reasonable consumer believes he is purchasing. That is to say, a manufacturer who would be negligent in marketing a given product, considering its risks, would necessarily be marketing a product which fell below the reasonable expectations of consumers who purchase it. The foreseeable uses to which a product could be put would be the same in the minds of both the seller and the buyer unless one of the parties was not acting reasonably. The advantage of describing a dangerous defect in the manner of Wade and Keeton is that it preserves

2. Wade, On the Nature of Strict Tort Liability for Products, 44 Miss.L.J. 825, 830 (1973) (including failure to warn as a design defect).

5. See generally, P. Keeton, Manufacturer's Liability: The Meaning of "Defect" in the Manufacture and Design of Products, 20 Syracuse L.Rev. 559, 568 (1969); P. Keeton, Products Liability—Inadequacy of Information, 48 Tex.L.Rev. 398, 403–404 (1970); Wade, Strict Tort Liability of Manufacturers, 19 Sw.L.J. 5, 15–16 (1965).

6. Cf. Welch v. Outboard Marine Corp., 481 F.2d 252, 254 (5th Cir.1973). See generally, Wade, supra note 2, at 834–835; P. Keeton, Products Liability—Some Observations About Allocation of Risks, 64 Mich.L. Rev. 1329, 1335 (1966).

8. 481 F.2d 252, 254 (5th Cir.1973).

the use of familiar terms and thought processes with which courts, lawyers, and jurors customarily deal.

While apparently judging the seller's conduct, the test set out above would actually be a characterization of the product by a jury. If the manufacturer was not acting reasonably in selling the product, knowing of the risks involved, then the product would be dangerously defective when sold and the manufacturer would be subject to liability.

In the case of a product which is claimed to be dangerously defective because of misdesign, the process is not so easy as in the case of mismanufacture. All the products made to that design are the same. The question of whether the design is unreasonably dangerous can be determined only by taking into consideration the surrounding circumstances and knowledge at the time the article was sold, and determining therefrom whether a reasonably prudent manufacturer would have so designed and sold the article in question had he known of the risk involved which injured plaintiff. The issue has been raised in some courts concerning whether, in this context, there is any distinction between strict liability and negligence. The evidence which proves the one will almost always, if not always, prove the other. We discussed this matter recently in the case of Roach v. Kononen, 99 Or.Adv.Sh. 1092, 525 P.2d 125 (1974), and pointed out that there is a difference between strict liability for misdesign and negligence. We said:

> "However, be all this as it may, it is generally recognized that the basic difference between negligence on the one hand and strict liability for a design defect on the other is that in strict liability we are talking about the condition (dangerousness) of an article which is designed in a particular way, while in negligence we are talking about the reasonableness of the manufacturer's actions in designing and selling the article as he did. The article can have a degree of dangerousness which the law of strict liability will not tolerate even though the actions of the designer were entirely reasonable in view of what he knew at the time he planned and sold the manufactured article. As Professor Wade points out, a way of determining whether the condition of the article is of the requisite degree of dangerousness to be defective (unreasonably dangerous; greater degree of danger than a consumer has a right to expect; not duly safe) is to assume that the manufacturer knew of the product's propensity to injure as it did, and then to ask whether, with such knowledge, something should have been done about the danger before it was sold. In other words, a greater burden is placed on the manufacturer than is the case in negligence because the law assumes he has knowledge of the article's dangerous propensity which he may not reasonably be expected to have, had he been charged with negligence." 99 Or.Adv.Sh. at 1099, 525 P.2d at 129.

To some it may seem that absolute liability has been imposed upon the manufacturer since it might be argued that no manufacturer could reasonably put into the stream of commerce an article which he realized might result in injury to a user. This is not the case, however. The manner of injury may be so fortuitous and the chances of injury occurring so remote that it is reasonable to sell the product despite the danger. In design cases the utility of the article may be so great, and the change of design necessary to alleviate the danger in question may so impair such utility, that it is reasonable to market the product as it is, even though the possibility of injury exists and was realized at the time of the sale. Again, the cost of the change necessary to alleviate the danger in design may be so great that the article would be priced out of the market and no one would buy it even though it was of high utility. Such an article is not dangerously defective despite its having inflicted injury.

In this case defendant contends it was Pope and Talbot's choice to purchase and use the sander without an automatic feeder, even though it was manufactured to be used with one, and, therefore, it was Pope and Talbot's business choice which resulted in plaintiff's injury and not any misdesign by defendant. However, it is recognized that a failure to warn may make a product unreasonably dangerous. * * *

It is our opinion that the evidence was sufficient for the jury to find that a reasonably prudent manufacturer, knowing that the machine would be fed manually and having the constructive knowledge of its propensity to regurgitate thin sheets when it was set for thick ones, which the courts via strict liability have imposed upon it, would have warned plaintiff's employer either to feed it automatically or to use some safety device, and that, in the absence of such a warning, the machine was dangerously defective. It is therefore unnecessary for us to decide the questions that would arise had adequate warnings been given.

* * *

It is apparent that the language being used in the discussion of the above problems is largely that which is also used in *negligence* cases, i.e., "unreasonably dangerous," "have reasonably anticipated," "reasonably prudent manufacturer," etc. It is necessary to remember that whether the doctrine of negligence, ultrahazardousness, or strict liability is being used to impose liability, the same process is going on in each instance, i.e., weighing the utility of the article against the risk of its use. Therefore, the same language and concepts of reasonableness are used by courts for the determination of unreasonable danger in products liability cases. * * *

* * *

The case is reversed and remanded for a new trial.

NOTES

1. In applying the risk-benefit (or cost-benefit) approach to particular products, many courts (including *Kimwood* in an omitted footnote) have been guided by the following considerations proposed by Dean Wade, On the Nature of Strict Tort Liability for Products, 44 Miss.L.J. 825, 837–38 (1973):

> (1) The usefulness and desirability of the product—its utility to the user and to the public as a whole.
>
> (2) The safety aspects of the product—the likelihood that it will cause injury, and the probable seriousness of the injury.
>
> (3) The availability of a substitute product which would meet the same need and not be as unsafe.
>
> (4) The manufacturer's ability to eliminate the unsafe character of the product without impairing its usefulness or making it too expensive to maintain its utility.
>
> (5) The user's ability to avoid danger by the exercise of care in the use of the product.
>
> (6) The user's anticipated awareness of the dangers inherent in the product and their avoidability, because of general public knowledge of the obvious condition of the product, or of the existence of suitable warnings or instructions.
>
> (7) The feasibility, on the part of the manufacturer, of spreading the loss by setting the price of the product or carrying liability insurance.

See, e.g., Roach v. Kononen, 269 Or. 457, 525 P.2d 125, 129 (1974) ("We agree that these factors should be considered by a court before submitting a design defect case to the jury. Also, proof of these factors bears on the jury's determination of whether or not a given design is defective."); Cepeda v. Cumberland Engineering Co., Inc., 76 N.J. 152, 386 A.2d 816 (1978).

Professor Vetri, in Products Liability: The Developing Framework for Analysis, 54 Or.L.Rev. 293 (1975), proposes that the jury be instructed on the relevant risk-benefit considerations. *Roach* adopted Dean Wade's proposal that the factors be explicitly addressed only by the court. Which approach is best?

Which of Dean Wade's factors is inconsistent with the imputed-knowledge-of-risk idea?

2. In Camacho v. Honda Motor Co., 741 P.2d 1240 (Colo.1987), the purchaser of a Honda Hawk motorcycle injured his legs in a collision with a car. His defective design suit was based on the theory that the motorcycle should have been equipped with tubular steel leg protection bars, which other manufacturers offered as optional equipment. Applying the consumer contemplation test of liability under § 402A, the trial court dismissed the action, and the Court of Appeals affirmed. In the Supreme Court, *held* (4–3), reversed:

> A consumer is justified in expecting that a product placed in the stream of commerce is reasonably safe * * *. Of course, whether a given product is reasonably safe and, therefore, not unreasonably dangerous, necessarily depends upon many circumstances. Any test, therefore, to determine whether a particular product is or is not actionable must consider several factors. While reference to "reasonable" or "unreasonable" standards introduces certain negligence con-

cepts into an area designed to be free from those concepts, [citations], that difficulty is much less troublesome than are the problems inherent in attempting to avoid dealing with the competing interests always involved in allocating the risk of loss in products liability actions, see generally W.P. Keeton, D. Dobbs, R. Keeton & D. Owen, Prosser and Keeton on the Law of Torts § 99 (5th ed. 1984); Wade, On Product "Design Defects" and Their Actionability, 33 Vand.L.Rev. 551, 570–71 (1980). In this regard, comment c to section 402A [observes that strict liability is premised on the grounds that the manufacturer has "assumed a special responsibility" toward consumers who buy its products and are thereby injured; that the public, "forced to rely upon the seller," has the right to expect "that reputable sellers will stand behind their goods; that * * * the burden of accidental injuries caused by products" should be "placed on those who market them, and be treated as a cost of production against which liability insurance can be obtained; and that the consumer * * * is entitled to the maximum of protection" by "those who market the products."]

These considerations strongly suggest that the consumer contemplation concept embodied in comment i, while illustrative of a particular problem, does not provide a satisfactory test for determining whether particular products are in a defective condition unreasonably dangerous to the user or consumer. In the final analysis, the principle of products liability contemplated by section 402A is premised upon the concept of enterprise liability for casting defective products into the stream of commerce. Jackson v. Harsco Corp., 673 P.2d 363 (Colo. 1983). The primary focus must remain upon the nature of the product under all relevant circumstances rather than upon the conduct of either the consumer or the manufacturer. [Citations.] Total reliance upon the hypothetical ordinary consumer's contemplation of an obvious danger diverts the appropriate focus and may thereby result in a finding that a product is not defective even though the product may easily have been designed to be much safer at little added expense and no impairment of utility. W.P. Keeton, D. Dobbs, R. Keeton & D. Owen, Prosser and Keeton on The Law of Torts § 99 at [698] (5th ed. 1984). * * *

In Ortho Pharmaceutical Corp. v. Heath, 722 P.2d 410 (Colo.1986), we recently recognized that exclusive reliance upon consumer expectations is a particularly inappropriate means of determining whether a product is unreasonably dangerous under section 402A where both the unreasonableness of the danger in the design defect and the efficacy of alternative designs in achieving a reasonable degree of safety must be defined primarily by technical, scientific information.[8] Moreover, manufacturers of such complex products as motor vehicles invariably have greater access than do ordinary consumers to the information

8. Honda asserts that the application of the consumer expectation test is particularly appropriate in the context of motorcycle design defect claims because the motorcycle purchaser who is injured in an accident has bargained for the condition about which he complains and because the element of conscious consumer choice is invariably present in contradistinction to those claims involving accidents occurring in the workplace. We cannot agree that the purchaser of a motorcycle bargains for the risk of serious leg injury; rather, the purchaser bargains for a motorized vehicle the purpose of which is to provide an economical, open-air, maneuverable form of transportation on the roadways.

necessary to reach informed decisions concerning the efficacy of potential safety measures. Harris, Enhanced Injury Theory: An Analytical Framework, 62 N.C.L.Rev. 643, 675 (1984). The principles that have evolved in the law of products liability have in part been developed to encourage manufacturers to use information gleaned from testing, inspection and data analysis to help avoid the "massive problem of product accidents." Palmer v. A.H. Robins Co., Inc., 684 P.2d 187 (Colo.1984) (quoting Owen, Punitive Damages in Products Liability Litigation, 74 Mich.L.Rev. 1257, 1258 (1976)).

* * * In *Ortho* we noted that the [Wade] factors are of value in balancing the attendant risks and benefits of a product to determine whether a product design is unreasonably dangerous * * *. The factors enumerated in *Ortho* are applicable to the determination of what constitutes a product that is in a defective unreasonably dangerous condition. By examining and weighing the various interests represented by these factors, a trial court is much more likely to be fair to the interests of both manufacturers and consumers in determining the status of particular products.

The question of the status of the motorcycle purchased by Camacho involves in part the interpretation of mechanical engineering data derived from research and testing—interpretation which necessarily includes the application of scientific and technical principles. * * * The record contains some evidence to support the conclusion that Honda could have provided crash bars at an acceptable cost without impairing the motorcycle's utility or substantially altering its nature and Honda's failure to do so rendered the vehicle unreasonably dangerous under the applicable danger-utility test.

3. In Helicoid Gage Div. of American Chain & Cable Co. v. Howell, 511 S.W.2d 573, 577 (Tex.Civ.App.1974), a pressure gage manufactured by the defendant burst, throwing a piece of the gage lens into plaintiff's eye. The jury rendered verdict for the plaintiff, and defendant appealed: "To determine whether a product is unreasonably dangerous, * * * it is necessary to weigh the risk of harm against the utility of the product, considering whether safety devices would unreasonably raise the costs or diminish the utility of the product. The evidence at trial showed that shatterproof glass would have increased the cost of each gage by approximately one dollar and would not have reduced the gage's utility. Further, there was testimony that this injury would not have occurred had shatterproof glass been used." Moreover, an "inexpensive" safety shield, that would not have diminished the utility of the gage, could have been added for about $2.50. *Held,* plaintiff's verdict affirmed.

4. Roach v. Kononen, 269 Or. 457, 525 P.2d 125 (1974), discussed in *Kimwood,* was an action against Ford Motor Company for injuries from a crash occurring when the hood on a Ford automobile suddenly flew up and blocked the driver's vision. Plaintiff's expert testified that the hood could have been designed to permit substantially better visibility in such situations. Another witness testified that Ford was aware of six or seven inadvertent hood openings occurring over a seven or eight year period. Ford's design engineer testified that the proposed design would require the addition of certain reinforcements to the hood and its hinges that would cost $5–10 per car. *Held,* jury verdict for defendant affirmed.

5. The operator's hand and arm were caught and drawn into a metal slitter machine in Dorsey v. Yoder Co., 331 F.Supp. 753 (E.D.Pa.1971), aff'd 474 F.2d 1339 (3d Cir.1973). In an action against the manufacturer for failing to install a guard on the machine, the jury returned a verdict for the plaintiff, and the defendant moved for judgment n.o.v. The court first noted that a relevant factor in the calculus of risk, weighing against a finding of defective design, was the fact that the absence of a guard was obvious to the operator. "On the other hand, a guard would not eliminate the machine's usefulness, nor would the cost of $200 to $500 on an $8,000 machine be unreasonable. Moreover, the seriousness of the potential harm was great. Ultimately, all of these facts were questions to be weighed by the jury in making their ultimate determination as to whether, under all of the circumstances, the machine was 'defective.' The jury found the balance tipped in favor of plaintiff. Considering the evidence in this case, this court could not possibly rule otherwise." 331 F.Supp. at 760.

6. Some courts look at risk-benefit analysis broadly as involving more than a comparison of the direct dollar costs of safety devices, on the one hand, and consumer injuries, on the other. Thibault v. Sears, Roebuck & Co., 118 N.H. 802, 395 A.2d 843 (1978), was a strict tort action against the manufacturer of a rotary lawn mower for injuries sustained by plaintiff when his foot slipped under the rear of the mower. Plaintiff claimed that the absence of a rear trailing guard rendered the mower's design unreasonably dangerous. The jury returned a verdict for the defendant, and the Supreme Court affirmed:

> In a strict liability case alleging defective design, the plaintiff must first prove the existence of a "defective condition unreasonably dangerous to the user." [Citations.] In determining unreasonable danger, courts should consider factors such as social utility and desirability. * * * In weighing utility and desirability against danger, courts should also consider whether the risk of danger could have been reduced without significant impact on product effectiveness and manufacturing cost. * * *
>
> Inquiry into the dangerousness of a product requires a multifaceted balancing process involving evaluation of many conflicting factors. A court will rarely be able to say as a matter of law that a product has no social utility, or that the purpose or manner of its use that caused the injury was not foreseeable. * * * Reasonableness, foreseeability, utility, and similar factors are questions of fact for jury determination.

If the testimony had revealed that the addition of the rear guard would have added $4 to the $100 price of the mower, could the jury reasonably have found for the plaintiff? What if it would have cost an additional $20? What if the guard would hang up on rocks and tree roots? What if it would detract from the overall "sleekness" of the design?

7. How broadly should the law view the *benefits* from a product? Cipollone v. Liggett Group, Inc., 644 F.Supp. 283 (D.N.J.1986), was a suit against cigarette manufacturers for the death of plaintiff's wife from lung cancer. The defendants sought to introduce evidence of the collateral social benefits flowing from the *production* of cigarettes, as opposed to their *consumption*:

> In essence, defendants argue that in determining liability, a jury engaged in the risk utility analysis may take into consideration profits made, employees hired, benefits to suppliers of goods and services, taxes generated and even charitable activities or contributions made

> by the defendant manufacturer. The analysis was never meant to balance the risk to the consumer against the general benefit to society. * * * It is the benefit and utility to the cigarette smoker which is here in issue, and not the benefit to the cigarette industry or those in turn, who benefit from its existence.

8. **Imputing Knowledge of the Danger: *Cost*-Benefit Analysis.** "All of these propositions can be stated perhaps in one general proposition: if the sale of the product under all the circumstances under which it was marketed subjected the consumer or others to an unreasonable risk of harm, the seller is subject to liability, and it is not relevant that he neither knew nor could have known nor ought to have known in the exercise of ordinary care that the unreasonable risk actually existed. It is enough that had he known of the risk and dangers he would not have marketed the product at all or he would have done so differently." P. Keeton, Products Liability—Inadequacy of Information, 48 Tex.L.Rev. 398, 404 (1970). "As thus refined, the unreasonable danger model transforms the somewhat subjective risk-benefit approach of negligence law—which is bounded by the limits of reasonable foreseeability—into an objective evaluation of the true *costs* and benefits of the product as marketed in its particular condition. The reasonable-seller-with-full-knowledge test gives an important additional perspective to the meaning of 'unreasonably dangerous' * * *." Montgomery & Owen, Reflections on the Nature and Administration of Strict Tort Liability for Defective Products, 27 S.C.L.Rev. 803, 844 (1976).

9. Two years after *Kimwood* the Oregon court decided Johnson v. Clark Equipment Co., 274 Or. 403, 547 P.2d 132, 142 n. 12 (1976). Verdict for defendant upon the following instruction:

> A product is said to be dangerously defective when it presents an unreasonable danger when used by persons expected to use it in the ordinary variety of ways in which the manufacturer or seller could reasonably expect it to be used by such persons. By "reasonably expected" I simply mean "foreseeability." Should the manufacturer or the seller have foreseen the product would present an unreasonable danger to the user?

Held, reversed. The court remarked as follows:

> Although this instruction was correct as to the governing law at the time this case was tried, the actual foreseeability of the danger presented by the product is no longer an issue after *Kimwood* and *Roach.* As these decisions pointed out, the law of strict products liability *assumes* that the particular danger presented was foreseeable by the manufacturer.
>
> Foreseeability is a negligence concept; a standard for assessing culpability. As such, it is not an appropriate consideration when determining whether a manufacturer should be held liable without fault. If, however, we *assume* foreseeability of the danger and ask only whether it would be reasonable to market the product in that condition with full knowledge of the risks involved, then that inquiry will reflect the proper focus of the law of products liability and center on the condition of the product, rather than on the culpability of the particular manufacturer.
>
> This focus is preserved in the jury instruction which this court suggested in the *Kimwood* case:

> "The law imputes to a manufacturer [supplier] knowledge of the harmful character of his product whether he actually knows of it or not. He is presumed to know of the harmful characteristics of that which he makes [supplies]. Therefore, a product is dangerously defective if it is so harmful to persons [or property] that a reasonable prudent manufacturer [supplier] with this knowledge would not have placed it on the market." 269 Or. at 501, n. 16, 525 P.2d at 1040.

10. The next year the court decided Newman v. Utility Trailer & Equipment Co., Inc., 278 Or. 395, 564 P.2d 674, 675–77 (1977), where plaintiff was injured when the tractor-trailer rig in which he was riding overturned as it was negotiating a sharp curve. Plaintiff's expert theorized that the upset was attributable to a reinforcing brace of inadequate strength on the frame. The jury was instructed to consider whether the defendants should have "foreseen the harm which the product would cause to the user under the circumstances of the case". *Held,* verdict for defendant reversed:

> It is obvious that trial courts are experiencing difficulty in distinguishing *foreseeability of use* from *foreseeability of the risk of harm.* Before a manufacturer or other seller is strictly liable for injury inflicted by a product, the product must have been put to a foreseeable use. As an example: if a shovel is used to prop open a heavy door, but, because of the way the shovel was designed, it is inadequate to the task and the door swings shut and crushes the user's hand, no responsibility for the injury results by reason of the shovel's not being designed to prop open doors since it was not reasonably foreseeable by the manufacturer or seller that it would be so used. Whether or not the article was put to a foreseeable use is a jury question unless, as in the above hypothetical case of the shovel, reasonable minds could not differ, in which instance the case would be at an end. On the other hand, if it is decided as a matter of law by the court or as a matter of fact by the jury that the article was being put to a foreseeable use at the time of the injury, it is assumed that the manufacturer or seller was aware of the risk involved which caused harm to plaintiff, whether or not the manufacturer or seller actually had such knowledge or reasonably could have been expected to have it. As a further illustration: if the shovel is being used to dig a ditch, and, while it is being so used, the blade strikes a rock in the soil and a piece of steel from the blade flies up and injures plaintiff's eye, the manufacturer or seller is assumed to have had knowledge of the risk of injury to plaintiff occasioned by the use of the shovel. The shovel was being used for a purpose for which it was manufactured. Whether the article is defective is then determined by whether a reasonably prudent manufacturer or seller, knowing of the risk which the shovel presented, would have put the article into the stream of commerce.

11. How important really is the distinction between risk-benefit and cost-benefit analysis in the typical design or warnings case? And to what extent have the courts been applying true cost-benefit analysis in cases where the distinction really does make a difference? Consider 4 Final Report of the Legal Study, Interagency Task Force on Product Liability 109–10 (1977):

> It is by now well recognized that the difference between negligence and strict liability in design defect cases is that the element of *scienter*—knowledge of the dangerous propensities of the product—is imputed to the manufacturer when strict liability is applied. Because, however,

the manufacturer is held to the standard of expert in its field, it will be a rare case indeed where the manufacturer "should not" have known of the dangers in its product although those dangers were knowable at the time of the marketing.

Recognizing the convergence of the theories of negligence and strict liability in design cases, the commentators have argued that, for strict liability to be of any consequence in such cases, knowledge of risks that were unknowable at the time of marketing should be imputed to manufacturers. This, however, the courts have consistently failed to do. Although there is language in some cases which appears to indicate a leaning toward imputation of knowledge of unknowable risks upon the manufacturer, the overwhelming majority of courts have evaluated the product on the basis of what dangers could have been known at the time of marketing.

12. The constructive knowledge, "*cost*-benefit," definition of strict liability—often referred to as the "Wade–Keeton test"—is particularly relevant to the state-of-the-art issue, examined in § 5(D), below.

13. Perfect quality control is often impossible, and the cost of improving the search for manufacturing flaws at some point becomes prohibitive. Should the defendant in a manufacturing flaw case be permitted to demonstrate that the benefits from improved quality control procedures (including the prevention of the plaintiff's injuries) were in fact less than the costs of improving the procedures? See Brown v. General Foods Corp., 117 Ariz. 530, 573 P.2d 930 (1978). Why or why not?

14. **Cost-Benefit Analysis in Governmental Safety Regulation.** Governmental product safety agencies, like the courts, make extensive use of risk-benefit analysis in regulatory decision-making. For purposes of § 15 of the Consumer Product Safety Act, which requires sellers promptly to report to the CPSC suspected defects in their products which could create substantial product hazards, the Commission initially proposed defining "defect" as follows:

> A "defect" within the meaning of section 15 of the CPSA is any aspect of a product which creates an unnecessary risk of injury. Such aspects include, but are not limited to the following: Performance, composition, contents, design, construction, finish, packaging, warnings, and instructions. A product presents an unnecessary risk if the aspect which creates the risk is not necessary for the product to perform its functional purpose. A risk is also unnecessary if the benefits (including recreational and aesthetic benefits) to be gained from use of the product do not justify the risk of injury. A product defect within the meaning of Section 15 includes both unintended manufacturing errors and/or imperfections and intended product aspects.

Many commentators on the proposed definition objected to the risk-benefit approach, and so it was dropped in the final version. See 16 CFR § 1115.4 (1978). In commenting upon the omission, however, the Commission remarked as follows: "Although [the risk-benefit] sentence has been deleted from final § 1115.4, the Commission believes that some kind of balancing is implicit in the concept of defect." 1 Cons.Prod.Saf. Guide (CCH) ¶ 12,300, at 10,289–5. Consider also the defect notification provisions of the National Traffic and Motor Vehicle Safety Act of 1966, where the concepts of "motor vehicle safety" and "defect" have been held "to signify a 'common-sense' balancing of safety benefits and economic costs." See United States v. General Motors Corp., 518 F.2d 420, 435 (D.C.Cir.1975).

Notwithstanding the widespread, perhaps inevitable, use of cost-benefit analysis in safety regulation, it remains a highly politicized issue in the CPSC and other agencies, and in the Congress. "A recent Consumer Product Safety Commission cost-benefit analysis on recliner chairs, which concluded that solving a hazard resulting in deaths to small children would be cost effective only if a solution could be found that cost less than 25 cents a chair, was 'not only stupid, but wrong,' Rep. Henry A. Waxman (D–Calif) said Feb. 25." Prod. Saf. & Liab.Rep. (BNA) 134 (Feb. 28, 1986). A more recent House bill barred the CPSC from using cost-benefit analysis in determining product safety. See Prod.Saf. & Liab.Rep. (BNA) 941, 942 (Sept. 30, 1988).

But far more controversial than the choice of an appropriate cost for safety improvements is the difficult task of determining an appropriate value for a statistical human life. While different agencies in differing contexts use widely varying figures, a recent study finds substantial use in the agencies of values in the range of $1–2 million per life. See C. Gillette & T. Hopkins, Federal Agency Valuations of Human Life (Report to the Admin. Conf. of the U.S.) (Oct. 1988).

15. Some commentators have noted that, unlike consumer expectancy analysis, risk-benefit analysis suffers from a lack of richness and humanism since it is predicated upon stark economic efficiency. See Klemme, The Enterprise Liability Theory of Torts, 47 U.Colo.L.Rev. 153, 191 n. 106 (1976). Professor Balkin, in Too Good to Be True: The Positive Economic Theory of Law, 87 Colum.L.Rev. 1447, 1475–76 (1987), faults efficiency tests for being incomplete:

> Human values and goals may take wealth maximization into account, but they may not be exclusively or even primarily concerned with it. Human action and human decision may rest only in part on [efficiency analysis. Thus,] the greatest problem with wealth maximization as a theory of human practical reason may be that it is insufficiently rich.

Compare Hubbard, Reasonable *Human* Expectations: A Normative Model for Imposing Strict Liability for Defective Products, 29 Mercer L.Rev. 465, 468–69 (1978):

> Which is more important—efficiency or expectation? The answer would seem to depend on the state of society. If the society had such a limited economy that efficiency were necessary for the subsistence of its members, then efficiency would be at least a prima facie candidate to prevail. However, this situation is certainly not the case in the United States. While inefficiency is not desirable in our circumstances, even a considerable amount of inefficiency need not be disastrous. A denial of expectations, on the other hand, would be equally offensive in both a hand-to-mouth and an "affluent" society because such a denial results in a negation of the right of persons to be viewed as ends rather than as mere factors of production involved in achieving an efficient society. From a more general perspective, the entire notion of individual rights becomes highly problematic if social benefit, no matter how slight, can justify a denial of any such right. Thus, human expectation ought to prevail over efficiency in our society.

Do you agree? Which test on balance is the better?

C. THE CONTINUING SEARCH FOR A VIABLE TEST OF "DEFECTIVENESS"

In searching for a workable test of "defectiveness," most courts focused initially upon the "defective condition unreasonably dangerous" phrase in § 402A. The evolution of this phrase is thus helpful in understanding some of the problems that have arisen in its application.

In 1958 the Reporter for the Restatement, Dean Prosser, prepared a first draft of § 402A imposing strict liability for the sale of food "in a condition dangerous to the consumer." Restatement (Second) of Torts § 402A (Prelim. Draft No. 6, 1958). Another draft was presented to the Council two years later without any change in the crucial "dangerous" condition language. Id. (Council Draft No. 8, 1960). In an effort to address the concern of certain members of the Council that the "dangerous" condition language was overbroad, Dean Prosser changed it to its present form by modifying "dangerous" with the word "unreasonably" and "condition" with the word "defective;" hence, "*defective condition unreasonably dangerous* to the user or consumer." This was the form in which the section was presented for consideration to the American Law Institute. Id. (Tent. Draft No. 6, 1961). See generally Wade, On the Nature of Strict Tort Liability for Products, 44 Miss.L.J. 825, 830 (1973).

Consider the following debate over the wording of the section that transpired on the floor of the Institute in 1961.

THE BIRTH OF "DEFECTIVE CONDITION UNREASONABLY DANGEROUS"

38 ALI Proceedings 86–89 (1961).

PRESIDENT TWEED: Now, as to possible language on Section 402A, I think the reporter has run down—

PROFESSOR DICKERSON: Mr. Chairman, may I make a small point? In this discussion of substantive issues I hesitate to bring up a mere question of draftsmanship, but I think this may have some significance.

I am a little bothered by the phrase "defective condition unreasonably dangerous to the consumer * * *." This signifies some nondefective conditions unreasonably dangerous to the consumer, and if there are, I would be interested in hearing an example of a product which was at the same time unreasonably dangerous but not defective.

I had always thought that "unreasonably dangerous" was simply the best possible test for what was legally defective. It seems to me * * * that everything we might want to cover here is subsumed under the words "unreasonably dangerous."

Now, the addition of the words "defective condition"—it would seem to me that this involves unnecessary questions of meaning. For example, in addition to "unreasonably dangerous," what would a purchaser have to show in order to make out a defective product? I would think that if he showed that it was unreasonably dangerous, it would per se be legally defective, and it is only gilding the lily to add the word "defective."

For these reasons I move that we strike the word "defective," and consolidate Comments *e* and *f*.

DEAN PROSSER: Mr. Dickerson has stated an original point of view which I first brought into the Council of The American Law Institute in connection with this section. " * * * food in a condition unreasonably* dangerous to the consumer" was my language. The Council then proceeded to raise the question of a number of products which, even though not defective, are in fact dangerous to the consumer—whiskey, for example [laughter]; cigarettes, which cause lung cancer; various types of drugs which can be administered with safety up to a point but may be dangerous if carried beyond that—and they raised the question whether "unreasonably dangerous" was sufficient to protect the defendant against possible liability in such cases.

Therefore, they suggested that there must be something wrong with the product itself, and hence the word "defective" was put in; but the fact that the product itself is dangerous, or even unreasonably dangerous, to people who consume it is not enough. There has to be something wrong with the product.

Now, I was rather indifferent to that. I thought "unreasonably dangerous," on the other hand, carried every meaning that was necessary, as Mr. Dickerson does; but I could see the point, so I accepted the change. "Defective" was put in to head off liability on the part of the seller of whiskey, on the part of the man who consumes it and gets delirium tremens, even though the jury might find that all whiskey is unreasonably dangerous to the consumer.

PROFESSOR DICKERSON: I rest my case entirely on the word "unreasonably." Whenever we gild the lily, I think we just invite difficulty.

PRESIDENT TWEED: The motion is to eliminate "defective" in the black letter * * *.

* * *

DEAN LOCKHART: * * *

It seems to me this ought to come out. I don't know how I voted in the Council.

DEAN PROSSER: Well, I can tell Dean Lockhart that he voted in favor of the word "defective." [Laughter]

* Dean Prosser apparently either misremembered or misspoke in stating that the "*unreasonably* dangerous" language was his.—Eds.

PROFESSOR JOINER: I would like to support Mr. Dickerson and Dean Lockhart. It seems to me that the Reporter's case of whiskey is taken care of by the words "unreasonably dangerous."

* * *

We merely confuse the law by adding "defective."

PRESIDENT TWEED: Well, let's have a vote. We have been two hours and twenty-two minutes on this section. The motion is to omit "defective."

[The motion was put to a voice vote.]

PRESIDENT TWEED: The noes seem to me to have it. Does anybody want to keep score?

DIRECTOR GOODRICH: I think the noes have it, but if anybody calls for a division, of course, we will count.

[Nobody called for a division, the motion to strike "defective" failed, and the entire phrase "defective condition unreasonably dangerous" was retained.]

NOTES

1. Of the two hours and twenty-two minutes devoted to § 402A, the vast bulk of the time had been spent on issues unrelated to the phraseology of its black letter provision.

2. Earlier in the discussion Dean Prosser had indicated that the "unreasonably dangerous" language too had been added "to head off liability for a product which is sold where there is nothing wrong with the product as a product, but nevertheless it is going to injure some people. A good many individuals are allergic to strawberries and eggs. That doesn't mean that there is anything wrong with the food. There is something wrong with the individual. 'Defective condition' and 'unreasonably dangerous' are deliberately designed to protect the defendant against undue liability." 38 ALI Proceedings 55 (1961).

3. The coverage of § 402A was broadened in 1962 to include "other products for intimate bodily use" in addition to food. Restatement, Second, Torts § 402A (Tent. Draft No. 7, 1962). Two years later the section was submitted to the Institute in its final form, in which liability was extended to the sale of "*any product* in a defective condition unreasonably dangerous to the user or consumer." Id. (Tent. Draft No. 10, 1964) (emphasis added). The section was approved by the Institute at its meeting that year, and the section was published a year later in volume 2 of the Second Restatement.

CRONIN v. J.B.E. OLSON CORP.

Supreme Court of California, 1972.
8 Cal.3d 121, 104 Cal.Rptr. 433, 501 P.2d 1153.

SULLIVAN, JUSTICE. In this products liability case, the principal question which we face is whether the injured plaintiff seeking recovery upon the theory of strict liability in tort must establish, among other facts, not only that the product contained a defect which proximately caused his injuries but also that such defective condition made the product unreasonably dangerous to the user or consumer. We have concluded that he need not do so. Accordingly, we find no error in the trial court's refusal to so instruct the jury. * * *

[The court reviewed the development of the strict tort doctrine in California, particularly its 1963 decision in Greenman v. Yuba Power Products, Inc., which held that "A manufacturer is strictly liable in tort when an article he places on the market, knowing that it is to be used without inspection for defects, proves to have a defect that causes injury to a human being." This language in *Greenman* was compared to § 402A's standard of liability for selling products in a "defective condition unreasonably dangerous to the user or consumer."]

The almost inextricable intertwining of the *Greenman* and Restatement standards in our jurisprudence was inevitable, considering the simplicity of *Greenman* and the fuller guidance for many situations offered by the Restatement and its commentary. Nevertheless, the issue now raised requires us to examine and resolve an apparent divergence in the two formulations.

* * * Prosser, the reporter for the Restatement, suggests that the "unreasonably dangerous" qualification was added to foreclose the possibility that the manufacturer of a product with inherent possibilities for harm (for example, butter, drugs, whiskey and automobiles) would become "automatically responsible for all the harm that such things do in the world." (Prosser, Strict Liability to the Consumer in California (1966) 18 Hastings L.J. 9, 23.)

The result of the limitation, however, has not been merely to prevent the seller from becoming an insurer of his products with respect to all harm generated by their use. Rather, it has burdened the injured plaintiff with proof of an element which rings of negligence. As a result, if, in the view of the trier of fact, the "ordinary consumer" would have expected the defective condition of a product, the seller is not strictly liable regardless of the expectations of the injured plaintiff. * * * In fact, it has been observed that the Restatement formulation of strict liability in practice rarely leads to a different conclusion than would have been reached under laws of negligence. * * *

Of particular concern is the susceptibility of Restatement section 402A to a literal reading which would require the finder of fact to conclude that the product is, first, defective and, second, unreasonably dangerous. (Note, supra, 55 Geo.L.J. 286, 296.) A bifurcated standard is of necessity more difficult to prove than a unitary one. But merely proclaiming that the phrase "defective condition unreasonably dangerous" requires only a single finding would not purge that phrase of its negligence complexion. We think that a requirement that a plaintiff also prove that the defect made the product "unreasonably dangerous" places upon him a significantly increased burden and represents a step backward in the area pioneered by this court.

* * *

In summary, we have concluded that to require an injured plaintiff to prove not only that the product contained a defect but also that such defect made the product unreasonably dangerous to the user or consumer would place a considerably greater burden upon him than that articulated in *Greenman.* We believe the *Greenman* formulation is consonant with the rationale and development of products liability law in California because it provides a clear and simple test for determining whether the injured plaintiff is entitled to recovery. * * *

* * *

[Affirmed.]

NOTES

1. The *Cronin* court's purge of the "unreasonably dangerous" phrase from strict liability in tort was followed in a very few cases. Butaud v. Suburban Marine & Sporting Goods, Inc., 543 P.2d 209 (Alaska 1975); Berkebile v. Brantly Helicopter Corp., 462 Pa. 83, 337 A.2d 893 (1975); Glass v. Ford Motor Co., 123 N.J.Super. 599, 304 A.2d 562 (Law.Div.1973). Noting that "Cronin has been widely criticized as providing no useful definition of an actionable defect, particularly in relation to a case of a product of unsafe design," the Supreme Court of New Jersey repudiated *Glass* on this point in Cepeda v. Cumberland Engineering Co., Inc., 76 N.J. 152, 386 A.2d 816 (1978). Like *Cepeda,* most courts that have passed on the question have rejected the *Cronin* approach. See, e.g., Byrns v. Riddell, Inc., 113 Ariz. 264, 550 P.2d 1065 (1976); Heldt v. Nicholson Mfg. Co., 72 Wis.2d 110, 240 N.W.2d 154 (1976). Commentary in the law reviews was generally critical of *Cronin.* E.g., Fischer, Products Liability—The Meaning of Defect, 39 Mo.L.Rev. 339 (1974); Keeton, Product Liability and the Meaning of Defect, 5 St. Mary's L.J. 30 (1973); Wade, On the Nature of Strict Tort Liability for Products, 44 Miss.L.J. 825 (1973).

2. Contrast Judge Wisdom's pre-*Cronin* observation in Ross v. Up–Right, Inc., 402 F.2d 943, 947 (5th Cir.1968), that "to speak in terms of 'defect' only causes confusion. * * * The key * * * is whether the product is 'unreasonably dangerous'."

3. **Alternative Verbalisms.** Some states which have rejected the entire Restatement phrase, "defective condition unreasonably dangerous," have also rejected its component parts, refusing to embrace either "defective" or the "unreasonably dangerous" phrase as the liability standard. Instead, various courts have substituted phrases such as "dangerously defective," or "not reasonably safe," or "unduly unsafe," or "not reasonably fit, suitable and safe."

4. In Azzarello v. Black Bros. Co., Inc., 480 Pa. 547, 391 A.2d 1020, 1027 n. 12 (1978), the court approved the following standard jury instruction:

> The [supplier] of a product is the guarantor of its safety. The product must, therefore, be provided with every element necessary to make it safe for [its intended] use, and without any condition that makes it unsafe for [its intended] use. If you find that the product, at the time it left the defendant's control, lacked any element necessary to make it safe for [its intended] use or contained any condition that made it unsafe for [its intended] use, then the product was defective, and the defendant is liable for all harm caused by such defect.

See Notes, 81 Dick.L.Rev. 374 (1977); 21 Vill.L.Rev. 794 (1976).

CATERPILLAR TRACTOR CO. v. BECK

Supreme Court of Alaska, 1979.
593 P.2d 871.

CONNER, JUSTICE.

On June 24, 1973, Derald Allen Beck was killed when the Caterpillar 944 front-end loader which he was operating rolled over an embankment. Decedent's widow, Paula Beck, brought this action against Caterpillar Tractor Company (hereinafter Caterpillar) for the wrongful death of her husband. Beck contended that Caterpillar's failure to equip the 944 loader with a roll-over protective shield (hereinafter ROPS) constituted a design defect in the loader * * *. [Verdict and judgment for the plaintiff, and Caterpillar appeals.]

* * *

A ROPS is an overhead protective canopy which is constructed to withstand a roll-over and, thus, protect the operator from being crushed. In addition, a ROPS can decrease the risk of a roll-over. There was no dispute at trial that a ROPS, as developed at the time of the accident, would have saved Derald Beck's life. Beck would not have been crushed and a ROPS may have even prevented the loader from overturning. * * *

* * *

II. DESIGN DEFECT

Caterpillar contends that the trial court erred in instructing the jury that "[a] design defect is one in which the product, however perfectly manufactured, incorporates or fails to incorporate a design feature with the result that injury is proximately caused thereby." Caterpillar argues that the instruction misconstrues the law of strict liability in that it essentially instructs the jury on absolute liability: it does not instruct the jury that they must first find a defect in the product nor does it give the jury guidance in determining whether a defect exists. In addition, Caterpillar urges that we define the term "defective" for cases involving design defect, preferably by use of a standard which balances the risk presented by the product in light of the product's utility. Beck, in response, argues that the jury was properly instructed on the necessity of finding a defect before it could fix liability and that the term "defect" need not be defined beyond its inherent meaning. Because this issue poses so substantial a question in a nascent body of law, we believe it would be helpful, before turning to the particulars of this instruction, to briefly summarize the development of products liability.

Strict products liability evolved from two separate bases: implied warranty and strict liability in tort.[8] In the process whereby the courts

8. See, e.g., Greenman v. Yuba Power Products, Inc., 59 Cal.2d 57, 27 Cal.Rptr. 697, 377 P.2d 897 (1962) (discussing both theories); Henningsen v. Bloomfield Motors, Inc., 32 N.J. 358, 161 A.2d 69 (1960) (warranty). [Citations.]

have combined these theoretical bases and have fashioned from them a new species of product liability, it has become apparent that several policy considerations have been at work.[9] First, greater efficiency and justice would be achieved by eliminating the necessity for plaintiffs to prove fault by manufacturers of defective products. Second, frustration of consumer expectation would still be the underlying basis of recovery. Third, incidence of harm from unsafe products would be reduced by imposing strict liability and thus providing an incentive to produce safer products. Fourth, risks would be allocated and losses spread by requiring a manufacturing enterprise to accept responsibility in strict liability for harm attributable to a defect in its product. The concept of risk allocation has been the primary policy rationale convincing courts to adopt strict products liability.[10]

* * *

Although courts and commentators have struggled with diverse approaches to strict products liability, most authorities appear to agree that manufacturers are not absolute insurers of their products. Strict liability will not impose legal responsibility simply because a product causes harm.[18] A product must be defective as marketed if liability is to attach, and "defective" must mean something more than a condition causing physical injury.

The instruction at issue stated that plaintiff Beck alleged that a design defect caused the death of Derald Beck and then proceeded to state that a product is defectively designed when an injury results from a design feature (or the lack of a design feature). Essentially, the jury was instructed that there must be proof of a defect in the product's design in order for liability to attach, and that proof of an injury could suffice to prove a defect. If such defect proximately caused the injury, strict liability is imposed. This is a tautology and tantamount to an instruction of absolute liability.

* * *

Caterpillar also contends that the jury was inadequately instructed on the meaning of design defect. Since a manufacturer's strict liability depends upon the meaning of defective, Caterpillar urges us to develop particular standards for assessing a product's defectiveness.

Design defects present the most perplexing problems in the field of strict products liability because there is no readily ascertainable external measure of defectiveness. While manufacturing flaws can be evaluated against the intended design of the product, no such objective standard exists in the design defect context. Beck argues that, despite

9. See generally, Keeton, Product Liability and the Meaning of Defect, 5 St. Mary's L.J. 30, 34–35 (1973).

10. See, e.g., Greenman v. Yuba Power Products, Inc., supra, note 8; Henningsen v. Bloomfield Motors, Inc., supra, note 8; Goldberg v. Kollsman Instrument Corp., 12 N.Y.2d 432, 240 N.Y.S.2d 592, 191 N.E.2d 81 (1963).

18. See Keeton, supra note 9, 5 St. Mary's L.J., at 33; Lascher, Strict Liability in Tort for Defective Products: The Road to and Past Vandermark, 38 S.Cal.L.Rev. 30, 47 (1965); Traynor, The Ways and Meanings of Defective Products and Strict Liability, 32 Tenn.L.Rev. 363, 366–67 (1965); Wade, Strict Tort Liability of Manufacturers, 19 Sw.L.J. 5, 13 (1965).

the lack of an external standard in design defect cases, the word "defect" has an inherent meaning; i.e., a flaw or incompleteness. Therefore, when jurors are instructed that they must find a defect to impose liability, they realize that the product must be faulty. However, we believe that the dictionary meaning of the word "defect" is insufficient to fully explain to the jury when a manufacturer should incur legal responsibility for his product's design.

> "[The] natural application [of the word 'defective'] would be limited to the situation in which something went wrong in the manufacturing process, so that the article was defective in the sense that the manufacturer had not intended it to be in that condition. To apply it also to the case in which * * * the design turns out to be a bad one or the product is likely to be injurious in its normal condition * * * [and] [t]o use it without defining it to the jury is almost to ensure that they will be misled." (footnotes omitted)

Wade, On the Nature of Strict Tort Liability for Products, 44 Miss.L.J. 825, 831–32 (1973). Since we are unwilling to view any product which causes an injury while being used properly as defectively designed, we must formulate a test which will guide the jury in design defect cases.

In the strict liability context, the term "defect" is "neither self-defining nor susceptible to a single definition applicable in all contexts." Barker v. Lull Engineering Co., Inc., 20 Cal.3d 413, 143 Cal. Rptr. 225, 235, 573 P.2d 443, 453 (1978). The varied purposes and the theoretical underpinnings of implied warranty and strict liability in tort have generated [a variety of] tests for product defectiveness * * *.

* * *

[The court discussed various shortcomings in the different liability tests, including the failure of the consumer expectations test to provide redress in the context of obvious dangers.] Consumer expectations are a factor to be considered in determining defectiveness, but the public policy supporting strict liability would be poorly served if consumer expectations were the sole boundary of liability.[35]

The Restatement (Second) of Torts, section 402A, provides a two-prong test for the seller's liability. Defectiveness is established if the product leaves the seller's hands in an "unreasonably dangerous" condition and such condition is not contemplated by the ultimate consumer. Thus, recovery would not be allowed for obvious or generally known dangers. Although the Restatement test improves upon the deficiencies of the above tests, we adhere to our previously expressed view that the "unreasonably dangerous" terminology of the Restate-

35. Consumer expectations cannot be the exclusive test because "[i]n many situations * * * the consumer would not know what to expect, because he would have no idea how safe the product could be made." Wade, On the Nature of Strict Tort Liability for Products, 44 Miss.L.J. 825, 829 (1973).

ment unnecessarily limits the scope of liability and unduly increases the plaintiff's burden of proof.[37]

Two commentators, Deans Page Keeton and John Wade,[38] have proposed similar risk/utility analysis tests. Their approaches recognized that evaluation of product defectiveness involves multiple factors, and they attempt to fulfill the purposes of strict products liability by creating a framework for balancing the relevant factors without shifting the inquiry to what the manufacturer should have foreseen at the time the product was sold.

* * *

Because a conclusion of "defectiveness" represents a determination that the design at issue is "wrong" in the sense that we will impose legal responsibility for harm caused therefrom, we are in agreement with Deans Wade and Keeton that the final assessment of "defectiveness" necessarily implies a weighing of diverse factors related to the product's desirability and to its dangerousness. Since evidence of these factors will be considered by the jury, we believe it is preferable to provide the jury with a proper framework in which to consider such evidence. However, we perceive no reason to reinsert negligence terminology into the analysis by instructing the jury, as suggested by Deans Wade and Keeton, to determine what a reasonable, prudent manufacturer would have done if aware of the harmful nature of the product. The focus of strict products liability is on the condition of the product, not on the manufacturing and marketing decision of the defendant. [Citation.] Therefore, indiscriminate use of reasonableness language will confuse the strict liability standard by introducing inessential attention to the conduct of the defendant, even if actual knowledge of the harmful condition is presumed rather than proven. Nor do we think it necessary to have a two-tier system where the trial judge, before giving the case to the jury, must first find that it would be reasonable for the jury to find for the plaintiff. Given proper instructions, we believe a jury can determine from the evidence whether a defect exists or not.

The California Supreme Court held in Barker v. Lull Engineering Co., Inc., supra, that:

> "[A] trial judge may properly instruct the jury that a product is defective in design (1) if the plaintiff demonstrates that the product failed to perform as safely as an ordinary consumer would expect when used in an intended or reasonably foreseeable manner, or (2) if the plaintiff proves that the product's design proximately caused his injury and the defendant fails to

37. See Butaud I, 543 P.2d 209 (Alaska 1975); Butaud v. Suburban Marine & Sporting Goods, Inc., 555 P.2d 42 (Alaska 1976) (hereinafter *Butaud II*).

38. See Keeton, supra note 9, 5 St. Mary's L.J., at 37. An earlier formulation appears in Keeton, Manufacturer's Liability: The Meaning of "Defect" in the Manufacture and Design of Products, 20 Syracuse L.Rev. 559, 568 (1969); Wade, On the Nature of Strict Tort Liability for Products, 44 Miss.L.J. 825, 834–35 (1973); Wade, Strict Tort Liability of Manufacturers, 19 Sw.L.J. 5, 15–17 (1965).

> prove * * * that on balance the benefits of the challenged design outweighed the risk of danger inherent in such design."

143 Cal.Rptr. at 239, 573 P.2d at 457–58.[43] * * *

In view of the diversity of product deficiencies which could fall within the notion of defect, we are persuaded that the *Barker* two-prong test provides the most comprehensive guidelines for instructing juries, without compromising any of the goals of strict liability.

The *Barker* test represents a composite of the most workable features of each of the other tests. The first prong of the *Barker* test—that a product is defectively designed if it fails "to perform as safely as an ordinary consumer would expect when used in an intended or reasonably foreseeable manner"—incorporates notions of the implied warranty of fitness for reasonable use, a primary concept in the evolution of strict products liability, but eases the burden of proof on the plaintiff. In a cause of action based upon a warranty of fitness and merchantability, the plaintiff would have to prove the breach by pinpointing the actual defect. Under the *Barker* test, the plaintiff need only show, for strict liability to apply, that he used the product in an intended or reasonably foreseeable fashion and the product failed to perform in that capacity as safely as expected. * * *

The second prong of the *Barker* definition encompasses those situations, such as the lack of a safety device which is presented here, where the product satisfies ordinary consumer expectations as to its general use but is still "defective" in that its design exposes the user or bystander to "excessive preventable danger." What is excessive preventable danger must turn on the facts of each case. With the focus off the ordinary consumer's expectations, the trier of fact balances the risk and the social utility of the product. This requires a weighing of various factors. Therefore, where necessary, the trial court may instruct the jury that if "on balance, the benefits of the challenged design outweigh the risk of danger inherent in such design," no liability will attach. *Barker,* supra, 143 Cal.Rptr. at 240, 573 P.2d at 458.

Although we believe that a balancing process is inevitable in certain design defect cases, we in no way intend to diminish our adherence to the goals of strict products liability. Therefore, we also agree with the position taken by *Barker* regarding the allocation of the burden of proof:

> "[I]nasmuch as * * * a manufacturer who seeks to escape liability for an injury proximately caused by the product's design on a risk-benefit theory should bear the burden of persuading the trier of fact that its product should not be judged defective, the defendant's burden is one affecting the burden of proof, rather than simply the burden of producing evidence." (citations omitted)

43. Other courts have adopted a similar test. See, e.g., Welch v. Outboard Marine Corp., 481 F.2d 252, 254 (5th Cir.1973); Henderson v. Ford Motor Co., 519 S.W.2d 87, 92 (Tex.1974).

143 Cal.Rptr. at 237, 573 P.2d at 455. We hold that the plaintiff need only show that he was injured and that the injury was proximately caused by the product's design. The defendant may then avoid liability for a defectively designed product by proving by a preponderance of the evidence that, "on balance, the benefits of the challenged design outweigh the risk of danger inherent in such design." *Barker,* supra, 143 Cal.Rptr. at 240, 573 P.2d at 458. This will require the fact-finder to consider and compare a number of competing factors, including but not limited to,

> "the gravity of the danger posed by the challenged design, the likelihood that such danger would occur, the mechanical feasibility of a safer alternative design, the financial cost of an improved design, and the adverse consequences to the product and to the consumer that would result from an alternative design."

143 Cal.Rptr. at 237, 573 P.2d at 455. Besides lessening the burdens of the plaintiff's prima facie case, this allocation puts the burden of producing the relevant complex and technical evidence on the party who has the most access to and is the most familiar with such evidence.[52]

* * *

In summary then, we hold that the instruction approved in *Clary* will in many cases suffice. However, in those cases where the meaning of "defect" will be unduly vague, particularly in design defect cases, the trial court may formulate instructions which define the legal concept of "defect" for the jury. Following the guidelines set by the *Barker* court, we hold that the trial court may instruct the jury that a product is defectively designed if:

> "(1) the plaintiff proves that the product failed to perform as safely as an ordinary consumer would expect when used in an intended or reasonably foreseeable manner, or (2) the plaintiff proves that the product's design proximately caused injury and the defendant fails to prove, in light of the relevant factors, that on balance the benefits of the challenged design outweigh the risk of danger inherent in such design."

143 Cal.Rptr. at 234, 573 P.2d at 452. Because the jury here was erroneously instructed on causation as the primary definition of defect, the judgment entered against appellant Caterpillar must be reversed.

* * *

REVERSED and REMANDED.

[Separate opinions of Dimond, S. J., and Burke, J., dissenting from certain rulings of the majority on comparative negligence, but concurring on issues of liability, omitted.]

52. The established rule is that the product must be shown to be defective when it left the defendant's possession or control. [Citations.] It follows that design defects must be measured by the knowledge and information which existed when the product left the hands of the manufacturer.

NOTES

1. "When the ghosts of case and assumpsit walk hand in hand at midnight, it is sometimes a convenient and comforting thing to have a borderland in which they may lose themselves." W. Prosser, The Borderland of Tort and Contract, in Selected Topics on the Law of Torts 380, 452 (1953).

2. The *Barker* court summarized its rationale as follows:

> [T]he test for defective design set out above is appropriate in light of the rationale and limits of the strict liability doctrine, for it subjects a manufacturer to liability whenever there is something "wrong" with its product's design—either because the product fails to meet ordinary consumer expectations as to safety or because, on balance, the design is not as safe as it should be—while stopping short of making the manufacturer an insurer for all injuries which may result from the use of its product. This test, moreover, explicitly focuses the trier of fact's attention on the adequacy of the product itself, rather than on the manufacturer's conduct, and places the burden on the manufacturer, rather than the plaintiff, to establish that because of the complexity of, and trade-offs implicit in, the design process, an injury-producing product should nevertheless not be found defective.

Barker v. Lull Engineering Co., 20 Cal.3d 413, 432, 143 Cal.Rptr. 225, 238, 573 P.2d 443, 456, 96 A.L.R.3d 1 (1978).

3. Reconsider Judge Wisdom's remarks in Welch v. Outboard Marine Corp., 481 F.2d 252, 254 (5th Cir.1973), relied upon in Phillips v. Kimwood Machinery Co., supra:

> We see no necessary inconsistency between a seller-oriented standard and a user-oriented standard when, as here, each turns on foreseeable risks. They are two sides of the same standard. A product is defective and unreasonably dangerous when a reasonable seller would not sell the product if he knew of the risks involved or if the risks are greater than a reasonable buyer would expect.

Welch is apparently the genesis of the alternative buyer-seller test of liability. See generally Montgomery & Owen, Reflections on the Theory and Administration of Strict Tort Liability for Defective Products, 27 S.C.L.Rev. 803, 843–45 (1976).

After quoting this excerpt from *Welch,* the *Phillips* court concluded that "the two standards are the same because a seller acting reasonably would be selling the same product which a reasonable consumer believes he is purchasing." Is this true?

4. A small number of courts have followed *Barker*'s two-pronged definition of product defect. In addition to Alaska in the principal case, the two-pronged aspect of the *Barker* test was explicitly adopted in Ontai v. Straub Clinic & Hosp., Inc., 66 Hawaii 237, 659 P.2d 734 (1983), and Knitz v. Minster Mach. Co., 69 Ohio St.2d 460, 432 N.E.2d 814 (1982). It was explicitly rejected in Lester v. Magic Chef, Inc., 230 Kan. 643, 641 P.2d 353 (1982). A couple of courts have danced around the issue, seemingly adopting the *Barker* alternative test approach, but without saying so explicitly. See Dart v. Wiebe Mfg., Inc., 147 Ariz. 242, 709 P.2d 876 (1985); Ortho Pharmaceutical Corp. v. Heath, 722 P.2d 410 (Colo.1986) (semble). Compare Baughn v. Honda Motor Co., Ltd., 107 Wash.2d

127, 727 P.2d 655, 660 (1986) (applying a "consumer expectation test with a risk-utility base").

PIETRONE v. AMERICAN HONDA MOTOR COMPANY, INC.

California Court of Appeal, 1987.
189 Cal.App.3d 1057, 235 Cal.Rptr. 137.

GATES, ASSOCIATE JUSTICE.

Defendant American Honda Motor Company, Inc., appeals from the judgment entered pursuant to a jury verdict in favor of plaintiff Alison Pietrone. It contends: "I. Because there was no evidence from which the jury could infer that the motorcycle performed less safely than the reasonable consumer could expect and no evidence that the motorcycle's design caused the injury, plaintiff failed to bear her burden of proving design defect under Barker v. Lull [Engineering Co. (1978) 20 Cal.3d 413, 143 Cal.Rptr. 225, 573 P.2d 443]. II. Plaintiff's counsel impermissibly argued the existence of alternative motorcycle wheel designs in closing argument despite the absence of any evidence of such designs. This argument allowed the jury to assume, without supporting evidence, such designs would have prevented the injury and to consider the 'benefits' of such designs without their 'risks.' "

Plaintiff presented evidence that she was a passenger on her husband's 1974 Honda CB 450 motorcycle on the afternoon of April 26, 1979. As they entered the intersection of Towne Avenue and Arrow Highway in the City of Pomona the driver of an on-coming automobile began a U-turn. Her husband moved to the right in an unsuccessful attempt to avoid the vehicle. The auto's bumper struck the lower portion of plaintiff's left leg, breaking it.

This impact was so slight it merely created a "wobbling sensation" in the motorcycle rather than causing it to overturn. Nonetheless, plaintiff's now unstable leg came into contact with the exposed spokes of its rear wheel behind the shock absorber * * *. [Her foot lodged in the] open area located in front of the shock absorber and above the chain guard.

So powerful were the forces that had been exerted upon plaintiff's foot, she was required to sit, helplessly trapped, for many agonizing minutes. In fact, she was freed only after firemen arrived armed with an instrument known as the "jaws of life" with which they were able to cut away the shock absorber. As a result of her experience, it was necessary for this 21-year old plaintiff to undergo a below the knee amputation of her leg.

After presenting the foregoing evidence, but before formally resting, counsel for plaintiff advised the court it was his "understanding of the law, as it exists now in product liability cases, that it is the responsibility of a plaintiff to meet her burden of proof that she present a prima facie case. [¶] That . . . a design feature, and in this case that would be the open, exposed, rotating wheel of this motorcycle, was a proximate cause of her injury. [¶] Having established a prima facie case to that extent, . . . the burden of proof then shifts to the defendant" who "must now prove and produce evidence that the benefit of this design feature outweighs the risk of injury, as has been presented by the plaintiff." Counsel expressed his belief that plaintiff had met this burden and sought the court's concurrence. He also informed the court that he had additional witnesses, specifically engineers, who could be called to defend "against whatever evidence the defendants present on their burden of proof."

[Defense counsel rested, without putting on any evidence, arguing that the plaintiff had failed to present a submissible case because of her failure to produce any evidence of alternative designs that would have prevented the harm. The trial court ruled, however, that the plaintiff had presented sufficient evidence to submit the design issue to the jury.]

In Barker v. Lull Engineering Co. (1978) 20 Cal.3d 413, 143 Cal. Rptr. 225, 573 P.2d 443, our highest court established that "a product may be found defective in design, so as to subject a manufacturer to strict liability for resulting injuries, under either of two alternative tests. First, a product may be found defective in design if the plaintiff establishes that the product failed to perform as safely as an ordinary consumer would expect when used in an intended or reasonably foreseeable manner. Second, a product may alternatively be found defective in design if the plaintiff demonstrates that the product's design proximately caused his injury and the defendant fails to establish, in light of the relevant factors [e.g., "the gravity of the danger posed by the challenged design, the likelihood that such danger would occur, the mechanical feasibility of a safer alternative design, the financial cost of an improved design, and the adverse consequences to the product and to the consumer that would result from an alternative design" (id. at p. 431, 143 Cal.Rptr. 225, 573 P.2d 443)], that, on balance, the benefits of the challenged design outweigh the risk of danger inherent in such design." (Id. at p. 432, 143 Cal.Rptr. 225, 573 P.2d 443.)

In the instant case the evidence conclusively established that a design feature of Honda's product—the open, exposed, rotating rear wheel in close proximity to the passenger's foot pegs—was a proximate cause of plaintiff's injury. Without more, the burden then shifted to Honda to justify its adoption and utilization of that particular design. (See BAJI No. 2.60 as modified in accordance with BAJI No. 9.00.5 (7th ed. 1986).) Further, even were it to be assumed that plaintiff's burden under *Barker* exceeded such a showing and required that she demonstrate the existence of some alternative design which would have prevented or lessened her injury, this burden was met by the jury's mere inspection of the photographs introduced into evidence. That is to say, no more than a cursory examination of this machine's configuration makes apparent both the danger of its design and potential solutions thereto.[2]

Given that such alternative designs were so self-evident as to obviate the need to present express testimony, expert or otherwise, on the subject, it is equally clear counsel for plaintiff did not commit misconduct by mentioning during argument that items which "would avoid contact" such as saddlebags, luggage racks, fairings, shields, etc., could be so placed as to partially enclose the motorcycle's rotating rear wheel. The existence of such devices on other models is a matter of general knowledge and their potential effectiveness in preventing the sort of accident which occurred here is patent.

Since Honda, apparently for unknown tactical reasons it regarded as sound, elected to make absolutely no effort "to establish that because of the complexity of, and trade-offs implicit in, the design process," (Barker v. Lull Engineering Co., supra, 20 Cal.3d at p. 432, 143 Cal. Rptr. 225, 573 P.2d 443), the risk of danger inherent in the particular design it selected for this model machine was outweighed by the benefits of that design, it failed to meet its burden of proof. (See the Use Note to BAJI No. 9.00.5 (7th ed. 1986).) Of course, had it sought to do so its efforts might well have proven successful for one can readily postulate potential economic, aesthetic and engineering reasons for the design selected. Nonetheless, in the complete absence of any evidence regarding such "beneficial" considerations, the jury's verdict was both understandable and proper.

Since we have determined, as did the trial court who actually heard the evidence and denied Honda's motion for a new trial, that plaintiff met her burden under the risk-benefit test, we need not consider whether or not she also would have prevailed under the consumer expectations test alone.

The judgment is affirmed.

COMPTON, ASSOCIATE JUSTICE.

I concur in the result solely under the compulsion of language in Barker v. Lull Engineering Co. (1978) 20 Cal.3d 413, 143 Cal.Rptr. 225, 573 P.2d 443. I must confess, however, that the result makes no practical sense to me. There is a fundamental flaw in the law governing product liability in California—a flaw which I am hopeful will be remedied by our newly-constituted Supreme Court.

The flaw is that under the prevailing concept, no consideration is given to the voluntary choice by a plaintiff to use a product which by its very nature is dangerous but highly utilitarian.

There is on the market today a wide variety of products, for example, chainsaws, "weedeaters" and other power tools which when used in their ordinary and expected manner can produce serious

2. Upon our own motion we ordered the exhibits introduced below transmitted to this court for review. (Cal.Rules of Court, rule 12(a).)

injuries. They have exposed blades which, when they strike some object or bind on a particular item, "kick back" and cause injury.

People voluntarily use these items knowing of their danger because they are useful for a particular job. Why should not that voluntary choice be an ingredient in determining liability for an injury resulting from such use?

Here, plaintiff's husband purchased this motorcycle because he apparently liked its design and appearance. He knew full well at the time that the rear wheel was exposed. If that exposure was of importance to him, he could have chosen another brand or purchased some other covering for the wheel.

Further, when plaintiff took her seat on the motorcycle, she knew that her feet were close to the exposed wheel. There was nothing secret about the fact that certain actions by herself or others could cause her foot to strike the wheel. Plaintiff accepted the configuration of the motorcycle and voluntarily elected to ride with her feet in that precarious position. Her foot was forced into the wheel by the negligence of another driver. Thus, the true cause of the injury was the combination of that driver's negligence and the plaintiff's position on the motorcycle.

Under these circumstances, why should the manufacturer of a popular and mechanically sound product be forced to justify its failure to install the various items, the existence of which Justice Gates says "is a matter of general knowledge and their potential effectiveness in preventing the sort of accident which occurred here is patent." Their absence was as patent to the plaintiff as to anybody else.

As I see it, if a manufacturer does everything necessary to make the machine function properly for the purpose for which it is designed, if the machine is without any latent defect, and if its functioning creates no danger or peril that is not known to the user, then the manufacturer has satisfied what the law ought to demand.

The concept of "socializing" the loss, which is at the heart of the present approach to product liability, is plainly and simply wrong. Unfortunately, as an intermediate appellate court, we are stuck with it. For this reason alone I concur in the result.

ROTH, PRESIDING JUSTICE, dissenting.

I respectfully dissent. The thrust of plaintiff's case is that defendant Honda, the distributor of the motorcycle, is strictly liable[1] to her based on her contention that the unenclosed spoked rear wheel of the motorcycle upon which she was a passenger was defectively designed (discussed infra). Her complete prima facie case consisted of evidence showing how the accident occurred (the injury to her leg) and the amputation of a portion thereof. Relying upon those bare bone facts

1. Although plaintiff's complaint had included other theories of liability, she abandoned them immediately before trial commenced and proceeded solely on a theory of strict liability.

and Barker v. Lull (1978) 20 Cal.3d 413, 143 Cal.Rptr. 225, 573 P.2d 443, she convinced the trial court she had completed a prima facie case of Honda's liability so that a showing of non-liability had shifted to defendant Honda. Hence, the narrow question before this court, as set forth by the record and fortified by the plaintiff's pretrial tactics, is when in the progress of a strict liability trial, such as the case at bench, does the burden of going forward shift?

* * *

* * * *Barker* makes clear that there is no absolute liability merely because a party is injured while using the defendant's product. There must be evidence of the design defect which proximately caused the injuries *and* evidence of how a safer product could have been manufactured. * * *

* * *

Here, plaintiff's evidence showed that while riding with her husband on his motorcycle, something she had done once or twice every week during the prior three years, she was injured following a collision with an automobile which broke her leg and pushed it into the motorcycle's unenclosed rear spinning spoked wire wheel. Plaintiff offered no evidence of similar prior accidents. Quite apart from the fact plaintiff presented no evidence as to what she or anyone else reasonably expected in regard to the safety of a motorcycle involved in a collision with a car, plaintiff offered no evidence, through either lay or expert testimony, on the significant question of safer alternative designs in regard to the unenclosed rear spoked wheel. Plaintiff attempted to elicit testimony from one of her medical witnesses as to how the motorcycle might have been modified so as to prevent the injury but was precluded from doing such because she was unable to lay a sufficient foundation for the witness' expertise on the question. Plaintiff's counsel, however, argued to the jury, over defendant's objection, about modifications to the motorcycle which might have prevented plaintiff's injuries. He pointed to items such as saddlebags, luggage racks, and fairings as examples of what could have been placed upon the rear wheel area of the motorcycle to enclose it. This argument was improper as there was no legally acceptable evidence in the record to support it (see, e.g., Malkasian v. Irwin (1964) 61 Cal.2d 738, 745–747, 40 Cal.Rptr. 78, 394 P.2d 822) and arguably those proposed designs might just as probably been design defects which could have caused more problems.

The naked facts before this court graphically illustrate why a plaintiff is required in its prima facie case to produce some evidence on a safer alternate design before a defendant is required to respond.

As Professor Schwartz has noted:

"The heart of the problem is this: one simply cannot talk meaningfully about a risk-benefit defect in a "product design until and unless one has identified some design alternative (including any design omission) that can serve as the basis for a risk-benefit analysis." (G. Schwartz, Foreward: Understanding Products Liability (1979) 67 Cal.L.Rev. 435, 468 and see also pp. 470–471.)

In my opinion, *Barker* holds, and common sense and pragmatic fairness dictate, that a plaintiff must set forth, through legally competent evidence, one or more proposed alternatives to the attacked design. (Accord: Cotchett and Cartwright, California Products Liability Actions (1985) § 7.02[1], p. 7–12.1.) Given that, defendant does have something tangible to rebut and is able to show plaintiff's proposals would either entail unreasonable cost, be practically unfeasible, interfere with the product's performance, or create (other) increased risks. (Barker v. Lull, supra, 20 Cal.3d at pp. 431–432, 143 Cal.Rptr. 225, 573 P.2d 443.) Following such a presentation by defendant, the trier of fact can then meaningfully engage in the balancing process known as the risk-benefit analysis to decide whether or not the product was defectively designed.

Absent such an approach, the defendant becomes an absolute insurer of the product. * * *

* * *

The pragmatic effect of the manner in which the present case was tried amounts to an inappropriate interjection into a strict liability lawsuit of the concept of res ipsa loquitor. * * *

It is well settled that res ipsa loquitor has no application to an action based solely upon a theory of strict liability in tort. * * *

Prophetically, one commentator noted this possibility over twenty years ago when he predicted res ipsa loquitor would be indirectly used to "prove" a product was defective. He warned: "If this practice grows, plaintiff may next be required only to connect up the injury with the product. He may not have to prove a defect. When and if this happens we shall have taken another step on the road toward making consumer's injuries into an equilibrium system, wherein the important question is not who *caused* the injury, but how should the harm be repaired." (T. Cowan, Some Policy Bases of Products Liability (1965) 17 Stan.L.Rev. 1077, 1094; emphasis added.)

The critical vice of the trial court's approach is to encourage lawsuits in which plaintiff's counsel alleges only two facts: (1) an accident occurred; and (2) the plaintiff was injured thereby. Instead of doing the requisite investigation, including the gathering of expert testimony, to prove a defendant's product was defective and that the product could have been more safely designed, a plaintiff, such as respondent herein, only establishes the twin facts of an accident and injuries. The consequent burden placed upon the judicial system and the tax-paying public which supports it is immense not to mention the dislocation it creates for all the parties plaintiff names in the action.

Exploding products liability litigation has created a fiscal crisis, fueled in part by such cases as this one where the effect of the jury's decision is to make any defendant, and especially deep pocket defendants, absolute and complete insurers for all injuries resulting from the use of their products even when a plaintiff has utterly failed to establish a design defect. At bench, clearly the driver of the car which hit the motorcycle was potentially culpable. Although served with plaintiff's complaint, he did not answer and pursuant to the parties' stipulation, a default was entered against him. Satisfying any judgment in part and/or in full against him would be futile. And although Honda cross-complained against plaintiff's husband for indemnification based upon a claim he had been negligent in his driving of the motorcycle, the court concluded otherwise in a bench trial conducted after plaintiff's trial had been completed. Hence, defendant Honda, the deep pocket defendant and the distributor of the motorcycle, is left holding the bag although, as Justice Compton cogently notes in his concurring opinion:

> "The true cause of the injury was the combination of [the automobile] driver's negligence and the plaintiff's position on the motorcycle."

I agree with Justice Compton that in an ill fated attempt to socialize the loss, the courts have expanded the concept of tort law and financial responsibility of any who may be embraced in the tort charged. I also agree that the original concept of strict liability is Gibraltar solid. However, socialization of the loss is not nor is the doctrine of strict liability the issue in this case. The fundamental question in this case is *due process* in a strict liability case. Acceptance of the trial court's approach eliminates due process. It permits any injured user of any product, including those mentioned in Justice Compton's concurring opinion, to sue a solvent defendant in strict liability merely by alleging purchase of the product and the sustaining of injuries while using the product. That result corrodes the rule of law as accepted since adversary trials have been an integral part of the administration of justice and substitutes an ad hoc judicial dispensation of justice. Such a judicial outlook undermines the concept of personal responsibility and the duty to exercise due care. Lack of legal necessity to personally use due care has reached the point at which the effort of a plaintiff to establish the liability of some conceivably solvent potential defendant corrodes the primary instinct of survival.

In brief, I suggest with humility the public is rapidly reaching the crossroads which present it with a choice between constitutional government as we have lived it or government by fifty judicial oligarchies.

The present judgment is in my opinion against the law in its present state of generous interpretation. I would reverse.

NOTES

1. "The rule places an enormous burden on the concept of a 'product design that proximately causes injury,' a burden which the concept seems ill-equipped to handle. * * * People fall off ladders all the time, and the fact that ladders are both high and in some general way unstable enables these falls to occur. Does it or doesn't it follow that in every case of a person's falling off a

ladder, the ladder's design proximately causes the fall?" G. Schwartz, Foreword: Understanding Products Liability, 67 Calif.L.Rev. 435, 466–67 (1979).

2. Except for Caterpillar Tractor Co. v. Beck, supra, the courts have rejected *Barker*'s second-prong shift in the burden of proof. Wilson v. Piper Aircraft Corp. (on rehearing), 282 Or. 411, 579 P.2d 1287 (1978); Hayes v. Ariens Co., 391 Mass. 407, 462 N.E.2d 273 (1984); Ontai v. Straub Clinic & Hosp. Inc., 66 Hawaii 237, 659 P.2d 734 (1983); Cremeans v. International Harvester Co., 6 Ohio St.3d 232, 452 N.E.2d 1281 (1983); Kallio v. Ford Motor Co., 407 N.W.2d 92 (Minn.1987). The commentators have also been critical of *Barker*'s shift in the burden of proof. See, e.g., Schwartz, supra note 1, at 467–68; Wade, On Product "Design Defects" and Their Actionability, 33 Vand.L. Rev. 551, 573 (1980); W.P. Keeton, D. Dobbs, R. Keeton & D. Owen, Prosser and Keeton on the Law of Torts 702 (5th ed. 1984).

3. The continuing search for a viable test for defectiveness goes on. Some courts continue to require a plaintiff to establish that the product was *both* defective *and* unreasonably dangerous. E.g., Patterson v. F. W. Woolworth Co., 786 F.2d 874 (8th Cir.1986) (Iowa law). By statute, Tennessee permits a plaintiff to recover upon a showing that the product was in a defective condition *or* unreasonably dangerous. See Smith v. Detroit Marine Engineering Corp., 712 S.W.2d 472, 474 (Tenn.App.1985).

How about different tests for different defects?

A. Some courts and commentators take the position that a consumer expectations, or deviation from specifications, test should be used in manufacturing flaw cases, while a risk-utility test should be used in design defect cases. See, e.g., McNeese v. Reading & Bates Drilling Co., 749 F.2d 270 (5th Cir.1985) (Tex. law); Bilotta v. Kelley Co., Inc., 346 N.W.2d 616 (Minn.1984).

B. What test is best for warnings cases? Is the *Barker* dual-pronged test appropriate? See Cavers v. Cushman Motor Sales, Inc., 95 Cal.App.3d 338, 157 Cal.Rptr. 142 (1979).

C. If the concepts of "defective" and "unreasonably dangerous" are too difficult to define, how about no test at all? Consider Nesselrode v. Executive Beechcraft, Inc., 707 S.W.2d 371, 377–78, 389, 393 (Mo.1986):

> Though Missouri has adopted the rule of strict tort liability as set forth in the *Restatement,* we have not yet formally incorporated, in any meaningful way, the *Restatement*'s consumer expectation test into the lexicon of our products liability law. [Citation.] Nor have we yet decided to travel or require plaintiffs to travel the path of risks and utilities. * * *
>
> Under our model of strict tort liability the concept of unreasonable danger, which is determinative of whether a product is defective in a design case, is presented to the jury as an ultimate issue without further definition.[11] [Citation.] Accordingly, our approved jury instruction which governs in a design defect case, MAI 25.04 (3rd) does

11. Most states, whether they apply a unitary definitional test or a multifactor analysis, define to some extent the appropriate standard to the jury. [Citations.] The subject of how the jury should be instructed and what is the proper role for the jury has been given attention by a number of commentators and courts. See Owens and Montgomery, Reflections on the Theory and Administration of Strict Tort Liability For Defective Products, 27 S.C.L.R. 803, 830–45 (1976) [double sic]; Wade, On the Nature of Strict Tort Liability for Products, 44 Miss.L.J. 825, 838–41 (1973); see also Phillips v. Kimwood Machine Co., 269 Or. 485, 525 P.2d 1033, 1039–40 (1974).

not contain as one of its component elements a definitional paragraph which gives independent content to the concept of unreasonable danger.

Notwithstanding the minority character of this approach, Professor Leon Green * * * explains why an approach that avoids the use of an external standard by which to determine unreasonable danger—i.e., defectiveness—is preferable to one which does use an external standard. He points out first that juries do not have "a fictitious standard by which to determine assault, battery, false imprisonment, nuisance, entry upon land, or the taking of a chattel" and then he suggests that "[n]or do juries need an external standard by which to determine the danger of a product in a unreasonably dangerous defective condition." Green, Strict Liability Under Sections 402A and 402B: A Decade of Litigation, 54 Tex.L.Rev. 1185, 1206 (1976). He concludes his discussion with the judgment that "the ritual indulged in by the giving of abstract, abstruse standards, impossible to comply with, only perpetuates the mystical trial by ordeal and *may conceal a hook in a transcendental lure that will snag an appellate court.*" Id. at 1206. (emphasis added)

As we noted previously, at the trial of a design defect case, the concept of unreasonable danger is treated as an ultimate issue. The jury gives this concept content by applying their collective intelligence and experience to the broad evidentiary spectrum of facts and circumstances presented by the parties. * * *

* * *

BLACKMAR, JUDGE, concurring.

* * *

I am not certain that the unadorned submission of unreasonable danger as an ultimate issue is appropriate for all products liability cases. I have particular reservation in cases in which a product has apparent social utility and cannot be made wholly safe. * * *

* * *

WELLIVER, JUDGE, dissenting.

* * *

* * * I am compelled to address [certain] glaring deficiencies in the principal opinion [including] its failure to adopt a test for "unreasonably dangerous" * * *.

I agree that the consumer expectation test, first developed in the area of contract law under an implied warranty theory, has come under increasing scrutiny and criticism by courts and commentators. Although not yet introduced into our law, it may well be that the prudent-manufacturer test or the risk-utility test (or the risk-utility test combined with a factor analysis) is the better reasoned approach. I cannot, however, agree with the principal opinion's limiting of its discussion to "edificatory" ends. The approach this Court sanctions, whether in the case *sub judice* or in future cases, will govern how cases shall be argued to the jury and then, if appropriate, briefed on appeal. This is a threshold matter inherent in every strict liability case and by not approving one of the tests, the principal opinion, in effect, leaves all future triers of strict product liability cases at their peril as to choosing a theory of proof at trial.

D. While the strict liability standard may well be appropriate for manufacturing flaw cases, should the courts acknowledge that negligence is really a better standard for design (and perhaps, warnings) cases after all? A few courts have so held. See Rix v. General Motors Corp., 723 P.2d 195 (Mont. 1986); Bilotta v. Kelley Co., Inc., 346 N.W.2d 616 (Minn.1984); Prentis v. Yale Mfg. Co., 421 Mich. 670, 365 N.W.2d 176 (1984). Products liability reform legislation often so provides. See Connor v. Skagit Corp., 30 Wash.App. 725, 638 P.2d 115, 121 (1981). See generally Foley v. Clark Equip. Co., 361 Pa.Super. 599, 523 A.2d 379 (1987) (extensive argument favoring negligence over strict liability in tort).

SECTION 2. DEFECTIVE MANUFACTURE

A manufacturer may breach its duty to manufacture "nondefective" products in two principal ways. First, the raw materials or components used in making the product may contain physical flaws. Second, although the components may individually be free of flaws, some mistake may be made in their assembly into the final product. When the manufacturing process goes awry in either manner, the product may fail to meet even the manufacturer's own specification standards. If such a product escapes the manufacturer's quality controls, its flawed condition may lead to its failure in use and possibly to injury of the user or another.

When a physically flawed product involved in an accident does end up on trial, its "defectiveness" is usually not contested in any theoretical sense. More typically, since the product may well have been damaged or destroyed in the accident, the crucial issue is whether the product's defective condition is attributable to mismanufacture or to some other cause—such as normal wear and tear, abuse by the user, or perhaps even to the accident itself.

A. IN GENERAL

POUNCEY v. FORD MOTOR CO.

United States Court of Appeals, Fifth Circuit, 1972.
464 F.2d 957.

LEWIS R. MORGAN, CIRCUIT JUDGE. C.L. Pouncey, the appellee, was injured while putting antifreeze in his 1966 Ford automobile. While he was accelerating the engine with the hood open, a blade broke off the radiator fan, cut through the water hose, and struck him in the face causing permanent facial disfigurement. Pouncey had purchased the car secondhand approximately six months before the accident from Clement Motor Company of Greenville, Alabama. The car had been driven approximately 62,000 miles at the time of the accident.

Pouncey brought this action below against Ford Motor Company, the appellant, seeking damages for the injury on a [negligence] theory. The case was tried to a jury which returned a verdict in favor of Pouncey in the amount of $15,000.00. Ford now appeals * * *. * * *

I.

As is frequently the case in products liability litigation, the trial produced a conflict in expert testimony. The main thrust of Pouncey's case was that the fan blade failure occurred because of a fatigue fracture in the metal fan blade. It was Pouncey's theory that the premature fatigue failure was caused by an excessive number of inclusions in the metal of the blade. An inclusion is a non-metallic impurity in the steel which weakens the metal.

To substantiate this theory, Pouncey called Dr. C. H. T. Wilkins, a metallurgical engineer, as an expert witness. Dr. Wilkins testified that he cut and mounted a specimen of metal from the failed blade. He also cut and mounted specimens from a blade which had not failed and from another Ford fan blade which had failed. On microscopic examination of this mount, Dr. Wilkins found a "surprising number of inclusions" which he did not expect to find in this type steel. These inclusions, he testified, were an identifiable defect in the metal which served as "stress concentrating areas" and "lowered the endurance limit of the fan".

Dr. Wilkins also testified concerning certain bends and deformations in the blade. He conceded that there appeared to be some bends in the blades but he expressed the opinion that the blade which actually failed was not bent. In his opinion, the bends in the blades were not the cause of the fatigue failure.

Not surprisingly, Ford's expert witnesses took a different view of the facts. Ford first called Dr. Robert Hochman, another metallurgical engineer. Dr. Hochman testified that he received and examined the metal specimen that had been mounted by Dr. Wilkins. It was his opinion that the specimen had been mounted in such a way that acid seeped into the cracks between the specimens of metal, causing an exaggerated appearance of large inclusions[.] Dr. Hochman remounted and polished the specimens and took photomicrographs of them. These photomicrographs showed an acceptable inclusion level, testified Dr. Hochman, which conformed with standards established by the Society of Automotive Engineers.

Dr. Hochman attributed the fracture to a different source. He testified that one arm of the blade was bent and that this would have a major effect in throwing the fan out of balance. He also noted that the ends of the blades were bent and cracked and that this condition would also tend to imbalance the fan. An out-of-balance condition, Dr. Hochman testified, could cause the blade to vibrate and set up a high stress pattern which would result in the acceleration of metal fatigue.

Dr. Hochman also noted a small notch in the fracture surface which could have been attributed to impact damage.

Ford also called two other expert witnesses, both of whom were Ford employees. Mr. Phillip Burch, a Ford design engineer, testified as to the testing procedures utilized by Ford on newly designed radiator fans. Mr. Robert Riding, another Ford engineer, testified concerning alleged bends in the fan blades. He stated in his opinion that the fan failed because of an unbalanced condition in the fan which may have been caused by a front end collision or by rough handling.

II.

* * *

Initially, Ford argues that the evidence was insufficient because Pouncey's expert testimony, viewed in its best light, does not make any one cause of the blade separation more probable than another. Ford places special emphasis on one portion of the record in which it is said that Dr. Wilkins declined to state that the level of inclusions which he found in the metal was unacceptable. The testimony in question is as follows:

"Q. From what you yourself saw, Doctor, of the inclusions that were in this radiator fan, Exhibit No. 1, that struck Mr. Pouncey, was that an acceptable level of inclusion in that material?

"A. In the sense that I found the number of inclusions that I did, sir, I was very much surprised.

"Q. You were surprised when you saw all that in there?

"MR. MATTHEWS: If the Court please, we move to exclude that answer. That is not what was asked. He said he was surprised. The question was whether it was accept—

"MR. MANCUSO: Why—

"THE COURT: Excuse me. Wait just a minute.

"MR. MATTHEWS: Whether it was an acceptable level of inclusion.

"THE COURT: I think it is appropriate if you can see if you can answer that question, whether it was an acceptable level of inclusion. Can you give an answer to it?

"A. No, sir. Because I do not know what they consider an acceptable level."

It is further contended that Dr. Wilkins' testimony as to the cause of the separation was speculative. Ford asserts that Dr. Wilkins merely stated that the inclusions "could" have caused the fatigue fracture and that he acknowledged that it might have been caused by imbalance of the blades or by other factors such as sludge build-up.

However, a careful reading of Dr. Wilkins' testimony in its entirety requires that we reject Ford's contentions. His testimony went far beyond mere speculation in pinpointing the cause of the fracture. He stated unequivocally that "enormous" inclusions not normally found in spring steel were an "identifiable defect" in the metal which caused premature fatigue failure.[1] Ford's assertion that Dr. Wilkins refused to

1. A sampling of Dr. Wilkins' testimony is as follows:

"Q. Is it true the presence of these substances, these foreign substances in metal premature, shorten the life of the metal?

A. Yes, sir, it can.

Q. Were these inclusions present and were they an identifiable defect in this particular radiator fan that has been marked as Exhibit No. 1 at the time the thing was installed on the automobile?

A. Yes, sir.

* * *

Q. But they [inclusions] were present in the metal?

A. Yes, sir. And should have been seen at an earlier time.

Q. Could they have been seen at an earlier time?

A. Yes, sir.

Q. If Ford, Dr. Wilkins, had the proper quality control tests run on that metal, would they have discovered that?

MR. MATTHEWS: Objection to the question, leads to conclusions on the jury.

THE COURT: I will sustain.

Q. Dr. Wilkins, with steel which is as you have testified, as dirty as what you saw, could they have reasonably expected this blade to have failed?

MR. MATTHEWS: Objection to the form of the question.

THE COURT: Overrule.

A. Yes, sir.

Q. All right. Now, Doctor, is it true that the presence of these inclusions would lower the endurance limit of this metal from what it would have been had not the inclusions been present in the metal?

A. Yes, sir.

Q. Now does this mean that the blade would break prematurely, and by prematurely I'm referring to what you would normally expect the length of the life of the blade to be?

MR. MATTHEWS: Objection.

THE COURT: Overruled.

A. Yes, sir.

Q. It would break prematurely with these type—

A. With respect to what might be considered normal life.

Q. Now, Doctor, is it true that the presence of these inclusions or these foreign substances or dirty matters, however you want to refer to it, would shorten the fatigue life of the metal in this particular Exhibit No. 1 that we are talking about from what you would expect it to be if it didn't have this matter in it?

A. Yes, sir.

* * *

Q. Did these inclusions constitute a stress concentrating area?

A. Yes, sir.

Q. All right. What are we referring to there?

A. When you apply a bending stress to a metal, and if an inclusion is located in a highly stressed area, particularly if it is in near the edge, which of course would be highly stressed, then you can have the stress itself concentrated in that particular area. And eventually have this develop into possibly a notch, which could lead into a fracture.

Q. Doctor, if everything you have testified to, does it have a bearing on what actually happened in this blade that struck Mr. Pouncey?

A. Yes, sir.

Q. Now, Doctor, is it true, with regard to these stress concentrated areas, that they did lower the endurance limit of this particular piece of metal that injured Mr. Pouncey from what it would have been had the inclusions or the stress concentrating areas not been in there?

A. Yes, sir.

Q. All right. And again would these—would the absence or is it true that the presence of these stress concentrating areas shorten the fatigue life of the metal from what it would have been had they not have been in there?

A. Yes, sir.

* * *

Q. You found inclusions in this metal that struck Mr. Pouncey, is that correct?

A. Yes, sir.

state that the level of inclusions which he found was "unacceptable" is unfounded. That refusal was merely based on his hesitancy to ascribe the label "unacceptable" to the level of inclusions which he found while not knowing how his questioner defined the term. As Dr. Wilkins stated, he declined to answer the question "[b]ecause I do not know what they consider an acceptable level".

* * *

Ford also contends that the evidence was insufficient to support an inference of negligence either on the part of Ford or Ford's supplier, Fram Corporation. Ford contends that the testimony is undisputed that even under the best quality control program there is always the possibility that isolated pockets of inclusions could be found in metal and that there is no practical means of discovering the particular fans which might have these impurities. Ford argues that the absence of any proof by Pouncey of inadequate quality control procedures on the part of Ford or its supplier bars submission of the issue of Ford's negligence to the jury. Again we disagree.

* * *

* * * Under Alabama law, it is settled that a manufacturer's liability for a defective product is predicated upon negligence in the manufacture or design of the product. [Citation.] However, the Alabama courts have freely permitted juries to infer manufacturer negligence from circumstantial evidence where there is in the record direct evidence of an actual defect in the product. For example, in Greyhound Corporation v. Brown, 269 Ala. 520, 113 So.2d 916 (1959), the plaintiff had been injured while riding in a bus when a tire manufactured by the defendant blew out. In an action against the manufacturer, the plaintiff produced expert testimony that the blowout was due to a defect in the tire, but there was apparently no evidence as to the quality control procedures employed by the manufacturer. The court permitted the jury to infer negligence from the direct evidence of the defect in the product. * * *

In the case at bar, there was direct evidence that Ford's supplier manufactured the blades with "dirty" spring steel. There is also testimony by Pouncey's expert that Ford and its supplier could reasonably expect a premature fatigue failure from steel with that level of inclusions. Finally, Ford itself offered no evidence as to the quality control procedures actually employed with regard to the radiator fans produced in 1966. The court below committed no error in permitting the jury to infer from this evidence negligence on the part of Ford in placing on the market a defective radiator fan which could reasonably have been expected to produce injury or damage.

* * *

Q. All right.

A. We found inclusions, and I might emphasize here, it is not merely a matter of finding inclusions. I think it is the number of them, and the distribution of them enters into it."

* * *

* * * The disputed evidence as to the cause of the blade fracture was such that reasonable men might reach different conclusions.

[Affirmed.]

WEINSTEIN, TWERSKI, PIEHLER & DONAHER, PRODUCT LIABILITY: AN INTERACTION OF LAW AND TECHNOLOGY

12 Duquesne L.Rev. 425, 430–31 (1974).

The determination of defect and its unreasonable danger is, in one sense, subjective because each product must be viewed in the particular context of its function and use. The use of the same product in two different environments, domestic and industrial, for example, may lead to different conclusions regarding its defectiveness and unreasonable danger. * * *

[T]he concept of defect is not self-defining when a product contains a flaw. Since all products are flawed at some technological level,[11] the decision must still be made as to when a flaw emerges as a defect. In order to make this decision, some judgmental standard must be utilized.

* * *

NOTES

1. Why was not more emphasis placed in *Pouncey* on the defendant's expert testimony that the inclusion level in the metal fan blade conformed to standards established by the Society of Automotive Engineers?

2. How would the plaintiff's case differ under strict tort? Implied warranty? Would evidence on the adequacy of defendant's quality control procedures be relevant?

3. Below are two photographs showing metallic flaws in a screw representative of the type discussed in the Weinstein et al. excerpt.

11. To a metallurgist all metallic structures contain flaws or irregularities at some size level. They range from dislocations at the atomic size level to cracks visible to the naked eye. * * * Since these flaws [unfortunately sometimes called *defects* by metallurgists] can be identified in all products, the critical question to be asked is when can these deviations from structural perfection really lead to a conclusion of [legal] defect.

* * *

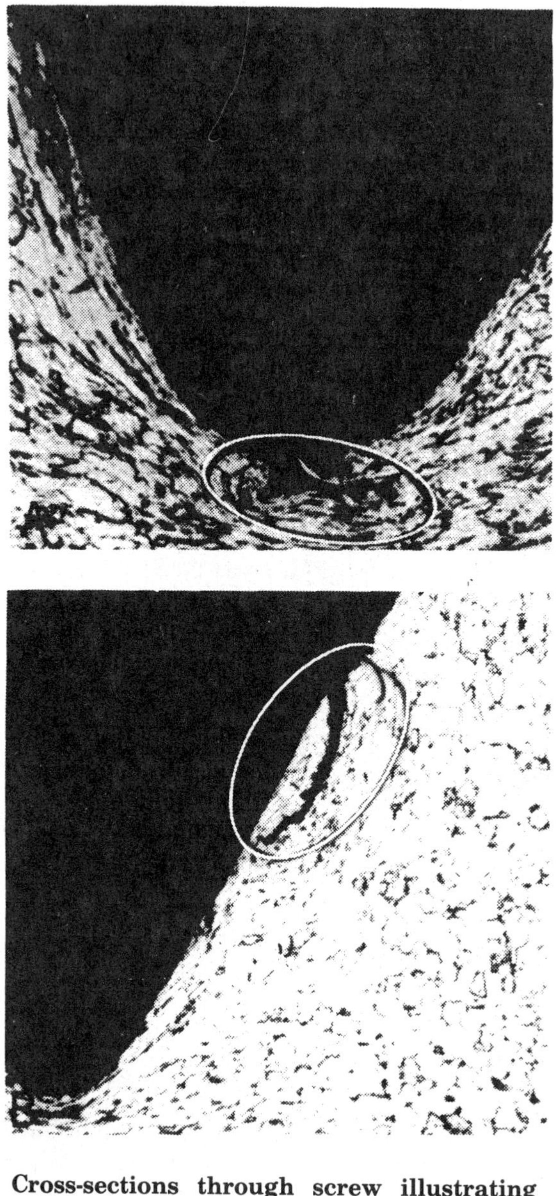

Cross-sections through screw illustrating roll-thread discontinuities at the root as well as the face of the threads. (A) Root discontinuities (250 X); (B) Face discontinuity (135 X).

4. In Keeler v. Richards Mfg. Co., Inc., 817 F.2d 1197 (5th Cir.1987), a surgeon inserted a compression hip screw into the plaintiff's broken hip to assist in the healing process. Several months later the screw broke, and plaintiff sued the manufacturer of the screw.

> Two of appellees' expert witnesses, John Harcourt and Dr. Gary Hansen, testified that the lag screw component of the compression hip screw contained at least four irregularities which they considered to be manufacturing defects. They also concluded that any one of the

identified defects could have been a producing cause of Mrs. Keeler's injuries. The first manufacturing defect they found concerned the length of the lag screw's internal threads. Appellants' design specifications required the lag screw's internal threads to be not more than 1.125 inches in length. John Harcourt testified that he measured the subject lag screw and found it to be 1.1875 inches in length. Dr. Hansen also examined the subject lag screw and confirmed that, in his opinion, the internal threads were "not in conformance with blueprint specifications."

Mr. Harcourt and Dr. Hansen testified that the presence of excess internal threads would weaken the lag screw by creating an area of unintentional stress concentration. They stated that, as a result of this defect, the lag screw's resistence to fatigue failure was decreased, which eventually caused the screw to break.

The second defect was evidenced by testimony that an unacceptable amount of metal debris was present in the lag screw at the time it was inserted into Mrs. Keeler's hip. John Harcourt testified that this debris would interfere with the surgeon's ability to compress the screw properly, thereby allowing the bones greater than normal movement. In turn, this failure to tighten properly would place a higher level of stress on the screw. Mr. Harcourt considered the resultant stress to be a producing cause of the screw's failure.

The claim of a third defect was based upon evidence that the subject screw's radius was slightly less than that of an exemplar hip screw furnished by Richards. John Harcourt testified that the smaller radius would result in greater stress concentration and that the subject screw was not as strong as it otherwise should have been. Finally, as a fourth defect, there was also some testimony that the hip screw failed to comply with the American Society of Testing Materials' (A.S.T.M.'s) standard of 35% ductility.

Held, jury verdict for plaintiff affirmed. 817 F.2d at 1200–01.

5. Other cases involving materials of inadequate strength or composition include O'Donnell v. Geneva Metal Wheel Co., 183 F.2d 733 (6th Cir.1950), cert. denied 341 U.S. 903, 71 S.Ct. 612, 95 L.Ed. 1342 (1951) (wheel barrow tire exploded because metal rivets holding rim together were weakened during assembly by pressing the metal too thin which generated visible radial cracks); Clark v. Zuzich Truck Lines, 344 S.W.2d 304 (Mo.App.1961) (truck's steering mechanism failed; evidence indicated that defendant's method of manufacturing, which differed from method recommended in Society of Automotive Engineers handbook, increased stress concentration on steering component which failed); Trowbridge v. Abrasive Co. of Philadelphia, 190 F.2d 825 (3d Cir.1951) (abrasive wheel disintegrated causing injury; manufacturing method trapped gases which generated internal fissures and cracks).

6. Manufacturing flaw cases often involve faulty product assembly. Many involve vehicles. For a representative sampling, see Hewitt v. B.F. Goodrich Co., 732 F.2d 1554 (11th Cir.1984) (tire bead bundle broke during manufacturing process); Hall v. Chrysler Corp., 526 F.2d 350 (5th Cir.1976) (misrouted transmission cable on truck came into contact with exhaust manifold, which melted cable and caused transmission to lock in "drive" position although gear lever indicated "park"); Reader v. General Motors Corp., 107 Ariz. 149, 483 P.2d 1388 (1971) (clip used to fasten speedometer cable to frame

incorrectly placed, causing cable to rub against and rupture brake fluid tube); Jenkins v. General Motors Corp., supra p. 53 (improperly torqued nut on bolt in suspension system worked loose, allowing bolt to fall out).

PROBLEMS OF PROOF

Most manufacturing flaw cases deal principally with problems of proof—of whether the accident was caused by a product defect or something else, and of whether any such responsible defect is attributable to the manufacturer. If a plaintiff is unable to prove by direct evidence that a manufacturing defect caused his accident, he must turn to circumstantial evidence and rely on inferences to prove his case. The following cases illustrate the principles and problems involved.

1. In Jakubowski v. Minnesota Mining & Mfg., 42 N.J. 177, 199 A.2d 826 (N.J.1964), the plaintiff was injured when the abrasive sanding disc on his grinding machine broke and struck him while he was working on the assembly line at Ford Motor Company. The disc was apparently discarded after the accident. Plaintiff sued the manufacturer of the disc in negligence and breach of warranty. The trial court dismissed both counts and, after an intermediate appeal, the Supreme Court (4–3) affirmed. Judge Proctor wrote for the majority:

> Plaintiff had worked for 17 years as a mechanic and body finisher on the production line at Ford and was experienced in the use of abrasive discs. On the day of the accident he was a relief operator for a crew of 15 grinders and solderers and had that morning as part of his duties brought from the stockroom a supply of 3M discs for the use of the grinders on the line. One of the grinders asked to be relieved and handed the plaintiff his pneumatic rotary-type grinding machine with a flexible sanding disc attached to its shaft. The grinder whom plaintiff relieved had been using the machine with the same disc attached, and plaintiff did not replace the disc before commencing his operation. The extent of the prior use of the disc does not appear. The grinding machine weighs about 7 pounds and is operated by air pressure which propels the disc on the shaft over a rubber or fiber backing plate with a diameter a few inches less than that of the disc. The machine is preset to rotate at 3600 revolutions per minute and with the 24-grit Type C disc attached is intended for rough sanding or snagging operations in which a braze, a "big gob" of brass, which may have sharp edges and abrupt corners, is cut down to a smooth surface by the action of the spinning disc applied under pressure by the operator. This type of snagging operation exposes the abrasive disc to a very punishing type of treatment. Plaintiff set the machine in operation at full speed by grasping its two handles and closing the valve in one of them to start the motor. He applied the spinning disc under pressure to a braze on an automobile body at the point where the windshield and door post are joined when the disc snapped in half and struck him in the abdomen. * * *
>
> The plaintiff testified that the discs "break often, and we change them as they break." Further, in response to the court's inquiry as to whether these discs had broken before, the plaintiff responded, "Yes; they break. We got hit many a time, but never thought nothing of it. A lot of fellows get hurt."
>
> * * *

The doctrine of *res ipsa loquitur,* where applicable, permits an inference that the plaintiff's injury was caused by the defendant's negligence. Generally, it cannot be invoked until it is shown that the instrumentality causing the injury was within the control of the defendant at the time of the mishap. However, if the instrumentality has left the control of the defendant prior thereto, the plaintiff may be permitted to invoke the doctrine if he introduces evidence that it was not improperly handled by himself or others, or its condition otherwise changed, after control was relinquished by the defendant. Bornstein v. Metropolitan Bottling Co., 26 N.J. 263, 273, 139 A.2d 404 (1958). When the doctrine of *res ipsa* is invoked the theory is that the type of accident which occurred does not happen in the absence of negligence, and where the defendant is in control of the instrumentality it is reasonable to infer that he was negligent. While a manufacturer is liable on its warranty irrespective of negligence, nevertheless it is necessary for the plaintiff to show that the dangerous condition which he contends constitutes a breach of warranty had its genesis when the instrumentality was within the control of the manufacturer. Accordingly, in the absence of direct evidence that the product is defective because of a manufacturing flaw or inadequate design, or other evidence which would permit an inference that a dangerous condition existed prior to sale, it is necessary to negate other causes of the failure of the product for which the defendant would not be responsible, in order to make it reasonable to infer that a dangerous condition existed at the time the defendant had control.

Plaintiff has shown that he used the disc in a proper manner and that it broke in use, and he contends that this evidence is sufficient to show a breach of warranty. The burden of proof was upon the plaintiff to show that the disc was unfit for its intended purpose when purchased from the manufacturer. "The test to be applied was whether the circumstances shown were such as to justify an inference of probability as distinguished from mere possibility." [Citation.] While it is possible that the disc broke because of a manufacturing flaw or because the design was inherently inadequate for rough snagging operations, it is just as possible that mishandling by the prior user or users or use beyond the expected life span of the disc was responsible.

* * *

Plaintiff has failed to introduce any evidence from which it is reasonable to infer that the expected useful life of the disc had not been exhausted at the time it broke. There is no hint in the record as to the manner and extent of use of the disc prior to plaintiff's use of it. Plaintiff failed to produce as a witness the workman he succeeded or to introduce other evidence which would exclude prior mishandling or overuse of the disc as a cause of the break. It is quite possible that a weakness in the backing was created by inexpert or careless use during the preceding operation, causing the disc to break when plaintiff subsequently used it. See Kramer v. R.M. Hollingshead Corp., 5 N.J. 386, 392, 75 A.2d 861 (1950).

Thus, we have here four possible causes of the break, viz.: manufacturing flaw, inadequate design, misuse, or overuse. The plaintiff has introduced no evidence which indicates that one of these causes is more probable than the others. In order to recover, he must present

> evidence from which it is reasonable to infer that more probably than not the cause of the break was one for which the defendant is responsible. [Citations.] We think that plaintiff has failed to show that it is more probable than not that the disc broke as a result of an unreasonably dangerous condition which existed at the time it was delivered by the defendant manufacturer to the plaintiff's employer. When a product can be damaged in the course of use and thereby become unreasonably dangerous, we cannot hold its manufacturer liable in warranty for the mere failure of the product in the absence of evidence tending to show that the product was not mishandled or used beyond its reasonably expected life span after it left the manufacturer's hands.

Dissenting, Chief Justice Weintraub responded: "My difficulty with the majority opinion is that it assumes that other possible causes for the disintegration of the disc are reasonably involved and hence that plaintiff to prevail was required to exclude them. So far as I know, those possibilities may be wholly imaginary."

2. Ten years later, the New Jersey Supreme Court had occasion to review the *Jakubowski* proof issues once again in Scanlon v. General Motors Corp., 65 N.J. 582, 326 A.2d 673, 681–85 (1974). Plaintiff's Chevrolet station wagon suddenly began to accelerate and crashed into a telephone pole before he could stop it. The road was dry and the weather clear at the time of the accident. The car had been purchased new 9 months earlier and had been driven 4000 miles before the accident. Although plaintiff had not himself had the carburetor adjusted, he did not know if his wife had; she did not testify at all. Plaintiff's expert, who had not examined the car or any of its parts, theorized that the sudden acceleration was caused by a piece of the carburetor cam breaking off and becoming jammed in the carburetor linkage. He conceded, however, that a photograph purporting to be of the cam in question showed it to be intact and unbroken. Plaintiff "admitted that after the accident he did not mention any malfunction of the vehicle in describing the occurrence to the investigating police officer whom he told he had simply lost control. Likewise, no mention of anything being wrong with the station wagon was made to [the dealer] upon a return visit some six months later." Defendant's theory was that plaintiff simply lost control of the vehicle, as he had told the police officer. At the close of all the evidence, the trial judge took the case from the jury and entered judgment for the defendant. The Appellate Division reversed. *Held,* judgment for defendant reinstated. Reaffirming the *Jakubowski* principles in a strict tort context, Judge Clifford wrote for the majority in part as follows:

> Plaintiff introduced evidence that the station wagon malfunctioned violently while being properly operated by him. This was sufficient to permit a finding that the vehicle was defective at the time of the accident.[7] [Citations.] However, this did not end plaintiff's burden with regard to the product itself. He still had to show that the

7. We note that it was the defendant manufacturer who produced the product at trial. Ordinarily it would be expected that production of the allegedly offending instrumentality would support plaintiff's position. Therefore, where it would be reasonable under all the circumstances for plaintiff to have produced the product which is claimed to suffer from a defect in the hands of defendant and plaintiff has failed to produce it or to offer any explanation or otherwise justify his failure to have done so, then the trier of fact is free to draw an adverse inference as to the existence of any defect. See Brownell v. White Motor Corp., 260 Or. 251, 490 P.2d 184, 187 (Sup.Ct.1971); McCormick, Evidence (2d ed. 1972) § 272, p. 656.

defective condition existed while in the control of the defendants. See Jakubowski v. Minnesota Mining & Manufacturing, supra, 42 N.J. at 182, 199 A.2d 826.

Plaintiff introduced no direct evidence that this defective condition existed while the vehicle was in the control of either defendant. He also failed to introduce "other evidence which would permit an inference that a dangerous condition existed prior to sale," Jakubowski v. Minnesota Mining & Manufacturing, supra, 42 N.J. at 184, 199 A.2d at 830. A motor vehicle is not a simple uncomplicated instrumentality. Its parts require periodic maintenance, minor adjustments and occasional major repairs or replacements. A nine-month old station wagon with 4000 miles on it is not the kind of product as to which human experience tells us an accident such as the one in question does not generally occur in the absence of a defect existing in the hands of the manufacturer. Relating its expected life span, durability and effective operability without maintenance to the age and prior usage of the Scanlon vehicle, we hold as a matter of substantive law that in the circumstances of this case the "other evidence" offered does not justify the drawing of an inference that any defect existed in the hands of the manufacturer or retailer.

It is equally clear that plaintiff failed to prove the defendants' responsibility for the defect by the negation of the other most likely possible causes of the accident. He attempted to do so by means of the testimony of an expert who had not examined the product and who testified in response to a hypothetical question. Quite properly, that hypothetical question contained within it an asserted negation of several possible alternative causes of the accident which would be obvious to a layman, *i.e.,* the car was not properly maintained and operated. But assuredly other possible causes existed, and given the complex nature of the product, plaintiff should have been required further to outline and discount the most likely of these in focusing upon the specific defect which he embraced.

As it was, plaintiff did not sufficiently negate even the possible alternative causes which he posed in his hypothetical. Specifically, he failed to establish that the defective condition was not the result of faulty maintenance. He showed that the vehicle was serviced twice by the defendant dealer, Demarest, and plaintiff testified that to the best of his knowledge no one adjusted the carburetor. However, he admitted that his wife was the principal driver. Her failure to appear as a witness to testify to the vehicle's maintenance was unexplained. *Jakubowski* requires at least that much, if not the testimony of the owner of the service station where they customarily traded, to negate the most likely possible alternative cause of improper maintenance. Alternatively, a subpoena of the station's records might have been sufficient to establish that no work was done on the carburetor by its employees. In this case improper maintenance or adjustment were conspicuous factors to be negated as most likely possible causes of malfunction. We conclude that those factors were not sufficiently negated to justify an inference that a defect existed while in the control of the defendants.

Pashman, J., dissented:

Our concern is not the ultimate conclusion to which each of us may come after reviewing plaintiff's factual proofs to show the elements of a strict liability action. That the absence of the wife's testimony could be considered "fatal to plaintiff's case" or that plaintiff could have subpoenaed service station records, indicates what plaintiff might have done differently to make a stronger case, but are irrelevant in deciding whether or not the case goes to the jury. It is not for this Court to decide how a case could be more convincingly presented.

* * *

In a strict liability action, plaintiff must show that the defect or dangerous condition originated when the instrumentality was in the manufacturer's control. This can be accomplished by direct evidence that the product is defective because of a manufacturing flaw, or by other evidence permitting such an inference, or by negating other causes of product failure. Jakubowski v. Minnesota Mining and Mfg. Co., 42 N.J. 177, 184, 199 A.2d 826 (1964). We are not faced here with merely the happening of an accident. Sudden uncontrolled acceleration followed by heavy brake application and 563 feet of skid marks surpass "mere surmise or conjecture." *Jakubowski,* supra at 182, 199 A.2d 826. These undisputed facts are consistent with a product defect and more than sufficient to support a finding by a jury in strict liability. * * *

3. Three and a half months after *Scanlon,* the New Jersey Supreme Court decided Moraca v. Ford Motor Co., 66 N.J. 454, 332 A.2d 599 (1975). "[P]laintiff heard a 'gink' in the front of his car and the steering mechanism suddenly locked," causing the car to skid off the road and into a tree. *Held,* the evidence was adequate to go to the jury. Distinguishing *Scanlon* on the basis of Scanlon's admissions and actions after the accident, the majority remarked as follows: "A new Lincoln Continental properly operated and maintained should not in normal experience develop a critical malfunction in the steering mechanism in six months and after being driven about 11,000 miles. When this happens a jury could reasonably infer that the malfunction was due to some manufacturing defect."

Clifford, J., dissented, in an opinion in which Mountain, J., joined:

With a nod in the direction of Scanlon v. General Motors Corp., 65 N.J. 582, 326 A.2d 673 (1974), the majority generously appraises today's holding as "quite consistent" with that recent effort to restate our formulation of the strict liability in tort doctrine. While the implication is that *Scanlon* is alive and robust in the fourth month of its life, in reality that decision is left reeling from the wounds inflicted upon it by the Court's opinion. I cannot reconcile the two cases.

* * *

The vehicle in question here was six months old with 11,000 miles of wear. If, as a matter of law, the critical inference cannot be drawn when the automobile is nine months old with 4,000 miles on it (the distance travelled is clearly more significant than a vehicle's age), *a fortiori* it cannot arise as to plaintiff's 11,000–mile Lincoln.

And if plaintiff's effort in *Scanlon* to negate other causes of the alleged defect fell short of what is required for the reason, among others, that his expert failed to "outline and discount the most likely of these [other causes] in focusing upon the specific defect which he embraced," then *a fortiori* where, as here, the experts did not even

> refer to any other possible causes, much less undertake to discount them, there is nothing for the jury to consider.

332 A.2d at 604–05.

4. Compare Holloway v. General Motors Corp., 403 Mich. 614, 271 N.W.2d 777 (1978), where plaintiff's car suddenly left the road and hit a utility pole. Plaintiff's theory was that a defective ball joint assembly in the front suspension broke when the car hit a chuckhole in the gravel road, causing the loss of control. The car was four years old at the time of the accident, had been driven 47,000 miles, and had two previous owners. The trial court directed a verdict for the defendant on the ground that Holloway had failed to establish a defect in the ball joint assembly. *Held,* reversed:

> A plaintiff has the burden of establishing that when the product left the manufacturer it was defective. He is not, however, obliged to eliminate all possible causes of the accident consistent with the view that there was no manufacturing defect. He sustains his burden when he establishes with direct or circumstantial evidence a reasonable probability that the defect is attributable to the manufacturer.
>
> * * *
>
> Where a failure is caused by a defect in a relatively inaccessible part integral to the structure of the automobile not generally required to be repaired, replaced or maintained, it may be reasonable, absent misuse, to infer that the defect is attributable to the manufacturer.
>
> The circumstantial evidence in the instant case adequately supports a reasonable inference that the accident was probably caused by a defect attributable to the manufacturer. Both the Holloways and General Motors agree that the break in the ball joint assembly was fresh, metallurgically clean, and due to an impact failure. This suggests that the failure was not a result of fatigue or wear, and, indeed, General Motors' experts testified that there were no signs of fatigue or wear. The fresh, metallurgically clean break, indicative of impact failure not attributable to fatigue or wear, tended also to negative lack of requisite maintenance, improper repair and even prior misuse as alternative causes. We are left with a reasonable probability that something was inherently wrong with the ball joint assembly such that it was unable to withstand an impact it should have withstood.
>
> * * *
>
> On rehearing, General Motors principally argues that a plaintiff does not sustain his burden of proof unless he identifies the specific cause of the defect. It contends that the Holloways must demonstrate which of the possible alternatives (design, material, assembly or a combination) was the precise cause of the failure, or be barred from recovery. It advances the policy argument that one of the purposes of the tort law is to encourage those engaged in activity which causes injury to adopt remedial measures to avoid so injuring other persons. If in truth there was a defect in manufacture, General Motors needs specific identification of the cause so that it can effect corrective measures.
>
> Acknowledging that encouraging tortfeasors to adopt corrective measures is one of the purposes of the tort law, another purpose is to compensate injured persons. It is the injury inflicted on the plaintiff that entitles him to a ,remedy, not his skill in discovering precisely where the defendant's manufacturing process went wrong.

> Just as a plaintiff injured in an automobile collision need not identify a character or other personality defect which caused the defendant to drive negligently, either to educate him or others so that remedial measures may be adopted or to facilitate governmental determination of whether he should be permitted to continue to drive, neither need a person injured by product failure identify the specific defect.

271 N.W.2d at 780, 782–83.

5. In accord, that plaintiff need not prove a specific defect, but may establish a prima facie case of defectiveness upon proof of a sudden malfunction, where other plausible causes are absent: Stackiewicz v. Nissan Motor Corp. in U.S.A., 100 Nev. 443, 686 P.2d 925 (1984) (steering on automobile with 2,400 total miles suddenly locked; routine maintenance performed at 1,000 miles); Dietz v. Waller, 141 Ariz. 107, 685 P.2d 744 (1984) (new speed boat "disintegrated" at high speed during normal operation); Perkins v. Trailco Mfg. & Sales Co., 613 S.W.2d 855 (Ky.1981) (new dump truck overturned; evidence of proper use and maintenance prior to malfunction). Liability on this basis is often referred to as the "malfunction theory" of recovery. See generally Annot., 65 A.L.R.4th (1988).

6. But the plaintiff has the burden of proof and must establish his case by the probabilities. "For circumstantial evidence to make out a prima facie case, it must tend to negate other reasonable causes, or there must be an expert opinion that the product was defective. [Citation.] Because liability in a products liability action cannot be based on mere speculation, guess or conjecture, the circumstances shown must justify an inference of probability as distinguished from mere possibility." Mateika v. LaSalle Thermogas Co., 94 Ill. App.3d 506, 49 Ill.Dec. 649, 418 N.E.2d 503 (1981). Thus, where there is an equal probability that an accident occurred for reasons other than a defect in the defendant's product, the plaintiff fails to make his case. E.g., Mays v. Ciba-Geigy Corp., 233 Kan. 38, 661 P.2d 348 (1983) (gas pipeline explosion).

B. FOOD AND DRINK

MATTHEWS v. CAMPBELL SOUP CO.

United States District Court, Southern District Texas, 1974.
380 F.Supp. 1061.

SEALS, DISTRICT JUDGE.

[Motion for summary judgment filed by defendant. Denied.] In this diversity suit, 28 U.S.C.A. § 1332(a)(1), Plaintiff seeks to recover for injuries to his teeth and gums which were allegedly suffered while he was eating the contents of a can of Defendant's Oyster Stew Soup. Plaintiff claims that the injuries were caused by a small deleterious object in the soup. Plaintiff surrendered this object to Defendant for examination and it has been identified as a small irregularly shaped oyster pearl.

Plaintiff sets forth two theories of recovery: strict liability in tort and negligence in the manufacture and labeling of this product. Defendant contends that on the undisputed facts before the Court, Plaintiff cannot prevail on a theory of strict liability and that there is no evidence in the record to raise an issue of negligence. * * *

* * *

Defendant argues that, as a matter of law, the can of Oyster Stew Soup at issue here was not unfit, unwholesome, defective, or unreasonably dangerous. * * *

Defendant's position is bottomed on what may be labeled the "foreign-natural" doctrine. This doctrine, which has been neither accepted nor rejected by Texas courts, apparently first emerged in Mix v. Ingersoll Candy Co., 6 Cal.2d 674, 59 P.2d 144 (1936). There plaintiff brought suit for injuries caused by a fragment of chicken bone contained in a chicken pie. The court held that the chicken pie was not unfit for human consumption as a matter of law:

> "* * * [W]e are of the opinion that despite the fact that a chicken bone may occasionally be encountered in a chicken pie, such chicken pie, in the absence of some further defect, is reasonably fit for human consumption. *Bones which are natural to the type of meat served cannot legitimately be called a foreign substance, and a consumer who eats meat dishes ought to anticipate and be on his guard against the presence of such bones.* At least he cannot hold the restaurant keeper whose representation implied by law is that the meat dish is reasonably fit for human consumption, liable for any injury occurring as a result of the presence of a chicken bone in such chicken pie." At 148 (Emphasis supplied)

Probably a majority of jurisdictions having occasion to treat the problem have adopted the Mix rationale. [Citations.]

* * *

Not all jurisdictions have followed the foreign-natural view; it has been rejected by several courts in favor of a "reasonable expectation" test. In Zabner v. Howard Johnson's Inc., 201 So.2d 824 (Fla.App.1967), a consumer was injured by a piece of walnut shell concealed in a dish of maple walnut ice cream. Following the foreign-natural test the trial court entered judgment for the defendant. After tracing the history of this doctrine and its application the appellate court opted in favor of a test of "reasonable expectation." "The test should be what is *'reasonably expected'* by the consumer in the food as served, not what might be natural to the ingredients of that food prior to preparation."

Observing that natural substances can often be as dangerous to the consumer as foreign objects such as a pebble or a piece of glass or wire, the *Zabner* court stated: "[The] naturalness of the substance to any ingredients in the food served is important only in determining whether the consumer may reasonably expect to find such substance in the particular type of dish or style of food served." The key question under the reasonable expectation test is whether the consumer ought to have anticipated the injury producing object in the final product not whether the object is foreign or natural. What the consumer might reasonably expect, the court noted, is a jury question in most cases.

* * *

Texas courts have never been in a position requiring an election between these two competing doctrines. A great number of cases involving harmful objects have been litigated but the objects were so obviously "foreign" that the issue did not arise. See, Athens Canning Co. v. Ballard, 365 S.W.2d 369 (Tex.Civ.App.1963), (burr in a can of purple hull peas); Brumit v. Cokins, 281 S.W.2d 154 (Tex.Civ.App.1955), (glass in a milk-shake); Campbell Soup Company, Inc. v. Ryan, 328 S.W.2d 821 (Tex.Civ.App.1959), (metal washer in a TV chicken dinner); Sweeney v. Cain, 243 S.W.2d 874 (Tex.Civ.App.1951), ("greenish brown slimy looking stuff with black spots on it" in a bottle of Coca–Cola).

Making an *Erie* educated guess, this Court holds that, if faced with the problem, Texas courts would follow the reasonable expectation rule as it is stated in *Zabner*. It is obvious that the "reasonable expectation" approach is considerably more compatible and consistent with Section 402A [noting consumer expectation tests in comments g and i].

* * *

* * * [T]he only way of avoiding misapplication of the foreign-natural theory is to focus on what the consumer might reasonably expect to find in the final product. This being the case it would make even more sense to discard the foreign-natural distinction and go directly to the reasonable expectation issue. The use of these labels does not advance the inquiry and unnecessarily increases the possibility of confusion on the ultimate issue.

* * *

Having settled on the "reasonable expectation" standard the question before this Court can be restated. Can it be said, as a matter of law, that the consumer can reasonably expect to encounter a pearl in a can of Defendant's Oyster Stew Soup. This Court thinks not. It is clearly an issue for the jury to decide. With the undisputed facts reflected in the pleadings, interrogatories and affidavits on file herein it would be impossible for this Court to ascertain what the common consumer experience is with respect to pearls in canned oyster stew. Defendant's Motion For Summary Judgment on the issue of strict liability is therefore denied.

[The court also found the evidence adequate to support a finding that defendant had been negligent in the manufacture and labeling of the soup.]

NOTES

1. "[T]he plaintiff was contentedly munching away one day on a piece of Roy Rogers take-out fried chicken (a wing) when she bit into something in the chicken that she perceived to be a worm." Yong Cha Hong v. Marriott Corp., 656 F.Supp. 445, 446 (D.Md.1987). In fact, it was not a worm, but "either one of

the chicken's major blood vessels (the aorta) or its trachea, both of which * * * would appear worm-like (although not meaty like a worm, but hollow) to a person unschooled in chicken anatomy." Id. at 447. Plaintiff sued in warranty, and defendants moved for summary judgment on the basis of the foreign/natural doctrine. *Held,* the reasonable expectation test should be applied, instead of the foreign/natural test; and (2) a jury, applying the test, could reasonably conclude that a piece of fast food fried chicken is unmerchantable if it contains an inedible item of the chicken's anatomy. Motion denied.

2. Betehia v. Cape Cod Corp., 10 Wis.2d 323, 103 N.W.2d 64, 68–69 (1960), was a bone-in-a-chicken-sandwich case:

> The "foreign-natural" test applied as a matter of law does not recommend itself to us as being logical or desirable. It is true one can expect a T-bone in T-bone steak, chicken bones in roast chicken, pork bone in a pork chop, pork bone in spare ribs, a rib bone in short ribs of beef, and fish bones in a whole baked or fried fish, but the expectation is based not on the naturalness of the particular bone to the meat, fowl, or fish, but on the type of dish served containing the meat, fowl, or fish. There is a distinction between what a consumer expects to find in a fish stick and in a baked or fried fish, or in a chicken sandwich made from sliced white meat and in roast chicken. The test should be what is reasonably expected by the consumer in the food as served, not what might be natural to the ingredients of that food prior to preparation. What is to be reasonably expected by the consumer is a jury question in most cases; at least, we cannot say as a matter of law that a patron of a restaurant must expect a bone in a chicken sandwich either because chicken bones are occasionally found there or are natural to chicken.

3. Fish bones, in particular, have stuck in the throats of the courts as well as in those of consumers. Assume a fish bone of one species ends up in a stew containing meat from other kinds of fish. Is the bone a "foreign" or "natural" substance? Cf. Arnaud's Restaurant, Inc. v. Cotter, 212 F.2d 883 (5th Cir.1954) (crab shell in pompano en papilotte).

4. See also Webster v. Blue Ship Tea Room, Inc., 347 Mass. 421, 198 N.E.2d 309 (1964), involving a fish bone in fish chowder. After framing the issue as whether the bone could be considered a foreign object, the court found no liability for breach of implied warranty, concluding that the occasional presence of fish bones in chowder is to be anticipated. The *Webster* opinion is well worth reading in full. Among other delights it contains a discourse on the history of chowder, several recipes for New England chowder, which the court characterizes as a "gustatory adventure," and a bald appeal to regional New England pride in the "hallowed tradition" of fish chowder. What if the chowder had been served in Nebraska? Should a Florida court confronted with a case involving a grapefruit seed in orange juice take the same approach?

5. How about a broken tooth on a kernel of corn in a box of corn flakes? See Adams v. Great Atlantic & Pacific Tea Co., 251 N.C. 565, 112 S.E.2d 92 (1960).

6. What result under the *Matthews* approach if the plaintiff purchases smoked pork, thinking it has already been cooked, eats it without further cooking, contracts trichinosis, and dies? What are the normal expectations of consumers of pork? A case on point is Scheller v. Wilson Certified Foods, Inc., 114 Ariz. 159, 559 P.2d 1074 (App.1976). On the above facts liability in both

strict tort and implied warranty was denied. The court noted that it is common knowledge that pork must be cooked before eating and, citing comment *i* to § 402A, concluded that uncooked pork is not dangerous to an extent beyond that contemplated by the ordinary consumer. If a person does cook the pork, yet still contracts trichinosis, should a jury be allowed to decide whether the meat was unfit, or should a court rule as a matter of law that the pork was not properly cooked? See Hollinger v. Shopper's Paradise of New Jersey, Inc., 134 N.J.Super. 328, 340 A.2d 687 (1975).

SHOSHONE COCA–COLA BOTTLING CO. v. DOLINSKI

Supreme Court of Nevada, 1966.
82 Nev. 439, 420 P.2d 855.

THOMPSON, JUSTICE.

* * *

1. Leo Dolinski suffered physical and mental distress when he partially consumed the contents of a bottle of "Squirt" containing a decomposed mouse. As a consequence he filed this action for damages against Shoshone Coca–Cola Bottling Company, the manufacturer and distributor of "Squirt."

* * * [T]he case was presented to the jury solely upon the doctrine of strict tort liability. The jury favored Dolinski with its verdict and fixed his damages at $2,500. This appeal by Shoshone ensued.

We affirm the verdict and judgment since, in our view, public policy demands that one who places upon the market a bottled beverage in a condition dangerous for use must be held strictly liable to the ultimate user for injuries resulting from such use, although the seller has exercised all reasonable care, and the user has not entered into a contractual relation with him.

* * *

2. Our acceptance of strict tort liability against the manufacturer and distributor of a bottled beverage does not mean that the plaintiff is relieved of the burden of proving a case. He must still establish that his injury was caused by a defect in the product, and that such defect existed when the product left the hands of the defendant. The concept of strict liability does not prove causation, nor does it trace cause to the defendant.

In the case at hand Shoshone contends that insufficient proof was offered to establish that the mouse was in the bottle of "Squirt" when it left Shoshone's possession. On this point the evidence was in conflict and the jury was free to choose. The Vice–President and General Manager of Shoshone testified, in substance, that had the mouse been in the bottle while at his plant, it would have been denuded because of the caustic solution used and extreme heat employed in the bottle washing and brushing process. As the mouse had hair when examined following the plaintiff's encounter, the Manager surmises that the rodent must have gotten into the bottle after leaving the defendant's possession. On the other hand, the plaintiff offered the expert testimony of a toxicologist who examined the bottle and contents on the day the plaintiff drank from it. It was his opinion that the mouse "had been dead for a long time" and that the dark stains (mouse feces) which he found on the bottom of the bottle must have been there before the liquid was added. The jury apparently preferred the latter evidence which traced cause to the defendant.

We turn to the question of tampering. Shoshone insists that a burden is cast upon the plaintiff to prove that there was no reasonable opportunity for someone to tamper with the bottle after it left Shoshone's control. * * *

The matter of tampering is inextricably tied to the problem of tracing cause to the defendant. This is so whether the claim for relief is based on negligence or strict liability. Whenever evidence is offered by the plaintiff tending to establish the presence of the mouse in the bottle when it left Shoshone's possession, the defense is encouraged to introduce evidence that the mouse must have gotten there after the bottle left Shoshone's control, thus interjecting the possibility that the bottle and its contents were tampered with by someone, perhaps as a practical joke or for some other reason. In this case, as in most cases, positive proof either way is not available. Inferences must be drawn from the best available evidence produced by each side. We have already alluded to that evidence.

It is apparent that the moment plaintiff produces evidence tending to show that the mouse was in the bottle while in the defendant's control, he has, to some degree, negated tampering by others. The converse is likewise true. A fortiori, once it is decided that enough evidence is present to trace cause to the defendant, that same evidence is sufficient to allow the jury to find an absence of tampering. For this reason, any notion that there is a burden of proof as to tampering, simply does not make sense. The sole burden is upon the plaintiff to prove that his injury was caused by a defect in the product and that such defect existed when the product left the hands of the defendant. The defendant, of course, may offer evidence suggesting tampering under a general denial of liability. * * *

* * *

[Affirmed.]

NOTES

1. Litigation in deleterious food and drink cases usually focuses on three major issues: whether the food or drink is wholesome or defective; whether the condition of the product in fact caused plaintiff's damages; and whether the product's condition can be attributed to the defendant.

2. As in *Shoshone,* the first two issues are not often seriously contested where the foreign substance in the product is so offensive that no one could doubt that the product is unwholesome and capable of causing injury, even without medical testimony. See Gentry v. Stokley–Van Camp, Prod.Liab.Rep.

(CCH) ¶ 9259 (Tenn.App.1982) (condom in can of pork and beans; plaintiff can meet burden with evidence of absence of tampering); Simmons v. Baton Rouge Coca–Cola Bottling Co., Ltd., 282 So.2d 827 (La.App.1973) (decomposed moth in bottle of Tab); Peryea v. Coca Cola Bottling Co. of New England, 109 R.I. 420, 286 A.2d 877 (1972) (slivers of glass in soft drink); Food Fair Stores of Fla., Inc. v. Macurda, 93 So.2d 860 (Fla.1957) (can of spinach infested with worms); Cernes v. Pittsburgh Coca Cola Bottling Co., 183 Kan. 758, 332 P.2d 258 (1958) (jelly substance in beverage, slimy like mud or insect); Pillars v. R.J. Reynolds Tobacco Co., 117 Miss. 490, 78 So. 365, 366 (1918) (decomposed human toe in chewing tobacco: "We can imagine no reason why, with ordinary care, human toes could not be left out of chewing tobacco, and if toes are found in chewing tobacco, it seems to us that somebody has been very careless.").

3. If the object is not necessarily offensive or commonly regarded as repulsive, the plaintiff must establish that the object's presence rendered the food or beverage unwholesome by in fact contaminating the product. Here, expert testimony will normally be required to establish the plaintiff's case. See Willis v. Safeway Stores, 199 Misc. 821, 105 N.Y.S.2d 9 (App.Div.1951) (pieces of cork from crushed bottle cap in beverage). But compare Martel v. Duffy–Mott Corp., 15 Mich.App. 67, 166 N.W.2d 541 (1968).

4. If there is no visible foreign substance in the food, the plaintiff will typically need expert testimony causally connecting his illness to the food. See, e.g., Gant v. Lucy Ho's Bamboo Garden, Inc., 460 So.2d 499 (Fla.App.1984) (food poisoning from egg rolls; doctor testified that the bacteria involved is usually transmitted from fecal matter of infected person, and that the egg rolls were the probable source).

5. If a person does not ingest the defective food, but is sickened by observing, touching or perhaps smelling, and thinking about it, he may be able to recover if he can establish the causal connection. See, e.g., Prejean v. Great Atlantic & Pacific Tea Co., Inc., 457 So.2d 60 (La.App.1984) (consumer nauseated by rotten roast that she saw was "green as grass" when she began to wash it; severe vomiting); Wallace v. Coca–Cola Bottling Plants, Inc., 269 A.2d 117 (Me. 1970) (unpackaged prophylactic in Coke).

6. See generally Bishop, Trouble in a Bottle, 16 Baylor L.Rev. 337 (1964), an interesting article classifying these cases in various respects. Glass is the most frequent intruder into beverage bottles, followed by mice in the following conditions and numbers: dead—16; dead, fur oozing Coca Cola—1; dead and putrid—2; dead, badly battered—1; decayed—2; decomposed—14; decomposed and swollen—1; skeleton only—1; small—1; unspecified—9. Flies, spiders, worms, and cockroaches also appear with some frequency. Led by Louisiana, the "top" nine states (by number of reported cases) are all in the South.

Just how does the proverbial mouse end up in the bottle? See Spangenberg, Exploding Bottles, 24 Ohio St.L.J. 516 (1963).

7. **Regulation.** The manufacture of food and drink is in some respects closely regulated. Food and drink marketed in the United States must comply with the Federal Food, Drug, and Cosmetic Act, 21 U.S.C.A. § 301 et seq., which prohibits the sale or distribution in interstate commerce of "adulterated" food or drink. A product may be adulterated under § 342 of the Act if it contains amounts of poisons, pesticide residues, additives, filth or decomposed matter in excess of administratively established tolerances. For obvious technical and economic reasons trace amounts of such materials are permitted even though larger amounts would clearly be dangerous to health. Many foods, especially

fruits and vegetables, that have been treated with pesticides contain some chemical residue. Some harmful substances cannot be removed during processing but are present at such low levels that they represent no real health hazard. Also, most processed foods contain preservatives or additives necessary for longer shelf life, color, or flavor. These compounds may not be entirely safe in large concentrations but involve little risk at low concentrations. Tolerance for some impurities reflects a judgment that the health risks from small concentrations of even possibly dangerous substances sometimes are outweighed by the benefits derived from their presence (including cost-savings from not removing them). See generally Merrill, Regulating Carcinogens in Food: A Legislator's Guide to the Food Safety Provisions of the Federal Food, Drug, and Cosmetic Act, 77 Mich.L.Rev. 171 (1978).

The states have pure food statutes imposing criminal penalties on those who sell adulterated food, regardless of the seller's knowledge of the adulteration or his ability to discover it. For products liability purposes, many jurisdictions treat violations of pure food statutes as negligence *per se.* See, e.g., Taylor v. B. Heller & Co., 364 F.2d 608 (6th Cir.1966); Coward v. Borden Foods, Inc., 267 S.C. 423, 229 S.E.2d 262 (1976).

8. See generally R. Dickerson, Products Liability and the Food Consumer (1951); Fasler, Food Poisoning and Product Liability, 41 Food, Drug, Cosm.L.J. 414 (1986); Saffir, FDA Regulations and Product Liability, 36 Food, Drug, Cosm.L.J. 478 (1981). For a historical view, see Perkins, Unwholesome Food as a Source of Liability (pts. 1 & 2), 5 Iowa L.Bull. 6 (1919), 86 (1920).

SECTION 3. DEFECTIVE DESIGN

What are the manufacturer's basic responsibilities in designing its products? What factors must be considered in determining whether enough safety has been built into the product? What should be the effect of proof that redesigning the product to make it safer would have been expensive or would have reduced its usefulness, or that the danger was obvious (or warned of), or that the consumer misused the product? In these and other contexts considered below, the underlying question will remain largely unchanged: How safe is safe enough?

Defective design is the area that has troubled the courts and commentators the most. "At present, questions related to 'design defects' and the determination of when a product is defective, because of the nature of its design, appear to be the most agitated and controversial issues before the courts in the field of products liability." Prentis v. Yale Mfg. Co., 421 Mich. 670, 365 N.W.2d 176, 182 (1984). This reflects the fact that the issues involved in this context more than others involve decisions of major importance concerning the allocation of social resources. Not surprisingly, this is the area where the propriety of judicial action has received the greatest scrutiny. It is also the area of greatest concern to manufacturers, since a judicial declaration that the design of the product on trial is "defective" condemns the entire product line.

Perhaps the most frequent allegation of design defectiveness is the absence of some type of safety device, such as a guard, an electrical interlock cut-off device, or a "safety" on a gun. In addition to this particular issue, there is a large variety of other ways in which products may be defectively designed, from fabrics that are inherently too flammable (and which have not been treated with an effective flame retardant chemical), to drain cleaners with chemical compositions that are excessively caustic, to products whose moving parts are made of metal too soft to last out the product's useful life. These are some of the issues addressed below.

A. IN GENERAL

MATTHEWS v. LAWNLITE CO.

Supreme Court of Florida, 1956.
88 So.2d 299.

TERRELL, JUSTICE.

[P]laintiff was in Dean's Tropical Furniture Shop examining furniture with the view of purchasing and sat in a lounge chair manufactured by defendant. "As plaintiff sat in said chair he laid his right hand on the right hand arm rest of said chair and the third finger of said right hand extended over the front of the right hand arm rest and under the front end thereof. Thereupon his said third finger of his right hand was completely severed by the moving parts of said chair and the finger fell upon the floor." A motion to dismiss the complaint was granted and this appeal was prosecuted from said order.

* * *

[Restatement of Torts § 398 provides:]

> "A manufacturer of a chattel made under a plan or design which makes it dangerous for the uses for which it is manufactured is subject to liability to others whom he should expect to use the chattel lawfully or to be in the vicinity of its probable use, for bodily harm caused by his failure to exercise reasonable care in the adoption of a safe plan or design."

* * *

The chair in question is a rocking chair with moving parts; it rocks back and forth. It was constructed of aluminum and was used for rest and recreation; it looks harmless, every aspect of it suggested ease and comfort. There was no notice of any kind that beneath its restful armrest there were moving metal parts so constructed that they would amputate the occupant's fingers with the ease that one clips a choice flower with pruning shears. It was designed, constructed and delivered to the public with these moving parts that were essential to its use. They were completely concealed from the user and as essential parts of the chair were inherently dangerous. No one would suspect that such a dangerous device would be concealed in such an innocent looking instrumentality.

* * * In our view the facts recited bring this case within the rule recited from Restatement of Torts. If such a mechanism is required for the chair, it should be protected by a housing. * * *

[Reversed and remanded.]

McCORMACK v. HANKSCRAFT CO.

Supreme Court of Minnesota, 1967.
278 Minn. 322, 154 N.W.2d 488.

ROGOSHESKE, JUSTICE. Plaintiff appeals from the judgment entered upon an order of the district court granting judgment n.o.v. and a conditional new trial in favor of defendant, Hankscraft Company, Inc.

Plaintiff, Andrea McCormack, brought this action for damages by Donald McCormack, her father and natural guardian, alleging that defendant's negligence and breach of implied and express warranties in the manufacture and sale of a steam vaporizer caused her to suffer substantial personal injuries. During the 3–week trial, defendant's motions for a directed verdict following the submission of plaintiff's evidence and at the close of all the evidence were denied. The court submitted the case to the jury on the questions of negligence and breach of express warranties, refusing to instruct on implied warranties. The jury returned a verdict against defendant, awarding plaintiff $150,000 damages.

* * *

[The] vaporizer had been used about a half dozen times without incident when, on November 20, 1960, it was again set up for use in a small bedroom in the northwest corner of the house, occupied by Andrea, then 3 years and 9 months old, and her baby sister, Alison, 1 year and 10 months old. Andrea slept in a regular single bed and Alison in a crib. To the east of the doorway of this bedroom is an adjoining bathroom, which Andrea frequently used during the night. The doors of the bedrooms and bathroom were habitually left open and a light was usually burning in the bathroom. * * * Andrea's mother set up the vaporizer at about 8 p.m. on a seat-step-type metal kitchen stool about 2½ feet high. * * *

At about 2:30 a.m., Mrs. McCormack heard a terrible scream and got out of bed. She found Andrea lying on the floor of her bedroom, screaming. The metal stool was upright, but the vaporizer was on the floor and the water had come out of the jar. The vaporizer had separated into its three component parts—a glass jar, a metal pan, and a plastic top-heating unit. The electric cord was still plugged into the electric outlet. In some manner, Andrea, while intending to go to the bathroom, had tipped over the vaporizer and caused the water in the jar to spill upon her body.

Andrea was rushed to the hospital for treatment. More than 30 percent of her body had severe burns; she was suffering from shock; and her condition was critical for some time. She had third-degree burns on her chest, shoulders, and back. Skin-graft surgery was performed on her twice. She was hospitalized for 74½ days. Ten days later she was admitted to the Kenny Institute for treatment. She remained there 102 days and thereafter was taken to the Mayo Clinic, where she had further surgery in August 1961. At the time of the trial, Andrea had heavy scar tissue on her chest, stomach, legs, arms, and neck; a deformed jaw; restricted movement of her head; an irregular posture; and the prospect of 6 to 12 more surgical procedures during her lifetime. Her condition is largely permanent.

The "automatic-electric" vaporizer in question is of normal design and consists of three component parts—an aluminum pan which serves as a base, a 1-gallon glass jar or water reservoir which is inserted into the pan, and a black plastic cap to which is fastened a black plastic heating-chamber tube.

* * *

* * * The cap and heating chamber assembly, by its own weight, rests loosely upon the glass jar with the black tube extending down into the jar. There are no threads inside the plastic cap or any other means provided to fasten the cap to the threaded neck of the jar. This design and construction were intended by defendant to serve as a safety measure to avoid any buildup of steam in the glass jar, but it also has the result of allowing the water in the jar to gush out instantaneously when the vaporizer is tipped over. This unit can be tipped over easily by a child through the exertion of about 2 pounds of force.

To operate the vaporizer in accordance with the instructions contained in defendant's booklet, the "entire plastic cover" is removed, the glass jar is filled to the filling marker with tap water containing minerals, and the cord is plugged into an electric outlet, whereupon "[t]he vaporizer will produce a gentle cloud of steam within a few minutes." The heating unit is designed so that it automatically turns off whenever the water in the jar decreases to a certain level. As the booklet pictorially illustrates, the water from the jar enters the lower section of the heating chamber through the small hole at the bottom. Here it is heated until it boils and is vaporized into steam, which passes out of the unit through the hole in the cap.

[The court noted that within 4 minutes of operation the water in the heating chamber reaches 212°, that the water outside the chamber reaches 172° after 1 hour and 182° after 5, and that water of 140° will burn and 180° water will cause third-degree burns on a small child.]

By touch, a user can determine that the water in the jar outside the heating unit, as well as the jar and the plastic cap, becomes hot during the operation of the vaporizer. However, there is no movement of the water in the jar and no means by which a user could discern by sight or touch that this reserve water in the jar became and remained scalding hot. Plaintiff's parents, relying upon their understanding of what defendant represented in its instruction booklet, were reasonably led to believe up to the time of plaintiff's injury that, since steam was generated only in the heating unit, the temperature of the water in the jar during the entire operation of the vaporizer remained the same as when put in. At all of the times when replenishing the water in either the first or second vaporizer, plaintiff's mother followed the routine of removing the entire plastic cover by using some "glove" or "mitt" as a precaution against the steam. She would leave the cord plugged in, add water to the jar, replace the cover, wait until steam appeared, and then leave the unit unattended in the room. As her testimony implied, she at no time discovered by touching or handling the unit when it was in use that the temperature of any part of the water in the jar became hot.

The instruction booklet furnished by defendant did not disclose the scalding temperatures reached by the water in the jar, nor was any warning given as to the dangers that could result from an accidental upset of the unit. While plaintiff's mother realized that the unit could be tipped over by a sufficient external force, she justifiably relied upon defendant's representations that it was "safe," "practically foolproof," and "tip-proof." She understood this to mean that the unit "was safe to use around [her] children" and that she "didn't have to worry" about dangers when it was left unattended in a child's room since this was the primary purpose for which it was sold.

In its booklet and advertising, defendant in fact made the representations relied upon by plaintiff's mother. In addition to the simple operating instructions and a pictorial "cut-away" indicating how the steam is generated by the electrodes in the heating chamber, the booklet stated:

> "WHY THE HANKSCRAFT VAPORIZER IS SUPERIOR TO OTHERS IN DESIGN.
>
> "Your vaporizer will run all night on one filling of water, directing a steady, gentle flow of medicated steam exactly where it is needed. No attention is necessary.
>
> "It's safe, too, and practically foolproof. Since the water itself makes the electric contact, the vaporizer shuts off automatically when the water is gone. The electric unit cannot burn out."

The booklet also had a picture of a vaporizer sending steam over a baby's crib, alongside which was printed:

> "For most effective use, the vaporizer should be placed at least four feet away from the person receiving treatment, and should not be placed above the patient's level."

Defendant's officers realized that the vaporizers would be primarily used in the treatment of children and usually would be unattended. They had knowledge that the water in the jar got scalding hot; that this water would cause third-degree burns on a small child; that the water in the jar would gush out instantaneously if the unit were tipped over; that the unit was not "tip-proof"; that the combination of the unsecured top and the hot water in the jar was dangerous because of the possibility that a child might tip it over during operation; and that, prior to plaintiff's injury, at least 10 to 12 children had been burned in this manner. Furthermore, defendant's officers realized that the fact the water in the jar got hot was not discernible during operation except by touching or handling the unit and that a user could conclude from their booklet that steam was generated in the plastic core and be led to believe that the reserve water in the jar did not itself become scalding hot.

Plaintiff called two expert witnesses, whose qualifications in the field of product design were unquestioned. Both testified that the design of the vaporizer was defective principally in that it failed to provide a means for securing the plastic cover to the jar in a manner which would prevent the water in the jar from instantaneously discharging when the unit was tipped over. In the opinion of both, the unit could be tipped over with little force and this defective design created a risk of bodily harm to a child if the unit were left operating and unattended in the room. This defect could have been eradicated by the adoption of any one of several practical and inexpensive alternative designs which utilized simple and well known techniques to secure the top to the jar. Any of these alternative designs could have been employed by defendant prior to its production of the second vaporizer by the application of sound product-design principles current at that time. Among these alternative designs was that of making threads on the inside of the plastic top so it could screw onto the jar and the putting of two or three small holes in the top, which would take care of any danger that steam would build up inside the jar. Both witnesses stated that such a change in design was essential to make the unit safe for its intended use because the presence of near-boiling water in the jar was not discernible by sight or touch and no warning of the risk of harm was contained in defendant's instruction booklet.

[The court considered the manufacturer's duty to warn and held that the evidence justified the jury's finding that the defendant had failed to use reasonable care to inform users of the scalding temperature of the water in the vaporizer.]

We similarly conclude and hold that the evidence is also sufficient to support the jury's verdict of liability on the ground that defendant was negligent in adopting an unsafe design. It is well established that a manufacturer, despite lack of privity of contract, has a duty to use reasonable care in designing its product so that those it should expect will use it are protected from unreasonable risk of harm while the product is being used for its intended use. A breach of such duty renders the manufacturer liable. [Citation.] Clearly, such a duty was owed to plaintiff for defendant admitted that the primary, intended use of the vaporizer was for the treatment of children's colds and croup.

The proof is sufficient to support plaintiff's claim of defective design in that, among other defects,[3] defendant failed to exercise reasonable care in securing the plastic cover to the jar to guard against the reasonably foreseeable danger that a child would tip the unit over when it was in use and be seriously burned by coming in contact with the scalding water that would instantaneously gush out of the jar.

* * *

To urge that a vaporizer is not a dangerous instrumentality is not persuasive to a reviewing court when the evidence reasonably permits a finding that a simple, practical, inexpensive, alternative design which fastened the top to the jar would have substantially reduced or eliminated the danger which caused plaintiff's injuries.[4] Defendant's experts testified that the design adopted was to guard against an explosion because of a buildup of steam in the heating unit and jar, but the jury could have accepted the testimony of plaintiff's experts which indicated the use of defendant's design was not necessary to accomplish this purpose. Moreover, the fact that at the time the second vaporizer was purchased many other brands of vaporizers on the market were designed in basically this same manner, while certainly relevant, did not necessarily bar the jury from concluding that the exercise of due care required the adoption of a different design.

[The court also found for the plaintiff on warranty and strict liability in tort, adopting the latter doctrine as the law of Minnesota.]

Reversed with directions to enter judgment upon the verdict.

3. Plaintiff claimed there were two other defects in design, but we believe the evidence insufficient to predicate liability upon either. It was argued that the water in the jar was rendered too hot because the design permitted steam and its condensate to escape from the eight ¼-inch holes in the upper section of the heating chamber into the water reservoir. But, plaintiff's experts failed to testify that if suggested changes had been adopted the water's temperature would have been reduced sufficiently so that it would not have caused third-degree burns to plaintiff. Plaintiff also argued that the vaporizer could be tipped too easily. While it was established that an alternative design would substantially increase the amount of force necessary to tip it over, the experts failed to testify as to how much force plaintiff likely would have exerted when she tipped the vaporizer over and therefore there was no indication whether the suggested changes would have prevented her from doing so. The matters which were omitted are not subjects of common knowledge, and in the absence of expert testimony, the jury could only speculate as to whether these suggested changes in design could have prevented plaintiff's injury. This constituted a failure of proof as to proximate cause. [Citations.]

4. Evidence of the existence of a feasible alternative design eliminating the unattached top renders the holding in Blissenbach v. Yanko, 90 Ohio App. 557, 107 N.E.2d 409, inapplicable to this case.

NOTE

1. The Hankscraft vaporizer is pictured below:

Hankscraft vaporizer design
at time of McCormack v. Hankscraft

Hankscraft vaporizer disassembled.

KNITZ v. MINSTER MACHINE COMPANY

Court of Appeals of Ohio, 1987.
1987 WL 6486 (WESTLAW).

PER CURIAM.

A. *Procedural History*

[The plaintiff lost two fingers when she accidentally activated the press she was operating. Her action against the press manufacturer was initially dismissed by the trial court but the Ohio Supreme Court reversed and remanded for trial. Knitz v. Minster Machine Co., 69 Ohio St.2d 460, 432 N.E.2d 814, cert. denied 459 U.S. 857, 103 S.Ct. 127, 74 L.Ed.2d 110 (1982). The jury returned a verdict for the plaintiff of $150,000 and defendant appealed to the Court of Appeals.]

B. *The Product*

During the week of August 16, 1976, appellee, Virginia Mae Knitz, was employed as a press operator at Toledo Die and Manufacturing Company (hereinafter referred to as TDM). After initial instructions on the operations of the plant's machinery, appellee began operation of various punch presses. On August 23, 1976, appellee was assigned to operate a sixty-ton OBI Press designed and manufactured by Minster Machine Company (hereinafter referred to as Minster).

The press, like those smaller in size, functioned in such a manner that the power was supplied in bringing two halves of a die together in order to manufacture variously formed items. The top half of the press, was attached to a ram, which, when activated, descended with sixty tons of force onto the bolster plate. The two die halves, when contact was made, shaped metal stock into various pieces. * * *

The press, which injured appellee, was delivered to TDM on October 15, 1971. As originally shipped, the press was delivered with a two-hand button tripping device.[a] This device permits activation of the press upon simultaneous depression of two buttons, which are placed at shoulder level above the die ram. The buttons, placed several feet apart, do not permit activation of the press unless both buttons are simultaneously depressed. Thus, activation of the press requires utilization of both hands, thereby preventing the operator from inadvertently placing his/her hand in the area where the ram descends.

Along with this device, TDM ordered an optional foot pedal tripping device,[4] designed and sold by Minster. The device attached to the press, permitted the operator to activate the press' ram by depressing a foot treadle. The operator was not then required to utilize the two-button, tripping device.

After the shipment of the press with the optional foot treadle, TDM installed a pull-back safeguard (possom type).[b] These guards were attached to [the] wrists of the operator and physically pull[ed] the operator's hands out of the die area when the ram descended to the bolster plate. Appellee, upon hiring, was briefly instructed in the operation of the presses and the pull-back safeguard.

C. *The Accident*

On August 23, 1976, appellee, while sitting on a stool as was acceptable, was operating the sixty-ton OBI press. The job required her to * * * place, with her hand, a block piece of metal stock in the space between the die halves. While performing this production run, appellee utilized the foot treadle to activate the ram, and the pull-back guards to provide safety against the erroneous insertion of her hands into the die area. After two hours, appellee, uncomfortable with the stool size, sought out a more comfortably-sized stool. Upon returning to her job station, she noticed that the scrap bin beneath the press had been emptied and the foot treadle had been moved. Appellee, without reattaching her pull-backs or deactivating the press, leaned on the shoulder bolster plate with her right hand, simultaneously attempting to manipulate the foot treadle with her foot into a more advantageous position. While moving the treadle, the ram was activated, severing appellee's two fingers.

Appellee, at trial, sought recompense claiming appellant's press was defectively manufactured for two reasons: (1) the press was defectively designed in that it did not have an adequately protected foot

a. See note 1 following case for diagram.—Eds.

4. Throughout the opinion, the use of the words "foot pedal" is synonymous with the words "foot treadle." [See note 1 following case for diagrams.—Eds.]

b. See note 1 following case for diagram.—Eds.

treadle which would have prevented against accidental activation of the press, and (2) the press was defectively designed since it failed to provide adequate safeguards which would have prevented activation of the press while a hand was in the die area. * * *

I.

TRIAL TESTIMONY

[Plaintiff-appellee used three expert witnesses,] Dennis Steinecker, staff technical specialist at Minster, Simon Tamny, consulting engineer, and James McCarthy, safety specialist. * * *

C. Foot Treadle

* * *

Simon Tamny, consulting engineer, * * * indicated that the foot pedal, as used with punch presses, had an uncharted history which would indicate that the device should not be used during the operation of a press. Mr. Tamny cited specifically that foot switches could be accidentally tripped causing injury to the hand by the descending ram, and second, that the use of foot pedals provided no safeguards to indicate whether the operator's hands were clear from the die area. He indicated that the use of foot switches should be avoided if at all possible. If the foot switches were to be used, they posed a danger to the operator's well-being; said danger being known in the industry for a period of years.

Mr. Tamny then evaluated three specific foot pedals. Mr. Tamny evaluated the Rees pedal, the Bradley pedal, and the Minster pedal.

Initially, Mr. Tamny made comparisons between the Rees and Bradley foot pedals with the Minster foot pedal. The Rees pedal was similar in design to the Minster pedal. The Rees pedal contained a metal box which covered the pedal which activated the press. At the base of the metal box was a large metal plate which was used as a foundation for the foot pedal in order to prevent the pedal from sliding on the floor. At the opening to the pedal, there was a metal flap which slanted down past the opening. Inside the metal flap was the pedal. This metal flap served to prevent accidental insertion of the foot against the pedal, thereby activating the ram. The primary advantage to the Rees model, as compared to the Minster model, concerned the fact that the activating pedal, was above the lowest surface of the covering flap. This prevented accidental activation of the pedal, since even if the operator's foot slid underneath the flap, the operator could not easily activate the ram by depression of the pedal, since the top of the pedal was above the lowest portion of the metal flap. Whereas, on the Minster model the metal flap protecting the opening area did not extend past the height of the inside foot pedal. With this design, an operator could accidentally slide his foot past the flap and depress the pedal.

The Bradley pedal, as compared with the Minster mechanism, was substantially different in style of operation. The Bradley pedal, designed after the accident occurred but available in form on the market, also contained a metal box surrounding the activating pedal. The Bradley mechanism also had a flap which covered access to the activating pedal. This flap, unlike the Minster pedal, did not operate by insertion of the foot underneath the flap, lifting the flap upwards and then placing the foot on the pedal. Instead, the Bradley pedal required the operator to place his entire foot past the top of the metal enclosure, pull the front flap back towards the operator with the heel, then insert the foot onto the activating pedal. In other words, the Bradley mechanism had a hinged door covering the access to the pedal. This hinged door opened towards the operator. As such, the operator had to make a specific movement past the door entrance, then back towards the operator until the front of the foot cleared the top of the casing and the access pedal, and then back into the box area where the pedal could be activated. This device, although not as convenient to the operator, prevented any accidental entry into the pedal activation device area, since entrance to the pedal required three specific movements.

After review of the differences between the Rees, Bradley and Minster foot pedals, Mr. Tamny concluded that the Minster foot pedal was the least desirable mechanism. He cited the fact that the Rees pedal was difficult to move and was more difficult to accidental[ly] trigger the ram. The Bradley device, although not available at the time of the accident, provided a design which, although lighter in structure and capable of being kicked about, prevented any accidental entry of an operator's foot into the pedal area. The Minster device did not have these basic safety features. The Minster device, as demonstrated by Mr. Tamny, could be easily activated by the slipping of a foot into the pedal area. Also because of the weight of the Minster pedal, the operator may be required to manipulate the foot pedal constantly due to its lightweight structure.

On cross-examination, Mr. Tamny indicated that there were many different designs for foot pedals on the market. He did note, however, that the Minster design was perhaps the third best design available to the consumer.

* * *

As rebuttal to Mr. Tamny's testimony, appellant, during its case, called as its expert witness, Robert Jordan, an engineering consultant, previously employed for twenty-five years at Minster Company. Mr. Jordan, while employed at Minster, was involved in the design of foot treadles and point of operation safeguards.

* * *

While noting that the Rees foot pedal was heavier and provided a more stable base, Mr. Jordan indicated that the device was more difficult to get into for the operator and, if necessary, the operator could easily bypass the safety precautions available on the foot pedal. The Bradley foot pedal had little weight to its foundation and did not provide a stable base. Although this mechanism did not permit inadvertent entry, the device required substantial effort by the operator to achieve entry to the pedal mechanism. This latter feature was both an advantage and disadvantage. While accidental entry was not likely to occur with the Bradley device, what could happen instead was that the operator, rather than withdraw his foot from the pedal while not operating the press might, instead, leave his foot in the triggering mechanism while he was not making a specific production run. In that case, the operator might trigger the ram by accident since he had left his foot in the Bradley foot pedal enclosure and, in so doing, the operator might subject himself to bodily harm. He further noted that the Bradley design could be easily bypassed by simply destroying the spring mechanism used to hold the outside access door up in front of the triggering pedal. He considered this a disadvantage when compared with the Minster foot pedal, since there was no spring mechanism in the Minster machine.[c]

D. Bolster Plate Safeguards

With respect to the defective nature of the bolster plate safeguards, appellee again relied upon the testimony of his expert witness Mr. McCarthy, a safety specialist, previously employed by the Pontiac Division of General Motors. Mr. McCarthy, while employed at Pontiac, was responsible for the development of programs to safeguard machines, including punch presses. Although Mr. McCarthy did not have an engineering degree, he had extensive background with press operations and the necessary safeguards for these machines. His responsibilities included research on how accidents occurred on press operations.

[Mr. McCarthy testified] that there were three specific systems which would be available at the point of operation of the press. These systems may be classified as mechanical, electrical, and pneumatic. The classifications concerned the type of safeguard which could be utilized to protect the operator. He then evaluated five specific safeguards and combinations thereof. These safeguards included the "sweep," the "interlock gate guard," the "moving/movable barrier," the "photoelectric system," and "pullbacks."

The sweep safeguard operates as a gate in front of the tool die area, which sweeps the operator's hands to the side when the ram is in operation. This device was originated in the late nineteenth century. Essentially, the sweep operates similar to the gate protection mechanism seen at a bowling alley. However, there is a significant danger to the uses of the sweep device in that there has been a history of operator accidents directly caused by the force generated by the use of the sweep. The sweep would often operate with such force that an opera-

c. One author's research assistant spoke with an employee of Allen–Bradley who stated that the company ceased manufacturing foot switches in 1977 due to products liability lawsuits. Later, counsel for the company stated that the decision was based more on the competitive climate than on liability concerns.—Eds.

tor's hand, caught in the die area, would be struck, breaking or fracturing the operator's arm or disabling it in some manner.

The next available safeguard is the interlock gate guard,[d] developed at the turn of the twentieth century. It served as an enclosure around the entire die area when the punch press was in operation. Although capable of being removed by the operator, the principle of the interlock gate guard was that it would not allow the ram to be in operation when [the] operator's hand was within the die area. This device acted as a safeguard regardless of any machine or human error involved. The primary disadvantage to this safeguard is that the operator's production rate was substantially reduced by the operation of the safeguard, thus reducing the quickness and efficiency of the operator.

Another safeguard available was the moving/movable barrier, developed in the early 1900s, which protected the point of operation. While the movable barrier would have prevented an operator's insertion of his hands into the die area, its primary disadvantage did not permit the flexibility of the operator to use different dies in the machine. Essentially, then, the barrier denied the operator the use of different dies in the machines, which was a primary advantage of buying a Minster press.

* * *

The next safeguard involves the use of a photo-electric system[e] to protect the operator. This system set forth an electrical field around the die area, which would detect when an operator's hand was within the die area. In such cases, the system with the use of its sensing devices, would prevent the operation of the die area until the operator removed his hand. This system, developed around 1950, is similar to that seen in the typical grocery store door, which operates when a consumer steps on a mat which contains sensing devices. There are two primary disadvantages to this system, the cost associated with the system, and second the operator's lack of knowledge as to whether the system is properly working. The operator would have no knowledge of whether the system is working until after an accident has occurred, only then, would the operator have full knowledge that a system did not work. At this point in time, obviously, it would be too late to prevent the injury.

The next safeguard available, which was in fact used on the Minster press, was the possom pull-backs. This safeguard required the operator to strap his wrists into a harness, which, when the press was in operation, pulled the operator's hands out of the die area. While this safeguard was one of the cheapest mechanisms available, it had the decided disadvantage that it required the operator to attach the pull-backs in order to prevent injury. Unlike the foregoing mentioned safeguards, which would have prevented injury regardless of human

d. See Note 1 following case for diagram.—Eds.

e. See Note 1 following case for diagram.—Eds.

error, the pull-backs required that the operator specifically act in order for the safeguard to properly prevent injury. That act required the operator to attach his wrist to the pull-backs.

Upon review of the various safeguards available, Mr. McCarthy concluded that had the alleged defective press utilized the interlock gate guard, the sweep, or the photoelectric system, the injury to appellee would not have occurred. These devices, Mr. McCarthy argues, could have also been placed on the machine by appellant, Minster Machine Company. Mr. McCarthy further notes that adequate safeguards were needed since the press was the most dangerous machine in the plant. Recognizing this fact, Mr. McCarthy developed his own safeguard which he opined could have been attached to the Minster machine to protect an operator's well-being. This device was a combination of an interlock guard and a barrier guard. The "McCarthy" guard would have served essentially the same purposes of those previously mentioned. This alternatively designed guard would [move vertically and provide] an enclosure around the press area which would have deactivated the ram when an operator's hand was within the die area. * * *

On cross-examination, Mr. McCarthy indicated that his designed guard was not in use anywhere in the country, and that if it was to be utilized, it would require considerable amount of work by the manufacturer to install the guard and to manufacture it. Counsel for appellant also noted on cross-examination the discrepancy in Mr. McCarthy's testimony from other cases in which he had been called to be an expert witness. Specifically, appellant's counsel noted that Mr. McCarthy had testified in the past that his specific form of safeguard was not always necessary and that adequate safeguarding could be utilized if there were shields on all sides of the die area. Only in this case had Mr. McCarthy required the use of his design mechanism in order to prevent all accidents from occurring. In retort to appellant's position, Mr. McCarthy indicated that * * * an adequate safeguard *must* be designed, developed and utilized in order to protect the health and well-being of the operator; and that his design met this desired outcome.

[In rebuttal, Mr. Jordan testified for the defendant-appellant] that the pullback had the disadvantage that the operator's arm would be jerked out of the way when the ram was in operation and as a result injury may occur[;] more importantly, he noted that there were several advantages including ease of inspection and maintenance of the pull-backs and the reliability of the pull-backs when utilized, which offset any disadvantage.

Mr. Jordan then addressed the question as to why Minster did not ship the press with any point of operation safeguards, other than a two-button tripping device. Mr. Jordan indicated initially that the press, when shipped, generally was not subject to a specific purpose. As such, the press may be utilized for a variety of dies which would need to be attached to the press. The difference in the size of the dies would affect the operations of the press, in particular the number of strokes per minute that the ram would be in operation and the type of metal stock used for feed into the die area. The differences in the operation of the press as well as the dies to be attached to the press did not permit the attachment of various safeguards, since the specific safeguards may prevent the user from utilizing the press in the desired manner. Therefore, no specific safeguard could be designed for the press.

Of the available safeguards presented in plaintiff's case, he stated the moving/movable barrier was said to be expensive, complex, and required additional supervision and maintenance to work properly. However, Mr. Jordan, in a telling comment, noted that the expense of the movable barrier would be irrelevant if it accomplished the purpose of providing the operator with better protection. He did further note that the movable barrier would significantly cut down the production rate available to the operators. As the final point, Mr. Jordan indicated that if the presses were to be sold with the movable barrier, then in all likelihood no presses could be sold since the additional cost associated with manufacturing and maintenance of the press as well as the sales price of the press would be substantially increased.

Turning his attention to the McCarthy guard, Mr. Jordan testified that to his knowledge no manufacturer in the country used the device designed by appellee's expert witness.

On cross-examination, appellee's counsel specifically pointed to the feasible operation of the press with various safeguards attached. In particular, Mr. Jordan conceded that the interlocking gate guard, sweep guard, and the photoelectric guard had been available prior to the sale of the Minster press. However, Mr. Jordan specifically stated that the sweep guard was not an acceptable means of point of operation safeguarding since it had often caused injury to the operator.

Upon further cross-examination, Mr. Jordan indicated that * * * while he would not recommend the use of pull-backs, he noted that they have been consistently used throughout the industry. As a final point, he pointed out that when a press company would ship a press with a foot pedal, it is normally expected that there would be additional point of operation safeguarding available.[11]

* * *

[The court traced the development of products liability law in Ohio, including the earlier appeal of this case, Knitz v. Minster Machine Co., 69 Ohio St.2d 460, 432 N.E.2d 814, cert. denied 459 U.S. 857, 103 S.Ct. 127, 74 L.Ed.2d 110 (1982), where the court adopted the *Barker* two-pronged test for design defect, but not the shift in the burden of proof. The Supreme Court in *Knitz*] concluded that a product design was in a defective condition for the user or consumer if it met either the consumer expectation test or the risk-benefit analysis test. In evaluat-

11. In recounting Mr. Jordan's testimony, the court is cognizant of the general statement of law which provides that a manufacturer has a nondelegable duty to safeguard the product.

ing whether the product design was defective, factors relevant to the determination included: (1) the likelihood that the product design would cause injury, (2) the gravity of the danger posed, and (3) the mechanical and economic feasibility of an improved design. Id., at 466.

* * *

Throughout the foregoing rationale, the judiciary has been ever cognizant of the dangers caused by an unduly liberal approach to strict products liability; said approach potentially leading to catastrophic economic and financial repercussions for manufacturers. So informed, the courts readily and willingly indicate that the law does not require the manufacturer to produce a perfect product, but only one reasonably safe for its intended use, Briney v. Sears, Roebuck & Co. (C.A. 6 1986), 782 F.2d 585, nor do the courts require the manufacturer to act as an "insurer" of products. * * *

B. Development of the Risk Benefit Analysis Test and Factors

* * *

In *Barker* * * * the court indicated several factors that a jury may consider in making its analysis:

> "[A] jury may consider, among other relevant factors, [1] the gravity of the danger posed by the challenged design, [2] the likelihood that such danger would occur, [3] the mechanical feasibility of a safer alternative design, [4] the financial cost of an improved design, and [5] the adverse consequences to the product and to the consumer that would result from an alternative design. [Citations omitted.]"

Other factors, somewhat repetitive to those mentioned in *Barker,* supra, have been cited by the Oregon Supreme Court in Johnson v. Clark Equipment Co. (Or.1976), 547 P.2d 132, 136–137 fn 1. Therein the court referred to (1) the utility of the product to the user and the public as a whole, (2) the availability of substitute products, (3) the safety aspects of available safeguards, (4) the manufacturer's ability to eliminate the unsafe character of the product without impairing its usefulness or making it too expensive to maintain, and (5) the user's awareness of the dangers, and the ability to spread the cost. [Citations.] An additional factor, discussed later in this text, is the admissibility of [relevant] governmental and industry standards as a part of the criteria of the risk benefit analysis.

From the many listed factors, it is clear not only from the trial of this case but from other cases that a key factor in plaintiff's proof is the availability of an alternative design. While the availability of an alternative design is a key factor in the plaintiff's case, it is equally clear that manufacturers, in defending their action, must consider their best defense to be the costs associated with the alternative design as well as the benefits of the existing design. However, in so defending, the manufacturers are placed in the unenviable position of arguing that the costs of any safety device outweigh the injury to the person's well being. A jury often confronted with the plaintiff, injured, agonizing in pain and perhaps dismembered, will then have to justify that the costs and the benefits outweigh the injury to the plaintiff; not an easy situation for a manufacturer, regardless of its actions in the development and design of the product.

* * *

IV.

ASSIGNMENTS OF ERROR

SUBSTANTIVE ISSUES

[Following *Barker,* the trial court instructed the jury on the two-pronged alternative test for design defect and further instructed that the burden of proof on the risk-benefit prong was on the defendant. The jury found for the defendant on the consumer expectations prong, and for the plaintiff on the risk-benefit prong. *Held,* shift in burden of proof to the defendant was reversible error.]

V.

ASSIGNMENTS OF ERROR

EVIDENTIARY ISSUES

* * *

A. *Governmental & Industry Regulations*

[A]ppellant argues that the trial court erred when it refused to permit the introduction of governmental and industry regulations concerning available safety devices for presses. Appellant argues that the regulations are part and parcel of determining the defectiveness under the risk-benefit analysis.

[A]ppellee filed a motion *in limine* requesting that the court prohibit the introduction of regulations by the Ohio Industrial Commission,[32] the Occupational Safety and Health Administration, and the American National Standards Institute, ANSI. Appellee urged as support for the motion that the basis for the exclusion of said regulations was that the regulations were irrelevant and would unduly prejudice her case. Appellee, in so urging, argued that the essence of the case concerned the alleged defectiveness of the product and the availability and feasibility of safety devices. The introduction of regulations, which were promulgated and applied to employers and not manufacturers, cast an unnecessary cloud over the issue of the defective design of the product. The jury, instead, would be misdirected into focusing on who had the responsibility for supplying the safety devices, i.e., manufacturer or employer, instead of whether the product was defectively designed. Appellant, in rebuttal to appellee's motion *in limine,* vociferously argued that the regulations were a necessary component of the risk-benefit analysis test. Conceding as appellant's counsel must, that

32. See Appendix B.

compliance or noncompliance with the governmental regulations does not absolutely determine the issue of liability, appellant appeals to this court stating that the manufacturer's reliance on governmental and industry regulations is a *relevant* factor in analyzing whether the risks of the product outweighed its benefits.

* * *

Congress passed the Occupational Safety and Health Act of 1970 to increase safety in the workplace and prevent workers' injuries. * * * This goal was accomplished by imposing civil and criminal penalties against employers failing to comply with OSHA standards.

OSHA was not designed to change common law or statutory rights or duties in the workplace. Congress's intent to prevent OSHA standards from becoming independent causes of action was obviously stated in 29 U.S.C. § 653(b)(4) which states:

> "(4) Nothing in this chapter shall be construed to supersede or in any manner affect any workmen's compensation law or to enlarge or diminish or affect in any other manner the common law or statutory rights, duties, or liabilities of employers and employees under any law with respect to injuries, diseases, or death of employees arising out of, or in the course of, employment."

Thus, several courts have refused to admit OSHA standards when the purpose of the proposed admission was at odds with the legislative directive cited above in § 653. [Citations.]

* * *

Although there is little agreement among the courts, the general trend seems to allow the admission of OSHA standards as long as the standards do not serve as the basis of the cause of action; i.e., violation of OSHA does not equate to a claim for strict products liability. Admission of the standards in the present case would allow the manufacturer to rebut the plaintiff's assertion that the press was unreasonably dangerous. Use of the OSHA standards in this manner appears entirely within the mandates set by Congress in 29 U.S.C. § 653(b)(4).

[Thus, evidence of compliance with OSHA standards, while not conclusive of nonliability, is relevant and admissible (subject to appropriate limiting instructions) to prove feasibility of design, availability of alternative safeguards, and other factors relevant to a risk-benefit determination of defectiveness. Similar principles apply to the admissibility of the Ohio Industrial Commission regulations and ANSI standards. Hence, their exclusion from evidence in this case was error.]

C. Prior and Subsequent Acts

[A]ppellant contends that the trial court erred when it permitted plaintiff to introduce evidence of prior and subsequent acts/accidents which were not substantially similar to the case at bar. At trial, appellee's counsel questioned Mr. Jordan, a Minster employee, and Mr.

Steinecker[43] about separate accidents, both prior to and subsequent to Ms. Knitz's mishap. To most questions on the accidents, Jordan responded that he could not recall the specific incident relating to the accident. The best that could be discerned from Jordan's testimony, as determined by the leading questions tendered, was that some, if not all of the machine accidents involved Minster presses, without a sweep device, electronic guard, or interlocking gate, and that an injury occurred by some inadvertent hand entry into the die area. No evidence appears to have been adduced as to whether the device which caused the accident was accidentally triggered by the foot pedal.

Appellant, while conceding that the trial court may exercise its discretion in permitting the introduction of evidence on prior accidents, argues that the evidence of prior acts as well as subsequent acts was inadmissible since they were not substantially similar and therefore did not warrant introduction into evidence at trial.

Evidence of *prior acts* is said to be admissible when it is narrowly restricted for the purpose of showing the hazardous nature of the product or to show the manufacturer's knowledge of other accidents as bearing on the question of notice to manufacturer of the product's dangerousness or possibly dangerous nature. [Citations]; Annotation, Products Liability: Admissibility of Evidence of Other Accidents to Prove Hazardous Nature of Product, 402 A.L.R.3d 780.

In admitting evidence of this nature, the trial court ordinarily is required to determine that the accidents occurred in substantially similar circumstances, so that the evidence is probative, and has a reasonable proximity in time before or after the accident. The factors are then compared with the defendant's potential for unfair surprise and the possibility of confusion of the jury to determine admissibility of the evidence. Annotation, Products Liability, supra.

With reference to *subsequent* accidents, the evidence has little relevance as to the issue of notice or knowledge on the part of the manufacturer, but it may have a limited role in establishing the dangerousness or hazardousness of the product, [citations], as well as the likelihood of injury, relevant factors under the risk-benefit analysis.

* * *

We find that both prior and subsequent acts may be probative as to determining the defectiveness of the product, and, therefore, are admissible. [Citation.] In so holding, we note that it has been said that where evidence is presented on prior accidents, and we relate this to subsequent accidents, that the opposing party can present evidence on the alleged dissimilarities of the subject occurrences, and any evidence

43. Dennis Steinecker, an employee of Minster Machine Co., investigates press-related injuries. He testified that Minster produces predominantly power presses, which do not contain dies, interlocking gate guards, sweep guards or photoelectric guards. He further testified he was aware of approximately 20 hand injuries on the presses, and another 32 injuries where no interlock gate guards were utilized or installed.

to this point of substantial similarity reflects upon the weight of the evidence and not the admissibility of the accidents. [Citations.]

At issue in both the questioning of Steinecker and Jordan, was appellee's attempt to show substantial similarity between injuries in other accidents and Ms. Knitz's injury. The similarity was based upon the fact that the injury that had occurred to all parties was an inadvertent hand injury on a mechanical press, which contained no bolster plate safeguards, such as an interlock guard, sweep guard or photoelectric guard. [Plaintiff-appellee argues] that the purpose for both introduction of the prior and subsequent accidents was to establish that Minster had notice of the defect and danger present, as well as knowledge of feasible designs which would prevent the injury. Appellee further cries fowl [sic] in that the manufacturer appears to have either destroyed, lost or mysteriously misplaced records of prior accidents which may have had greater similarity in relationship to the alleged defect, evidence which would have established the defectiveness. [W]e find that the introduction of the evidence was admissible and that appellant, through introduction of its own evidence or by its own questioning, may diminish the credibility of the evidence concerning the prior accidents. For these reasons, we agree with the trial court and, hold that under the facts of this case, evidence of both prior and subsequent accidents by appellee was admissible.

[H]olding that a product is substantially similar still requires that the evidence be admissible on the basis of relevance in the absence of undue prejudice to the parties. [Evidence Rule 403 provides that relevant evidence should be excluded if "its probative value is substantially outweighed by the danger of unfair prejudice, of confusion of the issues, or of misleading the jury."]

In this case, we recognize that it was within the trial court's discretion to determine what evidence is relevant and admissible in the case at bar. However, we are concerned with the undue prejudice that had befallen defendant-manufacturer in this case, for the transcript of proceedings indicates that Mr. Jordan was questioned on well over 30 separate accidents. Similarity of the accidents, bearly [sic] demonstrated by the leading questions of appellee's counsel, was certainly less than desirable and may well have produced undue prejudice to appellant's case. While such evidence, as stated before, is admissible, the constant onslaught of questions, without the plaintiff-appellee making some corresponding attempt at relating the accidents to the case at hand, is unduly prejudicial to defendant-appellant's case.

* * *

[On similar reasoning the *defendant* may introduce evidence of the *absence* or small number of similar accidents in an attempt to show that its product was not defective.]

[Reversed and remanded.]

HANDWORK, P.J., and CONNERS, J., concur; WILKOWSKI, J., dissents.

APPENDIX B

SPECIFIC SAFETY REQUIREMENTS OF THE INDUSTRIAL COMMISSION OF OHIO

* * *

POWER PRESSES, HAMMERS AND MACHINES

IC–5–08.02 DEFINITIONS

(B) Danger zone. (on power press operations *only*) means the area between the platen and bolster plate.

(C) Ram. Ram means the moving part of the machine referred to as the punch, plunger, ram or slide.

(D) Guards—Power Press:

(1) Electronic. Electronic guard means an electronic safety device so designed and installed that when the operator's hand or any part of body is in the danger zone, the press cannot be tripped and if the hand or any part of the body is inserted while the ram is descending, it will immediately stop the ram.

(2) Fixed Barrier. A fixed barrier guard means an enclosure to prevent the hands or fingers of the operator from entering the danger zone. It may be attached to the dies.

(3) Gate. A gate guard means a movable gate operated by the tripping device which interposes a barrier between the operator and the danger zone, and remains closed until the ram has completed the down stroke.

(4) Magnetic. A magnetic guard means a magnetic safety device so designed and installed that when the operator's hand or any part of body is in the danger zone, the press cannot be tripped and if the hand or any part of the body is inserted while the ram is descending, it will immediately stop the ram.

(5) Photoelectric or Selenium. A photoelectric or selenium guard means a source of light rays together with receiver and other electronic equipment so designed and installed that when the operator's hand or any part of body is in the danger zone the press cannot be tripped and if the hand or any part of the body is inserted while the ram is decending it will immediately stop the ram.

(6) Pull. A pull guard means a device actuated by the ram and attached below the Pittman screw so that movement of the ram will pull the operator's hand or hands from the area between the punch and die (danger zone).

(7) Restraint or Hold–Back. A restraint or hold-back guard means a device with attachment to the hands or wrists of the operator which shall keep the fingers of the operator from entering a pinch point.

(8) Sweep. A sweep guard means a device actuated by some moving part of the press and shall effectively sweep the hands of the operator from the danger zone when the ram or plunger descends.

(9) Two–Hand Tripping Device. A two-hand tripping device means a device designed and constructed to require the simultaneous use of both hands of the operator to trip the press.

(E) Power Press. Power press means a power-driven machine fitted with a ram and dies for the purpose of blanking, trimming, drawing, punching, stamping, coining or forming material. (See IC–5–01.02(G) Feeding: (1) Automatic, (2) Hand or Manual and (3) Semi–Automatic).

IC–5–08.03 POWER PRESSES

(A) GUARDING

(1) **Construction**

Every power press in use shall be constructed, or shall be guarded to prevent the hands or fingers of the operator from entering the danger zone during the operating cycle.

(B) ACCEPTABLE METHODS OF GUARDING

(1) **Manual Feed Presses,** by:

(a) Gate Guard

(b) Fixed Barrier Guard

(c) Sweep Guard

(d) Pull and Restraint or Hold–Back Guard

(e) Two–Hand Tripping Device

(f) Limitation of ram stroke

(g) Electronic Guard

(h) Photoelectric or Selenium Guard

(i) Magnetic Guard

(j) Use of Special Tools

* * *

(I) PREVENTION OF ACCIDENTAL TRIPPING

* * *

(2) **Foot Treadles**—Guarding

Foot treadles used to activate power presses shall be guarded.

NOTES

1. Consider the various machine guarding approaches illustrated below:

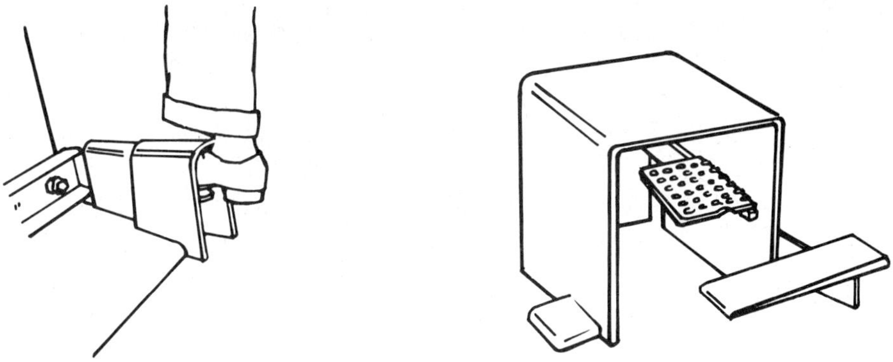

Treadle guards for presses and shears to prevent unintentional tripping

Gate guard on punch press. Guard is interlocked with tripping device of press so that plunger cannot descend until gate is in closed position

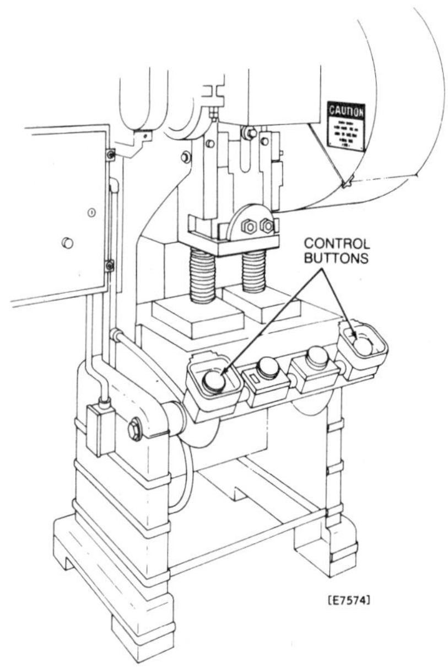

Two-hand control buttons on part-revolution clutch power press

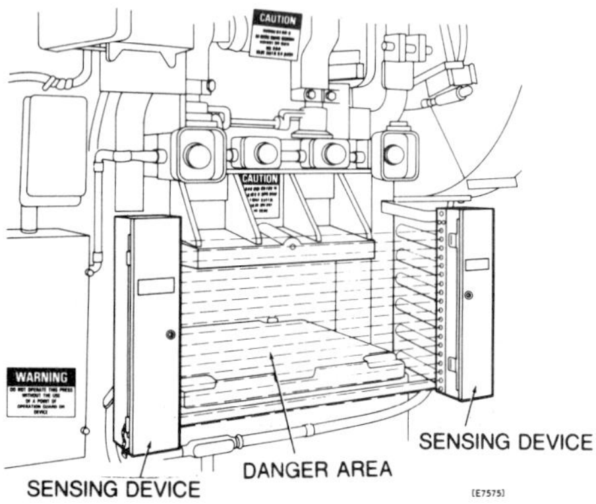

Photoelectric presence-sensing device on power press

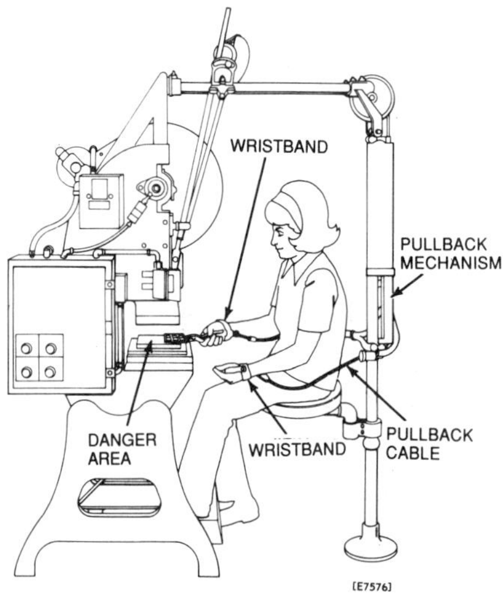

Pull-away Guard. Operator's hands are pulled away from danger zone before ram descends

2. In Wilson v. Piper Aircraft Corp., 282 Or. 61, 577 P.2d 1322 (1978), the plaintiffs' decedents died as a result of the crash of a small aircraft, a Piper Cherokee. Theorizing that the cause of the crash was engine failure due to carburetor icing when the plane entered a cloud, plaintiffs sued the manufacturer, alleging that the airplane engine was dangerously defective because of its susceptibility to carburetor icing. Plaintiffs alleged several specific design defects including the use of a carbureted rather than a fuel-injected engine. Jury verdicts for the plaintiffs were appealed. The court first rejected the defendant's assertion that the Cherokee design should be ruled safe as a matter of law because it had been specifically approved by the Federal Aviation Administration: "We have, in other contexts, refused to hold compliance with statutory or administrative safety standards to be conclusive on the question of tort liability * * *." The court thereupon proceeded to examine the requirements of a plaintiff's prima facie design defect case:

> We have * * * found suggestions in the reported decisions that the plaintiff's burden in a design defect case includes a showing that there was an available "alternative, safer design, practicable under the circumstances," [citation], or that "in terms of cost, practicality and technological possibility, the alternative design was feasible," [citations].
>
> In Roach v. Kononen/Ford Motor Co., supra, 269 Or. at 464, 525 P.2d 125, and Phillips v. Kimwood Machine Co., supra, 269 Or. at 501, 525 P.2d 1033, we said that the court should balance the utility of the risk against its magnitude in deciding whether to submit a design defect case to the jury. One of the factors to be weighed in making this determination is the manufacturer's ability to eliminate the unsafe character of the product without impairing its usefulness or making it too expensive to maintain its utility. In other words, the court is to determine, and to weigh in the balance, whether the proposed alternative design has been shown to be practicable. The trial court should not permit an allegation of design defect to go to the

jury unless there is sufficient evidence upon which to make this determination. If liability for alleged design defects is to "stop somewhere short of the freakish and the fantastic," plaintiffs' prima facie case of a defect must show more than the technical possibility of a safer design.

In some cases, because of the relatively uncomplicated nature of the product or the design feature in question, evidence of the dangerous nature of the design in question or of a safer alternative design may be sufficient to permit the court to consider this factor adequately. * * *

* * *

In other instances, however, the question of practicability cannot be properly weighed solely on the basis of inference and common knowledge. That is the case with the allegations we are considering here. Plaintiffs' allegations amount to a contention that an airplane furnished with a standard aircraft engine is defective because an engine of a different type, or with a different carburetor system, would be safer in one particular. It is not proper to submit such allegations to the jury unless the court is satisfied that there is evidence from which the jury could find the suggested alternatives are not only technically feasible but also practicable in terms of cost and the over-all design and operation of the product. It is part of the required proof that a design feature is a "defect" to present such evidence. In at least some instances in the present case, that requirement has not been met.

We consider, because it well illustrates the problems involved, plaintiffs' contention that defendant's airplane was defective because it was provided with a carbureted engine rather than an engine with a fuel injection system. There was evidence that carbureted airplane engines are characteristically subject to icing of a kind which can result in engine failure and that fuel injected engines are not nearly so subject to dangerous icing. There was also evidence that, at the time this airplane was manufactured, fuel injected engines of appropriate horsepower were available, and expert testimony that FAA approval of an airplane like this one with a fuel injected engine could probably have been obtained.

There is not, however, any evidence about what effect the substitution of a fuel injected engine in this airplane design would have had upon the airplane's cost, economy of operation, maintenance requirements, over-all performance, or safety in respects other than susceptibility to icing. Plaintiffs' own expert witnesses testified that a carbureted engine of the type used in this airplane was, except for its susceptibility to icing, a highly satisfactory, dependable engine. There was also undisputed evidence that 80 to 90 per cent of all small airplanes comparable to this one are manufactured with carbureted engines rather than with fuel injected engines. There was no explanation of why this is the case.

We also think it is significant that both in 1966, when this airplane was manufactured, and at the present time the FAA safety standards disclose that the agency was aware of the carburetor icing problems and provided for them in its regulations and yet determined that the use of carbureted engines was not unduly dangerous. Although we have held that compliance with the FAA safety standards does not preclude the possibility of liability for a design defect, we nevertheless believe that in a field as closely regulated as aircraft design and manufacture, it is proper to take into consideration, in determining whether plaintiffs have produced sufficient evidence of defect to go to the jury, the fact that the regulatory agency has approved the very design of which they complain after considering the dangers involved.

Taking into account all of the evidence, including the FAA determination that this aircraft design included adequate protection against carburetor icing, we hold that plaintiffs did not produce sufficient evidence that a reasonably prudent manufacturer who was aware of the risks of carburetor icing would not have designed this model of aircraft with a carbureted engine, or that substitution of a fuel injected engine was practicable.

Held, reversed and remanded for new trial.

3. Garst v. General Motors Corp., 207 Kan. 2, 484 P.2d 47 (1971), was a negligent design action against the manufacturer of the 40–ton "Euclid" earthmoving scraper pictured below, that ran into and injured a worker at a construction site. The operator saw the plaintiff shortly before he hit him but was unable to brake the scraper to a stop or steer it away to avoid the collision.

[A3964]

Euclid TS–24 Earth–Moving Scraper

Plaintiff claimed that the defendant had been negligent in the design of both the braking and steering systems on the scraper, alleging that they both should have been more effective. The jury returned a verdict for the plaintiff, and defendant appealed.

Plaintiff's expert was John B. Sevart, an assistant professor of mechanical engineering at Wichita State University studying for his doctorate, whose specialty was in systems and design:

Sevart had a limited amount of experience on hydraulic systems. On cross-examination he testified he was not a member of the Society of Automotive Engineers (SAE), and was not familiar with its standards relating to earth-moving equipment. He was not familiar with the portion of that society known as the Construction and Industrial Machines Technical Committee, or any of the standards that the committee has promulgated relating to heavy equipment. But he did know it had such standards.

* * *

Sevart considered the braking system of the scraper here in question reasonably designed and entirely adequate for use under dry conditions. Under those circumstances, he considered it a very standard design and had no complaints about the strength of the drums or the shoes. His challenge to the braking system related only to the open-type construction that allows mud to freely get in the system.

He knew of no other manufacturer, mentioning seven, that had other than "open" brakes on its similar equipment. He recognized there were some considerations which favored open brakes.

Sevart's theory was that "there should be a shield or a guard on the braking system as standard equipment." He proposed a flexible seal over the brake. The substance of his testimony was that such structure would not keep water out, nor would it keep mud or other foreign materials out. It would merely reduce the build-up time so that maintenance would not be required every day or every half a day, but probably on a weekly or biweekly basis. The build-up "would be over a longer period of time." * * *

Sevart knew of no flexible material that could be used to provide the seal over the brake which his theory postulated.

When cross-examined concerning several materials available which he mentioned could be used, it was disclosed that these materials would break down at temperatures of 250° Fahrenheit, and therefore, could not withstand either the brake temperatures of 500 to 800° Fahrenheit developed almost constantly when the scraper was in use, or the cherry-red temperatures of 1300° Fahrenheit to which the brakes heat under severe operating conditions in mountainous terrain. The flexible materials he mentioned would be subject to abrasion.

The substance of Sevart's testimony relative to sealing the braking units was that he could not specify a definite material that should have been used in the flexible seal at the time the TS–24 was designed between 1955 and 1962. He explained he was not a "materials expert."

* * *

Sevart also testified regarding the steering system of the TS–24 scraper. * * * "My theory is that the steering system is reasonably well designed." His only complaint was that "it steers too slow at low engine rpm. The way the machine is now designed, the speed of the steering depends upon engine speed." Sevart thought he could improve the steering system on the TS–24 scraper. He made three proposals which he claimed would have improved the steering. He had never constructed the steering systems he envisioned in his theory. * * *

The changes in steering that Sevart thought would make the turn more rapid were, first, to double the pump size and add a bypass. * * *

Sevart thought this system was in use on the Michigan scraper, but it turned out he had misunderstood and, on rebuttal, admitted: "I do not know of an example of this double size pump and the bypass valve on a scraper or heavy construction equipment."

[A General Motors expert testified that Sevart's proposal to double the pump size would divert 20% of the engine's horsepower and cause serious heat build-up problems.]

Sevart did not think the heat problem would be so serious but he did agree "the heat might go up, oh, 40, 50 percent." To solve the heat problem Sevart said he would increase "the size of the reservoir." Sevart agreed the "power bleed" was a problem, but he considered it would not prove "an insurmountable problem."

These problems, according to Sevart, would be avoided by his second alternative—a two-speed drive. * * *

Sevart admitted: "I don't know of any application of this type of arrangement on a scraper or any comparable heavy equipment."

To avoid the criticized *sudden shift* at some point from one gear to the other, thereby creating a safety hazard in steering, Sevart proposed a third alternative—that of a variable-speed cone drive. This alternative proposed by Sevart to improve the steering "would have been to put some form of continuous gear ratio between the pump and the engine. * * *"

[Defendant's experts testified that no manufacturer had ever used a cone drive on any comparable heavy equipment.]

With respect to the steering system utilized by the General Motors scraper, the record discloses no better solution was known to the industry. The steering system utilized by General Motors on the scraper in question is the standard type equipment in the heavy construction field. It is used by all manufacturers of like equipment except only Westinghouse–LeTourneau which in some models had electric steering. The evidence discloses the electric steering was slower than the hydraulic steering even at low engine rpm. Sevart admitted the steering system is, except for his complaint that it is not as fast as he would have made it, "reasonably well designed."

* * *

The courts are nearly unanimous in saying the product-design duty of a manufacturer *is that of reasonable care,* but it is not an insurer that its product, from a design standpoint, be accident-proof or incapable of producing injury. [Citation.]

In the instant case it is not enough to say that the scraper did not stop or turn quickly enough. In 42 Wash.L.Rev. 601, "Manufacturer's Liability for Defective Automobile Design," it was said:

> "To prove defective design, it is insufficient merely to assert that a different design would have alleviated or averted the plaintiff's injuries, since it may be assumed that any particular accident involving man and machine might have been avoided through a variation in the design of the machine. However, such a variation might greatly magnify the chances of other sorts of mishaps taking place, or else render the machine incapable of reasonably efficient performance of its function. * * *" (p. 608.)

* * *

All courts agree that as a matter of law, a manufacturer is not obligated to adopt only those features which represent the ultimate in safety or design. [Citations.]

* * *

In the determination of whether or not a manufacturer has in fact exercised the care and skill of an expert, several matters are to be considered. One of the most significant factors is whether others in the field are using the same design, or a safer design. Other factors to be considered are whether a safer design not yet in use is known to be feasible, and whether in the case of a new product there has been adequate testing. [Citations.]

* * *

The alternatives suggested by the appellees' expert witness were neither available nor feasible.

* * *

The appellees attack the position of General Motors to retain a competitive position in the manufacture of earth-moving equipment and their interest in economy. In our free enterprise system the ability of a manufacturer to remain competitive is a prerequisite to any manufacturer at all, and rules of law cannot be fashioned without giving due consideration to the economic factors involved. For example, General Motors in the manufacture of earth-moving equipment is not required to expend exorbitant sums of money in research to devise a sophisticated braking system which would price its product completely out of the market. The TS–24 scraper here in question is shown to have cost approximately $90,000.

* * *

In our opinion the evidence upon which the appellees rely to prove negligence in the design of the braking and steering systems of the TS–24 scraper was not of sufficient dignity to warrant its submission to the jury for consideration. In other words, there was no substantial competent evidence, as a matter of law, upon which the jury could find the appellant negligent in designing the braking and steering systems of the TS–24 scraper.

Held (5–2), judgment for plaintiff reversed.

4. In Acord v. General Motors Corp., 669 S.W.2d 111 (Tex.1984), the trial court instructed the jury that a manufacturer is not an insurer of the product it designs, that an adopted design need not be perfect nor render the product accident-proof, nor must the manufacturer incorporate the ultimate safety features in the product. *Held,* reversible error as an improper comment on the evidence.

5. **Feasible Design Alternatives.** The cases in this section show the importance the courts place on the feasibility of the alternative, safer designs proposed by the plaintiff.

A. What factors determine whether an alternative design is feasible? How does feasibility differ from reasonableness? From statutory or privately adopted design standards? Is feasibility an economic or engineering concept, or some hybrid of the two? Is it part of the plaintiff's case, or of the defendant's? Must an alternative design be proved by an expert?

B. Feasibility may include such factors as technological capability, commercial practicability, cost, commercial availability of materials or components, and the likelihood of consumer acceptance. See, e.g., Rix v. General Motors Corp., ___ Mont. ___, 723 P.2d 195 (1986); Troja v. Black & Decker Mfg. Co., 62 Md.App. 101, 488 A.2d 516 (1985); Oberst v. International Harvester Co., Inc., 640 F.2d 863 (7th Cir.1980).

Should the concept include all the disadvantages of the proposed design, including decreased utility and increased risks of harm from other dangers? Cf. Hagans v. Oliver Machinery Co., 576 F.2d 97 (5th Cir.1978) (multi-purposed table circular saw equipped with removable—instead of permanent—blade guard).

C. Many courts hold that proof of a feasible design alternative is a necessary part of the plaintiff's case, except perhaps in the case of simple products where the feasibility of the alternative design is self-evident to the jury. "Since plaintiff failed to present evidence that there was a safe and reasonably feasible alternative to defendants' product, the trial court properly concluded that there was no issue of design defect for the jury to determine." Macri v. Ames McDonough Co., 211 N.J.Super. 636, 512 A.2d 548, 551 (1986) (hammer which chipped); Voss v. Black & Decker Mfg. Co., 59 N.Y.2d 102, 463 N.Y.S.2d 398, 450 N.E.2d 204 (1983).

D. A number of courts, recognizing that there are rare products that cannot feasibly be redesigned and which are so dangerous that they should be removed from the market, have held that proof of a feasible design alternative is not technically part of the plaintiff's case: "Although normally evidence of a safer design alternative will be presented initially by the plaintiff, it is not necessarily required in all cases." Kallio v. Ford Motor Co., 407 N.W.2d 92, 96–97 (Minn.1987) (noting, however, that "as a practical matter, successful plaintiffs, almost without fail, introduce evidence of a safer alternative design"). See also Rahmig v. Mosley Mach. Co., 226 Neb. 423, 412 N.W.2d 56 (1987), overruling Nervd v. Haybuster Mfg., Inc., 215 Neb. 604, 340 N.W.2d 369, 375 (1983).

E. Reconsider Caterpillar Tractor Co. v. Beck, supra p. 228, endorsing the California *Barker* opinion. What, if anything, have California and Alaska done to the role of feasibility in design defect litigation?

F. What should be the role of alternative design proof in a state defining design defectiveness in terms of consumer expectations?

6. **Safety Standards.** Design safety standards from a variety of sources may be admissible on the issues both of design defectiveness and on design negligence.

A. **Governmental standards.** Compliance with a relevant governmental safety standard is generally considered probative of non-defectiveness or non-negligence. See Kaufman v. Meditec, Inc., 353 N.W.2d 297, 301 (N.D.1984) (setting forth products liability reform act provision establishing rebuttable presumption "that a product is [not defective] where the alleged defect in the plans or designs * * * were in conformity with government standards established for that industry"). Conversely, breach of such standards may show defectiveness or negligence per se. See Elsworth v. Beech Aircraft Corp., 37 Cal.3d 540, 208 Cal.Rptr. 874, 691 P.2d 630 (1984).

B. **Quasi-public standards organizations.** Some quasi-public organizations, such as Underwriters' Laboratories (UL) and the American National Standards Institute (ANSI), set product safety standards. Both compliance and breach of relevant standards of this type are generally considered probative on the issues of design defectiveness and negligence.

C. **Industry standards; Custom.** Evidence of compliance and breach of customary standards are some evidence, but not conclusive, of due care or negligence. The courts have split, however, on whether a manufacturer's adoption of a customary design is evidence of non-defectiveness. Compare Carter v. Massey–Ferguson, Inc., 716 F.2d 344 (5th Cir.1983) ("evidence of industry custom is relevant in a strict liability case [but] has a low probative value when * * * neither the feasibility of an alternative design nor the foreseeability of harm is at issue"), with Eldridge v. Firestone Tire & Rubber Co., 24 Ohio App.3d 94, 493 N.E.2d 293 (1985) (fact that most other lawn mowers did not have trailing guard in 1968 irrelevant to whether defendant's mower without guard "embodied excessive preventable danger").

Both sides of the argument were presented in Lewis v. Coffing Hoist Division, 515 Pa. 334, 528 A.2d 590 (1987), where plaintiff was injured when he fell against and accidentally activated a push-button control box that operated a hoist. His expert testified that the buttons should have been recessed into the box rather than protruding therefrom, or that they should have been surrounded by metal flanges. The trial court barred the defendant from introducing (1) an American Society of Mechanical Engineers (ASME) publication on electric hoist standards (which made no mention of control box design), and (2) expert testimony that at least 90% of the electric hoist control boxes made in this country are unguarded. *Held* (4–1–2), judgment on verdict for plaintiff affirmed. For the majority, Chief Justice Nix concluded that evidence on industry design standards, and the widespread use of the design throughout the industry, would have diverted the jury's attention from the adequacy of the control box design to the reasonableness of the defendant's conduct in choosing the design, and hence "would have improperly brought into the case concepts of negligence law." Dissenting, Justice Flaherty observed:

> [C]onsidering evidence of industry-wide acceptance in connection with the position of the American Society of Mechanical Engineers that, in fact, the switch was safely designed, the jury could properly conclude that the widespread use is at the least probative of the industry's acceptance of appellant's design as a safe one. * * * I would admit the evidence, not to show the reasonableness of appellant's use of the switch, but to show that users of the switch widely regard it as safe and so perhaps it is.

Justice Hutchinson, also dissenting, found himself, "compelled, in the words of a popular song, to 'speak out against the madness.' The instant madness is a creeping consensus among us judges and lawyers that we are more capable of designing products than engineers." In particular, Justice Hutchinson argued as follows:

> Industry standards are written by individuals considered by their peers in industry, academia and research to be especially knowledgeable in a particular technical specialty. These standards contain their collective expert wisdom. The committees who prepare the standards are as respected in their fields as the American Law Institute, on whose formulation of the law of strict liability the majority relies, is in ours. Their collective opinion is at least as valuable as any individual expert witness's. Of course, these industry standards would not be conclusive, but their relevance and competence is clear.

7. **Similar Accidents.** As in both *McCormack* and *Knitz,* plaintiffs often seek to introduce evidence of similar accidents. See also Exum v. General Electric Co., supra p. 64. Such evidence is admissible, in the discretion of the court, provided that it is substantially similar to the case at bar. Compare Brooks v. Chrysler Corp., 786 F.2d 1191 (D.C.Cir.1986) (prior occurrences admissible since virtually identical; however, NHTSA brake failure study excluded since less than 2% of data involved comparable accidents); Ponder v. Warren Tool Corp., 834 F.2d 1553 (10th Cir.1987) (evidence of other tire explosions from tire mounting bead seater properly excluded where not shown to have resulted from failure of bead seater properly to disengage).

"The evolving law of product liability now recognizes that evidence of defective design may be circumstantial. That is, the defect may be inferred by the behavior of the product." Koski v. Automatic Heating Service, 75 Mich. App. 180, 254 N.W.2d 836 (1977). Even a single prior similar occurrence may be admissible. See Warn Industries v. Geist, 343 So.2d 44 (Fla.App.1977), in which evidence that a winch which injured the plaintiff had failed on one prior occasion was ruled admissible as showing that something was wrong with the product.

The Consumer Product Safety Commission maintains a National Information Clearinghouse which collects data on injury-producing products. As part of this system, the National Electronic Surveillance System receives data from major hospital emergency rooms throughout the United States. Information collected through this system may be useful in documenting the frequency and nature of injuries associated with the use of particular products. Similar information may be obtained through the products liability exchange service of the Association of Trial Lawyers of America, the principal professional association of plaintiffs' lawyers. See Zackey, The ATLA Exchange—Professional Cooperation and Product Safety, Trial 63 (Nov.1978).

8. **Post-Accident Remedial Measures.** Assume that, prior to trial, the *Hankscraft* plastic top had been redesigned with threads so that it could be screwed securely onto the glass container. Should the plaintiff be permitted to introduce evidence of the redesign to prove that the earlier design was defective, or that the manufacturer had been negligent in originally designing the top without threads? The traditional evidentiary rule is reflected in the federal rule:

> **F.R.Evid. 407, Subsequent Remedial Measures:**
>
> When, after an event, measures are taken which, if taken previously, would have made the event less likely to occur, evidence of the subsequent measures is not admissible to prove negligence or culpable conduct in connection with the event. This rule does not require the exclusion of evidence of subsequent measures when offered for another purpose, such as proving ownership, control, or feasibility of precautionary measures, if controverted, or impeached.

The Advisory Committee Note gives two reasons in support of the rule: (1) "the rule rejects the notion that 'because the world gets wiser as it gets older, therefore it was foolish before' "; and (2) an attempt not to discourage persons from making safety improvements.

Whether the exclusionary rule should apply to strict liability cases has split the courts. Since the rule on its face applies only to negligence cases, many courts have refused to apply it to strict liability cases. The classic case adopting this view is Ault v. International Harvester Co., 13 Cal.3d 113, 117

Cal.Rptr. 812, 528 P.2d 1148 (1974), which rejected the empirical assumptions underlying the rule in the modern products liability context: "The contemporary corporate mass producer of goods, the normal products liability defendant, manufactures tens of thousands of units of goods; it is manifestly unrealistic to suggest that such a producer will forego making improvements in its product, and risk innumerable additional lawsuits and the attendant adverse effect upon its public image, simply because evidence of adoption of such improvement may be admitted in an action founded on strict liability for recovery on an injury that preceded the improvement." See also Sanderson v. Steve Snyder Enterprises, Inc., 196 Conn. 134, 491 A.2d 389, 395 (1985) ("it is unlikely that any evidentiary use of subsequent remedial measures will discourage a designer or manufacturer from taking them").

Many other courts apply the exclusionary rule to the strict liability context as well as to negligence, reasoning that the use of such evidence will discourage safety improvements in this context as any other. "The overwhelming trend in the federal courts has been to exclude evidence of subsequent remedial measures in products liability cases." Gauthier v. AMF, Inc., 788 F.2d 634, 637 (9th Cir.1986) ("there is no practical difference between strict liability and negligence in defective design cases and the public policy rationale to encourage remedial measures remains the same"). *Held,* admission of such evidence improper where manufacturer conceded economic and technological feasibility of safety devices but argued that "the safety problem was not great enough to warrant the trade-off of consumer frustration, increased complexity of the product, and risk of consumer efforts to disconnect the safety device." Id. at 638. See also Rix v. General Motors Corp., ___ Mont. ___, 723 P.2d 195, 202 (1986) (applying state evidence rule 407 to strict tort claim: "evidence of subsequent design modification is not probative of whether a product was defectively designed").

In New York, subsequent modifications may be shown in manufacturing defect cases but not in design or warnings cases. Cover v. Cohen, 61 N.Y.2d 261, 473 N.Y.S.2d 378, 461 N.E.2d 864 (1984). Many states have evidence rules similar or identical to Fed.R.Evid. 407, although some state statutes specifically exclude such evidence in strict liability cases. See generally Henderson, Product Liability and Admissibility of Subsequent Remedial Measures: Resolving the Conflict by Recognizing the Difference Between Negligence and Strict Tort Liability, 64 Neb.L.Rev. 1 (1985).

9. **Expert Testimony.**

A. **In general.** In a design case of any complexity, such as Knitz v. Minster Machine Co., above, expert testimony—from an engineer, mechanic, chemist, or other technical specialist—is necessary for the plaintiff to establish design defectiveness, particularly the availability of a feasible design alternative. (An expert often will be necessary to prove causation as well.) On the other hand, if the design defect was an obvious one, easy for the jury to understand—as in Matthews v. Lawnlite Co., above—expert testimony on defectiveness may not be necessary. This is because the purpose of expert testimony is to educate the jury on matters beyond ordinary experience. See, e.g., Pietrone v. American Honda Motor Co., Inc., 189 Cal.App.3d 1057, 235 Cal. Rptr. 137, 139 (1987) (expert testimony not required on defectiveness of exposed rear motorcycle wheel that could have been guarded: "alternative designs were so self-evident as to obviate the need to present express testimony, expert or otherwise"); Lynd v. Rockwell Mfg. Co., 276 Or. 341, 554 P.2d 1000, 1005 (1976) ("when the issues presented relate to matters which require only common knowledge and experience to understand them, the testimony of experts is not essential").

The role of plaintiff's expert in identifying one or more feasible alternative designs that could have prevented the accident is well illustrated by Hylton, et ux. v. John Deere Co., 802 F.2d 1011 (8th Cir.1986), where plaintiff's arm was pulled into the leveling auger in the grain bin of a combine he was operating when he sought to retrieve an address book that fell from his pocket into the bin. His expert proposed four separate design defects: (1) the absence of a guard over the auger; (2) the absence of a lid over the grain bin to prevent the auger from turning when opened; (3) the ability of the auger to engage even when the clutch was in neutral; and (4) the absence of an emergency stop system to permit a person to stop the motor in case of an accident. A principal role of the defendant's expert often is to explain how the plaintiff's expert's design alternatives are not feasible. Thus, John Deere's expert testified on the first alleged defect that a guard would (a) diminish the auger's ability to level the grain, and (b) damage the grain kernels. *Held,* judgment for defendant affirmed.

B. **Testing.** The value of an expert's opinion is increased, of course, if it is based upon an examination or testing of the product in question. See, e.g., Gillespie v. R.D. Werner Co., Inc., 71 Ill.2d 318, 17 Ill.Dec. 10, 375 N.E.2d 1294 (1978) (ladder which collapsed). Although most courts will not disqualify an expert witness for failing to acquire such first-hand knowledge about the product's relevant characteristics, such a failure will of course reduce the value of the testimony: "It is true that McCoy did not run metal hardness tests or examine the grease to substantiate his abnormal wear theory and that he did not examine the vehicle's spindle. These matters, however, go to the weight which the trier of fact should accord the evidence [but] do not make the testimony incredible." Wylie v. Ford Motor Co., 502 F.2d 1292, 1294 (10th Cir. 1974). But see Cosgrove v. Estate of Delves, 35 A.D.2d 730, 315 N.Y.S.2d 369 (1970) (expert measured but did not test plastic champagne cork which popped out of bottle; *held,* testimony insufficient to support verdict for plaintiff).

C. **Rules of evidence.** Consider the following Federal Rules of Evidence:

Fed.R.Evid. 702, Testimony by Experts:

If scientific, technical, or other specialized knowledge will assist the trier of fact to understand the evidence or to determine a fact in issue, a witness qualified as an expert by knowledge, skill, experience, training, or education, may testify thereto in the form of an opinion or otherwise.

Fed.R.Evid. 703, Bases of Opinion Testimony by Experts:

The facts or data in the particular case upon which an expert bases an opinion or inference may be those perceived by or made known to the expert at or before the hearing. If of a type reasonably relied upon by experts in the particular field in forming opinions or inferences upon the subject, the facts or data need not be admissible in evidence.

"[T]he rule is designed to broaden the basis for expert opinions * * * and to bring the judicial practice into line with the practice of the experts themselves when not in court." Advisory Comm. Note to Fed.R.Evid. 703. See generally Maietta v. International Harvester Co., 496 A.2d 286 (Me.1985).

Courts traditionally prohibited expert (and other) witnesses from usurping the function of the jury by giving opinions on the ultimate issue in the case. For various reasons, in recent years the rule has been breaking down. Consider the following:

Fed.R.Evid. 704, Opinion on Ultimate Issue:

> [T]estimony in the form of an opinion or inference otherwise admissible is not objectionable because it embraces an ultimate issue to be decided by the trier of fact.

The Advisory Committee Notes qualify Rule 704 by pointing out the requirement of Rules 701 & 702 that the opinion be helpful to the trier of fact. Those provisions "stand ready to exclude opinions phrased in terms of inadequately explored legal criteria." In Aller v. Rodgers Mach. Co., Inc., 268 N.W.2d 830, 840 (Iowa 1978), the court held that an expert may not opine that a product is unreasonably dangerous, because it is a question of law. Curiously, in the next paragraph, the court acknowledged that the issue was one for the jury. See also Strong v. E.I. DuPont de Nemours, Co., Inc., 667 F.2d 682, 685 (8th Cir.1981) (trial court did not err in excluding expert's opinion that defendant's warnings were inadequate and made product unreasonably dangerous). Contra Karns v. Emerson Elec. Co., 817 F.2d 1452, 1459 (10th Cir.1987) (appellate court labored to justify trial court's ruling permitting plaintiff's expert to testify that a product was "unreasonably dangerous beyond the expectation of the average user" and that the defendant "acted recklessly" in manufacturing it).

D. **Human factors experts.** Plaintiffs in products liability cases sometimes use "human factors" experts. One such expert, holding a Ph.D. in experimental psychology with an emphasis on human factors, testified in Prentis v. Yale Mfg. Co., 421 Mich. 670, 365 N.W.2d 176, 179 n. 4 (1984). The plaintiff was injured when the battery-powered walking-type fork lift he was operating experienced a power surge and knocked him down. Plaintiff claimed that this type of fork lift was defective because it did not provide a seat or platform for the operator on the lift itself but instead required the operator to operate the vehicle by lifting its handle up, like a wagon, and walking along with it. The plaintiff's human factors expert testified as follows:

> [T]he idea is that man was not properly integrated into this design. A man had to use it. It was designed for a man to use. It was improperly designed for a man to use safely. I think [the warnings booklet shows] that they realized that they had a very dangerous design here. They had to issue all kinds of warnings in this pamphlet and so on.
>
> Very essentially, you should not allow man to control this kind of power over the machine. He should have been on a platform on the machine that was properly guarded and so on. If it had been designed that way, he would not be in court today.

See generally Bliss, Human Factors Specialists, Trial 52 (Oct. 1984); Messina, The Human Factors Expert in Tort Litigation, Trial 38 (Jan. 1984); Ryan, Human Factors Engineering for Consumer Safety: A Perspective, Trial 86 (Nov. 1982).

E. **Abuse of expert testimony.** Some judges have expressed concern over the misuse of expert testimony in design defect litigation. In Lamon v. McDonnell Douglas Corp., 19 Wash.App. 515, 576 P.2d 426 (1978), aff'd 588 P.2d

1346 (Wash.1979), an airline stewardess stepped into an open emergency hatch in the galley floor. On defendant's motion for summary judgment, plaintiff introduced the affidavit of her expert to the effect that the hatch was unreasonably dangerous because the cover was not equipped with a spring to close it automatically as on other aircraft. *Held,* 2–1, summary judgment reversed and case remanded for trial. Dissenting, Judge Anderson remarked:

> * * * The use of expert witnesses in products liability cases is often helpful and, indeed, is sometimes essential. In modern day trial practice, such witnesses are frequently used. Advertising by expert witnesses in legal periodicals is now also common practice. Hundreds of expert witnesses who, for a fee, will testify in most fields of expertise are listed in at least one national publication, H. Philo, D. Robb and R. Goodman, Lawyers Desk Reference: Technical Sources for Conducting a Personal Injury Action (5th ed. 1975).
>
> In this jurisdiction, as in many others opinion testimony which is otherwise admissible is not objectionable just because it embraces an ultimate issue to be decided by the trier of fact. This does not mean, however, that a jury case is automatically made out every time an expert witness states an opinion that a given product is defective, dangerous or not reasonably safe. If that were so, there might very well be as a practical matter that which the law otherwise denies, and every manufacturer, processor and seller of a product would be absolutely liable and an insurer that no one under any circumstances would ever sustain damage or be injured by the product—or, at least, that a jury issue could always be made out to that effect.
>
> * * *
>
> In order to bring this issue into focus, some rhetorical questions should be posed.
>
> If a person walks into the edge of an open door and is injured, is a jury case made out if an engineer testifies that the injured person had to use the room where the door was located, that some doors close automatically and in his opinion the door which did not automatically close was not reasonably safe?
>
> If a person who has to use a particular room where a square table is located walks into the corner of a table in that room and is injured, is a jury case made out if an engineer points out that some tables are round and in his opinion the square table is not reasonably safe? Or to use the converse, if the square table in the room is then replaced by a round table, and an object falls off of the round table that probably would not have fallen from the square table and injures someone's foot, is a jury case made out by an engineer testifying that some tables are square and in his opinion the round table was not reasonably safe?
>
> It should not be held that a jury case is made out in any of these illustrative situations.
>
> Unless factual evidence in the record supports an expert witness' opinion, the opinion by itself should not be legally sufficient to get the issue on which it was expressed past an appropriate challenge.
>
> * * *
>
> In its final analysis, the fallacy of letting an expert witness' unsupported opinion create a fact issue in a case is perhaps better answered by logic than by legal precedent. Illustrative of this is a

> story told of Abraham Lincoln during his trial lawyer days. Lincoln is said to have cross-examined a witness as follows:
>
> "How many legs does a horse have?"
>
> "Four," said the witness.
>
> "Right," said Abe.
>
> "Now, if you call the tail a leg, how many legs does a horse have?"
>
> "Five," answered the witness.
>
> "Nope," said Abe, "callin' a tail a leg don't make it a leg."
>
> So it is here that merely calling a product unreasonably dangerous does not, without more, make it so.

576 P.2d at 426.

Compare Evers v. General Motors Corp., 770 F.2d 984 (11th Cir.1985), where plaintiff's car was broadsided near the driver's door by a car that ran a stop sign. Plaintiff sued the manufacturer of her own car alleging that it was defective in design due to the absence of an air bag. Defendant moved for summary judgment on the basis of deposition testimony that air bags do not work in side-impact collisions. Two days before the summary judgment hearing, plaintiff filed an affidavit of her expert stating that he had reviewed the evidence and concluded that the absence of an air bag rendered the car's design defective. *Held,* summary judgment for defendant affirmed. "[A] party may not avoid summary judgment solely on the basis of an expert's opinion that fails to provide specific facts from the record to support its conclusory allegations. * * * Most importantly, there is no specific mention of how an 'air bag' would have aided in a side-impact collision." Id. at 986. See Fed.R.Civ.P. 56(e).

That some expert witnesses will testify with less than complete candor is evident in Sanchez v. Black Brothers Co., 98 Ill.App.3d 264, 53 Ill.Dec. 505, 423 N.E.2d 1309 (1981), in which the trial court barred plaintiff from impeaching the credibility of defendant's expert witness on cross-examination with a speech he had given to a group of engineers on how to testify as an expert.

> During that speech, Mr. Barnett stated, *inter alia,* that:
>
> "The way I counteracted the thing, I used another technique. I used the technique as (sic) science as a foreign language. I made a statement to the attorney that absolutely nobody could understand. Now, what it amounts to, it's going to terminate the cross examination, and it's going to terminate it in a hurry.
>
> "*I want the jury to understand what I say when I feel there are certain conditions. Under direct examination, the jury understands everything that I say. Under cross examination, there are some things I will allow the jury to understand and there are some things which I will not allow the jury to understand.*
>
> "If you don't want the jury to understand something, then what you do is you answer the question precisely, you see. If somebody is working with a form of inertia, why I use a form of inertia. I say, 'Do you mean the second bolt above the first bolt,' you know. Just get into something which is a very precise way of saying something.

> "The interval of minus infinity to plus infinity of X times X, X^2, and you know the—no one is going to be able to do much with that kind of thing.
>
> "And he says, 'Can you simplify it?' You say, 'See, there's too much simplification already. This is the only way that I can state it to you so there will be no misunderstanding.'" (Emphasis added.)
>
> The bias or prejudice of a witness is always relevant [citation], and evidence "elicited on cross-examination or offered as impeachment is admissible if it tends to show a witness' bias and lack of credibility." [Citation.] Evidence of Barnett's speech, if believed by the jury, would tend to show his bias in favor of a party calling him to testify, in this case defendant. In evaluating Barnett's veracity and the weight to be given to his testimony, the jury was entitled to know of the speech.

423 N.E.2d at 1315, 1320 (concurring opinion). *Held,* precluding use of the speech for impeachment was reversible error. The majority opinion stated that "the expert witness is usually a hired partisan. Moreover, it is unlikely that he could be successfully prosecuted for perjury on the basis of his opinion testimony. * * * For these reasons, counsel must be given the widest possible latitude during cross examination * * *." Id. at 1315. Compare Harre v. A.H. Robins Co., Inc., 750 F.2d 1501 (11th Cir.1985) (judgment for defendant reversed and remanded since verdict based in part on perjured testimony by defense expert).

F. See generally Epstein & Klein, The Use and Abuse of Expert Testimony in Product Liability Actions, 17 Seton Hall L.Rev. 656 (1987); Carlson, Policing the Bases of Modern Expert Testimony, 39 Vand.L.Rev. 577 (1986) (discussing Agent Orange litigation); Hoenig, Drawing the Line on Expert Opinion, 8 J.Prod.L. 335 (1985); Broder, Strategies for Expert Witnesses, Trial 42 (May 1987); Cartwright & Phillips, The Expert in a Product Case: Preparation and Cross-examination, Trial 22 (Nov. 1986).

10. **Design Defects in Other Contexts.** While industrial machinery and durable consumer goods are the typical products giving rise to design defect allegations, such claims are asserted in other contexts too. See, e.g., Toner v. Lederle Laboratories, 828 F.2d 510 (9th Cir.1987) (DPT vaccine should have been formulated in safer manner); Boyer v. Empiregas, Inc. of Chillicothe, 734 S.W.2d 828 (Mo.App.1987) (inadequately odorized propane gas exploded); Cipollone v. Liggett Group, Inc., 649 F.Supp. 664 (D.N.J.1986) (cigarettes could have been more safely designed); Abels v. Murjani Int'l, Inc., Prod.Liab.Rep. (CCH) ¶ 11,229 (D.Kan.1988) (composition of blouse fabric, 80% cotton and 20% polyester, excessively flammable); Hilliard v. A.H. Robins Co., 148 Cal.App.3d 374, 196 Cal.Rptr. 117 (1983) (Dalkon Shield IUD, with multifiliment tail string, facilitated migration of bacteria into uterus); Drayton v. Jiffee Chemical Corp., 395 F.Supp. 1081 (N.D.Ohio 1975), modified 591 F.2d 352 (6th Cir.1978) (formulation of drain cleaner as 26% lye unnecessarily caustic); West v. Johnson & Johnson Products, Inc., 174 Cal.App.3d 831, 220 Cal.Rptr. 437 (1985) (extra-high absorbency tampons caused TSS).

B. REGULATION

Several federal agencies regulate product design safety, notably the CPSC (consumer products), NHTSA (automobiles), and OSHA (industrial products). When an agency promulgates a significant design safety regulation, it is likely to be challenged in court, as in the following case.

SOUTHLAND MOWER COMPANY v. CONSUMER PRODUCTS SAFETY COMMISSION

United States Court of Appeals, Fifth Circuit, 1980.
619 F.2d 499.

Petitions for Review of an Order of the Consumer Product Safety Commission.

Before JONES, GEE and REAVLEY, CIRCUIT JUDGES.

GEE, CIRCUIT JUDGE:

Approximately 77,000 people are injured each year in the United States by contacting the blades of walk-behind power mowers.[1] Of these injuries, an estimated 9,900 involve the amputation of at least one finger or toe, 11,400 involve fractures, 2,400 involve avulsions (the tearing of flesh or a body part) 2,300 involve contusions, and 51,400 involve lacerations. The annual economic cost inflicted by the 77,000 yearly blade-contact injuries has been estimated to be about $253 million. This figure does not include monetary compensation for pain and suffering or for the lost use of amputated fingers and toes.[2]

To reduce these blade-contact injuries, the Consumer Product Safety Commission ("CPSC" or "the Commission") promulgated[3] a Safety

1. 44 Fed. Reg. 9990, 10030 (1979). The estimates are based on 1977 data.

2. Id.

3. The gestation period for the safety standard was long and complex. The administrative process was initiated on August 15, 1973, when, pursuant to § 10 of the CPSA, 15 U.S.C. § 2059, the Outdoor Power Equipment Institute, Inc. (OPEI) petitioned the CPSC to begin a proceeding to develop a consumer product safety standard addressing the hazards of power lawn mowers and asked the Commission to adopt a voluntary standard, ANSI B71.1–1972, "Safety Specifications for Power Lawn Mowers, Lawn & Garden Tractors, & Lawn Tractors," approved by the American National Standards Institute, Inc. as the proposed consumer product safety standard. On November 16, 1973, the Commission, after considering information about injuries associated with power lawn mowers, granted that portion of OPEI's petition that requested a proceeding to develop the power lawn mower safety standard. The Commission denied OPEI's request to publish ANSI B71.1–1972, with amendments, as a proposed consumer product safety standard, however.

Instead, the Commission solicited offers to develop a standard pursuant to § 7(b) of the CPSA, 15 U.S.C. § 2056(b). Subsequently, the Commission selected Consumers Union of United States, Inc. (CU) to develop the safety standard. See 39 Fed. Reg. 37803 (1974). As the offeror, CU gave representatives of industry, consumers, and other interests the opportunity to participate in developing the standard. It submitted the resulting proposal to the Commission on July 17, 1975. The recommended standard comprehensively addressed all types of lawn mowers and lawn mower injuries and contained requirements relating to blade-contact and thrown-object injuries, as well as injuries resulting from lawn mowers' slipping, rolling, overturning, or failing to steer or brake, injuries caused by burns from direct contact with exposed heated surfaces of mowers or from fires ignited by lawn mower ignition fluids, and injuries caused by

Standard for Walk-Behind Power Lawn Mowers, 16 C.F.R. Part 1205 (1979), 44 Fed. Reg. 9990–10031 (Feb. 15, 1979), pursuant to section 7 of the Consumer Product Safety Act ("CPSA" or "the Act"), 15 U.S.C. § 2056 (1976).[4] In the present case we consider petitions by the Outdoor Power Equipment Institute ("OPEI"), manufacturers of power lawn mowers,[5] and an interested consumer to review[6] the Safety Standard for Walk-Behind Power Lawn Mowers.

The standard consists of three principal provisions: a requirement that rotary walk-behind power mowers pass a foot-probe test, 16 C.F.R. § 1205.4, 44 Fed. Reg. 10025–26, a requirement that rotary machines have a blade-control system that will stop the mower blade within three seconds after the operator's hands leave their normal operating position, 16 C.F.R. § 1205.5(a), 44 Fed. Reg. 10029, and a requirement, applicable to both rotary and reel-type mowers, that the product have a label of specified design to warn of the danger of blade contact, 16 C.F.R. § 1205.6, 44 Fed. Reg. 10029–30. * * *

* * *

Foot-Probe and Shielding Requirements

The standard mandates that walk-behind power rotary mowers pass a foot-probe test designed to assure that the machine guards the operator's feet against injuries caused by contact with the moving

electric shock from electrically powered lawn mowers or electric ignition systems.

After analyzing the recommended CU standard, on May 5, 1977, the Commission published a proposed comprehensive power lawn mower safety standard for public comment. 42 Fed. Reg. 23052 (1977). The proposal elicited more than 100 initial comments, and the Commission solicited and received further comments on these already submitted comments. 42 Fed. Reg. 34892 (1977). On June 7, 1978, the Commission published a notice that it would issue requirements addressing injuries from blade contact with walk-behind power mowers before issuing separate standards dealing with injuries associated with thrown objects, fuel and electrical hazards, and riding mowers. 43 Fed. Reg. 24697 (1978). In November 1978, the Commission requested additional comments on the safety and reliability of brake-clutch mechanisms. 43 Fed. Reg. 51638 (1978). On February 26, 1979, Part 1205—Safety Standard for Walk-Behind Power Lawn Mowers, applying only to blade-contact injuries from walk-behind power lawn mowers, was issued, to become effective December 31, 1981.

4. 15 U.S.C. § 2056(a) (1976) provides:

(a) The Commission may by rule, in accordance with this section and section 2058 of this title, promulgate consumer product safety standards. A consumer product safety standard shall consist of one or more of any of the following types of requirements:

(1) Requirements as to performance, composition, contents, design, construction, finish, or packaging of a consumer product.

(2) Requirements that a consumer product be marked with or accompanied by clear and adequate warnings or instructions, or requirements respecting the form of warnings or instructions.

Any requirement of such a standard shall be reasonably necessary to prevent or reduce an unreasonable risk of injury associated with such product. The requirements of such a standard (other than requirements relating to labeling, warnings, or instructions) shall, whenever feasible, be expressed in terms of performance requirements.

5. For convenience, we shall refer to the lawn mower industry petitioners collectively as OPEI.

6. Review of a safety standard by this court is authorized by § 11 of the CPSA, 15 U.S.C. § 2060 (1976).

blade. The test requires that a probe simulating a human foot be inserted along the rear 120 degrees of the mower and at the discharge chute without coming into contact with the blade when inserted. 16 C.F.R. § 1205.4, 44 Fed. Reg. 10025–26. See also Fed.Reg. 10001–10002. Mowers meet the foot-probe test by having shields that prevent the probe from entering the blade's path. 16 C.F.R. § 1205(a)(1), 44 Fed. Reg. 10025.

OPEI does not deny that a foot-probe test for the rear area of the mower is reasonably necessary to reduce injuries. Rather, it asserts that application of the test to the discharge chute is not supported by substantial record evidence. It alleges that the injury data does not show that foot injuries occur at that location and that it would be theoretically impossible for an operator to suffer a foot injury at the discharge chute while holding the "deadman's" blade-control[17] switch on the mower handle.[18]

The Act requires that safety standards be supported by "substantial evidence on the record as a whole." 15 U.S.C. § 2060(c). The foot-probe provision can be sustained only if the record contains " 'such relevant evidence as a reasonable mind might accept as adequate to support a conclusion' " that an unreasonable risk of foot injury exists from blade-contact at the discharge chute, that the foot-probe test will ameliorate it, and that the benefits of this proposed reform make it reasonable in light of the burdens it imposes on product manufacturers and consumers. Aqua Slide 'N' Dive v. Consumer Product Safety Commission, 569 F.2d 831, 838–40 (5th Cir.1978) [hereinafter cited as *Aqua Slide*] (quoting Consolidated Edison Co. v. NLRB, 305 U.S. 197, 229, 59 S.Ct. 206, 216, 83 L.Ed. 126 (1938)).

The determination of whether an unreasonable risk of discharge-chute injury exists involves "a balancing test like that familiar in tort law: The regulation may issue if the severity of the injury that may result from the product, factored by the likelihood of the injury, offsets the harm the regulation imposes upon manufacturers and consumers." *Aqua Slide*, 569 F.2d at 839 [citations]. Thus, under the unreasonable risk balancing test, even a very remote possibility that a product would inflict an extremely severe injury could pose an "unreasonable risk of injury" if the proposed safety standard promised to reduce the risk effectively without unduly increasing the product's price or decreasing

17. A deadman control refers to a device on the mower handle that requires continuous pressure to sustain rotation of the mower blades. Only if the operator can reach the discharge chute with his foot while holding the mower handle can he suffer blade-contact injuries at the discharge chute by mowers meeting the blade-stop requirement. Discharge-chute foot injuries suffered after the operator has released the mower handle and deadman's controls are addressed in the standard's blade-stop provision.

18. The rear 120 degrees of the mower and the discharge chute were selected for the foot-probe test because the Commission found that they are "areas where foot contact injuries are known to occur while the operator is holding the [mower] handle. Foot contact injuries that occur while the operator is not holding the handle will be addressed by the blade control . . . ." 44 Fed. Reg. 9993.

its availability or usefulness. *Aqua Slide,* 569 F.2d at 839–40.[22] Conversely, if the potential injury is less severe, its occurrence must be proven more likely in order to render the risk unreasonable and the safety standard warranted.

In the present case, the discharge-chute probe is intended to reduce the risk of such injuries as amputation of toes, fractures of bones in the feet or toes, avulsions, deep lacerations, and contusions. While the seriousness of these injuries cannot be gainsaid, it does not rise to the level of gravity that would render almost any risk, however remote, unreasonable if the risk could be reduced effectively by the proposed regulation.[23] Substantial evidence that such injury is significantly likely to occur is therefore necessary to sustain this portion of the lawn mower safety standard.

Our examination of the record has failed to reveal substantial evidence that injury at the discharge chute was sufficiently probable that it made the risk addressed by the foot probe of this area unreasonable. In a study of 36 blade-contact foot injuries conducted for the CPSC by the National Electronic Injury Surveillance System (NEISS),[24] one injury occurred when the operator inserted his foot into the blade path at the discharge chute while holding the mower handle. This injury represented almost three percent of the blade-contact foot injuries in the sample. However, the study did not involve a random sample, and it is not possible to extrapolate the percentage of total blade-contact injuries represented by discharge-chute incidents involv-

22. For example, in *Aqua Slide* this court ruled that the severity of paraplegic injury from swimming pool slides was so great that a one in ten million risk of such injury, which is less than the risk that an average person will be killed by lightning, would be an "unreasonable risk" if the proposed safety standard "actually promised to reduce the risk without unduly hampering the availability of the slides or decreasing their utility . . . ." 569 F.2d at 840. The court found, however, that the necessary showing of the standard's effectiveness had not been made and that the burdens the regulation would impose had not been adequately evaluated. Id. at 840–44.

23. Cf. *Aqua Slide,* 569 F.2d at 840 (remote risk of paraplegia could be unreasonable under CPSA); Bunny Bear, Inc. v. Peterson, 473 F.2d at 1006–07 (harm of burns or smoke inhalation, including death, from crib fires was sufficiently great to justify requirement that crib mattress pass a "cigarette test" by not igniting when touched with cigarette, when possibility existed that adult attending child might drop lighted cigarette on mattress) [although possibility of babies smoking, and dropping cigarettes, remote].

24. NEISS collects data from selected hospitals and reports them to the CPS. The system, which has been operational since July 1, 1972, was designed to develop statistically valid, rationally representative product-related injury data. It employs a computer-based network of 119 statistically selected hospital emergency rooms located throughout the country. 15 U.S.C. §§ 2054, 2055. See "Draft Hazard Analysis of Power Mower Related Injuries & Analysis of Proposed Power Mower Standard," U.S. CPSC, Bureau of Epidemiology (March 1977), at pp. 3–5. The Commission also obtains injury information from in-depth investigations (IDI's) of particular accidents reported through the NEISS network. IDI's conducted by the Commission, unlike basic NEISS accident data, are not statistically representative of all injuries in a particular product category. IDI's do, however, provide details concerning the sequence of events involved in the injury not available from NEISS surveillance information. Id. at 5. To overcome this deficiency, the Commission weighted IDI cases involving specified types of injuries to derive an adjusted IDI sample that conforms to NEISS data.

ing the operator's feet from the limited information furnished in the record. In any event, trustworthy statistical inferences cannot be drawn from a single incident of discharge-chute injury. Without reliable evidence of the likely number of injuries that would be addressed by application of the foot-probe test to the discharge chute, we are unable to agree that this provision is reasonably necessary to reduce or prevent an unreasonable risk of injury.

* * * We therefore vacate that part of the standard requiring the discharge-chute area of power lawn mowers to pass a foot-probe test.

[The court reviewed and upheld certain shielding requirements that supplemented the foot-probe test.]

Blade-Control System

The second key element of the standard requires a blade-control system that (1) will prevent the blade from rotating unless the operator activates a control, (2) allows the blade to be driven only if the operator remains in continuous contact with the "deadman's" control, and (3) causes the blade to stop moving within three seconds after the deadman's control is released. 16 C.F.R. § 1205.5. * * *

The blade-control system is intended to protect the operator against blade-contact injuries to both hands and feet by stopping the blade before the operator can contact it after he or she leaves the normal operating position and thus releases the deadman's control.[31] The Commission estimates that the blade-control provisions will eliminate approximately 46,500 operator blade-contact injuries a year. This figure represents approximately 60 percent of all blade-contact injuries and nearly 80 percent of all injuries claimed to be reduced by the standard. As OPEI acknowledges, the blade-contact requirements thus are the "centerpiece" of the Commission's strategy for reducing blade-control injuries.

Perhaps as befits its importance in the regulatory scheme promulgated by the Commission, the blade-control system is vigorously attacked by both OPEI and consumer proponents of stricter safety requirements. OPEI asserts that the blade-control system provision is expressed as a design requirement, rather than as a performance requirement, in violation of the Act. It argues that a number of alternative requirements are available that are less design restrictive and more performance oriented than the blade-stop criterion and that the Commission therefore erred in adopting the blade-stop approach. OPEI further contends that the standard is unreasonable because it requires the use of mechanisms that allegedly are not safe or reliable. And, OPEI claims, the three-second stopping time is unreasonably

31. For example, when the operator releases the deadman's control and approaches the blade area to clear the path of the mower, unclog a blocked discharge chute, adjust the wheels, or empty a grass catcher, the blade will stop rotating within three seconds. According to the Commission, by the time the operator reached the danger zone the blade would have stopped, or significantly slowed, thus preventing or minimizing injury.

short. In contrast, consumer advocate John O. Hayward maintains that the three-second blade-stopping time is too lax and that substantial evidence demonstrates that only a two-second or shorter blade-stopping time is justified.

The CPSA directs that a safety standard's provisions "shall, whenever feasible, be expressed in terms of performance requirements." 15 U.S.C. § 2056(a). The statutory preference[32] for performance requirements is rooted in the belief that this mode of regulation stimulates product innovation, promotes the search for cost-effective means of compliance, and fosters competition by offering consumers a range of choices in the marketplace, while design-restrictive rules tend to freeze technology, stifle research aimed at better and cheaper compliance measures, and deprive consumers of the opportunity to choose among competing designs. See S.Rep.No.92–835, 92d Cong., 2d Sess. 30 (1972), U.S.Code Cong. & Admin.News 1972, p. 4573; H.R. Rep.92–1153, 92d Cong., 2d Sess. 189 (1972).

Although only a limited number of designs can satisfy the blade-stop provision, we find this part of the standard is nonetheless a performance requirement. While the standard mandates that mower blades stop within a specified time period, it does not dictate a specific means of fulfilling this condition. Manufacturers are neither formally nor practically restricted to employing a particular design, since two existing mechanisms, a blade-disengagement system employing a brake-clutch device and an engine-stop system, are capable of passing the blade-stop test.

We also find that the Commission did not act improperly in failing to formulate a safety standard that would have allowed lawn mowers to be equipped with safety devices based on concepts of blade inaccessibility or blade harmlessness[33] as alternatives to blade-stop safety mechanisms. The CPSC did consider blade harmlessness and blade inaccessibility requirements but did not develop and adopt these alternative measures as part of the standard because it found that they were not feasible means of reducing or eliminating the risk of blade-contact injury at the time the standard was issued. * * *

32. While the statute favors performance requirements when feasible, it does not prohibit design standards when they are appropriate. 15 U.S.C. § 2056(a)(1) provides in part that:

> The Commission may by rule, in accordance with this section and section 2058 of this title, promulgate consumer product safety standards. A consumer product safety standard shall consist of one or more of any of the following types of requirements:
>
> (1) Requirements as to performance, composition, contents, design, construction, finish, or packaging of a consumer product.

(emphasis added).

33. As their names imply, safety mechanisms based on "blade inaccessibility" are designed to prevent contact with the moving blade by making it virtually impossible for a consumer to reach the blade with hands or feet by removing all controls from the blade area and eliminating the discharge chute. Devices based on "blade harmlessness" would employ grass-cutting means other than the standard rigid or semi-rigid blades that would not inflict serious injury if touched while in operation. It should be noted that the present standard already exempts such innovative, blade-harmless mowers as those using monofilament "blades" from the standard's safety requirements. 16 C.F.R. § 1205.3(a)(1); 44 Fed.Reg. at 9993.

* * *

We turn now to the issue of whether substantial evidence supports the selection of three seconds as the time limit within which blades must stop. The Commission based the three-second blade-stop time limit primarily upon four time-motion studies of operator-blade access time. These experiments were designed to measure the interval between the moment the operator released the deadman's control and the instant he or she reached the mower blade. One study of operator-blade access data collected at the University of Iowa in 1971 and analyzed by the National Bureau of Standards in 1975 showed that operators reached the blade hazard point after moving directly to it from the mower's rear in times ranging from 2.0 to 3.5 seconds.[38] A second operator-blade access study, using 100 subjects ranging in age from 16–62 with a mean age of 35, was conducted by Consumer's Union at Eckerd College in St. Petersburg, Florida, on March 5–7, 1975. The participants were tested using a reaction-time device designed to simulate a walk-behind power lawn mower. Each participant underwent 25 trials, for a total of 2,500 time-motion incidents. A December 7, 1976, summary of this Eckerd College Study reported that operator access time ranged from 1.66 to 4.90 seconds[39] for normal, as opposed to intentionally fast, movements. This summary cited data from trials using 12 and 15 subjects, aged 18–21. The Final Report on the Eckerd College Study, issued in May 1977, shows operator access time for the 100 participants as ranging from .6 to 3.3 seconds. The discrepancy is not explained. A third blade-access study using five subjects was conducted by the Office of the Medical Director (OMD) of the CPSC. In this experiment, direct, "casual" approach time ranged from 2.35 to 3.3 seconds, with an average time of 2.81 seconds.[40] OMD also recorded intentionally fast direct access times. These ranged from 1.26 to 2.5 seconds, with an average access time of 1.79 seconds.[41] In addition, OMD tested subjects' access times when they approached the discharge chute blade area by going around the opposite side and front of the

38. In eight trials, as analyzed in 1975, operators reached the blade in the following times (in seconds): 2, 3, 3, 2.5, 3.5, 2, 2.5, 3. (An earlier analysis performed by the NBS in 1974 and revised by the 1975 analysis had found that the access time ranged from 2.5 to 7.0 seconds. More accurate measurement methods used in the later study appear to account for the discrepancy.) It was recognized that the Iowa study was of limited value, however, because it employed machines that did not conform to the industry's voluntary standard in that they had shorter discharge chutes than the ANSI code now permits for current models. As a result, these blade-access times may have been shorter than access to the blades of current mower models. It should be noted, however, that figures derived from the other studies are in reasonable agreement with those of the University of Iowa test and that the test was not without some evidentiary value.

39. The data table attached to the summary shows that the longest blade-access time was 5.65 seconds, not 4.90 seconds. The discrepancy is not explained.

40. Blade-access times for the direct, casual approach test were: for subject A, 2.89 and 2.75 seconds; for subject B, 3.14 and 2.95 seconds; for subject C, 2.43 seconds; for subject D, 2.60 and 2.35 seconds; and for subject E, 2.90 and 3.30 seconds.

41. Blade-access times for the direct, intentionally fast approach test were: for subject A, 1.26 and 1.59 seconds; for subject B, 2.21 and 2.20 seconds; for subject C, 1.43 and 1.35 seconds; for subject D, 1.80 and 1.49 seconds; and for subject E, 2.52 and 2.05 seconds.

mower. The access time in the indirect, casual approach test ranged from 3.64 to 4.70 seconds, with an average time of 4.25 seconds.[42] Operator-access time in the indirect, hurried approach test fell between 2.48 and 3.68 seconds, with an average of 2.98 seconds.[43] The record contains only preliminary findings from the fourth empirical examination of operator blade-access times. This study was undertaken by the National Bureau of Standards. "[A] superficial examination of the limited observational data" was reported to show an average blade-access time of under three seconds.

In setting the blade-stop time, the Commission considered not only the time in which an operator could reach the blade after releasing the deadman's control but also the incremental cost of successively faster blade-stop times. The record contains substantial evidence that the cost of blade-stop mechanisms varies inversely with the length of time in which the device stops the blade,[44] so that a three-second blade-stop requirement will be cheaper to implement than a one- or two-second time limit.

We find that the three-second blade-stop requirement is not too lax, contrary to petitioner Hayward's claim. The three-second measure will protect consumers against many, although certainly not all, blade-contact injuries. While the Commission may not rely upon mere "common sense" or speculation to establish the *existence* of an *unreasonable risk* of injury, it may exercise considerable discretion in determining an appropriate *remedy.* The Commission was entitled to consider the incremental cost of requiring a shorter blade-stop time in rejecting a one- or two-second blade-stop solution. The standard need not guarantee protection for all consumers; it is sufficient that it promises greater safety for consumers and is reasonably necessary to *reduce* the risk of blade-contact injuries.

42. In this test, subject A had access times of 3.64 and 3.88 seconds; subject B, 4.52 and 4.18 seconds; subject C, 4.39 seconds; subject D, no recorded time; and subject E, 4.42 and 4.70 seconds.

43. Here access times were 2.60 and 2.48 for subject A; none recorded for subject B; 3.45 and 3.02 for subject C; 2.63 for subject D; and 3.68 for subject E.

44. A report by the Stanford Research Institute (SRI), "An Economic Analysis of the Proposed Consumers Union Power Mower Safety Standard" (April 1975), stated that the projected cost increases for walk-behind power mowers attributable to the blade-stop requirement would be $90–115 if the stop time were 3.0–4.9 seconds but only $75–100 per mower if the stop time were 5.0–6.0 seconds. In another 1977 study, SRI estimated that a 3-second blade-stop requirement would cost $16.50 more per mower than a 5-second test for manual start rotary mowers and $10.50 more per mower for electric start mowers. The Consumers Union Economic Support Study estimated roughly that the marginal per mower cost of a mechanism would be $10, while a 5-second blade-stop requirement would permit a $2 per mower savings over a 3-second blade clutch. OPEI submitted comparative incremental retail costs in September 1977 that stated that, for gas-powered rotary mowers with electric start mechanisms, a 7-second stop requirement would cost $5 per mower without "easy restart," and a 3-second brake-clutch device would cost $13.50 per mower. For gas-powered rotary mowers with manual starts, OPEI's cost estimate was $10 for a mower meeting a 7-second stop requirement, $15 for a mower having a 5-second engine kill with easy restart, and $34.50 for a 3-second brake-clutch system.

Correspondingly, we find no merit in OPEI's contention that the requirement of a three-second stopping time is unreasonably demanding. OPEI strenuously urges that the empirical studies cannot support a three-second blade-stop limit because they unrealistically fail to account for such psychological factors as a person's fear of a noisily operating machine and resulting reluctance to approach it. OPEI argues that these conditions would tend to make the operator stay away from the blade area for a longer time than was recorded in the artificial tests and perhaps until all noise and vibration from a moving blade ceases. OPEI also argues that the three-second requirement is not reasonable because a blade that is not moving under power would be decelerating and thus would inflict less damage than a fully powered blade.

The Commission properly rejected these contentions. The record contained neither suggestions for devising a test to measure psychological factors nor evidence indicating that in more "realistic" circumstances operator access to blades would be slower than registered in the time-motion studies. No deceleration curve information was cited to substantiate the claim that between three and seven seconds after power shut-off a blade would be coasting slowly, and no available test can accurately determine the blade velocity at which a risk of injury is reasonable.

We are also unpersuaded by OPEI's contention that current technology is inadequate safely to achieve a three-second blade-stop time. OPEI asserts that this requirement can only be met by using brake-clutch systems, which it alleges are unreliable and unsafe. * * *

* * *

Most convincing proof that safe and reliable three-second blade-stop mowers are currently feasible is the fact that, at the time the standard was issued, at least two mower manufacturers were currently producing and marketing mowers that had a brake-clutch mechanism complying with the standard. As one of these manufacturers declared, that such mowers are offered for sale demonstrates their manufacturer's belief in the safety and reliability of this type of brake-clutch mechanism. In addition, the evidence established that a brake clutch is basically a simple device that is widely used with safety and reliability in the production of automobiles and other types of machinery, such as chainsaws. The technology associated with brake clutches is therefore highly developed, and comments presented to the Commission made clear that potential difficulties with the particular application of various types of brake-clutch devices to power lawn mowers can be identified and resolved with present technical knowledge.

This evidence provides substantial support for the Commission's judgment that technology is available to design, produce, and assemble brake-clutch power lawn mowers that are unlikely to fail in an unsafe manner. * * * The three-second blade-stop time is therefore valid. [Citations.]

Labeling Requirement

The safety standard directs that both reel-type and rotary-power walk-behind lawn mowers carry a label of specified design. The label, which is to be placed on the blade housing or other blade shielding, states "DANGER, KEEP HANDS and FEET AWAY." It also contains a pictorial representation of a red, blade-like object cutting into the forefinger of an extended, black hand. 16 C.F.R. § 1205.6. The portrait of the blade and hand does not depict the hand as bleeding or dismembered.

* * *

[T]he Commission acted permissibly under section 7 in ordering manufacturers to furnish mowers with warning labels. The record clearly establishes that an unreasonable risk of blade-contact injury exists. The warning label directly addresses this risk of injury by warning operators and bystanders to keep hands and feet from the area in which the blade is accessible. It is true that the standard's shielding and blade-stop requirements also address the risk of blade-contact injury, but there is no claim that these prophylactic measures will be fail-safe. Thus, the Commission properly concluded that there was a *need* for labeling as a safety measure.

The *reasonableness* of the labeling requirement is also supported by the record. The Commission systematically tested various warning labels, and those with designs similar to the label required by the standard were found effective in communicating the risk of danger from moving blades. Significantly, the Commission found that the labeling requirement would impose little, if any, additional cost. The industry's voluntary standard already requires a warning label, and the mandatory label would be no more burdensome. Its contents are not shocking or gruesomely explicit and would not pose an unwarranted deterrent to potential purchasers of lawn mowers. [Citations.]

* * *

* * * On this record, we hold that the labeling requirement is reasonably necessary to reduce an unreasonable risk of injury.

Finding of Reasonable Necessity and Public Interest

In the preceding discussion, we have examined the petitioners' challenges to specific provisions of the standard and have found several of the complaints unfounded. However, OPEI also contends that the standard as a whole is not supported by substantial record evidence. It claims that the Commission based its determination that the standard was "reasonably necessary" and would produce a net benefit to society upon a document, "Economic Impact of Blade Contact Requirements for Power Mowers" ("the economic report"), which was unreliable because its methodology was fatally flawed, and its findings had never been exposed to public scrutiny in the administrative rulemaking process. Petitioner Hayward also criticizes the Commission's evaluation of the standard's net social benefit. He argues that the CPSC undervalued the safety benefits of the standard by erroneously failing to place a monetary value on the pain and suffering inflicted by the injuries that the rule was expected to reduce.

The Commission seeks to counter OPEI's broad attack on the standard by defending the final economic report's data and methodology and by asserting that the report was, in essence, merely a revision of earlier cost-benefit analyses of shielding and blade-stop requirements in light of additional evidence introduced into the record by OPEI. The Commission further contends that it adequately considered pain and suffering in evaluating the standard's benefits and that it was not required to quantify these aspects of the cost of lawn mower accidents.

We have carefully scrutinized the record and find that substantial evidence supports the conclusion that the safety benefits expected from the standard bear a reasonable relationship to its costs and make the standard reasonably necessary and in the public interest. The cost-benefit analysis contained in the final economic report and adopted by the standard, 44 Fed.Reg. at 10020–21, 10030, is not methodologically flawed. The Commission estimated that the regulations would raise the retail price of a complying lawn mower $35, costing the consumer $4.40 per year over the projected eight-year life of the mower. Total yearly compliance costs were believed to be $189 million for 5.4 million mower units (1978 production estimate). Blade-contact injuries were calculated to cost $253 million annually, exclusive of pain and suffering. Since, as we have noted, there are approximately 77,000 blade-contact injuries from walk-behind power mowers each year, each injury costs about $3,300, without counting the cost of pain and suffering. Currently there are some 40 million mowers in use by consumers, so that a consumer has about one chance in 500 (1/520) of incurring an injury costing $3,300, exclusive of pain and suffering. The standard's injury cost associated with each mower without the safety features is thus $6.35 per year. The Commission anticipated that implementation of the standard would reduce this injury cost by 83 percent, for an annual savings of $5.30 per mower, exclusive of the savings of pain and suffering costs. Because the standard would result in a net benefit of $.90, a mower meeting the standard's safety requirements would represent a worthwhile investment for the consumer, and the standard's implementation is in the best interests of society.

OPEI questions this analysis by asserting that, given an eight-year mower life, full compliance with the standard will take eight years because only one-eighth of all mowers will be replaced each year. As a result, only one-eighth of the total 83 percent estimated injury cost reduction attributed to the standard will be achieved after the standard's first year, with an additional one-eighth of the projected savings being achieved for each succeeding year until full compliance is had. From this observation, OPEI reasons that a complying mower will reduce injury costs by a mere $.70 after one year and not by the $5.30 projected by the Commission in justifying the standard. OPEI derived the $.70 per mower savings figure by reducing both the number of annual injuries and their total costs by one-eighth in determining a $5.65 per mower injury costs after one year, rather than the Commission's estimated annual injury cost of $6.35 per mower. OPEI then subtracted the $5.65 from the $6.35 to ascertain the savings in per mower injury cost after one year. On the basis of this calculation, OPEI claims that after one year a consumer will have paid $4.40 to reduce his mower injury costs by only $.70 and that the standard thus imposes an unreasonable expense on the consumer.

OPEI's attack on the cost-benefit analysis underpinning the standard is misconceived. It fails to recognize that only purchasers of complying mowers will pay the $4.40 annual cost for the standard's safety features and that these owners will receive the full benefit of the standard's anticipated effectiveness in reducing their injury costs for each year of the mower's life. OPEI's cost-benefit assessment thereby erroneously substitutes a figure representing the injury savings per mower in use, whether complying or not, for the amount of injury savings for owners of complying mowers, which is the relevant calculation. The correct analysis employed by the Commission to support the standard demonstrates its reasonable necessity in reducing the risk of blade-contact accidents. Because the economic findings establish that the standard is in the public interest even absent reliance upon the costs of pain and suffering, we need not determine whether the Commission must assign a dollar value to these aspects of the cost of accidents when precise calculation of their cost is not crucial for determining whether a standard is reasonably necessary and in the public interest. The methodology of the standard's supporting findings as to the costs and benefits of its requirements is sustained.

We also find that the evidence in the 1979 final economic report supporting the standard's cost effectiveness is reliable. In this report the Commission ultimately found that the standard would cost $189 million annually to implement, would prevent $211 million in yearly injury costs when full compliance was achieved, and would save $26.4 million after one year, assuming that the costs of accidents remained constant. The Commission's final economic analysis of the standard used data from fiscal year 1977 to compute an annual blade-contact injury cost of $253 million, exclusive of pain and suffering costs, caused by an estimated 77,000 injuries.

* * *

In summary, the standard's scope and its requirements that mowers pass a rear foot-probe test, shield-strength and obstruction tests, satisfy a three-second blade-stop criterion, and carry a prescribed warning label are upheld. The Commission's conclusion that the standard is reasonably necessary and in the public interest is also valid. The standard's requirement that mowers pass a discharge chute foot-probe test is not justified by substantial evidence on the record as a whole and is therefore vacated.

AFFIRMED IN PART, VACATED IN PART.

NOTES

1. The power mower regulations are set forth in 16 CFR § 1205 (1988). Do they appear to be in the public interest? What do you suppose really motivated the industry to challenge them in court?

2. Burch v. Sears, Roebuck and Co., 320 Pa.Super. 444, 467 A.2d 615 (1983), held that the absence of a deadman's device could render a power mower defective in design.

3. Reconsider the design defect accident cases previously considered. Might some of these accidents have been prevented by safety regulations? What might such regulations have provided? How should an agency go about determining (a) what type of safety regulations are needed, and (b) what, specifically, such regulations should provide?

4. Since its inception in the early 1970s, the CPSC has promulgated only a small number of design safety standards. In view of the vast number of product hazards, why do you suppose this is so? Should society devote more resources to accident prevention through product safety regulation?

5. Who should set product safety standards? Governmental regulators, subject to judicial review on rationality and fairness grounds? Manufacturers, subject to judicial review on products liability grounds? Both? Or do the existing legal mechanisms need a fundamental restructuring? See generally Pierce, Encouraging Safety: The Limits of Tort Law and Government Regulation, 33 Vand.L.Rev. 1281 (1980); Sugarman, Doing Away with Tort Law, 73 Calif.L.Rev. 555 (1985).

SECTION 4. DEFECTIVE MARKETING: WARNINGS AND INSTRUCTIONS

The manufacturer has certain informational obligations with respect to the products it sells. Thus, a product is "reasonably" safe (or non-"defective") only if it carries adequate informational "software" to permit the consumer to use it with reasonable safety.

From the manufacturer's perspective, it usually is less costly to warn of a danger than to improve quality assurance or to design the problem entirely out of the product. As representatives of the broader social point of view, courts as well often make the assumption that supplying warnings and instructions is the easy—and inexpensive—way for a manufacturer to fulfill its overall duty to market products that are reasonably safe. Consumers, too, in the form of injured plaintiffs, often reinforce the importance of the informational duties since proving a warning "defective" is often a much easier (and less expensive) task than successfully attacking a product's design.

While the direct economic costs of supplying "adequate" warnings and instructions with most products may be minimal, there are some less obvious "costs" involved which raise some subtle issues of substantial importance. First may be the problems from providing too much information—the risk of over-warning and "warnings pollution." Moreover, the decision on how much and what types of information a manufacturer must provide with a product can only be answered intelligently if the goals sought to be achieved by the legal requirements are fully understood. Probably the most generally accepted goal in this area is that of deterrence, or risk reduction, predicated on the notion that the consumer who is informed of dangers and methods of safe use will act to protect himself. Behind deterrence lies the far more complex goal of economic efficiency, which seeks to maximize social resources.

Another reason for requiring warnings and instructions, but one which reflects a different social value, has surfaced in recent years and is receiving increasing attention. This is the objective of promoting individual autonomy in decision-making. Thus, a consumer who is fully informed of the dangers in a product, and methods of safe use, may choose to use it in only a limited manner. Or he may choose not to use or buy it at all. Unlike the risk-reduction rationale, which reflects a utilitarian perspective rooted in economic efficiency, this kind of informed consent idea focuses on protecting the user's individual rights, specifically, his right "to determine his own fate." Pavlides v. Galveston Yacht Basin, Inc., 727 F.2d 330 (5th Cir.1984). "The rationale * * * is that the user or consumer is entitled to make his own choice as to whether the product's utility or benefits justify exposing himself to the risks of harm. Thus, a true choice situation arises, and a duty to warn attaches, whenever a reasonable man would want to be informed of the risk in order to decide whether to expose himself to it." Borel v. Fibreboard Paper Products Corp., 493 F.2d 1076, 1089 (5th Cir.1973), cert. denied 419 U.S. 869, 95 S.Ct. 127, 42 L.Ed.2d 107 (1974) (asbestos insulation worker contracted asbestosis and mesothelioma). Finally, concerns with paternalism, and efforts to promote individual responsibility, are additional policy factors involved in some warnings cases.

Policy issues of other types must also be addressed in the warnings context. Thus, if a substantial danger may be designed out of a product at little cost, perhaps even an "adequate" warning should not insulate a manufacturer who refuses to change the design. Uloth v. City Tank Corp., 376 Mass. 874, 384 N.E.2d 1188 (1978); Sturm, Ruger & Co. v. Day, 594 P.2d 38, 44 (Alaska 1979) ("Where the most stringent warning does not protect the public, the defect itself must be eliminated if the manufacturer is to avoid liability."). These and other considerations raised in this section suggest the need for critically examining the tempting conclusion that adding "adequate" warnings and instructions to all dangerous products is a simple panacea for achieving optimal product safety. Nevertheless, providing adequate danger and safe-use information with a product is indeed a key obligation of the manufacturer.

The most fundamental, recurring question in this area is whether the information supplied was "adequate," given the nature of the individual product and its probable environments of use. First, the manufacturer must provide sufficient instructions with the product to permit it to be used with reasonable safety. It is clear, however, that supplying even adequate instructions will not satisfy the manufacturer's duty to warn if the user is not thereby alerted to hidden dangers in the product.

This section will consider what types of information the manufacturer must convey to the user, how that information must be communicated, and to whom it must be given. Increasingly, this area is being addressed by Congress. The Occupational Safety and Health Act, the Consumer Product Safety Act, the Toxic Substances Control Act, and the Federal Food, Drug and Cosmetic Act are among the more prominent statutes mandating warnings in certain situations. See, for example, section 6 of the Toxic Substances Control Act, 15 U.S.C.A. § 2605(a), providing that the Environmental Protection Agency may require that chemical substances or mixtures regulated by the Act "be marked with or accompanied by clear and adequate warnings and instructions * * *. The form and content of such warnings and instructions shall be prescribed by the Administrator." Most of the law on warnings and instructions, however, has come from the courts.

MICHAEL v. WARNER/CHILCOTT

Court of Appeals of New Mexico, 1978.
91 N.M. 651, 579 P.2d 183.

OPINION

SUTIN, JUDGE. This is an interlocutory appeal granted defendant McKesson–Robbins, Foremost–McKesson, Skaggs Drug Centers, and third party defendant, U.S. Nuclear, Inc. These parties will be designated as defendants. The trial court denied defendants' motion for summary judgment and defendants appeal. We affirm.

A. *Facts.*

Plaintiff suffered with sinus congestion symptoms since about 1952. Over the years, he took a variety of medicines as initially prescribed by physicians. Around 1965, his physician prescribed "Sinutab" in writing to be ingested four a day on a daily basis. Plaintiff purchased this over-the-counter drug at Skaggs. He read the dosage requirements, the precautions and the printed literature on the label. He saw his doctor intermittently until 1970.

In 1970, plaintiff went to Skaggs to make another purchase of "Sinutabs" and was informed by the cashier that Skaggs had their own house brand called "Sinus Congestion Tablets." Plaintiff compared the ingredients on the label with those of "Sinutab" and determined that they were identical and purchased the bottle of "Sinus Congestion Tablets." On the front of the label is the name of Skaggs, Sinus Congestion Tablets, and the ingredients. One of the ingredients is phenacetin, a dangerous drug. The left side of the label is titled "SOLD WITH MONEY BACK GUARANTEE" and contains the "DOSAGE." On the right side, are "CAUTION" and "WARNING," the contents of which appear in small letters. A copy of the label is attached as Appendix "A".

The "WARNING" reads:

> *This medication may damage the kidneys when used in large amounts or for a long period of time. Do not take more than the recommended dosage, nor take regularly for longer than 10 days without consulting your physician.* KEEP THIS AND ALL MEDICATIONS OUT OF THE REACH OF CHILDREN. IN CASE OF ACCIDENTAL OVERDOSE, CONTACT A PHYSICIAN IMMEDIATELY. [Emphasis added.]

Plaintiff read the label. He did not recall reading either side of the label *while he was taking the drug.* He thought that if he had noted that kind of warning he would have consulted a doctor. He saw his personal physician intermittently with reference to his sinus and allergy problems and thought his doctor knew of his dosage of Sinus Congestion Tablets. He did not rely on the warning. He did not think an over-the-counter drug was harmful.

Plaintiff continued ingestion of this over-the-counter drug, four a day, on a regular daily basis, until April, 1973, when his kidney failure was first diagnosed. Plaintiff's physician ordered him to stop all medication.

* * *

The trial court found "that it *cannot* conclude as a matter of law that the warnings furnished by defendants on 'Sinus Congestion Tablets' * * * *did constitute as a matter of law adequate warnings as to the use of Sinus Congestion Tablets to preclude liability of these defendants* and that therefore the motion should be denied." [Emphasis added.]

* * *

* * * [D]efendants argue that plaintiff didn't bother to read the full label on Sinutabs; that if there was a warning, he did not rely on it; that when suit was filed, plaintiff was under the impression there was no warning on the label of "Sinus Congestion Tablets"; that if he had read the warning he would have quit using the tablets or asked the doctor about it. These are matters that relate to the conduct of plaintiff and bear upon his contributory negligence. They may test the credibility of plaintiff. These facts, however, do not relate to the issue of the adequacy of the warning given.

Defendants argue that the serious abuse of the product "is so extreme as to be almost beyond belief." Upon what basis this exaggeration is stated, we do not know. Defendants do not point to any evidence that plaintiff ingested more than the recommended dosage. Perhaps defendants mean that plaintiff took these tablets regularly for more than 10 days without consulting a physician. This fact, if true, does not bear upon the adequacy of the warning. It may constitute a factor relative to contributory negligence of the plaintiff.

* * *

The warning on the label was adopted verbatim from the warning promulgated by FFDC in 1964. The regulation is still in effect. 21 C.F.R. § 201.309 (1977). Defendants cite no authority to support a contention that this warning is adequate as a matter of law. In fact, it is not.

* * *

What is an adequate warning on a drug label? "Adequate" is defined as "sufficient for a specific requirement." Nissen v. Miller, 44 N.M. 487, 490, 105 P.2d 324, 326 (1940) says:

> The word "sufficient" is defined to mean adequate, enough, equal to the end proposed, and that which may be necessary to accomplish an object; it embraces no more than that which furnishes a plenitude, which, when done, suffices to accomplish the purpose intended in light of present conditions and viewed through the eyes of practical and cautious men.

"Warning" is defined to mean previous notice; caution against danger. [Citation.] The purpose of a "warning" is to apprise a party of the existence of danger of which he is not aware to enable him to protect himself against it, and where the party is aware of the danger, the warning will serve no useful purpose and is unnecessary, and there is no duty to warn against risks which are open and obvious. [Citation.]

An "ample warning" has been stated as a warning that would discharge the duty of reasonable care or fully sufficient to apprise those entitled thereto. [Citation.]

A "reasonable warning" is one which is reasonable under the circumstances, by one exercising ordinary care under the circumstances. [Citation.]

In First Nat. Bk., Albuquerque v. Nor–Am Agr. Prod., Inc., 88 N.M. 74, 537 P.2d 682 (Ct.App.1975) summary judgment was granted. Two theories of recovery were sought by plaintiff against defendant:

> (1) Negligence as to the warning, provided by the seller, of dangers associated with the use of the seller's product;
>
> (2) Special liability of the seller of a product for physical harm to a user or consumer, pursuant to Restatement, Torts, 2d § 402A, v. 2 (1965), at 347–348. [88 N.M. at 79, 537 P.2d at 687.]

In reversing the case, we held that adequacy of the warning given by a manufacturer in a negligence action presents an issue of fact for the jury. In making this determination, we said:

> The warning must adequately indicate the scope of the danger.
>
> * * *
>
> "The warning must reasonably communicate the extent or seriousness of harm that could result from the danger * * *"

* * *

> The physical aspects of the warning—conspicuousness, prominence, relative size of print, etc.,—must be adequate to alert the reasonably prudent person. [88 N.M. at 83–84, 537 P.2d at 691.]

From this potpourri, we hold that an "adequate warning" in this case means a notice placed on a label of "Sinus Congestion Tablets," reasonably readable, that apprises a consumer exercising reasonable care under the circumstances, of the existence and seriousness of the danger, sufficient to enable the consumer to protect himself against it, and sufficient to accomplish the purpose intended by the seller in the light of present conditions.

The "warning" given by defendants states that "This medication *may* damage the kidneys." [Emphasis added.] It does not apprise the consumer of the fact that it *will* damage the kidneys. It states "when used in *large* amounts." [Emphasis added.] The term "large" is vague and indefinite to a consumer. It does not state that "Phenacetin" is a dangerous drug. The lettering is so tiny it might require a consumer to read the words with a magnifying glass.

As a result, we conclude that a genuine issue of material fact exists on the adequacy of the warning.

Affirmed.

[Special concurrence of HERNANDEZ, J., omitted.]

APPENDIX A

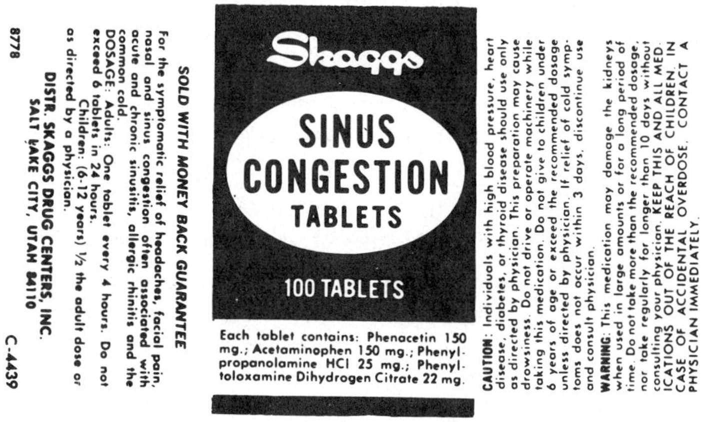

NOTES

1. "[I]n order for a warning to be adequate, it must provide 'a complete disclosure of the existence and extent of the risk involved' [citation]. A warning must (1) be designed so it can reasonably be expected to catch the attention of the consumer; (2) be comprehensible and give a fair indication of the specific risks involved with the product; and (3) be of an intensity justified by the magnitude of the risk." Pavlides v. Galveston Yacht Basin, Inc., 727 F.2d 330, 338 (5th Cir.1984).

2. In Burch v. Amsterdam Corp., 366 A.2d 1079 (D.C.App.1976), the plaintiff was badly burned in an explosion and flash fire that occurred while he was applying a floor tile adhesive sold by the defendant. The label on the can of mastic adhesive read as follows:

DANGER! EXTREMELY FLAMMABLE:

See Cautions elsewhere on label.

CAUTION: FLAMMABLE MIXTURE. DO NOT USE NEAR FIRE OR FLAME N.Y.F.D.C. of A. No. 2381

USE WITH ADEQUATE VENTILATION

MAY BE HARMFUL OR FATAL IF SWALLOWED—DO NOT INDUCE VOMITING, CALL PHYSICIAN—KEEP AWAY FROM CHILDREN

Plaintiff read the instructions on the label of the can of mastic adhesive, opened the windows, and turned on ductal fans and a large air conditioner. He checked the area to be sure there were no flames but did not think of the gas stove pilot lit in the kitchen where he was working. After plaintiff applied a first coat of adhesive to the floor, the vapors reached the pilot light and exploded. Plaintiff heard a "whoosh," "had a sense of time being elongated, felt searing heat and saw the skin peeling from his body." The trial court granted summary judgment for the defendant on plaintiff's claim of inadequate warnings, and the Court of Appeals reversed:

> The seller or manufacturer of a product whose use could result in foreseeable harm has a duty to give a warning which adequately advises the user of attendant risks and which provides *specific* directions for safe use. The sufficiency of a particular warning is ordinarily a question for the jury.
>
> The particular hazard encountered by appellants in using VICO–102 was that fumes or vapors from the product could ignite on contact with a pilot light, resulting in a violent fire or explosion. * * * Given the potential for serious injury we cannot say as a matter of law that this warning adequately alerted users of the dangers inherent in the product. Among other things, an ordinary user might not have realized that "near fire or flame" included nearby pilot lights or that fumes and vapors, as well as the adhesive itself, were extremely flammable.

Chief Judge Reilly dissented:

> Apparently my colleagues think that lack of the required degree of care might be inferred from the absence from the label of any specific mention of pilot lights "in light of the extreme flammability" of the product. But as the big lettering on the container described its contents in precisely those terms, I regard this position as untenable. If there was a duty to advert expressly to pilot lights in addition to "fire and flame", it would seem equally incumbent upon the vendors to devise a label warning against lighted pipes, cigars and cigarettes, vigil lights, candles, sparks from an electric lamp switch, a running fan or motor, and the other myriad of things which could possibly ignite vapors. If this is what the law requires, big lettering would have to be discarded for smaller print enumerating details at such length that few users would bother to read it—the warning then lacking the requisite "intensity". See DiArienzo v. Clairol, Inc., 125 N.J.Super. 224, 310 A.2d 106 (1973), where it was held that a pamphlet of instructions was

so detailed that a particular hazard was insufficiently highlighted, and Palace Laundry Dry Cleaning Co. v. Cole, D.C.Mun.App., 41 A.2d 231 (1945), holding that plaintiff was under no duty to read fine print (disclaimers of liability on a laundry slip).

In accord with *Burch,* Fiorentino v. A.E. Staley Mfg. Co., 416 N.E.2d 998, 1004 (Mass.App.1981) (jury "could have found that the critical warning ('near fire or flame') was too oblique to alert someone that a closed pilot light about eight feet away was an imminent source of peril"). The concurring opinion noted "the qualitative insufficiency of the warning to inform the user of the gasoline-like tendency of the cement to form heavier-than-air vapors which, unless dispersed, will flow in an invisible stream to distant sources of ignition." Id. at 1006.

3. Compare Murray v. Wilson Oak Flooring Co., 475 F.2d 129, 130–33 (7th Cir.1973), where plaintiff was burned in a fire that erupted when the vapors from the mastic flooring adhesive he was applying were ignited by the pilot light of a water heater or stove. In a negligence action against the manufacturer for supplying inadequate warnings, the jury gave verdict for the plaintiff, but the court granted the defendant's motion for j.n.o.v. The labels on the can stated in part as follows:

Keep
AWAY
From Fire,
HEAT and OPEN flame LIGHTS

CAUTION

LEAKING Packages Must be Removed to a Safe Place

DO NOT DROP

Another label was affixed to the opposite side of the can. White with red lettering, it set forth, in part, this message:

CAUTION: INFLAMMABLE MIXTURE
DO NOT USE NEAR FIRE OR FLAME

N. Y. F. D. C. of A. No. 2360
CONTAINS HEPTANE — USE IN WELL VENTILATED AREA
Do not smoke — Extinguish flame — including pilot lights
KEEP LID TIGHTLY CLOSED KEEP AWAY FROM CHILDREN

"Expert witnesses for both sides testified that Latex '45' emits a heavy and highly combust[i]ble vapor capable (1) of traveling for some distance along a floor from the point at which the mastic is spread, (2) of burning with explosive force upon encountering any form of exposed flame, and (3) of transmitting that flame back to the body of spread adhesive." Reversing the j.n.o.v. and reinstating plaintiff's verdict, the Court of Appeals remarked: "We cannot say as a matter of law that the term 'near' was sufficient to inform Murray that his spreading of adhesive within four feet of a pilot light *located behind a closed door* and within eight feet of stove pilot lights three feet off the floor exposed him to the risk of an explosion."

Do you agree?

4. **Overwarning—Warnings "Pollution."** With the preceding cases, contrast Cotton v. Buckeye Gas Products Co., 840 F.2d 935, 937–39 (D.C.Cir. 1988). Plaintiff worked for a construction company as a night heater watcher. His job was to monitor portable heaters used to cure concrete in cold weather and to change the propane cylinders supplied by the defendant as they ran low on gas. The areas being cured were wrapped in polyethylene curtains to contain the heat. Plaintiff neglected to close the valves on the used cylinders and stored them in the vicinity of the active heaters within the polyethylene enclosed areas. Gas escaping from the used cylinders ignited and severely burned the plaintiff. The jury ruled for the plaintiff on his inadequate warnings claim, but the trial court granted the defendant's motion for j.n.o.v. On appeal, *held,* affirmed:

> The cylinders supplied to plaintiff's employer by Buckeye bore labels clearly and conspicuously warning that the cylinders contained "flammable" gas and should not be used or stored in "living areas." App. at 5 (Def. Exh. 5). According to plaintiff, this warning was inadequate because it failed (1) to warn about the explosive properties of propane; (2) to instruct users to shut the valves on used cylinders; (3) to advise users not to use or store the cylinders in enclosed, unventilated areas; and (4) to warn that gas might escape from used cylinders believed to be empty.
>
> Failure-to-warn cases have the curious property that, when the episode is examined in hindsight, it appears as though addition of warnings keyed to a particular accident would be virtually cost free. What could be simpler than for the manufacturer to add the few simple items noted above? The primary cost is, in fact, the increase in time and effort required for the user to grasp the message. The inclusion of each extra item dilutes the punch of every other item. Given short attention spans, items crowd each other out; they get lost in fine print. Here, in fact, Buckeye responded to the information-cost problem with a dual approach: a brief message on the cannisters themselves and a more detailed one in the NLPGA pamphlet delivered to Miller & Long (and posted on the bulletin board at the Leesburg Pike construction site where Cotton was employed, Tr. at 761).
>
> Plaintiff's analysis completely disregards the problem of information costs. He asserts that "it would have been neither difficult nor costly for Buckeye to have purchased or created for attachment to its propane cylinders a clearer, more explicit label, such as the alternatives introduced at trial, warning of propane's dangers and instructing how to avoid them." Brief for Appellant at 25. But he offers no reason to suppose that any alternative package of warnings was preferable. He discounts altogether the warnings in the pamphlet,

without even considering what the cannister warning would have looked like if Buckeye had supplemented it not only with the special items he is personally interested in—in hindsight—but also with all other equally valuable items (*i.e.*, "equally" in terms of the scope and probability of the danger likely to be averted and the incremental impact of the information on user conduct). If every foreseeable possibility must be covered, "The list of foolish practices warned against would be so long, it would fill a volume." Kerr v. Koemm, 557 F.Supp. 283, 288 n. 2 (S.D.N.Y.1983). Unlike plaintiff, we must review the record in light of these obvious information costs.

Cotton's first complaint is that in neglecting to mention that propane is explosive, as well as flammable, the label failed to "convey a fair indication of the nature and extent of the danger to the mind of a reasonably prudent person." Brief for Appellant at 21 (quoting Spruill v. Boyle–Midway, Inc., 308 F.2d 79, 85 (4th Cir.1962)). True, warnings must identify the nature of a product's risks to ensure that the user is apprised of their seriousness. But the record here gives no suggestion of any relevant difference between "flammable" and "explosive." Cotton admitted that he knew propane was flammable and could ignite and burn him. Tr. at 640–41. That is precisely what happened. His injuries were exclusively burns, deriving exclusively from the gases' burning. Although the gas "exploded," Tr. 361–62, he suffered no injury from that fact insofar as it may be different from simply igniting. Cotton was thus fully aware of the relevant essential consequences of allowing gas to escape from the cylinders.

Although the other warnings that plaintiff contends should have been given were not contained in the cylinder labels, they were embodied in the NLPGA pamphlet. It warned that the cylinders should be used only in ventilated areas and that the cylinder valves should be closed. App. at 6–7 (Def. Exh. 1). (While the pamphlet did not explicitly warn that the valves should be closed on cylinders withdrawn from use because they might still have propane left in them, this was inferable as a matter of common sense from the pamphlet's insistence on keeping valves shut, on specific safety criteria for valves, and on proper use of valves. Again, a warning need not dot every i.)

The Virginia case most on point suggests that its courts would not allow a jury to find the warning defective on this record. In Sadler v. Lynch, 192 Va. 344, 64 S.E.2d 664, 667–68 (1951), plaintiff's decedent was killed when electric current ran from a power cable through a crane (and its bucket) to a truck. He had been told that he should "stay clear of the truck and get out of the way of it," and that it was dangerous to be around the crane while it was operating under power lines. 64 S.E.2d at 666. Instead, he approached and touched the truck. The court concluded that the warning was enough, even though it did not spell out the point that the truck would be charged with a deadly current "if the crane touched the wire at the same time as the bucket touched the truck." Id. at 667. Obviously an imaginative and sympathetic jury could have a flight of fancy by which omission of this detail rendered the warning unreasonable. Virginia said No.

Plaintiff relies substantially on appellate and district court decisions in the Fourth Circuit allowing juries wide leeway in finding warnings inadequate. See, e.g., Spruill v. Boyle–Midway, Inc., 308 F.2d 79 (4th Cir.1962) (infant dies from swallowing small quantity of furniture polish; adequacy of warning, "May be harmful if swallowed especially by children," in small print on bottle, was question for jury); Whitehurst v. Revlon, Inc., 307 F.Supp. 918, 921 (E.D.Va.1969) (smoker burned when her cigarette ignited fumes from fingernail polish; question for jury whether warning, "DO NOT HEAT OR USE NEAR FIRE," was adequate).

We think these cases distinguishable. In *Spruill*, for example, the court emphasized that the warning that was given "was placed so as to conceal it from all but the most cautious users. It is located in the midst of a body of print of the same size and color, with nothing to attract special attention to it except the words 'Safety Note'." 308 F.2d at 86. By contrast, Buckeye's label warned in large, bold letters that the propane was flammable. In *Whitehurst*, the gap between the injunction not to "use near fire" and the reality that a mere cigarette near the fingernail polish could be hazardous seems greater than any shortfall claimed here.

But even if not distinguishable, these cases seem untrue either to the agreed-on standard for sufficiency of the evidence or to Virginia substantive law. The cases show little concern that the jury verdict be one that *reasonable* jurors could have reached, or for *Sadler's* recognition that warnings need not spell out the risk in intricate detail.

5. Compare the following excerpt from Twerski, Weinstein, Donaher, Piehler, The Use and Abuse of Warnings in Products Liability—Design Defect Litigation Comes of Age, 61 Cornell L.Rev. 495, 514–16 (1976):

> Warnings, in order to be effective, must be selective. They must call the consumer's attention to a danger that has a real probability of occurring and whose impact will be significant. One must warn with discrimination since the consumer is being asked to discriminate and to react accordingly. The story of the boy who cried wolf is an analogy worth contemplating when considering the imposition of a warning in a case of rather marginal risk. * * * The warning process, in order to have impact, will have to select carefully the items which are to become part of the consumer's mental apparatus while using the product. Making the consumer account mentally for trivia or guard against risks that are not likely to occur imposes a very real societal cost. Even when the risks are significant, one must consider whether the consumer will perceive them as significant. If the only way to ensure that the consumer will consider them significant is to oversell the warning by increasing its intensity, one may again face the problem that all warnings will come into disrepute as overly alarming. * * *
>
> * * *
>
> In short, when calculating the burden of precaution which is part of the risk-utility calculus, it will be necessary to focus on costs other than the cost of label printing. The efficacy of warning is a societal cost of substantial importance. Thus, it will not be possible for the courts to rely on warnings alone to ensure product safety. The range of risks are so broad, and the type of consumer response so varied, that the courts cannot avoid asking "what is a reasonably safe product" or "how much product safety is enough." The answers will sometimes lie

> with an adequate warning, sometimes with redesign of the product, but most often with warning and design blended together to give an adequate level of safety.

But see Grether, Schwartz & Wilde, The Irrelevance of Information Overload: An Analysis of Search and Disclosure, 59 S.Cal.L.Rev. 277 (1986).

6. **Instructions.** "A duty to warn actually consists of two duties: One is to give adequate instructions for safe use, and the other is to give a warning as to dangers * * *." Ontai v. Straub Clinic & Hosp. Inc., 66 Hawaii 237, 659 P.2d 734, 743 (1983). While warnings and directions for use often blend into each other, Antcliff v. State Employees Credit Union, 414 Mich. 624, 327 N.W.2d 814 (1982), they involve separate types of information: A warning provides information on the danger itself; an instruction provides information on how to *avoid* it. In any particular case, either or both forms of information may be necessary. A plane may crash or a house may burn down if an airplane part or a woodstove chimney pipe is inadvertently installed upside down. See Nesselrode v. Executive Beechcraft, Inc., 707 S.W.2d 371 (Mo.1986) (plane); Duford v. Sears, Roebuck & Co., 833 F.2d 407 (1st Cir.1987) (woodstove). Even the best of instructions will not fulfill the duty to warn. See *Nesselrode,* supra. Nor will adequate warnings satisfy the duty to instruct the consumer on how to assemble or use the product safely. See Midgley v. S.S. Kresge Co., 55 Cal.App. 3d 67, 127 Cal.Rptr. 217 (1976) (K–Mart telescope had inadequate written instructions, and no diagrammatic illustrations, on proper method of attaching sun filter).

7. **Overpromotion.** An otherwise adequate warning may be nullified by assurances of safety. The classic case is Maize v. Atlantic Refining Co., 352 Pa. 51, 41 A.2d 850 (1945), where a 33-year-old wife and mother died from inhaling the tetrachloride fumes from a cleaning fluid she used to clean her rugs. The label on the can twice stated, "CAUTION: Do not inhale fumes. Use only in a well ventilated place." However, in letters that were several times larger, the cleaner's name—"Safety–Kleen"—was emblazoned all around the container. *Held,* verdict in the amount of $2500 for Mrs. Maize's estate and $7500 for her husband, upheld:

> [T]he conspicuous display on each of the four sides of a can of the words "Safety–Kleen" would naturally lull the user * * * into a false sense of security * * *. * * * The word "Safety" was so conspicuously displayed * * * as to make the word "Caution" and the admonition against inhaling fumes and as to use only in a well ventilated place seem of comparatively minor import. In fact, it is understandable that a woman busily engaged in the task of cleaning rugs might not take time to read everything on the can, particularly since the word "Safety" was so prominently featured as to exclude from her mind that "provident fear" which has been characterized as "the mother of safety."

Accord, Incollingo v. Ewing, 444 Pa. 263, 282 A.2d 206 (1971) (pharmaceutical company's detail men minimized drug's hazards and stressed its benefits and widespread acceptance).

8. **"Procedural" Adequacy—Method of Conveyance.** Even if the substantive content of a warning is fair, full, and accurate, it will do no good unless it reaches the user, catches his attention, and penetrates his mind. Hence, the method of conveying warnings and instructions must itself be adequate. The variety of issues here include:

A. **Conspicuousness.** Like disclaimers, warnings must be printed in type of a sufficient size, style, and color; they must be headed by appropriate signal words: "Warning," "Danger," "Caution," "Hazard," "Adverse Reactions," "Contraindications," etc.; and they must be located in a prominent position on the label, pamphlet, or other warning medium. See, e.g., Brown v. Gulf Oil Corp., Prod.Liab.Rep. (CCH) ¶ 10,474 (Tenn.App.1985) (size and location of warnings and instructions on label were adequate).

B. **Location on product.** If feasible, important warnings should be permanently located on the product itself rather than in a pamphlet, booklet, or information sheet that can be damaged, lost or destroyed. Hence, the warning may be located on the container's label; on a warning plate attached near the ram of a press or other danger point of the machine; or etched permanently into the product. See, e.g., West v. Broderick & Bascom Rope Co., 197 N.W.2d 202 (Iowa 1972) (metal tag with load limit could have been bonded to collar of metal rope or "sling" that broke); Griggs v. Firestone Tire & Rubber Co., 513 F.2d 851 (8th Cir.), cert. denied, 423 U.S. 865, 96 S.Ct. 124, 46 L.Ed.2d 93 (1975) (warning against mismatching multipiece tire rims to prevent violent explosions could have been stamped on rim components); Gordon v. Niagara Machine & Tool Works, 574 F.2d 1182, 1194 (5th Cir.1978) ("[A] direct warning attached to the press and conspicuously displayed at eye level would surely be a more effective warning than oral words [in a] manual.").

C. **Nonverbal warnings.** A gauge or warning light may be necessary to inform the user that a crane is about to tip or that a rear mounted aircraft engine has stopped operating. See Kay v. Cessna Aircraft Co., 548 F.2d 1370 (9th Cir.1977) (warning light not necessary because engine gauges on Skymaster instrument panel would have indicated dead engine). A buzzer, bell or rearview mirror may be necessary for the safe operation of a vehicle in reverse with poor rear visibility. Pike v. Frank G. Hough Co., 2 Cal.3d 465, 85 Cal. Rptr. 629, 467 P.2d 229 (1970). Color may have to be added to a dangerous, clear, chemical fluid to distinguish it from water. Hayes v. Kay Chemical Co., 135 Ill.App.3d 932, 90 Ill.Dec. 632, 482 N.E.2d 611 (1985) (McDonald's employee wiped face with towel saturated with caustic grill cleaner). Or odor added to propane gas. Jones v. Hittle Service, Inc., 219 Kan. 627, 549 P.2d 1383 (1976) (odorized to smell like rotten eggs or dead mice); Donahue v. Phillips Petroleum Co., 866 F.2d 1008 (8th Cir. 1989).

9. **Pictorial Warnings.** Diagrams and pictures are becoming an increasingly important form of communicating hazards.

A. **Standardized danger symbols—Adults.**

Consider Hubbard–Hall Chemical Co. v. Silverman, 340 F.2d 402 (1st Cir.1965), where two Spanish-speaking farm workers died from inhalation of insecticide dust. The insecticide bag contained written warnings only. The jury was charged that an adequate warning is one "calculated to bring home to a reasonably prudent person, a reasonably prudent user of the product, the nature and extent of the danger of the product involved." *Held,* a jury could reasonably conclude that even the best of written warnings might not be good enough, since the information foreseeably would be needed by persons of limited education, and that a skull and crossbones or other comparable symbols might fairly be required under the circumstances. See also Campos v. Firestone Tire & Rubber Co., 98 N.J. 198, 485 A.2d 305, 310 (1984).

With the traditional skull and crossbones pictured above, compare the following stylized version used by the Palmetto Poison Center in South Carolina:

Which version is preferable? Why?

B. **Standardized danger symbols—Children.**

MR. YUK

Research at the Pittsburgh Poison Center of the Children's Hospital of Pittsburgh in 1971 revealed that the traditional skull and crossbones symbol tended to attract rather than repel small children to hazardous substances so labelled. The children associated the symbol with cartoon pirates, adventure, excitement and, at least in Pittsburgh, with the Pittsburgh Pirates baseball team. So researchers sought a new symbol that would deter young children from playing with (or consuming) toxic substances in the home. Children at daycare centers were shown six bottles of mouthwash, separately labelled with different symbols, and asked to identify bottles they might not like to play with. The symbols included a red stop sign, a skull and crossbones, a scowling green face, and three others. The least popular was the scowling face, which one of the youngsters said "looks yukky." And so "Mr. Yuk" was born. The green-faced Mr. Yuk stickers, to be affixed by parents to toxic substances around the home, are now widely available from poison centers across the nation. He is a registered trademark and has been copyrighted by the Children's Hospital of Pittsburgh. Mr. Yuk stickers are credited in part with a substantial drop in child poisonings in recent years.

Should the warnings on toxic chemicals used in the home, such as drain cleaners, be considered defective if pictures of Mr. Yuk are not included on the label?

Should Mr. Yuk be made to look even more revolted? The variation on Mr. Yuk shown below, a registered New Zealand trademark of Quick Stil International, was found in a large field trial to be ineffective in preventing child poisonings. Many of the parents believed the symbol *attracted* children to the labelled substances. 5 Prod.Liab.International 190 (Dec. 1983).

[E7579]

C. **Particularized danger symbols—Adults.** Empirical research indicates that symbols may be necessary to alert even literate adults to product dangers. See the rather startling article by Dorris and Purswell, Warnings and Human Behavior: Implications for the Design of Product Warnings, 1 J.Prod. Liab. 254 (1977), suggesting that it matters little how completely a warning is worded, or even whether it is given at all, since few people will read or heed it anyway. See also Goldhaber & deTurk, Effects of Consumers' Familiarity With a Product on Attention To and Compliance With Warnings, 11 J.Prod.Liab. 29 (1988). For whatever reasons, people frequently fail to process danger information in a manner that will avoid accidents.

A powerful anti-acne drug called Accutane, a synthetic derivative of Vitamin A, has been found to cause birth defects in about 25% of children born to women taking the drug. Rather than totally banning the drug, the FDA has required the manufacturer to provide strong and specific written warnings and instructions, in both the patient and physician information labeling, together with the following diagram on each page of the patient leaflet

and on each side of the drug's packaging. In addition, the patient information labeling is to include a drawing of a deformed baby. Willis, New Warning About Accutane and Birth Defects, FDA Consumer 27 (Oct. 1988).

Several companies and industry associations have been working for some time to improve communications on product hazards in the workplace. The leader in this area has been FMC Corporation, which has developed a sophisticated industrial product warnings system, portions of which follow.

PRODUCT SAFETY SIGN AND LABEL SYSTEM

Written communication can have serious limitations. The same words used by different people can have entirely different meanings. Differences in terminology, intellect, and literacy can inhibit effective communication. Comprehension of a specific language can complicate effective communication even further. When written words are used to help prevent the occurrence of accidents, the limitations associated with words present serious communication problems.

One method of increasing communication effectiveness between a greater cross-section of population, both nationally and internationally, is to use pictorial or symbolic language in place of, or as a supplement to, written words.

This manual contains a graphic design system for safety signs and labels that uses pictorials as a principal means of communication. The pictorials are combined with words and colors in carefully designed formats intended to present comprehensive hazard information in an orderly and understandable manner.

When such safety signs and labels are placed on products in appropriate locations, they should help to reduce the occurrence of accidents through more effective communication.

* * *

The preferred format for product safety labels is a vertically oriented rectangle consisting of three panels encircled by a narrow border. The panels contain four messages which communicate:

1. The level of hazard seriousness.
2. The nature of the hazard.

3. The consequence of human interaction with the hazard.
4. The instructions on how to avoid the hazard.

The top panel of the format contains a signal word (DANGER, WARNING or CAUTION) which communicates the level of hazard seriousness. [DANGER is printed in white letters, against a red background; WARNING, in black on orange; and CAUTION, in black on yellow.]

The center panel contains the pictorial which communicates the nature of the hazard, and the possible consequence of human interaction with the hazard. In some instances the pictorial may, instead, depict what preventive measures to take, such as wearing protective equipment.

The bottom panel contains the instruction message on how to avoid the hazard. In some situations, the message may also contain a more precise definition of the hazard than can be communicated by the pictorial. [Sometimes a separate box, entitled SAFETY INSTRUCTIONS (white letters on green), is necessary to provide more information on safe use. Examples of each are as follows:]

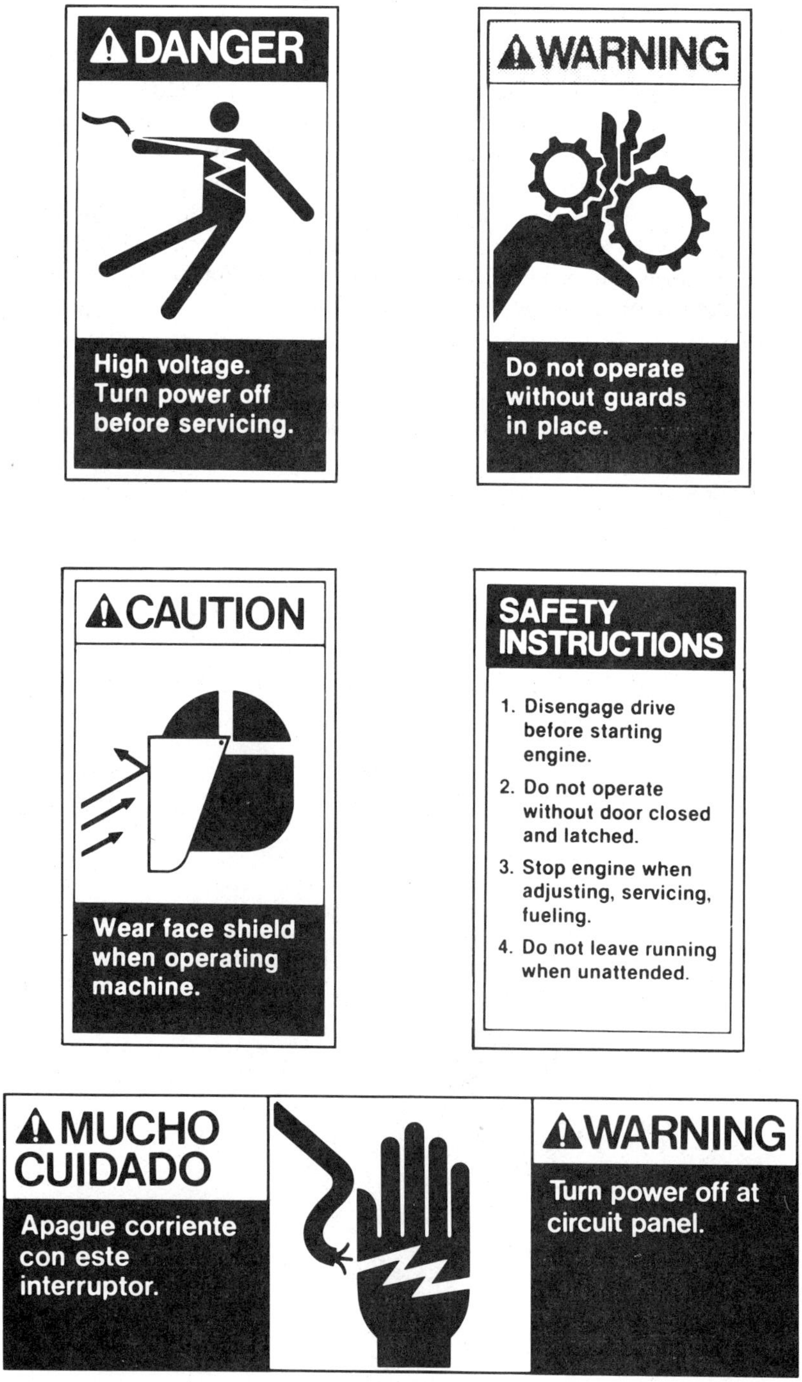
DANGER
High voltage.
Turn power off
before servicing.
WARNING
Do not operate
without guards
in place.
CAUTION
Wear face shield
when operating
machine.
SAFETY
INSTRUCTIONS
1. Disengage drive before starting engine.
2. Do not operate without door closed and latched.
3. Stop engine when adjusting, servicing, fueling.
4. Do not leave running when unattended.
MUCHO
CUIDADO
Apague corriente
con este
interruptor.
WARNING
Turn power off at
circuit panel.

[E7580]

SELECTED PICTORIAL EXAMPLES

[E7581]

What do you think of this form of warning? Do you think it would be more effective than a written warning alone? Is it too paternalistic toward the worker? Should OSHA require such warnings? Should similar, pictorial warnings be required for hazardous consumer products such as lawnmowers?

Should the absence of a pictorial representation make a written warning alone legally "defective"?

How might a plaintiff who confronted only a written warning *prove* that the absence of a pictorial representation made the warning inadequate?

10. **Expert Testimony.** Some courts have refused to admit expert testimony on the ultimate issue of the adequacy of a warning. E.g., Shell Oil Co. v. Gutierrez, 119 Ariz. 426, 581 P.2d 271 (App.1978) (expert opinion admissible on the properties of chemicals, but not on adequacy of warning). Other courts permit testimony on this issue by experts with various backgrounds, such as pharmacological labelling, communications psychology, human factors engineering, and others. See, e.g., Long v. Deere & Co., 238 Kan. 766, 715 P.2d 1023 (1986); Smith v. United States Gypsum Co., 612 P.2d 251 (Okl.1980) (testimony of chemical engineer and psychiatrist, that warning of flammability of heptane "inadequate" and "vague," admissible); Prevatt v. Pennwalt Corp., 192 Cal. App.3d 438, 237 Cal.Rptr. 488 (1987) (cognitive psychologist: labels failed to attract user's attention or to warn appropriately of the danger); Roddy, Expert Testimony on the Adequacy of a Product's Warning: Recent Cases, 12 Prod. Liab.Trends 109 (Oct. 1987).

11. **Post–Sale Warnings.**

A. **Continuing duty to warn.** Many courts, particularly in the context of prescription pharmaceuticals, have held that the manufacturer or other seller has a duty to provide warnings of dangers discovered after the product is sold. See, e.g., Wooderson v. Ortho Pharmaceutical Corp., 235 Kan. 387, 681 P.2d 1038, cert. denied, 469 U.S. 965, 105 S.Ct. 365, 83 L.Ed.2d 301 (1984) (prescription drug); Cover v. Cohen, 61 N.Y.2d 261, 473 N.Y.S.2d 378, 461 N.E.2d 864 (1984) (auto); Gracyalny v. Westinghouse Elec. Corp., 723 F.2d 1311 (7th Cir.1983) (circuit breaker). But see Lynch v. McStome and Lincoln Plaza Associates, ___ Pa.Super. ___, 548 A.2d 1276 (1988) (negligence; no duty to warn users of development of safer design). See generally Allee, Post–Sale Obligations of Product Manufacturers, 12 Fordham Urban L.J. 625 (1983–84); Schwartz, The Post–Sale Duty to Warn: Two Unfortunate Forks in the Road to a Reasonable Doctrine, 58 N.Y.U.L.Rev. 892 (1983).

B. **Admissibility of subsequent warnings.** The subsequent remedial measure admissibility issue, considered in the design context above, arises in warnings cases where the manufacturer adds or improves a warning after the plaintiff buys the product or suffers the accident. See, e.g., Shelbauer v. Butler Mfg. Co., 35 Cal.3d 442, 198 Cal.Rptr. 155, 673 P.2d 743 (1984) (admissible); Jacobson v. Manfredi, 100 Nev. 226, 679 P.2d 251 (1984) (admissible on feasibility); Fiorentino v. A.E. Staley Mfg. Co., 11 Mass.App.Ct. 428, 416 N.E.2d 998, 1005 (1981) (admissible, but concurring opinion questioned significance of feasibility issue in warnings context, since "it is obviously always 'feasible' to employ a more prominent or more urgent-sounding or more particularized form of warning").

12. On warnings generally, see Madden, The Duty to Warn in Products Liability: Contours and Criticism, 89 W.Va.L.Rev. 221 (1987) (comprehensive review); Gershonowitz, The Strict Liability Duty to Warn, 44 Wash. & Lee L.Rev. 71 (1987); Sales, The Duty to Warn and Instruct for Safe Use in Strict Tort Liability, 13 St. Mary's L.Rev. 521 (1982); Twerski, Weinstein, Donaher & Piehler, The Use and Abuse of Warnings in Products Liability—Design Defect Litigation Comes of Age, 61 Cornell L.Rev. 495 (1976); Noel, Products Defective Because of Inadequate Directions or Warnings, 23 Sw.L.J. 256 (1969); Noel,

Manufacturer's Negligence of Design or Directions for Use of a Product, 71 Yale L.J. 816 (1962).

HIGGINS v. E.I. DuPONT de NEMOURS & CO., INC.

United States District Court, District of Maryland, 1987.
671 F.Supp. 1055.

SMALKIN, DISTRICT JUDGE.

[Plaintiffs sued DuPont, the manufacturer of a paint called Imron, and two suppliers of chemical ingredients (glycol ether acetates) used therein, Eastern and Union Carbide, for failing to warn of the possible teratogenic [1] effects of the paint. The Baltimore City Fire Department purchased Imron from DuPont and distributed it in unmarked cans to its various fire stations throughout the city for use on fire-fighting equipment. The plaintiffs, fire fighters who used the paint, alleged that the glycol ether components of Imron interfered with the fetal development of their children who died at birth. Defendants Eastman and Union Carbide moved for summary judgment.]

Movants' legal position is that, as bulk suppliers of commodity chemicals to a sophisticated chemical and coatings company (DuPont), they had no duty to warn any DuPont customer (much less a customer's employees), of any possible teratogenic effects of the commodity chemicals or the product in which they were incorporated. Plaintiffs claim that the defendants Eastman and Union Carbide have not shown that this defense precludes their negligence claims and that the defense is not "material" to the strict liability claims.

In Goodbar v. Whitehead Bros., 591 F.Supp. 552 (W.D.Va.1984), aff'd sub nom. Beale v. Hardy, 769 F.2d 213 (4th Cir.1985), the United States District Court for the Western District of Virginia recognized the availability of a sophisticated user/bulk supplier defense in a negligent failure to warn claim, asserted under Restatement (Second) Torts § 388 (1965). *Goodbar* involved three diversity actions asserting negligence, strict liability, and warranty claims. 591 F.Supp. at 554. Specifically, some 132 present and former employees of the Lynchburg Foundry brought suit against 12 defendants who had supplied silica sand to the Foundry. Id. The sand was supplied unpackaged in railroad car lots, which were emptied onto conveyor belts or pneumatic transporters, where the material was conveyed to large tanks or silos for storage, ultimately to be used in various stages of metal castings production. Id. at 554–55. The suppliers in *Goodbar* were accused of "fail[ing] to advise the Foundry's employees with respect to the dangerous characteristics of silica products and how to protect themselves from them," resulting in the employees' exposure to silica and their eventual illness with silicosis. Id. at 555.

1. A teratogen is a compound that can cause birth defects, fetal death, or stillbirth.

In *Goodbar,* Judge Kiser noted that Virginia had not adopted § 402A strict liability, and that the focus therefore was on negligent failure to warn and breach of the implied warranty of merchantability. Id. With respect to the negligent failure to warn claim, Judge Kiser employed the analysis suggested by Restatement § 388.* Judge Kiser began by stating that the matter before him turned "upon whether the requirements of clause (c) [of § 388] have been met, namely whether the Defendants failed to exercise reasonable care in relying upon the Foundry to supply its employees with the necessary information to satisfy the duty to warn." Id. at 557. Judge Kiser thereafter looked to comment *n* of § 388, entitled "Warnings given to third person," which delineates factors that must be balanced in determining what precautions the supplier must take to satisfy the clause (c) requirement of reasonable care including

> (1) the dangerous condition of the product; (2) the purpose for which the product is used; (3) the form of any warnings given; (4) the reliability of the third party as a conduit of necessary information about the product; (5) the magnitude of the risk involved; and (6) the burden imposed on the supplier by requiring that he directly warn all users.

Id. at 557. * * *

On the basis of § 388 and comment *n* thereto, Judge Kiser recognized the sophisticated user/bulk supplier defense, holding that "there is no duty on product suppliers to warn employees of knowledgeable industrial purchasers as to product-related hazards." Id. at 559. Finding "that a plethora of material exists on the Lynchburg Foundry's extensive knowledge of the hazards of inhaling silica dust, the disease of silicosis and proper dust control methods," Judge Kiser granted the defendant suppliers' motion for summary judgment regarding the sophisticated user/bulk supplier defense on the § 388 negligent failure to warn claim. Id. at 561–62. Judge Kiser additionally noted that the defendant suppliers had no duty to warn Foundry employees, given that the Foundry was the only one in a position to communicate an effective warning to its employees. Id. at 566. The Court then listed a number of difficulties faced by the suppliers in trying to warn Foundry employees of silicosis, including "(1) the identification of the users or those exposed to its products would require a constant monitoring by

* Restatement (2d) of Torts § 388 (1965) provides:

§ 388. Chattel Known to be Dangerous for Intended Use

One who supplies directly or through a third person a chattel for another to use is subject to liability to those whom the supplier should expect to use the chattel with the consent of the other or to be endangered by its probable use, for physical harm caused by the use of the chattel in the manner for which and by a person for whose use it is supplied, if the supplier

(a) knows or has reason to know that the chattel is or is likely to be dangerous for the use for which it is supplied, and

(b) has no reason to believe that those for whose use the chattel is supplied will realize its dangerous condition, and

(c) fails to exercise reasonable care to inform them of its dangerous condition or of the facts which make it likely to be dangerous.

the suppliers in view of the constant turnover of the Foundry's large work force; (2) the manner in which the sand products are delivered in bulk (i.e. unpackaged railroad car lots or truck); (3) no written product warnings placed on the railroad cars would ever reach the workers involved in casting or those in the immediate vicinity due to the way the loose sand is unloaded, conveyed, and kept in storage bins until needed; (4) only the Foundry itself would be in a position to provide the good housekeeping measures, training and warnings to its workers on a continuous and systematic basis necessary to reduce the risk of silicosis; (5) the sand suppliers must rely on the Foundry to convey any safety information to its employees; (6) the confusion arising when twelve different suppliers and the Foundry each try to cope with the awesome task of instructing the Foundry workers; and (7) in a commercial setting, it would be totally unrealistic to assume that the suppliers would be able to exert pressure on a large, industrial customer such as the Foundry to allow the suppliers to come in and educate its workers about the hazards of silicosis." Id. (citations omitted).

In the absence of any controlling Maryland decision, this Court is confident that the Court of Appeals of Maryland would recognize the sophisticated user/bulk supplier defense in a negligent failure to warn case. * * *

This Court is similarly confident that the Court of Appeals of Maryland would also recognize the sophisticated user/bulk supplier defense in a failure to warn claim asserted on the ground of strict liability under Restatement (Second) Torts § 402A (1965). The parties have not cited, nor has the Court independently discovered, a Maryland case recognizing any doctrinal distinction between § 388 negligent, and § 402A strict liability, failure to warn cases. * * * The latest edition of the venerable Prosser work on torts states, with respect to failure to warn, that:

> It is commonly said that a product can be defective in the kind of way that makes it unreasonably dangerous by failing to warn or failing adequately to warn about a risk or hazard related to the way a product is designed. But notwithstanding what a few courts have said, a claimant who seeks recovery on this basis must according to the generally accepted view, prove the manufacturer-designer was negligent. There will be no liability without a showing that the defendant designer knew or should have known in the exercise of ordinary care of the risk or hazard about which he failed to warn. Moreover, there will be no liability unless manufacturer failed to take the precautions that a reasonable person would take in presenting the product to the public. *Although this ground of recovery is sometimes referred to as strict liability, it is really nothing more than a ground of negligence liability described as the sale of a product in a defective condition, subject, however, only to the defenses and other limitations or liability applicable to strict liability rather than negligence.*

W.L. Prosser and W.P. Ke[e]ton, Torts § 99, at 697 (5th ed. 1984) (emphasis supplied). It therefore appears clear that, in failure to warn cases, whether asserted on negligence or strict liability grounds, there is but one unitary theory of liability which is negligence based—the duty to use reasonable care in promulgating a warning. It logically follows, then, that the Court of Appeals of Maryland would recognize the sophisticated user/bulk supplier defense in any failure to warn claim.

In addition to the fact that the authorities reviewed above have concluded that the standards for negligent and strict liability failure to warn are essentially the same, this Court independently finds nothing about failure to warn in the context of strict liability that is inconsistent with the principles encompassed in comment *n* to § 388. Quite simply, both negligent and strict liability failure to warn involve the same questions of scope of duty and causation: (1) To what extent did the supplier act reasonably in communicating or failing to communicate a warning? (2) Given information provided by a supplier, was the failure of a sophisticated user to communicate an effective warning to an employee or other ultimate user an intervening cause of injury? As Prosser points out, it is really only the immunity of strict liability to negligence-based defenses (like contributory negligence) that distinguishes strict liability from negligence in failure to warn cases. This distinction does not militate against making the sophisticated user/bulk supplier defense available in a § 402A strict liability failure to warn claim.

Having determined that the Court of Appeals of Maryland would recognize the sophisticated user/bulk supplier defense to both negligent and strict liability failure to warn claims, this Court now addresses whether Eastman and Union Carbide are entitled to prevail, as a matter of law, on this defense against plaintiffs' failure to warn claims. It is worthwhile to restate the essential premise of this defense: There is no duty on product suppliers to warn ultimate users (whether employees or customers) of product-related hazards in products supplied in bulk to a knowledgeable user.[4] The corollary, of course, is that this is especially the case when the knowledgeable industrial purchaser is the only one in a position to communicate an effective warning to the ultimate user. It is clear from the "plethora of material" before this Court that the possible teratogenic effects of the chemicals were equally within the technical knowledge of DuPont, a very knowledgeable industrial purchaser of the constituent chemicals for its Imron paint, and Eastman and Union Carbide, the suppliers of said chemicals. DuPont acquired its knowledge of the possible teratogenic effects of the chemicals known collectively as glycol ether acetates through independent

4. Plaintiffs argue against reliance on *Goodbar,* stating that the sophisticated user/bulk supplier defense should not be expanded beyond cases of employee plaintiffs. Paper # 46, at 9–10. The Court does not find plaintiffs' position logically compelling. If anything, the bulk supplier would face an even more impossible task in communicating a warning to true consumers, *viz.,* those not in its customer's employ.

inquiry, as well as from various outside sources including Eastman and Union Carbide. As stated by the plaintiffs themselves, "DuPont was aware of the possible teratogenic effects of the glycol ether acetates used by it in Imron paint as early as 1980 * * *." * * * A DuPont memorandum dated April 23, 1981 makes clear that DuPont at that early date had within its possession reports regarding teratogenicity prepared by Japanese researchers, Dow Chemical, and the National Institute for Occupational Safety and Health (NIOSH). Those reports would be promptly evaluated by DuPont's own Haskell Laboratory. Id., Exhibit 2. More information on the possible teratogenic effects of glycol ether acetates came to DuPont in the ensuing years. * * * DuPont, then, clearly qualifies as a knowledgeable industrial purchaser with respect to bulk chemicals in general and the possible teratogenic effects of glycol ether acetates in particular. There was, thus, no duty on Eastman and Union Carbide as commodity chemical suppliers to DuPont to warn ultimate purchasers of Imron paint, or the employees thereof, as to teratogenic hazards. Goodbar v. Whitehead Bros., 591 F.Supp. at 559.

It is patently clear that DuPont was in a far better position than either of the bulk suppliers to communicate an effective warning to its customers, including the Baltimore City Fire Department, and to their customers' employees, including the plaintiff fire fighters. DuPont manufactured (from various chemicals including the glycol ether acetates supplied by Eastman and Union Carbide), packaged, labelled, and distributed the finished product denominated Imron paint. The facility with which DuPont could communicate an effective labelling warning to its customers is apparent. By comparison, Eastman and Union Carbide supplied in bulk, *via* railroad tank cars and tank trucks, vast amounts of liquid chemicals which were subsequently reprocessed and repackaged by DuPont as Imron paint, rendering these bulk suppliers unable, as a practical matter, to communicate any warning to the ultimate purchasers. Contrary to plaintiffs' assertion, there is simply no question of material fact as to whether Eastman and Union Carbide, as suppliers, reasonably relied on the knowledgeable industrial purchaser DuPont to warn customers like Baltimore City. Paper # 47, at 1; Paper # 46, at 6. The suppliers' apparent reliance upon DuPont to communicate an effective warning to its customers was also clearly reasonable. In short, there was no duty upon either Eastman or Union Carbide to communicate any warning to ultimate purchasers of Imron paint, given that only DuPont was ever in any reasonable position to communicate any effective warning. See Goodbar v. Whitehead Bros., 591 F.Supp. at 566.

* * *

[Eastman's and Union Carbide's motions for summary judgment granted.]

NOTES

1. Comment *n* to § 388 provides in part as follows:

> *n. Warnings given to third person.* Chattels are often supplied for the use of others * * *. In all such cases the question may arise as to whether the person supplying the chattel is exercising that reasonable care, which he owes to those who are to use it, by informing the third person through whom the chattel is supplied of its actual character.
>
> Giving to the third person through whom the chattel is supplied all the information necessary to its safe use is not in all cases sufficient to relieve the supplier from liability. It is merely a means by which this information is to be conveyed to those who are to use the chattel. The question remains whether this method gives a reasonable assurance that the information will reach those whose safety depends upon their having it. * * *
>
> * * *
>
> * * * [I]f the danger involved in the ignorant use of a particular chattel is very great, it may be that the supplier does not exercise reasonable care in entrusting the communication of the necessary information even to a person whom he has good reason to believe to be careful. Many such articles can be made to carry their own message to the understanding of those who are likely to use them by the form in which they are put out, by the container in which they are supplied, or by a label or other device, indicating with a substantial sufficiency their dangerous character. Where the danger involved in the ignorant use of their true quality is great and such means of disclosure are practicable and not unduly burdensome, it may well be that the supplier should be required to adopt them. * * *

2. DuPont was also a defendant in *Higgins.* How might the plaintiffs' own proofs against DuPont have undercut their case against Eastman and Union Carbide? Could plaintiffs' counsel have avoided this dilemma?

3. In Purvis v. PPG Industries, Inc., 502 So.2d 714, 722 (Ala.1987), a dry cleaner employee was poisoned by a cleaning solvent manufactured by defendant. PPG shipped the solvent in tank trucks to various distributors who then sold the solvent in drums to users such as plaintiff's employer. PPG provided its distributors with warning labels and all relevant danger information in Material Safety Data Sheets. Plaintiff claimed that PPG should have provided the warnings directly to her. *Held,* summary judgment for defendant affirmed:

> [Recent decisions] recognize that the manufacturers of some products have no effective way to convey product information or warnings to the ultimate consumer or user of the product. Whether because of bulk sales, repackaging, or product combinations, these manufacturers must rely upon downstream distributors and suppliers to do this. The law has properly evolved to the point where such reliance is permitted, so long as the manufacturer has a reasonable basis to believe that the distributor will pass along the product information or warnings.

4. In Adams v. Union Carbide Corp., 737 F.2d 1453 (6th Cir.1984), a General Motors assembly line worker developed a respiratory ailment from inhaling the vapors of a chemical used in making seat cushions. *Held* (2–1), summary judgment affirmed for the chemical manufacturer who provided warnings to General Motors and shipped the chemical in bulk. The dissenting

judge argued that the question under § 388 was one of fact for the jury which could reasonably have concluded that the defendant should have (1) verified that General Motors was implementing an appropriate safety program; (2) overseen such a program; and (3) undertaken to warn employees directly, perhaps through the labor union.

5. Some courts reject the sophisticated user and bulk supplier no-duty doctrines. See, e.g., Hall v. Ashland Oil Co., 625 F.Supp. 1515 (D.Conn.1986); Whitehead v. St. Joe Lead Co., Inc., 729 F.2d 238 (3d Cir.1984). Such courts hold that whether there is an obligation to provide warnings directly to ultimate users is a factual question, for jury determination, based on a balance of risk versus feasibility. See, e.g., Bryant v. Technical Research Co., 654 F.2d 1337 (9th Cir.1981) (bulk supplier might have obtained distributor's customer list and directly warned end users); Shell Oil Co. v. Gutierrez, 119 Ariz. 426, 581 P.2d 271 (App.1978).

6. As discussed above, if the product is a durable good on which a warning may be attached or embossed, the manufacturer will usually have a ready means to provide warnings directly to end users—regardless of whether there is a knowledgeable or "sophisticated" employer or other intermediary involved.

How might the manufacturer of fabric, sold in bulk to clothing manufacturers, warn end users of the fabric's flammability characteristics? See Gryc v. Dayton–Hudson Corp., 297 N.W.2d 727 (Minn.), cert. denied, 449 U.S. 921, 101 S.Ct. 320, 66 L.Ed.2d 149 (1980).

Further consideration of the obligations of component part suppliers is contained in Chapter 7, § 2.

7. **Theory of Liability.** Most courts apply ordinary negligence principles to "strict" liability warnings cases, including the principles of comment *n* to § 388. See, e.g., Whitehead v. St. Joe Lead Co., Inc., 729 F.2d 238 (3d Cir.1984). A few, however, have held that the duty to warn in strict tort is nondelegable as a matter of law. See, e.g., Neal v. Carey Canadian Mines, Ltd., 548 F.Supp. 357, 368 (E.D.Pa.1982), aff'd sub nom. Van Buskirk v. Carey Can. Mines, Ltd., 760 F.2d 481, 497 (3d Cir.1985).

As in other contexts, implied warranty is often considered the functional equivalent of strict tort liability in warnings cases, and "the scope of liability imposed under a breach-of-warranty theory in many if not most duty-to-warn cases will be identical to that imposed under a negligence theory." Bly v. Otis Elevator Co., 713 F.2d 1040, 1045 n. 8 (4th Cir.1983).

8. **Bystanders.** The broader question in *Higgins* is whether the manufacturer owes a duty to persons not in privity but foreseeably endangered by the product—whether the duty to warn extends to bystanders. In a variety of contexts, courts have extended the duty to such persons. See, e.g., Hayes v. Kay Chemical Co., 135 Ill.App.3d 932, 90 Ill.Dec. 632, 482 N.E.2d 611 (1985) (McDonald's employee wiped face with towel saturated with colorless, odorless, caustic grill cleaner used by another employee; duty extended beyond user to foreseeable persons and "nonusers"); Karns v. Emerson Electric Co., 817 F.2d 1452, 1457 (10th Cir.1987) (hand-held "Weed Eater" brush-cutting device, with exposed 10-inch circular steel sawblade "capable of suddenly flinging itself through an uncontrolled, 180 degree arc poses a danger to bystanders like Pearce that exceeds the expectations of the ordinary consumer"; blade struck something near ground, causing machine to swing violently around and cut off arm of user's nephew standing 6–10 feet to the rear); Givens v. Lederle, 556 F.2d 1341 (5th Cir.1977) (mother contracted polio, possibly from contact with

diapers of child recently administered vaccine manufactured by defendant). But see Kirk v. Michael Reese Hosp. & Med. Center, 117 Ill.2d 507, 111 Ill.Dec. 944, 513 N.E.2d 387 (1987) (drug manufacturer had no duty to passenger injured in car accident resulting when driver, who was taking defendant's drug and had been drinking, lost control of car).

9. **Regulation.** The Hazard Communication Standard promulgated by the Occupational Safety and Health Administration now requires manufacturers and importers to label all containers of hazardous chemicals and to provide Material Safety Data Sheets to purchasing employers. In turn, employers must make the MSDS information available to employees, and to train their employees in the safe handling of such substances. 29 C.F.R. § 1910.1200 (1988). The impact of this standard on workplace safety and products liability actions is difficult to predict. See Green, When Toxic Worlds Collide: Regulatory and Common Law Prescriptions for Risk Communication, 13 Harv.Envt'l L.Rev. 209 (1989); O'Reilly, Risks of Assumptions: Impacts of Regulatory Label Warnings Upon Industrial Products Liability, 37 Cath.U.L.Rev. 85 (1987).

10. See generally Faulk, Products Liability and the Chemical Manufacturer: Limitations on the Duty to Warn, 38 Okla.L.Rev. 233 (1985); Note, Failures to Warn and the Sophisticated User Defense, 74 Va.L.Rev. 579 (1988); Comment, Duty to Warn and the Sophisticated User Defense in Products Liability Cases, 15 Balt.L.Rev. 276 (1986).

MacDONALD v. ORTHO PHARMACEUTICAL CORPORATION

Supreme Judicial Court of Massachusetts, 1985.
394 Mass. 131, 475 N.E.2d 65, cert. denied, 474 U.S. 920, 106 S.Ct. 250, 88 L.Ed.2d 258 (1985).

ABRAMS, JUSTICE.

This products liability action raises the question of the extent of a drug manufacturer's duty to warn consumers of dangers inherent in the use of oral contraceptives. The plaintiffs brought suit against the defendant, Ortho Pharmaceutical Corporation (Ortho), for injuries allegedly caused by Ortho's birth control pills, and obtained a jury verdict in their favor. The defendant moved for a judgment notwithstanding the verdict. The judge concluded that the defendant did not owe a duty to warn the plaintiffs, and entered judgment for Ortho. The plaintiffs appealed. We transferred the case to this court on our own motion and reinstate the jury verdict.

We summarize the facts. In September, 1973, the plaintiff Carole D. MacDonald (MacDonald), who was twenty-six years old at the time, obtained from her gynecologist a prescription for Ortho–Novum contraceptive pills, manufactured by Ortho. As required by the then effective regulations promulgated by the United States Food and Drug Administration (FDA), the pill dispenser she received was labeled with a warning that "oral contraceptives are powerful and effective drugs which can cause side effects in some users and should not be used at all by some women," and that "[t]he most serious known side effect is abnormal blood clotting which can be fatal."[3] The warning also referred MacDonald to a booklet which she obtained from her gynecologist, and which was distributed by Ortho pursuant to FDA requirements. The booklet contained detailed information about the contraceptive pill, including the increased risk to pill users that vital organs such as the brain may be damaged by abnormal blood clotting.[4] The word "stroke" did not appear on the dispenser warning or in the booklet.

MacDonald's prescription for Ortho–Novum pills was renewed at subsequent annual visits to her gynecologist. The prescription was filled annually. On July 24, 1976, after approximately three years of using the pills, MacDonald suffered an occlusion of a cerebral artery by a blood clot, an injury commonly referred to as a stroke.[5] The injury caused the death of approximately twenty per cent of MacDonald's

3. FDA regulations in effect during the time period relevant to this litigation required that the following warning be included in or with the pill dispenser:

> "Do Not Take This Drug Without Your Doctor's Continued Supervision.
>
> "The oral contraceptives are powerful and effective drugs which can cause side effects in some users and should not be used at all by some women. The most serious known side effect is abnormal blood clotting which can be fatal.
>
> "Safe use of this drug requires a careful discussion with your doctor. To assist him in providing you with the necessary information, ________ (Firm name) has prepared a booklet (or other form) written in a style understandable to you as the drug user. This provides information on the effectiveness and known hazards of the drug including warnings, side effects and who should not use it. Your doctor will give you this booklet (or other form) if you ask for it and he can answer any questions you may have about the use of this drug.
>
> "Notify your doctor if you notice any unusual physical disturbance or discomfort."

21 C.F.R. § 130.45(d)(1), 35 Fed.Reg. 9002–9003 (1970), recodified at 21 C.F.R. § 310.501(a)(4), 39 Fed.Reg. 11680 (1974), 40 Fed.Reg. 5354 (1975).

4. Applicable FDA regulations required that the booklet contain "information in lay language, concerning effectiveness, contraindications, warnings, precautions, and adverse reactions," including a warning "regarding the serious side effects with special attention to thromboembolic disorders and stating the estimated morbidity and mortality in users vs. nonusers." 21 C.F.R. § 130.45(e) & (e)(3), 35 Fed.Reg. 9002, 9003 (1970), recodified at 21 C.F.R. § 310.501(a)(6) & (a)(6)(iii), 39 Fed.Reg. 11680 (1974), 40 Fed.Reg. 5353 (1975). Ortho's booklet contained the following information:

> "About blood clots
>
> "Blood clots occasionally form in the blood vessels of the legs and the pelvis of apparently healthy people and may threaten life if the clots break loose and then lodge in the lung or if they form in other vital organs, such as the brain. It has been estimated that about one woman in 2,000 on the pill each year suffers a blood clotting disorder severe enough to require hospitalization. The estimated death rate from abnormal blood clotting in healthy women under 35 not taking the pill is 1 in 500,000; whereas for the same group taking the pill it is 1 in 66,000. For healthy women over 35 not taking the pill, the rate is 1 in 200,000 compared to 1 in 25,000 for pill users. Blood clots are about three times more likely to develop in women over the age of 34. For these reasons it is important that women who have had blood clots in the legs, lungs or brain not use oral contraceptives. Anyone using the pill who has severe leg or chest pains, coughs up blood, has difficulty breathing, sudden severe headache or vomiting, dizziness or fainting, disturbances of vision or speech, weakness or numbness of an arm or leg, should call her doctor immediately and stop taking the pill."

5. MacDonald's hospital records refer to her injury as a "cerebral vascular accident," terminology likewise descriptive of brain damage attributable to blood clotting.

brain tissue, and left her permanently disabled. She and her husband initiated an action in the Superior Court against Ortho, seeking recovery for her personal injuries and his consequential damages and loss of consortium.

MacDonald testified that, during the time she used the pills, she was unaware that the risk of abnormal blood clotting encompassed the risk of stroke, and that she would not have used the pills had she been warned that stroke is an associated risk.[6] The case was submitted to a jury on the plaintiffs' theories that Ortho was negligent in failing to warn adequately of the dangers associated with the pills and that Ortho breached its warranty of merchantability. These two theories were treated, in effect, as a single claim of failure to warn. The jury returned a special verdict, finding no negligence or breach of warranty in the manufacture of the pills. The jury also found that Ortho adequately advised the gynecologist of the risks inherent in the pills;[7] the jury found, however, that Ortho was negligent and in breach of warranty because it failed to give MacDonald sufficient warning of such dangers. The jury further found that MacDonald's injury was caused by Ortho's pills, that the inadequacy of the warnings to MacDonald was the proximate cause of her injury, and that Ortho was liable to MacDonald and her husband.[8]

After the jury verdict, the judge granted Ortho's motion for judgment notwithstanding the verdict, concluding that, because oral contraceptives are prescription drugs, a manufacturer's duty to warn the consumer is satisfied if the manufacturer gives adequate warnings to the prescribing physician, and that the manufacturer has no duty to warn the consumer directly.

The narrow issue, on appeal, is whether, as the plaintiffs contend, a manufacturer of birth control pills owes a direct duty to the consumer to warn her of the dangers inherent in the use of the pill. We conclude that such a duty exists under the law of this Commonwealth.

1. *Extent of duty to warn.* Ordinarily, "a manufacturer of a product, which the manufacturer knows or should know is dangerous by nature or is in a dangerous condition," is under a duty to give

6. Subsequent to the events in this case, the FDA regulation was amended by 43 Fed.Reg. 4221 (1978), which replaced the regulation requirement of a specified warning on the pill dispenser, see note 3 supra, with a requirement that the dispenser contain a warning "of the serious side effects of oral contraceptives, such as thrombophlebitis, pulmonary embolism, myocardial infarction, retinal artery thrombosis, *stroke,* benign hepatic adenomas, induction of fetal abnormalities, and gallbladder disease" (emphasis added). See 21 C.F.R. § 310.501(a)(2)(iv) (1984).

7. MacDonald stated at trial that her gynecologist had informed her only that oral contraceptives might cause bloating, and had not advised her of the increased risk of stroke associated with consumption of birth control pills. The physician was not joined as a defendant in this action, and no questions relating to any potential liability on his part are before us.

MacDonald further testified at trial that she had read both the warning on the Dialpak tablet dispenser as well as the booklet which she received from her gynecologist. See notes 3 and 4, supra.

8. The only issue before us concerns the scope of Ortho's duty to the plaintiffs. The defendant does not contest the damages but relies solely on its claim that it owes no duty to warn the plaintiffs directly.

warning of those dangers to "persons who it is foreseeable will come in contact with, and consequently be endangered by, that product." H.P. Hood & Sons v. Ford Motor Co., 370 Mass. 69, 75, 345 N.E.2d 683 (1976). The element of privity being long discarded, a manufacturer's warning to the immediate purchaser will not, as a general matter, discharge this duty. However, "there are limits to that principle." Carter v. Yardley & Co., 319 Mass. 92, 98, 64 N.E.2d 693 (1946). Thus, "a manufacturer may be absolved from blame because of a justified reliance upon . . . a middleman." Id. at 99, 64 N.E.2d 693. This exception is applicable only in the limited instances in which the manufacturer's reliance on an intermediary is reasonable. See Restatement (Second) of Torts § 388, comment n (1965). In such narrowly defined circumstances, the manufacturer's immunity from liability if the consumer does not receive the warning is explicable on the grounds that the intermediary's failure to warn is a superseding cause of the consumer's injury, or, alternatively, that, because it is unreasonable in such circumstances to expect the manufacturer to communicate with the consumer, the manufacturer has no duty directly to warn the consumer.[9] See generally 1A Frumer and Friedman, Products Liability §§ 8.01, 8.03[3] (1983 & Supp. 1984); Restatement (Second) of Torts, supra at § 452, comment f.

The rule in jurisdictions that have addressed the question of the extent of a manufacturer's duty to warn in cases involving prescription drugs is that the prescribing physician acts as a "learned intermediary" between the manufacturer and the patient, and "the duty of the ethical drug manufacturer is to warn the doctor, rather than the patient, [although] the manufacturer is directly liable to the patient for a breach of such duty." McEwen v. Ortho Pharmaceutical Corp., 270 Or. 375, 386–387, 528 P.2d 522 (1974). Oral contraceptives, however, bear peculiar characteristics which warrant the imposition of a common law duty on the manufacturer to warn users directly of associated risks. Whereas a patient's involvement in decision-making concerning use of a prescription drug necessary to treat a malady is typically minimal or nonexistent, the healthy, young consumer of oral contraceptives is usually actively involved in the decision to use "the pill," as opposed to other available birth control products, and the prescribing physician is relegated to a relatively passive role.[10]

Furthermore, the physician prescribing "the pill," as a matter of course, examines the patient once before prescribing an oral contraceptive and only annually thereafter. J. Willson, E. Carrington, & W.

9. Ortho points out that a number of courts have reached this result in oral contraceptive cases. [Citing 15 cases.]

10. According to the American Medical Association, "the medical profession regards the pill, in most cases, as a convenience rather than a traditional medication." Statement of American Medical Association, published in Science News, March 14, 1970, quoted in Comment, Liability of Birth Control Pill Manufacturers, 23 Hastings L.J. 1526, 1532 (1972). These distinguishing features have been recognized by legal commentators as well as by the medical profession. See Merrill, Compensation for Prescription Drug Injuries, 59 Va.L.Rev. 1, 91, 93 (1973); Comment, Liability of Birth Control Pill Manufacturers, 23 Hastings L.J. 1526, 1538–1543 (1972).

Ledger, Obstetrics and Gynecology 184 (7th ed. 1983). D. Danforth, Obstetrics and Gynecology 267 (4th ed. 1982). T. Green, Gynecology; Essentials of Clinical Practice 593 (3d ed. 1977). At her annual checkup, the patient receives a renewal prescription for a full year's supply of the pill.[11] Thus, the patient may only seldom have the opportunity to explore her questions and concerns about the medication with the prescribing physician. Even if the physician, on those occasions, were scrupulously to remind the patient of the risks attendant on continuation of the oral contraceptive, "the patient cannot be expected to remember all of the details for a protracted period of time." 35 Fed. Reg. 9002 (1970).

Last, the birth control pill is specifically subject to extensive Federal regulation. The FDA has promulgated regulations designed to ensure that the choice of "the pill" as a contraceptive method is informed by comprehensible warnings of potential side effects.[12] See notes 3 and 4 supra. These regulations, and subsequent amendments, have their basis in the FDA commissioner's finding, after hearings, that "[b]ecause oral contraceptives are ordinarily taken electively by healthy women who have available to them alternative methods of treatment, and because of the relatively high incidence of serious illnesses associated with their use, . . . users of these drugs should, without exception, be furnished with written information telling them of the drug's benefits and risks." 43 Fed.Reg. 4215 (1978). The FDA also found that the facts necessary to informed decisions by women as to use of oral contraceptives are "too complex to expect the patient to remember everything told her by the physician," and that, in the absence of direct written warnings, many potential users of "the pill" do not receive the needed information "in an organized, comprehensive, understandable, and handy-for-future-reference form." 35 Fed.Reg. 9002 (1970).

The oral contraceptive thus stands apart from other prescription drugs in light of the heightened participation of patients in decisions relating to use of "the pill"; the substantial risks affiliated with the product's use; the feasibility of direct warnings by the manufacturer to the user; the limited participation of the physician (annual prescriptions); and the possibility that oral communications between physicians and consumers may be insufficient or too scanty standing alone fully to apprise consumers of the product's dangers at the time the initial selection of a contraceptive method is made as well as at subsequent points when alternative methods may be considered. We conclude that the manufacturer of oral contraceptives is not justified in relying on warnings to the medical profession to satisfy its common law duty to

11. MacDonald saw her gynecologist once in the summer of 1973, once in the summer of 1974, and once in August of 1975. At each appointment, she received a prescription for birth control pills. Thus, eleven months had elapsed between her last gynecological checkup and her stroke in July, 1976.

12. See 21 C.F.R. § 130.45(a), 35 Fed. Reg. 9002 (1970) (oral contraceptives "are used for long periods of time by large numbers of women who, for the most part, are healthy and take them as a matter of choice for prophylaxis against pregnancy, in full knowledge of other means of contraception"); 43 Fed.Reg. 4215 (1978).

warn, and that the manufacturer's obligation encompasses a duty to warn the ultimate user. Thus, the manufacturer's duty is to provide to the consumer written warnings conveying reasonable notice of the nature, gravity, and likelihood of known or knowable side effects, and advising the consumer to seek fuller explanation from the prescribing physician or other doctor of any such information of concern to the consumer.[13]

2. *Adequacy of the warning.* Because we reject the judge's conclusion that Ortho had no duty to warn MacDonald, we turn to Ortho's separate argument, not reached by the judge, that the evidence was insufficient to warrant the jury's finding that Ortho's warnings to MacDonald were inadequate. Ortho contends initially that its warnings complied with FDA labeling requirements, and that those requirements preempt or define the bounds of the common law duty to warn. We disagree. The regulatory history of the FDA requirements belies any objective to cloak them with preemptive effect. In response to concerns raised by drug manufacturers that warnings required and drafted by the FDA might be deemed inadequate by juries, the FDA commissioner specifically noted that the boundaries of civil tort liability for failure to warn are controlled by applicable State law. 43 Fed. Reg. 4214 (1978). Although the common law duty we today recognize is to a large degree coextensive with the regulatory duties imposed by the FDA, we are persuaded that, in instances where a trier of fact could reasonably conclude that a manufacturer's compliance with FDA labeling requirements or guidelines did not adequately apprise oral contraceptive users of inherent risks, the manufacturer should not be shielded from liability by such compliance. Compliance with FDA requirements, though admissible to demonstrate lack of negligence, is not conclusive on this issue, just as violation of FDA requirements is evidence, but not conclusive evidence, of negligence. [Citations.] We therefore concur with the plaintiffs' argument that even if the conclusion that Ortho complied with FDA requirements were inescapable, an issue we need not decide, the jury nonetheless could have found that the lack of a reference to "stroke" breached Ortho's common law duty to warn.

The common law duty to warn, like the analogous FDA "lay language" requirement, necessitates a warning "comprehensible to the average user and . . . convey[ing] a fair indication of the nature and extent of the danger to the mind of a reasonably prudent person." Ortho Pharmaceutical Corp. v. Chapman, 180 Ind.App. 33, 49, 388 N.E.2d 541 (1979), quoting Spruill v. Boyle–Midway, Inc., 308 F.2d 79, 85 (4th Cir.1962). Whether a particular warning measures up to this standard is almost always an issue to be resolved by a jury; few

13. This opinion does not diminish the prescribing physician's duty to "disclose in a reasonable manner all significant medical information that the physician possesses or reasonably should possess that is material to an intelligent decision by the patient whether to" take "the pill." Harnish v. Children's Hosp. Medical Center, 387 Mass. 152, 155, 439 N.E.2d 240 (1982).

questions are "more appropriately left to a common sense lay judgment than that of whether a written warning gets its message across to an average person." Ferebee v. Chevron Chem. Co., 552 F.Supp. 1293, 1304 (D.D.C.1982). * * *

Ortho argues that reasonable minds could not differ as to whether MacDonald was adequately informed of the risk of the injury she sustained by Ortho's warning that the oral contraceptives could cause "abnormal blood clotting which can be fatal" and further warning of the incremental likelihood of hospitalization or death due to blood clotting in "vital organs, such as the brain." We disagree. "The fact finder may find a warning to be unreasonable, hence inadequate, in its factual content, its expression of the facts, or the method or form in which it is conveyed. . . . The adequacy of such warnings is measured not only by what is stated, but also by the manner in which it is stated. A reasonable warning not only conveys a fair indication of the nature of the dangers involved, but also warns with the degree of intensity demanded by the nature of the risk. A warning may be found to be unreasonable in that it was unduly delayed, reluctant in tone or lacking in a sense of urgency." Seley v. G.D. Searle Co., 67 Ohio St.2d 192, 198, 423 N.E.2d 831 (1981). We cannot say that this jury's decision that the warning was inadequate is so unreasonable as to require the opposite conclusion as a matter of law. The jury may well have concluded, in light of their common experience and MacDonald's testimony, that the absence of a reference to "stroke" in the warning unduly minimized the warning's impact or failed to make the nature of the risk reasonably comprehensible to the average consumer. Similarly, the jury may have concluded that there are fates worse than death, such as the permanent disablement suffered by MacDonald, and that the mention of the risk of death did not, therefore, suffice to apprise an average consumer of the material risks of oral contraceptive use. Cf. Hubbard–Hall Chem. Co. v. Silverman, 340 F.2d 402, 405 (1st Cir.1965).

[Judgment for plaintiffs.]

O'CONNOR, JUSTICE (dissenting).

The court reverses the judgment below and holds Ortho Pharmaceutical Corporation (Ortho) liable to Carole and Bruce MacDonald even though the jury found that Ortho adequately informed Carole MacDonald's physician of the risks associated with the use of its contraceptive pills, and regardless of whether Ortho complied with the applicable Federal Food and Drug Administration (FDA) regulations governing the provision of printed information to users of oral contraceptives. I would hold that, as a matter of law, by adequately informing physicians of the risks associated with its product and by complying with applicable FDA regulations, a contraceptive pill manufacturer fulfils the duty to warn that it owes consumers. * * *

In order to fulfil its duty to warn consumers of risks associated with its product, a manufacturer of a nonprescription ("over-the-counter") drug must place on the drug's package printed warnings.

That duty "derives from the basic marketing predicate of the over-the-counter drug industry, namely, that nonprescription drugs are purchased by consumers for the purpose of self-medication *typically without any intended or actual intervention by a physician.*" Torsiello v. Whitehall Laboratories, 165 N.J.Super. 311, 322, 398 A.2d 132 (1979) (emphasis added). In contradistinction, a manufacturer of a prescription drug fulfils its duty to warn a consumer by adequately informing the consumer's physician—a "learned intermediary between the purchaser and the manufacturer"—of the drug's associated risks. Sterling Drug, Inc. v. Cornish, 370 F.2d 82, 85 (8th Cir.1966). That rule results from the fact that, by definition, before a consumer uses a prescription drug, that consumer must have some interaction with a doctor. See 21 U.S.C. § 353(b)(1) (1982). In cases involving manufacturers of contraceptive pills, every court but one has adhered to the "prescription drug" rule. [Citing 15 cases.] But see Lukaszewicz v. Ortho Pharmaceutical Corp., 510 F.Supp. 961, 963, amended by order, 532 F.Supp. 211 (D.Wis. 1981). The one court that went beyond the prescription drug rule, see Lukaszewicz v. Ortho Pharmaceutical Corp., supra, [decided on grounds of negligence per se]. To my knowledge, no other court has embraced the rule laid down today by the court.

Before prescribing any drug, whether on the doctor's initiative or at the patient's request, the doctor must exercise professional judgment as to the medical propriety of that patient's taking that drug and, in exercising that judgment, the doctor must conform to the standards of good medical practice laid down in Brune v. Belinkoff, 354 Mass. 102, 109, 235 N.E.2d 793 (1968). Furthermore, this court has held that a doctor must "disclose in a reasonable manner all significant medical information that the physician possesses or reasonably should possess that is material to an intelligent decision by the patient whether to undergo a proposed procedure." Harnish v. Children's Hosp. Medical Center, 387 Mass. 152, 155, 439 N.E.2d 240 (1982). That rule applies when a physician prescribes a drug just as it does when a physician performs any other medical procedure. * * *

Unless doctors have current, accurate, and complete information about a drug's risks, they cannot properly perform their vital role. Therefore, courts have imposed on drug manufacturers the duty to provide doctors with that information. See, e.g., Brochu v. Ortho Pharmaceutical Corp., [642 F.2d 652 (1st Cir.1981)]. A drug manufacturer who fails properly to fulfil that duty must respond in damages to a patient who suffers an injury as a result. See, e.g., McEwen v. Ortho Pharmaceutical Corp., [270 Or. 375, 528 P.2d 522 (1974)].

I believe that the "prescription drug" rule, combined with the *Harnish* rule, most fairly and efficiently allocates among drug manufacturers, physicians, and drug users, the risks and responsibilities involved with the use of prescription drugs. Furthermore, I believe that those rules best ensure that a prescription drug user will receive in the most effective manner the information that she needs to make an informed decision as to whether to use the drug. The rules place on drug manufacturers the duty to gather, compile, and provide to doctors data regarding the use of their drugs, tasks for which the manufacturers are best suited, and the rules place on doctors the burden of conveying those data to their patients in a useful and understandable manner, a task for which doctors are best suited. Doctors, unlike printed warnings, can tailor to the needs and abilities of an individual patient the information that that patient needs in order to make an informed decision whether to use a particular drug. Manufacturers are not in position to give adequate advice directly to those consumers whose medical histories and physical conditions, perhaps unknown to the consumers, make them peculiarly susceptible to risk. Prescription drugs—including oral contraceptives—differ from other products because their dangers vary widely depending on characteristics of individual consumers. Exposing a prescription drug manufacturer to liability based on a jury's determination that, despite adequately informing physicians of the drug's risks and complying with FDA regulations, the manufacturer failed reasonably to warn a particular plaintiff-consumer of individualized risks is not essential to reasonable consumer protection and places an unfair burden on prescription drug manufacturers.

* * *

Furthermore, even if there be a common law duty necessitating a direct warning to the consumer with respect to the "nature and extent of the danger" of contraceptive pills, as the court declares, the MacDonalds presented no evidence that Ortho failed to fulfil that duty. The court states only that the jury "could have found that the lack of a reference to 'stroke' breached Ortho's common law duty to warn." *Ante* at 71. Surely, the statement in Ortho's booklet that the contraceptive pill could cause life threatening blood clots to form in the brain, even though it did not contain the word "stroke," satisfied the court's requirement that Ortho provide "written warnings conveying reasonable notice of the nature, gravity, and likelihood of known or knowable side effects." *Ante* at 70. I would affirm the judgment for Ortho.

NOTES

1. **Learned Intermediary Doctrine.** As a general rule of products liability law, a manufacturer is bound to take all reasonable steps to provide necessary warnings to the ultimate user of a hazardous product. Like the bulk sale/sophisticated user doctrines examined above, the learned intermediary doctrine is an exception to that general rule. Its rationale was perhaps best described by Judge Wisdom in Reyes v. Wyeth Laboratories, 498 F.2d 1264 (5th Cir.), cert. denied, 419 U.S. 1096, 95 S.Ct. 687, 42 L.Ed.2d 688 (1974):

> [W]here *prescription* drugs are concerned, the manufacturer's duty to warn is limited to an obligation to advise the prescribing physician of any potential dangers that may result from the drug's use. This special standard for prescription drugs is an understandable exception to the Restatement's general rule that one who markets goods must warn foreseeable ultimate users of dangers inherent in his products. See Restatement (Second) of Torts, Section 388 (1965). Prescription drugs are likely to be complex medicines, esoteric in formula and

> varied in effect. As a medical expert, the prescribing physician can take into account the propensities of the drug, as well as the susceptibilities of his patient. His is the task of weighing the benefits of any medication against its potential dangers. The choice he makes is an informed one, an individualized medical judgment bottomed on a knowledge of both patient and palliative. Pharmaceutical companies then, who must warn ultimate purchasers of dangers inherent in patent drugs sold over the counter, in selling prescription drugs are required to warn only the prescribing physician, who acts as a "learned intermediary" between manufacturer and consumer.

498 F.2d at 1276. All jurisdictions have accepted the learned intermediary doctrine as an exception to the general rule.

2. In addition to prescription drugs, the learned intermediary doctrine has been applied to a cardiac pacemaker, Brooks v. Medtronic, Inc., 750 F.2d 1227 (4th Cir.1984); an intrauterine device, McKee v. Moore, 648 P.2d 21 (Okl.1982); a catheter inserted into a patient's heart, Phelps v. Sherwood Medical Industries, 836 F.2d 296 (7th Cir.1987); and an x-ray machine, Kirsch v. Picker International, Inc., 753 F.2d 670 (8th Cir.1985).

Efforts to apply the doctrine outside the medical field have generally failed. See, e.g., Hall v. Ashland Oil Co., 625 F.Supp. 1515 (D.Conn.1986) (differences between doctor-patient relationship and employer-employee relationship precluded application of learned intermediary doctrine to chemical manufacturer who warned decedent's employer but not decedent himself).

3. **Exceptions to the Doctrine.** If a prescription drug is dispensed under circumstances where the doctor does not render the type of individualized balancing of risks and benefits contemplated by the learned intermediary doctrine, the manufacturer may have to provide warnings directly to the patient.

A. **Mass immunization programs.** Most courts thus refuse to apply the learned intermediary rule to the mass immunization context, where patients are vaccinated in assembly-line fashion, often by persons other than physicians. See, e.g., Davis v. Wyeth Laboratories, Inc., 399 F.2d 121 (9th Cir.1968) (polio); Givens v. Lederle Laboratories, 556 F.2d 1341 (5th Cir.1977) (same); Brazzell v. United States, 788 F.2d 1352 (8th Cir.1986) (swine flu); Petty v. United States, 740 F.2d 1428 (8th Cir.1984) (same). How if at all could such warnings effectively be given to each participant? See Petty v. United States, 740 F.2d 1428, 1433–34 n. 3 (8th Cir.1984).

Might the provision of truly "effective" warnings directly (and without a doctor's explanation) to every person vaccinated in a mass immunization program needlessly scare many people out of participating in the program? Might such warnings increase the incidence of the disease in the community and thereby undercut the effectiveness of the immunization program? Is the legal rule therefore at odds with social policy? See Reyes v. Wyeth Laboratories, supra. See generally Franklin & Mais, Tort Law and Mass Immunization Programs: Lessons from the Polio and Flu Episodes, 65 Calif.L.Rev. 754 (1977).

B. **Birth control pills.** *MacDonald* created a new common-law exception to the learned intermediary rule for birth control pills. Two federal court judges followed *MacDonald.* See Stephens v. G.D. Searle & Co., 602 F.Supp. 379 (E.D. Mich.1985); Odgers v. Ortho Pharmaceutical Corp., 609 F.Supp. 867 (E.D.Mich. 1985). Many prior cases had applied the learned intermediary doctrine to birth control pills.

Is this new exception a good one?

4. **Over warning?** A Gallup poll in 1985 showed that "Americans greatly overestimate the risks and understate the effectiveness of birth control methods, particularly the pill, leaving them vulnerable to unintended pregnancies." According to the American College of Obstetricians and Gynecologists, unwanted pregnancies and more than a million abortions each year needlessly threaten women's lives. "The society's survey found that people are particularly misinformed about the birth control pill, which the group said is the most effective and safest contraceptive for many women." Three quarters of the women surveyed thought that the pill presents substantial health risks, despite the fact that the risk of death from taking the pill is about half the mother's risk of death from childbirth. Pill Poll—National Survey Finds Many Have Bad Information, The State (Columbia, S.C.), March 6, 1985, p. 2A, col. 2.

5. In drug litigation, the courts have addressed many of the same warnings issues arising in other products liability contexts.

A. **Adequacy.** All material information on possible risks must be conveyed to the doctor, comprehensible to the general practitioner as well as to the specialist. Risks must not be unduly downplayed, nor safety "overpromoted"; instead, the manufacturer's communications to the doctor must present a reasonably balanced portrayal of the effectiveness and dangers of the drug. Compare Stevens v. Parke, Davis & Co., 9 Cal.3d 51, 107 Cal.Rptr. 45, 507 P.2d 653 (1973) (overpromotion of Chloromycetin, a broad-spectrum antibiotic, downplaying risk of fatal aplastic anemia), with Spinden v. Johnson & Johnson, 177 N.J.Super. 605, 427 A.2d 597 (App.1981) (AMA Journal ads did not amount to overpromotion).

B. **Timeliness.** A long series of cases involving Aralen, a drug used in the treatment of rheumatoid arthritis and eventually linked to irreversible eye damage in some users, established the following general principles:

(1) A warning of side effects to be timely must be made promptly upon discovery of the coexistence of the side effect and use of the drug, even though a causal relationship has not been clearly proved. Basko v. Sterling Drug, Inc., 416 F.2d 417 (2d Cir.1969).

(2) The warning is required as soon as the side effect is documented even in only a very small percentage of users. Sterling Drug, Inc. v. Cornish, 370 F.2d 82 (8th Cir.1966).

(3) Since the drug company is held to have the knowledge of an expert, a warning to be timely must be given as soon as the risks are pointed out in reputable scientific journals. Schenebeck v. Sterling Drug, Inc., 423 F.2d 919 (8th Cir.1970).

C. **Method of conveyance.** There are several standard avenues of communication between drug companies and physicians for transmitting information about drugs. The Physician's Desk Reference (PDR), updated periodically, contains copies of package inserts for many prescription drugs. Another source of information, perhaps more complete than the PDR and updated monthly, is Facts and Comparisons. Information on warnings and contraindications is readily available to the physician from the reference works, and ordinarily the warning in the package insert and the PDR will be adequate to alert physicians to drug risks. However, the information provided in the PDR may become out of date due to new developments, and failure promptly to update the medical profession may subject the company to liability.

The manufacturer must select the best method reasonably available to convey important new information on drug dangers to the doctors who need the information. Thus, if information is critical, the manufacturer may be required to send

"Dear Doctor" letters to individual physicians to advise them of the new information. As to the standards of adequacy for such letters, see, e.g., Lawson v. G.D. Searle & Co., 64 Ill.2d 543, 1 Ill.Dec. 497, 356 N.E.2d 779 (1976). However, the typically busy physician may not regularly consult the PDR or even routinely read "Dear Doctor" letters. If the need to warn is compelling enough, the company may be required to use its "detail" men, salesmen who regularly call on physicians, to warn doctors specifically of a particular risk. A leading case on the factors which bear on whether the company must warn doctors in this manner is Sterling Drug, Inc. v. Yarrow, 408 F.2d 978 (8th Cir.1969) (Aralen; failure to use detail men to alert doctors of possible eye damage was unreasonable in light of the fact that the PDR and letters might not warn fast enough).

6. **Allergic Reactions.** Consider the following observations from Panel Discussion, Medico–Legal Aspects of Allergies, 24 Tenn.L.Rev. 840–42 (1957):

> * * * The term *allergy* or *hypersensitivity* refers to the condition or state of an individual who reacts specifically and with unusual symptoms to the administration of, or to contact with, a substance which when given in similar amounts to the majority of all other individuals proves harmless or innocuous. For example, the ingestion of egg-white produces no ill effects in most individuals. In the few persons, however, who might be allergic to egg white, a minute amount may cause either violent gastrointestinal disturbances, urticaria, eczema, or asthma. * * *
>
> * * *
>
> An allergic reaction is a chemical one, in which certain substances called antibodies are attached to the tissue cells. The substance producing the allergic reaction is called the *antigen* or *allergen.* It is the chemical union of this antigen and the antibody attached to the tissue cells that produces the allergic reaction. The antigen may be one of many thousands of substances; it may be a cosmetic, a metal, drug, dye, insecticide, cement, fabric, vegetable, inhalant, plant, or many others too numerous to mention.
>
> It should be emphasized that before one will have an allergic reaction to one of these, or other substances, he must possess the abnormal trait of having the antibody for that particular substance attached to his tissue cell. Such a tendency may be inherited or acquired—acquired by repeated exposure. * * *
>
> * * *
>
> Products liability in the field of allergy assumes great proportions because of the ever-increasing number of substances to which the average individual is exposed. This is true in industrial workers as well as those who purchase the products for personal use. Anticipation of adverse reactions on the part of the manufacturers and management is receiving greater attention than ever before. Attempts are being made to eliminate exposure to those products, substances, or inhalants which are commonly known to produce allergic reactions.
>
> A person suffering an allergic reaction to a product is, by definition, abnormal or hypersensitive. The resulting harm, therefore, is arguably more fairly attributable to some "defect" in the person's body rather than to a "defect" in the product—a product that is entirely safe for all normal ("nondefective") people.

Two lines of cases address the duty to warn of allergic reactions. One line requires a warning only if the manufacturer can foresee a risk of allergy in *a substantial number of persons.* See Kaempfe v. Lehn & Fink Products Corp., 21 A.D.2d 197, 249 N.Y.S.2d 840 (1964), aff'd 20 N.Y.2d 818, 284 N.Y.S.2d 708, 231

N.E.2d 294 (1967) (dermatitis from aluminum sulphate in deodorant; no liability where manufacturer received only 4 sensitivity complaints in 600,000 sales—plaintiff not one "of a substantial number or of an identifiable class" of allergic persons: "the manufacturer is [not] to be held under an absolute duty of giving special warning against a remote possibility of harm due to an unusual allergic reaction from use by a miniscule percentage of the potential customers"). Accord, Griggs v. Combe, Inc., 456 So.2d 790 (Ala.1984) (first known case of systemic illness from benzocaine in vaginal itch ointment). This is the position of comment *j* to § 402A of the Second Restatement of Torts. See also, comment *i* ("unreasonably dangerous" means dangerous to extent beyond contemplation of "ordinary" consumer). See also Adelman–Tremblay v. Jewel Companies, Inc., 859 F.2d 517 (7th Cir.1988).

Another line of cases rejects the no-duty approach for "insignificant" or "insubstantial" numbers of allergy victims and instead imposes a duty to warn of *any* foreseeable allergy that may be serious. See Wright v. Carter Products, Inc., 244 F.2d 53 (2d Cir.1957) (dermatitis from deodorant; manufacturer might have duty to warn, despite only 373 complaints in 82,000,000 sales, depending on foreseeability of allergy, frequency and seriousness thereof, and feasibility of providing a warning). "In failure-to-warn cases, as in strict liability cases generally, liability does not turn on whether the risk of harm runs to a substantial number of persons. Rather, * * * courts inquire whether the manufacturer knew that there were even a relatively few persons who could not use its product without serious injury, and whether a proper warning would have helped prevent harm to them." Kehm v. Procter & Gamble Mfg. Co., 724 F.2d 613 (8th Cir.1983) (user of defendant's extra absorbent Rely tampon died from toxic shock syndrome; court rejected defense of user's idiosyncratic allergic reaction as inapplicable to strict liability claim).

See generally Mobilia, Allergic Reactions to Prescription Drugs: A Proposal for Compensation, 48 Alb.L.Rev. 343 (1984); Schattman, A Cause of Action for the Allergic Consumer, 8 Houston L.Rev. 827 (1971); Noel, Products Defective Because of Inadequate Directions or Warnings, 23 Sw.L.J. 256 (1969); Comment, Strict Liability and Allergic Drug Reactions, 47 Miss.L.J. 526 (1976).

7. **Regulation.**

A. **FDA regulation of drugs.** Drugs are extensively regulated. The principal federal statute regulating the quality of drugs is the Federal Food, Drug and Cosmetic Act, 21 U.S.C.A. §§ 301–392, originally enacted by Congress in 1938. The Act's key provisions are § 331(a), prohibiting the sale of "any food, drug, device, or cosmetic that is adulterated or misbranded," and § 355, requiring the approval of the Food and Drug Administration (FDA) to the marketing of any new drug. The issue of drug warnings and instructions is addressed in the Act, from the perspective of whether drug labels are "misbranded," in §§ 352 and 353.

The general thrust of these sections is to require that adequate information on proper use (including dosage) and possible dangers be conveyed to the consumer, in the case of over-the-counter drugs, or to the physician, in the case of prescription drugs. A prescription drug is one which "because of its toxicity or other potentiality for harmful effect, or the method of its use, or the collateral measures necessary to its use, is not safe for use except under the supervision of a practitioner licensed by law to administer such drug." Such drugs must bear a label stating, "CAUTION: Federal law prohibits dispensing without prescription," § 353(b)(4), and providing any special directions for use and cautionary statements contained in the prescription. § 353(b)(2). Drug labels must contain "(1) adequate directions for use; and (2) such adequate warnings against use in those pathological conditions or by children where its use may be dangerous to health, or against unsafe dosage or methods or duration of administration or application, in such manner and form, as are necessary for the protection of users * * *." § 352(f). The drug's active ingredients and established name must be indicated, § 352(e), as must the drug's side effects, contraindications and effectiveness. § 352(n).

B. **Birth control pills.** The FDA has on occasion deviated from this general pattern and required that information on certain prescription drugs be transmitted directly to users. See, for example, 21 CFR § 310.501 (1988), providing in part as follows:

> (a) *Oral contraceptives.* (1) The Commissioner of Food and Drugs concludes that the safe and effective use of oral contraceptive drug products requires that patients be fully informed of the benefits and risks involved in the use of these drugs. Information in lay language concerning effectiveness, contraindication, warnings, precautions, and adverse reactions shall be furnished to each patient receiving oral contraceptives. This information shall be given to the patient by the dispenser in the form of a brief summary of certain essential information included in each package dispensed to each patient, and in a longer, detailed labeling piece in or accompanying each package dispensed to each patient. * * *
>
> (2) The brief summary shall specifically include the following:
>
> (i) A statement that oral contraceptives are effective, but that any failure to take them in accordance with the recommended dosage increases the chance of pregnancy.
>
> (ii) A statement of the specific items of history to be told the physician that would lead the physician not to prescribe oral contraceptives (i.e., the contraindications to use).
>
> (iii) A statement that oral contraceptives should be taken only under the continued supervision of a physician.
>
> (iv) A listing of the serious side effects of oral contraceptives, such as thrombophlebitis, pulmonary embolism, myocardial infarction, retinal artery thrombosis, stroke, benign hepatic adenomas, induction of fetal abnormalities, and gallbladder disease.
>
> (v) A statement in the form of a boxed warning that cigarette smoking increases the risks of serious side effects on the heart and blood vessels from oral contraceptive use, and advising women who use oral contraceptives not to smoke.
>
> (vi) A statement of the most common side effects, such as nausea and vomiting, weight change, change in menses, and breast tenderness.
>
> (vii) A statement that the estrogen in oral contraceptives has been found to cause breast cancer and other cancers in certain animals and that these findings suggest that oral contraceptives may also cause cancer in humans but that studies to date in women taking currently marketed oral contraceptives have not confirmed that oral contraceptives cause cancer in humans.
>
> (viii) A statement that oral contraceptives are of no value in the prevention or treatment of venereal disease.
>
> (ix) A statement calling attention to the detailed patient labeling and a recommendation that it be carefully read.

Subsection (3) prescribes the information which must be set forth in the detailed patient pamphlet, including more specific information about the risks described in the summary sheet, and various other information, such as instructions on proper use, "what to do in the event of one or two missed periods," and a comparison of the risk of death (in smokers and nonsmokers) from the pill, alternative means of contraception, abortion, and the use of no contraception at all.

The FDA has provided the following tables and graph as satisfying certain of the specified warning requirements. See § 310.501(a)(8); 43 Fed.Reg. 4223–26 (Jan. 31, 1978):

TABLE 1

SUMMARY OF RELATIVE RISK OF THROMBOEMBOLIC DISORDERS AND OTHER VASCULAR PROBLEMS IN ORAL CONTRACEPTIVE USERS COMPARED TO NONUSERS

	Relative risk, times greater
Idiopathic thromboembolic disease	4-11
Post surgery thromboembolic complications	4-6
Thrombotic stroke	4-9.5
Hemorrhagic stroke	2
Myocardial infarction	2-12

TABLE 2

Estimated annual mortality rate per 100,000 women from myocardial infarction by use of oral contraceptives, smoking habits, and age (in years):

	Myocardial infarction			
	Women aged 30-39		Women aged 40-44	
Smoking habits	Users	Non Users	Users	Non Users
All smokers	10.2	2.6	62.0	15.9
Heavy[1]	13.0	5.1	78.7	31.3
Light	4.7	.9	28.6	5.7
Nonsmokers	1.8	1.2	10.7	7.4
Smokers and nonsmokers	5.4	1.9	32.8	11.7

[1]Heavy smoker: 15 or more cigarettes per day. From Jain AK; Studies in Family Planning, 8:50, 1977.

Figure 1. Estimated annual number of deaths associated with control of fertility and no control per 100,000 nonsterile women, by regimen of control and age of woman.

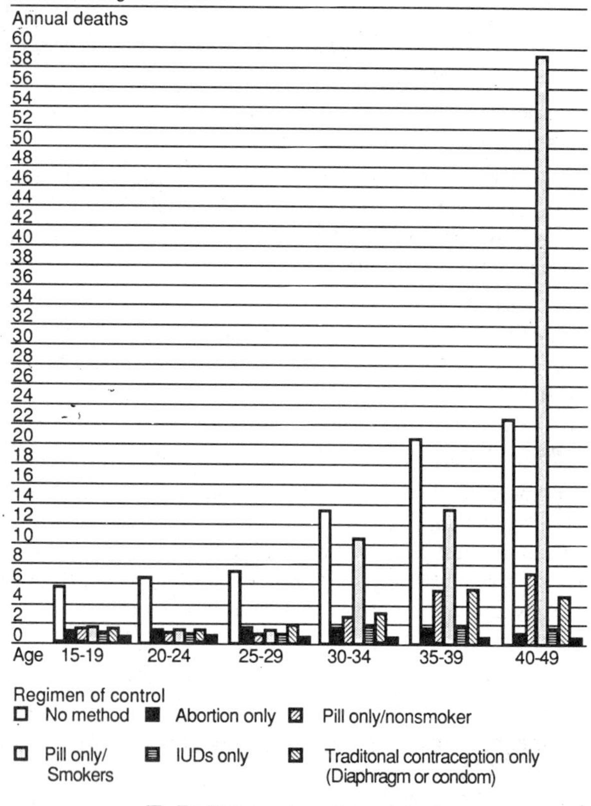

[E7582]

Recent Detailed Patient Labeling sheets for Ortho–Novum and other birth control pills summarize some of the information in Tables 2 and 3, above, and reproduce the bar graph in Figure 1. With respect to the increased risk of stroke, the patient information sheets state that "it has been estimated that women taking oral contraceptives are twice as likely as nonusers to have a stroke due to rupture of a blood vessel in the brain." Tables 2 and 3 are provided in the more detailed (and more technical) physician labeling that is included on the same sheet as the patient labeling that accompanies some birth control pills, but not Ortho-Novum.

Why does the FDA require that users be directly alerted to the dangers of oral contraceptives but not to those of other drugs, say, minor tranquilizers? Are the risks, usage patterns, public knowledge, or ability of the physician to supervise use significantly different in the two cases?

Why not require user information on *all* prescription drugs? Would such labeling make prescription drugs safer? More dangerous? Would people as readily follow their doctor's orders if they had routine access to information on the dangers associated with their prescription drugs? More readily? Are there other issues than safety involved? One may question whether the government should require—or even permit—that health information on the most serious risks be monopolized by the physicians. Just what is the proper role of government regulation in this area? See generally Gardner, Increasing Patient Awareness in Drug Therapy: Ramifications of a Patient Package Insert Requirement, 66 Geo.L.J. 837 (1978).

C. **Violation of regulation.** In many jurisdictions, violation of a state safety statute or regulatory provision may be negligence per se. See, e.g., Palmer v. A.H. Robins Co., Inc., 684 P.2d 187 (Colo.1984) (manufacturer of Dalkon Shield IUD negligent per se for advertising product as "safe" in violation of misbranding prohibition of state food and drug act); Stanton v. Astra Pharmaceutical Products, Inc., 718 F.2d 553 (3d Cir.1983) (Pa. law) (manufacturer of Xylocaine anesthetic negligent per se for failing to file adverse reaction reports required by FDA regulation; violation also rendered drug defective under § 402A, since FDA was unable to assure that warnings of adverse reactions were disseminated to doctors); Lukaszewicz v. Ortho Pharmaceutical Corp., 510 F.Supp. 961 (E.D.Wis.1981) (manufacturer of Ortho-Novum birth control pills negligent per se, and liable under § 402A, for failure to warn user directly of side effects pursuant to FDA regulation, 21 CFR § 310.501).

Whether a private right of action is expressly or impliedly created under a particular federal statute is another matter, dependent on the language of the statute and the intent of Congress. See, e.g., Sparks v. Metalcraft, Inc., 408 N.W.2d 347 (Iowa 1987) (no express or implied cause of action, for neurological damage from exposure to toxic solvents, under federal Hazardous Substances Act). Compare Swenson v. Emerson Electric Co., 374 N.W.2d 690 (Minn.1985), cert. denied, 476 U.S. 1130, 106 S.Ct. 1998, 90 L.Ed.2d 678 (1986) (private cause of action for violation of CPSC's substantial product hazard reporting regulations), with Drake v. Honeywell, Inc., 797 F.2d 603 (8th Cir.1986) (contra). See generally Comment, Private Causes of Action Under the Reporting Rules of the Consumer Product Safety Act, 70 Minn.L.Rev. 955 (1986).

D. **Compliance with regulation.** Reasoning that governmental safety requirements are generally set at minimum levels, the great majority of courts have agreed with *MacDonald* that providing such a mandated warning is evidence of due care and nondefectiveness but is not conclusive of either issue. After considering all the evidence, the jury is still free to find the manufacturer negligent or the warning "defective." See, e.g., Stevens v. Parke, Davis & Co., 9 Cal.3d 51, 65, 107 Cal.Rptr. 45, 53, 507 P.2d 653, 661 (1973) (FDA); Burch v. Amsterdam Corp., 366 A.2d 1079 (D.C.Ct.App.1976) (Federal Hazardous Substances Act); Ferebee v. Chevron Chemical Co., 736 F.2d 1529 (D.C.Cir.1984) (EPA-approved label for paraquat herbicide, under Federal Insecticide, Fungicide, and Rodenticide Act).

In recent years, manufacturers have increasingly been arguing that certain federal labeling requirements preempt state tort law. While the preemption argument has been rejected by many courts in many contexts, e.g., *Ferebee,* supra; Abbot v. American Cyanamid Co., 844 F.2d 1108, 1112 n. 1 (4th Cir.1988) (FDA-approved labeling of DPT vaccine: "The overwhelming majority of courts considering federal preemption of state law as regards vaccines have found no preemption."), some recent decisions have found preemption in certain contexts. E.g., Moore v. Kimberly–Clark Corp., 676 F.Supp. 731 (W.D.La.1987) (FDA-mandated tampon warning of TSS); Cipollone v. Liggett Group, Inc., 789 F.2d 181 (3d Cir.1986) (cigarette hazards labeling statute). The complex preemption issue is addressed further in Chapter 10, § 1, below.

Some jurisdictions have enacted legislation on point. See, e.g., Colo.Rev. Stat. § 13–21–403, and Utah Code Ann. § 78–15–16(3), which create a *presumption* of non-defectiveness and non-negligence if the product complies with applicable governmental standards. (The Colorado statute creates a converse presumption for noncompliance). Which is the better approach? Of what relevance is the fact that some regulatory agencies, the federal Consumer Product Safety Commission being a prime example, solicit proposals for standards from private industry and sometimes use these proposals as the basis for the standards promulgated?

E. **Other agencies.** As seen above, agencies other than the FDA require warnings of product hazards in various contexts. The Consumer Product Safety Commission is authorized to promulgate product safety standards requiring products to be accompanied by "clear and adequate" warnings. See 15 U.S.C.A. § 2056. An instructive case brought by a manufacturer against the Commission challenging a proposed warnings requirement was Aqua Slide 'N' Dive Corp. v. Consumer Product Safety Comm., 569 F.2d 831 (5th Cir.1978). In 1973, the Commission was petitioned by industry representatives to establish a safety standard for swimming pool slides. In January of 1976, the Commission proposed such a standard, citing the fact that adult users of swimming pool slides who slide headfirst into the water encounter a one in 10 million risk of spinal injury and paralysis as a result of striking the bottom of the pool. The proposed standard required that such slides be installed in water greater than four feet in depth and that various warning signs be provided. Because use of the slides in deeper water gave rise to a risk of drowning, the standard also prescribed that ladder chains be installed on such slides, together with an appropriate warning sign concerning the risk of drowning, to discourage use by smaller children. The warnings proposed in the standard provided in part as follows:

FIG U
SIGN ON TRANSOM FOR SLIDES PLACED IN WATER LESS THAN 4 FT DEEP

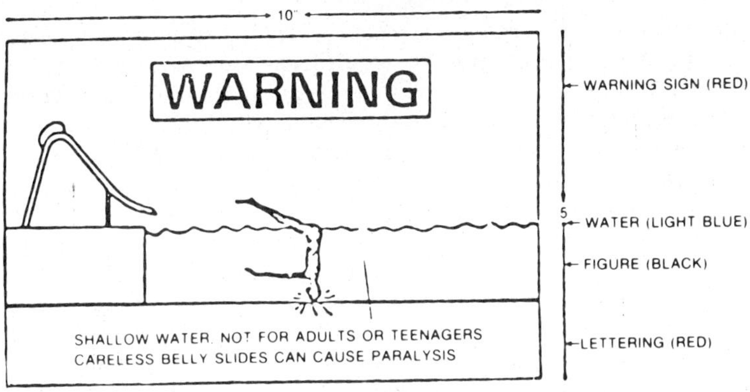

FIG V
SIGN ON TRANSOM FOR SLIDES PLACED IN 4 FT OF WATER OR DEEPER

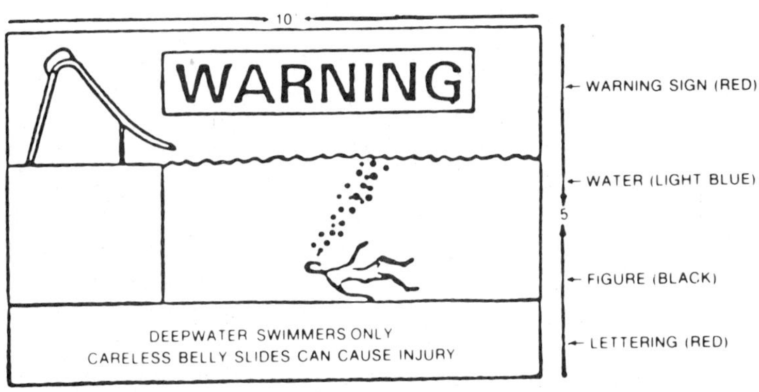

Subsequent to the promulgation of this safety standard, Aqua Slide 'N' Dive Corporation, manufacturer of 95% of the 350,000 swimming pool slides then in use in the United States, challenged the standards in court. Arguing that the Commission had failed to show that the standard was "reasonably necessary to eliminate or reduce an unreasonable risk of injury," as required by § 2058(c)(2), Aqua Slide alleged that neither the warning signs nor the ladder chain had been adequately tested for effectiveness and that the warnings themselves were so explicit as to deter people unnecessarily from using the slide. Despite the fact that the risk of injury was remote (there being a greater risk of being struck and killed by lightning), the seriousness of the injuries in such accidents led the court to conclude that some kind of safety standard for swimming pool slides might be "reasonably necessary." However, since the Commission had failed to produce "substantial evidence" demonstrating the effectiveness of the warnings proposed, the court concluded that they were not justified.

Specific Commission shortcomings included its failure to explain adequately why warnings were chosen over public education campaigns, its failure to extend the warning requirements to slides already in use, and its failure to conduct any meaningful tests to show that the warnings would be effective. The Court also agreed with Aqua Slide that the warnings may have been unnecessarily explicit since they failed to convey the fact that paralysis was only a one in 10 million risk and since there had been no tests to determine whether the warnings would needlessly deter slide use.

The one aspect of the safety standard which most clearly promised to reduce the risk of spinal injury was the requirement that large slides be placed for use in deep water. Unfortunately, this magnified the risk of drowning for small children and created a new safety problem. To counter this danger, the Commission developed the ladder chain requirement. The sign warning of the risk of drowning had never been tested for effectiveness although the ladder chain had been subjected to a limited "evaluation" by one of the Commission's consultants who "tried one out on his neighbors' children at a pool in his own back yard." The court held that such testing failed to produce any meaningful results and was "not the stuff of which substantial evidence is made." Reasoning that the Commission had failed to evaluate adequately the effect of the standard on the utility, cost and availability of the product (in addition to the effectiveness of the standard in reducing risks of injury), the court concluded that the proposed warnings and ladder chain requirements had to be set aside.

SECTION 5. LIMITATIONS ON DEFECTIVENESS

The inquiry to this point has centered on the factors and rationales used to support a determination that an injury-producing product should be declared legally defective. In this section, the focus shifts back in the other direction to a variety of issues arguing *against* a determination of defectiveness. Thus, while the underlying issues—of manufacturer accountability, feasibility, economic efficiency, consumer autonomy, and individual responsibility—remain largely the same, the cases collected here look past the questions of when and why liability may be in order to the knotty questions of when and why manufacturer liability for product-caused harm may *not* be appropriate.

A. OBVIOUS DANGERS

> [W]e hardly believe it is anymore necessary to tell an experienced factory worker that he should not put his hand into a machine that is at that moment breaking glass than it would be necessary to tell a zookeeper to keep his head out of a hippopotamus' mouth.

Bartkewich v. Billinger, 432 Pa. 351, 356, 247 A.2d 603, 606 (1968).

Many products liability cases involve dangers that are hidden or "latent." Reconsider Matthews v. Lawnlite Co., supra page 266. While shopping for outdoor furniture, the plaintiff sat in the defendant's aluminum lounge chair and placed his hand on the arm rest, extending his fingers around and underneath it. "[W]ith the ease that one clips a choice flower with pruning shears," the moving metal parts hidden under the rest amputated his finger. Emphasizing the unexpected nature of the danger, and indicating that a simple and inexpensive housing over the moving parts would have prevented the accident, the court held that the manufacturer should be responsible.

Consider whether the balance of social goals listed above might have altered the result if the plaintiff had known of the shearing action of the moving parts that lurked beneath the arm rest, or if the moving parts had been on top of the arm rest and hence open, "patent," and obvious to view. This section examines the effect of these factors on the issues of the manufacturer's duty and breach thereof. Their effect on the issues of causation and affirmative defenses is examined in Chapters 4 and 5, below.

CAMPO v. SCOFIELD

Court of Appeals of New York, 1950.
301 N.Y. 468, 95 N.E.2d 802.

FULD, JUDGE.

Plaintiff, working on his son's farm, was [dumping a crate of] onions into an "onion topping" machine, when his hands became caught in its revolving steel rollers and were [so] badly injured [that they required amputation]. He brought suit against defendants, manufacturers of the machine, alleging that they had been negligent in failing to equip it with a guard or stopping device. * * *

[The trial court denied the defendants' motion to dismiss, the Appellate Division reversed, and the plaintiff appealed. *Held,* plaintiff's failure to allege that the danger was latent or unknown was fatal to the complaint.]

If a manufacturer does everything necessary to make the machine function properly for the purpose for which it is designed, if the machine is without any latent defect, and if its functioning creates no danger or peril that is not known to the user, then the manufacturer has satisfied the law's demands. We have not yet reached the state where a manufacturer is under the duty of making a machine accident proof or foolproof. Just as the manufacturer is under no obligation, in order to guard against injury resulting from deterioration, to furnish a machine that will not wear out, [citation], so he is under no duty to guard against injury from a patent peril or from a source manifestly dangerous. To illustrate, the manufacturer who makes, properly and free of defects, an axe or a buzz saw or an airplane with an exposed propeller, is not to be held liable if one using the axe or the buzz saw is cut by it, or if someone working around the airplane comes in contact with the propeller. In such cases, the manufacturer has the right to expect that such persons will do everything necessary to avoid such contact, for the very nature of the article gives notice and warning of the consequences to be expected, of the injuries to be suffered. In other words, the manufacturer is under no duty to render a machine or other article "more" safe—as long as the danger to be avoided is obvious and patent to all.

[Affirmed; complaint dismissed.]

MICALLEF v. MIEHLE CO.

Court of Appeals of New York, 1976.
39 N.Y.2d 376, 384 N.Y.S.2d 115, 348 N.E.2d 571.

COOKE, JUDGE. The time has come to depart from the patent danger rule enunciated in Campo v. Scofield, 301 N.Y. 468, 95 N.E.2d 802.

This action was initiated to recover damages for personal injuries, allegedly resulting from negligent design and breach of an implied warranty. Paul Micallef, plaintiff, was employed by Lincoln Graphic Arts at its Farmingdale plant as a printing-press operator. For eight months he had been assigned to operate a photo-offset press, model RU 1, manufactured and sold by defendant Miehle–Gross Dexter, Inc., to his employer. The machine was 150 feet long, 15 feet high and 5 feet wide and was capable of printing at least 20,000 sheets an hour. Then, while working on January 22, 1969, plaintiff discovered that a foreign object had made its way onto the plate of the unit. Such a substance, known to the trade as a "hickie", causes a blemish or imperfection on the printed pages. Plaintiff informed his superior of the problem and told him he was going to "chase the hickie" whereupon the foreman warned him to be careful. "Chasing a hickie" consisted of applying, very lightly, a piece of plastic about eight inches wide to the printing plate, which is wrapped around a circular plate cylinder which spins at high speed. The revolving action of the plate against the plastic removes the "hickie". Unsuccessful in his first removal attempt, plaintiff started anew but this time the plastic was drawn into the nip point between the plate cylinder and an ink-form roller along with his hand. The machine had no safety guards to prevent such occurrence. Plaintiff testified that while his hand was trapped he reached for a shut-off button but couldn't contact it because of its location.

Plaintiff was aware of the danger of getting caught in the press in "chasing hickies." However, it was the custom and usage in the industry to "chase hickies on the run", because once the machine was stopped, it required at least three hours to resume printing and, in such event, the financial advantage of the high speed machine would be lessened. Although it was possible to have "chased the hickie" from another side of the machine, such approach would have caused plaintiff to be in a leaning position and would have increased the chances of scratching the plate. Through its representatives and engineers, defendant had observed the machine in operation and was cognizant of the manner in which "hickies were chased" by Lincoln's employees.

Samuel Aidlin, a professional engineer, had inspected the machine subsequent to the mishap. In his opinion, based upon the custom in the printing industry, it would have been good custom and practice to have placed guards near the rollers where plaintiff's hand entered the machine, the danger of human contact being well known. Moreover, he testified that at least three different types of guards were available, two for over 30 years, that they would not have impeded the practice of "chasing hickies," and that these guards would have protected an employee from exposure to the risk. * * *

[A jury verdict for the plaintiff was reversed by the Appellate Division, relying in part on Campo v. Scofield. This appeal followed.]

Directing our attention to the cause of action for negligence in design, defendant asserts, citing Campo v. Scofield (supra), that the action must be dismissed because the danger created by the absence of safeguards on the machine was open and obvious and, therefore, as the manufacturer it was under no duty to protect plaintiff from such a patent defect. * * *

The requirement that a latent defect be proved, before there could be a recovery against a manufacturer in a negligence action, has retained its vitality [citations]. The underlying rationale of the court's decision in *Campo* apparently is founded on the notion that it should be the task of the Legislature, not the judiciary, to compel manufacturers to install possible safety devices (Campo v. Scofield, supra, 301 N.Y. p. 472, 95 N.E.2d p. 804; see Marschall, An Obvious Wrong Does Not Make a Right: Manufacturers' Liability For Patently Dangerous Products, 48 N.Y.U.L.Rev. 1065, 1081). *Campo* has been the subject of sustained attack [citations]. The major thrust of criticism stems from the belief that, in our highly complex and technological society, we fall victim to the manufacturer who holds himself out as an expert in his field. It is argued that the *Campo* doctrine is "a vestigial carryover from pre-*MacPherson* [1] days when deceit was needed for recovery" (2 Harper & James, Torts, § 28.5).

More specifically, it is contended that the application of *Campo* amounts to an assumption of risk defense as a matter of law "with the added disadvantage that the defendant was relieved of the burden of proving that plaintiff had subjectively appreciated a known risk" (Rheingold, Expanding Liability of the Product Supplier: A Primer, 2 Hofstra L.Rev. 521, 541). *Campo* is viewed as inconsistent because, on the one hand, it places a duty on the manufacturer to develop a reasonably safe product yet eliminates this duty, thereby granting him immunity from answering in damages, if the dangerous character of the product can be readily seen, irrespective of whether the injured user or consumer actually perceived the danger. As Professors Harper and James succinctly assert: "The bottom does not logically drop out of a negligence case against the maker when it is shown that the purchaser knew of the dangerous condition. Thus if the product is a carrot-topping machine with exposed moving parts or an electric clothes wringer dangerous to the limbs of the operator, and if it would be

1. (MacPherson v. Buick Motor Co., 217 N.Y. 382, 111 N.E. 1050.)

feasible for the maker of the product to install a guard or safety release, it should be a question for the jury whether reasonable care demanded such a precaution, though its absence is obvious. Surely reasonable men might find here a great danger, even to one who knew the condition; and since it was so readily avoidable they might find the maker negligent". (2 Harper & James, Torts, § 28.5.)

Other jurisdictions have taken a more liberal position. For example, in Palmer v. Massey–Ferguson, 3 Wash.App. 508, 476 P.2d 713 [citation], the plaintiff brought an action against the manufacturer of a hay baler for injuries sustained while adjusting a drawbar. In response to the defendant's allegations that the patent peril precluded liability, the court said (p. 517, 476 P.2d p. 719): "The manufacturer of the obviously defective product ought not to escape because the product was obviously a bad one. The law, we think, ought to discourage misdesign rather than encouraging it in its obvious form." (See, also, Pike v. Hough Co., 2 Cal.3d 465, 85 Cal.Rptr. 629, 467 P.2d 229, supra; Byrnes v. Economic Mach. Co., 41 Mich.App. 192, 200 N.W.2d 104.) * * * We find the reasoning of these cases persuasive. *Campo* suffers from its rigidity in precluding recovery whenever it is demonstrated that the defect was patent. Its unwavering view produces harsh results in view of the difficulties in our mechanized way of life to fully perceive the scope of danger, which may ultimately be found by a court to be apparent in manufactured goods as a matter of law. * * * Apace with advanced technology, a relaxation of the *Campo* stringency is advisable. A casting of increased responsibility upon the manufacturer, who stands in a superior position to recognize and cure defects, for improper conduct in the placement of finished products into the channels of commerce furthers the public interest. To this end, we hold that a manufacturer is obligated to exercise that degree of care in his plan or design so as to avoid any unreasonable risk of harm to anyone who is likely to be exposed to the danger when the product is used in the manner for which the product was intended [citations] as well as an unintended yet reasonably foreseeable use [citations].

What constitutes "reasonable care" will, of course, vary with the surrounding circumstances and will involve "a balancing of the likelihood of harm, and the gravity of harm if it happens, against the burden of the precaution which would be effective to avoid the harm" [citations]. * * * ["]If the product would be unworkable when the alleged missing feature was added, or would be so expensive as to be priced out of the market, that would be relevant defensive matter" (Rheingold, Expanding Liability of the Product Supplier: A Primer, 2 Hofstra L.Rev. 521, 537); [citations]. In this case, there was no evidence submitted at trial to show the cost of guards that could have been attached in relation to the entire cost of the machine.

* * *

We next examine the duty owing from a plaintiff or, in other words, the conduct on a plaintiff's part which will bar recovery from a manufacturer. As now enunciated, the patent-danger doctrine should not, in and of itself, prevent a plaintiff from establishing his case. That does not mean, however, that the obviousness of the danger as a factor in the ultimate injury is thereby eliminated, for it must be remembered that in actions for negligent design, the ordinary rules of negligence apply [citations]. * * * Rather, the openness and obviousness of the danger should be available to the defendant on the issue of whether plaintiff exercised that degree of reasonable care as was required under the circumstances.

* * *

[Appellate Division order reversed; new trial granted.]

NOTES

1. The *Campo* obvious danger rule had been one of the most firmly entrenched doctrines in products liability law. One court, for example, while recognizing that the rule had been criticized as a vestigial carryover from pre-*MacPherson* days, nevertheless opted to align itself with other "vestigial jurisdictions in adhering to the distinction." Blankenship v. Morrison Machine Co., 255 Md. 241, 257 A.2d 430 (1969). See also Bartkewich v. Billenger, 432 Pa. 351, 247 A.2d 603 (1968) (no duty to supply guards or to locate emergency cut-off switches strategically around glass-breaking machine for benefit of worker whose hand was crushed when he reached in to free a piece of glass that was jamming and thought to be damaging the machine: "If he thought the machine was being damaged, what did he think would happen to his hand?").

The rule still obtains in some jurisdictions. See, e.g., Estrada v. Schmutz Mfg. Co., Inc., 734 F.2d 1218, 1220 (7th Cir.1984) (Ind. law) (Posner, J.) (factory worker's hand caught while brushing ink on rollers: if you "go to the zoo and put your hand through the lion's cage, and the lion bites your hand off, * * * you do not have an action against the zoo"); Gray v. Manitowoc Co., Inc., 771 F.2d 866 (5th Cir.1985) (Miss. law) (construction worker struck by boom of crane whose operator had blind spot that was common knowledge in industry); Branton v. Draper Corp., 185 Ga.App. 820, 366 S.E.2d 206 (1988) (weaver dragged into machinery when apron caught on exposed flywheel of loom).

2. The *Micallef* approach had been adopted earlier by some courts. E.g., Pike v. Frank G. Hough Co., 2 Cal.3d 465, 85 Cal.Rptr. 629, 467 P.2d 229 (1970) (obviousness of absence of rear-view mirrors and blind spot behind earthmoving machine relevant largely to defense of assumption of risk). Its approach has been enthusiastically endorsed in a good number of subsequent decisions. See, e.g., Holm v. Sponco Mfg., Inc., 324 N.W.2d 207 (Minn.1982); Owens v. Allis–Chalmers Corp., 414 Mich. 413, 326 N.W.2d 372 (1982). "The patent danger rule encourages manufacturers to be outrageous in their design, to eliminate safety devices, and to make hazards obvious. For example, if the cage which is placed on an electric fan as a safety device were left off and someone put his hand in the fan, under this doctrine there would be no duty on the manufacturer as a matter of law." Auburn Machine Works Co., Inc. v. Jones, 366 So.2d 1167, 1170 (Fla.1979).

3. If a manufacturer fully and fairly warns the consumer of all latent hazards, should the risk of injury shift to the consumer such that the manufacturer is absolved of any duty to design out the hazards? See comment *j* to Rest. (2d) of Torts § 402A:

> Where warning is given, the seller may reasonably assume that it will be read and heeded; and a product bearing such a warning, which is

safe for use if it is followed, is not in [a] defective condition, nor is it unreasonably dangerous.

Compare Uloth v. City Tank Corp., 376 Mass. 874, 384 N.E.2d 1188, 1192 (1978) (garbageman's foot slipped into compaction area and severed by descending packer blade):

> An adequate warning may reduce the likelihood of injury to the user of a product in some cases. We decline, however, to adopt any rule which permits a manufacturer or designer to discharge its total responsibility to workers by simply warning of the dangers of a product. Whether or not adequate warnings are given is a factor to be considered on the issue of negligence, but warnings cannot absolve the manufacturer or designer of all responsibility for the safety of the product. [I]n some circumstances a warning may not reduce the likelihood of injury. For example, where the danger is obvious, a warning may be superfluous. A designer may have no duty to warn of such dangers. [Citations.]
>
> Moreover, a user may not have a real alternative to using a dangerous product, as where a worker must either work on a dangerous machine or leave his job. [Citations.] Further, a warning is not effective in eliminating injuries due to instinctual reactions, momentary inadvertence, or forgetfulness on the part of a worker. One of the primary purposes of safety devices is to guard against such foreseeable situations. [Citation.]
>
> Balanced against the somewhat limited effectiveness of warnings is the designer's ability to anticipate and protect against possible injuries. If a slight change in design would prevent serious, perhaps fatal, injury, the designer may not avoid liability by simply warning of the possible injury. We think that in such a case the burden to prevent needless injury is best placed on the designer or manufacturer rather than on the individual user of a product. * * * Micallef v. Miehle Co., 39 N.Y.2d 376, 385, 384 N.Y.S.2d 115, 121, 348 N.E.2d 571, 577 (1976). [Citations.]

BELLING v. HAUGH'S POOLS, LTD.

Supreme Court of New York, Appellate Division, 1987.
126 A.D.2d 958, 511 N.Y.S.2d 732.

MEMORANDUM:

Plaintiff sustained serious injuries when he dove through an inner tube floating in the four-foot, above-ground swimming pool in a friend's yard. Plaintiff, who was 33 years old, 6 feet, 1 inch tall and 215 pounds at the time, was an experienced swimmer and familiar with above-ground pools including the pool in question, having been swimming in it for several hours on the day the accident occurred. Indeed, he had assisted the owner of the pool in its installation. He commenced this action on several theories of liability, principally products liability, claiming that defendants as the manufacturer and retailer failed to give adequate warnings of the dangers inherent in diving into a four-foot pool. Defendants moved for summary judgment * * *. The court denied the motion.

A manufacturer will be held liable under a theory of strict products liability where the product is defective and the defect may include a mistake in manufacturing, an improper design or the absence or inadequacy of warnings [citations]. Plaintiff must establish, of course, that the failure to warn was a proximate cause of the injury, i.e., "a substantial cause of the events which produced the injury" (Derdiarian v. Felix Contr. Corp., 51 N.Y.2d 308, 315, 434 N.Y.S.2d 166, 414 N.E.2d 666). Accordingly, there is no liability for failing to warn of obvious dangers, those that would be appreciated by the user to the same extent the warning would have provided (Prosser & Keeton on Torts [5th ed.], p. 686; [citations]).

Other jurisdictions have addressed the proximate cause issue raised herein and have concluded that the manufacturer cannot be liable because "a warning would have merely informed him [plaintiff] of risks of which he was already aware" ([citations]; see generally, Anno. 6 A.L.R. 4th 492).

Although proximate cause is usually a question for the jury, where only one conclusion may be drawn from established facts, "the question of legal cause may be decided as a matter of law" (Derdiarian v. Felix Contr. Co., 51 N.Y.2d 308, 315, 434 N.Y.S.2d 166, 414 N.E.2d 666). This is such a case.

[Order reversed; defendants' summary judgment motions granted.]

GREEN, J., dissenting:

I must dissent. I cannot conclude, as a matter of law, that defendants had no duty to warn, or that defendants' negligence was not a proximate cause of plaintiff's serious injuries. At the outset it is important to recall that "[t]he failure to warn is essentially a case of negligence and the drastic remedy of summary judgment is rarely granted since the very question of whether a defendant's conduct amounts to negligence is inherently a question for the trier of fact in all but the most egregious instances" [citations].

Defendants maintain that they had no duty to warn plaintiff of the dangers in diving off a deck or ladder into the pool because the dangers are obvious. The obviousness of a danger or the discoverability of it upon inspection, however, does not militate against a duty to warn, but rather is one of many factors for the jury to take into account in assessing comparative fault (see, Micallef v. Miehle Co., 39 N.Y.2d 376, 387, 384 N.Y.S.2d 115, 348 N.E.2d 571; New York Pattern Jury Instructions, Vol I, 2:135; [citations]).

"[T]he imposition of the duty to give a warning of some kind involves a balancing test which weighs the seriousness of potential harm to the consumer against the costs to the manufacturer. Since the cost of providing warnings is often minimal, the balance usually weighs in favor of an obligation to warn" (Cooley v. Carter–Wallace, Inc., supra, 102 A.D.2d at p. 644, 478 N.Y.S.2d 375).

This record reveals that defendants knew, or should have known, that similar dives into similar pools had resulted in over 100 quadriplegic injuries per year during the past ten years. Plaintiff's claim is that had defendants adequately warned him of this danger, he would not have taken the dive into the pool. Plaintiff established that it was foreseeable to defendants that people will dive from decks and ladders into the pool. Indeed, the owner's manual, under the heading "Safety Hints for Pool Owners", cautions that the pool "contains large quantities of water, however, and is deep enough to present inherent dangers to life and health unless the following safety rules are strictly observed." One such rule is "Do not dive or permit diving or jumping into the pool from the deck or pool rail. Serious injuries can be caused by failure to strictly follow this rule." Moreover, plaintiff established that the defendant manufacturer provided small warning decals to the pool owner to be attached in an "appropriate place." There is then a question of fact precluding summary judgment whether the warnings given were adequate, giving due consideration to the fact that plaintiff was a non-owner of the pool who could not be expected to read the owner's manual before using the pool [citations]. Assuming defendants breached their duty to warn, there also is an issue of fact whether defendants' negligence was the proximate cause of plaintiff's injuries. * * *

* * *

NOTES

1. Compare Smith v. Hub Mfg., Inc., 634 F.Supp. 1505 (N.D.N.Y.1986). While at a party, plaintiffs' 4–year–old son climbed up the ladder of an above-ground pool, fell in, lost consciousness, and died two years later. In an action against the manufacturers of the pool and the ladder, the defendants moved for summary judgment. *Held,* the defective design claim could go to the jury because of testimony by plaintiffs' expert "that other swimming pools have ladders that are more effective in preventing pool accidents." Summary judgment was ordered, however, on the failure-to-warn claim:

> [T]here is no duty to warn if the plaintiff knows of the danger or if the danger is well known and should be obvious to anyone. [Citations.] In such situations a warning would be superfluous. Moreover, the elements of a tort claim would not be satisfied in such situations because no plaintiff could establish that the failure to warn caused harm. Whether the danger of a product is obvious is a question for the court. [Citation.]
>
> The danger of swimming pools to small children is obvious and well known. Everyone should know that an accident like the one in this case is liable to happen if a child is left alone near a pool for even a short time. If some pools have ladders that prevent access by small children, such ladders are uncommon enough that parents should assume that a pool is dangerous unless they are told otherwise or find out otherwise by inspection.
>
> In addition, the plaintiffs in this case had personal knowledge of the danger of the pool to their son. First, on their way to the party

they told him that he was not allowed near the pool without an adult. They repeated this warning at the party. See Deposition of G. Smith, Aug. 16, 1984, pp. 47–48. Second, before the accident, Mr. Smith climbed up to the pool with Adam on the Lincoln ladder, and Mr. and Mrs. Smith saw Adam climbing on the ladder alone. See id. at 56, 62–64, 66–67; Deposition of L. Smith, Aug. 16, 1984, p. 128. Because the Smiths knew of this way of climbing to the pool, even if Hub or Lincoln breached a duty to warn of the dangers of their products to small children, such a breach would not make them liable for the accident.

2. Compare also Corbin v. Coleco Industries, 748 F.2d 411 (7th Cir.1984). The 27–year–old plaintiff jumped up onto the flat, 6–inch rim surrounding the top edge of his above-ground pool, "balanced himself, and dove in. He intended to do a 'belly flopper,' but for some reason his waist bent in mid-air and he entered the water head first. He hit his head on the bottom and suffered a fracture dislocation at vertebras C–5 and C–6. From that moment on, he has been quadriplegic."

The plaintiff's negligence and strict liability claims against the manufacturer, Coleco, were dismissed by the trial court, which ruled that "it was obviously dangerous for a six-foot man to dive into four feet of water, and that Corbin knew it. The court held additionally that Coleco had no duty to warn of open and obvious dangers and that a product is not defectively designed when its dangerous properties are patent. The district court found that the cause of Corbin's injuries was his own error of judgment in executing a shallow dive." Plaintiff appealed, claiming that there were disputed questions of fact on whether the risk of diving was latent or patent, whether Corbin in fact knew of the risk, and on the contemplations of an ordinary consumer toward the risk. *Held,* reversed and remanded:

> Corbin's expert, Gene D. Litwin, testified in his deposition * * * that even though people are generally aware of the danger of diving into shallow water, they believe that there is a safe way to do it, namely, by executing a flat, shallow dive. If people do in fact generally hold such a belief, then it cannot be said, as a matter of law, that the risk of spinal injury from diving into shallow water is open and obvious. Whether a danger is open and obvious depends not just on what people can see with their eyes but also on what they know and believe about what they see. In particular, if people generally believe that there is a danger associated with the use of a product, but that there is a safe way to use it, any danger there may be in using the product in the way generally believed to be safe is not open and obvious.
>
> * * *
>
> The district court also held (implicitly) that the absence of a warning was not a proximate cause of Corbin's injury, because he already knew of the danger. The rationale for this conclusion is apparently that one who already knows of a danger would not be informed or deterred by a warning, and so the absence of a warning could not be the cause of the subsequent injury. * * * Corbin testified in his deposition as follows:
>
> Q. Were you aware of the depth of the pool when you dove in?
>
> A. Yes.

> Q. Did it ever cross your mind that it might be too shallow to dive?
>
> A. I would say yes.
>
> Q. What did you think? I mean, how did this cross your mind? What went through your mind at the time?
>
> A. The time I did it?
>
> Q. Well, at the time it crossed your mind that it might be too shallow.
>
> A. Well, just I'm six foot tall and the water's four feet deep, you know. I guess an assumption that one would make, you know, you're deeper than the water is.

Corbin Deposition at 41–42. This testimony makes it clear that Corbin knew of some general danger in diving into shallow water. But it is inconclusive on the crucial points: whether he knew that he risked serious spinal cord injury, possibly resulting in paraplegia or quadriplegia, and whether he believed that it was safe to dive as long as the dive was flat and shallow.

Corbin's deposition also contains the following testimony:

> Q. At one point you stated that you jumped wrong.
>
> A. Yes.
>
> Q. What did you mean by that?
>
> A. Well, the intentions were to just kind of jump in and do a belly flopper, you know, just make a big splash and cool off and get back out of the pool, but for some unknown reason—nobody knows why, I don't know why—when I got in the air, I bent in the middle and went straight in the pool instead of on my stomach.
>
> A. So you didn't intend to jump the way you did?
>
> A. No. It was just something that did [sic] when it shouldn't have, I guess.

Corbin Deposition at 69–70. It is clear from this testimony that Corbin intended to do a flat and shallow dive—a "belly flopper." This clear intention, together with the Litwin testimony that people generally believe that flat, shallow dives into shallow water are safe, creates a genuine issue of material fact as to whether Corbin knew that he risked spinal injury by diving into shallow water, even if he attempted a flat, shallow dive. If he did not know this, then a conspicuous warning on the side of the pool could very well have deterred him from diving. Thus summary judgment for Coleco on the basis of Corbin's knowledge of the danger was inappropriate.

On the strict tort liability claim, the court reasoned as follows:

The district court found that Corbin's injuries were caused by his own error of judgment in executing a shallow dive that he knew to be dangerous, thus implicitly concluding as a matter of law that his injuries were not caused by a defect in the pool unreasonably dangerous to users. We think this was error, for there is evidence in the record that the pool was in a condition that made it exceptionally dangerous, well beyond what the ordinary user of swimming pools would contemplate and well beyond any danger that Corbin actually contemplated, and that this defect was the cause of Corbin's injury.

Corbin's theory is that the lip and sides of the pool are insufficiently rigid, so that a diver attempting a belly flopper from a standing position on the lip is thrown off balance and enters the water at a steeper angle than intended. The theory is supported in the record by the deposition testimony of Corbin's expert witness, Mr. Litwin:

> The lip is a sheet metal structure, and on the bottom side is supported by the vertical wall of the pool. Since the vertical wall of the pool is curved, the place where it intersects the underside of the lip varies as you move across the lip from one end of the lip to another. . . . The result of that is that the lip can be thought of as a teeter-totter, pivoting about the vertical wall with the pivot changing from place to place on the lip. The result of that not only is a wobble, but a wobble that changes according to where you happen to place your foot on the lip, and that will have the effect of increasing the difficulty in controlling the dive to someone that dives from the lip.

Litwin Deposition at 112. This testimony is sufficient to bar the district court from finding as a matter of law on the record before it that Corbin's pool was not in a defective condition unreasonably dangerous to the user or that such a condition did not cause Corbin's injury.

Nor did Indiana's *Campo*-type obvious danger rule bar recovery on the strict tort liability claim: "Even if it were open and obvious that there is some danger in diving into shallow water (a proposition put into question in the preceding section), we cannot say on this record as a matter of law that it was open and obvious that the lip of Corbin's pool wobbled or that a wobbly pool lip increases the danger of a dive from it."

LAAPERI v. SEARS, ROEBUCK & CO., INC.

United States Court of Appeals, First Circuit, 1986.
787 F.2d 726.

LEVIN H. CAMPBELL, CHIEF JUDGE.

[Plaintiff Laaperi purchased a Pittway smoke detector from Sears and installed it in the upstairs bedroom of his three sons. Several months later, an electrical cord in the boys' closet developed a short circuit that started a fire in which all three boys died. The smoke detector, attached to the same circuit that had the short, failed to sound an alarm because it was receiving no power when the fire began.]

[Claiming that he was unaware "that the very short circuit which might ignite a fire in his home could, at the same time, incapacitate the smoke detector," the plaintiff sued both Sears and Pittway for, among other things, negligent failure to warn. He contended that, had he known of the danger, he would have installed a battery-powered smoke detector as a back-up precaution or done something else to better protect his family. The jury returned verdicts for the plaintiff; the defendants' motions for summary judgment and j.n.o.v. were denied, and defendants appealed.]

Defendants contend that the district court * * * erred in denying their motions because, they claim, the danger that an electrical fire will incapacitate an electric-powered smoke detector is obvious. They point out that anyone purchasing a device powered by house electrical current will necessarily realize that if the current goes off for any reason, the device will not work.

In Massachusetts, as elsewhere, a failure to warn amounts to negligence only where the supplier of the good known to be dangerous for its intended use "has no reason to believe that those for whose use the chattel is supplied will realize its dangerous condition." Restatement (Second) of Torts § 388 (1965). [Citations.] Where the risks of the product are discernible by casual inspection, such as the danger that a knife can cut, or a stove burn, the consumer is in just as good a position as the manufacturer to gauge the dangers associated with the product, and nothing is gained by shifting to the manufacturer the duty to warn. Thus, a manufacturer is not required to warn that placing one's hand into the blades of a potato chopper will cause injury, Plante v. Hobart Corp., 771 F.2d 617 (1st Cir.1985), that permitting a three-year-old child to ride on the running board of a moving tractor risks injury to the child, Kerr v. Koemm, 557 F.Supp. 283 (S.D.N.Y.1983), or that firing a BB gun at another at close range can injure or kill, Sherk v. Daisy–Heddon, 498 Pa. 594, 450 A.2d 615 (1982). If a manufacturer had to warn consumers against every such obvious danger inherent in a product, "[t]he list of obvious practices warned against would be so long, it would fill a volume." Plante, 771 F.2d at 620.

Defendants ask us to declare that the risk that an electrical fire could incapacitate an AC-powered smoke detector is so obvious that the average consumer [3] would not benefit from a warning. This is not a

3. Defendants appear to claim that the obviousness standard should necessarily take into account the knowledge and experience of the individual consumer who is injured. The Massachusetts courts have made clear, however, that warnings are to be construed with the "average user" or "reasonably prudent person" in mind. MacDonald v. Ortho Pharmaceutical Corp., 394 Mass. 131, 475 N.E.2d 65, 71, cert. denied, ___ U.S. ___, 106 S.Ct. 250, 88 L.Ed.2d 258 (1985). See also Restatement (Second) of Torts § 388 comment a (1965). It is true that where a manufacturer reasonably expects only those with a certain degree of knowledge and expertise to come into contact with a product, the obviousness standard should be considered in light of the reasonable person with that knowledge or expertise. See, e.g., McIntyre v. Everest & Jennings, 575 F.2d 155 (8th Cir.), cert. denied, 439 U.S. 864, 99 S.Ct. 187, 58 L.Ed.2d 173 (1978) (risk of tipping in specially designed commode chair obvious to paraplegic); Martinez v. Dixie Carriers, Inc., 529 F.2d 457 (5th Cir. 1976) (dangers of chemical obvious to professional users to whom it is exclusively marketed); Restatement (Second) of Torts § 388 comment k (supplier must warn of product's dangers if there is "no reason to believe that those who will use it will have such special experience as will enable them to perceive the danger"). This rule is not relevant to the present case, however, for the smoke detector was marketed through Sears flyers and catalogs to individuals who could not be expected to have any particular expertise in electrical matters. The fact that Laaperi in fact had some such expertise was therefore purely fortuitous, and does not bear on the legal standard for obviousness.

trivial argument; in earlier—some might say sounder—days, we might have accepted it. Compare Jamieson v. Woodward & Lothrop, 247 F.2d 23 (D.C.Cir.1957). Our sense of the current state of the tort law in Massachusetts and most other jurisdictions, however, leads us to conclude that, today, the matter before us poses a jury question; that "obviousness" in a situation such as this would be treated by the Massachusetts courts as presenting a question of fact, not of law. To be sure, it would be obvious to anyone that an electrical outage would cause this smoke detector to fail. But the average purchaser might not comprehend the specific danger that a fire-causing electrical problem can simultaneously knock out the circuit into which a smoke detector is wired, causing the detector to fail at the very moment it is needed. Thus, while the failure of a detector to function as the result of an electrical malfunction due, say, to a broken power line or a neighborhood power outage would, we think, be obvious as a matter of law, the failure that occurred here, being associated with the very risk—fire—for which the device was purchased, was not, or so a jury could find.

Our conclusion finds support in a number of Massachusetts cases stating that a court should be extremely reluctant to take from the jury issues regarding the adequacy of warnings. The recent decision of the Massachusetts Supreme Judicial Court in MacDonald v. Ortho Pharmaceutical Corp., 394 Mass. 131, 475 N.E.2d 65, cert. denied, 474 U.S. 920, 106 S.Ct. 250, 88 L.Ed.2d 258 (1985) is instructive:

> The common law duty to warn . . . necessitates a warning "comprehensible to the average user and . . . convey[ing] a fair indication of the nature and extent of the danger to the mind of a reasonably prudent person." Whether a particular warning measures up to this standard is almost always an issue to be resolved by a jury; few questions are "more appropriately left to a common sense lay judgment than that of whether a written warning gets its message across to an average person." * * *

Id., 475 N.E.2d at 71 (citations omitted). Applying this standard, we think that the issue of obviousness to the average consumer of the danger of a fire-related power outage was one for the jury, not the court, to determine. In the present case, the jury was specifically instructed that if it found this danger to be obvious it should hold for defendants. It failed to do so.

B. *Causation*

While, as just discussed, the danger the detector would fail in these circumstances was not so obvious as to eliminate, as a matter of law, any need to warn, we must also consider whether Laaperi's specialized electrical knowledge constituted a bar to his own recovery. As pointed out in note 3, supra, plaintiff's specialized knowledge is immaterial to whether defendants had a duty to warn, since that duty is defined by the knowledge of the average purchaser. But plaintiff's expertise *is* relevant to whether defendants' failure to warn caused plaintiff's damages. Even though defendants may have been required to provide a warning, plaintiff may not recover if it can be shown that because of his above-average knowledge, he already appreciated the very danger the warning would have described. In such event there would be no connection between the negligent failure to warn and plaintiff's damages.

Defendants here presented considerable evidence suggesting that Laaperi, who was something of an electrical handyman, knew of the danger and still took no precautions. Laaperi, however, offered evidence that he did *not* know of the danger, and that he would have guarded against it had he been warned. The following exchange, between Laaperi and his counsel on direct examination, tends to support the jury's determination of liability:

> MR. SWARTZ: Sir, did you ever consider when purchasing this smoke detector that an electric outage would render it inoperable?
>
> THE WITNESS [LAAPERI]: I did not.
>
> Q: Did you ever consider or contemplate at any time installing a separate circuit for the smoke detector in and of itself?
>
> A: I did not.
>
> Q: Did you ever read the owner's manual?
>
> A: Yes, I did.
>
> Q: If the owner's manual had indicated to you to place this on a separate circuit, would you have done it?
>
> A: Yes, I would have.
>
> Q: Were you ever advised by any literature or any written instructions to purchase a back-up battery system?
>
> A: No.
>
> Q: If you were alerted to that, would you have done it?
>
> A: I think I would have, yes.
>
> Self-serving as this testimony was, the jury was free to credit it. * * * [W]e cannot say that the district court erred in denying defendants' motions for directed verdict and judgment n.o.v., for the jury could have believed Laaperi's testimony in the colloquy quoted above, among other evidence, and concluded that had he been properly warned, Laaperi would have instituted different fire detection methods in his home to protect his family against the danger that his smoke detector would be rendered useless in the event of a fire-related power outage.

* * *

[Affirmed.]

NOTES

1. A classic obvious danger warnings case is Jamieson v. Woodward & Lothrop, 247 F.2d 23 (D.C.Cir.), cert. denied, 355 U.S. 855, 78 S.Ct. 84, 2 L.Ed.2d 63 (1957) in which plaintiff was injured while lying on the floor when the defendant's rubber "Lithe–Line" exercise rope slipped off her feet and hit her in the eye. *Held* (5–4), summary judgment for defendants affirmed: "Surely every adult knows that, if an elastic band, whether it be an office rubber band or a rubber rope exerciser, is stretched and one's hold on it slips, the elastic snaps back. There was no duty on the manufacturer to warn of that simple fact." The dissenting judges thought that there was a jury issue on the obviousness of the danger, reasoning that "the resiliency of rubber generally may be assumed to be a fact known to all, but reasonable minds can differ as to whether the danger that lurks in this condition in performing the [Tummy Flattener] exercise recommended by the manufacturer here—a striking force which can hit the eye and detach a retina—was readily apparent to all users of the device."

2. The law on this point has remained largely unchanged, such that most courts hold that there simply is no duty to warn of obvious dangers. See, e.g., Van Dettum v. K–Mart Corp., 133 Ill.App.3d 861, 89 Ill.Dec. 98, 479 N.E.2d 1104 (1985) (elastic strap on automobile seat cover snapped back during installation, striking plaintiff in the eye); Emerick v. United States Suzuki Motor Corp., 750 F.2d 19 (3d Cir.1984) (riding motorcycle with kickstand down); Mach v. General Motors Corp., 112 Mich.App. 158, 315 N.W.2d 561 (1982) (jump-starting bulldozer while kneeling on its track); Kerr v. Koemm, 557 F.Supp. 283 (S.D.N.Y.1983) (riding 3–year–old child on running board of tractor over bumpy ground); Morgan v. Bethlehem Steel Corp., 135 Ill.App.3d 242, 90 Ill. Dec. 36, 481 N.E.2d 836 (1985) (driving into side of moving train; no duty to light or add reflectors to train cars); Dickens v. Avanti Research & Devel., Inc., 161 Ill.App.3d 565, 113 Ill.Dec. 399, 515 N.E.2d 208 (1987) (electrocution from CB antenna hitting power line); Complaint of Diehl, 610 F.Supp. 223 (D.Idaho 1985) (electrocution from sailboat mast hitting power line); Brown v. Sears, Roebuck & Co., 136 Ariz. 556, 667 P.2d 750 (App.1983) (electrocution from frayed extension cord); Plante v. Hobart Corp., 771 F.2d 617 (1st Cir.1985) (sticking hand in potato grinder); Kuras v. International Harvestor Co., 820 F.2d 15 (1st Cir.1987) (sticking hand under power lawn mower).

3. **Known Dangers.** The same is true, in many jurisdictions, with respect to dangers known to the user, whether obvious or not. See, e.g., Sprankle v. Bower Ammonia & Chem. Co., 824 F.2d 409 (5th Cir.1987) (hazards to worker's respiratory system from inhaling ammonia gas; plaintiff had earlier refused to clean storage tanks because of risk); Sherk v. Daisy–Heddon, 498 Pa. 594, 450 A.2d 615 (1982) (BB gun fired into friend's head at close range could kill); Garrett v. Nissen Corp., 84 N.M. 16, 498 P.2d 1359, 1364 (1972) (danger of falling off trampoline); Hagans v. Oliver Machinery Co., 576 F.2d 97 (5th Cir.1978) (danger of cutting knotted wood with power circular saw).

4. Compare Campos v. Firestone Tire & Rubber Co., 98 N.J. 198, 485 A.2d 305 (1984), where the court (a) rejected the no-duty-to-warn-of-obvious-dangers doctrine, holding that the obviousness of the hazard was only one factor in the liability analysis, and (b) held that the user's knowledge was relevant to whether the absence of an adequate warning was a cause in fact of the injury, but not to the duty to warn: "Since the duty is to place on the market a product free of defects, and this duty attaches at the time the product is

introduced into the stream of commerce, a particular user's subjective knowledge of a danger does not and cannot modify the manufacturer's duty." 485 A.2d at 311.

On the first aspect of *Campos,* very few courts have similarly applied the *Micallef* doctrine to the warnings context. Was *Campos* right on this point, or did it miss the mark?

Many courts agree with the second aspect of *Campos,* regarding the user's knowledge of the danger as relevant to cause in fact. Should the user's knowledge go to duty? To cause in fact? To proximate cause? To affirmative defenses, such as assumption of risk, based on the user's misconduct?

5. **Specificity of Risk.** Courts disagree on how specific the plaintiff's knowledge of the danger must be before his warnings claim is defeated, on whatever ground. Compare Tacke v. Vermeer Mfg. Co., ___ Mont. ___, 713 P.2d 527 (1986) (duty to warn of specific risk of getting caught in machine's rollers; worker's general knowledge that machines were dangerous insufficient), with Shaffer v. AMF, Inc., 842 F.2d 893 (6th Cir.1988) (since general dangers of motorcycle riding are open and obvious, no duty to warn of specific risks), and Lister v. Bill Kelley Athletic, Inc., 137 Ill.App.3d 829, 92 Ill.Dec. 672, 485 N.E.2d 483 (1985) (helmet manufacturer had no duty to warn football player of risk of broken neck and quadriplegia where coaches told him "not to use his head in making a tackle and that he could injure himself if he used the top of the helmet to make a tackle").

6. What if the danger is known but forgotten? Should there be a duty to *remind*? Compare *Tacke,* supra n. 5 (yes), with Berry v. Eckhardt Porsche Audi, Inc., 578 P.2d 1195 (Okl.1978) (seat belt warning buzzer is "valiant attempt on the part of manufacturer's to nag an occupant into fastening his seat belt," but its absence or failure is not a defect since function of seat belts is generally known).

7. **Alcohol.**

A. **Champagne corks.** What if a person, who knows that a champagne cork can pop out when the bottle is opened, is distracted by the festivities while opening a bottle. With two-thirds the momentum of a .22 caliber pistol, the cork or plastic stopper shoots out unexpectedly and injures her eye. Should there have been a warning of the pop? See generally Shuput v. Heublein Inc., 511 F.2d 1104 (10th Cir.1975); Dechello v. Johnson Enterprises, 74 Md.App. 228, 536 A.2d 1203 (Spec.App.1988); Pollack, . . . And No–Risk Bubbly, N.Y. Times, May 4, 1988, at 46, col. 1 (noting development by industrial design company of 4–inch tethered polyethylene stopper that adds to safety while preserving the "pop").

B. **Drinking—The courts.** Because the general dangers of alcohol are so widely known, plaintiffs injured by the excessive consumption of alcohol, or in car accidents caused thereby, have uniformly been denied recovery on claims against manufacturers for failure to warn. See, e.g., Pemberton v. American Distilled Spirits Co., 664 S.W.2d 690 (Tenn.1984) (death by single overdose of grain alcohol; Tenn. Products Liability Act provided no duty to warn of dangers apparent to ordinary user). "The ordinary consumer in today's society * * * knows of the dangers of driving while intoxicated." Morris v. Adolph Coors Co., 735 S.W.2d 578, 583 (Tex.App.1987) (injuries in car accident caused by driver drunk on beer; tort, warranty and statutory claims all dismissed). See Restatement (2d) of Torts § 402A, comments *i* and *j*.

In Hon v. Stroh Brewery Co., 835 F.2d 510 (3d Cir.1987), plaintiff's 26–year–old husband died from pancreatitis as the result of drinking 2 or 3 cans of Old Milwaukee Beer on an average of 4 nights per week for about 5 years. Plaintiff sued the manufacturer for failing to warn that even moderate consumption may be harmful. One of plaintiff's experts, a medical doctor, filed an affidavit stating that "small amounts of alcohol taken for a relatively brief period of time are occasionally lethal." Id. at 511. Another expert, a toxicologist and pharmacologist, stated by affidavit:

> Members of the public generally believe that the excessive and prolonged use of alcohol results in the development of disease. In my experience, laymen consider liver disease to be the principal or sole malady associated with such excessive and prolonged use of alcoholic beverages. Such is not the case, however, as clearly demonstrated by the case of Mr. Hon. His use of alcohol appears to have been prolonged, but was not, in my view, excessive. Additionally, Mr. Hon died as a result of pancreatitis, not hepatic disease. The general public's concept of alcohol-related disease is archaic. Medical science has clearly established that liver, pancreatic, gastrointestinal, and neurological disease are the result of either excessive or prolonged consumption of alcoholic beverages.

Id. at n. 2.

Held, summary judgment for defendant reversed, and case remanded for trial. The court concluded that the risks from moderate consumption of alcohol may not be generally known. It noted, however, that the consumer need not be informed of "the particular etiology by which the risk is created," nor must he be alerted to every malady to each organ endangered by prolonged consumption, provided that he knows generally that his consumption creates a substantial risk of injury. 835 F.2d at 516 n. 8. At trial, the court held that the plaintiff could introduce Stroh's commercials to show that the public is unaware of the dangers from moderate consumption. "If a jury finds that Stroh's marketing of its product has effectively taught the consuming public that consumption of beer on the order of eight to twelve cans of beer per week can be part of the 'good life' and is properly associated with health, robust activities, this [would be relevant to] whether an express warning was necessary to make Old Milwaukee beer safe for its intended purpose." 835 F.2d at 514–15. How about express warranty?

Compare, with *Hon,* three failure-to-warn claims filed on behalf of children suffering from fetal alcohol syndrome. The lawsuits, the first of their kind in the nation, allege that the syndrome, caused by the consumption of alcohol during pregnancy, is characterized by birth defects including mental retardation, damage to the brain and nervous system, and heart, limb and facial defects. The U.S. Surgeon General has issued a warning of these dangers. Prod.Saf.&.Liab.Rep. (BNA) 11 (Jan. 1, 1988).

Should every can and bottle of every kind of alcoholic beverage be required to warn of danger? If so, who should impose such a requirement? The courts? The state legislatures? The Congress? What should the warnings say? See Notes, 53 Mo.L.Rev. 555 (1988), (noting *Hon*); 63 Wash.L.Rev. 979 (1988).

C. **Legislation.** S. 2047, 100th Cong., 2d Sess. (1988), would have required every alcoholic beverage container to be labeled, on a rotating basis, with one of the following statements:

(1) WARNING: THE SURGEON GENERAL HAS DETERMINED THAT THE CONSUMPTION OF THIS PRODUCT, WHICH CONTAINS ALCOHOL, DURING PREGNANCY CAN CAUSE MENTAL RETARDATION AND OTHER BIRTH DEFECTS.

(2) WARNING: DRINKING THIS PRODUCT, WHICH CONTAINS ALCOHOL, IMPAIRS YOUR ABILITY TO DRIVE A CAR OR OPERATE MACHINERY.

(3) WARNING: THIS PRODUCT CONTAINS ALCOHOL AND IS PARTICULARLY HAZARDOUS IN COMBINATION WITH SOME DRUGS.

(4) WARNING: THE CONSUMPTION OF THIS PRODUCT, WHICH CONTAINS ALCOHOL, CAN INCREASE THE RISK OF DEVELOPING HYPERTENSION, LIVER DISEASE, AND CANCER.

(5) WARNING: ALCOHOL IS A DRUG AND MAY BE ADDICTIVE.

A similar bill, introduced by Senator Dodd of Connecticut in 1986, included the following in lieu of the "addictive" warning:

WARNING: RAPID CONSUMPTION OF THIS PRODUCT, WHICH CONTAINS ALCOHOL, CAN CAUSE IMMEDIATE DEATH.

This form of legislation is receiving increasing attention. Bills were recently filed (and rejected) in Florida and California, and one passed the Massachusetts house in 1987 and was refiled in 1988. More than 60 national health organizations supported S. 2047, and a Gallup poll found that nearly 80% of Americans favor the labeling of alcoholic beverages with health warnings. A recent editorial contends: "Consumers need to be able to make informed choices about everything they eat or drink or take as medicine. Especially alcoholic beverages. They need to know what's in them. And to be alerted to any possible hazards." USA Today, April 8, 1988, at 10A, col. 1. Citing statistics that 100,000 Americans die from alcohol use each year, that thousands of children are born each year with alcohol-related birth defects, that "18 million Americans and their families are torn apart by addiction and related problems," and that the annual loss to the nation exceeds $100 billion, the House and Senate sponsors of the warning label legislation noted that they had "waited more than a decade for the industry to heed the Food and Drug Administration's call for warning labels." They concluded: "What the alcohol marketers fear is information. What the public needs is that information. If marketers will not act responsibly to educate consumers about the real risks and costs, then Congress should." Conyers & Thurmond, We Can't Wait for Industry to Act, id. at col. 3.

Do you agree, or is this an excess of paternalism for risks that are generally known?

In late 1988, Congress enacted a compromise bill, H.R. 5210, requiring warnings that consumption of alcoholic beverages during pregnancy may cause birth defects, that it impairs the ability to drive a car or operate machinery, and that it may cause health problems. States are prohibited from requiring additional warnings. See 16 Prod.Saf. & Liab.Rep. (BNA) 1039 (Oct. 28, 1988).

8. **Judge or Jury.** The obviousness of a risk, and hence the duty to warn, is sometimes held to be a question of law for the court, particularly with respect to obviously obvious dangers. See, e.g., Smith v. Hub Mfg., Inc., supra p. 368 (young child fell into above-ground pool—no duty); Morgan v. Bethlehem Steel Corp., 135 Ill.App.3d 242, 90 Ill.Dec. 36, 481 N.E.2d 836, 838 (1985) (decedent drove into side of train—no duty). However, when the nature of the risk is more complex, obviousness may become a jury question. See, e.g., Corbin v. Coleco Indus., supra p. 369 (risk of spinal injury to adult from attempted belly flopper in above-ground pool); *Laaperi,* supra p. 371 (smoke detector short circuit).

Do you think this issue is largely a legal technicality, or might it have some practical relevance to the success of a failure to warn case? How might defense counsel try to dispose of warnings cases? How might plaintiffs' counsel respond? Cf. n. 5, supra p. 376.

9. **Theory of Liability.** Apart from their roles as separate doctrines or as bearing on cause in fact, how might the obviousness of a danger, or the plaintiff's knowledge of it, affect the following theories of recovery:

A. **Negligence.**

B. **Tortious misrepresentation.** See Rest. (2d) of Torts § 541; cf. id. § 402B, com. *j.*

C. **Warranty.** See U.C.C. § 2–316(3)(b) and com. 8.

D. **Strict liability in tort.**

(1) *Consumer expectations test.*

(2) *Risk-benefit test.*

(3) *Cost-benefit test.*

(4) *Calabresi's "cheapest cost avoider" test:* liability on the person who was in the best position to make a correct cost-benefit analysis. See Calabresi & Hirschoff, Toward a Test for Strict Liability in Torts, 81 Yale L.J. 1055 (1972).

10. Many courts and commentators criticize the consumer expectations test as being unfair to consumers in the context of obvious dangers. See, e.g., Delvaux v. Ford Motor Co., 764 F.2d 469 (7th Cir.1985) (rollover of convertible without roll bar); W.P. Keeton, Products Liability—Design Hazards and the Meaning of Defect, 10 Cum.L.Rev. 293, 300–05 (1979). At least one court appears for this reason to have abandoned the consumer expectations test altogether. See Camacho v. Honda Motor Co., 741 P.2d 1240 (Colo.1987) (motorcycle without crash bars; risk-benefit inquiry proper test). Is this necessary?

11. **Reform.** Statutes provide for a bar to recovery or reduction in damages in the case of obvious dangers, or generally known and inherent dangers, at least in Calif., Idaho, Kan., Mont., N.J., Ohio, Tenn. & Utah. See Prod.Liab.Rep. (CCH) ¶¶ 90,000 et seq.

12. See generally Pardieck & Hulbert, Is the Danger Really Open and Obvious?, 19 Ind.L.Rev. 383 (1986); Phillips, Products Liability: Obviousness of Danger Revisited, 15 Ind.L.Rev. 797 (1982); Leibman & Sandy, Can the Open and Obvious Danger Rule Coexist with Strict Tort Product Liability?: A Legal and Economic Analysis, 20 Am.Bus.L.J. 299 (1982); Henderson, The Demise of the Patent Danger Rule, 3 Corp.L.Rev. 78 (1980); Darling, The Patent Danger Rule: An Analysis and a Survey of Its Vitality, 29 Mercer L.Rev. 583 (1978);

Marschall, An Obvious Wrong Does Not Make A Right: Manufacturers' Liability for Patently Dangerous Products, 48 N.Y.U.L.Rev. 1065 (1973).

B. MISUSE

> We cannot charge the manufacturer of a knife when it is used as a toothpick and the user complains because the sharp edge cuts.

General Motors Corp. v. Hopkins, 548 S.W.2d 344, 349 (Tex.1977).

An original premise of manufacturer liability was that the injury arose out of the proper use of the product. Thus, in Greenman v. Yuba Power Products, Inc., 59 Cal.2d 57, 64, 27 Cal.Rptr. 697, 701, 377 P.2d 897, 901 (1963):

> Implicit in the machine's presence on the market * * * was a representation that it would safely do *the jobs for which it was built.* * * * To establish the manufacturer's liability it was sufficient that plaintiff proved that he was injured while using the Shopsmith *in a way it was intended to be used* as a result of the defect in design and manufacture of which plaintiff was not aware that made the Shopsmith *unsafe for its intended use.* (Emphasis added.)

What if the plaintiff in *Greenman* had been injured while using the lathe on a piece of wood that was too big for the machine? Or on a piece of metal, contrary to instructions? Or was running the lathe over its safe maximum speed? These are some of the issues of product "misuse" explored in this section.

VENEZIA v. MILLER BREWING COMPANY

United States Court of Appeals, First Circuit, 1980.
626 F.2d 188.

LEVIN H. CAMPBELL, CIRCUIT JUDGE.

[While playing with friends, the 8-year-old plaintiff found a discarded Miller Beer bottle and threw it against a telephone pole. The bottle shattered, and particles of glass injured his eye. His suit asserting warranty and negligence claims against Miller Brewing Company and three glass manufacturers was dismissed by the trial court for failure to state a claim, under Fed.R.Civ.P. 12(b)(6), and plaintiff appealed.] Plaintiff's basic premise is that Miller and the bottle manufacturers should have been aware of the dangers inherent in their "thin walled" "non-returnable" bottles and should have accordingly designed and marketed a product better able to safely withstand such foreseeable misuse as breakage in the course of improper handling by children.

* * *

Plaintiff's allegation of breach of warranty is based upon Mass.G.L. c. 106 § 2–314, which provides that a merchant impliedly warrants that his goods are, *inter alia,* "fit for the *ordinary* purposes for which such goods are used." (Emphasis added.) The linchpin of the warranty claim (and, as will be seen, the negligence claim also) is thus the proper scope of the term ordinary purpose. While at first blush it might appear beyond dispute that throwing a glass container into a telephone pole is by no means an "ordinary" use of that product, some brief examination of recent authority relied on by plaintiff in support of the contrary view may be helpful in explaining just why the initial impression is, in fact, sound.

In Back v. Wickes Corp., ___ Mass. ___, 378 N.E.2d 964 (1978), the Massachusetts Supreme Judicial Court explored the contours of section 2–314's "ordinary purpose" concept and concluded that the " 'ordinary purposes' contemplated by [that warranty] section include both those uses which the manufacturer intended and those which are reasonably foreseeable." 378 N.E.2d at 969. "It is no more than a play on words," the court concluded, "to charge that goods must be fit for 'ordinary' purposes, but not for 'extraordinary' or 'different' or 'unusual' purposes. Such [language] fails to inform . . . as to whether the defendant has warranted the goods to be free from the propensity that caused the plaintiff's injuries." 378 N.E.2d at 968.

Seizing on these passages and the Supreme Judicial Court's further admonition that a manufacturer must, in designing a product, "anticipate the environment in which [that] product will be used," plaintiff urges that the present defendants might reasonably be found by a jury to have broken a fitness warranty by designing and manufacturing glass bottles unable to safely withstand the arguably foreseeable product abuse that occurred here.

[But] we believe the *Back* court held only that a manufacturer's warranty of product fitness for ordinary use includes a guarantee that such product will withstand, in a reasonably safe manner, foreseeable "misuse" incident to or arising out of the product's intended use. See W. Prosser, The Law of Torts, § 96, p. 646 (1971). We think it would be stretching too far to believe that the Massachusetts courts are presently prepared to expand their definition of "ordinary purposes" to include the deliberate misuse of an otherwise reasonably safe container in a manner totally unrelated to any normal or intended use of that item. The Massachusetts Supreme Judicial Court previously has found no breach of a warranty of merchantability where a plaintiff was injured by glass breakage sustained in an attempt to pry the cover off a glass baby food jar with a beer-type can opener.[2] Vincent v. Nicholas E. Tsiknas Co., 337 Mass. 726, 151 N.E.2d 263 (1958). A *fortiori,* we can see no possible implied fitness warranty that an empty glass bottle

2. While the jar had included directions to open "gently," the court emphasized in reaching its decision that "glass jars are not sold, or bought, in the expectation that they will be subjected to pressures" of the sort as were in fact exerted. 151 N.E.2d at 265. If a glass container has not been warranted to withstand an attempt to open it with an improper opening device, it hardly could be warranted to safely survive impact with a telephone pole.

discarded by unknown persons would more safely withstand being intentionally smashed against a solid stationary object. Under Massachusetts law the question of fitness for ordinary purposes is largely one centering around reasonable consumer expectations. *Back,* supra, 378 N.E.2d at 970; *Vincent,* supra, 151 N.E.2d at 265. "The propensity of glass to break under pressure is common knowledge," *Vincent,* 151 N.E.2d at 265. No reasonable consumer would expect anything but that a glass beer bottle, apparently well suited for its immediate intended use, would fail to safely withstand the type of purposeful abuse involved here. In fact, one would suspect that the present eight year old plaintiff knew well the expected result, if not the potential injury, of his conduct. What, if not the possibility of shattering the bottle, would lead him to throw it against the pole in the first place? [Citation.]

* * *

[With respect to his negligence claim, plaintiff] again, as he did in his warranty argument, attempts to expand the scope of the "intended" use concept by resort to the familiar, and sometimes misleading, rubric of "foreseeability." But reliance on such generality is of limited assistance, for "In a sense, in retrospect almost nothing is unforeseeable." Green v. Volkswagen of America, Inc., 485 F.2d 430, 438 (6th Cir.1973) [quoting Mieher v. Brown, 54 Ill.2d 539, 301 N.E.2d 307 (Ill.1973)], see also Prosser, supra, § 43, p. 267–68. One with the time and imagination and aided by hindsight no doubt can conjure up all sorts of arguably "foreseeable" misuses of a variety of otherwise reasonable safe products. We see no evidence that the Massachusetts courts have abandoned their previously expressed view that "a common or straightforward product, if safe for normal uses reasonably to be anticipated at the time of manufacture, is not defective [i.e., unfit for its intended use] simply because it is foreseeable that it may cause injury to someone using it improperly." Tibbets v. Ford Motor Co., 4 Mass.App. 738, 358 N.E.2d 460, 462 (Appeals Ct.1976). Indeed, the Supreme Judicial Court has recently cited with approval previous decisions of this and other circuit courts which have defined the scope of the concept of "intended use" as encompassing the "probable ancillary consequences of normal use," and the consequences "incident to the normal and expected use" of a particular product. [Citations.] Certainly the present product misuse falls far outside that definition.

Even under the most expansive theories of products liability, a "manufacturer is not an insurer and cannot be held to a standard of duty of guarding against all possible types of accidents and injuries" in any way causally related to the design and manufacture of its products. Schneider v. Chrysler Motors Corp., 401 F.2d 549, 557 (8th Cir.1968). The world, as the Massachusetts Appeals Court has noted, is "full of rough edges." *Tibbets,* supra, 358 N.E.2d at 462. Review of the relevant authority convinces us that the Massachusetts courts would not be prepared to hold a manufacturer liable for injuries sustained by an individual coming into contact with such "rough edges" created by his own intentional misuse of an otherwise "fit" product in a manner in no reasonable way related to the immediate intended uses for which the product was designed, manufactured and marketed. As the district court properly observed, the impact of endorsing a contrary conclusion would be overwhelming, with every discarded glass object holding the potential for generating a future lawsuit.

Affirmed.

ELLSWORTH v. SHERNE LINGERIE, INC.

Court of Appeals of Maryland, 1985.
303 Md. 581, 495 A.2d 348.

McAuliffe, Judge.

[Plaintiff was severely burned when the nightgown she was wearing inside out, with the pockets protruding, ignited when it came in contact with her electric range. She had placed a tea kettle on the burner set on "high" and was reaching for a coffee filter in the cupboard over the stove when her pocket touched the edge of the burner and ignited. The gown was designed and manufactured by Sherne Lingerie which bought the cotton flannelette material from a fabric manufacturer, Cone Mills. Plaintiff sued both Sherne and Cone, alleging negligence and strict liability in tort for failing to flame retard the fabric and failing to warn of the flammability hazard. Defendants claimed that the plaintiff had misused the gown, and the judge instructed the jury on the doctrine of misuse. The jury returned a verdict for the defendants, which was upheld by the intermediate appellate court, and plaintiff appealed.]

* * *

The problem of understanding the issue of misuse in strict liability cases is * * * compounded by the absence of agreement as to the meaning of the word. Misuse has been defined as: a use not reasonably foreseeable, Payne v. Soft Sheen Products, Inc., 486 A.2d 712, 725 (D.C.1985); Ford Motor Company v. Matthews, 291 So.2d 169, 174 (Miss. 1974); a use of the product in a manner which defendant could not reasonably foresee, McGowne v. Challenge–Cook Bros., Inc., 672 F.2d 652, 661 (8th Cir.1982); Hughes v. Magic Chef, Inc., 288 N.W.2d 542, 545 (Iowa 1980); * * * a use or handling so unusual that the average consumer could not reasonably expect the product to be designed and manufactured to withstand it—a use which the seller, therefore, need not anticipate and provide for, Findlay v. Copeland Lumber Co., 265 Or. 300, 509 P.2d 28, 31 (1973); use of the product which constitutes wilful or reckless misconduct or an invitation of injury, Gangi v. Sears, Roebuck & Co., 33 Conn.Sup. 81, 360 A.2d 907, 909 (1976). The Fifth Circuit, in Jones v. Menard, 559 F.2d 1282, 1285 n. 4 (5th Cir.1977) (applying the law of Louisiana), defined misuse in the context of the three types of products cases. That court said,

> [i]n inadequate warning cases misuse means that the seller had no duty to warn against unforeseeable uses of its products, while in design cases misuse means that the manufacturer had no duty to design a product so as to prevent injuries arising from unforeseeable uses of that product. . . . In defective manufacture cases, however, misuse means that the injury was not caused by some inherent defect in the product but by the consumer's abnormal use of it. . . .[5]

It has been suggested that misuse means any use not intended by the manufacturer, but this is too narrow and fails to take into account a variety of uses reasonably foreseeable although not subjectively intended. It has also been suggested that virtually anything is possible, and thus arguably foreseeable, so that foreseeability as a test is too broad.

We conclude, as have most courts which have considered the issue, that "reasonable foreseeability" is the appropriate test, and thus a seller is required to provide a product that is not unreasonably dangerous when used for a purpose and in a manner that is reasonably foreseeable.[6] * * *

* * *

Applying these principles to the facts of this case, we conclude the evidence was insufficient to generate an issue of misuse, and that the trial judge erred in allowing the jury to consider misuse of the product as a possible bar to recovery. Clearly, and concededly, Appellant was using the nightgown for a reasonably foreseeable purpose. We conclude that her manner of use of the nightgown, though possibly careless, was reasonably foreseeable as a matter of law. It certainly may be foreseen that wearing apparel, such as nightgowns and robes, will occasionally be worn inside out. It is also foreseeable that a loosely fitting gown will come into contact with sources of ignition in the environment where it may be expected to be worn, and particularly when worn in the kitchen and near a stove. Momentary inattention or carelessness on the part of the user, while it may constitute contributory negligence, does not add up to misuse of the product under these circumstances.

* * *

[Reversed and remanded for new trial.]

---

5. See also, W. Prosser & W. Keeton, The Law of Torts § 102 (5th ed. 1984) (misuse is defined as a use different in a kind from what was intended, and unforeseeable misuse in the sense of a use that could not reasonably have been anticipated by the manufacturer); J. Dooley, Modern Tort Law § 32.79 (1983 & Cum.Supp.1984) (misuse is using it for a purpose neither intended nor foreseeable by the defendant); L. Frumer & M. Friedman, Products Liability § 15.01 (1984) (misuse is the abnormal or unintended use of the product if such use was not reasonably foreseeable); P. Sherman, Products Liability for the General Practitioner § 9.06 (1981) (misuse is an unintended and unforeseeable use of a product, by a user, consumer, or third party, that is not in accord with the purpose for which the product was intended).

6. [Citing Moran v. Fabergé, infra.]

MORAN v. FABERGE, INC.

Court of Appeals of Maryland, 1975.
273 Md. 538, 332 A.2d 11.

DIGGES, JUDGE.

[Negligence action by petitioner, Nancy Moran, against cologne manufacturer for personal injuries sustained when a bottle of the cologne caught fire. The jury returned a verdict for the petitioner, but the trial court entered a j.n.o.v. for the defendant. The Court of Special Appeals affirmed, Moran v. Williams, 19 Md.App. 546, 313 A.2d 527 (1974), and plaintiff appealed.]

* * * [O]n the fateful night of June 8, 1969, Nancy Moran, then 17 years old, visited the home of Mr. and Mrs. Louis P. Grigsby in Hillcrest Heights, Maryland, to meet with a number of friends, including Randy Williams, a young lady of 15 years, who was residing with the Grigsbys at the time. The group congregated in the basement which was being maintained partly as a family clubroom and partly as a laundry room. After listening to music for some time on that warm summer night (estimated to be 72–73° F.), everyone left the basement, except Nancy and Randy. Apparently these two girls were at a loss for entertainment as eventually they centered their attention on a lit Christmas-tree-shaped candle which was positioned on a shelf behind the couch in the clubroom. Possibly because "the idle mind knows not what it is it wants" [3] the girls began to discuss whether the candle was scented. After agreeing that it was not, Randy, while remarking "Well, let's make it scented," impulsively grabbed a "drip bottle" of Fabergé's Tigress cologne, which had been placed by Mrs. Grigsby in the basement for use as a laundry deoderant, and began to pour its contents onto the lower portion of the candle somewhat below the flame. Instantaneously, a burst of fire sprang out and burned Nancy's neck and breasts as she stood nearby watching but not fully aware of what her friend was doing.

During the trial the petitioner introduced evidence, which was not disputed, tending to show that, though no warning of the fact was attached to the bottle or otherwise given, Fabergé's Tigress cologne was highly flammable and, therefore, inherently dangerous.[4] To demonstrate this the petitioner produced scientific experimental evidence revealing that this cologne, composed of, by volume, 82.06% alcohol, 5.1% perfume and oils, and 12.84% water, is a dangerously combustible product with a flash point of 73° Fahrenheit, approximately room temperature.[5]

3. Cicero, De Divinatione, bk. II, ch. 13, quoting the poet Quintus Ennius.

4. Such a warning, however, is placed on Fabergé's Tigress aerosol spray cologne. According to the respondent, the spray container has a warning while the "drip bottle" does not because the spray has a freon propellant and thus is chemically different.

5. Utilizing the American Standard Testing Materials' scientific method of determining the flash point, the tester proceeds as follows: the liquid to be tested is poured into a glass cup surrounded by a

Additionally, the petitioner evoked testimony from two Fabergé officials, Carl Mann, its Vice President and Chief Perfumer, and Stephen Shernov, a company aerosol chemist, which indicated that not only was the manufacturer aware of this hazardous quality but also Fabergé foresaw that its product might well be dangerous when placed near flame.

Having produced evidence as to this inherently dangerous characteristic of Tigress cologne, which was known to the company though not to the public generally, as well as the fact that the manufacturer knew it might come in contact with fire and be hazardous in that circumstance, the petitioner contends that a jury question was presented as to whether Fabergé was negligent for failing to warn against its product's latent flammability characteristic. * * *

[The court observed that a determination of negligence involves a balancing of the risk of injury against the cost of precautions, and it noted that the balance almost always tips in favor of liability in warnings cases since the cost of providing an adequate warning usually is minimal. On the question of whether such a duty to warn arises in the first place, the court first looked to Rest. (2d) of Torts § 388] which instructs that a manufacturer is liable for harm "caused by the use of the chattel in the manner for which * * * it is supplied." Strictly speaking these words would lead one to believe that the manufacturer's responsibility extends only to those intended uses for which the product was supplied. However, this is misleading since such is not the case. As most courts and legal authors agree, the duty of the manufacturer to warn of latent dangers inherent in its product goes beyond the precise use contemplated by the producer and extends to all those which are reasonably foreseeable. Spruill v. Boyle–Midway, Inc., 308 F.2d 79, 83–84 (4th Cir.1962); [citations].

Even though there is a vast middle ground of product uses about which reasonable minds could disagree as to whether they are or should be foreseeable to the manufacturer, thus requiring resolution by the trier of fact, * * * there are extremes, abutting this wide in-between group, about which reasonable minds would not differ as to whether there is a duty to warn, making the determination of this issue one of law.

A review of the many cases on this subject discloses that courts have not had an easy time agreeing as to which uses by consumers require submission to the trier of fact for determination of the foreseeability issue, and those about which reasonable minds would not disagree, so that the foreseeability issue can be decided as a matter of law;

water bath; a thermometer is kept in the fluid to check its temperature as the water bath is slowly heated; and, starting at 40° Fahrenheit but increasing the temperature by increments of 2 degrees at a time, the tester passes a wand with an eighth of an inch gas-fed bead flame over the liquid in the cup at a height of one-quarter inch above the surface of the liquid being tested. The temperature of the liquid at which its vapors are ignited constitutes its flash point. In this case the test was run six times by an expert in order to obtain an average flash point.

not only have they applied differing ratiocinations but they have also arrived at apparently inconsistent determinations. For example, some courts have ruled that a jury may hold a manufacturer to a duty to warn because it is foreseeable that a baby might consume furniture polish, Spruill v. Boyle–Midway, Inc., 308 F.2d 79 (4th Cir.1962); that a body rub gives off a vapor which could be ignited under a user's clothing as he attempted to light a cigarette, [citation]; that a boy of fifteen might dive into a vinyl lined swimming pool thirty inches deep, [citation]; that paint might in some way be splashed into the eye of a painter's helper, [citation]; or that use of an automobile includes involvement in collisions, [citations]. On the other hand, there are courts which have decided that certain uses in which dangers arose (often uses very similar to those which other courts have submitted to the jury) are as a matter of law not foreseeable by the manufacturer so that he is not liable for failing to warn the consumer of the hazard involved. Cases of this ilk have included those where the court held that the manufacturer could not, as a matter of law, foresee that a housewife would splash cleaning fluid into her eye, [citation]; that the magnesium alloy legs of its product, a bathinette, when made hot by a fire in a residence would begin to blaze intensely, sending flames across a hallway and thereby greatly increasing the danger to the property and persons present, [citation]; that an automobile would participate in collisions, [citations]; or that a window casement with steel crossbars might be used either as a handrest or as a ladder by iron and steel workmen, [citation].

* * *

[Quoting from Professor Harper's treatise,]

> "the courts are perfectly accurate in declaring that there can be no liability where the harm is unforeseeable, if *'foreseeability' refers to the general type of harm sustained.* It is literally true that there is no liability for damage that falls entirely outside the *general threat of harm* which made the conduct of the actor negligent. *The sequence of events, of course, need not be foreseeable. The manner in which the risk culminates in harm may be unusual, improbable and highly unexpectable, from the point of view of the actor at the time of his conduct. And yet, if the harm suffered falls within the general danger area, there may be liability, provided other requisites of legal causation are present.*" Harper, A Treatise on the Law of Torts, § 7 (1933) (emphasis added).

See Pease v. Sinclair Refining Co., 104 F.2d 183, 185 (2d Cir.1939); [citations]. And, once the product is used in this "general field of danger," if the manufacturer's conduct is a significant factor in causing harm to another, the fact that the manufacturer neither foresaw nor should have foreseen the severity of the harm or the exact manner in which it occurred, does not prevent it from being liable.

Based on this negligence law we think that in the products liability domain a duty to warn is imposed on a manufacturer if the item it produces has an inherent and hidden danger about which the producer knows, or should know, could be a substantial factor in bringing injury to an individual or his property when the manufacturer's product comes near to or in contact with the elements which are present normally in the environment where the product can reasonably be expected to be brought or used. Spruill v. Boyle–Midway, Inc., 308 F.2d 79, 83–84 (4th Cir.1962); Comment, Foreseeability in Product Design and Duty to Warn Cases—Distinctions and Misconceptions, supra. Under this analysis the unusual and bizarre details of accidents, which human experience shows are far from unlikely, are only significant as background facts to the individual case; it is not necessary that the manufacturer foresee the exact manner in which accidents occur. Thus, in the context of this case, it was not necessary for a cologne manufacturer to foresee that someone would be hurt when a friend poured its product near the flame of a lit candle; it was only necessary that it be foreseeable to the producer that its product, while in its normal environment, may be brought near a catalyst, likely to be found in that environment, which can untie the chattel's inherent danger. For example while seated at a dressing table, a woman might strike a match to light a cigarette close enough to the top of the open cologne bottle so as to cause an explosion, or that while seated in a similar manner she might turn suddenly and accidentally bump the bottle of cologne with her elbow, splashing some cologne on a burning candle placed on the vanity. So, in the words of the Supreme Court of Missouri: "If there is some probability of harm sufficiently serious that ordinary men would take precautions to avoid it, then failure so to do is negligence." Bean v. Ross Manufacturing Co., 344 S.W.2d 18, 25 (Mo. 1961); [citations].

In applying this test here, we hold that it was unnecessary, to support a verdict in favor of the petitioner, that there be produced evidence, as demanded by the Court of Special Appeals, "which would tend to show or would support a rational inference that Fabergé foresaw or should have foreseen that its [Tigress] cologne would be used in the manner [(pouring the cologne on the lower portion of a lit candle in an attempt to scent it)] which caused the injuries to Nancy Moran," Moran v. Williams, supra, 19 Md.App. at 561–562, 313 A.2d at 536; rather, it was only necessary that the evidence be sufficient to support the conclusion that Fabergé, knowing or deemed to know that its Tigress cologne was a potentially dangerous flammable product, could reasonably foresee that in the environment of its use, such as the home of the Grigsbys, this cologne might come close enough to a flame to cause an explosion of sufficient intensity to burn property or injure bystanders, such as Nancy.

* * *

* * * Therefore, we are constrained to believe and hold that, in the instant case, especially considering the economic and social climate

of our day, the issue of Fabergé's negligence was for the jury and that Judge Couch should not have granted the motion for judgment n.o.v.

[Reversed and remanded for entry of judgment on verdict for plaintiff.]

O'DONNELL, JUDGE (dissenting).

* * *

It must be emphasized that upon the record there was no evidence whatsoever of such a use as was here made of the cologne ever having previously occurred; in fact, the use of Tigress cologne had a 27 year accident-free history. * * *

* * *

Assuming, *arguendo,* that Fabergé may have a duty to warn of a general risk because of a latent danger of flammability of its cologne—where its vapors might be brought within one-quarter of an inch of an open flame—it does not follow that this duty to warn is owed to everyone, howsoever the product might be used or abused. It may well be true that the manufacturer owes a duty to warn of the general risk of fire to a young lady who, while applying the cologne, accidentally should knock over the container and spill it upon a burning candle, but such are not the facts here. * * *

* * *

All the cases cited by the majority in support of their conclusion contain the element—conspicuously absent in this case—that there was a reasonable foreseeability on the part of the manufacturer that the use which was being made of the product at the time of the injury was itself reasonably foreseeable by the manufacturer.

As the counsel for Fabergé observed succinctly:

> "There may be some iconoclast who would like their [sic] candles to smell like rum, but if someone were to pour 150 proof rum [75% alcohol] on a lighted candle to give it a rum scent and the vapors of that rum were to catch fire and injure someone, the manufacturer of the rum would not be liable because this is idiosyncratic and unforeseeable use of the product."

A fortiori, if someone undertakes to use a skin freshener or body cologne to perfume a lighted candle and its vapors, in juxtaposition to the open flame, should ignite, its manufacturer should not be liable because of this palpably unanticipated and unforeseeable misuse of its product.

* * *

It seems to me that the majority has fallen into the pitfall, recognized by Professor Prosser, who, in undertaking to analyze the treatment by the various courts of the illusory concept of "foreseeability" and noting the confusion resulting therefrom, states:

> "Some 'margin of leeway' has to be left for the unusual and the unexpected. But this has opened a very wide door; and the

courts have taken so much advantage of the leeway that it can scarcely be doubted that a great deal of what the ordinary man would regard as freakish, bizarre, and unpredictable has crept within the bounds of liability by the simple device of permitting the jury to foresee at least its very broad, and vague, general outlines." W. Prosser, Torts, § 43, at 269 (4th ed. 1971).

* * *

NOTES

1. The doctrine of product misuse has been around for many years. "It seems quite clearly established where the purchaser, actually knowing the defective nature of the article, puts it to a use for which it is unfit and unsafe, any injury received therefrom is due to his misuse and not to the act of him who created the defect." Bohlen, The Basis of Affirmative Obligations in the Law of Tort (pt. 3), 53 U.Pa.L.Rev. 337, 343 (1905).

2. "If a consumer employs a product in some extraordinary manner, and encounters a known danger in the course of his conduct, the doctrine of product misuse will bar recovery from the manufacturer. The adventurous consumer has voluntarily placed himself in a category distinct from the normal consumer who foregoes the pleasure and convenience of using products in novel but dangerous ways. The rationale of loss distribution does not reach his case because it is unfair to force consumers who forego these additional benefits to subsidize those individuals who voluntarily take the additional risks. [The misuse defense] fall[s] into the general category of assumption of risk." Holford, The Limits of Strict Liability for Product Design and Manufacture, 52 Tex. L.Rev. 81, 89 (1973).

3. The misuse doctrine is built into the concept of merchantability, in U.C.C. § 2–314(2)(c) (fitness for "ordinary" purposes), and into the concept of negligence, in Rest. (2d) of Torts § 388 (negligent warnings—liability for harm from "use of the chattel in the manner for which * * * it is supplied"); § 395 (negligent manufacture—liability for harm caused by chattel's "lawful use in a manner and for a purpose for which it is supplied"); and § 398 (negligent design—liability for harm from "probable use," special application of § 395). It also defines the limits of strict liability in tort under § 402A, com. *g* (defectiveness not established by harm from "mishandling"); com. *h* (product not defective when safe for "normal handling"); com. *i* (unreasonable danger not established by harm from "over-consumption"); and com. *j* (no duty to warn of generally known risks of excessive use; seller may assume warnings will be read and heeded, and product with adequate warning is neither defective nor unreasonably dangerous).

4. **Quacking Like a Duck: Classifying the Misuse "Defense."** It is the defendant, of course, who will try to establish that the plaintiff misused the product. Does this mean, therefore, that misuse is an affirmative defense, on which the defendant has the burden of pleading and proof? This question was considered by the *Ellsworth* court in a portion of the opinion omitted above. The trial court had charged the jury:

> [I]n the strict liability theory, it is for the plaintiff to show by a preponderance of the evidence that the defendants manufactured a defective product, which was unreasonably dangerous and that the defect was a proximate cause of the plaintiff's injuries.

* * *

> The burden is then upon the defendant to show that the plaintiff misused the product.

495 A.2d at 352. The appellate court considered the plaintiff's claim that this instruction was in error:

> Comment *h* to § 402A provides a basis for the "misuse" defense. It states:
>
>> A product is not in a defective condition when it is safe for normal handling and consumption. If the injury results from abnormal handling, as where a bottled beverage is knocked against a radiator to remove the cap; or from abnormal preparation for use, as where too much salt is added to food; or from abnormal consumption, as where a child eats too much candy and is made ill, the seller is not liable.
>
> Most jurisdictions have adopted the Restatement view that misuse or abnormal use is a factor in a strict liability action.
>
> The courts, however, are split on the question of whether the issue of misuse properly arises as a part of a plaintiff's case, or is an affirmative defense. Some courts have referred to misuse as an affirmative defense or part of the defendant's burden of proof. [Citing cases from Ala., Colo., Conn., Fla., Idaho, Neb., N.M., Ohio, Okla., Tenn., Tex., Utah & Wash.]
>
> The recent trend in a number of courts has been to consider the question of misuse as a part of the plaintiff's case, and as being directly related to the issues of defectiveness, or of proximate cause, or both. [Citing cases from Ariz., Ill., Iowa, Miss., Mo. & N.D.] Commentators have agreed. See L. Frumer & M. Friedman, Products Liability § 15.01 (1984); J. Dooley, Modern Tort Law § 32.79 (1983 & Cum.Supp. 1984); Noel, Defective Products: Abnormal Use, Contributory Negligence, and Assumption of Risk, 25 Vand.L.Rev. 93, 96 (1972).
>
> Other courts have referred to the "defense" of misuse without specifying whether it is an affirmative defense, or evidence that tends to negate the plaintiff's case. See for example Young v. Up–Right Scaffolds, Inc., 637 F.2d 810 (D.C.Cir.1980).
>
> * * *
>
> We conclude, as have most courts which have considered the issue, that "reasonable foreseeability" is the appropriate test, and thus a seller is required to provide a product that is not unreasonably dangerous when used for a purpose and in a manner that is reasonably foreseeable. If a product is unreasonably dangerous for such use it is "defective" within the meaning of § 402A of the Restatement, and if that defect is a cause of damage the seller will be responsible. On the other hand, if the product is not unreasonably dangerous when used for a purpose and in a manner that is reasonably foreseeable, it simply is not defective, and the seller will not be liable.[7]

7. Whether foreseeability of use relates to the requirement of proof of "defective condition" or to proof of being "unreasonably dangerous" the result is the same, for both must be proven as a part of a plaintiff's case. Comments g and h of § 402A support the prevailing view that misuse relates to the existence *vel non* of a defect.

> Misuse of a product may also bar recovery where the misuse is the sole proximate cause of damage, or where it is the intervening or superseding cause. For example, a high speed electric drill may be defective because a manufacturing defect causes it to short circuit and produce a shock during normal usage. A plaintiff who attaches a brush to that drill and in attempting to clean his teeth suffers injury to his mouth from the high speed of the brush will lose because his misuse is the sole cause of his misfortune, and the defect in the drill is not in any way related to the harm.[9]
>
> Misuse may also embrace the concept of mishandling. As Comment g of § 402A states "the seller is not liable when he delivers the product in a safe condition, and subsequent mishandling . . . make[s] it harmful by the time it is consumed." The burden of proof is upon the plaintiff to show that the product was in a defective condition when it left the hands of the seller.
>
> From what we have said it is apparent that questions of misuse of the product are involved in the determination of whether the product was defective, and whether a defect was the proximate cause of the injury. Because defectiveness and causation are elements which must be proved by the plaintiff, we conclude that misuse is not an affirmative defense. Misuse, therefore, is a "defense" only in the sense that proof of misuse negates one or more essential elements of a plaintiff's case, and may thereby defeat recovery.

Id. at 353–56.

Compare Uptain v. Huntington Lab, Inc., 723 P.2d 1322, 1325 (Colo.1986): "[T]he defense of misuse * * * is a particularized defense requiring that the plaintiff's use of the product be unforeseeable and unintended as well as the cause of the injuries." Further, "[m]isuse * * * is a question of causation. Regardless of the defective condition, if any, of a manufacturer's product, a manufacturer will not be liable if an unforeseeable misuse of the product caused the injuries." Id. at 1325. The dissent referred to misuse as an "affirmative defense." Id. at 1332.

So, what is misuse? Part of plaintiff's case on defect? On cause in fact? On proximate cause? Part of defendant's case as an affirmative defense? Some of the above? All of the above? For one approach, see Hughes v. Magic Chef, Inc., 288 N.W.2d 542, 545–47 (Iowa 1980).

5. Although the courts have described the manufacturer's design responsibility for product misuse in a variety of ways, there is general agreement that the underlying principle of limitation is one of "reasonable foreseeability"—as elastic as that concept may be. Reconsider the distinction between the foreseeability of *use* and the foreseeability of *harm,* made by the court in Newman v. Utility Trailer & Equipment Co., Inc., 278 Or. 395, 397, 564 P.2d 674, 676 (1977), supra p. 220. Is foreseeability of "use" specific enough? Is there a difference between the *type* of use and the *manner* of use? Does it matter, or is all this a trivial play on words?

6. Are the principal cases correctly decided? Are they consistent?

9. For a discussion of a similar hypothetical situation see Vargo, The Defenses to Strict Liability in Tort: A New Vocabulary With An Old Meaning, 29 Mercer L.Rev. 447, 459 (1978).

7. Under the *Moran* majority's rationale, is there any set of facts which would not support a judgment for the plaintiff, assuming the cologne had somehow been ignited in a home environment? What if plaintiff, after cutting grass with a gasoline powered mower on a hot day, decides to splash cologne on her face while standing over the power mower; some of the cologne strikes the hot engine, ignites, and causes serious burns? What result if plaintiff pours cologne into her backyard incinerator because she hopes it will control the odors?

8. Is it reasonably foreseeable, as a matter of fact, or as a matter of law, that:

A. A person will insist on buying shoes that are too small for his feet? See Rest. (2d) of Torts § 395 comment *j*.

B. A person will insist on buying automobile tires that are too large for his rims? See McDevitt v. Standard Oil Co. of Tex., 391 F.2d 364 (5th Cir.1968).

C. A person will sit in a chair too small for his posterior (300 pounds)? See Horne v. Liberty Furniture Co., 452 So.2d 204 (La.App.1984).

D. A person will stand on an ordinary chair? See Rest. (2d) Torts § 395, comment *k*.

E. A car will be driven at 115 m.p.h., go out of control and injure a third party? See Schemel v. General Motors Corp., 384 F.2d 802 (7th Cir.1967).

F. A tire, designed for speeds to 85 m.p.h., equipped on a car designed for speeds to 100 m.p.h., will blow out at 100 m.p.h.? See LeBouef v. Goodyear Tire & Rubber Co., 451 F.Supp. 253 (W.D.La.1978).

G. The emergency brake on a car will be left on during operation, long enough to vaporize the hydraulic brake fluid, causing a brake failure? Knapp v. Hertz Corp., 59 Ill.App.3d 241, 17 Ill.Dec. 65, 375 N.E.2d 1349 (1978).

H. A person will attempt suicide by closing himself in a car trunk without an inside release latch, and be trapped inside for 9 days after changing his mind? Daniell v. Ford Motor Co., Inc., 581 F.Supp. 728 (D.N.M.1984).

I. An empty Clorox container will be used to store gasoline, will tip over, and the gasoline will be ignited by a spark from the motor of an electric appliance in another room? See Taylor v. General Elec. Co., 208 N.J.Super. 207, 505 A.2d 190 (1986).

J. A patient will walk, against doctor's orders, on his broken leg held together with a defective surgical pin designed only to stabilize the fracture, not to support the weight of a man? See Stewart v. Von Solbrig Hosp., Inc., 24 Ill. App.3d 599, 321 N.E.2d 428 (1974).

K. A machine will not be maintained? See Wilson v. Crouse–Hinds Co., 556 F.2d 870 (8th Cir.), cert. denied, 434 U.S. 968, 98 S.Ct. 513, 54 L.Ed.2d 455 (1977).

L. A person will pour hot Wesson Oil from the skillet back into the bottle, and then recap the bottle, causing it to explode? See Chandler v. Hunt Food & Indus., Inc., Prod.Liab.Rep. (CCH) ¶ 5969 (Tenn.1968).

M. Burning alcohol, sold only for professional dental use, will be drunk by penal farm inmate dental assistants, who then will go blind? See Barnes v. Litton Indus. Prod., Inc., 555 F.2d 1184 (4th Cir.1977).

N. A doctor will transplant synthetic fibers, normally used for rugs and "astroturf," into a patient's scalp as a treatment for baldness, causing irritation and infection? Berg v. Underwood's Hair Adaption Process, Inc., 751 F.2d 136 (2d Cir.1984).

Is the legal "test" adequate to resolve these cases in a principled, predictable manner?

9. **Common Practice.** If persons regularly use the product in a dangerous, unintended manner, the use was probably a foreseeable one. See Gootee v. Colt Industries, Inc., 712 F.2d 1057, 1065 (6th Cir.1983) (use of revolver half-cock as safety virtually universal practice); Lamer v. McKee Industries, Inc., 721 P.2d 611, 615 (Alaska 1986) ("a manufacturer should not be relieved of responsibility simply because it closes its eyes to the way its products are actually used by consumers").

10. **Children.** Both manufacturers and courts have had an especially difficult time with the misuse of products by children. If the children are so young that they fail to appreciate danger, they can be expected to eat, poke, climb into, throw, and otherwise abuse about anything in the household, and the courts have held that many such risks are foreseeable. Spruill v. Boyle–Midway, Inc., 308 F.2d 79 (4th Cir.1962), is the classic case. Plaintiff's infant decedent died from drinking some of the defendant's cherry-red furniture polish that had been left open momentarily on the bureau beside his crib. Plaintiff argued that the "harmful if swallowed, especially by children" warning on the label was inadequate. Defendant countered by arguing that the product was not intended to be consumed. Remarking that, " 'Intended use' is but a convenient adaptation of the basic test of 'reasonable foreseeability,' " the court observed that in addition to the literally intended uses of a product a seller "must also be expected to anticipate the environment which is normal for the use of his product and where, as here, that environment is the home, he must anticipate the reasonably foreseeable risks of the use of his product in such an environment. These are risks which are inherent in the proper use for which his product is manufactured. Thus where such a product is an inherently dangerous one, and its danger is not obvious to the average housewife," the manufacturer must warn of the reasonably foreseeable hazards, "though such risks may be incidental to the actual use for which the product was intended." Affirming a judgment for the plaintiff, the court concluded that the manufacturer could fairly have been held to foresee that such a product might be found and drunk by unattended children.

Compare Victory Sparkler & Specialty Co. v. Latimer, 53 F.2d 3 (8th Cir. 1931) (small child ate "spit devil" firework that was wrapped in plain red wrapper and looked like candy); Sherk v. Daisy–Heddon, 498 Pa. 594, 450 A.2d 615 (1982) (thinking safety was on, 14–year–old pointed BB gun at friend's head and pulled trigger, killing friend); Ritter v. Narragansett Elec. Co., 109 R.I. 176, 283 A.2d 255 (1971) (4–year–old opened and stood on oven door to see what was cooking on stove, causing range and pot of boiling water to topple over); Larue v. National Union Elec. Corp., 571 F.2d 51 (1st Cir.1978) (11–year–old boy, riding canister vacuum cleaner like toy car, injured when his penis slipped through opening of filter support into fan whirling at 15,000 r.p.m.); Simpson v. Standard Container Co., 72 Md.App. 199, 527 A.2d 1337 (Spec.App.1987) (children played with gas can designed without child-proof top—no duty); Keller v. Welles Dept. Store of Racine, 88 Wis.2d 24, 276 N.W.2d 319, 324 (App.1979) (same—contra):

> Children are incurably curious about their environment. A gasoline can * * * is commonly stored either on the floor or on a low shelf.

> These are areas readily accessible to children in their "explorations." It is not unforeseeable that a child might attempt to taste the liquid in the can [or,] in the course of playing "mow the lawn" or "gas station," a child might pour the gasoline from the can.

What is a manufacturer to do? What is a court to do?

11. **Failure to Follow Directions.** What if the user fails to read or heed the warnings or instructions?

"I had a very bad headache. Bad pain of various kinds. The childproof bottle top gave me some trouble, but by the time a little wave of rage had swept over me, I had defeated it. I tilted some tablets into my left palm, carefully counted off three with my right forefinger, and pushed them into my mouth. I always take three, because the directions say to take one or two." H.F. Saint, Invisible Man 58 (Atheneum 1987).

Many courts follow the approach of Rest. (2d) Torts § 402A comment *j:*

> Where warning is given, the seller may reasonably assume that it will be read and heeded; and a product bearing such a warning, which is safe for use if it is followed, is not in a defective condition, nor is it unreasonably dangerous.

See, e.g., Peterson v. Parke Davis & Co., 705 P.2d 1001 (Colo.App.1985) (doctor failed to read or heed warnings and instructions in package insert, leaving patient on toxic drug despite contraindications); Sturm, Ruger & Co. v. Bloyd, 586 S.W.2d 19 (Ky.1979) (owner of six-shooter revolver left hammer resting on firing pin in line with loaded cartridge, contrary to explicit instructions and warnings; gun discharged when dropped on floor); Uptain v. Huntington Lab, Inc., 723 P.2d 1322, 1326 (Colo.1986) (housekeeper used bare hands to wring out mop used to apply bathroom cleaning solution containing 23% hydrochloric acid); Watson v. Uniden Corp. of America, 775 F.2d 1514 (11th Cir.1985) (warranty—failure to follow instructions is not use in "normal" manner, but jury question on warnings adequacy on negligence and strict liability counts).

But what if the warning or instruction disregarded is itself inadequate? "[I]f the injury resulting from foreseeable misuse of a product is one which an adequate warning concerning the use of the product would likely prevent, such misuse is no defense." Bristol–Myers Co. v. Gonzales, 548 S.W.2d 416, 422–23 (Tex.Civ.App.1976), rev'd on other grounds 561 S.W.2d 801 (1978). See also Harless v. Boyle–Midway Div., American Home Prod., 594 F.2d 1051, 1055 (5th Cir.1979) ("It seems both confusing and internally inconsistent to ask a jury who has previously concluded that the label was inadequate to consider the defense of failure to read an adequate label.").

Should it matter whether the inadequacy is one of "substance," or instead is "procedural" in the sense of failing to catch the user's attention? Should it make a difference whether plaintiff read the message and failed to heed it, or simply failed to read it in the first place? See generally Uptain v. Huntington Lab, Inc., 723 P.2d 1322, 1333 (Colo.1986) (dissenting opinion).

12. **Type of Defect.** Should the "rule" be the same for all three types of defect? In Bryan v. John Bean Div. of FMC Corp., 566 F.2d 541 (5th Cir.1978), the court noted that "the unforeseeable misuse defense has developed in cases alleging defective design rather than manufacturing defect. [Citations.] We question whether the misuse has as wide a scope in cases of manufacturing defect, which, by definition, present a flaw in the product not intended to occur. In these circumstances, misuse relates only to causation of the accident, rather

than tending to prove the absence of a defect in the product as manufactured. See General Motors Corp. v. Hopkins, [548 S.W.2d 344 (Tex.1977)]."

How about claims of inadequate warnings? See note 10, above. Considering the slight direct cost of providing a warning, why should there be any misuse limitations at all on the manufacturer's duty to warn?

13. **Trial Tactics.** What if defense counsel in *Moran* was convinced that the perfume was not particularly flammable and, hence, doubted the veracity of the girls' story as to how the accident occurred? In Howard v. Faberge, Inc., 679 S.W.2d 644 (Tex.App.1984), the plaintiff claimed that, after dousing his upper body with Brut 33 Splash–On Lotion, he dropped a match into his waistband, igniting the Brut and burning his body. Plaintiff sued for failure to warn of the lotion's flammability. In closing argument, defense counsel emphasized the weaknesses in the plaintiff's evidence on the lotion's supposed flammability. Suddenly, he produced a bottle purporting to be Brut, poured it over his arm, waved a lit match over his arm, and called on God to burn him if he were wrong. The jury returned a verdict for the defendant. On appeal, *held,* counsel's improper experiment was incurably prejudicial, requiring reversal and a new trial.

14. **Reform.** At least Arizona, Idaho, Indiana and Montana by statute bar or reduce recovery of a person injured due to misuse. Arizona's statute includes conduct in violation of adequate warnings or instructions; Idaho defines misuse in terms of the conduct of an ordinary reasonably prudent person, and Montana treats "unreasonable misuse" as an affirmative defense. See 2 Prod. Liab. Rep. (CCH) ¶¶ 90,312; 91,314; 91,514; 92,711. See Gosewisch v. American Honda Motor Co., Inc., 153 Ariz. 400, 737 P.2d 376 (1987).

15. See generally Twerski, The Many Faces of Misuse: An Inquiry Into the Emerging Doctrine of Comparative Causation, 29 Mercer L.Rev. 403 (1978); Vargo, The Defenses to Strict Liability in Tort: A New Vocabulary with an Old Meaning, 29 Mercer L.Rev. 447 (1978); Noel, Defective Products: Abnormal Use, Contributory Negligence, and Assumption of Risk, 25 Vand.L.Rev. 93 (1972); Note, 57 Neb.L.Rev. 817 (1978); Annot., 65 A.L.R.4th 263 (1988).

C. DETERIORATION

> There is no duty upon a manufacturer to furnish a machine that will not wear out.

Auld v. Sears, Roebuck & Co., 261 App.Div. 918, 25 N.Y.S.2d 491, 493 (1941), aff'd, 288 N.Y. 515, 41 N.E.2d 927 (1942).

SAVAGE v. JACOBSEN MANUFACTURING COMPANY

District Court of Appeal of Florida, 1981.
396 So.2d 731.

[Plaintiff, an operator of lawn-mowing tractors at a golf club, slipped and fell from the platform beneath the driver's seat as she was dismounting a tractor manufactured by the defendant and sold to the club a little over three years before. At the time of initial purchase, the platform was covered with a gritty, nonskid paint, but the surface had worn off over time. Several weeks before her accident, the plaintiff's husband, a mechanic who serviced the tractor, had noticed that the platform was slippery from morning dew and hydraulic fluid which had leaked from a reservoir behind the seat, as often happened on such tractors. He asked their supervisor to purchase some nonskid paint to recoat several pieces of equipment, including the tractor in question, but the supervisor had not done so. Plaintiff's suit against the manufacturer, alleging that her injury was due to the absence of a nonskid surface on the tractor's platform, was dismissed on the defendant's motion for summary judgment. Plaintiff appealed.]

The issue before us here is whether * * * there is a genuine issue of material fact, Holl v. Talcott, 191 So.2d 40 (Fla.1966), as to whether the absence of a nonskid surface on the tractor at the time of appellant's injury constituted a defect. We hold that the trial court properly concluded that there was no showing of a defect. The record before us discloses no evidence that the nonskid painted surface in any way constituted a deviation from the norm, failed to meet the standard of the industry, or constituted a latent, functional defect. In fact, the evidence showed that the purchaser of the tractor was aware at the time of the purchase of the fact that the painted surface would eventually wear off and was aware prior to appellant's accident that the nonskid surface had, in fact, worn off. Thus the platform did not constitute an "unexpected danger" as to such purchaser. In short, there was no showing of a "defect" which would give rise to the application of § 402A. The nonskid surface merely wore off.

Although we have not found any Florida cases dealing specifically with a manufacturer's duty to produce products with component parts or surfaces that do not wear out with normal use, that issue has been decided several times by the courts of Louisiana. In the area of strict products liability Louisiana has adopted the substantial equivalent of § 402A. [Citation.]

In Foster v. Marshall, 341 So.2d 1354 (La.App.), cert. refused, 343 So.2d 1067, cert. denied, 343 So.2d 1077 (La.1977), a bolting assembly on the left front axle of a trailer separated, causing the trailer to veer into an oncoming lane of travel and collide with the plaintiff's automobile. The evidence showed that the bolting assembly on the trailer failed primarily because a cotter pin had worn out over time. In affirming the portion of the trial court's decision in favor of the manufacturer, the court of appeal held that the wearing out of a cotter pin did not constitute a "defect," stating:

> A manufacturer cannot be expected to design products with component parts which will never wear out, regardless of the nature of use or maintenance. A manufacturer is entitled to anticipate that a consumer purchasing its product will use reasonable care in maintaining it. The product in this case was a relatively simple piece of agricultural equipment for use by farmers or harvesters who generally have some degree of experience in the maintenance of agricultural equipment. All

persons who dealt with this particular wagon testified they knew that cotter keys will wear out and need to be replaced periodically. * * *

* * *

A product is defective when the risks are greater than a reasonable buyer would expect. Welch v. Outboard Marine Corp., 481 F.2d 252 (5th Cir.1973). A reasonable buyer of a piece of agricultural equipment such as a cotton wagon should expect the product to contain consumable parts which require inspection and maintenance.

Id. at 1361. [Citations.]

We are in accord with the reasoning set out in *Foster.* For us to hold otherwise would be tantamount to saying that a manufacturer is an insurer of his product. * * *

[Summary judgment affirmed.]

NOTES

1. Compare Blair v. Martin's, 78 A.D.2d 895, 433 N.Y.S.2d 221, 222 (1980). Plaintiff purchased a pair of plastic boots from the defendant for under $10, wore them for months, had new "lifts" installed by her shoemaker, and wore them for several more months. She fell one day, as she was descending the subway steps, and found that the heel had come off one of the boots. *Held,* judgment for defendant, after jury trial, affirmed:

> [W]e believe plaintiffs failed to establish, beyond the barest conclusory allegation, that the accident was caused by a defect present in the boots at the time plaintiff purchased them and not by a defect caused as a result of alteration by her shoemaker (who was unavailable to testify at the trial) or by the boots' simply having worn out.

2. In *Savage,* assume that a weld attaching the platform to the tractor frame had failed, causing the platform to shift and the plaintiff to fall. Same result? What if the failure occurred 10 years after manufacture? 30 years?

3. In Pryor v. Lee C. Moore Corp., 262 F.2d 673, 675 (10th Cir.1958), the mast or derrick of a drilling rig collapsed after 15 years of good service. A weld failed at the foot of one leg of the derrick, indicating that the weld was improperly fused at the point of failure, according to expert testimony. *Held,* prolonged safe use would not bar a negligence claim altogether, but would be considered as "one factor, albeit an important one, in the determination of the factual issue whether the negligent manufacture proximately caused the harm."

4. In Mickle v. Blackmon, 252 S.C. 202, 166 S.E.2d 173, 188–90 (1969), the plaintiff was riding in the front passenger seat of a 1949 Ford automobile hit by another car in 1962. The force of the collision threw her against the gearshift lever mounted on the steering wheel, shattering the protective knob and causing the plaintiff's body to become impaled on the spear-like lever. Ford knew that the white plastic material it had selected for the knob weakened from exposure to ultraviolet rays, but did not switch to the black material (resistant to such rays) until 1950. In plaintiff's suit against Ford for negligent design, the jury returned a verdict for the plaintiff. The trial court granted Ford's motion for j.n.o.v., and plaintiff appealed. *Held,* reversed:

It is implicit in the verdict that the gearshift lever presented an unreasonable risk of injury if not adequately guarded. At the time of plaintiff's injury the knob on the Hill car continued to serve its functional purpose as a handhold, but it had become useless as a protective guard. It is inferable that the condition of the knob did not arise from ordinary wear and tear, but from an inherent weakness in the material of which Ford was aware when the selection was made. In the light of the insidious effect on this material of exposure to sunlight in the normal use of an automobile, it could reasonably be concluded that Ford should have foreseen that many thousands of the one million vehicles produced by it in 1949 would, in the course of time, be operated millions of miles with gearshift lever balls which, while yet serving adequately as handholds, would furnish no protection to an occupant who might be thrown against the gearshift lever. The jury could reasonably conclude that Ford's conduct, in manufacturing a needed safety device of a material which could not tolerate a frequently encountered aspect of the environment in which it would be employed, exposed many users of its product to unreasonably great risk of harm. * * *

* * *

In a products liability case against the manufacturer, plaintiff does, of course, have the burden of establishing that the defect complained of existed at the time the product was sold by the defendant. "There is no duty on a manufacturer to furnish a machine that will not wear out." Auld v. Sears, Roebuck & Co., 261 App.Div. 918, 25 N.Y.S.2d 491, aff'd, 288 N.Y. 515, 41 N.E.2d 927. We subscribe to the following statement of the law which is applicable to the facts of this case:

> "If the chattel is in good condition when it is sold, the seller is not responsible when it undergoes subsequent changes, or wears out. The mere lapse of time since the sale by the defendant, during which there has been continued safe use of the product, is always relevant, as indicating that the seller was not responsible for the defect. There have been occasional cases in which, upon the particular facts, it has been held to be conclusive. It is, however, quite certain that *neither long continued lapse of time nor changes in ownership will be sufficient in themselves to defeat recovery when there is clear evidence of an original defect in the thing sold.*" (Emphasis added.) Prosser on Torts, 667 (3d ed. 1964).

Here, * * * there was evidence of an original weakness in the gearshift assembly which caused the collapse of the protective knob. The deterioration of the product and its consequent failure was the very risk created by the negligent choice of material, or the jury could so find. The rule relied upon, that a manufacturer is not liable for the failure of a product due to deterioration from ordinary wear and tear or misuse, simply does not fit these facts.

We readily concede that the passage of thirteen years between the marketing of a product and its injury-producing failure is a formidable obstacle to fastening liability upon the manufacturer. However, it may reasonably be inferred in this case that the advanced age of the ball was coincidental with its failure rather than the cause of it, and that the knob would have shattered upon a comparable impact had it occurred much earlier in the life of the car. The important inquiry is not how long the knob lasted but what caused its failure. Mere passage of time should not excuse Ford if its negligence was the cause. Since this conclusion finds support in the evidence, the issue was for the jury.

5. Reconsider the problem raised in Ford Motor Co. v. Moulton, supra p. 147, of an automobile manufacturer's warranty limitation to 12 months or 12,000 miles. If a defect in the steering causes an accident 13 months after purchase, should a limitation of the implied warranty's duration to 12 months be considered "reasonable" and "conscionable" for purposes of § 108 of the Magnuson–Moss Act? See p. 156, supra. How about 3 years after purchase? Ten?

6. As indicated by the cases above, the life expectancy issue is often treated by the courts as a factual question of cause in fact, or proximate causation, rather than as a question of duty. Consider Balido v. Improved Machinery, Inc., 29 Cal.App.3d 633, 105 Cal.Rptr. 890, 896–97 (1972), involving an injury due to the failure of a non-moving part in a press about 14 years old:

> Passage of time, then, bears only on the third essential of plaintiff's proof—the causal connection between injury and design. The problem arises as a by-product of the inevitability of change, for change brought about by time unravels the connection between prior cause and later effect. Did the product fail because it was badly designed or because it was badly manufactured? Because badly manufactured or badly maintained? Badly maintained or abused in use? Abused in use or because it wore out? Here, we find ourselves deep in the labyrinth of causation, where passage of time almost inevitably brings its concomitant of multiple cause and multiple effect. In working our way out of this labyrinth legal rules, inferences, presumptions furnish little help, for the basic problem is one of reliability of proof.
>
> In areas where the problem of time, change, and causation has proved particularly troublesome the legislature has provided the courts with arbitrary mechanical solutions, often in the form of statutes of limitation. These statutes, although couched as procedural limitations on the time within which to bring suit, in effect terminate substantive liability by decreeing that after the passage of a specified time the causal connection between defect and injury will no longer be legally recognized. But no such legislative aids for evaluating causation have been adopted in product liability, and the courts have been required to work out their own solutions.
>
> In substance, the basic rule in current use declares that the effect of lapse of time on causation is a question for determination by the trier of fact within the limitations of legal cause. Concededly, so loose a rule may not be wholly satisfactory to lawyers advising clients, but for courts and judges it suggests that in most cases the issue of causation should be submitted to the trier of fact, at least whenever a theory of causation can be plausibly sustained.

HODDER v. GOODYEAR TIRE & RUBBER COMPANY

Supreme Court of Minnesota, 1988.
426 N.W.2d 826.

SIMONETT, J.: This products liability case raises a variety of issues, including interpretation of the statutory "useful life defense," the duty to warn, and entitlement to punitive damages. * * *

On December 19, 1981, plaintiff Dale Hodder, age 17, was seriously injured when the metal rim of a truck tire explosively separated while he was mounting the tire of a customer's logging truck. Hodder was then employed by Remer Oil Company, a service station in the small community of Remer in northern Minnesota. Hodder remembers he was to fix a flat tire on the truck but remembers little else.

The tire that exploded was mounted on a KWX multi-piece rim assembly made by defendant Goodyear Tire & Rubber Company. This assembly consists of a heavy metal rim base, about which the tire with an inner tube is placed, plus a separate metal side ring that attaches to the rim. The rim base is split to facilitate getting the tire on and off; on assembly, the split ends must be carefully realigned and the side ring then fastens to and helps lock the rim base. * * *

The K-rim which injured Hodder was manufactured in 1955, 26 years before the accident. The rim was corroded and worn but there was also evidence the component parts were in serviceable condition at the time of the explosion. Goodyear had been making K-rims since the 1920's, and possibly a quarter million are still in circulation. Manufacture of the KWX was discontinued in 1962. After 1955, Goodyear became aware of the danger of pressurized separation of its multi-piece rim assemblies. By the 1970's, Goodyear was using safety films, posters, manuals, advertising, and promotion of OSHA standards to make known information on maintenance and repair of K-rims and to warn about dangers associated with misassembly or use of worn parts. Hodder never saw any of this material.

[Hodder sued Goodyear (and a subsidiary) who in turn brought in Hodder's employer, Remer Oil, as a third party defendant. The jury found that the K-rim was not defectively designed but that Goodyear was negligent and subject to punitive damages for failing to warn, and awarded Hodder $3.4 million in compensatory damages and $12.5 million in punitive damages. The allocation of fault was 85% to Goodyear, 15% to Remer, and none to Hodder. The jury also concluded that the K-rim's "useful life" had expired, and that Hodder was not negligent in failing to so determine. Goodyear appealed.]

I.

Minn.Stat. § 604.03, subd. 1 (1986), provides that in a products liability action, "it is a *defense* to a claim against a designer, manufacturer, distributor or seller of the product or a part thereof, that the injury was sustained following the expiration of the *ordinary useful life* of the product." (Emphasis added.) Subdivision 2 states, "The useful life of a product is not necessarily the life inherent in the product, but is the period during which with reasonable safety the product should be useful to the user." The subdivision goes on to say this period "shall be determined by reference to the experience of users of similar products," and then lists some of the factors to be taken into account.[2]

In this case the statute was read to the jurors, and, in answer to special questions, the jury found that the K-rim's useful life had expired and Hodder was not negligent in failing to have determined the useful life had expired. In denying Goodyear's post-trial motions, the trial court ruled that the useful life defense was inapplicable because, the jury having found the K-rim was not accompanied by adequate warnings, there never was a period during which with reasonable safety the rim was useful to the user. In other words, by the statute's own definition, the K-rim never had a useful life.

Hodder, of course, agrees with the trial court's ruling. Alternatively, Hodder argues the useful life defense is simply one factor for the jury to consider in determining fault. Goodyear, on the other hand, says the useful life defense is just that, a defense, a complete bar to any injury occurring after the useful life of the product has expired. Both parties select remarks made in the legislative hearings on the useful life defense which support their position. We think the legislative history is inconclusive, but this much is certain: The legislature was concerned about expanding products liability and intended to limit open-ended liability for aging products. The question for us is to what extent that purpose has been accomplished.

Section 604.03 is not a typical statute of repose. A statute of repose starts the limitation period for bringing an action from the date of manufacture or sale of the product, unlike a statute of limitations which starts from the date of injury. A typical statute of repose will specify a presumptive number of years after which an action cannot be brought.[3] Here, however, the limitation period is determined by the

2. Subdivision 2 of section 604.03 reads in its entirety:

> The useful life of a product is not necessarily the life inherent in the product, but is the period during which with reasonable safety the product should be useful to the user. This period shall be determined by reference to the experience of users of similar products, taking into account present conditions and past developments, including but not limited to (1) wear and tear or deterioration from natural causes, (2) the progress of the art, economic changes, inventions and developments within the industry, (3) the climatic and other local conditions peculiar to the user, (4) the policy of the user and similar users as to repairs, renewals and replacements, (5) the useful life as stated by the designer, manufacturer, distributor, or seller of the product in brochures or pamphlets furnished with the product or in a notice attached to the product, and (6) any modification of the product by the user.

3. Six states have useful or anticipated life provisions in their products liability statutes. In five states, the useful life is coupled with a presumptive period (or, in Connecticut, is an exception to a statute of repose) and expiration of the useful life unambiguously bars recovery. Conn.Gen. Stat. § 52–577a (1987); Idaho Code, § 6–1403(2) (Supp.1987); Kan.Stat.Ann. § 60–3303 (1983); Tenn.Code Ann. § 29–28–103 (1980); Wash.Rev.Code § 7.72.060 (Supp. 1987). Arkansas explicitly provides that use of a product beyond its "anticipated life" is an element of comparative fault. Ark.Stat.Ann. § 16–116–105 (1987). Min-

trier of fact after injury occurs. The jury makes this determination by "reference to users of similar products," and takes into account, among other things, natural deterioration, progress of the art, climatic and other peculiar local conditions, repair practices, the useful life as specified by the manufacturer, and any user modification.

The statute's useful life concept is ambiguous. It is not clear if useful life refers to the life of the particular product involved which caused the injury, or if the life of that particular product is to be measured by the useful life of all like products made by that particular manufacturer, or by the life of some generic product or industry norm. The statute seemingly tries to encompass all three approaches, but this presents problems. The particular product involved in the accident may conceivably have several different life spans depending on which measurement is used.

There are other problems. The statute surely is meant to cover a product originally nondefective but which becomes "defective" with age. But how long must a product last to avoid being labelled originally defective? Does the statute also cover an originally defective product? A product may be defective *ab initio,* but not cause injury until the normal life span of a nondefective like product expires. If these products are not covered, as the trial court ruled, the useful life statute is irrelevant to most products liability claims.

These problems, in turn, raise questions about the role of the user of the product (who may be the owner, a temporary user, or a hypothetical average person) in determining the product's useful life. Hodder points out the useful life definition relies on many of the same factors used to prove design defect, manufacturing defect and failure to warn, with the odd result that the same evidence is used to support a cause of action and to defeat it. Nevertheless, this may be exactly what the legislature intended. But Hodder also seems to say that the useful life defense incorporates a "reasonable person" standard of care, i.e., the defense is not operative unless the plaintiff user knows or should know the product is no longer reasonably safe to use. Goodyear counters by saying section 604.03 must be viewed as a statute of repose, *i.e.,* the defense focuses entirely on the condition of the product and has "nothing to do with a person's conduct." Further, because the defense applies to "any action," even a user's injury attributable to a manufacturer's failure to warn is barred after the product's useful life has expired.

Notwithstanding Goodyear's claim, it seems to us that section 604.03 does have something to do with the particular person who is using the particular product. Useful life is the period the product is "useful to the user." *Id.,* subd. 2. A factor to be considered is "the

nesota appears to be the only state that simply labels expiration of useful life as a "defense."

One effect of a statute of repose is that it has the potential of barring recovery even before the cause of action accrues. This raises constitutional questions, briefed by the parties, but which we do not reach.

policy of the user * * * as to repairs, renewals and replacements." *Id.* Another factor is "any modification of the product by the user." *Id.* A review of the legislative hearings also suggests that the legislature thought the obviousness of a product's deterioration to the particular user might be a consideration in determining useful life.[4] Significant, too, is the fact that the legislature first considered and abandoned a true 15–year statute of repose, H.F. 338, § 3, 70th Legis., 1977 (second House reading, April 18, 1977), and instead adopted a useful life concept derived from a 1977 federal task force study on products liability. See U.S. Dept. of Commerce, *Final Report, Interagency Task Force on Product Liability* (1977). The final report, with cursory analysis, endorsed the useful life concept, but the task force's legal study specifically recommended only that manufacturers utilize a notice disclaiming liability for a product after a specific period of time. The legal study contrasted the "useful-life-disclaimer approach" with more "drastic" statutes of repose, reasoning that "[i]f a claim is to be barred before the injury occurs, it seems more equitable to ensure that the employee or consumer knows that he is using the product at his own risk, and that if he is injured, there will be no recovery against the manufacturer." Id. at 28–29. Interestingly, section 604.03, subd. 2, includes among the factors determining useful life the manufacturer's notice of the product's useful life.

This much is clear. There will be cases where a reasonably prudent user should know a product's useful life has expired and instances where the user has no reason to know nor way of knowing. Goodyear argues that in either case, the user is barred from recovery. We decline to adopt this construction. Expiration of useful life is a defense but we think the legislature has stopped short of saying it is an absolute defense, and it is not for us to take that step, especially in view of the mixed signals given by the statute.

We hold, therefore, that the expiration of a product's useful life under section 604.03 is a factor to be weighed by the jury in determining the fault of the manufacturer and the fault of the user. In other words, the statute emphasizes to the trier of fact the importance, in determining comparative liability, of considering whether the product has outlived its useful life. Section 604.03 should be read to the jury as part of its instructions, perhaps with a prefatory statement that the statutory defense, if found to be applicable, is to be considered, along with other factors, in evaluating the conduct of the manufacturer and the user. There is no need for separate special verdict questions as

4. For example, Senator Spear inquired in committee how the consumer determines when useful life ends, and "what * * * a prudent consumer [does] under this kind of a provision to take reasonable precautions not to use a product when useful life has worn out." (Committee Hearing, Feb. 1, 1978). Senator Davies responded with a hypothetical lawnmower user who allows the muffler to rust off but continues using the mower until he becomes deaf. The user would have no claim for ear damage against the lawnmower or muffler manufacturer. The clear implication is that the deterioration was obvious to the user, who failed to exercise reasonable care in continuing to use the product.

were given in this case on useful life. The jury's evaluation of the useful life defense will be reflected in its answers to the special verdict questions on fault.

In this case, the jury found, in answer to a superfluous question, that the K-rim's useful life had expired. This answer is not consistent with the jury's finding of fault. The jury would have weighed the useful life expiration along with all the other liability aspects of the case in finding Hodder not negligent, Goodyear negligent, and in comparing Goodyear's fault with Remer Oil's fault. This was proper.

How to limit open-ended liability for aging products is perplexing. The useful life approach seems, at first glance, attractive, but as one commentator has noted, on closer study, these statutes "seem incoherent both theoretically and operationally." Schwartz, New Products, Old Products, Evolving Law, Retroactive Law, 58 N.Y.U.L.Rev. 796, 848 (1983). Indeed, the author wonders if it is possible to devise a workable repose statute that measures the time period by a useful life concept. It may be that such a statute is feasible, but until that time arrives, the courts apparently, as Professor Schwartz suggests, will simply have to monitor motions for directed verdicts closely in cases of aging products.

II.

* * *

If safety hazards in the use of K-rims did not become known to Goodyear until after 1955, after the K-rim which injured Hodder was made and sold, did Goodyear have a post-sale duty to warn Hodder and other similar users? We have not had occasion to deal with this question before. * * *

On the facts of this case, we hold that a continuing post-sale duty to warn existed and was adequately submitted. Cf. Comstock v. General Motors Corp., 358 Mich. 163, 99 N.W.2d 627 (1959). Hundreds of thousands of K-rims have been used in millions of tire changes over the years without incident; of the 134 or so K-rim explosions which did occur, many are explained by improper servicing or misuse. Goodyear steadfastly maintains its K-rim is a safe product if used properly. Nevertheless, it became evident by the late 1950's that K-rims could be temperamental; that the margin for error in servicing the K-rim assembly was dangerously small and it might explosively separate with seemingly little provocation; that when explosions did occur, serious injury or death usually resulted; and, therefore, that great care was required in the handling and servicing of K-rims. Further, Goodyear has continued over the years in the tire rim business, and, although all K-rim production was discontinued by 1969, Goodyear continued to advertise its K-rims as late as 1977, and has continued to sell tires and tubes for use with used K-rims. Finally, Goodyear undertook a duty to warn of K-rim dangers. Under these circumstances, it seems to us that Goodyear had a continuing duty to instruct and to warn, so that users of used K-rims would be apprised of safety hazards which, at an earlier time, were not fully appreciated. A continuing duty to warn arises only in special cases. We think this is such a case.

* * *

Goodyear also says it had no duty to warn because Hodder knew or should have known of the K-rim danger. While Hodder had received training in the servicing of multi-piece rims, his appreciation of the inherent dangers involved was not so perfect as to absolve Goodyear as a matter of law of its duty to warn.[6]

Goodyear did, in fact, recognize a continuing duty to warn and, by the late 1970's, before Hodder's accident, it distributed warnings and instructions by means of safety films, posters, manuals, and advertising. The jury, however, could have found that Goodyear's warnings were inadequate to reach K-rim users. We hold the jury's finding that Goodyear was negligent in performing its duty to warn is sustained by the evidence. While a closer question, we also hold the jury could find that breach of this duty was a cause of Hodder's injuries. [Citation.]

[Affirmed on point and remanded.]

NOTES

1. Lawsuits filed many years after the product was manufactured and sold involve a large number of problems for the courts and parties. Apart from the fact that all products eventually do wear out, there are increasing problems with the availability and reliability of evidence as time goes on: skid marks fade; burn marks are painted over; debris from the accident is cleaned up and thrown away; the product is repaired, disposed of, or lost; files are destroyed; witnesses forget, move away, get ill, and die. "There comes a time when [a potential defendant] ought to be secure in his reasonable expectation that the slate has been wiped clean of ancient obligations, and he ought not to be called on to resist a claim when 'evidence has been lost, memories have faded, and witnesses have disappeared.'" Raymond v. Eli Lilly & Co., 117 N.H. 164, 371 A.2d 170, 173–74 (1977) (Kenison, C.J.).

2. **Statutes of Limitation.** The traditional legislative way for addressing these problems has been through statutes of limitation, which bar claims that are brought more than a certain time—from 1 to 6 years, typically 2 or 3—after the claim accrues. Thus, the crucial question is when the claim first "accrues."

6. The 1973 Smith internal company report states in part:

"In the eyes of the user community, the [K-rim] part is a secondary component. It is a sturdy, heavy part, made of steel. He, therefore, thinks it has an unlimited useful life. * * *

"We have expert knowledge with regard to maintenance. Such information is published, but the information may not reach the involved user. If it does, he apparently doesn't see any reason for it. We do not follow up published information with personal contact to show how and the reason why.

"We have expert knowledge with regard to serviceability (possibly negative type of knowledge). Such information is not detailed in our publications. The involved user cannot tell a "good" part from a "bad". He doesn't believe the part won't function (provide support for the tire). He doesn't believe it will endanger him. Even if he feels it is unserviceable, he may not be able to replace it due to owner['s] or his bosses['] instructions; or a replacement may not be available. He may be willing to take a chance because he can't afford a new rim, or he's in a hurry."

A. **Tort.** Traditionally courts have held that tort claims accrue at the time of the wrong or injury. E.g., Cannon v. Sears, Roebuck & Co., 374 Mass. 739, 374 N.E.2d 582 (1978).

B. **Warranty.** Under U.C.C. § 2–725(2), warranty actions accrue on breach—upon tender of delivery—which usually is the date of sale. Patterson v. Her Majesty Industries, Inc., 450 F.Supp. 425 (E.D.Pa.1978), held that the relevant sale is retail rather than wholesale. While an express warranty may possibly "extend to future performance" under § 2–725(2), as for example "lifetime" guarantees, most courts have held that implied warranties by their very nature cannot "explicitly" extend to future performance under subsection (2). See Holdridge v. Heyer–Schulte Corp. of Santa Barbara, 440 F.Supp. 1088 (N.D.N.Y.1977).

C. **Wrongful death.** Such actions generally accrue at the date of death. See Arrowood v. General Motors Corp., 539 F.2d 1321 (4th Cir.1976).

3. In the event of a violent injury, such as the explosion of a gas canister or the loss of fingers in a press, the plaintiff will know that he has been injured (and often that he may have a legal claim against the defendant) from the moment the limitation period begins to run. But if the damage is a latent disease or condition, caused by a drug, asbestos, or other toxic substance, the plaintiff may not discover his injury until after the limitation period has lapsed. In warranty, he may not even suffer an injury until after the statute has run. Patterson v. Her Majesty Industries, Inc., 450 F.Supp. 425 (E.D.Pa.1978), quoted approvingly from Judge Frank's dissenting opinion in Dincher v. Marlin Firearms Co., 198 F.2d 821, 823 (2d Cir.1952), where he described the "Alice in Wonderland" effect of such a result:

> Except in topsy-turvy land, you can't die before you are conceived, or be divorced before ever you marry, or harvest a crop never planted, or burn down a house never built, or miss a train running on a nonexistent railroad. For substantially similar reasons, it has always heretofore been accepted, as a sort of legal "axiom," that a statute of limitations does not begin to run against a cause of action before that cause of action exists, i.e., before a judicial remedy is available to the plaintiff.

4. This problem has been addressed by both the courts and the legislatures of many states by the adoption of the "discovery rule," providing that the statute is tolled until the plaintiff discovers, or reasonably should have discovered, his injury (or, in some states, his legal claim):

> There are at least four points at which a tort cause of action may accrue: (1) when the defendant breaches his duty; (2) when the plaintiff suffers harm; (3) when the plaintiff becomes aware of his injury; and (4) when the plaintiff discovers the causal relationship between his harm and the defendant's misconduct. * * *
>
> * * *
>
> * * * We believe that the proper formulation of the rule and the one that will cause the least confusion is the one adopted by the majority of courts: A cause of action will not accrue under the discovery rule until the plaintiff discovers or in the exercise of reasonable diligence should have discovered not only that he has been injured but also that his injury may have been caused by the defendant's conduct.

Raymond v. Eli Lilly & Co., 117 N.H. 164, 371 A.2d 170, 172, 174 (1977).

5. **"Reform."** But the discovery rule proves a hardship on defendants who thus become vulnerable to lawsuits indefinitely, sometimes decades after the product was originally manufactured. As part of the products liability "reform" movement of the 1970s and 1980s, many states have responded by adopting "useful life" statutes, as addresed by *Hodder* in Minnesota, or, more commonly, "statutes of repose." A statute of repose is simply a statute of limitation—typically for 8, 10, or 12 years—which begins to run at the date of manufacture or, alternatively, initial sale. The thought is to give manufacturers a time certain after which they may be confident that their legal obligations have ended. Plaintiffs, however, once again become subject to the "Alice in Wonderland" effect of having their rights cut off before they arise. Yet such statutes often have exceptions for longer time periods if: (1) so warranted by the defendant; (2) the defendant is guilty of fraud; or (3) the injury was caused by asbestos, or by some other toxic substance generating a latent disease.

At the end of the period, the repose statutes variously provide for: (1) an absolute bar to all products liability actions; (2) a rebuttable presumption of non-defectiveness and non-negligence, rebuttable by a preponderance of the evidence or, alternatively, by clear and convincing evidence; (3) a bar to strict liability actions only; (4) a limitation of liability to the product's "useful life"; or (5) both a useful life provision and some form of repose provision.

Which of the above approaches best balances the interests of plaintiffs and defendants? Which is the most workable?

A small number of courts have held their state statutes of repose to be unconstitutional. See, e.g., Kennedy v. Cumberland Engineering Co., Inc., ___ R.I. ___, 471 A.2d 195 (1984). Contra, Tetterton v. Long Mfg. Co., Inc., 314 N.C. 44, 332 S.E.2d 67, 75 (1985) (listing states both ways). See generally McGovern, The Variety, Policy and Constitutionality of Product Liability Statutes of Repose, 30 Am.U.L.Rev. 579 (1981); Annot., 25 A.L.R. 4th 641 (1983).

6. Since the tort and warranty statutes of limitations are often different, a plaintiff's lawyer handling a claim arising out of an older accident will have to be cautious in framing his complaint. Cf. Salvador v. Atlantic Steel Boiler Co., 256 Pa.Super. 330, 389 A.2d 1148 (1978) (two year tort statute, not U.C.C. § 2–725, applicable to all third party personal injury actions whether or not pleaded under U.C.C.; "It takes a very strained reading of Section 2–725 to conclude that it was ever meant to apply to persons other than the contracting parties").

7. A John Doe complaint may be filed against an unknown manufacturer during the statute of limitations and amended, to add the manufacturer's name, after the statute has run. Although this procedure is permissible in some states, which hold that the replacement of the John Doe designation with the manufacturer's real name relates back to the original timely suit, it is unclear whether the procedure is permitted in federal courts under Fed.R.Civ. P. 15(c). Compare Britt v. Arvanitis, 590 F.2d 57 (3d Cir.1978) (not permitted), with Lindley v. General Elec. Co., 780 F.2d 797 (9th Cir.), cert. denied, 476 U.S. 1186, 106 S.Ct. 2926, 91 L.Ed.2d 554 (1986) (procedure, permitted under state law, not prohibited by Rule 15(c)).

8. The passage of time gives rise to an enormous web of interrelated issues examined throughout this book, including foreseeability, defectiveness, changes in the state of the art, consumer abuse, cause in fact, proximate cause (third party abuse), proof (admissibility of recall campaign letters; evidence of subsequent improvements in warnings or design), statutes of limitations, and statutes of repose.

9. **Conflict of Laws.** Important issues involving the conflict of laws are raised by the many variations in statutes of limitations and repose among the states. See generally R. Leflar, L. MacDougal, & R. Felix, American Conflicts Law 348–56 (4th ed. 1986). A recent case of importance is Shewbrooks v. A.C. & S. Inc., 529 So.2d 557 (Miss.1988) (5–4), in which the Mississippi Supreme Court refused to dismiss an asbestos personal injury suit, brought by a Delaware couple in Mississippi, because the statute for such an action had run in Delaware (2 years) but not in Mississippi (6 years). Since the defendants were engaged in business in Mississippi, and hence had sufficient contacts to satisfy due process, the court held that the case should not be dismissed on forum non conveniens grounds, although the parties had no other connection with the state. A dissenting Judge lamented: "We have doomed Mississippi to become a dumping ground for the nation's homeless tort litigation." It may not remain so for long, since both houses of the state legislature have passed bills reducing the statute of limitations, although they have not yet agreed on a new time limit. Prod. Saf. & Liab. Rep. (BNA) 510 (June 3, 1988). See generally Sun Oil Co. v. Wortman, 486 U.S. ___, 108 S.Ct. 2117, 100 L.Ed.2d 743 (1988) (states may constitutionally apply their own statutes of limitations to claims governed by law of other states).

10. See generally Phillips, An Analysis of Proposed Reform of Products Liability Statutes of Limitations, 56 N.C.L.Rev. 663 (1978); Birnbaum, "First Breath's" Last Gasp: The Discovery Rule in Products Liability Cases, 13 Forum 279 (1977); Massery, Date-of-Sale Statutes of Limitation—A New Immunity for Product Suppliers, 1977 Ins.L.J. 535.

D. UNAVOIDABLE DANGERS AND "STATE OF THE ART"

> A consumer would not expect a Model T to have the safety features which are incorporated in automobiles made today.

Bruce v. Martin–Marietta Corp., 544 F.2d 442, 447 (10th Cir.1976).

Some product defects are discoverable under prevailing technology, but only upon the expenditure of resources in excess of what is demanded by economic prudence. In production flaw cases of this type, manufacturers are generally held responsible for resulting injuries under strict liability, but not negligence. Other products contain dangerous conditions that are completely undiscoverable—regardless of the resources employed—until after the injury has resulted. Blood infected with serum hepatitis is a prime example. And there are some products—cigarettes being a good illustration—where the dangers are now recognized but unavoidable. The terms "undiscoverable," "unknowable," and "unavoidable" have often been used interchangeably by the courts and commentators in describing these types of cases. Another phrase used with some frequency by the courts is "state of the art," as in the state of the art defense, or, state of the art evidence. Although the phrase is variously defined by different courts in differing contexts, the basic idea is that a product risk was generally unknown, or the means of avoiding it unknown or unavailable, at the time the product was manufactured and sold.

Although these concepts have been developed only loosely by most courts, and so have not generally crystallized into formal rules, they share a common theme: the inability of the manufacturer to control the risk. The resulting legal issues go to the heart of the meaning of "defectiveness" and "strict liability" and force a reexamination of the central goals of products liability law. Among the fundamental questions raised in this area are: Who should bear the risks and benefits of changes in technology that develop over time? How should the law deal with changes in public attitudes toward risk, toward institutions such as manufacturers, toward individual responsibility, and toward products liability doctrine? Are present-day juries capable of judging products made before they were born according to the technology, standards and values of long ago? Is the judicial system capable of addressing these problems in a principled manner, or is the legislature a preferable forum for making the fundamental choices? These are some of the perplexing issues, with which the courts, legislatures and commentators are now just beginning to grapple, that are on the cutting edge of modern products liability law.

PONTIFEX v. SEARS, ROEBUCK & CO.

United States Court of Appeals, Fourth Circuit, 1955.
226 F.2d 909.

PER CURIAM. This is an appeal from a judgment on a directed verdict for defendant in a personal injury case. Plaintiff was injured when she was struck in the eye by a rope pulled to start the gasoline engine of a lawn mower. Plaintiff contends that there was negligence in the design of the lawn mower in that the rope was not permanently attached to a spring recoil mechanism, such as is found in the latest models of these machines, and that no warning was given of the danger of using it. We do not think, however, that it can be held to be negligence to sell an old model machine not equipped with a safety device of later models, and we find no evidence of negligence in the design or construction of the machine or of any need for warning or of any other negligence upon which a verdict for plaintiff could have been based.

Affirmed.

BRUCE v. MARTIN–MARIETTA CORP.

United States Court of Appeals, Tenth Circuit, 1976.
544 F.2d 442.

BREITENSTEIN, CIRCUIT JUDGE. These consolidated appeals relate to a product liability case arising out of an airplane crash. Plaintiffs-appellants are persons injured, and representatives of persons killed, in the crash. Defendant-appellee Martin–Marietta Corporation manufactured the plane. Defendant-appellee Ozark Airlines was an intermediate owner and seller of the plane. Jurisdiction is based on diversity. The district court gave summary judgment for the defendants. We affirm.

The airplane, a Martin 404, was chartered to carry the Wichita State University team and some of its supporters to a football game in Logan, Utah. On October 2, 1970, the plane crashed into a mountain west of Silver Plume, Colorado. The plane first struck trees at an altitude of approximately 10,800 ft. and then travelled 425 ft. before coming to rest. Seats in the passenger cabin broke loose from their floor attachments, were thrown forward against the bulkhead of the plane, and blocked exit. A fire then developed. Of the 40 persons on the plane, 32 died in the crash.

Martin manufactured the plane and sold it to Eastern Airlines in March, 1952. Eastern used the plane about ten years and in 1962 sold it to Mohawk Airlines which used it about three years and sold it to Ozark Airlines in 1965.

In 1967, Ozark sold the plane to Fairchild–Hiller Corporation, a manufacturer of aircraft. The plane was in storage until sometime in 1970 when it was sold to Jack Richards Aircraft Company. Golden Eagle Aviation contracted with Wichita State University to provide transportation for its football games away from home. Golden Eagle supplied the crew and used the Richards aircraft. Eastern, Mohawk and Ozark are all carriers providing scheduled services under pertinent federal aviation regulations. The defendants in the instant suit are Martin and Ozark.

On these appeals the plaintiffs do not contend that any action of either defendant caused the plane to crash. Their claims are that the defendants' failures to design, manufacture, or maintain the plane in crashworthy condition caused the deaths, or enhanced the injuries, of the passengers. The alleged defects are the inadequacy of the seat fastenings and the lack of protection against fire. Plaintiffs seek recovery on theories of negligence, implied warranty, and strict liability in tort.

* * *

In support of its motion for summary judgment, Martin submitted the affidavit of its Assistant Secretary [stating that the plane conformed to all Civil Aeronautics Administration requirements concerning seats and fire protection].

In response, plaintiffs presented the affidavit of an aircraft accident investigator whose qualifications are not questioned. He said:

> "My studies thus far indicate that there were airline passenger seats in common use on October 2, 1970, which, if installed in the subject Martin 404 aircraft, would have remained in place throughout this otherwise survivable accident

and would not have trapped the occupants in the burning aircraft. An occupant in this crash should not have had his escape from the burning aircraft impeded by seat failures. In the crash in question the seat failures constituted an unreasonable dangerous condition to the passengers because the seat failures prevented them from exiting the burning aircraft."

* * *

Plaintiffs do not controvert the Martin affidavit that the plane which crashed was designed "to meet or exceed" all applicable CAA requirements. They emphasize that the 1938 Act refers to "minimum standards" but they do not present any more stringent standards which might have been applicable at the time of manufacture.

The plaintiffs' specific allegations relate to the fire hazard and the adequacy of the seat fastenings. On the fire hazard, plaintiffs do not contest the Martin affidavit which shows not only compliance with air safety regulations but also specific design features for protection against fire. The only fact shown by plaintiffs with regard to the seats is that in 1970, 18 years after Martin made and sold the plane, airplane passenger seats, which would have withstood the crash, were in use. The record establishes that when the plane was made and first sold, its design was within the state of the art. The plaintiffs' affidavit that 18 years after the manufacture and sale of the plane safer passenger seats were in use is not relevant to the determination of whether Martin, by satisfying the 1952 state-of-art requirements, exercised reasonable care and, hence, was not negligent.

Plaintiffs say that state-of-art evidence is not material when the claim is based on strict liability. They argue that a showing of a design defective in 1970 establishes that the plane was defective in 1952, the time of the original sale, absent a subsequent alteration of the plane. For support of their position, plaintiffs rely on Pryor v. Lee C. Moore Corp., 10 Cir., 262 F.2d 673, and Mickle v. Blackmon, 252 S.C. 202, 166 S.E.2d 173. These cases hold that prolonged safe use of a product is evidence of lack of defect but is not conclusive. We have no quarrel with the rule but have no need to apply it here.

There is authority that state-of-art evidence is not relevant to a strict liability claim. Cunningham v. MacNeal Memorial Hospital, 47 Ill.2d 443, 226 N.E.2d 897, 902, 904; and Gelsumino v. E.W. Bliss Co., 10 Ill.App.3d 604, 295 N.E.2d 110, 113. The basic reasoning is that the principles noted in § 402A(1) are, by subsection (a), made applicable although "the seller has exercised all possible care in the preparation and sale of his product." To our knowledge, none of the states whose laws might apply to the instant case have adopted the Illinois rule. We respectfully reject it.

* * *

[T]here is "general" agreement that to prove liability under § 402A the plaintiff must show that the product was dangerous beyond the expectation of the ordinary customer. State-of-art evidence helps to determine the expectation of the ordinary consumer. A consumer would not expect a Model T to have the safety features which are incorporated in automobiles made today. The same expectation applies to airplanes. Plaintiffs have not shown that the ordinary consumer would expect a plane made in 1952 to have the safety features of one made in 1970. State-of-art evidence was properly received and considered by the trial court.

* * *

The judgments in favor of Martin and Ozark are severally affirmed.

BOATLAND OF HOUSTON, INC. v. BAILEY

Supreme Court of Texas, 1980.
609 S.W.2d 743.

McGEE, JUSTICE.

This is a product defect case involving an alleged defect in the design of a 16–foot bass boat. The plaintiffs were the widow and adult children of Samuel Bailey, who was killed in a boating accident in May of 1973. They sued under the wrongful death statute, alleging that Samuel Bailey's death occurred because the boat he was operating was defectively designed. The boat had struck a partially submerged tree stump, and Bailey was thrown into the water. With its motor still running, the boat turned sharply and circled back toward the stump. Bailey was killed by the propeller * * *.

Bailey's wife and children sought damages under a strict liability theory from the boat's seller, Boatland of Houston, Inc. At trial, they urged several reasons why the boat was defectively designed, including inadequate seating and control area arrangement, unsafe stick steering and throttle design, and the failure of the motor to automatically turn off when Bailey was thrown from the boat.

The trial court rendered a take-nothing judgment based on the jury's failure to find that the boat was defective * * *. The court of civil appeals, with one justice dissenting, reversed and remanded * * *. 585 S.W.2d 805. We reverse the judgment of the court of civil appeals and affirm that of the trial court.

EVIDENCE OF DESIGN DEFECT

* * *

In Turner v. General Motors Corp., [584 S.W.2d 844, 848 (Tex. 1979)], this court discussed the strict liability standard of "defectiveness" as applied in design defect cases. Whether a product was defectively designed requires a balancing by the jury of its utility against the likelihood of and gravity of injury from its use. The jury may consider many factors before deciding whether a product's usefulness or desirability are outweighed by its risks. Their finding on defectiveness may be influenced by evidence of a safer design that would have prevented the injury.[2] Turner v. General Motors Corp., supra at 849. See Keeton, Product Liability and the Meaning of Defect, 5 St. Mary's L.J. 30, 38 (1973); Wade, Strict Tort Liability of Manufacturers, 19 Sw.L.J. 5, 17 (1965). Because defectiveness of the product in question is determined in relation to safer alternatives, the fact that its risks could be diminished easily or cheaply may greatly influence the outcome of the case.

Whether a product was defectively designed must be judged against the technological context existing at the time of its manufacture. Thus, when the plaintiff alleges that a product was defectively designed because it lacked a specific feature, attention may become focused on the feasibility of that feature—the capacity to provide the feature without greatly increasing the product's cost or impairing usefulness. This feasibility is a relative, not an absolute, concept; the more scientifically and economically feasible the alternative was, the more likely that a jury may find that the product was defectively designed. A plaintiff may advance the argument that a safer alternative was feasible with evidence that it was in actual use or was available at the time of manufacture. Feasibility may also be shown with evidence of the scientific and economic capacity to develop the safer alternative. Thus, evidence of the actual use of, or capacity to use, safer alternatives is relevant insofar as it depicts the available scientific knowledge and the practicalities of applying that knowledge to a product's design. This method of presenting evidence of defective design is not new to the Texas law of product liability. [Citations.]

As part of their case-in-chief, the Baileys produced evidence of the scientific and economic feasibility of a design that would have caused the boat's motor to automatically shut off when Bailey fell out. According to the Baileys, the boat's design should have incorporated an automatic cut-off system or the boat should have been equipped with a safety device known as a "kill switch."

The deposition of J.C. Nessmith, president of Boatland, was read, in which he stated that there were presently several types of "kill switches" available, and that they were now installed by Boatland when it assembled and sold bass boats.

* * *

The deposition testimony of George Horton, the inventor of a kill switch designed for open-top carriers, was also introduced. Horton began developing his "Quick Kill" in November of 1972 and applied for a patent in January of 1973. According to Horton, his invention required no breakthroughs in the state of the art of manufacturing or production. He stated that his invention was simple: a lanyard con-

2. In *Turner*, this court stated that a number of evidentiary factors may be considered in determining whether a product's design is defective. The product's usefulness and desirability, the likelihood and gravity of injury from its use, the ability to eliminate the risk without seriously increasing the product's usefulness or cost, and the expectations of the ordinary consumer are some of these factors. Turner v. General Motors Corp., 584 S.W.2d 844, 849 (Tex.1979).

nects the operator's body to a device that fits over the ignition key. If the operator moves, the lanyard is pulled, the device rotates, and the ignition switch turns off. When he began to market his "Quick Kill," the response by boat dealers was very positive, which Horton perceived to be due to the filling of a recognized need. He considered the kill switch to be a necessary safety device for a bass boat with stick steering. If the kill switch were hooked up and the operator thrown out, the killing of the motor would prevent the boat from circling back where it came from. Horton also testified that for 30 years racing boats had been using various types of kill switches. Thus, the concept of kill switches was not new.

* * *

Boatland elicited evidence to rebut the Baileys' evidence of the feasibility of equipping boats with kill switches or similar devices in March of 1973, when the boat was assembled and sold. The Baileys had been granted a running objection to all evidence of this nature. In response to the Baileys' evidence that kill switches were presently used by Boatland, Nessmith testified that he did not know of kill switches until the spring of 1973, and first began to sell them a year later.

In response to the Baileys' evidence that the "Quick Kill" was readily available at the time of trial, Horton stated on cross-examination that until he obtained the patent for his "Quick Kill" in 1974 he kept the idea to himself. Before he began to manufacture them, he investigated the market for competitive devices and found none. The only applications of the automatic engine shut-off concept in use at the time were homemade, such as on racing boats. He first became aware of competitive devices in August of 1974.

Boatland introduced other evidence to show that kill switches were not available when Bailey's boat was sold. The deposition of Jimmy Wood, a game warden, was read in which he stated that he first became aware of kill switches in 1975. He testified that he had a "Quick Kill" on his boat since 1976, and he thought it was the only kill switch made. Willis Hudson, who manufactured the boat operated by Bailey, testified that he first became aware of kill switches in 1974 or 1975 and to his knowledge no such thing was available before then. Ralph Cornelius, the vice-president of a marine appliance dealership, testified that kill switches were not available in 1973. The first kill switch he saw to be sold was in 1974, although homemade "crash throttles" or foot buttons had long been in use.

Apart from evidence of the feasibility of an automatic motor cut-off design, evidence was introduced pertaining to whether such a design would have prevented Bailey's injuries. After considering the feasibility and effectiveness of an alternative design and other factors such as the utility and risk, the jury found that the boat was not defective. The trial court rendered judgment for Boatland. The Baileys complained on appeal that the trial court erred in admitting Boatland's evidence that kill switches were unavailable when Bailey's boat was assembled and sold. The court of civil appeals agreed, holding that the evidence was material only to the care exercised by Boatland and thus irrelevant in a strict liability case.

In its appeal to this court, Boatland contends that the court of civil appeals misconstrued the nature and purpose of its evidence. According to Boatland, when the Baileys introduced evidence that kill switches were a feasible safety alternative, Boatland was entitled to introduce evidence that kill switches were not yet available when Bailey's boat was sold and thus were not a feasible design alternative at that time.

The primary dispute concerning the feasibility of an alternative design for Bailey's boat was the "state of the art" when the boat was sold. The admissibility and effect of "state of the art" evidence has been a subject of controversy in both negligence and strict product liability cases. In negligence cases, the reasonableness of the defendant's conduct in placing the product on the market is in issue. Evidence of industry customs at the time of manufacture may be offered by either party for the purpose of comparing the defendant's conduct with industry customs. An offer of evidence of the defendant's compliance with custom to rebut evidence of its negligence has been described as the "state of the art defense." See generally 2 L. Frumer & M. Friedman, Products Liability § 16A[4][i] (1980). In this connection, it is argued that the state of the art is equivalent to industry custom and is relevant only to the issue of the defendant's negligence and irrelevant to a strict liability theory of recovery.

In our view, "custom" is distinguishable from "state of the art." The state of the art with respect to a particular product refers to the technological environment at the time of its manufacture. This technological environment includes the scientific knowledge, economic feasibility, and the practicalities of implementation when the product was manufactured. Evidence of this nature is important in determining whether a safer design was feasible. The limitations imposed by the state of the art at the time of manufacture may affect the feasibility of a safer design. Evidence of the state of the art in design defect cases has been discussed and held admissible in other jurisdictions. See, e.g., Raney v. Honeywell, Inc., 540 F.2d 932 (8th Cir.1976); Caterpillar Tractor Co. v. Beck, 593 P.2d 871 (Alaska 1979); Barker v. Lull Engineering Co., 20 Cal.3d 413, 573 P.2d 443, 143 Cal.Rptr. 225 (1978); Kerns v. Engelke, 76 Ill.2d 154, 28 Ill.Dec. 500, 390 N.E.2d 859 (1979); Cepeda v. Cumberland Engineering Co., Inc., 76 N.J. 152, 386 A.2d 816 (1978). [Citations.] In this case, the evidence advanced by both parties was relevant to the feasibility of designing bass boats to shut off automatically if the operator fell out, or more specifically, the feasibility of equipping bass boats with safety switches.

The Baileys offered state of the art evidence to establish the feasibility of a more safely designed boat: They established that when Bailey's boat was sold in 1973, the general concept of a boat designed so that its motor would automatically cut off had been applied for years on racing boats. One kill switch, the "Quick Kill," was invented at that time and required no mechanical breakthrough. The Baileys were also allowed to show that other kill switches were presently in use and that the defendant itself presently installed them.

Logically, the plaintiff's strongest evidence of feasibility of an alternative design is its actual use by the defendant or others at the time of manufacture. Even if a safer alternative was not being used, evidence that it was available, known about, or capable of being developed is relevant in determining its feasibility. In contrast, the defendant's strongest rebuttal evidence is that a particular design alternative was impossible due to the state of the art. Yet the defendant's ability to rebut the plaintiff's evidence is not limited to showing that a particular alternative was impossible; it is entitled to rebut the plaintiff's evidence of feasibility with evidence of limitations on feasibility. A suggested alternative may be invented or discovered but not be feasible for use because of the time necessary for its application and implementation. Also, a suggested alternative may be available, but impractical for reasons such as greatly increased cost or impairment of the product's usefulness. When the plaintiff has introduced evidence that a safer alternative was feasible because it was used, the defendant may then introduce contradictory evidence that it was not used.

Thus in response to the Baileys' evidence of kill switch use in 1978, the time of trial, Boatland was properly allowed to show that they were not used when the boat was sold in 1973. To rebut proof that safety switches were possible and feasible when Bailey's boat was sold because the underlying concept was known and the "Quick Kill," a simple, inexpensive device had been invented, Boatland was properly allowed to show that neither the "Quick Kill" nor any other kill switch was available at that time.

It could reasonably be inferred from this evidence that although the underlying concept of automatic motor cut-off devices was not new, kill switches were not as feasible an alternative as the Baileys' evidence implied. Boatland did not offer evidence of technological impossibility or absolute nonfeasibility; its evidence was offered to show limited availability when the boat was sold. Once the jury was informed of the state of the art, it was able to consider the extent to which it was feasible to incorporate an automatic cut-off device or similar design characteristic into Bailey's boat. The feasibility and effectiveness of a safer design and other factors such as utility and risk, were properly considered by the jury before it ultimately concluded that the boat sold to Bailey was not defectively designed.[3]

3. This opinion, insofar as it holds that certain evidence of the state of the art is admissible on the issue of defectiveness in product design cases, is not intended to suggest that such evidence constitutes a defense, such as do misuse and assumption of the risk. Nor does evidence of the state of the art entitle the defendant to a defensive issue inquiring whether it complied with the state of the art at the time of manufacture.

In cases involving strict liability for defective design, liability is determined by the product's defective condition; there is no need to prove that the defendant's conduct was negligent. Considerations such as the utility and risk of the product in question and the feasibility of safer alternatives are presented according to the facts as they are proved to be, not according to the defendant's perceptions. Thus, even though the defendant has exercised due care his product may be found defective. When the Baileys introduced evidence of the use of kill switches, Boatland was entitled to introduce rebuttal evidence of non-use at the time of manufacture due to limitations imposed by the state of the art. Evidence offered under these circumstances is offered to rebut plaintiff's evidence that a safer alternative was feasible and is relevant to defectiveness. It was not offered to show that a custom existed or to infer the defendant's compliance therewith. We would be presented with a different question if the state of the art in 1973 with respect to kill switches had not been disputed and Boatland had attempted to avoid liability by offering proof that Bailey's boat complied with industry custom.

* * *

CONCLUSION

For the reasons stated above the judgment of the court of civil appeals is reversed. The judgment rendered by the trial court, that the Baileys take nothing against Boatland, is affirmed.

ON REHEARING

CAMPBELL, JUSTICE, dissenting.

I dissent.

"State of the art" does not mean "the state of industry practice." "State of the art" means "state of industry knowledge." At the time of the manufacture of the boat in question, the device and concept of a circuit breaker, as is at issue in this case, was simple, mechanical, cheap, practical, possible, economically feasible and a concept seventy years old, which required no engineering or technical breakthrough. The concept was known by the industry. This fact removes it from "state of the art."

Boatland is a retail seller. It is not the manufacturer. From the adoption of strict liability in this case, and consideration of public policy, each entity involved in the chain of commercial distribution of a defective product has been subject to strict liability for injuries thereby caused, even though it is in no way responsible for the creation of a defective product or could not cure the defect. The remedy for a faultless retail seller is an action for indemnity against the manufacturer.

In products liability, the measure is the dangerously defective quality of the specific product in litigation. The focus is on the product, not the reasoning behind the manufacturer's option of design or the care exercised in making such decisions. Commercial availability or defectiveness as to Boatland is not the test. Defectiveness as to the product is the test. If commercial unavailability is not a defense or limitation on feasibility to the manufacturer, it cannot be a defense to the seller.

The manufacturer of the boat, Mr. Hudson, testified as follows as concerns the concept of a "kill switch." It is practically without dispute that this is one of the simplest mechanical devices and concepts known to man. Its function is, can be, and was performed by many and varied simple constructions. It is more a concept than an invention. The concept has been around most of this century. It is admittedly an easily incorporated concept. Was an invention required in order to incorporate a circuit breaker on a bass boat? Absolutely not! Did the manufacturer have to wait until George Horton invented his specific "Quick Kill" switch before it could incorporate a kill switch of some sort on its bass boats? Absolutely not! Mr. Hudson uses an even simpler electrical circuit breaker on his boats.

Mr. Hudson testified he could have made a kill switch himself, of his own, and of many possible designs, but simply did not do it. Why didn't he do it? He didn't think about it. He never had any safety engineer examine his boats. He hadn't heard of such, he puts them on now, but still thinks people won't use them.

Was the manufacturer faced with a limitation or state of the art due to commercial unavailability? No. If the manufacturer of this boat were the defendant in this case, would the majority hold under this evidence that the commercial unavailability of someone else's simple product is a limitation on the manufacturer's capability (feasibility) to incorporate a device performing the same safety function on its boat? Not if any semblance of strict product liability is to be preserved.

The test for defectiveness of a given product is the same, whether the defendant is the manufacturer, wholesaler or retail seller. The focus is upon the product and not the care or conduct of the particular defendant. * * *

* * *

NOTE

"State of the art" means quite different things to different people. To some (especially manufacturers), the phrase refers to the customary practice in the industry. See Phillips, The Standard for Determining Defectiveness in Products Liability, 46 U.Cin.L.Rev. 101, 115 n. 71 (1977). To others (especially plaintiffs' counsel), it means the ultimate in existing technology, including all knowledge pertinent to the problem existing at the time, regardless of its source, that is published and accessible to researchers in libraries.

Nebraska's "reform" act defines state of the art as "the best technology reasonably available at the time." See Prod.Liab.Rep. (CCH) ¶ 92,812. Would a journal article on point, published in another country in a foreign language, be "reasonably available" to an American manufacturer?

BESHADA v. JOHNS–MANVILLE PRODUCTS CORP.

Supreme Court of New Jersey, 1982.
90 N.J. 191, 447 A.2d 539.

PASHMAN, J.

The sole question here is whether defendants in a product liability case based on strict liability for failure to warn may raise a "state of the art" defense. Defendants assert that the danger of which they failed to warn was undiscovered at the time the product was marketed and that it was undiscoverable given the state of scientific knowledge at that time. The case comes to us on appeal from the trial court's denial of plaintiffs' motion to strike the state-of-the-art defense. For the reasons stated below, we reverse the trial court judgment and strike the defense.

I

These six consolidated cases are personal injury and wrongful death actions brought against manufacturers and distributors of asbestos products. Plaintiffs are workers, or survivors of deceased workers, who claim to have been exposed to asbestos for varying periods of time. They allege that as a result of that exposure they contracted asbestosis (a non-malignant scarring of the lungs), mesothelioma (a rare cancer of the lining of the chest, the pleura, or the lining of the abdomen, the peritoneum) and other asbestos-related illnesses.

* * *

There is substantial factual dispute about what defendants knew and when they knew it. A trial judge in the Eastern District of Texas, the forum for numerous asbestos-related cases, has concluded that "[k]nowledge of the danger can be attributed to the industry as early as the mid–1930's. . . ." Hardy v. Johns–Manville Sales Corp., 509 F.Supp. 1352, 1355 (E.D.Texas 1981) (footnote omitted). Defendants respond, however, that it was not until the 1960's that the medical profession in the United States recognized that a potential health hazard arose from the use of insulation products containing asbestos. Before that time, according to defendants, the danger from asbestos was believed limited to workers in asbestos textile mills, who were exposed to much higher concentrations of asbestos dust than were the workers at other sites, such as shipyards. Defendants claim that it was not discovered until recently that the much smaller concentrations those workers faced were also hazardous.

We need not resolve the factual issues raised. For purposes of plaintiffs' motion to strike the defense, we assume the defendants' version of the facts. The issue is whether the medical community's presumed unawareness of the dangers of asbestos is a defense to plaintiffs' claims.

* * *

III

Our inquiry starts with the principles laid down in Freund v. Cellofilm Properties, Inc., [87 N.J. 229, 432 A.2d 925 (1981)], Suter v. San Angelo Foundry & Machine Company, [81 N.J. 150, 406 A.2d 140 (1979)], and Cepeda v. Cumberland Engineering Company, Inc., 76 N.J. 152, 386 A.2d 816 (1978). In Suter, we summarized the principle of strict liability as follows:

> If at the time the seller distributes a product, it is not reasonably fit, suitable and safe for its intended or reasonably foreseeable purposes so that users or others who may be expected to come in contact with the product are injured as a result thereof, then the seller shall be responsible for the ensuing damages. [Id. at 169, 406 A.2d 140 (footnote omitted)]

The determination of whether a product is "reasonably fit, suitable and safe" depends on a comparison of its risks and its utility (risk-utility equation).

> Central to this theory is the risk-utility equation for determining liability. The theory is that only safe products should be marketed—a safe product being one whose utility outweighs its inherent risk, provided that risk has been reduced to the greatest extent possible consistent with the product's continued utility. [Freund, 87 N.J. at 238, n. 1, 432 A.2d 925]

In *Cepeda,* we explained that in the context of design defect liability, strict liability is identical to liability for negligence, with one important caveat: "The only qualification is as to the requisite of foreseeability by the manufacturer of the dangerous propensity of the chattel manifested at the trial—this being imputed to the manufacturer." Cepeda, 76 N.J. at 172, 386 A.2d 816. See Freund v. Cellofilm Properties, Inc., 87 N.J. at 239, 439 A.2d 925. In so holding, we adopted the explication of strict liability offered by Dean Wade:

> The time has now come to be forthright in using a tort way of thinking and tort terminology [in cases of strict liability in tort]. There are several ways of doing it, and it is not difficult. The simplest and easiest way, it would seem, is to assume that the defendant knew of the dangerous condition of the product and ask whether he was then negligent in putting it on the market or supplying it to someone else. In other words, the scienter is supplied as a matter of law, and there is no need for the plaintiff to prove its existence as a matter of fact. Once given this notice of the dangerous condition of the chattel, the question then becomes whether the defendant was negligent to people who might be harmed by that condition if they came into contact with it or were in the vicinity of it. Another way of saying this is to ask whether the magnitude of the risk created by the dangerous condition of the product was outweighed by the social utility attained by putting it out in this fashion. [Wade, "On the Nature of Strict Tort Liability for

Products," 44 Miss.L.J. 825, 834–35 (1973), quoted in Cepeda, 76 N.J. at 172, 386 A.2d 816]

Stated differently, negligence is conduct-oriented, asking whether defendant's actions were reasonable; strict liability is product-oriented, asking whether the product was reasonably safe for its foreseeable purposes. Freund, 87 N.J. at 238, 432 A.2d 925.[3]

"Warning" cases constitute one category of strict liability cases. Their relation to the strict liability principles set forth above can best be analyzed by focusing on the definition of safe products found in footnote 1 of *Freund.* See supra at 544. For purposes of analysis, we can distinguish two tests for determining whether a product is safe: (1) does its utility outweigh its risk? and (2) if so, has that risk been reduced to the greatest extent possible consistent with the product's utility? Id. at 238, n. 1, 432 A.2d 925. The first question looks to the product as it was in fact marketed. If that product caused more harm than good, it was not reasonably fit for its intended purposes. We can therefore impose strict liability for the injuries it caused without having to determine whether it could have been rendered safer. The second aspect of strict liability, however, requires that the risk from the product be reduced to the greatest extent possible without hindering its utility. Whether or not the product passes the initial risk-utility test, it is not reasonably safe if the same product could have been made or marketed more safely.[4]

Warning cases are of this second type.[5] When plaintiffs urge that a product is hazardous because it lacks a warning, they typically look to the second test, saying in effect that regardless of the overall cost-benefit calculation the product is unsafe because a warning could make it safer at virtually no added cost and without limiting its utility. *Freund* recognized this, noting that in cases alleging "an inadequate warning as to safe use, the utility of the product, as counter-balanced against the risks of its use, is rarely at issue." Id. at 242, 432 A.2d 925.

3. The imputation of knowledge is, of course, a legal fiction. It is another way of saying that for purposes of strict liability the defendant's knowledge of the danger is irrelevant. See Freund v. Cellofilm Products, Inc., 87 N.J. at 239, 432 A.2d 925, quoting Keeton, "Products Liability—Inadequacy of Information," 48 Tex.L.Rev. 398, 407–08 (1970). The imputation of knowledge does not represent any presumption that defendants knew or even that they could have known of the product's dangers.

4. This dichotomy is created only for purposes of analysis, because it will help explain the role of state-of-the-art in strict liability cases. In actuality, the only test for product safety is whether the benefit outweighs the risk. However, in calculating the benefit from any product, one must consider alternate products that can yield the same benefit at lower risk. Wade, 44 Miss.L.J. at 837–38.

5. This two-part distinction can best be clarified by looking at how it would apply to automobiles without seatbelts. Because of the great utility of cars, few would dispute that even without seatbelts, a car's utility to society outweighs its risks. Thus, cars would be considered safe under the first aspect of the test. However, since seatbelts make cars safer without hindering utility, cars without seatbelts are deemed unsafe by virtue of the second part of the *Freund* test. Warnings are like seatbelts: regardless of the utility and risk of a product without warnings, a warning can generally be added without diminishing utility. Freund v. Cellofilm Properties, Inc., 87 N.J. at 238–39, n. 1, 432 A.2d 925.

Freund is our leading case on strict liability for failure to warn. In *Freund,* Justice Handler applied the principles set forth above, initially laid down in *Suter* and *Cepeda,* to warning cases. The issue there was whether there is any difference between negligence and strict liability in warning cases. We stated unequivocally that there is. That difference is the same difference that we noted in *Suter* and *Cepeda* concerning other design defect cases:

> when a plaintiff sues under strict liability, there is no need to prove that the manufacturer knew or should have known of any dangerous propensities of its product—such knowledge is imputed to the manufacturer. [Freund v. Cellofilm Properties, Inc., 87 N.J. at 239, 432 A.2d 925]

* * *

IV

As it relates to warning cases, the state-of-the-art defense asserts that distributors of products can be held liable only for injuries resulting from dangers that were scientifically discoverable at the time the product was distributed. Defendants argue that the question of whether the product can be made safer must be limited to consideration of the available technology at the time the product was distributed. Liability would be absolute, defendants argue, if it could be imposed on the basis of a subsequently discovered means to make the product safer since technology will always be developing new ways to make products safer. Such a rule, they assert, would make manufacturers liable whenever their products cause harm, whether or not they are reasonably fit for their foreseeable purposes.

Defendants conceptualize the scientific unknowability of the dangerous propensities of a product as a technological barrier to making the product safer by providing warnings. Thus, a warning was not "possible" within the meaning of the *Freund* requirement that risk be reduced "to the greatest extent possible."

In urging this position, defendants must somehow distinguish the *Freund* holding that knowledge of the dangers of the product is imputed to defendants as a matter of law. A state-of-the-art defense would contravene that by requiring plaintiffs to prove at least that knowledge of the dangers was scientifically available at the time of manufacture.

Defendants argue that *Freund* did not specify precisely what knowledge is imputed to defendants. They construe *Freund* to impute only that degree of knowledge of the product's dangerousness that existed at the time of manufacture or distribution.[6]

6. Defendants seek support in this regard from the following passage in *Suter:*

> Depending upon the proofs, some factors which may be considered by the jury in deciding the reasonableness of the manufacturer's conduct include the technological feasibility of manufacturing a product whose design would have prevented or avoided the accident, given the known state of the art; and the likelihood that the product will cause injury and the probable seriousness of the injury. We observe in passing that the state of the art refers not only to the common practice and standards

While we agree that *Freund* did not explicitly address this question, the principles laid down in *Freund* and our prior cases contradict defendants' position. Essentially, state-of-the-art is a negligence defense. It seeks to explain why defendants are not culpable for failing to provide a warning. They assert, in effect, that because they could not have known the product was dangerous, they acted reasonably in marketing it without a warning. But in strict liability cases, culpability is irrelevant. The product was unsafe. That it was unsafe because of the state of technology does not change the fact that it was unsafe. Strict liability focuses on the product, not the fault of the manufacturer. "If the conduct is unreasonably dangerous, then there should be strict liability without reference to what excuse defendant might give for being unaware of the danger." Keeton, 48 Tex.L.Rev. at 408.

When the defendants argue that it is unreasonable to impose a duty on them to warn of the unknowable, they misconstrue both the purpose and effect of strict liability. By imposing strict liability, we are not requiring defendants to have done something that is impossible. In this sense, the phrase "duty to warn" is misleading. It implies negligence concepts with their attendant focus on the reasonableness of defendant's behavior. However, a major concern of strict liability—ignored by defendants—is the conclusion that if a product was in fact defective, the distributor of the product should compensate its victims for the misfortune that it inflicted on them.

* * *

The most important inquiry, however, is whether imposition of liability for failure to warn of dangers which were undiscoverable at the time of manufacture will advance the goals and policies sought to be achieved by our strict liability rules. We believe that it will.

Risk Spreading. One of the most important arguments generally advanced for imposing strict liability is that the manufacturers and distributors of defective products can best allocate the costs of the injuries resulting from those products. The premise is that the price of a product should reflect all of its costs, including the cost of injuries caused by the product. This can best be accomplished by imposing liability on the manufacturer and distributors. Those persons can insure against liability and incorporate the cost of the insurance in the price of the product. In this way, the costs of the product will be borne by those who profit from it: the manufacturers and distributors who profit from its sale and the buyers who profit from its use. "It should

in the industry but also to other design alternatives within practical and technological limitations at the time of distribution. [81 N.J. 171–72, 406 A.2d 140 (citation omitted)]

* * *

We hold in this case that a state-of-the-art defense should not be allowed in failure to warn cases. There are strong conceptual similarities between warning and safety device cases. See n. 3 above. Thus, the reasoning applied here may be equally applicable to cases involving failure to include appropriate safety devices in products. However, there may be distinctions between the two situations. We specifically decline to address whether a state-of-the-art defense is appropriate to safety device cases.

be a cost of doing business that in the course of doing that business an unreasonable risk was created." Keeton, 48 Tex.L.Rev. at 408. See Prosser, The Law of Torts, § 75, p. 495 (4th Ed.1971).

Defendants argue that this policy is not forwarded by imposition of liability for unknowable hazards. Since such hazards by definition are not predicted, the price of the hazardous product will not be adjusted to reflect the costs of the injuries it will produce. Rather, defendants state, the cost "will be borne by the public at large and reflected in a general, across the board increase in premiums to compensate for unanticipated risks." There is some truth in this assertion, but it is not a bad result.

* * * [S]preading the costs of injuries among all those who produce, distribute and purchase manufactured products is far preferable to imposing it on the innocent victims who suffer illnesses and disability from defective products. This basic normative premise is at the center of our strict liability rules. It is unchanged by the state of scientific knowledge at the time of manufacture.

Finally, contrary to defendants' assertion, this rule will not cause the price and production level of manufactured products to diverge from the so-called economically efficient level. Rather, the rule will force the price of any particular product to reflect the cost of insuring against the possibility that the product will turn out to be defective.

Accident Avoidance. * * * Defendants urge that this argument has no force as to hazards which by definition were undiscoverable. Defendants have treated the level of technological knowledge at a given time as an independent variable not affected by defendants' conduct. But this view ignores the important role of industry in product safety research. The "state-of-the-art" at a given time is partly determined by how much industry invests in safety research. By imposing on manufacturers the costs of failure to discover hazards, we create an incentive for them to invest more actively in safety research.

Fact finding process. The analysis thus far has assumed that it is possible to define what constitutes "undiscoverable" knowledge and that it will be reasonably possible to determine what knowledge was technologically discoverable at a given time. In fact, both assumptions are highly questionable. The vast confusion that is virtually certain to arise from any attempt to deal in a trial setting with the concept of scientific knowability constitutes a strong reason for avoiding the concept altogether by striking the state-of-the-art defense.

Scientific knowability, as we understand it, refers not to what in fact was known at the time, but to what *could have been* known at the time. In other words, even if no scientist had actually formed the belief that asbestos was dangerous, the hazards would be deemed "knowable" if a scientist could have formed that belief by applying research or performing tests that were available at the time. Proof of what could have been known will inevitably be complicated, costly, confusing and time-consuming. Each side will have to produce experts in the history of science and technology to speculate as to what knowledge was feasible in a given year. We doubt that juries will be capable of even understanding the concept of scientific knowability, much less be able to resolve such a complex issue. Moreover, we should resist legal rules that will so greatly add to the costs both sides incur in trying a case.

* * *

In addition, discussion of state-of-the-art could easily confuse juries into believing that blameworthiness is at issue. Juries might mistakenly translate the confused concept of state-of-the-art into the simple question of whether it was defendants' fault that they did not know of the hazards of asbestos. But that would be negligence, not strict liability.

For precisely this reason, Professor Keeton has urged that negligence concepts be carefully avoided in strict liability cases.

> My principal thesis is and has been that theories of negligence should be avoided altogether in the products liability area in order to simplify the law, and that if the sale of a product is made under circumstances that would subject someone to an unreasonable risk in fact, liability for harm resulting from those risks should follow. [Keeton, 48 Tex.L.Rev. at 409 (footnote omitted)]

* * *

V

For the reasons expressed above, we conclude that plaintiffs' position is consistent with our holding in *Freund* and prior cases and will achieve the various policies underlying strict liability. The burden of illness from dangerous products such as asbestos should be placed upon those who profit from its production and, more generally, upon society at large, which reaps the benefits of the various products our economy manufactures. That burden should not be imposed exclusively on the innocent victim. Although victims must in any case suffer the pain involved, they should be spared the burdensome financial consequences of unfit products. At the same time, we believe this position will serve the salutary goals of increasing product safety research and simplifying tort trials.

Defendants have argued that it is unreasonable to impose a duty on them to warn of the unknowable. * * * [Yet] defendants' products were not reasonably safe because they did not have a warning. Without a warning, users of the product were unaware of its hazards and could not protect themselves from injury. We impose strict liability because it is unfair for the distributors of a defective product not to compensate its victims. As between those innocent victims and the distributors, it is the distributors—and the public which consumes their products—which should bear the unforeseen costs of the product.

The judgment of the trial court is reversed; the plaintiff's motion to strike the state-of-the-art defense is granted.

OWEN, RETHINKING THE POLICIES OF STRICT PRODUCTS LIABILITY

33 Vanderbilt L.Rev. 681, 703–07 (1980).

Compensation, Loss Shifting, and Loss Spreading

Sanctioned by generations of repetition in the law reports and journals, these three purported "goals" of tort law were embraced enthusiastically by courts and commentators seeking to justify the development of strict products liability. It is often heard that a central purpose of strict liability is to "compensate" the accident victim, to "shift the loss" (or risk) from the person who suffered it to the one who caused it, or to "spread the loss" (or risk) among others on whom it will fall less heavily. As variants of the same misconception, each of these three stock phrases is in need of the closest scrutiny.

Each of these concepts begins with the premise that the economic burden of an accident should for some reason be shifted away from the person on whom it falls, and to somebody else. A threshold danger with such a premise is that it presumptively sets in motion, without some independent showing of good cause, the intrusive and expensive machinery of governmental adjudication. Holmes may well have been right a century ago in arguing for an opposite approach. These "rationales," moreover, are mostly bootstrap explanations for an end result; they do indeed explain the *consequence* of a judgment requiring the defendant to pay the claimant for his loss, but they provide little guidance for deciding whether a defendant fairly should be made to pay for someone else's loss in the first place. The result, of course, of finding for the plaintiff under any rule of civil liability—whether in contract, property, tort, or antitrust—is usually to compensate the claimant and thus to shift his loss to the defendant who in turn will almost always somehow "spread" at least some of it among other people. So, while explanatory of an end result, the loss-shifting group of rationales do little to assist in making or justifying a decision to achieve that result. As decisional tools, all three rationales thus suffer incurably from being one-directional—they argue only that payment should be made. If it be assumed that about one-half the time the defendant should not in principle be made to pay, reliance on the loss-shifting rationales will thus be as likely to produce a wrong result as one that is correct. They therefore suffer as a group from structural inadequacy as decisional tools.

The risk-shifting goals do reflect certain values. At one level, the principal value advanced by shifting a loss away from an injured person, thus helping him regain his economic feet, is compassion. Yet losses shifted away from injured persons must necessarily be shifted onto other persons who may well deserve compassion, too. If the resource pot were big enough, it surely would be monstrous to deny economic rehabilitation to any person suffering an accidental loss, whether from product accident, earthquake, flood, automobile collision or any other calamity. Indeed, the sooner this nation can truly afford a total system of compensation and rehabilitation for all victims of all accidents, as New Zealand put in place a few years ago, and all *disease* victims as well, the better off we all will be. The costs of such compensation plans are enormous, however, and we would do well to reflect upon just how much of our collective resources are at stake. There simply is, unhappily, no great accident pit into which losses may be thrown and from which resources may be retrieved.

With a bit of help from [OPEC], we have passed in about a decade from a general perception that our economy would soon be able to produce enough to satisfy the basic wants of almost all our citizens to a realization of the very limited nature of many of our important resources. Until some dramatic breakthrough occurs in energy technology, which may not be within this century or even in our lifetimes, we may in fact be facing a reality of decreasing resources—of fewer and fewer goods to go around. When faced squarely with the question, many persons in such a world might want to rethink the value of compassion as a basis for allocating scarce resources. One might well doubt whether a principle that shifts all the losses of product accidents to manufacturers, and thus which serves to deplete the resources of the producers and employers, is well suited to the economic realities of the 1980s. It may be, to the contrary, that what is really needed in times of increasing scarcity are principles that give stimulus rather than disincentive to those who are in a position to make new discoveries and to increase productivity. Compassion, then, though a value to respect, may well compete with other important social goals.

At a fundamental level, the "compassionate" loss shifting rationale masks somewhat a scheme of "social engineering" or "distributive justice," the principal feature of which is wealth equalization—the shifting of wealth from rich to poor. This is disturbing for several reasons. First, one may question whether the judicial arm of government ought to be permitted to use the arguably fortuitous occasion of a product accident to achieve a kind of "taking" of a person's wealth because he has more of it than does the plaintiff. An accident may be a legitimate occasion for decisions of distributive justice if there are other good reasons for forcing a wealth transfer as well, but the question whether the relative wealth of the parties *alone* should determine accident compensation decisions is a fundamental one of social policy that should be made in the open through the collective legislative will of the people. If such questions of "taxation" policy for some reason must be made by courts, they should at least make clear the stakes at issue and the choices made.

Still another problem with the compassionate wealth equalization rationale is the assumption that the loss is shifted away from some "real" person to a mere institutional company. Since business entities are thought to promote the general public good in this country by providing goods and services desired by the people, a bias against institutional defendants may not make much sense. Such entities, moreover, are made up of real people, too—from the shareholders, who are at bottom almost always "small" investors, to employees and creditors. Ultimately, through more expensive, fewer, or less useful products, the public whom such entities exist to serve are the ones to whom at least part of the loss is passed. To say that the consuming public is thereby only paying for another cost involved in making the product again begs the question of on whom the loss should fairly fall.

"Spreading the loss" to many such persons does in fact relieve uninsured accident victims of a sudden, crushing economic blow that may tear apart the fabric of the victim's life. Compassion for such persons might indeed be chosen by the public, especially if forced to choose through some kind of Rawlsian "veil of ignorance." When constructing at the start the basic social compact, a rational person might well be risk-averse and so might choose to "chip in" a bit of wealth to insure himself and his neighbors against the risk of losing all. But America in the 1980s has come far indeed from such a primal stage. Today, most persons are insured under private plans against accidental losses, at least for the expenses of health care that may result. Free medical care on a welfare basis is often available for those who are not so covered, and a variety of private and public wage-continuation plans help to take some of the economic sting out of accidental injuries. For the large proportion of product accidents that occur in the workplace, workers' compensation helps at least to some extent. Since the very *raison d'etre* of such compensation plans is to insure against such losses, they are probably more efficiently administered than are accident insurance "plans" imposed judicially on product manufacturers. Nor may it be fair (or efficient) to penalize the prudent consumer who insures himself through health and wage insurance plans by forcing him to pay again through higher prices to overinsure himself and also to insure his less prudent neighbors. The risk shifting rationales may thus be misguided in the premises on which they rest.

Compensation and risk shifting should very probably be abandoned altogether as "rationales" of social policy for products liability decisionmaking. Such arguments are "structurally" inadequate as decisional tools, since they point in one direction only—toward liability. They mask social value judgments of the highest order that may well be better left to formal legislation. Moreover, the hidden values themselves rest on premises that grow shaky with analysis. Although loss spreading is a more justifiable social goal than the other two, it too suffers from many of the same weaknesses and thus should be turned to as a policy guide only with studied care. When the loss-shift clouds have cleared away, the difficult choices of social policy will appear more clearly, and princip[led] decisionmaking should be enhanced.

HENDERSON, COPING WITH THE TIME DIMENSION IN PRODUCTS LIABILITY

69 Calif.L.Rev. 919, 939–949 (1981).

Should Courts Rely on Post–Distribution Increases in Knowledge of Product Hazards?

Of the types of hindsight * * * reliance on post-distribution increases in knowledge of hazards is the most widely recognized. A growing number of courts and commentators is urging that time-of-trial knowledge of hazards be imputed to manufacturers when judging the reasonableness of their design and marketing choices. That some courts and commentators have refused to join this trend and that the Commerce Department's Model Uniform Product Liability Act refuses to condone this type of judicial reliance on hindsight emphasizes the need for analysis of this issue.

1. Would Such Reliance Promote Utility?

An argument frequently advanced in support of this form of judicial reliance on hindsight is that it will help to achieve the "risk control" objective. Imposing strict liability for unknown hazards should pressure manufacturers to invest more heavily in testing products before releasing them. Since strict liability eliminates some of the practical difficulties of establishing negligence-based liability, manufacturers will not be so willing to gamble on escaping liability by forgoing pre-distribution testing and research. However, imposing strict liability may create disincentives for manufacturers to reduce risks. For one thing, manufacturers may be discouraged from testing after distribution to discover whether products are causing harm. Under traditional negligence rules of liability, a manufacturer who discovers previously unknown hazards can escape liability by sharing that information with the public—as when the manufacturer warns prescribing physicians about prescription drugs. Under strict liability based on hindsight, a manufacturer helps to establish its liability by sharing such information, since greater knowledge raises the standard by which the manufacturer will be judged. To be sure, the longer the manufacturer distributes a product that turns out to be hazardous, the greater will be its total exposure to liability; therefore, the manufacturer might have an incentive to continue to test, to find out if the product should be discontinued or recalled. However, the manufacturer might decide that it is better to discontinue or reduce post-distribution efforts to determine whether its products are hazardous, so that it will be judged by a low standard of knowledge in the future. Although some increases in knowledge of hazards come from other sources, such as government studies, much of the research comes from private enterprise. Strict liability may discourage this important source of research and development.

Moreover, if manufacturers are held strictly liable based on knowledge acquired after the distribution of the product, they may be pressured to be too cautious in bringing new products to market. Manufacturers are under economic pressures to market their new products quickly. However, this pressure may be countered if manufacturers believe that strict liability exposes them in fact to greater liability than in theory they should bear. This can occur in cases where the question of whether a previously unknown product hazard caused the plaintiff's harm must be resolved on the basis of circumstantial evidence such as a statistical correlation between use of the defendant's product and the type of harm suffered by the plaintiff. Since a direct causal link cannot be shown between the product and the harm, the defendant may be found liable in cases where the product did not in fact cause the harm. If such excess liability were likely, manufacturers would invest too heavily in testing products prior to marketing, resulting in the waste of scarce resources. This excessive investment in testing would delay the marketing of new products. The costs of delay would be borne in part by consumers denied the benefits of these products.

The point here is not that manufacturers held strictly liable for unknown hazards necessarily would abandon post-distribution efforts to test for hazards, or that important new products would never reach the market. More modestly, the point is that the answer to the question of how manufacturers would alter their behavior in testing and marketing products is less clear than proponents of strict liability for unknown hazards have claimed. It is possible that the net effect of imposing strict liability in the form of judicial hindsight would be an increase, rather than a decrease, in social waste.

* * *

Would imposing strict liability for unknown hazards reduce the transaction costs represented by the costs of litigation? In theory, such reliance on hindsight might simplify trials and thereby reduce transaction costs of each claim. As a practical matter, however, transaction costs might not change. Although the Wade–Keeton strict liability test would eliminate the question of whether a reasonable manufacturer would have discovered the hazard, it would retain the question of whether a reasonable consumer in the plaintiff's position would have acted differently. Moreover, the plaintiff might introduce much the same evidence in a negligence case and a strict liability case. For example, the plaintiff probably would have to use statistical correlations relied on as circumstantial proof of causation for strict liability, and could have used the same facts to prove that a prudent manufacturer would have discovered the hazards and warned of them. The jury instructions would probably be shorter under strict liability; but the proof at trial, and hence the important transaction costs, would be substantially the same.

It remains to consider whether imposing strict liability for unknown hazards would accomplish the objective of spreading accident losses as a means of reducing dislocation costs. If one assumes that defendants can adequately insure against liability, or are financially strong enough to survive uninsured liability, the loss spreading objective would be achieved more readily with judicial reliance on hindsight than with liability based on negligence. Indeed, on these assumptions, almost any change in liability rules that increases defendants' exposure would promote loss spreading. However, one problem with justifying liability for unknown hazards on notions of loss spreading is the assumption that defendants will be able to insure or to survive without insurance. It is doubtful that liability for unknown risks could adequately be insured against. Moreover, although some manufacturers are financially strong enough to survive substantial liability in excess of coverage, many are not. Certainly, some losses are large enough to crush even the strongest manufacturers. Thus, although producers are much more efficient insurers than are consumers with respect to manufacturing defects, they may be no more, or perhaps even less, efficient than consumers with respect to unknown design hazards.

On balance, it is difficult to see how judicial reliance on post-distribution increases in knowledge of product design hazards would promote social utility. Clearly, such a form of strict liability would not achieve the objectives of market deterrence or transaction cost reduction. Whether it would reduce accident costs by increasing incentives for manufacturers to invest in product testing, or whether it would reduce dislocation costs by spreading losses effectively, are questions to which the answers are not so clear as proponents of strict liability for unknown hazards have claimed.

NOTES

1. The defendant in *Beshada,* Johns–Manville ("Manville"), filed for bankruptcy in 1983. See infra, Chapter 10.

2. Compare the concluding observations in A. Schwartz, Products Liability, Corporate Structure and Bankruptcy: Toxic Substances and the Remote Risk Relationship, 14 J.Leg.Stud. 689, 736 (1985):

> Courts should not impose remote risks on firms. A remote risk is a risk whose full extent a cost-justified research program would not reveal. To impose such risks is unfair, for it makes firms responsible for what they would not prevent. Also, firms have incentives to pursue inefficient strategies, such as liquidating when their going concern value exceeds their liquidation value, just to avoid the surprising liability that a remote risk imposition creates. The use of these strategies apparently underlies the extraordinary problems that bankruptcy and corporate law face in situations such as the asbestos disaster. These bodies of law can conveniently resolve the problems that products liability accidents create, when firms can anticipate the risk of those accidents. But corporate and bankruptcy law can never cope with the chaos that can result when firms are made to bear large liabilities for which they could not plan.
>
> The fairness and efficiency objections to imposing remote risks on firms imply the error of such impositions unless strong instrumental or

> justice reasons exist to hold firms liable. But there are no such reasons. Imposing remote risks advances none of the instrumental goals that tort law pursues, nor is it implied by any justice-based tort theory. This is not to say that society owes no obligation to the victims of remote risks. Our country routinely honors the humanitarian claims of persons harmed by unexpected disasters. The private law suit, however, has traditionally been regarded as an impermissible method of meeting such obligations. That the victims of some remote risks can conveniently cast their claims in the form of private law suits is a contingent fact, not a justification for altering this practice.

Contrast Page, Generic Product Risks: The Case Against Comment *k* and for Strict Tort Liability, 58 N.Y.U. L.Rev. 853, 891 (1983): "Both the satisfaction of justifiable expectations on the part of product victims and the achievement of modest advances in safety justify the application of strict liability to harm from unknownable generic hazards."

3. One year after *Beshada,* the New Jersey Supreme Court decided O'Brien v. Muskin Corp., 94 N.J. 169, 463 A.2d 298 (1983). The 23–year–old plaintiff was injured when he dove—from the platform by the pool on the roof of the garage—into 3½ feet of water in an above-ground swimming pool manufactured by the defendant. As his hands hit the vinyl-lined pool bottom, they slid apart, and his head struck the bottom. A decal on the side of the pool, in letters one-half inch high, stated "DO NOT DIVE." Plaintiff claimed that the warning was inadequate and that the material used for the pool bottom was too slippery. The trial court ruled that he had failed to prove a design defect in the pool and so instructed the jury only on the warnings claim. A judgment for the defendant was reversed by the Appellate Division, which remanded for a new trial, and the defendant appealed. *Held,* affirmed:

> * * * [W]e conclude that state-of-the-art evidence is relevant to risk utility analysis and admissible in a strict liability case involving a defectively designed product.
>
> * * *
>
> Although the appropriate [defectiveness] standard might be variously defined, one definition, based on a comparison of the utility of the product with the risk of injury that it poses to the public, has gained prominence. To the extent that "risk-utility analysis," as it is known, implicates the reasonableness of the manufacturer's conduct, strict liability law continues to manifest that part of its heritage attributable to the law of negligence. * * *
>
> * * *
>
> By implication, risk-utility analysis includes [considerations in addition to Wade's seven factors] such as the "state-of-the-art" at the time of the manufacture of the product. [Citation.] The "state-of-the-art" refers to the existing level of technological expertise and scientific knowledge relevant to a particular industry at the time a product is designed. Robb, "A Practical Approach to Use of State of the Art Evidence in Strict Products Liability Cases," 77 Nw.U.L.Rev. 1, 4–5 & n. 15 (1977). Although customs of an industry may be relevant, Suter, 81 N.J. at 171–72, 406 A.2d 140, because those customs may lag behind technological development, they are not identical with the state-of-the-art. See Michalko, 91 N.J. at 397–98, 451 A.2d 179; Robb, supra, 77 Nw.U.L.Rev. at 4–5. A manufacturer may have a duty to make

products pursuant to a safer design even if the custom of the industry is not to use that alternative. Michalko, 91 N.J. at 397, 451 A.2d 179.

State-of-the-art relates to both components of the risk-utility equation, Suter, 81 N.J. at 171–72, 406 A.2d 140. Although the focus is on the product, our attention is drawn to the reasonableness of the manufacturer's conduct in placing the product on the market. Id. In that regard, the risk side of the equation may involve, among other factors, risks that the manufacturer knew or should have known would be posed by the product, as well as the adequacy of any warnings. The utility side generally will include an appraisal of the need for the product and available design alternatives. Furthermore, some products are unavoidably unsafe: the need for a product may be great, but the existing state of human knowledge may not make it safe. Restatement § 402A, comment k. With those products, the determination of liability may be achieved more appropriately through an evaluation of the adequacy of the warnings. In brief, risk-utility analysis is not a petrified, but a dynamic process. Where a particular product falls on the risk-utility continuum will depend on the facts of each case. A toy that poses undue risks to infants may be viewed differently from a therapeutic device that protects or prolongs life. As we proceed, as we must, on a case-by-case basis, risk-utility analysis provides the flexibility necessary for an appropriate adjustment of the interests of manufacturers, consumers, and the public.

Although state-of-the-art evidence may be dispositive on the facts of a particular case, it does not constitute an absolute defense apart from risk-utility analysis. See Beshada v. Johns–Manville Products Corp., 90 N.J. 191, 202–05 & n. 6, 447 A.2d 539 (1982). The ultimate burden of proving a defect is on the plaintiff, but the burden is on the defendant to prove that compliance with state-of-the-art, in conjunction with other relevant evidence, justifies placing a product on the market. Compliance with proof of state-of-the-art need not, as a matter of law, compel a judgment for a defendant. State-of-the-art evidence, together with other evidence relevant to risk-utility analysis, however, may support a judgment for a defendant. In brief, state-of-the-art evidence is relevant to, but not necessarily dispositive of, risk-utility analysis. That is, a product may embody the state-of-the-art and still fail to satisfy the risk-utility equation.

The assessment of the utility of a design involves the consideration of available alternatives. If no alternatives are available, recourse to a unique design is more defensible. The existence of a safer and equally efficacious design, however, diminishes the justification for using a challenged design.

The evaluation of the utility of a product also involves the relative need for that product; some products are essentials, while others are luxuries. A product that fills a critical need and can be designed in only one way should be viewed differently from a luxury item. Still other products, including some for which no alternative exists, are so dangerous and of such little use that under the risk-utility analysis, a manufacturer would bear the cost of liability of harm to others. That cost might dissuade a manufacturer from placing the product on the market, even if the product has been made as safely as possible. Indeed, plaintiff contends that above-ground pools with vinyl liners are

> such products and that manufacturers who market those pools should bear the cost of injuries they cause to foreseeable users.
>
> A critical issue at trial was whether the design of the pool, calling for a vinyl bottom in a pool four feet deep, was defective. The trial court should have permitted the jury to consider whether, because of the dimensions of the pool and slipperiness of the bottom, the risks of injury so outweighed the utility of the product as to constitute a defect. In removing that issue from consideration by the jury, the trial court erred. To establish sufficient proof to compel submission of the issue to the jury for appropriate fact-finding under risk-utility analysis, it was not necessary for plaintiff to prove the existence of alternative, safer designs. Viewing the evidence in the light most favorable to plaintiff, even if there are no alternative methods of making bottoms for above-ground pools, the jury might have found that the risk posed by the pool outweighed its utility.

Justice Schreiber wrote a concurring and dissenting opinion, critical of *Beshada,* to which Justice Clifford responded in a concurring opinion:

> More troublesome however, is Justice Schreiber's reading of the majority opinion, particularly his assertion that today's decision takes Beshada v. Johns–Manville Prod. Corp., 90 N.J. 191, 447 A.2d 539 (1982), a step farther along an intolerably extreme path. I share Justice Schreiber's thinly-disguised discomfort with *Beshada;* and if I believed for one moment that our decision today advanced *Beshada's* exotic theory, I would jump ship. It does not, so I do not.
>
> State-of-the-art evidence is implicitly included in the factors employed in the risk/utility analysis adopted in Cepeda v. Cumberland Eng'g Co., Inc., 76 N.J. 152, 172–75, 386 A.2d 816 (1978), whose use is reaffirmed today, *ante* at 304–305.[1] Whereas *Beshada* foreclosed the use of state-of-the-art as a defense to a design-defect-warning case, today's majority opinion could scarcely be more unambiguous in pointing out that state-of-the-art evidence is just one type of proof that may be relevant on the central issue of defect and that it may, in certain instances, support a judgment for defendant. *Ante* at 305.

Justice Pashman, the author of *Beshada,* had retired in 1982, shortly after that opinion was rendered.

FELDMAN v. LEDERLE LABORATORIES

Supreme Court of New Jersey, 1984.
97 N.J. 429, 479 A.2d 374.

SCHREIBER, J.

In this case defendants and *amici* drug manufacturers argued that the doctrine of strict products liability should not apply to prescription drugs. We hold otherwise and conclude that drug manufacturers have

1. The third and fourth factors embody state-of-the-art considerations:

(3) The availability of a substitute product which would meet the same need and not be as unsafe.

(4) The manufacturer's ability to eliminate the unsafe character of the product without impairing its usefulness or making it too expensive to maintain its utility.

a duty to warn of dangers of which they know or should have known on the basis of reasonably obtainable or available knowledge.

Plaintiff, Carol Ann Feldman, has gray teeth as a result of taking a tetracyline drug, Declomycin. Plaintiff's father, a pharmacist and a medical doctor, prescribed and administered the drug to her when she was an infant to control upper respiratory and other secondary types of infections. Since Dr. Feldman claimed that he had administered Declomycin, suit was instituted against defendant, Lederle Laboratories, which manufactured and marketed Declomycin. The action was presented to the jury on the theory that the defendant was strictly liable, not because the drug was ineffective as an antibiotic, but because defendant had failed to warn physicians of the drug's side effect, tooth discoloration.

Defendant contended that * * * it had complied with the state of the art in its warning literature. It had not warned of possible tooth discoloration because, the defendant claimed, the possibility of that side effect was not known at the time its literature was disseminated.

The jury found for the defendant. The Appellate Division affirmed in an unreported opinion. Plaintiff petitioned for certification and we summarily remanded the cause to the Appellate Division to reconsider in light of Beshada v. Johns–Manville Prods. Corp., 90 N.J. 191, 447 A.2d 539 (1982), which was decided after the Appellate Division decision. 91 N.J. 266, 450 A.2d 579 (1982). The Appellate Division reaffirmed the judgment for the defendant, holding that prescription drugs are a special category of products and that drug manufacturers would not be strictly liable for failing to warn of a side effect that was unknown when the drug was sold. 189 N.J.Super. 424, 460 A.2d 203 (1983). We granted plaintiff's petition for certification. 94 N.J. 594, 468 A.2d 230 (1983). We permitted the following *amici* to participate in the proceeding before us: ATLA–NJ, The New Jersey Affiliate of the Association of Trial Lawyers of America; the Pharmaceutical Manufacturers Association; and numerous drug manufacturers.

I

Most facts are undisputed, although there are some sharply disputed conclusions and opinions by the respective experts. Tetracyclines are a group of antibiotics that was first introduced in 1948. They were produced by different drug manufacturers that marketed the drugs under various trade names.

Defendant first marketed Declomycin in 1959. The Physicians' Desk Reference (PDR), a book used by doctors to determine effects of drugs, contains data furnished by drug manufacturers about drugs, their compositions, usages, and reactions. The 1959 PDR entry for Declomycin stated that it had a greater antibiotic potency that made it possible to achieve therapeutic activity with less weight of antibiotic; it had a reduced renal clearance rate that produced a prolongation of the antibacterial levels in the body; and it was therapeutically equally effective as other tetracyclines in infections caused by organisms sensitive to the tetracyclines. The PDR is produced annually. Until the 1965 or 1966 edition, the PDR did not mention that tooth discoloration was a possible side effect of Declomycin. Since 1965 or 1966 the PDR has stated that the drug, when administered to infants and children, could cause tooth discoloration that would be permanent if the drug were given during the developmental stage of the permanent teeth.

Plaintiff, Carol Ann Feldman, was born on February 8, 1960. Her father, Dr. Harold Feldman, asserted that he prescribed Declomycin for her approximately seven or more times from September or October, 1960, when she was eight or nine months old, until the end of 1963. She was given this drug to prevent secondary infections when she had different childhood diseases.

* * *

Plaintiff's baby teeth were discolored gray-brown. Her permanent teeth were more deeply discolored, being primarily gray. The parties agreed that this discoloration had resulted from use of a tetracycline, although they disputed whether Declomycin was the particular tetracycline involved. * * *

The respective experts, Dr. Bonda for the plaintiff and Dr. Guggenheimer for the defendant, agreed that scientific literature existed by 1960 that referred to tooth staining being caused by tetracycline. Dr. Bonda specifically mentioned a 1956 article by Dr. Andre reciting that tetracycline accumulated in mineralized portions of growing bones and teeth of mice; an article by Dr. Milch in the July, 1957 Journal of the National Cancer Institute reporting that laboratory animals had yellow fluorescents in bones, including teeth, following dosages of tetracycline; [and several other articles published from 1958–61.] Dr. Bonda concluded the defendant should have begun to investigate the possible effects of all forms of tetracycline on teeth no later than 1956, when the Andre article appeared.

Defendant's expert, Dr. Guggenheimer, on the other hand, noted that before 1962 the literature on tooth discoloration concerned only patients with cystic fibrosis who had been receiving massive doses of tetracyclines. He pointed out that Dr. Milch's papers described only fluorescents, not tooth staining. He testified that Declomycin did not become available until 1959 and that it would take 2½ years for permanent teeth developing in 1959 to erupt. The completion of accurate controlled studies of multiple well-documented cases would have been the only way one could really know whether Declomycin caused tooth discoloration in permanent teeth. Dr. Guggenheimer's testimony is unclear as to whether a correlation between tetracycline and tooth discoloration had been established in 1962. One reading of his testimony indicates that such a correlation was not known to exist and that only by hindsight could that conclusion be drawn. It is also possible to interpret his opinion to be that such correlation had been established in 1962. In any event it is significant that Dr. Guggenheimer gave no opinion as to 1963.

* * *

In 1963, the defendant received complaints from eight doctors that Declomycin was causing tooth staining. In May, 1963 the defendant referred the FDA again to the side effect of Declomycin. Commencing in mid-December, 1963, after receipt of FDA approval, it included the same warning in the Declomycin literature as in other tetracyclines.

* * *

The trial court's charge to the jury * * * stated that if the defendant did not know of the danger of tooth discoloration, and if the application of reasonably developed human skill and foresight consistent with the state of the art and the knowledge of the scientific community existing during the periods in question would not have alerted defendant to the danger, then there would have to be a finding for the defendant. * * *

II

Does Strict Liability Apply to Manufacturers of Prescription Drugs?

The defendant never contended in its answer or at trial that the doctrine of strict liability should not apply to prescription drugs. It first raised this proposition after we had remanded the matter to the Appellate Division for reconsideration in light of *Beshada,* supra, 90 N.J. 191, 447 A.2d 539. The defendant and the drug manufacturing *amici curiae* urged that public policy as explicated in comment k to section 402A of the Restatement (Second) of Torts (1965) [hereinafter cited as Restatement] should immunize drug manufacturers from liability for side effects of prescription drugs. Comment k suggests that strict liability should not apply to certain unavoidably unsafe products. We do not agree that the protective shield of comment k immunizes all prescription drugs. Moreover, we are of the opinion that generally the principle of strict liability is applicable to manufacturers of prescription drugs.

There are some circumstances in which as a matter of public policy this Court has determined that strict liability should not be applied. [Citations;] Brody v. Overlook Hosp., 66 N.J. 448, 332 A.2d 596 (1975). Most recently we acknowledged that principle in O'Brien v. Muskin Corp., 94 N.J. 169, 186, 463 A.2d 298 (1983).

Certain principles may be distilled from these cases. When the essential nature of the transaction involves a service rather than a product, public policy may dictate, in view of the status of the provider, that the general welfare is served better by inapplicability of the strict liability doctrine. Further, when the provider is a nonprofit institution that supplies a product and that product is vital to the public health, the doctrine may similarly be inapplicable. The common thread that runs through these cases is that in each of those situations there is a strong public policy rooted in the general welfare that justifies imposing responsibility only on the basis of a want of due care (negligence) rather than on the basis of a defective product (strict liability).

* * *

The last occasion a comparable issue was raised in this Court was in Brody v. Overlook Hosp., supra, 66 N.J. 448, 332 A.2d 596, in 1975. There the blood used in a transfusion in a hospital was defective because it was infected with viral hepatitis. The presence of hepatitis was not discoverable by the county blood bank, a charitable nonprofit organization that supplied the blood, 121 N.J.Super. at 309, 296 A.2d 668, or by the hospital. 66 N.J. at 450, 332 A.2d 596. We held * * * that strict liability was not appropriate. The primary reason for our decision was the public policy advocating the inapplicability of the strict liability doctrine. * * *

Drug manufacturers do not fall within the policy exceptions expressed in the foregoing cases. Drug manufacturers, unlike doctors and dentists, do not render to consumers professional services involving skills in judgment and diagnosis. They produce goods and place them into the stream of commerce. Although their products may be valuable to the public, the drug manufacturers are not nonprofit or charitable institutions. They are commercial profit-making enterprises upon which product responsibility properly rests.

* * *

The defendant has not presented any evidence to support the proposition that strict liability should not be applied to drug manufacturers that produce and distribute prescription drugs including Declomycin. Further, as observed previously, this proposition was not raised at trial. The record understandably has little, if any, evidence pertinent or material to that issue. For example, the record shows that before offering new drugs to the public, drug companies furnish certain material to scientists or doctors engaged in research. There is no evidence of the extent and nature of research that drug companies usually perform or that the defendant actually performed with respect to Declomycin. The evidence throws no light on whether all drugs should be treated alike, some being more vital to the public health and human survival than others. The evidence does not demonstrate why the drug-manufacturing industry should be placed in a different category from other manufacturers and suppliers of mass-produced products in which the enterprise bears the liability for a product that is not fit, suitable, or safe for its intended use. [Citation.]

* * *

Defendant and drug manufacturing *amici* also contend that all prescription drugs are unavoidably unsafe and therefore that drug manufacturers of these products fall within the protective aegis of comment k of the Restatement, supra. Comment k reads as follows:

> *Unavoidably unsafe products.* There are some products which, in the present state of human knowledge, are quite incapable of being made *safe* for their intended and ordinary

> use. These are especially common in the field of drugs. An outstanding example is the vaccine for the Pasteur treatment of rabies, which not uncommonly leads to very serious and damaging consequences when it is injected. Since the disease itself invariably leads to a dreadful death, both the marketing and the use of the vaccine are fully justified, notwithstanding the unavoidable high degree of risk which they involve. Such a product, properly prepared, *and accompanied by proper directions and warning,* is not defective, nor is it *unreasonably* [emphasis in original] dangerous. The same is true of many other drugs, vaccines, and the like, many of which for this very reason cannot legally be sold except to physicians, or under the prescription of a physician. It is also true in particular of many new or experimental drugs as to which, because of lack of time and opportunity for sufficient medical experience, there can be no assurance of safety, or perhaps even of purity of ingredients, but such experience as there is justifies the marketing and use of the drug notwithstanding a medically recognizable risk. The seller of such products, *again with the qualification that they are properly prepared and marketed, and proper warning is given,* where the situation calls for it, is not to be held to strict liability for unfortunate consequences attending their use, merely because he has undertaken to supply the public with an apparently useful and desirable product, attended with a known but apparently reasonable risk. [Emphasis added.]

Comment k immunizes from strict liability the manufacturers of some products, including certain drugs, that are unavoidably unsafe. However, we see no reason to hold as a matter of law and policy that all prescription drugs that are unsafe are unavoidably so. Drugs, like any other products, may contain defects that could have been avoided by better manufacturing or design. Whether a drug is unavoidably unsafe should be decided on a case-by-case basis; we perceive no justification for giving all prescription drug manufacturers a blanket immunity from strict liability manufacturing and design defect claims under comment k.

Moreover, even if a prescription drug were unavoidably unsafe, the comment k immunity would not eliminate strict liability for failure to provide a proper warning. As Justice Pollock stated in *O'Brien,* supra, "[w]ith those products, the determination of liability may be achieved more appropriately through an evaluation of the adequacy of the warnings." 94 N.J. at 183, 463 A.2d 298. Thus, a manufacturer who knows or should know of the danger or side effects of a product is not relieved of its duty to warn. Rather, as the comment expressly states, it is only the unavoidably unsafe product "*accompanied by proper* * * * *warning*" that is not defective. (Emphasis added.) * * * Irrespective of whether a court or a jury decides that the drug falls within the special category of comment k, that finding may not absolve the manufacturer of its failure to warn the physician or consumer of the condition within the manufacturer's actual or constructive knowledge affecting the safety, fitness, or suitability of the drug. See Wade, "On the Effect in Product Liability of Knowledge Unavailable Prior to Marketing," 58 N.Y.U.L.Rev. 734, 745 (1983) [hereinafter cited as Wade (1983)].

In sum, we hold that none of the policy reasons for exempting certain products from strict liability is applicable to this case. Production and marketing of drugs do not fit within the public policy exemptions for doctors, dentists, and nonprofit or charitable health care institutions. There is insufficient evidence to find that Declomycin's utility so outweighs its risks that the manufacturer should be immune from strict liability under a risk-utility analysis. Finally, Declomycin would not be exempt from strict liability under comment k to the Restatement, supra, if the defendant failed to provide an adequate warning of the possible tooth-discoloration effect of administering the drugs to infants.

III

* * *

This is a strict-liability-warning case. * * * The crux of the plaintiff's complaint is that her doctor should have been warned of a possible side effect of the drug in infants, discoloration of teeth.

The failure-to-warn strict liability classification is similar to the improper design category. *O'Brien,* supra, 94 N.J. at 181, 463 A.2d 298; Freund v. Cellofilm Properties, Inc., 87 N.J. 229, 242, 432 A.2d 925 (1981). The manufacturer is under a duty to produce and distribute a product that is reasonably fit, suitable, and safe. It has not met that obligation if it puts a defective article into the stream of commerce that causes injury or damage. * * * Generally speaking, the doctrine of strict liability assumes that enterprises should be responsible for damages to consumers resulting from defective products regardless of fault. The doctrine differs from a negligence theory, which centers on the defendant's conduct and seeks to determine whether the defendant acted as a reasonably prudent person. This difference between strict liability and negligence is commonly expressed by stating that in a strict liability analysis, the defendant is assumed to know of the dangerous propensity of the product, whereas in a negligence case, the plaintiff must prove that the defendant knew or should have known of the danger. * * *

When the strict liability defect consists of an improper design or warning, reasonableness of the defendant's conduct is a factor in determining liability. [Citations.] The question in strict liability design-defect and warning cases is whether, assuming that the manufacturer knew of the defect in the product, he acted in a reasonably prudent manner in marketing the product or in providing the warnings given. Thus, once the defendant's knowledge of the defect is imputed, strict liability analysis becomes almost identical to negligence analysis in its focus on the reasonableness of the defendant's conduct. In [Cepeda v. Cumberland Eng'g Co., 76 N.J. 152, 172, 386 A.2d 816 (1978), and Suter v. San Angelo Foundry & Mach. Co., 81 N.J. 150, 171, 406 A.2d 140 (1979)], we quoted approvingly Prosser's treatise on torts: "Since proper design is a matter of reasonable fitness, the strict liability adds little or nothing to negligence on the part of the manufacturer * * *." W. Prosser, Law of Torts 659 n. 72 (4th ed. 1971).

Generally, the state of the art in design defect cases and available knowledge in defect warning situations are relevant factors in measuring reasonableness of conduct. Thus in *Suter*, supra, we explained that other than assuming that the manufacturer knew of the harmful propensity of the product, the jury could consider "the technological feasibility of manufacturing a product whose design would have prevented or avoided the accident, given the known state of the art." Id. at 172, 406 A.2d 140. We observed that "the state of the art refers not only to the common practice and standards in the industry but also to the other design alternatives within practical and technological limits at the time of distribution." Id. Moreover, in *O'Brien*, supra, we again referred to the state of the art as an appropriate factor to be considered by the jury to determine whether feasible alternatives existed when the product was marketed. 94 N.J. at 183–84, 463 A.2d 298.

Similarly, as to warnings, generally conduct should be measured by knowledge at the time the manufacturer distributed the product. Did the defendant know, or should he have known, of the danger, given the scientific, technological, and other information available when the product was distributed; or, in other words, did he have actual or constructive knowledge of the danger? The Restatement, supra, has adopted this test in comment j to section 402A, which reads in pertinent part as follows:

> *Directions or warning.* In order to prevent the product from being unreasonably dangerous, the seller may be required to give directions or warning, on the container, as to its use. * * * Where the product contains an ingredient * * * whose danger is not generally known, or if known is one which the consumer would reasonably not expect to find in the product, the seller is required to give warning against it, *if he has knowledge, or by the application of reasonable, developed human skill and foresight should have knowledge,* of the presence of the ingredient and the danger. [Emphasis added.]

Under this standard negligence and strict liability in warning cases may be deemed to be functional equivalents. [Citations.] Constructive knowledge embraces knowledge that should have been known based on information that was reasonably available or obtainable and should have alerted a reasonably prudent person to act. Put another way, would a person of reasonable intelligence or of the superior expertise of the defendant charged with such knowledge conclude that defendant should have alerted the consuming public? See Restatement, supra, § 12(2).

Further, a manufacturer is held to the standard of an expert in the field. [Citations.] A manufacturer should keep abreast of scientific advances.

* * *

Furthermore, a reasonably prudent manufacturer will be deemed to know of reliable information generally available or reasonably obtainable in the industry or in the particular field involved. Such information need not be limited to that furnished by experts in the field, but may also include material provided by others. Thus, for example, if a substantial number of doctors or consumers had complained to a drug manufacturer of an untoward effect of a drug, that would have constituted sufficient information requiring an appropriate warning. [Citations.]

This test does not conflict with the assumption made in strict liability design defect and warning cases that the defendant knew of the dangerous propensity of the product, if the knowledge that is assumed is reasonably knowable in the sense of actual or constructive knowledge. A warning that a product may have an unknowable danger warns one of nothing. Neither *Cepeda* nor *Suter* stated that the manufacturer would be deemed to know of the dangerous propensity of the chattel when the danger was unknowable. See Ferrigno v. Eli Lilly and Co., 175 N.J.Super. 551, 576, 420 A.2d 1305 (Law Div.1980). In our opinion *Beshada*, supra, would not demand a contrary conclusion in the typical design defect or warning case. If *Beshada* were deemed to hold generally or in all cases, particularly with respect to a situation like the present one involving drugs vital to health, that in a warning context knowledge of the unknowable is irrelevant in determining the applicability of strict liability, we would not agree. Many commentators have criticized this aspect of the *Beshada* reasoning and the public policies on which it is based. See, e.g., Page, "Generic Product Risks: The Case Against Comment K and for Strict Tort Liability," 58 N.Y.U.L.Rev. 853, 877–82 (1983); Schwartz, "The Post–Sale Duty to Warn: Two Unfortunate Forks in the Road to a Reasonable Doctrine," 58 N.Y.U.L.Rev. 892, 901–05 (1983); Wade (1983), supra, at 754–56; Comment, "Requiring Omniscience: The Duty to Warn of Scientifically Undiscoverable Product Defects," 71 Geo.L.J. 1635 (1983); Comment, "Beshada v. Johns Manville Products Corp.: Adding Uncertainty to Injury," 35 Rutgers L.Rev. 982, 1008–15 (1983); Note, "Products Liability—Strict Liability in Tort—State-of-the-Art Defense Inapplicable in Design Defect Cases," 13 Seton Hall L.Rev. 625 (1983). But see Hayes v. Ariens Co., 391 Mass. 407, 413, 462 N.E.2d 273, 277–78 (1984) (citing *Beshada* with approval for the proposition that in strict liability the seller "is presumed to have been informed at the time of sale of all risks whether or not he actually knew or reasonably should have known of them"). The rationale of *Beshada* is not applicable to this case. We do not overrule *Beshada*, but restrict *Beshada* to the circumstances giving rise to its holding. [Citations.] We note, in passing, that, although not argued and determined in *Beshada,* there were or may have been data and other information generally available, aside from scientific knowledge, that arguably could have alerted the manufacturer at an early stage in the distribution of its product to the dangers associated with its use.

In strict liability warning cases, unlike negligence cases, however, the defendant should properly bear the burden of proving that the information was not reasonably available or obtainable and that it therefore lacked actual or constructive knowledge of the defect. [Citations.] The defendant is in a superior position to know the technological material or data in the particular field or specialty. The defendant is the expert, often performing self-testing. It is the defendant that injected the product in the stream of commerce for its economic gain. As a matter of policy the burden of proving the status of knowledge in the field at the time of distribution is properly placed on the defendant. [Citations.]

One other aspect with respect to warnings based on subsequently obtained knowledge should be considered. Communication of the new warning should unquestionably be given to prescribing physicians as soon as reasonably feasible. Although a manufacturer may not have actual or constructive knowledge of a danger so as to impose upon it a duty to warn, subsequently acquired knowledge, both actual and constructive, also may obligate the manufacturer to take reasonable steps to notify purchasers and consumers of the newly-discovered danger. [Citations.]

The timeliness of the warning issue is obliquely present in this case. It is possible that Dr. Feldman already had Declomycin on hand when defendant became aware of Declomycin's side effect. If that state of affairs existed, defendant would have had an obligation to warn doctors and others promptly. This most assuredly would include those to whom defendant had already furnished the product. See Schenebeck v. Sterling Drug, Inc., 423 F.2d 919, 922 (8th Cir.1970); Basko, supra, 416 F.2d at 426. See generally Note, "The Manufacturer's Duty to Notify of Subsequent Safety Improvements," 33 Stan.L.Rev. 1087 (1981). The extent and nature of post-distribution warnings may vary depending on the circumstances, but in the context of this case, the defendant at a minimum would have had a duty of advising physicians, including plaintiff's father, whom it had directly solicited to use Declomycin.

* * *

V

* * *

The trial court erred in fixing the date at which defendant's actual or constructive knowledge was to be measured. It was undisputed that plaintiff had received Declomycin or another tetracycline from approximately September, 1960 until the end of 1963. When the trial court considered the motion, it referred to the conflict in the evidence on whether defendant knew or should have known of the correlation between an infant's ingestion of Declomycin and tooth discoloration in *1960,* when the plaintiff first began receiving the drug.

However, the evidence is overwhelming that at least by mid-November, 1962, defendant had sufficient information to warrant that it warn doctors of the possible tooth discoloration effects of Declomycin when administered to infants. According to Dr. Swanzey, then defendant's Director of Regulatory Agency Relations, defendant had "strong suspicions" of the connection between tetracyclines and the discoloration of the teeth by the end of 1962. However, the defendant's actions indicate that its awareness at that time went beyond the stage of suspicion. There was no equivocation in its letter to the FDA on November 16, 1962. The letter proposed that defendant add to the labels on all its tetracycline products, including Declomycin, the following warning: "Use of *any* tetracycline during teeth development in the neonatal period or early childhood may cause discoloration of the teeth." (Emphasis added.) Lloyd Carr, defendant's Product Service Manager, explained in a letter to Dr. Feldman that "[w]hen the causal relationship between tooth staining and tetracycline became *unquestionably* demonstrated by our Company, we notified the Food and Drug Administration by letter of November 16, 1962." (Emphasis added.) Mr. Carr testified that he was referring in his letter to all of defendant's tetracycline drugs, including Declomycin. Viewing the testimony of Dr. Guggenheimer, defendant's expert witness, from the viewpoint most favorable to defendant, he testified that a manufacturer could not have been expected to draw a correlation between tooth discoloration and Declomycin in 1962, although, at the time of trial, in hindsight, it was clear that the correlation in fact existed in 1962.

Apart from plaintiff's evidence to the effect that defendant should have known of the side effect as early as 1960, the record overwhelmingly demonstrates that defendant actually knew of the danger by the end of 1962. Defendant nonetheless continued to market the drug in 1963 and plaintiff continued to ingest the drug that year. Insofar as that period of time is concerned, a jury determination based on defendant's lack of knowledge would be "a miscarriage of justice under the law." See R. 2:10–1. In that event defendant would be responsible at least for the enhancement of the condition.

We reverse and remand for a new trial.

BROWN v. SUPERIOR COURT

Supreme Court of California, 1988.
44 Cal.3d 1049, 245 Cal.Rptr. 412, 751 P.2d 470.

MOSK, JUSTICE.

In current litigation several significant issues have arisen relating to the liability of manufacturers of prescription drugs for injuries caused by their products. Our first and broadest inquiry is whether such a manufacturer may be held strictly liable for a product that is defective in design.

* * *

A number of plaintiffs filed actions in the San Francisco Superior Court against numerous drug manufacturers which allegedly produced DES, a substance plaintiffs claimed was used by their mothers to prevent miscarriage. They alleged that the drug was defective and they were injured *in utero* when their mothers ingested it.

* * *

The trial court * * * determined that defendants could not be held strictly liable for the alleged defect in DES but only for their failure to warn of known or knowable side effects of the drug.

[The Court of Appeal affirmed.] We granted review to examine the conclusions of the Court of Appeal and its potential conflict with Kearl v. Lederle Laboratories (1985) 172 Cal.App.3d 812, 218 Cal.Rptr. 453, on the issue of strict liability of a drug manufacturer for a defect in the design of a prescription drug.

I. *Strict Liability*

A. *Strict Liability in General*

Barker [v. Lull Engineering Co. (1978) 20 Cal.3d 413, 143 Cal.Rptr. 225, 573 P.2d 443 (hereafter Barker)] identified three types of product defects. (20 Cal.3d at p. 428, 143 Cal.Rptr. 225, 573 P.2d 443.) First, there may be a flaw in the manufacturing process, resulting in a product that differs from the manufacturer's intended result. The archetypal example of such a defect was involved in *Escola,* supra, 24 Cal.2d 453, 150 P.2d 436, a Coca Cola bottle that exploded. Such a manufacturing defect did not exist in the heavy equipment that caused the injury in *Barker,* and is not alleged in the present case.

Second, there are products which are "perfectly" manufactured but are unsafe because of the absence of a safety device, i.e., a defect in design. This was the defect alleged in *Barker.* It held that a product is defectively designed if it failed to perform as safely as an ordinary consumer would expect when used as intended or reasonably foreseeable, or if, on balance, the risk of danger inherent in the challenged design outweighs the benefits of the design. (20 Cal.3d at p. 430, 143 Cal.Rptr. 225, 573 P.2d 443.) Plaintiff asserts this test should be applied in the present case because DES contained a design defect.

The third type of defect identified in *Barker* is a product that is dangerous because it lacks adequate warnings or instructions. According to plaintiff, defendants here failed to warn of the dangers inherent in the use of DES. We are concerned, therefore, with the second and third types of defects described in *Barker.*

B. *Strict Liability and Prescription Drugs*

[T]he members of the American Law Institute, in considering whether to adopt a rule of strict liability, pondered whether the manufacturer of a prescription drug should be subject to the doctrine. (38 ALI Proc. 19, 90–92, 98 (1961).) During a rather confusing discussion of a draft of what was to become section 402A, a member of the institute proposed that drugs should be exempted from strict liability on the ground that it would be "against the public interest" to apply the doctrine to such products because of "the very serious tendency to stifle medical research and testing." Dean Prosser, who was the reporter for the Restatement Second of Torts, responded that the problem was a real one, and that he had it in mind in drafting section 402A. A motion to exempt prescription drugs from the section was defeated on the suggestion of Dean Prosser that the problem could be dealt with in the comments to the section. However, a motion to state the exemption in a comment was also defeated. (38 ALI Proc. 19, 90–98, supra.) At the next meeting of the institute in 1962, section 402A was approved together with comment k thereto. (41 ALI Proc. 227, 244 (1962).)

The comment provides that the producer of a properly manufactured prescription drug may be held liable for injuries caused by the product only if it was not accompanied by a warning of dangers that the manufacturer knew or should have known about.

* * *

Comment k has been analyzed and criticized by numerous commentators. While there is some disagreement as to its scope and meaning, there is a general consensus that, although it purports to explain the strict liability doctrine, in fact the principle it states is based on negligence. (E.g., Schwartz, Unavoidably Unsafe Products: Clarifying the Meaning and Policy Behind Comment K (1985) 42 Wash. & Lee L.Rev. 1139, 1141; McClellan, Drug Induced Injury (1978) 25 Wayne L.Rev. 1, 2; Kidwell, the Duty to Warn: A Description of the Model of Decision (1975) 53 Tex.L.Rev. 1375, 1377–1378; Merrill, Compensation for Prescription Drug Injuries (1973) 59 Va.L.Rev. 1, 50.) That is, comment k would impose liability on a drug manufacturer only if it failed to warn of a defect of which it either knew or should have known. This concept focuses not on a deficiency in the product—the hallmark of strict liability—but on the fault of the producer in failing to warn of dangers inherent in the use of its product that were either known or knowable—an idea which "rings of negligence," in the words of *Cronin,* * * * 8 Cal.3d 121, 132, 104 Cal.Rptr. 433, 501 P.2d 1153.[4]

4. The test stated in comment k is to be distinguished from strict liability for failure to warn. Although both concepts identify failure to warn as the basis of liability, comment k imposes liability only if the manufacturer knew or should have known of the defect at the time the product was sold or distributed. Under strict liability, the reason why the warning was not issued is irrelevant, and the manufacturer is liable even if it neither knew nor could have known of the defect about which the warning was required. Thus, comment k, by focussing on the blameworthiness of the manufacturer, sets forth a test which sounds in negligence * * *.

Comment k has been adopted in the overwhelming majority of jurisdictions that have considered the matter. [Citations.] In California, several decisions of the Courts of Appeal have embraced the comment k exemption [citations], but this court has never spoken to the issue.

We are aware of only one decision that has applied the doctrine of strict liability to prescription drugs. (Brochu v. Ortho Pharmaceutical Corp. (1st Cir.1981) 642 F.2d 652, 654–657.)[6] Most cases have embraced the rule of comment k without detailed analysis of its language. A few, notably Kearl v. Lederle Laboratories, supra, 172 Cal.App.3d 812, 218 Cal.Rptr. 453 (hereafter *Kearl*), have conditioned application of the exemption stated therein on a finding that the drug involved is in fact "unavoidably dangerous," reasoning that the comment was intended to exempt only such drugs from strict liability. (Accord, Toner v. Lederle Laboratories (1987) 112 Idaho 328, 732 P.2d 297, 303–309; see also Feldman v. Lederle Laboratories (1984) 97 N.J. 429, 479 A.2d 374, 382–383 [involving allegations of a failure to warn, but stating that "whether a drug is unavoidably unsafe should be decided on a case-by-case basis."].) And in Collins v. Eli Lilly Co. (1984) 116 Wisc.2d 166, 342 N.W.2d 37, 52, it was held that comment k was applicable only if the drug in question was placed on the market without adequate testing because of exigent circumstances.[7]

We appear, then, to have three distinct choices: (1) to hold that the manufacturer of a prescription drug is strictly liable for a defect in its product because it was defectively designed, as that term is defined in Barker, or because of a failure to warn of its dangerous propensities even though such dangers were neither known nor scientifically knowable at the time of distribution;[8] (2) to determine that liability attaches only if a manufacturer fails to warn of dangerous propensities of which it was or should have been aware, in conformity with comment k; or (3) to decide, like Kearl and Toner v. Lederle Laboratories, supra, 732 P.2d 297, 303–309, that strict liability for design defects should apply to prescription drugs unless the particular drug which caused the injury is found to be "unavoidably dangerous."

We shall conclude that (1) a drug manufacturer's liability for a defectively designed drug should not be measured by the standards of strict liability; (2) because of the public interest in the development, availability, and reasonable price of drugs, the appropriate test for

6. In *Brochu,* the plaintiff had taken an oral contraceptive which contained 100 milligrams of estrogen as well as other ingredients. According to the evidence at trial, estrogen posed a serious risk of harm to her, and the defendant manufactured another contraceptive pill containing only 50 milligrams of estrogen which was equally effective.

7. In her dissenting opinion in Finn v. G.D. Searle & Co. (1984) 35 Cal.3d 691, 705, 200 Cal.Rptr. 870, 677 P.2d 1147, Chief Justice Bird advocated a strict liability rule for prescription drugs based on the test set forth in *Barker.*

8. We agree with the suggestion of a commentator that a manufacturer's knowledge should be measured at the time a drug is distributed because it is at this point that the manufacturer relinquishes control of the product. (Wade, On the Effect in Product Liability of Knowledge Unavailable Prior to Marketing (1983) 58 N.Y. U.L.Rev. 734, 753–754.)

determining responsibility is the test stated in comment k; and (3) for these same reasons of policy, we disapprove the holding of *Kearl* that only those prescription drugs found to be "unavoidably dangerous" should be measured by the comment k standard and that strict liability should apply to drugs that do not meet that description.

1. *Design defect*

Barker, as we have seen, set forth two alternative tests to measure a design defect: first, whether the product performed as safely as the ordinary consumer would expect when used in an intended and reasonably foreseeable manner, and second, whether, on balance, the benefits of the challenged design outweighed the risk of danger inherent in the design. In making the latter determination, the jury may consider these factors: "the gravity of the danger posed by the challenged design, the likelihood that such danger would occur, the mechanical feasibility of a safer alternative design, the financial cost of an improved design, and the adverse consequences to the product and to the consumer that would result from an alternative design." (20 Cal.3d at p. 431, 143 Cal.Rptr. 225, 573 P.2d 443.)

Defendants assert that neither of these tests is applicable to a prescription drug like DES. As to the "consumer expectation" standard, they claim, the "consumer" is not the plaintiff but the physician who prescribes the drug, and it is to him that the manufacturer's warnings are directed. A physician appreciates the fact that all prescription drugs involve inherent risks, known and unknown, and he does not expect that the drug is without such risks. We agree that the "consumer expectation" aspect of the *Barker* test is inappropriate to prescription drugs.

[The court examined whether the second test, balancing the risks and benefits, is appropriate for prescription drugs.]

Of course, the fact that a drug with dangerous side effects may be characterized as containing a defect in design does not necessarily mean that its producer is to be held strictly liable for the defect. The determination of that issue depends on whether the public interest would be served by the imposition of such liability. As we have seen, the fundamental reasons underlying the imposition of strict liability are to deter manufacturers from marketing products that are unsafe, and to spread the cost of injury from the plaintiff to the consuming public, which will pay a higher price for the product to reflect the increased expense of insurance to the manufacturer resulting from its greater exposure to liability.

These reasons could justify application of the doctrine to the manufacturers of prescription drugs. It is indisputable, as plaintiff contends, that the risk of injury from such drugs is unavoidable, that a consumer may be helpless to protect himself from serious harm caused by them, and that, like other products, the cost of insuring against strict liability can be passed on by the producer to the consumer who buys the item. Moreover, as we observe below, in some cases additional testing of drugs before they are marketed might reveal dangerous side effects, resulting in a safer product.

But there is an important distinction between prescription drugs and other products such as construction machinery (Barker; Pike v. Frank G. Hough Co. (1970) 2 Cal.3d 465, 85 Cal.Rptr. 629, 467 P.2d 229), a lawnmower (Luque v. McLean (1972) 8 Cal.3d 136, 104 Cal.Rptr. 443, 501 P.2d 1163), or perfume (Moran v. Faberge, Inc. (1975) 273 Md. 538, 332 A.2d 11), the producers of which were held strictly liable. In the latter cases, the product is used to make work easier or to provide pleasure, while in the former it may be necessary to alleviate pain and suffering or to sustain life. Moreover, unlike other important medical products (wheelchairs, for example), harm to some users from prescription drugs is unavoidable. Because of these distinctions, the broader public interest in the availability of drugs at an affordable price must be considered in deciding the appropriate standard of liability for injuries resulting from their use.

Perhaps a drug might be made safer if it was withheld from the market until scientific skill and knowledge advanced to the point at which additional dangerous side effects would be revealed. But in most cases such a delay in marketing new drugs—added to the delay required to obtain approval for release of the product from the Food and Drug Administration—would not serve the public welfare. Public policy favors the development and marketing of beneficial new drugs, even though some risks, perhaps serious ones, might accompany their introduction, because drugs can save lives and reduce pain and suffering.

If drug manufacturers were subject to strict liability, they might be reluctant to undertake research programs to develop some pharmaceuticals that would prove beneficial or to distribute others that are available to be marketed, because of the fear of large adverse monetary judgments. Further, the additional expense of insuring against such liability—assuming insurance would be available—and of research programs to reveal possible dangers not detectable by available scientific methods could place the cost of medication beyond the reach of those who need it most.

Dean Prosser summed up the justification for exempting prescription drugs from strict liability as follows: "The argument that industries producing potentially dangerous products should make good the harm, distribute it by liability insurance, and add the cost to the price of the product, encounters reason for pause, when we consider that two of the greatest medical boons to the human race, penicillin and cortisone, both have their dangerous side effects, and that drug companies might well have been deterred from producing and selling them.

"Thus far the courts have tended to hold the manufacturer to a high standard of care in preparing and testing drugs of unknown potentiality and in giving warning; but in the absence of evidence that this standard has not been met, they have refused to hold the maker liable for unforeseeable harm." (Prosser, Torts (4th ed. 1971) § 99, at p. 661, fns. omitted.)

The possibility that the cost of insurance and of defending against lawsuits will diminish the availability and increase the price of pharmaceuticals is far from theoretical. Defendants cite a host of examples of products which have greatly increased in price or have been withdrawn or withheld from the market because of the fear that their producers would be held liable for large judgments.

For example, according to defendant E.R. Squibb & Sons, Inc., Bendectin, the only antinauseant drug available for pregnant women, was withdrawn from sale in 1983 because the cost of insurance almost equalled the entire income from sale of the drug. Before it was withdrawn, the price of Bendectin increased by over 300 percent. (132 Chemical Week (June 12, 1983) p. 14.)

Drug manufacturers refused to supply a newly discovered vaccine for influenza on the ground that mass innoculation would subject them to enormous liability. The government therefore assumed the risk of lawsuits resulting from injuries caused by the vaccine. (Franklin & Mais, Tort Law and Mass Immunization Programs (1977) 65 Cal.L.Rev. 754, 769 et seq.; Feldman v. Lederle Laboratories (1983) 189 N.J.Super. 424, 460 A.2d 203, 209.) One producer of diptheria-tetanus-pertussis vaccine withdrew from the market, giving as its reason "extreme liability exposure, cost of litigation and the difficulty of continuing to obtain adequate insurance." (Hearing Before Subcom. on Health and the Environment of House Com. on Energy and Commerce on Vaccine Injury Compensation, 98th Cong., 2d Sess. (Sept. 10, 1984) p. 295.) There are only two manufacturers of the vaccine remaining in the market, and the cost of each dose rose a hundredfold from 11 cents in 1982 to $11.40 in 1986, $8 of which was for an insurance reserve. The price increase roughly paralleled an increase in the number of lawsuits from one in 1978 to 219 in 1985. (232 Science (June 13, 1986) p. 1339.) Finally, a manufacturer was unable to market a new drug for the treatment of vision problems because it could not obtain adequate liability insurance at a reasonable cost. (N.Y.Times (Oct. 14, 1986) p. 10.)

There is no doubt that, from the public's standpoint, these are unfortunate consequences. And they occurred even though almost all jurisdictions follow the negligence standard of comment k. It is not unreasonable to conclude in these circumstances that the imposition of a harsher test for liability would not further the public interest in the development and availability of these important products.[10]

We decline to hold, therefore, that a drug manufacturer's liability for injuries caused by the defective design of a prescription drug should be measured by the standard set forth in *Barker.*

10. We express no opinion whether the products to which these examples relate were in fact beneficial to the public health. Our purpose is to demonstrate that there is a rational connection between the cost and availability of pharmaceuticals and the liability imposed on their manufacturers for injuries resulting from their use.

2. *Failure to warn*

For these same reasons of policy, we reject plaintiff's assertion that a drug manufacturer should be held strictly liable for failure to warn of risks inherent in a drug even though it neither knew nor could have known by the application of scientific knowledge available at the time of distribution that the drug could produce the undesirable side effects suffered by the plaintiff.

Numerous cases have recognized that a product may be defective because of the absence of a warning that was necessary to allow its safe use. [Citations.] While some decisions apply strict liability principles to such a defect by holding that it is irrelevant whether the manufacturer knew of the danger or should have known of it (e.g., Halpern v. Johns–Manville Sales Corp. (La.1986) 484 So.2d 110, 114; Elmore v. Owens–Illinois, Inc. (Mo.1984) 673 S.W.2d 434, 438; Carrecter v. Colson Equipment Co. (1985) 346 Pa.Super. 95, 499 A.2d 326, 330–331; Little v. PPG Industries, Inc. [Wash.App.1978] 579 P.2d 940, 947; Haugen v. Minnesota Mining and Manufacturing Co. (1976) 15 Wash.App. 379, 550 P.2d 71, 76–77), most jurisdictions hold to the contrary. That is, liability is conditioned on the actual or constructive knowledge of the risk by the manufacturer as of the time the product was sold or distributed. [Citations.] This rule is consistent with comment j to section 402A, which confines the duty to warn to a situation in which the seller "has knowledge, or by the application of reasonable, developed human skill and foresight should have knowledge of . . . the danger."

It has been said that to "hold the manufacturer liable for failure to warn of a danger of which it would be impossible to know based on the present state of human knowledge would make the manufacturer the virtual insurer of the product. . . ." (Woodill v. Parke Davis & Co. [Ill.1980] 402 N.E.2d 194, 199; accord, Leibowitz v. Ortho Pharmaceutical Corp. (1973) 224 Pa.Super. 418, 307 A.2d 449, 458; see Schwartz, The Post–Sale Duty to Warn: Two Unfortunate Forks in the Road to a Reasonable Doctrine (1983) 58 N.Y.U.L. Rev. 892, 894–905.) The likelihood of the producer's liability would increase with significant advances in scientific knowledge, discouraging the development of new and improved drugs to combat disease. Thus, we disagree with plaintiff's assertion that defendants should be held liable for failing to warn the physician who prescribed DES to plaintiff's mother of alleged defects in the drug that were neither known by defendants nor scientifically knowable at the time the drug was distributed.

3. *The Kearl test*

One further question remains in this aspect of the case. Comment k, as we have seen, provides that the maker of an "unavoidably unsafe" product is not liable for injuries resulting from its use if the product is "properly prepared, and accompanied by proper directions and warning." With the few exceptions noted above, the courts which have adopted comment k have viewed all prescription drugs as coming within its scope.

Kearl suggested that not all drugs are "unavoidably dangerous" so as to merit the protection of the negligence standard of comment k, and it devised a test to separate those which meet that description from those which do not. It held that the question whether a drug should be exempt from strict liability as "unavoidably dangerous" presents a mixed question of law and fact which should be decided on the basis of evidence to be taken by the trial judge out of the presence of the jury. The judge should determine, after hearing the evidence, "(1) whether, when distributed, the product was intended to confer an exceptionally important benefit that made its availability highly desirable; (2) whether the then-existing risk posed by the product was both 'substantial' and 'unavoidable'; and (3) whether the interest in availability (again measured as of the time of distribution) outweighs the interest in promoting enhanced accountability through strict liability design defect review." (172 Cal.App.3d at pp. 829–830, fn. omitted, 218 Cal.Rptr. 453.) If these questions are answered in the affirmative the liability of the manufacturer is tested by the standards of comment k; otherwise, strict liability is the applicable test.

We acknowledge that there is some appeal in the basic premise of *Kearl*. It seems unjust to grant the same protection from liability to those who gave us thalidomide as to the producers of penicillin. If some method could be devised to confine the benefit of the comment k negligence standard to those drugs that have proved useful to mankind while denying the privilege to those that are clearly harmful, it would deserve serious consideration. But we know of no means by which this can be accomplished without substantially impairing the public interest in the development and marketing of new drugs, because the harm to this interest arises in the very process of attempting to make the distinction.

Under the "mini-trial" directed by Kearl, a drug manufacturer has no assurance that a product he places on the market will be measured by the liability standard of comment k because a trial judge could decide that [the drug failed the three-factor test for determining whether it was "unavoidably dangerous"].

Kearl gives the manufacturer a chance to avoid strict liability. But the eligibility of each drug for favorable treatment must be tested at a trial, with its attendant litigation costs, and the drug must survive two risk/benefit challenges, first by the judge and then by the jury. In order to vindicate the public's interest in the availability and affordability of prescription drugs, a manufacturer must have a greater assurance that his products will not be measured by a strict liability standard than is provided by the test stated in *Kearl*. Therefore, we disapprove the portion of *Kearl* which holds that comment k should not be applied to a prescription drug unless the trial court first determines that the drug is "unavoidably dangerous." [11]

In conclusion, and in accord with almost all our sister states that have considered the issue, we hold that a manufacturer is not strictly liable for injuries caused by a prescription drug so long as the drug was properly prepared and accompanied by warnings of its dangerous propensities that were either known or reasonably scientifically knowable at the time of distribution.[12]

* * *

The judgment of the Court of Appeal is affirmed.

NOTES

1. "An outstanding example" of an unavoidably dangerous drug, which according to comment *k* should be exempted from strict tort liability, is rabies vaccine, "which not uncommonly leads to very serious and damaging consequences when it is injected. Since the disease itself invariably leads to a dreadful death, both the marketing and use of the vaccine are fully justified, notwithstanding the unavoidable high degree of risk which they involve." Restatement, Second, of Torts § 402A, comment *k* (1965). See Calabresi v. Trenton State College, 162 N.J.Super. 145, 392 A.2d 600 (App.Div.1978) (brain damage resulting in inability to concentrate on economics such that plaintiff had to drop out of college; manufacturer not liable, but case against doctor remanded for trial on issue of informed consent).

2. The great majority of courts applying the comment *k* unavoidable danger concept have done so in the context of prescription drugs and vaccines, blood, and medical devices. A few infrequent cases have applied the doctrine to other products. See, e.g., Purvis v. PPG Industries, Inc., 502 So.2d 714 (Ala. 1987) (dry cleaning solvent); Payne v. Soft Sheen Products, Inc., 486 A.2d 712 (D.C.App.1985) (permanent wave solution).

---

11. While *Kearl* does not place great emphasis on the language of comment k as the basis of its holding, plaintiff as well as amici curiae focus on the language of the comment in support of their assertion that it cannot be interpreted to grant blanket immunity from strict liability to all prescription drugs, but only to those which are "unavoidably dangerous." We concede that the language of the comment is unclear in this respect. * * *

Nevertheless, we are of the view that the comment was intended to and should apply to all prescription drugs. As we note above, almost all jurisdictions that have adopted the rule stated in the comment view its provisions as granting immunity from strict liability to all such drugs. In addition, as we make clear from our discussion of *Kearl*, the benefit of the negligence standard stated in the comment would be greatly diminished if all drugs were required to run the gauntlet of a risk/benefit analysis in order to qualify for application of the standard.

12. Our conclusion does not mean, of course, that drug manufacturers are free of all liability for defective drugs. They are subject to liability for manufacturing defects, as well as under general principles of negligence, and for failure to warn of known or reasonably knowable side effects.

It should also be noted that the consumers of prescription drugs are afforded greater protection against defects than consumers of other products, since "the drug industry is closely regulated by the Food and Drug Administration, which actively controls the testing and manufacture of drugs and the method by which they are marketed, including the contents of warning labels." (Sindell, 26 Cal.3d at p. 609, 163 Cal.Rptr. 132, 607 P.2d 924.)

McKEE v. MILES LABORATORIES, INC.

United States District Court, Eastern District Kentucky, 1987.
675 F.Supp. 1060.

SILER, CHIEF JUDGE.

This matter is before the Court on the motion by defendant Miles Laboratories, Inc. and its division, Cutter Laboratories, for summary judgment. * * *

This action arose from the circumstances surrounding the blood transfusion of plaintiff's decedent, David Allen McKee. David McKee suffered from Hemophilia A, which meant he lacked a protein necessary for the normal coagulation of his blood. That missing protein is called Factor VIII. A method used by pharmaceutical companies for the treatment of hemophiliacs involved producing Factor VIII by combining (or pooling) plasma collected from thousands of individuals all over the United States. The Factor VIII is precipitated out of the combined plasma and then it is lyophilized (or freeze dried). David McKee used defendant's concentrated Factor VIII Product by the pooled lyophilized method. As a result of its use he contracted acquired immune deficiency syndrome ("AIDS"). Decedent was so diagnosed as having AIDS in October 1983 and subsequently died in 1984. His Administratrix and wife, Stella Mae McKee, brought this action for damages as representative of his estate and on her own behalf.

Defendants move for summary judgment as to plaintiff's strict liability claims, contending that these claims are barred by Kentucky's Blood Shield statute, K.R.S. 139.125. Defendants also move for summary judgment as to the merits of the case, contending that at the time plaintiff's decedent contracted AIDS there was no test which would have revealed the presence of this dreaded disease. In opposition to the motion for summary judgment, plaintiff argues that there is a genuine issue of material fact as to whether an alternative testing method was available in 1983 when decedent contracted AIDS. Plaintiff also asserts that Kentucky's blood shield statute did not bar product liability claims and that, in any event, the statute is not applicable to this situation, but, if applicable, then unconstitutional.

The two central issues before the Court are: (1) whether strict liability applies to defendant's conduct; and (2) whether there existed, at the time plaintiff's decedent contracted the disease, a plausible alternative testing for determining the AIDS virus.

* * *

The relevant statute in question provides:

> Procurement, processing or distribution of blood or human tissue deemed service and not sale. The procurement, processing, distribution or use of whole blood, plasma, blood products, blood derivatives and other human tissues such as corneas, bones or organs for the purpose of injecting, transfusing or transplanting any of them into the human body is declared to

> be, for all purposes, the rendition of a service by every person participating therein and, whether or not any remuneration is paid therefor, is declared not to be a sale of such whole blood, plasma, blood products, blood derivatives or other tissues, for any purpose, subsequent to enactment of this section.

K.R.S. 139.125.

Only one Kentucky case has been found discussing this statute. In McMichael v. American Red Cross, 532 S.W.2d 7 (Ky.1975), the Court of Appeals (then Kentucky's highest Court) declined to address the applicability or constitutionality of K.R.S. 139.125. The case involved a plaintiff encountering serum hepatitis from a blood transfusion. Rather than discussing the above two issues, the Kentucky Court sustained the lower court's directed verdict on the basis that "there were no alternative methods available at the time by which hepatitis virus could effectively be excluded from blood or the presence of the virus determined." *Id.* at 9. However, the trial court granted a directed verdict in favor of the defendant, the blood supplier, relying upon K.R.S. 139.125. Although this Court sought certification as to the issues of strict liability and constitutionality of the above statute, the Supreme Court of Kentucky declined the request, relying upon its holding in *McMichael,* supra.

There is nothing within the provisions of Kentucky's Constitution which would make K.R.S. 139.125 contrary to the framers' intent. * * *

The Court is guided as well by defendants' authority under Coffee v. Cutter Biological and Miles Laboratories, Inc., 809 F.2d 191 (2d Cir. 1987). In that case the Court analyzed a blood shield statute similar to Kentucky's blood shield statute. Based upon the analysis of that opinion and the plain language of the statute, this Court concludes that Kentucky's blood shield statute was intended to preclude the assertion of [strict] product liability claims arising out [of] the sale of blood components. The plain and unambiguous words of the statute clearly state that supplying blood or blood derivatives is to be considered a service by every person participating therein. Only four jurisdictions in the nation have not legislatively barred the application of [strict] products liability theories to blood and blood products. Kentucky is not listed as one of those four states. See Greif, Hospital and Blood Bank Liability to Patients Who Contract Aids Throug[h] Blood Transfusions, 23 San Diego L.Rev. 875, 882 n. 36 (July–Aug. 1986) (listing Kentucky as having enacted such a statute); Kozup v. Georgetown University, 663 F.Supp. 1048 (D.D.C.1987). Because transactions involving blood and blood components are to be considered services, as opposed to sales, they are outside the purview of Kentucky's product liability statute. K.R.S. 411.300; 411.320; 411.340; *McMichael,* supra.

As was noted in *Coffee,* blood shield statutes in other states uniformly have been interpreted as barring strict liability claims. To permit the plaintiff to circumvent the exemption of blood and blood derivatives by pursuing claims under the product liability statute would defeat the obvious legislative intent of K.R.S. 139.125. Consequently, plaintiff's claims against defendants arising under strict liability should be dismissed.

The Court now turns its attention to the second issue, that is, whether at the time plaintiff's decedent contracted the AIDS virus a plausible alternative testing method existed to detect its presence within the blood derivatives. In reaching this answer, the Court is guided by the well-reasoned decision in Kozup v. Georgetown University, 663 F.Supp. 1048 (D.D.C.1987), which analyzed existing methods available for the testing of AIDS during the early 1980s. *Kozup* involved a newborn receiving a blood transfusion for hypovolemia, a condition associated with premature birth, in January 1983. The child received three transfusions which were contaminated with the virus now known to transmit AIDS. The contaminated blood was supplied by the American Red Cross, which received it from an individual in 1982, and was administered by the Georgetown University Hospital. The child subsequently died from complications related to the AIDS infection.

In its analysis, the District Court reviewed the medical chronology of the AIDS virus to determine exactly what was known about AIDS by the scientific and medical communities and when. As in the present case, much of what the plaintiffs claimed in *Kozup* turned on allegations that defendants knew or should have known certain facts related to AIDS. This Court [need] not rehash the same chronolog[ical] medical history of AIDS which the *Kozup* Court so methodically composed. It is suffic[ient] to conclude that it was not until 1984 that the medical community reached a consensus as to the proposition that AIDS was transmittable by blood. *Kozup,* supra; Curran, Acquired Immune Deficiency Syndrome (AIDS) Associated With Transfusions, 310 New Eng.J.Med. 69, 70 (1984). In April, 1984, scientists identified the virus HTLV–III as the cause of AIDS. Fischinger, Acquired Immune Deficiency Syndrome: The Causative Agent and the Evolving Perspective, 9 Current Problems in Cancer 4 (1985). By May, 1985, an enzyme-linked immunosorbent assay (ELISA) test was made available, which screens for the antibodies sensitive to HT[LV]–III. Hermann, AIDS: Malpractice and Transmission Liability, 58 U.Colo.L.Rev. 63, 77 (Winter 86–87). Once it was available, the Center for Disease Control issued guidelines for implementing the ELISA test. This laboratory test has proven 98.6 percent effective in detecting exposure to AIDS. Comment, Transfusion Associated Acquired Immune Deficiency Syndrome (AIDS): Blood Bank Liability?, 16 U.Balt.L.Rev. 81, 86 & n. 36 (Fall 1986). When coupled with a second test, the Western Blot Analysis, the rate of detection for exposure to AIDS rises to 100 percent. Id. at n. 37.

However, there is still no test for presence for the virus itself, nor is there a cure for the disease. *Kozup,* supra at 1053. As no recent breakthrough has been cited to the Court for the diagnosis, testing or treatment of AIDS, it can rely upon the Court's analysis and conclusions in *Kozup.*

As in *Kozup,* plaintiff alleges negligence as a basis for recovery from defendant. In short, plaintiff alleges that Cutter was negligent in failing to take measures designed to protect her husband from being infected with AIDS. Specifically, plaintiff contends that alternatives existed for the testing of the AIDS virus in defendant's product, citing the procedure of heat treatment. However, a review of the medical chronology set forth in *Kozup* reveals this contention inaccurate. As of 1983, no pharmaceutical company, blood bank, hospital or federal health care regulator in the United States took special AIDS-related measures in connection with transfusions. *Kozup,* supra at 1055. Doctors diagnosed plaintiff's decedent with AIDS in the Fall of 1983 before any specialized measures existed. Furthermore, plaintiff can point to no organization, government entity or medical association within the United States which advocated the use of plaintiff's alternative testing as a means of screening defendant's product for AIDS. Instead, plaintiff offers testimony of an expert whose current opinion is that pharmaceutical companies should have used a heat treating method to exclude viruses such as AIDS. This expert cannot alone create a standard of care or a prima facie case of negligence, where he is entirely in opposition to the standard prevailing in 1982–83. His opinion cannot be permitted to supplant the standard of care as established by the conduct of the pharmaceutical community which plaintiff's expert criticizes. To permit this hindsight opinion to preclude summary judgment would violate the United States Supreme Court's mandate that Rule 56 be construed with due regard to defendants who have shown by competent evidence that a plaintiff's claims have no factual basis. Celotex Corp. v. Catrett, 477 U.S. 317, 106 S.Ct. 2548, 2555, 91 L.Ed.2d 265 (1986).

It is clear that in order to prevail on the theory of negligence, plaintiff must show that defendant, Cutter Laboratories, violated a standard of care. That standard is established by looking to the conduct of the industry or profession in similar circumstances as of that date. *Ulrich v. Kasco Abrasives Co.,* 532 S.W.2d 197 (Ky.1976). The standard of care for pharmaceutical companies at the time of decedent's transfusions did not require defendant to screen or perform plaintiff's suggested alternative testing to eliminate the risk of AIDS contamination. Consequently, no negligence occurred as defendants met the standard of care as then existed within the industry.

As stated in *Kozup,* this Court is mindful of the terrible personal tragedy that David McKee's struggle with AIDS must have been for the McKee family, especially in light of the recent breakthroughs in AIDS research. However, because plaintiff fails to make out a prima facie case of negligence, summary judgment for defendant on the issue of negligence is proper as well. An appropriate Order shall be entered.

NOTES

1. Historically, most of the contaminated blood cases concerned serum hepatitis, which is the disease that most of the blood shield statutes sought to address. (California has an analogous AIDS vaccine shield statute providing manufacturers of such vaccines limited immunity from strict liability. See Prod.Liab.Rep. (CCH) ¶ 90,540.) There is still no reliable blood test for serum hepatitis, which is fatal in 5–10% of the cases, making that risk truly both "undiscoverable" and "unavoidable." However, as *McKee* points out, laboratory tests developed in the mid–1980s now permit the detection of AIDS in blood.

Prior to 1986, Maryland's blood shield law was explicitly limited to serum hepatitis; thereafter, it was broadened to address all types of blood contamination by declaring the supplying of blood products to be a "service" rather than a "sale." Doe v. Miles Laboratories, Inc., 675 F.Supp. 1466, 1479–80 (D.Md.1987), was a case in which the plaintiff contracted AIDS from a transfusion in 1983, when the Maryland statute was still limited to hepatitis. The court, therefore, had to determine as a matter of common law whether to allow a strict liability claim against the supplier of the blood at a time when the risk was allegedly unknown, unknowable, and beyond the state of the scientific art:

> Do policy considerations warrant exempting blood and blood products from strict products liability in tort? Defendant argues that the "unavoidably unsafe products" exemption provided to § 402A by Comment *k* applies to it. * * *
>
> * * *
>
> This Court is not prepared to find that HTLV–III carrying blood presents a "reasonable danger" as Comment *k* requires. It is estimated that up to 95% of severe hemophiliacs test positive for exposure to the HTLV–III virus. Ray v. School District of Desoto County, 666 F.Supp. 1524, 1527 (M.D.Fla.1987). The nearly complete exposure by the group most in need of coagulant-factors and the inevitably fatal nature of the disease for those who actually develop it are stark facts. The fact the virus was indetectible prior to 1985 is not a mitigating factor. The best view is to consider blood containing indetectible diseases to be a defective product and therefore that strict liability is applicable. * * *
>
> It is argued that providers of blood and blood products are promoting the general welfare by making possible improved health. It is argued that it is a fundamental social policy of the State of Maryland to promote the supply of blood and blood products. And it is argued that to allow strict products liability, which given the wide exposure to AIDS due to transfusions could create potentially substantial liability, would so raise costs of production that the supply of blood could be choked off.
>
> The arguments are unpersuasive. One can agree with John Stuart Mill that poetry provides a higher type of pleasure than does pushpin without accepting defendant Miles' argument that it is a provider of poetry and therefore should be exempt from the seemingly Benthamite calculus providers of pushpins are subject to. Nor should it be. Those who choose to operate in the economic marketplace play by the rules applicable to all.

> The arguments in favor of strict products liability apply as persuasively to blood and blood products as they do to any other product. First, there is no reason why victims of defective blood should bear the costs where victims of other defective products do not. Second, strict liability would provide the incentive to promote all possible accident prevention, for it is a rational business decision to keep costs down. Third, the producers are in a better position to spread the costs than are individual consumers. Finally, it makes for a more efficient allocation of social resources when the price of a transfusion of blood or blood products reflects its true costs.
>
> Entrepreneurs by their nature are risk taking individuals. To the extent they need an incentive to engage in socially beneficial activities, the law already provides it in the form of a corporate shield on personal liability. To do as defendant argues, and exempt blood from strict liability would be to subsidize the product by forcing either victims or government through its social welfare programs to bear accident costs. In the absence of a clear expression on the part of the legislature of an intent to subsidize a particular product, it is not this Court's role to create the subsidy indirectly by carving out a Judge made exemption to strict products liability.

Held, summary judgment denied. For a thorough review of the developments in AIDS research, see Kozup v. Georgetown University, 663 F.Supp. 1048 (D.D.C.1987), rev'd on other grounds, 851 F.2d 437 (D.C.Cir.1988). For a listing of citations to the blood shield laws in 48 states, see Roberts v. Suburban Hosp. Ass'n, Inc., 73 Md.App. 1, 532 A.2d 1081, 1086 n. 3 (1987) (AIDS) (stating that the only jurisdictions without such statutes are New Jersey, Vermont, and the District of Columbia).

How can you assist a potential client, who contracted AIDS or hepatitis from a blood transfusion, in the face of a blood shield statute? Do you decline the case? See generally both *Kozup* and *Roberts,* above.

2. The courts have split on the central question of whether "state-of-the-art evidence" may be introduced by a defendant on a strict liability claim—in other words, whether a supplier may successfully defend such a case by showing that the risk was unknowable or otherwise unavoidable. A number of courts, often in the asbestos context, have followed the *Beshada* approach and ruled that such evidence is irrelevant to a strict liability claim. See, e.g., Johnson v. Raybestos–Manhattan, Inc., ___ Hawaii ___, 740 P.2d 548 (1987); Kisor v. Johns–Manville Corp., 783 F.2d 1337 (9th Cir.1986) (Wash. law); Elmore v. Owens–Illinois, Inc., 673 S.W.2d 434 (Mo.1984); Hayes v. Ariens Co., 391 Mass. 407, 462 N.E.2d 273 (1984). However, many courts have ruled to the contrary, often relying on comment *j,* and allowed such evidence and a "state-of-the-art defense." See, e.g., Lohrmann v. Pittsburgh Corning Corp., 782 F.2d 1156 (4th Cir.1986); Bernier v. Raymark Industries, Inc., 516 A.2d 534 (Me. 1986).

3. In the design context, the issue is often fought on whether the plaintiff must establish a feasible design alternative and, alternatively, whether the defendant may defend by showing the absence of such an alternative. "Manufacturers are not to be held strictly liable for failure to design safety features, if the technology to do so is unavailable at the time the product is made." Rexrode v. American Laundry Press Co., 674 F.2d 826 (10th Cir.1982). While most courts apparently agree, some hold that the feasibility of alternative

designs is only one factor in the analysis. Norton v. Snapper Power Equip., 806 F.2d 1545 (11th Cir.1987) (state-of-the-art evidence is relevant both to plaintiff's case and defense). Compare Adams v. Fuqua Industries, Inc., 820 F.2d 271 (8th Cir.1987) (lawn mower manufacturer should have been permitted to offer rebuttal evidence that safety devices proposed by plaintiff not feasible since not developed at time of manufacture). However, since requiring proof of feasibility conflicts with the consumer expectations test of defectiveness, a few courts have ruled that the plaintiff need not prove the existence of a feasible alternative design. See Rahmig v. Mosley Machinery Co., 226 Neb. 423, 412 N.W.2d 56 (1987). See generally supra, p. 293.

4. Who should have the burden of proof on state of the art, plaintiff or defendant? Why?

5. **The "Wade–Keeton" Test, Scienter, and "Strict" Liability.** Reconsider the "Wade–Keeton" or "cost"-benefit test of defectiveness, examined above at pp. 219–21. How does *Beshada* reason that this test precludes the unknowable danger "defense"? How does *Feldman* deal with the issue of constructive knowledge? How does *Brown* handle it? Which court is correct?

Both Dean Wade and Dean Keeton have repudiated "their" test(s)—Dean Wade who never meant what he said, and Dean Keeton, who no longer believes what he said. See Wade, On the Effect in Product Liability of Knowledge Unavailable Prior to Marketing, Postscript, 58 N.Y.U.L.Rev. 734, 761 (1983); W.P. Keeton, D. Dobbs, R. Keeton & D. Owen, Prosser and Keeton on the Law of Torts 697–98 n. 21 (5th ed. 1984). Is the test such a bad one?

6. Some courts distinguish warnings from design cases in ruling on the state-of-the-art defense. Others distinguish between strict liability in tort and warranty. See Spartanburg County Sch. Dist. Seven v. National Gypsum Co., 805 F.2d 1148 (4th Cir.1986) (state-of-the-art defense available in strict tort, but not warranty, claim; property damage). Do these distinctions make sense?

7. **Disaggregating Products Liability Law.** How about using true strict liability for some products, but not for others? Perhaps strict liability should apply only to the "worst" products, such as asbestos. This, of course, is what *Feldman's* restriction of *Beshada* to its facts effectively did. See also Halphen v. Johns–Manville Sales Corp., 484 So.2d 110 (La.1986). Or perhaps strict liability should apply to all products except the "best"—such as prescription drugs, as *Brown* did, or the *very* best, as *Feldman* held.

Are drugs and blood really so socially beneficial that they deserve special treatment? How about pacemakers? Glasses? Automobiles? Is asbestos really so socially objectionable as to deserve special treatment? How about cigarettes? Alcohol? Cheap handguns? Agent Orange? And how about dangerous prescription drugs, like Thalidomide? Or the Dalkon Shield IUD?

What do you think about the courts (and legislatures—i.e., blood shield laws, statutes protecting gun manufacturers, laws favoring victims of asbestos) adopting special rules of products liability for "special" products? Are not the underlying social policies always the same? Is not this form of special treatment offensive to fundamental notions of equality of treatment by the law?

Or has the law of products liability painted with too broad of a brush? Is the word "product" so broad that it captures some situations where the traditional goals of products liability law are overshadowed by other considerations? Is the disaggregation of "products" liability law a positive development? Should it be accomplished broadly, as a matter of law, like *Brown*, or narrowly, on a case-by-case basis, like *Feldman*?

"Numerous courts have flatly rejected Equal–Protection-based attacks on blood shield statutes." Samson v. Greenville Hosp. System, 295 S.C. 359, 368 S.E.2d 665, 667 (1988). The constitutionality of the *Beshada–Feldman* special treatment of asbestos was narrowly upheld in In re Asbestos Litigation, 829 F.2d 1233, 1244 (3d Cir.1987) (1–1–1) ("the policies of risk spreading, compensation for victims, and simplification of trials in the highly unusual circumstances of asbestos claims furnish an adequate, albeit minimal, basis for eliminating the state-of-the-art defense in these cases"). Concurring, Judge Becker reasoned that "the New Jersey Supreme Court has determined a legislative fact—that the hazards of asbestos exposure were knowable to the industry at all relevant times." Id. at 1245. Judge Hunter concluded: "Today this court has ruled that the manufacturers of one product may not use the state-of-the-art defense. That product is asbestos. * * * This is just plain wrong and I dissent." Id. at 1252.

8. **The Politics of Tort Law.**

A. **In general.** Does the *Brown* opinion sound like it came from the same court that decided *Greenman, Cronin* and *Barker?* Did it? It was decided within a few months after Chief Justice Rose Bird and two other "liberal" justices were denied reelection and replaced by judges with more "moderate" views. At least in the Chief Justice's case, the campaign against her centered on her refusal to uphold death penalty convictions.

B. **Tort "reform."** As the 1980s progressed, insurers and manufacturers pressed harder and harder for tort and products liability reform in the state legislatures and the Congress. An important issue in the debate has been the question of "state of the art," and liability for unavoidable dangers, and many states have passed statutes on point. Which of the following approaches are the most reasonable?

(1) Evidence of technological feasibility may be considered by the trier of fact. *Washington,* 2 Prod.Liab.Rep. (CCH) ¶ 94,992;

(2) Evidence of post-sale advancements in the state of the art is not admissible. *Arizona,* id. at ¶ 90,315;

(3) Evidence that the product conformed to the state of the art, as distinguished from industry standards, raises a rebuttable presumption that the product was not defective and the defendant not negligent. *Colorado,* id. at ¶ 90,612;

(4) A supplier is not liable if the product is unavoidably unsafe and a warning is given that a reasonably prudent person would give in similar circumstances. *New Jersey,* id. at ¶ 93,153–54;

(5) Undiscoverability of the risk, using prevailing research and scientific techniques under the state of the art, is an affirmative defense. *New Hampshire,* id. at ¶ 93,013; or

(6) Conforming to the state of the art is an affirmative defense, defined as the technical, mechanical and scientific knowledge in existence and reasonably feasible for use at the time of manufacture. *Arizona,* id. at ¶ 90,310–12.

Note the web of interrelationships between state of the art, product deterioration, and the multitude of related issues mentioned in note 8, p. 408, above.

9. Each year increasing numbers of substances are newly discovered to be carcinogenic. Should the manufacturers, or consumers, of such products bear the "unavoidable" losses from previously unknown and "undiscoverable" hazards?

10. Whatever happened to "strict" liability?

11. **Cogitating on the Limitations of Law.**

> A mature understanding of and respect for law includes an appreciation of its limitations. Law would be reduced to tyranny, and its purposes deprived of a vital dimension, if it were viewed one dimensionally as a good. It is only the most insightful judge who truly understands that law, like most everything known to man, is an evil in excess. Although law must by nature move into the human comedy from time to time to referee disputes between the players, it should cut narrowly and precisely while inside and should move out swiftly when the job is done. Since the job to be accomplished can properly be defined only in terms of the purposes behind the law, a mature respect for the purposes of the law includes a keen respect for its proper limits.

Owen, "Respect For Law and Man: The Tort Law of Chief Justice Frank Rowe Kenison," 11 Vt.L.Rev. 389, 407 (1986).

12. See generally V. Schwartz, Unavoidably Unsafe Products: Clarifying the Meaning and Policy Behind Comment *k,* 42 Wash. & Lee L.Rev. 1139 (1985); Birnbaum & Wrubel, "State of the Art" and Strict Products Liability, 21 Tort & Ins. L.J. 30 (1985); Wade, On the Effect in Product Liability of Knowledge Unavailable Prior to Marketing, 58 N.Y.U.L.Rev. 734 (1983); Page, Generic Product Risks: The Case Against Comment *k* and for Strict Tort Liability, 58 N.Y. U.L.Rev. 853 (1983); Robb, A Practical Approach to Use of State of the Art Evidence in Strict Products Liability Cases, 77 Nw.U.L.Rev. 1 (1982); O'Donnell, Design Litigation and the State of the Art: Terminology, Practice and Reform, 11 Akron L.Rev. 627 (1978); Willig, The Comment *k* Character: A Conceptual Barrier to Strict Liability, 29 Mercer L.Rev. 545 (1978).

Chapter 4

CAUSATION

> The search for causes must have been an incident of the early awakening of primordial man. There is no human who hesitates to identify the cause of any calamity that touches his life. In the highest echelons of social and scientific research, the vain attempts to reduce to control the causes of war, crime, poverty, cancer, and other barriers to man's happy existence continue with unabated zeal. The attraction of causes is as magnetic for people as flames are for insects, and it is frequently as deadly.

Green, Strict Liability Under Sections 402A and 402B: A Decade of Litigation, 54 Tex.L.Rev. 1185, 1208 (1976).

Two distinct topics are examined in this chapter, cause in fact and legal or "proximate" cause. While many courts reserve the term "proximate cause" exclusively for issues concerning the scope of legal duty, others use it in a broader sense to include the concept of cause in fact as well. See, e.g., Kerns v. Engelke, 54 Ill.App.3d 323, 12 Ill.Dec. 270, 369 N.E.2d 1284, 1292 (1977), rev'd in part on other grounds, 76 Ill. 2d 154, 28 Ill.Dec. 500, 390 N.E.2d 859 (1979): " 'Proximate cause' is a term of art which encompasses the distinct concepts of cause in fact and legal cause. Determining whether defendant's conduct was a cause of plaintiff's injury involves nothing more than an analysis of the facts. Once it is established that the defendant's conduct has in fact been a cause of the injury, however, there remains the question whether the defendant should be legally responsible for what he has caused. As otherwise stated, the question is whether the policy of the law will extend defendant's responsibility to the consequences which have in fact occurred."

SECTION 1. CAUSE IN FACT: CONNECTING PLAINTIFF'S HARM TO DEFENDANT'S BREACH OF DUTY

A. GENERAL PRINCIPLES

The principles of cause in fact are basically the same in the products liability context as in other areas of tort law. See, e.g., Kerns v. Engelke, supra, where the court outlined the fundamental principles: "Two tests are generally applied in determining the issue of causation in fact. Under the 'substantial factor' test, the defendant's conduct is a cause of an event if it was a material element and a substantial factor in bringing it about. Under the second test, commonly called the 'but for' rule, the defendant's conduct is not a cause of an event if the event would have occurred without it." The court observed further that "causation in fact is a question 'upon which all the learning, literature and lore of the law are largely lost. It is a matter upon which any layman is quite as competent to sit in judgment as the most experienced court.' (W. Prosser, Law of Torts at 237 (4th ed. 1971).) For that reason, causation in fact is usually a question for the jury."

DRAYTON v. JIFFEE CHEMICAL CORP.

United States District Court, Northern District of Ohio, 1975.
395 F.Supp. 1081, modified and aff'd, 591 F.2d 352 (6th Cir.1978).

FINDINGS OF FACT AND CONCLUSIONS OF LAW

BATTISTI, CHIEF JUDGE. This action arose out of the severe facial disfigurement incurred by the infant plaintiff, Terri Drayton, as a result of a chemical burn. After a trial to the court, the following facts have been established.

The incident in question occurred on December 21, 1968. At that time both plaintiffs, the infant Terri Drayton and her mother Bernice Drayton, lived in a boarding house in Cleveland, Ohio. The house was occupied by several other tenants including James Henderson, the putative father of Terri Drayton.

At approximately 7:00 p.m. on the night of December 21, 1968 Bernice Drayton and her daughter were on the first floor of the boarding house readying it for Christmas by decorating the Christmas tree and retrieving toys and decorations from the basement. At about that time Henderson returned home and obtained a bottle of "liquid-plumr" from his landlady, Mrs. Sorrell, for the purpose of clearing a clogged drain in the second floor bathroom sink. As he ascended the stairs, Henderson had his daughter, Terri, in one arm and the bottle of liquid-plumr in the other. Henderson testified that as he climbed the stairs he read a portion of the label.

At the top of the stairs, Henderson put Terri on the floor in the hall and entered the bathroom alone. According to the testimony, he then poured half of the bottle of liquid-plumr into the drain and placed the uncapped bottle on the back of the sink adjacent to the left faucet. Henderson then placed a towel over the open drain and stepped back from the sink. At that moment Terri grabbed his leg and screamed. When Henderson looked down at the child, she had been doused with the liquid drain cleaner. Henderson testified that he was unaware of the child's presence in the bathroom until the instant he heard her scream.

Immediately after the accident, Henderson took the child downstairs where both Bernice Drayton and Mrs. Sorrell were present.

Recalling that the label said "something about burns" and "something about water" Henderson wet his handkerchief and dabbed at Terri's face. After some confusion, Henderson, Mrs. Drayton, Mrs. Sorrell, and Terri drove to Forest City Hospital so that the child might be treated. Apparently the physicians at Forest City were not equipped to adequately cope with the extensive burns suffered by Terri Drayton. For that reason she was referred to University Hospitals for admission, a transfer that entailed an additional twenty-five minute delay. As a result of the injuries sustained on December 21, 1968, Terri Drayton has been hospitalized on eight separate occasions, undergone eleven operative procedures, and compiled a 190 page hospital record—all at the age of seven.

The product that allegedly caused Terri Drayton's injuries, liquid-plumr, is designed, manufactured, and marketed by defendant Jiffee Chemical Corporation, an Indiana corporation. * * *

* * *

[Among other contentions,] Jiffee denies that it was their product (liquid-plumr) that was being used by Henderson at the time of the accident.

III. *Alleged Misidentification of the Product.*

With regard to this last contention, it is significant to note that the container which Henderson used to clear the bathroom drain was never recovered nor were the circumstances of its disposal ascertained. Given the emotional atmosphere that surrounded the accident and its aftermath it is most likely that the container was disposed of without regard to what role it might play in possible future litigation. Thus the identity of the injury-causing product must be determined from the testimony of those who were present in the boarding house at the time of the accident.

The landlady of the boarding house, Mrs. Sorrell, testified that she bought a bottle of liquid-plumr in 1966, more than a year before the incident that is the subject of the instant action. She was quite definite in her testimony as was Mrs. Drayton who said that she remembered the name "liquid-plumr" because "those words were large."

Defendant argues that the injury-producing product was not "liquid-plumr" but rather "Mister Plumber", a drain cleaner composed of 92–93% sulfuric acid. The basis for such argument is certain behavior by Henderson that is arguably inconsistent with the recommended procedures for employing liquid-plumr. Great emphasis is placed on Henderson's covering of the drain with a towel immediately after pouring in the drain cleaner. At a 1972 deposition Henderson testified:

> Q. You said, as I understand it, you poured some liquid-plumr into the sink and then put a towel on top of it?
>
> A. Right.
>
> Q. Why did you do that?

A. As I remember reading the label, it said something about odors, you know, giving off a bad odor or something, so I placed a towel over it.

At trial, Henderson's testimony was substantially identical.

The reason for defendant's reliance on Henderson's covering the drain with a towel emanates from the precise wording of the liquid-plumr and Mister Plumber labels. The liquid-plumr label is virtually devoid of any reference to odors. On the front of the label it says merely "No Odor." The Mister Plumber label, however, specifically directs that the drain be covered with a wet cloth. It also states "have plenty of VENTILATION as unpleasant odors may arise. Covering drain with wet cloth will help." Inasmuch as Henderson testified that he had had no prior experience with drain cleaners such behavior is certainly more consistent with having read the Mister Plumber directions than those contained on the liquid-plumr label. Such an inference, however, is not sufficient to offset the uncontroverted (albeit self-serving) testimony of Henderson, Mrs. Drayton, and Mrs. Sorrell. For such an inference to prevail, this Court would have to find the unequivocal testimony of all three of the above witnesses to be incredible—something which it is not prepared to do.

Similarly, defendant finds great significance in Henderson's *dabbing* Terri's face with a wet handkerchief rather than *flushing* it with water. Resort, again, is had to the exact wording of the respective labels. The liquid-plumr label calls for the affected area to be flushed or flooded with large amounts of water. Mr. Plumber, on the other hand, directs that the area be wiped gently prior to being flooded with water. This act by Henderson, which was reasonable and prudent under the circumstances, is too fragile an underpinning upon which to find a misidentification of the injurious product.

At trial defendant also made reference to the rapidity with which the liquid drain cleaner burned Terry Drayton as well as the fact that Mrs. Sorrell's shirt was eaten through as a result of holding Terri Drayton's head to her chest while enroute to the hospital. Mr. Levy, who is president of Krobaugh Laboratories, testified that sulfuric acid acts much more quickly on human tissue than does sodium hydroxide. Similarly, Mr. Summerfelt, the manager of specialty products for Clorox, testified that the effect of the chemical on Mrs. Sorrell's shirt was inconsistent with exposure to a 30% solution of sodium hydroxide and, in fact, was more consistent with exposure to sulfuric acid.

Such empirical observations, however, are of little significance absent a factual frame of reference. To say that sulfuric acid burns human tissue more quickly than sodium hydroxide is not to say that sodium hydroxide doesn't burn it at all. At trial it was impossible to accurately fix the total elapsed time that the liquid drain cleaner was on Terri Drayton's face. Considering only the twenty-five minute delay in driving from Forest City Hospital to University Hospitals such exposure to the liquid drain cleaner was not insubstantial.

It is also impossible to identify the brand of drain cleaner by its effect on Mrs. Sorrell's shirt. Absent precise information about the shirt's fiber and composition and the duration of the chemical contact any attempt to correlate corrosive effect with a specific chemical compound would be purely speculative. Thus plaintiffs have proven, by a preponderance of the evidence, that it was, in fact, liquid-plumr that came in contact with Terri Drayton and caused her injuries.

[The court found the defendant liable.]

NOTES

1. An essential element of the plaintiff's case is identification of the named defendant as the manufacturer or supplier of the defective product. Many of the cases on this point have involved beverage manufacturers. See, for example, Baker v. Coca–Cola Bottling Works of Gary, 132 Ind.App. 390, 177 N.E.2d 759 (1961).

2. One method of identification is proof that the product bears the defendant's name, as by a label or decal of some sort. See, e.g., Smith v. Ariens Co., 375 Mass. 620, 377 N.E.2d 954 (1978) ("Ariens" decal affixed to defective snowmobile); Helm v. Pepsi–Cola Bottling Co. of St. Louis, Inc., 723 S.W.2d 465 (Mo.App.1986) (plaintiff's wife and lawyer both read "Mead Corporation" on bottom of defective carton subsequently lost by another lawyer).

3. Another method of identification is testimony by the retailer that it had purchased the type of product sold to the consumer from a particular supplier. See, e.g., Amin v. Knape & Vogt Co., Inc., 148 Ill.App.3d 1075, 102 Ill. Dec. 561, 500 N.E.2d 454 (1986) (shelf clips sold to college); Payton v. Abbott Labs, 780 F.2d 147 (1st Cir.1985) (pharmacist purchased generic drug from supplier who generally purchased that type of drug from defendant).

4. Where there is no direct identifying information, other evidence may point toward the defendant, such as the product's composition or method of construction (like a garment's stitching) that is unique to the defendant. Cf. C.K.S., Inc. v. Helen Borgenicht Sportswear, Inc., 25 A.D.2d 218, 268 N.Y.S.2d 409 (1966) (appearance and composition of blouse).

5. In the absence of proof establishing the probability that the defendant manufactured the product, the plaintiff's case will ordinarily fail. See, e.g., Brown by Brown v. Stone Mfg. Co., Inc., 660 F.Supp. 454, 458 (S.D.Miss.1986) (child's pink nightgown that caught fire, the remnants of which were discarded at hospital, was purchased from store that carried several similar brands; child thought defendant's gown purchased by mother at same store one year after accident was "sort of like" accident gown, but had different color design; washing instructions remembered by mother differed from those on defendant's subsequently purchased gown—*held,* jury would not be permitted "to resort to guesswork in identifying * * * proper manufacturer").

6. **Multiple Defendants.**

A. **Concurrent causes—Liability.** If the actions or products of two or more persons combined to cause the plaintiff's harm, then each such person who was a "substantial factor" in causing the harm may be liable. See, e.g., Basko v. Sterling Drug, Inc., 416 F.2d 417 (2d Cir.1969) (two drugs). All that the plaintiff must establish is that the defendant's negligence, or the defective condition in its product, was "a"—rather than "the"—substantial factor in causing the accident. See, e.g., Vlahovich v. Betts Mach. Co., 101 Ill.App.2d 123, 242 N.E.2d 17, 20 (1968) (concurring opinion), aff'd, 45 Ill.2d 506, 260 N.E.2d 230 (1970).

B. **Concurrent causes—Apportionment of damages.** It is often difficult to determine which portions of a plaintiff's injuries are attributable to each of two or more responsible parties. If the trier of fact is able to determine which aspects of the plaintiff's loss are attributable to each defendant, then damages ordinarily will be apportioned on that basis. But where no fair and practicable method for apportioning the loss is available, then each defendant whose breach of duty was a substantial factor in producing the damage may be held jointly and severally responsible for the total loss. See, e.g., Smith v. J.C. Penny Co., Inc., 269 Or. 643, 525 P.2d 1299 (1974) (plaintiff suffered severe burns from her excessively flammable imitation fur coat which caught fire when service station operator negligently sprayed gasoline on floor heater).

Plaintiffs were injured in a fire following a two car collision which occurred when their car was hit by another vehicle driven by Whalen. They sued Whalen for negligent driving and the manufacturer of the car in which they were riding (Ford) for designing an uncrashworthy automobile. Judgments for plaintiffs were affirmed on appeal in Buehler v. Whalen, 70 Ill.2d 51, 15 Ill.Dec. 852, 374 N.E.2d 460 (1977). Whalen argued that the jury should have been instructed to apportion all of the damages to Ford since plaintiff's only injuries were burns caused by the uncrashworthy design of the car's fuel system. The court thought otherwise: "What defendant Whalen would overlook is her obviously negligent driving which caused the collision, the precipitating cause of the fire. We have here a classic case of concurrent tortfeasors whose separate acts combine to produce a single individual injury. Under these circumstances there is no apportionment." 15 Ill.Dec. at 857, 374 N.E.2d at 465.

The doctrine of joint and several liability has come under increasing scrutiny in recent years as part of the tort reform movement, and many states have modified or abolished the doctrine. The general approach of the reform statutes is to correlate a defendant's liability to his proportionate fault, although the variations between the statutes are significant. See, e.g., *Alaska*—parties less than 50% at fault may not be jointly liable for more than twice the percentage of fault allocated to them, Prod.Liab.Rep. (CCH) ¶ 90,225; *Arizona*—"the liability of each defendant for damages is several only and is not joint," id. at ¶ 90,332; *California*—"the liability of each defendant for non-economic damages shall be several only and shall not be joint," id. at ¶ 90,573.

C. **One cause—Two or more possible culprits.**

(1) If the plaintiff's harm was caused by a single product or person, but can be traced only to two or more possible culprits, the plaintiff generally will be unable to meet his burden of proof on identifying the tortfeasor. In Garcia v. Joseph Vince Co., 84 Cal.App.3d 868, 148 Cal.Rptr. 843, 846–47 (1978) ("Hamlet II"), a college student's eye was injured during a fencing match when his opponent's sabre penetrated his mask because its tip was thin and sharp instead of round. The sabre was thereafter placed back in the team bag with all the other sabres and was not produced at trial because it had either been lost or "mixed up with the others in the shuffle." The coach had purchased the sabres from two manufacturers. Since there was no evidence pointing to either manufacturer in particular, plaintiff sued both. *Held,* nonsuit affirmed: "The

jury on the basis of such evidence would be purely speculating as to who should be liable. * * * The evidence was evenly divided * * *."

Plaintiff argued "that when the evidence is evenly balanced * * *, under the rule of Summers v. Tice, 33 Cal.2d 80, 199 P.2d 1, the burden of proof should shift to [the defendants] to establish who sold the product. This argument has no merit." Why not?

(2) Compare Snider v. Bob Thibodeau Ford, Inc., 42 Mich.App. 708, 202 N.W.2d 727 (1972), where plaintiff was injured when the brakes on his delivery truck failed. Since plaintiff was unable to prove whether the defect had been caused by the manufacturer or the dealer, the trial court dismissed his action against the manufacturer. *Held,* reversed:

> True, the burden of proving which of two possible wrongdoers is responsible is generally assigned to the plaintiff. The courts have, however, shown a willingness to consider special circumstances when allocating the burden of proof. This accords with the general view that the placing of that burden is "merely a question of policy and fairness" based on experience in the different situations.
>
> * * *
>
> In this case, because of the technical problems involved in a brake system, the superior knowledge and expertise of a manufacturer like Ford, and the close relationship between the manufacturer and retailer Thibodeau, we conclude that the burden of negating individual responsibility for the brake failure should be placed on the defendants.

202 N.W.2d at 732–33.

(3) *Holding two or more defendants liable for harm caused by only one.* In certain circumstances, some courts permit the plaintiff injured by a single product who is unable to prove the identity of the manufacturer to recover against two or more manufacturers of the same kind of product. Four principle approaches have been used to allow recovery on this basis: (1) concert of action; (2) alternative liability; (3) enterprise liability; and (4) market share liability. These theories are discussed below in Chapter 10, § 2, in the context of toxic substance litigation.

7. On product identification, see generally Annot., 51 A.L.R.3d 1344 (1973).

CALHOUN v. HONDA MOTOR COMPANY, LTD.

United States Court of Appeals, Sixth Circuit, 1984.
738 F.2d 126.

KEITH, CIRCUIT JUDGE.

* * *

I. Facts

On July 18, 1978 plaintiff, Richard Calhoun was driving his Honda 750 CB motorcycle to work when he collided with the rear of a stationary tractor trailer truck. There were no witnesses to the accident and as a result of his injuries Calhoun does not recall what happened. A Kentucky state policeman was called to the scene and he later testified that the motorcycle had left forty feet of skid marks on the pavement.

Plaintiff filed an action against Honda alleging strict liability for his injuries under Restatement (Second) of Torts § 402A (1974). The alleged product defect was poor wet braking performance due to a design defect present in all 1977 Honda 750 CB motorcycles. In support of his allegation, plaintiff relied upon a recall letter issued by Honda five months prior to the accident. The letter stated that the performance of the rear brake pad was reduced by heavy rain conditions. Although it had not rained the day of the accident, plaintiff had visited a car wash approximately thirty minutes prior to the collision.

* * *

At the conclusion of all evidence, Honda made a motion for a directed verdict which was denied. The jury found for plaintiff and awarded him $1,250,000.

Nine months later, the district court granted Honda a judgment notwithstanding the verdict or a new trial if this court reversed the judgment notwithstanding the verdict. It is from this order that plaintiff appeals.

II. Judgment Notwithstanding the Verdict

Calhoun argues that the district court's grant of a judgment notwithstanding the verdict was erroneous because the jury's verdict was supported by substantial evidence. Regretfully, we disagree.

* * *

A. The Evidence Did Not Support the Verdict Because Plaintiff Failed to Establish Causation.

The jury found Honda liable for Calhoun's injuries on the theory of strict liability in torts. Restatement (Second) of Torts § 402A. In order to find a manufacturer liable for injury sustained by his product, the jury must have found that the product in question was defective and that this defect was the cause of plaintiff's injury.

Calhoun alleges that there was a defect in the rear brake of the motorcycle. Although Calhoun cannot remember what took place because of his injuries, he hypothesized that when he applied the brakes they did not perform properly. He claims this failure was the result of the brake pads becoming wet when he took his motorcycle to a car wash.

Plaintiff relied upon a recall letter sent by Honda to all owners of Honda 750 CB motorcycles as proof of a braking defect. The letter stated:

> Honda Motor Co., Ltd., has determined that a defect which related to motor vehicle safety exists in the rear brake pads of certain Honda motorcycles.

> When the rear disc brake is applied during operation in heavy rain, there may be noticeable initial reduction in effectiveness of the brake followed by gradual recovery to normal, dry condition effectiveness. If pedal force is not increased to compensate for the reduced initial effectiveness, a longer stopping distance will result. If pedal force is increased to compensate for the reduced initial effectiveness and then maintained despite the recovery of the brake, available tire traction may be exceeded, resulting in skidding of the rear wheel. If the rear wheel remains in a skidding condition, loss of control and vehicle crash can occur. (Plaintiff's Exhibit # 5).

Although it was reversible error to admit this letter into evidence,[2] if we were to assume arguendo that the letter was admissible and established the existence of a defect, Calhoun failed to show where the defect was the cause of the accident. Causation is an element which may be proved either by direct or circumstantial evidence. However, if a party seeks to establish causation by circumstantial evidence "the evidence must be sufficient to tilt the balance from possibility to probability." Perkins v. Trailco Mfg. & Sales Co., 613 S.W.2d 855 (Ky. 1981); Midwestern V.W. Corp. v. Ringley, 503 S.W.2d 745 (Ky.1973); Fields v. Western Kentucky Gas Co., 478 S.W.2d 20 (Ky.1972); Holbrook v. Rose, 458 S.W.2d 155 (Ky.1970).

In Perkins v. Trailco Mfg. & Sales Co., supra, the plaintiff was injured when in the process of operating a dump truck it overturned. He brought an action based on products liability and alleged that a defect in the truck's hydraulic hoist assembly caused his injury. The trial court directed a verdict on grounds that plaintiff had failed to establish causation. The Kentucky Supreme Court reversed. The court found that although plaintiff had failed to submit direct proof of a specific defect, he had successfully negated other possible causes for the trailer's failure to function properly. Therefore, a reasonable inference of probability rather than a mere possibility of respondent's culpability existed. 613 S.W.2d at 857–58.

By contrast, where an accident could have resulted for any number of reasons, the plaintiff has failed to establish the necessary proximate cause. Plaintiff, in Midwestern V.W. v. Ringley, supra, brought a suit in strict liability against the manufacturer of her Volkswagen. Plaintiff claimed that as she was driving along a wet road she attempted to apply her brakes but the right front wheel grabbed, causing her to spin out of control. On three previous occasions plaintiff had taken her car to the dealer's service department for a condition she described as "pulling to the right", whenever she applied the brakes. Each time the service department told her the problem had been repaired. After the accident, the problem was diagnosed as an "out of round" right front disc brake. Plaintiff claimed this was a defect in the manufacturing process and the cause of the accident. The testimony at trial, however,

2. See discussion, Part III infra.

indicated that the car could have pulled to the right for any number of reasons:

> [a]ll of Wanda's witnesses testified that an "out of round" brake drum on the right front would cause the automobile to pull to the right when the brakes were applied. On cross-examination they testified that dirt and dust in the left brake lining would cause the automobile to pull to the right. They further testified on cross-examination that water in the left brake lining would cause the automobile to pull to the right; that improper adjustment of the right-front brake drum would cause the automobile to pull to the right. There was testimony by one of the witnesses that an examination of the right-front brake after the accident revealed that it was adjusted too tightly. Wanda's witnesses further testified on cross-examination that improper tire pressure and improper alignment could cause pulling.

503 S.W.2d at 747.

The Kentucky Court of Appeals reversed the trial judge's verdict in favor of plaintiff because the "plaintiff had failed to prove that the defect in manufacturing was the probable cause of the accident." Id.

Of course a plaintiff need not establish beyond all doubt a specific cause of an accident. For example, in Fields v. Western Kentucky Gas, supra, the plaintiff was injured when, in the process of laying sewer pipes underground, he lit a match and an explosion occurred. The plaintiff alleged that the probable cause of the accident was the explosion of natural gas, resulting from a leak in [defendant] gas company's line. The court, in finding the existence of probable cause, stated:

> [t]he plaintiff need not establish a case beyond a reasonable doubt. Although a jury may not be permitted to speculate when the probabilities of an event's having happened in one of two or more ways are equal and there is no evidence as to which way it did happen, it is neither legal "speculation" nor "conjecture" when a jury finds as a fact that an event happened by reason of a particular cause when the evidence on behalf of a party, if believed, is sufficient to show that it is more likely than not that the event occurred as a result of the cause so found.

478 S.W.2d at 22.

Calhoun's evidence never went further than to show that the claimed defect was a possible, not probable cause of the collision. This is insufficient to establish liability. The recall letter stated that the motorcycle's braking performance was reduced by heavy rain. However, it was not raining the day of the accident nor did plaintiff successfully prove that washing the motorcycle at a car wash was tantamount to a condition of heavy rain.

B. The Expert's Testimony Was Insufficient to Establish Causation.

Although plaintiff's expert opined that the brakes were wet at the time of the accident, the evidence does not support his conclusion.

Before giving his testimony as to the cause of the accident, Stanley Klein, a consulting engineer, related that he had investigated motorcycle safety in the past. He stated that he had viewed the motorcycle after the accident and was aware of the events preceding the accident including the visit to the car wash. Based upon his engineering experience, education and the investigation of the accident, he concluded that plaintiff's motorcycle deviated from generally accepted standards of safety engineering practice and that the cause of the accident was uncontrolled braking performance which led to the brakes locking up. Klein testified under cross-examination that he assumed that the brakes were wet when applied by Calhoun due to the fact that the motorcycle had been washed some time before hand. His assumption, however, is not supported by the type of evidence necessary to reach this conclusion. For example, he did not know the amount of time that passed from when plaintiff washed his bike until he had his accident. He did not know how many stops plaintiff made before the accident. He did not know the material out of which the brake pad was made and therefore did not know the brake pad's drying time. Without knowledge of these facts, his assumption that the brakes were wet and therefore in a condition equivalent to that created by heavy rain, is baseless. An expert's testimony which expresses an opinion must be based on the evidence. As the court said in Polk v. Ford Motor Co., 529 F.2d 259 (8th Cir.1976), cert. denied, 426 U.S. 907, 96 S.Ct. 2229, 48 L.Ed.2d 832 (1976): "[t]here must, of course, be sufficient facts already in evidence or disclosed by the witness as a result of his investigation to take the testimony out of the realm of guesswork and speculation." 529 F.2d at 261.

Also, the evidence presented by Honda's experts did not aid plaintiff in establishing causation. To the contrary, their testimony supported an inference that the alleged defect was *not* the proximate cause of the accident. Honda's experts performed certain tests using a motorcycle identical to plaintiff's. The experts placed the brake pads taken from the rear wheel of Calhoun's motorcycle onto the demonstration motorcycle. They applied a mixture from the car wash directly onto the rear wheel and then tested the brake deceleration. The same test was again performed, minus the washing. According to expert Gambardella, "there was no significant difference in the rear brake performance between the pre-wash and post-wash." (Transcript at 50–17). "There were no control problems." (Transcript at 87–17).

Although it is within the jury's province to determine which expert to believe, plaintiff's expert's opinion as to the cause of the accident was supported by nothing more than conjecture and supposition. It was not based upon evidence which entitled it to be credited by the jury.

Unfortunately, plaintiff does not recall the accident and there were no witnesses. Calhoun relies upon the fact that there were forty feet of skid marks which proved that he applied his brakes before the collision. These skid marks however are not dispositive of a brake defect. It is just as probable that they were the result of inattentiveness, as of brake failure. This fact was brought out during cross-examination of Mr. Klein:

> Q. But you don't know whether it was [rear brake lock up which caused the accident] as opposed to Mr. Calhoun just not reacting to the situation, do you?
>
> A. I have no way of knowing. (Transcript at 46–10).

Mr. Klein surmised that the brakes must have malfunctioned because failure to pay attention would have been suicidal. Such an assumption, although possessing a certain common sense appeal, is insufficient to prove that the defect was the probable cause of the accident. Mr. Klein, on cross-examination, also conceded that it would have been possible for the motorcycle to have left forty feet of skid marks with perfectly dry brakes. (Transcript at 40).

The record reveals that very little is known about this tragic accident. It was estimated that approximately twenty minutes passed from the time plaintiff left the car wash until he had his accident. After leaving the car wash he drove to his aunt's house. The motorcycle sat outside his aunt's house for twenty minutes while he went inside to change clothes. Honda's expert, who retraced plaintiff's route, estimated he applied his brakes at least two times before the accident. Calhoun's mother estimated that it was several miles from the aunt's house to the scene of the accident; part of this distance retraced the route Calhoun had taken from the car wash. There was undisputed testimony at trial that the brake pads were in constant contact with the discs and therefore would be rubbed dry in approximately 125 feet. It would seem highly unlikely that the brake pads would still be wet after the aforementioned sequence of events. Even more unlikely is the possibility that they would be as wet as pads which were exposed to heavy rain conditions.

The evidence in this case has never risen to the level of establishing that the alleged defect was the probable cause of the accident. At best, it was a possible cause in a series of possibilities, of which plaintiff's inattentiveness cannot be excluded. Simply establishing a defect as the possible cause of an accident is not, however, sufficient to prove liability. The law in this area is clear. In Midwestern V.W. Corp. v. Ringley, 503 S.W.2d 745, 747 (Ky.1973), the Court said:

> [a]lthough the jury may draw reasonable inferences from the evidence of a defect in manufacturing, it is incumbent on the plaintiff to introduce evidence that will support a reasonable inference that the defect was the "probable" cause of the accident as distinguished from a "possible" cause among other

possibilities; otherwise, the jury verdict is based on speculation and surmise.

Plaintiff failed to prove that the defect was the proximate cause of the accident and therefore the jury's verdict in his favor was not supported by the evidence.

This decision is a difficult one for our Court. It is not without heartfelt sympathy for Mr. Calhoun that we affirm the district court. We realize that as a result of his injury, plaintiff is of unsound mind and may be unable to care for himself the remainder of his days. However, the evidence failed to establish that the alleged defect was anything but a possible cause of his injury. * * *

III. New Trial

The trial judge's opinion stated that in the event our Court reversed the grant of JNOV, then defendants should be given a new trial. The judge's conditional grant was based on his belief that it was prejudicial error to allow the recall letter into evidence. * * *

* * *

The trial judge was not in error in ruling this letter inadmissible both on grounds of irrelevancy and prejudice. * * *

The recall letter was placed into evidence before independent evidence as to defect and causation were established. As we have already discussed, plaintiff failed to show where the conditions described in the letter were present when plaintiff had his accident. Failure to establish this fact made the letter irrelevant. Farner v. Paccar, 562 F.2d 518, 525–26 (8th Cir.1977).

* * *

Finally, to allow this letter into evidence worked a grave prejudice to defendant Honda. Its admission into evidence may have been interpreted by the jury as a ruling by the court that car washing had the same effect as operating under heavy rain. Such an inference is not supported by the evidence. Accordingly, the judgment * * * is in all respects, Affirmed.

NOTES

1. What, other than defective brakes, might have caused the plaintiff's accident? The court refers to plaintiff's "inattentiveness" as a possible cause. What do you suppose that means? Contributory negligence (then a defense in Kentucky)? Would it have made any difference had a comparative negligence rule been in force at the time? Or was the court thinking along different lines?

2. Compare Schwartz v. Macrose Lumber & Trim Co., 29 A.D.2d 781, 287 N.Y.S.2d 706, 707–08 (1968), aff'd 24 N.Y.2d 856, 301 N.Y.S.2d 91, 248 N.E.2d 920 (1969), where a judgment for the plaintiff was reversed:

> Plaintiff sued, on theories of negligence and breach of warranty, to recover damages for an injury to his eye claimed to have been sustained while he was hammering a nail through a stud into a concrete basement wall. In our opinion, his proof was not sufficient to establish

> that his injury was caused by the shattering of the nail and the effect of the head of the nail striking his eye. Plaintiff himself testified that he did not know what had struck his eye; though the nail was found with its head missing, the nailhead was not found; nor was the portion of the nail retained after the accident or submitted into evidence at the trial.
>
> The injury to plaintiff's eye could have resulted from a wood splinter from the stud or a piece of concrete from the wall. "Where the facts proven show that there are several possible causes of an injury, for one or more of which the defendant was not responsible, and it is just as reasonable and probable that the injury was the result of one cause as the other, plaintiff cannot have a recovery, since he has failed to prove that the negligence of the defendant caused the injury" [citations]. Thus, in our view, plaintiff's evidence was insufficient to demonstrate a causal relation between his injury and the asserted defect in the nail sold to him.

Accord, Price v. Ashby's Inc., 11 Utah 2d 54, 354 P.2d 1064 (1960) (hole in airlift line caused one side of automobile to sink lower than the other, but there was no proof that this defect—rather than driver error—caused car to continue straight at bend in road: "With two or more possible causes such as an inattentive driver and a mechanical defect * * *; proof that it may have been either is not proof that it was in fact either."); Crocker v. Sears, Roebuck & Co. 346 So.2d 921 (Miss.1977) (fire that destroyed plaintiff's house could just as plausibly have been started by recent rewiring of house, or by defective installation of stove, as by defect in the stove itself; Church v. Martin–Baker Aircraft Co., Ltd., 643 F.Supp. 499 (E.D.Mo.1986) (death of fighter pilot who ejected from plane could have been caused by defective ejection seat or external wind blasts).

3. **Product Malfunction.** Note the *Calhoun* court's recognition that proof of defect and causation may sometimes be established by a showing that the product malfunctioned, together with the negation of other possible causes. This form of proof is discussed in Chapter 3 above, pp. 252–58. Why did not the malfunction theory of causation help the plaintiff in *Calhoun?*

4. If the causal connection between the use of a product and an injury is apparent to a layperson, many courts will permit the case to go to the jury even without expert testimony on causation. Thus, in Coca Cola Bottling Co. v. Cromwell, 203 Ark. 933, 159 S.W.2d 744 (1942), something stuck in plaintiff's throat as she took a swallow of Coke, and so she took another swig to wash it down. She immediately became ill and was hospitalized. The remaining contents of the bottle were strained and found to contain six spider legs. *Held,* jury verdict for plaintiff affirmed. See also Dickson v. National Supermarkets, Inc., 728 S.W.2d 736 (Mo.App.1987) (family members all became ill shortly after eating gooey butter cake, the only food they shared in common, between 5 p.m. and 6:30 p.m., to tide them over until dinner; cake left bitter after-taste and turned dark brown in middle by 11 p.m.).

By contrast, if the causal connection between the defendant's product and the plaintiff's harm is not self-evident, expert testimony will usually be necessary. See, e.g., Muniz Nunez v. American Home Products Corp., 582 F.Supp. 459 (D.Puerto Rico 1984) (no expert testimony that drug caused plaintiff's penis to become permanently erect, but bent). But even expert testimony may not establish a cause that is not proved to a reasonable degree of scientific certainty. See McCann v. Amy Joy Donut Shops, 325 Pa.Super. 340, 472 A.2d 1149 (1984) (excessively greasy cruller "apparently" caused plaintiff's ulcer to flare up; insufficient expert testimony which should have been based on a reasonable medical certainty).

5. Even if plaintiff is successful in tracing his injury to a product defect, he must further prove that the defect was in the product at the time it left the defendant's hands. See, e.g., Ford Motor Co. v. Matthews, 291 So.2d 169 (Miss. 1974) (plaintiff proved that part of tractor's starting mechanism was defective at time of sale even though tractor was subsequently damaged in fire); Bombardi v. Pochel's Appliance & T.V. Co., 9 Wash.App. 797, 515 P.2d 540 (1973) (plaintiff traced defect in used TV set to manufacturer although set had been serviced seven or eight times during first ownership). Compare Maher v. General Motors Corp., 370 Mass. 231, 346 N.E.2d 833 (1976) (testimony that steering suddenly locked failed to establish car defective at time of sale since dealer had serviced steering on three occasions).

6. Both the principal case and the note cases above show that the cause in fact issue usually involves practical problems of proof much more than metaphysical inquiries into causal connection. Consider the following observations:

> The more typical factual causation issue in [the products liability] context is one of proof: is the circumstantial evidence of how the accident happened adequate to support the inferences that a defect existed in the product and that it was a substantial factor in producing the misadventure? This is a very different issue from "but for" causation; it is a question of *degree* of the certainty of proof, of the *likelihood* that a product defect was an appreciable factor in producing the accident. This is in fact the primary form of proof of causation available in a good number of products cases, particularly where the plaintiff is killed in the accident, and where the evidence on causation is circumstantial and admits of alternative explanations of how the accident occurred. A workable rule applied to this type of cause in fact problem in some torts cases outside of the products liability area is that to prevail, the plaintiff must only show that the defendant's conduct substantially increased the risk of the type of harm he suffered. This concept of causation is sometimes called a "causal linkage."

Owen, The Highly Blameworthy Manufacturer: Implications on Rules of Liability and Defense in Products Liability Actions, 10 Ind.L.Rev. 769, 779 (1977).

Apply the "causal linkage" test to an equal plausibility case such as *Schwartz* in note 2 above. Same result? What is your opinion of this test?

7. The but for issue does arise quite clearly in some cases. A stainless steel surgical pin made by defendants was implanted in plaintiff's broken leg to help align and stabilize the bone, and the leg was put in a cast. When the fracture did not heal in the cast, plaintiff's doctor removed it but instructed plaintiff not to walk on the leg. Plaintiff disobeyed, and the pin broke, causing various complications. Plaintiff presented evidence "that the Rush pin in question had inclusions and scratches which reduced the pin's strength [by a factor of one third]. However, none of the evidence pointed to the fact that this alleged defect was the cause of the break. Even if the pin had no defects whatsoever, the evidence showed that the pin would have broken if the plaintiff walked on it after his cast was removed." *Held,* for defendant: the cause of the break was misuse, not any defect in the pin. Stewart v. Von Solbrig Hosp.,

Inc., 24 Ill.App.3d 599, 321 N.E.2d 428, 432 (1974). See also Gordon v. Goldman Bros., Inc., 130 A.D.2d 457, 515 N.Y.S.2d 39 (1987) (novice hiker wearing defendant's boots slipped on sharply sloped and gravel-covered hill; complaint dismissed in absence of evidence that different boots would have prevented fall); Norton v. Snapper Power Equip., 806 F.2d 1545 (11th Cir.1987) (dead man device, that could have stopped power mower blades in less than one second after handle was released, might have prevented accident).

8. The *sine qua non* issue is apt to arise in cases where the product is seriously abused or mishandled. So, even if the gas tank on an automobile is located too close to the rear of the car, this defect in design is not the cause of an explosion following a high speed collision that would have exploded the tank even had it been located in a "proper" position. Cf. Self v. General Motors Corp., 42 Cal.App.3d 1, 116 Cal.Rptr. 575 (1974). A defect in the design of an automobile door latch, that pops open too easily when scraped along a metal divider fence, is not the cause of the door opening if the force of the impact is so great that no latch could have kept it shut. Cf. Daly v. General Motors Corp., 20 Cal.3d 725, 144 Cal.Rptr. 380, 383, 575 P.2d 1162 (1978).

9. Should the manufacturer of a defective fire extinguisher be liable for the destruction of a building by a fire that was discovered only after it was so large that even a properly functioning extinguisher would have been useless against it? Cf. Caplaco One, Inc. v. Amerex Corp., 435 F.Supp. 1116 (E.D.Mo. 1977), aff'd, 572 F.2d 634 (8th Cir.1978).

B. RELIANCE ON WARNINGS

GREINER v. VOLKSWAGENWERK AKTIENGESELLSCHAFT

United States District Court, Eastern District Pennsylvania, 1977.
429 F.Supp. 495.

JOSEPH S. LORD, III, CHIEF JUDGE.

[Plaintiff was injured when the Volkswagen beetle in which she was riding rolled over. The jury found that the vehicle was not defectively designed, and plaintiff appealed the withholding from the jury of her theory on failure to warn. Holding that the jury should have been permitted to pass on this theory, the Court of Appeals vacated the judgment for the defendant and remanded the case for further consideration. 540 F.2d 85 (3d Cir.1976). Following is the trial court's decision on remand.]

* * * As we see it, the precise question is: Assuming the necessity of a warning of the Volkswagen's propensity to overturn on sharp steering maneuvers, how did the absence of a warning cause the accident? Or conversely, how would its presence have prevented the accident?

Except for the widely varying estimates of the Volkswagen's speed, the facts of the accident are really not in dispute. Finding herself on her own wrong side of the road facing an oncoming car, the plaintiff's driver, Nickel, turned to her right. She immediately found herself headed for a concrete bridge railing approximately ten feet away. Her speed was between 30 and 60 miles per hour. To avoid the bridge railing, Nickel turned sharply to the left and the Volkswagen overturned. Under these circumstances, warning or not, there was no conceivable way that an accident could have been avoided. Even giving Nickel the best possible reading of the evidence, at 30 miles per hour, she would cover ten feet in approximately one-fourth of a second. It is simply not within the bounds of human reason to suppose that, had there been a warning, Nickel would have recalled it, considered it and then intentionally crashed head-on into a concrete rail. We do not, however, rest our determination on this conclusion.

It is true that the Restatement of Torts, § 402(a), comment j, states:

> "Where warning is given, the seller may reasonably assume that it will be read and heeded; * * *" (P. 353).

Implicit in that comment, however, is the assumption that the warning *could* have been heeded to avoid the peril. Here, it could not. Here, when Nickel found herself ten feet from the railing, a serious accident was inevitable, warning or no warning, and plaintiff made no showing that one would have been less devastating than the other. * * *

Plaintiff points to several cases where recovery was held allowable absent specific evidence of proximate cause. Their factual patterns may be summarized as follows:

1. Berkebile v. Brantly Helicopter Corp., 225 Pa.Super. 349, 311 A.2d 140 (1973). Plaintiff's decedent was killed when a seven foot piece of one of the rotor blades of his helicopter flew off after a power failure, causing the copter to crash. Plaintiff alleged, *inter alia,* an inadequate warning of the need for an instantaneous shift to autorotation in the event of power failure. A judgment for defendant was reversed.

2. Tomao v. A.P. De Sanno & Son, 209 F.2d 544 (3d Cir.1954). A grinding wheel disintegrated, partially blinding the plaintiff. The wheel was being operated at 10,000 revolutions per minute. The maximum safe speed was less than 6,000 revolutions per minute, but the wheel had no warning to this effect. A verdict for plaintiff was sustained.

3. Maize, Admr. v. Atlantic Refining Company, 352 Pa. 51, 41 A.2d 850 (1945). A can of cleaning fluid called Safety-Kleen bore a legend that was held insufficient to warn a user to use it in a well-ventilated space. A verdict for plaintiff was sustained.

4. Hopkins v. E.I. Du Pont DeNemour & Co., 199 F.2d 930 (3d Cir. 1952). A stick of dynamite exploded when it was inserted into a freshly drilled hole. There was no warning that such an explosion could occur because of the heat generated by the drilling. A judgment for defendant was reversed.

Defendant argues that in all of those cases, there was no specific proof that the absence or inadequacy of warning was a causative factor in bringing about the harm. Those cases, however, are distinguishable. In the first place, the nature of the required warning was both specific and easily followed—push the autorotation button immediately on engine failure, do not operate in excess of 6,000 revolutions per minute, use only in well-ventilated area, and do not insert dynamite in freshly drilled hole. It requires no guess or conjecture to determine how the accident could have been avoided by following the warnings. In this case, on the other hand, although the propensity to overturn on sudden maneuvers could be described, whether such description could have avoided this accident would call for pure speculation.

Secondly, in the four cases referred to by plaintiff, it was reasonable to infer from the evidence that the simple, easily understood directions and limitations could and would be followed had they been given.

* * * No such inference can be made here, because under the circumstances of this case, a warning, even if read, could not have been heeded.

At oral argument, plaintiff's counsel suggested a more remote causal connection between the failure to warn and the accident: that had the warning been given Nickel might not have bought the car. Such a suggestion, in our opinion, would have invited the jury "to indulge in 'pure conjecture or guess' ". Greiner v. Volkswagenwerk Aktiengesellschaft, 540 F.2d 85, 94 (3d Cir.1976). The fine line between "conjecture" on the one hand, and "reasonable inference" on the other, is sometimes hard to draw. As we have said, it is reasonable to infer that a simple warning such as "Do not operate in excess of 6,000 revolutions per minute" would be followed. It is an inference that arises from the factual situation.

In Commonwealth v. Whitman, 199 Pa.Super. 631 at page 634, 186 A.2d 632 at page 633 (1962) the court said:

> "Inference is a process of reasoning by which a fact or proposition sought to be established * * * is deduced as a logical consequence from other facts, or a state of facts, already proved or admitted."

* * *

There are no proven facts in this record which would lend the dignity of an inference as opposed to a guess, that Nickel would not have purchased the Volkswagen in the face of a warning. Indeed, the impropriety of permitting the jury to make such a finding is intensified by the fact that Nickel testified in plaintiff's case and was totally silent about the effect such a warning would have had. In the face of available, but unproduced evidence, we think it would have been totally improper to permit the jury to guess what Nickel would have said if asked about the effect of the presence of a warning.[2] * * *

Plaintiff also argues that defect means the existence of a characteristic or limitation on the use of a product of which no warning is given, and that causation is proven if a cause and effect relationship between the condition and the harm is established. Plaintiff says: "It is erroneous to consider the non-warning per se as being the causative factor. The question is not whether the warning, if given, would have caused the consumer to act differently." Plaintiff's Brief on Remand, p. 11, n. 6. We disagree. We find more persuasive the article of Professor Keeton, Products Liability, 48 Tex.L.Rev. 398, 414 (1970):

> "If the basis for recovery under strict liability is inadequacy of warnings or instruction about dangers, then plaintiff would be required to show that an adequate warning or instruction would have prevented the harm."

For the foregoing reasons, we are convinced that the record would not justify submission to the jury of the proximate cause of the failure to warn. Pursuant to the instructions on remand, we will reinstate the judgment for defendant.

NOTES

1. Accord, Roy v. Volkswagenwerk Aktiengesellschaft, 600 F.Supp. 653 (C.D.Cal.1985) (VW van rolled over when driver swerved to avoid hitting dog). Compare Staymates v. ITT Holub Industries, 364 Pa.Super. 37, 527 A.2d 140 (1987) (warning could not have prevented "instinctive, knee-jerk reaction").

2. What do you think of the *Greiner* court's summary rejection of the plaintiff's claim that, had she been adequately warned, she might not have purchased the beetle at all? Accord, American Motors Corp. v. Ellis, 403 So.2d 459 (Fla.App.1981); Baughn v. Honda Motor Co., Ltd., 107 Wash.2d 127, 727 P.2d 655 (1986). But see Larsen v. General Motors Corp., 391 F.2d 495, 505–06 (8th Cir.1968); Spruill v. Boyle–Midway, Inc., 308 F.2d 79, 87 (4th Cir.1962) ("had the warning * * * convey[ed] a conception of the true nature of the danger, this mother * * * might not have purchased the product at all"); Kavanaugh v. Kavanaugh, 131 Ariz. 344, 641 P.2d 258, 265 (App.1981).

By rejecting this argument, does the court frustrate the autonomy-promotion goal of the law of warnings? How can a consumer meaningfully choose whether to accept a product's hazards, in exchange for the product's benefits, unless he is warned of the hazards prior to purchase so that he may decide whether to buy it at all?

3. In Powell v. J.T. Posey Co., 766 F.2d 131, 134–35 (3d Cir.1985), the plaintiff-nurse helped an 84–year–old geriatric patient bathe and dress and then secured him to his armchair by tying the straps of a restraint vest (part of the "Posey Houdini Security Suit") to the back of the chair. Later, when the plaintiff returned to the patient's room, she found that he had untied himself from the chair and was moving toward the bed. The patient appeared to be falling, and as the plaintiff grasped him, they both fell upon the bed. Plain-

2. Indeed, the more reasonable inference is that her testimony would have been unfavorable to plaintiff's case. 2 Wigmore on Evidence (3rd Ed.) § 285.

tiff's back was injured, and she sued the manufacturer of the vest for failing to warn that a patient might be able to untie the vest. The hospital policy was to use the vests on all patients over 65 and to add wrist straps only if the patient was violent, prone to escape, or otherwise appeared to need greater restraint. The patient involved in this case had given no prior indication that the wrist straps might be needed. The trial court rendered judgment for the plaintiff, and the defendant appealed:

> Overall, there was no proof that, "but for" the absence of an adequate warning, the harm would not have resulted. The jury apparently based its contrary conclusion on the mere speculation that a warning might have induced the plaintiff to contravene hospital policy and apply wrist straps to Adams. This circuit has held that such speculation is not a sufficient basis on which to impose liability. See Conti v. Ford Motor Co., 743 F.2d 195 (3d Cir.1984). In *Conti,* the plaintiff sustained injuries when her husband started his standard transmission car without disengaging the clutch. The car lurched backwards and the plaintiff, who was in the process of entering the car at the time, lost her balance and fell. The *Conti* court held that the defendant was "entitled to judgment in its favor as a matter of law because the Contis [had] failed to prove that the existence of any additional warning may have forestalled Mr. Conti's 'momentary inadvertence' * * * in failing to disengage the clutch while starting the car in gear." 743 F.2d at 197. The court stated that "mere speculation that if Mr. Conti's eyes had caught a sticker warning him to depress the clutch * * * he may have remembered [to do so]" was not a sufficient basis on which to impose liability. Id. at 198.
>
> In the instant case, as in *Conti,* there is insufficient evidence in the record to support a reasonable inference that a warning would have made the plaintiff act differently. She would have placed Adams in the hand-tied vest without any additional restraint, warning or no warning, because he was over sixty-five years of age, non-violent, and not known to need further restraint. She would have rushed to grasp Adams, warning or no warning, when he appeared to her to be falling, because that was her instinctive reaction. The manufacturer could have placed a warning in its literature, on the vest itself, or even on the door of Adams' room, and yet this accident still would have occurred.

Held, reversed.

4. Compare Salk v. Alpine Ski Shop, Inc., 115 R.I. 309, 342 A.2d 622, 626 (1975). Ski bindings manufactured and sold by defendants failed to release when plaintiff fell, and he broke his leg. *Held,* there was no causal relationship between plaintiff's injury and defendants' failure to warn that the bindings would not release under all conditions. "[P]laintiff did not allege that had he been warned of the inevitable dangers of skiing, he would not have skied; nor did he allege that he would have purchased other bindings and that other bindings would have prevented his injury. Quite to the contrary, * * * plaintiff has continued to ski."

5. Consider also Shell Oil Co. v. Gutierrez, 119 Ariz. 426, 581 P.2d 271, 280–81 (App.1978). Plaintiffs were injured in an explosion when the vapors in an "empty" drum of xylene were ignited as one plaintiff began welding nearby. The xylene had been purchased from the defendants by plaintiffs' employer in 55

gallon drums for use as a cleaning solvent. After the xylene was drained from the drums, the "empties"—which always contained a residue of xylene and highly explosive vapors—were stored in the yard. The drum which exploded had for some reason been moved to within a few feet of where plaintiffs were working, but since such drums were often used for trash, plaintiffs gave it little thought. As soon as one of them began to weld, the drum exploded.

Plaintiffs claimed that: "(1) the product was defective because the label did not give adequate warning of the danger of explosion of vapor in a barrel drained of liquid and (2) the product was defective for failure to give adequate instructions for safe handling." The drum, which had a red body and yellow ends, did have a 4″ X 4″ diamond-shaped "FLAMMABLE LIQUID" label with a picture of a shooting flame, in black against a red background. Plaintiffs did not see the label, however, and testified that they would not have welded in the area if they had. The jury gave verdicts for the plaintiffs, and defendants appealed.

Ruling that the adequacy issue had properly been submitted to the jury, the court addressed the issue of cause in fact:

> Flint's third point is that any inadequacy in labeling was not a cause in fact of the injuries, since appellees did not read the warning which was given. That the party who is injured might not have read or heeded a warning is not always sufficient to disprove the existence of a causal relationship between the injury and the defect. Adequate warning could have actuated a policy in handling "empties" which would have prevented the accident. DeSantis v. Parker Feeders, Inc., 547 F.2d 357 (7th Cir. 1976). Had the label stated that the barrel should be washed with an inert solvent, stored with the bung holes covered, and returned immediately, presumably the barrel would not have been where it was.
>
> Furthermore, the adequacy of a warning label is not determined solely by reference to the words on the label but also by reference to the physical aspects of the warning, such as conspicuousness, prominence, and relative size of print. All of these physical aspects must be adequate to alert the reasonably prudent person. [Citation]. Here, the only label attached to the barrel was small in size, approximately 4″ X 4″. The jury could have determined that the physical aspects of this label were inadequate in light of the foreseeable risk of injury, and that if a larger and more conspicuous label was attached, it would have been seen, read and heeded.
>
> There was substantial evidence from which the jury could have concluded that the failure of the defendants to provide an adequate warning was a factor in producing the injuries. Cause in fact was an issue for the jury.

Judgment for the plaintiffs was affirmed.

6. Consider also Jones v. Hittle Service, Inc., 219 Kan. 627, 549 P.2d 1383 (1976), where plaintiffs' decedents were killed in an explosion of gas sold by the defendants. Plaintiffs contended that the defendants had been negligent in adding only one pound of odorant to 10,000 gallons of gas, rather than the nine pounds claimed to be necessary to make the gas reasonably safe. The gas, however, had seeped through the soil prior to passing into the basement where it exploded, and much of the odorizing agent had been leached out as a result. Plaintiffs' expert admitted that even at the nine pound level there would not have been enough odor left in the gas after it had passed through the soil to have been smelled by the victims. *Held*, the inadequate odorization was not a cause of the explosion.

NISSEN TRAMPOLINE CO. v. TERRE HAUTE FIRST NATIONAL BANK

Court of Appeals of Indiana, 1975.
332 N.E.2d 820 (Ind.App.1975), rev'd, 265 Ind. 457, 358 N.E.2d 974 (1976).

LYBROOK, JUDGE. Defendant-appellant Nissen Trampoline Company appeals from a granting of a new trial following a jury verdict in its favor in a products liability action initiated by plaintiff-appellee Terre Haute First National Bank as guardian of the estate of Bruno Garzolini, Jr., a minor.

The record reveals that defendant Nissen was the manufacturer of a product know as "Aqua Diver", a circular trampoline with a metal frame thirty-six (36) inches in diameter and a bed of approximately sixteen (16) inches in diameter. The bed is attached to the frame by a network of elastic cables. This circular structure is then attached to a larger metal frame which has a platform approximately twenty-two (22) inches above the bed of the trampoline. The platform is accessible by a ladder attached at the rear. The entire structure, Aqua Diver, was designed and marketed by defendant for use as a diving apparatus at a swimming pool and/or lake. According to literature distributed by defendant, Aqua Diver was "twice as much fun as an old-fashioned diving board at half the cost."

Herbert A. Mason d/b/a Southlake Beach, purchased an Aqua Diver from Nissen and installed it upon a wooden platform at the beach. On June 28, 1970, while attempting to use the Aqua Diver for his first time, plaintiff Bruno Garzolini, Jr., a thirteen (13) year old boy, was injured. Although unable to recall all the specifics of the occurrence, Garzolini testified that he intended to jump from the platform of the Aqua Diver onto the bed of the trampoline and thereby catapult himself into the water. However, plaintiff landed with only one foot on the bed of the trampoline. His other foot either missed or slipped off the bed and passed through the open space between the bed and circular frame, becoming entangled in the elastic cables. As a result, plaintiff fell from the structure and became suspended by his left leg which remained ensnarled in the cables. Ultimately, plaintiff's injuries required amputation of the leg above the knee. Evidence at trial established that in tests conducted prior to marketing the Aqua Diver, defendant had determined that it was possible for a user's foot to pass through the elastic cables which connected the bed to the frame. Nevertheless, Nissen marketed the product without accompanying it with any warnings or instructions for use.

Plaintiff initiated this action, naming both Nissen and Mason as co-defendants, maintaining that Nissen was liable under the doctrine of strict liability, and that Mason was liable for negligence in failing to furnish supervision and instruction for use of the Aqua Diver. Trial by jury resulted in verdicts in favor of both defendants. Thereafter, pursuant to plaintiff's motion to correct errors and Ind.Rules of Procedure, Trial Rule 59(E), the trial judge granted a new trial as to Nissen only, thereby prompting this appeal. * * *

* * *

In the case at bar, the trial court's findings, which are supported by uncontradicted evidence, reveal that prior to marketing the Aqua Diver, Nissen had discovered through testing that it was possible for a user's foot to pass between the elastic cables connecting the bed of the trampoline to the circular frame and thereby cause injury. Additionally, the undisputed evidence reveals that notwithstanding the knowledge of this danger involved in the use of Aqua Diver, Nissen marketed the product without a warning. This undisputed evidence * * * is substantial evidence to support the trial court's conclusion that the Aqua Diver was a defective product dangerous to the user without a warning within the purview of § 402A. We therefore conclude that there were sufficient special findings to establish that Aqua Diver was defective. * * *

* * *

The issue of causation in both negligence and strict liability cases wherein the defect is in design or manufacture differs fundamentally from causation in failure to warn cases. In the former, it is generally required that the plaintiff establish a causal connection in fact by proof that the harm resulted from the condition or ingredient that made the product defective. In the latter case, however, the difference arises in that the factor rendering the product defective is separable from the product itself. Applying the causation in fact test to the failure to warn case would give rise to a doctrine that liability is predicated upon a showing by the plaintiff that he would have suffered no injury but for the absence of warning. Stated differently, the plaintiff would be required to show that he would have heeded a warning had one been given. In our opinion, such an approach would undermine the purpose behind the doctrine of strict tort liability since any such testimony would generally be speculative at best. A more reasonable approach which represents a compromise within the framework of strict liability as suggested in Technical Chemical Co. v. Jacobs (Supreme Court of Texas 1972), 480 S.W.2d 602, and discussed at 53 A.L.R.3d 239 and 50 Texas L.Rev. 577 (1972); is that the law should supply the presumption that an adequate warning would have been read and heeded, thereby minimizing the obvious problems of proof of causation. We find such an approach to be meritorious, workable, and desirable.

Comment *j* of Restatement (2d) Torts, § 402A (1965), provides a presumption protecting the manufacturer where a warning is given:

> "Where warning is given, the seller may reasonably assume that it will be read and heeded; * * *"

However, where there is no warning, as in the case at bar, the presumption of comment *j* that the user would have read and heeded an adequate warning works in favor of the plaintiff user. In other words, the presumption of causation herein is that Garzolini would have read an adequate warning concerning the danger of a user's foot slipping between the elastic cables of Aqua Diver and heeded it, resulting in his not using the Aqua Diver. This presumption may, however, be rebutted by the manufacturer Nissen with contrary evidence that the presumed fact did not exist. As the Texas Supreme Court said in Technical Chemical Co. v. Jacobs, supra:

> "Depending upon the individual facts, this may be accomplished by the manufacturer's producing evidence that the user was blind, illiterate, intoxicated at the time of use, irresponsible or lax in judgment or by some other circumstance tending to show that the improper use was or would have been made regardless of the warning."

480 S.W.2d at 606.

Placing the burden of rebutting the presumption of causation on the manufacturer in failure to warn cases is not inconsistent with the policies behind strict liability. It would encourage manufacturers to provide safe products and to warn of the known dangers in the use of the product which might cause injury. Such a presumption would also discourage those manufacturers who would rather risk liability than provide a warning which would impair the marketability of the product. The presumption of causation in failure to warn cases is not to be taken as an abrogation of the issue of causation, thereby subjecting a manufacturer to liability for almost any injury caused by his product. Rather, it merely shifts to the manufacturer the burden of proof where the fact-finder could only speculate as to whether the injury could have been prevented by a warning.

* * *

Affirmed.

NOTES

1. Nissen was reversed on procedural grounds in 358 N.E.2d 974, 981 (Ind. 1976), where the following picture of the Aqua Diver was set forth:

2. **Presuming Causation.** Several other courts have similarly "adopted" a rebuttable presumption that the plaintiff would have read and heeded an adequate warning. See, e.g., Payne v. Soft Sheen Products, Inc., 486 A.2d 712 (D.C.App.1985). Some courts, without expressly adopting such a presumption, appear to do so implicitly. See, e.g., DeLuryea v. Winthrop Laboratories, 697 F.2d 222 (8th Cir.1983) (no need for testimony from prescribing doctors that they would have heeded adequate warnings); Wooderson v. Ortho Pharmaceutical Corp., 235 Kan. 387, 681 P.2d 1038 (1984). Other courts have noted but avoided deciding the issue. Kallio v. Ford Motor Co., 407 N.W.2d 92 (Minn. 1987); Gosewisch v. American Honda Motor Co., Inc., 153 Ariz. 400, 737 P.2d 376 (1987). And at least one court has rejected the presumption approach. Potthoff v. Alms, 41 Colo.App. 51, 583 P.2d 309, 311 (1978).

3. In a typical case, how legitimate really is a presumption that the plaintiff would have read and heeded an adequate warning? Will such a presumption be inherently speculative in every case? Reconsider note 9(c), supra page 329. If a presumption is not generally true, is it rationally based? May a court properly employ such a presumption?

4. **Rebutting the Presumption.** Consider Craven v. Niagara Mach. & Tool Works, Inc., 417 N.E.2d 1165, 1171 (Ind.App.1981) (tool and die maker's hand injured in punch press):

> A rebuttable presumption does not shift the burden of proof but it does impose upon the opposing party a burden of producing evidence. Sumpter v. State, (1974) 261 Ind. 471, 306 N.E.2d 95. If the opponent produces evidence which rebuts the presumption, it serves no further purpose. Id. Niagara offered evidence to rebut the presumption through testimony that Craven had been warned and reminded to use safety blocks, which he failed to do. Once this evidence was offered Craven was then obligated to prove, by direct and circumstantial evidence and reasonable inference therefrom, the ultimate fact that he would have heeded the warning. [Citation.] Craven testified that he would heed a warning of a different nature and that he did use safety blocks when he recognized a danger with heavy dies. He also testified that he heeded warnings on "Roll-in" saws. Other witnesses testified that he was extremely cautious in carrying out his work in terms of safety. From this evidence, a jury could reasonably infer that Craven would have heeded a warning; thus, the issue of cause in fact was ultimately for the jury.

Compare Magro v. Ragsdale Bros., Inc., 721 S.W.2d 832 (Tex.1986) (presumption of inattentiveness not rebutted by single instance of inattentiveness, "unrelated to the plaintiff's ability to perceive or heed warnings or instructions and which does not rise to the level of habit" under evidence rule 406); Overpeck v. Chicago Pneumatic Tool Co., 823 F.2d 751, 756 (3d Cir.1987) (presumption rebutted by proof that plaintiff knew the danger; once rebutted "it fell completely from the case," disappearing like the proverbial bat in the light); Gosewisch v. American Honda Motor Co., Inc., 153 Ariz. 400, 737 P.2d 376 (1987) (plaintiff disregarded other warnings); Seley v. G.D. Searle & Co., 67 Ohio St.2d 192, 423 N.E.2d 831 (1981) (doctor would have prescribed birth control pills for plaintiff even if warning had been adequate).

Plaintiff was struck in the eye in a BB gun fight and sued the manufacturer of the gun for failing to warn of this risk. The father of the boy who shot the gun had instructed him in its proper use. *Held,* summary judgment for defendant affirmed. "Once [the boy] ignored his father's instructions, no warning Daisy could have given would have prevented the accident, thus the presumption disappeared and there was no genuine issue of fact as to causation." Menard v. Newhall, 135 Vt. 53, 373 A.2d 505 (1977).

5. **Plaintiff's Testimony on Hypothetical Reliance.** In Blue v. Drackett Products Co., 143 So.2d 897 (Fla.App.1962), the seven-year-old plaintiff was injured in an explosion when he took a can of Drano off the shelf, put water in it, and recapped the can. The manufacturer was sued for failing to warn that the product formed an explosive gas when mixed with water. The mother testified that she had noticed only three words on the label—"Drano," "poison," and "antidotes"—and that she had read neither the admonition to keep the product out of the reach of children nor the words "Keep water out of can." The trial court excluded the mother's testimony that she would have kept the product out of plaintiff's reach had she known it would explode if water were added to the can, and the jury ruled for the defendant. *Held,* reversed:

> "[P]laintiffs were denied their right to prove by direct evidence a material issue raised by the pleadings as to whether the injury was directly caused by the claimed insufficiency of the label to warn the mother that the can had an explosive potential in addition to its danger as a poison. While the question propounded required testimony of what would have been done under circumstances that never existed, the real character of such evidence was the present knowledge of the only witness who knew and could say what would have been done had the explosive propensities of the product been known."

Id. at 898.

The dissent disagreed, arguing that since she had read only three words on the label, her testimony as to what she would have done had she read the entire label would be "highly improper and conjectural." On appeal to the Florida Supreme Court, *held,* reversed again: "Conjecture has no place in proceedings of this sort." Drackett Prod. Co. v. Blue, 152 So.2d 463, 465 (Fla.1963).

Right result? What result if:

A. Mother had seen only the two words "Drano" and "Poison"?

B. Mother had read the entire label and instructed plaintiff not to add water to the can?

C. Mother had read the entire label and had put the can on the top shelf to keep it out of plaintiff's reach, but plaintiff had climbed up after it?

Compare Reyes v. Wyeth Laboratories, 498 F.2d 1264, 1281 (5th Cir.1974), where Judge Wisdom adopted a presumption that an adequate warning would have been heeded by the infant-plaintiff's mother, noting that her testimony as to what she would have done had proper warnings been given would have been "both speculative and self-serving."

The courts have split on the admissibility of a plaintiff's self-serving testimony as to whether and how, hypothetically, he would have heeded an adequate warning. *Inadmissible:* Van Dike v. AMF, Inc., 146 Mich.App. 176, 379 N.W.2d 412, 415 (1985) (evidence rule 701 limits lay witness opinion testimony to opinions or inferences rationally based on witness's perceptions and helpful to a clear understanding of his testimony or determination of a fact in issue); Messenger v. Bucyrus–Erie Co., 507 F.Supp. 41, 43 (W.D.Pa.1980) (same). *Admissible:* Laaperi v. Sears, Roebuck & Co., Inc., 787 F.2d 726, 732 (1st Cir.1986) ("Self-serving as this testimony was, the jury was free to credit it."); Kavanaugh v. Kavanaugh, 131 Ariz. 344, 641 P.2d 258, 265 (App.1981) (5–year–old's father testified that he would not have purchased power lawn mower had he been warned of danger).

Should such testimony be allowed or excluded?

6. **"Reform."** The Connecticut product liability statute provides that "the claimant shall prove by a fair preponderance of the evidence that if adequate warnings or instruction had been provided, the claimant would not have suffered the harm." Prod.Liab.Rep. (CCH) ¶ 90,717. May a Connecticut court apply a *Nissen* presumption?

7. Assume that a smoker who knows the risk of contracting lung cancer from smoking cigarettes succumbs to the disease and dies. Should the smoker's estate be able to recover against the manufacturer for failing to warn of other significant diseases of which the smoker was not aware? See Cipollone v. Liggett Group Inc., Prod.Liab.Rep. (CCH) ¶ 11,637 (D.N.J.1987).

8. **Failure to Read Warnings or Instructions.** Will a plaintiff's inadequate warnings claim be defeated for lack of causation if he admits that he failed even to *read* the warnings given? See Johnson v. Niagara Mach. & Tool Works, 666 F.2d 1223, 1225 (8th Cir.1981) ("an issue as to the adequacy of a warning necessarily presupposes that the [plaintiff] has read the warning"). What if someone connected with the plaintiff—his supervisor, fellow employee, teacher, parent, child, or friend—had read the warning? See Nesselrode v. Executive Beechcraft, Inc., 707 S.W.2d 371, 385 (Mo.1986) (aircraft maintenance director, who had read maintenance manual, testified "that had he known of any warnings concerning the actuators, he would have alerted his mechanics"); Ferebee v. Chevron Chem. Co., 736 F.2d 1529, 1538–39 (D.C.Cir.1984) (Md. law).

Should the effect of a plaintiff's failure to *read* a warning depend on how the warning was allegedly inadequate? See E.R. Squibb & Sons, Inc. v. Cox, 477 So.2d 963 (Ala.1985).

9. **Failure to Heed Warnings or Instructions.** What should be the result if the plaintiff reads but refuses to *heed* the warnings given? See Baughn v. Honda Motor Co., Ltd., 107 Wash.2d 127, 727 P.2d 655 (1986) (two children rode mini-trail bike in street contrary to label on gas tank and warnings from parents—no causation); Van Dike v. AMF, Inc., 146 Mich.App. 176, 379 N.W.2d 412 (1985) (plaintiff tried to perform double back somersault on trampoline after being told to get off because of danger involved—no causation).

Should the effect of a plaintiff's failure to *heed* a warning depend on how the warning was allegedly inadequate? Cf. Petty v. United States, 740 F.2d 1428, 1438–39 (8th Cir.1984).

10. **Known and Obvious Dangers.** What happens to the cause in fact issue when the risk is known or obvious to the plaintiff? Reconsider Laaperi v. Sears, Roebuck & Co., Inc., 787 F.2d 726 (1st Cir.1986), supra p. 371. See also McCormick v. Custom Pools, Inc., 376 N.W.2d 471, 476 (Minn.App.1985) ("a warning would not have deterred McCormick from diving since a warning would have merely informed him of risks of which he was already aware"); Plummer v. Lederle Laboratories, 819 F.2d 349, 359 (2d Cir.1987) (doctor testified that he knew the risk plaintiff claimed should have been in package insert but, as a matter of practice, chose not to inform patients thereof: " 'no harm could have been caused by failure to warn of a risk already known' "); Sherk v. Daisy–Heddon, 498 Pa. 594, 450 A.2d 615 (1982):

> [I]t is clear that the alleged "defect" in the warnings accompanying the Power King air rifle did not cause James Sherk's death. Robert Saenz had possession of the Power King [BB gun] only because he had disobeyed his parents' directions not to use the rifle. Notwithstanding his own knowledge of [its] lethal propensity, his knowledge that [it] should never be pointed at anyone, and his failure to check the position of the safety mechanism, he directed the Power King from close range at James Sherk's head.

Id. at 620.

But what if a "known" risk is momentarily forgotten? See Conti v. Ford Motor Co., 743 F.2d 195, 198–99 (3d Cir.1984) (experienced driver injured wife when he started standard transmission car in reverse without engaging clutch):

> [T]he jury's conclusion was based on the mere speculation that if Mr. Conti's eyes had caught a sticker warning him to depress the clutch pedal as he was talking to his wife, he may have remembered to either shift the car to neutral or to disengage the clutch prior to starting the car. Ford cannot be held liable on a failure-to-warn theory merely because a jury concludes that more warnings are needed to remind drivers of the intricacies of standard transmissions.

Compare Vallillo v. Muskin Corp., 212 N.J.Super. 155, 514 A.2d 528, 530 (1986):

> Clearly, if the user of a product knows at the moment of use the very danger of which the warning would have apprised him, but chooses to disregard that conscious knowledge, then the presence or absence of the warning is irrelevant. * * *
>
> Conversely, if * * * the danger had been even momentarily forgotten by the user and there is some reasonable possibility that the warning would have triggered his recollection of the danger and thus changed his conduct, then the absence of a warning is a proper ingredient in a proximate cause analysis.

11. Consider Zemsky v. City of New York, 821 F.2d 148, 152 (2d Cir.1987): "The company's alleged failure to warn can hardly have been a cause of the [student's] assault during which the disappearing ink was thrown in [the teacher's] eyes."

SECTION 2. PROXIMATE CAUSE: LIMITING RESPONSIBILITY FOR HARM

The issue that is usually called "proximate cause" is a very different one from "cause in fact." As most courts use the former term, it presupposes (or inquires separately into) some factual connection between defendant's breach of duty and plaintiff's injury and addresses instead the policy question of whether in fairness the defendant ought to be held legally accountable for the plaintiff's harm which is in some manner "remote" from the defendant's breach. Noting that "[p]roximate cause cannot be reduced to absolute rules," Prosser and Keeton quote 1 Street, Foundations of Legal Liability 110 (1906) on the role of proximate cause: "It is always to be determined on the facts of each case upon mixed considerations of logic, common sense, justice, policy and precedent." See W.P. Keeton, D. Dobbs, R. Keeton & D. Owen, Prosser & Keeton on the Law of Torts 279 (5th ed. 1984). Consider also Craig v. Burch, 228 So.2d 723, 728–30 (La.App.1969):

> We believe cases of this nature can be more properly adjudicated when the alleged negligence of the defendant or contributory negligence of plaintiff are considered in the light of four basic concepts, namely: (1) duty of care owed; (2) breach of the duty of care; (3) whether the breach of duty found is a cause in fact of the accident, and (4) proximate cause. Authorities are in unanimous agreement that the question of duty of care owed is determined in view of two elementary factors: (1) Does plaintiff have an interest which is protected at all, and (2) is plaintiff's interest protected against the type of conduct with which he can charge defendant? In determining breach of duty, the question is the reasonableness of the care taken by defendant in the light of the attending circumstances including the interest of the plaintiff and the social utility of defendant's conduct.
>
> Cause in fact is a purely factual inquiry which poses the "but for" test, meaning but for defendant's action the accident would not have occurred. * * *
>
> * * *
>
> Proximate cause, however, is not a factual consideration. It is a legal tool, a legislative and judicial policy. Dartez v. City of Sulphur, La.App., 179 So.2d 482. From time immemorial courts have customarily applied two well known tests in determining proximate cause. These are: (1) Was the accident the natural and probable consequences of defendant's act, and (2) Were the results of defendant's conduct reasonably foreseeable? As thusly applied, it appears the proximate cause concept has been employed by the courts to extend or restrict liability at the court's discretion depending upon the circumstances of each case rather than on the basis that the action of the defendant was or was not a cause in fact of the accident. Such application is one of policy as evidenced in cases where the negligent defendant is not held for all losses causally related to his negligent act but only those that are the result of the force he set in motion while that force is of substantial moment. [Citations.]
>
> Proximate cause presupposes breach of a duty constituting a cause in fact of the accident. Dartez v. City of Sulphur, La. App., 179 So.2d 482. When considering proximate cause in connection with a statutory violation, the basic inquiry is what kind of risk or risks does the statute seek to protect against? Dixie Drive It Yourself System New Orleans Co. v. American Beverage Co., 242 La. 471, 137 So.2d 298. Stated otherwise,

> proximate cause involves a determination of what statutory duties extend to what risks. In the absence of statutory duty, proximate cause is determined in the light of the query whether plaintiff's particular interest is protected against defendant's particular conduct. Dartez v. City of Sulphur, above. It appears, therefore, proximate cause is but a third facet of the duty formula utilized as a means of determining when liability attaches to a cause in fact or to one or more of several causes in fact. [Citations.]
>
> The term proximate cause must be used with caution because it does not concern an inquiry into cause. Rather it involves an inquiry into duty, more particularly, the extent of defendant's duty with respect to plaintiff's interest to be protected.

While proximate cause is dealt with here as a separate doctrine, it should be noted that the issue permeates not only duty concepts but indeed *most* of the crucial elements of a products liability case. So, typically, the ultimate issue in the case will be whether, or the degree to which, some ("defective") condition of the product, the plaintiff himself, or some third party "caused" the injury. The court in Palmer v. Ford Motor Co., 498 F.2d 952, 953 (10th Cir.1974), was thus not far off the mark in noting that the labeling of plaintiff's unreasonable encounter of a known danger as contributory negligence or assumption of risk was of little significance since "[t]he controlling factor is causation." Thought of in this broader sense, proximate cause is at the core of every products liability suit. "The issues of a 402A action lie as close together as the fingers of one hand, and one issue cannot be considered without holding the other issues in conscious suspense; for all the issues are essential to liability, and each has a part to play in the functioning of all the others. Causal connection runs as a thread through the seller's duty, the violation of its duty, and the use made of the product in its consumption that results in the consumer's injury." Green, Strict Liability Under Sections 402A and 402B: A Decade of Litigation, 54 Tex.L.Rev. 1185, 1208 (1976).

A. FORESEEABILITY AND DUTY LIMITATIONS ON LIABILITY

The scope of a seller's liability is often limited through application of the principle of ("reasonable") "foreseeability." This is indeed the principal "test" of proximate cause used by courts to determine whether responsibility for the defendant's breach of duty should extend to the plaintiff's harm. A few courts, however, hold that foreseeability is relevant only to the breach of duty issue and that proximate cause extends to all direct, or "natural and probable," consequences of the breach. See, e.g., Koski v. Automatic Heating Service, 75 Mich.App. 180, 254 N.W.2d 836 (1977). Still other courts recognize that, while the foreseeability of injury is one important factor to consider in deciding upon the proper reach of liability, other duty-type policy issues should play an important role as well. See, e.g., Van Skike v. Zussman, 22 Ill. App.3d 1039, 318 N.E.2d 244 (1974). The cases in this section should be read against the admonition of Dean Wade and others that policy issues are better dealt with in the open, perhaps in the context of duty, than hidden behind a smokescreen of foreseeability and proximate cause. See Wade, On the Nature of Strict Tort Liability for Products, 44 Miss. L.J. 825, 847 (1973).

CRANKSHAW v. PIEDMONT DRIVING CLUB, INC.

Court of Appeals of Georgia, 1967.
115 Ga.App. 820, 156 S.E.2d 208.

Plaintiff Elizabeth Crankshaw seeks damages against Piedmont Driving Club, Inc., alleging that on January 15, 1966, she in company with R.M. Harris and Miss Arlene Harris patronized the dining room of the defendant; that Miss Harris ordered shrimp and began eating same at which time she noticed a peculiar odor emanating from the shrimp dish causing her to feel nauseated; that Miss Harris excused herself and proceeded toward the rest room; shortly thereafter plaintiff proceeded toward the rest room to give aid and comfort to Miss Harris and as plaintiff entered the rest room she saw Miss Harris leaning over one of the bowls; that "unbeknownest to plaintiff, Miss Harris had vomited just inside the entrance to the rest room" and that as she hurried toward her she "stepped into the vomit, and her feet flew out from under her," causing her to fall and break her hip. The petition alleged negligence of the defendant in selling unwholesome, deleterious food and in failing to clean up the floor of the rest room or to warn plaintiff of the condition of the floor.

The trial court sustained the defendant's general demurrer to the petition, from which judgment the plaintiff appeals.

JORDAN, PRESIDING JUDGE. Appellant in her brief properly abandons the allegation of negligence due to defendant's failure to clean the regurgitated substance from the floor since under the facts alleged the defendant had no notice, actual or constructive, of its presence on the floor prior to plaintiff's fall. Appellant contends, however, that "the heart of the legal question presented" is whether or not the negligent serving of unwholesome food to Miss Harris was the proximate cause of her (appellant's) injury. Viewing the case from this posed question we conclude that the trial court was correct in sustaining the general demurrer.

"If the damages are only the imaginary or possible result of the tortious act, or other and contingent circumstances preponderate largely in causing the injurious effect, such damages are too remote to be the basis of recovery against the wrongdoer." Code, § 105–2008. Damages must flow from the "legal and natural result of the act done." Code,

§ 105–2009. The question of proximate cause is one for a jury except in palpably clear and indisputable cases. We think the facts alleged in this petition bring it within the exception and subject it to be ruled upon as a matter of law. The court must assume this burden where a jury can draw but one reasonable conclusion if the facts alleged are proved, that conclusion being that the acts of the defendant were not the proximate cause of the injury. Stallings v. Georgia Power Co., 67 Ga.App. 435, 20 S.E.2d 776. In our opinion a jury could not reasonably conclude that the plaintiff's injury was proximately caused by the defendant's negligence in serving unwholesome food to another person.

Judgment affirmed.

NOTES

1. Right result? Whatever happened to the "Danger invites rescue" doctrine? See Wagner v. International Ry. Co., 232 N.Y. 176, 133 N.E. 437 (1921) (Cardozo, J.).

2. Same result if the sickened person injured *herself* when she slipped on her *own* vomit?

3. Plaintiff was driving at 45–50 mph when he hit a horse that suddenly appeared in front of his car. The horse was thrown into the air and onto the roof, collapsing the roof rail (called the "header") on the passenger side of the car, which instantly killed plaintiff's wife. Plaintiff and his son, who was sitting in the back seat, were uninjured; plaintiff's daughter, sitting on her mother's lap in the front, sustained minor cuts and bruises. Plaintiff sued the car manufacturer for defective roof design:

> Defendant argues that the accident was freak and bizarre in that it involved an unusual concentration of forces and an abnormal load on the header, which resulted in the failure of the roof structure. It argues that the support structure is designed to work as a whole but that the horse hit the header at a point where the other roof components could not contribute to its support. * * * In sum, defendant contends that the design was not defective, because the force and impact of the accident were so unusual that it could not have reasonably been anticipated.
>
> Product liability for defective design does not extend to cases where the risk of injury from the product's failure is so remote that a reasonable manufacturer would not consider it in design decisions. [Citation.] Plaintiff offered evidence that collisions with large animals, including horses, are common and foreseeable. Defendant countered that it was not foreseeable that such a collision would produce an impact on the roof concentrated at a particular point rather than being more evenly distributed. The problem with that argument is that its converse is equally true: It was just as unpredictable that the impact from a collision would fall evenly on the entire roof rather than land with greater force on its weakest part. That the horse landed with its full weight on the header did not make the accident any more a freak occurrence than if the weight had been distributed evenly.
>
> There was evidence that the [car's roof design could and should have been made stronger].

Held, "that the accident and the manner of injury were not unforeseeable, as a matter of law, and that plaintiff presented sufficient evidence of defective design to justify submission of the case to the jury." Judgment for plaintiff affirmed. Green v. Denney, 87 Or.App. 298, 742 P.2d 639 (1987). Not mentioned in the opinion, the jury verdict was for $1.5 million. See Insight, p. 62, col. 3, March 7, 1988. Mentioned in the opinion, the car was a Ford Pinto.

4. Plaintiff was wearing a dress while her mother placed a hem in it with brittle, hardened-steel dressmaker pins manufactured by the defendant. Plaintiff bumped a coffee table with her knee, driving a pin into her knee bone where it broke into three pieces. *Held,* no duty to warn of a danger that could not be foreseen. "[T]he manufacturer is asked to anticipate, not only that pins will pierce, but they will be driven into the body with such force as to strike a bone and shatter." The event was "a freak accident that probably could not be duplicated under any condition." One judge dissented: "The 'freak accident' argument might prove not in the least persuasive to a jury." Sidwell v. William Prym, Inc., 112 Idaho 76, 730 P.2d 996, 999, 1003 (1986).

5. While changing a flat tire, plaintiff popped the hubcap off with a screwdriver, and the hubcap flew into the air. As he grabbed for it in mid-air, "his fingers entered a port hole and were severely cut by the sharp edge of this hole." In Kikis v. Ford Motor Co., 386 So.2d 306 (Fla.App.1980), the plaintiff appealed a j.n.o.v. for the defendant. "A foreseeable consequence is not what possibly might occur, or always occurs, but rather is a consequence which may be reasonably anticipated as a likely result of an act." *Held,* reversed and remanded: "These facts raise a question about whether the accident was a foreseeable consequence of defendant's negligence in designing or manufacturing the hubcap [with sharp edges]."

6. What rule of law should be applied to these cases? Whether the connection between the breach of duty and the harm is "proximate" or "remote"? Whether the result is "legal and natural"? A "freak accident"? "Likely"? "Foreseeable"? See Prosser, Palsgraf Revisited, 52 Mich.L.Rev. 1, 19 (1953) ("too cockeyed and far-fetched").

WINNETT v. WINNETT

Supreme Court of Illinois, 1974.
57 Ill.2d 7, 310 N.E.2d 1.

UNDERWOOD, C.J. Four-year-old Teresa Kay Winnett was injured when she placed her hand on a moving conveyor belt or screen on a forage wagon then being operated on her grandfather's farm. [She settled a suit against her grandfather and pursued a strict tort action against the manufacturer of the forage wagon, alleging that it was defectively designed because of the absence of rear view mirrors and of a guard or shield to prevent persons from coming in contact with the moving conveyor belt. The circuit court granted the defendant's motion to dismiss for failure to state a cause of action, the Appellate Court reversed, 9 Ill.App.3d 644, 292 N.E.2d 524, and defendant appealed.]

The arguments of the parties here have focused largely upon whether "use" of this forage wagon by a four-year-old child was "foreseeable" by the manufacturer. Plaintiff urges that foreseeability has no place in strict-tort-liability doctrine but that, in any event, the likelihood of small children being in the vicinity of operating farm equipment is not so unforeseeable as to warrant taking the case from the jury; defendant contends that the product was being "used" by a child for whose use it was not intended and whose use of it was not foreseeable. Consequently, argues defendant, no liability for the injury may be imposed upon the manufacturer.

* * * Whether this forage wagon was unreasonably dangerous when operated for its intended purpose by one for whose use it was intended is simply not a relevant consideration unless plaintiff is a person entitled to the protections afforded by the concepts of strict-tort-liability actions against manufacturers.

The large majority of courts which have considered the question of recovery in a strict-tort-liability action by persons other than those for whose use the product was intended have found the terms "bystander" or "innocent bystander" a convenient means of categorizing an additional group of persons for whose injuries courts have allowed recovery. * * *

We, however, find this categorization of plaintiffs as users, consumers or innocent bystanders helpful only in a general sense [since harm to "bystanders," while often foreseeable, is not always so.]

* * *

Whether the plaintiff here is an individual who is entitled to the protections afforded by the concepts of strict tort liability depends upon whether it can be fairly said that her conduct in placing her fingers in the moving screen or belt of the forage wagon was reasonably foreseeable. A foreseeability test, however, is not intended to bring within the scope of the defendant's liability every injury that might possibly occur. "In a sense, in retrospect almost nothing is entirely unforeseeable." (Mieher v. Brown, 54 Ill.2d 539, 544, 301 N.E.2d 307, 309.) Foreseeability means that which it is *objectively reasonable* to expect, not merely what might conceivably occur. Cf. Williams v. Brown Mfg. Co., 45 Ill. 2d 418, 425, 261 N.E.2d 305.

* * * While in retrospect it can be asserted that the manufacturer of the forage wagon should have foreseen that the unfortunate event in this case might conceivably occur, we do not believe its occurrence was objectively reasonable to expect. It cannot, in our judgment, fairly be said that a manufacturer should reasonably foresee that a four-year-old child will be permitted to approach an operating farm forage wagon or that the child will be permitted to place her fingers in or on the holes in its moving screen. We believe the trial court properly dismissed plaintiff's amended complaint.

* * *

Appellate court reversed; circuit court affirmed.

GOLDENHERSH, JUSTICE (dissenting).

* * *

The majority recognizes that the only foreseeability question presented on this record is whether it is reasonably foreseeable that someone might be injured by reason of coming into contact with the inadequately protected and unreasonably dangerous mechanism. This question is properly one for a jury and should not be decided as a question of law. [Citation.]

* * *

RICHELMAN v. KEWANEE MACHINERY AND CONVEYOR COMPANY

Appellate Court of Illinois, Fifth District, 1978.
59 Ill.App.3d 578, 16 Ill.Dec. 778, 375 N.E.2d 885.

MORAN, JUSTICE.

Defendant appeals from a judgment in the amount of $75,000 entered by the circuit court of St. Clair County after a jury found the issues in favor of the plaintiff in a suit based upon strict liability and negligence.

On November 17, 1972, Mark Richelman, then 2 years 9 months of age, suffered a traumatic amputation of his right leg when he became entangled in a grain auger located in his grandfather's farm yard. In response to special interrogatories the jury indicated that its verdict was founded upon both theories of the case.

In 1965 the Kewanee Machinery and Conveyor Company designed what became known as the Model 260 Auger to be used, *inter alia,* to convey grain from a hopper located on the ground to a storage silo. The auger consists of a 41–foot metal tube, or sleeve, within which revolves a screw-like mechanism extending from a 25–foot high storage bin down to a gravity hopper which sits on the ground. * * *

[Mark and his cousin had been put down for their customary mid-day nap.] Upon learning that the children were napping, Donald Richelman started the auger and proceeded to feed some cattle approximately 50 feet away from the operating machinery. As the children were unable to sleep, Mrs. Richelman dressed them and took them to their grandmother's house nearby. This activity went unnoticed by Donald Richelman. While Mrs. Richelman spoke with her mother-in-law in the living room, the children played on an enclosed porch. Less than five minutes later both parents heard Mark's screams and rushed to the grain elevator in time to pull their son from the hopper. The minor plaintiff's right leg had been amputated by the grain auger. However, no one had witnessed precisely how the young child had become entangled in the machinery.

There was a great deal of evidence adduced at trial concerning the methodology employed in testing the various guard designs. James Suhr, who had been instrumental as a design engineer in the employ of Kewanee during the 1965 tests was called as a witness for the plaintiff. He testified that in designing the guards he considered only the safety of the implement operator; the safety of a by-stander was not even a factor. He explained that he anticipated that anyone, male or female, of high school age could be an operator of the auger. Nevertheless, in determining the width of the gap between the guard bars, Suhr measured only the width of his own size 12–B shoe and accordingly spaced the bars 4⅝″ apart. This decision was made with full knowledge that men and women of high school age generally have narrower feet than his own. Suhr admitted that he did not contemplate an operator tripping so that another part of the body could become engaged in the auger. Finally, he stated that although the engineers were fully cognizant that augers are generally located in a farmhouse complex where small children often play, their safety was not a consideration in designing the auger guard. In short, the guard was designed for the safety of "the majority of users." * * *

* * *

The only issue for review is whether Mark Richelman's injury was foreseeable as a matter of law under the rationale of Winnett v. Winnett, 57 Ill.2d 7, 310 N.E.2d 1.

* * *

We find it helpful to review those cases which have relied upon *Winnett* in holding that a particular injury was not reasonably foreseeable. In Wenzell v. MTD Products, Inc., 32 Ill.App.3d 279, 336 N.E.2d 125, the four-year-old plaintiff was injured when a gasoline-powered lawn mower driven by a seven-year-old came into contact with plaintiff's foot. The First District denied liability commenting that the "mower was being used by a group of children virtually as a toy." (32 Ill.App.3d 279, 291, 336 N.E.2d 125, 134.) In our opinion, these cases indicate nothing more than a reluctance by the judiciary to hold a manufacturer liable when children are allowed to play with dangerous objects. The acts precipitating injury in both cases were basically intentional. * * * In this case, however, there is no positive evidence that the minor plaintiff was actively playing with or attempting to operate the grain auger. Thus, the jury could have inferred that Mark inadvertently tripped or fell into the open hopper.

Moreover, the undisputed evidence disclosed that most adults could have been similarly injured because of the 4⅝″ gap between the bars of the vertical-type auger guard in this case; whereas, the indication in the *Winnett* pleading cited in the Supreme Court opinion was that the holes in the conveyor belt were only of a sufficient size to admit the fingers of a small child. The fact that the individual injured is a child should not preclude recovery where an adult, albeit one with a narrower foot than that of the design engineer, could likewise have sustained injury. Thus, the real question is not so much whether the defendant could "objectively expect" that Mark Richelman would not take a nap on the day in question but instead would venture outdoors and become entangled in the grain auger, but rather whether the defendant could "objectively expect" that if one with a smaller than 4⅝″ shoe width were to trip or fall near the auger he could be injured because of the inadequate safety guard.

* * *

A detailed recitation of the evidence regarding foreseeability would serve no purpose here. We need only repeat that questions of foreseeability as well as questions whether a product is defective or unreasonably dangerous are ordinarily for the jury to resolve. * * * We cannot say as a matter of law that injury to the plaintiff in this case was not objectively reasonable to expect. For reasons stated earlier in this opinion, we do not find the *Winnett* case and its progeny controlling on this issue.

Affirmed.

JONES, JUSTICE, DISSENTING.

* * *

It would be difficult to find a case factually more similar to Winnett v. Winnett, 57 Ill.2d 7, 13, 310 N.E.2d 1, 5, than this one and the decision here should consequently be controlled by *Winnett.* * * * We need only change the age of the child to two years and nine months and the type of machine to a grain auger and the similarity of this case to *Winnett* is complete.

The majority ignores the similarity of the facts, and the basis of the decision in *Winnett,* and seeks to distinguish this case from *Winnett* upon the grounds that there was "no positive evidence that the minor plaintiff was actively playing with or attempting to operate the grain auger." When the basis of the *Winnett* decision is considered the distinction advanced by the majority is irrelevant; it would not be objectively reasonable for the manufacturer to expect plaintiff to be injured by the auger either while playing with it or by accidentally falling into it. As the court stated in Gille v. Winnebago County Housing Authority, 44 Ill.2d 419, 426, 255 N.E.2d 904, 908: "The responsibility for a child's safety lies primarily with its parents, whose duty is to see that his behavior does not involve danger to himself. Others can be held responsible for injuries only if they are at fault under some recognized theory of liability."

It is likewise irrelevant that an adult might be injured by the machine in question. We are to consider only whether the defendant could reasonably foresee that the plaintiff in question would be injured by the auger. Foreseeability of injury in general simply does not enter into a determination of this particular case. The only question can be whether this particular plaintiff's injury was reasonably foreseeable. The *Winnett* case held that it was not and we should follow it.

NOTES

1. Are *Winnett* and *Richelman* consistent? Are they explainable on the "reasonable foreseeability" of the injuries? On whether the accidents were "objectively reasonable to expect"? How useful are these tests in deciding whether manufacturers of farming machinery or the injured children (and their parents) should bear the economic burden of such accidental losses?

What considerations appear to have really influenced the majority and dissenting judges in these cases? Should these factors have been made more explicit? Should the jury have been told to consider them? Whether told to or not, *do* juries consider them?

Is there any connection at all between the real considerations at work in such cases and the "test" of reasonable foreseeability? Need there be?

2. Compare Forrest City Mach. Works, Inc. v. Aderhold, 273 Ark. 33, 616 S.W.2d 720, 723 (1981), where an 8–year–old boy's leg was caught in the power take-off shaft attached to a grain cart on which he was climbing. *Held,* judgment for plaintiff affirmed: "The record shows that farming in Arkansas is frequently a family operation and all family youngsters may be expected to come into contact with the family's farm machinery."

3. Consider Passwaters v. General Motors Corp., 454 F.2d 1270, 1276 n. 5 (8th Cir.1972), which broadened the scope of a manufacturer's liability to foreseeable risks to foreseeable bystanders: "The difficulty is that 'foreseeability' is a hazardous term to define in the abstract and, like so many other doctrines, must turn on the judgmental process." The court quoted the following observations of a leading torts scholar:

> "It all depends upon what factors in the evidence a court is willing to isolate and emphasize for the purpose of making this decision, which process in turn depends pretty much on what outcome the court wishes to achieve or thinks to be politic. This factor in the judgment process, in turn, is not usually a matter of conscious choice but may be a function of the judge's accumulated experience in and observations of the world he lives in." Gregory, Proximate Cause in Negligence—A Retreat from "Rationalization." 6 U.Chi.L.Rev. 36, 50 (1938).

The court continued: "Generally, whether a duty exists is a question of law, yet when a difficult determination depends on policy values underlying the 'common affairs of life,' it is generally thought that the jury is the best d[i]viner of such values."

4. Compare Yassin v. Certified Grocers of Illinois, Inc., 150 Ill.App.3d 1052, 104 Ill.Dec. 52, 502 N.E.2d 315 (1986) (3–year–old wandered away from mother to work area in rear of grocery store where she caught her hand in meat tenderizer left on and unattended; *held,* injury *not* objectively reasonable to expect), with Pierce v. Hobart Corp., 159 Ill.App.3d 31, 111 Ill.Dec. 110, 512 N.E.2d 14 (1987) (10–year–old, who helped around restaurant after school, caught hand in meat grinder while pushing in piece of cheese; *held,* reversing summary judgment for manufacturer, foreseeability for jury).

5. Recall the distinction, in determining defectiveness in strict tort, between the foreseeability of *harm* and the foreseeability of *use.* See supra, p. 220, and infra n. 10(A). The plaintiff in a strict tort action need not establish the former, but only the latter. A manufacturer "is not required to foresee, for example, that a lawnmower—which is designed to cut grass—will be used to cut logs or to cut pipe. Yet he is required to foresee an injury resulting from a defect * * * during the use of the mower for a purpose for which it was intended * * *." Eshbach v. W.T. Grant's & Co., 481 F.2d 940, 943 (3d Cir. 1973) (while riding on back of riding lawnmower driven by her 9–year–old brother, child passenger's foot slipped into unguarded chain and sprocket; *held,* verdict for defendant reversed for error in foreseeability instructions).

6. Occasional decisions use a direct consequences "test" rather than (or in addition to) the doctrine of foreseeability. See, e.g., Koski v. Automatic Heating Service, 75 Mich.App. 180, 254 N.W.2d 836 (1977) (plaintiff contracted rare

form of pneumonia from inhaling fungus; summary judgment for seller of humidifier reversed and remanded).

7. Consider the role of foreseeability within the doctrine of proximate causation in the Second Restatement of Torts:

§ 435. Foreseeability of Harm or Manner of Its Occurrence

(1) If the actor's conduct is a substantial factor in bringing about harm to another, the fact that the actor neither foresaw nor should have foreseen the extent of the harm or the manner in which it occurred does not prevent him from being liable.

(2) The actor's conduct may be held not to be a legal cause of harm to another where after the event and looking back from the harm to the actor's negligent conduct, it appears to the court highly extraordinary that it should have brought about the harm.

8. **Manner of Harm.** It generally is agreed that the precise manner in which the harm occurs need not be foreseeable. So, a meat packing company which negligently applied a rubber band to bind a shank of lamb need not have foreseen that a butcher would be hit in the eye when the band flew off as he grasped the lamb to pull it forward along a conveyor rail. Katz v. Swift & Co., 276 F.2d 905, 906 (2d Cir.1960) ("It was, of course, not necessary that defendant should have been able to anticipate the particular chain of events that would result in injury in order to be held liable. [Citation.] It was sufficient that it was foreseeable that injury might result if the rubber bands were improperly attached * * *."). Nor must it have been foreseen by the seller of an improperly designed rotary power lawn mower that a stick would be ejected at high velocity through the open window of a passing police patrol car 26 feet away and into the eye of the officer within. Swearngin v. Sears Roebuck & Co., 376 F.2d 637, 642 (10th Cir.1967).

In Noonan v. Buick Co., 211 So.2d 54 (Fla.App.1968), plaintiff's three-year-old son grabbed the steering wheel which caused the automobile to begin to skid. When plaintiff quickly turned the wheel to adjust for the skid, the inadequately secured driver's seat catapulted plaintiff into the roof, rendering him unconscious.. The car thereupon left the road and rolled over, seriously injuring the plaintiff. *Held,* the jury could properly have found that plaintiff's injury was a foreseeable result of the inadequately secured seat.

Consider, however, the observation of the court in Kerns v. Engelke, 54 Ill. App.3d 323, 12 Ill.Dec. 270, 369 N.E.2d 1284, 1293 (1977), rev'd in part 76 Ill.2d 154, 28 Ill.Dec. 500, 390 N.E.2d 859 (1979), that "certain accidents may occur in such a 'tragically bizarre' and 'unique' manner that no legal duty to guard against them will be imposed upon the defendant." Plaintiff farmhand's eye was struck by a piece of bailing wire used by his employer to tie up the power take-off shaft to the body of the forage blower for ease in transport. The jury found for the plaintiff, on grounds that a warning or safe transport device should have been provided with the machine, and defendant-manufacturer appealed. *Held,* affirmed. "Seeing nothing freakish or fantastic in the sequence of events which led to plaintiff's accident here, we feel no hesitation in holding that appellants had a legal duty to provide against it. Whether plaintiff's injuries were the natural and probable result of the defective forage blower was for the trier of fact to determine." Id.

9. **Extent of Harm.** Myrtle Poplar pricked her finger on the jagged point of a silvery metal star adorning a cosmetic gift box she had received for

Christmas. An infection developed, and the finger had to be amputated. The manufacturer argued that it should not be held to anticipate "so extraordinary and unpredictable a result" as an amputation "from the otherwise trivial puncturing of her skin." The court disagreed: "[I]f the plaintiff's injury is traceable to the defendant's negligence without intervention of any other independent, legally operative event—the injured person is entitled to recover for the harm actually suffered even though the precise nature and extent of those injuries, as they finally developed, were more severe than could ordinarily have been foreseen. [Citations.] In other words, a defendant is chargeable for all the harm and suffering which his negligent act brought on even though the plaintiff's injuries were aggravated by his own predisposition or weakness [citations] or by the intervening mistake or negligence of a physician who treated the original injury." Poplar v. Bourjois, 298 N.Y. 62, 80 N.E.2d 334, 336–37 (1948) (dictum). See also Smith v. J.C. Penney Co., Inc., 269 Or. 643, 525 P.2d 1299, 1306–07 (1974).

10. **Type of Harm.**

A. **In general.** In contrast to the manner and extent of harm, the foreseeability vel non of the *type* of harm suffered by the plaintiff—or the *type* of *risk* that caused the harm—figures prominently in the proximate cause determination of many courts. See Rest. (2d) Torts § 442(a), infra p. 517.

Plaintiff purchased an ordinary, portable space heater from the defendant retailer in order to control the temperature in a house trailer he used for raising chinchillas. Because the heater was not designed for use in tightly-enclosed, poorly-ventilated areas such as trailers, the trailer became overheated and 330 of plaintiff's 360 "rare and unusual chinchilla herd" perished as a result. Should the manufacturer have foreseen this loss? Frey v. Montgomery Ward & Co., 258 N.W.2d 782 (Minn.1977), held this to be a jury question.

Is the foreseeability issue here one of type of *harm* or type of *use?* Does it matter?

Suppose plaintiff purchases a space heater, specifically designed and sold for chinchilla house-heating purposes, which malfunctions one winter night when plaintiff is sleeping with the chinchillas because he is locked out of his house. Should the manufacturer be liable if plaintiff suffers frostbite?

B. **Emotional distress.** Should a manufacturer be expected to foresee that some consumers will become distressed, and perhaps even suffer illness as a result, if its products are defective? Compare Caputzal v. Lindsay Co., 48 N.J. 69, 222 A.2d 513 (1966) (no: heart attack from fright at sight of rusty brown water caused by defect in defendant's water softener; plaintiff's emotional hypersensitivity was idiosyncratic and hence unforeseeable), with Barnette v. Dickens, 205 Va. 12, 135 S.E.2d 109 (1964) (yes: plaintiff became hysterical, and ultimately suffered traumatic neurosis, when she witnessed her washing machine vibrating violently, like a "robot gone crazy"). Compare Way v. Tampa Coca Cola Bottling Co., 260 So.2d 288 (Fla.App.1972) (yes: mental distress from sucking on rat in bottle of Coke).

Plaintiff became embarrassed, upset, angry, nervous, perspirey, sluggish, depressed, and suffered a "beastly headache" when, upon getting out of a swimming pool containing her neighbors, friends and fellow PTA members, her new bathing suit was seen to be transparent such that "her personal and private parts were exposed to view." Thereafter, at picnics and other functions, the subject was "always brought up" and her friends would say, " 'Let's turn a hose on Evelyn', or 'Let's throw her in the water and see what kind of bathing suit she has on'." Holden v. Kayser Roth Corp., 92 Ill.App.2d 240, 235 N.E.2d 426 (1968).

If you were a judge or juror, what would you think of Evelyn's suit? Would you provide her with a modest recovery?

Liability for emotional distress is treated further below, in chapter 6, § 2.

C. **Suicide.** Should the manufacturer be liable for a suicide caused by a defective product? See Saxton v. McDonnell Douglas Aircraft Co., 428 F.Supp. 1047 (C.D.Cal.1977) (no: mother of passenger killed in plane crash committed suicide from stress of son's death and subsequent products liability trial).

What if the accident victim *himself* commits suicide from remorse over his injuries? Cf. Fuller v. Preis, 35 N.Y.2d 425, 363 N.Y.S.2d 568, 322 N.E.2d 263 (1974) (yes, if caused by irresistible impulse: surgeon suffered brain damage in car accident).

B. INTERVENING CAUSES

The connection between the defendant's breach of duty and the plaintiff's injury may appear tenuous or "remote" because of the intervention of some force other than the plaintiff or defendant. Someone other than the plaintiff may abuse the product, or ignore its warnings or instructions, in a manner that might give rise to a contributory negligence, assumption of risk, or misuse defense had the conduct been that of the plaintiff. As with the problem of product misuse by the plaintiff, whether from the vantage point of duty or defense, the principal criterion used to determine whether an intervening cause will be held to "supersede" the seller's breach of duty—and hence relieve him of liability—is one of "foreseeability." Yet, as seen in the preceding section, the foreseeability "doctrine" is at best a slippery and incomplete basis for deciding cases. This problem, moreover, is magnified in the context of intervening causation. "There is no area of tort law that has generated more confusion than the question of superseding or intervening cause [especially] where the claim is based on products liability." Montgomery Elevator Co. v. McCullough, 676 S.W.2d 776 (Ky.1984).

DUGAN v. SEARS, ROEBUCK & COMPANY

Appellate Court of Illinois, 1983.
113 Ill.App.3d 740, 73 Ill.Dec. 320, 454 N.E.2d 64.

LORENZ, JUSTICE delivered the opinion of the court upon rehearing:

Plaintiff, Steve Dugan, a minor, filed a strict liability action (by his father and next friend) to recover for injuries suffered when a power lawnmower manufactured and sold by the defendants, Roper Corporation and Sears, Roebuck & Company, picked up a small piece of plastic and ejected it at high velocity, blinding plaintiff's right eye.

A jury returned a verdict in favor of the defendants, and plaintiff appeals * * *.

* * *

Carol Favia testified that on May 20, 1974, she was mowing the front lawn of her home while five-year-old Steve Dugan, a neighbor, sat on the steps of her front porch. The power mower, which had been manufactured by Roper and purchased from Sears, came with an owner's manual. Favia testified she read the manual, including the following warning:

> "Do not allow anyone in the area while cutting. Keep children and pets in the backyard while mowing the front yard. Keep a wary eye out for children or passersby. Stop the engine while they are in the vicinity of your mower * * *. [A]lthough the area mowed should be completely cleared of all foreign objects, a small object could be accidentally thrown by the mower."

The manual further warned that "[i]t is imperative in [the mower's] use and maintenance that the operator always follow the normal precautions set forth in the Rules for Safe Operation as well as other instructions contained in the Owner's Manual in order to prevent injury or damage."

Despite having read these warnings, Favia continued to mow the lawn while plaintiff sat nearby on the porch steps. Suddenly, while she was about 10 feet from plaintiff, Favia heard a click, then "Stevie cried out and he put his hand over his eye." She took him for first aid, and when she returned she found, on the porch steps, the piece of plastic which hit plaintiff in the eye.

At trial plaintiff asserted that the mower was unreasonably dangerous on the grounds that its design permitted it to randomly discharge foreign objects. In support of this theory plaintiff presented expert opinion evidence that alternative product designs were feasible, and were safer than the designs used by the manufacturer.

The defendants responded by presenting evidence, and arguing, that the conduct of Carol Favia constituted the sole proximate cause of plaintiff's injury. They also presented expert opinion evidence that the mower was not unreasonably dangerous.

The jury was instructed, among other things, that plaintiff had the burden of proving that an unreasonably dangerous condition in the mower was a "proximate cause" of plaintiff's injury. (See Illinois Pattern Jury Instructions, Civil (2d ed. 1977 Supp.) § 400.02.) The jury was also instructed that: "If you decide that the sole proximate cause of the injury to the plaintiff was the conduct of some person other than the defendants, then your verdict should be for the defendants." See Illinois Pattern Jury Instructions, Civil (2d ed. 1971) § 12.04.

OPINION

First we shall consider whether the trial court erred by permitting the defendants to present evidence that Carol Favia's conduct was the sole proximate cause of plaintiff's injury.

For an injured plaintiff "[t]o recover in strict liability, the injury must result from a condition of the product, the condition must be unreasonably dangerous and the condition must have existed at the time the product left the manufacturer's control." Hunt v. Blasius (1978), 74 Ill.2d 203, 210, 23 Ill.Dec. 574, 384 N.E.2d 368.

Among the justifications for imposing liability without proof of negligence (i.e., strict liability) on the manufacturers and sellers of products is that "public policy demands that the burden of accidental injuries caused by products intended for consumption be placed upon those who market them, and be treated as a cost of production against which liability insurance can be obtained * * *." (Restatement (Second) of Torts (1965) § 402A, com. *c*, at 350.) Therefore, liability is imposed even though "the seller has exercised all possible care in the preparation and sale of his product * * *." (Restatement (Second) of Torts (1965) § 402(A)(2)(a).) Nevertheless, strict liability is not absolute liability, and a manufacturer "is not an absolute insurer who is responsible for all physical hurts occurring in the course of using the product." Helene Curtis Industries, Inc. v. Pruitt (5th Cir.1967), 385 F.2d 841, 849, cert. denied, 391 U.S. 913, 88 S.Ct. 1806, 20 L.Ed.2d 652. See also Winnett v. Winnett (1974), 57 Ill.2d 7, 11, 310 N.E.2d 1.

The difficulty is in where to draw the line between strict liability and absolute liability. This involves a clash between the policy which favors compensating injured consumers, and the policy against imposing on manufacturers and sellers the heavy burden of becoming absolute insurers of the safety of their products. Therefore, "[u]ntil Americans have a comprehensive scheme of social insurance, courts must resolve by a balancing process the head-on collision between the need for adequate recovery and viable enterprises." Helene Curtis Industries, Inc. v. Pruitt (5th Cir.1967), 385 F.2d 841, 862, cert. denied, 391 U.S. 913, 88 S.Ct. 1806, 20 L.Ed.2d 652.

One of the mechanisms used to draw the line between these competing interests is the doctrine of proximate cause. As the trial court instructed the jury, "proximate cause" is a "cause which, in natural or probable sequence, produced the injury complained of." (Illinois Pattern Jury Instructions, Civil (2d ed. 1977 Suppl.) § 400.–04.) And, as developed in negligence cases, the concept of proximate cause is used "to limit responsibility for legal or policy reasons for the consequences of negligent conduct." Dooley, Modern Tort Law § 8.03, at 232 (Lindahl Rev.1982).

The same need to limit liability for policy reasons exists with strict liability actions, and "[i]n any product action, the product must be a proximate cause of the damages. This requisite is universally recognized, whether the theory be negligence, warranty, or strict liability in tort." Dooley, Modern Tort Law § 32.03, at 243 (Lindahl Rev.1982). See Williams v. Brown Manufacturing Co., Inc. (1970), 45 Ill.2d 418, 431, 261 N.E.2d 305.

In the present case the defendants argued that Carol Favia's conduct was the "sole proximate cause" of plaintiff's injuries, and that he therefore failed to meet his burden of proving that his injuries were proximately caused by defendants' product. Clearly, plaintiff would not have been injured if Favia had complied with the warnings she was admittedly aware of. Therefore, even if a cause-in-fact of plaintiff's injury was an unreasonably dangerous condition in defendants' product, it was relevant to consider whether Favia's conduct was a superseding cause which became the sole proximate cause of plaintiff's injury.

"A superseding cause is an act of a third person or other force which by its intervention prevents the actor from being liable for harm to another which his antecedent [tortious conduct] is a substantial factor in bringing about." (Restatement (Second) of Torts (1965) § 440.) "The concept is that there has intervened between the original wrong and the final injury a new and independent force. The injury is imputed to the new force and not the first and more remote cause." Dooley, Modern Tort Law, § 8.05, at 235 (Lindahl Rev.1982).

According to plaintiff, however, Favia's conduct was so foreseeable that, as a matter of law, it could not be considered a superseding cause. Thus, plaintiff concludes the trial court erred when it admitted evidence and argument concerning Favia's conduct in disregarding defendants' warnings.

"The intervention of independent, concurrent or intervening forces will not break the causal connection if the intervention of such independent force was itself *probable and foreseeable.*" (Lewis v. Stran Steel Co. (1974), 57 Ill.2d 94, 100, 311 N.E.2d 128 (emphasis added).) "The test that should be applied in all cases in determining the question of proximate cause is whether the first wrongdoer might have reasonably anticipated the intervening cause as a *natural and probable result* of the first party's own [tortious conduct]." Merlo v. Public Service Co. of Northern Illinois (1942), 381 Ill. 300, 317, 45 N.E.2d 665 (emphasis added).

Moreover, "[t]he debatable quality of issues such as * * * proximate cause, the fact that fair minded men might reach different conclusions, emphasize the appropriateness and necessity of leaving such questions to a fact-finding body." (Ney v. Yellow Cab Co. (1954), 2 Ill.2d 74, 84, 117 N.E.2d 74.) Consequently, "If different minds might reasonably draw different inferences from the facts given, then the court must defer to the judgment of the jury on the accompanying issues of foreseeability and the effect of an intervening cause." Peck v. Ford (7th Cir.1979), 603 F.2d 1240, 1243.

Applying these principles to the present case, and assuming for the sake of argument that plaintiff's injury was caused by an unreasonably dangerous condition in defendants' product, the pertinent question is this: could reasonable people disagree about whether the intervening force (Carol Favia's conduct in knowingly disregarding defendants' warnings) was so probable, natural, and foreseeable that the defendants should remain strictly liable for the injury.

There is no doubt that with any given product somebody will eventually disregard the manufacturer's warnings, thereby causing injuries. Nevertheless, as noted above, defendants in strict liability cases are not absolutely liable as insurers, and we find that reasonable people can disagree over whether Favia's conduct was so probable, natural, and foreseeable that the defendants should be held strictly liable for the alleged unreasonably dangerous condition in their product. We therefore find that it was not against the manifest weight of the evidence for the jury to decide that Favia's conduct was a superseding cause which became the sole proximate cause of plaintiff's injuries.

* * *

Affirmed.

ANDERSON v. DREIS & KRUMP MANUFACTURING CORPORATION

Court of Appeals of Washington, 1987.
48 Wash.App. 432, 739 P.2d 1177.

MUNSON, JUDGE.

Steve Anderson brought this products liability action to recover damages for personal injuries received while operating a Chicago Press Brake (press) manufactured by Dreis & Krump Manufacturing Corporation (Dreis). Mr. Anderson alleged Dreis was liable under theories of breach of warranty, negligence, and strict liability. The trial court entered summary judgment for Dreis, dismissing the action. [Plaintiff appealed.]

Mr. Anderson was injured on July 3, 1979, while operating a press owned by his employer, Comet Corporation. The press was manufactured by Dreis, an Illinois corporation in the business of designing and manufacturing such industrial equipment. Dreis sold the press to Niblock Machine, Inc., a distributor who, in turn, sold the press to Comet. Comet installed the press in its Spokane facility. Neither Comet nor Niblock is a party to this action.

A detailed description of the press is necessary for an understanding of our ruling. It was designed as a general purpose or "multifunctional" press, capable of performing a variety of functions. Comet used the press for corrugating metal.[2] During operation, the press' "ram," or vertically movable upper section, would descend upon the "bed" or lower section. Shaping tools or "dies" are attached to the ram as well

2. As utilized by Comet, sheets of aluminum, approximately 100 inches long, were fed into the press from the back of the press moving through the point of operation toward the operator.

as the bed. When the ram descends, the metal is bent into the desired shape by the upper die pressing the metal against the lower die. The area between the ram die and the bed die is referred to as the "point of operation."

The press, as originally designed, manufactured, and sold to Comet, could be activated by either of two means: the first was a 2–button control located at shoulder level above the ram. These buttons had to be pressed simultaneously, using both hands, to start the press, causing the ram to descend. The 2–button system was also the press' principal safety feature because the operator's hands were on the buttons, and thus prevented from entering the point of operation when the ram descended. The second means of activation was by depressing a foot treadle connected to a rod which ran along the base of the press. The treadle's position could be moved right and left along the length of the press to accommodate the position of the operator. This movement allowed the treadle to be positioned so the operator was within arms reach of the point of operation. Accidental depression of the treadle could be prevented by engaging a "treadle lock"; however, that device apparently was not automatic, but rather had to be manually engaged. Dreis provided no accompanying safety device to prevent the operator's hands from entering the point of operation when the press was activated by the treadle. The operator could choose either the 2–button control or the treadle by flipping a lever on the side of the press.

When the press was delivered, Comet received safety and operator manuals provided by Dreis, instructing prospective operators how to use the press safely. One of these safety manuals instructed purchasers never to eliminate or bypass any safety device installed on the press. Moreover, that manual requested purchasers to contact Dreis with respect to the continued use of the press after any modification.

Additionally, Dreis attached the following warning sign to the front of the press near the point of operation:

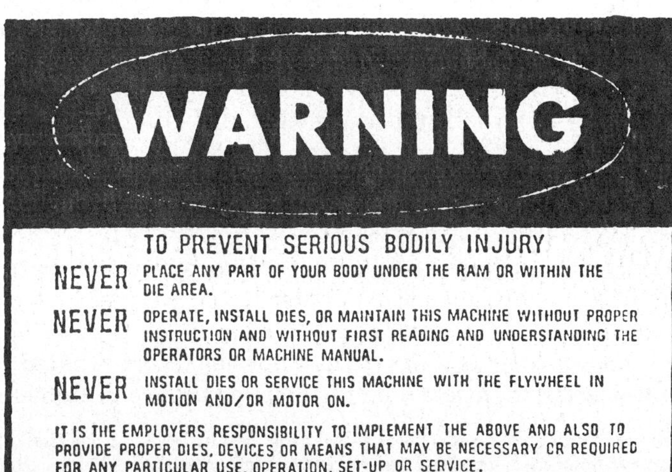

When delivered, the 2–button device was the operational activation system. Thereafter, Comet disconnected that control and rewired the press so that it could be activated by pushing a single button attached to the end of a long, flexible electric cord. This flexible cord, like the adjustable treadle, allowed the operator to move along the length of the press' bed. Because this method of activation required the use of only one hand, the operator's other hand was left free to enter the dangerous point of operation.

After modifying the activation system, Comet did not install "point-of-operation" guards.[3] Comet was aware of the danger to operators from use of the unguarded press and discussed these dangers at company meetings prior to the accident. Additionally, the Washington State Department of Labor & Industries inspected the press prior to the accident and found the press to be unsafe. Although not clear from the record, Dreis contends Comet was fined for lack of point-of-operation safety devices on the press.

This accident occurred when Mr. Anderson reached into the point-of-operation area to brush away small circles of aluminum that had accumulated during the stamping process. He was leaning into the die area when his stomach accidently hit the single button activator, the cord of which had been laid nearby. As a result, the ram cycled downward, severely injuring one of his hands.

In moving for summary judgment, Dreis argued: (1) the press was not defective as manufactured and sold since the press included the 2–button (activator) safety feature; (2) adequate warnings were attached to and accompanied the press when it was sold; and (3) Comet's modification of the activation system was the superseding cause of Mr. Anderson's injury.

In response, Mr. Anderson argued the press was designed to be used with the treadle activator. Because use of the treadle allowed the operator to place his hands within the point-of-operation area, the press should have included corresponding point-of-operation or barrier-type guards. He asserted the single button activator, though a modification, did not cut off Dreis' liability because that activation method was no more dangerous than the foot treadle, and the kind of harm which occurred, i.e., accidental injury to hands, was no different than the kind of harm which would have occurred if the treadle had been used.

Mr. Anderson's arguments were supported by three experts familiar with this type of industrial equipment. These experts stated the press was defectively designed because of lack of point-of-operation guards and inadequate warnings. The Superior Court granted summary judgment, dismissing the action, primarily because of Comet's modi-

3. The record indicates that several types of point-of-operation guards were available, including: (a) barrier guards, and (b) "light curtains." Either of these guards would have prevented the press from cycling while the operator's hands were in the point-of-operation area.

fication; Mr. Anderson appeals. Additional facts will be incorporated below as necessary.

A. Breach of Warranty

* * * Because contractual privity does not exist between Mr. Anderson and Dreis, the court properly dismissed the breach of warranty action. RCW 62A.2–318; [citation].

B. Duty to Warn

Mr. Anderson next * * * argues the warnings, as given, inadequately informed Mr. Anderson of the full extent of the dangers associated with the press. He maintains his experts' affidavits raise genuine issues of material fact as to the adequacy of the warnings. We disagree.

* * *

C. Design Defect

Mr. Anderson next contends the court erred in not permitting a jury to decide whether the press was reasonably safe as designed under theories of strict liability and negligence. We agree. A manufacturer is required under both strict liability and negligence principles to design and produce a reasonably safe product. * * *

We find * * * that whether (1) the press was defective because it lacked point-of-operation guards and/or (2) Dreis negligently failed to design a reasonably safe press given the lack of guards both are questions properly resolved by a jury. Dreis contends, however, its installation of point-of-operation guards or other safety devices, such as interlocks, was not feasible because installation of those devices on the multipurpose press would have unduly restricted the myriad uses for which the press was designed. We are not persuaded.

First, Dreis presented no evidence demonstrating that barrier guards or interlock devices would actually have interfered with the press operation *as used here.* Second, a manufacturer cannot delegate to the buyer its responsibility to equip an otherwise dangerous machine with safety guards. [Citations, including Bexiga v. Havir Mfg. Corp., 60 N.J. 402, 290 A.2d 281, 286, (1972)]. We conclude whether the press was defective and/or Dreis negligent in designing and selling a press without point-of-operation safety devices are questions of fact for the jury.

D. Employer's Modification

The court held Comet's modification from the 2–button device to the single button switch was the superseding cause of Mr. Anderson's injury thereby relieving Dreis of liability as a matter of law. Consequently, the crucial issue is whether the trial court was correct in passing on superseding cause as a matter of law or whether a jury should do so as a matter of fact.

Proximate cause is an essential element of both negligence and products liability theories; it consists of two elements: (1) factual or "but for" causation and (2) legal causation. [Citations.] Factual causation is established between a defendant's act and a subsequent injury only where it can be said the injury would not have occurred "but for" the defendant's act. W. Keeton, D. Dobbs, R. Keeton, and D. Owen, Torts § 42, at 273 (5th ed. 1984). * * * Dreis does not question the existence of factual causation here.

Assuming Dreis' failure to equip the press with point of operation guards can be said to be a factual cause of Mr. Anderson's injury, such a determination does not necessarily lead to the conclusion Dreis' failure was also the legal cause of the injury. W. Keeton, D. Dobbs, R. Keeton, & D. Owen, at 272–73. Unlike factual causation, legal causation "hinges on principles of responsibility, not physics," Van Buskirk v. Carey Canadian Mines, Ltd., 760 F.2d 481, 492 (3rd Cir.1985), and the determination of legal causation rests on policy considerations as to how far the legal consequences of a defendant's act should extend. * * *

The doctrine of superseding cause, however, limits the situations in which legal causation can be held to exist between two events. The doctrine applies where the act of a third party intervenes between the defendant's original conduct and the plaintiff's injury such that the defendant may no longer be deemed responsible for the injury. Campbell v. ITE Imperial Corp., 107 Wash.2d 807, 813, 733 P.2d 969 (1987); Restatement (Second) of Torts § 440 (1965). Superseding cause thus prevents a determination of legal causation between a defendant's actions and a plaintiff's injuries where the intervening act breaks the otherwise natural and continuous causal connection between events. [Citation.]

Whether an act may be considered a superseding cause sufficient to relieve a defendant of liability depends on whether the intervening act can reasonably be foreseen by the defendant; only intervening acts which are *not* reasonably foreseeable are deemed superseding causes. [Citation.] The foreseeability of an intervening act, unlike the determination of legal cause in general, is ordinarily a question of fact for the jury. [Citations.] However, foreseeability is a flexible concept, and a defendant will not be relieved of responsibility simply because the exact manner in which the injury occurred could not be anticipated. Rikstad v. Holmberg, 76 Wash.2d 265, 269, 456 P.2d 355 (1969); Smith v. Acme Paving Co., 16 Wash.App. 389, 396, 558 P.2d 811 (1976). Rikstad, 76 Wash.2d at 269, 456 P.2d 355 (quoting McLeod v. Grant Cy. Sch. Dist., 42 Wash.2d 316, 321–22, 255 P.2d 360 (1953)), provides:

> It is not, however, the unusualness of the [intervening] act that resulted in injury to plaintiff that is the test of foreseeabil-

ity, but whether the result of the act is within the ambit of the hazards covered by the duty imposed upon defendant.

* * *

* * * It is literally true that there is no liability for damage that falls entirely outside the general threat of harm which made the conduct of the actor negligent. The sequence of events, of course, need not be foreseeable. *The manner in which the risk culminates in harm may be unusual, improbable and highly unexpectable, from the point of view of the actor at the time of his conduct. And yet, if the harm suffered falls within the general danger area, there may be liability, provided other requisites of legal causation are present.*

(Italics ours.)[6] See also W. Keeton, D. Dobbs, R. Keeton, D. Owen, at 316. In this context our Supreme Court has held that generally an intervening act is not a superseding cause where the intervening act (1) does not bring about a different type of harm than otherwise would have resulted from the defendant's conduct; and (2) does not operate independently of the situation created by the defendant's conduct. Campbell, 107 Wash.2d at 813–14, 733 P.2d 969; Herberg v. Swartz, 89 Wash.2d 916, 927–28, 578 P.2d 17 (1978); Restatement (Second) of Torts §§ 442–45 (1965). The above principles are equally applicable to negligence and strict products liability theories. Campbell, 107 Wash.2d at 814, 733 P.2d 969.

Dreis primarily contends Comet's deactivation of the 2–button device and installation of an alternative activation system destroyed the efficacy of the press' safety features. Dreis maintains, and the court found, the deactivation of this safety feature was unforeseeable and constituted a superseding cause of the accident as a matter of law. We disagree.

Contrary to Dreis' argument, a jury could find it was reasonably foreseeable to Dreis that a purchaser of the press would choose an alternative method of activation given the press' myriad uses, see Jiminez v. Dreis & Krump Mfg. Co., 736 F.2d 51 (2d Cir.1984), and because an alternative activation system, i.e., the treadle, was designed into the press and delivered with it to Comet. Obviously, use of an alternative activation method, such as the treadle, rendered the 2–button activation system superfluous and its safety features ineffective since the press operator's hands were no longer occupied.

We are cognizant that the activation method chosen by Comet was not originally designed into the press by Dreis and thus the precise manner in which this accident occurred may not have been foreseeable to Dreis. See Rikstad, 76 Wash.2d at 269, 456 P.2d 355; Restatement (Second) of Torts § 442B comments *a* and *b* (1965). However, the single button switch, like the treadle, foreseeably allowed the press to be accidentally activated while the operator's free hands were in the

6. [See] Restatement (Second) of Torts § 442B comment[s *a* and *b* (1965)].

unguarded point-of-operation area. Under these circumstances, a jury could find the accidental activation of the press, while Mr. Anderson's hand was in the die area, was within the foreseeable scope of danger created by Dreis' failure to incorporate guards around the point-of-operation area. In the absence of any evidence that Comet's modification enhanced the danger of accidental activation above that found in the treadle,[7] we decline to hold that Comet's modification constitutes a superseding cause as a matter of law. Accord, [Citations;] Balido v. Improved Mach., Inc., 29 Cal.App.3d 633, 105 Cal.Rptr. 890, 901 (1972).

Two additional considerations bolster our conclusion that a jury should properly determine whether Comet's alteration of the press was a superseding cause of Mr. Anderson's injury. First, the modification did not result in a different type of harm than otherwise would have occurred from Dreis' failure to supply point-of-operation guards with the press. The harm caused by this deficiency, i.e., injury to hands or other body parts, remained the same regardless of the alternative activation method chosen. Second, the intervening modification cannot be said to have operated independently from Dreis' failure to equip the press with guards. Rather, if the guards had been present, Mr. Anderson's hand could not have entered the die area while the press cycled, no matter which activation method was employed. See Rhoads v. Service Mach. Co., 329 F.Supp. 367, 377 (E.D.Ark.1971). Thus, a jury could determine that Comet's intervening alteration, rather than superseding Dreis' failure to supply guards, instead concurred with that failure to bring about the harm. As Smith v. Acme Paving Co., supra 16 Wash.App. at 396, 558 P.2d 811 notes:

> There may, of course, be more than one proximate cause of an injury, and the concurring negligence of a third party does not necessarily break the causal chain from original negligence to final injury. Where a defendant's original negligence continues, and contributes to the injury, the mere fact another's intervening negligent act is a further cause of the accident does not prevent defendant's act from constituting a cause for which he is liable.

(Citations omitted.)

7. Cf. Hanlon v. Cyril Bath Co., 541 F.2d 343, 345 (3d Cir.1975). In *Hanlon*, the plaintiff's employer modified the press activation mechanism from a treadle which required 65 pounds of downward pressure before activation to an electric switch at the end of a flexible cable. The court, at 346, held this modification caused the accident, stating:

> Clearly, the substitution of the easily depressed mobile electrical foot switch for the original fixed elevated mechanical treadle that was responsive only to some 65 pounds of downward pressure removed a safeguard against accidental activation that had been incorporated in the original structural design and would have been adequate to prevent this accident.

Here, however, no evidence was presented indicating the necessary pressure needed to depress the foot treadle. In fact, there is no evidence comparing the respective risks of accidental activation created by these two activation methods. An affidavit of one of Mr. Anderson's experts provides "the thumb operated control provided a safer control for the intended [activation] function than would a foot activator." * * *

We conclude reasonable persons could disagree as to whether Comet's modification broke the causal chain between Dreis' design choice and Mr. Anderson's injury. Consequently, the court erred in holding the modification of the activation system was a superseding cause of Mr. Anderson's injury as a matter of law.

E. Comet's Failure to Supply Guards

Notwithstanding the foregoing analysis, Dreis argues, relying on *Campbell v. ITE Imperial Corp.*, supra, that Comet had actual, specific knowledge of the danger created by the press' lack of guards and thus had a duty to itself supply such guards. Dreis argues Comet's failure to supply such guards was a negligent act sufficient to constitute a superseding cause as a matter of law. We disagree.

The Restatement (Second) of Torts § 449, at 482 (1965) provides the negligence of a third party does not constitute a superseding cause "[i]f the likelihood that a third person may act in a particular manner is * * * one of the hazards which makes the [original] actor negligent." See also Campbell, 107 Wash.2d at 814–15, 733 P.2d 969. This court has previously held it is foreseeable a small company which purchases dangerous industrial machinery will not install guards on that machinery when the manufacturer delivers that equipment without them. [Citations.] Not only is the manufacturer's duty to supply safety guards on dangerous industrial equipment nondelegable, *Bexiga v. Havir Mfg. Corp.*, supra, but the failure of the purchaser to supply guards is so likely that it constitutes one of the hazards which makes a manufacturer's failure to supply such guards negligent. Restatement (Second) of Torts § 449 (1965). Moreover, the public interest in assuring that appropriate safety devices be installed on industrial machinery would be undermined if installation was left to the "haphazard conduct of the ultimate purchaser." Bexiga, 290 A.2d at 285.

* * *

Thus, we hold a question of fact exists as to whether Comet's failure to supply guards was a negligent act sufficient to relieve Dreis of responsibility.

F. Comet's Continued Use of the Press After the Department of Labor & Industries' Warning

Dreis further contends Comet's continued use of the guardless press after being warned by the Department of Labor & Industries that the press was dangerous without guards constitutes a superseding cause of the injury. To the extent this argument is related to the one set out immediately above, we need not address it further. Notwithstanding, Rhoads v. Service Mach. Co., supra, is particularly apt here.

In *Rhoads*, the press, like the one in question here, had been shipped with dual hand controls and a warning sign; it possessed no point of operation guards. Prior to the accident, the Arkansas Department of Labor ordered the purchaser (employer) to install safety guards on the press. The purchaser failed to install the guards, deactivated the dual hand control, and installed an alternative activation device. That device was accidentally activated, resulting in the plaintiff's injury. The court rejected the contention such conduct on the part of the purchaser-employer amounted to a superseding cause, immunizing the manufacturer from liability as a matter of law; the court declared at 376:

> While the defendant may have thought that Al–Craft would have taken adequate precautions to protect its employees, or that it would be required to do so by its workmen's compensation insurance carrier or by regulatory agencies of the State of Arkansas, the Court does not think that as a matter of law defendant had a right to assume that protective devices would be provided.

Accord, *Balido,* 105 Cal.Rptr. at 900 ("an owner's lack of compliance with a state safety order does not release a manufacturer from liability for injuries attributable to deficient safety design"); Bexiga v. Havir Mfg. Corp., supra; Finnegan v. Havir Mfg. Corp., 60 N.J. 413, 290 A.2d 286 (1972). We agree with the reasoning manifested in those decisions. and likewise hold Comet's failure to heed the Department's warning does not immunize Dreis as a matter of law.

G. Summary

In conclusion, we affirm the trial court's summary judgment on the issues of breach of warranty and breach of the duty to warn. We reverse the trial court's determination that the press was not defectively designed as a matter of law and that Dreis' design was not the legal cause of Mr. Anderson's injury as a matter of law. Therefore, we reverse and remand for trial.

MCINTURFF, C.J., concurs.

GREEN, JUDGE (dissenting).

In my view the trial judge was correct in ruling the modification of the activation mechanism of the press was the intervening proximate cause of Mr. Anderson's injuries and dismissing the complaint.

The press was designed to be activated by the use of two buttons or a foot treadle. When the buttons were used, it was impossible for the operator's hands to be under the press. The purchaser, Comet, elected to activate the press by use of buttons. However, instead of using the two buttons as the machine was designed, Comet not only modified the press so it could be activated by one button, but placed that button in a position where it could be accidentally activated by the operator's body rubbing against it. That is what happened here. The operator, while removing metal from beneath the press, rubbed against the dangling button setting off the press and injuring his hand.

It is apparent that the sole and proximate cause of this accident was Comet's negligent modification of the button activation system, creating the danger of accidental activation.

If the accident had happened while using the foot treadle, then the issue of defective design as the proximate cause of the injury would create a question for the trier of fact. Here, the treadle was not used and the question of defective design for treadle use is not an issue.

I would affirm.

NOTES

1. In *Dugan,* do you think that the manufacturer or Sears could foresee that someone might read the operator's manual quickly, when she first purchased the mower, and thereafter forget much of what she read? Might there be something, perhaps one or two minor points, that a student read earlier in this book which has now been forgotten? Is it "foreseeable" that product users will not always remember to, be able to, want to, or know to obey every warning and instruction that accompanies a product? If so, is *Dugan* wrongly decided?

2. In *Anderson,* why should the manufacturer of a multi-purpose press equipped with a perfectly safe (2–button control) safety device be liable for an accident caused by the employer's destruction of the safe device and replacement with a dangerous one? Is *Anderson* wrongly decided?

3. As both *Dugan* and *Anderson* illustrate, many courts rely substantially on the Second Restatement of Torts for a formulation of principles for intervening and superseding causation. Consider the following:

RESTATEMENT (SECOND) OF TORTS (1965)

§ 442. Considerations Important in Determining Whether an Intervening Force is a Superseding Cause

The following considerations are of importance in determining whether an intervening force is a superseding cause of harm to another:

(a) The fact that its intervention brings about harm different in kind from that which would otherwise have resulted from the actor's negligence;

(b) the fact that its operation or the consequences thereof appear after the event to be extraordinary rather than normal in view of the circumstances existing at the time of its operation;

(c) the fact that the intervening force is operating independently of any situation created by the actor's negligence, or, on the other hand, is or is not a normal result of such a situation;

(d) the fact that the operation of the intervening force is due to a third person's act or to his failure to act;

(e) the fact that the intervening force is due to an act of a third person which is wrongful toward the other and as such subjects the third person to liability to him;

(f) the degree of culpability of a wrongful act of a third person which sets the intervening force in motion.

Consider also the following section on whether and when a third person's nonfeasance will amount to a superseding cause of the plaintiff's harm:

§ 452. **Third Person's Failure to Prevent Harm**

(1) Except as stated in Subsection (2), the failure of a third person to act to prevent harm to another threatened by the actor's negligent conduct is not a superseding cause of such harm.

(2) Where, because of lapse of time or otherwise, the duty to prevent harm to another threatened by the actor's negligent conduct is found to have shifted from the actor to a third person, the failure of the third person to prevent such harm is a superseding cause.

Comment *f* to § 452 provides: A court may "find that all duty and responsibility for the prevention of the harm has passed to the third person. It is apparently impossible to state any comprehensive rule as to when such a decision will be made." Relevant factors include "the degree of danger and the magnitude of the risk of harm, the character and position of the third person who is to take the responsibility, his knowledge of the danger and the likelihood that he will or will not exercise proper care, his relation to the plaintiff or to the defendant, the lapse of time, and perhaps other considerations."

Consider the following, recurring forms of third-party intervening misconduct.

4. **Parent Misconduct.**

A. **Passive: Negligent supervision.** Many, perhaps most, products liability cases in which young children are injured involve "inadequate" supervision on the part of a parent or other person having custody of the child at the time of the accident. Reconsider *Winnett* and *Richelman* from this perspective. Today, there are virtually no decisions expressly holding that a parent's negligent supervision supersedes the responsibility of a manufacturer of a defective product. In a sense, however, this is implicitly what the court did in *Winnett,* and what the dissent argued should have been done in *Richelman.* Nevertheless, at least with respect to products intended for use in the home, most courts consider parental neglect—and the resulting wandering and mischief of curious youngsters—part of the "foreseeable environment of use" of such products. See, e.g., Spruill v. Boyle–Midway, Inc., 308 F.2d 79 (4th Cir. 1962) (unattended infant drank furniture polish that mother left on bureau beside crib); Eshback v. W.T. Grant's & Co., 481 F.2d 940 (3d Cir.1973) (unbeknownst to father, 9–year-old son drove riding mower with sister riding on back). But see Wenzell v. MTD Products, Inc., 32 Ill.App.3d 279, 336 N.E.2d 125, 134 (1975) (unforeseeable that riding mower would be used by group of young children "virtually as a toy").

B. **Active: Injuring child with the product.** Some of the cases involve more affirmative misconduct by the parent, such as falling asleep at the wheel of a car in which the child is riding, Rossell v. Volkswagen of America, 147 Ariz. 160, 709 P.2d 517 (1985), or knocking over a bottle of liquid drain cleaner onto the child, Drayton v. Jiffee Chemical Corp., 395 F.Supp. 1081 (N.D. Ohio 1975), aff'd, 591 F.2d 352 (6th Cir.1978). Rarely is such conduct held to be a superseding cause.

5. **Doctor Misconduct.**

A. **Failing to pass on manufacturer's warnings.** Recall that under the "learned intermediary" doctrine, the manufacturer of a prescription drug generally is obligated to warn the doctor, not the patient. See supra, p. 350. What if the doctor negligently, or intentionally, fails to pass along to the patient an important warning or instruction that eventuates into harm?

In Kirk v. Michael Reese Hosp. & Medical Center, 117 Ill.2d 507, 111 Ill. Dec. 944, 513 N.E.2d 387 (1987), plaintiff was injured when the driver of the car in which he was a passenger lost control of the vehicle and crashed into a tree. Earlier in the day, the driver had been discharged from a hospital where he had been a psychiatric patient. His doctors had prescribed two drugs, Thorazine and Prolixin, but had failed to warn him of the dangers of mixing alcohol with the drugs. After leaving the hospital, he consumed an alcoholic drink which may have interacted with the drugs to cause the loss of control later in the day. *Held,* the manufacturers could not reasonably have foreseen the injury and, hence, were not strictly liable in tort:

> [I]t cannot be said that Squibb and SmithKline should have reasonably foreseen that their drugs would be dispensed without warnings by the physicians, that the patient would be discharged from the hospital, drink alcohol, drive a car, lose control of the car, hit a tree, and injure the passenger, Kirk, on the same day. This sequence would be triggered by an element that we have determined that the pharmaceutical companies did not have to foresee under the circumstances shown here: that the drugs would be dispensed without the warnings that the two companies provided to the physicians.

111 Ill.Dec. at 951, 513 N.E.2d at 394.

B. **Active misconduct.** What should be the effect of more affirmative misconduct by a doctor or other medical care provider? A doctor's use of a drug contrary to express warnings will generally terminate the manufacturer's responsibility. See, e.g., Dyer v. Best Pharmacal, 118 Ariz. 465, 577 P.2d 1084 (1978).

Compare Pharmaseal Laboratories, Inc. v. Goffe, 90 N.M. 753, 568 P.2d 589 (1977). As treatment for an internal obstruction, an intestinal tube weighted with a small balloon of mercury was inserted through plaintiff's nostril, down through his stomach, and into his intestines. As the tube began to be removed, it stuck, and the doctor tugged at it forcefully several times to pull it out. The balloon was broken, and plaintiff was discovered to have inhaled the mercury into his lungs. Plaintiff was placed head-down on a tilt table, and "[t]he hospital employees pounded on [his] back for several hours in an attempt to remove the mercury. His head constantly hit the foot of the bed and he experienced chest pain. The next morning he suffered a myocardial infarction." Should the actions of the doctor and hospital employees shield the manufacturer from liability as a matter of law for selling a balloon of inadequate strength? *Held,* no; summary judgment reversed and case remanded for trial.

6. **Employer Misconduct.**

A. **Failing to pass on manufacturer's warnings.** As examined in Chapter 3 above, the manufacturer of an industrial product may have a duty to communicate warnings and instructions directly to employees. If the manufacturer has such a duty, and if the manufacturer provides a warning only to the employer (as in an information sheet or a technical data manual) and not to the employees (as in a label on the product's container or a warning plate on a machine), the employer's failure to pass along the warning to its employees will not generally supersede the manufacturer's duty to warn them directly. See, e.g., Gordon v. Niagara Mach. & Tool Works, 574 F.2d 1182 (5th Cir.1978). But cf. Little v. PPG Industries, Inc., 19 Wash.App. 812, 579 P.2d 940 (1978) (plaintiff's husband lost consciousness from inhaling fumes of defendant's defectively labeled solvent and drowned when he fell face down in shallow water; jury should be permitted to find that defendant's responsibility was superseded by employer's failure to pass on warnings of two incidents of lost consciousness).

B. **Failing to maintain the product.** If an industrial machine malfunctions due to improper maintenance by the employer, should the manufacturer be liable? "The manufacturer is not liable for lack of normal maintenance." Rogers v. Unimac Co., Inc., 115 Ariz. 304, 565 P.2d 181, 184 (1977) (failure to replace worn and cracked parts in automatic car wash mechanism). See also Conder v. Hull Lift Truck, Inc., 435 N.E.2d 10 (Ind.1982) (jury could find that employer's failure to repair known accelerator sticking problem on forklift was unforeseeable). But cf. Johnson v. Salem Corp., 97 N.J. 78, 477 A.2d 1246, 1255 (1984) (where a machine is defective without a guard, the employer's negligent maintenance—that may have caused a risk of injury that would have been prevented by the guard—does not relieve the manufacturer of responsibility).

C. **Failing to add guards.** Prior to the 1970s, the custom was for employers—rather than manufacturers—to install appropriate guards on industrial machinery. Yet Bexiga v. Havir Mfg. Corp., 60 N.J. 402, 290 A.2d 281 (1972), infra p. 645, established the manufacturer's nondelegable duty to equip its machinery with sufficient safety devices. Thus, if the manufacturer fails to provide adequate guards, the employer's failure to remedy the danger will not generally shield the manufacturer. This is true even if the employer blithely ignores warning letters from the manufacturer urging the employer to cure the defect, explaining how to do so, and offering to provide the employer with the necessary material, for a fee. Balido v. Improved Machinery, Inc., 29 Cal.App. 3d 633, 105 Cal.Rptr. 890 (1973). See also Montgomery Elevator Co. v. McCullough, 676 S.W.2d 776 (Ky.1984).

D. **Removing or altering guards.**

(1) *In general.* A recurring problem for manufacturers attempting to comply with the *Bexiga* nondelegable duty doctrine occurs when the employer removes or alters a guard provided by the manufacturer. Guards are modified or removed for a variety of reasons: because they malfunction; to facilitate cleaning or maintenance of the machinery; to enhance the usefulness of the machine, as by permitting stock or a particular size or shape to enter the machine; or to speed up production.

Most courts hold the manufacturer accountable for injuries attributable to "foreseeable" modifications, provided that a feasible remedy—such as an electrical interlock—was available. See, e.g., Cepeda v. Cumberland Engineering Co., Inc., 76 N.J. 152, 386 A.2d 816 (1978), rev'g 70 N.J. 274, 351 A.2d 22 (1976) (guard attached to machine with four bolts was not reattached to machine after cleaning; since interlock installation would have cost $25–30, and frequent cleaning was necessary, *held,* foreseeability of removal for jury). Accord, Marois v. Paper Converting Mach. Co., 539 A.2d 621 (Me.1988); Brown v. United States Stove Co., 98 N.J. 155, 484 A.2d 1234, 1240 (1984) ("a design defect inherent in a safety feature of a product that foreseeably leads to a substantial alteration and an increased risk of danger can be a basis for strict products liability").

In a small number of jurisdictions, even foreseeable alterations may bar recovery. See Hines v. Joy Mfg. Co., 850 F.2d 1146, 1151 (6th Cir.1988) (interpreting Kentucky product liability statute barring recovery for injuries caused by product modifications: "we are not inclined to read the common law concept of foreseeability" into the act). Compare Robinson v. Reed–Prentice Div. of Package Machinery Co., 49 N.Y.2d 471, 426 N.Y.S.2d 717, 721, 403 N.E.2d 440, 444 (1980), where the employee was injured when he stuck his hand through a hole in the safety guard cut by the employer:

> The manufacturer's duty, however, does not extend to designing a product that is impossible to abuse or one whose safety features may not be circumvented. A manufacturer need not incorporate safety features into its product so as to guarantee that no harm will come to every user no matter how careless or even reckless [citations]. Nor must he trace his product through every link in the chain of distribution to insure that users will not adapt the product to suit their own unique purposes. The duty of a manufacturer, therefore, is not an open-ended one. It extends to the design and manufacture of a finished product which is safe at the time of sale. Material alterations at the hands of a third party which work a substantial change in the condition in which the product was sold by destroying the functional utility of a key safety feature, however foreseeable that modification may have been, are not within the ambit of a manufacturer's responsibility. Acceptance of plaintiff's concept of duty would expand the scope of a manufacturer's duty beyond all reasonable bounds and would be tantamount to imposing absolute liability on manufacturers for all product-related injuries (see Henderson, Judicial Review of Manufacturer's Conscious Design Choices: The Limits of Adjudication, 73 Col.L.Rev. 1531).
>
> Unfortunately, as this case bears out, it may often be that an injured party, because of the exclusivity of workers' compensation, is barred from commencing an action against the one who exposes him to unreasonable peril by affirmatively rendering a safe product dangerous. However, that an employee may have no remedy in tort against his employer gives the courts no license to thrust upon a third-party manufacturer a duty to insure that its product will not be abused or that its safety features will be callously altered by a purchaser * * *.

Held, judgment for plaintiff reversed. See also Huber v. Niagara Mach. & Tool Works, 430 N.W.2d 465 (Minn.1988) (no duty to warn of danger in removing safety devices). But see Lopez v. Precision Papers, Inc., 107 A.D.2d 667, 484 N.Y.S.2d 585 (1985), aff'd 67 N.Y.2d 871, 501 N.Y.S.2d 798, 492 N.E.2d 1214 (1986), in which a claim was upheld for injuries attributable to the removal of a removable overhead guard on a forklift. The design defect alleged by the plaintiff was the failure to provide an interlock mechanism, that would have been activated by the removal of the guard, preventing the lift from rising above the operator's head.

(2) *Substantial change.* As these decisions show, the courts often examine the modification question in terms of whether the product was "substantially changed" after it left the manufacturer. This derives from Rest. (2d) Torts

§ 402A(b) which provides for liability only if the product "is expected to and does reach the user or consumer without substantial change in the condition in which it is sold." See also caveat (2) and comments *p* and *q*. See, e.g., Temple v. Wean United, Inc., 50 Ohio St.2d 317, 364 N.E.2d 267 (1977) (employer held to have made "substantial change" in punch press by substituting two waist-high buttons in an upward position for the shoulder-level buttons facing outward that had been equipped on the side of the press by the manufacturer; ram descended when stock to be stamped fell on buttons). See generally Soler v. Castmaster, 98 N.J. 137, 484 A.2d 1225 (1984). Unlike *Robinson,* most courts deny effect to even a substantial change unless it was "unforeseeable." See, e.g., *Brown,* supra D.(1); Eck v. Powermatic Houdaille, 364 Pa.Super. 178, 527 A.2d 1012 (1987).

E. **Dangerous use of products by other employees**. Employees hurt one another with industrial machinery in a large variety of ways. A fellow employee's misconduct may or may not supersede the manufacturer's design responsibilities depending on the nature ("foreseeability") of the misconduct and the availability to the manufacturer of a feasible means to prevent it. See Wieder v. Towmotor Corp., 568 F.Supp. 1058 (E.D.Pa.1983), in which a worker left a forklift on an incline and forgot to set the handbrake. Plaintiff was injured when the forklift rolled down the incline and struck him. His theory of liability was that the forklift should have had a passive, "back-up" brake system. *Held,* verdict for plaintiff sustained.

Compare Union Carbide Corp. v. Holton, 136 Ga.App. 726, 222 S.E.2d 105 (1975). Defendant sold plaintiff's employer a cylinder of refrigerant labeled: "This is a no deposit, disposable cylinder. Illegal to refill." After the refrigerant had been used up, other employees refilled it with compressed air for use in blowing out drains. Plaintiff was injured when the cylinder, apparently refilled to an excessive pressure, exploded as he picked it up. "Even if appellant could have foreseen that its disposable cylinders might be reused, it had no control over how they might be refilled, what and how much substance would be used in them, how long they could be safely refilled, and what gauges or release valves should be used on them. No amount of labeling on the original container can instruct the consumer in all aspects of how to safely modify and reuse the cylinders, considering the myriad of conceivable reuses to which such cylinders might be put." Union Carbide Corp. v. Holton, 136 Ga. App. 726, 222 S.E.2d 105 (1975). *Held,* judgment for plaintiff reversed: "It was not the duty of appellant to provide equipment on the cylinder that would make it safe for refilling because it did not sell it for that purpose. It was instead the duty of the person reusing it to make it safe for the purpose for which *he* intended to use it. In effect, appellant had no 'duty to protect the plaintiff against such an intervening cause.' Prosser on Torts, (4th Ed.1971), p. 283."

F. **Doctrine: Shifting responsibility.** Particularly in the industrial setting, a proximate cause sub-doctrine relied upon occasionally in the products liability decisions is the notion that full responsibility for product safety may sometimes be shifted to the employer after the passage of many years and the integration of the product into the employer's operations. See Rest. (2d) of Torts § 452, above.

In Mueller v. Jeffrey Mfg. Co., 494 F.Supp. 275 (E.D.Pa.1980), the plaintiff fell through a three foot square hole in a concrete floor of his employer's foundry building. The opening was part of a sand handling system consisting of a collection of conveyors, elevators and other equipment. Plaintiff's employer had purchased the sand handling equipment and installation design plans (which prescribed the location of the hole) from the defendant, but had done the installation, including the construction of the slab floor and the hole, itself. The plaintiff claimed that the system was defectively designed and that the defendant should have warned of the risk. Relying on § 452, the court stated:

> Particularly where a substantial amount of time intervenes, the overtness of the danger, the nature of the product sold, the identity of the consumer, the relative abilities of the manufacturer and the employer to remedy the alleged defect and the nature and availability of the remedy should be considered as well as any other consideration which comports with the universally accepted policy of assigning and imposing ultimate liability for negligence upon the person primarily responsible therefor. * * *
>
> * * *
>
> * * * In the case at bar the intervention of fifteen years between the date of sale and injury, the atypical nature of the § 402A product and sale, the obvious nature of the danger, the ready ability of the employer to remedy the danger without technical assistance or advice from the manufacturer, the indisputable duty of the employer to keep the workplace safe and the employer's sole possession and control of the equipment for fifteen years created circumstances which shifted the duty from the manufacturer to the employer. As a matter of law, defendant's conduct cannot be said to be the proximate cause of plaintiff's injury. Therefore, defendant's motion for summary judgment will be granted.

494 F.Supp. at 278–79.

7. **Other Party Misconduct.** Although intervening misconduct in products liability cases usually involves parents, doctors, or employers, other parties are sometimes involved. The lawnmower case, *Dugan,* is a good example. Most courts use a foreseeability approach in these cases, too. In Bigbee v. Pacific Tel. & Tel. Co., 34 Cal.3d 49, 192 Cal.Rptr. 857, 665 P.2d 947 (1983), plaintiff was standing in a telephone booth 15 feet from the street when it was struck by a drunken driver. Plaintiff saw the car coming but could not flee because the door jammed. Plaintiff sued various defendants in connection with the design, location, installation, and maintenance of the booth, and the defendants moved to dismiss, arguing that the drunk driver's conduct was a superseding cause. The trial judge dismissed the complaint and plaintiff appealed. *Held,* reversed and remanded: "the risk that a car might hit the telephone booth could be found to constitute one of the hazards to which plaintiff was exposed."

See also Peck v. Ford Motor Co., 603 F.2d 1240, 1244–45 (7th Cir.1979) (plaintiff's vehicle struck rear of defective Ford truck 3 hours after it had stalled and been left by its driver unattended in the highway): Ford's "tort had 'spent its force.' That duty had passed to the driver who was clearly in the best position to prevent further harm." Compare Hill v. General Motors Corp., 637 S.W.2d 382, 386 (Mo.App.1982), in which a Chevrolet Blazer overturned because the owners had modified its suspension system with lifts and installed oversized tires. A suit against GM by two passengers injured in the accident was dismissed by the trial judge. Relying on *Robinson v. Reed–Prentice,* supra, the appellate court upheld the dismissal, ruling that GM had no duty to warn even of a foreseeable risk "that a user will alter its product so as to make it dangerous."

8. **Statutory Reform.** Product alteration is one of the key products liability reform issues. Several of the state reform acts passed in the late 1970s and 1980s have provisions making product alteration a defense to products liability suits. Illustrative are the following:

Kentucky, Prod.Liab.Rep.(CCH) ¶ 91,812:

> *Circumstances under which defendant is liable.*—(1) In any product liability action, a manufacturer shall be liable only for the personal injury, death or property damage that would have occurred if the product had been used in its original, unaltered and unmodified condition. For the purpose of this section, product alteration or modification shall include failure to observe routine care and maintenance, but shall not include ordinary wear and tear. This section shall apply to alterations or modifications made by any person or entity, except those made in accordance with specifications or instructions furnished by the manufacturer.

Tennessee, id. at ¶ 94,417:

> *Alteration of Product.* If a product is not unreasonably dangerous at the time it leaves the control of the manufacturer or seller but was made unreasonably dangerous by subsequent, unforeseeable alteration, change, improper maintenance or abnormal use, the manufacturer or seller is not liable.

Oregon, id. at ¶ 93,813:

> *Defenses.* It shall be a defense to a product liability civil action that an alteration or modification of a product occurred under the following circumstances:
>
> (1) The alteration or modification was made without the consent of or was made not in accordance with the instructions or specifications of the manufacturer, distributor, seller or lessor;
>
> (2) The alteration or modification was a substantial contributing factor to the personal injury, death or property damage; and
>
> (3) If the alteration or modification was reasonably foreseeable, the manufacturer, distributor, seller or lessor gave adequate warning.

Which approach do you think is preferable? How about simply providing that evidence of an alteration is admissible? *Michigan,* id. at ¶ 92,312. How about reducing the plaintiff's damages on a comparative basis, rather than barring recovery altogether, for product alteration or other abuse? *Idaho,* id. at ¶ 91,314.

Or should the legislatures stay out of this area, and leave it to the courts?

WILLIAMS v. RCA CORPORATION

Appellate Court of Illinois, 1978.
59 Ill.App.3d 229, 17 Ill.Dec. 144, 376 N.E.2d 37.

SULLIVAN, PRESIDING JUSTICE. Plaintiff appeals from an order granting a motion to dismiss his complaint, and the propriety of that order is the only question presented on review.

The complaint, sounding in strict tort liability, alleges that plaintiff was employed by an investigative service as a security guard. In connection with his duties, his employer provided him with a two-way portable receiver manufactured by RCA Corporation (defendant). He was assigned the duty of watching a certain restaurant and, when a robbery occurred there, pursuant to his employer's instructions he used the receiver to communicate with automobile patrols in the area to converge and assist him in the apprehension of the offender. Unknown to plaintiff at that time, the receiver did not function—so that his request for assistance was not received and, when he attempted to make the arrest by himself, he was wounded by the robber. The complaint also alleges that there were certain defects in the receiver which rendered it unreasonably dangerous; that these defects existed when the receiver left the control of defendant; and that the defective condition of the receiver was the proximate cause of his having been wounded.

* * *

In its motion to dismiss, as in its brief here, defendant asserts that as a matter of law the shooting was an independent, intervening cause which broke any causal connection between the receiver and plaintiff's injury. Plaintiff argues that defendant "should have foreseen that a security guard would be imperiled if [the receiver] failed to function properly."

* * * An intervening criminal act does not necessarily break the causal connection if that criminal act is probable and foreseeable. (Downs v. Camp (1969), 113 Ill.App.2d 221, 252 N.E.2d 46; Restatement (Second) of Torts § 448 (1965).) Whether an intervening criminal act is foreseeable depends upon the circumstances of the case. Ney v. Yellow Cab Co. (1954), 2 Ill.2d 74, 117 N.E.2d 74.

* * * Foreseeability means that which is objectively reasonable to expect, not what might conceivably occur. Winnett v. Winnett (1974), 57 Ill.2d 7, 12, 310 N.E.2d 1, 5.

The parties have referred us to no case in the United States where a manufacturer has been held liable for injuries from use of a product where a criminal act has intervened, and we have found only one. In Klages v. General Ordinance Equipment Corp. (1976), 240 Pa.Super. 356, 367 A.2d 304, a plaintiff suffered severe gunshot wounds when a mace weapon manufactured by defendant failed to function during a confrontation between plaintiff and an armed robber. The court held that since the product was an instrument of crime prevention, the manufacturer could foresee the specific injuries accruing to a user if the product failed to function and, under those circumstances, the intervening criminal act was not a superseding cause absolving the manufacturer from liability. We view this case as distinguishable on two grounds—(1) the plaintiff in *Klages* brought the action under § 402B of the Restatement (strict liability by misrepresentation) and not § 402A; and (2) that the product in *Klages* was designed to prevent criminal attack, and therefore the manufacturer could reasonably foresee the injury if it did not function. In the instant case, the portable two-way receiver was a product designed for communication purposes, not the prevention of criminal attack, and therefore the purpose and expected result in the manufacture and use of the respective products are inherently different.

* * *

* * * While it might be said that the manufacturer of the two-way receiver could have foreseen that the shooting might conceivably occur, we do not believe its occurrence was objectively reasonable to expect, for the following reasons: (1) Under ordinary circumstances, the manufacturer may reasonably assume that no one will violate the criminal law (Restatement (Second) of Torts § 302B, comment d, at 89 (1965)); (2) the portable two-way receiver is a product designed for short-range, out-of-presence communication between individuals possessing such units and not the prevention of criminal attack; and (3) it cannot fairly be said, under the circumstances here, that the manufacturer should reasonably foresee that the security guard would approach the armed robber before he became aware of the presence of his support—whether or not he had knowledge of the malfunctioning of the receiver.

For the reasons stated, we conclude that the trial court properly found that the intervening criminal act was unforeseeable [as] a matter of law, and we affirm this judgment.

Affirmed.

NOTES

1. Compare Hollenbeck v. Selectone Corp., 131 Ill.App.3d 969, 87 Ill.Dec. 44, 476 N.E.2d 746 (1985), where the plaintiff police officer was issued a mobile pager manufactured by the defendant. Plaintiff tried unsuccessfully to activate the pager to call for assistance to help make an arrest, and he was injured in the course of the arrest. The products liability claims were dismissed by the trial court, and plaintiff appealed. *Held,* dismissal of the § 402B claim reversed and remanded:

> We find that the intervening criminal acts were not so improbable and unforeseeable as to break the causal connection. As the *Williams* court stated, probable and foreseeable means "objectively reasonable to expect." In the instant case, the plaintiff has alleged that the defendant represented that its product was suitable for use by police agencies and that it marketed its product specifically for use by such agencies. It was, therefore, objectively reasonable to expect that [pagers] would be used by police officers in emergency situations where communication by pager was necessary. Given the undisputable fact that one of the critical functions of a police officer is to deal with persons violating the law, it was objectively reasonable to expect that the pager would be utilized in a situation involving a criminal offense. In short, we cannot say, as the court in *Williams* did, that the defendant manufacturer could assume that no one will violate the law.
>
> It was also objectively reasonable to expect that the plaintiff, after activating the pager, would proceed to make the arrest. It is a police officer's duty to apprehend and arrest those violating the law. The

> defendant knew or should have known of this duty when it marketed its product to police departments. Thus, the instant case is distinguishable from *Williams* in that the defendant manufacturer should have foreseen that the plaintiff would act after activating his pager.

476 N.E.2d at 747–48. The concurring judge thought that the case was indistinguishable from *Williams,* such that the *Williams* decision was effectively overruled.

2. In Bellotte v. Zayre Corp., 531 F.2d 1100 (1st Cir.1976), the 5–year–old plaintiff suffered burns when his pajamas caught fire from a match. Believing testimony that his 12–year–old brother had tossed the match on him, the jury in an action against the seller returned a verdict for the defendant. *Held,* affirmed. Although many clothing flammability accidents are caused by children playing with matches, "[t]he deliberate setting afire of a child's pajamas by another would not appear to fall within those acts that ought to be anticipated by a clothing supplier." The court approved the trial court's instruction that such a deliberate act constituted an "absolute defense."

But see d'Hedouville v. Pioneer Hotel Co., 552 F.2d 886 (9th Cir.1977), in which the court applied "the general principle of foreseeability to a case where plaintiff's decedent and 27 others perished in a hotel fire set by an arsonist. *Held,* manufacturer of excessively flammable acrylic fiber used in carpeting not relieved of liability where it "was aware of the danger of fire, knew fires are often the result of arson, and knew that in all likelihood its carpeting would be installed in buildings without sprinkler systems, smoke sensors, or fire alarms, and in multi-story homes lacking the safety features the Pioneer Hotel also lacked." Id. at 894.

Which is right, *Bellotte or dHedouville?* Or are they reconcilable?

3. Crowther v. Ross Chemical & Mfg. Co., 42 Mich.App. 426, 202 N.W.2d 577 (1972), was a defective warnings case against the manufacturer of airplane glue for the deaths of two young girls killed by a person under the effects of "glue sniffing." Plaintiff alleged that defendant knew or should have known that its glue would be sniffed by some users and that sniffers could lose self-control and become insane, thus giving rise to a duty to warn of the dangers involved. Citing to §§ 448 and 449 of the Second Restatement of Torts, the court held that defendant's motion for summary judgment had properly been denied. Section 448 provides that a third person's intentionally tortious or criminal act is a superseding cause, although the defendant's negligence afforded the opportunity for such misconduct, unless the misconduct was a foreseeable risk of the defendant's negligence. Section 449 provides that an intentionally tortious or criminal act is not a superseding cause if the likelihood of such behavior is one of the hazards which makes the actor negligent.

4. Should a dealer, who sells an escaped criminal a used gun, without first obtaining information on the purchaser's identity as required by the federal gun control law, be held liable for the deaths of persons on whom the gun is subsequently used? See Franco v. Bunyard, 261 Ark. 144, 547 S.W.2d 91 (1977). Cf. Hetherton v. Sears, Roebuck & Co., 593 F.2d 526 (3d Cir.1979) (ammunition sold in violation of state law requiring positive identification).

Should the manufacturer of a cheap, small, easily concealed handgun be liable to the victim of a criminal assault? Compare Kelley v. R.G. Industries, 304 Md. 124, 497 A.2d 1143 (1985) (yes) with, e.g., Knott v. Liberty Jewelry & Loan, Inc., 50 Wash.App. 267, 748 P.2d 661 (1988) (no).

Should the manufacturer of an ignition lock system that is particularly easy for a thief to pick be responsible for injuries to a person injured several hours later when his car is hit by the stolen car, driven at the time by a person to whom the thief had given it? See Hampshire v. Ford Motor Co., 155 Mich. App. 143, 399 N.W.2d 36 (1986).

Should the manufacturer of a pharmacy product deliberately contaminated by a third person be liable to the purchaser for failing to seal the product to render it tamper-proof? See Wheeler v. Andrew Jergens Co., 696 S.W.2d 326 (Ky.App.1985). Cf. Elsroth v. Johnson & Johnson, 700 F.Supp. 151 (S.D.N.Y. 1988) (no liability for providing packaging that was merely tamper-resistant, rather than tamper-proof). See Annot., 67 A.L.R.4th 964 (1989).

5. On proximate cause, see generally Fischer, Products Liability—Proximate Cause, Intervening Cause, and Duty, 52 Mo.L.Rev. 547 (1987).

6. **Problems.**

A. Plaintiff is out walking her dog, wearing her trusty whistle (purchased from the local sporting goods store) on a chain around her neck for protection, when a rapist attacks. She blows on the whistle, but it fails to work because the little ball gets stuck in the opening. Should the whistle manufacturer be liable?

B. What if an old person is assaulted at home when the assailant finally breaks into the bedroom 10 minutes after the victim's attempt to phone to a neighbor proves unavailing because a defect in the telephone causes it to be unexpectedly out of order? Should the telephone manufacturer be liable?

Chapter 5

DEFENSES BASED ON PLAINTIFF'S CONDUCT

"[O]ver 2/3 of all injuries related to consumer products have nothing to do with the design or the performance of the product. They relate to the misuse or abuse of the product."

Byington, Chairman, Consumer Product Safety Commission, Trial Magazine 25 (Feb. 1978)

SECTION 1. CONTRIBUTORY AND COMPARATIVE NEGLIGENCE

REED v. CARLYLE & MARTIN, INC.

Supreme Court of Virginia, 1974.
214 Va. 592, 202 S.E.2d 874, cert. denied, 419 U.S. 859, 95 S.Ct. 108, 42 L.Ed.2d 93 (1974).

CARRICO, J., delivered the opinion of the court.

The plaintiff, Grayson C. Reed, was injured when he fell into the moving parts of a piece of farm equipment. He brought [products liability actions against the manufacturer, retailer, and repairer of the equipment. The trial court granted defendants' motions for summary judgment on the basis of plaintiff's contributory negligence, and plaintiff appealed. The question before the court was whether the plaintiff was contributorily negligent as a matter of law.]

The depositions disclose that on September 29, 1970, the date of the accident, the plaintiff, then 50 years of age, was employed as a laborer on a farm owned by Robert L. Hardy in Loudoun County. The plaintiff, in his words, had "always been a farmer."

Shortly before the date in question, Hardy had purchased from the defendant Carlyle & Martin, Inc., of Hagerstown, Maryland, a used ensilage wagon manufactured by the defendant Grove Manufacturing Company of Greencastle, Pennsylvania. The wagon was designed to be pulled by a tractor, from which it also received power to operate its unloading mechanism. In the unloading operation, two moving drag chains carried ensilage forward to the front of the wagon into a pair of exposed beaters—metal rods to which metal spikes were attached. The revolving beaters deposited the ensilage onto a moving conveyor belt, which then discharged the ensilage from the side of the wagon.

After the wagon was brought to the farm, it was loaded with ensilage and towed to a silo. When an attempt was made to unload the wagon, it would not operate properly. The defendant Carlyle & Anderson, Inc., of Purcellville, Virginia, in response to a call from the farm, sent a repairman who examined the wagon and found that the drag chains were broken. He stated that the wagon would have to be unloaded before it could be repaired. He then departed.

The plaintiff and a fellow employee, Edward Moten, towed the wagon to a nearby field with a tractor. Leaving the tractor running and the beaters and conveyor belt in operation, the two employees climbed atop the load of ensilage, estimated to be five feet deep.

Moten proceeded to unload the ensilage by throwing it with a pitchfork from the rear of the wagon. The plaintiff, however, "decided" to throw the ensilage with a pitchfork into the beaters because, in his words, that was the "easiest" and "quickest" way. In unloading the ensilage, which contained "a good bit of sap" and was "right slippery," the plaintiff created a bank, upon which he was standing, sloping toward the beaters. Suddenly, the ensilage under his feet gave way, and he fell into the beaters. Moten, hearing the plaintiff's cry for help, stopped the beaters by turning off the tractor's engine. The plaintiff was injured severely.

The plaintiff testified that although he had not before used a Grove wagon, the type in which he was injured, he had previously worked with a John Deere wagon. The two, he said, were "basically the same." And, when asked if he "had been fully familiar with this type wagon and the way it operated before this accident happened," the plaintiff replied, "Yes, I'd worked with them before." He insisted, however, that he "didn't feel any danger about" working near the beaters.

It is this last bit of testimony, that he "didn't feel any danger about" working near the beaters, upon which the plaintiff places emphasis in his argument that he was not negligent. But the test is not whether the plaintiff actually knew of the danger confronting him, but whether, in the exercise of reasonable care, he should have known he was in a situation of peril. See Budzinski v. Harris, 213 Va. 107, 110, 189 S.E.2d 372, 375 (1972). We think reasonable men would not differ upon the proposition that the plaintiff should have known of his peril.

The plaintiff, an experienced farmer, admitted that he was familiar with the operation of the type ensilage wagon in which he was working. Moreover, the revolving beaters were exposed to his plain view. The danger posed by the turning, spike-like mechanism was, therefore, open and obvious to the plaintiff. In exposing himself to this obvious danger, he failed to exercise reasonable care for his own safety. [Citation.]

* * *

The plaintiff's final argument is that he created a jury issue concerning his negligence by showing that it was the "established custom and usage among farm laborers to use the same or similar procedure" he used in unloading the ensilage wagon. The ready answer to this argument is that the existence of a custom or usage cannot excuse conduct which is otherwise negligent where, as here, the custom or usage itself is not "reasonably safe or adequate for its purpose and occasion."

[Summary judgment for defendants affirmed.]

PARRIS v. M.A. BRUDER & SONS, INC.

United States District Court, Eastern District Pennsylvania, 1966.
261 F.Supp. 406.

LUONGO, DISTRICT JUDGE. This matter is before me on plaintiff's motion for new trial.

Harry Parris, a professional spray painter, sued M.A. Bruder & Sons, Inc. (Bruder) seeking to recover damages for a disabling asthmatic condition allegedly contracted from exposure to fumes or vapors created in the spray application of an epoxy base surface coating product manufactured by Bruder. It is Parris' contention that the product (Ply-tile) was dangerous and that Bruder was negligent in failing to give adequate instructions as to its use and in failing to give warning of the dangers it knew or should have known were involved in the use of the product.

[Through his experts, plaintiff contended that certain ingredients in the Ply–tile were irritants or sensitizers that caused his asthmatic condition. The defendants contended that the plaintiff's failure to use a mask while spray painting was contributory negligence.]

* * *

The jury returned a verdict in favor of the defendant.

Plaintiff's motion for new trial is based almost entirely upon his contention that the question of plaintiff's contributory negligence should not have been submitted to the jury, that contributory negligence is not available as a defense in cases where defendant's negligence consists of a failure to warn. The main support for this very general proposition appears to be a statement from a much cited article, Dillard and Hart, Product Liability: Directions for Use and the Duty To Warn, 41 Va.L.Rev. 145, 163 (1955):

> "Though these time-honored defenses [contributory negligence and assumption of risk] are frequently invoked to defeat recovery, they are theoretically inapplicable when the defendant's breach of duty is based on a failure to warn. To allow these defenses is to indulge in circular reasoning, since usually the plaintiff cannot be said to have assumed a risk of which he was ignorant or to have contributed to his own injury when he had no way of reasonably ascertaining that the danger of injury existed."

The portion of that paragraph which was not quoted by plaintiff reads as follows:

"On the other hand, if the plaintiff knew of the danger from an independent source, the manufacturer's failure to warn would not be the proximate cause of the injury. Nevertheless, many courts hold that the issue of contributory negligence is involved, and is a question for the jury."

* * *

Parris had been a spray painter for more than 20 years. He testified that he was aware that a mask must be worn at all times during spray painting, particularly if the spraying was being done indoors as it was here. Parris' employer furnished for his use a mask together with as many replacement filter cartridges as needed. It was clear that there was substantial risk of harm from spray painting without a mask although the precise nature of the harm was not testified to. There was ample evidence that on a number of occasions, on this and on other job sites, Parris had sprayed without a mask.

It appears to be plaintiff's position that there was a *different* risk of harm from some of the ingredients of Ply-tile than from the use of oil or water base paints, and since plaintiff was unaware of the *specific* risk of harm, he is not chargeable with contributory negligence. This position cannot be sustained. As noted in 2 Harper and James, Torts § 20.5(6) (1956):

"Foreseeability does not mean that the precise hazard or the exact consequences which were encountered should have been foreseen. * * * '[W]hen it is found that a man ought to have foreseen in a general way consequences of a certain kind, it will not avail him to say that he could not foresee the precise course or the full extent of the consequences, being of that kind, which in fact happened.' "

* * * The same principle is applicable in assessing contributory negligence, see Prosser, Torts § 64 (3d ed. 1964); Restatement, Torts 2d §§ 463–64 (1965), and is controlling here. Since there was evidence that plaintiff was aware of risk of harm from failure to wear a mask while spray painting, the defense of contributory negligence became available. It was for the jury to determine whether plaintiff's failure to wear the mask contributed to the harm he sustained.

* * *

[Plaintiff's motion for new trial denied.]

NOTES

1. What result if an asbestos insulation installer or remover failed occasionally to wear his mask and contracted asbestosis, a seriously debilitating lung disorder? What if he knew of the risk of contracting asbestosis, but not the risk of mesothelioma (a particularly lethal form of cancer), and he eventually contracted and died from the latter disease?

2. All forms of imprudent behavior are demonstrated in the cases. See, e.g., Lee v. Crest Chemical Co., 583 F.Supp. 131 (M.D.N.C.1984) (plaintiff failed to wear rubber gloves, contrary to label instructions, and splattered some of defendant's caustic rust stain remover on her hand; defendant's motion for

summary judgment granted, pursuant to statutory provision barring recovery for use of product contrary to instructions); Ford Motor Co. v. Bartholomew, 297 S.E.2d 675 (Va.1982) (gear shift lever, not fully engaged in park, slipped into reverse with motor running; jury's finding of no contributory negligence upheld); J.P.M. & B.M. v. Schmid Laboratories, Inc., 178 N.J.Super. 122, 428 A.2d 515 (1981) (negligent use of condom); Duke v. American Olean Tile Co., 155 Mich.App. 555, 400 N.W.2d 677 (1986) (in slip and fall action against manufacturer of quarry tile used for flooring in fast food restaurant, jury could find that plaintiff was walking unreasonably fast).

3. **Children.** In Porter v. United Steel & Wire Co., 436 F.Supp. 1376 (N.D.Iowa 1977), the 5–year–old plaintiff fell and was injured when she attempted to climb into a grocery shopping cart manufactured by the defendant. *Held,* plaintiff was too young to be contributorily negligent, and the parents' negligence in failing to instruct or supervise the child would not be imputed to her.

Compare Siemer v. Midwest Mower Corp., 286 F.2d 381 (8th Cir.1961), where a 13–year–old child was mowing a lawn with the defendant's rotary power lawn mower. The mower hit a pipe imbedded in the ground that protruded 1¾ inches above ground level. The mower bounced back and over her foot which was injured by the revolving blade. In an action against the manufacturer for failing to guard the rear of the mower, the jury gave verdict for the defendant, and plaintiff appealed. *Held,* affirmed:

> The jury could have found under the evidence that Deanne saw the pipe in question or could have found that she did not look carefully enough or she would have seen it. She had mowed past the pipe three or four times before coming in contact with it. She was aware of the danger of running into such an obstruction.

Id. at 384. Contrast Phillips, Products Liability for Personal Injury to Minors, 56 Va.L.Rev. 1223, 1225 (1970): "The assumption that children will expose themselves to danger in ways that a reasonable adult would not precludes the manufacturer's reliance on the obviousness of the product's danger to the child plaintiff." Should this principle be applied to adult-type products like power lawn mowers, or just to toys? Professor Phillips concludes that "even the best of educational efforts cannot be expected to change the essential nature of children, and, unless we are prepared to ignore this fact, in many instances better product design presents the only realistic means available for protecting children against injuries." Id. at 1240–41. On children and product safety, see generally Field, The Young Consumer: A Paradigm Analysis of the Roles of Public and Private Law in Preventing and Redressing Injuries, 29 Mercer L.Rev. 523 (1978).

4. **Employees.** When a person's job is especially dangerous some courts may " 'lessen the amount of caution required of him by law in the exercise of reasonable care.' " Young v. Aro Corp., 36 Cal.App.3d 240, 111 Cal.Rptr. 535, 537 (1973) (worker knowingly operating grinding wheel at excessive speed killed when wheel exploded). Moreover, the employer's knowledge of a product danger will not be imputed to its workers for purposes of contributory negligence. See Jackson v. Coast Paint & Lacquer Co., 499 F.2d 809 (9th Cir.1974).

5. **Warranty.** Plaintiff purchased some groceries including a Hershey "Mr. Goodbar" at the defendant's food store. When she arrived back home, she sat down in a chair to read the newspaper beside a table on which she placed the candy bar. "While reading, she reached with one hand and took the candy

bar from the table. Without looking, and with one hand, she opened one end of the wrapper and slid the bar partially out from it. Using this one-handed method, she broke off pieces, one after another, and put them into her mouth.

"From the outset she noticed that the bar 'didn't taste just right,' but she assumed this was because she hadn't eaten all day. She had consumed about one-third of the candy bar by the time she bit into a mushy worm. When she looked at the bar, she saw that it was covered with worms and webbing; worms were crawling out of the chocolate and the webbing had little eggs 'hanging onto it.' " Mrs. Kassouf was sickened and suffered a chronic ulcerative colitis as a result of ingesting the contaminated candy.

In an action against the grocery store for breach of warranty of merchantability, the jury returned a verdict for the plaintiff. Defendant appealed the trial court's refusal to instruct the jury that plaintiff had a duty "to take reasonable precautions for her own safety in the handling, inspection, and consumption" of the candy bar. *Held,* affirmed. There is no duty to look at and feel a candy bar prior to biting into it. Kassouf v. Lee Brothers, Inc., 209 Cal.App.2d 568, 26 Cal.Rptr. 276 (1962).

6. The warranty provisions of UCC Article 2 do not speak in terms of "contributory negligence" but instead address the issue as one of scope of warranty or proximate cause. See Erdman v. Johnson Bros. Radio & Television Co., 260 Md. 190, 271 A.2d 744 (1970) (scope of merchantability warranty did not extend to owners' continued use of cantankerous television set which emitted heavy smoke, sparks, and crackling sounds; use of set in such condition, and failure to unplug it before going to bed with knowledge that it sometimes turned itself on, was not "normal" use and supported finding of contributory negligence—defined as using product known to be dangerously defective).

Comment 13 to § 2–314 provides in part: "Action by the buyer following an examination of the goods which ought to have indicated the defect complained of can be shown as matter bearing on whether the breach itself was the cause of the injury."

Section 2–316(3)(b) provides that "when the buyer before entering into the contract has examined the goods * * * as fully as he desired or has refused to examine the goods there is no implied warranty with regard to defects which an examination ought in the circumstances to have revealed to him." Comment 8 explains further that "if the buyer discovers the defect and uses the goods anyway, or if he unreasonably fails to examine the goods before he uses them, resulting injuries may be found to result from his own action rather than proximately from a breach of warranty."

Section 2–715(2)(b) defines "consequential damages" (allowable under § 2–714) to include "injury to person or property proximately resulting from any breach of warranty." Comment 5 provides in part: "Where the injury involved follows the use of goods without discovery of the defect causing the damage, the question of 'proximate' cause turns on whether it was reasonable for the buyer to use the goods without such inspection as would have revealed the defects. If it was not reasonable for him to do so, or if he did in fact discover the defect prior to his use, the injury would not proximately result from the breach of warranty."

7. **Express Warranty.** If the manufacturer warrants the safety of a product, the user's failure to guard against the falsity of the warranty should not bar recovery if an injury results. See Hensley v. Sherman Car Wash Equip.

Co., 33 Colo.App. 279, 520 P.2d 146, 148 (1974) (car wash employee stepped in hole at end of conveyor; equipment manufacturer's information sheet stated that pivoting safety hood "eliminates all possibility of persons stepping into an open pit"): "Contributory negligence is not a defense where plaintiff's conduct only puts the warranty to the test." See also Hansen v. Firestone Tire & Rubber Co., 276 F.2d 254, 258 (6th Cir.1960) ("If the manufacturer chooses to extend the scope of his liability by certifying certain qualities as existent, the negligent acts of the buyer, bringing about the revelation that the qualities do not exist, would not defeat recovery.").

A consumer's negligent reliance on tortious misrepresentations is usually treated as an issue of the justifiability of reliance, sometimes called the right to rely. Cf. Klages v. General Ordinance Equip. Corp., 240 Pa.Super. 356, 367 A.2d 304 (1976).

McCOWN v. INTERNATIONAL HARVESTER CO.

Supreme Court of Pennsylvania, 1975.
463 Pa. 13, 342 A.2d 381.

JONES, CHIEF JUSTICE. Appellant, manufacturer of large over-the-road tractors, was held liable under Section 402A of Restatement (Second) of Torts (1965) for the injuries sustained by the appellee in a one-vehicle accident. The Superior Court affirmed and we granted allocatur limited to the issue of the availability of contributory negligence as a defense to a 402A action.

Appellee was injured while driving a tractor manufactured by appellant. The design of the steering mechanism of the tractor made the vehicle unusually difficult to maneuver. Specifically, twelve to fifteen percent more mechanical effort than that normally expended had to be applied to the steering wheel to accomplish any given turn. Appellee, after driving the vehicle for several hours, stopped for an equipment check on the blacktopped shoulder of the Pennsylvania Turnpike. After completing the inspection the appellee proceeded to reenter the Turnpike.

Unrelated to any steering difficulty appellee struck a guardrail adjoining the shoulder with the right front tire of the tractor. This collision caused the steering wheel to spin rapidly in the direction opposite to the turn. The spokes of the spinning steering wheel struck appellee's right arm, fracturing his wrist and forearm. Evidence adduced at trial indicated that the force and speed of the steering wheel's counterrotation were directly related to the design of the steering mechanism.

For the purposes of this appeal appellant concedes the defect in the steering system's design, but argues that appellee's contributory negligence in colliding with the guardrail should at least be considered in determining appellee's recovery. We disagree and affirm.

In Webb v. Zern, 422 Pa. 424, 220 A.2d 853 (1966), this Court adopted Section 402A of the Restatement and in Ferraro v. Ford Motor

Co., 423 Pa. 324, 223 A.2d 746 (1966), permitted the assertion of assumption of the risk as a defense to a 402A action, citing with approval comment *n* to Section 402A. Today, we complete our acceptance of the principles delineated in comment *n* [1] by rejecting contributory negligence as an available defense in 402A cases.

Appellant's position that contributory negligence should affect 402A liability could have two possible applications. Either contributory negligence should serve to diminish any recovery in an amount adjudged equal to a plaintiff's lack of care or, as in most other tort actions, contributory negligence should be available as a complete defense to liability.

Acceptance of the appellant's first alternative would create a system of comparative assessment of damages for 402A actions. Neither the General Assembly by statute nor this Court by case law has established such a scheme of comparative negligence in other areas of tort law. Without considering the relative merits of comparative negligence, we think it unwise to embrace the theory in the context of an appeal involving Section 402A.[3]

Adoption of contributory negligence as a complete defense in 402A actions would defeat one theoretical basis for our acceptance of Section 402A. "Our courts have determined that a manufacturer by marketing and advertising his products impliedly represents that it is safe for its intended use." Salvador v. Atlantic Steel Boiler Co., 457 Pa. 24, 32, 319 A.2d 903, 907 (1974). Based on that implied representation is the consumer's assumption that a manufacturer's goods are safe. Recognition of consumer negligence as a defense to a 402A action would contradict this normal expectation of product safety. One does not inspect a product for defects or guard against the possibility of product defects when one assumes the item to be safe. The law should not require such inspection or caution when it has accepted as reasonable the consumer's anticipation of safety. We reject contributory negligence as a defense to actions grounded in Section 402A.

Judgment affirmed.

Mr. Justice Roberts did not participate in the consideration or decision of this case.

Mr. Justice Pomeroy filed a concurring opinion.

POMEROY, JUSTICE (concurring).

I agree with the Court that negligence by the plaintiff should not necessarily bar recovery in a products liability action brought pursuant to Section 402A of the Restatement (Second) of Torts; I also agree that

1. The portion of comment *n* relevant to this opinion is as follows:

"Contributory negligence of the plaintiff is not a defense when such negligence consists merely in a failure to discover the defect in the product, or to guard against the possibility of its existence."

3. To initially apply a theory of comparative negligence to an area of the law in which liability is not premised on negligence seems particularly inappropriate.

McCown's conduct in the instant case—misjudging whether the tractor he was driving would clear a guard rail as he was leaving the parking area—should not bar his recovery from the appellant. The purpose of this opinion is to place the Court's decision in what I perceive as its proper perspective.

Contrary to what the opinion of the Court seems to suggest, the answer to the question presented by this appeal is not to be found altogether in the language of Comment [*n*] to Section 402A. Comment *n* provides, on the one hand, that the negligent failure to discover a defect in a product or to guard against the possibility of its existence is not [a] defense to a strict liability action, and, on the other hand, that assumption of risk is a defense. But the conduct of John McCown, the appellee, fits into neither of the above categories. His negligence, if any, was the manner of his operation of an International Harvester tractor. Although Comment *n* is silent with regard to the consequences of negligent use of a product, it points to a resolution of the issue by referring to Section 524 of the Restatement (Second) of Torts. That section provides that in general "the contributory negligence of the plaintiff is not a defense to the strict liability of one who carries on an abnormally dangerous activity." [2] Neither the Comments to Section 524 nor Comment *n* to Section 402A offer a rationale for the application of this rule in products liability cases, but I am satisfied that the elimination of the defense of plaintiff's negligence is in accord not only with the weight of authority in other jurisdictions but also with the policy which underlies the concept of strict liability in tort.

The strict liability of Section 402A is founded in part upon the belief that as between the sellers of products and those who use them, the former are the better able to bear the losses caused by defects in the products involved. See Bialek v. Pittsburgh Brewing Company, 430 Pa. 176, 187 n. 2, 242 A.2d 231, 236 n. 2 (1968); Restatement (Second) of Torts § 402A, Comments c & f. This greater loss-bearing capacity is unrelated to negligence in the manufacture or marketing of products. Indeed, retail and wholesale sellers of chattels are themselves often in no position to discover or avoid defects in their inventories, even by the exercise of a high degree of care. Thus, defendants in Section 402A actions are subjected to liability without regard to fault. It is a proper corollary to this principle that the lesser loss-bearing capacity of product users exists independently of their negligence or lack of it. It follows that such negligence should not ordinarily or necessarily oper-

2. In their treatise on the law of Torts, Professors Harper and James state as follows the rationale for the rule that contributory negligence is not a defense to the strict liability of one engaged in an extrahazardous activity:

> "Society has, in effect, permitted defendant's activity on the condition that he compensate those injured by its peculiar hazards and has thereby transferred some of the duty that protects potential victims from the victims themselves to the entrepreneur. In such a context ordinary questions of negligence on either side of the scale become irrelevant. Human failings like inadvertence are simply part of the setting that makes a toll of the enterprise inevitable." (Footnotes omitted).

2 F. Harper & F. James, The Law of Torts, § 22.7 at 1216–17 (1956).

ate to preclude recovery in a strict liability case. On the other hand, where assumption of risk is involved, the "loss-bearing" policy underlying Section 402A is outweighed by a countervailing policy, one which refuses recovery to persons who consciously expose themselves to known dangers. This policy is deemed stronger than the one, reflected in the normal law of contributory negligence, which denies recovery to individuals whose conduct is merely lacking in due care under the circumstances.

* * *

NOTES

1. In Sheehan v. Anthony Pools, 440 A.2d 1085, 1090–92 (Md.Ct.Spec.App. 1982), the plaintiff was injured when, during a swimming party at his new pool, he fell off the side of the diving board onto the concrete coping of the alcove from which the board projected. The pool was shaped as follows:

In the plaintiff's strict tort action against the swimming pool company, the plaintiff claimed that the non-skid material on the board should have extended to and over the edges of the board and that the design of the pool's diving board-coping area was unsafe. The trial judge denied the defendant's request to instruct the jury that contributory negligence *was* a defense and also denied the plaintiff's request for a charge that the plaintiff's inadvertence in using the board was *not* a defense. The jury returned a verdict for the defendant, and plaintiff appealed:

> In closing argument, * * * Anthony Pools' counsel was permitted, over objection, to argue as follows:
>
> > "You must find that this defect proximately caused the accident. The clear testimony here from Mr. Weiner and using your common sense is that *if someone steps on the board with about an inch of their foot on it, they will fall off the side. That was the proximate cause, the way the board was used, not the design of the board.* I am not willing to concede for a moment that there is anything defective about the board when you use the standards which are customary in the industry and any governmental regulations. Even if you feel there was, I ask you to find that the proximate cause was *the way Mr. Sheehan used it, not the way it was designed.*
> >
> > Mr. Kane, I think, added another element to this as did Mrs. Christinat. *Mr. Kane said he saw the witness taking his arms back.* That describes to me what a witness does in a running event. *What he did is he turned the corner, he got ready, and just went right off the side, and no other design of this board would have prevented that unless perhaps a railing along the side of the board.*
> >
> > He had a little discrepancy in his testimony. He at first said on direct that he didn't teeter. Then I read to him from his

deposition where he said *he teetered*, and I asked him what that meant, and I said, did it mean this, and he just threw his arms up and went off.

Mrs. Christenat said that Mr. Sheehan *turned and talked to someone*. That isn't my testimony, it is their witness. She said he turned to talk to someone on the right of the pool. *That again shows that he wasn't looking where he was going*." (Emphasis added.)

We think there is substance to the Sheehans' claim that the jury was left without guidance on a point of critical importance, i.e., the type of conduct on the part of the consumer in the use of the product which could or could not afford a valid defense to the seller; the prejudicial effect of this omission was compounded when Anthony Pools' counsel was permitted to argue contributory negligence on the part of Mr. Sheehan under the guise of proximate cause.

To begin with, Comment n. to § 402A explicitly states that the contributory negligence of the consumer is *not* a defense in strict liability cases

> "*when such negligence consists merely in a failure to discover the defect in the product, or to guard against the possibility of its existence*. On the other hand the form of contributory negligence which consists in voluntarily and unreasonably proceeding to encounter a known danger, *and commonly passes under the name of assumption of risk, is a defense under this Section* as in other cases of strict liability." (Emphasis added.)

Comment n. then concludes:

> "If the user or consumer discovers the defect and is aware of the danger, and nevertheless proceeds unreasonably to make use of the product and is injured by it, *he is barred from recovery*." (Emphasis added.)

The Restatement definition has been followed in numerous appellate opinions. In a leading case, Cepeda v. Cumberland Engineering Co., Inc., 76 N.J. 152, 386 A.2d 816 (1978), the court stated with respect to Comment n:

> "However, it is implicit in Comment n. and the generality of the cases that *only a limited range of a plaintiff's conduct—not contributory negligence in the sense of mere carelessness or inadvertence—can be a defense to an action for strict liability in tort for injuries sustained as the result of a product defect, particularly if the defect is one of unsafe design*. [Citations.] We agree that acceptance of 'ordinary' contributory negligence as a defense in actions for strict liability in tort would be incompatible with the policy considerations which led to the adoption of strict tort liability in the first instance. [Citation.] *The manufacturer's duty is imposed precisely to avert foreseeable inadvertent injury to a user of a product*. * * *

Id. 386 A.2d at 832.

Held, reversed and remanded: "On the basis of the facts involved and of the Sheehans' specific request, an instruction should have been granted that Mr.

Sheehan's inadvertent or careless use of the diving board and pool would not bar his recovery."

2. Alabama has likened its doctrine of strict liability in tort to negligence per se and has thus held that ordinary contributory negligence—in addition to assumption of risk—acts as a total bar to recovery. Atkins v. American Motors Corp., 335 So.2d 134, 143 (Ala.1976).

3. In a state where contributory negligence bars recovery in strict tort, should a plaintiff who negligently encounters a known risk be barred from recovery against the manufacturer of a product which is defective precisely because of its failure to prevent such negligent encounters? See Bexiga v. Havir Mfg. Co., 60 N.J. 402, 290 A.2d 281 (1972), infra p. 645, where plaintiff's hand was crushed in a punch press:

> * * * We think this case presents a situation where the interests of justice dictate that contributory negligence be unavailable as a defense to either the negligence or strict liability claims.
>
> The asserted negligence of plaintiff—placing his hand under the ram while at the same time depressing the foot pedal—was the very eventuality the safety devices were designed to guard against. It would be anomalous to hold that defendant has a duty to install safety devices but a breach of that duty results in no liability for the very injury the duty was meant to protect against.

290 A.2d at 286. See also Suter v. San Angelo Foundry & Mach. Co., 81 N.J. 150, 406 A.2d 140 (1979). Cf. Rivera v. Westinghouse Elevator Co., 107 N.J. 256, 526 A.2d 705 (1987).

4. **Reform Legislation.** Many states have enacted products liability "reform" statutes providing various defenses based on a plaintiff's misconduct. The conduct is sometimes defined in terms of "reasonable care," which effectively reintroduces contributory negligence as a defense. Arizona's statute, for example, provides a defense for the use of the product contrary to its instructions or warnings "if the injured person knew or with the exercise of reasonable or diligent care should have known of such instructions or warnings." Prod. Liab.Rep. (CCH) ¶ 90,312. Kentucky enacted a contributory negligence defense to products liability actions in 1978, held constitutional in Reda Pump Co. v. Finck, 713 S.W.2d 818 (Ky.1986), but superseded it with a comparative fault act in 1988. Compare id. at ¶ 91,812(3) with ¶ 91,820(1).

5. **Sole Proximate Cause.** The plaintiff's contributory negligence will bar recovery even in strict liability in tort if it is the *sole* proximate cause of the injury. See McCarty v. F.C. Kingston Co., 22 Ariz.App. 17, 522 P.2d 778 (1974). For the sole proximate cause defense in comparative negligence, see p. 551 n. 8, below.

DALY v. GENERAL MOTORS CORP.

Supreme Court of California, 1978.
20 Cal.3d 725, 144 Cal.Rptr. 380, 575 P.2d 1162.

RICHARDSON, JUSTICE. The most important of several problems which we consider is whether the principles of comparative negligence expressed by us in Li v. Yellow Cab Co. (1975) 13 Cal.3d 804, 119 Cal.

Rptr. 858, 532 P.2d 1226, apply to actions founded on strict products liability. We will conclude that they do. * * *

THE FACTS AND THE TRIAL

* * * In the early hours of October 31, 1970, decedent Kirk Daly, a 36–year–old attorney, was driving his Opel southbound on the Harbor Freeway in Los Angeles. The vehicle, while travelling at a speed of 50–70 miles per hour, collided with and damaged 50 feet of metal divider fence. After the initial impact between the left side of the vehicle and the fence the Opel spun counterclockwise, the driver's door was thrown open, and Daly was forcibly ejected from the car and sustained fatal head injuries. It was equally undisputed that had the deceased remained in the Opel his injuries, in all probability, would have been relatively minor.

At trial the jury heard conflicting expert versions as to the functioning of the latch mechanism during the accident. Plaintiffs' principal witness testified that the Opel's door was caused to open when the latch button on the exterior handle of the driver's door was forcibly depressed by some protruding portion of the divider fence. It was his opinion that the exposed push button on the door constituted a design "defect" which caused injuries greatly in excess of those which Daly would otherwise have sustained. * * *

Over plaintiffs' objections, defendants were permitted to introduce evidence indicating that: (1) the Opel was equipped with a seat belt-shoulder harness system, and a door lock, either of which if used, it was contended, would have prevented Daly's ejection from the vehicle; (2) Daly used neither the harness system nor the lock; (3) the 1970 Opel owner's manual contained warnings that seat belts should be worn and doors locked when the car was in motion for "accident security"; and (4) Daly was intoxicated at the time of collision, which evidence the jury was advised was admitted for the limited purpose of determining whether decedent had used the vehicle's safety equipment. After relatively brief deliberations the jury returned a verdict favoring all defendants, and plaintiffs appeal from the ensuing adverse judgment.

STRICT PRODUCTS LIABILITY AND COMPARATIVE FAULT

In response to plaintiffs' assertion that the "intoxication-nonuse" evidence was improperly admitted, defendants contend that the deceased's own conduct contributed to his death. Because plaintiffs' case rests upon strict products liability based on improper design of the door latch and because defendants assert a failure in decedent's conduct, namely, his alleged intoxication and nonuse of safety equipment, without which the accident and ensuing death would not have occurred, there is thereby posed the overriding issue in the case, should comparative principles apply in strict products liability actions?

From its inception, however, strict liability has never been, and is not now, *absolute* liability. * * *

In Li v. Yellow Cab Co., supra, 13 Cal.3d 804, 119 Cal.Rptr. 858, 532 P.2d 1126, we introduced the other doctrine with which we are concerned, comparative negligence. We examined the history of contributory negligence, the massive criticism directed at it because its presence in the slightest degree completely barred plaintiff's recovery, and the increasing defection from the doctrine. * * * [W]e announced in *Li* the adoption of a "pure" form of comparative negligence which, when present, reduced but did not prevent plaintiff's recovery. (Pp. 828–829, 119 Cal.Rptr. 858, 532 P.2d 1126.) We held that the defense of assumption of risk, insofar as it is no more than a variant of contributory negligence, was merged into the assessment of liability in proportion to fault. * * *

We stand now at the point of confluence of these two conceptual streams * * *.

Those counseling against the recognition of comparative fault principles in strict products liability cases vigorously stress, perhaps equally, not only the conceptual, but also the semantic difficulties incident to such a course. The task of merging the two concepts is said to be impossible, that "apples and oranges" cannot be compared, that "oil and water" do not mix, and that strict liability, which is not founded on negligence or fault, is inhospitable to comparative principles. The syllogism runs, contributory negligence was only a defense to negligence, comparative negligence only affects contributory negligence, therefore comparative negligence cannot be a defense to strict liability. * * *

The inherent difficulty in the "apples and oranges" argument is its insistence on fixed and precise definitional treatment of legal concepts. In the evolving areas of both products liability and tort defenses, however, there has developed much conceptual overlapping and interweaving in order to attain substantial justice. The concept of strict liability itself, as we have noted, arose from dissatisfaction with the wooden formalisms of traditional tort and contract principles in order to protect the consumer of manufactured goods. * * *

Furthermore, the "apples and oranges" argument may be conceptually suspect. It has been suggested that the term "contributory negligence," one of the vital building blocks upon which much of the argument is based, may indeed itself be a misnomer since it lacks the first element of the classical negligence formula, namely, a duty of care owing to another. * * *

We think, accordingly, the conclusion may fairly be drawn that the terms "comparative negligence," "contributory negligence" and "assumption of risk" do not, standing alone, lend themselves to the exact measurements of a micrometer-caliper, or to such precise definition as to divert us from otherwise strong and consistent countervailing policy considerations. Fixed semantic consistency at this point is less important than the attainment of a just and equitable result. The interweaving of concept and terminology in this area suggests a judicial posture that is flexible rather than doctrinaire.

We pause at this point to observe that where, as here, a consumer or user sues the manufacturer or designer alone, technically, neither fault nor conduct is really compared functionally. The conduct of one party in combination with the product of another, or perhaps the placing of a defective article in the stream of projected and anticipated use, may produce the ultimate injury. In such a case, as in the situation before us, we think the term "equitable apportionment or allocation of loss" may be more descriptive than "comparative fault."

* * * We imposed strict liability against the manufacturer and in favor of the user or consumer in order to relieve injured consumers "from *problems of proof* inherent in pursuing negligence * * * and warranty * * * remedies, * * * " [Citations.] As we have noted, we sought to place the burden of loss on manufacturers rather than " * * * injured persons *who are powerless to protect themselves* * * *." [Citations.]

The foregoing goals, we think, will not be frustrated by the adoption of comparative principles. Plaintiffs will continue to be relieved of proving that the manufacturer or distributor was negligent in the production, design, or dissemination of the article in question. Defendant's liability for injuries caused by a defective product remains strict. The principle of protecting the defenseless is likewise preserved, for plaintiff's recovery will be reduced *only* to the extent that his own lack of reasonable care contributed to his injury. The cost of compensating the victim of a defective product, albeit proportionately reduced, remains on defendant manufacturer, and will, through him, be "spread among society." However, we do not permit plaintiff's own conduct relative to the product to escape unexamined, and as to that share of plaintiff's damages which flows from his own fault we discern no reason of policy why it should, following *Li,* be borne by others. Such a result would directly contravene the principle announced in *Li,* that loss should be assessed equitably in proportion to fault.

* * *

A second objection to the application of comparative principles in strict products liability cases is that a manufacturer's incentive to produce safe products will thereby be reduced or removed. While we fully recognize this concern we think, for several reasons, that the problem is more shadow than substance. First, of course, the manufacturer cannot avoid its continuing liability for a defective product even when the plaintiff's own conduct has contributed to his injury. The manufacturer's liability, and therefore its incentive to avoid and correct product defects, remains; its exposure will be lessened only to the extent that the trier finds that the victim's conduct contributed to his injury. Second, as a practical matter a manufacturer, in a particular case, cannot assume that the user of a defective product upon whom an injury is visited will be blameworthy. * * * Finally, we must observe that under the present law, which recognizes assumption of risk as a complete defense to products liability, the curious and cynical message is that it profits the manufacturer to make his product so defective that in the event of injury he can argue that the user had to be aware of its patent defects. To that extent the incentives are inverted. We conclude, accordingly, that no substantial or significant impairment of the safety incentives of defendants will occur by the adoption of comparative principles.

* * *

A third objection to the merger of strict liability and comparative fault focuses on the claim that, as a practical matter, triers of fact, particularly jurors, cannot assess, measure, or compare plaintiff's negligence with defendant's strict liability. We are unpersuaded by the argument and are convinced that jurors are able to undertake a fair apportionment of liability.

* * *

We note that the majority of our sister states which have addressed the problem, either by statute or judicial decree, have extended comparative principles to strict products liability.

Our research discloses that of the more than 30 states which have adopted some form of comparative negligence, three (including California) have done so judicially. The two other states, Alaska (Butaud v. Suburban Marine & Sport. Goods, Inc., supra, 555 P.2d 42, 46) and Florida (West v. Caterpillar Tractor Company, Inc., supra, 336 So.2d 80, 89–90) have likewise, judicially, extended comparative principles to strict liability actions. At least five states have adopted comparative fault statutes which are not limited in their language to negligence actions: Arkansas (Ark.Rev.Stat. §§ 27–1763–65 (1975); Maine (M.S.A., tit. 14, § 156 (1965)); Mississippi (3 Miss.Code Ann. § 11–7–15 (1917); New York (CPLR, art. 14A, § 1411 (1975)); and Rhode Island (2A R.I. Gen.Laws, § 9–20–4 (1971)). The New York statute expressly applies to strict liability actions. (See CPLR, supra, art. 14A, § 1411, Practice Commentaries, C 1411:1.) The Mississippi statute has been judicially construed as extending to suits founded on strict products liability. (Edwards v. Sears, Roebuck and Company (5th Cir.1975) 512 F.2d 276, 290.) On the other hand one state, Connecticut, has statutorily prohibited the use of comparative fault as a defense in strict liability actions. (Pub.L. 77–335, eff. July 1, 1977.)

Of the three decisions which have declined to apply comparative negligence to strict liability, two have noted their reliance on state comparative negligence statutes which are expressly confined to "negligence" actions. (Melia v. Ford Motor Co. (8th Cir.1976) 534 F.2d 795, 802 [Nebraska "slight-gross" comparative negligence statute]; Kirkland v. General Motors Corporation (Okla.1974) 521 P.2d 1353, 1367–1368 [noting the limiting statutory language but holding that driving while intoxicated was product misuse barring recovery]; see also Kinard v. The Coats Company, Inc. (Colo.App.1976) 553 P.2d 835, 837.) At least three jurisdictions have applied comparative negligence statutes to strict liability actions, despite language arguably limiting the statute application to negligence. (Dippel v. Sciano, supra, 37 Wis.2d 443, 155 N.W.2d 55, 64; Sun Val. Airlines, Inc. v. Avco–Lycoming Corp. (D.Idaho 1976) 411 F.Supp. 598, 602–603; Hagenbuch v. Snap–On Tools Corp. (D.N.H.1972) 339 F.Supp. 676, 681–683.) * * *

Moreover, we are further encouraged in our decision herein by noting that the apparent majority of scholarly commentators has urged adoption of the rule which we announce herein. [Citations.]

We find additional significance in the provisions of the proposed Uniform Comparative Fault Act (Act), authored by Professor Wade * * * We quote portions of section 1 of the proposed Act: "Section 1. [Effect of Contributory Fault.] [¶] (a) In an action based on fault to recover damages for injury or death to person or harm to property, any contributory fault chargeable to the claimant diminishes proportionately the amount awarded as compensatory damages for an injury attributable to the claimant's contributory fault, but does not bar recovery * * *. [¶] (b) 'Fault' includes acts or omissions that are in any measure negligent or reckless toward the person or property of the actor or others, *or that subject a person to strict tort liability.*" (Italics added.) * * *

Having examined the principal objections and finding them not insurmountable, and persuaded by logic, justice, and fundamental fairness, we conclude that a system of comparative fault should be and it is hereby extended to actions founded on strict products liability. In such cases the separate defense of "assumption of risk," to the extent that it is a form of contributory negligence, is abolished. While * * * the term "equitable apportionment of loss" is more accurately descriptive of the process, nonetheless, the term "comparative fault" has gained such wide acceptance by courts and in the literature that we adopt its use herein.

For the guidance of trial courts, we do note the existence, under rule 49(a), Federal Rules of Civil Procedure, of a form of special verdict tailored to cases applying the maritime doctrine of strict liability for unseaworthiness * * *. Under this form, the jury is first required to answer "yes" or "no" to a series of questions setting forth possible bases for a finding that vessel unseaworthiness was a proximate cause of the plaintiff's injuries. If the jury indicates that unseaworthiness was a contributing cause, it then moves on to a second group of similar questions seeking to determine whether, and in what particulars, the plaintiff's own negligence was also a contributing factor. If the answers to these questions establish a finding of contributory negligence, the jury is told to "state in percentage the extent to which the plaintiff's own negligence contributed to his injuries. (___%)." Finally, the jury is instructed to indicate the amount of plaintiff's damages *without reference* to his own negligence. The *court* then reduces the damage award by the percentage figure the jury has supplied. [Citations.] We cite this form as illustrative of one technique by which the court and jury may approach the task of apportionment.

[The court held that its ruling on comparative fault would be applied prospectively only, but it reversed the judgment because the intoxication and seat belt nonuse evidence was inadmissible under the then-prevailing law.]

TOBRINER, CLARK and MANUEL, JJ., concur.

CLARK, JUSTICE, concurring.

* * *

[I prefer] a uniform index factor, such as 30, 50 or 70 percent[.] A uniform discount of the negligent plaintiff's recovery would eliminate the necessity of the often impossible task of comparing fault. A discount system would bring about consistency and predictability where neither now exists, permitting evaluation and settlement of claims.

* * *

JEFFERSON, JUSTICE, concurring and dissenting.

* * *

I consider the majority conclusion a case of wishful thinking and an application of an impractical, ivory-tower approach. The majority's assumption that a jury is capable of making a fair apportionment between a plaintiff's negligent conduct and a defendant's defective product is no more logical or convincing than if a jury were to be instructed that it should add a quart of milk (representing plaintiff's negligence) and a metal bar three feet in length (representing defendant's strict liability for a defective product), and that the two added together equal 100 percent—the total fault for plaintiff's injuries * * *. * * *

* * *

[T]he percentage assessed will represent nothing more substantial or reasonable than that which results from the application of the jurors' instincts, speculations, conjectures and guesses.

* * *

The guessing game that will be imposed on juries by the application of comparative negligence principles to defective product liability cases will be further enhanced in those cases in which several defendants are joined in an action—some being sued on a negligence theory and others on the defective product theory and where there are several plaintiffs whose conduct may range from no negligence at all to varying degrees of negligence. The jury will be required to determine percentages of fault with respect to all the parties (and perhaps some nonparties) by seeking to compare and evaluate the *conduct* of certain parties with the *product* of other parties to produce 100 percent of fault * * *.

With all due deference to the scholarly analysis and discussion found in the majority opinion, I must conclude, nevertheless, that the majority's view constitutes a glaring failure to appreciate the limitations on, and the realities of, our jury trial system. * * * There is no common denominator by which factors such as pounds, circles, quarts, triangles, inches, and squares can be added together for a total so that a determination can be made of the percentage contribution of each to the total. * * *

* * *

It appeals to my sense of reason, justice and equity that we continue the existing legal principle which permits manufacturers to spread through society the costs of compensating injured plaintiffs *fully,* rather than the adoption of an untenable legal principle which will result in *reducing* the total costs to be spread by manufacturers, but at the expense of injured plaintiffs by reducing their recovery *below* the full losses sustained through the necessarily fortuitous, conjectural and haphazard determinations to be made by juries.

[ROSE] BIRD, C.J., concurs.

MOSK, JUSTICE, dissenting.

I dissent.

This will be remembered as the dark day when this court, which heroically took the lead in originating the doctrine of products liability (Greenman v. Yuba Power Products, Inc. (1963) 59 Cal.2d 57, 27 Cal. Rptr. 697, 377 P.2d 897) and steadfastly resisted efforts to inject concepts of negligence into the newly designed tort (Cronin v. J.B.E. Olson Corp. (1972) 8 Cal. 121, 104 Cal.Rptr. 433, 501 P.2d 1153), inexplicably turned 180 degrees and beat a hasty retreat almost back to square one. The pure concept of products liability so pridefully fashioned and nurtured by this court for the past decade and a half is reduced to a shambles.

The majority inject a foreign object—the tort of negligence—into the tort of products liability by the simple expedient of calling negligence something else: on some pages their opinion speaks of "comparative fault," on others reference is to "comparative principles," and elsewhere the term "equitable apportionment" is employed, although this is clearly not a proceeding in equity. But a rose is a rose[!] and negligence is negligence * * *.

* * *

Transferring the liability, or part of the liability, from the party responsible for putting the article in the stream of commerce to the consumer is precisely what the majority propose to do. They do this by employing a euphemism: the victim's recovery is to be "proportionately reduced." The result, however delicately described, is to dilute the defect of the article by elevating the conduct of the wounded consumer to an issue of equal significance. * * *

* * *

The defective product is comparable to a time bomb ready to explode; it maims its victims indiscriminately, the righteous and the evil, the careful and the careless. Thus when a faulty design or otherwise defective product is involved, the litigation should not be diverted to consideration of the negligence of the plaintiff. The liability issues are simple: was the product or its design faulty, did the defendant inject the defective product into the stream of commerce, and did the defect cause the injury? The conduct of the ultimate consumer-victim who used the product in the contemplated or foreseeable manner is wholly irrelevant to those issues.

* * *

The majority deny their opinion diminishes the therapeutic effect of products liability upon producers of defective products. [Yet] the motivation to avoid polluting the stream of commerce with defective products increases in direct relation to the size of potential damage awards.

In sum, I am convinced that since the negligence of the defendant is irrelevant in products liability cases, the negligence—call it contributory or comparative—of the plaintiff is also irrelevant. The majority, by considering the comparative negligence of a plaintiff in an action in which defendant's negligence is not an issue, apply an untenable double standard. Their error is grievously unsettling to the law of torts. More significantly, this decision seriously erodes the pattern of the law which up to now reflected a healthy concern for consumers victimized by defective products placed on the market in this mechanized age through the dynamics of mass production, national and international distribution, and psychologically subtle marketing.

* * *

COULTER v. AMERICAN BAKERIES COMPANY

District Court of Appeal of Florida, 1988.
530 So.2d 1009.

WIGGINTON, J.

This appeal is from a jury verdict and final judgment awarding damages in a products liability action which damages were reduced due to the jury's finding of comparative negligence. The issue presented is whether the trial court erred in allowing the defendant/appellee to raise comparative negligence as a defense and by instructing the jury on comparative negligence. We reverse.

The uncontroverted evidence presented at trial revealed that appellant had purchased doughnuts manufactured by appellee and sealed in their original package. She opened the package in her automobile and in the course of driving to her destination consumed several pieces of one doughnut by breaking them off with her fingers and popping them into her mouth. Because of an abscessed tooth and sore jaw, instead of chewing the doughnut with her teeth appellant would sip milk through a straw allowing the doughnut to dissolve in her mouth. In fact, it was the dissolving nature of the doughnut which had prompted appellant to purchase that particular product. Shortly after she began consuming the doughnut, she felt something stick in her throat and immediately ceased ingestion. It was later discovered through x-rays the same day that appellant had consumed a piece containing a metal wire and causing her subsequent injury.

A complaint was filed alleging breach of implied warranty in that the doughnuts were unfit for human consumption. Appellee asserted the affirmative defense of comparative negligence, alleging that appellant was negligent in the manner in which she had consumed the doughnut by not "chewing" it. At trial, appellant objected to a proposed instruction on comparative negligence which objection was overruled.

The jury returned a verdict in favor of appellant awarding $12,500 in damages. However, based on the instruction on comparative negligence, the jury assessed negligence against appellant in the amount of 80 percent, thereby reducing her damages to $2,500.

It is settled that comparative negligence is a defense in an implied warranty action. West v. Caterpillar Tractor Company, Inc., 336 So.2d 80 (Fla.1976); Coleman v. American Universal of Florida, Inc., 264 So. 2d 451 (Fla. 1st DCA 1972). However, it is equally settled that where there is no evidence tending to prove comparative negligence, the issue should not be submitted to the jury. [Citation.]

In a breach of an implied warranty action based on the presence of a harmful substance in food, the test of whether the presence of the harmful substance constitutes a breach of implied warranty is whether the consumer can reasonably expect to find the substance in the food as served. [Citation.] Moreover, when asserting the defense of comparative negligence in an implied warranty action, the issue pertains to the misuse of the product as opposed to the failure to discover or guard against a defect. Coleman v. American Universal of Florida, Inc., 264 So.2d at 453–54.

Applying the foregoing to the instant case, there was simply no evidence that appellant could have expected to find a wire in the doughnut or that she used the doughnut in an abnormal, unintended, or unforeseen way. Indeed, appellant was essentially protecting herself—that is, her abscessed tooth—as best she could by choosing a doughnut that was soft and could easily dissolve with the milk. In that sense, by her use of the milk she was "chewing" the doughnut. Consequently, there being no evidence tending to prove comparative negligence, the trial court erred in submitting the issue to the jury. [Reversed and remanded for entry of judgment for full amount of the damages.]

NOTES

1. Justice Richardson suggests that a change in labels from "comparative fault" to something like "equitable apportionment of loss" might help to allay concerns over the apparent inconsistency of mixing apples and oranges, defectiveness and contributory negligence. Do you agree? Are additional problems with the entire scheme highlighted by the new label? How about "comparative causation"? See Butaud v. Suburban Marine & Sporting Goods, Inc., 555 P.2d

42, 47 (Alaska 1976) (Rabinowitz, J., concurring); Duncan v. Cessna Aircraft Co., 665 S.W.2d 414, 427 (Tex.1984): "We choose comparative *causation* instead because it is conceptually accurate in cases based on strict liability and breach of warranty theories in which the defendant's 'fault,' in the traditional sense of culpability, is not at issue."

2. Many courts have followed the *Daly* approach of applying comparative fault principles to strict tort actions, reducing a plaintiff's damages in proportion to his fault. See, e.g., Coney v. J.L.G. Industries, 97 Ill.2d 104, 73 Ill.Dec. 337, 454 N.E.2d 197 (1983); Kaneko v. Hilo Coast Processing, 65 Hawaii 447, 654 P.2d 343 (1982); Duncan v. Cessna Aircraft Co., 665 S.W.2d 414 (Tex.1984). Other courts have disagreed, refusing to reduce a plaintiff's damages on account of his negligence in strict tort actions. See, e.g., Bowling v. Heil Co., 31 Ohio St.3d 277, 511 N.E.2d 373 (1987); Lippard v. Houdaille Industries, 715 S.W.2d 491 (Mo.1986); Staymates v. ITT Holub Industries, 364 Pa.Super. 37, 527 A.2d 140 (1987).

Comparative negligence statutes generally provide that the parties' "negligence" or "fault" are to be compared, and the courts have split on whether such language covers *strict* liability actions. Louisiana has adopted a functional approach, applying comparative fault where it will encourage product users to be more careful, but not where manufacturers need to be encouraged to make safer products. Bell v. Jet Wheel Blast, 462 So.2d 166, 171–72 (La.1985).

Daly and *Coulter* were decided in jurisdictions with "pure" comparative fault, where a plaintiff is entitled to recover (diminished damages) even if his fault exceeded that of the defendant(s). Most states instead have some form of "modified" comparative fault, permitting recovery only if the plaintiff's fault was less than (or, in other states, less than or equal to) the defendant's. In such states, the plaintiff who is more at fault will be barred from recovering any damages whatsoever.

3. **Warranty.** The courts have also split on whether comparative fault applies to warranty actions. See generally H. Woods, Comparative Fault §§ 14:16, 14:17 (2d ed. 1987). Are the arguments pro and con entirely the same as in strict tort? Are the arguments the same in implied warranty as in express warranty?

4. **Failure to Discover a Defect or Guard Against Its Existence.** Suppose that for several weeks prior to total steering failure on plaintiff's car, the steering had been causing difficulty, yet plaintiff had failed to have it checked. Should plaintiff's award be reduced on this account? See generally Busch v. Busch Const. Inc., 262 N.W.2d 377, 394 (Minn.1977) ("a consumer's negligent failure to inspect a product or to guard against defects is not a defense and thus may not be compared with a distributor's strict liability"). Would Justice Richardson agree?

Like *Coulter,* some courts that generally apply comparative fault to strict liability and warranty actions refuse to reduce a plaintiff's damages for this form of negligence. See also Simpson v. General Motors Corp., 108 Ill.2d 146, 90 Ill.Dec. 854, 856, 483 N.E.2d 1, 3 (1985) ("consumer's unobservant, inattentive, ignorant, or awkward failure to discover or guard against a defect should not be compared as a damage-reducing factor").

5. Why do you suppose the *Coulter* jury assigned 80% of the fault to the plaintiff?

6. Some examples of comparative fault in application include Busch v. Busch Const., Inc., 262 N.W.2d 377 (Minn.1977) (defect causing steering to lock,

85%; plaintiff's negligent failure to apply brakes thereafter, 15%); West v. Caterpillar Tractor Co., Inc., 336 So.2d 80 (Fla.1976) (road construction grading machine with poor rear visibility, no rear view mirrors, and no audible warning system for operating in reverse, 65%; failure to maintain proper lookout around such a machine, 35%); Blaw-Knox Food & Chemical Equip. Corp. v. Holmes, 348 So.2d 604 (Fla.App.1977) (tendency of rotating flow wheel shaft to pop out of bearing in potato chip cooker kettle, 52%; Frito Lay employee's attempt to replace shaft manually while standing on board placed across kettle of hot oil, and slipping in, 48%); Delisa v. Stewart Agency, Inc., 515 So.2d 426 (Fla.App.1987) (defective seat belts, 40%; riding with intoxicated driver, knowing seat belts did not work, 60%).

7. Multiple parties multiply the problems. As plaintiff attempted to exit from the rear seat of an automobile driven by D–1 and manufactured by D–2, her foot caught in the safety belt causing her to fall. She sued D–1, for negligently failing to turn the light on, and D–2, for defective design. The jury apportioned total causal negligence as follows: 50% to plaintiff; 25% to D–1; and 25% to D–2. The Vermont comparative negligence statute provided in part: "Contributory negligence shall not bar recovery * * * if the negligence was not greater than the causal negligence of the defendant * * *." *Held,* since plaintiff's negligence exceeded that of the defendants individually, plaintiff could not recover against either one. Stannard v. Harris, 135 Vt. 544, 380 A.2d 101 (1977). Cf. Cartel Capital Corp. v. Fireco of New Jersey, 81 N.J. 548, 410 A.2d 674 (1980), (restaurant owner 41% at fault for allowing paper plates to fall on grill; retailer-installer of fire sprinkler system 30% at fault for inserting screw in wrong place in the activating handle mechanism; manufacturer 29% at fault for designing system presenting risk that installer would make such a mistake).

8. **Sole Proximate Cause.** As with contributory negligence, n. 5 supra p. 540, at least one court has held that a plaintiff's fault may be the sole proximate cause of an accident, even in a comparative fault jurisdiction. Kroon v. Beech Aircraft Corp., 628 F.2d 891 (5th Cir.1980) (2–1) (Fla. law) (pilot attempted to take off without removing gust lock pin from steering control column).

9. Among the many articles on comparative fault in products liability litigation, see, e.g., Leff & Pinto, Comparative Negligence in Strict Products Liability: The Courts Render the Final Judgment, 89 Dick.L.Rev. 915 (1985); Woods, The Trend Toward Comparative Fault, 7 J.Prod.Liab. 399 (1984); Thode, Some Thoughts on the Use of Comparisons in Products Liability Cases, 1981 Utah L.Rev. 3; Westerbeke & Meltzer, Comparative Fault and Strict Products Liability in Kansas: Reflections on the Distinction Between Initial Liability and Ultimate Loss Allocation, 28 Kan.L.Rev. 25 (1979); Fischer, Products Liability—Applicability of Comparative Negligence, 43 Mo.L.Rev. 431 (1978); Wade, Products Liability and Plaintiff's Fault—The Uniform Comparative Fault Act, 29 Mercer L.Rev. 373 (1978); Twerski, The Use and Abuse of Comparative Negligence in Products Liability, 10 Ind.L.Rev. 797 (1977); Schwartz, Strict Liability and Comparative Negligence, 42 Tenn.L.Rev. 171 (1974). See also V. Schwartz, Comparative Negligence ch. 12 (2d ed. 1986); H. Woods, Comparative Fault ch. 14 (2d ed. 1987).

SECTION 2. ASSUMPTION OF RISK

MORAN v. RAYMOND CORP.

United States Court of Appeals, Seventh Circuit, 1973.
484 F.2d 1008, cert. denied, 415 U.S. 932, 94 S.Ct. 1445, 39 L.Ed.2d 490 (1974).

PELL, CIRCUIT JUDGE. Defendant, The Raymond Corporation (Raymond), appeals from a judgment for $250,000.00 entered on a jury verdict in favor of plaintiff, Juan Moran, on his complaint for personal injuries he had allegedly received while he was an employee of Central Steel and Wire Company (Central).

Raymond manufactured a lift truck, known as a sideloader, which was designed to operate in narrow aisles. It differs from the standard fork lift truck, on which the load is carried fully beyond the front wheels in that, as the name sideloader indicates, the load-lifter is located on one side of the equipment and extends equidistant over the front and rear sets of wheels. At one end of the equipment there is located an operator's cage with the controls inside. Moran had operated a sideloader at Central for approximately three months. On the night in question, he was in the process of returning a tray to a rack approximately eight or nine feet above the ground when some wire rods on the tray slipped therefrom. In attempting to correct this situation, Moran left the operator's cage and first stood on the movable forks and eventually on a platform below the forks. Still not achieving the desired result, he attempted to lower the forks but rather than returning to the cage and while standing on the platform on the lift side of the equipment, he reached through an opening into the cage and pulled the control lever to lower the forks. Although he tried to bring his hand back quickly, it became stuck because of a bandage he had on his wrist. When the cross bar came down with a shearing action, Moran's right arm was seriously injured.

Moran's complaint was based on both negligence and strict liability theories. Among Raymond's defenses were that the lift truck was not defectively manufactured (and therefore could not be the basis of a strict liability in tort claim), that Moran had assumed the risk, and that Moran had misused the sideloader so as to bar recovery as a matter of law. The jury rejected all of the defenses and answered special interrogatories finding no assumption of the risk or misuse.

* * *

We do not have to determine whether Raymond is correct in its contention that its lift truck was not "defective" as that term is used to invoke the doctrine of strict liability in tort actions since we find it clear * * * that Moran assumed the risk. The Illinois Supreme Court adopted the doctrine of strict liability in tort in Suvada v. White Motor Co., 32 Ill.2d 612, 210 N.E.2d 182 (1965). In Williams v. Brown Manufacturing Co., 45 Ill.2d 418, 261 N.E.2d 305 (1970), the court held that simple contributory negligence, which would bar recovery by a plaintiff in a tort action based on negligence, would not preclude recovery in a suit based on a strict liability theory, 45 Ill.2d at 426, 261 N.E.2d 305.

The court held, however, "that a plaintiff who knows a product is in a dangerous condition and proceeds in disregard of this known danger (often termed 'assumption of risk') may not recover for resulting injuries." 45 Ill.2d at 426, 261 N.E.2d at 309.[2] The test which the jury was to apply was

> "* * * whether a user has assumed the risk of using a product known to be dangerously defective is fundamentally a subjective test, in the sense that it is *his* knowledge, understanding and appreciation of the danger which must be assessed, rather than that of the reasonably prudent person (Restatement (Second) of Torts, § 496D, comment (c)), it must also be remembered that this is ordinarily a question to be determined by the jury. That determination is not to be made solely on the basis of the user's own statements but rather upon the jury's assessment of all of the facts established by the evidence. No juror is compelled by the subjective nature of this test to accept a user's testimony that he was unaware of the danger, if, in the light of all of the evidence, he could not have been unaware of the hazard (Restatement (Second) of Torts, § 496D, comments (d) and (e)); and the factors of the user's age, experience, knowledge and understanding, as well as the obviousness of the defect and the danger it poses, (Wade, Strict Tort Liability of Manufacturers, 19 Sw.L.J. 5 (1965), see Pitts v. Basile, 35 Ill.2d 49, 219 N.E.2d 472) will all be relevant to the jury's determination of the issue, if raised." 45 Ill.2d at 430–431, 261 N.E.2d at 312. (Emphasis in original.) * * *

Although the test of assumption of risk is a subjective one, depending on the knowledge of the injured party, it is apparent that the question need not always go to the jury. The language in *Williams,* supra, that the defense of assumption of the risk ordinarily presents a question to be determined by the jury while permitting the jury to disbelieve the injured party's testimonial denial of knowledge of the danger, even though the test is a subjective one, does not mean that a jury question is presented when the testimony is clear that he did know of the danger.

In Fore v. Vermeer Manufacturing Co., 7 Ill.App.3d 346, 287 N.E.2d 526 (3d Dist., 1972), the court affirmed the grant of summary judgment against the plaintiff when the plaintiff admitted in his deposition that he had had numerous past difficulties with the machine: "It appears to be clear that the plaintiff had actual knowledge of the danger; that he

2. The court also held that "plaintiffs who 'misuse' a product—use it for a purpose neither intended nor 'foreseeable' (objectively reasonable) by the defendant—may be barred from recovery." 45 Ill.2d at 425, 261 N.E.2d at 309.

understood and appreciated the risk, and that he deliberately exposed himself to such risk, all while he was of full age, well experienced, with complete knowledge and understanding of an obvious defect, and an obvious danger." 287 N.E.2d at 527–528. * * *

If we now turn to Moran's own testimony and apply the Illinois standards for assumption of the risk, it becomes clear that Moran, on the testimony in this record, assumed the risk. Moran testified that he had been working at Central for approximately five months at the time of the accident. During the first two months he did not drive a sideloader. During the next three months, following a week of training including how to operate the machine, he had filled many orders daily, all with the help of a Raymond sideloader. Although at one point he testified that he had never been told not to operate the machine from outside the driver's cage, he later admitted that he had been instructed to stand in the cage "when you are operating the controls." He clearly knew that there was a substantial risk involved in working with the machine. Particularly, however, and most significantly, he recognized the danger in operating the machine in the way he was at the time he was injured since he testified that he knew the bar would hit him if he did not move out of the way: "That's why I pulled the control fast and I withdrew the hand quickly." The bar was about a foot and a half above his head when he pulled the lever to lower the forks.

While one who stands under the guillotine blade with knowledge of the fact that there will be a descent of the operational part upon activation of the controlling lever would scarcely seem to be in a position to claim that the blade fell faster than he anticipated, nevertheless, we find no support in the record for Moran's contention that the lowering speed of the sideloader he had been operating for several hours at the time of the accident was greater than was that of the sideloader he had previously operated.

By way of summary, Moran, standing out of the operator's cage in a position where he would be in the path of the equipment if it was caused to become operative, reached with some effort on his part into the control area and pulled the control lever down as far as it would go. He knew when he did that, the forks would start coming down and would go all the way to the bottom unless he pushed the lever back. This was clearly proven subjective evidence and the verdict * * * cannot stand. Plaintiff argues that "[t]o say that Juan Moran consciously assumed the risk of his own injury would, under the circumstances, be to say that he intended to maim himself, or he was bent upon suicide." This conclusion does not follow. What is clear is that Moran was in a hurry and that he took a calculated risk that he could get his hand out of the way before the forks hit him. Workmen often take risks which they should not take and are fortunate enough to avoid injury. In finding that Moran assumed the risk, we are not dealing with the waiver of a constitutional right designed to protect fair trial, *cf.* Schneckloth v. Bustamonte, 412 U.S. 218, 93 S.Ct. 2041, 36 L.Ed.2d 854 (1973), but rather with a hasty, but nonetheless knowing, decision. Obviously Moran, who had operated the machine from the front of the forks before without misadventure, *thought* he could do so again. But that is not the test applied in Illinois. The test, although subjective, relates to knowledge of the risk and not to whether it was a good risk. [Citations.]

[Reversed.]

NOTE

In Johnson v. Mid–South Distrib., Inc., Prod.Liab.Rep. (CCH) ¶ 7984 (Tenn. Ct.App.1977), a farmhand was injured when his pants leg became entangled in a rotating shaft behind a tractor as he attempted to mount the tractor. The shaft ran from the power take-off (PTO) outlet at the rear of the tractor to a fertilizer spreader pulled behind the tractor and powered by the rotating shaft. Johnson filed suit against the fertilizer dealer which had supplied the spreader, alleging that the spreader was in a defective condition "because, although originally furnished with a shield device by the manufacturer covering the area where the shaft coupled to the tractor power take-off, there was no shield at the coupling area where Johnson became entangled and that Mid–South had superior knowledge of that defect and danger and failed to warn of it." Mid–South pleaded assumption of risk.

The court noted that "assumption of the risk acts in bar of recovery when the proof shows that the plaintiff has (1) knowledge of the danger, (2) an appreciation of that danger, and (3) voluntarily exposed himself to that danger. [Citations.] Knowledge on the part of the plaintiff is the keystone of the doctrine." At trial, plaintiff had testified in part as follows:

> Q. Now, tell us, if you will, how you go about hooking up this spreader or distributor to the tractor?
>
> A. Well, you back into the tongue of it, put a pin in it, and take the shaft and put it onto the tractor PTO shaft, I recon (sic) is what you call it.
>
> * * *
>
> Q. All right; Mr. Johnson, on the spreader that was delivered to Mr. Taylor's house that morning and which you hooked up behind this tractor, did it have any kind of shield around this shaft?
>
> A. No, sir.
>
> Q. Have you ever seen—well, let me ask you this—have you spread fertilizer with this type of spreader before?
>
> A. Yes, sir.
>
> Q. Have you ever seen one that did have a shield on it?
>
> A. Yes, sir.
>
> Q. Do all of them that come out have shields on them?
>
> A. No, sir.
>
> * * *
>
> Q. Mr. Johnson, I believe you said you tried to be careful around machinery all your life? Is that right?
>
> A. Yes, sir.
>
> * * *

Q. Had you warned people about the dangers of the PTO shaft without a shield?

A. Yes, sir, such as Mr. Henry and hands on the place.

* * *

Q. Did you realize that you might be hurt if you got involved with or got into that turning shaft?

A. Yes, sir, you would get hurt if you got in it.

Q. Did you think that in the way that you were going to use it that it was particularly dangerous?

A. Not particularly, unless you put yourself into it.

Q. Mr. Johnson, the PTO shaft without a shield is not dangerous unless you come in contact with it, is it? Or your clothing comes in contact with it?

A. If you come in contact with it, yes, sir.

Q. But, other than that it's not dangerous, is it?

A. No sir, it's not dangerous if you don't come in contact with it—it is dangerous if you come in contact with it, just like anything else.

Q. So, you knew and understood, full well, when you hooked up to that thing, didn't you?

A. Yes, sir, I did,—anything.

* * *

Q. All right, sir; now when you came back to get on your tractor you knew the PTO was going, didn't you?

A. Yes, sir, I knew it.

Q. You knew it didn't have a shield on it?

A. Yes, sir.

Q. And, you knew it was dangerous if you got up against it?

A. If you got against it or stuck your hand in it or foot in it, it was dangerous.

Q. Or caught your pants leg in it?

A. Yes, sir.

* * *

Q. And, at that time, when you hooked it up, I believe you said a while ago, you knew that it would be dangerous if you got up next to it, didn't you?

A. Yes, sir, if you got against it it would be dangerous. If you stuck your hand in it it would be dangerous.

Q. Just like going in a saw-mill and sticking your hand in a buzz saw?

A. Yes, sir, that's right.

* * *

Q. The next question I want to ask you, Mr. Johnson, is, you can put the tractor in neutral, leave it running, and stop the PTO shaft from running, and not cut off the tractor?

A. Yes, sir, you can do it.

Q. All right; but you didn't do that?

A. No, sir. Never had.

What result?

Compare the plaintiff's testimony in O'Neal v. Carolina Farm Supply of Johnston, Inc., 309 S.E.2d 776, 780 (S.C.App.1983) (Bell, J.), where his pigs allegedly died from eating toxic corn supplied by the defendant:

> Q. But you went ahead and ground it up and fed it to your hogs knowing it was moldy and knowing it was the worse [sic] corn you had ever bought, is that right?
>
> A. I did.

What result?

See also Hedgepeth v. Fruehauf Corp., 634 F.Supp. 93 (S.D.Miss.1986) (oil tanker truck driver, who slipped while walking on top of tanker, testified that top was covered with oil and that he had known it was "real slick and real cruddy"); Bishop v. Firestone Tire & Rubber Co., 814 F.2d 437, 446 (7th Cir. 1987) (truck tire repairman stated, prior to explosion of multi-piece rim, "that he hoped the tire would not explode").

HEIL CO. v. GRANT

Court of Civil Appeals of Texas, 1976.
534 S.W.2d 916.

DUNAGAN, CHIEF JUSTICE. This is a products liability [action for the death of James Grant, the Decedent, brought by his widow and children against] the Heil Company, a major manufacturer of hydraulic hoists.

Decedent was killed on February 18, 1972, while assisting his brother, Vernon Grant, in making repairs on Vernon Grant's dump truck. The dump truck was equipped with a telescopic sleeve hoist designed and sold by the Heil Company for the purpose of raising the bed of the truck. The hoist is operated by a mechanism consisting basically of a control valve with levers inside the cab, a hydraulic pump and a partially exposed "pullout" cable which runs lengthwise beneath the bed. The injection of oil into the telescopic sleeve raises the bed until the pullout cable becomes taut and pulls a valve in the control assembly into a neutral position. The bed is lowered by pushing the valve into another position. This is normally accomplished with the levers inside the cab but can occur when the exposed portion of the pullout cable is struck.

Decedent and Vernon were working beneath the raised bed when it somehow descended. Vernon jumped away but Decedent did not. Heil Company's engineer found no malfunction in the hoist mechanism and concluded that the pullout cable had been tripped. Immediately before the accident, Vernon told Decedent that if he hit the pullout cable, the bed would come down. This portion of Vernon's testimony was preserved in appellant's bill of exception as it was excluded under the Dead Man's Statute. In this same bill, Vernon testified that he would not normally work under the raised bed without bracing it with some wooden blocks which he had at home.

Plaintiffs sued the Heil Company under a theory of strict liability for defective design of the hoist mechanism and for failure to warn of the hazard. * * *

The jury found that the producing causes of the death were: (1) the pullout cable which was defectively designed because it was not accompanied by adequate warnings * * *; (2) the control valve, which was defectively designed for the same reason * * *; (3) Heil Company's failure to supply a brace * * *; and (4) Heil Company's failure to provide bracing instructions * * *. * * *

The Heil Company pleaded, offered evidence of and requested Special Issues on the defenses of assumption of risk and misuse. The trial court, applying the Dead Man's Statute, excluded that portion of Vernon Grant's testimony which related to those defenses and refused to submit Special Issues thereon since there was no other evidence to support such issues. Heil Company's primary contention before this court is that the exclusion of Vernon Grant's testimony was harmful error because that testimony was admissible and established or raised fact issues of those defenses.

* * *

* * * Plaintiffs first contend that "no evidence raised the necessary elements of assumption of risk." The theory of the assumption of risk defense is that a person may not recover for an injury received when he voluntarily exposes himself to a known and appreciated danger. Halepeska v. Callihan Interests, Inc., 371 S.W.2d 368, 379 (Tex.1963). The doctrine of assumed risk is harsh and will not be extended. Ellis v. Moore, 401 S.W.2d 789, 794 (Tex.1966). Clearly, if there was no evidence of one or more of the elements of the doctrine, any error in excluding the portions of Vernon Grant's testimony relating thereto was harmless.

Plaintiffs contend that Vernon Grant's warning to Decedent ("I stated * * * that if he hit the cable, the bed would come down") did not constitute evidence that Decedent "knew" of the risk. Plaintiffs argue that Decedent might not have heard, understood or remembered the warning and that Vernon Grant's testimony was merely evidence that Decedent *could* have known of the risk.

An injured person's knowledge of a dangerous condition or defect is measured subjectively; i.e., by that person's actual, conscious knowledge. Massman–Johnson v. Gundolf, 484 S.W.2d 555, 557 (Tex.1972). The fact that the injured person *should have known* of the danger will not support the assumption of risk defense. Halepeska v. Callihan Interests, Inc., supra. Sometimes, however, that person may know such facts as to be charged with knowledge of the danger. Halepeska v. Callihan Interests, Inc., supra. This standard would be applied when it was difficult or impossible to determine the state of the injured person's mind; as it was in the instant case of a fatal injury. * * *

Whether an injured person actually knew of the danger is peculiarly within the province of the jury. [Citation.] Here, there was some evidence from which the jury could have found that Decedent "knew" of the danger, to-wit: the fact that he had been told of the effect of hitting the pullout cable. Although the jury could also have found that Decedent did not know of the danger because he did not hear, understand or remember the warning, we are not able to say, as a matter of law, that he did not know of that danger.

Plaintiffs argue that even if Decedent had knowledge of some danger, there is no evidence that he knew of the specific defect involved. Knowledge of the general hazard involved in operating a punch-press machine will not support the assumption of risk defense. Rhoads v. Service Machine Co., 329 F.Supp. 367 (E.D.Ark.1971). The general hazard in the instant case was working beneath the raised bed of the dump truck. Vernon Grant and Heil Company's engineer both concluded that the bed descended because the pullout cable was tripped. This evidence indicates that the specific danger was that striking the pullout cable would cause the bed to descend. The jury, upon consideration of Vernon Grant's testimony, could have found that Decedent knew of this specific hazard. Plaintiffs also contend that the requisite knowledge must be of a "defect" and that "knowledge that a phenomenon will occur in a product * * * is not knowledge that the product is dangerously defective." * * * It is clear, however, that the assumption of risk defense is premised upon knowledge of the dangerous condition of a product rather than recognition of its defectiveness. [Citations.]

Plaintiffs argue that even if Decedent knew of the danger of the pullout cable, there is no evidence that he knew of the other dangerous defects, to-wit: the defectively designed control valve; the failure to supply a support brace; and the failure to instruct as to proper bracing procedures. These defects may well have been producing or proximate causes of the death. In our opinion, however, all of the above producing causes were part of the same danger. The assumption of risk defense is based upon the injured person's awareness of the danger of injury rather than an awareness of the producing causes of the injury. Since there was some evidence that Decedent knew of the specific danger in hitting the pullout cable, plaintiffs' argument is without merit.

The danger encountered must [also be] appreciated to raise the assumption of risk defense. Ellis v. Moore, supra. Again, the test is subjective. Massman–Johnson v. Gundolf, supra. We look for some evidence that Decedent actually appreciated the risk or was in possession of facts from which he would be legally charged with appreciation of the danger. [Citation.] If by reason of age, or lack of information, experience, intelligence or judgment, Decedent did not understand the risk involved, he will not be taken to have assumed that risk. Restatement (Second) of Torts, Section 496D, comment c.

Decedent was approximately 53 years old at the time of the accident. His formal education had stopped at the 5th or 6th grade but he had been to a trade or mechanical school. He had been a sergeant in the army. Decedent had previously made a living by building airplanes, moving houses and doing construction work. He had not previously worked upon Vernon Grant's dump truck.

Plaintiffs argue that Decedent, after hearing Vernon Grant's warning, might have thought that the bed would descend only until the cable was released. Plaintiffs' expert testified that a construction laborer who had not previously owned or operated a dump truck probably would not appreciate the hazard from looking at the hoist mechanism. Heil Company's engineer testified that he had been involved in the hoist industry for 4 years before he became completely aware that a dump bed would descend when the pullout cable was struck.

There is some evidence that Decedent might not have appreciated the danger of hitting the pullout cable. However, by reason of Decedent's information, age and experience, we conclude that there was some evidence of probative force that he did appreciate that danger. Thus, an issue for the jury exists.

Plaintiffs' final point in support of their contention of no evidence of the necessary elements of the assumption of risk defense is that Decedent's encounter of the risk was not shown to have been voluntary. A voluntary encounter means by free and intelligent choice. [Citation.]

Plaintiffs argue as follows: that there was no evidence that Decedent did not forget the warning; that there was no evidence that the tripping of the pullout cable was not accidental; that Decedent chose to encounter the risk in the face of unreasonable alternatives; or that Decedent was exercising a legal right when he encountered the danger. We have thoroughly considered each of these arguments and find them to be without merit. We conclude that there was some evidence that would support a jury finding that Decedent's encounter with the risk was by free and intelligent choice.

Plaintiffs' second contention * * * is that any error in excluding the testimony of Vernon Grant which related to assumption of risk was harmless because that defense is inapplicable when strict liability is based upon a failure to warn of a dangerous condition. Plaintiffs rely upon statements to the effect that when there is a breach of the duty to warn, there is no assumption of the risk. See: McClanahan v. California-Spray Chemical Corp., 194 Va. 842, 75 S.E.2d 712, 725 (1953); Wright v. Carter Products, Inc., 244 F.2d 53, 60 (2d Cir.1957); R. Keeton, Assumption of Risk in Products Liability Cases, 22 La.L.Rev. 122, 145 (1961). These statements were made in situations in which no warning had been given to the injured person. The function of the warning is to give that person knowledge and an opportunity to appreciate the danger. Ellis v. Moore, supra, 401 S.W.2d at 793. The supplier of a defective product is usually in the best position to supply this warning but there is no reason why the warning cannot come from another source. "One who voluntarily chooses to use a chattel with a complete realization, *regardless of how it was acquired,* of the risks to which he thus exposes himself voluntarily assumes such risks * * *." 1 Hursh & Bailey, American Law of Products Liability 2d, sec. 2:107 (Emphasis added.) * * * We hold that since Vernon Grant may have warned Decedent of the danger, the jury's finding of Heil Company's failure to do so did not render the assumption of risk defense inapplicable.

Plaintiffs' final argument * * * is that any error in excluding evidence of assumption of risk was harmless because that defense is inapplicable when strict liability is based upon the defective design of a product being used in a manner reasonably foreseeable to the supplier. Plaintiffs argue that the supplier is in the best position to discover a design defect and should not be permitted to avoid liability on the ground that the injured person made a foolish judgment to encounter the danger. The thrust of this argument is that assumption of risk *should* not be applicable in any case when strict liability is based upon the defective design of a product. The defense of assumption of risk was held available in such a case in Rourke v. Garza, 530 S.W.2d 794 [Tex.1975]. Plaintiffs' contention is overruled.

* * *

[The court ruled that the Dead Man's Statute was inapplicable to the plaintiffs' wrongful death action since they were suing in their own right and not as representatives for the decedent.]

[Judgment for widow and children reversed, and case remanded for new trial.]

NOTES

1. As plaintiff was mowing his grass up an incline with a rotary lawn mower manufactured by defendant, he approached a barrel in his path. He disengaged the driving clutch and stopped pushing the mower, but did not release the clutch controlling the blades. As he worked to move the barrel, his feet slipped on the newly mown grass and into the machine. Plaintiff sued, claiming that the mower was defective because it was not equipped with a "deadman's throttle" that would have stopped the blade automatically when the forward motion of the machine was stopped. *Held,* plaintiff had assumed the risk; directed verdict for defendant affirmed. Denton v. Bachtold Bros., Inc., 8 Ill.App.3d 1038, 291 N.E.2d 229 (1972).

Compare Burch v. Sears, Roebuck and Co., 320 Pa.Super. 444, 467 A.2d 615, 620 (1983). Plaintiff's electric mower shut off twice and would not restart until he pushed the reset button. The third time the motor shut off, plaintiff leaned the mower on its side, without disturbing the reset button, and reached into the blade area to remove the accumulated clumps of grass. The motor unexpectedly restarted and severely injured plaintiff's hand. Plaintiff's suit was based upon the mower's failure to have a deadman's device. *Held,* the jury could reasonably find that the plaintiff had not assumed the risk because he believed that the motor was stopped and could be restarted only if the reset button were depressed.

2. In Green v. Sanitary Scale Co., 431 F.2d 371 (3d Cir.1970), plaintiff's hand was caught and injured in a meat grinder. Although it was equipped with a metal stomper, plaintiff would use his hand to push the meat down until the meat was caught in the worm gear. One time his hand was caught in the gear along with the meat. The trial judge refused to charge on assumption of risk; *held,* reversed. The jury could find that he knew of the risk yet voluntarily assumed it "because, as he testified, it was more convenient to use his hand."

Compare Venturelli v. Cincinnati, Inc., 850 F.2d 825 (1st Cir.1988). Plaintiff pushed a sheet of metal into a plate shearing machine, but neglected to remove his finger from under one of the metal "hold-down" cylinders ("dogs") before he activated the machine with the foot pedal. The dogs descended and crushed his finger. In his action against the manufacturer for failure to provide adequate guards, he admitted that he knew the machine was dangerous without guards and that he knew his hand might be injured if he hit the pedal while his hand was under the dog. *Held,* no assumption of risk. Plaintiff's encounter with the risk was not *voluntary:* although he knew the risk of activating the machine with his finger under a dog, he did not voluntarily encounter the risk if he believed that his hand was out of the danger area on this particular occasion.

3. An intelligent adult familiar with the product is more likely to be found to have assumed a risk than an inexperienced or dim-witted adult, or a child. Compare Mackowick v. Westinghouse Elec. Corp., 373 Pa.Super. 434, 541 A.2d 749 (1988) (experienced electrician stuck screwdriver into energized capacitor box—assumption of risk); Barnes v. Harley–Davidson Motor Co., Inc., 182 Ga.App. 778, 357 S.E.2d 127 (1987) (motorcyclist of nearly 20 years, who collided with stalled car at night, claimed that motorcycle should have been equipped with crash bars, as standard equipment, and that headlamp provided too little light at high speed—assumption of risk); and Bakunas v. Life Pack, Inc., 531 F.Supp. 89 (E.D.La.1982) (movie stuntman performed free fall from 323 feet into air-inflated cushion rated only to 200 feet—assumption of risk) with Nettles v. Electrolux Motor AB, 784 F.2d 1574 (11th Cir.1986) (experienced but dim-witted woodcutter, injured when chain saw kicked back, had been injured by kick backs before, and knew that he could use a saw equipped with a chain brake—no assumption of risk); and Forrest City Mach. Works, Inc. v. Aderhold, 616 S.W.2d 720 (Ark.1981) (climbing off grain cart, 8–year–old caught pants in rotating PTO shaft attached to tractor—no assumption of risk).

4. **Awareness of Specific Risks.** In Haugen v. Minnesota Min. & Mfg. Co., 15 Wash.App. 379, 550 P.2d 71 (1976), plaintiff was blinded in one eye when the grinding wheel he was working on exploded into three pieces, one of which hit him in the eye. Plaintiff was not wearing safety goggles at the time of the accident, although two pair were available in the shop, and he knew of their importance from his prior safety training. The trial court instructed the jury as follows: "It is not enough to bar recovery by the plaintiff on the defense of assumption of risk that the plaintiff knew that there was a general danger connected with the use of the product, but rather it must be shown that the plaintiff actually knew, appreciated, and voluntarily and unreasonably exposed himself to the specific defect and danger which caused his injuries." On appeal, *held,* instruction was proper; judgment for plaintiff affirmed:

> [P]laintiff testified that he was aware that dust or small particles of wood were likely to be thrown from the dashboard while he was grinding on it. He further testified that he did not deem it necessary

> to wear the available safety goggles because he felt that his eyeglasses would provide adequate protection from this danger. If plaintiff assumed any risk at all, it was the risk of having dust or small particles of wood or metal lodged in his eye during the grinding process. He was obviously not aware of the latent defect in the structural integrity of the disc itself and the danger posed by that defect. This latent defect was not and probably could not have been known by the plaintiff. Plaintiff, therefore, could not have assumed the risk engendered by the defect.

550 P.2d at 75.

In Pennsylvania, the plaintiff must be proved to have known of the specific "*defect*" which caused his injury. This was explained in Mackowick v. Westinghouse Elec. Corp., 373 Pa.Super. 434, 541 A.2d 749, 753 (1988) (dissenting opinion):

> However, use of the term "defect", with its mechanical and technological connotations, has caused much confusion among members of the bench and bar. Some have argued that a plaintiff is aware of a specific defect only if he understands the mechanical process which causes the item to be dangerous. This interpretation is an overly technical misstatement of the law. For assumption of the risk to apply, a plaintiff needn't understand the mechanical process, but must be subjectively aware of the nature, character, and extent of the danger posed *by the specific attribute* which is allegedly defective; this requires more than a general awareness by the plaintiff that the product is somehow dangerous. [Citations.]

Compare Lonon v. Pep Boys, Manny, Moe & Jack, 371 Pa.Super. 291, 538 A.2d 22 (1988), where plaintiff was injured while attempting to jump-start his battery from another battery. As he was attaching the jumper cables to his battery, the battery exploded, splashing sulfuric acid into his eyes. His expert theorized that the explosion was caused by a defective weld in the battery; the defendant's expert opined that the explosion was due to the plaintiff's failure to use the spark-free jump-starting procedures specified in the instructions referred to by a warning on the battery.

The plaintiff had worked at a service station, knew that batteries contain acid, had jump-started cars fifty times or more, had witnessed sparks created during jump starts, and had heard of batteries exploding. *Held,* he could *not* have assumed the risk of the defect in the battery, because he did not know about it. However, he *may* have assumed the more general risk that the battery might explode if he did not use the jumper cables properly.

JOHNSON v. CLARK EQUIPMENT CO.

Supreme Court of Oregon, 1976.
274 Or. 403, 547 P.2d 132.

HOWELL, JUSTICE. This is a products liability case in which plaintiff seeks to recover damages for injuries he sustained while operating a forklift truck manufactured and designed by defendant Clark Equipment Company and sold to plaintiff's employer by defendant Topline Equipment Co. Plaintiff appeals from a jury verdict for defendants.

Plaintiff assigns as error the giving of certain instructions relating to the concept of strict liability as well as those concerning assumption of risk. The plaintiff also assigns as error the court's failure to give his requested instructions on those issues.

Plaintiff was employed as a forklift operator at the Warrenton Lumber Company in Warrenton. His job entailed moving bundles of lumber about the Warrenton plant. Because of his various responsibilities, the job was a rather hectic one. The accident occurred on June 24, 1971, shortly after plaintiff's shift began and while he was engaged in feeding the random planer. Plaintiff was in a hurry and was carrying two banded bundles of 2 × 4's which were to be placed on the chains leading into the planer. Before the bundles could be placed on the chains, it was necessary to cut the metal bands around them. Normally, these bands were cut either by the forklift driver himself or by another Warrenton employee. On the day of the accident, plaintiff had no one to help him by cutting the bands. Although he normally dismounted his machine and moved to the front to cut the bands on this occasion plaintiff remained in the cab of the forklift and reached through the uprights with the cutters. While he was cutting the bands, his body came in contact with the ascent/descent lever controlling the movement of the forks. The forklift carriage descended and severed his arms just below the elbows.

Essentially, the forklift consists of a cab attached to uprights along which the forks are raised and lowered. The uprights consist of inner and outer masts: the inner mast is hydraulically raised and lowered within the outer mast. The forks themselves are attached to a chain and sprocket device which causes them to follow the movements of the inner mast. Each mast is tied together at various points with horizontal crossbars. As the inner mast moves within the outer mast, the crossbars of the inner mast pass within 3/8 of an inch of the crossbars of the outer mast. At the time of the accident, plaintiff's arms were between the uprights, and, as the forks descended, the horizontal crossbars of the inner mast sheared plaintiff's arms against the crossbars of the outer mast and severed them.

The ascent/descent lever which caused the inner mast to descend when plaintiff's body came in contact with it is one of three levers controlling the movement of the forks. These levers are located at the front of the cab and to the right of the steering wheel. The ascent/descent lever is the nearest of the three to the steering wheel. The operator pushes this lever forward to raise the forks and pulls it back to lower them. Once the lever is released, a spring device returns it to a neutral position. Whenever the ascent/descent lever returns to a neutral position, the movement of the inner mast and forks ceases, and the load remains in mid-air.

In his complaint, plaintiff alleged faulty design * * * in that (a) the uprights and cross members were positioned in a manner which allowed them to sever plaintiff's arms; (b) no guard or screen was placed between the cab and the uprights; (c) the ascent/descent lever was located so as to permit the operator's body to unintentionally come in contact with it; (d) the lever was not designed to remain in a neutral position until manually released; and (e) no adequate signs were included to warn the operator of the dangers posed by the machine. At the trial, there was conflicting evidence as to each of these alleged defects as well as to their combined effect.

* * *

The concept of assumption of risk in a products liability case differs somewhat from the traditional tort doctrine of assumption of risk. Accordingly, in Findlay v. Copeland Lumber Co., 265 Or. 300, 509 P.2d 28 (1973), we adopted the definition of assumption of risk for products liability cases which is contained in Comment *n* to § 402A of the Restatement of Torts 2d (1965). In contrast to the more traditional defense which includes only two elements—subjective knowledge and voluntary encounter—Comment *n* sets forth three elements which must be shown before the plaintiff can be barred from recovery. The defendant must show, first, that the plaintiff *himself* actually knew and appreciated the particular risk or danger created by the defect; second, that plaintiff voluntarily encountered the risk while realizing the danger; and, third, that plaintiff's decision to voluntarily encounter the known risk was unreasonable. * * *[5]

In this case, although the trial court properly began by distinguishing assumption of risk from contributory negligence, the court's definition of assumption of risk was not complete. There was no discussion of the element of unreasonableness as it relates to plaintiff's decision to encounter the risk. Although the court did at least mention the other two elements, proof of all three elements is essential to the assumption of the risk defense outlined in Comment *n* * * *. * * *

* * *

The reasonableness of any decision to encounter a known danger must depend upon the circumstances surrounding that decision as well as on the relative probability and gravity of the risk incurred. Whenever the jury attempts to ascertain whether a plaintiff's decision to encounter a known risk was reasonable, it will be necessary for them to consider the conditions which motivated the decision, the pressures which were operating on the plaintiff, and the amount of time which he had to make the decision.

It should be emphasized that this element of unreasonableness pertains only to the nature of plaintiff's decision to encounter the known danger. We are not concerned with the apparent reasonable-

5. The Comment *n* defense represents a hybrid of contributory negligence and assumption of the risk. It combines both the subjective elements of the traditional assumption of the risk defense and the objective element of contributory negligence. The jury must find that the plaintiff had subjective knowledge and appreciation of the risk and voluntarily assumed it. The jury must also find that plaintiff's decision to assume the risk was objectively unreasonable. Whether the plaintiff's conduct constitutes a defense will depend upon the particular facts and circumstances of each individual case.

ness or unreasonableness of the physical conduct through which plaintiff encountered the danger, but rather the reasonableness of his decision to do so. This distinction, while seemingly theoretical, is significant. * * *

We feel that working conditions and related circumstances are a particularly relevant consideration in an inquiry into the reasonableness of a decision to encounter a job-related danger. Such factors often will have a strong influence on that decision, and, in some cases, they may represent the most important motivational factors. For example, a worker might fear that a slowdown in his individual production would slow down the entire production team and thereby draw the attention of his boss. If he has a history of such slowdowns, or of causing excessive spoilage or ruining machine parts, he may have good cause to fear dismissal. The job market could be tight, and he may have little hope of being able to find a new job. Moreover, the situation may demand an immediate, hurried decision. It is certainly possible that, under such circumstances, a reasonable jury could find that his decision to encounter a known risk was not unreasonable. See [citations]; Brown v. Quick Mix Co., 75 Wash.2d 833, 836, 454 P.2d 205, 208 (1969) ("It could never be said as a matter of law that a workman whose job requires him to expose himself to a danger, voluntarily and unreasonably encounters the same."). Cf. Rhoads v. Service Mach. Co., 329 F.Supp. 367, 381 (E.D.Ark.1971) ("The 'voluntariness' with which a worker assigned to a dangerous machine in a factory 'assumes the risk of injury' from the machine is illusory.") [citations].

Hindsight is always better than foresight, and the reasonableness of a decision to encounter a risk should be determined as of the time that decision is made. In this case there was considerable testimony about the hectic nature of the forklift driver's job from both the plaintiff himself and from a former driver who had been doing the same work plaintiff was doing at the time of the injury, and who had asked for another position when he found that he was no longer able to keep up that job's demands. Plaintiff indicated that if his forklift had been able to keep up with the heavy loads and the fast pace which he was required to maintain, he would not have been in a rush, time would not have been so important, and he would have been able to get off the machine to cut the wire bands. Plaintiff testified that all he was thinking of at the time of the accident was "[t]he time that I had to do the job in, and the job I was doing." He also stated that if he had had time to think about it he would not have reached through the uprights. Significantly, the defendants' brief concedes that plaintiff encountered the risk only because of his working conditions, and at trial defendants even argued that such factors were the sole cause of plaintiff's injury.[11]

11. Defendants, while conceding that plaintiff encountered the risk "only because he was in a hurry to keep up with the work assigned by his employer," contend that it would be unfair to allow the jury to consider these working conditions since neither defendant had any control over them. That argument, however, assumes that working conditions would be relevant in this case only if they were somehow related to defendants' own conduct. The assumption is incorrect. The

Therefore, even if the jury disbelieved plaintiff's testimony and concluded that he knew and appreciated the danger that the carriage might somehow start to descend while his arms were through the uprights, and, further, that his actions in reaching through the uprights were voluntary, there would still remain an issue for the jury's consideration—whether, under the evidence in this case, his decision to do so was unreasonable. The issue is not whether it might have been more reasonable to have selected another method of cutting the bands around the lumber but rather, whether it was unreasonable, under all the circumstances, for plaintiff to have selected the method he did.

Thus, considering all these circumstances, we find that the requested instruction should have been given. * * *

Reversed and remanded for a new trial.

[Concurring opinion of Holman, J., omitted.]

NOTES

1. Compare *Johnson* with *Moran,* supra p. 552. Are the cases inconsistent?

2. With *Johnson,* compare McCalla v. Harnischfeger Corp., 215 N.J.Super. 160, 521 A.2d 851, 856 (1987) ("'[A]n employee engaged in his assigned task * * * has no meaningful choice.'"). In some jurisdictions, however, a third party employer's compulsion will not defeat the voluntariness of an employee's assumption of risk asserted by the manufacturer. See Hedgepeth v. Fruehauf Corp., 634 F.Supp. 93, 99 n. 3 (S.D.Miss.1986) (relying on Rest. (2d) Torts § 496E (comment *b*)).

3. Many courts have followed the approach of comment *n* to § 402A in strict liability cases, requiring that the plaintiff's decision to encounter the risk be shown to have been *unreasonable,* in addition to knowledgeable and voluntary. See, e.g., Allen v. Chance Mfg. Co., Inc., 398 Mass. 32, 494 N.E.2d 1324 (1986) (implied warranty).

4. **Warranty.** Some courts treat assumption of risk as a defense to warranty claims. See, e.g., Allen v. Chance Mfg. Co., Inc., 398 Mass. 32, 494 N.E.2d 1324 (1986) (implied warranty); Lust v. Clark Equip. Co., Inc., 792 F.2d 436 (4th Cir.1986) (Va. law) (same); Pritchard v. Liggett & Myers Tobacco Co., 350 F.2d 479 (3d Cir.1965) (express warranty). It may be preferable to inquire whether the conduct falls outside of the warranty, is not in reliance on the warranty, or to examine the issue from the perspective of proximate causation. See Hensley v. Sherman Car Wash Equip. Co., 33 Colo.App. 279, 520 P.2d 146 (1974), citing Erdman v. Johnson Bros. Radio & Television Co., supra p. 534, n.6.

In tortious misrepresentation cases, assumption of risk is treated as part of the issue of justifiable reliance. See Klages v. General Ordnance Equip. Corp., 240 Pa.Super. 356, 367 A.2d 304 (1976), supra p. 91 n.3.

5. **Bystanders.** Assumption of risk has been held applicable to bystanders. See Baker v. Chrysler Corp., 55 Cal.App.3d 710, 127 Cal.Rptr. 745 (1976) (pedestrian, hit by allegedly uncrashworthy car with protruding metal headlight protector, ran across street trying to beat oncoming car); Brown v. Link

working conditions are relevant to the inquiry into the reasonableness of plaintiff's decision to encounter an allegedly known danger. * * *

Belt Corp., 565 F.2d 1107 (9th Cir.1977) (worker run over by crane with bad visibility and no warning signal devices). But see Barr v. Rivinius, Inc., 58 Ill. App.3d 121, 15 Ill.Dec. 591, 373 N.E.2d 1063 (1978) (2–1) (worker hit by roadgrader-shoulder spreader machine).

6. Some states have abolished assumption of risk by statute. See Hornbeck v. Western States Fire Apparatus, Inc., 280 Or. 647, 572 P.2d 620 (1977). Other states have abolished it by judicial decision. One such state, New Jersey, has had an interesting struggle dealing with aggravated user misconduct without this defense in products liability cases. Its solution was to recognize "a defense of contributory negligence to strict liability in tort based upon a voluntary and unreasonable encountering by the plaintiff of a known safety hazard of a machine where proximately contributive to the accident." Cepeda v. Cumberland Engineering Co., Inc., 76 N.J. 152, 386 A.2d 816, 833 (1978).

7. "A basic enigma inherent in [the assumption of risk doctrine] is its dependence upon the notion of full appreciation of risk. 'Risk' implies a degree of want of appreciation of the forces that are at work in a given factual setting, since if one knew and understood all these forces he would know that injury was certain to occur or that it was certain not to occur. Thus the expression 'fully appreciated risk' may seem to be a self-contradiction." R. Keeton, Assumption of Risk in Products Liability Cases, 22 La.L.Rev. 122, 124 (1961).

See Campbell v. ITE Imperial Corp., 107 Wash.2d 807, 733 P.2d 969, 976 (1987) (wireman received severe electrical shock when he began to clean electrical equipment that was not deenergized due to defect in configuration of equipment): "To conclude that Campbell was aware of the specific defect in this configuration would be tantamount to believing that he intended to commit suicide."

Is the enigma posed by Professor Keeton resolvable?

8. **Express Assumption of Risk—Releases.** In Diedrich v. Wright, 550 F.Supp. 805 (N.D.Ill.1982), plaintiff was severely injured when her parachute failed to open fully because the lines were crossed. In her suit against the parachute center for supplying her with an unsafe parachute, the defendant asserted that she had waived her rights by signing a release form that generally exculpated the defendant from liability for injuries from parachuting. *Held*, that the release could not bar a strict liability action, and that it did not bar the negligence action because it failed clearly to state that the plaintiff was relieving the defendant of liability for *negligence*.

9. **Fireman's Rule.** Most states hold that a fireman injured in fighting a fire may not recover against a party who tortiously caused the fire because the fireman had assumed the normal risks incident to the job. See, e.g., Brown v. General Elec. Corp., 648 F.Supp. 470 (M.D.Ga.1986) (while fighting fire caused by defective coffee pot, fireman injured from jumping off roof of burning building that exploded).

10. **Comparative Fault.** Even with the advent of comparative fault, many states have retained assumption of risk as a complete bar to recovery, at least for purposes of strict liability. See, e.g., Duncan v. Cessna Aircraft Co., 665 S.W.2d 414, 423 (Tex.1984). Ohio's experience has been interesting. The Supreme Court merged assumption of risk into its statutory comparative negligence scheme in 1983. Then, in Bowling v. Heil Co., 31 Ohio St.3d 277, 511 N.E.2d 373 (1987), the court declined to apply comparative fault principles in any respect to products liability claims based on *strict liability* in tort, ruling

that an unreasonable assumption of risk under comment *n* to § 402A remained an absolute defense to strict tort actions. In Onderko v. Richmond Mfg. Co., 31 Ohio St.3d 296, 511 N.E.2d 388 (1987), the majority reaffirmed this doctrine:

> At first blush, this absolute bar to recovery may seem unnecessarily or insupportably harsh. It must be remembered, however, that this foreclosure of recovery on a strict liability theory does not deprive an injured plaintiff of all possible remedies. A plaintiff injured by a product is not limited to the theory of strict liability as the sole means of redress. An action in negligence may also be available to compensate the plaintiff for his injury.

Id. at 392. In dissent, Justice Sweeney argued that the majority's approach denies a person injured by a defective product recovery for any damages, "no matter how slight the plaintiff-victim assumed the risk." Further, applying comparative fault principles to assumption of risk would "dissuade the legal gymnastics that courts and juries endure in [the lawyer's attempts] to categorize a plaintiff-victim's conduct as 'assumption of risk' or 'contributory negligence' where a plaintiff's conduct plays a significant role * * *." Id. at 394.

An increasing number of jurisdictions, both by statute and judicial opinion, have merged the assumption of risk doctrine into comparative fault, treating it as a type of fault for damage-reducing purposes, rather than as a complete defense. See, e.g., South v. A.B. Chance Co., 96 Wash.2d 439, 635 P.2d 728 (1981) (7–2); Zahrte v. Sturm, Ruger & Co., Inc., 203 Mont. 90, 661 P.2d 17 (1983); Austin v. Raybestos–Manhattan, Inc., 471 A.2d 280 (Me.1984); Blackburn v. Dorta, 348 So.2d 287, 292 (Fla.1977):

> We find no discernable basis analytically or historically to maintain a distinction between the affirmative defense of contributory negligence and assumption of risk. * * * [Would the fault principles of tort law and comparative negligence be advanced by] a doctrine which would totally bar recovery by one who voluntarily, but reasonably, assumes a known risk while one whose conduct is unreasonable but denominated "contributory negligence" is permitted to recover a proportionate amount of his damages for injury? Certainly not. Therefore, we hold that the affirmative defense of implied assumption of risk is merged into the defense of contributory negligence and the principles of comparative negligence * * * shall apply * * *.

Contrast Justice Mosk's observations in a portion of his dissenting opinion in *Daly* omitted above:

> The majority note one "felicitous result" of adopting comparative negligence to products liability: the merger of assumption of risk—which they term a "bizarre anomaly"—into their innovative defense. I find that result neither felicitous nor tenable. * * * If a consumer elects to use a product patently defective when other alternatives are available, or to use a product in a manner clearly not intended or foreseeable, he assumes the risks inherent in his improper utilization and should not be heard to complain about the condition of the object. One who employs a power saw to trim his fingernails—and thereafter finds the number of his fingers reduced—should not prevail to any extent whatever against the manufacturer even if the saw had a defective blade. I would retain assumption of risk as a total defense to products liability, as it always has been.

575 P.2d 1162 at 1185.

Which approach is preferable, bar or merger? Even if assumption of risk is merged into comparative fault, note that in most jurisdictions the conduct will probably continue to serve as a total bar—like any other type of plaintiff "fault"—when it exceeds the defendant's fault.

11. Is the assumption of risk doctrine cost efficient? See Nelson v. Brunswick Corp., 503 F.2d 376 (9th Cir.1974).

12. See generally Twerski, Old Wine in a New Flask—Restructuring Assumption of Risk in the Products Liability Era, 60 Iowa L.Rev. 1 (1974); Note, Assumption of Risk and Strict Products Liability, 95 Harv.L.Rev. 872 (1982).

SECTION 3. MISUSE

If a plaintiff's injury results in substantial part from his misuse of a product, he may be barred from recovery. This important concept was examined above, at p. 380 et seq., as a limitation on product defectiveness. Those materials should be reviewed here. We saw there that a plaintiff in most jurisdictions will be unable to recover if his injury resulted from his *unforeseeable* misuse of the product. Although the plaintiff in most states must prove, as part of his prima facie case, that his injuries arose from a foreseeable use of the product, a number of jurisdictions (mostly by statute) treat product misuse as an affirmative defense.

Whether "product misuse" should be merged into comparative fault, and treated as a damage-reducing factor rather than as a total bar, is a difficult question yet to be addressed by most courts and legislatures. One might expect that injuries produced by unforeseeable misuse should remain outside of the scope of recovery, since manufacturers would appear to have no duty to prevent them. At least a couple of courts, however, have ruled to the contrary: "[W]e hold that where an unreasonably dangerous defect of a product and the plaintiff's assumption of risk or *unforeseeable misuse* of the product are concurring proximate causes of the injury suffered, the trier of fact must compare those concurring causes to determine the respective percentages" for the apportionment of damages. Mauch v. Manufacturers Sales & Service, Inc., 345 N.W.2d 338, 348 (N.D.1984) (emphasis added), citing General Motors v. Hopkins, 548 S.W.2d 344 (Tex.1977) (heroic attempt to explicate and justify this nonsense). See generally Fischer, Products Liability—Applicability of Comparative Negligence to Misuse and Assumption of the Risk, 43 Mo.L.Rev. 643 (1978); Twerski, The Many Faces of Misuse: An Inquiry Into the Emerging Doctrine of Comparative Causation, 29 Mercer L.Rev. 403 (1978).

Regardless of how the burden of proof and comparative fault issues are resolved in any particular jurisdiction, product misuse is certain to remain an important "defense" in products liability litigation.

PROBLEMS ON CONSUMER MISCONDUCT

Consider how the various defenses based on user misconduct might apply to the following situations:

1. Plaintiff purchases a lightweight vacuum cleaner designed and manufactured by the defendant. After several hours of intermittent use, it appears to be losing suction. Leaving the vacuum on, plaintiff takes off the detachable mouthpiece, leaving exposed the tubular opening into the machine. Plaintiff inserts his fingers into the opening to extract some dirt which is blocking the tube. His fingers are injured when they are struck by blades of the motor fan hidden behind the dirt.

2. The label on the "Drainclean" can, that contains highly corrosive crystals, warns: "Caution. Not for internal consumption. Keep out of reach of children." Plaintiff is a 10–year–old child who eats a spoonful on a friend's dare, and is badly sickened.

3. Plaintiff operates a large punch press manufactured by the defendant. Every 30–40 minutes plaintiff must clear the accumulated metal debris off the press, which involves leaving the point of operation (where the press is activated by means of a foot switch) and going to the other side of the press where there is much better access to the surface area containing the debris. Plaintiff leaves the machine on during these clearing operations to avoid the 5–minute warm-up period necessary if the machine is turned off. When performing this operation, he normally kicks the foot switch under the machine to get it out of the way of traffic. One time he forgets, and another employee accidentally activates the foot control while walking by the press. Plaintiff's hands are injured.

4. Plaintiff takes a sleeping pill and gets into bed to read, wearing an excessively flammable nightgown manufactured by the defendant. While smoking a cigarette, she falls asleep and drops the cigarette on the nightgown which ignites, burning her severely. Cf. Ross v. Spiegel, Inc., 53 Ohio App.2d 297, 373 N.E.2d 1288 (1977).

5. Plaintiff is a lawyer who knows that many persons are injured annually by projectiles thrown by rotary lawnmowers, sometimes at great distances. While her teenage son is mowing the lawn, plaintiff washes the outside windows on her house, 20 feet from the nearest portion of the lawn. Plaintiff's eye is injured when a pebble is hurled by the lawnmower 30 feet away.

6. Plaintiff is a drunken driver hit by another car when plaintiff goes through a red light at high speed. She is injured in two respects: (1) brain damage, worth $1 million, resulting from her head hitting the roof, which would have been prevented had she been wearing her seat belt, and (2) severe burn injuries, worth $500,000, caused by the uncrashworthy design of the fuel system on the plaintiff's car. The defendant is the manufacturer of plaintiff's car.

7. Plaintiff's wife goes into labor and he helps her into their car to transport her to the hospital. As he hurries around the front of the car to take his seat behind the wheel, he notices that his right front tire has a large bubble in it. As a tire salesman, he knows that this presents a serious risk of blowout and that the tire could fail at any time, which could cause him to lose control of the car. His wife, however, has had various complications with her pregnancy, and the doctor had advised him that both the mother's and child's lives would be substantially endangered if his wife were not taken to the hospital immediately once she went into labor. Apart from the car, no other means of transportation is available. Plaintiff jumps into the car and proceeds to drive the two miles to the hospital very cautiously, at 25 m.p.h. Unhappily, the tire blows out, the car goes over an embankment, and plaintiff is injured.

Chapter 6

DAMAGES

SECTION 1. PERSONAL INJURY AND DEATH

ANDERSON v. SEARS, ROEBUCK & CO.

United States District Court, Eastern District of Louisiana, 1974.
377 F.Supp. 136.

CASSIBRY, DISTRICT JUDGE. On April 23, 1970 the Britains' home was completely consumed by a fire which was ignited by a defective Sears' heater. Both Mildred Britain and her infant daughter, Helen Britain, were severely burned and Helen Britain suffered multiple permanent injuries. Thereafter, Mildred Britain and Harry Britain, individually and as administrator of the estate of Helen Britain, brought suit against Sears, Roebuck and Company, Preway, Inc., and Employers Mutual Liability Insurance Company of Wisconsin. Preway, Inc. and its insurer, Employers Mutual Liability Insurance Company of Wisconsin, third-partied Employers Liability Assurance Corporation, Ltd., the insurer of Controls Company of America, and plaintiffs then amended their complaint to add Employers Liability Assurance Corporation, Ltd. as an additional defendant. Plaintiffs ground their quest for recovery on two distinct theories. They allege that Sears was negligent in the installation, maintenance, and repair of the heater, and that Sears, Preway, and Employers Liability Assurance Corporation, the insurer of Controls Company of America, are liable as the manufacturers of the heater and its component parts.

The case was fairly and properly tried, over a period of eight days, before a competent and attentive jury. After having received comprehensive and impartial charges, the jury deliberated a reasonable length of time and returned a verdict in favor of Mildred Britain, Harry Britain, individually, and Harry Britain, as administrator of the estate of Helen Britain, and against Sears, Preway and Preway's insurer, Employers Mutual of Wausau, for two hundred fifty thousand dollars, twenty three thousand dollars, and two million dollars respectively. The defendant, Employers Liability Assurance Corporation, the insurer of Controls Corporation of America, received a favorable verdict.

The cast defendants have moved for post-trial relief via motions for a judgment notwithstanding the verdict, a new trial, and/or alternatively, a remittitur. All of these motions save one have been disposed of. The sole issue presently before the court is whether the damages awarded to Helen Britain were excessive.

Although the case defendants contend that the damages awarded to Helen Britain were excessive, none of them have referred me to any evidence which infers or establishes that the award was excessive, nor have they been able to establish that passion, prejudice or any other improper motive influenced the jury in making its award. Defendants ground their argument of excessiveness merely on the size of the verdict. The reasonableness of quantum, however, is not to be decided in a vacuum but rather is to be considered in light of the evidence as to the injuries and actual damages sustained and the future effects thereof. In this context, defendants have not offered any evidence at trial nor have they directed any cogent arguments in their briefs to sustain their burden of proving that the verdict was excessive.

The legal standard on which to gauge a jury verdict for remittitur purposes is the "maximum recovery rule," Gorsalitz v. Olin Mathieson Chemical Corp., 429 F.2d 1033 (5th Cir.1970); Glazer v. Glazer, 278 F.Supp. 476 (E.D.La.1968). This rule directs the trial judge to determine whether the verdict of the jury exceeds the maximum amount which the jury could reasonably find and if it does, the trial judge may then reduce the verdict to the highest amount that the jury could properly have awarded. Functionally, the maximum recovery rule both preserves the constitutionally protected role of the jury as finder of facts and prevents the predilections of the judge from infecting the jury's determination. Thus, the court's task is to ascertain, by scrutinizing all of the evidence as to each element of damages, what amount would be the maximum the jury could have reasonably awarded. In this case there are five cardinal elements of damages: past physical and mental pain; future physical and mental pain; future medical expenses; loss of earning capacity and permanent disability and disfigurement.

PAST PHYSICAL AND MENTAL PAIN

The infant child Helen Britain, was almost burned to death in the tragic fire that swept her home. She was burned over forty per cent of her entire body; third degree burns cover eighty per cent of her scalp and second and third degree burns of the trunk and of her extremities account for the remainder. Helen Britain's immediate post-trauma treatment required hospitalization for twenty-eight days, during which time the child developed pneumonia, required numerous transfusions, suffered fever, vomiting, diarrhea, and infection, and underwent skin graft surgery, under general anesthesia, to her scalp, which was only partially successful. Keloid scarring caused webbing and ankylosis of the child's extremities and severely limited their motion. The child's fingers became adhered together; scarring bent the arm at the elbow in a burdensome, fixed position; and thick scarring on the thighs and on the side of and behind the knees impaired walking.

This child had to undergo subsequent hospitalizations for further major operations and treatment. The second major operation under general anesthesia was undertaken to graft new skin from the back and stomach to the remaining bare areas of the scalp. The third operation under general anesthesia was an attempt to relieve the deformity of her left hand caused by the webbing scars which bound down the fingers of that hand. A fourth operation under general anesthesia was performed to reduce scars which had grown back on the left hand again webbing the fingers. I cannot envisage the breadth and intensity of the pain experienced by Helen Britain throughout this ordeal.

The undisputed testimony reveals that one of the most tragic aspects of this case is that the horrible mental and emotional trauma caused to this child occurred at an age which medical experts maintain is crucial to a child's entire psyche and personality formation. Helen Britain's persistent emotional and mental disturbance is evidenced by bed wetting, nightmares, refusing to sleep alone, withdrawal, and speech impediments. Dr. Cyril Phillips, a psychiatrist, and Dr. Diamond both indicated that the child manifested to them, even at this early age, emotional illness and retarded mental growth.

The evidence reflects that an award of six hundred thousand dollars for this element of damages alone would not be unreasonable.

FUTURE PHYSICAL AND MENTAL PAIN

There is clear evidence that the stretching, pulling, and breaking down of scars inherent in growth will continue to cause severe pain and a crippling limitation of motion in varying degrees to all of Helen Britain's upper and lower extremities. Very little can be done to improve the condition of the scalp which will never be able to breathe, sweat or grow hair. There will be risks, trauma and pain, both physical and mental, with each of the recommended twenty-seven future operations which will extend over most of the child's adult life, if she is in fact fortunate enough to be able to risk undergoing these recommended surgeries. Furthermore, Helen Britain must vigilantly guard against irritation, infection and further injury to the damaged and abnormal skin, scars and grafts because any injury, however slight, can generate cancer in these adynamic areas.

The inherent stresses and tensions of each new phase of life will severely tax this little girl's debilitated and delicate mental and emotional capacity. Throughout her future life expectancy of seventy-five years, it is reasonable to expect, that she will be deprived of a normal social life and that she will never find a husband and raise a family. On top of this, Helen Britain will always be subjected to rejection, stares and tactless inquiries from children and adults.

The court concludes that an award of seven hundred fifty thousand dollars for this element of damages alone would not be excessive.

FUTURE MEDICAL EXPENSES

A large award for future medical expenses is justified. The uncontradicted testimony was that Helen Britain would need the guidance, treatment and counselling of a team of doctors, including plastic surgeons, psychiatrists and sociologists, throughout her lifetime. Add to this the cost of the twenty-seven recommended operations and the cost of private tutoring necessitated by the child's mental and emotional needs and the jury could justifiably award a figure of two hundred and fifty thousand dollars to cover these future expenses.

LOSS OF EARNING CAPACITY

The evidence of Helen Britain's disabilities both physical, mental and emotional was such that this court holds that the jury could properly find that these disabilities would prevent her from earning a living for the rest of her life. Not only do the physical impairments to her extremities disable her but her emotional limitations require avoiding stress and the combined effect is the permanent incapacity to maintain serious employment.

The jury was provided with actuarial figures which accurately calculated both the deduction of interest to be earned and the addition of an inflationary buffer, on any award made for future loss of earning capacity. In view of these incontrovertible projections at trial, it was within the province of the jury to award as much as $330,000.00 for the loss of earning capacity.

PERMANENT DISABILITY AND DISFIGUREMENT

The award for this element of damage must evaluate in monetary terms the compensation due this plaintiff for the permanent physical, mental and emotional disabilities and disfigurements proved by the evidence adduced at trial. A narration treating Miss Britain's permanent disabilities and disfigurements would be lengthy and redundant; therefore, I resort to listing.

1. The complete permanent loss of 80% of the scalp caused by the destruction of sweat glands, hair follicles and tissue—all of which effects a grotesque disfigurement and freakish appearance.
2. The permanent loss of the normal use of the legs.
3. The permanent impairment of the left fingers and hand caused by recurring webbing and resulting in limited motion.
4. The permanent impairment of the right hand caused by scars and webbing of the fingers.
5. The permanent injury to the left elbow and left arm with ankylosis and resulting in a crippling deformity.

6. The permanent destruction of 40% of the normal skin. As a result of this a large portion of the body is covered by "pigskin." Pigskin resembles the dry, cracked skin of an aged person and is highly susceptible to irritation from such ordinary things as temperature changes and washing.
7. Permanent scars over the majority of the body where skin donor sites were removed.
8. The permanent impairment of speech.
9. The loss of three years of formative and impressionable childhood.
10. Permanently reduced and impaired emotional capacity.
11. The permanent impairment of normal social, recreational and educational life.
12. The permanent imprint of her mother's hand on her stomach.

Considering each of the foregoing items, the court concludes that the jury had the prerogative of awarding up to one million, one hundred thousand dollars for this element of damages.

By totaling the estimated maximum recovery for each element of damages, the jury's actual award is placed in proper perspective. According to my calculations the maximum jury award supported by the evidence in this case could have been two million, nine hundred eighty thousand dollars. Obviously, the jury's two million dollar verdict is well within the periphery established by the maximum award test.

The defendants assert three other grounds for a remittitur. They contend that there was error in the verdict since the verdict exceeded the amount prayed for in the plaintiff's pleadings. This contention fails because the plaintiffs' pleadings were amended subsequent to the jury verdict to conform to the evidence and the verdict of the jury. This amendment was permitted by the court in accordance with law. Stewart v. Banks, 397 F.2d 798 (5th Cir.1968); Riggs, Ferris, and Geer v. Lillibridge, 316 F.2d 60 (2nd Cir.1963); Wendy v. McLean Trucking Co., 279 F.2d 958 (2nd Cir.1960); Fed.R.Civ.P. 54(c).

Preway and its insurer argue that the introduction of photographs of the plaintiff was inflammatory. Since a part of plaintiff's claim for damages is for disfigurement and the humiliation and embarrassment resulting therefrom, I hold that these photographs were properly admitted to show the condition of the plaintiff as she appeared to others, at the time they were taken. Warrington v. Employers Group Insurance Companies, 207 So.2d 207 (La.App. 4th Cir.1968); Presley v. Upper Mississippi Towing Corp., 153 So.2d 416 (La.App. 1st Cir.1963); Bonner v. General Accident Fire & Life Assurance Corp., 136 So.2d 412 (La. App. 1st Cir.1961), Fed.R.Civ.P. 43.

The defendants suggest that the presence of the child in the courtroom and in the corridors of the courthouse in some way inflamed or prejudiced the jury. This allegation is unfounded; the defendants have not pointed out any wrongful conduct on the part of Helen Britain, her parents, or counsel for plaintiffs. Helen Britain was well behaved and quiet the entire time she was in the courtroom.

Accordingly I hold that there was not any bias, prejudice, or any other improper influence which motivated the jury in making its award.

The defendants' motions for a remittitur are denied.

NOTES

1. The effect of inflation on the calculation of future earnings loss is receiving increasing attention. Whether specific evidence on the effect of inflation on future earnings is allowable is the subject of disagreement. In Huddell v. Levin, 537 F.2d 726 (3d Cir.1976), expert testimony on this issue was ruled admissible in a crashworthiness case:

> Finally, G.M. argues that the district court erred in admitting evidence that the inflationary trend of the general economy would cause Dr. Huddell's earnings to increase by 6 per cent per annum. We have had occasion to consider this issue in other contexts, [citation] but this is our first occasion to consider the issue in the context of New Jersey law. Again, Tenore v. Nu Car Carriers, Inc., supra, 67 N.J. at 481, 341 A.2d at 621, controls: "in wrongful death actions, the jury should be instructed that it is permissible for them to consider the impact of inflation upon the survivor's future losses." Expressing concern that expert evidence on this question might be "unduly speculative", the Court set forth guidelines for the reception of such evidence:
>
> > To reduce the possibility of undue conjecture on the part of the jury, plaintiff should also have an opportunity to offer expert economic testimony on the question to provide them with informed guidelines in their deliberations. See Evid.R. 56; Rempfer v. Deerfield Packing Corp., 4 N.J. 135, 141–42, 72 A.2d 204 (1950). Of course, we recognize that economists may differ in their analyses of past trends and future projections and consequently we anticipate that defendants in wrongful death cases will want to offer the testimony of their own experts in rebuttal. This is a familiar practice in other contexts and we see no reason why the same procedure cannot be resorted to in order to give the jury in death cases the benefit of all available points of view.
> >
> > In holding that expert economic testimony is admissible in actions for wrongful death on the issue of the effect of inflation on the survivor's future pecuniary loss, we are aware that not all courts share this view. In our judgment, however, it is simply unrealistic to ignore the problem of inflation in this context. Given the enormity of the potential impact of rising costs over a long period of time, we conclude that evidence of informed estimates of future inflationary trends will result in damage awards that are fair and just.

> We return to the matter of introduction in evidence of tables prepared by the expert witness purporting to show plaintiff's aggregate damages. This is improper for two reasons. In the first place, the tables assume fact findings not within the peculiar expertise of the economic expert. In the second place, the projection of a gross figure before the jury submitted by an expert tends to exert an undue psychological impact leading to the danger of its uncritical acceptance by the jury in the place of its own function in evaluating the proofs.
>
> * * *
>
> What we do expect is that the experts will provide the jury with their analyses of trends of future wage increases and discount interest rates generally and that then, giving due regard to credibility, the jury will use those trends and rates in arriving at their own independent single-figure appraisal of plaintiff's pecuniary loss.

Ibid., 67 N.J. at 481–84, 341 A.2d at 621–23 (footnotes omitted).

Upon retrial the *Tenore* inflation rule and guidelines will apply.

537 F.2d at 743. This approach is consistent with the trend of decisions which have generally approved the consideration of inflation in calculating lost future income. The issues are also explored in Riha v. Jasper Blackburn Corp., 516 F.2d 840 (8th Cir.1975).

2. Plaintiff suffers a serious back injury from a defective product. His future disability can be reduced and pain and suffering minimized if he undergoes elective surgery. He refuses because there is no guarantee the operation will be successful and a small risk that he might be permanently paralyzed or even die. Must he either submit to the operation or have his damages reduced? Cf. Lorenc v. Chemirad Corp., 37 N.J. 56, 179 A.2d 401 (1962).

3. **Wrongful Death.** Since wrongful death actions in most jurisdictions are creatures of statute, the statutory language (as interpreted by the courts) governs the coverage of particular claims. Thus, the statute of limitations for death actions may be shorter than for personal injury actions. See Prod.Liab. Rep. (CCH) ¶ 3370. Warranty actions may not be allowed. See Necktas v. General Motors Corp., 357 Mass. 546, 259 N.E.2d 234 (1970). Nor may claims for punitive damages. See Eisert v. Greenburg Roofing & Sheet Metal Co., 314 N.W.2d 226 (Minn.1982).

4. **Valuation.** There is perhaps the least law on what may be the most elusive of all issues confronting juries and courts—monetizing injuries and deaths. For example, what would be the *minimum* value a jury should be permitted to find for severe injuries to the penis and testicles? See J.I. Case Co. v. McCartin–McAuliffe Plumbing & Heating, Inc., 118 Ill.2d 447, 114 Ill.Dec. 105, 516 N.E.2d 260 (1987) (plaintiff's clothing caught in machine and pulled him in, causing traumatic amputation of one testicle, loss of skin on the penis and other testicle, and eventual surgical removal of second testicle, rendering him sterile). What is the *maximum* value a jury should be permitted to find for the death of a 15–year–old girl killed in a rollover of a microbus? See MacCuish v. Volkswagenwerk A.G., 22 Mass.App.Ct. 380, 494 N.E.2d 390 (1986), aff'd mem. by an equally divided court, 400 Mass. 1003, 508 N.E.2d 842 (1987).

5. **Loss of Consortium and Companionship.** As in other contexts, a spouse may have a claim for loss of consortium arising out of a product accident. Timms v. Verson Allsteel Press Co., 520 F.Supp. 1147 (N.D.Ga.1981) (husband's fingers crushed in press). Compare Klein v. Sears Roebuck & Co., 773 F.2d 1421 (4th Cir.1985) (wife's recovery of $104,000 for loss of consortium, arising out of husband's hand injury from lawnmower, reversed for insufficient evidence). Yet most courts have refused, in this context as in others, to permit claims by parents and by children for the loss of companionship arising out of injury to the other. See Siciliano v. Capitol City Shows, Inc., 124 N.H. 719, 475 A.2d 19 (1984) (4–1) (denying parents' claim for loss of society of minor children injured and killed on amusement ride); Kershner v. Beloit Corp., 611 F.Supp. 943 (D.Me.1985) (denying children's claim for loss of injured parent's society); Green v. A.B. Hagglund and Soner, 634 F.Supp. 790 (D.Idaho 1986) (same).

6. **Noneconomic Damages.** By the late 1980s, about a dozen states had enacted statutory caps on "noneconomic" damages, defined variously to include pain and suffering, inconvenience, physical impairment, disfigurement, loss of enjoyment of life, emotional distress, loss of consortium, and other nonpecuniary damage. Most of the caps range from $250–500,000; the highest to date is $875,000 in New Hampshire. Washington has a formula based on the plaintiff's annual wage and life expectancy.

Do you think such caps are constitutional?

7. **Ad Damnum Clauses.** Some states, such as Arizona and Utah, prohibit the plaintiff from including a specific damages demand in the complaint. By contrast, at least Tennessee requires such a clause. Compare Prod. Liab.Rep. (CCH) ¶¶ 90,314 and 94,613 with 94,414.

SECTION 2. EMOTIONAL DISTRESS

KROGER CO. v. BECK

Court of Appeals of Indiana, 1978.
176 Ind.App. 202, 375 N.E.2d 640.

STATON, JUDGE. Phyllis Beck sued The Kroger Company in the St. Joseph Superior Court, Small Claims Division; Beck recovered $2700. Kroger appeals. Two issues are before us:

(1) Was there sufficient evidence of a contemporaneous physical injury to support the trial court's award of damages for mental anguish?

(2) Was $2700 an excessive damage award for mental anguish and suffering?

We have reviewed the record, and we find that the judgment of the trial court is supported by the evidence. We affirm.

I.

Injury

Phyllis Beck purchased a sirloin steak for her family at a Kroger grocery store on October 31, 1976. The steak had been prepackaged by Kroger for its customers. Later the same day, she prepared the steak for dinner by cutting it into portions and broiling it. After serving the steak to her family for dinner, Phyllis Beck felt a sharp pain in the back of her throat when she placed the second bite of the steak into her mouth. She yanked the piece of steak from her mouth, ran into the bathroom, and vomited violently. In the steak, she found an inch-long piece of metal which was the tip end of a large hypodermic needle used for injecting animals. This sharp end of the hypodermic needle had punctured her throat.

Phyllis Beck testified at trial that she could not swear that she bled as a result of the puncture because of the location of the wound (soft palate at the back of the throat) and the vomiting. She did not go to a doctor, but rather administered first aid to herself for a month by gargling with Listerine. Although her mouth has healed and she does not have a scar, she is afraid that such an incident will reoccur. She further testified that she has not been able to enjoy eating steak or any other kind of meat since.

Her husband was present when she was injured by the needle. He told the court that at one point during dinner his wife screamed and went into the bathroom and vomited. She showed him the needle which she had removed from her mouth. He testified that after the incident "having meat or not having meat" was "a bone of contention." The incident "took, quite frankly, the fun out of eating for some time. * * *"

II.

Contemporaneous Physical Injury

Kroger argues, on appeal, that Beck failed to show any contemporaneous physical injury which would justify an award for the psychological injury. Kroger suggests that the "pricking" of Phyllis Beck's throat did not constitute an appreciable physical injury. Kroger maintains that the psychological injury she claims is only related to a fear of what might have happened had the needle been swallowed and was not directly related to the contemporaneous physical "pricking."

* * *

Kroger characterizes her injury as a "prick" followed by an unconnected fear. This framing of the factual basis of the complaint is not even remotely supported by the evidence. Moreover, Kroger's attempt to show that her fear of eating meat was not related to the "prick" of the needle presupposes that a contemporaneous physical injury (which was uncontradicted, in that a "prick" is an injury) must be permanent or substantial to spawn mental distress. A cursory review of mental anguish decisions shows that permanent or substantial physical injury is not required and has not been required by the law.[1]

Coca–Cola Bottling Co. of Arkansas v. Langston (1939), 198 Ark. 59, 127 S.W.2d 263, concerned a man who drank a beverage in which he found two or three teaspoonfuls of finely ground or powdered glass. He discovered particles of glass in his mouth and became frightened. Examination revealed that his mouth was roughened, cut, and bleeding. The court, in allowing a recovery of $1000, stated that "[i]t is possibly true that the tiny cuts or scratches made by the glass in the man's throat did not amount to very much." But, the court added, "we must recognize the principle that one who takes into his mouth some matter which he thinks is deleterious, injurious, poisonous, that there may be ensuing fright, there may be great mental and consequent physical suffering." [sic] 127 S.W.2d at 264. Phyllis Beck's testimony detailed physical injury, month-long pain, nausea, vomiting, fright, and loss of ability to eat meat.

* * *

Once it has been shown that injury occurred, it is for the trier of fact to determine whether that injury was the catalyst producing the mental distress.

* * * Kroger does not maintain that a sharp object in a steak which "pricks" the throat and causes vomiting could not engender emotional distress. Phyllis Beck's testimony was unrefuted, and it established the legally required injury as well as the causal connection. The trial court did not commit error when it considered mental distress which had been based on an uncontroverted contemporaneous physical injury.[5]

III.

Damages

Kroger asserts that even if damages for mental distress were proper, $2700 is an excessive amount in that Phyllis Beck did not offer specific evidence supporting that amount. A damage judgment will

1. In Clark Restaurant Co. v. Rau (1931), 41 Ohio App. 23, 179 N.E. 196, a man swallowed some glass which scratched the walls of his stomach; he suffered pain and mental distress. The court held that "[i]f as a proximate result of such negligence * * * [plaintiff] swallowed particles of glass contained in the food, this fact in itself establishes an injury even though there be no other injury." Id. at 197. * * *

In allowing recovery for mental distress, the courts have uniformly stated that there must be a contemporaneous physical injury which can serve as a predicate to recovery for the ensuing fright, apprehension, and mental anguish suffered. See Tuttle v. Meyer Dairy Products Co. (1956), 75 Ohio App. 587, 138 N.E.2d 429. In *Meyer* there was no recovery because the plaintiff "expelled said glass [which had been in cottage cheese] from her mouth *without being cut or scratched thereby* * * *." (Emphasis added.) But, there is no requirement that the injury be severe to support the parasitic mental anguish claim. A causal connection is all that is mandated. * * *

5. The contemporaneous physical injury analysis has been generally accepted as the proper test for mental anguish liability.

only be reversed by this Court after we have examined the evidence concerning the injuries, and it is apparent that the amount of damages assessed by the fact-finder is so small or so great as to indicate that the fact-finder was motivated by prejudice, passion, partiality, corruption, or considered some improper element. * * *

* * *

Phyllis Beck's husband corroborated her account of what happened when she encountered the needle. The anxiety that she experienced was manifested immediately. She stated that she came back from the bathroom and "pulled everything off the table and was worried that someone else possibly might have had another part of maybe the same thing in their meat." She has had nightmares about the incident. Her husband testified that after the occurrence his wife "wasn't in the state of mind that she wanted to [prepare meat]." The trial judge specifically held that he did not consider the mental anguish to be "unreasonable." He stated, "I think we have substantial enough injury." After deciding the issue of liability, the judge considered the damages for a couple of days before awarding the $2700.

* * *

A fact-finder has the right to consider the mental suffering caused by the anxiety and fear of the ensuing consequences. Phyllis Beck stated, "It lodge up there kind of almost—it almost gagged me. And for a few seconds, which seemed like hours to me, I thought I was going to choke to death. And this is why I vomited." Where realization of the physical effects which *can* be produced by the foreign object *did* produce the total emotional and physical result, recovery is allowed even if there is no showing that the fatal or deleterious consequence resulted in the particular case.

Phyllis Beck's fear of eating meat was also worthy of consideration by the court. She testified that meat had been a staple in her family's diet. She averred that she was on a high protein diet and that meat as a source of protein and as a pleasure had been taken from her. We believe that her loss should be compensable.

[Affirmed.]

NOTES

1. Many of the products liability mental anguish cases, like *Beck,* involve psychological reactions to foreign or deleterious substances in food and drink. In Way v. Tampa Coca Cola Bottling Co., 260 So.2d 288 (Fla.App.1972), plaintiff was sucking the partially frozen contents out of a bottle of Coke when he encountered something that "resembled a rat with the hair sucked off." He thereupon became nauseated and vomited. His physical discomfort lasted two days, and he suffered a lasting aversion to dark colored drinks. The court, in allowing recovery, quoted approvingly from the following:

> We have examined various texts in this area and R. Dickerson, PRODUCTS LIABILITY AND THE FOOD CONSUMER (1951) makes the following observation:

"Whenever the plaintiff's condition is directly related to the *discovery* of the offending condition, it may be taken for granted that psychological factors have played the preponderate part.

"As for the mental and nervous distress itself, the courts have universally allowed it as a legitimate damage item where some of the food is eaten and the distress is caused by or accompanied by illness or physical injury." (Emphasis theirs.)

2. **Physical Injuries.** The great majority of courts require plaintiff to establish that the emotional distress caused, or was caused by, some injury, illness or other physical condition. See Payton v. Abbott Labs, 386 Mass. 540, 437 N.E.2d 171, 181 (1982) (suit by DES daughters for emotional distress due to increased likelihood of suffering future cancer): "[T]o recover for negligently inflicted emotional distress, [a plaintiff] must allege and prove she suffered physical harm as a result of the conduct which caused the emotional distress. [In addition, such] harm must either cause or be caused by the emotional distress * * *." Accord, Ellington v. Coca Cola Bottling Co. of Tulsa, Inc., 717 P.2d 109 (Okl.1986) (plaintiff permitted to recover for emotional distress from observing piece of "Good-n-Plenty" candy, which she thought was a worm, in her bottle of Coke; distress caused nausea, diarrhea, dehydration, kidney infection, and fever).

3. The *Payton* court, supra note 2, outlined the elements of a negligent infliction of emotional distress claim as follows:

(1) negligence;

(2) emotional distress;

(3) causation;

(4) physical harm manifested by objective symptomatology; and

(5) that a reasonable person would have suffered emotional distress under the circumstances of the case.

437 N.E.2d at 181. Not all courts subscribe to elements (4) and (5).

4. In Wilson v. Redken Laboratories, Inc., 562 S.W.2d 633 (Ky.1978), plaintiff's hair fell out after it was treated with a defective hair conditioner made by the defendant. "Louise had to purchase wigs to cover the ugliness. The damage to her hair made her nervous and upset. When she was asked about it, Louise would cry. She was so distressed about her appearance that she slept in a wig." The jury awarded her $45 for medical expenses, $200 for the cost of wigs, and $30,000 for mental anguish. Reversing as to damages, the intermediate appellate court concluded that the amount awarded for mental anguish appeared at "first blush" to be a product of passion and prejudice. *Held,* reversed and judgment entered on jury verdict: "[I]f any person had a right to a 'first blush' in the real sense of the * * * phrase, that person was Louise * * *."

5. Long-term psychological or personality changes may be associated with the sudden trauma of a product-related injury. If the causal connection can be established, damages for such psychological damage may be recovered. In DeSantis v. Parker Feeders, Inc., 547 F.2d 357 (7th Cir.1976), for example, a 12–year–old boy was caught in the auger blades of a cattle feeder manufactured by the defendant. As a result, he lost his left leg below the knee and a portion of his right foot. A psychiatrist testified that the child was, after the accident, inordinately preoccupied with physical injuries and with feet and that it would be difficult for the child to have satisfactory emotional and sexual relationships

as he grew older. The defendant objected to the psychiatrist's description of the child's condition as a "neurosis" and to compensation for emotional injuries which were outside the general realm of pain and suffering. The trial court allowed the jury to consider whether the defective product had caused "post-traumatic personality disorder." The jury found the plaintiff's physical and emotional harm, past and future, to be $800,000, and made no attempt to separate the physical from the emotional pain and suffering. *Held,* affirmed on appeal.

6. **Pre-Impact Emotional Distress.** Should passengers in a defective airliner be permitted to recover damages for their terror prior to an impending crash? What if the plane, shaking violently and hurtling toward the ground at speeds approaching the speed of sound, is pulled out of the impending disaster at the last moment by a skillful pilot? Should it make a difference, in other words, whether the impact actually occurs? Which is the stronger case? See Quill v. Trans World Airlines, Inc., 361 N.W.2d 438 (Minn.App.1985); Shu–Tao Lin v. McDonnell Douglas Corp., 742 F.2d 45, 53 (2d Cir.1984); Platt v. McDonnell Douglas Corp., 554 F.Supp. 360 (E.D.Mich.1983); In re Air Crash Disaster Near Chicago, Illinois on May 25, 1979, 507 F.Supp. 21 (N.D.Ill.1980). See generally Turezyn, When Circumstances Provide a Guarantee of Genuineness: Permitting Recovery for Pre–Impact Emotional Distress, 28 B.C.L.Rev. 881 (1987).

7. **Strict Liability in Tort.** So far the analysis has concerned the *negligent* infliction of emotional distress. How about *strict liability* for emotional distress resulting from a defective product? What are the arguments pro and con? Cf. Shepard v. Superior Court, 76 Cal.App.3d 16, 142 Cal.Rptr. 612 (1977) (2–1) (warranty and strict tort; bystanders). A number of courts have allowed recovery without much analysis. See, e.g., Jeanelle v. Thompson Medical Co., Inc., 613 F.Supp. 346 (E.D.Mo.1985); Gnirk v. Ford Motor Co., 572 F.Supp. 1201 (D.S.D.1983). But see Rahn v. Gerdts, 119 Ill.App.3d 781, 74 Ill. Dec. 378, 455 N.E.2d 807 (1983).

How significant is the black letter language of § 402A, which subjects a product seller to liability for "physical harm"? See Walters v. Mintec/International, 758 F.2d 73 (3d Cir.1985), and Sease v. Taylor's Pets, Inc., 74 Or.App. 110, 700 P.2d 1054 (1985), both holding that emotional distress is recoverable in strict tort if, but only if, physical harm is also suffered. Although one may assume that most jurisdictions would in any event carry over to strict tort the physical injury requirement from negligence, at least a couple of § 402A jurisdictions have dropped the physical injury requirement in claims for negligent infliction of emotional distress. See, e.g., Culbert v. Sampson's Supermarkets Inc., 444 A.2d 433 (Me.1982).

How about allowing recovery for emotional distress in strict liability actions, but limiting such damages to economic loss? See Mead, Recovery for Psychic Harm in Strict Products Liability: Has the Interest in Psychic Equilibrium Come the Final Mile?, 59 St. John's L.Rev. 457, 500 (1985).

PEARSALL v. EMHART INDUSTRIES, INC.

United States District Court, Eastern District Pennsylvania, 1984.
599 F.Supp. 207.

KATZ, DISTRICT JUDGE.

[Plaintiff sued the manufacturers of heat and smoke alarms installed in her home, claiming that defects in the alarms were substantial factors in causing the deaths of her husband and two children who died in a fire in their home. The jury found for the plaintiff and awarded substantial damages, including $400,000 for the plaintiff's emotional distress. By post-trial motions, defendants challenged several rulings, including the submission of the emotional distress claim to the jury.]

* * *

Defendants argue that plaintiff's claim for emotional distress should not have been submitted to the jury since the plaintiff did not witness the deaths of her husband and children from the fire. In recent years Pennsylvania has expanded the right of a bystander who "witnesses" a traumatic event to recover for emotional distress. In Sinn v. Burd, 486 Pa. 146, 404 A.2d 672 (1979) the Pennsylvania Supreme Court held that a mother who saw her own child struck and killed by a negligently operated vehicle could recover. The Court's decision placed much emphasis on its conclusion that the injuries to the bystander were foreseeable. The Supreme Court has applied a three factor test to determine whether injuries to a bystander from witnessing a wrongful death are foreseeable:

> (1) Whether plaintiff was located near the scene of the accident as contrasted with one who was a distance away from it. (2) Whether the shock resulted from a direct emotional impact upon plaintiff from the sensory and contemporaneous observance of the accident, as contrasted with learning of the accident from others after its occurrence. (3) Whether plaintiff and the victim were closely related, as contrasted with an absence of any relationship or the presence of only a distant relationship.

Yandrich v. Radic, 495 Pa. 243, 247, 433 A.2d 459, 461 (1981); Sinn v. Burd, 486 Pa. 146, 170–71; 404 A.2d 672, 684 (1979) (quoting from Dillon v. Legg, 68 Cal.2d 728, 69 Cal.Rptr. 72, 441 P.2d 912 (1968)). In *Sinn,* the Court found that "[w]here the bystander is a mother who witnessed the violent death of her small child and the emotional shock emanated directly from personal observation of the event, we hold as a matter of law that the mental distress and its effects is a foreseeable injury." 486 Pa. at 173, 404 A.2d at 686. The Court specifically noted that it was not considering the case of a parent who was merely notified of an accident but was not present at the scene of the injury or death. 486 Pa. at 173 n. 21, 404 A.2d at 686 n. 21.

In Yandrich v. Radic, 495 Pa. 243, 433 A.2d 459 (1981) the Pennsylvania Supreme Court addressed the issue it had expressly left open in *Sinn*—whether a parent who was neither a witness to the accident nor in the immediate vicinity thereof, but arrived at the scene after his son had already been taken to the hospital could maintain an action for negligent infliction of emotional distress. Applying the foreseeability standards enunciated in *Sinn* the Court found that the father could not bring such an action. The Court found that the plaintiff was not located near the scene of the accident and that the shock to the plaintiff did not result from the sensory and contemporaneous observance of the accident. 495 Pa. at 247, 433 A.2d at 463.

I find that the facts of the instant case support a claim by Mrs. Pearsall for infliction of emotional distress. Upon arriving home, Mrs. Pearsall witnessed the fire-fighters bringing the blaze under control. She testified that she stood near the bodies of her husband and children at the scene of the fire. She arrived at the hospital shortly before the ambulance arrived and witnessed the bodies of her husband and daughter being carried off the ambulance. She testified that she couldn't pick up her daughter because "she [Laurie] was real hot." Mrs. Pearsall also offered substantial evidence proving her claims of subsequent emotional distress.

That Mrs. Pearsall arrived at the scene of the fire shortly after her husband and children had actually died in no way diminishes the foreseeability of her emotional distress. Upon arriving home she witnessed the fire and had no idea whether her husband and children were alive or dead. She saw and later touched the bodies of her family as the fire that took their lives was still smoldering. Her emotional distress was not caused merely by others notifying her of the accident. Instead, plaintiff's shock and emotional distress resulted from the direct impact upon her senses of the fire and its aftermath. I am satisfied that the emotional distress of this mother witnessing the fire and its carnage is foreseeable to a manufacturer of defective alarms and, therefore, meets the standards enunciated in Sinn v. Burd and Yandrich v. Radic. See also Bliss v. Allentown Public Library, 497 F.Supp. 487 (E.D.Pa.1980) (direct visual observation of accident unnecessary to state claim for negligent infliction of emotional distress); General Motors Corp. v. Grizzle, 642 S.W.2d 837 (Tex.App.1982) (mother arriving upon scene moments after accident may recover for infliction of emotional distress); Nazaroff v. Superior Court, 80 Cal.App.3d 553, 145 Cal. Rptr. 657 (1978) (same).

* * *

[Defendants' post-trial motions denied.]

NOTES

1. **"Bystanders."** Like Pennsylvania, roughly half the states have adopted some form of the *Dillon v. Legg* foreseeability guidelines for the emotional distress of bystanders, although there are only a small number of cases applying the guidelines in the products liability context. See Culbert v.

Sampson's Supermarkets Inc., 444 A.2d 433 (Me.1982) (while spoon feeding her infant some Beech Nut turkey and rice baby food, mother observed him choke and gag on, and then spit up, hard object); Shepard v. Superior Court, 76 Cal. App.3d 16, 142 Cal.Rptr. 612 (1977) (after being side-swiped by another car, rear door popped open, throwing brother and sister onto highway; parents and brother observed sister being run over and killed by other car).

Some courts instead still apply the "zone of danger" test to bystander cases. See, e.g., Jeannelle v. Thompson Medical Co., Inc., 613 F.Supp. 346 (E.D.Mo. 1985) (brother in zone of danger could assert claim for emotional distress from observing mother and brother violently attacked by person deranged by defective drug); Levit v. General Motors Corp., 682 F.Supp. 386 (N.D.Ill.1988) (claim denied where plaintiff was away from home when refrigerator burst into flames); Smith v. Hub Mfg., Inc., 634 F.Supp. 1505 (N.D.N.Y.1986) (claim denied where parents found young son floating unconscious in above-ground pool). And bystanders must prove the other elements of an emotional distress claim, including in most jurisdictions physical impact or injury. Gilbert v. WMATA, Prod.Liab.Rep. (CCH) ¶10,586 (D.D.C.1985) (grandmother and twin sister observed other twin strangled to death in escalator); Brown v. Cadillac Motor Car Div., 468 So.2d 903 (Fla.1985) (driver struck and killed his mother).

2. **"Users."** A couple of decisions have allowed third party recovery, even where the *Dillon* test could not be met, on the theory that the plaintiff was a *user* of the product and hence really a first party to whom a duty was directly owed rather than a bystander. Kately v. Wilkinson, 148 Cal.App.3d 576, 195 Cal.Rptr. 902 (1983) (father and daughter were towing daughter's best friend on water skis when steering locked, causing boat to circle and hit skier, partially dismembering her; father and daughter, whose presence was legally required to watch skier, were both foreseeable users); Gnirk v. Ford Motor Co., 572 F.Supp. 1201 (D.S.D.1983) (when mother left infant in car to open gate, transmission slipped from park to reverse, and car travelled into pond where it disappeared).

3. A dentist administers nitrous oxide to a patient, thinking it is oxygen because the valves on her anesthesia machine are mislabeled. The patient dies. The dentist is sued for malpractice, subjected to a criminal investigation, loses her practice, and as a consequence of all this suffers a deep depression. Should she be permitted to maintain a strict tort action for her emotional distress against the manufacturer of the anesthesia machine? Cf. Kennedy v. McKesson Co., 58 N.Y.2d 500, 462 N.Y.S.2d 421, 448 N.E.2d 1332 (1983).

4. May tort law's historical reluctance to give full recognition to emotional stability reflect a sexist failure to protect interests possessed by women more than men? See generally M. Chamallas with L. Kerber, Women, Mothers and the Law of Fright: A History (forthcoming).

5. Emotional distress concerning future consequences, such as cancerphobia from exposure to toxic substances, is examined in Chapter 10, below.

6. See generally Mead, Recovery for Psychic Harm in Strict Products Liability: Has the Interest in Psychic Equilibrium Come the Final Mile?, 59 St. John's L.Rev. 457, 500 (1985); Silverman, Recovery for Emotional Distress in Strict Products Liability, 61 Chi.-Kent L.Rev. 545 (1985); Bohrer, Fear and Trembling in the Twentieth Century: Technological Risk, Uncertainty and Emotional Distress, 1984 Wis.L.Rev. 83; Joseph, Dillon's Other Leg: The Extension of the Doctrine Which Permits Bystander Recovery for Emotional

Trauma and Physical Injuries to Actions Based on Strict Liability in Tort, 18 Duq.L.Rev. 1 (1979).

SECTION 3. ECONOMIC LOSS AND PROPERTY DAMAGE

SPRING MOTORS DISTRIBUTORS, INC. v. FORD MOTOR COMPANY

Supreme Court of New Jersey, 1985.
98 N.J. 555, 489 A.2d 660.

POLLOCK, J.

The fundamental issue on this appeal concerns the rights of a commercial buyer to recover for economic loss caused by the purchase of defective goods. More specifically, the question is whether the buyer should be restricted to its cause of action under the Uniform Commercial Code (hereinafter U.C.C. or the Code) or should be allowed to pursue a cause of action predicated on principles of negligence and strict liability. The difference is important because the buyer in the present case instituted its action beyond the four-year period provided by the U.C.C., N.J.S.A. 12A:2–725, but within the six-year period applicable to tort actions, N.J.S.A. 2A:14–1.

The defendants are a motor vehicle manufacturer, its dealer, and a supplier of transmissions. The gravamen of the complaint is that defects in the transmissions, which were installed in commercial trucks, caused the buyer to sustain a loss in the benefit of its bargain and consequential damages. Specifically, the buyer sought recovery for repair, towing, and replacement parts, as well as for lost profits and a decrease in the value of the trucks.

* * *

[The trial court decided the plaintiff's claim was one in contract and applied the UCC statute of limitations. The Appellate Division, holding that the action was better characterized as strict liability in tort, reversed. Defendants appealed.]

We hold that a commercial buyer seeking damages for economic loss resulting from the purchase of defective goods may recover from an immediate seller and a remote supplier in a distributive chain for breach of warranty under the U.C.C., but not in strict liability or negligence. We hold also that the buyer need not establish privity with the remote supplier to maintain an action for breach of express or implied warranties. Accordingly, the four-year period of limitations provided by the Code, N.J.S.A. 12A:2–725, not the six-year general statute of limitations, N.J.S.A. 2A:14–1, determines the time within which an action must be commenced against the immediate seller and remote supplier.

* * *

Economic loss can take the form of either direct or consequential damages. A direct economic loss includes the loss of the benefit of the bargain, i.e., the difference between the value of the product as represented and its value in its defective condition. Consequential economic loss includes such indirect losses as lost profits. J. White & R. Summers, Handbook of the Law Under the Uniform Commercial Code §§ 11–4 to 11–6 at 405–10 (2d ed. 1980) [hereinafter cited as White & Summers]; Note, "Economic Loss in Products Liability Jurisprudence," 66 Colum.L.Rev. 917, 918 (1966); Note, "Manufacturer's Liability to Remote Purchasers for 'Economic Loss' Damages—Tort or Contract?," 114 U.Pa.L.Rev. 539, 542 (1966). Because it presents a claim for economic loss, which is not normally recoverable in a tort action, rather than a claim for physical harm, this case probes the boundary between strict liability and the UCC. [The court reviewed *Henningsen v. Bloomfield Motors*, supra p. 128.]

Underlying the *Henningsen* decision was the Court's recognition that consumers were in an unequal bargaining position with respect to automobile manufacturers and dealers, who required them to sign standard contracts. *Henningsen,* supra, 32 N.J. at 389–404, 161 A.2d 69. One of the main purposes of strict liability, as declared in *Henningsen,* is the allocation of the risk and distribution of the loss to the better risk-bearer. Id. at 379, 161 A.2d 69; Suter v. San Angelo Foundry & Mach. Co., 81 N.J. 150, 173, 406 A.2d 140 (1979). Generally, the manufacturer, who is better able to eliminate defects from its product and who can spread the cost of the risk among all of its customers, is the better risk-bearer. Restatement, supra, § 402A comment c. By contrast, the individual consumer is poorly situated to bear the entire risk of loss from injuries caused by a defective product. Through allocation of the risk of loss to the manufacturer, strict liability achieves its objective of protecting the consumer who, because of unequal bargaining power, cannot protect him or herself.

The year after the *Henningsen* decision, 1961, the Legislature adopted the U.C.C., effective January 1, 1963. L.1961, c. 120. Then in 1965 this Court decided Santor v. A. & M. Karagheusian, Inc., 44 N.J. 52, 207 A.2d 305, which, like *Henningsen,* involved facts that occurred before the adoption of the U.C.C. In *Santor,* a carpet manufacturer sold a defective carpet to a consumer through its wholly-owned distributor. The Court found that the consumer could recover against the manufacturer, although there was no privity between the parties and the action was for an economic loss.

The action was couched in terms of a breach of implied warranty of merchantability, id. at 63, 207 A.2d 305, but the Court acknowledged that the action could be described better as one in strict liability. Id. at 63–67, 207 A.2d 305. In *Santor,* Justice Francis made clear that neither mass advertising by the manufacturer nor personal injuries to the consumer was essential to the invocation of strict liability. Id. at

65, 207 A.2d 305. Echoing his words in *Henningsen,* he stated that the purpose of a strict liability action was to shift the risk of loss so that it was borne by "the makers of the products who put them in the channels of trade, rather than by the injured or damaged persons who ordinarily are powerless to protect themselves." Id. Like the plaintiff in *Henningsen,* the plaintiff in *Santor* was an individual consumer. Furthermore, the action was for a direct economic loss, and the Court limited recovery to the lost benefit of the bargain, i.e., "the difference between the price paid by the plaintiff and the actual market value of the defective carpeting at the time when plaintiff knew or should have known it was defective * * *." Id. at 68–69, 207 A.2d 305.

* * *

As the preceding cases demonstrate, the U.C.C. rules pertaining to the sale of goods overlap the doctrine of strict liability for placing a defective product in the stream of commerce. One reason for the overlap is that strict liability, in this regard, evolved from implied warranties of fitness and merchantability under the U.C.C. and its predecessor, the Uniform Sales Act. Those warranties originated as a matter of social policy to compensate consumers who sustained personal injuries from defective food. Prosser & Keeton [on the Law of Torts], § 97 at 690 (4th ed.1984). Neither the A.L.I., which published the Restatement (Second) of Torts, nor the permanent editorial board of the U.C.C., which operates as a joint project of the A.L.I. and the Commissioners on Uniform State Laws, has undertaken to resolve the overlap between strict liability as declared in section 402A and the breach of warranty provisions under the U.C.C. 112 N.J.L.J. 700 (1983).

From the perspective of the injured party, strict liability generally provides a more congenial environment than contract principles, which may prevent recovery because of a lack of privity with the manufacturer. In addition to privity, the Code retains two other requirements that may pose considerable obstacles to a buyer. The first requirement is that of notice to a seller of a breach of warranty, N.J.S.A. 12A:2–607(3); the second arises from the seller's ability to limit or disclaim liability to an innocent purchaser. N.J.S.A. 12A:2–316. A buyer who does not deal directly with a manufacturer cannot negotiate over the terms of a disclaimer and might find it impossible to give the manufacturer notice of the breach of warranty following an injury. Prosser & Keeton, supra, § 97 at 691–92. Strict liability, on the other hand, circumvents the technical requirements of the U.C.C. with respect to privity, notice, and limitation of damages. Avoiding those requirements is particularly important for persons outside the distributive chain who sustain physical damage caused by a defective product.

By comparison, the U.C.C. emphasizes the simplification of the law governing commercial transactions and the expansion of commercial practices through agreement. N.J.S.A. 12A:1–102. Underlying the U.C.C. policy is the principle that parties should be free to make contracts of their choice, including contracts disclaiming liability for breach of warranty. Once they reach such an agreement, society has an interest in seeing that the agreement is fulfilled. Consequently, the U.C.C. is the more appropriate vehicle for resolving commercial disputes arising out of business transactions between persons in a distributive chain.

The problem is ascertaining where on the spectrum to place a cause of action brought by a commercial entity, or even a consumer, for purely economic loss. One gains perspective by reviewing the decisions of this Court and those of the Supreme Court of California.

As explained earlier, this Court's decision in *Henningsen* was couched in warranty terms. In Greenman v. Yuba Power Prods., Inc., 59 Cal.2d 57, 27 Cal.Rptr. 697, 701, 377 P.2d 897, 901 [1963], which involved personal injuries sustained by a husband from a defective power saw purchased by his wife, the California court drew on *Henningsen,* but declared that the cause of action could be more appropriately denominated as strict liability in tort.

The cross-pollination between the two jurisdictions continued through our *Santor* decision, which relied on *Greenman.* Five months later, however, when the California court was confronted with an individual's claim for economic loss resulting from the purchase of a defective truck, that court rejected *Santor* and held that the consumer could not recover in strict liability for economic loss. Seely v. White Motor Co., 63 Cal.2d 9, 45 Cal.Rptr. 17, 403 P.2d 145 (1965).

In *Seely,* an individual owner-driver purchased a truck for use in his heavy duty hauling business. From the time the purchaser took possession, the truck bounced violently, but the dealer was unable to correct the defect. Thereafter, a brake failure caused the truck to overturn. The truck sustained property damage, and Seely, who stopped making payments after the accident, sued the dealer and the manufacturer for lost profits and the money paid on the purchase price of the truck.

Chief Justice Traynor, writing for the majority of the court, affirmed a judgment for Seely. The absence of privity did not preclude judgment against the manufacturer for the breach of an express warranty that the truck was "free from defects in material and workmanship under normal use and service * * *." Seely, supra, 63 Cal.2d at 13, 45 Cal.Rptr. at 20, 403 P.2d at 148. After reaching that result, the court rejected plaintiff's alternative contention of strict liability. The court ruled that in the absence of personal injuries or property damage strict liability was inapplicable. Although the truck had been damaged, the court sustained a finding of the trial court that defendant had not created the defect that caused the damage.

While rejecting plaintiff's right to recover in strict liability, Chief Justice Traynor observed that the law of sales has been carefully articulated to govern economic relationships between suppliers and consumers. He stated further that strict liability was not intended to undermine the warranty provisions of the U.C.C., but "to govern the distinct problem of physical injuries." Seely, supra, 63 Cal.2d at 15, 45 Cal.Rptr. at 21, 403 P.2d at 149.

In a concurring and dissenting opinion, Justice Peters embraced *Santor,* and stated that an individual consumer should be allowed to recover in strict liability for economic damages such as those sustained by Seely. Seely, supra, 63 Cal.2d at 20–22, 45 Cal.Rptr. at 25–27, 403 P.2d at 153–55. According to Justice Peters, the roles played by the parties and the nature of the transaction, not the nature of the damage, were important. Id. He also distinguished transactions involving consumers from those "*within* the world of commerce, where parties generally bargain on a somewhat equal plane and may be presumed to be familiar with the legal problems involved when defective goods are purchased." Seely, supra, 63 Cal.2d at 27, 45 Cal.Rptr. at 29, 403 P.2d at 157 (emphasis in original).

Over the intervening years, *Seely* has emerged as representing the majority view. [Citations.]

Santor, however, has attracted the support of a few jurisdictions. [Citations.]

Commentators likewise have been critical of *Santor,* and wary of extending strict liability to encompass claims for purely economic loss. See, e.g., White & Summers, supra, § 11–9 at 418 (in claims for economic loss, better solution than in *Santor* would be to hold strict liability inapplicable and apply statute of limitations under the Code); Franklin, "When Worlds Collide: Liability Theories and Disclaimers in Defective Product Cases," 18 Stan.L.Rev. 974, 989–90 (1966) (criticizing courts as defiant or unaware of relevance of sales law to products liability law); Speidel, "Products Liability, Economic Loss and the U.C.C.," 40 Tenn.L.Rev. 309, 316–18, 327 (1973) (social needs justify strict liability where product is so dangerous that personal injury or property damage may occur, but case is less compelling where other commercial losses occur; U.C.C. is ideally suited for resolution of commercial loss claims); Wade, "Tort Liability for Products Causing Physical Injury and Article 2 of the U.C.C.," 48 Mo.L.Rev. 1, 26 n. 87 (1983) (substantial majority rule, in accord with *Seely,* is that economic loss is not actionable in tort); [citations].

In the present case, which involves an action between commercial parties, we need not reconsider the *Santor* rule that an ultimate consumer may recover in strict liability for direct economic loss. To determine whether a commercial buyer may recover economic loss, however, we must reconsider the policies underlying the doctrine of strict liability and those underlying the U.C.C. Those policy considerations include, among others, the relative bargaining power of the parties and the allocation of the loss to the better risk-bearer in a modern marketing system. As a general rule, the rights and duties of a buyer and seller are determined by the law of sales, which throughout this century has been expressed first in the Uniform Sales Act and more recently in the U.C.C. As indicated, however, strict liability evolved as a judicial response to inadequacies in sales law with respect to consumers who sustained physical injuries from defective goods made or distributed by remote parties in the marketing chain.

The considerations that give rise to strict liability do not obtain between commercial parties with comparable bargaining power. Iowa Elec. Light & Power Co. v. Allis–Chalmers Mfg. Co., [360 F.Supp. 25, 32 (S.D.Iowa 1973)] (stating doctrine of strict liability loses all meaning when plaintiff is a large company suing for commercial loss). Furthermore, perfect parity is not necessary to a determination that parties have substantially equal bargaining positions. Cf. Moreira Constr. Co., Inc. v. Moretrench Corp., 97 N.J.Super. 391, 394–95, 235 A.2d 211 (App. Div.1967), aff'd o.b., 51 N.J. 405, 241 A.2d 236 (1968) (refusing to apply rule of *Santor* to suit between corporations even though plaintiff was a small company and defendant was the world's largest well point company). Suffice it to state that Spring Motors had sufficient bargaining power to persuade Ford to install Clark transmissions in the trucks that were the subject of the contract.

Insofar as risk allocation and distribution are concerned, Spring Motors is at least as well situated as the defendants to assess the impact of economic loss. Indeed, a commercial buyer, such as Spring Motors, may be better situated than the manufacturer to factor into its price the risk of economic loss caused by the purchase of a defective product. See Note, "Economic Loss in Products Liability Jurisprudence," supra, 66 Colum.L.Rev. at 952–58.

Presumably the price paid by Spring Motors for the trucks reflected the fact that Ford was liable for repair or replacement of parts only. By seeking to impose the risk of loss on Ford, Spring Motors seeks, in effect, to obtain a better bargain than it made. In such a context, the imposition of the risk of loss on the manufacturer might lead to price increases for all of its customers, including individual consumers. Id. at 956–57. As between commercial parties, then, the allocation of risks in accordance with their agreement better serves the public interest than an allocation achieved as a matter of policy without reference to that agreement.

Delineation of the boundary between strict liability and the U.C.C. requires appreciation not only of the policy considerations underlying both sets of principles, but also of the role of the Legislature as a coordinate branch of government. By enacting the U.C.C., the Legislature adopted a carefully-conceived system of rights and remedies to govern commercial transactions. Allowing Spring Motors to recover from Ford under tort principles would dislocate major provisions of the Code. For example, application of tort principles would obviate the statutory requirement that a buyer give notice of a breach of warranty, N.J.S.A. 12A:2–607, and would deprive the seller of the ability to exclude or limit its liability, N.J.S.A. 12A:2–316. In sum, the U.C.C. represents a comprehensive statutory scheme that satisfies the needs of the world of commerce, and courts should pause before extending judicial doctrines that might dislocate the legislative structure.

* * *

* * * [W]e hold that a commercial buyer seeking damages for economic loss only should proceed under the U.C.C. against parties in the chain of distribution. Hence, we reverse that part of the judgment of the Appellate Division that permitted Spring Motors to maintain against the defendants an action in strict liability for economic loss.

III

What we have said about Spring Motors' strict liability claim applies substantially to its negligence claim. Underlying that conclusion is the principle that a seller's duty of care generally stops short of creating a right in a commercial buyer to recover a purely economic loss. Thus viewed, the definition of the seller's duty reflects a policy choice that economic losses inflicted by a seller of goods are better resolved under principles of contract law. In that context, economic interests traditionally have not been entitled to protection against mere negligence. [Citations.]

The demarcation of duties arising in tort and those arising in contract is often indistinct, but one difference appears in the interest protected under each set of principles. Prosser & Keeton, supra, § 92 at 655–56. The purpose of a tort duty of care is to protect society's interest in freedom from harm, i.e., the duty arises from policy considerations formed without reference to any agreement between the parties. A contractual duty, by comparison, arises from society's interest in the performance of promises. Generally speaking, tort principles, such as negligence, are better suited for resolving claims involving unanticipated physical injury, particularly those arising out of an accident. Contract principles, on the other hand, are generally more appropriate for determining claims for consequential damage that the parties have, or could have, addressed in their agreement.

Although the nature of the damage may be a useful point of distinction, it also signals more subtle differences in the roles that tort and contract play in our legal system. The differences include judicial evaluation of the status, relationship, and expectations of the parties; the ability of the parties to protect themselves against the risk of loss either by contractual provision or by insurance; and the manner in which the loss occurred. See Pennsylvania Glass Sand Corp. v. Caterpillar Tractor Co., 652 F.2d 1165, 1173 (3rd Cir.1981) (allowing recovery for damage to defective machinery resulting from fire caused by defect). This evaluation reflects, among other things, policy choices about the relative roles of contracts and tort law as sources of legal obligations. As among commercial parties in a direct chain of distribution, contract law, expressed here through the U.C.C., provides the more appropriate system for adjudicating disputes arising from frustrated economic expectations.

Some courts, however, have rejected the distinction between physical harm and economic loss as arbitrary, thereby allowing recovery in tort for repair costs and lost profits. See, e.g., Berg v. General Motors Corp., 87 Wash.2d 584, 555 P.2d 818, 822–23 (1976) (purely economic loss, including lost fishing profits, recoverable in negligence against remote manufacturer of diesel engine); cf. Emerson G.M. Diesel, Inc. v. Alaskan Enterprise, 732 F.2d 1468, 1474 (9th Cir.1984) (recovery under strict liability for economic loss available in admiralty against manufacturer of diesel engine parts). Other courts have rejected the requirement of an accident as a prerequisite to recovery in negligence. See, e.g., State ex rel. Western Seed Prod. Corp. v. J.R. Campbell, 250 Or. 262, 442 P.2d 215, 218 (1968) (recovery in negligence allowed against remote supplier for crop losses caused by defective seed); see also, Nobility Homes of Texas v. Shivers, supra, 557 S.W.2d at 78, 83 (purchaser of defectively designed and constructed mobile homes may recover in negligence and for breach of implied warranties under U.C.C., but not in strict liability).

Nonetheless, the weight of authority supports the proposition that economic expectations that are protected by the U.C.C. are not entitled to supplemental protection by negligence principles. See Arrow Leasing Corp. v. Cummins Arizona Diesel, Inc., supra, 136 Ariz. [444,] 549, 666 P.2d [544,] 549 [1983] ("our conclusion that economic losses are best handled by contract law rather than tort law is applicable whether the theory involved is strict liability or negligence"); Clark v. International Harvester Co., supra, 99 Idaho 326, 581 P.2d 784, 794 (1978) (the law of negligence does not impose a duty to "build a tractor that plows fast enough and breaks down infrequently enough" for plaintiff to make a profit); Moorman Mfg. Co. v. National Tank Co., supra, 91 Ill.2d [69,] 86, 61 Ill.Dec. [746,] 754, 435 N.E.2d [443,] 451 (purchaser may not recover in strict liability or negligence against manufacturer of defective grain storage tank); Superwood Corp. v. Siempelkamp Corp., 311 N.W.2d 159, 162 (Minn.1981) (no recovery in strict liability or negligence for lost profits or damage to hot plate press); Wade, "Tort Liability for Products Causing Physical Injury and Article 2 of the U.C.C.," supra, 48 Mo.L.Rev. at 26 n. 87 (substantial majority rule has come to be that economic losses are not actionable in negligence); Note, "Manufacturers' Liability for Economic Loss," supra, 66 Colum.L.Rev. at 929–31 (negligence is one of the least fruitful avenues of recovery for economic loss). Stated otherwise, the U.C.C. "is generally regarded as the *exclusive source* for ascertaining when a seller is subject to liability for damages if the claim is based on intangible economic loss not attributable to physical injury to person or harm to a tangible thing other than the defective product itself." Prosser & Keeton, supra, § 95A at 680. In the present case, the commercial buyer understandably was disappointed in its purchase. The point remains, however, that the U.C.C. provides an adequate set of rights and remedies to resolve the differences between Spring Motors and the Ford defendants.

It follows from our determination that Spring Motors should be restricted to its U.C.C. remedies as against Ford and Turnpike Ford that the appropriate statute of limitations is the four-year time bar contained in N.J.S.A. 12A:2–725. More than four years elapsed between the date of the delivery of the trucks and the institution of this action against Ford and Turnpike Ford. Consequently, Spring Motors' suit against them is time-barred.

[Reversed; complaint dismissed.]

HANDLER, J., concurring.

In this case the Court rules that common-law causes of action sounding in strict products liability and negligence against the supplier of a product are no longer available to "commercial buyers" who incur economic loss attributable to a defective condition in the product. * * * The concern that prompts me to write specially is not so much the application of this holding to the facts of this case but its possible reach to situations different from that presented by this litigation.

I agree with the Court that under the particular circumstances of this case, resort to the Uniform Commercial Code is appropriate. Spring Motors Distributors, Inc. (Spring Motors) is a commercial entity engaged in the business of leasing trucks, which it purchases for use in the regular course of its business. Spring Motors maintains a fleet of 300 trucks. In this case it purchased 14 trucks from Ford Motor Co. (Ford). There is nothing in the record to suggest that the transaction was anything but a regular and typical commercial undertaking for Spring Motors or that the transaction between these experienced parties was other than a common commercial event for them. Further, the contract between Spring Motors and Ford specified that the trucks would be supplied with transmissions manufactured by Clark Equipment Co. (Clark). Thus, Spring Motors apparently had the commercial experience, economic status, and bargaining power to be able to specify to its principal supplier, Ford, that it required a particular transmission and to designate Clark as the supplier of that component.

* * *

It is also important to emphasize that the selection by the Court of a particular remedy does not turn on a label. It would not be correct to consider the U.C.C. remedy to be exclusively applicable to a purchaser's claim simply because the transaction can be viewed as "commercial" or having occurred in the course of business, or because the ultimate purchaser is in business or is itself a commercial entity. For example, the ultimate purchaser of a vehicle could be a travelling salesperson or a small-scale trucker, or a carpenter, plumber, electrician, or landscape gardener. It does not follow automatically that if the vehicle proves to be defective, the U.C.C. shall apply as the exclusive remedy to govern the recovery of direct or consequential economic loss solely because such purchaser is in business or bought the vehicle for use in business. Rather, the analysis should turn on whether a purchase made in that kind of setting, even if for a business or commercial purpose, is sufficiently distinguishable from a purchase for personal use by an ordinary private consumer to justify a difference in remedial treatment.

* * *

In its determination of the available causes of action and remedies for economic loss attributable to a defective product, a court should consider not only that the transaction or the purchase is "commercial" but that the parties, among other things, are commercially experienced and have comparatively equal bargaining power in dealing with one another with respect to the underlying transaction. * * *

* * *

Another consideration in determining what avenues of relief are open to parties for loss occasioned by defective products is risk allocation. In further support of an exclusive U.C.C. remedy, the Court states that Spring Motors is "at least as well situated as the defendants to absorb the impact of economic loss, perhaps even better situated." Ante at 671. Other purchasers, however, may not be so situated even though their ultimate use of the product may be "commercial." * * * Where the parties do not bargain with comparable economic strength, as distinguished from the circumstances of this case, the inferior risk-bearing position of the aggrieved purchaser may militate in favor of continuing common-law avenues of relief.

* * *

This analysis, I would emphasize, is not inconsistent with the Court's opinion, which focuses on the reasons in this case for applying the U.C.C., particularly, equal bargaining power and ability to allocate risks. Logically, if those reasons are not present in a given case, alternative modes of recovery, such as found in the law of strict products liability or negligence, should be available. These theories of law have developed over the years to provide just relief and adequate redress to innocent persons who have been victimized by the wrongful conduct of others. Consumers who are not in a position reasonably to protect themselves against economic loss attributable to a defective product should not be insulated from the ameliorative reach of the law simply because they are also commercial purchasers.

We have recognized in an appropriate context the propriety of recovery by a purchaser-consumer based on strict products liability for economic losses attributable to a defective product. Santor v. Karagheusian, 44 N.J. 52, 207 A.2d 305 (1965). The Court's opinion in this case suggests an acceptable narrowing of the breadth of our holding in *Santor*. It does not, however, serve to displace that decision or to signal a different rule in cases in which the requirements of sound public policy and fairness call for its continued application.

NOTES

1. What, precisely, is the holding of *Spring Motors?* Is *Santor* effectively overruled?

2. *Spring Motors* appears to treat alike two types of damages that may be separately classified: (1) economic loss, and (2) damage to the product itself.

When damage to the product itself is in the nature of deterioration or, as in *Spring Motors,* the failure to function as expected, almost all courts now reject the *Santor* approach and confine the buyer (apart from fraud) to his commercial law remedies.

Yet, what if the defective transmissions had caused several of the trucks to crash? A few courts have allowed negligence and strict tort actions for recovery of damage to the defective product itself in this context. See, e.g., Cloud v. Kit Mfg. Co., 563 P.2d 248 (Alaska 1977) (flammable rug pad caught fire, "a sudden calamitous occurrence"; strict tort claim allowed); Russell v. Ford Motor Co., 281 Or. 587, 575 P.2d 1383 (1978) (pick-up truck damaged when "man-endangering" defective weld in axle housing fractured, causing loss of control and crash; strict tort claim allowed); Corfab, Inc. v. Modine Mfg. Co., 641 F.Supp. 448 (N.D.Ill.1986) ("sudden and calamitous" breakdown of heating units, releasing toxic gases into factory building; negligence and strict tort claims allowed).

Most courts, however, hold simply that damage to the product itself, of whatever type, is recoverable only in warranty:

> [S]ince by definition no person or other property is damaged, the resulting loss is purely economic. Even when the harm to the product itself occurs through an abrupt, accident-like event, the resulting loss due to repair costs, decreased value, and lost profits is essentially the failure of the purchaser to receive the benefit of its bargain—traditionally the core concern of contract law.

East River Steamship Corp. v. Transamerica Delaval, Inc., 476 U.S. 858, 106 S.Ct. 2295, 2302, 90 L.Ed.2d 865 (1986) (admiralty; commercial transaction). See also Mid Continent Aircraft Corp. v. Curry County Spraying Service, Inc., 572 S.W.2d 308 (Tex.1978).

3. A couple of decisions have applied a multi-factored balancing approach for determining the appropriateness of tort recovery for damage to a defective product and (other) economic loss. See Salt River Project Agr. Improvement & Power Dist. v. Westinghouse Elec. Corp., 143 Ariz. 368, 694 P.2d 198 (1984), and Pennsylvania Glass Sand Corp. v. Caterpillar Tractor Co., 652 F.2d 1165 (3d Cir. 1981) (Pa. law), examining (1) the nature of the product defect, (2) the manner in which the loss occurred, and (3) the type of loss (or type of risk).

The last two factors are analyzed in *Spring Motors.* With respect to the first, a couple of courts have held that a negligence action could be maintained for economic losses based on the failure to warn of discovered dangers, as opposed to manufacturing or design claims. See, e.g., McConnell v. Caterpillar Tractor Co., 646 F.Supp. 1520 (D.N.J.1986); Miller Industries v. Caterpillar Tractor Co., 733 F.2d 813, 818 (11th Cir.1984):

> Whatever the merits of adopting a rule that views defects in a product as part of the parties' bargain and thus within the law of sales, it is much less tenable to presume that the buyer has bargained away the manufacturer's obligation to warn of defects that later come to the manufacturer's attention. A duty to warn of a product's defects of which the seller becomes aware goes not to the quality of the product that the buyer expects from the bargain, but to the type of conduct which tort law governs as a matter of social and public policy.

The multi-factored balancing approach was rejected by the Supreme Court as "unsatisfactory" in *East River Steamship,* supra, for being "too indeterminate to enable manufacturers easily to structure their business behavior." *Penn-*

sylvania Glass Sand, relied upon in *Spring Motors* but criticized in *East River Steamship,* was overruled in Aloe Coal Co. v. Clark Equip. Co., 816 F.2d 110 (3d Cir.1987).

4. The courts have had a much easier time dealing with damage to property other than the product itself. The widely prevailing view allows recovery for such damage in tort law as well as warranty. See generally Cloud v. Kit Mfg. Co., 563 P.2d 248 (Alaska 1977), where the court noted that most courts apply the doctrine of strict liability in tort to claims for damage to other property:

> In Seely v. White Motor Co., 63 Cal.2d 9, 403 P.2d 145, 152 (1965), Chief Justice Traynor, writing for the Supreme Court of California, stated:
>
> > Plaintiff contends that, even though the law of warranty governs the economic relations between the parties, the doctrine of strict liability in tort should be extended to govern physical injury to plaintiff's property, as well as personal injury. We agree with this contention. Physical injury to property is so akin to personal injury that there is no reason for distinguishing them.
>
> We agree that direct physical injury to property and personal injury should be treated similarly in the resolution of products liability litigation. As we noted in Clary v. Fifth Avenue Chrysler Center, Inc., 454 P.2d 244, 248 (Alaska 1969), that "[t]he purpose of imposing such strict liability on the manufacturer and retailer is to insure that the cost of injuries resulting from defective products are borne by the manufacturers that put such products on the market rather than by the injured persons who are powerless to protect themselves." A similar need arises when the consumer's property rather than person is damaged due to a defect in the manufacture of the particular product.

Id. at 250–51. The court noted that § 402A provides for strict liability for harm "to the ultimate user or consumer, or to his property."

5. May a school board recover from the manufacturer the costs of removing asbestos insulation, installed in the schools many years before, which now must be removed to avoid health risks to the children? The asbestos abatement problem is examined in ch. 10, infra p. 999.

6. **Reform.** The comprehensive products liability reform statutes generally address the recoverability of economic loss and property damage, at least indirectly, in the definition of "product liability action [or claim]," or "harm." E.g., *Ariz.:* action for "bodily injury, death or property damage," Prod.Liab.Rep. (CCH) ¶ 90,310; *Colo.:* action for "personal injury, death, or property damage," id. at ¶ 90,610; *Conn.:* claim for "personal injury, death or property damage"; " 'Harm' includes damage to property, including the product itself * * *. As between commercial parties, 'harm' does not include commercial loss." Id. at ¶ 90,713; *N.J.:* "Harm" includes (a) "physical damage to property, other than to the product itself," (b) injury, illness or death, (c) pain and suffering and emotional distress, and (d) loss of consortium or services, id. at ¶ 93,151; *Ohio:* claim for "death, physical injury to person, emotional distress, or physical damage to property other than the product in question," id. at ¶ 93,610.

7. See generally, Speidel, Warranty Theory, Economic Loss and the Privity Requirement: Once More Into the Void, 67 B.U.L.Rev. 9 (1987); Gaebler, Negligence, Economic Loss, and the U.C.C., 61 Ind.L.J. 593 (1986); Solomine,

Recovery of Economic Damages in Product Liability Actions and the Reemergence of Contractual Remedies, 51 Mo.L.Rev. 977 (1986); Schwartz, Economic Loss in American Tort Law: The Examples of J'Aire and of Products Liability, 23 San Diego L.Rev. 37 (1986); Rabin, Tort Recovery for Negligently Inflicted Economic Loss: A Reassessment, 37 Stan.L.Rev. 1513 (1985); Notes, 70 Marq.L.Rev. 320 (1987); 28 B.C.L.Rev. 383 (1987); 84 Mich.L.Rev. 517 (1985).

Spring Motors is noted in 17 Rut.L.J. 381 (1986), and 17 Seton Hall L.Rev. 330 (1987). *East River Steamship* is noted in 32 Loy.L.Rev. 1007 (1987), 18 Rut. L.J. 375 (1987), and 61 Tul.L.Rev. 1229 (1987).

PROBLEM

Rural Power Company (RPC), a small electric utility, purchased 5 gas turbine generators from General Electric Company (GE), which GE installed in RPC's 5 separate generating stations. Within six months, each of the 5 generators malfunctioned, due to an internal defect, with the following results:

At Station # 1, the generator exploded, injuring an engineer.

At Station # 2, the generator overheated, which ignited some oil, starting a fire that destroyed the station and its contents but not the generator.

At Station # 3, the generator itself ignited and was destroyed, but nothing else was damaged.

At Station # 4, the generator regularly overheated, and wore out prematurely within 6 months.

At Station # 5, the generator failed for several days during peak demand, when alternative sources of power were unavailable, causing RPC (1) to lose $25,000 in peak-time profits, and (2) to become liable for $50,000 in penalties to its industrial customers pursuant to their contracts for the supply of electricity.

RPC and the engineer sue GE in negligence and strict liability in tort for each of these separate losses. GE defends on the basis of a Limitation of Remedies clause in the Purchase and Sale Agreement, which RPC had tried unsuccessfully to delete during contract negotiations, that provides as follows:

> "The sole and exclusive remedy available to RPC and its employees for breach of any provision under this Agreement, breach by GE of any implied warranty, or the commission by GE of any tort in connection with the turbines that are the subject of this Agreement, shall be for GE to repair or replace the turbine, or any defective part(s) therein, at GE's option."

Before the lawsuit, GE did in fact offer to replace each of the 5 turbines, in total satisfaction of the claims against it, but RPC and the engineer both refused the offer and filed suit. Discovery reveals that after the sale of the turbines, but before the problems began, GE engineers discovered the defect but neglected to inform RPC.

What result on each claim?

SECTION 4. PUNITIVE DAMAGES

GRYC v. DAYTON–HUDSON CORP.

Supreme Court of Minnesota, 1980.
297 N.W.2d 727, cert. denied, 449 U.S. 921, 101 S.Ct. 320, 66 L.Ed.2d 149 (1980).

* * *

TODD, JUSTICE.

On December 8, 1969, Lee Ann Gryc, then 4 years of age, was clothed in pajamas made from a cotton material manufactured by defendant Riegel Textile Corporation (Riegel). The material was commercially known as "flannelette." It was not treated but did meet the minimum federal standards of product flammability. Lee Ann reached across the electric stove in her home to shut off a timer. Her pajamas were instantly ignited and she received severe burns over her upper body. The jury found Riegel liable for these injuries and awarded Lee Ann $750,000 in compensatory damages and $1,000,000 in punitive damages. We affirm.

* * *

The pajamas worn by Lee Ann were two-piece, loose-fitting, and the pajama top flared out at the waist. The flannelette used in the pajamas was manufactured by Riegel and distributed to [a clothing manufacturer which made and sold the pajamas to the representative of the defendant retailer, Dayton–Hudson.]

The flannelette used in Lee Ann's pajamas was woven material made from yarns spun from natural cotton fiber. The fabric was brushed on one side which created a nap. Flannelette is light weight, warm, and absorbent. It has a soft feel or "hand", breathes well, and is launderable and durable. It is relatively inexpensive. Flannelette was very popular during the relevant time period because of these qualities and was the dominant fabric used in children's winter sleepwear.

The flannelette used in Lee Ann's pajamas was not treated with any flame retardant. Its flammable characteristics were demonstrated by one of plaintiffs' expert witnesses, Dr. Robert Johnson, by film at trial. Dr. Johnson reconstructed Lee Ann's accident by making a copy of Lee Ann's pajamas, placing them on a mannequin the size of Lee Ann, and using an ignition source similar to the Gryc electric burner. The film showed that the fabric ignited instantaneously when the hem of the pajama top was placed in contact with the ignition source. The front of the pajama top burned from hem to neck in 4 to 5 seconds. The same experiment was performed on a pair of pajamas of the same design but constructed of newsprint. The newsprint pajamas burned only slightly faster than did the untreated flannelette pajamas.

Plaintiff's experts concluded that the untreated cotton flannelette was unreasonably dangerous for use in children's sleepwear because of the instantaneous manner in which the fabric ignited, the speed at which it burned, the amount of heat produced when it burned, and the difficulty of extinguishing the flames. Defendant's experts characterized these burning characteristics as "normal" for the mass of the fabric and as a "natural" phenomenon for cotton, the characteristics of which had not changed for hundreds of years. They concluded, therefore, that the fabric used in the Gryc pajamas was not defective.

* * *

It was shown at trial that the safety of cotton flannelette could be significantly increased by applying [a chemical flame retardant] to the fabric. Dr. Johnson, by film, demonstrated the flammable characteristics of flame retarded cotton flannelette. He created a pair of pajamas like those which Lee Ann had worn, except that they were treated with a flame-retardant process available in 1967. The pajamas were placed against a heat source similar to an electric burner for 30 seconds. The pajamas blackened, burned, and charred but did not flame in an area 6 inches wide and 8 inches long in that 30 seconds. When the fabric was removed from the heat source, the blackening and charring stopped.

The serious dispute between the experts concerned the availability of flame-retardant processes during the relevant time period which would not destroy the desirable characteristics of cotton flannelette. Plaintiffs' experts testified that, as early as 1962, there were flame-retardant processes which could be applied to the fabric without adversely affecting its qualities enough to make it unsaleable. Plaintiffs also showed that, in England, flannelette-like sleepwear was required by law to be flame retarded since the 1950's.

Defendant's experts were of the opposite view. They testified that there were no durable flame retardant chemicals which could be applied to the fabric without severely reducing its tensile and tear strength, its soft feel, increasing its weight and cost, and adversely affecting the color of the fabric.

Plaintiffs' witnesses admitted that there were no mills producing flame retarded flannelette for public consumption in any volume in 1967. However, both of plaintiffs' experts testified that the flame retardant chemicals and the process for applying them could have been made commercially available as early as 1962–1966, if only the textile mills had so desired.

* * *

Defendant's experts contended that no warning of the flammable characteristics of cotton flannelette was necessary on the Gryc pajamas because its burning characteristics are obvious and natural for the mass of the fabric. However, plaintiffs introduced a great amount of testimony tending to show that garment manufacturers, wholesalers, retailers, and consumers were not aware of the highly flammable characteristics of untreated cotton flannelette. Their evidence tended to show that Riegel and other garment manufacturers were uniquely aware of these characteristics.

Defendant's experts were also of the opinion that a warning would not be feasible or practical because Riegel could not be assured that such a warning would get beyond the garment manufacturers. However, there was testimony that for other purposes Riegel could and did use hang tags which were sent through the chain of commerce and did reach consumers.

Defendant's experts were also of the opinion that a warning would "stigmatize" Riegel's flannelette and make it unmarketable as compared with identical flannelette from competitor mills.

Plaintiffs also claimed that defendant Riegel should have instructed consumers of a home remedy which would temporarily flame retard flannelette pajamas. This remedy, a water base solution of boric acid and borax, would come out in the wash, but could be simply sprinkled on clothing after each washing. Dr. Johnson conducted a test with a pair of flannelette pajamas treated with such a solution. The pajamas did not ignite when they were held against a hot plate for 5 seconds.

The issues presented on this appeal are:

(1) Whether the award of punitive damages is an appropriate remedy in a products liability case;

(2) Whether defendant's compliance with an applicable federal safety standard precludes a punitive damages award;

(3) Whether the imposition of punitive damages on a defendant who has complied with the federal Flammable Fabrics Act is prohibited by the preemption provision of that Act or by the Supremacy Clause of the United States Constitution;

(4) Whether the trial court applied the proper legal standard in instructing the jury on the issue of punitive damages;

(5) Whether there was sufficient evidence to support the award of punitive damages in this case;

(6) Whether policy considerations dictate against an award of punitive damages in this case;

(7) Whether the award of $1,000,000 in punitive damages is excessive; * * *.

1. This case presents the question, not heretofore considered by this court, of whether punitive damages may be appropriately awarded in the context of a strict liability action. There is ample authority from many jurisdictions approving this remedy in strict liability cases. An exhaustive article, Owen, Punitive Damages in Products Liability Litigation, 74 Mich.L.Rev. 1258 (1976), discusses the pros and cons of allowing such an award. The author concludes that punitive damages are an appropriate remedy in such cases based on the following rationale:

> Manufacturers have a powerful hold over the means for discovering and correcting product hazards. Through the processes of design, testing, inspection and collection of data on

product safety performance in the field, the manufacturer has virtually exclusive access to much of the information necessary for effective control of dangers facing product consumers. * * *

Most manufacturers, both from a desire to avoid liability and from a generalized sense of social responsibility, prudently use their resources to prevent excessively hazardous products from reaching or staying on the market. On occasion, however, manufacturers abuse their control over safety information and market defective products in flagrant disregard of the public safety. * * * A legal tool is needed that will help to expose this type of gross misconduct, punish those manufacturers guilty of such flagrant misbehavior, and deter all manufacturers from acting with similar disregard for the public welfare. The punitive damages remedy is such a tool.

Id. at 1258–60.

Based on this rationale, we recognize today that punitive damages, in an appropriate case, may properly be awarded in a strict liability action.

2. The Flammable Fabrics Act of 1953, Chap. 164, § 4, 67 Stat. 111, as amended, Chap. 833, 68 Stat. 770 (1954), in effect at the time this cause of action arose,[2] applied to fabrics sold in interstate commerce for wearing apparel. This statute sets forth a test [termed the CS 191–53] to determine whether a fabric is dangerous when used in clothing. * * *

The fabric in the Gryc pajamas passed the CS 191–53 test. * * *

Riegel argues that its compliance with the federal Act precludes, as a matter of law, a finding of that guilty state of mind which is a necessary prerequisite to a punitive damages award. It argues that it was justified in relying on the Act in determining which fabrics were safe for dissemination in the marketplace. The trial court addressed this issue in its post-trial memorandum and found:

The difficulty with [Riegel's] argument is that it does not assess the validity of the test. It was proven almost conclusively at trial that this test did not and could not properly determine the flammability of fabrics such as cotton flannelette. Moreover, it was almost conclusively established, in addition, that defendant Riegel knew not only that the test was invalid but that it could not evaluate the flammability of its products * * *. Knowing full well at all times after the passage of the Flammable Fabrics Act that CS 191–53 was unreliable, the defendant cannot today say that punitive damages should not be allowed simply because its cotton flannelette passed an unreliable test. Riegel's argument that it had a right to act on

2. The Flammable Fabrics Act was subsequently amended to provide for more stringent regulation of fabric used for children's sleepwear. However, these revisions are inapplicable to this cause of action.

> the basis of the legislation * * * is a specious one, because such actions were not taken in good faith and must be viewed in the context of the knowledge that Riegel had that its cotton flannelette was extremely dangerous to the public because of its racing flammability.

On reviewing the record, we have determined that the trial court's findings are supported by the evidence and that its conclusions are correct. There was substantial evidence at trial which established that the CS 191–53 test was not a valid indicator of the flammable characteristics of fabrics and did not take into account the uses to which a fabric would be put in determining its safety.[3] It was shown that newspaper passed the CS 191–53 test with a 48–percent margin of safety.

It was also shown that the original intent of Congress in passing the CS 191–53 test into law was primarily to protect the public against certain highly flammable synthetic products, not all unreasonably dangerous clothing. 1953 U.S.Code Cong. & Admin.News, p. 1723.

Furthermore, there was evidence that the test was adopted as a result of industry influence and, therefore, served to protect the textile industry rather than the public. * * *

The evidence established that Riegel knew of the invalidity of the CS 191–53 test and was aware that unreasonably dangerous fabrics passed the test. Riegel's head of research, Linton C. Reynolds, knew that newspaper and 19 other samples of paper passed the CS 191–53 test and communicated this to a Riegel top official. In addition, Riegel knew that persons were suffering severe burn injuries when Riegel's flannelette ignited. In 1956, one of Riegel's top officials wrote in a memorandum, "We are always sitting on somewhat of a powder keg as regards our flannelette being so inflammable." The memorandum was entitled "Flammability—Liability."

Several courts have addressed the issue of whether compliance with the CS 191–53 test precludes liability for compensatory damages as a matter of law and have concluded that it does not. [Citations.] These courts reasoned that since it was shown that the test was invalid, compliance with that test did not preclude a finding that a product was unreasonably dangerous. For the same reason, we conclude that while compliance with this test may be relevant to the issue of punitive damages, it does not preclude such an award as a matter of law.

3. In 1967, the Flammable Fabrics Act was amended to include the following preemption provision:

> This Act is intended to supersede any law of any State or political subdivision thereof inconsistent with its provisions.

3. The commentators have agreed. See Swartz, Product Liability: The Torch Cases, 76 Case & Comment, No. 1, p. 3 (1971); [citations]; Campbell & Vargo, The Flammable Fabrics Act and Strict Liability in Tort, 9 Ind.L.Rev. 395 (1976).

Flammable Fabrics Act, Pub.L. No. 90–189, § 16, 81 Stat. 568. Riegel contends that the imposition of punitive damages on a defendant who has complied with the Flammable Fabrics Act constitutes an inconsistent state law which is preempted by the Act. Riegel argues, therefore, that the punitive damages award in this case is violative of the Act and the Supremacy Clause of the United States Constitution.

* * *

The stated purpose of this preemption provision was to preclude the multiple regulation of textile manufacturers by providing a "uniform" federal regulation. Report of the Senate Commerce Committee, 113 Cong.Rec. 20328 (1967). Riegel argues that the punitive damages remedy serves to frustrate this stated purpose by imposing a higher duty on a textile manufacturer than is required by the federal Act. * * *

* * *

* * * The original 1967 preemption provision is ambiguous in that it does not expressly state which types of state action are preempted by the Act. It merely states that all inconsistent state *laws* are preempted. However, the 1976 amendment clarifies this ambiguity by replacing the term "law" with "flammability standard or regulation." This suggests that Congress merely intended to preempt inconsistent state statutory enactments rather than all state laws. This conclusion is bolstered by the legislative history under both the 1967 and 1976 preemption amendments. * * * Therefore, we find that Congress did not expressly intend to preempt state private civil remedies by its preemption provision.

However, this does not end our inquiry. We must also determine whether preemption of the punitive damages remedy may be implied from the federal Act. There is some indication that Congress specifically did not intend to preempt any private civil remedies. First, 15 U.S. C.A. § 1199 (West, 1974), a subdivision of the Flammable Fabrics Act, provides in part:

> The provisions of this chapter shall be held in addition to, and not in substitution for or limitation of, the provisions of any other law.

It is arguable that this provision seeks to leave intact any state law which is not expressly precluded by the preemption provision. [Citation.]

* * *

The United States Supreme Court has stated that where a challenged state law concerns the vital state interest of protecting its citizens from injury, it cannot be inferred that Congress deprived the states of the power to act in the absence of compelled congressional direction. San Diego Building Trades Council v. Garmon, 359 U.S. 236, 79 S.Ct. 773, 3 L.Ed.2d 775 (1959); [citations]. * * *.

In this case, the state punitive damages remedy concerns the vital state interest of protecting persons against personal injury. It seeks to protect state citizens from the willful, wanton, and reckless manufacture of a dangerously flammable fabric for use in children's sleepwear. The 1953 Flammable Fabrics Act did not seek to protect persons from this particular risk. As stated earlier, the purpose underlying the original Act was primarily to prohibit the sale of highly flammable synthetic materials, not all unreasonably dangerous fabrics.

* * *

Since there is no clear congressional intent to preempt the private state remedy of punitive damages, we find that such preemption cannot be implied. We, therefore, reject Riegel's preemption arguments.

4. [The court refused to consider Riegel's arguments on the proper legal standard and burden of proof for punitive damages since these issues had not been raised at trial.]

5. In instructing the jury on the issue of punitive damages, the court listed several factors which the jury was to take into account in determining whether Riegel had acted in willful or reckless disregard of plaintiffs' rights:

> 1. The existence and magnitude of the product danger to the public;
>
> 2. The cost or feasibility of reducing the danger to an acceptable level;
>
> 3. The manufacturer's awareness of the danger, the magnitude of the danger, and the availability of a feasible remedy;
>
> 4. The nature and duration of, and the reasons for, the manufacturer's failure to act appropriately to discover or reduce the danger;
>
> 5. The extent to which the manufacturer purposefully created the danger;
>
> 6. The extent to which the defendants are subject to federal safety regulation;
>
> 7. The probability that compensatory damages might be awarded against defendants in other cases; and, finally,
>
> 8. The amount of time which has passed since the actions sought to be deterred.

We have reviewed the entire record and, after taking into consideration the above-listed factors, have concluded that there was sufficient, in fact substantial, evidence for the jury to find that Riegel acted in willful, wanton and/or malicious disregard of the rights of others in marketing its flannelette.

The Danger

Plaintiffs introduced substantial evidence to show that thousands of people were dying or being seriously injured from clothing fires involving highly flammable fabrics each year. It was shown that the young and the very old were the most susceptible to these injuries. Furthermore, Dr. Johnson, at trial, demonstrated the instantaneous ignition and rapid burning rate of the untreated cotton flannelette manufactured by Riegel.

The Feasibility of Reducing the Hazard

As previously indicated, plaintiffs introduced a large amount of evidence showing that flame retardant products could have been applied to cotton flannelette well before Riegel manufactured the flannelette used in Lee Ann's pajamas. Of course, there was contrary evidence presented on this point by Riegel's witnesses, but plaintiffs' experts provided credible evidence.

However, even if such evidence had not been sufficient, there was sufficient evidence from which the jury could conclude that Riegel was strictly liable for its failure to warn. * * * The high flammability of Riegel's cotton flannelette is itself evidence of its duty in this regard. Furthermore, there was substantial evidence that Riegel was uniquely aware of these flammable characteristics.

Riegel did not seriously argue at trial that it was unable to provide a warning to the consumer, nor could it because plaintiffs introduced evidence that Riegel was able to send advertising information concerning the positive attributes of its product through the chain of commerce.

Riegel mainly argued at trial and argues here on appeal that it was not feasible to warn consumers because such a warning would "stigmatize" its product, thereby seemingly admitting that it was protecting the marketing of a product consumers might deem unreasonably hazardous.

Riegel's Knowledge

Riegel's knowledge of the hazard involved and its reason for not taking feasible measures to reduce this hazard was demonstrated at trial. In 1956, one of Riegel's top officials sent to the Riegel head of research a memorandum listing a number of clothing fires and consequent injuries which occurred to persons wearing Riegel flannelette garments. This memorandum stated that the company was sitting on a "powder keg" with respect to the flammability of their flannelette. It was also proven at trial that between 1960 and 1967, Riegel was on notice that approximately 6 lawsuits were brought against it for accidents involving its cotton flannelette.

Riegel introduced a great amount of evidence showing its communications with several chemical companies concerning the availability of flame retardant products and the application of these products to its cotton flannelette. Riegel apparently introduced these items in an effort to show its good faith in attempting to find and apply a viable flame retardant to its cotton flannelette. However, one of Riegel's own letters evidences the reason for its failure in this area. In April 1968, a letter from an official of Riegel explained that satisfactory runs were made with flame-retarded flannelette using various chemicals, but that Riegel was not going to use these products until federal law so required because of the cost factor. Plaintiffs' witnesses testified that the cost of flame-retardant fabrics would not make them unmarketable. Thus, it may be inferred from this letter that the decision not to use flame-retardant cotton flannelette was merely an economic one for the benefit of Riegel.

Plaintiffs' evidence also tended to prove that while Riegel conducted some surveillance of developments in the flame-retardant field, its efforts were minimal. Plaintiffs introduced evidence that prior to 1965, Riegel kept no records on its research and development of nonflammable products and fabrics. Furthermore, from 1967 to 1969, $140,000 was spent on research in this area while the entire research and development spending of the company amounted to $1,831,731.

6. [The court addressed Riegel's arguments on the risk of overpunishment.]

Riegel * * * argues that there is no need for the deterrent of punitive damages in this case. Riegel contends that compensatory damages and loss of sales and reputation act as an adequate deterrent. Riegel also posits that since it no longer manufactures cotton flannelette and since the Flammable Fabrics Act presently has more stringent standards for children's sleepwear, no deterrent is needed. This argument ignores the fact that Riegel was shown to have acted in reckless disregard of the public for purely economic reasons in the past. A punitive damages award serves to deter Riegel from acting in a similar manner with respect to other products manufactured by it in the future. Furthermore, since the potential of compensatory damages awards and loss of sales and reputation did not serve to deter Riegel in the past, Riegel cannot now argue that these considerations act as an adequate deterrent.

Riegel also overlooks the fact that one of the functions of a punitive damages award is to punish past misconduct. This function is well served by a punitive damages award in this case.

7. Riegel contends that the punitive damages award of $1,000,000 was clearly excessive. This court has stated that it will not disturb a punitive damages award unless it appears that the award was actuated by passion and prejudice and is so excessive as to be deemed unreasonable. Hammerstein v. Reiling, 262 Minn. 200, 115 N.W.2d 259 (1962). We have reviewed the record in this case and find that the punitive damages award is not unreasonable in light of the evidence presented.

The evidence shows that Riegel created a substantial danger to the public by marketing its highly flammable cotton flannelette. Riegel continued to market this product even though there were economically feasible measures which could have been taken to reduce this danger to a fairly acceptable level. The evidence also showed that Riegel was aware of the danger and the means for reducing this danger. Furthermore, Riegel is a multi-million dollar corporation which reaped substantial profits through the sale of its highly flammable cotton flannelette. We, therefore, do not find that the punitive damages award was excessive as a matter of law.

* * *

[Affirmed.]

NOTE

Consider Tetuan v. A.H. Robins Co., 241 Kan. 441, 738 P.2d 1210 (1987), which involved the sale of an IUD contraceptive device called the "Dalkon Shield," marketed by A.H. Robins from 1970 to 1974. The shield was a piece of plastic, roughly oval in shape, which was less than two inches in diameter. Four phalanges on either side, giving it a crab-like appearance, secured it within the uterus. Attached to the bottom of the shield, like most IUDs, was a tailstring, descending from the uterus through the cervix and into the vagina, that permitted the user to know that the device was in place. Unlike other IUDs, which all had monofilament strings, the Dalkon Shield's string was comprised of 200–400 individual filaments covered by a nylon sheath. Unfortunately, the shield's multifilament string, much more so than the monofilament string, acted as a wick for bacteria to travel from the vagina into the uterus, which sometimes resulted in a serious malady called pelvic inflammatory disease (PID).

Robins was barraged with complaints and finally took the shield off the market at the urging of the FDA in 1974. In 1980, the company issued a "Dear Doctor" letter recommending the removal of the shield from asymptomatic users, but refused to pay for such removal. In 1984, Robins sent out its final "Dear Doctor" letter, recommending the removal of any remaining Dalkon Shields, and offering to pay for removal.

The plaintiff's doctor fitted her with a shield in 1971. In September 1979, she began to experience fever and severe pain from PID, caused by the shield. Her doctor, who had received no warnings from A.H. Robins, was unable to diagnose the problem. After antibiotic treatment and hospitalization, the shield was finally removed in March 1980, but the pain persisted. Plaintiff's doctor referred her to a specialist who found it necessary in June 1980 to perform a total hysterectomy—the removal of her uterus, Fallopian tubes, and ovaries. Plaintiff sued Robins, and the jury found in her favor, awarding $1.7 million in compensatory damages, and assessing punitive damages of $7.5 million. Robins appealed:

> Robins stresses that no Kansas appellate court has ever upheld a punitive damage award of this magnitude. Neither has any been presented with corporate misconduct of such gravity and duration. We note that, in Palmer v. A.H. Robins Co., Inc., 684 P.2d 187 (Colo. 1984), the Colorado Supreme Court upheld an award of punitive damages of $6.2 million * * *.
>
> * * * In the present case, the jury made a specific finding of fraud. A review of the record indicates that there was substantial evidence tending to show Robins knew the Dalkon Shield was not safe or effective; that Robins knew of the wicking nature of the tail string; that Robins knew of a high rate of PID and septic abortion associated

with the Dalkon Shield; that Robins misled doctors through claims of safety and efficacy while it knew there was no basis for a claim of safety, and all responsible tests for the Dalkon Shield's effectiveness showed a much higher pregnancy rate than Dr. Davis' "1.1%" figure; that Robins similarly misled consumers through a misleading lay promotional campaign; that Robins never publicly retracted its claims of "effectiveness" even though it had privately acknowledged the 1.1% rate as invalid; and that Robins knew there were serious problems with its open-ended nylon multifilament string in maintaining its integrity within the body. But not only was there substantial evidence to conclude that Robins fully comprehended, by 1974 at the latest, the enormity of the dangers it had created, but that it deliberately and intentionally concealed those dangers; that it put money into "favorable" studies; that it tried to neutralize any critics of the Dalkon Shield; that Robins was motivated by a desire to avoid litigation judgments rather than a concern for the safety of the users of the Dalkon Shield; that it consistently denied the dangers of the Dalkon Shield for nearly fifteen years after its original marketing of the Dalkon Shield; that it commissioned studies on the Dalkon Shield which it dropped or concealed when the results were unfavorable; and, ultimately, that it consigned hundreds of documents to the furnace rather than inform women that the Dalkon Shield carried inside their bodies was a bacterial time bomb which could cause septic abortions, PID, and even death.

* * *

The $6.2 million punitive damage award against Robins in *Palmer* was rendered by the jury on July 30, 1979. Loretta Tetuan first experienced symptoms of PID in late September of that year. It is entirely possible that plaintiff's injuries could have been avoided if the company had reacted to the verdict by immediately moving to recall the product or to at least warn of its dangers. Instead, Robins responded with the same position it had taken for the last decade—that the Dalkon Shield was "safe and effective." Robins issued a statement on July 31, 1979, that the verdict was "an aberration" and that it was confident "this unwarranted verdict will not survive" on appeal.

The first Dalkon Shield case to proceed to trial on the merits occurred in Kansas in Deemer v. A.H. Robins Co., Case No. C–26420. On March 1, 1975, the jury awarded punitive damages against Robins in the amount of $75,000. Robins did not recall the product; it did not warn users of the Dalkon Shield's dangers; it did not warn physicians. It certainly did not warn Loretta Tetuan or the physicians who treated her. Instead, it reacted to the modest punitive damages award in *Deemer* by promptly attempting to destroy all evidence of its knowledge of the Dalkon Shield's dangers, consigning hundreds of documents to the draft furnace. To punish Robins for its conduct and to discourage others from committing like wrongs in the future, the punitive damages award is justified.

The judgment is affirmed.

738 P.2d at 1239–40, 1246.

ACOSTA v. HONDA MOTOR COMPANY, LTD.

United States Court of Appeals, Third Circuit, 1983.
717 F.2d 828.

BECKER, CIRCUIT JUDGE.

* * * This case presents the important question whether Virgin Islands law permits the award of punitive damages against defendants who have been found strictly liable under section 402A of the Restatement (Second) of Torts for having marketed defective products. * * *

In early 1976, plaintiff purchased a used Honda CB750 motorcycle. At that time the motorcycle was six years old; plaintiff was its third owner. Approximately two months after he bought the motorcycle, plaintiff was injured when he was thrown from the motorcycle while riding at night on a lighted road in St. Thomas. According to his testimony, he was driving at approximately 30–35 miles per hour when he saw in the road a repair ditch approximately four inches deep and ten feet long. He testified that he slowed down, retained control of the motorcycle, and maneuvered it straight through the ditch. As he was exiting the ditch, however, the motorcycle's rear wheel hit the back edge of the ditch and collapsed. Despite plaintiff's efforts to maintain control, the collapsed rear of the motorcycle jerked into the air, tossing him to the ground. Plaintiff sustained multiple injuries, including four fractured vertebrae, a broken femur, and a punctured liver.

[Plaintiff sued the motorcycle manufacturer, Honda, the wheel manufacturer, Daido Kogyo, and another, alleging defects in design and manufacture and failure to warn. The jury returned verdicts against Honda and Daido Kogyo for $175,000 in compensatory damages and assessed each $210,000 in punitive damages. Noting that he was surprised at the modest level of the compensatory award, the trial court denied the defendants' motions for judgment n.o.v. Defendants appealed.]

* * *

Defendants' principal contention on appeal is that the evidence was insufficient as a matter of law to sustain the award of punitive damages and that the district court erred in submitting the issue to the jury in the first place. Before turning to that question, however, we first must address their argument that punitive damages are unavailable in this case because, no matter what the evidence, punitive damages are fundamentally inconsistent with a regime of strict products liability in general, and with section 402A in particular.

A. *The Availability of Punitive Damages in the Strict Liability Context.*

* * *

The Restatement (Second) of Torts does include a generally applicable provision regarding punitive damages. Section 908(2) declares:

> Punitive damages may be awarded for conduct that is outrageous, because of the defendant's evil motive or his reckless

> indifference to the rights of others. In assessing punitive damages, the trier of fact can properly consider the character of the defendant's act, the nature and extent of the harm to the plaintiff that the defendant caused or intended to cause and the wealth of the defendant.

Nowhere in that section or the comments did the drafters suggest that these principles should not apply to strict products liability, and we concur with the considered opinion of the Court of Appeals for the Fifth Circuit that "[p]unishment and deterrence, the basis for punitive damages * * *, are no less appropriate with respect to a product manufacturer who knowingly ignores safety deficiencies in its product that may endanger human life" than in other cases in which "the defendant's conduct shows wantonness or recklessness or reckless indifference to the rights of others." Dorsey v. Honda Motor Co., 655 F.2d 650, 658 (5th Cir.1981) (construing Florida law), opinion modified on rehearing, 670 F.2d 21 (5th Cir.), cert. denied, ___ U.S. ___, 103 S.Ct. 177, 74 L.Ed. 2d 145 (1982).

Some courts and commentators, however, have suggested that the policies underlying punitive damages are so incompatible with those animating strict products liability that punitive damage awards should not be permitted against defendants found liable under 402A. These arguments essentially break down into three groups: contentions that punitive damages will upset the delicate balance struck in the creation of a strict products liability regime, assertions that the goals of punitive damages are unachievable in the strict products liability context, and arguments that the imposition of punitive damages in 402A cases will have extremely undesirable economic and social consequences. We disagree that these considerations warrant our precluding the award of punitive damages, and we discuss each in turn.

1. *Would the Availability of Punitive Damages Disrupt the Regime of Strict Products Liability?*

* * *

We reject the notion that punitive damages are theoretically inconsistent with strict products liability. While it is true that section 402A eschews the culpability of defendants' conduct as a factor in determining liability, it does not do so because focusing on culpability is always inappropriate. Indeed the drafters of the Restatement explicitly noted that 402A "does not preclude liability based upon the alternative ground of negligence of the seller, where such negligence can be proved." Comment a. Rather, the rule is intended to expand recovery by circumventing the restrictions imposed by fault-based standards. [Citation.] The fact that some sellers therefore will be found liable in the absence of fault does not mean that those who are at fault—and outrageously so—should not be punished.[10] [Citations.]

10. Defendants also contend that a jury is likely to be confused by the presence of the two concepts in the same case. Accord Gold v. Johns–Manville Sales Corp., 553 F.Supp. 482, 485, (D.N.J.1983). But that argument ignores the fact that many plain-

One court, however, recently has advanced an economics-based objection to allowing punitive damages in a 402A action:

> [T]he allowance of punitive damages would warp the valuation process which is implicit in the litigation process. That is, the product's price should reflect the cost of accidents or the cost of accident avoidance mechanisms in order that the market may assess the usefulness of the product. * * * The assessment of punitive damages upon the manufacturer and distributors can be analyzed as the imposition of costs for poor managerial decisions. These costs should not be spread to the buying public through an adjustment of the product's price. To do so will deflate the usefulness of the product on the basis of facts which do not relate to the product itself.

Gold v. Johns–Manville Sales Corp., 553 F.Supp. 482, 484 (D.N.J.1983) (citations omitted). Although the argument is attractive, it is predicated on a questionable premise, for it is not necessarily true that an award of punitive damages will be spread to the public through an adjustment of the price. In order for such spreading to occur, not only would a manufacturer have to be able to forecast punitive damages awards against him, but the market structure also would have to be such that he had sufficient unutilized market power to pass on the increased costs. Unless an entire competitive industry was behaving similarly (i.e., engaging in the same kind of opprobrious conduct and forecasting), a manufacturer would seem to be unable to afford to pass on the costs.[11] Accord Wangen v. Ford Motor Co., 97 Wis.2d 260, 294 N.W.2d 437, 452 (1980).

2. *Does the Strict Liability Context Limit the Effectiveness of Punitive Damages?*

Section 908(1) of the Restatement (Second) of Torts makes clear that

> [p]unitive damages are damages, other than compensatory or nominal damages, awarded against a person *to punish him for his outrageous conduct and to deter him and others like him from similar conduct* in the future.

tiffs plead alternative theories of negligence and strict products liability. Thus juries are frequently asked, as was the case here, simultaneously to consider both fault and nonfault based standards of liability. Moreover, we are convinced that a properly instructed jury will be able to distinguish between the standards applicable to awards of compensatory and punitive damages.

11. Law-and-economics scholars are divided on the effect and appropriateness of punitive damages. See generally Punitive Damages, 56 So.Cal.L.Rev. 1 (1982). While the debate focuses on the availability of punitive damages generally, a number of the proponents of punitive damages have endorsed their use in the strict products liability context. See, e.g., Cooter, Economic Analysis of Punitive Damages, 56 So.Cal.L.Rev. 79, 95 ("[T]o recover punitive damages, the economic model suggests that the consumer should also be required to prove that the manufacturer knowingly caused the defect."); Owen, Punitive Damages in Products Liability Litigation, 74 Mich.L.Rev. 1257 (1976) (concluding that "punitive damages may be usefully employed in products liability litigation to punish and to deter the marketing of defective products in flagrant disregard of the public safety").

(Emphasis added.); [citation]. While few, if any courts, have challenged these goals, some courts and commentators have suggested that the connection between punitive damages and the goals of punishment and deterrence will be attenuated in the strict products liability context.

Proponents of this argument point out that the magnitude of recent jury verdicts, coupled with the potential for a single design defect to serve as the template for hundreds or thousands of defective, injury-causing products, means that a manufacturer may be liable for many millions of dollars merely as compensation to injured victims. See 3 L. Frumer & M. Friedman, Products Liability § 33.01[7]. Thus, the argument runs, compensatory damages have reached such a level in products-liability litigation that, despite their more limited purpose, they have begun to perform the functions heretofore performed by punitive damages. Manufacturers, the argument concludes, therefore already have every incentive to insure that their products are as safe as possible. Indeed the Court of Appeals for the Second Circuit observed as early as 1967:

> Many awards of compensatory damages doubtless contain something of a punitive element, and more would do so if a separate award for exemplary damages were eliminated. Even though products liability insurance blunts the deterrent effect of compensatory awards to a considerable extent, the total coverage under such policies is often limited, bad experience is usually reflected in future rates, and insurance affords no protection to the damage to reputation among [users, consumers, and distributors] which an instance like the present must inevitably produce.

Roginsky v. Richardson–Merrell, Inc., 378 F.2d 832, 841 (2d Cir.1967). Thus the *Roginsky* court concluded that punitive damages were unnecessary to punish and deter the reckless marketing of defective products.

We are not persuaded that limiting recovery to compensatory damages will, in all cases, provide an effective deterrent against the type of wrongful conduct for which punitive damages are usually available. For example, the cost of litigation relative to the likely recovery may deter victims of product defects from suing the manufacturer, even under a regime of strict liability, where products causing numerous minor injuries are involved. The availability of punitive damages to those who do sue may offset the decreased deterrence attributable to those who thus could but do not. Similarly, consumers will not always be aware of the source of an injury caused by a product defect, see Sturm, Ruger & Co. v. Day, 594 P.2d 38, modified, 615 P.2d 621 (1980) on rehearing, 627 P.2d 204 (Alaska), cert. denied, 454 U.S. 894, 102 S.Ct. 391, 70 L.Ed.2d 209 (1981); Owen, Punitive Damages in Products Liability Litigation, 74 Mich.L.Rev. 1258, 1287–95 (1976) (also noting the expense of litigation), or they may wrongfully attribute the accident to their own clumsiness; the manufacturer's reprieve in such cases will be offset by the availability of punitive damages in other cases. Finally, under existing doctrine, compensatory damages may prove an inadequate deterrent even when victims do bring suit. Current doctrine does not, for example, allow the estate of a decedent killed by a defective product to recover the value of life to the decedent himself; recovery is instead limited to the pecuniary loss to those immediately surrounding the decedent. In many instances, this doctrine may lead to inadequate compensation. In addition, those peripherally injured by accidents to another generally are not allowed to bring suit, yet their loss may be, in moral or practical terms, extremely substantial. See Owen, Civil Punishment and the Public Good, 56 So. Cal.L.Rev. 103, 113 (1982). While punitive damages may not be a logically perfect method of remedying these perhaps unavoidable flaws in our system of justice, they are a useful surrogate not necessarily precluded by a strict products liability regime.

3. *Will Punitive Damages Have Undesirable Economic and Social Consequences?*

Perhaps recognizing that mere redundancy would not be sufficient to supersede considerations in favor of allowing punitive damages, the *Roginsky* court predicted that the availability of such damages would have unfortunate results. The court noted that there are frequently numerous potential plaintiffs with claims arising from the same defect in design or manufacture; if each such plaintiff can recover punitive damages, the court warned, the aggregate recovery could be "catastrophic."

> If liability policies can protect against this risk as several courts have held, the cost of providing this probably needless deterrence, not only to the few manufacturers from whom punitive damages for highly negligent conduct are sought but to the thousands from whom it never will be, is passed on to the consuming public; if they cannot, as is held by other courts and recommended by most commentators, a sufficiently egregious error to one product can end the business life of a concern that has wrought much good in the past and might otherwise have continued to do so in the future, with many innocent stockholders suffering extinction of their investments for a single management sin.

Id. at 841.

Although we recognize that the effect of punitive damages may be harsh, we find somewhat excessive the *Roginsky* court's dire predictions about the consequences of allowing punitive damages. First, even assuming that policy considerations would permit manufacturers to insure against punitive damages,[14] it is not clear that such insurance

14. It would seem obvious that the availability of insurance to cover awards of punitive damages would undercut their punitive and deterrent effect. Indeed the Court of Appeals for the Fifth Circuit has so recognized in refusing to enforce such provisions of automobile insurance policies:

> Where a person is able to insure himself against punishment he gains a freedom of misconduct inconsistent with the es-

would necessarily emasculate the effectiveness of the remedy or result in "needless deterrence." Rather, a 1976 study by the Department of Commerce noted that recent increases in the number of products liability claims, policy cancellations, insurance premiums, and average loss per claim have contributed to a situation in which * * * many manufacturers are making stronger efforts to improve design and quality control. [Citation.] As one commentator has noted, "these developments compel the conclusion that products liability litigation is increasingly forcing manufacturers to improve product safety even when they are insured against claims for product injuries." Owen, supra, 74 Mich.L.Rev. at 1310.

More importantly, we do not share *Roginsky's* in terrorem vision of the consequences of punitive damages for which insurance is unavailable. It is, of course, possible that "a sufficiently egregious error as to one product" could result in the demise of its manufacturer, but such a result is not inevitable.[15] [For one thing, prior punitive damages awards may be considered in determining the amount of a subsequent award.] [16] Moreover, this court has previously recognized that both the wealth of the defendant, [citation],[17] and the size of compensatory

> tablishment of sanctions against such misconduct. It is not disputed that insurance against criminal fines or penalties would be void as violative of public policy. The same public policy should invalidate any contract of insurance against the civil punishment that punitive damages represent.

Northwestern National Casualty Co. v. McNulty, 307 F.2d 432, 440 (5th Cir.1962); accord Smith v. Merchant Mut. Bonding Co. (In re Guardianship of Smith), 211 Kan. 397, 405, 507 P.2d 189, 196 (1973); Owen, supra, 74 Mich.L.Rev. at 1312–13; Ellis, Fairness and Efficiency in the Law of Punitive Damages, 56 So.Cal.L.Rev. 1, 74, 75 (1982). Some courts, however, have permitted such insurance. See, e.g., Lazenby v. Universal Underwriters Ins. Co., 214 Tenn. 639, 383 S.W.2d 1 (1964); cases cited Owen, supra, 74 Mich.L.Rev. at 1312 n. 267.

15. Nor is such a result necessarily untenable. See infra note 17. We note, however, that no empirical evidence has been offered that Roginsky's forebodings have been realized in the sixteen years since it was written. See State ex rel. Young v. Crookham, 290 Or. 61, 618 P.2d 1268 (1980) (apprehension of corporate annihilation by awards of punitive damages is exaggerated).

16. At least one court has questioned whether these practical problems can be overcome. See *Roginsky,* supra, 378 F.2d at 839–40. In light of our conclusion that plaintiff did not adduce evidence sufficient to sustain his claim for punitive damages, however, see infra Part III.C., we need not determine whether or to what extent a court, before submitting the claim to the jury, should consider prior awards of punitive damages against a defendant for recklessly marketing the same defective product. See generally Owen, supra, 74 Mich. L.Rev. at 1319 (suggesting increased judicial control in the assessment of punitive damages).

17. Although *Herman* involved a situation in which evidence of the defendant's wealth was introduced by plaintiff in order to get higher punitive damages, such evidence can cut both ways. For example, a jury might decide that a defendant's financial position, as a result of other awards of punitive damages for the same conduct, is so precarious that a sizeable award of punitive damages would be inappropriate.

Of course, a jury might reasonably decide, when faced with such information, that a bankrupting award is nevertheless appropriate. Although the Second Circuit posited the case in which an otherwise "good" manufacturer is thereby driven out of business, the situation is equally likely in which the manufacturer is one whose success and financial health is directly attributable to its willingness recklessly to market an unsafe, but therefore cheaper and more popular, product. Thus an award of punitive damages may have the effect of redressing an unfair and socially undesirable competitive advantage.

damages, [citation], should be taken into account in assessing punitive damages. "Thus, corporate defendants are protected from excessive punitive damage awards through judicial control both at the district court and appellate levels." Neal v. Carey Canadian Mines, supra, 548 F.Supp. at 377.

B. *Standard of Proof*

Although we reject each of the various arguments against awarding punitive damages in the strict liability context, we agree with Judge Friendly's observation in *Roginsky,* supra, that "the consequences of imposing punitive damages in a case like the present are so serious" that "particularly careful scrutiny" is warranted. 378 F.2d at 852 (denying petition for rehearing); cf. Comment, Criminal Safeguards and the Punitive Damages Defendant, 34 U.Chi.L.Rev. 408, 417 (1967) ("If one accepts the proposition that the consequences of punitive damages can be 'momentous and serious,' then justice requires increasing the burden of persuasion of the plaintiff in a punitive damages action.") We therefore hold under Virgin Islands law that a plaintiff seeking punitive damages, at least in an action in which liability is predicated on section 402A, must prove the requisite "outrageous" conduct by clear and convincing proof.[18] Accord Wangen v. Ford Motor Co., supra; Model Uniform Product Liability Act § 120(A), 44 Fed.Reg. 62748 (1979).

C. *The Standard Applied*

Applying the "clear and convincing" standard to the facts of this case, we conclude that the [evidence was insufficient to support the punitive damages awards.]

Plaintiff's evidence allegedly supporting his claim for punitive damages essentially consisted of the following:

1. The rear wheel of his motorcycle collapsed from a thirty-five mile per hour impact with a ditch four inches deep;

2. The particular wheel of plaintiff's motorcycle suffered from an inherent lack of strength as evidenced by the fact that

We also take issue with the Second Circuit's hypothesis that the innocent victim of a punitive damages award will be the manufacturing corporation's innocent shareholders. It is true, of course, that the shareholders may ultimately bear the burden of such an award, see supra pp. 837–838, and it is also true that they are innocent to the extent that it was actually management or an employee who was responsible for the conduct justifying the award. At the same time, it *is* the shareholders who have benefited from any such conduct that has redounded to the manufacturer's fiscal advantage. Moreover, the loss of investment and the decline in value of investments are risks which investors knowingly undertake, and investors should not enjoy ill-gotten gains. There is a public interest to encourage shareholders and corporate management to exercise closer control over the operations of the entity, and the imposition of punitive damages may serve this interest.

Wangen v. Ford Motor Co., 97 Wis.2d 260, 294 N.W.2d 437, 453–54 (1980).

18. Even with such proof, however, a plaintiff is not entitled to recover such damages as a matter of right. Rather the Restatement is quite clear that the award is discretionary with the trier of fact. See § 908 comment d.

it weighed sixteen percent less than several other randomly sampled rear wheels of motorcycles of the same model;

3. The owner's manual represented the CB750 as a high-speed touring motorcycle but provided no warning that the rear wheel might collapse upon the type of impact that occurred in this case;

4. Although the owner's manual instructed users to set and maintain the tension of the motorcycle's shock absorbers and wheel spokes, the manual did not warn that the failure to do so might result in the collapse of the wheel;

5. Defendants merely spot-checked rear wheels during the assembly process and did not crush test or weigh each wheel;

6. Plaintiff's expert witness testified that the above evidence constituted defective manufacture and a failure adequately to inspect or to warn; and

7. Plaintiff's expert concluded that defendant's conduct manifested a "colossal disregard for the safety of the users of the motor vehicle," App. II at 125–26.[20]

Plaintiff contends that the jury was entitled to infer from this evidence that defendants recklessly disregarded his rights and safety as a user of the motorcycle. We cannot agree. As we have suggested above, section 908 of the Restatement declares that reckless or outrageous conduct on the part of the defendant is the touchstone of punitive damages. [Citations.] Although section 908 does not elaborate on the kind of conduct for which punitive damages are appropriate, comment b refers to section 500 * * *.

The commentary accompanying section 500 provides:

> Recklessness may consist of either of two different types of conduct. In one the actor knows, or has reason to know . . . of facts which create a high degree of risk of physical harm to another, and deliberately proceeds to act, or to fail to act, in conscious disregard of, or indifference to, that risk. In the other the actor has such knowledge, or reason to know, of the facts, but does not realize or appreciate the high degree of risk involved, although a reasonable man in his position would do so. An objective standard is applied to him and he is held to the realization of the aggravated risk which a reasonable man in his place would have, although he does not himself have it.
>
> * * *

For either type of conduct, to be reckless it must be unreasonable; but to be reckless, it must be something more than negligent. It must not only be unreasonable, but it must involve a risk of harm to others substantially in excess of that necessary to make the conduct negligent.

20. Although not raised on appeal, the admissibility of this statement under Fed. R.Evid. 702 or 704 is open to serious question.

It must involve an easily perceptible danger of death or substantial physical harm, and the probability that it will so result must be substantially greater than is required for ordinary negligence.

We have examined the evidence; viewed in the light most favorable to plaintiff, it does not show that the conduct of any defendant was outrageous or reckless. Indeed we discern no basis upon which the jury could have concluded that defendants knew or had reason to know that the rear wheel of Acosta's motorcycle was defective in design or manufacture and that they decided not to remedy the defect in conscious disregard of or indifference to the risk thereby created. Although the wheel had been used in over 275,000 motorcycles, and the model first offered in 1970 (six years before plaintiff's accident), there was no evidence of previous consumer complaints or lawsuits that might have called to defendants' attention that there might be a problem. Moreover, plaintiff offered no proof that defendants developed or failed to modify the engineering designs for the rear wheel of the CB750 with any knowledge or reason to know of its alleged lack of safety.[21] Such matters would have been admissible on the punitive damages issues.

In short, a jury could not have reasonably concluded that the evidence by the clear and convincing standard showed defendants to have acted with reckless disregard for the safety of users of the CB750.[22] Accordingly, we hold that the district court should have granted defendants' motions for directed verdicts on the punitive damage claim and that it was error to deny the subsequent motions for judgment n.o.v. on behalf of Honda and Daido Kogyo.

[Punitive damages awards reversed; remanded.]

NOTES

1. In addition to punishment and deterrence, punitive or "exemplary" damages also serve to maximize compliance with the rules of law and to compensate plaintiffs. They are often criticized for giving plaintiffs undeserved windfalls since they are awarded in addition to compensatory damages. They are, indeed, a powerful tool in the hands of a skillful plaintiff's lawyer. How appropriate are such damages in the products liability context? In *strict* liability cases?

21. In fact, defendants adduced evidence, which was not contradicted, that pre-production testing followed standard procedures, including on-the-road testing and laboratory testing (including wheel crushing to determine durability), and that samples from each production run of completed motorcycles were subjected to final dynamometer tests before shipping. Apparently, none of these tests suggested that a problem might exist.

22. The clear and convincing standard of proof we announce today pertains to the degree of proof needed to be found by the trier of fact before it assesses punitive damages. The standard is not applicable to an appellate court in reviewing the determination of the trier of fact that there was or was not clear and convincing evidence of outrageous conduct. Rather the applicable standard of review on appeal is whether the record "is critically deficient of that minimum quantum of evidence from which a jury might reasonably afford relief." Denneny v. Siegel, 407 F.2d 433, 439 (3d Cir.1969).

2. Most courts hold that punitive damages will not lie in warranty cases, applying the general rule prohibiting such awards in contract cases. See U.C.C. § 1–106(1): "[N]either consequential or special nor penal damages may be had except as specifically provided in this Act or by any other rule of law."

3. Although punitive damages awards were quite rare in products liability cases until the 1980s, they are now fairly common. Such awards are not uncommon in automotive litigation and are considered further in that context in ch. 9, below.

4. The threat of punitive damages judgments may have played a role in the bankruptcy of Johns–Manville, in connection with its sale of asbestos products over many years without warning of the risks of asbestosis and other lung disorders. The problems of punitive damages in the context of toxic substances such as asbestos are examined in ch. 10, § 3, below.

Another company that chose the bankruptcy route (in 1984–85) in the face of massive claims for punitive (and compensatory) damages was A.H. Robins, in connection with the Dalkon Shield litigation, discussed above. A federal court confirmed a reorganization plan for the company in 1988, providing for a $2 billion claimants' trust fund for compensatory damages. Stating that the company's punitive damages liability was "staggering" and "unpredictable," and that such damages would have been a "wild card" undermining a realistic reorganization plan, the court ruled that punitive damages claims would be disallowed. See 16 Prod.Saf.&Liab.Rep. (BNA) 793 (Aug. 19, 1988). The *Tetuan* court, among others, questioned whether Robin's bankruptcy petition might have been more of a strategic maneuver, in the management of the thousands of pending cases it confronted around the country, than a true reflection of insolvency (which is not required under Chapter 11). See 738 P.2d at 1244.

5. **Expert Testimony.** The plaintiff's expert in *Acosta* testified that the defendant's conduct reflected "a colossal disregard for * * * safety." 717 F.2d at 840. This form of "expert" testimony on manufacturer reprehensibility is increasing in products liability trials as plaintiffs' counsel seek to lay a foundation for a punitive damages award. See also American Cyanamid Co. v. Roy, 498 So.2d 859, 862 (Fla.1986) ("terrible misrepresentation"); Chrysler Corp. v. Wolmer, 499 So.2d 823, 827 (Fla.1986) ("an atrocious violation of accepted practices in safety engineering" reflecting "a reckless disregard for safety"); Sliman v. Aluminum Co. of America, 112 Idaho 277, 731 P.2d 1267, 1275 (1986) ("extreme deviation from the customary practice in the industry"); Airco, Inc. v. Simmons First Nat. Bank, 276 Ark. 486, 638 S.W.2d 660, 662–63 (1982) (product was "grossly in violation of safety engineering principles and never should have been put on the market"); Ford Motor Co. v. Stubblefield, 171 Ga.App. 331, 319 S.E.2d 470 (1984) (defendant's actions were "conscious," "deliberate," and "callous").

The last two cases involved the same expert, a "system safety and human factors enginee[r]" who is stated to have testified "in over 100 cases with products ranging from toys to airplanes" and whose "field of expertise" is said to be "punitive damages based on engineering management negligence" in a Technical Expert Directory. Products Liability and Transportation Legal Directory 196 (1983). Having apparently made such testimony on corporate "malice" his specialty, this particular expert has proved successful in his efforts: in *Airco,* the jury returned a $3 million punitive damages verdict for the sale of a defective anesthesia ventilator and, in *Stubblefield,* the jury assessed punitive damages of $8 million for the sale of an uncrashworthy car.

Most courts, in the few opinions reflecting such expert testimony on corporate malice, either pay little or no attention to its propriety (as in *Airco* and *Stubblefield*), or reason that it is proper. Karns v. Emerson Elec. Co., 817 F.2d 1452, 1459 (10th Cir.1987) ("reckless"). In *Acosta,* supra, 717 F.2d at 840 n. 20, Judge Becker expressed serious doubts as to its admissibility. What is the problem? What are the relevant rules of evidence? What are the policy issues?

As a plaintiff's lawyer, would you seek to have your expert so testify? As a court, would you permit such testimony?

6. **Judicial Control.** *Acosta* is an example of the courts that have "begun to exert stricter control over the process of determining such awards, from discovery safeguards and pretrial rulings through remittitur or reversal on appeal. Several courts that recently have approved for the first time awards of punitive damages in products liability cases have emphasized the importance of firm trial and appellate court control to reduce the added risks of abuse—particularly the threat of over-punishment from multiple awards for a single product mistake. This development is of crucial importance, one that may well be necessary to prevent such awards from violating a corporation's due process rights." Owen, Problems in Assessing Punitive Damages Against Manufacturers of Defective Products, 49 U.Chi.L.Rev. 1, 50 (1982).

7. **Constitutional Issues.** Defendants and commentators have long questioned the fairness of a civil penalty system, based on standards as vague as "malice," "reckless," or "willful and wanton," with no real ceiling on the size of the assessments, which has none of the procedural safeguards designed to assure the propriety of punishment in criminal cases. See, e.g., Comment, Criminal Safeguards and the Punitive Damages Defendant, 34 U.Chi.L.Rev. 408 (1967). Due process challenges to punitive damages claims have traditionally fared poorly in the courts. Yet a renewed interest in the fairness of punitive damages law and procedures has sparked a reconsideration of the constitutional issues. See, e.g., Massey, The Excessive Fines Clause and Punitive Damages: Some Lessons From History, 40 Vand.L.Rev. 1233 (1987); Lawrence, Fines, Penalties, and Forfeitures: An Historical and Comparative Analysis, 65 N.C.L. Rev. 49 (1986); Jeffries, A Comment on the Constitutionality of Punitive Damages, 72 Va.L.Rev. 139 (1986); Wheeler, The Constitutional Case for Reforming Punitive Damages Procedures, 69 Va.L.Rev. 269 (1983); Notes, 75 Calif.L.Rev. 1433 (1987) (8th Amendment excessive fines clause), 85 Mich.L.Rev. 1699 (1987) (same).

As this book goes to press, the first federal court has ruled (in an asbestos case) that multiple punitive damages judgments for a single course of conduct violate a manufacturer's due process rights in the mass tort litigation context. Juzwin v. Amtorg Trading Corp., No. 87–3876 (D.N.J. March 9, 1989).

The United States Supreme Court twice ducked the constitutional issues in recent years in Bankers Life & Cas. Co. v. Crenshaw, ___ U.S. ___, 108 S.Ct. 1645, 100 L.Ed.2d 62 (1988), and Aetna Life Ins. Co. v. Lavoie, 475 U.S. 813, 106 S.Ct. 1580, 89 L.Ed.2d 823 (1986). It has granted certiorari in Kelco Disposal, Inc. v. Browning-Ferris Industries of Vermont, Inc., 845 F.2d 404 (2d Cir.1988), on the issue of whether a $6 million punitive damages award, far in excess of the compensatory award, is excessive under the 8th Amendment or otherwise.

VOSSLER v. RICHARDS MANUFACTURING COMPANY, INC.

California Court of Appeal, 1983.
143 Cal.App.3d 952, 192 Cal.Rptr. 219.

ANDREEN, ASSOCIATE JUSTICE.

Defendant Richards Manufacturing Company, Inc. (Richards) appeals from a judgment following jury trial in a products liability case. No attack is made on the sufficiency of evidence except as to the matter of punitive damages. The judgment was for compensatory damages of $25,000 and punitive damages of $500,000. We affirm.

* * *

In the period from 1970 through 1972, Dr. Leonard Marmor, an orthopedic surgeon working with the defendant corporation, developed a prosthetic device known as the Marmor Modular Knee, which permitted treatment of certain diseases of the knee by inserting specially crafted pieces of metal and plastic onto the surfaces of the bones that make up the knee joint. The metal components of the modular knee were originally produced in three sizes—small, medium and large—and each size included three elements (a template, a trial and a final component), each perfectly matched within a size for implantation. When implanting a metal component, the surgeon used the template to mark and prepare the bone, the trial component to insure that preparation of the bone was accurate, and then cemented the final component permanently in place. An important part of the surgical technique involved placing the final component so that it did not protrude forward of its proper location and impinge upon the kneecap when the knee was flexed.

During 1973 defendant, through engineering error, began manufacturing final metal components of the medium category which were larger than originally designed and which therefore did not match the medium template and trial components. It was thus possible that a surgeon could prepare a bone for insertion of the medium metal component using properly sized medium template and trial components (which were reused from surgery to surgery) and then cement into place a too-large medium final component.

Defendant had no procedure for insuring that the final components it produced were of the proper size, and so it manufactured and sold the larger-than-proper medium final components for some time without discovering the error. In January of 1974, defendant discovered its error, but in order to prevent its competitors from gaining a larger share of the market for such devices, concealed it from the medical profession, from its own sales personnel and from Dr. Marmor. Defendant attempted to replace, on a pretext, all of the properly sized medium template and trial components with newly manufactured larger components, and later attempted to resell the originally designed medium components as a supposedly new "small-medium" size, all without informing anyone outside the defendant corporation of the reason for its actions.

On October 15, 1974, a Marmor Modular Knee was implanted in the right knee of the then 67-year-old plaintiff. One of the metal components used by the surgeon was a medium, and in the subsequent complications and treatment thereof it was revealed that the discrepancy between the older, smaller template and trial components and the larger final component had resulted in improper positioning of the final component, causing impingement on the plaintiff's kneecap which necessitated eventual removal of the kneecap, and other damages.

On the issue of punitive damages, plaintiff proved that the components of the modular knee were actually manufactured by a subsidiary of the defendant and "sold" to defendant for approximately $23 per component, of which 10 percent reflected profit to the subsidiary. Defendant sold the modular knee components to the medical profession for prices ranging during the relevant period from $108 to $140 per component. From January 10, 1973, through April 2, 1973, 4,042 of the medium trial and final components were manufactured. The modular knee components comprised about one-third of the output of the subsidiary that manufactured it. Defendant's sales revenues were approximately $50 million in 1979, and the modular knee was one of 7,000 different products sold by defendant during the relevant period. * * *

* * *

During plaintiff's closing argument, defense counsel objected to the statement of plaintiff's counsel that defendant was " * * * doing over fifty million dollars a year in sales * * *," on the grounds that it was unsupported by evidence, irrelevant and prejudicial. The objection was overruled on all grounds.

* * *

NECESSITY OF INTRODUCING EVIDENCE OF DEFENDANT'S WEALTH AS PREREQUISITE FOR PUNITIVE DAMAGES

Citing Neal v. Farmers Ins. Exchange, supra, 21 Cal.3d 910, 148 Cal.Rptr. 389, 582 P.2d 980, Richards contends that punitive damages may not be awarded unless a plaintiff introduces evidence of defendant's wealth or profit from wrongdoing. However, *Neal* holds only that in determining whether a punitive damages award was excessive as a matter of law, the court should consider the wealth of the defendant. *Neal* did not hold that a punitive damages claim would fall if plaintiff did not introduce evidence of defendant's wealth.

* * *

The trend of modern decisions in other jurisdictions is to place the burden of producing evidence of wealth on the wrongdoer, permitting the defendant to establish its financial inability to pay punitive damages.

For instance, in Rinaldi v. Aaron (Fla.1975) 314 So.2d 762, the Supreme Court of Florida reversed a trial court's order removing consideration of punitive damages from the jury where the plaintiff had not introduced any evidence of the defendant's financial ability to pay. The court noted that such evidence of ability to pay was always admissible, but held that it was not a requisite to such an award, following the decisions of many other jurisdictions, including California. (Id., at p. 764.)

* * *

We recognize that since the purpose of punitive damages is to punish and deter wrongdoing by fashioning a monetary penalty tailored to the wealth of the defendant and to the reprehensibility of his conduct, absence of any evidence about the defendant's wealth significantly impairs a rational effectuation of this purpose. However, in view of direct California authority for the principle that the *plaintiff* need not introduce evidence of the defendant's wealth in order to be awarded punitive damages [citations], it is consonant with stare decisis and consistent with the modern trend to require the wrongdoer to demonstrate at the trial level that a particular award of punitive damages will exact too great a penalty because of his financial condition. Presumably, in the great majority of cases it will be to the plaintiff's advantage to show that the defendant is capable of absorbing a substantial penalty, and in those situations where it is otherwise, the defendant will be motivated to show its penury. The defendant is in the best position to provide the most accurate data concerning its financial condition, and need not decide whether to introduce such information until after the plaintiff has presented a sufficient case for the punitive damages issue to go to the trier of fact. If the defendant wishes to challenge an award of exemplary damages on appeal, its production of financial data will provide the basis for appellate review as mandated by the Supreme Court in *Neal* and other cases.

Richards contends that "* * * to require a defendant to present 'mitigating' financial condition evidence would be, for all intents and purposes, requiring the defendant to make a tacit admission that some award of punitive damages is appropriate. * * * The unfairness of placing such a burden on the defendant is manifest." * * * Defendants have developed techniques which permit them to introduce mitigating evidence without diminishing the force of their contest as to liability.

For all these reasons, we hold that the plaintiff has no obligation to introduce evidence of the defendant's financial condition when seeking punitive damages.

INSTRUCTIONS TO THE JURY

In the course of instructing the jury, the trial court stated as follows:

"The law provides no fixed standard as to the amount of such punitive damages, but leaves the amount to the jury's sound discretion, exercised without passion or prejudice.

"Any amount awarded for punitive damages should bear a reasonable relation to the actual damages, although no fixed ratio exists." [5]

The jury was [properly instructed].

DEFENDANT'S CONDUCT AS JUSTIFYING AN AWARD OF PUNITIVE DAMAGES

Defendant's attempt on appeal to suggest that its conduct exhibited a concern for the safety of the public via careful monitoring of its manufacture and sale of the modular knee is patently ludicrous. It was undisputed at trial that defendant purposely concealed the discrepancy in size between the medium final component as originally designed and as later produced by defendant from the medical profession, from Dr. Marmor—the inventor of the modular knee—and from its own sales personnel solely to protect its market position. The jury evidently disbelieved the self-serving testimony of defendant's corporate officers regarding their purported tests as to the medical significance of the larger-than-proper medium final component. Defendant further attempted to capitalize on its concealment of its manufacturing error by marketing the originally designed medium components as a purportedly "new" size. The comments of the Court of Appeal in Grimshaw v. Ford Motor Co. (1981) 119 Cal.App.3d 757, 174 Cal.Rptr. 348 are particularly appropriate here:

> "In assessing the propriety of a punitive damage award, as in assessing the propriety of any other judicial ruling based upon factual determinations, the evidence must be viewed in the light most favorable to the judgment. [Citation.] Viewing the record thusly in the instant case, the conduct of Ford's management was reprehensible in the extreme. It exhibited a conscious and callous disregard of public safety in order to maximize corporate profits. Ford's self-evaluation of its conduct is based on a review of the evidence most favorable to it instead of on the basis of the evidence most favorable to the judgment. Unlike malicious conduct directed toward a single specific individual, Ford's tortious conduct endangered the lives of thousands of Pinto purchasers. Weighed against the factor of reprehensibility, the punitive damage award as reduced by the trial judge was not excessive." (Id., at pp. 819–820, 174 Cal.Rptr. 348.)

Defendant's conduct in the present case was marginally less monstrously inhumane than the conduct of the defendant in *Grimshaw,* since concealment of Richards' manufacturing error for the sole pur-

5. BAJI No. 14.71 (1980 revision).

pose of protecting its profits merely threatened excruciating pain and crippling immobility to thousands of arthritic patients and anguish to their physicians and their families, not the fiery death that the auto manufacturer visited upon its customers. However, insofar as reprehensibility of conduct was concerned, the jury's award of punitive damages was fully justified.

PLAINTIFF'S CLOSING ARGUMENT

Richards contends that the court should not have permitted plaintiff's counsel to argue the amount of Richards' gross sales and a calculation of Richards' profit from its manufacture of the mismatched modular knee.

Counsel established the cost of the knee to Richards from its subsidiary and the sales price to its customers. From this he calculated an alleged profit margin and, using the number of operations of Dr. Jennings, constructed an argument of how much profit Richards had made from the sale of the mismatched knee.

* * * [T]he sole defense objection was that there was no evidence in the record that the defendant was doing over $50 million a year in sales. And that, if supported by the evidence, such was irrelevant and prejudicial. This was the extent of the objection.

Net, not gross, figures are the best yardstick to be used in determining punitive damages. [Citation.] Plaintiff's counsel purported to argue net income from the sales of the medium-sized components. Although the argument was superficial, there was no objection as to that portion of it. The issue is waived. [Citation.]

As to the objection as to the amount of gross sales, that figure was in evidence. Read in context, the gross sales amount was used in part to demonstrate to the jury that Richards was a sophisticated company and that when it made its marketing decision to conceal its product defect from its salesmen and the physicians who were to implant it, it should be held responsible for its actions. The gross sales figure was also used to bolster the amount of punitive damages claimed. However, there was no objection to this line of argument; the only objection made was to the use of the gross sales amount in the first context.

Evidence of gross sales figures is relevant, even if entitled to less weight than net profit. See, for example, Neal v. Farmers Ins. Exchange, supra, 21 Cal.3d 910, 148 Cal.Rptr. 389, 582 P.2d 980 which stated at page 929: "Finally, we note that the amount of punitive damages represented by the reduced judgment (i.e., approximately $740,000) represents less than one-tenth of 1 percent of defendant's *gross* assets. * * *" (Emphasis added.) * * *

Even in cases in which other evidence of net wealth appeared in the record, courts have indicated that figures on gross sales, gross income, or gross wealth are at least relevant to the issue of punitive damages. [Citations.]

We conclude that to the extent the issue was preserved for appeal, there was no prejudicial misconduct.

RATIO BETWEEN PUNITIVE AND COMPENSATORY DAMAGES

The jury's award of $500,000 in punitive damages represents a ratio of 20:1 between punitive and compensatory damages. Richards does not argue that such a ratio is disproportionate in punitive damage cases generally—indeed it cannot. It limits its argument to products liability actions, and contends that in the special circumstances of such litigation, the ratio is too high. It states that no punitive/compensatory ratio in a products case has ever exceeded 2:1 in California or 7:1 in any jurisdiction.

Products liability cases may be distinguished from typical punitive damage cases in several respects. The definition of proscribed conduct is malice, which may be established if the defendant acted with a "conscious disregard for the safety of others." A manufacturer designing a product must take trade-offs in terms of product safety against cost and utility. A design engineer necessarily makes cost-benefit analyses many times in the production of a complex product. Such a definition of malice may operate unfairly in some cases, and may tend to discourage product development. However, that consideration is of no moment here. Richards was not punished for a design decision; it had a well-designed product. Due to a manufacturing error, the product did not fit the template for which it was made. Richards knew of this defect, but in order to protect its competitive position against other manufacturers of prosthetic devices, decided to continue to market the defective product anyway. The public policy in favor of product development is unaffected by the award of punitive damages in this case.

* * *

The requirement of a reasonable relationship between compensatory and punitive damages is a useful tool in guarding against juror excess. So applied in this case, the ratio of 20:1 is not too high. The actual damages were limited; Richards' conduct was egregious. A ratio of 20:1 would be excessive in a case like *Grimshaw.* It is appropriate here because the jury could logically determine that any less would not sufficiently punish and deter.

[Affirmed.]

NOTES

1. **Determining Amount.** One of the most perplexing problems for courts and juries has been the determination of appropriate amounts for punitive damages awards. The Restatement formulation is widely accepted, but not too helpful, in directing the factfinder to consider: (1) the character of the defendant's act, (2) the nature and extent of the plaintiff's harm, and (3) the defendant's wealth. Rest. (2d) of Torts § 908(2).

A number of courts have found useful the following list of considerations applicable to the products liability context:

(1) the amount of the plaintiff's litigation expenses;

(2) the seriousness of the hazard to the public;

(3) the profitability of the marketing misconduct (increased by an appropriate multiple);

(4) the attitude and conduct of the enterprise upon discovery of the misconduct;

(5) the degree of the manufacturer's awareness of the hazard and of its excessiveness;

(6) the number and level of employees involved in causing or covering up the marketing misconduct;

(7) the duration of both the improper marketing behavior and its cover-up;

(8) the financial condition of the enterprise and the probable effect thereon of a particular judgment; and

(9) the total punishment the enterprise will probably receive from other sources.

Owen, Punitive Damages in Products Liability Litigation, 74 Mich.L.Rev. 1257, 1319 (1976). What do you think of these factors? What do you think of the "ratio rule" applied in *Vossler?*

2. **Reversal and Remittitur.** Because large awards of punitive damages often reflect passion or prejudice by the jury, they are frequently reversed or remitted by the trial or appellate court. Perhaps the most famous award of this type was the $125 million punitive damages verdict against Ford Motor Company in a Pinto fuel system case, discussed in *Vossler,* Grimshaw v. Ford Motor Co., 119 Cal.App.3d 757, 174 Cal.Rptr. 348 (1981), infra p. 829. The trial court's remittitur to $3.5 million was upheld on appeal. See also Ford Motor Co. v. Durrill, 714 S.W.2d 329 (Tex.App.1986), vac'd and remanded on settlement of parties 754 S.W.2d 646 (1988) (Mustang II fuel system) ($100 million punitive damages verdict, remitted by trial court to $20 million, further remitted on appeal to $10 million); Hodder v. Goodyear Tire & Rubber Co., 426 N.W.2d 826 (Minn.1988) (multi-piece tire rim exploded) ($12.5 million punitive damages verdict reduced to $4 million). "[I]t is because of the unique, public aspect of punitive damages that the court exercises a much closer supervision over these awards than is the case with compensatory awards." Id. at 837.

3. Perhaps the most imaginative remittitur order was entered by the trial court in O'Gilvie v. International Playtex, Inc., 609 F.Supp. 817 (D.Kan.1985), in which the jury returned a $10 million punitive damages verdict against the defendant for selling a high-absorbency tampon that sometimes caused toxic shock syndrome (TSS). The court offered to reduce or eliminate the punitive verdict if the defendant would remove the product from the market. Playtex promised to do so, and Judge Kelly remitted the verdict to $1.35 million. *Held* (2–1), the defendant's post-trial conduct was irrelevant to the issue, and the court had no authority to remit on that basis. Reversed, and the $10 million judgment reinstated. 821 F.2d 1438 (10th Cir.1987).

4. **Reform.** Punitive damages have been the subject of substantial recent reform. Consider the following approaches:

A. **Raising the standard of proof to "clear and convincing evidence."** E.g., *Acosta,* supra; Kan.Stat.Ann. § 60–3701; Ohio Rev.Code Ann. § 2307.80.

B. **Capping punitive awards.** E.g., Ala.Acts 87–185 (1987) ($250,000 unless misconduct was "highly aggravated"); Colo.Rev.Stat. 13–21–102 (punitive damages may not exceed compensatory damages).

C. **Payment of portion of award to public treasury.** E.g., Colo.Rev. Stat. 13–21–102 (60%); Iowa Code § 668A.1 (75%).

D. **Bifurcating trials.** E.g., N.J.Laws ch. 197, S.B. 2805 (1988) (bifurcated trial required); Mo.Laws H.B. 700 § 39 (1988) (same; net worth evidence admissible only in punitive damages portion of trial).

E. **Shifting determination of amount from jury to judge.** E.g., Kan. Stat.Ann. § 60–3701; Ohio Rev.Code Ann. § 2307.80.

F. **Barring punitive damages where defendant complied with government regulations.** E.g., N.J.Laws ch. 197, S.B. 2805 (1988) (FDA regulations); Ohio Rev.Code Ann. § 2307.80 (same); Tex.Laws 1987, S.B. 5 § 81.008 (same).

G. **Allowing punitive damages to be pleaded only upon proper showing and amendment to complaint.** E.g., Minn.Stat. § 549.191; Fla. Stat. § 768.72.

H. **Constitutional limitations.** Courts may shortly begin limiting punitive damages in various respects on constitutional grounds. See supra, p. 623 n. 7.

5. Punitive damages are examined further below in the contexts of automotive litigation, p. 829, and toxic substance litigation, p. 959.

6. See generally Ausness, Retribution and Deterrence: The Role of Punitive Damages in Products Liability Litigation, 74 Ky.L.J. 1 (1986); Seltzer, Punitive Damages in Mass Tort Litigation: Addressing the Problems of Fairness, Efficiency and Control, 52 Fordham L.Rev. 37 (1983); Ellis, Fairness and Efficiency in the Law of Punitive Damages, 56 So.Cal.L.Rev. 1 (1982); Owen, Problems in Assessing Punitive Damages Against Manufacturers of Defective Products, 49 U.Chi.L.Rev. 1 (1982); Owen, Punitive Damages in Products Liability Litigation, 74 Mich.L.Rev. 1257 (1976); Annot., 13 A.L.R.4th 52 (1982).

Chapter 7

SPECIAL TYPES OF DEFENDANTS

To this point, the focus has been on problems arising from litigation involving product manufacturers. Yet parties in the distribution chain other than the manufacturer play important roles in providing consumers with defective products. While in many respects the principles of liability are identical regardless of the defendant's position in the distributional chain, a number of variations and special considerations need to be examined.

As you consider the materials in this chapter, bear in mind the diversity of interests, concentrations of economic power, and methods of doing business of the various non-manufacturing defendants. Retailers, for example, vary in size from small, corner stores to major and even multi-national enterprises; in function from serving primarily as conduits for products made by others to imposing on manufacturers their own design specifications and quality control programs; and in range of services from sale alone to sale plus substantial services. Wholesalers, distributors, and component part manufacturers exhibit corresponding diversities. One step further removed from the distribution chain are advertisers and product endorsers who help to convey the product's image to consumers and to shape their expectations. Other defendants examined in this chapter include the federal government, government contractors, apparent manufacturers, employers, and successor corporations.

Despite the variations among these and other parties participating in the sale of new chattels, some common problems have occupied the attention of the courts. One is the extent to which strict liability in tort should be applied to defendants other than the manufacturer. It will be seen that negligence principles have retained a significant role where the liability of non-manufacturing defendants is involved. Suits against non-manufacturers inevitably foster attempts to shift the losses back up the distributional chain to the manufacturer. Accordingly, courts in recent years have increasingly focused upon various complex issues involved in the adjustment of losses among defendants.

SECTION 1. RETAILERS, WHOLESALERS, AND DISTRIBUTORS

ZAMORA v. MOBIL CORPORATION

Supreme Court of Washington, 1985.
104 Wash.2d 199, 704 P.2d 584.

PEARSON, JUSTICE.

The primary issue presented by this appeal is whether a seller of propane, who never had physical possession or control of the gas, should be held liable under either common law negligence or strict product liability theories for injuries resulting from a propane explosion and fire. We hold that as a matter of law respondent was not negligent, but that the principles of common law strict liability do place respondent in the chain of distribution of the propane. * * *

* * *

[A propane gas leak in the house of plaintiff-appellants went undetected because insufficient odorant had been added to the gas. A resulting fire killed 5 of appellants' children. Appellants sued the manufacturer (Mobil), distributor (Cal Gas, the respondent), and retailer (Northwest). The trial judge granted respondent's motion for summary judgment. Appellants settled with the other parties and appealed the entry of summary judgment for Cal Gas.]

Mobil manufactured the propane involved here at its Ferndale, Washington refinery. Propane is an odorless, colorless, highly flammable gas; a foul-smelling odorant is added to increase the safety of the product. Pennwalt manufactured this odorant (thiophane) and sold it to Mobil for use at Mobil's Ferndale refinery. Respondent Cal Gas, a Delaware corporation headquartered in California, bought the propane from Mobil and sold it to Northwest Propane, a retailer who delivered the propane directly to appellants. Significantly, respondent never had possession or control of the propane here. It bought and sold the gas completely as a paper transaction. Northwest Propane took delivery of the gas it purchased from respondent directly from Mobil's Ferndale refinery.

The fact that respondent never physically handled, modified, altered, transported, or refined the propane ultimately sold to appellants is uncontroverted. At issue here is the legal effect of respondent's role in the marketing of the gas.

I

Negligence

Appellants allege that respondent was negligent in failing to inspect the propane for odorization and in failing to warn appellants of the dangers of the propane. We find that because respondent never had possession or control of the gas and had no reason to believe that the gas was not properly odorized, it had no duty to inspect or warn appellants.

The general rule is that where a product is sold in the original package or container, in the condition in which it was received from a reputable manufacturer, and the seller had no opportunity to inspect or test before resale, no liability attaches to that seller for such failure to test or inspect. Annot., Seller's Duty to Test or Inspect as Affecting His Liability for Product–Caused Injury, 6 A.L.R.3d 12, 25 (1966); Davis v. Siloo, Inc., 47 N.C.App. 237, 267 S.E.2d 354 (1980); Sam Shainberg Co. v. Barlow, 258 So.2d 242 (Miss.1972). The rationale of that rule fully applies to respondent, who never handled the product and therefore had no opportunity to test or inspect it.

Further, a seller of an item which was manufactured by a third party is not generally liable for harm caused by the dangerous character of the item *if* the seller did not know or had no reason to know that the item was, or was likely to be, dangerous. Restatement of Torts § 402 (1948 Supp.); Ringstad v. I. Magnin & Co., 39 Wash.2d 923, 239 P.2d 848 (1952); Continental Cas. Co. v. Belknap Hardware & Mfg. Co., 281 S.W.2d 914 (Ky.Ct.App.1955). A seller is not obligated to test a product unless he has notice that it may be dangerous or defective. Ringstad, 39 Wash.2d at 926, 239 P.2d 848.

In the present case Mobil, from whom respondent purchased the propane, had contracted with respondent to odorize the propane in accordance with governmental regulations or industry practice. Because respondent could reasonably rely on Mobil, a reputable manufacturer, to odorize the propane and because respondent had no opportunity to inspect the gas itself, respondent cannot be held to have known or to have had reason to know that the propane was unreasonably dangerous by virtue of inadequate odorization.

Appellants, however, urge that because propane is an inherently dangerous product, respondent should be held to have a duty to *obtain* control or possession in order to inspect it. We disagree.

Unquestionably, propane gas is an inherently dangerous product. Andrews v. Del Guzzi, 56 Wash.2d 381, 353 P.2d 422 (1960). Nonetheless, the manufacturer (Mobil) and the retailer (Northwest Propane) each had possession and control of the gas and were in a position to inspect it. Generally, the seller of gas is under no duty to test for odorant where it has no facility for odorizing and where it is shown that the manufacturer had the equipment to odorize. Likewise, the seller of the gas has no duty to test or inspect where the manufacturer has certified that malodorant has been added. Davis v. Aetna Ins. Co., 291 So.2d 486 (La.Ct.App.1974).

The rule stated in Martin v. Schoonover, 13 Wash.App. 48, 54–55, 533 P.2d 438 (1975), applicable not only to retailers, but also to other product sellers, is appropriate here:

> The more the retailer [seller] is only a conduit for the product, the less likely he can be held in negligence * * * Conversely, the more the [seller] takes an active part in preparing the product for final use and takes the role of a manufacturer or assembler, the more likely he can be found liable in negligence. * * * If a [seller] adopts a product as his own, he is subject to the same liability for negligence as is the manufacturer * * * The [seller] can be found negligent in cases where he has failed to make an inspection * * * prior to sale when it was reasonable for him to do so in light of the nature of the product, the reputability of the supplier and the scope of the risk.

(Citations omitted.)

Here, respondent never touched the product, took no active part in its manufacture, did not adopt the product as its own, and was dealing with reputable manufacturers (Mobil and Pennwalt). In spite of the inherently dangerous nature of propane, it appears respondent had no notice that the product was unreasonably dangerous due to a defect (inadequate odorization). Thus, respondent had no duty to test or inspect in this case.

A duty to warn arises when the supplier "knows or has reason to know that the chattel is or is likely to be dangerous for the use for which it is supplied". Restatement (Second) of Torts § 388(a) (1965); Jones v. Hittle Serv., Inc., 219 Kan. 627, 549 P.2d 1383 (1976).

In *Hittle,* the distributors of propane gas sold the gas in bulk to the retailer, who in turn sold it to the ultimate consumer. An explosion occurred and the distributors/manufacturers were sued. That court held that the distributors of bulk propane to a retailer had no independent duty to warn the ultimate consumer. Rather, the distributor had only a duty to insure that the *retailer* was knowledgeable regarding the dangers and was able to warn the ultimate buyers. Thus, a seller of bulk propane can delegate to the retailer its duty to warn the ultimate consumer.

Furthermore, the bulk seller has no duty to warn the retailer of the dangers of a product if that retailer is already aware "through common knowledge or learning" of a specific hazard. Lancaster Silo & Block Co. v. Northern Propane Gas Co., 75 A.D.2d 55, 427 N.Y.S.2d 1009 (1980); Parkinson v. California Co., 255 F.2d 265 (10th Cir.1958) (holding that manufacturer had no duty to warn its purchasers (retailer and transporter of gas) of dangers where those purchasers had operated a gas business for years, were familiar with the trade journals, and already knew the dangers).

Accordingly, respondent could rely on Northwest Propane to warn the ultimate consumer (appellants). Additionally, because Northwest Propane is a well-established propane distributor, the largest in Whatcom County and in business for many years, respondent had no duty to warn Northwest Propane of the obvious dangers of its business.

II

Strict Liability

The product liability act is inapplicable to this case because the fire occurred prior to the effective date of that act. See RCW 7.72.060 and 4.22.920. Applying only the common law principles of strict liability for a defective product, we hold that respondent is properly regarded as a member in the chain of distribution of the propane. * * *

This court adopted section 402A as the law of this state and applied it to claims against manufacturers in Ulmer v. Ford Motor Co., 75 Wash.2d 522, 452 P.2d 729 (1969). In a broad interpretation of section 402A, this court later extended strict liability beyond manufacturers to all others in the chain of distribution. Seattle–First Nat'l Bank v. Tabert, 86 Wash.2d 145, 542 P.2d 774 (1975).

Section 402A, by its literal terms, imposes strict liability for *any* sale of a defective product. Thus, the sale itself of a defective product may trigger strict liability. See LaRosa v. Superior Court of Santa Clara, 122 Cal.App.3d 741, 176 Cal.Rptr. 224 (1981).

Additionally, the policies underlying the imposition of strict liability justify its imposition in this case. The primary policy justification recognized by this court for the extension of strict liability to all sellers in the chain of distribution is provision of the "maximum of protection" to the consumer. The sellers are then required to argue among themselves any questions as to their respective liability. *Seattle–First Nat'l Bank v. Tabert, supra.* That policy rationale is as applicable to sellers who never handle or control the product as it is to those sellers who do possess or control the product. * * *

Accordingly, the fact that respondent never physically handled the gas is not dispositive of the question whether it should be regarded to be a member in the chain of distribution. Respondent has not provided this court with any case, nor has our research revealed any case, which holds that handling or possession of the product is a requisite of strict liability. Respondent's reliance on Lyons v. Premo Pharmaceutical Labs, Inc., 170 N.J.Super. 183, 406 A.2d 185 (1979) to support such a proposition is misplaced.

In *Lyons,* the court held that a broker, who never had possession of the product, could not be held strictly liable. This holding was based on the fact that the product was subsequently sold in an *altered form* and for *unsafe uses,* those ultimate uses being beyond the broker's knowledge and control. Conversely, in the present case the gas was marketed exactly as sold by respondent and respondent had full knowledge of the uses to which the ultimate consumer would put the gas. Thus, the *Lyons* case is inapposite here.

Furthermore, respondent cannot be held to be merely a "passive conduit" in the marketing of the propane, as it claims. Respondent did agree to hold its buyer, Northwest Propane, harmless for liability resulting from improper odorization. Therefore, respondent's role in the marketing of the propane was certainly more active than that of an uninvolved conduit. Moreover, as we indicated in *Tabert,* the *degree* of a seller's participation in the marketing process is less important to our decision than the public protection consideration where, as here, a seller has had *some* identifiable role in placing a defective product on the market.

Accordingly, based upon the literal terms of section 402A and upon the public protection rationale for our broad interpretation of that section, we find that respondent is appropriately included within the chain of distribution of the propane sold to appellants.

[Reversed and remanded.]

NOTES

1. **Retailers—Negligence.** Most courts have held that the retailer does not have a duty to test or inspect in the absence of notice that the product is likely to be dangerous. See Rest. (2d) Torts § 402. But cf. Bower v. Corbell, 408 P.2d 307 (Okl.1965). Yet the courts have also generally held that the retailer does have a duty to warn if it knows or should know that the product is likely to be dangerous when put to normal use. See Frey v. Montgomery Ward & Co., 258 N.W.2d 782 (Minn.1977).

2. Should the retailer's economic power relative to that of the manufacturer bear on whether it should be required to test or inspect its products prior to sale? What if the retailer is a major national chain—such as Sears, K-Mart, or Toys-R-Us—which may be in a position to extract indemnification agreements from manufacturers as a condition of marketing their products? Conversely, what if the retailer is small and highly dependent on a single product manufactured by a large company? Do purchasers have different expectations when purchasing products from large chain stores versus small merchants?

3. **Negligent Entrustment.** Retailers may be liable for selling dangerous products to minors under the theory of negligent entrustment. That theory is examined in detail in Moning v. Alfono, 400 Mich. 425, 254 N.W.2d 759 (1977) (young boy hit in eye with pellet from friend's slingshot; jury might find sale of slingshot to 11-year-old friend created unreasonable risk of harm to plaintiff). Consider one commentator's opinion of Moning's implications: "[H]olding a marketing chain liable for all foreseeable injuries stemming from use of its products will have a devastating effect on the merchandisers of inexpensive toys and games. In effect the court has banned the marketing of any such products that have even a slight propensity to cause physical injury." Comment, 46 U.Cinn.L.Rev. 1047, 1054 (1977). Do you agree?

4. **Tortious Misrepresentation.** Many of the products liability cases involving tortious misrepresentation have involved retailers as defendants, as discussed in ch. 2, above. Note, however, that retailer communications to consumers ordinarily are not "public" representations for purposes of strict liability under Rest. (2d) Torts § 402B (1965).

5. **Express Warranty.** Retailers may of course expressly warrant the quality of the products they sell under U.C.C. § 2-313. In addition, a retailer will be liable under the manufacturer's express warranty if the retailer "adopts" the manufacturer's warranty. E.g., Scovil v. Chilcoat, 424 P.2d 87

(Okl.1967) (new VW engine). Mere resale of a product carrying a manufacturer express warranty does not alone constitute adoption, nor does explaining its terms to the buyer. See Import Motors, Inc. v. Matthews, 557 S.W.2d 807 (Tex. Civ.App.1977). Nor does making repairs on behalf of the manufacturer pursuant to the latter's warranty. Carbo Indus. Inc. v. Becker Chevrolet Inc., 112 A.D.2d 336, 491 N.Y.S.2d 786 (1985).

Section 2–314(2)(f) of the Code provides that goods carry an implied warranty of merchantability that they shall "conform to the promises or affirmations of fact made on the container or label if any." Does this section serve "to overturn the 'adoption' of warranty rule which sometimes has shielded the retailer"? See W. Hawkland, A Transactional Guide to the U.C.C. 69–70 (1964).

6. **Implied Warranty.**

A. **In general.** Retailers may be liable for breach of implied warranties under U.C.C. §§ 2–314 and 2–315. E.g., Pierce v. Liberty Furniture Co., Inc., 141 Ga.App. 175, 233 S.E.2d 33 (1977) (§ 2–314) (defective porch swing collapsed; retailer liable although swing kit purchased in sealed container from reputable manufacturer and resold to plaintiff in original package).

In the consumer goods products liability context, the § 2–315 warranty is principally applicable to retailers. Why?

B. **Restaurateurs.** As a holdover from days when an innkeeper would provide a traveler with food, lodging, and a stable for his horse all for a single fee, some courts used to hold that the sale of food for consumption on the premises was the provision of a service to which implied warranties did not attach. The modern rule is to the contrary. See U.C.C. § 2–314(1); Ray v. Deas, 112 Ga.App. 191, 144 S.E.2d 468 (1965); Sofman v. Denham Food Service, Inc., 37 N.J. 304, 181 A.2d 168 (1962).

Should a restaurant be liable under U.C.C. § 2–314 for injuries from a wine glass breaking in a patron's hand? What are the issues? See Shaffer v. Victoria Station, Inc., 91 Wash.2d 295, 588 P.2d 233 (1978), rev'g 18 Wash.App. 816, 572 P.2d 737 (1977).

7. **Strict Liability in Tort.** Strict liability in tort is widely applied to retailers. E.g., Mead v. Warner Pruyn Div., 57 A.D.2d 340, 394 N.Y.S.2d 483 (1977). Comment *f* to § 402A provides: "The rule stated in this Section applies to any person engaged in the business of selling products for use or consumption. It therefore applies to any manufacturer of such a product, to any wholesale or retail dealer or distributor, and to the operator of a restaurant."

An early, influential case on point was Vandermark v. Ford Motor Co., 61 Cal.2d 256, 37 Cal.Rptr. 896, 391 P.2d 168, 171–72 (1964) (Traynor, J.):

> Retailers like manufacturers are engaged in the business of distributing goods to the public. They are an integral part of the overall producing and marketing enterprise that should bear the cost of injuries resulting from defective products. (See Greenman v. Yuba Power Products, Inc., 59 Cal.2d 57, 63, 27 Cal.Rptr. 697, 377 P.2d 897.) In some cases the retailer may be the only member of that enterprise reasonably available to the injured plaintiff. In other cases the retailer himself may play a substantial part in insuring that the product is safe or may be in a position to exert pressure on the manufacturer to that end; the retailer's strict liability thus serves as an added incentive to safety. Strict liability on the manufacturer and retailer alike affords maximum protection to the injured plaintiff and works no

injustice to the defendants, for they can adjust the costs of such protection between them in the course of their continuing business relationship.

8. **Wholesalers and Distributors.** As illustrated by *Zamora,* and stated in comment *f* to § 402A above, the liability rules applicable to retailers have generally been applied to wholesalers and distributors as well. See also Beam v. Omark Indus., Inc., 143 Ga.App. 142, 237 S.E.2d 607 (1977) (negligence—wholesaler removed product from container and failed to pass along warnings and instructions); Smith v. Fiat–Roosevelt Motors, Inc., 556 F.2d 728 (5th Cir. 1977) (strict liability—importer-distributor subject to liability for uncrashworthy car).

9. **Reform.** Retailer liability has been an active area for legislative reform. The general approach has been to relieve the retailer of strict liability, except for express warranty (and possibly manufacturing flaws), unless the manufacturer cannot be identified, is insolvent, or is not subject to the jurisdiction of the court.

Such statutes sometimes include a "sealed container" defense, a common law doctrine that had withered away with the advent of U.C.C. § 2–314. See Pierce v. Liberty Furniture Co., supra note 6. This defense protects the retail seller (or other non-manufacturing seller) if the seller buys and resells the product in a sealed container and the seller has no reason to believe it is defective.

Retailer reform statutes have been adopted in *Del.,* Prod.Liab.Rep. (CCH) ¶ 90,810; *Idaho,* id. at ¶ 91,316 (detailed provisions); *Iowa,* id. at ¶ 91,610; *Kan.,* id. at ¶ 91,717; *Ky.,* id. at ¶ 91,814; *Md.,* id. at ¶ 92,111; *Minn.,* id. at ¶ 92,430; *N.C.,* id. at ¶ 93,411; *N.D.,* id. at ¶ 93,517; *Ohio,* id. at ¶ 93,617; *R.I.,* id. at ¶ 94,150; *S.D.,* id. at ¶ 94,321; *Tenn.,* id. at ¶ 94,415; and *Wash.,* id. at ¶ 94,920.

A couple of states have statutes restricting the liability of motor vehicle dealers, as between such dealers and the manufacturers. See *Idaho,* id. at ¶ 91,370; *Me.,* id. at ¶ 92,075.

10. See generally Cavico, The Strict Tort Liability of Retailers, Wholesalers, and Distributors of Defective Products, 12 Nova L.Rev. 213 (1987); Leete, Products Liability for Nonmanufacturer Product Sellers: Is It Time To Draw the Line?, 17 Forum 1250 (1982).

SECTION 2. COMPONENT PART MANUFACTURERS AND ASSEMBLERS

CITY OF FRANKLIN v. BADGER FORD TRUCK SALES, INC.

Supreme Court of Wisconsin, 1973.
58 Wis.2d 641, 207 N.W.2d 866.

* * *

ROBERT W. HANSEN, JUSTICE.

The municipality (Franklin) sued the sales company (Badger), the chassis maker (Ford), and the wheel maker (Gunite), alleging each liable under products liability for the sale to the city of a fire truck chassis with a defective wheel. The fire truck was damaged when it tipped over while negotiating a turn in responding to a fire call.

* * *

BASIS OF LIABILITY. The case against all three defendants went to the jury on the basis of strict liability. Ford and Gunite contend that they were manufacturers of component parts and, as such, were not subject to the rule of strict liability. Some states hold component manufacturers and suppliers subject to strict liability; some do not. Where there is no change in the component part itself, but it is merely incorporated into something larger, and where the cause of harm or injury is found, as here, to be a defect in the component part, we hold that, as to the ultimate user or consumer, the strict liability standard applies to the maker and supplier of the defective component part. Where the component part is subject to further processing or substantial change, or where the causing of injury is not directly attributable to defective construction of the component part, the result might be different. We agree with the comment: "* * * The question is essentially one of whether the responsibility for discovery and prevention of the dangerous defect is shifted to the intermediate party who is to make the changes. * * *"[6] In the case before us, we do not see responsibility for the defective construction of the wheel shifting from the maker of the wheel or from the assembler of wheel and chassis so as to make only the seller, who was in no position to detect the hidden defect, strictly liable.[7]

* * *

[Remanded for trial for determination of relative negligence of defendants for purposes of contribution.]

---

6. [Rest. (2d) Torts § 402A, comment *p.* See also comment *q*:] "*Component parts.* The same problem [referring to products requiring further processing] arises in cases of the sale of a component part of a product to be assembled by another, as for example a tire to be placed on a new automobile, a brake cylinder for the same purpose, or an instrument for the panel of an airplane. Again the question arises, whether the responsibility is not shifted to the assembler. It is no doubt to be expected that where there is no change in the component part itself, but it is merely incorporated into something larger, the strict liability will be found to carry through to the ultimate user or consumer. But in the absence of a sufficient number of decisions on the matter to justify a conclusion, the Institute expresses no opinion on the matter."

7. In Howes v. Hansen (1972), 56 Wis.2d 247, 201 N.W.2d 825, in extending strict liability protection beyond a user or consumer to a bystander, this court stated one of the reasons for the strict liability concept was stated in Dippel v. Sciano, supra, 37 Wis.2d page 451, 155 N.W.2d page 58, to be "* * * the manufacturer has the greatest ability to control the risk created by his products since he may initiate or adopt inspection and quality control measures thereby preventing defective products. * * *" See also: Frumer and Friedman, 2 Products Liability, sec. 16.04[2][f], pages 3–151–152, stating: "There seems to be no good reason why, if the lack of privity is not a consideration * * * the part manufacturer as well as the assembler should not be liable to the injured person. * * * While it may be true that the assembler is in a better position to distribute the risk in a particular case, and will ordinarily be the supplier to whom the injured person will look for redress, the part manufacturer did, after all, supply a defective product."

LEE v. BUTCHER BOY

California Court of Appeal, 1985.
169 Cal.App.3d 375, 215 Cal.Rptr. 195, review denied.*

[Plaintiff's hand was caught and injured in a meat grinding machine. In addition to suing the manufacturer of the grinder, plaintiff and her husband sued the manufacturer of the motor used in the grinder, contending that (1) the motor should have stopped immediately when turned off, and (2) the motor manufacturer should have warned that it took awhile for the motor to stop. The court granted the motor manufacturer's motion for summary judgment, and plaintiffs appeal.]

* * *

We have found no case in which a component part manufacturer who had no role in designing the finished product and who supplied a non-defective component part, was held liable for the defective design of the finished product. To the contrary, the cases relied on by defendant demonstrate a reluctance against imposing liability in this situation.

In Zambrana v. Standard Oil Co. (1972) 26 Cal.App.3d 209, 102 Cal. Rptr. 699, the plaintiff was injured when his car was struck by another vehicle that went out of control due to a sudden loss of tire pressure. The accident allegedly occurred when a metal valve stem and metal extension assembly on the tire broke. The plaintiff sued the manufacturer and retailer of the tire, Firestone, for defective manufacture or design of the metal valve stem. Firestone did not manufacture or sell the metal extension, which the purchaser of the tire had previously bought elsewhere. The plaintiff did not contend that either component in and of itself was defective, but that the combination of the two metal parts was dangerous.

The *Zambrana* court granted Firestone's motion for summary judgment, stating: "Plaintiff has cited no authority for the application of strict liability to this kind of situation. Under the circumstances shown, Firestone was neither a 'designer' nor 'manufacturer' of the combination of parts which is said to be 'defective.'" (Zambrana, supra, 26 Cal.App.3d at p. 217, 102 Cal.Rptr. 699.) The court noted that Firestone simply provided the purchaser who desired to use a valve stem extension, a choice between rubber and brass valve stems.

* * *

Similarly, in Fierro v. International Harvester Co., supra, 127 Cal. App.3d 862, 869, 179 Cal.Rptr. 923, the court stated that the component part manufacturer of the fuel tank installed in the truck manufactured by Luer, "could reasonably expect that Luer would take appropriate measures to insure proper design to cover and protect the fuel tanks."

We find the above cases relied on by defendant to be analogous and persuasive authority. The evidence establishes that defendant had no role in the design of the machine, and that defendant reasonably relied

* Bird, J., is of the opinion that the petition should be granted.

on Lasar to take appropriate measures to insure proper design and installation of the motor. We conclude that defendant's manufacture or design of the non-defective motor could not have proximately caused the injury.

Plaintiffs' reliance on DeLeon v. Commercial Manufacturing & Supply Co. (1983) 148 Cal.App.3d 336, 195 Cal.Rptr. 867, is misplaced. *DeLeon* does not impose a duty upon the manufacturer of a non-defective component part product to investigate the safety of the finished product that was solely designed and manufactured by another manufacturer. In *DeLeon,* the injured plaintiff urged "facts showing the [manufacturer of the finished product] relied on the expertise of [the defendant component part manufacturer] when it invited [the defendant's] employees to come to the plant to view the proposed bin configuration and to construct it properly as a part of the ongoing plant operation." (148 Cal.App.3d at p. 343, 195 Cal.Rptr. 867.) The *DeLeon* court thus concluded that the case was not "a clear-cut legal question of component part liability, but instead [presented] a factual issue of involvement in design which will permit variations in the applicable rules of law depending upon how the trier of fact determines the extent of [the component part manufacturer's] design responsibility." (Ibid.) The facts of this case are markedly different. Unlike *DeLeon,* here defendant had no design role in making the finished product. It is uncontradicted that the motors purchased from defendant were standard shelf items, and that Mr. Lasar, the sole designer of the machine, sought no advice from defendant, but instead told defendant which motors he desired to purchase.

2. *Failure to Warn.*

The manufacturer of a product may be held strictly liable and the product deemed defective, for the manufacturer's failure to warn: "[A] manufacturer or a supplier of a product is required to give warnings of any dangerous propensities in the product, or in its use, of which he knows, or should know, and which the user of the product would not ordinarily discover. [Citations.]" (Groll v. Shell Oil Co. (1983) 148 Cal. App.3d 444, 448, 196 Cal.Rptr. 52.)

* * *

On a motion for summary judgment in a case involving the manufacturer's failure to warn, the burden rests upon the moving party to show the absence of triable issues of fact concerning the existence of dangerous propensities in the product which the manufacturer knew or should have known, and which the user would not ordinarily discover.

We find this case to be factually analogous to Zambrana v. Standard Oil Co., *supra,* 26 Cal.App.3d 209, 102 Cal.Rptr. 699. The *Zambrana* court, in reviewing the summary judgment granted to defendant Firestone, concluded that the purchaser of the component part metal valve stem exercised free choice in selecting that stem rather than a rubber stem. There was, as in this case, no allegation that the component part metal valve stem was in itself defective. The plaintiff, as here, contended that it was the combination of the parts that was unreasonably dangerous. The *Zambrana* court refused to impose liability against the component part manufacturer for failing to warn the purchaser: "Nor is this a transaction in which the seller of the article (in this case the brass valve stem) is under a duty to warn the buyer by reason of dangers in use which are not generally known and recognized. [Citations.] One need not be an engineer to discern that a stem one and one-half inches in length offers six times the exposure to accidental blows as a stem one-quarter inch in length * * *. * * *

Similarly in this case, there is nothing to indicate that the motor in its use had unreasonably dangerous propensities not ordinarily discoverable by the user. The uncontradicted evidence shows that all motors, even "brake motors," do not stop immediately. There is no danger in the motor which would not have been obvious to a person of ordinary intelligence.

Moreover, we stress that defendant gave no input and had no control over the design, manufacture, and packaging of the finished product. The cases relied on by defendant demonstrate a reluctance against imposing liability for the component part manufacturer's failure to warn the consumer where the final product is subsequently packaged, labeled and marketed by another manufacturer. (Walker v. Stauffer Chemical Corp. (1971) 19 Cal.App.3d 669, 96 Cal.Rptr. 803; Groll v. Shell Oil Co., supra, 148 Cal.App.3d 444, 196 Cal.Rptr. 52.)

In *Walker,* the plaintiff was injured by "Clear–All" a drain cleaning product containing sulfuric acid. The plaintiff sued Stauffer, the component part manufacturer of sulfuric acid, in strict liability for failure to warn. Stauffer successfully moved for summary judgment, and the appellate court affirmed. *Walker* stated that it is not "realistically feasible or necessary to the protection of the public to require the manufacturer and supplier of a standard chemical ingredient such as bulk sulfuric acid, not having control over the subsequent compounding, packaging or marketing of an item eventually causing injury to the ultimate consumer, to bear the responsibility for that injury. The manufacturer (seller) of the product causing the injury is so situated as to afford the necessary protection." (Walker v. Stauffer Chemical Corp., supra, 19 Cal.App.3d 669, 674, 96 Cal.Rptr. 803.)

We agree with the *Walker* court that the manufacturer of the finished product is in the best position to protect against and warn of the danger that arises after the non-defective component part is installed in the finished product. And, as noted in *Walker:* "We are referred to no California case, nor has independent research revealed any such, extending the strict liability of the manufacturer (seller) to the supplier of a substance to be used in compounding or formulating the product which eventually causes injury to an ultimate consumer. On the contrary this dearth of authority indicates to us a reluctance on the part of the bench and bar to consider such an extension necessary or desirable for the protection of the ultimate consumer." (Id., at p. 673, 96 Cal.Rptr. 803.)

Accordingly, we conclude that defendant owed no duty to plaintiffs to warn that the motor did not stop immediately.

The summary judgment is affirmed.

NOTES

1. Troubled in part by the absence of privity of contract, some early decisions questioned whether strict liability should lie against the manufacturer of a defective component part. See Goldberg v. Kollsman Instrument Corp., 12 N.Y.2d 432, 240 N.Y.S.2d 592, 191 N.E.2d 81 (1963) (warranty) (defective altimeter caused crash of plane). See generally Hunt, A Reporter at Large: The Case of Flight 320, The New Yorker, (Apr. 30, 1960, at 119) (fascinating account of *Goldberg* crash and subsequent investigation into its cause).

Recent courts, however, have virtually all agreed with the *City of Franklin* approach holding the manufacturer of the defective component part liable for resulting harm. E.g., d'Hedouville v. Pioneer Hotel Co., 552 F.2d 886 (9th Cir. 1977) (flammable acrylic fiber made into carpeting).

2. However, the component part manufacturer will not be held responsible if the part is subjected to substantial change by an assembler, and the changed condition causes an accident. Liability in strict tort will lie only if the product "is expected to and does reach the user or consumer without substantial change in the condition in which it is sold." Rest. (2d) Torts § 402A(1)(b). See Union Supply Co. v. Pust, 196 Colo. 162, 583 P.2d 276 (1978).

Consider also comment *p* to § 402A, which provides in part:

> It seems reasonably clear that the mere fact that the product is to undergo processing, or other substantial change, will not in all cases relieve the seller of liability under the rule stated in this Section. * * * [T]he seller of an automobile with a defective steering gear which breaks and injures the driver, can scarcely expect to be relieved of the responsibility by reason of the fact that the car is sold to a dealer who is expected to "service" it, adjust the brakes, mount and inflate the tires, and the like, before it is ready for use. On the other hand, the manufacturer of pigiron, which is capable of a wide variety of uses, is not so likely to be held to strict liability when it turns out to be unsuitable for the child's tricycle into which it is finally made by a remote buyer. The question is essentially one of whether the responsibility for discovery and prevention of the dangerous defect is shifted to the intermediate party who is to make the changes.

3. Compare, with comment *p*'s pigiron tricycle example, States Steamship Co. v. Stone Manganese Marine, Ltd., 371 F.Supp. 500 (D.N.J.1973). This was a suit brought by a shipowner against the manufacturer of alloy ingots which were cast into propellers and installed on plaintiff's ships by a third party shipyard. The alloy was inadequate for the job, and several of the propeller blades fractured causing various damage. Defendant argued that casting the ingots into propellers was a "substantial change" in their condition, precluding liability under § 402A. The court thought this "too simplistic a reading of Section 402A(1)(b)," pointing out that at issue were "the qualities of the alloy, regardless of its shape". But compare Parker v. Warren, 503 S.W.2d 938 (Tenn.

App.1974) (seller of low-grade lumber who did not know of intended use for bleacher seats not strictly liable for collapse of bleachers).

4. Problems arise when an apparently safe component is assembled into the final product in a dangerous manner or the final product is marketed by the assembler without proper warnings of its dangers. Thus, no liability for selling dual operating buttons to plaintiff's employer who installed them on a power press, facing *upwards*, creating risk that stock could fall upon and accidentally activate the buttons. Temple v. Wean United, Inc., 50 Ohio St.2d 317, 364 N.E.2d 267, 4 O.O.3d 466 (1977). "[T]he obligation that generates the duty to warn does not extend to the speculative anticipation of how manufactured components, not in and of themselves dangerous or defective, can become potentially dangerous dependent upon the nature of their integration into a unit designed and assembled by another. Because of limited contact with [the employer], there is no indication that Square D could have known that its components were to be fashioned or fabricated into the power press in the particular manner that they were." 364 N.E.2d at 272.

Accord, Wenrick v. Schloemann–Siemag Aktiengesellschaft, 361 Pa.Super. 137, 522 A.2d 52 (1987) (dangerous location of switch on press); Searls v. Doe, 29 Ohio App.3d 309, 505 N.E.2d 287, 290 (1986) (injury from use of assembly line conveyor system): "[D]efendants, as manufacturers of component parts, had no duty to warn plaintiff of a potentially dangerous or defective design of a system, where defendants were not responsible for the design [of the system] and where the component parts, not in and of themselves dangerous or defective, were manufactured in accordance with specifications." But see Parkins v. Van Doren Sales, Inc., 45 Wash.App. 19, 724 P.2d 389 (1986); Beauchamp v. Russell & Mac Valves, Inc., 547 F.Supp. 1191 (N.D.Ga.1982) (component part manufacturer may have greatest access to information and hence be in best position to warn).

5. What advice would you have for a chemical company which sells hundreds of different compounds to several hundred commercial users? To a screw manufacturer who has thousands of commercial purchasers? Cf. Kennelly, Trial of a General Aviation Aircraft Case Against Manufacturer, Component–Part Maker, and Overhaul Company—Defective 5¢ Screws Result in $660,000 Aggregate Awards for Two Deaths, Trial Lawyers Guide 281 (1971).

BEXIGA v. HAVIR MANUFACTURING CORP.

Supreme Court of New Jersey, 1972.
60 N.J. 402, 290 A.2d 281.

PROCTOR, J.

This is a products liability case. Plaintiff John Bexiga, Jr., a minor, was operating a power punch press for his employer, Regina Corporation (Regina), when his right hand was crushed by the ram of the machine, resulting in the loss of fingers and deformity of his hand. [Plaintiff's action against the manufacturer, brought in negligence, warranty, and strict tort, was dismissed by the trial court at the close of plaintiff's case. The intermediate appellate court affirmed, 276 A.2d 590, and plaintiff appealed.]

The machine which caused the injuries was a 10–ton punch press * * *. With the exception of a guard over the flywheel there were no safety devices of any kind on the machine when it was shipped. [Plaintiff's] theory is that the punch press was so dangerous in design that the manufacturer was under a duty to equip it with some form of safety device to protect the user while the machine was being operated.

[Plaintiff's expert, Gass, testified that there were two basic types of safety devices available at the time, (1) a push-button device with buttons located so as to require the operator to place both hands on them away from the die area in order to activate the press, and (2) a simple guardrail or gate that would descend prior to the ram's descent and thus would act as a barrier keeping the operator's hands away from the moving ram. He further testified that the gate device would probably have to be modified when the press was put to certain uses but that the push-button device was appropriate for all of the machine's normal uses. On cross-examination, Gass conceded that the custom of the trade was to leave the selection and installation of safety devices to the ultimate user. He was of the opinion, however, that the custom was "improper in that the machine was defectively designed for safety and the purchasers 'almost never' provided safety devices."]

[In affirming the trial court's dismissal, the Appellate Division] reasoned that since it was the custom of the trade that purchasers, rather than manufacturers, provide safety devices on punch presses like the one in question, Havir "had no reason to believe that the press would be put to use without some additions, i.e., the installation by Regina of protective devices suitable to whatever manufacturing process the press was to be devoted." [Citations.] It also stated that N.J. S.A. 34:6–62, in effect at the time of the sale, required the factory owner to equip its power presses with proper guards. Id. at 404, 276 A.2d at 593. It held liability could not be imposed under [§ 402A] because the manufacturer did not expect the product to reach the user without substantial change. Id. at 403–04, 276 A.2d 590. [The Supreme Court disagreed, holding that the jury might reasonably have concluded that the defendant should have added a push-button device to the machine.]

As we previously said on the issue of strict liability, the Appellate Division applied the rule set forth in the Restatement. To the extent that that rule absolves the manufacturer of liability where he may expect the purchaser to provide safety devices (Restatement, supra, § 402A(1)(b)), it should not be applied. Where a manufacturer places into the channels of trade a finished product which can be put to use and which should be provided with safety devices because without such it creates an unreasonable risk of harm, and where such safety devices can feasibly be installed by the manufacturer, the fact that he expects that someone else will install such devices should not immunize him. The public interest in assuring that safety devices are installed demands more from the manufacturer than to permit him to leave such a critical phase of his manufacturing process to the haphazard conduct of the ultimate purchaser. The only way to be certain that such devices will be installed on all machines—which clearly the public interest requires—is to place the duty on the manufacturer where it is feasible for him to do so.

We hold that where there is an unreasonable risk of harm to the user of a machine which has no protective safety device, as here, the jury may infer that the machine was defective in design unless it finds that the incorporation by the manufacturer of a safety device would render the machine unusable for its intended purposes. As we have said, the jury could infer from plaintif[f's] evidence that it was feasible for Havir to install the push-button device. Therefore, it was error for the trial court to dismiss the strict liability claim at the close of plaintif[f's] case.

Of course the question of whether one is negligent depends on whether he acted reasonably under the circumstances of a particular case. Thus, aside from the question of the practicability of Havir's installation of a safety device on the press here involved as to negligence, we must consider whether Havir could reasonably foresee that Regina would not install a safety device. On this issue the custom of the trade—that the manufacturer did not install safety devices but relied on the purchaser to do so—while ordinarily evidential, is not conclusive. [Citation.] Nor would it be conclusive that N.J.S.A. 34:6–62 imposed the duty on the purchaser. While Havir may have thought that Regina would have taken adequate precautions to protect its employees or that it would be required to do so by statute, we do not think in view of the circumstances here that Havir had a right as a matter of law to assume such devices would be provided. * * *

* * *

The judgment of the Appellate Division is reversed and the cause is remanded for a new trial.

VERGE v. FORD MOTOR CO.

United States Court of Appeals, Third Circuit, 1978.
581 F.2d 384.

A. LEON HIGGINBOTHAM, JR., CIRCUIT JUDGE.

We must address, in this case, a little-litigated subtlety of products liability law: On whom to place design responsibilities where a product has been manufactured and assembled in more than one stage. Because we conclude that the Ford Motor Company was not responsible for the design defect here, we hold that the district court erred in denying Ford's Motion for Judgment n.o.v.

I.

The plaintiff, Jesus Garcia Verge, was an employee of the Government of the Virgin Island's Department of Public Works Sanitation Division. He worked on a garbage collection crew in St. Croix. On

February 23, 1973, while Mr. Verge was standing at the rear of a garbage truck, a co-worker placed a full can of garbage about three feet behind him. Then the driver of the truck, without having received a signal to proceed, without checking to locate the position of Mr. Verge and the other crew members and without any warning to them, put the truck into reverse gear. Mr. Verge was pinned between the truck and the garbage can that had been left behind him. As a result of this accident, he suffered a broken leg.

Mr. Verge filed a complaint against Ford, Leach Co. [and others, alleging that the truck was defectively designed and the defendants were negligent in that they] failed:

> to equip the truck with mirrors or other devices by which the operator of the truck would be able to ascertain the presence of individuals to its rear, prior to reversing the vehicle. The defendants further failed to equip the garbage truck with an operable buzzer or other device which would warn Jesus Garcia Verge and other persons foreseeably similarly situated that the garbage truck was to be reversed.

[Plaintiff settled with Leach Co. and the other defendants before trial.]

The case against Ford was based on Section 402A of the Restatement (2d) of Torts. The jury returned a verdict of $75,000.00 in Mr. Verge's favor. Ford moved for judgment n.o.v., the denial of which is the basis for this appeal.

II.

Plaintiff's central allegation is that Ford's cab and chassis was defective when it left Ford's hands because it did not contain a warning buzzer that would sound when the truck was put into reverse gear. Plaintiff's expert witness testified that a garbage truck without such a device is unreasonably dangerous.

Any design defect case of this type involves two primary issues: (1) Was there a defect?; (2) If so, who is responsible for it? In finding for the plaintiff, the jury obviously answered the first question in the affirmative, i.e., it found that the absence of a warning device on the garbage truck did render it unreasonably dangerous within the meaning of 402A. This is an issue properly submitted to the jury and we cannot say that its finding is not supported by the evidence. We confront, here, the second issue. More precisely, we must determine whether the responsibility for installing such a device should be placed solely upon the company that manufactured the cab and chassis, or solely upon the company who modified the chassis by adding the compactor unit or upon both.[2]

2. In order to more closely track the language of 402A the issue can be rephrased in terms of whether the truck reached the consumer without "substantial change" or whether the truck was in a "defective condition" when it left Ford's hands. Such rephrasing is, however, of little assistance in determining whether Ford should be held liable for not installing the warning device here.

This court has previously stated: "[W]e believe that the requirement that liability only be imposed where the manufacturer is responsible for the defective conditions is necessarily implicit in § 402A [citation]. Where, as here, the finished product is the result of substantial work by more than one party, we must determine responsibility for the absence of a safety device by looking primarily to at least three factors:

> 1. Trade Custom—at what stage is that device generally installed. [Citations]; Schipper v. Levitt and Sons, Inc., 44 N.J. 70, 207 A.2d 314 (1965).
>
> 2. Relative expertise—which party is best acquainted with the design problems and safety techniques in question. * * *
>
> 3. Practicality—at what stage is installation of device most feasible. [Citation.]; Bexiga v. Havir Mfg. Co., 60 N.J. 402, 290 A.2d 281 (1972); [citation].

As we analyze these factors, we will remain mindful of the words of New Jersey Supreme Court Justice Nathan L. Jacobs, in Schipper v. Levitt, supra, 44 N.J. at 99, 207 A.2d at 330: "In developing steps towards higher consumer and user protection through higher trade morality and responsibility, the law should view trade relations realistically rather than mythically."

* * *

* * * David Leach, the President of Leach Co. * * * testified that the cabs and chassis are generally purchased from Ford by a dealer. The cab and chassis unit is referred to as the F–700 Model. This model is a multi-purpose vehicle that can be converted for other uses beside garbage collection. Trucks are generally driven from Ford to Leach's plant in Oshkosh, Wisconsin, by "Drive-away" companies which are hired for this purpose. The trucks are accompanied by bills of lading prepared by the manufacturer. They contain Leach's address and are signed by Leach after it inspects the vehicle for damage. The bill of lading for the particular truck involved in the accident here was never entered into evidence. In fact, no documentation relating to any garbage trucks was ever entered into evidence.

When Leach receives the cabs and chassis, it converts them into garbage trucks. This conversion process involves cutting from four to six feet from the chassis, placing the compactor unit onto the chassis and making certain electrical hook-ups.

Leach bills the purchaser of the truck for the compactor unit and the assembly of the unit to the truck. Leach, except for rare occasions, does not itself purchase the trucks. After conversion the truck is shipped to a dealer or ultimate customer.

Leach disclaimed any personal knowledge of how the truck in question got to the Oshkosh plant. He believed that the purchaser of the truck was the Puerto Rico Iron Works which he believed to be a Ford truck dealer.

We will now examine what the record here reveals as to each of the three factors already delineated as crucial to our analysis.

1. TRADE CUSTOM

Plaintiff's counsel specifically asked plaintiff's expert witness whether it was the trade custom that the warning device be installed by the company that manufactured the cab and chassis or by the company that installed the compactor units onto the chassis. Unfortunately, the expert's reply did not answer the question and, when the subject was raised again on cross-examination, no clear answer emerged.

The only other evidence pertaining to this issue comes from the testimony of David Leach. He testified that his company has installed safety devices, but only when the order from the purchasing agent specifically requested the installation of such a device. Mr. Leach went on to say that such a device is generally installed by the truck manufacturer. Mr. Leach testified, however, only as to his company's experience. There is no evidence of whether his company's experience was shared by the garbage truck industry as a whole, or even of how substantial is Leach's share of that industry. Therefore, Mr. Leach's testimony is not an adequate basis for determining the trade custom in this regard.

2. EXPERTISE

Since the record is without persuasive evidence of trade custom, we must proceed to analyze the other two factors. The evidence relating to comparative expertise indicates that Leach is more expert than Ford in the design of refuse collection vehicles. David Leach testified that his company does install warning devices. He also testified that his company has been in the garbage collection vehicle business since 1932 and has installed compactor units on hundreds of trucks each year since at least 1954. Except for an unrelated hand tool business, Leach is involved solely in the manufacture and installation of compactor units. There was no testimony relating to Ford's expertise in the design of garbage collection vehicles. There is no evidence that Ford ever installed a warning device of the type in question. There is not even any direct evidence that Ford was aware that any of its F–700 trucks was being converted into refuse collection vehicles. Thus the evidence indicates that Leach is considerably more expert in the design of garbage trucks than is Ford.

3. PRACTICALITY

Finally it is clear from the record that it is considerably more practical for warning devices to be installed by Leach rather than by Ford. It is essential to recognize that, by the testimony of plaintiff's own expert witness, the Ford cab and chassis was a multi-purpose vehicle. As such, the topless chassis could be modified for a number of uses that would require no backup buzzer. Thus, if a flat bed were added that allowed unobstructed rear vision, it is difficult to conceive of a legal basis for finding that the absence of a warning device would constitute a design defect. Similarly, if a body were added that was lower than the rear view window or if a body were added that otherwise allowed adequate rear vision, there would be no basis for finding that a design defect was present because of the failure to incorporate a backup buzzer. Thus, we are dealing with a vehicle that was not inherently defective when manufactured, but that became defective solely because of additions made by a company with decades of experience in accomplishing just this type of modification.

A similar situation was addressed in Bexiga v. Havir Manufacturing Corp., supra. There, the trial court and intermediate appellate court had held that the manufacturer of a punch press was not liable for the failure to install a safety device because the machine could perform various tasks and it would be impractical for the manufacturer to install different safety devices for each separate use. The Supreme Court of New Jersey, however, concluded that there was evidence from which the jury could have found that one safety device could be installed for all uses of the machine. * * * Here, however, the evidence is that it would not be feasible to install the safety device in question on all F–700 trucks. Furthermore, there was no evidence that it would be feasible for Ford to determine which trucks were to be converted for refuse collection use. As mentioned, there is no direct evidence that Ford was even aware that the truck in question or any F–700 truck would be used for refuse collection. Since Ford manufactures the F–700 for a variety of uses and Leach's conversion business is solely concerned with garbage trucks, it seems much more practical for Leach to install the warning device. [Citations.] [6]

III.

Thus the evidence in this case shows that Leach is more expert in garbage vehicle design than Ford and that it would be more practical for Leach to install the warning device rather than for Ford to do so. On the facts of this case, plaintiff failed to prove that it was practical for Ford to install such a warning device on all of its vehicles when such a device would not be required for many uses of the vehicle. We recognize there might be different factual situations where a manufacturer could be obligated to install certain devices that have a limited use, but we, under the facts of this case, hold that plaintiff has failed to bring forth proof sufficient to warrant the imposition of liability on Ford. * * * We hold that Ford was not responsible for including a backup warning device or other safety device on the F–700 cab and chassis here and is not liable for injuries caused by the absence of such

6. We do not suggest that Ford could not foresee that its F–700 chassis would be converted for use as a garbage truck. We emphasize only that Leach was in a much better position than Ford to incorporate the safety features necessitated by such a use.

a device. Thus, the district court erred in denying Ford's motion for judgment n.o.v.

The judgment of the district court will be reversed with instructions to grant the judgment n.o.v. in favor of Ford.

NOTES

1. Are *Bexiga* and *Verge* consistent? Do you agree with *Verge* that it was more practical for Leach than Ford to install the buzzers?

2. Havir and Ford were both in a sense manufacturers of component parts. Does this change the analysis?

3. Same result in *Verge* if Ford had known that the cab and chassis units would be converted to garbage trucks? See Iannaccone v. Leach Co., Prod.Liab. Rep. (CCH) ¶ 11,641 (E.D.N.Y.1987).

4. Plaintiff's arm was caught in the "nip point" of a conveyor belt in Pust v. Union Supply Co., 38 Colo.App. 435, 561 P.2d 355 (1976), aff'd, 196 Colo. 162, 583 P.2d 276 (1978). Plaintiff's employer, Holly Sugar Corporation, "prepared bid drawings and sent them to potential manufacturers. Defendant Union, the low bidder, prepared its own drawings of the conveyor system and sent them back to Holly. Union's plans made certain changes in the component parts and added mechanical engineering specifications. Union had portions of the system built by various subcontractors, partially assembled the conveyor, and shipped it in sections to Holly. Holly provided the motor, conveyor belting, and supporting structure and assembled the entire system in its plant." Plaintiff brought a strict tort action against Union for defective design, based on the absence of guards at the nip points of the conveyor belt. Since Union had "merely manufactured what Holly had asked it to, Union argues that it could not be expected to add guards when none were requested." Relying upon *Bexiga,* the court rejected this argument:

> It would be anomalous, indeed, to adopt 402A, and yet permit a manufacturer to insulate itself from liability by categorizing the sale of its products as components simply because they have to be assembled, or to permit it to manufacture a product for which it delegates to the purchaser either the duty of designing or incorporating safety devices. Thus, we hold that a fabricator, who manufactures a product according to plans submitted by the ultimate user cannot avoid liability even if the design submitted is unsafe, provided it is feasible for him to install safety devices.

561 P.2d at 361. Accord, Parkins v. Van Doren Sales, Inc., 45 Wash.App. 19, 724 P.2d 389 (1986).

5. In Gordon v. Niagara Machine and Tool Works, 574 F.2d 1182, 1190 (5th Cir.1978), the court refused to follow *Bexiga,* stating: "[W]e decline to find a multifunctional, general purpose machine, like the Niagara press, was in [a] defective condition when marketed without guarding devices. The machine having been designed for many kinds of operation, it was incumbent upon the machine purchaser to select safety devices appropriate for his particular function." Compare Shawver v. Roberts Corp., 90 Wis.2d 672, 280 N.W.2d 226 (1979) (no strict tort liability for manufacturer of unassembled conveyor for absence of available safety devices since expectation was that the devices would later be added by the purchaser who was the assembler; no expectation that the product would reach the consumer without substantial change); Garrison v.

Rohm & Haas Co., 492 F.2d 346, 351 (6th Cir.1974) (fabricator that manufactured dolly to specifications not liable for "defective design so far as wheel placement and center of gravity were concerned").

6. **Optional Safety Devices.** What if the manufacturer offers safety guards as optional equipment which the purchaser-employer declines to purchase? Compare Helicoid Gage Div. of American Chain & Cable Co. v. Howell, 511 S.W.2d 573 (Tex.Civ.App.1974) (high pressure gage should have been equipped with safety shield, costing about $2, as standard rather than optional equipment), and Christopher v. Hyster Co., 58 Ill.App.3d 791, 16 Ill.Dec. 83, 374 N.E.2d 858 (1978) (nondelegable duty to supply guards, despite purchaser's insistence that forklift not have guards to permit its use in low-clearance areas, where evidence that retractable overhead guards were available at the time), with Murphy v. Eaton, Yale & Towne, Inc., 444 F.2d 317 (6th Cir.1971) (jury question whether forklift defectively designed where overhead guards not standard equipment but offered as accessories).

7. If the purchaser fails to add a safety device, or removes or alters one provided by the manufacturer, recovery against the manufacturer has occasionally been barred on grounds of proximate cause. See, e.g., State Stove Mfg. Co. v. Hodges, 189 So.2d 113 (Miss.1966) (5–4) (manufacturer supplied hot water heater without pressure relief valve, but with explicit instructions to installer to add one). See generally ch. 4, above.

8. In Vandermark v. Ford Motor Co., 61 Cal.2d 256, 37 Cal.Rptr. 896, 898–99, 391 P.2d 168, 170–71 (1964), Justice Traynor addressed the question whether an automobile manufacturer should be strictly liable in tort for injuries caused by defects that should have been discovered by the dealer under established inspection procedures:

> [The strict liability] rules focus responsibility for defects, whether negligently or nonnegligently caused, on the manufacturer of the completed product, and they apply regardless of what part of the manufacturing process the manufacturer chooses to delegate to third parties. It appears in the present case that Ford delegates the final steps in that process to its authorized dealers. It does not deliver cars to its dealers that are ready to be driven away by the ultimate purchasers but relies on its dealers to make the final inspections, corrections, and adjustments necessary to make the cars ready for use. Since Ford, as the manufacturer of the completed product, cannot delegate its duty to have its cars delivered to the ultimate purchaser free from dangerous defects, it cannot escape liability on the ground that the defect in Vandermark's car may have been caused by something one of its authorized dealers did or failed to do.

9. Some courts, including *City of Franklin,* supra, have used comparative responsibility principles to allocate fault among component part manufacturers, assemblers, and retailers. This approach is criticized in Comment, 49 U.Chi.L.Rev. 544 (1982), for diluting the incentives on the party best able to eliminate the defect.

10. **Reform.** An Arizona statute provides that a seller shall indemnify the manufacturer "if the seller provided the plans or specifications for the manufacture or preparation of the product and such plans or specifications were a substantial cause of the product's alleged defect * * *." Prod.Liab. Rep. (CCH) ¶ 90,313.

11. *Bexiga* is noted at 86 Harv.L.Rev. 923 (1973); *Verge* at 24 Vill.L.Rev. 406 (1978–79). On component part manufacturers, see Note, 54 J.Air L. & Com. 215 (1988).

SECTION 3. THE FEDERAL GOVERNMENT

BERKOVITZ v. UNITED STATES

United States Supreme Court, 1988.
486 U.S. ___, 108 S.Ct. 1954, 100 L.Ed.2d 531.

JUSTICE MARSHALL delivered the opinion of the Court.

The question in this case is whether the discretionary function exception of the Federal Tort Claims Act (FTCA or Act), 28 U.S.C. § 2680(a), bars a suit based on the Government's licensing of an oral polio vaccine and on its subsequent approval of the release of a specific lot of that vaccine to the public.

I

On May 10, 1979, Kevan Berkovitz, then a 2–month–old infant, ingested a dose of Orimune, an oral polio vaccine manufactured by Lederle Laboratories. Within one month, he contracted a severe case of polio. The disease left Berkovitz almost completely paralyzed and unable to breathe without the assistance of a respirator. The Communicable Disease Center, an agency of the Federal Government, determined that Berkovitz had contracted polio from the vaccine.

Berkovitz, joined by his parents as guardians, subsequently filed suit against the United States in Federal District Court.[1] The complaint alleged that the United States was liable for his injuries under the FTCA, 28 U.S.C. §§ 1346(b), 2674, because the Division of Biologic Standards (DBS), then a part of the National Institutes of Health, had acted wrongfully in licensing Lederle Laboratories to produce Orimune and because the Bureau of Biologics of the Food and Drug Administration (FDA) * had acted wrongfully in approving release to the public of the particular lot of vaccine containing Berkovitz's dose. According to petitioners, these actions violated federal law and policy regarding the inspection and approval of polio vaccines.

The Government moved to dismiss the suit for lack of subject-matter jurisdiction on the ground that the agency actions fell within the discretionary function exception of the FTCA. The District Court

1. Petitioners also sued Lederle Laboratories in a separate civil action. That suit was settled before the instant case was filed.

* In 1963, the DBS issued a license to Lederle to produce Orimune. The DBS was transferred in 1972 from the National Institutes of Health to the FDA and renamed the Bureau of Biologics, and in 1984 it was renamed the Office of Biologics Research and Review.—Eds.

denied this motion, concluding that neither the licensing of Orimune nor the release of a specific lot of that vaccine to the public was a "discretionary function" within the meaning of the FTCA. Civ. Action No. 84–2893 (WD Pa., Apr. 30, 1986). At the Government's request, the District Court certified its decision for immediate appeal to the Third Circuit pursuant to 28 U.S.C. § 1292(b), and the Court of Appeals accepted jurisdiction.

A divided panel of the Court of Appeals reversed. 822 F.2d 1322 (CA3 1987). * * *

We granted certiorari, 484 U.S. ___, 108 S.Ct. 692, 98 L.Ed.2d 645 (1988), to resolve a conflict in the Circuits regarding the effect of the discretionary function exception on claims arising from the Government's regulation of polio vaccines. * * *

II

The FTCA, 28 U.S.C. § 1346(b), generally authorizes suits against the United States for damages

> "for injury or loss of property, or personal injury or death caused by the negligent or wrongful act or omission of any employee of the Government while acting within the scope of his office or employment, under circumstances where the United States, if a private person, would be liable to the claimant in accordance with the law of the place where the act or omission occurred."

The Act includes a number of exceptions to this broad waiver of sovereign immunity. The exception relevant to this case provides that no liability shall lie for

> "[a]ny claim * * * based upon the exercise or performance or the failure to exercise or perform a discretionary function or duty on the part of a federal agency or an employee of the Government, whether or not the discretion involved be abused." 28 U.S.C. § 2680(a).

This exception, as we stated in our most recent opinion on the subject, "marks the boundary between Congress' willingness to impose tort liability upon the United States and its desire to protect certain governmental activities from exposure to suit by private individuals." United States v. Varig Airlines, 467 U.S., at 808, 104 S.Ct., at 2761–2762.

The determination of whether the discretionary function exception bars a suit against the Government is guided by several established principles. This Court stated in *Varig* that "it is the nature of the conduct, rather than the status of the actor, that governs whether the discretionary function exception applies in a given case." Id., at 813, 104 S.Ct., at 2764. In examining the nature of the challenged conduct, a court must first consider whether the action is a matter of choice for the acting employee. This inquiry is mandated by the language of the exception; conduct cannot be discretionary unless it involves an element of judgment or choice. See Dalehite v. United States, 346 U.S. 15, 34, 73 S.Ct. 956, 967, 97 L.Ed. 1427 (1953) (stating that the exception protects "the discretion of the executive or the administrator to act according to one's judgment of the best course"). Thus, the discretionary function exception will not apply when a federal statute, regulation, or policy specifically prescribes a course of action for an employee to follow. In this event, the employee has no rightful option but to adhere to the directive. And if the employee's conduct cannot appropriately be the product of judgment or choice, then there is no discretion in the conduct for the discretionary function exception to protect. [Citation.] Moreover, assuming the challenged conduct involves an element of judgment, a court must determine whether that judgment is of the kind that the discretionary function exception was designed to shield. The basis for the discretionary function exception was Congress' desire to "prevent judicial 'second-guessing' of legislative and administrative decisions grounded in social, economic, and political policy through the medium of an action in tort." United States v. Varig Airlines, supra, at 814, 104 S.Ct., at 2764–2765. The exception, properly construed, therefore protects only governmental actions and decisions based on considerations of public policy. * * *

This Court's decision in *Varig Airlines* illustrates these propositions. The two cases resolved in that decision were tort suits by the victims of airplane accidents who alleged that the Federal Aviation Administration (FAA) had acted negligently in certifying certain airplanes for operation. The Court characterized the suits as challenging the FAA's decision to certify the airplanes without first inspecting them and held that this decision was a discretionary act for which the Government was immune from liability. In reaching this result, the Court carefully reviewed the statutory and regulatory scheme governing the inspection and certification of airplanes. Congress had given the Secretary of Transportation broad authority to establish and implement a program for enforcing compliance with airplane safety standards. In the exercise of that authority, the FAA, as the Secretary's designee, had devised a system of "spot-checking" airplanes for compliance. This Court first held that the establishment of that system was a discretionary function within the meaning of the FTCA because it represented a policy determination as to how best to "accommodat[e] the goal of air transportation safety and the reality of finite agency resources." 467 U.S., at 820, 104 S.Ct., at 2767–2768. The Court then stated that the discretionary function exception also protected "the acts of FAA employees in executing the 'spot-check' program" because under this program the employees "were specifically empowered to make policy judgments regarding the degree of confidence that might reasonably be placed in a given manufacturer, the need to maximize compliance with FAA regulations, and the efficient allocation of agency resources." Ibid. Thus, the Court held the challenged acts protected from liability because they were within the range of choice accorded by federal policy and law and were the results of policy determinations.

In restating and clarifying the scope of the discretionary function exception, we intend specifically to reject the Government's argument, pressed both in this Court and the Court of Appeals, that the exception precludes liability for any and all acts arising out of the regulatory programs of federal agencies. That argument is rebutted first by the language of the exception, which protects "discretionary" functions, rather than "regulatory" functions. The significance of Congress' choice of language is supported by the legislative history. * * * The discretionary function exception applies only to conduct that involves the permissible exercise of policy judgment. The question in this case is whether the governmental activities challenged by petitioners are of this discretionary nature.

III

Petitioners' suit raises two broad claims. First, petitioners assert that the DBS violated a federal statute and accompanying regulations in issuing a license to Lederle Laboratories to produce Orimune. Second, petitioners argue that the Bureau of Biologics of the FDA violated federal regulations and policy in approving the release of the particular lot of Orimune that contained Kevan Berkovitz's dose. * * *

A

* * *

[The Court reviewed several specific statutory and regulatory provisions governing the development, testing, and licensure of vaccines. These provisions] require the DBS, prior to issuing a product license, to receive all data the manufacturer is required to submit, examine the product, and make a determination that the product complies with safety standards.

Petitioners' first allegation with regard to the licensing of Orimune is that the DBS issued a product license without first receiving data that the manufacturer must submit showing how the product, at the various stages of the manufacturing process, matched up against regulatory safety standards. See App. 12–13; Brief for Petitioners 5–6. The discretionary function exception does not bar a cause of action based on this allegation. The statute and regulations described above require, as a precondition to licensing, that the DBS receive certain test data from the manufacturer relating to the product's compliance with regulatory standards. See § 351(d), 58 Stat. 702–703, as amended, 42 U.S.C. § 262(d) (providing that a license shall issue "only upon a showing" by the manufacturer); 42 CFR § 73.3 (Supp.1964); 21 CFR § 601.2 (1987) (providing that application for license shall be deemed as filed only upon receipt of relevant test data). The DBS has no discretion to issue a license without first receiving the required test data; to do so would violate a specific statutory and regulatory directive. Accordingly, to the extent that petitioners' licensing claim is based on a decision of the DBS to issue a license without having received the required test data, the discretionary function exception imposes no bar.

Petitioners' other allegation regarding the licensing of Orimune is difficult to describe with precision. Petitioners contend that the DBS licensed Orimune even though the vaccine did not comply with certain regulatory safety standards. See App. 12; Brief for Petitioners 4–6.[9]

If petitioners aver that the DBS licensed Orimune either without determining whether the vaccine complied with regulatory standards or after determining that the vaccine failed to comply, the discretionary function exception does not bar the claim. Under the scheme governing the DBS's regulation of polio vaccines, the DBS may not issue a license except upon an examination of the product and a determination that the product complies with all regulatory standards. See 42 CFR § 73.5(a) (Supp.1964); 21 CFR § 601.4 (1987). The agency has no discretion to deviate from this mandated procedure. Petitioners' claim, if interpreted as alleging that the DBS licensed Orimune in the absence of a determination that the vaccine complied with regulatory standards, therefore does not challenge a discretionary function. Rather, the claim charges a failure on the part of the agency to perform its clear duty under federal law. When a suit charges an agency with failing to act in accord with a specific mandatory directive, the discretionary function exception does not apply.

If petitioners' claim is that the DBS made a determination that Orimune complied with regulatory standards, but that the determination was incorrect, the question of the applicability of the discretionary function exception requires a somewhat different analysis. In that event, the question turns on whether the manner and method of determining compliance with the safety standards at issue involves agency judgment of the kind protected by the discretionary function exception.[11] Petitioners contend that the determination involves the

9. Petitioners point to two specific regulatory standards that the product allegedly failed to satisfy. First, petitioners claim that an original virus strain from which the vaccine was made did not comply with the requirement that the strain be "free of harmful effect upon administration in the recommended dosage to at least 100,000 people susceptible to poliomyelitis." 42 CFR § 73.110(b)(2)(i) (Supp.1964); see 21 CFR § 630.10(b)(2)(i) (1987). Second, petitioners assert that the strain, a seed virus, a vaccine monopool, and the ultimate vaccine product failed to comply with the regulatory scheme's neurovirulence requirement. See 42 CFR §§ 73.110(b)(2)(ii), 73.110(b)(4), 73.114(b)(1) (Supp.1964); 21 CFR §§ 630.110(b)(2)(ii), 630.110(b)(4), 630.16(b)(1) (1987). Neurovirulence is the capacity of an infectious agent to produce pathologic effects on the central nervous system. In this context, it refers to the vaccine's ability to cause paralytic poliomyelitis. The neurovirulence of a vaccine product is tested by injecting the product into monkeys. The product meets the neurovirulence criterion only if a specified number of the animals survive and a "comparative analysis" demonstrates that the neurovirulence of the vaccine product "does not exceed" the neurovirulence of a reference product previously selected by the agency. 42 CFR § 73.114(b)(1)(iii) (Supp.1964); 21 CFR § 630.16(b)(1)(iii) (1987).

11. As noted, see n. 9, infra, the regulatory standards that petitioners claim were not satisfied in this case are the neurovirulence criterion and the requirement that virus strains be free from harmful effect. The question presented is thus application of objective scientific standards, see Brief for Petitioners 16–17, whereas the Government asserts that the determination incorporates considerable "policy judgment," Brief for United States 36. [The record is incomplete on this issue, and the District Court should decide] whether agency officials appropriately exercise policy judgment in determining that a vaccine product complies with the relevant safety standards.

B

The regulatory scheme governing release of vaccine lots is distinct from that governing the issuance of licenses. The former set of regulations places an obligation on manufacturers to examine all vaccine lots prior to distribution to ensure that they comply with regulatory standards. See 21 CFR § 610.1 (1978). These regulations, however, do not impose a corresponding duty on the Bureau of Biologics. Although the regulations empower the Bureau to examine any vaccine lot and prevent the distribution of a noncomplying lot, see 21 CFR § 610.2(a) (1978), they do not require the Bureau to take such action in all cases. The regulations generally allow the Bureau to determine the appropriate manner in which to regulate the release of vaccine lots, rather than mandating certain kinds of agency action. The regulatory scheme governing the release of vaccine lots is substantially similar in this respect to the scheme discussed in United States v. Varig Airlines, 467 U.S. 797, 104 S.Ct. 2755, 81 L.Ed.2d 660 (1984).

Given this regulatory context, the discretionary function exception bars any claims that challenge the Bureau's formulation of policy as to the appropriate way in which to regulate the release of vaccine lots. Cf. id., at 819–820, 104 S.Ct., at 2767–2768 (holding that discretionary function exception barred claim challenging FAA's decision to establish a spot-checking program). In addition, if the policies and programs formulated by the Bureau allow room for implementing officials to make independent policy judgments, the discretionary function exception protects the acts taken by those officials in the exercise of this discretion. Cf. id., at 820, 104 S.Ct., at 2767–2768 (holding that discretionary function exception barred claim that employees charged with executing the FAA's spot-checking program made negligent policy judgments respecting the proper inspection of airplanes). The discretionary function exception, however, does not apply if the acts complained of do not involve the permissible exercise of policy discretion. Thus, if the Bureau's policy leaves no room for an official to exercise policy judgment in performing a given act, or if the act simply does not involve the exercise of such judgment, the discretionary function exception does not bar a claim that the act was negligent or wrongful. Cf. Indian Towing Co. v. United States, 350 U.S., at 69, 76 S.Ct., at 126–127 (holding that a negligent failure to maintain a lighthouse in good

whether the determination that a vaccine product complies with each of these regulatory standards involves judgment of the kind that the discretionary function exception protects.

working order subjected Government to suit under the FTCA even though the initial decision to undertake and maintain lighthouse service was a discretionary policy judgment).

Viewed in light of these principles, petitioners' claim regarding the release of the vaccine lot from which Kevan Berkovitz received his dose survives the Government's motion to dismiss. Petitioners allege that, under the authority granted by the regulations, the Bureau of Biologics has adopted a policy of testing all vaccine lots for compliance with safety standards and preventing the distribution to the public of any lots that fail to comply. Petitioners further allege that notwithstanding this policy, which allegedly leaves no room for implementing officials to exercise independent policy judgment, employees of the Bureau knowingly approved the release of a lot that did not comply with safety standards. See App. 13; Brief for Petitioners 20–21; Reply Brief for Petitioners 15–17. Thus, petitioners' complaint is directed at a governmental action that allegedly involved no policy discretion. Petitioners, of course, have not proved their factual allegations, but they are not required to do so on a motion to dismiss. If those allegations are correct—that is, if the Bureau's policy did not allow the official who took the challenged action to release a noncomplying lot on the basis of policy considerations—the discretionary function exception does not bar the claim.[13] Because petitioners may yet show, on the basis of materials obtained in discovery or otherwise, that the conduct challenged here did not involve the permissible exercise of policy discretion, the invocation of the discretionary function exception to dismiss petitioners' lot release claim was improper.

IV

For the foregoing reasons, the Court of Appeals erred in holding that the discretionary function exception required the dismissal of petitioners' claims respecting the licensing of Orimune and the release of a particular vaccine lot. The judgment of the Court of Appeals is accordingly reversed, and the case is remanded for further proceedings consistent with this opinion.

It is so ordered.

NOTES

1. In the interest of justice, why does it matter whether the plaintiff's injury resulted from the government's erroneous policy or from the government's erroneous failure to follow its regulatory rule? Indeed, is not an error in policy the more objectionable of the two? Or are the courts in these cases concerned with something other than justice?

13. The Government's own argument before this Court provides some support for petitioners' allegation regarding the Bureau's policy. The Government indicated that the Bureau reviews each lot of vaccine and decides whether it complies with safety standards. See Tr. of Oral Arg. 42. The Government further suggested that if an employee knew that a lot did not comply with these standards, he would have no discretion to approve the release of the lot. See id., at 31–32.

2. The Court of Appeals decision in *Berkovitz* is noted at 61 Temp.L.Rev. 281 (1988).

SECTION 4. GOVERNMENT CONTRACTORS

BOYLE v. UNITED TECHNOLOGIES CORPORATION

Supreme Court of United States, 1988.
487 U.S. ___, 108 S.Ct. 2510, 101 L.Ed.2d 442.

JUSTICE SCALIA delivered the opinion of the Court.

This case requires us to decide when a contractor providing military equipment to the Federal Government can be held liable under state tort law for injury caused by a design defect.

I

On April 27, 1983, David A. Boyle, a United States Marine helicopter copilot, was killed when the CH–53D helicopter in which he was flying crashed off the coast of Virginia Beach, Virginia, during a training exercise. Although Boyle survived the impact of the crash, he was unable to escape from the helicopter and drowned. Boyle's father, petitioner here, brought this diversity action in Federal District Court against the Sikorsky Division of United Technologies Corporation (Sikorsky), which built the helicopter for the United States.

* * * [P]etitioner alleged that Sikorsky had defectively designed the copilot's emergency escape system: the escape hatch opened out instead of in (and was therefore ineffective in a submerged craft because of water pressure), and access to the escape hatch handle was obstructed by other equipment. The jury returned a general verdict in favor of petitioner and awarded him $725,000. The District Court denied Sikorsky's motion for judgment notwithstanding the verdict.

The Court of Appeals reversed and remanded with directions that judgment be entered for Sikorsky. * * * It * * * found, as a matter of federal law, that Sikorsky could not be held liable for the allegedly defective design of the escape hatch because, on the evidence presented, it satisfied the requirements of the "military contractor defense," which the court had recognized the same day in Tozer v. LTV Corp., 792 F.2d 403 (CA4 1986). 792 F.2d, at 414–415.

Petitioner sought review here, challenging the Court of Appeals' decision on three levels: First, petitioner contends that there is no justification in federal law for shielding government contractors from liability for design defects in military equipment. Second, he argues in the alternative that even if such a defense should exist, the Court of Appeals' formulation of the conditions for its application is inappropriate. Finally, petitioner contends that the Court of Appeals erred in not remanding for a jury determination of whether the elements of the defense were met in this case. We granted certiorari, 479 U.S. 1029 (1986).

II

Petitioner's broadest contention is that, in the absence of legislation specifically immunizing Government contractors from liability for design defects, there is no basis for judicial recognition of such a defense. We disagree. In most fields of activity, to be sure, this Court has refused to find federal pre-emption of state law in the absence of either a clear statutory prescription, [citations], or a direct conflict between federal and state law. [Citations.] But we have held that a few areas, involving "uniquely federal interests," Texas Industries, Inc. v. Radcliff Materials, Inc., 451 U.S. 630, 640 (1981), are so committed by the Constitution and laws of the United States to federal control that state law is pre-empted and replaced, where necessary, by federal law of a content prescribed (absent explicit statutory directive) by the courts—so-called "federal common law." [Citations.]

* * *

[T]he Federal Government's interest in the procurement of equipment is implicated by suits such as the present one—even though the dispute is one between private parties. * * * The imposition of liability on Government contractors will directly affect the terms of Government contracts: either the contractor will decline to manufacture the design specified by the Government, or it will raise its price. Either way, the interests of the United States will be directly affected.

That the procurement of equipment by the United States is an area of uniquely federal interest does not, however, end the inquiry. That merely establishes a necessary, not a sufficient, condition for the displacement of state law. Displacement will occur only where, as we have variously described, a "significant conflict" exists between an identifiable "federal policy or interest and the [operation] of state law," [citation], or the application of state law would "frustrate specific objectives" of federal legislation [citation]. * * *

* * *

* * * Here the state-imposed duty of care that is the asserted basis of the contractor's liability (specifically, the duty to equip helicopters with the sort of escape-hatch mechanism petitioner claims was necessary) is precisely contrary to the duty imposed by the Government contract (the duty to manufacture and deliver helicopters with the sort of escape-hatch mechanism shown by the specifications). Even in this sort of situation, it would be unreasonable to say that there is always a "significant conflict" between the state law and a federal policy or interest. If, for example, a federal procurement officer orders, by model number, a quantity of stock helicopters that happen to be equipped with escape hatches opening outward, it is impossible to say that the Government has a significant interest in that particular feature. That would be scarcely more reasonable than saying that a

private individual who orders such a craft by model number cannot sue for the manufacturer's negligence because he got precisely what he ordered.

In its search for the limiting principle to identify those situations in which a "significant conflict" with federal policy or interests does arise, the Court of Appeals, in the lead case upon which its opinion here relied, identified as the source of the conflict the *Feres* doctrine, under which the Federal Tort Claims Act does not cover injuries to armed service personnel in the course of military service. See Feres v. United States, 340 U.S. 135 (1950). Military contractor liability would conflict with this doctrine, the Fourth Circuit reasoned, since the increased cost of the contractor's tort liability would be added to the price of the contract, and "[s]uch pass-through costs would * * * defeat the purpose of the immunity for military accidents conferred upon the government itself." *Tozer,* 792 F.2d, at 408. Other courts upholding the defense have embraced similar reasoning. See, e.g., [citations]; *McKay v. Rockwell Int'l Corp.,* 704 F.2d 444, 449 (CA9 1983), cert. denied, 464 U.S. 1043 (1984). We do not adopt this analysis because it seems to us that the *Feres* doctrine, in its application to the present problem, logically produces results that are in some respects too broad and in some respects too narrow. Too broad, because if the Government contractor defense is to prohibit suit against the manufacturer whenever *Feres* would prevent suit against the Government, then even injuries caused to military personnel by a helicopter purchased from stock (in our example above), or by any standard equipment purchased by the Government, would be covered. Since *Feres* prohibits all service-related tort claims against the Government, a contractor defense that rests upon it should prohibit all service-related tort claims against the manufacturer—making inexplicable the three limiting criteria for contractor immunity (which we will discuss presently) that the Court of Appeals adopted. On the other hand, reliance on *Feres* produces (or logically should produce) results that are in another respect too narrow. Since that doctrine covers only service-related injuries, and not injuries caused by the military to civilians, it could not be invoked to prevent, for example, a civilian's suit against the manufacturer of fighter planes, based on a state tort theory, claiming harm from what is alleged to be needlessly high levels of noise produced by the jet engines. Yet we think that the character of the jet engines the Government orders for its fighter planes cannot be regulated by state tort law, no more in suits by civilians than in suits by members of the armed services.

There is, however, a statutory provision that demonstrates the potential for, and suggests the outlines of, "significant conflict" between federal interests and state law in the context of government procurement. In the Federal Tort Claims Act (FTCA), Congress authorized damages to be recovered against the United States for harm caused by the negligent or wrongful conduct of Government employees, to the extent that a private person would be liable under the law of the place where the conduct occurred. 28 U.S.C. § 1346(b). It excepted from this consent to suit, however,

> "[a]ny claim * * * based upon the exercise or performance or the failure to exercise or perform a discretionary function or duty on the part of a federal agency or an employee of the Government, whether or not the discretion involved be abused." 28 U.S.C. § 2680(a).

We think that the selection of the appropriate design for military equipment to be used by our Armed Forces is assuredly a discretionary function within the meaning of this provision. It often involves not merely engineering analysis but judgment as to the balancing of many technical, military, and even social considerations, including specifically the trade-off between greater safety and greater combat effectiveness. And we are further of the view that permitting "second-guessing" of these judgments, see United States v. Varig Airlines, 467 U.S. 797, 814 (1984), through state tort suits against contractors would produce the same effect sought to be avoided by the FTCA exemption. The financial burden of judgments against the contractors would ultimately be passed through, substantially if not totally, to the United States itself, since defense contractors will predictably raise their prices to cover, or to insure against, contingent liability for the Government-ordered designs. To put the point differently: It makes little sense to insulate the Government against financial liability for the judgment that a particular feature of military equipment is necessary when the Government produces the equipment itself, but not when it contracts for the production. In sum, we are of the view that state law which holds Government contractors liable for design defects in military equipment does in some circumstances present a "significant conflict" with federal policy and must be displaced.

We agree with the scope of displacement adopted by the Fourth Circuit here, which is also that adopted by the Ninth Circuit, see *McKay v. Rockwell Int'l Corp.*, supra, at 451. Liability for design defects in military equipment cannot be imposed, pursuant to state law, when (1) the United States approved reasonably precise specifications; (2) the equipment conformed to those specifications; and (3) the supplier warned the United States about the dangers in the use of the equipment that were known to the supplier but not to the United States. The first two of these conditions assure that the suit is within the area where the policy of the "discretionary function" would be frustrated—i.e., they assure that the design feature in question was considered by a Government officer, and not merely by the contractor itself. The third condition is necessary because, in its absence, the displacement of state tort law would create some incentive for the manufacturer to withhold knowledge of risks, since conveying that knowledge might disrupt the contract but withholding it would produce no liability. We adopt this provision lest our effort to protect discretionary functions perversely impede them by cutting off information highly relevant to the discretionary decision.

We have considered the alternative formulation of the Government contractor defense, urged upon us by petitioner, which was adopted by the Eleventh Circuit in Shaw v. Grumman Aerospace Corp., 778 F.2d 736, 746 (1985), cert. pending, No. 85–1529. That would preclude suit only if (1) the contractor did not participate, or participated only minimally, in the design of the defective equipment; or (2) the contractor timely warned the Government of the risks of the design and notified it of alternative designs reasonably known by it, and the Government, although forewarned, clearly authorized the contractor to proceed with the dangerous design. While this formulation may represent a perfectly reasonable tort rule, it is not a rule designed to protect the federal interest embodied in the "discretionary function" exemption. The design ultimately selected may well reflect a significant policy judgment by Government officials whether or not the contractor rather than those officials developed the design. In addition, it does not seem to us sound policy to penalize, and thus deter, active contractor participation in the design process, placing the contractor at risk unless it identifies all design defects.

* * *

[Judgment vacated; remanded to Court of Appeals for determination of whether a reasonable jury could have found for the petitioner, on the facts presented, consistent with the government contractor defense.]

JUSTICE BRENNAN, with whom JUSTICE MARSHALL and JUSTICE BLACKMUN join, dissenting.

Lieutenant David A. Boyle died when the CH–53D helicopter he was copiloting spun out of control and plunged into the ocean. We may assume, for purposes of this case, that Lt. Boyle was trapped under water and drowned because respondent United Technologies negligently designed the helicopter's escape hatch. We may further assume that any competent engineer would have discovered and cured the defects, but that they inexplicably escaped respondent's notice. Had respondent designed such a death trap for a commercial firm, Lt. Boyle's family could sue under Virginia tort law and be compensated for his tragic and unnecessary death. But respondent designed the helicopter for the Federal Government, and that, the Court tells us today, makes all the difference: Respondent is immune from liability so long as it obtained approval of "reasonably precise specifications"—perhaps no more than a rubberstamp from a federal procurement officer who might or might not have noticed or cared about the defects, or even had the expertise to discover them.

If respondent's immunity "bore the legitimacy of having been prescribed by the people's elected representatives," we would be duty bound to implement their will, whether or not we approved. United States v. Johnson, 481 U.S. ___, ___ (1987) (dissenting opinion of Scalia, J.). Congress, however, has remained silent—and conspicuously so, having resisted a sustained campaign by Government contractors to legislate for them some defense.[1] The Court—unelected and unaccountable to the people—has unabashedly stepped into the breach to legislate a rule denying Lt. Boyle's family the compensation that state law assures them. This time the injustice is of this Court's own making.

Worse yet, the injustice will extend far beyond the facts of this case, for the Court's newly discovered Government contractor defense is breathtakingly sweeping. It applies not only to military equipment like the CH-53D helicopter, but (so far as I can tell) to any made-to-order gadget that the Federal Government might purchase after previewing plans—from NASA's Challenger space shuttle to the Postal Service's old mail cars. The contractor may invoke the defense in suits brought not only by military personnel like Lt. Boyle, or Government employees, but by anyone injured by a Government contractor's negligent design, including, for example, the children who might have died had respondent's helicopter crashed on the beach. It applies even if the Government has not intentionally sacrificed safety for other interests like speed or efficiency, and, indeed, even if the equipment is not of a type that is typically considered dangerous; thus, the contractor who designs a Government building can invoke the defense when the elevator cable snaps or the walls collapse. And the defense is invocable regardless of how blatant or easily remedied the defect, so long as the contractor missed it and the specifications approved by the Government, however unreasonably dangerous, were "reasonably precise." [Ante.]

In my view, this Court lacks both authority and expertise to fashion such a rule, whether to protect the Treasury of the United States or the coffers of industry. Because I would leave that exercise of legislative power to Congress, where our Constitution places it, I would reverse the Court of Appeals and reinstate petitioner's jury award.

I

* * *

In pronouncing that "[t]here is no federal general common law," [Erie R. Co. v. Thompkins, 304 U.S. 64, 78 (1938)] put to rest the notion that the grant of diversity jurisdiction to federal courts is itself authority to fashion rules of substantive law. See United States v. Little Lake Misere Land Co. 412 U.S. 580, 591 (1973). As the author of today's opinion for the Court pronounced for a unanimous Court just two months ago, ["]we start with the assumption that the historic police powers of the States were not to be superseded . . . unless that was the clear and manifest purpose of Congress.["] Puerto Rico Dept of Consumer Affairs v. Isla Petroleum Corp. 485 U.S. ___, ___, (1988)

1. See, e.g., H.R. 4765, 99th Cong., 2d Sess. (1986) (limitations on civil liability of Government contractors); S. 2441, 99th Cong., 2d Sess. (1986) (same). See also H.R. 2378, 100th Cong., 1st Sess. (1987) (indemnification of civil liability for Government contractors); H.R. 5883, 98th Cong., 2d Sess. (1984) (same); H.R. 1504, 97th Cong., 1st Sess. (1981) (same); H.R. 5351, 96th Cong., 1st Sess. (1979) (same).

(citations omitted). Just as "[t]here is no federal pre-emption in vacuo, without a constitutional text or a federal statute to assert it," id., at ___, federal common law cannot supersede state law in vacuo out of no more than an idiosyncratic determination by five Justices that a particular area is "uniquely federal."

Accordingly, we have emphasized that federal common law can displace state law in "few and restricted" instances. Wheeldin v. Wheeler, 373 U.S. 647, 651 (1963). "[A]bsent some congressional authorization to formulate substantive rules of decision, federal common law exists only in such narrow areas as those concerned with the rights and obligations of the United States, interstate and international disputes implicating conflicting rights of States or our relations with foreign nations, and admiralty cases." Texas Industries, Inc. v. Radcliff Materials, Inc. 451 U.S. 630, 641, (1981) (footnotes omitted). "The enactment of a federal rule in an area of national concern, and the decision whether to displace state law in doing so, is generally made not by the federal judiciary, purposefully insulated from democratic pressures, but by the people through their elected representatives in Congress." Milwaukee v. Illinois, 451 U.S. 304, 312–313 (1981). [Citations.] State laws "should be overridden by the federal courts only where clear and substantial interests of the National Government, which cannot be served consistently with respect for such state interests, will suffer major damage if the state law is applied." United States v. Yazell, 382 U.S. 341, 352 (1966).

II

Congress has not decided to supersede state law here (if anything, it has decided not to, see n. 1, supra) and the Court does not pretend that its newly manufactured "Government contractor defense" fits within any of the handful of "narrow areas," *Texas Industries,* supra, at 641, of "uniquely federal interests" in which we have heretofore done so, 451 U.S., at 640. Rather, the Court creates a new category of "uniquely federal interests" out of a synthesis of two whose origins predate *Erie* itself: the interest in administering the "obligations to and rights of the United States under its contracts," [ante,], and the interest in regulating the "civil liability of federal officials for actions taken in the course of their duty," [ante.] This case is, however, simply a suit between two private parties. We have steadfastly declined to impose federal contract law on relationships that are collateral to a federal contract, or to extend the federal employee's immunity beyond federal employees. And the Court's ability to list two, or ten, inapplicable areas of "uniquely federal interest" does not support its conclusion that the liability of Government contractors is so "clear and substantial" an interest that this Court must step in lest state law does "major damage." [Citation.]

* * *

III

In a valiant attempt to bridge the analytical canyon between what [the precedent relied on by the Court] said and what the Court wishes it had said, the Court invokes the discretionary function exception of the Federal Tort Claims Act (FTCA), 28 U.S.C. § 2680(a). The Court does not suggest that the exception has any direct bearing here, for petitioner has sued a private manufacturer (not the Federal Government) under Virginia law (not the FTCA). Perhaps that is why respondent has three times disavowed any reliance on the discretionary function exception, even after coaching by the Court,[4] as has the Government.[5]

Notwithstanding these disclaimers, the Court invokes the exception, reasoning that federal common law must immunize Government contractors from state tort law to prevent erosion of the discretionary function exception's *policy* of foreclosing judicial " 'second-guessing' " of discretionary governmental decisions. [Ante,] quoting United States v. Varig Airlines, 467 U.S. 797, 814 (1984). The erosion the Court fears apparently is rooted not in a concern that suits against Government contractors will prevent them from designing, or the Government from commissioning the design of, precisely the product the Government wants, but in the concern that such suits might preclude the Government from purchasing the desired product at the price it wants: "The financial burden of judgments against the contractors," the Court fears, "would ultimately be passed through, substantially if not totally, to the United States itself." [Ante.]

Even granting the Court's factual premise, which is by no means self-evident, the Court cites no authority for the proposition that burdens imposed on Government contractors, but passed on to the Government, burden the Government in a way that justifies extension of its immunity. However substantial such indirect burdens may be, we have held in other contexts that they are legally irrelevant. [Citation.]

* * *

IV

At bottom, the Court's analysis is premised on the proposition that any tort liability indirectly absorbed by the Government so burdens governmental functions as to compel us to act when Congress has not. That proposition is by no means uncontroversial. The tort system is

4. * * *

"QUESTION: * * * [Y]our preemption argument, I want to be sure I understand it—does not depend at all on the Federal Tort Claims Act, as I understand it. * * *

"MR. LACOVARA: That's correct." Trans of Oral Arg 33–35 (reargument Apr. 27, 1988).

5. "QUESTION: Does the Government's position depend at all on the discretionary function exemption in the Federal Tort Claims Act?

"MR. AYER: Well, that's a hard question to answer. * * * I think my answer to you is, no, ultimately it should not." Id., at 40–41.

premised on the assumption that the imposition of liability encourages actors to prevent any injury whose expected cost exceeds the cost of prevention. If the system is working as it should, Government contractors will design equipment to avoid certain injuries (like the deaths of soldiers or Government employees), which would be certain to burden the Government. The Court therefore has no basis for its assumption that tort liability will result in a net burden on the Government (let alone a clearly excessive net burden) rather than a net gain.

Perhaps tort liability is an inefficient means of ensuring the quality of design efforts, but "[w]hatever the merits of the policy" the Court wishes to implement, "its conversion into law is a proper subject for congressional action, not for any creative power of ours." [Citation.] It is, after all, "Congress, not this Court or the other federal courts, [that] is the custodian of the national purse. By the same token [Congress] is the primary and most often the exclusive arbiter of federal fiscal affairs. And these comprehend, as we have said, securing the treasury or the Government against financial losses *however inflicted. . . .*" [Citations.] If Congress shared the Court's assumptions and conclusion it could readily enact "A BILL To place limitations on the civil liability of government contractors to ensure that such liability does not impede the ability of the United States to procure necessary goods and services," H.R. 4765, 99th Cong. 2d Sess. (1986); see also S. 2441, 99th Cong., 2d Sess. (1986). It has not.

Were I a legislator, I would probably vote against any law absolving multibillion dollar private enterprises from answering for their tragic mistakes, at least if that law were justified by no more than the unsupported speculation that their liability might ultimately burden the United States Treasury. Some of my colleagues here would evidently vote otherwise (as they have here), but that should not matter here. We are judges not legislators, and the vote is not ours to cast.

I respectfully dissent.

JUSTICE STEVENS, dissenting.

When judges are asked to embark on a lawmaking venture, I believe they should carefully consider whether they, or a legislative body, are better equipped to perform the task at hand. There are instances of so-called interstitial lawmaking that inevitably become part of the judicial process. But when we are asked to create an entirely new doctrine—to answer "questions of policy on which Congress has not spoken," United States v. Gilman, 347 U.S. 507, 511 (1954)—we have a special duty to identify the proper decisionmaker before trying to make the proper decision.

When the novel question of policy involves a balancing of the conflicting interests in the efficient operation of a massive governmental program and the protection of the rights of the individual—whether in the social welfare context, the civil service context, or the military procurement context—I feel very deeply that we should defer to the expertise of the Congress. That * * * is why I am so distressed by the majority's decision today. For in this case, as in *United States v. Gilman,* supra: "The selection of that policy which is most advantageous to the whole involves a host of considerations that must be weighed and appraised. That function is more appropriately for those who write the laws, rather than for those who interpret them." 347 U.S., at 511–513.

I respectfully dissent.

NOTES

1. If the government designs a product and puts it out to bid, and it is manufactured by the winning contractor according to the government's design specifications, should the manufacturer be liable for injuries caused by "defects" in the design? Should the government?

Same result if a manufacturer designs and builds a prototype of a complex product, say a helicopter, and successfully peddles it to the Pentagon?

Is the Court's rule sound?

2. How, if at all, do you think *Boyle* will affect the cost of products purchased by the government? The availability of such products? Their quality? Safety?

3. If you represent a government contractor, what procedures would you advise your client to adopt to maximize the value of *Boyle?*

4. What, precisely, did *Boyle* hold? How far does its reasoning extend?

A. Does the defense encompass nonmilitary products, such as lawnmowers, purchased by the military? Nonmilitary products purchased by other branches of government, such as mail trucks?

How persuasive is Justice Brennan's dissent, arguing that the holding is very wide?

B. Does it apply to nondeliberative approvals of "reasonably precise specifications"? To what extent does the Court's decision require reference to the difficult and uncertain boundaries of the discretionary function exception?

C. Does the defense apply when the "reasonably precise specifications" that are actually reviewed and approved do not include the design danger that causes the harm? In other words, if the government approves precise specifications for most aspects of a helicopter, but the specifications do not specify which way the doors open, does the defense apply?

D. Does the defense apply to manufacturing defect claims? Review carefully the three elements of the defense. See McGonigal v. Gearhart Indus., 851 F.2d 777 (5th Cir.1988). Inadequate warning claims?

5. What is the majority's reasoning in Boyle? Does it square with the just compensation clause of the 5th amendment?

6. Why is the third prong of the defense defined so narrowly? Should not the manufacturer be liable for failing to warn the government about all risks of which the manufacturer reasonably *should* have known?

7. See Ausness, Surrogate Immunity: The Government Contract Defense and Products Liability, 47 Ohio St.L.J. 1985 (1986); Note, 95 Yale L.J. 992 (1985).

SECTION 5. APPARENT MANUFACTURERS: PRODUCT SPONSORS, LICENSORS, AND FRANCHISERS

HEBEL v. SHERMAN EQUIPMENT

Supreme Court of Illinois, 1982.
92 Ill.2d 368, 65 Ill.Dec. 888, 442 N.E.2d 199.

CLARK, JUSTICE:

* * *

* * * On February 22, 1976, plaintiff, Rohn Hebel, then 16 years old, was working at the Glenbrook Standard Service Station and Car Wash in Northbrook when his foot was caught in the car conveyor and mangled by the conveyor's drive chain. Hebel's amended complaint, alleging that the "car washing machine" at the Glenbrook Standard Station had been designed, manufactured and sold by Sherman and that it was in a defective and unreasonably dangerous condition, was filed on July 31, 1978.

The Glenbrook Standard Station purchased its car-washing equipment in 1971 from Haverberg Auto Laundry Equipment Company in Chicago. Haverberg (which is sometimes referred to in the pleadings by its trade name, Flapan Car Wash Equipment Company) is primarily engaged in selling, installing and servicing automatic car-washing equipment, but it also manufactures some car-washing equipment itself. Haverberg is a distributor for Sherman Industries, Inc. (the actual corporate name of Sherman Equipment), a New Jersey-based manufacturer of automatic car-washing machinery. Apart from the conveyor, nearly all of the equipment purchased by Glenbrook from Haverberg was manufactured by Sherman. This included a large washer, shaped like an inverted "U," with enormous brushes, of the kind commonly seen at a tunnel-type car wash, as well as a similarly shaped rinser, dryer, and "wax actuator." Each of these machines prominently displayed Sherman's trade name and rather distinctive logo ("Sherman Supersonic Systems, Palmyra, N.J."). The conveyor—an 80–foot–long track with rollers that emerge from beneath the floor to push automobiles along under the various washing and rinsing units—bore no identifying name or serial number. Hebel admits in his brief that the conveyor was designed and manufactured by Haverberg, not by Sherman.

Sherman moved for summary judgment in the circuit court on the ground that it did not manufacture, design or sell the allegedly defective conveyor that injured the plaintiff. It supported the motion with the affidavits of employees of Sherman and Haverberg stating that Haverberg, not Sherman, designed and manufactured the conveyor. Hebel's response to the motion asserted that Sherman "had held itself out to be the manufacturer of the automatic car washing system" at the Glenbrook Standard Station, including the defective conveyor which was a "component of the system," and that Sherman was therefore liable as though it were the actual manufacturer. The appellate court, in reversing the summary judgment, found that a factual issue existed as to whether Sherman held itself out as the manufacturer of the conveyor, apparently on the basis of evidence from which the court thought it could be inferred that Sherman had authorized Haverberg's use of its name in advertising the conveyor. [Citation.]

Decision of this case requires us first to examine the "holding out" or "apparent manufacturer" doctrine. The imposition of tort liability based on a defendant's status as the "apparent manufacturer" of a harm-causing product predates by some years the advent of the doctrine of strict liability in tort of suppliers of unreasonably unsafe chattels. The rule evolved in cases in which a retailer or distributor of a product manufactured by another was found to have held itself out to the public as the product's manufacturer, and therefore to be subject to the same liability as the actual manufacturer. (2 Hursh & Bailey, American Law of Products Liability sec. 7:2 (2d ed. 1974), and cases there cited.) The rationale for imposing liability on the apparent manufacturer was a species of estoppel: the vendor who, through its labeling or advertising of a product, caused the public to believe that it was the manufacturer and to buy the product in reliance on the vendor's reputation and care in making it, was held to have assumed the obligations of a manufacturer and to be estopped to deny its identity as the manufacturer. [Citations.] The Restatement (Second) of Torts formulation of the rule states: "One who puts out as his own product a chattel manufactured by another is subject to the same liability as though he were its manufacturer." (Restatement (Second) of Torts sec. 400 (1965).) According to the Restatement comment: "The actor puts out a chattel as his own product in two types of cases. The first is where the actor appears to be the manufacturer of the chattel. The second is where the chattel appears to have been made particularly for the actor. In the first type of case the actor frequently causes the chattel to be used in reliance upon his care in making it; in the second, he frequently causes the chattel to be used in reliance upon a belief that he has required it to be made properly for him and that the actor's reputation is an assurance to the user of the quality of the product. * * * Thus, one puts out a chattel as his own product when he puts it out under his name or affixes to it his trade name or trademark. When such identification is referred to on the label as an indication of the quality or wholesomeness of the chattel, there is an added emphasis that the user can rely upon the reputation of the person so identified." (Restatement (Second) of Torts sec. 400, comment *d* (1965).) Another justification sometimes given for the rule is that where a defendant puts out a product as its own, the purchaser has no means of ascertaining the identity of the true manufacturer, and it is thus fair to impose liability on the party whose actions effectively conceal the true manufacturer's identity. [Citations.]

"Holding out" cases usually involve either (a) a defendant's labeling or affixing to the product its own name, trade name, or trademark; or (b) advertising identifying the defendant as the maker of the product. * * *

It is noteworthy that the apparent-manufacturer doctrine was developed in the context of suits by consumers against sellers of dangerous chattels. Nearly all the cases imposing liability on this basis involve defendants who were retailers or distributors. The aim of the doctrine clearly was to provide a remedy for consumers injured by unsafe products. Today, of course, this objective is achieved by the doctrine of strict products liability; all sellers of dangerously defective chattels are now strictly liable to injured purchasers—that is, they have the same liability as the manufacturer—without regard to whether or not they held themselves out to the public as the maker of the product. [Citation.] The function of the apparent-manufacturer doctrine has, as it were, been absorbed by the theory of sellers' strict liability in tort for injuries caused by unreasonably unsafe products.

Two questions thus arise: first, whether anything remains of the apparent-manufacturer rule; and, second, whether the rule applies to a defendant who, like Sherman, neither manufactured nor sold the product that injured the plaintiff. The doctrine, as noted above, was fashioned with reference to sellers; we have found only two cases in which it was applied to a nonseller. [Citations.] Even if we assume, however, that the apparent-manufacturer doctrine is properly applicable to Sherman, we find that the pleadings, depositions, affidavits and other materials introduced on the motion for summary judgment, considered in the light most favorable to the plaintiff, fail to reveal facts that amount to Sherman's holding itself out to the public as the manufacturer of Haverberg's conveyor.

It is undisputed that the greater part of the car-washing equipment in use at the Glenbrook Standard Station was manufactured by Sherman and was labeled with Sherman's name and logo, and that the allegedly defective conveyor, manufactured by Haverberg, bore no identifying insignia. The appellate court found that the reasonable person in plaintiff's position would view the entire assemblage at the Glenbrook car wash as one "system" and would infer that Sherman manufactured all of its "component parts," including the conveyor, and that this inference amounts to Sherman's holding itself out as the conveyor's manufacturer. We think that this belief, reasonable or not, has no bearing on the issue. The primary rationale for imposing liability on the apparent manufacturer of a defective product is that it has induced the *purchasing public* to believe that it is the actual manufacturer, and to act on this belief—that is, to *purchase the product in reliance* on the apparent manufacturer's reputation and skill in making it. [Citations.] It is thus apparent that whether a holding out has occurred must be judged from the viewpoint of the purchasing public, and in light of circumstances as of the time of purchase. It is clear, and plaintiff does not seriously dispute, that the various car-washing machines made by Sherman, as well as the conveyor made by Haverberg, were individual pieces of equipment which were purchased and sold as separate items, and apparently also were operated independently of one another. That a casual observer, viewing the machines after their purchase and installation, might think otherwise does not mean that a reasonable purchaser of car-washing equipment, such as Glenbrook, would rely on such an impression. This is not a case in which the defendant manufactures and sells a single machine that contains a defective component part not manufactured by it (compare Penn v. Inferno Manufacturing Corp. (La.App.1967), 199 So.2d 210 (defendant, manufacturer of fluid level gauge, had manufacturer's liability for injuries caused by explosion of sight glass; though sight glass manufactured by another, defendant held itself out as manufacturer by labeling gauge with its name and also labeling box in which separate glasses were shipped, and failing to indicate that glass had been manufactured by another)). The mere fact that Sherman's machines, which bore its name, were sold by Haverberg and used by Glenbrook in conjunction with a separate, unlabeled piece of equipment does not, we think, identify Sherman in the mind of the reasonable purchaser as the maker of the unlabeled machine, or render Sherman liable for injuries caused by it under the apparent-manufacturer rule.

We next consider plaintiff's contention that the use of Sherman's name on a promotional flyer, issued by Haverberg, advertising the conveyor amounted to Sherman's holding itself out as manufacturer of the conveyor.

Sherman prepared and issued a number of flyers advertising the equipment it made. Each of these one-page flyers describes one of its car-washing machines. On the front, each flyer has a photograph of the unit, on which the Sherman Supersonic Systems logo is clearly visible, with the name and model number of the unit at the top of the page. Text on both sides describes the machine's features and specifications. The name Sherman Car Wash Equipment Company (which was Sherman's official name prior to 1976), the name Sherman Industries, Inc., the Sherman Supersonic Systems logo, and Sherman's New Jersey address and phone number appear in large type at the bottom of each side of the page.

The brochure on which plaintiff seeks to base liability was prepared by Haverberg. At the top of one side in large type is printed "Jack Flapan's HAVERBERG Equipment Company"; the name "Haverberg" is on a separate line and is in print larger than the other wording. The reverse has text extolling the conveyor and describing its features. On both sides of the flyer appear two photos of the conveyor track and mechanism with no designation on the conveyor as to its manufacturer. At the bottom of the side of the sheet with the text is the single word "Sherman," followed on the next line by the name

"Haverberg Auto Laundry Equipment Company, Inc." and Haverberg's Chicago address and phone number.

As discussed above, a defendant that advertises itself as the maker of a product may be found to have held itself out to the public as the manufacturer, if the advertising was such as to lead a reasonable purchaser to believe that the defendant, and not some other party, was the actual manufacturer. * * * [H]owever, * * * the flyer was undisputedly prepared by Haverberg, not by Sherman. We have found no case in which a defendant was held to have a manufacturer's liability based on *another party's* representations in its advertising that defendant was the manufacturer.

The plaintiff argues, however, that Sherman should be liable if found to have authorized Haverberg's use of its name in promoting sales of its conveyor. Plaintiff relies primarily on Connelly v. Uniroyal, Inc. (1979), 75 Ill.2d 393, 27 Ill.Dec. 343, 389 N.E.2d 155. In *Connelly,* this court considered the issue of the liability of a licensor (Uniroyal) for injuries caused by a defective tire bearing the Uniroyal trademark which had been manufactured by the licensee—a Belgian corporation indirectly controlled by Uniroyal—under a licensing agreement pursuant to which Uniroyal provided the licensee with the plans, specifications and other technical know-how needed to produce the tires, authorized the licensee's use of the Uniroyal name and trademark in advertising, and in consideration received quarterly payments from the licensee. The court held that Uniroyal was strictly liable in tort, although it had neither manufactured nor sold the tire that injured the plaintiff.

The basis for the imposition of strict liability in *Connelly* was the defendant's integral involvement in the overall producing and marketing enterprise that placed the dangerous product in the stream of commerce, and its participation in the profits from the distribution of the product. (75 Ill.2d 393, 411, 27 Ill.Dec. 343, 389 N.E.2d 155.) This "enterprise theory" of liability has been recognized in a growing number of decisions dealing with trademark licensing and franchising agreements. (Sandrock, Tort Liability of a Non–Manufacturing Franchisor for Acts of its Franchisee, 48 U.Cin.L.Rev. 699 (1979).) One factor leading to the imposition of strict tort liability on the nonmanufacturing trademark owner in these cases is that the licensee's use of the trademark in advertising the product creates the public impression that the licensor is the actual maker and induces consumers to rely on the appearance that the trademark owner is responsible for the product and stands behind it. (Kosters v. Seven–Up Co. (6th Cir.1979), 595 F.2d 347, 353 (Michigan law).) However, the inducement of consumer reliance is not the only consideration in imposing strict liability. Rather, the decisions emphasize that liability arises from the same combination of considerations that underlie the doctrine of strict products liability generally: that the loss caused by unsafe products should be borne by those who create the risk of harm by participating in the manufacture, marketing and distribution of unsafe products; who derive economic benefit from placing them in the stream of commerce; and who are in a position to eliminate the unsafe character of the product and prevent the loss. [Citations.] As stated in the seminal case of Kasel v. Remington Arms, Inc. (1972), 24 Cal.App.3d 711, 101 Cal.Rptr. 314, strict liability arises, not because of the defendant's legal relationship with the manufacturer or with other entities in the manufacturing-marketing system, but because of its "participatory connection, for [its] personal profit or other benefit, with the injury-producing product and with the enterprise that created consumer demand for and reliance upon the product." 24 Cal.App.3d 711, 725, 101 Cal.Rptr. 314, 323.

The instant case does not come within the rule of *Connelly.* Comparing the facts of the two cases, it is evident that the circumstances that persuaded us that Uniroyal should be responsible for defective products manufactured by its licensee are absent here. Uniroyal specifically authorized its licensee to place the Uniroyal trademark, strongly identified with Uniroyal, on its tires and to use it in promoting sales—actions calculated to produce the impression in the purchaser's mind that the tires were a Uniroyal product. Uniroyal set up the arrangement and received both direct payments and indirect economic benefits from it. Haverberg, by contrast, did not place the "Sherman Supersonic Systems" trade name or logo on its conveyor or its promotional material but made what might almost be called incidental use of the name "Sherman" in conjunction with its own name—perhaps with some thought of suggesting its business relationship with Sherman, or trading a little on Sherman's business goodwill. There was no evidence to suggest that Sherman authorized or permitted Haverberg to place its name on the flyer. While it might well be possible to find, even in the absence of a formal, written agreement, that a defendant had authorized another party to use its name or trademark, there was no evidence here of even an informal understanding between Sherman and Haverberg as to Haverberg's advertising of Haverberg's products. Sherman did not receive payment from Haverberg for the use of its name, or any part of Haverberg's profit from the sales of the conveyor.

In short, we do not find that Sherman had the kind of participatory connection with the enterprise that produced and marketed the conveyor, or the economic benefit from placing it in the stream of commerce, that led to the imposition of strict liability in *Connelly.* While that opinion did state that a defendant's participation in the chain of distribution was not an essential element for strict liability to apply (75 Ill.2d 393, 410–11, 27 Ill.Dec. 343, 389 N.E.2d 155), the reference was to the fact that a defendant such as Uniroyal who is not in the direct chain of sale leading from manufacturer to consumer may nonetheless be so integrally involved in the overall producing and marketing enterprise that strict liability will follow.

For the foregoing reasons, the judgment of the appellate court is reversed, and the judgment of the circuit court of Cook County is affirmed.

NOTES

1. Whose reliance on the defendant's holding out should be relevant, the purchaser's or the plaintiff's?

2. **Franchisers.** If a franchiser consents to the use of its name on an unsafe product, its liability may hinge on the extent of its control over the creation of the unsafe condition. In Kosters v. Seven–Up Co., 595 F.2d 347 (6th Cir.1979), plaintiff was blinded in one eye when a bottle of 7–Up slipped out of a defectively designed carton that had been supplied to the franchisee bottling company from a third party. The Seven–Up Company contractually retained control over the design of the carton, and the particular carton involved had been submitted to and approved by Seven–Up.

Held, Seven–Up was subject to strict liability (in implied warranty) for the carton's design. Whether this duty arises depends upon a combination of factors: "(1) the risk created by approving for distribution an unsafe product likely to cause injury, (2) the franchis[e]r's ability and opportunity to eliminate the unsafe character of the product and prevent the loss, (3) the consumer's lack of knowledge of danger, and (4) the consumer's reliance on the trade name which gives the intended impression that the franchis[e]r is responsible and stands behind the product." 595 F.2d at 353. In sum, "Liability is based on the franchis[e]r's control and the public's assumption, induced by the franchis[e]r's conduct, that it does in fact control and vouch for the product." Id. Of course the case for liability is even stronger if the franchiser itself designs the product. See Cook v. Branick Mfg., Inc., 736 F.2d 1442 (11th Cir. 1984).

Contrast Better Beverages, Inc. v. Meschwitz, 643 S.W.2d 502 (Tex.App. 1982), in which a Dr. Pepper bottle top flew off the bottle into the plaintiff's eye. *Held,* the franchiser-trademark holder was not liable for an injury caused by the bottling or capping processes where it only supplied the syrup and was not involved in processing, bottling, or capping the bottle. See also Torres v. Goodyear Tire & Rubber Co., 857 F.2d 1293 (9th Cir.1988) (trademark licensor not subject to strict liability).

3. A related issue concerns the liability of a parent corporation for the acts of its subsidiary. If the parent and subsidiary are so closely related as to be essentially identical, the limited liability provided by incorporation may be disregarded. An important factor in determining whether the corporate veil may be pierced is the adequacy of the subsidiary corporation's capitalization. See Nelson v. International Paint Co., Inc., 734 F.2d 1084, 1091–93 (5th Cir. 1984) (attempt to impose liability on parent for defective paint sold by subsidiary). See generally Hackney & Benson, Shareholder Liability for Inadequate Capital, 43 U.Pitt.L.Rev. 837 (1982). See generally P. Blumberg, The Law of Corporate Groups—Substantive Law ch. 13 (1987).

On trademark licensors, see Goldstein, Products Liability and the Trademark Owner: "When a Trademark is a Warranty," 32 Bus.Law 957 (1977); Note, 55 Iowa L.Rev. 693 (1970). On franchisers, see Notes, 5 U.San.Fran.L. Rev. 118 (1970); 41 S.Cal.L.Rev. 143 (1968).

SECTION 6. CERTIFIERS, ENDORSERS, AND PUBLISHERS

HANBERRY v. HEARST CORPORATION

Court of Appeals of California, 1969.
276 Cal.App.2d 680, 81 Cal.Rptr. 519.

AULT, ASSOCIATE JUSTICE, PRO TEM.

[Plaintiff appeals from the trial court's order sustaining respondent Hearst Corporation's demurrer and entry of a judgment dismissing her complaint against Hearst.]

[Plaintiff] alleges she purchased a pair of shoes on March 30, 1966 at a retail store owned and operated by the defendant Akron; the shoes had been imported and distributed to Akron by the defendant Victor B. Handal & Bros., Inc.; the shoes were defective in manufacture and design and had a low co-efficient of friction on vinyl and certain other floor coverings commonly used in this area and were slippery and unsafe when worn on such floor coverings; she was unaware of the defect and in wearing the shoes on the same day she purchased them, she stepped on the vinyl floor of her kitchen, slipped, fell and sustained severe personal injuries.

Appellant further alleges respondent Hearst publishes a monthly magazine known as Good Housekeeping in which products, including the shoes she purchased, were advertised as meeting the "Good Housekeeping's Consumers' Guaranty Seal". With respect to the seal the magazine stated: "This is Good Housekeeping's Consumers' Guaranty" and "We satisfy ourselves that products advertised in Good Housekeeping are good ones and that the advertising claims made for them in our magazine are truthful." The seal itself contained the promise, "If the product or performance is defective, Good Housekeeping guarantees replacement or refund to consumer."

Appellant alleges further she had frequently read Good Housekeeping Magazine "and believed the products bearing the seal had been examined, tested and inspected by defendant and were good and safe for the use intended"; prior to purchasing the shoes she had seen an advertisement of them, either in Good Housekeeping Magazine or in a newspaper ad placed by defendant Handal which incorporated the contents of the Good Housekeeping endorsement; Good Housekeeping seal was affixed to the shoes and the container for the shoes with Hearst's consent; Hearst was paid for the advertising of the shoes which appeared in its magazine and for the use of its seal; appellant relied upon respondent's representation and seal and purchased the shoes because of them. Appellant further alleges Hearst made no examination, test or investigation of the shoes, or a sample thereof, or if such tests were made they were done in a careless and negligent manner and that Hearst's issuance of its seal and certification as to the shoes was not warranted by the information it possessed.

* * *

The basic question presented on this appeal is whether one who endorses a product for his own economic gain, and for the purpose of encouraging and inducing the public to buy it, may be liable to a purchaser who, relying on the endorsement, buys the product and is injured because it is defective and not as represented in the endorsement. We conclude such liability may exist and a cause of action has been pleaded in the instant case. In arriving at this conclusion, we are influenced more by public policy than by whether such cause of action can be comfortably fitted into one of the law's traditional categories of liability. [Citations.]

Appellant's third amended complaint alleges facts which support her argument respondent Hearst is not just a publisher of a magazine which accepts and publishes advertisements from manufacturers and retailers of consumer products. To enhance the value of its magazine as an advertising medium, to compete more favorably in the advertising market, it offers to those whose products meet such standards as it may impose and who choose to purchase its services, the "Good Housekeeping Consumers' Guaranty Seal" and its certification, "We have satisfied ourselves the products and services advertised in Good Housekeeping are good ones and the advertising claims made for them in our magazine are truthful."

Respondent's endorsement and approval of a product is not confined to the pages of its own magazine. It permits the manufacturer or retailer of a product which has been approved by Good Housekeeping Magazine to advertise that fact in other advertising media and permits its seal to appear in such ads and to be attached to the product itself. While the device used by respondent enhances the value of Good Housekeeping Magazine for advertising purposes, it does so because its seal and certification tend to induce and encourage consumers to purchase products advertised in the magazine and which bear that seal and certification. Implicit in the seal and certification is the representation respondent has taken reasonable steps to make an independent examination of the product endorsed, with some degree of expertise, and found it satisfactory. Since the very purpose of respondent's seal and certification is to induce consumers to purchase products so endorsed, it is foreseeable certain consumers will do so, relying upon respondent's representations concerning them, in some instances, even more than upon statements made by the retailer, manufacturer or distributor.

Having voluntarily involved itself into the marketing process, having in effect loaned its reputation to promote and induce the sale of a given product, the question arises whether respondent can escape liability for injury which results when the product is defective and not as represented by its endorsement. In voluntarily assuming this business relationship, we think respondent Hearst has placed itself in the position where public policy imposes upon it the duty to use ordinary care in the issuance of its seal and certification of quality so that members of the consuming public who rely on its endorsement are not unreasonably exposed to the risk of harm. [Citation.]

* * *

While we have held appellant has stated a cause of action for negligent misrepresentation against Hearst, we reject her contention she may also proceed in warranty or on the theory of strict liability in tort. She has cited no authority, and we have found none, which has extended either theory of recovery to one not directly involved in manufacturing products for, or supplying products to, the consuming public. To invoke either theory of recovery here would subject respondent to liability not warranted by the circumstances. Appellant does not contend, nor do respondent's representations permit the interpretation, it examined or tested the particular pair of shoes involved. The most that can be implied from respondent's representation is that it has examined or tested samples of the product and found the general design and materials used to be satisfactory. Application of either warranty or strict liability in tort would subject respondent to liability even if the general design and material used in making this brand of shoe were good, but the particular pair became defective through some mishap in the manufacturing process. We believe this kind of liability for individually defective items should be limited to those directly involved in the manufacturing and supplying process, and should not be extended through warranty or strict liability to a general endorser who makes no representation it has examined or tested each item marketed.

* * *

[Judgment of dismissal reversed as to negligent misrepresentation claim.]

NOTES

1. Compare Hempstead v. General Fire Extinguisher Corp., 269 F.Supp. 109 (D.Del.1967), where the defendant, Underwriters Laboratories, a nonprofit testing organization, allowed the use of its inspection and testing label on fire extinguishers manufactured by the General Fire Extinguisher Corporation. *Held,* U.L. could be held liable, for injuries from the explosion of an extinguisher carrying its label, for negligent approval of its design.

Should certifiers be subject to *strict* liability?

2. Insurance companies and gas utilities having the duty to inspect a product, such as industrial machinery, furnaces, or service lines, may be liable for negligent inspection. See, e.g., O'Laughlin v. Minnesota Natural Gas Co., 253 N.W.2d 826 (Minn.1977) (gas furnace); Jackson v. New Jersey Mfrs. Ins. Co., 166 N.J.Super. 448, 400 A.2d 81 (App.Div.1979) (insurer liable to third persons only if it has undertaken to make safety inspections upon which insured has relied). See generally Comment, 66 Ky.L.J. 910 (1977–78) (insurers); Annot., 26 A.L.R.2d 136 (1952) (gas companies). Should such an inspection be held to carry an implied warranty of sufficiency?

3. Assume that a movie or sports star or other public figure is paid to endorse a product which is defective in some respect. Plaintiff purchases it on the strength of the endorsement and is injured by the defect. Should the endorser be liable? For example, plaintiff suffers spinal injuries from hitting his head on the bottom of a swimming pool of insufficient depth beneath the diving board. If plaintiff purchased the pool in reliance upon an endorsement by Greg Louganis, an Olympic gold-medalist diver, should Louganis be subject to liability for the injuries? If so, on what theories of liability? Should Jim Palmer, the former Baltimore Orioles pitcher, be liable to a man who suffers an allergic reaction to a brand of underwear Palmer promoted? Are the issues the same?

4. **Publishers and Booksellers.** In Brocklesby v. United States, 767 F.2d 1288 (9th Cir.1985), plaintiffs brought wrongful death and property damage claims against the publisher of an aircraft instrument approach chart and the federal government. An error in the chart, based on inaccurate data supplied by the FAA to the chart publisher, caused an airline jet to crash into a mountain. Plaintiffs argued that strict liability should apply. The publisher obtained its information from the FAA but presented it in a unique graphic format. *Held,* the chart was a "product," the publisher its "manufacturer," and strict liability applied. Compare Lewin v. McCreight, 655 F.Supp. 282 (E.D.Mich.1987) (publisher of "how to" book who had no involvement in contents of book was not liable for failure to warn of "defective ideas" contained in book).

5. Cardozo v. True, 342 So.2d 1053 (Fla.Dist.Ct.App.1977), was a case against a retail book dealer for selling a cookbook containing a recipe that was allegedly defective for its failure to warn that an ingredient, Dasheen plant (commonly known as "elephant's ears"), is poisonous when eaten uncooked. Plaintiff nibbled on the ingredient while preparing a recipe from the cookbook and immediately became ill. *Held,* the bookseller could not be held liable in implied warranty for the recipe, defective or not. Analogizing to the defamation cases, where distributors of information prepared by others are not held liable if there is no opportunity to investigate, the court observed as follows:

> It is unthinkable that standards imposed on the quality of goods sold by a merchant would require that merchant, who is a book seller, to evaluate the thought processes of the many authors and publishers of the hundreds and often thousands of books which the merchant offers for sale. One can readily imagine the extent of potential litigation. Is the newsdealer, or for that matter the neighborhood news carrier, liable if the local paper's recipes call for inedible ingredients? We think not.
>
> * * *
>
> The common theme running through these decisions is that ideas hold a privileged position in our society. They are not equivalent to commercial products. Those who are in the business of distributing the ideas of other people perform a unique and essential function. To hold those who perform this essential function liable, regardless of fault, when an injury results would severely restrict the flow of the ideas they distribute.

The *Cardozo* court expressly avoided ruling on the liability of an author or publisher on similar facts. Are the policies the same in such cases?

6. Compare Eimann v. Soldier of Fortune Magazine, Inc., 680 F.Supp. 863 (S.D.Tex.1988), where plaintiffs sued the magazine in negligence for publishing the following ad:

> EX-MARINES—67-69 'Nam vets—ex-DI-weapons specialist—jungle warfare, pilot, M.E., high risk assignments U.S. or overseas. (404) 991-2684.

A husband hired the person who placed the ad to kill his wife, and the job was done. *Held,* a negligence action for failure to investigate could be maintained, in view of the nature of the magazine and the fact that other ads explicitly offered criminal services. The first amendment was not a bar because this form of commercial speech was not as stringently protected as core speech. (In March 1988, the jury awarded plaintiffs $9.4 million.) Accord, Norwood v. Soldier of Fortune Magazine, Inc., 651 F.Supp. 1397 (W.D.Ark.1987) (contract killer).

7. Contrast Herceg v. Hustler Magazine, Inc., 814 F.2d 1017 (5th Cir.1987), cert. denied, ___ U.S. ___, 108 S.Ct. 1219, 99 L.Ed.2d 420 (1988), where the parents of a 14-year-old boy sued the magazine for publishing an article entitled, "Orgasm of Death." The article described in detail the practice of autoerotic asphyxiation, which entailed masturbating while "hanging" oneself to cut off the blood supply to the brain at the moment of orgasm. Plaintiffs' son died while engaged in this activity; a copy of the magazine opened to the article was found lying at his feet. The jury awarded $69,000 to his mother, $3,000 to his friend who found him hanging, and assessed the defendant $110,000 in punitive damages, for "inciting" the decedent's act. *Held,* reversed: "Even if the article paints in glowing terms the pleasures supposedly achieved by the practice it describes, * * * no fair reading of it can make its content advocacy, let alone incitement to engage in the practice." Id. at 1022–23. The majority reasoned that the first amendment compelled this result:

> The extent of the danger created by a publication therefore is not immaterial in determining the state's power to penalize that publication for harm that ensues, but first amendment protection is not eliminated simply because publication of an idea creates a potential hazard. Whether the Hustler article, therefore, placed a dangerous idea into Troy's head is but one factor in determining whether the state may impose damages for that consequence. Against the important social goal of protecting the lives of adolescents like Troy, the Constitution requires us to balance more than Hustler's right to publish the particular article, subject to the possibility of civil liability should harm ensue, but also the danger that unclear or diminished standards of first amendment protection may both inhibit the expression of protected ideas by other speakers and constrict the right of the public to receive those ideas.

Id. at 1020. Concurring, Judge Jones remarked:

> What disturbs me to the point of despair is the majority's broad reasoning which appears to foreclose the possibility that any state might choose to temper the excesses of the pornography business by imposing civil liability for harms it directly causes. * * * To deny this possibility, I believe, is to degrade the free market of ideas to a level with the black market for heroin. Despite the grand flourishes of rhetoric in many first amendment decisions concerning the sanctity of

> "dangerous" ideas, no federal court has held that death is a legitimate price to pay for freedom of speech.

Id. at 1025.

Some authorities estimate that 500 to 1,000 deaths, most of which are erroneously misdiagnosed as suicide, occur each year due to teenagers engaged in the autoerotic practice involved in *Herceg.* N.Y. Times, March 27, 1984, at C1, col. 4.

8. See Baby, Liability of a Product Endorser as Certifier: A Tort Whose Time Has Come and Gone, 20 Trial 38 (1984); Comments, Tort Liability for Nonlibelous Negligent Statements: First Amendment Considerations, 93 Yale L.J. 744 (1984); Tort Liability of the Media for Audience Acts of Violence: A Constitutional Analysis, 52 S.Cal.L.Rev. 529 (1979); Note, Publisher Liability for Material that Invites Reliance, 66 Tex.L.Rev. 1155 (1988).

SECTION 7. EMPLOYERS

COMMENT, *BELL v. INDUSTRIAL VANGAS:* THE EMPLOYER-MANUFACTURER AND THE DILEMMA OF DUAL CAPACITY

34 Hastings L.J. 461, 463–70 (1982).

History of the Workers' Compensation System

Workers' compensation legislation in California, as in other states, arose out of the increased industrial hazards and changing employer-employee relationships attending the industrial revolution. With an increase in the number of industrial accidents came the development of the fellow-servant rule and the doctrines of assumption of the risk and contributory negligence, which served to protect employers from liability to injured employees. The scope of the employer's duty to employees was also limited, resulting in the risks of employment falling primarily upon the worker. The common law rules were predicated upon the assumption that workers voluntarily choose the hazards of their employment, thus waiving their right to recover damages for injuries arising from dangers that are normal incidents of their employment. The difficulty of proving the employer's negligence and the difficulty in overcoming the common law defenses left many injured workers uncompensated.

The social problems associated with the lack of remedies for injured workers gave rise to legislative attempts to aid such workers. Workers' compensation legislation in California first modified, and later abolished, the common law defenses of the employer. * * * The Workmen's Compensation, Insurance and Safety Act of 1917, with amendments, has become California's workers' compensation law. The Act is intended to provide a remedy for injured employees, regardless of fault, based upon the employment relationship, and not upon tort or contract principles.

Theory and Function of Workers' Compensation

The * * * workers' compensation system reflects a social policy of reallocating the burden of industrial injuries from the worker to society as a whole by allowing the cost of worker injuries to be included in the costs of production and later reflected in the prices consumers pay for products. * * *

The chief benefit of the workers' compensation system for the injured employee is that it provides a much speedier and more certain recovery than a suit at law. By abolishing the requirement of proving negligence on the part of the employer, workers' compensation also makes some recovery available for injured workers in a large number of cases where employer fault would be difficult to establish. In contrast, the benefits of the system for industrial employers lie in the protection from excessive liability in tort for employee injuries. In a more general sense, workers' compensation also benefits society by providing incentives for employers to run safe operations.

The quid pro quo of the workers' compensation system * * * is that an employee, injured within the course of his or her employment, gains a statutory no-fault remedy but sacrifices the right to pursue a potentially larger recovery in tort. Accordingly, the California workers' compensation statutes provide that where the "conditions of compensation" exist, workers' compensation provides the exclusive right of recovery against the employer for work-related injuries. Dissatisfaction with the scope of workers' compensation coverage and the average workers' compensation recovery, however, has led an increasing number of injured workers to argue that their injuries should be compensable outside of the workers' compensation system.

The increase in the number of common law suits by injured employees is also partially the result of changes in the historical "tradeoff" of rights associated with workers' compensation. Whereas the prospects for recovery for injured workers under the common law were slim at the time of the enactment of the first workers' compensation law, theories such as strict products liability and comparative negligence make actions at common law much more attractive to injured workers today. The result has been the creation of theories such as the dual capacity doctrine, which circumvent the exclusivity of workers' compensation and allow recovery at law as well.

DEVELOPMENT OF DUAL CAPACITY DOCTRINE

The dual capacity doctrine was first recognized in Duprey v. Shane, 39 Cal.2d 781, 249 P.2d 8 (1952). Defendant chiropractor treated his nurse for an injury. The treatment aggravated the injury, and the nurse sued for malpractice. The court permitted the suit, notwithstanding the exclusive remedy rule of the workers' compensation statute, because the defendant had assumed the obligations of a chiropractor when he undertook to treat his employee as a patient.

In 1977, the doctrine was extended to the products liability context in Douglas v. E. & J. Gallo Winery, 69 Cal.App.3d 103, 137 Cal.Rptr. 797 (1977). Plaintiffs were injured when the scaffolding on which they were working collapsed. Their employer had manufactured the scaffolding as well as other scaffolding sold to the general public. *Held,* plaintiffs could maintain a products liability action against their employer on the dual capacity doctrine:

> When an employer becomes a manufacturer for sale to the public, and assumes the risk of being a manufacturer, he has the opportunity to spread his costs for product liability and transfer it to the ultimate consumer. The fact that he himself as an employer may be one of those ultimate consumers is a factor he must consider in whether or not he becomes a manufacturer for sale to the public. The obligations of a manufacturer exist even if the manufacturer had not employed workers such as plaintiff.
>
> Limitations on the remedy of an injured employee should not be extended beyond the purposes of the Workers' Compensation Law. Failure to apply the dual capacity doctrine to the manufacturer who sells to the public would unduly restrict the injured person's remedy. There is no reason to relieve a manufacturer who sells to the public of liability *as a manufacturer* by the chance circumstance that the defendant manufacturer also happens to be an employer of the injured person. The deterrent value of a manufacturer's liability to promote the manufacture of safe products is effectively reduced if recovery is limited to Workers' Compensation.
>
> We limit the holding of this case to a defendant who engaged in manufacturing for sale to the general public. A single or occasional disconnected act does not constitute engaging in such manufacturing. * * * On the other hand, manufacturers' liability clearly arises where plaintiff employee is injured in using a product designed and manufactured by his employer primarily for sale to the general public and only incidentally used in the defendant's other activities.

137 Cal.Rptr. at 802–03.

In the same year as *Douglas,* Ohio also applied the doctrine to a products liability case, Mercer v. Uniroyal, Inc., 49 Ohio App.2d 279, 361 N.E.2d 492 (1976), in which a truckdriver for Uniroyal was injured in a crash when a defective Uniroyal tire on his truck blew out. Four years later, the doctrine was reaffirmed and extended in California, in Bell v. Industrial Vangas, Inc., 30 Cal.3d 628, 179 Cal.Rptr. 30, 637 P.2d

266 (1981). Outside of California and Ohio, however, the doctrine was experiencing quite a different reception.

RADER v. UNITED STATES RUBBER RECLAIMING CO., INC.

United States District Court, Southern District of Mississippi, 1985.
617 F.Supp. 1045.

BARBOUR, DISTRICT JUDGE.

* * *

FACTS

In September 1984, Rader, an employee of U.S. Rubber, was injured in the scope of his employment when the reclaimator which he was operating malfunctioned and emitted a large fireball which burned him. According to Rader, U.S. Rubber designed the reclaimator and is liable for the injuries he sustained as a result of the malfunction under the dual capacity doctrine.

Neither Rader nor U.S. Rubber states whether Rader has received workers' compensation benefits as a result of his injuries. Rader does admit, however, that he was injured in the course of his employment. Accordingly, there appears to be no question that Rader is entitled to recover workers' compensation.

U.S. Rubber moves for summary judgment on the basis that workers' compensation is Rader's exclusive remedy. Rader responds on the basis that the dual capacity doctrine, under which an employer assumes a role independent of his status as employer, permits recovery against U.S. Rubber despite the exclusive provisions of workers' compensation.

LAW

There is no question that workers' compensation is an employee's exclusive remedy for work-related injuries. Miss.Code Ann. § 71–3–9 (1972), entitled "Exclusiveness of liability," states that:

> [t]he liability of a employer to pay compensation shall be exclusive and in place of all other liability of such employer to the employee. * * *

The Mississippi Supreme Court has consistently rejected attempts to circumvent the exclusive remedy of workers' compensation. [Citations.] This Court is of the opinion that the Mississippi Supreme Court would likewise reject Rader's attempt to circumvent the workers' compensation act on the basis of the dual capacity doctrine.

The dual capacity doctrine provides that an employer may become liable in tort to an injured employee when the employer assumes an identity separate and apart from his role as employer. 2A Larson, Workmen's Compensation Law, § 72.81. The vast majority of courts have rejected the dual capacity doctrine and have held that an employer who designs, manufactures or distributes a product used by its employees cannot be held liable to an injured employee on the theory of products liability. 2A Larson, Workmen's Compensation Law, §§ 65.35, 72.83. Only Ohio and California have acknowledged the dual capacity doctrine. See, e.g., Duprey v. Shane, 39 Cal.2d 781, 249 P.2d 8 (1952); Mercer v. Uniroyal, 49 Ohio App.2d 279, 361 N.E.2d 492 (1977). Yet, even these states limit the applicability of the doctrine to products which are not only furnished to the employee but also sold to the public. See also 2A Larson, Workmens' Compensation Law, § 72.83.

Rader has not alleged that U.S. Rubber sold its reclaimator to the public. Even if he did, this Court's conclusion would be the same. As Larson states,

> [i]magine how much would remain of employer immunity if it were forfeited every time an employer adjusted or tinkered with a machine.

Id. at § 72.81. Accordingly, the Motion of U.S. Rubber for Summary Judgment is granted. A Final Judgment in accordance with this Memorandum Opinion will be entered pursuant to F.R.Civ.P. Rule 54.

NOTES

1. See Billy v. Consolidated Mach. Tool Corp., 51 N.Y.2d 152, 432 N.Y.S.2d 879, 412 N.E.2d 934 (1980):

> Having examined all of the pertinent precedent, we conclude that the "dual capacity" doctrine as it has been applied to permit common-law suits against employers in their capacities as property owners or manufacturers of plant equipment is fundamentally unsound. The Workers' Compensation Law was designed to spread the risk of industrial accidents through the vehicle of insurance coverage and, more specifically, to "provide a swift and sure source of benefits to the injured employee or to the dependents of [a] deceased employee" [citation], without regard to fault in most instances. In exchange for the security of knowing that fixed benefits will be paid without the need to resort to expensive and sometimes risky litigation, however, the employee has been asked to pay a price in the form of the loss of his common-law right to sue his employer in tort and perhaps to enjoy a more substantial recovery through a jury award. The legislative implementation of this "trade-off" is embodied in section 11 of the Workers' Compensation Law, which precludes suits against the employer and limits the employees to the recompense afforded under the statute when he is injured in the course of his employment.
>
> We cannot sanction the circumvention of this clear legislative plan by approving a theory which would permit the employer to be sued in his capacity as property owner or manufacturer of equipment used on the job site. As we have previously observed, "an employer remains an employer in his relations with his employees as to all matters arising from and connected with their employment. He may not be treated as a dual legal personality, 'a sort of Dr. Jekyl and Mr. Hyde' " [citations.] Employers are expected to provide their employees with a safe workplace that is reasonably free of hazards. This obligation to provide a safe workplace simply cannot be separated in a logical and

> orderly fashion from the duties owed by the employer to his employees by reason of his ownership of the premises or his manufacture of the equipment with which the employees must work. Indeed, these duties are merely subcategories within the complex of obligations that arise in connection with the employment relation. We would be seriously undermining the salutary social purposes underlying the existing workers' compensation scheme if we were to permit common-law recovery outside of that scheme on the basis of such illusory distinctions. This we decline to do.

432 N.Y.S.2d at 883, 412 N.E.2d at 939. Accord, Weber v. Armco, Inc., 663 P.2d 1221, 1226 (Okl.1983). See also Kaess v. Armstrong Cork Co., 403 N.W.2d 643 (Minn.1987).

2. "The dual capacity doctrine, in spite of widespread and varied attempts to invoke it as a way to defeat exclusiveness, flourished in only two states, Ohio and California, and even there for only a few years, from 1977 to 1983." 2A A. Larson, The Law of Workmen's Compensation § 72.81(c), at 14–236 (1988). In 1982, the California legislature effectively abolished the doctrine, see Cal.Lab. Code § 3602, and in 1983, the Ohio Supreme Court substantially restricted the doctrine. Freese v. Consolidated Rail Corp., 4 Ohio St.3d 5, 445 N.E.2d 1110 (1983). See also Bakonyi v. Ralston Purina Co., 17 Ohio St.3d 154, 478 N.E.2d 241 (1985).

Thus, the doctrine is essentially dead: "It is now held with virtual unanimity that an employer, who is also the manufacturer * * * of a product used in the work, cannot be held liable in damages to his own employee on a theory of products liability." 2 A. Larson, supra, § 72.83, at 14–252.

3. Is the doctrine really such a bad idea? See Note, 96 Harv.L.Rev. 1641, 1661 (1983):

> [M]ost courts have yielded to a perception that any breach in the exclusive remedy rule would betray the bargain implicit in the enactment of the original workers' compensation laws and thereby impair, if not destroy, the compensation system itself. In view of the outdated terms of the bargain and the inconsistency of these terms with major goals of compensation law, courts should not feel compelled to apply the exclusive remedy rule rigidly in the borderline cases not squarely within the scope of the bargain. Judicial recognition of reasonable exceptions to the rule would itself contribute to the achievement of safety, compensation, and equity goals while encouraging legislatures to undertake necessary reform of the workers' compensation system.

4. Another means of avoiding the exclusive remedy rule in some states, but not in others, is to demonstrate that the employer intentionally caused harm to the employee. Compare Blankenship v. Cincinnati Milacron Chemicals, Inc., 69 Ohio St.2d 608, 433 N.E.2d 572, cert. denied, 457 U.S. 857, 103 S.Ct. 127, 74 L.Ed.2d 110 (1982) (employees exposed to noxious chemicals; tort action allowed) with Poyser v. Newman & Co., Inc., 514 Pa. 32, 522 A.2d 548 (1987) (failure to guard sawblades; tort action barred). This type of claim generally arises in the toxic substance context. See p. 1001 n. 4, below.

5. Some economists argue that there is no need for the tort system to intervene in the employment context because market forces will require employers to pay higher wages for more dangerous work. See, e.g., Posner, A Theory of Negligence, 1 J. Legal Stud. 29, 69–70 (1972). Yet an employee may rationally minimize the risks he actually confronts. "If the psychological

benefit of suppressing one's fear in a particular activity exceeds the cost due to increased chances of accident, the worker will believe the activity to be safe." Akerlof & Dickens, The Economic Consequences of Cognitive Dissonance, 72 Am.Econ.Rev. 307, 308 (1982). See also Epstein, The Historical Origins and Economic Structure of Workers' Compensation Law, 16 Ga.L.Rev. 775 (1982), arguing that the workers' compensation system should (and basically does) mimic a contractual bargain between workers and employers to allocate workplace risks.

6. See Comments, 23 Hous.L.Rev. 945 (1986); 34 Hast.L.J. 461 (1982); Notes, 59 S.Cal.L.Rev. 205 (1985); 21 Duq.L.Rev. 995 (1983); Annot., 9 A.L.R.4th 873 (1981).

SECTION 8. SUCCESSOR CORPORATIONS

LEANNAIS v. CINCINNATI, INCORPORATED

United States Court of Appeals, Seventh Circuit, 1977.
565 F.2d 437.

MARKEY, CHIEF JUDGE. On April 20, 1973, appellant Raymond Leannais was injured while operating a coil slitter machine incident to his employment at Fullerton Metals Company in Milwaukee, Wisconsin.

In this diversity suit, Leannais and his wife (Leannais) sought damages from Cincinnati, Inc., and Cincinnati–Forte Co., (Cincinnati), the alleged corporate successors to the original manufacturer of the machine. The complaint alleges strict liability, negligence in the design and manufacture of the machine, and failure to warn potential users after serious injuries had occurred. In view of affidavits filed by both parties, the court granted summary judgment for Cincinnati.[2] We reverse and remand.

FACTS

The machine on which Leannais was injured had been manufactured by Forte Equipment Company (Forte) and sold to Fullerton in late 1964. In December, 1967, Forte sold its assets to Cincinnati, Inc., an Ohio corporation, for cash and certain employment agreements. Cincinnati, Inc., established a subsidiary named Cincinnati–Forte to accept the Forte assets. The subsidiary was dissolved in 1973 and the assets of Cincinnati–Forte were purchased by Cincinnati, Inc.

In the Forte–Cincinnati, Inc. agreement, Cincinnati expressly limited its liability for personal injury caused by Forte for a period of five years from the December 6, 1967 closing date of the contract, and

2. Cincinnati–Forte Co. was dismissed for want of service of process. Leannais does not appeal that action.

agreed to use its best efforts to secure a specific amount of insurance against such claims during that time.[3] No other liability for personal injury claims was assumed. Cincinnati was first notified of Leannais' injury in July, 1975, more than seven years after the acquisition of Forte's assets.

THE ISSUE

The issue before us is whether Cincinnati can be held liable for appellant's injury (1) under "corporate merger" or "continuation" theories, (2) under a "product line" theory of strict tort liability, or (3) because it negligently failed to warn of the potentially dangerous condition of the machines. The parties agree that Wisconsin law applies. That state being the situs of the injury and the residence of Leannais, it has the principal interest of any state in the rules of law to be applied.

3. The only liability for personal injury claims of this nature assumed by Cincinnati is set forth in paragraph 11(q) of the Purchase Agreement:

> (q) With respect to any claim by a third party, notice of which is given to Forte or Cincinnati within five (5) years of the Closing Date, based on personal injury allegedly caused by Forte Equipment as defined in Paragraph 3(b) above, whether such claims be made against Forte or Cincinnati, Cincinnati shall undertake to obtain, and shall use its best efforts to secure, insurance at its expense against such claims in the amount of Five Hundred Thousand ($500,000) Dollars. Toczyl and Rogalla shall apply and use their best efforts, experience and knowledge to aid in the investigation, defense and adjustment of such personal injury claims, with a view toward minimizing the effect of such claims and protecting the joint interests of the parties to this Agreement. As to each loss, damage or deficiency resulting from any such claim, or cost or expense in connection with the investigation, defense or adjustment thereof, to the extent not compensated by insurance and not assigned to Cincinnati or to Forte under Subparagraphs (b) and (c) of Paragraph 4, Forte, Toczyl or Rogalla, or any or all of them, jointly and severally, shall be liable to Cincinnati, and shall pay upon demand by Cincinnati, an amount equal to twenty-five percent (25%) of said loss, damage or deficiency and costs and expenses relating thereto. Nevertheless, the aggregated liability of Toczyl and Rogalla under this Subparagraph (q) shall not exceed the lesser of (i) $100,000 or (ii) the aggregate amount of the payments under subpart (4) of Paragraph 3(a) over the five-year period set forth in said subpart. Furthermore, in the event of termination of employment of either Toczyl or Rogalla or both pursuant to Paragraph 3(d), said liability of Toczyl and Rogalla for loss, damage, deficiency and costs and expenses relating thereto after such termination will be reduced to the lesser of (i) $50,000 for each determined separately and not jointly, or (ii) the aggregate amount of the payments under subpart (4) of Paragraph 3(d). Cincinnati's right of offset under this Subparagraph shall be limited to amounts otherwise payable under subpart (4) of Paragraph 3(a).
>
> Notwithstanding anything else set forth herein, no assumption by Cincinnati nor agreement or indemnification by Forte shall constitute a recognition that any third person is a proper creditor of or claimant against Forte or Cincinnati, nor shall any such agreement or assumption or indemnification revive or make valid, or operate as a recognition of the validity of, or as a waiver of any defense or counterclaim in respect of, any claim against any of such corporations, its assets, directors, officers or shareholders, whether such claim has been barred by any statute of limitations, or has become or is invalid or unenforceable for any cause, or in respect of which any such corporation, its officers, directors or shareholders has any defense or counterclaim.

OPINION

"MERGER" OR "CONTINUATION"

The general rule in the majority of American jurisdictions, including Wisconsin, is that a corporation which purchases the assets of another corporation does not succeed to the liabilities of the selling corporation. Bazan v. Kux Machine Co., 358 F.Supp. 1250 (E.D.Wis. 1973). Here, Cincinnati had no part in the design, manufacture, sale or distribution of the allegedly defective machine, and the general rule accords with the fundamental principle of justice and fairness, under which the law imposes responsibility for one's own act and not for the totally independent acts of others. There are, however, four well-recognized exceptions to the general rule under which liability may be imposed on a purchasing corporation: (1) when the purchasing corporation expressly or impliedly agreed to assume the selling corporation's liability; (2) when the transaction amounts to a consolidation or merger of the purchaser and seller corporations; (3) when the purchaser corporation is merely a continuation of the seller corporation; or (4) when the transaction is entered into fraudulently to escape liability for such obligations. [Citations.]

Leannais contends that the transaction here falls under exceptions (2) or (3), i.e., that there was a "merger" of the two corporations or that Cincinnati is a "mere continuation" of Forte. A merger, however, involves the actual absorption of one corporation into another, with the former losing its existence as a separate corporate entity. That did not happen here. When the seller corporation retains its existence while parting with its assets, a "de facto merger" may be found if the consideration given by the purchaser corporation be shares of its own stock. [Citations.] Here, no stock in Cincinnati or in Cincinnati–Forte was transferred as consideration for Forte's assets. A "consolidation" occurs when two combining corporations are dissolved and lose their identity in a new corporate entity. [Citation.] Cincinnati maintained its distinct corporate identity from a time prior to and throughout the transactions herein to the present day. The key element of a "continuation" is a common identity of the officers, directors and stockholders in the selling and purchasing corporations. Unlike the situation in which a new corporation merely takes over the assets of the selling corporation under the old management, the management of Forte was not carried over to Cincinnati. Nor did any shareholder of either corporation become an owner, director, or officer of the other.

We conclude, therefore, that the purchase of Forte's assets was not such as to bring it within either the "merger" or the "mere continuation" exception to the general rule. Cincinnati did not impliedly assume Forte's liability and its express assumption in paragraph 11(q) of the Purchase Agreement was limited to the five years stated. No allegation of fraudulent conduct having been made, the transaction must be viewed as a bona fide, arm's length bargain, valid under

Wisconsin law. It is thus clear that Cincinnati is not liable for the injury to Leannais under any of the traditional exceptions to the general rule respecting purchaser corporations.

"PRODUCT LINE"

Leannais also asserts a form of "tort" theory founded on "strict liability," and extension of the law of purchaser corporation liability exemplified by the recent case of Ray v. Alad Corp., [19 Cal.3d 22, 136 Cal. Rptr. 574, 560 P.2d 3 (1970)]. Ray sued a corporation which had purchased the assets of a ladder manufacturer, claiming injury from a defective ladder made by that manufacturer. Finding no basis for liability under the traditional exceptions discussed above, the California Supreme Court relied upon policy considerations. Drawing analogies from the treatment of certain labor law problems of successor corporations by the United States Supreme Court, Howard Johnson Co. v. Hotel Employees, 417 U.S. 249, 94 S.Ct. 2236, 41 L.Ed.2d 46 (1974), Golden State Bottling Co. v. NLRB, 414 U.S. 168, 94 S.Ct. 414, 38 L.Ed.2d 388 (1973), the court created a special "strict tort liability" exception to protect "otherwise defenseless victims of manufacturing defects" and to spread "*throughout society* * * * the cost of compensating them." (original emphasis)[7]

In essence, the court adopted a rule tied to the "product line":

> We therefore conclude that a party which acquires a manufacturing business and continues the output of its line of products under the circumstances here presented assumes strict tort liability for defects in units of the same product line previously manufactured and distributed by the entity from which the business was acquired. 136 Cal.Rptr. at 582, 560 P.2d at 11.

The record here contains not the slightest indication that Wisconsin courts have created, or would create, such a far-reaching exception to the non-liability of asset purchasers, so long the basis of economic decisions by its citizens. It is on occasion absolutely necessary, if justice be done, for courts to "legislate" within the "interstices" of a statute, or by analogy to other laws and judicial precedents. In recent years, for a variety of reasons, many have thought it necessary to turn to the courts in search of solutions to social problems. Courts are ill-equipped, however, to balance equities among future plaintiffs and defendants. Such forays can result in wide-ranging ramifications on society, the contemplation of which is precluded by the exigencies of

7. The court relied heavily on the underlying purpose stated in Greenman v. Yuba Power Products, Inc., 59 Cal.2d 57, 63, 27 Cal.Rptr. 697, 701, 377 P.2d 897, 901 (1963). With deference, grave risks arise from court adoption of policy considerations to effect a change in a law so fundamental to the interdependent economic segments of a complex society. Whether the mounting costs of such change can be absorbed by insurance, whether product liability costs may grow so high in one state as to encourage business emigration, whether the relationship of workmen's compensation laws to product liability laws should be adjusted, and whether the many other economic and social effects of such an exception can be justified, are questions difficult to answer by analysis of the facts of a particular case and, it would appear, are more amenable to legislative investigation and determination.

deciding a particular case presented on a limited record developed by present parties. Absent compelling necessity, therefore, a Federal Court should not impose the policy pronouncements of the Supreme Court of one state upon the citizens of another. Nor are we at liberty to impose our own view as to what the law of Wisconsin should be. As the Wisconsin Supreme Court has recognized, such broad public policy issues are best handled by legislatures with their comprehensive machinery for public input and debate. [Citation.]

Indeed, the 1977 Wisconsin legislature by Joint Resolution, has directed its legislative council to conduct a complete study of the problems here presented, i.e., those related to product liability, and to recommend necessary legislation. State of Wisconsin, 1977 Assembly Joint Resolution 16, January 19, 1977.

Under all the circumstances, therefore, we hold that there is no "product line" theory transferring to a purchaser corporation the liabilities of the seller under Wisconsin law.

As a matter of law, therefore, Cincinnati did not assume, by virtue of the Purchase Agreement, the obligation to insure against Forte's product liabilities beyond those of which notice was received within five years. Leannais' claim did not arise during that period. Cincinnati cannot be held liable under Wisconsin law in strict liability for injury resulting from defects in the coil slitter designed, manufactured, and delivered by Forte.

FAILURE TO WARN

Leannais alleges that Cincinnati received notice of injury claims, and thereafter had a duty to warn present and prior purchasers of the dangerous condition of the machine.

The trial judge was apparently of the view that the Purchase Agreement's limitation on assumed liability, supra note 3, disposed of this claim. The Agreement, however, has no application to this particular allegation. The claim is based upon *Cincinnati's own* alleged omission under traditional principles of tort law. The essential question is whether Cincinnati had, and breached, a legal *duty* to warn Leannais' employer. Resolution of this issue thus turned on material questions of fact, and summary judgment was improper.

In Chadwick v. Air Reduction Co., 239 F.Supp. 247 (E.D.Ohio, 1965), the claim alleged that Air Reduction had knowledge of other personal injury claims at the time of, and subsequent to, the acquisition of assets and that such knowledge imposed a duty to notify past purchasers of the product's danger. Analogizing to the tort principle of the "Good Samaritan," whereby the law has traditionally imposed no duty on an ordinary bystander to rescue others, the court held that Air Reduction had no duty to warn prior purchasers of the product's known defects. When the same issue arose in Shane v. Hobam, Inc., 332 F.Supp. 526 (E.D.Pa.1971), that court had difficulty accepting the reasoning of *Chadwick*. *Shane* was similar to the present case, although the purchase agreement there expressly stated that Hobam assumed *no* product liability for sales made before the acquisition. The court granted partial summary judgment to Hobam, finding no liability resulting solely from the purchase of assets, but the court was unwilling to classify Hobam as an innocent bystander free of any duty to warn. The transfer of the corporate name, goodwill, and servicing responsibility for machines made before the transfer, created questions which the court was unwilling to foreclose by summary judgment:

> Plaintiff is treading on uncharted precedential seas and while there may be a serious question as to whether he has tipped the balance of precedent in his favor, I am reluctant to, and therefore will not, grant a summary judgment before pertinent factual gaps in the present case are filled in, thereby permitting the above questions to be answered with greater precisio[n]. 332 F.Supp. at 530.

A duty to aid another has been found to arise from special relations between the parties, the most common being carrier-passenger and innkeeper-guest relationships. The law has been extended in recent years to include many others:

> During the last century, liability for "nonfeasance" has been extended still further to a limited group of relations, in which custom, public sentiment, and views of social policy have led the courts to find a duty of affirmative action. It is not likely that this process of extension has ended. For the most part such a duty has been imposed where the relation is of some actual or potential economic advantage to the defendant, and the expected benefit justifies the requirement of special obligations. Prosser, Law of Torts, § 56, p. 339 (4th Ed.1971).

On the record before us, there is indication of actual or potential economic benefit to Cincinnati, attributable to customers of Forte. Cincinnati assumed all service obligations of Forte. Maintaining service ties to Forte customers enables Cincinnati to influence future sales. Knowledge of when and where various customers may need additional machinery, and knowledge of the condition of equipment which may need replacement, are important sales resources. Whether Cincinnati's succession to the service contracts provides sufficient nexus to establish a legal duty to warn Leannais' employer of the dangerous condition of the particular machine here involved, or of prior serious injuries incurred on other machines, is unclear from the bare pleadings and affidavits of record, and must await determination on remand. The existence of such a duty may be dependent upon such unanswered factual questions as whether the particular machine involved was under a service contract, whether Cincinnati had ever serviced that machine, or whether Cincinnati had information on present or prior ownership of Forte–built machines.

We intimate no view as to whether a duty to warn is present or was breached in the case before us. There being outstanding issues of material fact touching upon Cincinnati's own acts or omissions, however, summary judgment was inappropriate. Accordingly, the judgment of the district court is reversed and the case is remanded for further proceedings consistent herewith.

FAIRCHILD, CHIEF JUDGE, concurring in part, dissenting in part.

I join that part of the court's opinion which holds that question of fact exists as to whether the defendant had received notice of claims of injury and, therefore, had a duty to warn earlier purchasers of a dangerous condition in the product.

But I respectfully dissent from the holding that a successor company can be held liable for injuries caused by the defective product of its predecessor only when (1) there is an express or implied agreement of assumption, (2) the successor company consolidated or merged with the predecessor, (3) the successor is a "mere continuation" of the predecessor, or (4) the transfer of assets had the fraudulent purpose to allow the predecessor to escape liability for its obligations. The rule relied on pre-dates Wisconsin's adoption of the policy of strict liability in tort, [citations], and, there seems to be no decision of the Wisconsin courts applying this rule to strict liability for harm caused to the user of an unreasonably dangerous product. [Citation.]

In this area, I find most persuasive the reasoning of the Supreme Court of California in Ray v. Alad Corp., 19 Cal.3d 22, 136 Cal.Rptr. 574, 560 P.2d 3 (1977), that only by extending strict liability to successor companies that carry on the product line of their predecessors and that trade on the good name and good will of their predecessors can the policy underlying the strict products liability rule be given full effect. In Ray v. Alad, supra, the California Court justified imposing strict liability upon a successor company continuing the product line on three grounds:

> (1) the virtual destruction of the plaintiff's remedies against the original manufacturer caused by the successor's acquisition of the business, (2) the successor's ability to assume the original manufacturer's risk-spreading role, and (3) the fairness of requiring the successor to assume a responsibility for defective products that was a burden necessarily attached to the original manufacturer's good will being enjoyed by the successor in the continued operation of the business.

I find this reasoning sound and assume that the courts of Wisconsin would concur.

NOTES

1. As discussed in *Leannais,* California has extended successor corporation responsibility to strict tort products liability claims from products of a type that the successor company continues to produce. Ray v. Alad Corp., 19 Cal.3d 22, 136 Cal.Rptr. 574, 560 P.2d 3 (1977). *Ray's* summary of the three policy reasons supporting its approach is set forth in Judge Fairchild's dissent in *Leannais.*

2. What do you think of *Ray's* first rationale, based on the destruction of the plaintiff's remedies? *Ray* explained the first rationale as follows:

> [T]he practical value of [plaintiff's right to recover in strict tort for damages caused by a defective product] against the original manufacturer was vitiated by the purchase of Alad I's tangible assets, trade name and good will on behalf of Alad II [citation] and the dissolution of Alad I within two months thereafter in accordance with the purchase agreement. The injury giving rise to plaintiff's claim against Alad did not occur until more than six months after the filing of the dissolution certificate declaring that Alad I's "known debts and liabilities have been actually paid" and its "known assets have been distributed to its shareholders." This distribution of assets was perfectly proper as there was no requirement that provision be made for claims such as plaintiff's that had not yet come into existence. Thus, even if plaintiff could obtain a judgment on his claim against the dissolved and assetless Alad I [citation] he would face formidable and probably insuperable obstacles in attempting to obtain satisfaction of the judgment from former stockholders or directors. [Citations.]

560 P.2d at 9.

How about amending the dissolution statutes to condition the corporation's ability to liquidate and dissolve upon its making adequate provision for future products liability claims? See Green, Successor Liability: The Superiority of Statutory Reform to Protect Products Liability Claimants, 72 Cornell L.Rev. 17 (1986); Roe, Mergers, Acquisitions, and Tort: A Comment on the Problem of Successor Corporation Liability, 70 Va.L.Rev. 1559 (1984).

3. How compelling is Ray's second rationale, based on the successor's ability to spread the risk?

4. What do you think of the third rationale, that the successor ought to bear the burdens along with the benefits of the predecessor's goodwill? Consider the views of one commentator:

> This reasoning is specious. Goodwill is simply an intangible property right. The successor has, by hypothesis, paid adequate compensation to obtain the goodwill and has put it to productive use. Unless the courts relying on this argument are creating a new concept of property rights, no justification exists for requiring a purchaser to pay more for an asset than the parties have agreed it is worth. Despite substantial criticism, courts blithely continue to rely on the goodwill justification to support [expanded] successor liability * * *.

Green, Successor Liability: The Superiority of Statutory Reform to Protect Products Liability Claimants, 72 Cornell L.Rev. 17, 29–30 (1986).

Might *Ray* have been referring to "goodwill" in a broader sense than the corporate-accounting law perspective of a property right in an intangible asset?

5. The court in Turner v. Bituminous Cas. Co., 397 Mich. 406, 244 N.W.2d 873 (1976), imposed liability on a purchaser of assets by expanding the continuation theory, justifying its holding in part as follows:

> Is there a reasonable legal or logical difference, all other things being equal, to justify products liability recovery where an acquisition is made through the transfer of some of the acquirer's stock but not where the acquisition is for cash?
>
> * * *

The reasoning behind this must be that shareholders of the first company, become, as a result of the stock transfer, shareholders of the second corporation. Technically, this argument is strong. The presence of stock as consideration should be one factor to use to determine whether there exists a sufficient nexus between the successor and predecessor corporations to establish successor liability. However, the absence of an exchange of stock should not be conclusive. The proportionate number of shares paid out by the acquiring corporation may be very small in a corporate assets purchase, and usually is, so that the strength of commonality of ownership is quite minimal. The continuity of shareholders is apt to be a paper one, more symbolic than real. The actual owners of shares at the time of manufacture of the alleged defective product and the actual owners at the time of sale of the corporation assets may be entirely different individuals.

Finally, it seems both unfair and unbelievable that a corporate combination or acquisition decision would be principally or exclusively made on the basis of cutting off the contingent right to sue of a products liability victim. From that, two conclusions suggest themselves. First, it would seem illogical that a merger or de facto merger be encumbered by liability for a products liability suit while a cash acquisition of corporate assets is free from such liability. Second, on the other hand, if there are no real business reasons for choosing a cash acquisition of corporate assets and the only real reason is to avoid products liability suits, then it would seem that the machinery of corporate law is unreasonably geared up to accomplish a purpose not really intended for it or in the public interest.

Summarizing then, logically and teleologically, there is no basis for treating a purchase of corporate assets different from a de facto merger. Both the injured party and the transferee corporation have common goals in each situation. It would make better sense if the law had a common result and allowed products liability recovery in each case.

244 N.W.2d at 879–880.

6. Most courts have followed the approach of the principal case, *Leannais,* and retained the conventional corporate law principles. See, e.g., Simoneau v. South Bend Lathe, Inc., 130 N.H. 466, 543 A.2d 407 (1988); Flaugher v. Cone Automatic Mach. Co., 30 Ohio St.3d 60, 507 N.E.2d 331 (1987). For a thorough discussion of the pros and cons of expanding successor liability, see Fish v. Amsted Indus., Inc., 126 Wis.2d 293, 376 N.W.2d 820 (1985) (4 opinions).

7. Consider how a court should handle a claim against the successor in the following situations:

A. The successor discontinues marketing the type of product that caused the injury because it appeared to be unprofitable. See Bullington v. Union Tool Corp., 254 Ga. 283, 328 S.E.2d 726 (1985).

B. The successor acquires only a division of the predecessor. The predecessor dissolves after the sale, but before the plaintiff is injured. Should it matter whether the division was the one that manufactured the product involved?

C. The predecessor is a retailer. See Kaminski v. Western MacArthur Co., 175 Cal.App.3d 445, 220 Cal.Rptr. 895 (1985).

D. The predecessor sells its assets piecemeal at an auction to several purchasers and then dissolves.

E. The predecessor is insolvent and sells its tangible assets to a successor which uses them to continue making the same product line with the same employees, management, and physical facilities. See Hall v. Armstrong Cork, Inc., 103 Wash.2d 258, 692 P.2d 787 (1984); Timmerman v. American Trencher, Inc., 220 Neb. 175, 368 N.W.2d 502 (1985).

F. The predecessor, faced with massive tort liabilities—for example, Johns–Manville before it filed for bankruptcy—liquidates as much of its assets as it can and distributes the proceeds through dividends to its shareholders. See Roe, Corporate Strategic Reaction to Mass Tort, 72 Va.L.Rev. 1 (1986).

G. The successor settles with the plaintiff and asserts an indemnification claim against the predecessor for the settlement amount. See Hydro–Air Equipment, Inc. v. Hyatt Corp., 852 F.2d 403 (9th Cir.1988).

8. See P. Blumberg, The Law of Corporate Groups—Substantive Law ch. 13 (1987); Green, Successor Liability: The Superiority of Statutory Reform to Protect Products Liability Claimants, 72 Cornell L.Rev. 17 (1986); Roe, Mergers, Acquisitions, and Tort: A Comment on the Problem of Successor Corporation Liability, 70 Va.L.Rev. 1559 (1984); J. Phillips, Product Line Continuity and Successor Corporation Liability, 58 N.Y.U.L.Rev. 906 (1983); D. Phillips, Products Liability of Successor Corporations: A Corporate and Commercial Law Perspective, 11 Hofstra L.Rev. 249 (1982); Comment, 87 Colum.L.Rev. 1048 (1987); Note, 58 Ind.L.J. 677 (1983).

SECTION 9. ALLOCATING RESPONSIBILITY AND LOSS: CONTRIBUTION AND INDEMNITY

Modern products liability litigation frequently involves multiple defendants, each of whom may bear some responsibility for a plaintiff's harm. The dramatic expansion of multi-party litigation may be attributed to the expanded liability of those within the chain of distribution (such as retailers, distributors, successors, and employers) and the broadened use of joinder of parties, including persons outside the chain of distribution who may have contributed to the plaintiff's harm.

Tactical considerations often induce plaintiffs' lawyers to join all potentially liable parties, and third party joinder rules afford defendants the opportunity to join others who may contribute to a settlement or judgment. With multiple defendants come important questions of how liability will be allocated among them. Even if a potentially liable person is not joined in the underlying action, the defendant(s) in that action may bring a subsequent action against him for indemnity or contribution.

Since the great majority of products liability cases result in settlement, loss allocation issues arise significantly in this context as well. The rights, duties and relationships of the plaintiff, settling defendants, and nonsettling defendants play a crucial role in the dynamics of pretrial settlement strategy in contemporary products liability litigation.

PHILLIPS, CONTRIBUTION AND INDEMNITY IN PRODUCTS LIABILITY

42 Tenn.L.Rev. 85, 87–94 (1974).

II. CONTRIBUTION AND INDEMNITY COMPARED

A. *Express Agreements*

Rights of contribution or indemnity may arise either by express contract or by implication of law. Where they are based on express contract, they are usually in the form of indemnity: one party agrees to hold another harmless from any damage arising out of use of a product, or to reimburse the other for liability he may incur as a result of such use. Such agreements are usually not held to be against public policy even when they provide for nonliability or reimbursement for injuries caused by the promisee's own negligence, although courts generally construe the agreement quite strictly and require that it make very clear that the promisee is being released from the consequences of his own fault.

* * *

Express agreements appear relatively rarely, however, and the lack of more frequent use may be explained in part by two significant considerations. As a practical matter it may not be good business to attempt to negotiate the shifting of risks at the bargaining stage, particularly where the agreement expressly releases one from liability for his own fault, thereby perhaps raising questions about the reliability of the product or of the contracting party. Also, the parties may not stand in a contractual relationship with one another, in which event no express agreement can be negotiated. More commonly indemnity or contribution is sought not on the basis of express agreement, but rather on principles of implied contract or equitable loss apportionment.

B. *Implied or Equitable Apportionment*

Implied indemnity or contribution is basically equitable in nature, although it is sometimes described in terms of implied contract. It is based on a determination that, where there is more than one party who may be liable for the same wrong or loss to another, liability should in fairness be apportioned between or among all such parties. There may of course be any number of joint tortfeasors, but the basic situation analyzed here will include only the injured party, A, and two cotortfeasors, X and Y, against whom A has a claim; X, in turn, has a claim over against Y for indemnity or contribution.

The amount of X's claim against Y will depend on whether X is asserting a claim for indemnity or contribution. Traditionally, a claim in indemnity by X against Y is for the full amount X has been required to pay A. In contribution, however, the claim is for less than the full amount. In Tennessee, for example, each tortfeasor shares equally with the other tortfeasors under the Contribution Among Tortfeasors Act adopted in this state. So, if there are only two tortfeasors, X and Y, each would bear one-half of the liability to A; if there are three tortfeasors, each would bear one-third, and so on. In other jurisdictions, however, shares of liability for contribution may be computed on the basis of comparative responsibility for the loss, rather than on a strict pro rata basis. This method of apportioning loss resembles that used in jurisdictions applying a comparative negligence approach to adjusting claims by the injured party, A, against either X or Y.

Whenever A is permitted to recover against X or Y for a single injury caused by both X and Y, the extent of A's judgment against the tortfeasors is normally for the full amount of his loss, subject to any reduction that may be made for A's own negligence in a comparative negligence jurisdiction. Although A can collect the entire judgment only once, either from X or Y or in part from both depending on the availability of executable assets, the judgment itself is for the full amount of recoverable damages against each. The apportionment of liability, either on the basis of contribution or indemnity, occurs if at all as between X and Y. It would be possible, of course, to apportion liability at the front end, in determining A's claim against X and Y, rather than in determining the latter parties's rights *inter sese,* but this is not usually done unless the damages can be reasonably allocated between X and Y on the basis of relative causation.

Essentially, then, there are three main approaches to allocating loss among several tortfeasors, each of whom is responsible for the same wrong to a third party: (1) pro rata division of liability, (2) allocation of liability on the basis of comparative fault, and (3) a complete shifting of liability from one tortfeasor to the other. The first and second approaches are typical of claims for contribution, and the third of claims in indemnity. The first approach can be criticized for its arbitrariness but defended for its predictability and ease of application. The second can be supported on the basis of its equitable orientation which is the theoretical basis for allocation of loss among tortfeasors, and conversely can be attacked for its uncertainty of application, especially where differences in degrees of fault are divided by very fine lines. The third is the subject of the following section.

III. The Role of Fault in Indemnity Recovery

The indemnity approach of completely shifting the loss from one tortfeasor to another would seem to make sense only where the entire actual fault lies with the indemnitor (Y), and the indemnitee (X) is free from actual fault and is held liable to the injured party (A) only because of some duty strictly imposed by statute or case law. In fact, many of the situations where indemnity is imposed involve nonfault, or only "technical" fault, on the part of the indemnitee, and actual fault on the part of the indemnitor. This indemnity pattern is not uniform, however, and there is a large body of cases where indemnity has been allowed even though both the indemnitee and the indemnitor are at fault. The courts' approach in such cases has been to characterize the indemnitee's fault as merely "passive" or secondary, while that of the indemnitor is described as "active" or primary.

A. LOSS ALLOCATION WITHIN THE DISTRIBUTION CHAIN

DIGREGORIO v. CHAMPLAIN VALLEY FRUIT CO.

Supreme Court of Vermont, 1969.
127 Vt. 562, 255 A.2d 183.

HOLDEN, CHIEF JUSTICE. The plaintiffs, who operate the Quality Market in Burlington, purchased some bananas from the defendant Champlain Valley Fruit Company. One of the bananas contained a glass fruit thermometer which had been inserted by the defendant wholesaler. The fruit that contained the thermometer, or fragments of the instrument, was retailed by the plaintiffs to Mrs. Barbara Malloy who injured her teeth when she undertook to eat the banana. She later brought an action to recover for the injury against the plaintiffs, alleging breach of warranty and negligence. The plaintiffs called upon the defendant Champlain Valley Fruit Company to enter and defend the action. Upon its refusal, it became necessary for the plaintiffs to employ counsel to defend them. The Champlain Valley Fruit Company was later joined as a party defendant. The personal injury action was settled without trial. Of the amount paid to compromise the claim, the plaintiffs contributed $300 and the defendant Champlain Valley paid $1,200.

On the strength of these facts, which were submitted as an agreed case, the plaintiffs seek to recover their contribution to the settlement and reasonable expenses. The lower court ordered judgment for the plaintiffs in the amount of $968.23. The defendants, who we refer to in the singular, bring this appeal.

The defendant challenges the plaintiffs' right to contribution on the contention that the plaintiffs have only the standing of joint tort feasors, relying on Spalding v. Administrator of Oakes, 42 Vt. 343. It seeks to support this position by stating that the evidence would have disclosed active fault by the plaintiffs had the Malloy action gone to full trial. The argument is based on facts beyond those agreed upon and entirely foreign to the record in this appeal. * * *

In this light the most that can be said for the plaintiffs' misconduct is a failure to discover, in its retail operation, the presence of the thermometer which the defendant Champlain Valley had inserted in the banana. This shortage, of itself, will not defeat the plaintiffs' right to indemnity against the seller who put the harmful cause in motion. Boston Woven Hose and Rubber Co. v. Kendall, 178 Mass. 232, 59 N.E. 657, 51 L.R.A. 781 (opinion by Holmes, C.J.).

Under the Uniform Sales Act, the sale of the bananas—first by the defendant Champlain Valley Fruit Company and later by the plaintiffs, as the Quality Market, carried an implied warranty that the food was wholesome and fit for human consumption at the time of purchase. O'Brien v. Comstock Foods, Inc., 125 Vt. 158, 161, 212 A.2d 69. The fact that the injured consumer had a right of action against either the wholesaler or retailer, or both, does not disrupt the defendant's undertaking with the plaintiffs. On the showing made in the stipulated facts, there is no policy of the law which prevents the plaintiffs from holding the defendant to its implied warranty for such damage as the plaintiffs sustained from the purchase and resale of the dangerous commodity. Manning Manufacturing Co. v. Hartol Products Corp. of New England, 2 Cir., 99 F.2d 813, 814.

In the framework of this appeal we are not concerned with the contributions among wrongdoers who have violated equivalent duties, as in Spalding v. Administrator of Oakes, supra, 42 Vt. at 349. See also Oakes v. Spaulding, 40 Vt. 347, 352–353. We are dealing with successive warranties implied by law which attended the initial, as well as the subsequent sale of defective foodstuff. Both parties to this controversy, as sellers, had duties and obligations to the injured consumer. O'Brien v. Comstock Foods, Inc., supra, 125 Vt. at 161, 212 A.2d 69. The plaintiffs were also buyers. And the defendant's warranty and duty extended to them, as well as to the person injured. Whether the original action was brought in contract or tort is of no consequence. [Citations.]

As between themselves, the parties to the present action are not in equal fault for the plaintiffs were entitled to rely on the defendant's warranty to them. In these circumstances indemnity is not precluded by the rule against contribution among wrongdoers. [Citations.] Since it appears that the plaintiffs' fault in its duty to the injured person was secondary to the initial negligence of the defendant, its right to restitution is established. Restatement, Restitution §§ 76, 93(1).

The defense offers further resistance. It urges that the plaintiffs' defense of the personal injury action and its contribution to the settlement were voluntarily undertaken and not subject to indemnity. The findings do not support the argument.

To protect the indemnitor's right to defend against liability, a voluntary payment by an indemnitee, without notice to the person sought to be charged, may foreclose restitution. Peerless Casualty Co. v. Cole, 121 Vt. 258, 266, 155 A.2d 866. The letter from plaintiffs' counsel to Champlain Valley, which is incorporated in the findings, fully protected its right to defend the action and called upon it to do so. According to the findings, the defendant's refusal to defend in the first instance, made it necessary for the plaintiffs to undertake the defense. At this point the plaintiffs were entitled to proceed in good faith to reach a reasonable settlement. Boston & Maine Railroad v. Howard Hardware Co., 123 Vt. 203, 210, 186 A.2d 184.

The fact that the defendant finally participated in the compromise indicates its acquiescence in the result it achieved. There is nothing in the findings to indicate the plaintiffs' contribution was unreasonable. And we cannot infer from the facts presented that the joint compromise with the claimant discharged the defendant from the obligation of its warranty to the retailer.

[Affirmed as modified per stipulation.]

NOTES

1. Consider the observations of Judge Kelly, concurring in Frey v. Montgomery Ward & Co., 258 N.W.2d 782, 790 (Minn.1977): "Retailers generally are at the mercy of manufacturers with respect to knowledge of dangers that inhere in the products they sell. Standing at the head of the stream of commerce, we may presume a manufacturer to be familiar with its product and the dangers it presents the public. Not only is it reasonable for a retailer to rely on the manufacturer's greater knowledge of its product, but that reliance is recognized by the law of implied warranties."

2. See U.C.C. § 2–314, comment 8, providing that the fitness for ordinary purposes aspect of the implied warranty of "merchantability" affords "protection [to] the person buying for resale to the ultimate consumer * * *, and merchantable goods must therefore be 'honestly' resalable in the normal course of business because they are what they purport to be." See also comment 1.

3. "It is not unusual for liability to move transactionally up the chain of distribution until the manufacturer ultimately pays for its breach of its implied warranty of merchantability to the distributor to whom it initially sold the goods. Indeed, * * * prior to the removal of the problems concerning the requirement of 'vertical' and 'horizontal' privity, this was precisely how everyone assumed the causes of action would develop. * * * Although the elimination of the privity requirements has made such a procedure unnecessary, it has not made it improper." Kelly v. Hanscom Bros., Inc., 231 Pa.Super. 357, 331 A.2d 737, 740 (1974) (retailer of defective toy could recover against wholesaler in warranty, and wholesaler could use same procedure against Japanese manufacturer; irrelevant that manufacturer might be insolvent or beyond reach of court, since wholesaler had assumed such risks by choosing to do business with it).

PROMAULAYKO v. AMTORG TRADING CORPORATION

Superior Court of New Jersey, Appellate Division, 1988.
224 N.J.Super. 391, 540 A.2d 893.

COLEMAN, J.H., P.J.A.D.

The novel question presented in this appeal is whether in a strict liability case, one distributor in a chain of distributors of a defective product is entitled to common law indemnification from another distributor where both are found to be vicariously liable to an injured party. Here, the primary liability or the defect in the product was the absence of a warning on a product which proximately caused asbestosis. The trial judge ordered common law indemnification. We now reverse.

The essential facts are not complicated. John Promaulayko was employed for more than 40 years by the Ruberoid Corporation, South Bound Brook Plant (Ruberoid). His job was to assist in the manufacture of asbestos shingles. His job exposed him to asbestos fiber which caused him to contract asbestosis. He died on October 1, 1980. Plaintiff filed a wrongful death and a survivor's action against the suppliers of asbestos fiber and asbestos containing products to Ruberoid during the 40 years John Promaulayko worked for Ruberoid. The claims were based on defective warnings on the effects of asbestos fiber. [Citations.]

At the conclusion of a jury trial, the jury found that defendants did not wrongfully cause the death of decedent. Based on the evidence, the jury apparently concluded that decedent died from a heart attack which was unrelated to his asbestosis. Thus, the wrongful death cause of action was dismissed. On the survivor's cause of action, however, the jury found that the estate and the widow, Marie Promaulayko, should recover from Asbestos Corporation Limited, Amtorg Trading Corporation (Amtorg) and Leonard J. Buck, Inc. (Buck). Buck and Amtorg were the brokers-distributors which sold Russian asbestos fiber and asbestos products to Ruberoid during decedent's employment. Asbestos Corporation Limited sold non-Russian made asbestos fiber to Ruberoid during decedent's employment.

The jury returned a verdict in favor of the estate for $60,000 and in favor of Marie Promaulayko for $40,000 on her *per quod* claim. The jury also answered the following special interrogatories:

> 6. Considering that all of the fault which proximately contributed to John Promaulayko's asbestosis is 100%, what percentage of that total fault is attributable to:
>
> | | |
> |---|---|
> | (a) Leonard J. Buck, Inc. | 25% |
> | (b) Amtorg Trading Corp. | 10% |
> | (c) Asbestos Corp., Ltd. (also known as Johnson's Company Ltd.) | 65% |
> | TOTAL | 100% |
>
> (Answer Questions 7A and 7B *only if* you have found fault on the part of *both* Leonard J. Buck, Inc. and Amtorg Trading Corp.)

7A. Was all (100%) of the asbestos fiber sold by Leonard J. Buck, Inc., which proximately contributed to John Promaulayko's asbestosis sold to Buck by Amtorg Trading Corp.?

Yes X No __

Based on the jury's conclusion that all of the asbestos which Buck sold to Ruberoid had been obtained by Buck from Amtorg, the trial judge ordered common law indemnification of Buck by Amtorg. In addition to the indemnification, Final Judgment was entered [for the estate for $60,000 and for Marie Promaulayko for $40,000 against each of the defendants].

* * *

In this appeal, Amtorg contends that Buck was not entitled to indemnification from it because the jury found that although Amtorg sold Buck all the asbestos fiber Buck sold Ruberoid, the jury nonetheless found that Buck was more responsible (25%) for causing John Promaulayko's asbestosis than Amtorg (10%). * * *

The right to common law indemnity amongst distributors held jointly liable in a products liability case poses a difficult issue. * * *

Ordinarily, a party who is at fault may not obtain indemnification for its own wrongdoing. [Citations.] One who is vicariously liable and seeks indemnification must be without fault. Cartel Capital Corp. v. Fireco of N.J., 81 N.J. 548, 566, 410 A.2d 674 (1980). In Cartel our Supreme Court observed:

> It is settled that indemnity may not ordinarily be obtained by a party who has been at fault. The general rule is set forth in Restatement, Restitution § 96 at 418 (1937):
>
>> A person who, *without personal fault,* has become subject to tort liability for the unauthorized and wrongful conduct of another, is entitled to indemnity from the other for expenditures properly made in the discharge of such liability. [emphasis supplied]
>
> * * * It would be inequitable to permit an active wrongdoer in the absence of a contractual understanding between the parties to obtain indemnity from another wrongdoer and thus escape any responsibility. We see no reason not to follow the general rule.

While a determination of whether a product was defective in a strict liability case is product-oriented rather than conduct-oriented, a determination of common law indemnification among distributors of a product is conduct oriented. Our research reveals one case that contains some discussion that is relevant to the issue presented here. In * * * Builders Supply Co. v. McCabe, 366 Pa. 322, 77 A.2d 368, 370–371 (Sup.Ct.1951), [the] court said:

> The right of *indemnity* rests upon a difference between the primary and secondary liability of two persons each of whom is made responsible by the law to an injured party. It is a right

> which enures to a person who, without active fault on his own part, has been compelled, by reason of some legal obligation, to pay damages occasioned by the initial negligence of another, and for which he himself is only secondarily liable. The difference between primary and secondary liability is not based on a difference in *degrees* of negligence or on any doctrine of *comparative* negligence, * * *. It depends on a difference in the *character* or *kind* of wrongs which cause the injury and in the nature of the legal obligation owed by each of the wrongdoers to the injured person * * *.
>
> * * * [T]he important point to be noted in all the cases is that secondary as distinguished from primary liability rests upon a fault that is imputed or constructive only, being based on some legal relation between the parties, or arising from some positive rule of common or statutory law or because of a failure to discover or correct a defect or remedy a dangerous condition caused by the act of the one primarily responsible. 77 A.2d, at pages 370, 371.

The trial court's order requiring Amtorg to indemnify Buck is not based on any primary fault of Amtorg. Instead, it is based on Amtorg's proximity to the manufacturer. The jury's finding that Amtorg sold to Buck all of the asbestos fiber Buck sold Ruberoid placed Amtorg closer to the manufacturer in the chain of distribution than was Buck. Both Amtorg and Buck, however, were blameless in terms of conduct that created the defect in the product. The fact that Amtorg supplied Buck with all of the asbestos Buck distributed to Ruberoid does not change the kind or character of Amtorg's liability from secondary to primary. Here, it is clear that the manufacturer, a Russian Company, created the defect by not placing a warning on the product. Common law indemnification is based on equitable principles designed to further the ends of justice by allowing a party whose liability is merely constructive, technical, imputed or vicarious to be indemnified by the party who caused the defect. A retailer or distributor is permitted to be indemnified by the manufacturer because the manufacturer created the defect and the distributor or retailer is generally blameless.

The purpose of indemnification is restitution to prevent an active wrongdoer from being unjustly enriched by having another party discharge the obligation of the active wrongdoer. See Restatement, Restitution, § 1, comments a and b (1936). "The unexpressed premise has been that indemnity should be granted in *any factual situation* in which, as between the parties themselves, it is just and fair that the indemnitor should bear the total responsibility, rather than to leave it on the indemnitee or to divide it proportionately between the parties by contribution." Restatement, Torts 2d, § 886B, comment on subsection (1) at 346 (1977). Indemnity provides flexibility in securing a fair apportionment of loss among tortfeasors in widely varying circumstances.

Where, as here, the distributors' liability is based upon a common failure to detect the defect in the product and this failure merely continued the defect created by the manufacturer, we perceive of no valid reason to shift the liability of one distributor to another distributor through common law indemnification. Because Buck and Amtorg were both without personal fault, indemnification would create, rather than prevent, unjust enrichment. A distributor or retailer held responsible based solely on principles of vicarious liability may not therefore be indemnified by another distributor or retailer whose fault is also vicarious in nature. In such circumstances, both are blameless distributors whose liability to the injured consumer is predicated on the manufacturer's defect. [Citation.] Consequently, we hold that common law indemnification was improperly allowed and is therefore reversed.[3]

Some may perceive that the rule announced today is harsh. But the apparent harshness can be mitigated by a proper application of existing law not advanced by Buck or Amtorg in this appeal. By the verdict of the jury, Asbestos Corporation Limited, Buck and Amtorg were found to share the responsibility for causing decedent's asbestosis. Yet the trial judge entered judgment, apparently without objection from counsel, requiring each of the three defendants to pay the entire $100,000 to the estate and the widow, thus ignoring the jury's percentage verdict.

The Comparative Negligence Act, [citations], required the judge to give credence to the jury's percentages. N.J.S.A. 2A:15–5.2c required the judge to "mold the judgment from the finding of fact made by the trier of fact." This means that the judgment should have been molded to require Asbestos Corporation to pay 65%, Buck to pay 25% and Amtorg to pay 10% of the total $100,000 verdict. By virtue of N.J.S.A. 2A:15–5.3, the estate and the widow "may recover the full amount of the molded verdict from any party against whom such recovering party is not barred from recovery." If Buck or Amtorg is required to pay more than its percentage share of the molded judgment, it "may seek contribution from the other joint tortfeasors." Ibid. * * * Buck and Amtorg are joint tortfeasors as to all of the Russian asbestos sold to

3. The principle employed here is reasonably easy to explain. If we assume a simple chain of distribution from manufacturer to wholesaler to retailer to consumer, and if the manufacturer who would be responsible to indemnify both the retailer and wholesaler cannot be found or is financially irresponsible, we must determine the respective responsibilities of the wholesaler and retailer. There are only three possible configurations: The first configuration would be if we apply the principle of common law indemnification, the retailer could obtain indemnification from the wholesaler and the wholesaler would pay the entire judgment. We have rejected that hypothosis here. The second configuration would be for the retailer alone to bear responsibility. We also reject this proposition since we have posited that all parties in the chain of distribution may be vicariously liable for distributing the defective product which injured the consumer. The third configuration which we have here accepted, is that the wholesaler and retailer both may be responsible and therefore subject to the application of the principles of comparative responsibility under the Comparative Negligence Act and the rights afforded them to receive contribution under the Joint Tortfeasors Contribution Law. N.J.S.A. 2A:15–5.1 et seq.; N.J.S.A. 2A:53A–1 et seq. The third configuration represents the present case.

Ruberoid by Buck. Thus, both are subject to the Joint Tortfeasors Contribution Law, N.J.S.A. 2A:53A–1, 2 and 3. [Citation.] Both Buck and Amtorg filed cross-claims for contribution pursuant to N.J.S.A. 2A:53A–1 et seq.

We recognize that computing Buck's potential contribution may appear to be made more difficult by the jury's determination that all of the asbestos Buck shipped to Ruberoid came from Amtorg and yet the jury found Buck more responsible than Amtorg. The trial judge nonetheless should have applied the Comparative Negligence Act and the Joint Tortfeasors Contribution Law rather than principles of common law indemnification in molding the verdict. Any attempt, however, to order contribution would be premature before one joint tortfeasor "pays such judgment in whole or in part." N.J.S.A. 2A:53A–3. After one joint tortfeasor has paid the entire judgment or any part thereof, such joint tortfeasor "shall be entitled to recover contribution from the other joint tortfeasor or joint tortfeasors for the excess so paid over his pro rata share. * * * " Ibid. The pro rata share of Buck or Amtorg for contribution is identical to its percentage of fault as determined by the jury. [Citations.] Consequently, we do not perceive that the preclusion of common law indemnification is too harsh.

The order requiring Amtorg to indemnify Buck is reversed.

NOTES

1. Were Amtorg and Buck as blameless as the court asserts? The "manufacturer" apparently provided raw asbestos that it had mined. Who within the distribution chain was best suited to provide adequate warnings of the dangers of asbestos fibers?

2. Why was the manufacturer not joined in the suit? "If the plaintiff sues the dealer alone, the dealer in his own interest should implead the manufacturer and thus avoid circuity of action. Service of process on the manufacturer may present a problem occasionally. But here recourse may be had to the long-arm service rule [which] may overcome the difficulty in most cases." Newmark v. Gimbel's Inc., 54 N.J. 585, 285 A.2d 697, 705 (1969).

Recent Supreme Court decisions have imposed increased constitutional limitations on the reach of state long-arm statutes. In Asahi Metal Industry Co., Ltd. v. Superior Court, 480 U.S. 102, 107 S.Ct. 1026, 94 L.Ed.2d 92 (1987), the Court held that California could not compel a Japanese component part manufacturer to respond to an indemnity claim by the Taiwanese manufacturer in California, where the plaintiff had been injured and filed suit against the manufacturer. The plaintiff did not sue the component part manufacturer and settled his case with the manufacturer. Whether the result in *Asahi* would have been the same had plaintiff had a live claim against the manufacturer is unclear. See generally Stravitz, Sayonara to Minimum Contacts: Asahi Metal Industry Co. v. Superior Court, 39 So.Car.L.Rev. 729 (1988). See also World-Wide Volkswagen Corp. v. Woodson, 444 U.S. 286, 100 S.Ct. 559, 62 L.Ed.2d 490 (1980) (retail auto dealer and regional distributor that did not sell in the forum state could not be sued there by injured consumers who had driven the automobile to the forum, where accident occurred).

3. The retailer will often want to follow the "vouching in" procedures of U.C.C. § 2–607(5): "Where the buyer is sued for breach of a warranty or other obligation for which his seller is answerable over (a) he may give his seller written notice of the litigation. If the notice states that the seller may come in and defend and that if the seller does not do so he will be bound in any action against him by his buyer by any determination of fact common to the two litigations, then unless the seller after seasonable receipt of the notice does come in and defend he is so bound."

Failure to give notice and to tender the defense of the suit to its supplier may thus increase the retailer's burdens in a subsequent indemnity action, especially if the first case is settled: "In the event that no offer is made to the indemnitor to either approve or defend, then the indemnitee should have the burden of showing actual [in lieu of potential] liability to the original plaintiff." Morrissette v. Sears, Roebuck & Co., 114 N.H. 384, 322 A.2d 7, 10 (1974). "In either event, the reasonableness of the amount of the settlement must be established by [the indemnitee]." 322 A.2d at 11. Compare Martinique Shoes, Inc. v. New York Progressive Wood Heel Co., 207 Pa.Super. 404, 217 A.2d 781 (1966) (voluntary settlement, or judgment without prior notice to indemnitor, increases indemnitee's burden of proof in indemnity suit) with St. Paul Fire & Marine Ins. Co. v. Michelin Tire Corp., 12 Ill.App.3d 165, 298 N.E.2d 289 (1973) (indemnitee not "mere volunteer"). On vouching in, see generally Squillante, "Vouching In" Letter, 78 Com.L.J. 415 (1973); Note, 29 Ark.L.Rev. 486 (1976).

Compare the 1978 enactment of Ariz.Rev.Stat. § 12–684(A): "In any product liability action where the manufacturer refuses to accept a tender of defense from the seller, the manufacturer shall indemnify the seller for any judgment rendered against the seller and shall also reimburse the seller for reasonable attorneys' fees and costs incurred by the seller in defending such action, unless [the seller (1) knew of the defect, or (2) improperly altered or installed the product]."

4. **Attorney's Fees.** Some jurisdictions hold that "generally an indemnitee is entitled to recover, as part of his damages, reasonable attorney's fees, and reasonable and proper legal costs and expenses, which he is compelled to pay as the result of suits by or against him in reference to the matter against which he is indemnified." Insurance Co. of North America v. King, 340 So.2d 1175, 1176 (Fla.App.1976). Contra, Kerns v. Engelke, 76 Ill.2d 154, 28 Ill.Dec. 500, 390 N.E.2d 859 (1979). The indemnitee should logically be permitted to recover such expenses even (or, especially) if judgment is rendered in his favor in the first action, leaving only the attorney's fees and litigation expenses to be recovered in the indemnity action. See Pender v. Skillcraft Industries, 358 So. 2d 45 (Fla.App.1978). Notice of the first action and tender of its defense to the supplier may be necessary to the recovery of such expenses. Yet even then the court may disallow attorney's fees if the indemnitee in the earlier suit defended against a separate wrongful act of its own. See Shaffer v. Honeywell, Inc., 249 N.W.2d 251 (S.D.1976).

5. **Express Indemnification Agreements.** A retailer may have enough bargaining power to require the manufacturer to agree contractually to indemnify it for losses resulting from defective products. Such agreements are generally enforced, and the retailer will not be required to establish the manufacturer's negligence if not so provided in the agreement. See Kelly Springfield Tire Co. v. Mobil Oil Corp., 551 P.2d 671 (Okl.App.1975) (agreement provided that retailer would be indemnified against "every claim" from defective workmanship in tires; retailer need only establish that it incurred liabili-

ty, and good faith settlement with consumer sufficient). See also Richards Mfg. Co. v. Aspromonte, 553 S.W.2d 169 (Tex.Civ.App.1977) (manufacturer entering into indemnification agreement with retailer created duty of care to retailer to provide safe product). Such agreements may be void as against public policy, however, if the retailer's liability is based upon violation of a statutory prohibition. See, e.g., Zerby v. Warren, 297 Minn. 134, 210 N.W.2d 58 (1973) (sale of glue containing hazardous substances to minor).

B. LOSS ALLOCATION OUTSIDE THE DISTRIBUTION CHAIN

SVETZ v. LAND TOOL COMPANY

Superior Court of Pennsylvania, 1986.
355 Pa.Super. 230, 513 A.2d 403.

WIEAND, JUDGE.

May a defendant who has been sued on theories of negligence and strict liability for damages allegedly caused by a defective product join as additional defendants those persons whose acts of negligence are alleged by him to be the sole or contributing causes of the plaintiff's injuries? The trial court held that such joinder was improper and granted the additional defendants' motions for summary judgment with prejudice. We reverse.

Ignatius Svetz, while operating a motorcycle in a westwardly direction on Route 422 in Montgomery County on June 5, 1980, lost control of his vehicle, fell, and struck his head on the pavement. The impact caused the helmet which he was wearing to split, and Svetz sustained head injuries which caused his death. His trustee ad litem, Jane Svetz, filed wrongful death and survival actions against Land Tool Company, the manufacturer of the helmet, and against Royal Auto Supply, the retailer. The complaint set forth, in separate counts, causes of action sounding in (1) negligence and (2) strict liability. Land Tool Company, the manufacturer, joined as additional defendants (1) V.J.L., Inc., t/a Orchard View Inn, where the decedent, prior to the accident, had allegedly consumed alcoholic beverages while visibly intoxicated, and (2) John Yorck, with whom the decedent allegedly had been racing at the time when the decedent lost control of his motorcycle. Because of independent acts of negligence, it was alleged in the defendant's complaint, the additional defendants were alone liable to the plaintiff, or jointly liable with Land Tool Company on the cause of action alleged by the plaintiff, or liable over to Land Tool Company on such cause of action. Subsequently, both additional defendants filed motions for summary judgment. They argued that in a case of strict liability for a defective product, a defendant manufacturer is barred from joining an additional defendant whose liability, if any, is premised upon negligence. The trial court accepted this argument and, by separate orders, granted the motions for summary judgment and dismissed "all claims" against the additional defendants "with prejudice."

The right to join one or more additional defendants is granted by Pa.R.C.P. 2252(a) in the following language:

> (a) In any action the defendant or any additional defendant may, as the joining party, join as an additional defendant any person whether or not a party to the action *who may be alone liable or liable over to him on the cause of action declared upon by the plaintiff or jointly or severally liable thereon with him,* or who may be liable to the joining party on any cause of action which he may have against the joined party arising out of the transaction or occurrence or series of transactions or occurrences upon which the plaintiff's cause of action is based. (emphasis added).*

* * * The rule permitting the joinder of additional defendants is to be broadly construed to effectuate its purpose of avoiding multiple lawsuits "by settling in one action all claims arising out of the transaction or occurrence which gave rise to the plaintiff's complaint." [Citations.]

In the instant case, the appellant-manufacturer asserted three separate bases for joining appellees as additional defendants: (1) that appellees were alone liable to the plaintiff; (2) that appellees were jointly or severally liable with appellant, i.e., for contribution; and (3) that appellees were liable over to the appellant-manufacturer by way of indemnification. The only substantive limitation placed upon the right to join an additional defendant on any of these grounds is that liability must be premised upon the same cause of action alleged by the plaintiff in his or her complaint. Pa.R.C.P. 2252(a). [Citations.]

"Cause of action" has been defined as

> [t]he fact or facts which give a person a right to judicial relief. The legal effect of an occurrence. A situation or state of facts which would entitle party to sustain action and give him right to seek a judicial remedy in his behalf.

Black's Law Dictionary (5th ed. 1979). The words "cause of action" as used in the rule must be construed "to mean 'damages or injuries.'" * * * This Court has favored the policy of broadly interpreting Rule 2252 "not only to compel every interested person to defend the action by the plaintiff, but also to save the original defendant from possible harm resulting from loss of evidence as might result if compelled to await the end of the suit before proceeding against those from whom he seeks contribution." Martinelli v. Mulloy, supra, at 135, 299 A.2d 21. Ragan v. Steen, 229 Pa.Super. 515, 525–526, 331 A.2d 724, 730 (1974).

* Compare Fed.R.Civ.P. 14(a): "[A] defending party, as a third-party plaintiff, may cause a summons and complaint to be served upon a person not a party to the action who is or may be liable to the third-party plaintiff for all or part of the plaintiff's claim against the third-party plaintiff."—Eds.

The cause of action alleged by the plaintiff in the case *sub judice* was for damages resulting from the death of her decedent when the motorcycle being operated by the decedent went out of control and crashed. The plaintiff's complaint averred that a defective helmet had been a substantial factor in causing death. The appellant-manufacturer denied that the helmet had been defective and alleged that the decedent's loss of control, and hence his death, had been caused by the decedent's engaging in a race, while intoxicated, with another motorcyclist. Therefore, appellant joined as additional defendants the tavern keeper who, allegedly, had served alcoholic beverages to the decedent while the decedent was visibly intoxicated and the motorcyclist who had engaged in a race with the decedent. Because the additional defendants' alleged liabilities arose from the same cause of action sued upon by the plaintiff, i.e., for the fatal injuries sustained by the decedent as a result of the motorcycle accident, joinder of appellees as additional defendants was expressly allowed by Pa.R.C.P. 2252(a). It may well be that for this reason alone joinder can be sustained in this case. The trial court's opinion, however, cites additional reasons for dismissing the joinder of appellees as additional defendants; and, therefore, we proceed to a consideration of those issues.

It will be recalled that the trial court held joinder improper because plaintiff's claim against the appellant-manufacturer was based on principles of strict liability; whereas, the appellant-manufacturer's claim for contribution from the additional defendants was based on negligence. However, the trial court overlooked the fact that plaintiff's cause of action against the appellant-manufacturer, as pleaded in separate counts of her complaint, was based on two theories, not one. The first count contained averments that the manufacturer had been guilty of negligence in designing and manufacturing the helmet worn by the decedent. Only the second count was based on principles of strict liability. In view of the averments of the first count of the complaint, joinder of additional defendants on theories of joint negligence was clearly proper. There was no reason for refusing to allow in one and the same action a claim by the defendant that the negligence of the additional defendants had contributed causally to the death of plaintiff's decedent.

The trial court's suggestion that a defendant who is liable under principles of strict liability is not entitled to seek contribution from one whose negligence combines to cause harm, moreover, is not consistent with the law in this Commonwealth. The Uniform Contribution Among Tortfeasors Act in Pennsylvania provides that a joint tortfeasor who has discharged more than his pro rata share of a common liability may seek contribution from any other tortfeasor who contributed to the loss. See: 42 Pa.C.S. § 8324(b). The doctrine of contribution is based on equity. * * *

In Puller v. Puller, 380 Pa. 219, 221, 110 A.2d 175, 177 (1955), the Supreme Court observed that "contribution is not a recovery for the tort [committed against the plaintiff,] but the enforcement of an equitable duty to share liability for the wrong done." Accord: Coniaris v. Vail Associates, Inc., 196 Colo. 392, 586 P.2d 224 (1978) (claim for contribution is separate and distinct from underlying tort; the rights and obligations of the defendants flow not from the tort, but from the judgment or settlement itself). Thus, a tortfeasor's right to receive contribution from a joint tortfeasor derives not from his liability to the claimant but rather from the equitable principle that once the joint liability of several tortfeasors has been determined, it would be unfair to impose the financial burden of the plaintiff's loss on one tortfeasor to the exclusion of the other. It matters not on which theory a tortfeasor has been held responsible for the tort committed against the plaintiff. So long as the party seeking contribution has paid in excess of his or her share of liability, it would be inequitable under the Act to deny that party's right to contribution from a second tortfeasor who also contributed to the plaintiff's injury.

This equitable consideration is confirmed expressly by the language of the Uniform Act. "Joint tortfeasors" are defined as "two or more persons jointly or severally liable in tort for the same injury to persons or property. * * *" 42 Pa.C.S. § 8322. The statutory language does not limit the right of contribution to tortfeasors who have been guilty of negligence. Contribution is available whenever two or more persons are jointly or severally liable in tort, irrespective of the theory by which tort liability is imposed. [Citation.] We hold, therefore, that defendants who are liable under principles of strict liability and defendants who are liable because of negligence may be joint tortfeasors. [Citations.]

It follows of necessity that where strictly liable and negligent defendants have acted as joint tortfeasors, contribution among them can properly be awarded. Although this precise issue has not previously been considered by the appellate courts of this Commonwealth, a majority of those courts which have considered the issue have reached the same result. * * * Of the twenty other states which have adopted a version of the Uniform Contribution Among Tortfeasors Act, the courts of eight have held that a common theory of recovery (e.g., all defendants liable to plaintiff for negligence or all defendants strictly liable) is not a prerequisite to contribution. * * * The same result has also been reached in at least five jurisdictions which have not adopted the Uniform Act. See: Safeway Stores, Inc. v. Nest–Kart, 21 Cal.3d 322, 579 P.2d 441, 146 Cal.Rptr. 550 (1978); Skinner v. Reed–Prentice Division Package Machinery Co., 70 Ill.2d 1, 15 Ill.Dec. 829, 374 N.E.2d 437 (1977), cert. denied, 436 U.S. 946, 98 S.Ct. 2849, 56 L.Ed. 2d 787 (1978); [citations.] Today, we join those courts which have permitted contribution among tortfeasors who are strictly liable and tortfeasors who are liable for negligence. Not only do these decisions represent the trend in modern legal thought, but they also reflect the better view.

This result is not in conflict with policy considerations which support strict liability for defective products. * * * Strict liability was based upon a policy determination that, as between an innocent consumer and a manufacturer of a defective product, the manufacturer should bear the loss. [Citation.] The focus of strict liability, therefore, must be upon the relationship existing between the plaintiff-consumer and the defendant-manufacturer. [Citation.] The focus of the Uniform Contribution Among Tortfeasors Act, on the other hand, is upon the relationship between tortfeasors after a determination has been made that they are jointly liable for the plaintiff's injury. Thus, it is only after plaintiff's loss has been assessed against joint tortfeasors and the policy goals of strict liability have been satisfied that the Act achieves significance. It then seeks to achieve an equitable apportionment of that loss among all tortfeasors who have contributed to the loss. By permitting a tortfeasor found strictly liable to recover contribution from a negligent joint tortfeasor we merely effectuate the Uniform Act's goal of achieving equity between tortfeasors without subverting policies of strict liability.

In addition to the claim for contribution, the complaint filed by the appellant-manufacturer against the appellee-additional defendants in this case contained an averment that the additional defendants were liable over to appellant for indemnification. This indemnity claim was also dismissed by the trial court. Although, as we have indicated, it was error to deny the appellant-manufacturer's right to seek contribution, we conclude that dismissal of appellant's claim for indemnification was proper.

"Indemnity, a common-law equitable remedy, shifts the entire loss from one defendant to another." Burch v. Sears, Roebuck and Co., 320 Pa.Super. 444, 456, 467 A.2d 615, 622 (1983). It is " 'recognized in cases where community opinion would consider that in justice the responsibility should rest upon one [defendant] rather than the other.' " Id. at 457, 467 A.2d at 622, quoting W. Prosser, Law of Torts 313 (4th ed. 1971). In general, indemnity is available to those who are secondarily or vicariously liable from those who are primarily liable. Builders Supply Co. v. McCabe, 366 Pa. 322, 77 A.2d 368 (1951).

In the instant case, the averments of appellant's complaint do not establish a legally recognizable claim for indemnity against the additional defendants. Appellant has been unable to demonstrate error in the trial court's dismissal of the general averment that the additional defendants were liable over to the appellant-manufacturer. This portion of the trial court's orders, therefore, will be affirmed.

[Summary judgment on indemnification claim affirmed; order dismissing joinder reversed; remanded.]

NOTES

1. For what reason might a court follow the opposite approach and prohibit the strictly liable (and, hence, "innocent") manufacturer from seeking contribution or indemnity against a negligent third party who caused an

accident in whole or in part? Is the *Svetz* result sound? See Seidelson, The 402A Defendant and the Negligent Actor, 15 Duq.L.Rev. 371 (1977).

2. **Dividing Damages: Computation of Defendants' Shares.** Regardless of whether some of the parties are outside the chain of distribution, and assuming that contribution is appropriate, how should responsibility for the damages be divided between multiple actors? Traditionally, contribution generally was prescribed on a pro rata, equal division basis. See Unif. Contribution Among Tortfeasors Act § 2, 12 U.L.A. 57, 87 (1955 rev.). With the advent of the comparative fault doctrine in recent years, many courts and legislatures have switched to a comparative approach for contribution purposes, dividing responsibility for damages in proportion to the defendants' fault, causation, or responsibility. See Unif. Comparative Fault Act § 4, 12 U.L.A. 37, 47 (1977, Supp.1988).

3. **Comparative ("Equitable") Indemnity.** Although indemnity traditionally shifted the loss entirely from one tortfeasor to another, some courts have applied comparative fault principles even here. Dole v. Dow Chemical Co., 30 N.Y.2d 143, 331 N.Y.S.2d 382, 282 N.E.2d 288 (1972); Missouri Pac. R. Co. v. Whitehead & Kales Co., 566 S.W.2d 466 (Mo.1978); Safeway Stores, Inc. v. Nest–Kart, 21 Cal.3d 322, 146 Cal.Rptr. 550, 579 P.2d 441, 445 (1978): "With the advent of the common law comparative indemnity doctrine, we achieve a more precise apportionment of liability in circumstances such as the instant case by allocating damages on a comparative fault or a comparative responsibility basis, rather than by fixing an inflexible pro rata apportionment pursuant to the contribution statutes."

4. **Non–Parties.** In allocating damages among those responsible for the plaintiff's loss, should the trier-of-fact consider the fault of a person not brought into the lawsuit? Compare Ladwig v. Ermanco Inc., 504 F.Supp. 1229 (E.D.Wis. 1981) (yes), with Ryden v. Johns–Manville Products, 518 F.Supp. 311 (W.D.Pa. 1981) (no). Since the non-party is not present to explain and defend its actions, how can the jury rationally allocate fault to it? Will the parties before the court have adequate *incentives* to present the jury with sufficient information about the non-party's participation in the accident? Will the parties have adequate *means* to find and prove these facts?

5. **Reform.** As *Svetz* points out, contribution is predicated upon the joint responsibility of two or more persons for a plaintiff's loss. Unless a defendant is held liable for more than its "share" of the damages, as under joint and several liability, there is no occasion for contribution. A significant effect of the legislative tort reform movement of the mid-late 1980s has been a dramatic curtailment in the joint and several liability rules in the various states. During 1986–88, slightly more than half of the states modified or abolished the doctrine of joint and several liability. See, e.g., *Ariz.*—abolished, 2 Prod.Liab. Rep. (CCH) ¶ 90,332; *Calif.*—abolished as to "non-economic damages," retained as to "economic damages," id. at ¶ 90,573; *Iowa*—abolished as to defendants less than 50% at fault, id. at ¶ 91,633; *N.Y.*—abolished as to "non-economic loss" for defendants 50% or less at fault, without considering fault of non-parties not subject to jurisdiction of court, id. at ¶ 93,311.

6. See Greenstone, Spreading the Loss—Indemnity, Contribution, Comparative Negligence and Subrogation, 13 Forum 266 (1977); Jensvold, A Modern Approach to Loss Allocation Among Tortfeasors in Products Liability Cases, 58 Minn.L.Rev. 723 (1974).

C. WORK-RELATED INJURIES

LARSON, WORKMEN'S COMPENSATION: THIRD PARTY'S ACTION OVER AGAINST EMPLOYER

65 Nw.U.L.Rev. 351 (1970).

Perhaps the most evenly-balanced controversy in all of workmen's compensation law is the question whether a third party in an action by the employee can recover over against the employer, when the employer's fault has caused or contributed to the injury.

WEISGALL, PRODUCT LIABILITY IN THE WORKPLACE: THE EFFECT OF WORKERS' COMPENSATION ON THE RIGHTS AND LIABILITIES OF THIRD PARTIES

1977 Wis.L.Rev. 1035, 1036.

At first consideration, the relevance of third party rights and liabilities to the workers' compensation system is not readily apparent. After all, workers' compensation, in theory, is a self-contained no-fault system under which the injured employee receives benefits pursuant to a set compensation schedule, and the costs related to an employee's benefits are treated by the employer as internalized costs of doing business. However, a second reparations system—product liability litigation against manufacturers and sellers of industrial machinery—is increasingly affecting the functions and objectives of the workers' compensation system. Employers, employees, and workers' compensation insurance carriers frequently engage in protracted litigation in attempts to obtain recovery beyond the amounts allowed by workers' compensation or to shift the economic costs to those beyond the direct employee-employer link.

The potential overlapping of and conflict between these two reparations systems arises with every workplace accident involving industrial products or equipment. The injured employee can file a claim under his state's workers' compensation program, but the amount of his recovery is specifically limited by statute. However, while he is barred by statute from bringing a lawsuit against his employer, he may seek additional recovery by bringing an action against a third party such as the manufacturer and/or seller of the machine or other product by which he was injured. The ability of the product manufacturer or other third party to defend himself and to seek to bring the employer into the action is directly controlled not by common law principles of negligence or strict liability, but by the workers' compensation statutes of the state in which the suit is brought. The interaction of these two systems—product liability and workers' compensation—directly affects the total costs and the allocation of the costs of the workers' compensation system. Both areas of law are in a state of dramatic change.

LAMBERTSON v. CINCINNATI CORP.

Supreme Court of Minnesota, 1977.
312 Minn. 114, 257 N.W.2d 679.

SHERAN, CHIEF JUSTICE.

Cincinnati Corporation, defendant and third-party plaintiff in a personal injury/product liability action, appeals from a judgment of the district court which awarded a worker $34,000 in damages but denied defendant manufacturer contribution from an employer which was partly at fault for the accident. We reverse in part and remand with instructions.

Cincinnati is the manufacturer of a press brake, a large machine used for bending metal. The brake has a large vertical ram which moves up and down. Dies are placed on the ram and on the bed of the machine, and metal to be bent is placed between the ram and the bed. When the ram comes down onto the metal, a bend, or brake, is made in the metal at the point where the die on the ram matches the die in the bed. The movement of the ram is controlled by the operator by means of a single foot pedal at the base of the machine.

Cincinnati sold a press brake to Hutchinson Manufacturing and Sales, Inc., plaintiff's employer. On April 25, 1972, plaintiff was assisting a coemployee in the operation of the press brake. The coemployee was controlling the foot pedal, and plaintiff was placing long metal strips between the ram and the bed and removing them after they had been bent. As the ram was being raised after one cycle, a piece of metal which had been bent fell to the side of the bed opposite to the side where plaintiff was working. Plaintiff reached through the jaws of the machine to retrieve the piece of metal, but his coemployee had kept his foot on the pedal, thus permitting the ram to descend again, crushing plaintiff's arm between the ram and the bed.

After recovering workers' compensation from Hutchinson, plaintiff brought this action against Cincinnati. Plaintiff testified that he had never operated the press brake before and did not know it was capable of double cycling, i.e., continuing through another cycle without the ram's stopping at the top. He testified that he knew he should not have put his arm between the jaws, but that he did not know that his coemployee still had his foot on the pedal or that the ram would descend again before he could retrieve the piece of metal.

Plaintiff introduced expert testimony and safety rules and regulations from which the jury could have found that certain safety devices and features could have been installed on the press brake at the time of its manufacture and sale to Hutchinson in 1967, and that such devices would have prevented the accident. Sufficiency of this evidence to support a finding of negligence on the part of Cincinnati is not contested on this appeal. Cincinnati does, however, ask for indemnity from Hutchinson based on events occurring after 1967.

In 1969, after representatives of Cincinnati viewed the particular uses to which the press brake was put at Hutchinson, Cincinnati offered to Hutchinson (at Hutchinson's expense) two changes in the machine: (1) Operation by two or more palm buttons or foot switches; (2) automatic stoppage of the ram at the top of the cycle—i.e., no double cycling. These changes apparently were declined. In 1971, Cincinnati sent out a sales pamphlet to all owners of its press brakes describing a Waveguard safety device, an electronic sensing device designed to detect foreign matter in the press and stop the press if such matter were present. Hutchinson did not order or install such a device. There was testimony by plaintiff's expert from which one could conclude that the absence of two of these offered features—the automatic stop and the electronic sensor—constituted defects in the machine that were causally related to this accident.

* * *

The case was submitted to the jury on special verdict on a theory of negligence. The jury found all parties causally negligent and apportioned their comparative negligence as follows: Plaintiff—15 percent; Cincinnati—25 percent; Hutchinson—60 percent. The jury found damages of $40,000. The trial court ordered judgment against Cincinnati for $34,000, the full amount of the verdict less 15 percent for plaintiff's negligence, and denied Cincinnati's claim for contribution or indemnity from Hutchinson.

* * *

[The] most important issue in this case concerns the claim of Cincinnati, a third-party tortfeasor, for indemnity or contribution from Hutchinson, plaintiff's employer. This issue is a troublesome one and has generated a substantial amount of debate in the bench and bar of this and other states. * * * The essence of the controversy is this: If contribution or indemnity is allowed, the employer may be forced to pay his employee—through the conduit of the third-party tortfeasor—an amount in excess of his statutory workers' compensation liability. This arguably thwarts the central concept behind workers' compensation, i.e., that the employer and employee receive the benefits of a guaranteed, fixed-schedule, nonfault recovery system, which then constitutes the exclusive liability of the employer to his employee. See, Minn.St. 176.031. If contribution or indemnity is not allowed, a third-party stranger to the workers' compensation system is made to bear the burden of a full common-law judgment despite possibly greater fault on the part of the employer. This obvious inequity is further exacerbated by the right of the employer to recover directly or indirectly from the third party the amount he has paid in compensation regardless of the employer's own negligence. Minn.St. 176.061, subds. 5, 6(d). [Citation.] Thus, the third party is forced to subsidize a workers' compensation system in a proportion greater than his own fault and at a financial level far in excess of the workers' compensation schedule.

The even balance in this controversy results from conflicts among the policies underlying workers' compensation, contribution/indemnity, and comparative negligence and the fault concept of tort recovery. Workers' compensation, a creature of Minnesota law since 1913, subjects almost all employers and employees to an essentially nonfault recovery system for accidents arising out of and in the course of employment. In exchange for guaranteed compensation for injury regardless of his own fault or the solvency of at-fault fellow employees, the employee is limited to a fixed schedule of recovery and gives up any right to a common-law action against the employer. See, Minn.St. 176.021, 176.031. This court has indicated on many occasions that the purpose of workers' compensation is broadly remedial and that workers' compensation laws are to be construed to favor employee recovery of benefits. [Citations.]

Despite its essential nonfault character, the workers' compensation system retains an important common-law aspect—the third-party action. See, Minn.St. 176.061. The employee, and in some instances the employer, is allowed to bring an action against a third party who is legally responsible for the employee's injury. Such an action accomplishes two beneficial results for the workers' compensation system: (1) The at-fault third party is made to reimburse the employer who has been forced to bear the cost of the third party's activity; and (2) the employee obtains a full common-law recovery against the third party, who is not subject to the benefits and burdens of the workers' compensation system. While some states have placed the former result first in importance and have decreed that the employer must be reimbursed for all compensation benefits before the employee receives anything from a third-party judgment (see, 2A Larson, Workmen's Compensation Law, § 74.31), Minnesota has given paramount importance to the latter object in mandating that the employee receive a third of the judgment after litigation expenses are paid and before the employer can collect compensation paid. * * *

In summary, the interests of the respective parties in the workers' compensation system are therefore as follows: The employer has a primary interest in limiting his payment for employee injury to the workers' compensation schedule and a secondary interest in receiving reimbursement when a third party has caused him to incur obligations to his employee. [Citation.] The employee has a primary interest in receiving full workers' compensation benefits and, to the extent a third party has caused him injury, a common-law recovery from that third party.

In contrast, the third party's interest is that of any other cotortfeasor—to limit its liability to no more than its established fault. This interest is vindicated through contribution or indemnity. Contribution and indemnity are variant common-law remedies used to secure restitution and fair apportionment of loss among those whose activities combine to produce injury. * * * When one tortfeasor has paid or is about to pay more than his equitable share of damages to an injured party, he has an interest in obtaining indemnity or contribution from his fellow tortfeasors.

Comparative negligence, which is embodied in Minn.St. 604.01 and was substantially borrowed from our sister state of Wisconsin in 1969, introduces yet another dimension to the third-party tortfeasor's predicament. By abolishing the defense of contributory negligence in cases where plaintiff's percentage of total causal negligence is less than defendant's, it permits an injured workman to recover against the third party more frequently. In addition, Minn.St. 604.01, subd. 1, specifies a rule for contribution:

> "* * * When there are two or more persons who are jointly liable, contributions to awards shall be in proportion to the percentage of negligence attributable to each, provided, however, that each shall remain jointly and severally liable for the whole award."

Thus, a jointly liable tortfeasor has an interest, at least where the other tortfeasors are solvent and otherwise available for contribution, in contributing no more to the plaintiff's recovery than the percentage of negligence attributable to him.

* * *

Cincinnati initially seeks indemnity from Hutchinson chiefly on the ground that it offered safety devices to Hutchinson which, if installed on the press brake, could have prevented the accident. The difficulty with this argument lies in the jury's unchallenged finding that Cincinnati was 25–percent negligent in the first instance, when it placed its press brake in the stream of commerce without certain kinds of safety devices. Since the independent acts of negligent manufacture and sale by Cincinnati and refusal of safety devices by Hutchinson combined to produce plaintiff's injury, liability should be apportioned between them, not shifted entirely to one or the other. Therefore, if Cincinnati is entitled to any remedy, that remedy is contribution.

Cincinnati's claim for contribution, however, confronts two further problems: (1) Our holding in Hendrickson v. Minnesota Power & Light Co., 258 Minn. 368, 104 N.W.2d 843 (1960), that contribution is not available because of the absence of a common liability; and (2) the policy interest of the employer in paying no more than his workers' compensation liability because of an employee injury and the other conflicting policies and statutes discussed earlier in this opinion.

Considering the first of these problems, we cannot find any continuing persuasive force in the reasoning of the court in *Hendrickson.* * * * While there is no common liability to the employee *in tort,* both the employer and the third party are nonetheless liable to the employee for his injuries; the employer through the fixed no-fault workers' compensation system and the third party through the variable recovery available in a common law tort action. Contribution is a flexible, equitable remedy designed to accomplish a fair allocation of loss among parties. Such a remedy should be utilized to achieve fairness on particular facts, unfettered by outworn technical concepts like common liability.

The second problem confronting Cincinnati's claim is a more formidable one. The equitable merit in Cincinnati's claim is plain: It has been forced to bear the entire burden of plaintiff's recovery despite the fact that it was only 25–percent negligent and has a 60–percent–negligent employer joined in the action and available for contribution. In contrast, granting contribution would result in substantial employer participation in its employee's common-law recovery despite the exclusive-remedy clause. This problem is, in large part, a legislative one which demands a comprehensive solution in statutory form. See, Note, 1 Wm. Mitchell L.Rev. 134, 160. The problem is discussed in Larson, Workmen's Compensation: Third Party's Action Over Against Employer, 65 Nw.U.L.Rev. 351, 419:

> "The phrase most frequently heard in arguments against recovery over by the third party against the employer is this: the allowance of such recovery over accomplishes indirectly what cannot be done directly and, therefore, evades the spirit of the legislation. This is not entirely accurate, for it does not tell the whole story. True, the end result is that a common-law size recovery proceeds from the employer to the employee. In the process, however, two things are accomplished, one of which is relevant to the purposes of the compensation provision and the other of which is independent of it. The relevant accomplishment is that of preserving the employee's common-law rights against negligent outsiders. This having been done, there still remains the job of adjusting rights fairly between the outsider and the negligent employer. The question here becomes very precise: did the compensation acts, in conferring immunity on the employer from common-law suits, mean to do so only at the expense of the injured employee, or also at the expense of outsiders? One answer is that whereas the injured employee got *quid pro quo* in receiving assured compensation payments as a substitute for tort recoveries, the third party has received absolutely nothing and, hence, should not be impliedly held to have given up rights which he had before. It is unfair, so the argument runs, to pull the third party within the principle of mutual sacrifice when his part is to be all sacrifice and no corresponding gain.
>
> "A situation like this ought to be dealt with legislatively. It is rather inconsiderate to force courts to speculate about legislative intention on the strength of statutory language, in the framing of which the draftsmen had not the remotest trace of the present question in their minds. The legislature should face squarely the question whether the third party who hap-

pens to be so unfortunate as to get tangled up with a compensable injury should, so to speak, individually subsidize the compensation system by bearing alone a burden which normally he could shift to the employer."

While the opinions of other jurisdictions must be read with caution on this issue because of different statutes and concepts of recovery in negligence cases, we have found direction in the approach taken by the Pennsylvania Supreme Court. That court has allowed contribution from the employer up to the amount of the workers' compensation benefits. [Citations.] This approach allows the third party to obtain limited contribution, but substantially preserves the employer's interest in not paying more than workers' compensation liability. While this approach may not allow full contribution recovery to the third party in all cases, it is the solution we consider most consistent with fairness and the various statutory schemes before us. If further reform is to be accomplished, it must be effected by legislative changes in workers'-compensation-third-party law.

For the reasons expressed above, the judgment is reversed and the case is remanded with instructions to grant contribution against Hutchinson in an amount proportional to its percentage of negligence, but not to exceed its total workers' compensation liability to plaintiff.

Affirmed in part, reversed in part and remanded with instructions.

NOTES

1. Contra, Thompson v. Stearns Chem. Corp., 345 N.W.2d 131 (Iowa 1984). Most courts faced with the issue have denied claims by manufacturers for contribution or indemnity from employers. The ordinary rationale given for this result is that the legislature has prescribed that an injured worker's exclusive remedy shall be the benefits provided by the statute. See, e.g., Outboard Marine Corp. v. Schupbach, 93 Nev. 158, 561 P.2d 450 (1977) (Nevada workers' compensation act is exclusive remedy against employer for workplace injuries). What policy arguments favor interpreting statutory compensation schemes as precluding contribution claims against employers? Is such an approach fair to manufacturers? See generally 2A A. Larson, The Law of Workmen's Compensation §§ 76.20 et seq. (1988).

Pennsylvania, which *Lambertson* cited as a jurisdiction permitting limited contribution, amended its workers' compensation statute in 1974 to prohibit contribution. 77 Pa.Cons.Stat.Ann. § 481(b) (Supp.1986). This has been interpreted as barring even the joinder of employers in actions by employees against third-parties. Heckendorn v. Consolidated Rail Corp., 293 Pa.Super. 474, 439 A.2d 674 (1981); Hamme v. Dreis & Krump Mfg. Co., 716 F.2d 152 (3d Cir.1982).

2. Although the manufacturer is generally barred from suing the employer, the converse is not true; that is, the employer typically *is* permitted to maintain a subrogation action against the manufacturer, for recovery of workers' compensation benefits, sometimes even though the employer's fault also contributed to the employee's injury. But cf. Schweizer v. Elox Div. of Colt Industries, 133 N.J.Super. 297, 336 A.2d 73 (1975), holding that all defenses which could have been raised against the employee can be asserted by the manufacturer against the employer's subrogation action. The typical proce-

dures of the Florida workers' compensation statute were explained in Sunspan Engineering & Constr. Co. v. Spring–Lock Scaffolding Co., 310 So.2d 4, 6 (Fla. 1975): "[T]he Act permits the employee to sue a third party tortfeasor. The employer is subrogated to the rights of the employee as against a third party tortfeasor to the extent of compensation benefits payable to the employee. The employer has a lien on any proceeds recovered by the employee from the tortfeasor which are equitably distributed. If employee does not sue the tortfeasor within one year, employer may sue."

3. Is there a potential conflict between the interests of the employer, in pursuing its subrogation rights, and the employee, in pursuing a favorable settlement from the manufacturer?

4. Some courts following the majority rule interpret their statutes to permit the reduction of a plaintiff's judgment against the manufacturer by the amount received in workers' compensation benefits. See Santisteven v. Dow Chemical Co., 506 F.2d 1216, 1220 (9th Cir.1974) (Nevada act). For a contrary interpretation of the Arkansas act, see Rhoads v. Service Mach. Co., 329 F.Supp. 367, 371 (E.D.Ark.1971) (motion for remittitur of this type "without merit and seems to the Court to be an effort to revive indirectly the effort of the defendant to secure contribution or indemnity from plaintiff's employer").

Is the practical effect of this approach any different from that taken by the court in *Lambertson?*

5. Is the majority approach fair? In Schuldies v. Service Mach. Co., Inc., 448 F.Supp. 1196 (E.D.Wis.1978), plaintiff was injured when she accidentally stepped on the foot switch while removing a die shoe from a punch press. The jury found that the defendant was 25% negligent in its design of the press with the footswitch (but, paradoxically, that the machine's design was not in a defective condition unreasonably dangerous to users), that the employer was 70% at fault, and that plaintiff herself was 5% negligent. Damages were found to be $338,600. *Held,* manufacturer was responsible for 95% of the damages, even though only 25% at fault; exclusive remedy doctrine prohibited contribution action against the employer. See also Outboard Marine Corp. v. Schupbach, 93 Nev. 158, 561 P.2d 450, 454 (1977) (manufacturer liable for total damages of $1.2 million although only 25% at fault; while admitting there was "some appeal" to defendant's contention that this was "manifestly inequitable," the court concluded that the argument should not be directed to the court but to the legislature which had adopted the exclusive remedy principle).

6. Decisions in New York and Illinois go beyond the *Lambertson* rule and allow contribution in an amount based upon the employer's proportionate fault regardless of the level of workers' compensation benefits. See Dole v. Dow Chemical Co., 30 N.Y.2d 143, 331 N.Y.S.2d 382, 282 N.E.2d 288 (1972); Skinner v. Reed–Prentice Div. Package Mach. Co., 70 Ill.2d 1, 15 Ill.Dec. 829, 374 N.E.2d 437, 443 (1977) (cause of action by manufacturer against employer stated for contribution "based on the relative degree to which the defective product and the employer's misuse of the product or its assumption of the risk contributed to cause plaintiff's injuries"); Doyle v. Rhodes, 101 Ill.2d 1, 77 Ill.Dec. 759, 461 N.E.2d 382 (1984) (adhering to *Skinner* despite subsequent enactment of joint tortfeasor contribution statute conditioning contribution on defendant being "subject to liability in tort.").

7. Professor Jeffrey O'Connell has proposed a comprehensive solution to the workers' compensation—products liability dilemma. His proposal calls for raising workers' compensation benefits to an adequate level and making them

the exclusive remedy against *any* party for work-related injuries from defective products. Manufacturers would not need to seek contribution or indemnification from employers since employees could not bring tort actions against manufacturers. Compensation benefits under this plan would be funded by employers and manufacturers on some equitable basis. See, e.g., O'Connell, Bargaining for Waivers of Third–Party Tort Claims: An Answer to Product Liability Woes for Employers and Their Employees and Suppliers, 1976 U.Ill. L.F. 435. Would barring employees' rights to recover from manufacturers in tort be constitutional? Compare Sunspan Eng'g & Const. Co. v. Spring-Lock Scaffolding Co., 310 So.2d 4 (Fla.1975) (manufacturer's indemnity suit against employer allowed; exclusive remedy provision violative of constitutional guarantee of access to courts and of equal protection) with Grove Mfg. Co. v. Cardinal Const. Co., 534 S.W.2d 153 (Tex.Civ.App.1976) (prohibition of contribution from employer constitutional). Professor O'Connell suggests these difficulties could be avoided by contract through collective bargaining between unions and employers. What additional problems might this create?

8. Contractual provisions whereby an employer agrees to indemnify a supplier for any liability it may incur as a result of the use of the product are generally enforced despite the exclusive remedy provision. See, e.g., Olsen v. Shell Oil Co., 595 F.2d 1099 (5th Cir.), cert. denied, 444 U.S. 979, 100 S.Ct. 480, 62 L.Ed.2d 405 (1979); Liberty Mutual Ins. Co. v. Westerlind, 374 Mass. 524, 373 N.E.2d 957 (1978); Rucker Co. v M & P Drilling Co., 653 P.2d 1239 (Okl. 1982). But see Aetna Cas. & Sur. Co. v. L.K. Comstock & Co., Inc., 684 F.2d 1267 (9th Cir.1982) (Nevada Worker's compensation statute voids express indemnification contract).

9. **Reform.** A number of statutory reforms have been proposed. A common proposal is to eliminate both the employer's subrogation rights against the manufacturer and the manufacturer's contribution or indemnity rights against the employer, coupled with a reduction in the employee's judgment against the manufacturer for any workers' compensation benefits paid or payable. See, e.g., S. 100, § 10, 99th Cong., 1st Sess. (1985).

10. See Davis, Third Party Tortfeasors' Rights Where Compensation–Covered Employers Are Negligent—Where Do Dole and Sunspan Lead?, 4 Hofstra L.Rev. 571 (1976); Bernstein, Third Party Claims in Workers' Compensation: A Proposal to Do More with Less, 1977 Wash.U.L.Q. 543; Weisgall, Product Liability in the Workplace: The Effect of Workers' Compensation on the Rights and Liabilities of Third Parties, 1977 Wisc.L.Rev. 1035 (1977); Mitchell, Products Liability, Workmen's Compensation and the Industrial Accident, 14 Duq.L.Rev. 348 (1976); Lynch, The Clash Between Strict Products Liability Doctrine and the Workers' Compensation Exclusivity Rule: The Negligent Employer and the Third–Party Manufacturer, 50 Ins.Coun.J. 35 (1983); Note, 96 Harv.L.Rev. 1641 (1983).

D. PARTIAL SETTLEMENTS

CARTEL CAPITAL CORPORATION v. FIRECO OF NEW JERSEY

Supreme Court of New Jersey, 1980.
81 N.J. 548, 410 A.2d 674.

SCHREIBER, J.

Plaintiff, Country Burger of Ramsey, Inc. (Country Burger), sued Fireco of New Jersey (Fireco), the retailer, installer and servicer of plaintiff's fire extinguishing equipment, and Ansul, Inc. (Ansul), manufacturer of that equipment, for property damage caused by a fire during which the equipment allegedly failed to operate. Plaintiff's cause of action against Ansul was based upon negligence and strict liability arising out of a design defect. The action against Fireco involved strict liability because of the same design defect and negligence in improperly servicing the system. The codefendants asserted cross-claims against each other under the Joint Tortfeasors Contribution Act, N.J.S.A. 2A:53A–1 et seq., and for indemnification.

At the outset of the trial Ansul settled with plaintiff for $50,000, voluntarily dismissed its cross-claims and successfully moved for dismissal of Fireco's cross-claims. Plaintiff then proceeded against Fireco alone. In response to a set of special interrogatories, the jury found that Fireco was negligent, that Ansul had defectively designed the equipment, and that both the negligence and defect were proximate causes of plaintiff's damages. The jury determined that plaintiff had also been guilty of negligence. It fixed damages due to the malfunctioning of the fire extinguishing equipment to operate at $113,400 and the percentages of fault as follows: Plaintiff—41%, Fireco—30%, and Ansul—29%. The trial court then entered a judgment in favor of plaintiff for $34,020, plus interest and costs.

[Plaintiff and Fireco both appealed, first to the Superior Court, which reversed, and then to the Supreme Court.]

* * *

The central legal issues are the effect to be given to plaintiff's settlement with defendant Ansul, the existence of plaintiff's negligence, and the propriety of dismissing Fireco's cross-claims for indemnification and contribution.

I.

Defendants Ansul and Fireco argue that Country Burger's settlement with Ansul eliminated plaintiff's strict liability cause of action against Fireco, on the theory that the release of Ansul operated to remove any basis for the derivative claim against Fireco. Additionally, it is contended that Country Burger had, in fact, abandoned its strict product liability claim against Fireco. We find neither of these arguments persuasive.

Ansul contends that when it settled plaintiff's strict product liability claim, any cause of action predicated on that defect had been extinguished. However, a plaintiff may be entitled to and obtain several judgments against different persons for the same obligation or liability so long as there is only one satisfaction or recovery. * * *

Even when liability of one defendant is wholly vicarious, settlement with the primarily liable defendant may not necessarily release the other. For example, when an employer is liable for an employee's negligence, both the employer and employee are jointly and severally liable to the injured party until full satisfaction is received. * * *

This rationale is also apposite when one joint tortfeasor has settled. Over 20 years ago Justice Jacobs in Breen v. Peck, 28 N.J. 351, 146 A.2d 665 (1958), discussed and rejected the common law doctrine that the release of one joint tortfeasor automatically released all. Instead the Court adopted the principle that the legal effect of a release on other parties should be determined by the intent of the parties to the release, with due consideration being given to whether the compensation paid was fully adequate. Id. at 367, 146 A.2d 665. That eminently more just rule has been consistently followed. * * *

* * *

It follows that we must look to the parties' intention when the settlement was made. Breen v. Peck, 28 N.J. at 367, 146 A.2d 665. Before the jury was impanelled and sworn, Ansul announced that it had settled with plaintiff for $50,000; its total damage claim exceeded $180,000. Ansul's attorney stated that he would "be receiving settlement papers probably in the nature of a covenant not to sue" and "that the settlement with Ansul is not intended to release the other defendant, Fireco of New Jersey." The general release delivered conformed with that intent. Recited therein was the following:

> It is the intention of this Release to release Ansul, Inc., only, and this Release shall not affect in any way any and all claims the Releasor has against Fireco of New Jersey.

Further, plaintiff relinquished its claim against Ansul for only partial satisfaction of its alleged damages. The settlement was less than one-third the amount of damages claimed. The jury award of $113,400 confirmed that plaintiff's losses substantially exceeded the $50,000 settlement figure. Thus, plaintiff's action against Fireco, in which plaintiff sought damages based upon strict liability and negligence, remained viable. Release of Ansul as a primary tortfeasor did not release Fireco from either its vicarious or direct responsibility.

* * *

II.

We pass next to the question of what legal effect, if any, should be given to plaintiff's conduct. * * * [The court concluded that the plaintiff's conduct was insufficient as a matter of law to diminish its recovery.]

III.

We turn next to Fireco's cross-claims for indemnity or contribution from Ansul as a joint tortfeasor. As we have seen Fireco was exposed to liability because it had distributed and sold a defective piece of fire extinguishing equipment. Since Ansul had manufactured and sold the apparatus to Fireco, Fireco had a viable cross-claim against Ansul for indemnity. * * *

* * *

Fireco's cross-claim also sought contribution under the Joint Tortfeasors Contribution Law, N.J.S.A. 2A:53A–1 et seq. That act established a right of contribution among joint tortfeasors, N.J.S.A. 2A:53A–2, when the "injury or damage is suffered by any person as a result of the wrongful act, neglect or default of joint tortfeasors * * *." N.J.S.A. 2A:53A–3. When that has occurred a joint tortfeasor can recover contribution from another tortfeasor for any excess paid in satisfaction of a judgment "over his pro rata share * * *." N.J.S.A. 2A:53A–3. That law applies here.

The statute defines "joint tortfeasors" to mean two or more persons jointly or severally "liable in tort for the same injury." N.J.S.A. 2A:53A–1. Ansul and Fireco satisfy that definition. Both were found to be at fault and liable in tort—Ansul because of its production and distribution of a defective product, Suter v. San Angelo Foundry & Machine Co., 81 N.J. at 162, 406 A.2d 140, and Fireco because of its negligent servicing and because of its role in the distributive chain of a defective product.

We have previously held that the Contribution Law does not require that joint tortfeasors be liable on the same theory of recovery, so that a defendant whose responsibility arises out of strict liability and another defendant whose responsibility is due to negligence may be joint tortfeasors under that law. * * *

As indicated previously a joint tortfeasor's recovery is limited under the Contribution Law to any excess paid over "his pro rata share." N.J.S.A. 2A:53A–3. In this respect it is important to note the effect on the Joint Tortfeasors Contribution Law of the Comparative Negligence Act, N.J.S.A. 2A:15–5.1 et seq. Under that act the percentage of each party's fault must be found and "[a]ny party who is so compelled to pay more than such party's percentage share may seek contribution from the other joint tortfeasors." N.J.S.A. 2A:15–5.3. Thus the Legislature has seen fit to redefine the "pro rata" allocation to be a party's "percentage share" in the contribution scheme between and among joint tortfeasors. Rogers v. Spady, 147 N.J.Super. 274, 277, 371 A.2d 285 (App.Div.1977).

Under the joint tortfeasors law we had held that a settlement with a joint tortfeasor, even though for less than a pro rata share of the total claim, reduced the plaintiff's total claim against the nonsettling codefendant or codefendants by the pro rata share and thus barred contribution from the settling tortfeasor. [Citations.] Now the effect on the plaintiff of a joint tortfeasor's settlement will depend upon the percentage of fault found against him. When one defendant settles, the remaining codefendant or codefendants are chargeable with the total verdict less that attributable to the settling defendant's percentage share.

Other jurisdictions have reached similar results. See Gomes v. Brodhurst, 394 F.2d 465, 468 (3 Cir.1968) (on rehearing) (applying law of the Virgin Islands); Bartels v. Williston, 276 N.W.2d 113 (N.Dak.Sup. Ct.1979). Cf. Frey v. Snelgrove, 269 N.W.2d 918 (Minn.Sup.Ct.1978) (involving a "Pierringer-type" release); Pierringer v. Hoger, 21 Wis.2d 182, 124 N.W.2d 106 (Sup.Ct.1963) (release of codefendant expressly states that nonsettling tortfeasors would not be liable for that percentage of fault to be attributed to settling tortfeasor). Our holding also comports with Section 6 of the Uniform Comparative Fault Act (1977).

Applying the foregoing principles, we find that the total relevant fault is that of Ansul and Fireco, there being no contributory negligence as a matter of law. Ansul's 29% and Fireco's 30%, or 59%, constitute the total fault in the case. In a sense, the 59% is 100%. Thus, Fireco's responsibility is 30/59ths or 50.8% and Ansul's is 29/59ths or 49.2%. It follows that Fireco's proportionate share of the entire damages of $113,400 is $57,661.01 and Ansul's proportionate share is $55,738.99. Ansul, however, had settled its obligation to the plaintiff for $50,000. Fireco remains liable for its share, namely $57,661.01.

Accordingly, the cause is remanded to the trial court for entry of a judgment in favor of the plaintiff and against Fireco in the sum of $57,661.01 plus costs and interest.

NOTES

1. In most jurisdictions, the basic settlement rules are now governed by statute. New Jersey's approach reflects that of § 6 of the Uniform Comparative Fault Act, which reduces a plaintiff's recovery against nonsettling defendants by the percentage fault ("equitable share") of any settling defendants. 12 U.L.A. 50 (Supp.1988). See also Duncan v. Cessna Aircraft Co., 665 S.W.2d 414 (Tex.1984).

By comparison, in California, the plaintiff's claim is reduced by the dollar value of a "good faith" settlement. See Abbott Ford, Inc. v. Superior Court, 43 Cal.3d 858, 239 Cal.Rptr. 626, 741 P.2d 124 (1987) (applying good faith standard to sliding-scale Mary Carter settlement agreement); American Motorcycle Ass'n v. Superior Court, 20 Cal.3d 578, 146 Cal.Rptr. 182, 578 P.2d 899, 916 (1978). In New York, the plaintiff's claim is reduced by the greater of the settlement amount or the settling defendant's equitable share of the damages.

Which approach is best?

2. Should the jury be informed of the fact of settlement and its effect on the remaining defendants? See Slayton v. Ford Motor Co., 140 Vt. 27, 435 A.2d 946 (1981) (no). See also Brewer v. Payless Stations, Inc., 412 Mich. 673, 316 N.W.2d 702 (1982) (unless the parties agree otherwise, crediting to be performed by the court). Should the answer depend on whether the settling defendant has remained in the case to have its liability and comparative share determined?

3. In a dollar-for-dollar credit jurisdiction, matters are complicated when the total award must be reduced by some percentage of a plaintiff's fault as well as by a prior settlement. How should such computations be made? See Rittenhouse v. Erhart, 424 Mich. 166, 380 N.W.2d 440 (1985).

4. **Mary Carter Agreements.** "Mary Carter" agreements, a type of settlement device used in multi-party litigation, owe their name to the case of Booth v. Mary Carter Paint Co., 202 So.2d 8 (Fla.App.1967), which approved their use in personal injury litigation. Since that case, the Florida courts have used the term to mean "any agreement between the plaintiff and some (but less than all) defendants whereby the parties place limitations on the financial responsibility of the agreeing defendants, the amount of which is variable and usually in some inverse ratio to the amount of recovery which the plaintiff is able to make against the nonagreeing defendant or defendants." Maule Indus., Inc. v. Rountree, 264 So.2d 445 (Fla.App.1972), remanded for new trial, 284 So. 2d 389 (Fla.1973) (parties entitled to discover such agreements). The Supreme Court of Florida described such agreements in Ward v. Ochoa, 284 So.2d 385 (Fla.1973):

> A "Mary Carter Agreement" * * * is basically a contract by which one co-defendant secretly agrees with the plaintiff that, if such defendant will proceed to defend himself in court, his own maximum liability will be diminished proportionately by increasing the liability of the other codefendants. Secrecy is the essence of such an arrangement because the court or jury as trier of the facts, if apprised of this, would likely weight differently the testimony and conduct of the signing defendant as related to the non-signing defendant. By painting a gruesome testimonial picture of the other defendant's misconduct or, in some cases, by admissions against himself and the other defendants, he could diminish or eliminate his own liability by use of the secret "Mary Carter Agreement."

One commentator has identified four characteristics of Mary Carter agreements:

(1) Secrecy, the parties usually agreeing to keep the arrangement confidential;

(2) The contracting defendant agrees to remain as a defendant in the action and may become an active proponent of the plaintiff's case;

(3) The contracting defendant "guarantees" the plaintiff a specific sum of money in the event the plaintiff loses the case or if the plaintiff recovers less than the agreed sum; and

(4) The contracting defendant obtains an interest in the litigation; the plaintiff may agree to refund the payment the defendant has made if the verdict from other defendants exceeds the sum guaranteed to the plaintiff or there may be some form of pro rata reduction.

Freedman, The Expected Demise of "Mary Carter": She Never Was Well, 1975 Ins.L.J. 602, 609.

These agreements resemble covenants not to sue in that the plaintiff releases his cause of action against the settling defendant. They have, however, two characteristics not found in covenants not to sue. First, the settling defendant remains as an active participant in the litigation, in appearance but not in fact a true adversary of the plaintiff. Second, because of the refund provision, the settling defendant has an incentive to increase the plaintiff's recovery by presenting damaging testimony against the nonsettling defendants.

Most states, including Florida, have required that such agreements be disclosed so that the bias of the settling defendant may be revealed. See, e.g., Ward v. Ochoa, 284 So.2d 385 (Fla.1973); General Motors Corp. v. Simmons, 558 S.W.2d 855 (Tex.1977); Gatto v. Walgreen Drug Co., 61 Ill.2d 513, 337 N.E.2d 23 (1975), cert. denied 425 U.S. 936, 96 S.Ct. 1669, 48 L.Ed.2d 178 (1976).

On Mary Carter agreements generally, see Entman, Mary Carter Agreements: An Assessment of Attempted Solutions, 38 U.Fla.L.Rev. 521 (1986); Note, 87 Colum.L.Rev. 368 (1987).

5. **Loan Receipts.** Loan receipts may take two forms, one of which is a variation on the Mary Carter agreement. One defendant may advance an interest-free loan to the plaintiff in return for a covenant not to sue. The plaintiff then pursues his claim against the nonsettling defendants and, if a recovery is obtained, repays the "loan" upon the conditions provided in the agreement. The settling defendant, as in a Mary Carter agreement, remains a party to the litigation. The other type of loan receipt transaction typically involves an insurance company advancing money to an injured plaintiff (usually the insured) who is obligated to repay only if he collects from the defendant. In return, the injured plaintiff agrees to initiate an action against the defendant or permits the insurer to bring an action in the insured's name. Both the insurer and the insured benefit from this arrangement since the insurance company's role in the litigation is kept from the jury.

An example of a loan receipt transaction in a products liability dispute is Biven v. Charlie's Hobby Shop, 500 S.W.2d 597 (Ky.1973). Plaintiff's child was accidentally shot and killed by another child, and plaintiff brought suit against the other child and his parents in negligence. The insurance company for the defendant parents entered into a loan receipt agreement with the plaintiff whereby plaintiff received a $20,000 "loan" repayable only out of any recovery plaintiff might recover against the manufacturer and retailer of the allegedly defective pistol involved in the accident, and assigning plaintiff's claims against such parties to the insurer "to the extent necessary to repay such loan." Plaintiff's suit against the child and parents was thereupon dismissed with prejudice, and plaintiff brought suit against the manufacturer and retailer for $200,000. *Held,* loan receipt was valid and, although it released one concurrent tortfeasor, it did not serve to release the others.

On loan receipts, see Comment, 10 Val.U.L.Rev. 231 (1976); Note, 25 DePaul L.Rev. 792 (1976).

6. Several of the issues considered here are addressed in the Uniform Comparative Fault Act which generally provides for contribution in proportion to fault. See generally Wade, Products Liability and Plaintiff's Fault—The Uniform Comparative Fault Act, 29 Mercer L.Rev. 373 (1978); Wade, A Uniform Comparative Fault Act—What Should It Provide?, 10 U.Mich.J.L.Ref. 220 (1977).

7. See Kaplan, From Contribution to Good Faith Settlements: Equity Where Are You? 49 J.Air.L. & Com. 771 (1984); Davis, Comparative Negligence, Comparative Contribution, and Equal Protection in the Trial and Settlement of Multiple Defendant Product Cases, 10 Ind.L.Rev. 831 (1977); Jensvold, A Modern Approach to Loss Allocation Among Tortfeasors in Products Liability Cases, 58 Minn.L.Rev. 723 (1974).

Chapter 8

SPECIAL TYPES OF PRODUCTS AND TRANSACTIONS

Some "products liability" litigation involves transactions other than the typical sale of a new chattel examined so far. The principal issue involved in many of these cases is whether the usual principles of products liability law, particularly the doctrine of strict liability in tort, should be extended from the new chattel sale situation to another transactional context. In some of these cases, the differing objectives and doctrinal borderlines of products liability, premises liability, professional malpractice, environmental protection, and other areas of the law are brought into sharp relief.

SECTION 1. LEASES AND BAILMENTS

PRICE v. SHELL OIL COMPANY

Supreme Court of California, 1970.
2 Cal.3d 245, 85 Cal.Rptr. 178, 466 P.2d 722.

SULLIVAN, JUSTICE. We hold in this case that the doctrine of strict liability in tort which we have heretofore made applicable to sellers of personal property is also applicable to bailors and lessors of such property. As appears infra, we find substantial evidence in the record that the lessor in the present matter falls within the reach of the doctrine. We therefore affirm the judgment entered on the verdicts in favor of plaintiff Merton Price and plaintiff in intervention Pacific Employers Insurance Company (Pacific) and against defendant Shell Oil Company (Shell). * * *

Plaintiff is an aircraft mechanic employed by Flying Tiger. In 1958 Flying Tiger leased from defendant Shell a gasoline tank truck with a movable ladder mounted upon the tank for refueling certain types of aircraft. * * *

[While plaintiff was climbing the ladder onto the wing of an aircraft, the ladder broke and plaintiff was injured. Plaintiff recovered in an action against Shell upon strict liability in tort, and Shell appealed.]

Application of the Rule of Strict Liability

Shell contends that the trial court erred in submitting the case to the jury on the issue of strict liability. It argues that it is not a manufacturer, distributor or retailer of gasoline trucks. On the contrary, Shell asserts that in the present circumstances it was a bailor or lessor and that its liability as such was governed solely by Civil Code, section 1955 which imposed on Shell no greater duty than that of exercising ordinary care. In support of this contention Shell notes that section 408 of the Restatement Second of Torts "continues to hold" *lessors* of personal property liable only for negligence although section 402A now imposes strict liability upon sellers of such property. From this premise Shell argues that the Restatement did not intend to apply strict liability to lessors.

The rule is now settled in California that "A manufacturer is strictly liable in tort when an article he places on the market, knowing that it is to be used without inspection for defects, proves to have a defect that causes injury to a human being." (Greenman v. Yuba Power Products, Inc. (1963) 59 Cal.2d 57, 62, 27 Cal.Rptr. 697, 700, 377 P.2d 897, 900, 13 A.L.R.3d 1049.) A retail dealer, being an "integral part of the overall producing and marketing enterprise" (Vandermark v. Ford Motor Co. (1964) 61 Cal.2d 256, 262, 37 Cal.Rptr. 896, 899, 391 P.2d 168, 171), is similarly liable. (See also Elmore v. American Motors Corp. (1969) 70 Cal.2d 578, 75 Cal.Rptr. 652, 451 P.2d 84; Prosser, Strict Liability to the Consumer in California (1966) 18 Hastings L.J. 9.) We have given this rule of strict liability a broad application. * * *

Such a broad philosophy evolves naturally from the purpose of imposing strict liability which "is to insure that the costs of injuries resulting from defective products are borne by the manufacturers that put such products on the market rather than by the injured persons who are powerless to protect themselves." (Greenman v. Yuba Power Products, Inc., supra, 59 Cal.2d 57, 63, 27 Cal.Rptr. 697, 701, 377 P.2d 897, 901.) Essentially the paramount policy to be promoted by the rule is the protection of otherwise defenseless victims of manufacturing defects and the spreading throughout society of the cost of compensating them. * * *

Similarly we can perceive no substantial difference between *sellers* of personal property and *non-sellers,* such as bailors and lessors. In each instance, the seller or non-seller "places [an article] on the market, knowing that it is to be used without inspection for defects, * * *." (*Greenman,* supra, 59 Cal.2d at p. 62, 27 Cal.Rptr. at p. 700, 377 P.2d at p. 900.) In the light of the policy to be subserved, it should make no difference that the party distributing the article has retained title to it. [Like manufacturers and retailers, lessors] are able to bear the cost of compensating for injuries resulting from defects by spreading the loss through an adjustment of the rental.

[R]ecent decisions support this view. In Cintrone v. Hertz Truck Leasing, etc. (1965) 45 N.J. 434, 212 A.2d 769, the court held that a lessor of trucks is liable upon the basis of strict liability in tort because "A bailor for hire, such as a person in the U-drive-it business, puts motor vehicles in the stream of commerce in a fashion not unlike a manufacturer or retailer," subjects such a leased vehicle "to more sustained use on the highways than most ordinary car purchasers," and by the very nature of his business, exposes "the bailee, his employees, passengers and the traveling public * * * to a greater *quantum* of potential danger of harm from defective vehicles than usually arises out of sales by the manufacturer." (222 A.2d at p. 777)

* * *

For the above reasons, we are of the opinion that the doctrine of strict liability in tort should be made applicable to bailors and lessors of personal property in the same manner as we have held it applicable to sellers of such property. * * * [W]e can find no significant difference between a manufacturer or retailer who places an article on the market by means of a sale and a bailor or lessor who accomplishes the same result by means of a lease. (See *Cintrone,* supra, 212 A.2d 769, 776.) In today's society with "the growth of the business of renting motor vehicles, trucks and pleasure cars" (*Cintrone,* supra) and the persistent advertising efforts to put one "in the driver's seat" (id. at p. 777) we have no difficulty in finding the doctrine peculiarly applicable to the lessor of motor vehicles. The very reasons which impelled us to apply the doctrine in *Greenman* urge us to apply it in the instant case.

However, since we reason by analogy, we make clear that the doctrine should be made applicable to lessors in the same way as we have made it applicable to sellers. * * * In *Cintrone,* supra, the court using a phrase somewhat like the one noted above in *Greenman,* observed that a "bailor for hire * * * puts motor vehicles *in the stream of commerce* in a fashion not unlike a manufacturer or retailer." (212 A.2d at p. 777; italics added.) * * * The same rule appears in the Restatement, and California has held in several cases that strict liability does not apply to isolated transactions. [Citations.] Our analysis of these authorities leads to the conclusion that for the doctrine of strict liability in tort to apply to a lessor of personalty, the lessor should be found to be in the business of leasing, in the same general sense as the seller of personalty is found to be in the business of manufacturing or retailing.

Shell contends that even if the issue of strict liability was properly submitted to the jury, nevertheless Shell cannot be held liable under such doctrine since there is no evidence in the record that it leased more than one tank truck. It argues in effect that, unlike the lessor in *Cintrone,* Shell was not in the business of leasing such trucks.

This contention is without merit. There is ample evidence in the record indicating that Shell was engaged in more than a single lease transaction. The testimony of Brendemuhl, Shell's plant superintendent in charge of the distribution of aviation fuel, established that Shell was engaged in organized and continuing operation. It also showed that trucks were leased to lessees other than Flying Tiger.

Finally, the lease agreement itself warrants the inference that Shell was engaged in the business of leasing gasoline tank trucks and that the lease now before us was not an isolated or occasional transaction. This document, which is a part of the record on appeal, is entitled "Automotive Equipment Lease" and consists of two pages of *printed*, single spaced, standard-form provisions concerning term, rent, lessee's maintenance duties, taxes and fees, indemnity insurance, assignments and subleasing, and notice. Significantly, the name "Shell Oil Company" or "Shell" appears in print throughout the document. The provisions for description of the exact type of chassis and tank indicate that the standard-form lease is used only for refueler trucks. The provision for description of the number, make, size and rating of ancillary equipment—filters, meters, hose reels, reel hoses, pumps and fire extinguishers—as well as a general provision for "other equipment" with spaces to be filled in, warrants the inference that Shell had a wide variety of refueler trucks which were leased under the provisions of its standard-form automotive equipment leases.

In view of the foregoing we are satisfied that there is substantial evidence showing, or from which it can be reasonably inferred, that Shell was a commercial lessor within the rule of strict liability applicable to this case.

* * *

The judgments are affirmed.

NOTES

1. The *Cintrone* case discussed in *Price* was the path-breaking case extending liability without fault to commercial lease transactions. It has been widely followed. E.g., Francioni v. Gibsonia Truck Corp., 472 Pa. 362, 372 A.2d 736 (1977) (reviewing the cases); Martin v. Ryder Truck Rental, Inc., 353 A.2d 581 (Del.1976); Stang v. Hertz Corp., 83 N.M. 730, 497 P.2d 732 (1972).

2. Compare Katz v. Slade, 460 S.W.2d 608 (Mo.1970) (strict liability claim against municipality dismissed where golf cart leased from municipal golf course malfunctioned; course was operated as a recreational resource for city residents, not a commercial venture).

3. Strict tort has been held not to apply to "private" lease transactions. See Brescia v. Great Road Realty Trust, 117 N.H. 154, 373 A.2d 1310 (1977) (lease arrangement of defective crane between two companies closely held by same person; "defendant does not deal in cranes, and its role as lessor was due solely to [lessee's] shortage of funds").

4. Should a laundromat be strictly liable in tort as a "lessor" of defective washers and dryers that injure its patrons? See Garcia v. Halsett, 3 Cal.App.3d 319, 82 Cal.Rptr. 420 (1970). A young boy's arm became entangled in clothing and was injured when a defective washing machine at defendant's laundromat unexpectedly began to spin. *Held,* although this was a license rather than a lease transaction, a strict tort action against the laundromat owner would lie:

"Although respondent is not engaged in the distribution of the product, in the same manner as a manufacturer, retailer or lessor, he does provide the product to the public for use by the public, and consequently does play more than a random and accidental role in the overall marketing enterprise of the product in question. Thus, the rationale of *Greenman* and *Vandermark* applies as logically and desirably to a licensor of chattels as to the manufacturers, retailers and lessors thereof." 82 Cal.Rptr. at 423.

5. See Ausness, Strict Liability for Chattel Leasing, 48 U.Pitt.L.Rev. 273 (1987); Henszey, Application of Strict Liability to the Leasing Industry, 33 Bus. Law. 631 (1978); Annot., 52 A.L.R.3d 121 (1973).

KEEN v. DOMINICK'S FINER FOODS, INC.

Appellate Court of Illinois, 1977.
49 Ill.App.3d 480, 7 Ill.Dec. 341, 364 N.E.2d 502.

McNamara, Justice. The plaintiff, Eleanore Keen, filed suit against the defendant, Dominick's Finer Foods, Inc., seeking to recover for injuries allegedly sustained while using a shopping cart in a Dominick's store located in Highland Park, Illinois. Plaintiff filed a four count complaint alleging theories of negligence, strict products liability, breach of implied warranty, and breach of duty of care by a bailor. The trial court granted Dominick's motion to strike all counts except that based upon negligence. * * * Plaintiff has appealed solely from that part of the trial court's order dismissing the count in which she alleged a cause of action in strict tort liability.

In her complaint plaintiff charged that on January 21, 1975, she was shopping in a grocery store owned and operated by Dominick's. As she was pushing a shopping cart supplied by the store, the cart allegedly tipped over onto its side. Plaintiff was injured when she attempted to prevent the cart from overturning. Plaintiff further charged that at the time she was using the shopping cart, it was not reasonably safe for the use intended in that it was inclined to collapse in a manner which would cause it to roll onto its side and injure its user. In moving to dismiss the count in question, Dominick's maintained that it was not liable under the principles of strict products liability since the shopping cart could not be deemed a product for which Dominick's was responsible for placing into the stream of commerce. The trial court agreed with Dominick's contention and entered an order dismissing the count. The propriety of that order is at issue before us.

The nature of a manufacturer's liability for placing a defective product into the stream of commerce was set out in Suvada v. White Motor Co. (1965), 32 Ill.2d 612, 623, 210 N.E.2d 182, 188:

> " * * * The plaintiffs must prove that their injury or damage resulted from a condition of the product, that the condition was an unreasonably dangerous one and that the condition existed at the time it left the manufacturer's control. * * * "

The rule promulgated in *Suvada* is in accordance with the Restatement (Second) of Torts § 402A (1964) * * *.

In Dunham v. Vaughan and Bushnell Mfg. Co. (1969), 42 Ill.2d 339, 247 N.E.2d 401, the court stated that *Suvada* applies with equal compulsion to all the parties in a chain who place the article into commerce. While liability does not depend upon whether there was an actual sales transaction [citation], it is necessary that the party to be charged with liability be in the business of placing the allegedly defective product into the stream of commerce. [Citation.] Accordingly, it becomes apparent that the cornerstone of liability rests upon the defendant's active participation in placing the product into commerce for use and consumption by others. One of the underlying reasons for imposing strict liability is to ensure that losses are borne by those who have created the risk and subsequently reaped the profit of marketing the allegedly defective product. Liability will not be imposed upon a defendant who is not a part of the original producing and marketing chain. Peterson v. Lou Bachrodt Chevrolet Co. (1975), 61 Ill.2d 17, 329 N.E.2d 785.

In the present case, plaintiff concedes that Dominick's is not in the business of either selling or renting shopping carts. She maintains, however, that although Dominick's gratuitously furnishes the carts to its customers, such is done as an incident of the sale of the items which constitutes Dominick's business. In attempting to hold Dominick's strictly liable, plaintiff relies upon the case of Bainter v. Lamoine LP Gas Co. (1974), 24 Ill.App.3d 913, 321 N.E.2d 744. In that case this court permitted a cause of action in strict products liability against a defendant who supplied a defective tank for storage of gas sold to the plaintiff. The tank was characterized as an incident of the sale of the gas and the consideration given for the gas was deemed to include the use of the tank.

The facts in *Bainter* differ demonstrably from those in the present case. In *Bainter* the fluidity of the product compelled supplying the tank as a necessary concomitant of the sale of gas. The shopping cart, on the other hand, can be classified only as a convenient receptacle which the customer may temporarily utilize to move groceries to the checkout or outside to the customer's automobile. Not every customer will use a shopping cart. It is our opinion that to hold Dominick's liable under the principles of strict products liability would require an extension of those principles which neither the supreme court in *Suvada* nor this court in *Bainter* envisioned. The instant case does not present the *Bainter* situation where an allegedly defective container which is an integral part of the product disseminated by defendant causes injury or damage. In such a case the container may well be deemed incident and necessary to the sale of the product. In the present case, plaintiff's use of the allegedly defective shopping cart could only be considered as a use of a convenience furnished by Dominick's to facilitate its customers' shopping. Any mishap which might occur from availing oneself of such a convenience does not render the store liable under the principles of strict products liability. In this case, the allegedly defective shopping cart was placed into the stream of commerce by the parties responsible for its distribution to Dominick's. The store, like its customer, is merely a user of the shopping cart.

Public policy considerations do not demand that the duty of a storekeeper to keep its premises in a safe condition be elevated beyond the traditional standard of reasonable care. Ryan v. Robeson's, Inc. (1969), 113 Ill.App.2d 416, 251 N.E.2d 545. Plaintiff is not denied a cause of action in negligence nor is she precluded from establishing a cause of action in strict products liability against the manufacturer of the shopping cart and others who placed the shopping cart into the stream of commerce and reaped the profits therefrom. We simply hold that Dominick's cannot be considered to be part of the distributive chain within the ambit of the principles of strict products liability.

* * *

For the reasons stated, the order of the circuit court of Cook County dismissing the count of the complaint founded on strict products liability is affirmed.

Order affirmed.

JIGANTI, J., concurs.

SIMON, PRESIDING JUSTICE, dissenting.

The plaintiff should be permitted to proceed to trial on her strict products liability count. Dominick's was part of the stream of commerce flowing from the cart's manufacturer to the plaintiff. The cart was intended for use by customers of grocery supermarkets. It reached the plaintiff through Dominick's. Therefore, the stream of commerce did not stop, as the majority views it, with the parties who distributed the cart to Dominick's, but continued until the cart reached the customers who were intended to use it and for whose use Dominick's supplied it. The approach of the majority is that Dominick's is the consumer or user of the carts. On the other hand, I regard Dominick's as the supplier of the carts to its customers and, therefore, as a conduit in the marketing chain which brought the carts to their ultimate users, Dominick's customers.

Although, as the majority points out, Dominick's neither sells nor rents shopping carts, it does supply them for its customers. It would be virtually impossible for a customer to make substantial purchases at Dominick's supermarts without the use of a cart. The customer may be regarded as paying for this use because the cart is a cost of doing business which no doubt is reflected in the charge Dominick's makes for its merchandise. The cart not only provides a convenience for Dominick's customers, but also increases Dominick's sales and profits. As the majority states, one of the reasons for imposing strict liability is to ensure that losses are borne by those who reap the profit of marketing an allegedly defective product. By supplying the carts, Dominick's fits within this rationale.

* * *

NOTES

1. Compare Wagner v. Coronet Hotel, 10 Ariz.App. 296, 458 P.2d 390, 395 (1969), where plaintiff was injured when he slipped on an allegedly defective rubber shower mat provided by the defendant hotel: "Of all the various policy views expressed for the theory of strict liability, none are applicable to the Coronet Hotel."

2. In Safeway Stores, Inc. v. Nest–Kart, 21 Cal.3d 322, 146 Cal.Rptr. 550, 579 P.2d 441 (1978), the supermarket shopping cart broke and fell on plaintiff's foot. The jury found the supermarket liable, in negligence and strict liability in tort, and the cart manufacturer strictly liable, apportioning 80% to the supermarket and 20% to the manufacturer. Without discussing the propriety of the strict liability claim against the supermarket, the Supreme Court approved the verdict.

3. In Armstrong Rubber Co. v. Urquidez, 570 S.W.2d 374 (Tex.1978), the court held that strict tort would not apply to an action brought for the death of a test driver as the result of a blowout of an allegedly defective tire manufactured by the defendant, Armstrong. Armstrong supplied the tire in question to plaintiff's employer, a tire-testing facility, as a "non-interest spare" to be used on test vehicles along with whatever tires were actually being tested at the time: "Armstrong never released the non-interest spare to an ordinary user or consumer within the meaning of the Restatement. The defective tire, although not itself the subject of the test, always remained within the industrial, testing process. Accordingly, the tire never entered the stream of commerce. The lower courts, therefore, inappropriately applied the doctrine of strict liability to the present industrial transaction." 570 S.W.2d at 377.

Compare First Nat. Bank v. Cessna Aircraft Co., 365 So.2d 966, 967 (Ala. 1978) (strict tort doctrine applies to the crash of a demonstrator airplane): "[H]aving placed the product on the market, if the manufacturer still retains some measure of control, he should be liable under the doctrine."

4. With Bainter v. Lamoine LP Gas Co., 24 Ill.App.3d 913, 321 N.E.2d 744 (1974), discussed in *Keen,* compare Shaffer v. Victoria Station, Inc., 91 Wash.2d 295, 588 P.2d 233 (1978) (restaurant liable in both warranty and strict tort for injuries to patron from wine glass shattering in his hand).

5. **Warranty.** In Garfield v. Furniture Fair–Hanover, 113 N.J.Super. 509, 274 A.2d 325 (1971), a woman was injured when a bed collapsed that had been loaned to her and her husband by the defendant furniture store pending the delivery of a new bed they had purchased. *Held,* since plaintiffs had never taken title to the loaned bed, and since they were bound to return it upon delivery of the purchased bed, the transaction was a bailment rather than a sale under U.C.C. § 2–106(1). Nor had the bailment become integrated into the sale of the new bed so as to extend the warranties attaching to the sale to the bailment as well.

A few courts have applied the Commercial Code warranties in the lease or bailment context. See e.g., Hawkins Const. Co. v. Matthews Co., Inc., 190 Neb. 546, 209 N.W.2d 643 (1973); Owens v. Patent Scaffolding Co.—Div. of Harsco, 77 Misc.2d 992, 354 N.Y.S.2d 778 (1974), rev'd on other grounds 50 A.D.2d 866, 376 N.Y.S.2d 948 (1975) (Article 2 warranty provisions applied to lease transactions, since "there is no real commercial or economic difference to a contractor-user of scaffolding equipment between buying equipment and leasing it for use on a job"). See generally Note, 27 Mercer L.Rev. 347 (1975).

6. In Hurley v. Larry's Water Ski School, 762 F.2d 925 (11th Cir.1985), plaintiff was injured while taking water skiing lessons from the defendant when the wooden tow handle he was holding broke. In his action against the ski school, the court held that since the tow rope or handle were at all times attached to the boat, he never had complete possession and control over them and so never had a bailment. Although plaintiff's strict liability in tort claim thus would not lie, his breach of warranty claim could. Implicit in the defendant's agreement to provide ski lessons to the plaintiff was "an implied warranty that the equipment supplied by Larry's was fit for the purpose of teaching an individual to ski." Id. at 929.

7. On bailments generally, see Notes, 28 Okla.L.Rev. 913 (1975); 57 Marq. L.Rev. 111 (1973); Annot., 48 A.L.R.3d 668 (1973).

SECTION 2. SERVICES

MURPHY v. E.R. SQUIBB & SONS, INC.

Supreme Court of California, 1985.
40 Cal.3d 672, 221 Cal.Rptr. 447, 710 P.2d 247.

MOSK, JUSTICE.

We consider issues relating to the liability of a manufacturer and a pharmacy for the production and sale of an allegedly defective drug, stilbestrol (DES). We will decide whether a pharmacy at which the drug was purchased may be held strictly liable for alleged defects in the product (as distinguished from ordinary negligence) * * *.

Plaintiff filed an action for personal injuries allegedly resulting from DES taken by her mother in 1951 and 1952 during pregnancy for the purpose of reducing the risk of miscarriage. The complaint sought damages on the theory of strict liability, alleging that the drug was defectively designed, with the result that plaintiff developed clear cell adenocarcinoma at the age of 23. As defendants, plaintiff joined Exclusive Prescription Pharmacy Corporation (Exclusive) where plaintiff's mother purchased the DES, and E.R. Squibb & Sons, Inc. (Squibb). * * *

* * *

The Action Against Exclusive

In the seminal case of Greenman v. Yuba Power Products, Inc. (1963) 59 Cal.2d 57, 27 Cal.Rptr. 697, 377 P.2d 897, Justice Traynor, writing for the court, held a manufacturer strictly liable in tort for injuries caused by a defective product which it knew would be used without inspection for defects. In Vandermark v. Ford Motor Co. (1964) 61 Cal.2d 256, 37 Cal.Rptr. 896, 391 P.2d 168, the strict liability doctrine was extended to retailers of defective products.

Plaintiff asserts that a pharmacy which sells prescription drugs is in the same position as a retailer of any other consumer product, and that the reasons advanced in *Greenman* and *Vandermark* for imposing strict liability necessarily apply to a pharmacy. Exclusive counters that a pharmacist who dispenses a prescription drug is primarily furnishing a service rather than selling a product, and that the rationale underlying imposition of strict liability does not justify application of the doctrine to him.

Before reaching the merits of these conflicting claims, we observe that pharmacists perform a broad range of tasks, from selling razor blades and dental floss to treating patients in a health care facility by ordering laboratory tests and administering drugs by injection (Bus. & Prof.Code, § 4046, subd. (c)(4)) and acting as consultants regarding medication prescribed for patients at such facilities (Cal.Admin.Code, tit. 22, § 72375). The discussion which follows relates only to the duties in a community pharmacy of a pharmacist who fills prescriptions for drugs on the order of a physician or other medical care provider, and who has used due care in compounding and labelling the drug.

There are no cases in California deciding whether a retail pharmacy is strictly liable for injuries caused by an inherent defect in a drug. In Florida (McLeod v. W.S. Merrell Co. (Fla.1965) 174 So.2d 736, 739), North Carolina (Batiste v. American Home Products Corp. (1977) 32 N.C.App. 1, 231 S.E.2d 269, 275) and New York (Bichler v. Willing (1977) 58 A.D.2d 331, 397 N.Y.2d 57, 59–60) a pharmacy is held not to be strictly liable for defects in a prescription drug. These cases rely on section 402A of the Restatement Second, of Torts, which declares that unavoidably unsafe products such as drugs are not defective if they are accompanied by an appropriate warning (id., com. k), and that a seller is only required to warn of defects of which he knew or should have known (id., com. j).

It is critical to the issue posed to determine if the dominant role of a pharmacist in supplying a prescription drug should be characterized as the performance of a service or the sale of a product. Both parties accept as a general rule that "those who sell their services for the guidance of others * * * are not liable in the absence of negligence or intentional misconduct." (Gagne v. Bertran (1954) 43 Cal.2d 481, 487, 275 P.2d 15.) This principle was applied in Carmichael v. Reitz (1971) 17 Cal.App.3d 958, 95 Cal.Rptr. 381, the primary authority on which the trial court relied. A doctor who prescribed a drug purchased by the patient at a pharmacy was held not to be strictly liable for injuries resulting from its use. In response to the argument of the plaintiff that the doctor was "in a sense a retailer" of the drug, the court stated that the doctor prescribed the medication only as an aid to effect a cure and was not in the business of selling the drug. The court observed, "[T]he distinction between a transaction where the primary objective is the acquisition of ownership or use of a product and one where the dominant purpose is to obtain services has not been obliterated. Where the services sought are professional in character, the distinction applies *a fortiori.*" (Id. at p. 978, 95 Cal.Rptr. 381.) On this theory, a hospital was held not strictly liable as the "supplier" for injuries arising out of the use of a surgical needle which broke during an operation. (Silverhart v. Mount Zion Hospital (1971) 20 Cal.App.3d 1022, 1027, 98 Cal. Rptr. 187.)

Magrine v. Krasnica (1967) 94 N.J.Super. 228, 227 A.2d 539, held that a dentist was not strictly liable for injuries caused by a needle which broke during the course of treatment due to a latent defect. The court characterized the difference between a sale and a service as follows: "[T]he *essence* of the transaction between the retail seller and the consumer relates to the *article sold.* The seller is *in the business* of supplying the product to the consumer. It is that, and that alone, for which he is paid. A dentist or physician offers, and is paid for, his professional services and skill. That is the *essence* of the relationship between him and his patient." (Id. 227 A.2d at p. 543.) (Accord: Babcock v. Nudelman (1937) 367 Ill. 626, 12 N.E.2d 635 [holding optometrists and oculists who examined eyes and sold eyeglasses, exempt from a tax imposed on retailers of tangible goods on the ground that their main objective was to provide a service and that the sale of eyeglasses was purely incidental to the service]; see also Barbee v. Rogers (Tex.1968) 425 S.W.2d 342.)

As might be anticipated, the parties differ sharply as to whether the main function of a pharmacist is to provide a service or to sell a product. Plaintiff asserts that the duties of a pharmacist in filling a prescription do not differ from those of any other retailer: he reads the prescription, fills the container with the proper type and dosage of the medication required, types up a label, attaches it to the container, and exchanges the medication for payment by the customer. In essence, argues plaintiff, a pharmacist is the functional equivalent of "an experienced clerk at a hardware store."

Exclusive and amici curiae paint a dramatically different picture of the role of the pharmacist, characterizing him as a professional who provides an important health service. They point out that with a few exceptions specified by statute, only a physician or a licensed pharmacist may compound or dispense prescription drugs (Bus. & Prof.Code, § 4050 et seq.). In order to obtain a license, a pharmacist must have graduated from a four-year college of pharmacy or the department of pharmacy of a university, have one year of practical experience under the supervision of a registered pharmacist, and pass a written examination given by the California State Board of Pharmacy (Board) (§§ 4085, 4087). He must comply with continuing education requirements as a condition to renewal of his license (§ 4098.5), and is subject to rules of professional responsibility and to disciplinary proceedings for violation of those rules (§ 4350 et seq.).

A pharmacist is required not only to assure that the drug prescribed is properly selected, measured and labelled but, according to the Board, he must be alert to errors in prescriptions written by doctors, and contact the doctor in case of doubts or questions regarding the drug prescribed. In addition, the pharmacist may discuss with the patient the proper use of the drug and the potential side effects, and must be aware of the possibility of harmful interaction between various medications which the pharmacist knows the patient is using. According to the Board, about 22 percent of patients are counseled by the pharmacist, who spends one and one-half to two hours a day in such consultation. (Citing Cal.Pharm. (Jan. 1985) 1984 Lilly Digest Rep., p. 33, table 19.)

It seems clear to us that the pharmacist is engaged in a hybrid enterprise, combining the performance of services and the sale of prescription drugs. It is pure hyperbole to suggest, as does plaintiff, that the role of the pharmacist is similar to that of a clerk in an ordinary retail store. * * * A key factor is that the pharmacist who fills a prescription is in a different position from the ordinary retailer because he cannot offer a prescription for sale except by order of the doctor. In this respect, he is providing a service to the doctor and acting as an extension of the doctor in the same sense as a technician who takes an X-ray or analyzes a blood sample on a doctor's order.

Nevertheless, it cannot be disputed that a sale in fact occurs. There is an obvious distinction between the doctor who provides a patient with a prescription for a defective drug (Carmichael, supra, 17 Cal.App.3d 958, 95 Cal.Rptr. 381), a dentist who uses a faulty drill (Magrine, supra, 227 A.2d 539) or a hospital that uses a defective needle during surgery (Silverhart, supra, 20 Cal.App.3d 1022, 98 Cal.Rptr. 187), and a pharmacist who fills a prescription. The pharmacist is in the business of selling prescription drugs, and his role begins and ends with the sale. His services are rendered only in connection with the sale, and a patient who goes to a pharmacy to have a prescription filled generally is seeking to purchase the drug rather than to obtain the advice of the pharmacist.

By contrast, the doctor, dentist and hospital in the cases cited above are not in the business of selling the drug or device; they use the product in the course of treatment as one element in their efforts to effect a cure, and furnishing the services does not depend on sale of a product.

Ordinarily, in deciding whether the sale or service aspect of an enterprise predominates, we would confine our consideration to the type of factors discussed above. In the case of a pharmacy, however, we must broaden our inquiry. The Legislature has provided in section 4046 that the practice of pharmacy is not only a profession (subd. (a)), but also a "dynamic patient-oriented *health service* that applies a scientific body of knowledge to improve and promote patient health by means of appropriate drug use and drug related therapy" (subd. (b)). (Emphasis added.)

This declaration that a pharmacist provides a health service is similar to section 1606 of the Health and Safety Code, which declares that the distribution or use of whole blood or plasma is a service for all purposes and shall not be construed to be a sale. The object of section 1606 is to avoid application of the doctrine of strict liability to those who make or sell blood or blood plasma, or to those who use it in blood transfusions, thereby promoting the constant availability of an adequate supply of blood. (McDonald v. Sacramento Medical Foundation Blood Bank (1976) 62 Cal.App.3d 866, 872, 133 Cal.Rptr. 444.) In keeping with this purpose, it is held that a hospital using blood in a transfusion (Shepard v. Alexian Brothers Hosp. (1973) 33 Cal.App.3d 606, 109 Cal.Rptr. 132), a blood bank supplying the blood (*McDonald*) and a manufacturer of blood plasma selling it for transfusion (Fogo v. Cutter Laboratories, Inc. (1977) 68 Cal.App.3d 744, 137 Cal.Rptr. 417), are immune from strict liability because the Legislature has declared in section 1606 that they are providing a service rather than making a sale.

It is true that section 1606 of the Health and Safety Code provides not only that the distribution and use of blood and blood plasma is a service, but also that they should be deemed not to constitute a sale, whereas section 4046, subdivision (b), does not expressly declare that a sale is not involved in the practice of pharmacy. Nevertheless, the Legislature could not have been unaware when it enacted this provision that a pharmacist's main function is to fill prescriptions for medications that are sold to the public. Indeed, from a comparative functional aspect, a pharmacist's role is more aptly characterized as the performance of a service than that of the manufacturer and seller of blood plasma. The Legislature must have intended, therefore, that even though a pharmacist is paid for the medication he dispenses, his conduct in filling a prescription is to be deemed a service, and, like the manufacturer of blood plasma, a pharmacy is immune from strict liability.

* * *

There is no definitive legislative history of subdivision (b), and we are not certain, therefore, of the Legislature's motivation in shielding pharmacies from strict liability. The Legislature may have determined that it is not in the public interest to subject them to strict liability, because (like the need to assure an adequate supply of blood plasma) the wide availability of a full range of prescription drugs at economical cost outweighs the advantage to the individual consumer of being able to recover for injuries on a strict liability basis rather than to be limited to claims arising from negligence.

If pharmacies were held strictly liable for the drugs they dispense, some of them, to avoid liability, might restrict availability by refusing to dispense drugs which pose even a potentially remote risk of harm, although such medications may be essential to the health or even the survival of patients. Furthermore, in order to assure that a pharmacy receives the maximum protection in the event of suit for defects in a drug, the pharmacist may select the more expensive product made by an established manufacturer when he has a choice of several brands of the same drug. As the Board's amicus brief warns, "Why choose a new company's inexpensive product, which has received excellent reviews in the literature for its quality, over the more expensive product of an established multinational corporation which will certainly have assets available for purpose of indemnification 10, 20, or 30 years down the line?"

The Legislature might have decided also that, since the doctor who ordered the drug provided by the pharmacy cannot be held strictly liable for its defects and in some circumstances the manufacturer who created the defect can also escape liability, it would be unfair and burdensome to expose the pharmacy alone to strict liability since it may provide the drug only on a doctor's prescription, which the pharmacist must strictly follow. Plaintiff emphasizes that some pharmacies are owned by large chain store operations which are as capable as large drug manufacturers to respond in damages. But most pharmacies are not in this category. According to the Board, approximately 3,385 pharmacy permits are held in California by independent operators of 3 or fewer pharmacies, many of which are single drugstores owned by the operating pharmacist. Only 1,165 permits are held by operators of 4 or more pharmacies, and 642 permits are held by hospital pharmacies.

Finally, plaintiff contends that even if the pharmacist is personally exempt from strict liability because he provides a service, the "merchandising organization which employs him * * * should not be so exempted." Plaintiff cites no authority in support of this claim, and we perceive no basis in law or rationale for accepting it. The fact that a pharmacy may be owned by an enterprise which also deals in ordinary merchandise does not justify the conclusion that it should be held strictly liable when it performs a service. Moreover, the policy justifying the grant of immunity from strict liability to the practice of pharmacy would only be effectuated if the pharmacy operation itself is exempted.

For the reasons stated above, we conclude that the trial court was correct in granting judgment on the pleadings to Exclusive.

* * *

The judgment is affirmed.

GRODIN, JUSTICE, concurring.

* * *

* * * I conclude that nothing in our previous decisions, nor the decisions of any other state, either directly or by analogy supports extension of strict liability to retail pharmacists who sell prescription drugs.

A pharmacist is not free to sell a prescription drug to anyone who merely requests the product and offers payment; unlike a car dealer or a tire vendor, a pharmacist may dispense his prescription drugs only after being authorized to do so by a prescribing physician or similar person. (Bus. & Prof.Code, § 4036, subd. (a).) In preparing the drug and selling it to his customer on the prescriber's authorization, the pharmacist simply carries out what the prescriber orders. Although he has some limited discretion in the matter—i.e., he may (i) under certain circumstances, fill the prescription with a less costly substitute containing the same ingredients, or (ii) consult the prescribing physician if he believes the prescription is mistaken or otherwise inappropriate in light of the patient's other prescriptions—final authority for ordering the prescription filled still rests exclusively with the prescribing physician. At the same time, the physician, whose responsibility it is to properly diagnose, counsel, prescribe and warn his patient about proper use and risks associated with the prescribed drug, is exempt under *Bertran* from strict liability for defects in the drug he orders the pharmacist to dispense. (Carmichael v. Reitz, supra, 17 Cal.App.3d at pp. 977–979, 95 Cal.Rptr. 381.) In this situation—in which policy considerations intervene to exempt the primarily responsible actor (the prescriber) from strict liability—basic fairness and common sense dictate it would be fundamentally unfair to treat pharmacists like any other retailer of any other product.

I conclude strict liability should not apply in the case of a retail pharmacist, whose authority to sell prescription drugs is closely regulated by statute, and who dispenses his product only at the direction of a prescriber who is himself exempt from such liability.

[The concurring opinion of Lucas, J., is omitted.]

BIRD, CHIEF JUSTICE, dissenting.

I dissent from the affirmance of the judgment in favor of defendant Exclusive Prescription Pharmacy Corporation (Exclusive). Under principles of products liability which are firmly established in this state, a retail druggist is strictly liable in tort for the sale of a defective prescription drug. Today's majority reach the opposite conclusion by retreating from sound principles which, in less turbulent times, were viewed as beyond serious challenge.

Specifically, the majority take a narrow and cramped view of the policies served by strict liability. Several of the most important policies, first articulated in the pioneering opinions of Chief Justice Roger Traynor, are not even mentioned. The majority's failure to address these policies has unfortunate consequences which go beyond their incorrect conclusion regarding liability.

As a result of this unfortunate opinion, doubts are cast on this court's past statements recognizing the applicability of the entire doctrine of strict liability to defective prescription drugs. In the process, the very foundations of the doctrine are called into question. I cannot join in a retreat from one of this court's most firmly established, highly acclaimed and beneficial adaptations of tort law to modern mass production and marketing methods.

The majority also embrace elitist distinctions based on the professional status of retail druggists and, thereby, draw utterly contradictory conclusions regarding the significance of this status. Contradictions aside, professionalism has nothing to do with the central question to be answered here.

The issue is whether retail druggists and pharmacies, which sell prescription drugs to consumers, are engaged primarily in selling a product or in performing a service. The simple answer is that in the marketing of prescription drugs by retail druggists, as in the marketing of automobiles and other consumer products, the sale aspect predominates over any incidental service provided to the consumer. For this reason, and because every one of the policies served by strict liability would be advanced by applying the doctrine to the sale of a defective prescription drug by a retail druggist, I would reverse the judgment in favor of defendant Exclusive.

[Justice Bird reviewed the court's development of products liability policies in *Escola, Greenman, Vandermark,* and Sindell v. Abbott Laboratories, 26 Cal.3d 588, 163 Cal.Rptr. 132, 607 P.2d 924 (1980), infra. p. 938. These decisions have identified] several major policies served by the doctrine of strict liability: (1) providing maximum compensation to helpless victims for the often catastrophic costs of injuries caused by defective products; (2) providing an incentive for better design, manufacturing and testing procedures by placing those costs on the parties responsible for defective products reaching the market, thereby reducing injuries; (3) spreading the costs of injuries that do occur among those who benefit from the marketing and use of the product.

* * *

Instead [of considering these policies], the majority cite with apparent approval opinions from other jurisdictions holding that a pharmacy cannot be held strictly liable for design defects in any prescription drug, absent proof that it failed to warn of known dangers.[2] [Citations.]

The opinions cited by the majority rely heavily on comment k to section 402A of the Restatement Second of Torts. Each interprets comment k as exempting prescription drugs from strict liability for design defects on the theory that all such drugs are unavoidably unsafe products which are useful to society. That interpretation is squarely inconsistent with decisions of this court spanning a quarter of a century which have affirmed the importance and breadth of the strict liability doctrine. (See ante, at pp. 449–451 of 221 Cal.Rptr., pp. 249–251 of 710 P.2d.)

2. Plaintiff here consciously rejected the "failure to warn" approach. As plaintiff explains, she "has not alleged in this case that DES was defective because defendants failed to warn of the risks attendant to the use of the drug. Quite [ ] the contrary, it was plaintiff's intention to prove that this drug should have never been marketed at all for use in pregnant women. It was ineffective for the indication promoted by Squibb and it caused cancer in the daughters of women who ingested the drug while pregnant. Suffice to say that a drug marketed for use in pregnant women bearing a warning that it is not to be used by pregnant women is conceptually ludicrous. Plaintiff refused to base her case on such thinly constructed logic, but rather elected to establish strict products liability on the manufacturer and retailer of this pharmaceutical product based on its defective design."

Specifically, it is inconsistent with *Sindell* 's recognition that strict liability policies are "particularly significant where medication is involved, for the consumer is virtually helpless to protect himself from serious, sometimes permanent, sometimes fatal, injuries caused by deleterious drugs." (*Sindell,* supra, 26 Cal.3d at p. 611, 163 Cal.Rptr. 132, 607 P.2d 924.) * * *

* * *

Under the test which the parties and the majority agree govern here, strict liability applies if the purchase of a product is the "primary objective" or "essence" of the transaction. (Carmichael v. Reitz (1971) 17 Cal.App.3d 958, 978, 95 Cal.Rptr. 381; see Magrine v. Krasnica (1967) 94 N.J.Super. 227 A.2d 539.) Strict liability is inapplicable only where the transaction is limited to the provision of a service and does not involve the sale of a product (Gagne v. Bertran (1954) 43 Cal.2d 481, 487, 275 P.2d 15 [defendant who performed soil tests not strictly liable]) or where the service aspect predominates and any sale included in the transaction is incidental to the provision of the service. (Silverhart v. Mount Zion Hospital (1971) 20 Cal.App.3d 1022, 1027, 98 Cal.Rptr. 187 [hospital that supplied surgical needle which broke during operation not strictly liable].)

Accepting the majority's characterization of the retail druggist's business as "a hybrid enterprise, combining the performance of services and the sale of prescription drugs" (maj. opn., at p. 451 of 221 Cal.Rptr., p. 251 of 710 P.2d), it is nonetheless abundantly clear that the sale aspect predominates.

The majority's own statistics bear this out. Only 22 percent of patients who purchase prescription drugs are counseled by the retail druggist, who spends an average of only one and one-half hours a day performing this service. (See maj. opn., at p. 451 of 221 Cal.Rptr., p. 221 of 710 P.2d.) Thus, in the vast majority of prescription drug sales transactions, the customer receives only a product and no services from the retail druggist.

The predominance of the sale is also reflected by the fixed prices the retail druggist charges for prescription drugs, based on a markup from wholesale cost rather than an hourly fee calculation. (Compare Gagne v. Bertran, supra, 43 Cal.2d at p. 487, 275 P.2d 15 [hourly fee charged by soil tester showed that he was selling a service, not a product].)

The majority dismiss as "pure hyberbole" plaintiff's suggestion that the retail druggist's role is similar to that of a clerk in an "ordinary" retail store. Yet, the average hardware store clerk probably devotes as much or more time to counseling customers on the applications and proper use of the items offered for sale by the store. I doubt that the majority would have any difficulty concluding that the essence of the transaction between the hardware clerk and the customer is a sale rather than a service.

The majority, diverging from the inquiry into the nature of the transaction, contend that the educational and professional standards which must be met to obtain a pharmacist's license somehow dictate the conclusion that the retail druggist and the pharmacy are primarily engaged in the provision of a service. (See maj. opn. at p. 451 of 221 Cal.Rptr., p. 251 of 710 P.2d.) An almost mystical significance is attributed to the retail druggist's admitted expertise and professional status.

* * * Nowhere do they explain how the retail druggist's professional status converts the business of selling prescription drugs, in which the provision of services plays a subordinate role, into a business in which the service aspect predominates.

* * *

The majority attempt to dispel any persisting doubts by referring to the language of Business and Professions Code section 4046. (See maj. opn., at pp. 451–453 of 221 Cal.Rptr., pp. 251–253 of 710 P.2d.) They conclude that the Legislature intended this provision to exempt retail druggists and pharmacies from strict liability in the same manner that Health and Safety Code section 1606 exempts all persons involved in the distribution of blood and blood products [citations]. However, when the two statutes are placed side by side, the differences are striking.

* * *

The foregoing comparison establishes that when the Legislature intends to exempt an occupational group or activity from strict liability, it knows how to say so. (See Johnson & Johnson v. Superior Court (1985) 38 Cal.3d 243, 249–250, 211 Cal.Rptr. 517, 695 P.2d 1058.) It did so for those engaged in supplying blood and blood products when it enacted the explicit language of Health and Safety Code section 1606.

No such intention can be gleaned from the vague and general language concerning the practice of pharmacy in Business and Professions Code section 4046. No amount of speculation by this court * * * can make up for the absence of a declaration by the Legislature of the intent which the majority seek to attribute to it.

The majority do not stop at speculation regarding the Legislature's intent. They also engage in the purest form of speculation, attempting to divine the motivation which underlay this supposed intent. It is fair to say that the concerns they settle on are their own rather than the Legislature's. These concerns range from a fear that imposing strict liability on retail druggists would lead to a scarcity of life-saving drugs to a fear of increased prices. (See maj. opn., at p. 451 of 221 Cal.Rptr., p. 251 of 710 P.2d.) The majority also express concern about the fairness of imposing strict liability on those retail druggists who are small, "independent operators," particularly because the prescribing doctor and, in some circumstances, the manufacturer, can escape liability. (Id., at p. 453 of 221 Cal.Rptr., p. 253 of 710 P.2d.)

Apart from the lack of evidence that the Legislature shared the majority's concern when it enacted Business and Professions Code section 4046, these arguments do not support the exemption of retail druggists from strict liability. There is no evidence that the imposition of strict liability would cause the supply of prescription drugs to dry up. Such fears are unfounded if one but reviews the experience with other retail sales businesses after they were made subject to strict liability.

For example, automobile dealers have been subject since *Vandermark* to strict liability for injuries caused by defects in the automobiles they sell. Although injuries from such defects are not uncommon, automobile dealers have continued in business, and there has been no noticeable decrease in the supply of cars for sale.

As to the concern that prices might rise, this possibility has long been recognized and accepted as an integral part of the strict liability doctrine. (See, e.g., Escola, supra, 24 Cal.2d at p. 462, 150 P.2d 436 (conc. opn. of Traynor, J.) ["the risk of injury can be insured by the manufacturer and distributed among the public as a cost of doing business"]; [citation]. * * *

The majority stress the small size of many pharmacy businesses. However, it cannot be denied that a high volume of prescription drugs are currently marketed by large-scale, modern commercial enterprises. The fact that there continue to be many single drugstores owned by the operating retail druggist does not justify an exception.

* * *

For all the reasons articulated above, retail druggists and pharmacies should be strictly liable for the sale of defective prescription drugs. The injured consumer should not assume that burden. The judgment on the pleadings in favor of defendant Exclusive should be reversed.

KAUS and BROUSSARD, JJ., concur.

NOTES

1. The classic case is Gagne v. Bertran, 43 Cal.2d 481, 275 P.2d 15 (1954) (Traynor, J.), involving the liability of a soil tester for an erroneous report:

> The evidence in the present case does not justify the imposition of the strict liability of a warranty. There was no express warranty agreement, and there is nothing in the evidence to indicate that defendant assumed responsibility for the accuracy of his statements. * * * The amount of his fee and the fact that he was paid by the hour also indicate that he was selling service and not insurance. Thus the general rule is applicable that those who sell their services for the guidance of others in their economic, financial, and personal affairs are not liable in the absence of negligence or intentional misconduct.
>
> * * *
>
> The services of experts are sought because of their special skill. They have a duty to exercise the ordinary skill and competence of members of their profession, and a failure to discharge that duty will subject them to liability for negligence. Those who hire such persons

> are not justified in expecting infallibility, but can expect only reasonable care and competence. They purchase service, not insurance.

275 P.2d at 20, 21.

2. What precisely is the holding in *Murphy*, and what are its rationales?

3. Same result if the customer discusses a malady with the pharmacist who deliberates and then selects a product which is defective in some manner that causes injury to the plaintiff, such as:

A. Calcium tablets, of a particular type and strength, that ultimately cause heel spurs?

B. An ointment, that causes dermatitis?

C. Talcum powder, inhaled by the customer over time, that causes a lung disorder?

D. A normally extra-safe type of razor blade, with a tiny manufacturing defect that cuts a hemophiliac user while shaving?

4. To what extent is *Murphy* reflective of a reluctance to impose heavy costs on the health care industry? To what extent might it reflect the trend toward relieving retailers from strict liability? See generally Vandall, Applying Strict Liability to Pharmacists, 18 U.Toledo L.Rev. 1 (1986) (arguing in favor of strict liability).

5. Compare Hector v. Cedars–Sinai Medical Center, 180 Cal.App.3d 493, 225 Cal.Rptr. 595 (1986) (hospital's provision of defective pacemaker implanted in patient was "integrally related to its primary function of providing medical services"; summary judgment proper on warranty and strict liability claims), with Thomas v. St. Joseph Hosp., 618 S.W.2d 791 (Tex.Civ.App.1981) (strict liability appropriate where hospital provided patient with flammable gown).

6. **Professionals.** Should doctors, dentists, architects, engineers, lawyers, and law professors be exempted from the normal rules? There is broad agreement that such "professionals" should not be strictly liable for their errors. The architect cases are illustrative. In Audlane Lumber & Builders Supply, Inc. v. D.E. Britt Associates, Inc., 168 So.2d 333, 335 (Fla.App.1964), the court remarked:

> With respect to the alleged "implied warranty of fitness," we see no reason for application of this theory in circumstances involving professional liability. Unlike the lower court, however, we do not base our decision on the narrow ground of privity. An engineer, or any other so-called professional, does not "warrant" his service or the tangible evidence of his skill to be "merchantable" or "fit for an intended use." These are terms uniquely applicable to goods. Rather, in the preparation of design and specifications as the basis of construction, the engineer or architect "warrants" that he will or has exercised his skill according to a certain standard of care, that he acted reasonably and without neglect. Breach of this "warranty" occurs if he was negligent. Accordingly, the elements of an action for negligence and for breach of the "implied warranty" are the same. The use of the term "implied warranty" in these circumstances merely introduces further confusion into an area of law where confusion abounds.

Consider also City of Mounds View v. Walijarvi, 263 N.W.2d 420, 424–25 (Minn. 1978), reconsidering the majority rule:

The reasoning underlying the general rule as it applies both to architects and other vendors of professional services is relatively straightforward. Architects, doctors, engineers, attorneys, and others deal in somewhat inexact sciences and are continually called upon to exercise their skilled judgment in order to anticipate and provide for random factors which are incapable of precise measurement. The indeterminate nature of these factors makes it impossible for professional service people to gauge them with complete accuracy in every instance. Thus, doctors cannot promise that every operation will be successful; a lawyer can never be certain that a contract he drafts is without latent ambiguity; and an architect cannot be certain that a structural design will interact with natural forces as anticipated. Because of the inescapable possibility of error which inheres in these services, the law has traditionally required, not perfect results, but rather the exercise of that skill and judgment which can be reasonably expected from similarly situated professionals. * * *

We have reexamined our case law on the subject of professional services and are not persuaded that the time has yet arrived for the abrogation of the traditional rule. Adoption of the city's implied warranty theory would in effect impose strict liability on architects for latent defects in the structures they design. That is, once a court or jury has made the threshold finding that a structure was somehow unfit for its intended purpose, liability would be imposed on the responsible architect in spite of his diligent application of state-of-the-art design techniques. If every facet of structural design consisted of little more than the mechanical application of immutable physical principles, we could accept the rule of strict liability which the city proposes. But even in the present state of relative technological enlightenment, the keenest engineering minds can err in their most searching assessment of the natural factors which determine whether structural components will adequately serve their intended purpose. Until the random element is eliminated in the application of architectural sciences, we think it fairer tha[t] the purchaser of the architect's services bear the risk of such unforeseeable difficulties.

The city suggests that many of the design-related tasks performed by modern architects are routine and carry no risk of error if they are performed with professional due care. It is argued that with respect to such tasks, the premise on which the traditional rule rests is inoperative, making the adoption of the implied warranty theory fully proper. We note, however, that architectural errors in relatively simple matters are quite easily handled under the existing cause of action for professional negligence.

Moreover, if implied warranties are held to accompany only uncomplicated architectural endeavors, the finder of fact will be forced in every case to determine, as a preliminary matter, whether the alleged architectural error was made in the performance of a sufficiently simplistic task. * * * We think the net effect would be the interjection of substantive ambiguity into the law of professional malpractice without a favorable trade-off in procedural expedience.

In addition, we observe that the ills which spurred the creation and expansion of the implied warranty/strict liability doctrine are not really present in this case or in the architect-client relationship generally. The implied warranty of fitness originated primarily as a means of facilitating the legitimate interests of the consuming public and bringing common-law remedies into step with the practicalities of modern industrialism. The outmoded requirement of contractual privity, coupled with manufacturers' sweeping disclaimers of liability, frequently operated to deny effective remedies to those who purchased commercial products at the bottom of a multi-tiered production and distribution network. See, generally, Prosser, Torts (4 ed.) §§ 97, 98. The introduction of the implied warranty doctrine created an effective remedy by allowing plaintiffs to proceed directly against the offending party without reliance on express contractual warranties.

The relationship between architect and client is markedly different. For a client, architectural services are hardly produced by a faceless business entity, insulated by a network of distributors, wholesalers, and retailers. Architects and clients normally enjoy a one-to-one relationship and communicate fairly extensively during the course of the relationship. When a legal dispute arises, the client has no trouble locating the source of his problem, and a remedial device like the implied warranty is largely unnecessary.

Finally, while it is undoubtedly fair to impose strict liability on manufacturers who have ample opportunity to test their products for defects before marketing them, the same cannot be said of architects. Normally, an architect has but a single chance to create a design for a client which will produce a defect-free structure. Accordingly, we do not think it just that architects should be forced to bear the same burden of liability for their products as that which has been imposed on manufacturers generally.

For these reasons, we decline to extend the implied warranty/strict liability doctrine to cover vendors of professional services. Our conclusion does not, of course, preclude the city from pursuing its standard malpractice action against the architects and proving that the basement area of the new addition was negligently designed.

Contra, holding that a design professional impliedly warrants that the structure will be reasonably fit for its intended use, Broyles v. Brown Engineering Co., 275 Ala. 35, 151 So.2d 767 (1963) (as to routine engineering survey of subdivision drainage requirements); Bloomsburg Mills, Inc. v. Sordoni Const. Co., 401 Pa. 358, 164 A.2d 201 (1960); Hill v. Polar Pantries, 219 S.C. 263, 64 S.E.2d 885 (1951).

Doctors uniformly have been held not subject to strict liability for medical accidents. Barton v. Owen, 71 Cal.App.3d 484, 139 Cal.Rptr. 494 (1977); Hoven v. Kelble, 79 Wis.2d 444, 256 N.W.2d 379 (1977).

Except perhaps for law professors, professionals are liable of course for their negligent mistakes.

7. Was (former) Chief Justice Bird correct in asserting that the *Murphy* majority's reasoning was "elitist"? If true, does that characterization illuminate or obscure the significant issues?

8. Compare Newmark v. Gimbel's Inc., 102 N.J.Super. 279, 246 A.2d 11 (1968), where the customer of a beauty parlor lost her hair and developed contact dermatitis due to a permanent wave solution applied by the defendant beautician. Plaintiff's warranty claims were dismissed by the trial court, and plaintiff appealed:

[T]he transaction here in question consisting of the supplying of a product for use in the administration of a permanent wave to plaintiff, carried with it an implied warranty that the product used was reasonably fit for the purpose for which it was to be used. N.J.S. 12A:2–315, N.J.S.A.

Mrs. Newmark was a regular customer of defendant and had a weekly appointment to have her hair washed and set. On the day in question she received something in addition—a permanent wave. In essence, it involved application of a permanent wave lotion or solution and thereafter a neutralizer. The lotion was selected by one of defendant's operators who was familiar with her scalp and hair from current examination and prior visits. The product was secured from sources known to defendant and only defendant knew of any special instructions concerning its use. The risk from use of the lotion was incident to the operation of defendant's business, a business which yielded it a profit and placed it in a position to promote safety through pressure on suppliers. It was in a position to protect itself by making inquiry or tests to determine the susceptibility of customers to the use of the product, or by using another lotion which did not present the possibility of an adverse effect. It could secure indemnity from its suppliers through legal proceedings or otherwise. The fact that there was no separate charge for the product did not preclude its being considered as having been supplied to the customer in a sense justifying the imposition of an implied warranty against injurious defects therein.

The facts in Magrine v. Krasnica, [94 N.J.Super. 228, 227 A.2d 539 (1967)], on which defendant principally relies, are clearly distinguishable. That case involved a hypodermic needle, a tool of the dental profession, which was never intended to be supplied to the patient or consumed in the course of dental treatment. Here the product supplied to Mrs. Newmark was used up in the process of giving her a permanent wave. While it was later rinsed out, its effect was intended to remain and be part of the finished product. * * *

Held, reversed and remanded. The Supreme Court of New Jersey affirmed. 54 N.J. 585, 258 A.2d 697 (1969) (Francis, J.):

Defendants suggest that there is no doctrinal basis for distinguishing the services rendered by a beauty parlor operator from those rendered by a dentist or a doctor, and that consequently the liability of all three should be tested by the same principles. On the contrary there is a vast difference in the relationships. The beautician is engaged in a commercial enterprise; the dentist and doctor in a profession. The former caters publicly not to a need but to a form of aesthetic convenience or luxury, involving the rendition of non-professional services and the application of products for which a charge is made. The dentist or doctor does not and cannot advertise for patients; the demand for his services stems from a felt necessity of the patient. In response to such a call the doctor, and to a somewhat lesser degree the dentist, exercises his best judgment in diagnosing the patient's ailment or disability, prescribing and sometimes furnishing medicines or other methods of treatment which he believes, and in some measure hopes, will relieve or cure the condition. His performance is not mechanical or routine because each patient requires indi-

> vidual study and formulation of an informed judgment as to the physical or mental disability or condition presented, and the course of treatment needed. * * * Practitioners of such callings, licensed by the State to practice after years of study and preparation, must be deemed to have a special and essential role in our society, that of studying our physical and mental ills and ways to alleviate or cure them, and that of applying their knowledge, empirical judgment and skill in an effort to diagnose and then to relieve or to cure the ailment of a particular patient. Thus their paramount function—the essence of their function—ought to be regarded as the furnishing of opinions and services. Their unique status and the rendition of these *sui generis* services bear such a necessary and intimate relationship to public health and welfare that their obligation ought to be grounded and expressed in a duty to exercise reasonable competence and care toward their patients. In our judgment, the nature of the services, the utility of and the need for them, involving as they do, the health and even survival of many people, are so important to the general welfare as to outweigh in the policy scale any need for the imposition on dentists and doctors of the rules of strict liability in tort.

258 A.2d at 702–03.

9. Drawing the line between professional and nonprofessional services is not always easy. Should the prescription, fitting and sale of contact lenses result in strict liability on the optometrist for eye damage caused by an improper curvature in the lenses? Is it relevant that optometrists must be licensed? That the defendant operates a chain of 84 offices throughout the state? That it advertises in newspapers, radio and television? That a standard fee is charged, regardless of the complexity of the individual's eye problems or the number of fittings required? See Barbee v. Rogers, 425 S.W.2d 342 (Tex. 1968); W.P. Keeton, Torts, 23 Sw.L.J. 1, 6–9 (1969).

10. **Installers and Repairers.** Do the policies underlying strict liability for sellers of defective goods apply to those who install the goods in a faulty manner? Many courts hold not. See Hunt v. Guarantee Elec. Co. of St. Louis, 667 S.W.2d 9 (Mo.App.1984); Hinojasa v. Automatic Elevator Co., 92 Ill.App.3d 351, 48 Ill.Dec. 150, 416 N.E.2d 45 (1980). Others hold that strict liability in warranty or tort should apply, particularly if the installer participates in the product's design or manufacture. See Gunderson v. Sani–Kem Corp., 674 S.W.2d 665 (Mo.App.1984) (conveyor system); O'Laughlin v. Minnesota Natural Gas Co., 253 N.W.2d 826 (Minn.1977) (defective installation of home furnace).

Should strict liability principles apply to faulty repair? See Hoffman v. Simplot Aviation, Inc., 97 Idaho 32, 539 P.2d 584 (1975) (private plane: no); Winans v. Rockwell Internat'l Corp., 705 F.2d 1449 (5th Cir.1983) (jet plane: no); Barry v. Stevens Equipment Co., 176 Ga.App. 27, 335 S.E.2d 129 (1985) (repairer and refurbisher of alligator shearer machine: no). Contra, perhaps, if the repairer was the original seller or manufacturer and alters the product. Young v. Aro Corp., 36 Cal.App.3d 240, 111 Cal.Rptr. 535 (1973). Or if repairs create a deceptive appearance of safety. Anderson v. Glynn Const. Co., 421 N.W.2d 141 (Iowa 1988).

In this context, too, the question of whether strict liability in tort or warranty applies may also turn on whether the essential nature of the transaction is predominantly a sale, with the defendant's services provided only incidentally, or vice versa. See, e.g., Air Heaters, Inc. v. Johnson Elec., Inc., 258 N.W.2d 649 (N.D.1977).

LEWIS v. BIG POWDERHORN MOUNTAIN SKI CORP.

Court of Appeals of Michigan, 1976.
69 Mich.App. 437, 245 N.W.2d 81.

R.B. BURNS, JUDGE.

Plaintiff Theresa Lewis claims to have been injured while riding a rope-tow at defendant's ski facility. Plaintiffs' second amended complaint contained three counts reflecting alternative legal theories of liability. The trial judge granted defendant's motion to dismiss on all counts except negligent operation of the rope-tow, and the jury returned a verdict of no cause of action on that theory. This appeal focuses its challenge on the trial court's dismissal of plaintiffs' count for breach of implied warranties.

The parties agree that a sale of goods is not involved and, therefore, that Article 2 of the Uniform Commercial Code and the implied warranties contained therein do not apply. Instead, plaintiffs contend that "[a]part from statute, implied warranties may apply," Insurance Co. of North America v. Radiant Electric Co., 55 Mich.App. 410, 412, 222 N.W.2d 323, 324 (1974), and base their argument on a dicta pronouncement of this Court in Buckeye Union Fire Insurance Co. v. Detroit Edison Co., 38 Mich.App. 325, 196 N.W.2d 316 (1972).

Buckeye Union involved a "service," the sale of electricity, inseverably linked to a tangible (and defective) "product", electricity, sold by the kilowatt. Similarly, the two cases upon which *Buckeye Union* relied, Hoffman v. Misericordia Hospital of Philadelphia, 439 Pa. 501, 267 A.2d 867 (1970), and Newmark v. Gimbel's Inc., 54 N.J. 585, 258 A.2d 697 (1969), involved defective products which were administered to the respective plaintiffs as part of an alleged sale of a service. None of these cases constitute authority for the proposition that implied-at-law warranties arise from the sale of a service unattached to a product. *Buckeye Union* recognized that a product was involved in the service (38 Mich.App. p. 331, 196 N.W.2d p. 319):

"The record is lacking in any substantive proof that the fire in plaintiffs' house was caused by a defect in the manufacture or delivery of the electricity."

The only product in this case that could conceivably be divined by the exercise of ingenuity is "a weekend of skiing", presumably to necessarily include use of a rope tow. We cannot consider this to be a product within the plain and common meaning of the term.

In what way may sale of a pure service logically be distinct from sale of a good or product? The law of *products* liability provides the fiction of implied warranties to enable a "consumer [to] sue a manufacturer directly for economic loss resulting from a defect in a product attributable to the manufacturer *without proving negligence".* Cova v. Harley Davidson Motor Co., 26 Mich.App. 602, 609, 182 N.W.2d 800, 804 (1970). (Emphasis added.) What, however, *is* an implied warranty in a nonproduct situation? For one, it is clearly meaningless to consider a warranty of merchantability in this context. Neither, on the facts of this case, can it be a warranty of fitness for purpose: plaintiffs were unable to provide any evidence as to defectiveness or unfitness of the rope-tow apparatus.

Plaintiffs, rather, find a *defect in service* and contend the existence of "implied warranties as to safety in the operation of [the] rope tow". But as it is not (and cannot seriously be) contended that "strict liability" should lie for operation of the rope tow, any "implied warranty of safety" can be nothing other than an implied promise not to operate the rope tow in a negligent manner. And this question, negligent operation, is precisely that which the jury was properly allowed to determine.

"Products liability" has carved a wide and confusing swath across the law of tort and contract. Judge, now Justice, Levin has acutely recognized the complications spawned by the "misleading terminology of warranty" and the "amalgam of all those concepts". Cova v. Harley Davidson Motor Co., supra, 614–15, 182 N.W.2d 800. In Spence v. Three Rivers Builders & Masonry Supply, Inc., 353 Mich. 120, 131, 90 N.W.2d 873, 879 (1958), the Supreme Court concluded that products liability actions for breach of implied warranty are, in the last analysis, "bottomed on negligence". We can see nothing to be gained by further obscuring the procedures of pleading and proof by encouraging plaintiffs to couch the identical argument in alternative theoretical forms, one valid and one imaginative. The judgment is affirmed.

Costs to defendant.

T.M. BURNS, PRESIDING JUDGE (dissenting).

I cannot agree with the majority's interpretation of my opinion in Buckeye Union Fire Insurance Co. v. Detroit Edison Co., 38 Mich.App. 325, 196 N.W.2d 316 (1972).

For implied warranties to arise from the sale of a good there must be a "sale" of a "good". For implied warranties to arise from the provision of a service, there must be a providing of a service. The perceived requirement that the sale of a product must accompany the provision of a service before implied warranties will arise does not make sense to me.

The purchaser of services rightfully may expect that those services will be properly provided. If a homeowner contracts to have his house painted, he should legitimately expect that the painter will do a reasonably adequate job whether the painter provides the paint or not. The painter's "product", if there must be one, is the performance of his work. If a skier purchases a ticket to ride a tow rope, she legitimately expects that the tow will be operated in a reasonably safe manner. To require the injured skier to prove that the towing mechanism itself is defective is without reason. It is when the rendition of the service does not meet the legitimate expectations of the person being served that a proper cause of action arises.

The confusion caused by the very use of the term "implied warranty" arises once again. The term essentially connotes an action resting upon a contractual relation between the parties. Its use in describing an action more suitably designated "products liability" or "manufacturer's liability", while misdescriptive, relates ultimately to the same legal policy of holding liable one whose actions have done damage to another by failing to meet one's reasonable expectations. Whether the cause of action arises *ex contractu* or *ex delicto* or is implied in law or in fact, however, is irrelevant to its legitimacy. The object is to provide just compensation to the person suffering damage as the result of another's breach of a legal duty. That legal duty may arise from the defendant's wrongful affirmative act, negligence, occupation of land, sale of a good, manufacture of a product, or provision of a service.

The cause of action of breach of implied warranty in the provision of services is closely related to the same cause of action arising from the sale of goods. The action is contractual in foundation. It is indeed distinct from the negligence action. The liability of neither the seller of the defective goods nor the manufacturer of defective products depends upon a showing of negligence. The policy underlying the liability of the seller and manufacturer applies with equal logic to that of the provider of a service. I find no compelling distinction.

I would reverse.

NOTES

1. Do you agree with Judge Burns?

2. Compare Bolduc v. Herbert Schneider Corp., 117 N.H. 566, 374 A.2d 1187 (1977) (no implied warranty or strict tort liability for fall from ski lift tramway; moreover, statute prohibited holding ski lift operator as common carrier with specially high duty of care).

3. Should an amusement park be strictly liable to a patron for a pinched finger caught in the restraining bar of a ride cubicle? See Sergermeister v. Recreation Corp. of America, Inc., 314 So.2d 626 (Fla.App.1975). What if the ride collapses altogether? See Rekab, Inc. v. Frank Hrubetz & Co., 261 Md. 141, 274 A.2d 107 (1971). See also Siciliano v. Capitol City Shows, Inc., 124 N.H. 719, 475 A.2d 19 (1984). Should a department store be strictly liable to an infant who falls off a power-operated horse which is excessively fast and jerky? Cf. Savoia v. F.W. Woolworth Co., 88 N.J.Super. 153, 211 A.2d 214 (App.Div. 1965) (negligence).

The Consumer Product Safety Commission asserted jurisdiction over a dangerous amusement ride, the "Zipper," resulting in corrective action in 1978 in the form of installation of safety lap bars. See 2 Cons.Prod.Saf.Guide (CCH) ¶ 44,172.

4. **Electricity.** The courts have had substantial difficulty in deciding whether power companies should be subject to strict liability, in tort or warranty, for electrical accidents. Many courts now hold that electricity is a

"product" or "good" that can be "sold" to consumers, but that the sale does not occur until it reaches the consumer's house or place of business. Thus, electricity in powerlines is generally not considered to have entered the "stream of commerce." See generally Houston Lighting & Power Co. v. Reynolds, ___ S.W.2d ___ (Tex.1988); Otte v. Dayton Power & Light Co., 37 Ohio St.3d 33, 523 N.E.2d 835 (1988); Smith v. Home Light & Power Co., 734 P.2d 1051 (Colo.1987); Pierce v. Pacific Gas & Elec. Co., 166 Cal.App.3d 68, 212 Cal.Rptr. 283 (1985); Carbone v. Connecticut Light and Power Co., 40 Conn. Supp. 120, 482 A.2d 722 (1984); Annot., 60 A.L.R.4th 732 (1988). Contrast Otte v. Dayton Power & Light Co., 37 Ohio St.3d 33, 523 N.E.2d 835, 840 (1988) (electricity is a service, not a product—"electricity is not manufactured and * * * undergoes a substantial change in form before entering the home").

Compare Moody v. City of Galveston, 524 S.W.2d 583 (Tex.Civ.App.1975) (city strictly liable in tort for providing plaintiff "defective" water accompanied by flammable gas that ignited cigarette in plaintiff's house).

5. **Lending Transactions.** Courts have refused to apply strict liability principles to those who finance sales or leases of products, including lease-for-purchase transactions. See, e.g., Rivera v. Mahogony Corp., 145 Ill.App.3d 213, 98 Ill.Dec. 538, 494 N.E.2d 660 (1986) (lease-purchase of plastic molding machine); Agristor Leasing v. Meuli, 634 F.Supp. 1208, 1216 (D.Kan.1986) ("A distinction is drawn * * * between 'commercial' lessors and 'finance' lessors, with strict liability being imposed on the former but not the latter."); Wynn v. Kensington Mortgage and Finance Corp., 697 S.W.2d 47 (Tex.App.1985) (consumer lender financed purchase of mobile home); Annot., 28 A.L.R.4th 326 (1984).

Nor have the courts allowed negligence claims against lenders, provided that the lender does not involve itself with the product other than is necessary to protect its interests as a lender. See, e.g., Rice v. First Federal Sav. & Loan Ass'n of Lake County, 207 So.2d 22 (Fla.App.1968) (lender charged borrower 1% inspection and supervision fee; *held,* lender not liable to owner-borrower for failing to discover construction defects since inspections were to protect its own interests, not the owner's). But cf. Connor v. Great Western Sav. & Loan Ass'n, 69 Cal.2d 850, 73 Cal.Rptr. 369, 447 P.2d 609 (1968) (lender's extensive participation in real estate development project amounted to assumption of duty of care toward buyers of poorly constructed homes). *Connor* prompted the enactment the following year of Cal.Civ.Code § 3434 (West) which relieved lenders of liability for construction defects unless the lender acts "outside the scope of the activities of a lender of money."

Compare Wright v. Newman, 735 F.2d 1073 (8th Cir.1984), where a collision resulted from a defective towing ball on a repossessed truck that was towing a car. The car came off the towing ball and crashed head on into plaintiff's car. Ford Motor Credit Company had purchased the finance contract on the truck from the dealer and had hired a driver to return the truck to the dealer from the place of repossession. In an action against FMCC, *held,* (1) FMCC was not a distributor of the product and, hence, was not subject to strict tort liability; but that (2) FMCC was subject to liability as a supplier in negligence for failing to inspect the truck for defects so that it could inform the driver.

6. Should a bank which provides clerking and cashiering services at an auction be liable for injuries from a defective product purchased there? See Meyers v. Robb, 82 Mich.App. 549, 267 N.W.2d 450 (1978).

Should a bank that issues a MasterCard be liable to a person injured by a defective product purchased with one of its cards? See Comment, 21 U.C.L.A.L. Rev. 278 (1973).

7. **Reform.** The Idaho Products Liability Reform Act excludes from its definition of "product sellers":

> A provider of professional services who utilizes or sells products within the legally authorized scope of its professional practice. A nonprofessional provider of services is not included unless the sale or use of a product is the principal part of the transaction, and the essence of the relationship between the seller and purchaser is not the furnishing of judgment, skill, or services.

2 Prod.Liab.Rep. (CCH) ¶ 91,311. "Finance lessors" are also excluded. Id.

8. **Miscellaneous Transactions.** Should common carriers be strictly liable for injuries from "defective" transport by plane, train, bus, or subway? See Schmidt, Ince & Richbourg, Piercing the Aluminum Overcast: A Case for Strict Liability for Commercial Air Carriers, 9 Lincoln L.Rev. 37 (1974). Should there be strict liability for defective computer programming? See Smith, Suing the Provider of Computer Software: How Courts Are Applying U.C.C. Article Two, Strict Tort Liability, and Professional Malpractice, 24 Willamette L.Rev. 743 (1988); Comment, 53 J.Urb.L. 279 (1975). For providing a defective investigative report on a prospective employee? See Strong v. Retail Credit Co., 38 Colo.App. 125, 552 P.2d 1025 (1976). For a defective insurance policy? See Recent Cases, 9 Akron L.Rev. 584 (1976). For defective settlement decisions by the plaintiff's insurer? See Crisci v. Security Ins. Co., of New Haven, 66 Cal.2d 425, 58 Cal.Rptr. 13, 426 P.2d 173 (1967); Schwartz, Statutory Strict Liability For an Insurer's Failure to Settle: A Balanced Plan for an Unresolved Problem, [1975] Duke L.J. 901. For defective driving? See Hammontree v. Jenner, 20 Cal.App.3d 528, 97 Cal.Rptr. 739 (1971). For defective psychiatric treatment? See Furrow, Defective Mental Treatment: A Proposal For the Application of Strict Liability to Psychiatric Services, 58 B.U.L.Rev. 391 (1978).

9. Should lawyers be strictly liable for providing "defective" legal services? For making mistakes only of certain types? See generally Green, The Duty to Give Accurate Information, 12 U.C.L.A.L.Rev. 464 (1965).

10. Reconsider the various tests used by the courts in determining whether to extend strict liability to different types of service transactions, including whether the service involved the "sale" of a "product," whether the defendant participated in moving the product along the stream of commerce, whether the object was mass-produced, whether the characteristics of the transaction looked more like a sale or more like a service, and whether the services were professional or nonprofessional. Which tests are best? What policy choices do they reflect? Would the courts do better to focus instead on the variety of policy issues involved in each case? Would such an ad hoc approach be administratively practicable?

11. Consider Comment, 22 U.C.L.A.L.Rev. 401 (1974):

> The extension of enterprise liability to all services would have a sound basis in economic and justice considerations. Enterprise liability would achieve deterrence, compensation, reduced administrative costs and efficient allocation of resources. These achievements are made possible not by the deep pockets of the defendant performers, but rather by the strategic position of the performer in the commercial structure. Further, it is a good deal more equitable to let all users pay

> for the risk inherent in the activity they find useful, than to force a randomly selected victim to bear the cost alone. These reasons compel the extension of enterprise liability to consumer service transactions.

Id. at 450. Do you agree?

12. See Baldwin, Products Liability as It Applies to Service Transactions, 43 J.AirL. & Comm. 323 (1977); Crump & Maxwell, Should Health Service Providers be Strictly Liable for Product Related Injuries? A Legal and Economic Analysis, 36 Sw.L.J. 831 (1982); Greenfield, Consumer Protection in Service Transactions—Implied Warranties and Strict Liability in Tort, 1974 Utah L.Rev. 661; Mallor, Liability Without Fault for Professional Services: Toward a New Standard of Professional Accountability, 9 Seton Hall L.Rev. 474 (1978); Powers, Distinguishing Between Products and Services in Strict Liability, 62 N.Car.L.Rev. 415 (1984); Reynolds, Strict Liability for Commercial Service—Will Another Citadel Crumble?, 30 Okla.L.Rev. 298 (1977); Sales, The Services-Sales Transaction: A Citadel Under Assault, 10 St. Mary's L.J. 13 (1978); Vandall, Applying Strict Liability to Pharmacists, 18 Toledo L.Rev. 1 (1986); Note, 125 U.Pa.L.Rev. 365 (1976) (implied warranties).

SECTION 3. USED PRODUCTS

JORDAN v. SUNNYSLOPE APPLIANCE PROPANE & PLUMBING SUPPLIES COMPANY

Arizona Court of Appeals, 1983.
135 Ariz. 309, 660 P.2d 1236.

MEYERSON, JUDGE.

The sole issue on this appeal from summary judgment is whether the trial court correctly held that dealers in used products cannot be held strictly liable for harm resulting from defective goods which may be unreasonably dangerous. We hold that a dealer in used goods may be held strictly liable under the Restatement (Second) of Torts § 402A (1965) (hereinafter cited as § 402A) as adopted by our supreme court.

I. FACTS

In December, 1975, the father of plaintiff J.B. Jordan purchased a used propane storage tank from Canyon Gas and Appliance Co. (Canyon Gas), a dealer in new and used propane tanks. The tank had been manufactured by American Pipe and Steel Co. (American Pipe) in 1947. The tank was sold without guarantees or representations regarding its condition. Jordan's father inspected the tank before buying it, removed the tank from Canyon Gas's premises and had it installed at his rental property located adjacent to his son's home. The tank was filled regularly and used for a year and a half after its purchase without incident.

On August 17, 1977, the tank was serviced by Sunnyslope Appliance Propane and Plumbing Supplies Co. (Sunnyslope). While the tank was being filled with liquid propane, the hose used in filling the tank disconnected. The propane exploded, totally destroying the plaintiff's house next door.

Plaintiffs filed a complaint alleging strict liability in tort against American Pipe and Canyon Gas. Plaintiffs alleged that the shut-off valve in the tank malfunctioned by failing to close, thereby allowing the propane to escape from the tank when the hose disconnected. They alleged that the valve was defective in design, material, construction or workmanship. Plaintiffs also sued Sunnyslope for negligently filling the tank and allowing the propane to escape.

American Pipe sought summary judgment on the grounds that it had not manufactured the valve and because there was no evidence that the valve had been installed on the tank when it left the manufacturer. The trial court granted American Pipe's motion for summary judgment and dismissed American Pipe as a defendant. No appeal was taken from that judgment.

Sometime thereafter Canyon Gas moved for summary judgment, arguing that the doctrine of strict liability in tort did not extend to a seller of used goods. The trial court granted the motion and dismissed Canyon Gas from the case. Plaintiffs have appealed from the granting of Canyon Gas's motion for summary judgment.

II. CONTENTIONS OF THE PARTIES

The dispute between the parties centers on the scope and extent of protection we are to afford those injured by unreasonably dangerous and defective products. * * *

In arguing that strict liability should be imposed on dealers in used goods, plaintiffs urge that § 402A and the comments thereto can be read to show the drafters meant to include used goods or at least did not mean to exclude them from the section. Section 402A states that one who sells "any" product is liable, not one who sells "any new" product. Comment (f) specifies there is an exception for one who is an "occasional" seller, not engaged in the business of selling the particular kind of product. It does not state that an exception applies to those in the business of selling particular used goods.

Plaintiff urges that the requirement that the product be "unreasonably dangerous" allows the trier of fact to inquire into the age and condition of the product and the knowledge of the buyer, and serves to limit liability to those cases where injury was caused by a defect below the degree of safety which the ordinary purchaser of a used product could reasonably expect. Plaintiff points out that strict liability is a cost spreading device to shift the cost of injuries from the injured party to those responsible for placing the product on the market and who are more aware and better able to control the actual risks involved.

Plaintiff contends that the seller is able to adjust the cost of products he sells to include the cost of liability, insure against losses, and choose whether to place any particular product on the market at all. Plaintiff urges that a seller of used goods, just like a seller of new goods, is able to distribute the cost of doing business among his customers or shift liability to others in the chain of production.

In urging this court not to impose the doctrine of strict liability on used good dealers, Canyon Gas stresses the differences between dealers in used and new goods. It argues that the dealer in used products is not an integral part of the producing and marketing chain, having had no part in placing the product into the hands of consumers in the first instance. Because he has no continuing relationship with the manufacturer, Canyon Gas argues that a dealer in used products cannot exert pressure on the manufacturer nor adjust the cost of liability imposed upon him during the course of such relationship. Furthermore, according to Canyon Gas, the dealer in used goods cannot obtain indemnity because the product has changed hands since leaving the manufacturer. Finally, Canyon Gas argues that the cost of insurance would be prohibitive and trying to pass liability and insurance costs on to customers would drive used good dealers out of the market.

III. DECISIONS FROM OTHER JURISDICTIONS

Most of the arguments proffered by the parties have been discussed at length by those courts which have faced this issue to date. The question of whether or in what circumstances a dealer in used products should be held strictly liable for a defect attributable to the initial design or manufacturing of the used product has produced a split in authority. Annot., 53 A.L.R.3d 337 (1973).

In Hovenden v. Tenbush, 529 S.W.2d 302 (Tex.Ct.App.1975), a plaintiff sought to impose strict liability upon a dealer in used brick. Relying on its understanding of the language in § 402A and the policy behind it as set forth in the official comments, the court held that a seller of used products is not insulated from liability. * * *

The court concluded that because enterprise liability is the basis for the rule, dealers in used goods should be treated the same for strict liability purposes as dealers in new goods. According to the court, both obtain profit from selling the product and often are able to distribute the cost and shift liability. The court observed that "Sec. 402A imposed liability on sellers of used products where the evidence showed that the injury resulted from an inherent defect in the product, rather than from a condition brought about by normal use of the chattel." 529 S.W.2d at 309.

In Turner v. International Harvester Company, 133 N.J.Super. 277, 336 A.2d 62 (1975) a New Jersey court held that § 402A applied to dealers in used goods; the plaintiff was fatally injured when a truck collapsed on him. The court found enterprise liability to be the justification for the products liability doctrine and found that the same considerations for holding sellers of new goods strictly liable applied to dealers in used goods:

> An economic analysis of enterprise liability, which includes direct as well as indirect costs, would charge those in the business of selling a defective product with responsibility for all harms, physical and economic, which result from its use. To a considerable extent—with respect to *new* goods—the manufacturer bases the cost of his product on his expenses, which include damages caused by the product and insurance to cover those damages. This cost is spread among all the customers for that product; it reflects the justifiable expectations of customers regarding safety, quality and durability of new goods. Sellers of used goods may similarly distribute their costs of doing business which, in turn, will reflect what is considered by the public to be justifiable expectations regarding safety, quality and durability of used goods.

Id. at 288–89, 336 A.2d at 69 (citations omitted).

The *Turner* court rejected the notion that the public did not expect used products to be safe from manufacturing and design defects when purchasing a serviceable product as opposed to junk parts. The court observed that while buyers of used products could not expect the same quality and durability as would be found in a new product, their expectations of *safety* were not generally lessened simply because the product is used:

> [R]ealistic expectations of quality and durability will be lower for used goods, commensurate with their age, appearance and price. However, safety of the general public demands that when a used motor vehicle, for example, is sold for use *as a serviceable motor vehicle* (and not as junk parts), absent special circumstances, the seller be responsible for safety defects whether known or unknown at time of sale, present while the machine was under his control. Otherwise, the buyer and the general public are bearing the enterprise liability stemming from introduction of the dangerously defective used vehicle onto the public highways. Public policy demands that the buyer receive a used chattel safe for the purpose intended (where no substantial change will occur prior to reaching the buyer or foreseeable consumer).

Id. at 289, 336 A.2d at 69.

Finally, the *Turner* court observed that the requirement that the defect in the product be "unreasonably dangerous" permits the court or jury to inquire into the nature of the product, its age and condition, creating a standard against which the defect can be measured. The unreasonably dangerous standard also allows an inquiry into the particular relationship of the parties or the degree of sophistication of the purchaser which might show that the product did not present an unreasonable danger in the particular situation. As the court said:

> It is only when there is unreasonable danger * * * in the defective product that recovery can be founded on the rule of

> strict liability in tort, and this should be especially so when dealing with used goods. Only by this word 'unreasonable' is the court or jury permitted an inquiry into the nature of the product, its age and condition, and thus able to set a standard against which the defect can be measured.
>
> * * *
>
> Use of the 'unreasonably dangerous' standard, whether viewed from the general statement of the rule or the definition of a dangerous condition, permits a court to look both at the sophistication of the injured purchaser and the reasonable expectations of the seller to determine whether the strict liability rule should be applied.

Id. at 291–92, 336 A.2d at 70–71. As explained in Section IV, infra, we agree with the reasoning of the court in *Turner* and find strict liability equally applicable to damage caused to property as well as personal injury. See Rocky Mountain Fire and Casualty Co. v. Biddulph Oldsmobile, 131 Ariz. 289, 640 P.2d 851 (1982).

One of the first courts to conclude that sellers of used goods should not be strictly liable for defects created by the manufacturer was the Oregon court in Tillman v. Vance Equipment Co., 286 Or. 747, 596 P.2d 1299 (1979). The plaintiff sought to impose strict liability on the seller for injuries from a defect in a used crane. The court noted that "*if a jurisdiction has adopted the principle of strict liability on the basis of enterprise liability, the liability of the seller of either a new or used product would logically follow.*" Id. at 753, 596 P.2d at 1302 (emphasis added). The court noted, however, that it had never been willing to rely on enterprise liability alone as a justification for strict liability for defective products. Along with enterprise liability, the Oregon court identified three other justifications for the doctrine—implied representation of safety made by the seller to the consumer, risk reduction and compensation.

The court first considered whether an inference can be made that a dealer makes any representation with regard to safety when selling a used product. The court decided that a buyer of used goods does not expect the same quality as a buyer of new goods:

> Those markets, generally speaking, operate on the apparent understanding that the seller, even though he is in the business of selling such goods, makes no particular representation about their quality simply by offering them for sale. If a buyer wants some assurance of quality, he typically either bargains for it in the specific transaction or seeks out a dealer who routinely offers it. * * *

Id. at 755, 596 P.2d at 1303. The court then concluded that the sale of a used product, without more, does not generate the kind of expectations of safety which are created when the product is first put on the market. Id. at 755–56, 596 P.2d at 1304. In our view, this reasoning misses the mark because we have found no empirical evidence to warrant the conclusion that the purchaser of a used product from a commercial dealer engaged in the business of selling that product, necessarily expects the product to contain *unreasonably dangerous* defects. Furthermore, this contention ignores the plight of the innocent bystander, such as the plaintiffs herein, who may suffer loss or injury without ever having purchased the product themselves.

The Oregon court also noted that the risk-reduction aspect of strict liability would not be served where a used product was sold. The court observed that a dealer in used products is normally outside the original chain of distribution of the product. It saw no ready channel of communication by which the dealer and the manufacturer may exchange information about possible or actual dangerous defects with a view to eliminating the defects.

Admittedly, the relationship between a dealer in used products and the manufacturer is more attenuated than the relationship between the dealer in new products and the manufacturer. But we reject the view that the seller of used goods is outside the chain of distribution. He offers the goods for sale and profits therefrom. Thus, he is an integral part of the marketing system. At any rate, imposing strict liability on the commercial dealer of used products should result in increased maintenance and inspection of such products before they are offered for sale. See Escola v. Coca Cola Bottling Co., 24 Cal.2d 453, 462, 150 P.2d 436, 440–41 (1944).

In Tauber–Arons Auctioneers Co. v. Superior Court, 101 Cal.App.3d 268, 161 Cal.Rptr. 789 (1980) the plaintiff sought to impose strict liability on an auctioneer for a defective product sold in an auction. The court concluded that the connection between the auctioneer and the product sold in the auction was "random and accidental," and therefore the auctioneer should not be held strictly liable. The court went on to embrace the Oregon rule from *Tillman* limiting liability of secondhand dealers with respect to defects created by the original manufacturer. The California court approved the conclusion that the representation of safety in new products is greater than in used products. The court was also persuaded that because the dealer in used goods is usually outside the original marketing chain, he cannot play a role in risk reduction and cannot adjust the cost with the manufacturer as easily. The court agreed with Oregon's conclusion that strict liability should not be imposed on dealers in used goods absent some representation of quality beyond the sale itself or other special circumstances.

In La Rosa v. Superior Court, 122 Cal.App.3d 741, 176 Cal.Rptr. 224 (1981) the court reaffirmed the position it took in *Tauber–Arons*. *Importantly, the court indicated that it believed that if § 402A were wholly embraced in California, strict liability should be imposed on dealers in used goods.* The court went on to point out that California courts have not deemed themselves to be invariably bound by § 402A. It cited the decision in Cronin v. J.B.E. Olson Corp., 8 Cal.3d 121, 104 Cal.Rptr. 433,

501 P.2d 1153 (1972), in which the court rejected the "unreasonably dangerous" element of § 402A. The court considered various policy considerations similar to those discussed in *Tillman* and *Tauber–Arons* and concluded that strict liability should not be imposed on dealers in used goods.

IV. ARIZONA CASES

Arizona courts have touched on the question of whether strict liability is to be imposed on dealers in used goods in only one case. In Rix v. Reeves, 23 Ariz.App. 243, 532 P.2d 185 (1975) this court was asked to impose strict liability on an auto salvage yard operator from whom the plaintiff had obtained a used wheel which later caused injury. Although this court found no strict liability in that particular case, we do not find *Rix* controlling on whether Arizona should impose strict liability on dealers in used goods as a general rule. We limited the holding in *Rix* to the particular facts of that case. We found "no justification * * * for extending the strict liability in tort theory to the operator of an auto salvage yard where a tire rim of unknown age and use fails." Id. at 245, 532 P.2d at 187.[3] In *Rix* we observed that it would be a severe economic blow to force dealers in junk parts—parts which are often obviously worn and damaged—to inspect and repair the parts, warn against dangers, and insure against possible liability. We pointed out, though, that "[b]y used products we do not refer to products rebuilt by a manufacturer, nor do we mean to imply that there is never any liability when used products are sold."

Because the Arizona Supreme Court has embraced the rule of strict liability as expressed in § 402A, we conclude that a dealer engaged in the business of selling used goods of the type in question may be held strictly liable under the terms of the Restatement rule. We note that whereas California has held that a plaintiff need not prove that a defect in a product made the product unreasonably dangerous, thus making sellers absolute insurers against defects causing injury, our supreme court has rejected that position. Byrns v. Riddell, Inc., 113 Ariz. 264, 550 P.2d 1065 (1976). Because California courts have removed the unreasonably dangerous element in strict liability cases, they have a proper concern that dealers in used goods should not be made insurers of their products like dealers in new goods. We need not have this concern because the unreasonably dangerous standard is intact in Arizona. It is the plaintiff's burden in Arizona, in a strict liability case, to prove that the product is unreasonably dangerous; thus, the nature of the good—whether it is new or used—becomes relevant. As the *Turner* court found, the unreasonably dangerous standard which allows inquiry into matters such as age and condition of a used product, specific representations made, and sophistication of the buyer, provides sufficient protection to the dealer in used goods. Rix v. Reeves, 23 Ariz. App. at 245–46, 532 P.2d at 187–88; see Brady v. Melody Homes Mfg.,

3. In addition to salvage yard sales, strict liability should not extend to "random and accidental" sales such as garage sales or swap meets. § 402A comment (f).

121 Ariz. at 257, 589 P.2d at 900 (unreasonably dangerous means " 'dangerous to an extent beyond that which would be contemplated by the ordinary consumer who purchases it, with the ordinary knowledge common to the community as to its characteristics.' ") (quoting from § 402A comment (i)).

* * *

* * * There is no justification for finding that used good dealers as a class cannot shift losses, distribute costs, or insure against losses.

Canyon Gas cites one additional reason to withhold imposition of strict liability on sellers of used goods—that the dealer will not be able to obtain indemnity from the manufacturer if there has been a substantial change in the product since it left the manufacturer. This is true, however, whether the product is new or used. A.R.S. § 12–683(2). Admittedly, the longer the product is in the marketplace, the greater the likelihood that it will be altered or modified. We reject the notion that in all cases it will be impossible for the seller of used goods to seek indemnification from the manufacturer. Indeed, Arizona law authorizes a seller to seek indemnity from a manufacturer without any limitation on whether the product is new or used. A.R.S. §§ 12–681–86. In addition, no product liability action may be filed more than twelve years after the product was first sold. A.R.S. § 12–551.

Accordingly, we reverse the summary judgment in favor of Canyon Gas and return the matter to the trial court for the parties to litigate the factual questions which they may show to exist.

NOTES

1. Compare Peterson v. Lou Bachrodt Chevrolet Co., 61 Ill.2d 17, 329 N.E.2d 785 (1975). Two child pedestrians were killed when the brakes failed on a car purchased used three months before from the defendant car dealer. *Held,* strict tort action would not lie. Plaintiffs had not proved that the defect in the brakes had been caused either by the manufacturer or by the used car dealer. "If strict liability is imposed upon the facts alleged here, the used car dealer would in effect become an insurer against defects which had come into existence after the chain of distribution was completed, and while the product was under the control of one or more consumers." Justice Goldenhersh dissented: "[T]here is no basis for distinguishing a defect resulting from repairs made by a used car dealer and a defect which exists by reason of his failure to make a reasonable inspection, and * * * both should be the basis for imposing strict liability." Id. at 788.

2. Reconsider the policies underlying strict liability in tort, summarized above at p. 181. Do they argue for applying strict tort to the sale of used goods? See Tillman v. Vance Equipment Co., 286 Or. 747, 596 P.2d 1299 (1979), concluding that strict tort policies fail to support liability for sellers of used goods. Compare the following:

> Clearly, * * * the implied representation-consumer expectations rationale [should be a focal point. A] consumer's expectations of safety are generally much lower for used products than for new ones. Moreover, since a principal reason for purchasing a product used rather than new is to save money, it is doubtful that such buyers would want

to pay a surcharge for a forced purchase of accident insurance, especially not for accidents resulting from obvious design hazards. Yet if the issue were framed in terms of a used car dealer's responsibility to test or inspect the brake shoes or the steering linkage, it is not so clear just what a typical consumer's safety expectations might be. * * *

The * * * risk reduction [rationale deserves consideration, too.] Dealers in used goods do not, in fact, have much ability to apply economic sanctions to manufacturers and thereby induce a higher level of design safety. Compared to consumers, however, they often are far better able to control the risk. It may thus make good economic sense to apply an efficiency-inducing legal doctrine to such cases. In the used car situation described above, for example, it may be a sound economic decision to encourage used car dealers to perform routine safety tests on those parts of the brakes and steering systems that are subject to wear and that may not have received proper maintenance.

Owen, Rethinking the Policies of Strict Products Liability, 33 Vand.L.Rev. 681, 698 (1980).

3. Probably most courts have refused to apply strict liability in tort to used goods transactions. E.g., Grimes v. Axtell Ford Lincoln–Mercury, 403 N.W.2d 781 (Iowa 1987); Keith v. Russell T. Bundy & Associates, Inc., 495 So.2d 1223 (Fla.App.1986). The result may well be contra, however, if the seller also overhauls or rebuilds the product. See, e.g., Crandell v. Larkin & Jones Appliance Co., Inc., 334 N.W.2d 31 (S.D.1983) (dealer, who reconditioned and guaranteed used clothes dryer which caught fire, liable in strict tort, express warranty, and implied warranty of merchantability).

4. **Negligence.** The seller of a used product may be liable in negligence, Gaidry Motors v. Brannon, 268 S.W.2d 627 (Ky.1953) (used car dealer has duty to make reasonable inspection). But cf. Harison–Gulley Chevrolet, Inc. v. Carr, 134 Ga.App. 449, 214 S.E.2d 712 (1975) (dealer has no duty to inspect used car for latent defects before resale if vehicle has valid inspection sticker).

5. **Warranty.** Early courts held that the sale of a used product did not carry an implied warranty. See Bayer v. Winton Motor Car Co., 194 Mich. 222, 160 N.W. 642 (1916). Today, however, an implied warranty of merchantability will attach in certain situations. See U.C.C. § 2–314, comment 3: "A contract for the sale of second-hand goods, however, involves only such obligation as is appropriate to such goods * * *"; Roupp v. Acor, 253 Pa.Super. 46, 384 A.2d 968 (1978) (both implied warranties accompanied sale of used truck). But see Valley Datsun v. Martinez, 578 S.W.2d 485 (Tex.Civ.App.1979), where the court held that there is no implied warranty of merchantability where the purchaser knows the goods are used. See generally Note, 13 Tulsa L.J. 627 (1978). On used car sales, see Annots., 22 A.L.R.3d 1387 (1968) (implied warranties); 36 A.L.R.3d 125 (1971) (express warranties).

6. See Notes, 19 Cal.W.L.Rev. 330 (1983); 20 San Diego L.Rev. 399 (1983) (used cars); 33 Stan.L.Rev. 535 (1981); 52 S.Cal.L.Rev. 805 (1979); Annot., 53 A.L.R.3d 337 (1973).

SECTION 4. REAL ESTATE

BECKER v. IRM CORPORATION

Supreme Court of California, 1985.
38 Cal.3d 454, 213 Cal.Rptr. 213, 698 P.2d 116.

BROUSSARD, JUSTICE.

In this personal injury action plaintiff's complaint asserted causes of action of strict liability and negligence against defendant landlord. Defendant moved for summary judgment urging that a landlord is not liable to a tenant for a latent defect of the rented premises absent concealment of a known danger or an expressed contractual or statutory duty to repair. The trial court granted the motion and denied a motion for reconsideration. Plaintiff appeals.

We have concluded that the trial court erred as to both causes of action.

The complaint alleged that plaintiff was injured when he slipped and fell against the frosted glass shower door in the apartment he leased from defendant. The door was made of untempered glass. It broke and severely lacerated his arm. It is undisputed that the risk of serious injury would have been substantially reduced if the shower door had been made of tempered glass rather than untempered glass.

Defendant's affidavits in support of the motion for summary judgment may be summarized as follows: Plaintiff's apartment is part of a 36–unit apartment complex built in 1962 and 1963 and acquired by defendant in 1974. Prior to the acquisition, two officers of defendant walked through most of the apartments and observed that all of the shower doors were of frosted glass and appeared to be the same. The officials, one of whom managed the property from the time of its acquisition, stated that prior to plaintiff's accident in 1978 there were no accidents involving the shower doors and that they were not advised that any of the shower doors were made of untempered glass. They first learned that some of the shower doors were of untempered glass after the accident. Their inspection of shower doors after the accident provided "no visible difference between the tempered and untempered glass in terms of visible appearance."

Defendant's maintenance man stated that after the accident he examined the glass doors, and that 31 of the doors with untempered glass were replaced by him. He also stated that in looking for the untempered glass shower doors "there was no way that a layperson could tell any difference by simply looking at the shower doors. The only way that I was able to differentiate * * * was by looking for a very small mark in the corner of each piece of glass."

* * *

STRICT LIABILITY

[The court reviewed the development of strict tort liability in California.]

We follow a stream of commerce approach to strict liability in tort and extend liability to all those who are part of the "overall producing and marketing enterprise that should bear the cost of injuries from defective products." (Vandermark v. Ford Motor Co. (1964) 61 Cal.2d 256, 262 et seq.) The doctrine of strict liability in tort has been applied not only to manufacturers but to the various links in the commercial marketing chain including a retailer (id.), a wholesale-retail distributor (Barth v. B.F. Goodrich Tire Co. (1968) 265 Cal.App.2d 228, 251 et seq.), personal property lessors and bailors (Price v. Shell Oil Co. (1970) 2 Cal. 3d 245, 251–253), and a licensor of personalty (Garcia v. Halsett (1970) 3 Cal.App.3d 319, 324–326). In holding that strict liability in tort was applicable to lessors and bailors in Price v. Shell Oil Co., supra, 2 Cal.3d at page 254, it was pointed out that strict liability does not apply to isolated transactions such as the sale of a single lot.

Application of warranty doctrine has not been limited to those engaged in commerce in personalty but has been applied where appropriate to those engaged in the real estate business. Traditionally, the courts applied the doctrine of caveat emptor with the buyer assuming the risk on quality unless there was express warranty, fraud or misrepresentation. (E.g., Gustafson v. Dunman, Inc. (1962) 204 Cal.App.2d 10, 13.)

However, the courts have recognized that a contract to build is in effect one of material and labor, that implied warranties are not limited to sales transactions, and that building contracts give rise to a warranty of merchantability and suitability for ordinary use. (Aced v. Hobbs–Sesack Plumbing Co. (1961) 55 Cal.2d 573, 580–583; Pollard v. Saxe & Yolles Dev. Co. (1974) 12 Cal.3d 374, 378; Green v. Superior Court (1974) 10 Cal.3d 616, 626.) And in Pollard v. Saxe & Yolles Dev. Co., supra, 12 Cal.3d 374, 377–380, it was held that an implied warranty of quality attaches to the sale of new construction. The court pointed out that the doctrine of implied warranty in a sales contract is based on the actual and presumed knowledge of the seller, reliance on the seller's skill and judgment, and the ordinary expectations of the parties. The court reasoned that "the builder or seller of new construction—not unlike the manufacturer or merchandiser of personalty—makes implied representations, ordinarily indispensable to the sale, that the builder has used reasonable skill and judgment in constructing the building. On the other hand, the purchaser does not usually possess the knowledge of the builder and is unable to fully examine a completed house and its components without disturbing the finished product." (12 Cal.3d at p. 379.) The court concluded that "builders and sellers of new construction should be held to what is impliedly represented—that the completed structure was designed and constructed in a reasonably workmanlike manner." (Id. at p. 380.)

Similarly, application of strict liability in tort has not been limited to those engaged in commerce in personalty but has been applied where appropriate to those engaged in real estate businesses who impliedly represent the quality of their product. In Kriegler v. Eichler Homes, Inc. (1969) 269 Cal.App.2d 224, a builder who mass-produced homes was held strictly liable when the heating system placed in a home failed. The court relied upon Schipper v. Levitt & Sons, Inc. (N.J.1965) 207 A.2d 314, 325–326, where the court pointed out that when in our modern society a person purchases a tract house from an advertised model, he relies upon the skill of the developer and the implied representation that the house will be erected in a reasonably workmanlike manner and reasonably fit for habitation, that the purchaser ordinarily does not have the means to protect himself either by hiring experts to supervise and inspect or by provision in the deed, and that the public interest dictates that the cost of injury from defects should be borne by the developer who created the danger and who is in a better economic position to bear the loss rather than the injured party who relied on the developer's skill and implied representation. In Avner v. Longridge Estates (1969) 272 Cal.App.2d 607, 615, it was held that a manufacturer of a residential lot may be held strictly liable in tort for damages suffered by the owner as the result of defect in the manufacturing process causing subsidence.

A similar development appears with respect to the landlord-tenant relationship. The earlier legal concepts regarded the lease as an equivalent to a sale of the premises for the term and under traditional common law rules the landlord owed no duty to place leased premises in a habitable condition and no obligation to repair absent an agreement. (Green v. Superior Court (1974) 10 Cal.3d 616, 622; McNally v. Ward (1961) 192 Cal.App.2d 871, 878.) "The common law placed the risk on the tenant as to whether the condition of the leased property made it unsuitable for the use contemplated by the parties. In recent years, the definite judicial trend has been in the direction of increasing the responsibility of the landlord, in the absence of a valid contrary agreement, to provide the tenant with property in a condition suitable for the use contemplated by the parties. This judicial trend has been supported by the statutes that deal with this problem. This judicial and statutory trend reflects a view that no one should be allowed or forced to live in unsafe and unhealthy housing." (Rest.2d Property, Landlord and Tenant, ch. 5, introductory note, p. 150.)

The Restatement draws a distinction as to defective conditions in leased dwellings existing at the time of the lease and those arising thereafter. In the former situation the tenant may recover damages in the absence of lessor fault while in the latter damages are recoverable only if the landlord is at fault. (Compare id., § 5.1, subd. (2)(a), pp. 168–169 with §§ 5.2, subd. (2)(a), p. 184, and 5.4, subd. (2)(a), pp. 194–195.)

Departures from the traditional common law rule applicable to landlords evolved in California both by statute and judicial decision. * * *

Pointing out that the traditional common law rule that the landlord had no duty to make the dwelling habitable arose in the agrarianism of the Middle Ages and is incompatible with contemporary social conditions and modern legal values, California courts have recognized that a lease for a dwelling contains an implied warranty of habitability. (Hinson v. Delis (1972) 26 Cal.App.3d 62, 68–71; Green v. Superior Court (1974) 10 Cal.3d 616, 622 et seq.; Knight v. Hallsthammar (1981) 29 Cal.3d 46, 51–53.) In *Green,* the court reasoned that the typical city dweller leasing an apartment cannot realistically be viewed as merely acquiring an interest in land but rather contracts for a place to live, that modern apartment buildings are complex, difficult and expensive to repair and adequate inspection by tenants is a virtual impossibility, that repairs will often be outside the reach of abilities or finances of tenants, that the scarcity of adequate low-cost housing has left tenants with little bargaining power and rendered the common law remedies inadequate, and that the widespread enactment of comprehensive housing codes show that public policy compels landlords to bear "the primary responsibility for maintaining safe, clean and habitable housing in our state." (10 Cal.3d at pp. 623–628.)

Green analogized to the parallel dramatic changes in the law of commercial transactions where modern decisions have recognized that the consumer in an industrial society should be entitled to rely on the skill of the supplier to assure that goods and services are of adequate quality and, discarding the caveat emptor approach, have implied a warranty of merchantability and fitness. Pointing out that the modern urban tenant is in the same position as any normal consumer of goods, it was concluded that a tenant may reasonably expect that the product purchased is fit as a living unit and that since the lease specifies a term the tenant may reasonably expect that the premises will be fit for habitation for the term. (10 Cal.3d at p. 627.)

Green held that breach of the implied warranty of habitability may be urged as a defense in an unlawful detainer proceeding and that in such cases the court could determine that the breach warranted a partial or total reduction in rent. (10 Cal.3d at p. 631 et seq.) Neither *Green* nor our subsequent decision in Knight v. Hallsthammar, supra, 29 Cal.3d 46, discussed whether or to what extent breach of the implied warranty of habitability might provide a basis for recovery of tort damages for injuries caused by the breach.

Developments in the law of landlord liability for injuries due to defective condition of the demised premises have not lagged far behind. The traditional common law rule was that a landlord is not liable to the tenant for injuries due to a defective condition or faulty construction of the demised premises in the absence of fraud, concealment or covenant in the lease. (E.g., Del Pino v. Gualtieri (1968) 265 Cal.App.2d 912,

919–920; Forrester v. Hoover Hotel & Inv. Co. (1948) 87 Cal.App.2d 226, 232.) The rule was not only based on traditional property concepts and caveat emptor but also on the landlord's lack of possession and control. (E.g., Brennan v. Cockrell Investments, Inc. (1973) 35 Cal.App.3d 796, 799–801.) A number of exceptions have developed to the rule of landlord nonliability—where the landlord voluntarily undertakes to repair, where the landlord had knowledge of defects, where a safety law was violated, where the landlord retained a part of the premises for common use, and where the lease was for a semi-public purpose. (3 Witkin, Summary of Cal.Law (8th ed. 1973) pp. 2135–2136.)

Strict liability for the conditions of the demised premises has been applied to landlords. Prior to *Greenman*, it was held that where a landlord represented that a wall-bed was safe, secure and in fit condition at the time of the letting, the plaintiff could maintain an action based on the express warranty. (Shattuck v. St. Francis Hotel & Apts. (1936) 7 Cal.2d 358, 360–361.) Also, prior to *Greenman*, it was held that a lessee could recover for breach of an implied warranty of fitness for use when a door to which a folding bed was attached fell and injured him. (Fisher v. Pennington (1931) 116 Cal.App. 248, 249–251.) *Fisher* was followed in Charleville v. Metropolitan Trust Co. (1934) 136 Cal.App. 349, 355 which also involved a folding bed and Hunter v. Freeman (1951) 105 Cal.App.2d 129, 131 et seq., involving an explosion of a detachable heater. In all four cases, the accident occurred shortly after the tenant went into possession, and it was also held that the warranty liability was limited to "the condition of the premises at the beginning of the term and not to conditions which, unknown to the lessor, subsequently arise." (Forrester v. Hoover Hotel & Inv. Co. (1948) 87 Cal.App.2d 226, 232, 196 P.2d 825). Each of the above cases involved a furnished apartment and the accident was arguably attributable to the furnishings as well as the condition of the demised premises.

Subsequent to *Greenman*, strict liability in tort was applied to landlords for injuries to tenants in Fakhoury v. Magner (1972) 25 Cal. App.3d 58, 62–63 and Golden v. Conway (1976) 55 Cal.App.3d 948, 960–963. In *Fakhoury*, a couch in a furnished apartment collapsed, and the court held that the landlord is strictly liable in tort for defective furniture, pointing out that the liability was not for defective premises. (25 Cal.App.3d at p. 63.) In *Golden*, the landlord employed a contractor to install a heater, and because of defective manufacture of installation there was a fire. Although acknowledging the distinction made in *Fakhoury* between defective fixtures and defective furniture, the court rejected it and held that the landlord engaged in the business of leasing property is strictly liable in tort when he equips the premises with an appliance which proves to have defects causing injury. (55 Cal.App.3d at pp. 960–963.) Defendant points out that *Fakhoury* differs from the instant case because injury resulted from defective personalty rather than the condition of the premises and that *Golden* differs because the landlord installed the heater whereas the shower door was apparently installed by the builder.

We are satisfied that the rationale of the foregoing cases, establishing the duties of a landlord and the doctrine of strict liability in tort, requires us to conclude that a landlord engaged in the business of leasing dwellings is strictly liable in tort for injuries resulting from a latent defect in the premises when the defect existed at the time the premises were let to the tenant. It is clear that landlords are part of the "overall producing and marketing enterprise" that makes housing accommodations available to renters. (Cf. Vandemark v. Ford Motor Co., supra, 61 Cal.2d at p. 262; Green v. Superior Court, supra, 10 Cal. 3d at pp. 623, 627.) A landlord, like defendant owning numerous units, is not engaged in isolated acts within the enterprise but plays a substantial role. The fact that the enterprise is one involving real estate may not immunize the landlord. Our courts have long recognized that contracts relating to realty may give rise to implied warranties. (Aced v. Hobbs–Sesack Plumbing Co., supra, 55 Cal.2d 573, 580–583.)

Absent disclosure of defects, the landlord in renting the premises makes an implied representation that the premises are fit for use as a dwelling and the representation is ordinarily indispensible to the lease. (Pollard v. Saxe & Yolles Dev. Co., supra, 12 Cal.3d 374, 377–380.) The tenant purchasing housing for a limited period is in no position to inspect for latent defects in the increasingly complex modern apartment buildings or to bear the expense of repair whereas the landlord is in a much better position to inspect for and repair latent defects. (Green v. Superior Court, supra, 10 Cal.3d at p. 626.) The tenant's ability to inspect is ordinarily substantially less than that of a purchaser of the property. (Cf. Pollard v. Saxe & Yolles Dev. Co., *supra,* 12 Cal. 3d at p. 379.)

The tenant renting the dwelling is compelled to rely upon the implied assurance of safety made by the landlord. It is also apparent that the landlord by adjustment of price at the time he acquires the property, by rentals or by insurance is in a better position to bear the costs of injuries due to defects in the premises than the tenants.

In these circumstances, strict liability in tort for latent defects existing at the time of renting must be applied to insure that the landlord who markets the product bears the costs of injuries resulting from the defects "rather than the injured persons who are powerless to protect themselves." (Greenman v. Yuba Power Products, Inc., supra, 59 Cal.2d at p. 63.)

Defendant argues that a landlord who purchases an existing building which is not new should be exempt from strict liability in tort for latent defects because, like dealers in used personalty, he assertedly is not part of the manufacturing and marketing enterprise. Defendant relies on a statement in Vandermark v. Ford Motor Co., supra, 61 Cal. 2d 256, 262–263: "Strict liability on the manufacturer and retailer alike affords maximum protection to the injured plaintiff and works no injustice to defendants, for they can adjust the costs of such protection between them in the course of their continuing business relationship." Defendant states that it has never been in a business relationship with the builder and that purchasers of used rental properties do not have a continuing business relationship with builders permitting adjustments of the costs of protecting tenants.

In several cases, it has been held that a seller of used machinery who does not rebuild or rehabilitate the machinery is not strictly liable in tort. (Wilkinson v. Hicks (1981) 126 Cal.App.3d 515, 520 et seq.; LaRosa v. Superior Court (1981) 122 Cal.App.3d 741, 748 et seq.; Tauber–Arons Auctioneers Co., Inc. v. Superior Court (1980) 101 Cal. App.3d 268, 273 et seq.) Each of these cases relied at least in part on the theory that the used machinery dealer simply by offering machinery for sale does not make any representation as to quality or durability and thus does not generate the expectation of safety involved in the sale of new goods. (*Wilkinson, supra,* 126 Cal.App.3d at pp. 520–521; *LaRosa, supra,* 122 Cal.App.3d at pp. 760–761; *Tauber–Arons,* supra, 101 Cal.App.3d at p. 278 et seq.) When the seller of the used goods makes extensive modifications or reconditions, he is treated as a manufacturer—there is an expectation that the safety of the product has been addressed. (Green v. City of Los Angeles (1974) 40 Cal.App.3d 819, 838.)

LaRosa v. Superior Court, supra, 122 Cal.App.3d 741, 756–757 and Tauber–Arons Auctioneers Co., Inc. v. Superior Court, supra, 101 Cal. App.3d 268, 282, also suggested that the used machinery dealer ordinarily is not part of the manufacturing and marketing enterprise.

However, a continuing business relationship is not essential to imposition of strict liability. The unavailability of the manufacturer is not a factor militating against liability of others engaged in the enterprise. The paramount policy of the strict products liability rule remains the spreading throughout society of the cost of compensating otherwise defenseless victims of manufacturing defects. [Citations] If anything, the unavailability of the manufacturer is a factor militating in favor of liability of persons engaged in the enterprise who can spread the cost of compensation. * * *

Landlords are an integral part of the enterprise of producing and marketing rental housing. While used machinery is often scrapped or discarded so that resale for use may be the exception rather than the rule, landlords are essential to the rental business. They have more than a random or accidental role in the marketing enterprise. In addition, landlords have a continuing relationship to the property following the renting in contrast to the used machinery dealer who sells. As we have seen, in renting property the landlord, unlike the used machinery dealer, makes representations of habitability and safety.

The cost of protecting tenants is an appropriate cost of the enterprise. Within our marketplace economy, the cost of purchasing rental housing is obviously based on the anticipated risks and rewards of the purchase, and thus it may be expected that along with numerous other factors the price of used rental housing will depend in part on the quality of the building and reflect the anticipated costs of protecting tenants, including repairs, replacement of defects and insurance. Further, the landlord after purchase may be able to adjust rents to reflect such costs. The landlord will also often be able to seek equitable indemnity for losses.

We conclude that the absence of a continuing business relationship between builder and landlord does not preclude application of strict liability in tort for latent defects existing at the time of the lease because landlords are an integral part of the enterprise and they should bear the cost of injuries resulting from such defects rather than the injured persons who are powerless to protect themselves. (Greenman v. Yuba Power Products, Inc., supra, 59 Cal.2d 57, 63.)

NEGLIGENCE

[The court proceeded to plaintiff's cause of action asserting the landlord was negligent in its role as owner of the property.]

Accordingly, a landlord in caring for his property must act toward his tenant as a reasonable person under all of the circumstances, including the likelihood of injury, the probable seriousness of injury, the burden of reducing or avoiding the risk, and his degree of control over the risk-creating defect. [Citations.]

* * *

A person contemplating purchase of rental property, in the exercise of due care, will examine its condition. Maintenance of rental property in a safe and habitable condition is the primary responsibility of the landlord. (Green v. Superior Court, supra, 10 Cal.3d 616, 627, 111 Cal.Rptr. 704, 517 P.2d 1168.) In the exercise of ordinary care, the purchaser of rental property may be expected to inspect the premises not only to determine whether they are aesthetically pleasing but also to determine whether they meet bare living standards, including whether they are safe. The prospective purchaser may be expected to make such inspection in the absence of knowledge of any existing defects or of any prior accidents. Similarly, a landlord at time of letting may be expected to inspect an apartment to determine whether it is safe.

* * *

The duty to inspect should charge the defendant only with those matters which would have been disclosed by a reasonable inspection. In the instant case, the undisputed affidavits are to the effect that there was "no visible difference between the tempered and untempered glass in terms of visible appearance," but that there was a "very small mark" in the corner of each piece of glass which apparently showed that the glass was untempered. The glass was not before the trial court when it granted the motion for summary judgment, and the record does not disclose the nature of the "mark." If the "mark" was "untempered" a trier of fact could properly conclude that a reasonable inspection would have, at least, included a visual inspection which disclosed the danger. In resolving doubts in favor of the party opposing the motion for summary judgment (Rowland v. Christian, supra, 69 Cal.2d 108, 111), defendant's failure to fully identify the "mark" requires us to assume that it would have disclosed the danger to a reasonable inspection.

As to each cause of action the trial court erred in granting summary judgment in favor of defendant.

The judgment is reversed.

KAUS, REYNOSO and GRODIN, JJ., concur.

BIRD, CHIEF JUSTICE, concurring.

* * *

It is vigorously argued as a reason for exclusion of respondent from liability as a matter of law, that it was not the owner of the building when the allegedly defective product was installed. Once IRM became the landlord, however, it acted in effect as distributor or supplier of housing, with authority and ability to monitor all products so furnished, including appliances and fixtures in the apartments. And by failing to remove shower doors made of untempered glass, respondent maintained the distribution of these appliances to its tenants.

* * *

LUCAS, JUSTICE, concurring and dissenting.

I concur in that portion of the majority opinion which holds that a landlord may be held liable for dangerous conditions of which he knew or should have known. However, I cannot join in imposing upon landlords strict liability for latent defects in any component of their property no matter who built or installed the defective item.

Taking an unprecedented leap, the majority imposes "an unusual and unjust burden on property owners * * *. [T]he landlord [will] be faced with liability for every injury claim resulting from any untoward condition in every cranny of the building, whether it is reasonably foreseeable or not." (Dwyer v. Skyline Apartments, Inc. (N.J.App.1973) 123 N.J.Super. 48, 301 A.2d 463, 467, affd. obiter dictum, 63 N.J. 577, 311 A.2d 1.) Any landlord, even one renting the family home for a year, will now be insurer for defects in any wire, screw, latch, cabinet door, pipe or other article on and in his premises at the time they are let despite the fact that he neither installed the item nor had any knowledge or reason to know of the defect. I believe, in conformance with the almost unanimous judgment of other jurisdictions considering this issue, that such imposition of liability is inappropriate. * * *

* * *

Discounting other crucial and long-recognized justifications for imposition of strict liability, my colleagues focus primarily on the "risk-spreading" function of this form of liability. Essentially they ignore the fact that landlords of used property have no special position with regard to original manufacturers and sellers and thus have no influence to wield in order to improve product safety. Moreover, contrary to the majority's implication, the landlord, while impliedly representing that the premises are habitable, is not representing to tenants that he has expertise and guarantees the perfection of every item forming the premises. Instead of considering what role landlords of used property realistically play with regard to that property, the majority concentrates narrowly on the advancement of "The paramount policy of the strict products liability rules [namely] the spreading throughout society of the cost of compensating otherwise defenseless victims of manufacturing defects." (Ante, p. 220 of 213 Cal.Rptr., at p. 123 of 698 P.2d.) * * *

* * *

Unlike retailers, lessors, bailors, wholesalers or others in the original chain of distribution of the product, the landlord owning used property cannot adjust the costs of protection up the chain. He may only do it, at best, *down* the chain of "distribution," namely by charging more to his tenants. Unlike the others mentioned above, such a "merchant" has no opportunity to enter into indemnification agreements with those more closely linked with the making of the product—he will have little idea if any when he buys the property as to the origin of items such as the wiring found in the walls, and without doubt even if he has such knowledge will have no bargaining power to enter into any agreements with such suppliers. Moreover, his responsibility extends to a myriad of products, unlike the situation faced by a retailer of a particular line of goods. Landlords henceforth are in a risky business. No matter how carefully they inspect, and no matter how impossible to discern the defect, they are now the last outpost of liability for countless unrelated products in which they have no particular expertise.[4]

* * *

I would hold that a subsequent purchaser of property who has not installed, altered or created the item or condition which is claimed to be defective, and who has no actual or constructive knowledge of any defect therein, should not be held strictly liable. If the landlord knows or should know of the defect, then he has a duty to take appropriate action to correct or warn of the problem. However, where the landlord has no continuing relationship with the chain of marketing leading back to the manufacturer of the defective product, and thus has no way of influencing the production or design of the product or of adjusting

4. One court summed up the difference between extending strict liability to lessors of commercial products and to motel owners in a manner which has general application in our context as well: "A major consideration in holding lessors of commercial products strictly liable was that such lessors possessed expert knowledge of the characteristics of the equipment or machines they leased. [Citations.] Another consideration is that such lessors, like retailers, deal continually with their suppliers, giving them an enduring relationship which permits them to seek contribution and indemnification. These considerations do not apply when a motel operator makes a one-time purchase of furnishings and fixtures about which he has no special expertise. Therefore, we hold that a motel operator is not strictly liable for defects in the fixtures and furnishings of the rooms he held out to the public." (Livingston v. Begay (1982) 98 N.M. 712, 652 P.2d 734, 738–739.)

potential costs of the *manufacturer's* enterprise or others in the business of marketing the item at issue, imposition of strict liability is inappropriate. The only rationales supporting such responsibility are ease of proof for the injured party and "distributing" the risk of damages to the landlord. The costs of such an extension of liability to those *without* expertise or continuing relationships for the multiple products and parts for which they may now bear responsibility will entail a significant shift in how our tort system has heretofore operated. It amounts, in effect, to insurance for tenants, because it does nothing to aid in the goals of deterrence or product safety.

I would affirm the trial court's decision to the extent that it granted summary judgment to defendant on the cause of action sounding in strict liability, while joining in the majority's reversal as to the negligence cause of action.

MOSK, J., concurs.

NOTES

1. The year after *Becker* was decided, three out of the four justices who concurred in the majority opinion were voted out of office, and the fourth (Kaus, J.) retired. The two dissenting justices have remained on the court, and Lucas is now Chief Justice.

2. Contra, Armstrong v. Cione, ___ Hawaii ___, 738 P.2d 79 (1987) (on identical facts, relying in part on Lucas dissent).

3. **Negligence and Warranty.** The rule of caveat emptor, or more precisely "caveat lessee," dominated for centuries the law of real estate leases as it did the law of real estate sales. Because of the dominant position of the landowner in medieval society, the landlord was cloaked at an early date in a mantle of immunity from liability for injuries caused by defective conditions in the leased premises. As time progressed, however, various exceptions grew up around the general rule of nonliability, so that landlords became subject to liability in negligence for (1) hidden dangers known to the lessor but not to the lessee, (2) injuries to persons off the premises, (3) defects in premises leased for admission of the public, (4) defects in "common areas" retained under the landlord's control, (5) failure to keep the premises in good repair when the landlord had covenanted so to do, (6) negligence in making repairs, and (7) defects constituting violations of building or housing code provisions. Then, in 1973, the New Hampshire Supreme Court turned the general rule of nonliability on its head and held that landlords would be subject to the general principles of negligence liability. Sargent v. Ross, 113 N.H. 388, 308 A.2d 528 (1973) (Kenison, C.J.).

On the warranty side of the matter, while a warranty of habitability had been implied into short-term leases of furnished dwellings by a few courts for some time, courts began to find a general implied warranty of habitability in leases of residential premises in the 1960s and early 1970s. E.g., Pines v. Perssion, 14 Wis.2d 590, 111 N.W.2d 409 (1961); Lemle v. Breeden, 51 Hawaii 426, 462 P.2d 470 (1969); Javins v. First Nat. Realty Corp., 138 U.S.App.D.C. 369, 428 F.2d 1071, cert. denied 400 U.S. 925, 91 S.Ct. 186, 27 L.Ed.2d 185 (1970). While most of the cases are essentially contractual disputes surrounding the nonpayment of rent, at least one was a more typical products liability suit involving personal injuries. Old Town Development Co. v. Langford, 349 N.E.2d 744 (Ind.App.1976), set aside without opinion, 369 N.E.2d 404 (Ind.1977) (explosion of defective furnace in apartment building). See also Rivera v. Selfon Home Repairs and Improvements Co., 294 Pa.Super. 41, 439 A.2d 739 (1982).

4. How should disclaimers of liability be treated in the leasehold context? See Henrioulle v. Marin Ventures, Inc., 20 Cal.3d 512, 143 Cal.Rptr. 247, 573 P.2d 465 (1978) (landlord negligence exculpation clause violated public policy).

5. **Sales of Real Estate.** A growing majority of states has replaced the traditional rule of caveat emptor in the sale of new homes with an implied warranty of reasonable quality, or "habitability." See, e.g., Vincent v. Jim Walter Homes, Inc., Prod.Liab.Rep. (CCH) ¶ 8278 (Tenn.App.1978); McDonald v. Mianecki, 159 N.J.Super. 1, 386 A.2d 1325 (App.Div.1978), aff'd 79 N.J. 275, 398 A.2d 1283 (1979) (water with high iron content stained fixtures "chocolaty brown," had offensive odor, fizzled like "Alka–Seltzer," and emitted methane gas); Lane v. Trenholm Bldg. Co., 267 S.C. 497, 229 S.E.2d 728, 729 (1976) (summarizing policy reasons: "the transaction was primarily a sale of a house and not a conveyance of land, the disparity of bargaining positions between the seller and purchaser, reliance by the purchaser on the skill of the builder, and the inability of the purchaser to inspect the house for latent defects"); Hartley v. Ballou, 286 N.C. 51, 209 S.E.2d 776 (1974) (basement flooded; implied warranty of freedom from major, latent structural defects); Rutledge v. Dodenhoff, 254 S.C. 407, 175 S.E.2d 792 (1970) (overflowing septic tank); Humber v. Morton, 426 S.W.2d 554 (Tex.1968) (fire from defective fireplace); Carpenter v. Donohoe, 154 Colo. 78, 388 P.2d 399 (1964) (cracking walls).

Contra, Bruce Farms, Inc. v. Coupe, 219 Va. 287, 247 S.E.2d 400, 403–404 (1978) (cracking bricks), the court reasoning that the "modern rule" would open too many questions: "Should it apply only when the seller is the builder? Should it be confined to the sale of houses under construction or those newly constructed or extended to the sale of renovated homes? Should it be limited to single-family detached dwellings or should it also reach owner-occupied condominium units or duplex houses? Should the warranty cover materials, fixtures, and other physical appurtenances?" The court also saw troubles in determining the duration of such warranties and damages for their breach. "[T]he decision * * * is one properly within the province of the General Assembly. The issue involves a multitude of competing economic, cultural, and societal values which courts are ill-equipped to balance, a fact best illustrated by the disparate conclusions reached by the several courts which have tinkered with the common law rule." 247 S.E.2d at 404.

6. There is also growing authority for applying strict tort principles to the sale of new homes, especially those constructed by mass production developers as was the case in the landmark decision, Schipper v. Levitt & Sons, Inc., 44 N.J. 70, 207 A.2d 314 (1965) (infant severely scalded by excessively hot water from faucet in bathroom sink due to failure of developer to add inexpensive mixing valve to reduce temperature of water drawn from boiler). Should a medium-sized builder which constructs 6 or 8 houses be strictly liable in tort? See Patitucci v. Drelich, 153 N.J.Super. 177, 379 A.2d 297 (Law Div.1977) (defective sewage disposal system; yes). How about the custom builder who works on only two or three houses at a time? For a case refusing to follow *Schipper,* see Chapman v. Lily Cache Builders, Inc., 48 Ill.App.3d 919, 6 Ill.Dec. 176, 362 N.E.2d 811 (1977) (building contractors generally not as financially capable as manufacturers of mass produced chattels to act as insurers).

Strict tort has been applied to "defective" house lots which subsided from inadequate compaction of the fill, Avner v. Longridge Estates, 272 Cal.App.2d 607, 77 Cal.Rptr. 633 (1969); and to the defective "design" of a house through placement of the hot water heater in the garage. Hyman v. Gordon, 35 Cal. App.3d 769, 111 Cal.Rptr. 262 (1973).

7. The court refused to apply strict tort to the design of a parking garage in Lowrie v. Evanston, 50 Ill.App.3d 376, 8 Ill.Dec. 537, 365 N.E.2d 923 (1977). Plaintiff's decedent was killed when he fell from an upper level of an open air parking garage which allegedly had insufficient walking space around the vehicles and no railings to prevent such falls. *Schipper* and *Kriegler* were distinguished: "[T]hese cases do not deal with a defect in the home *per se* but with a defect with some product installed therein. Thus, it appears to us that these builder-vendor cases apply strict liability to a contractor who sells a defective product along with the home, as distinguished from holding that a home is itself a product." See also Cox v. Shaffer, 223 Pa.Super. 429, 302 A.2d 456 (1973) (plaintiff asphyxiated in silo from lack of ventilation; strict tort applicable only to defective components of building, not entire building).

8. Products liability principles have been held applicable to the sale of an interest in a cooperative apartment, Berman v. Watergate West, Inc., 391 A.2d 1351 (D.C.App.1978), a condominium, Gable v. Silver, 258 So.2d 11 (Fla.App.), aff'd 264 So.2d 418 (1972), and a mobile home. Gautheir v. Mayo, 77 Mich.App. 513, 258 N.W.2d 748 (1977).

9. See Love, Landlord's Liability for Defective Premises: Caveat Lessee, Negligence, or Strict Liability?, 1975 Wis.L.Rev. 19 (excellent overview); Ursin, Strict Liability for Defective Business Premises—One Step Beyond Rowland and Greenman, 22 U.C.L.A.L.Rev. 820 (1975); Moscovitz, Implied Warranty of Habitability: A New Doctrine Raising New Issues, 62 Calif.L.Rev. 1444 (1974); Notes, 99 Harv.L.Rev. 1861 (1986) (real estate broker liability for defective housing); 17 Land & Water L.Rev. 467 (1982) (unsafe homesites); 32 Stan.L. Rev. 607 (1980) (used homes); 25 S.D.L.Rev. 333 (1980) (new and used housing); Annot., 25 A.L.R.4th 351 (1983) (strict liability for defects in buildings and land). The whole matter is examined comprehensively in J. Page, The Law of Premises Liability (2d ed. 1988).

SECTION 5. DISPOSAL AND DESTRUCTION

KALIK v. ALLIS-CHALMERS CORPORATION

United States District Court, Western District of Pennsylvania, 1987.
658 F.Supp. 631.*

TEITELBAUM, DISTRICT JUDGE.

This is an action by the owners of a site contaminated by hazardous substances against the manufacturers and suppliers of the products containing the hazardous substances to recover clean-up costs and

* References to the complaint have been omitted.—Eds.

damages under the Comprehensive Environmental Response Compensation and Liability Act of 1980 (CERCLA) and under state law.

The action was brought by the Kaliks, the owners of a site from which plaintiff Ben Kalik operated the Swissvale Auto Surplus Parts Company (SASPC), a scrap metal business. There are 27 defendants: 3 manufacturers of electrical components containing PCB's, a hazardous substance, 23 suppliers of junk electrical components containing PCB's, and 1 defendant which is both a manufacturer of electrical components containing PCB's and a supplier of junk electrical components containing PCB's.

The complaint makes the following allegations. Between 1970 and 1984 SASPC purchased junk electrical components for use as scrap. The junk electrical components contained PCB's, a hazardous substance. During the course of storage, handling and dismantling of the junk electrical components, PCB contaminated oil spilled or leaked onto the site. The combustion of PCB's under certain circumstances may produce dioxins, a highly toxic substance. As a furnace was used in dismantling and processing the junk electrical components, dioxins polluted the site. The United States Environmental Protection Agency (EPA) has spent $1.9 million to clean up the site; the plaintiffs have spent $22,000 to remove PCB contaminated oil from the site.

Plaintiffs seek recovery of clean-up costs, damages for injuries to the site and to the business, and a declaration of rights. Federal jurisdiction over the manufacturer defendants is based on diversity of citizenship. Federal jurisdiction over the supplier defendants is based on CERCLA, 42 U.S.C. §§ 9601–57.

* * *

1. *General Electric*

The complaint identifies GE as a manufacturer of electrical components containing PCB's. GE is named as a defendant in two counts: Count 1 sets forth a products liability claim under § 402A of the Restatement (2d) of Torts, Count 5 sets forth a claim for a negligent failure to warn.

a. *failure to state a claim—reasonably foreseeable use*

GE moves to dismiss for failure to state a claim. GE's position derives from the fact that it manufactured *new* electrical components, but that SASPC dealt in *junk* electrical components. Based on these facts, GE makes a three part argument.

First, GE argues that the plaintiffs are not within the class of *persons protected* under § 402A or the duty to warn. Specifically, GE contends that the allegations of the complaint that SASPC dealt in junk electrical components establishes as a matter of law that the plaintiffs are not "users" of the new electrical components manufactured by GE entitled to the protection of § 402A or to warnings.

Second, GE argues that it is not a *person subject to liability* under § 402A. Specifically, GE contends that there are no allegations that it sold junk electrical components which would be necessary to impose liability under § 402A.

Third, GE argues that its *product* has been substantially changed precluding liability under § 402A. Specifically, GE contends that there are no allegations that the new electrical components it manufactured were not substantially changed and, in fact, the allegations that SASPC dealt in junk electrical components suggest that GE's product was substantially changed, thereby precluding liability under § 402A.

Although GE has framed its argument in three parts focusing on the persons protected, the persons subject to liability, and the product, these three parts can all be subsumed within the broader inquiry of whether plaintiff's use of defendant's product was reasonably foreseeable by defendant manufacturer. It is to this question that the Court now turns.

Liability exists under § 402A or for a negligent failure to warn only if there was a use of the product reasonably foreseeable to the manufacturer. * * *

Nevertheless, it has been held, as a matter of law, that the recycling of a product, after it has been destroyed, is not a use of the product reasonably foreseeable to the manufacturer. Johnson v. Murph Metals, Inc., 562 F.Supp. 246 (N.D.Tx.1983). In *Johnson* the defendant manufactured automotive batteries. After the useful life of the batteries, the batteries were often resold in order to recycle the lead in the batteries. In the recycling process, the batteries were first destroyed, then the lead was extracted, and then the lead was introduced into a lead smelting process. The plaintiffs, employees of lead smelting companies, alleged that during the lead smelting process, they were exposed to harmful lead fumes and lead dust. It was stipulated that the employees did not sustain any harm while the batteries were intact or while the batteries were being destroyed. The employees asserted the battery manufacturer was liable under § 402A and for a negligent failure to warn. The Court held, as a matter of law, that it was "untenable to find that the creation of dangerous gases due to the smelting of scrap metal is a 'use' of defendant's automotive batteries." 562 F.Supp. at 249.

It has also been held, as a matter of law, that the destruction of a product is not a use of the product reasonably foreseeable to the manufacturer. Wingett v. Teledyne Industries, Inc., 479 N.E.2d 51 (Ind.1985). In *Wingett* the defendant manufactured ductwork used to collect sand and dust from machinery. The plaintiff, a member of a demolition crew, alleged that during the removal of the ductwork, he sustained injury when the connection between two segments of ductwork gave way. The plaintiff asserted the ductwork manufacturer was liable under § 402A. The Court held, as a matter of law, that the dismantling or demolishing of the ductwork was not a reasonably foreseeable use.

> While the question of foreseeability is generally one of fact for the jury, we hold that appellant's "use" of the ductwork was not reasonably foreseeable as a matter of law, notwithstanding appellant's allegation that he was employing the standard trade procedure for duct removal. Because the dismantling and demolition of the ductwork was not a reasonably foreseeable use of the product [the manufacturer] * * * owed no duty to [appellant] to warn of any risks related to his work as part of the demolition crew. 479 N.E.2d at 56.

The parties have not cited, and the Court's research has not disclosed, any cases reaching contrary results on similar facts. Thus, although the Pennsylvania courts have not yet addressed this issue, there is no reason to believe that they would reach a contrary result.

In the present case the plaintiffs allege injuries sustained during the course of storage and handling of junk electrical components, and also injuries sustained during the course of dismantling and processing junk electrical components. The decisions discussed above provide no basis for concluding, as a matter of law, that the storage and handling of junk electrical components was not a reasonably foreseeable use of GE's product. On the other hand, these decisions do provide a persuasive basis for concluding, as a matter of law, that the dismantling and processing of junk electrical components was not a reasonably foreseeable use of GE's product, and the Court so finds. Accordingly, the allegations of injury as a result of the dismantling and processing of junk electrical components will be dismissed.

* * *

4. *Max Berman and Edward P. Green*

The complaint identifies Max Berman and Edward P. Green as suppliers of junk electrical components containing PCB's. Berman and Green are named as defendants in Counts 1–4 and 6–9. Federal jurisdiction over Berman and Green is based on CERCLA.

* * *

CERCLA creates a private cause of action against statutorily defined "responsible parties" for recovery of response costs incurred by any other person. [Citations.] However, at least one court has recognized that the equitable defense of unclean hands is available in a private response cost recovery action under CERCLA. [Citations.]

Berman and Green assert the unclean hands defense. They contend plaintiffs were actively responsible for the release of hazardous substances and therefore cannot maintain this action under CERCLA. In response, plaintiffs concede the availability of the unclean hands defense, but assert that they were innocent victims of the release of hazardous substances on their site.

* * * In the complaint the plaintiffs allege they were innocent victims of the release of hazardous substances on their site. Thus, assuming without deciding, that the defense of unclean hands is available in a private response cost recovery action under CERCLA, the face of the complaint does not establish the defense.

* * *

An appropriate order will be entered.

NOTES

1. Within the context of the growing waste disposal problem, *Kalik* illustrates the confluence of products liability and environmental law. Long after products have outlived their useful lives, "junked" products continue to pose hazards to the community.

2. Consider Ashland Oil, Inc. v. Miller Oil Purchasing Co., 678 F.2d 1293 (5th Cir.1982), holding that a waste disposal contractor was not subject to liability under § 402A, for its disposal of a highly dangerous chemical waste product, because it was not in the business of selling such waste. The contractor tried to incinerate the waste, but it turned into hydrochloric acid which damaged the incinerator. In an attempt to disguise and dispose of the waste, the contractor mixed it with crude oil and had it trucked away. This mixture was eventually sold through wholesale and retail vendors of petroleum products as good crude oil to the plaintiff, whose refinery was damaged when the mixture caught fire and exploded. The two vendors of "crude oil" were both held liable under § 402A.

3. While the disposal problem is most severe for toxic substances, it exists as well for durable goods. Should General Electric be liable for the suffocation of a child playing in a dump who climbs inside a long-abandoned G.E. refrigerator, manufactured with a latching mechanism in the 1940s, who cannot get out when the door swings shut?

3. How logical is *Kalik* 's holding that the processing and disposal of worn-out products is unforeseeable, as a matter of law?

4. See Tucci v. Bossert, 53 A.D.2d 291, 385 N.Y.S.2d 328 (1976), where the purchasers of a can of Drano drain cleaner disposed it, with some of the contents remaining in the can, in a trash bag placed outside their house. Two children came along, removed the can from the bag, and poured water into the can. The can exploded and injured one of the children. Plaintiffs sued the manufacturer for selling a defectively packaged product with inadequate warnings. The trial court dismissed the complaint. On appeal, *held,* complaint reinstated. See also Hall v. E.I. Du Pont De Nemours & Co., Inc., 345 F.Supp. 353 (E.D.N.Y.1972) (children found and injured by lost or abandoned blasting caps; defendants' motion to dismiss denied).

Contrast Venezia v. Miller Brewing Co., 626 F.2d 188 (1st Cir.1980), treated above in connection with misuse, supra p. 380, where a child threw a discarded beer bottle against a telephone pole and suffered injury to his eye. *Held,* dismissal of complaint affirmed: "[T]he impact of endorsing a contrary conclusion would be overwhelming, with every discarded glass object holding the potential for generating a future lawsuit." Right result? Right reasoning? What if plaintiff cuts her foot when she steps on and breaks a discarded beer bottle hidden in the sand at the beach?

5. General Electric purchased a machine in 1962, used it for 11 years, and sold it as surplus property, "as is-where is," at a price set by its weight as scrap. It was resold, reconditioned, and put back into use without the original safety devices. Should G.E. be subject to strict liability in tort to a subsequent purchaser's employee injured while using the machine? See Sukljian v. Charles Ross & Son Co., Inc., 69 N.Y.2d 89, 511 N.Y.S.2d 821, 503 N.E.2d 1358 (1986). See also Galindo v. Precision American Corp., 754 F.2d 1212 (5th Cir. 1985) (business sold its used equipment on occasional basis).

6. See G. Nothstein, Toxic Torts Litigation of Hazardous Substance Cases (1984); DiBenedetto, Generator Liability Under the Common Law and Federal and State Statutes, 39 Bus.Law. 611 (1984); Hall, The Problem of Unending Liability for Hazardous Waste Management, 38 Bus.Law. 593, 606 (1983); Johnson, Hazardous Waste Disposal: Is There Still a Role for Common Law?, 18 Tulsa L.J. 448 (1983); Seltzer, Personal Injury Hazardous Waste Litigation: A Proposal for Tort Reform, 10 B.C.Envtl.Aff.L.Rev. 797 (1983); Developments in the Law—Toxic Waste Litigation, 99 Harv.L.Rev. 1458, 1462 (1986); Note, The Inapplicability of Traditional Tort Analysis to Environmental Risks: The Example of Toxic Waste Pollution Victim Compensation, 35 Stan.L.Rev. 575 (1983).

Chapter 9

SPECIAL ISSUES IN AUTOMOTIVE LITIGATION

A considerable proportion of products liability litigation involves claims against manufacturers of cars, vans, trucks, and motorcycles alleging that defects in the vehicles caused injuries to the plaintiffs. The usual victims in such accidents are the drivers and passengers, but sometimes bystanders are struck by the vehicle or some component thereof—such as a runaway tire from an 18–wheeler truck.

The automotive cases examined so far have for the most part involved manufacturing flaws: MacPherson v. Buick Motor Co., supra p. 48, involved a wheel made of defective wood; Jenkins v. General Motors Corp., supra p. 53, involved an improperly tightened nut in the suspension system; Ford Motor Co. v. Zahn, supra p. 60 involved a jagged edge or burr on the corner of the ash tray. One of the cases involved a warnings claim: Greiner v. Volkswagenwerk A.G., supra p. 479, where there was no warning of the VW beetle's propensity to roll over on sharp steering maneuvers. Most of the cases examined so far have involved claims of defect that caused the accident.

Not yet examined are automotive products liability cases involving defects in design. There are two principal types of automotive design cases: (1) those where the design defect *causes the accident,* and (2) those where the design defect *aggravates the injuries* in an accident caused by something else, such as driver error. Examples of the first type of case are design defects in the vehicle's steering, e.g., Halvorsen v. Ford Motor Co., 132 A.D.2d 57, 522 N.Y.S.2d 272 (App.Div.1987), or

* From The N.Y. Times. See p. 1020, infra.

brakes, e.g., Brooks v. Chrysler Corp., 786 F.2d 1191 (D.C.Cir.1986) (lip-in dust boot permitted junk to enter caliper bore). Since design defects by their nature infect the entire product line, threatening the safety of thousands of persons, some have become quite notorious. The control problems with the Corvair, publicized by Ralph Nader in "Unsafe at Any Speed" in the 1960s, is one example. Examples from the 1980s include the accelerator sticking problems of the Audi, in particular, and the roll-over tendencies of the Suzuki Samurai.

An example from the 1970s, that continues to the present, e.g., Narciso v. Ford Motor Co., 137 A.D.2d 508, 524 N.Y.S.2d 251 (1988), involves the tendency of the transmissions in certain Ford vehicles to slip from Park to Reverse. Accidents can occur when the driver tries to place the gear shift in Park but mispositions the lever on the gatepost between Park and Reverse. If the driver then leaves the car with the engine running, the vibration from the engine or the door slamming may cause the transmission to slip into Reverse. Plaintiffs' experts have testified that the shape and height of the gatepost, and the design of the springs involved, make it much more likely that the Ford FMX transmission will accidentally slip into Reverse than the transmissions in other cars. See, e.g., Ford Motor Co. v. Nowak, 638 S.W.2d 582 (Tex. App.1982) (5–1) (affirming $400,000 pecuniary damages and $4,000,000 punitive damages awards for death of person run over when she went behind the car to close the driveway gate); Ford Motor Co. v. Bartholomew, 224 Va. 421, 297 S.E.2d 675 (1982) (affirming but remitting damages to $16,500 awarded to person slightly injured when she fell while chasing car that slipped into reverse while she was loading groceries). See generally Branton, From "Park" to "Reverse"—The Costly Slip, Trial 42 (Nov. 1978).

The second type of design defects, examined in the cases that follow, cause the injuries of the occupant in an accident vehicle to be unnecessarily severe. This type of defect can also become quite notorious, as illustrated by the Ford Pinto fuel tank problem in the 1970s and early 1980s. These "second collision" or "crashworthiness" cases are the focus of this chapter because they involve a variety of special issues that are unique. In addition, they involve many of the problems of law and proof present in virtually every serious automotive product case.

SECTION 1. CRASHWORTHINESS

"Crashworthiness" is defined in the Motor Vehicle Information and Cost Savings Act, 15 U.S.C.A. § 1901(14), as "the protection that a passenger motor vehicle offers its passengers against personal injury or death as a result of a motor vehicle accident." The concept focuses on the vehicle's capacity to withstand the physical stresses of a collision and its ability to minimize the additional or "enhanced" injuries the passengers may sustain as a result of the "second collision" between the occupants and the interior of the vehicle. The cause of the accident (the first collision, or roll-over in a one car accident) is largely irrelevant to the crashworthiness issue and, specifically, the accident need not have been caused by a defect in the car.

Whether manufacturers should be obligated to design crashworthy vehicles was one of the major debates in products liability law in the late 1960s and early 1970s. The origin of the controversy was Evans v. General Motors Corp., 359 F.2d 822 (7th Cir.), cert. denied 385 U.S. 836, 87 S.Ct. 83, 17 L.Ed.2d 70 (1966), where the driver was killed when another vehicle struck the side of his vehicle which collapsed in on him. Plaintiff alleged that the death was attributable to the "X" frame design of his vehicle which afforded occupants less protection than the side frame rail design used by other manufacturers as shown in the advertisement of a rival manufacturer set forth below.

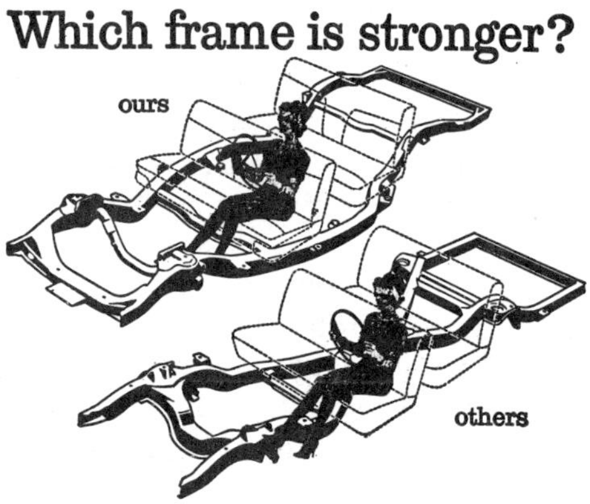

Observing that the intended purpose of a car does not include its participation in collisions, the court held, 2–1, that the manufacturer had breached no duty in failing to design a safer car. A contrary position was taken by the Eighth Circuit in Larsen v. General Motors Corp., 391 F.2d 495 (8th Cir.1968). In that case plaintiff was involved in a head-on collision and was injured when the steering mechanism, the front shaft of which protruded 2.7 inches in front of the forward tires, was propelled back into his head. In view of the clear foreseeability of automobile accidents, and data demonstrating that many if not most vehicles are involved in at least one accident which causes injury or death, the court ruled that car manufacturers must be held accountable for vehicular safety in the crash environment. "The sole function of an automobile is not just to provide a means of transportation, it is to provide a safe means of transportation or as safe as is reasonably possible under the present state of the art." Id. at 502.

Although a small handful of cases followed the *Evans* no-duty approach, the vast majority followed *Larsen.* If there was any doubt as to the final outcome of the issue, it was put to rest in 1977 when the Seventh Circuit repudiated its decision in *Evans,* in Huff v. White Motor Corp., 565 F.2d 104 (7th Cir.1977) (death by fire from rupture of fuel tank). The court concluded that there "is no rational basis for limiting the manufacturer's liability to those instances where a structural defect has caused the collision and a resulting injury. * * * Since collisions for whatever cause are foreseeable events, the scope of liability should be commensurate with the scope of foreseeable risks." Id. at 109.

Settling the crashworthiness duty issue does not of course resolve the more difficult problem of deciding just what the limits of the manufacturer's design obligations should be. What kinds of accidents should a vehicle reasonably be able to withstand? How severe and what types of injuries are acceptable? In some situations these questions are easy to resolve. Thus, if a low-speed collision causes the covering of the hub to the steering wheel to pop off, exposing sharp prongs that injure a passenger's face, the car could hardly be found to be reasonably crashworthy. See Ellithorpe v. Ford Motor Co., 503 S.W. 2d 516 (Tenn.1973). Yet, as developed in the materials that follow, difficult issues arise when the initial impact is more severe.

The difficult problem of apportioning damages gives rise to certain problems of proof. Since usually the uncrashworthy design does not cause the initial accident, the defendant should logically be liable only for those additional ("aggravated" or "enhanced") injuries caused in the "second collision." Yet what if the plaintiff dies or cannot otherwise make a reasoned demonstration of the extra injuries attributable only to the defect in design?

Finally, what if plaintiff's death could have been prevented, or his injuries reduced, if the car had been equipped with an air bag? If such a device could feasibly and inexpensively have been installed in the car, should its absence render the design defective?

BURGOS v. LUTZ

New York Supreme Court, Appellate Division, 1987.
128 A.D.2d 496, 512 N.Y.S.2d 424.

[PER CURIAM.]

* * *

The plaintiff's decedent was killed while driving his Honda Civic 1200 when he made a left turn at an intersection and his car was struck by an oncoming vehicle, a Ford LTD. The decedent suffered a transection (laceration) of his thoracic aorta, and apparently died instantly. The plaintiff brought this action against the driver of the Ford, alleging negligence, and against the respondents herein, alleging, inter alia, defective design of the steering column and seat belt system of the Honda.

After a three-month trial, the jury returned a special verdict in favor of the driver and the owner of the Ford. * * *

The plaintiff's evidence concerning the defective seatbelt system consisted of expert testimony to the effect that, upon inspection of the actual seatbelt in the decedent's Honda, the locking device performed erratically. The plaintiff failed to establish that the erratic performance was caused by the design of the locking device. Furthermore, the plaintiff's expert did not testify that there was an alternative, safer design of the seatbelt locking system. Moreover, none of the plaintiff's evidence established, either directly or circumstantially, that the decedent was wearing his lap or shoulder belts at the time of the collision. Thus, the plaintiff failed to meet her obligation to present evidence that it was feasible to design a seatbelt system in a safer manner (see, Voss v. Black & Decker Mfg. Co., 59 N.Y.2d 102, 108, 463 N.Y.S.2d 398, 450 N.E.2d 204), or that the alleged defect was the cause in fact of the decedent's death. Accordingly, the plaintiff failed to establish a prima facie case of a defectively designed seatbelt system.

The plaintiff's theory with respect to her claim of a defectively designed steering column was that the system lacked an adequate energy absorbing capability, and that when the decedent came into contact with the steering wheel, his chest sustained an intolerable impact from the force of the collision, causing the injuries which resulted in his death. Although the plaintiff's expert testified to the characteristics and qualities of an alternative, feasible steering column energy absorption system, the expert failed to explain how the proposed design would have prevented any of the decedent's injuries under the circumstances of the actual collision. Significantly, the plaintiff's expert failed to indicate how the alternative design would have absorbed more energy than the steering column design used in the decedent's vehicle. Thus, the plaintiff failed to show that the alternative design was any safer or more capable of preventing the harm that the decedent suffered than Honda's design * * *. * * *

Because the plaintiff failed to establish a prima facie case with respect to either of her defective design claims, the trial court properly granted the respondents' motions to dismiss those claims.

[Affirmed.]

NOTES

1. This "short" case, which took *three months* to try, raises many of the issues in litigation involving automobiles. Consider, in studying the cases and materials in this chapter, why it would take so long to try such a case. Consider also the resources consumed in this type of litigation.

2. The typical automobile defect case usually involves a complex interrelationship of proof of design defect, including the feasibility of alternative designs, the role of safety devices such as seatbelts, and difficult issues of causation. All require extensive expert testimony on what are frequently speculative questions, about which there is little hard evidence and much uncertainty. For example, how can anyone really know what would have happened had the plaintiff been wearing a seat belt? Or had the steering column absorbed more energy? How much certainty should be required from the evidence, and who should bear the risk of the evidence being insufficient?

If you had represented plaintiff in *Burgos,* what might you have done differently?

3. There is extensive federal regulation of automotive design by the National Highway Traffic Safety Administration (NHTSA) of the Department of Transportation. How should this pervasive regulatory system affect the common law process of products liability litigation?

SUMNICHT v. TOYOTA MOTOR SALES, U.S.A., INC.

Wisconsin Supreme Court, 1984.
121 Wis.2d 338, 360 N.W.2d 2.

CECI, JUSTICE.

* * *

This case arises from an automobile accident which occurred sometime after 2:00 a.m. on May 16, 1976, when the vehicle in which Vernon C. Sumnicht was a passenger left the roadway on a curve and collided with a tree. Sumnicht was rendered a quadriplegic as a result of this accident.

The accident occurred on Highway 89, approximately five miles south of Whitewater, Wisconsin. The evidence is clear that immediately prior to the accident, Sumnicht was lying down, with his head behind the driver's seat, in the back seat of a 1975 Toyota Corolla two-door sedan operated by Edmund C. O'Connor, Jr. Sumnicht was not using the available seat belt. Jack Vallerugo was riding in the front passenger's seat of the Toyota, which was equipped with bucket seats. Sumnicht, O'Connor, and Vallerugo were returning to the University of Wisconsin–Whitewater, where they were students.

The vehicle headed north on Highway 89, when it entered a large curve in the roadway. The Toyota drifted off the highway, traveling approximately 303 feet along the shoulder. It then crossed a drainage ditch and climbed a grass incline before hitting the tree head-on. At the moment of impact with the tree, the Toyota was estimated to be traveling between thirty and fifty miles per hour.

O'Connor sustained chest injuries, from which he fully recovered. Vallerugo also received chest injuries and died en route to the hospital. Sumnicht suffered a fractured dislocation of his cervical spine at C6–7, which caused his quadriplegia. Other than his severed spinal cord, Sumnicht had relatively minor injuries, which consisted of two chipped teeth, a possible fractured rib, and two leg lacerations.

Sumnicht initially commenced suit against the driver of the Toyota, his father, and their insurers, later amending his complaint to include three sellers and distributors of the 1975 Toyota involved in the accident (collectively referred to herein as "Toyota"). The complaint alleged causes of action on the theories of strict products liability and negligence.

The trial commenced on January 31, 1983, lasting over three weeks. Sumnicht's liability case revolved around the theories that the front seat system of the Toyota was both defective and unreasonably dangerous and negligently designed and manufactured. His liability experts included an accident reconstructionist, a mechanical engineer, a biomedical engineer, a safety engineer, a neurosurgeon, and a metallurgist.

These experts testified that, at the time of the collision, Sumnicht was lying down in the back seat, with his head toward the driver's side of the Toyota. They theorized that upon impact of the car with the tree, Sumnicht was propelled forward and his head became entrapped in the cutout portion of the back of the driver's seat, while his lower torso swung forward, smashing into the back of the front passenger's seat. The inboard hinge on the passenger's seat broke loose, allowing Sumnicht's lower torso to wrap around the seat. The continued movement forward of his lower torso, while his head was stationary, created the shearing forces which injured his spinal cord and resulted in his quadriplegic condition.

Sumnicht's experts opined that the 1975 Toyota was defective and unreasonably dangerous and negligently designed and manufactured insofar as the back of the bucket seat did not have any energy-absorbing material beneath the vinyl seat cover. Instead of the bucket seat's serving as a shock absorber, it permitted Sumnicht's head to become captured in the hollow cutout portion of the back of the driver's seat.

The hinges on the passenger's seat which connect the bottom of the seat to the seat back were also criticized. There was testimony that the inboard bracket on the passenger's seat broke upon impact because it was made of the weakest steel available. This allowed Sumnicht's lower torso to propel around and enter the front seat area of the Toyota. Sumnicht's experts concluded that had the seat backs not been so designed and had the bracket not broken, Sumnicht would not have sustained the paralyzing injuries.

Conversely, Toyota was of the opinion that the seat system was not defective and did not cause Sumnicht's injuries. Toyota's liability experts included an engineer specializing in crash analysis, a biomechanical engineer, an accident reconstructionist, and a metallurgist. These experts theorized that Sumnicht's head did not become entrapped in the seat at all. It was reasoned that just prior to the collision, Sumnicht sat up and was injured when he was thrown over and between the front bucket seats, striking his head on the dashboard area of the automobile.

At the verdict formulation phase of the trial, the court dismissed the negligence claim at Toyota's request, and the case went to the jury solely on the theory of strict liability. The jury found that the 1975 Toyota automobile contained such a defect in the design of the seat system as to be unreasonably dangerous to a prospective passenger in the rear seat of the automobile and found that such defective design was a cause of injuries to the plaintiff over and above those injuries which he probably would have sustained as a result of the collision without such defective design. The jury also found that O'Connor was negligent at the time of the collision and that his negligence was also a cause of plaintiff's injuries. The jury found that plaintiff was not negligent in his own conduct prior to the collision. The jury apportioned the negligence at fifty percent to the defective seat system and fifty percent to the driver, Edmund C. O'Connor, Jr. The jury awarded 4.7 million dollars for the plaintiff's personal injuries, including his pain and suffering, past and future; his permanent disability; his loss of earnings, past and future; and his medical, hospital, drugs, and nursing care, past and future. These damages were awarded specifically for injuries which plaintiff sustained over and above injuries which he would have probably sustained from the collision without the defective design in the seat system. The trial court reduced the damage award by the percentage of negligence attributed to O'Connor, denied Toyota's motions after verdict, and entered judgment against Toyota in the amount of 2.35 million dollars. Toyota now appeals.

I.

A. *Introduction*

This suit falls within a class of cases commonly referred to as "second collision" or "crashworthy" cases. The crashworthiness doctrine imposes liability upon a manufacturer in a vehicular collision case for design defects which do not cause the initial accident but which cause additional or more severe injuries when the driver or passenger subsequently impacts with the defective interior or exterior of the vehicle. This double-collision distinction is clarified by the following:

> "An automobile collision is really two collisions. In the first phase of the accident, the plaintiff's automobile collides with another automobile or with a stationary object. Most of the property damage results from the first collision, but the occupants of the vehicle usually sustain little or no injury at this stage. Personal injuries occur most frequently in the second collision, in which the occupants are thrown against or collide with some part of their automobile. Courts will hold the manufacturer liable for the plaintiff's loss in the second collision only if defective design of the automobile caused or exacerbated the plaintiff's injury. Yet, if a court finds that defective automobile design did cause some injury, determining where one defendant's liability ends and another's begins may be virtually impossible. Both those injuries for which the manufacturer should be liable and those attributable to other causes, such as another driver's negligence, occurred during the very brief time span of the second collision." Note, Apportionment of Damages in the "Second Collision" Case, 63 Va.L. Rev. 475, 476 (1977) (footnotes omitted).

The instant case can be termed a "second collision" case because the respondent's claim is not that Toyota's defective seat system caused the accident ("first collision"), but, rather, that as a result of his impact with the defective seats ("second collision"), he sustained injuries which he otherwise would not have sustained.

The case generally credited with extending liability to manufacturers for injuries resulting from a defectively designed automobile that is uncrashworthy is Larsen v. General Motors Corporation, 391 F.2d 495 (8th Cir.1968). That court pioneered the benchmark that,

> "Any design defect not causing the accident would not subject the manufacturer to liability for the entire damage, but the manufacturer should be liable for that portion of the damage or injury caused by the defective design over and above the damage or injury that probably would have occurred as a result of the impact or collision absent the defective design." Id, at 503. (Emphasis added.)

This ruling is consistent with the basic premise behind all tort law which limits a defendant's liability to that portion of harm which he has in fact caused, as distinguished from harm arising from other sources.

The issue of a manufacturer's liability in a "second collision" case was first decided by this court in Arbet v. Gussarson, 66 Wis.2d 551, 225 N.W.2d 431 (1975), a case arising out of an automobile accident in which the plaintiffs were burned following the rupture of their vehicle's gasoline tank and ignition of the fuel. The plaintiffs alleged in their complaint that the defectively designed gasoline tank, although not a cause of the accident, was the proximate cause of their burns. The trial court dismissed the complaint, and we reversed, holding that the automobile manufacturer may incur liability for injuries to occupants of a vehicle arising from its negligence in designing the vehicle such that it is unreasonably unsafe in an accident. Id. at 553, 225 N.W.2d 431.

* * *

B. *Burden of Proof*

The standard of proof issue in "second collision" products liability cases has been phrased by some as being an issue of which party bears the burden of proving the apportionment of damages. Apportionment of damages should not be confused with plaintiff's burden of proving causation. One author explains,

> "Once it is determined that the defendant's conduct has been a cause of some damage suffered by the plaintiff, a further question may arise as to the portion of the total damage sustained which may properly be assigned to the defendant, as distinguished from other causes. The question is primarily not one of the fact of causation, but of the feasibility and practical convenience of splitting up the total harm into separate parts which may be attributed to each of two or more

causes." Prosser and Keeton on Torts section 52 at 345 (footnote omitted).

The Arbet decision tells us that Sumnicht has a cause of action in strict liability against Toyota for all injuries which the defective seat system was a substantial factor in causing. Arbet, 66 Wis.2d at 557, 225 N.W.2d 431. This premise forecloses recovery against Toyota for injuries sustained solely in the "first collision," because Toyota's defective seat system was not a proximate cause of the accident. Requiring Sumnicht to distinguish between the damages sustained in the "first collision" and the "second collision" is part and parcel of his burden of proving causation. However, only after Sumnicht has proven what injuries were caused by Toyota is the issue of apportionment of damages properly raised. The precise issue here is not which party bears the burden of apportioning damages in cases involving joint tortfeasors, but what quantum of evidence must a plaintiff bring forth in a "second collision" products liability case to prove that his injuries were proximately caused by the manufacturer's defect.

A divergence in opinion on this issue stems from the following language in Larsen v. General Motors Corporation, 391 F.2d 495:

> "[T]he manufacturer should be liable for that portion of the damage or injury caused by the defective design over and above the damage or injury that probably would have occurred as a result of the impact or collision absent the defective design." Id. at 503. (Emphasis added.); cited in Arbet, 66 Wis. 2d at 561, 225 N.W.2d 431.

Based on this language, appellants take the position that in a "second collision" case the plaintiff must not only prove that the defective product was a substantial factor in causing the injuries, but also must prove what the injuries would have been had there been no defect. Toyota asserts that its liability is nonexistent until Sumnicht shows the extent to which the injuries were enhanced by the defect.

Two opposing views on the plaintiff's standard of proof are set forth in Huddell v. Levin, 537 F.2d 726 (3d Cir.1976), and Fox v. Ford Motor Co., 575 F.2d 774 (10th Cir.1978). Toyota relies on *Huddell,* wherein that court held that the plaintiff must prove three elements in order to recover in a crashworthy case.

> "We have set forth, supra, the basic elements of proof in an orthodox strict liability case under New Jersey law: a *defective* product *causing* injury. The simplicity of the general formulation belies the difficulty of applying it in the infinite variety of cases that arise. Unlike orthodox products liability or negligence litigation, crashworthy or second collision cases impugning the design of an automobile require a highly refined and almost invariably difficult presentation of proof in three aspects. First, in establishing that the design in question was defective, the plaintiff must offer proof of an alternative, safer design, practicable under the circumstances. * * *

> Second, the plaintiff must offer proof of what injuries, if any, would have resulted had the alternative, safer design been used. * * * We agree in this regard with Judge Barlow in Yetter v. Rajeski, 364 F.Supp. 105, 109 (D.N.J.1973) that 'it is absolutely necessary that the jury be presented with some evidence as to the extent of injuries, if any, which would have been suffered * * * had the plaintiff's hypothetical design been installed. * * *' Third, as a corollary to the second aspect of proof, the plaintiff must offer some method of establishing the extent of enhanced injuries attributable to the defective design." Id. at 737–38. (Emphasis in original.)

The *Huddell* court has been criticized for requiring the plaintiff to assume an impossible burden of proving a negative fact. The United States Court of Appeals for the Eighth Circuit declares,

> "The primary difficulty we have with [the *Huddell*] analysis is that it forces not only the parties but the jury as well to try a hypothetical case. Liability and damage questions are difficult enough within orthodox principles of tort law without extending consideration to a case of a hypothetical victim. More realistically, the parties and juries should direct their attentions to what actually happened rather than what might have happened.
>
> " * * * We write to reaffirm that *Larsen* was not intended to create a rule which requires the plaintiff to assume an impossible burden of proving a negative fact. A rule of law which requires a plaintiff to prove what portion of indivisible harm was caused by each party and what might have happened in lieu of what did happen requires obvious speculation and proof of the impossible. This approach converts the common law rules governing principles of legal causation into a morass of confusion and uncertainty." Mitchell v. Volkswagenwerk, AG, 669 F.2d 1199, 1204–05 (8th Cir.1982).

Sumnicht relies on a second approach to the standard of proof in a "second collision" case, enumerated in *Fox*, 575 F.2d 774, which places a significantly lesser burden of proof on a plaintiff. In *Fox,* the tenth circuit found no reason to require plaintiffs in second collision cases to bring forth proof in addition to that required of plaintiffs in all tort cases, i.e., that the plaintiff suffered a legally cognizable injury proximately caused by the defendant. The court reasoned,

> "Generally this duty to prove so-called enhanced damages is simply a part of the plaintiff's responsibility to prove proximate cause, that is, that the defendant in such a case is liable only for those damages which are within the orbit of risk created by him, but Ford would have us say that the plaintiffs were required to prove with specificity the injuries which flowed specifically from its deficiencies.

"The case which is relied on by Ford to illustrate its position is Huddell v. Levin, 537 F.2d 726 (3d Cir.1976). There the holding was that plaintiff in a collision case such as the present one had the burden of proving enhanced injuries and that the presentation of evidence that the accident was survivable did not meet this burden. The thesis of this case was that collision cases are to be treated differently from other liability or negligence cases as far as the specificity of proof is concerned. It refused to follow the orthodox doctrines of joint liability of concurrent tort-feasors for injuries which flow from their concurring in one impact.

> "We fail to see any difference between this type of case and the other case in which two parties, one passive, the other active, cooperate in the production of an injury. Each one's contribution in a causal sense must be established. Damages may be apportioned between the two causes if there are distinct harms or a reasonable basis for determining the causes of injury. Restatement of Torts, Second, section 433 A." Id. at 787.

The tenth circuit then addressed the issue of apportionment of damages, holding that death "is not a divisible injury in which apportionment is either appropriate or possible." Id.

For the reasons set out in *Mitchell* and *Fox,* this court also rejects the two requirements enumerated in *Huddell* that the plaintiff in a "second collision" case must offer proof of what injuries, if any, would have resulted had an alternative, safer design been used and that the plaintiff must offer some method of establishing the extent of enhanced injuries attributable to the defective design.

* * * The rule of strict liability, as adopted in Wisconsin, requires proof that the product was in a defective condition, unreasonably dangerous, which caused the plaintiff's harm. The long-standing test for cause in Wisconsin is whether the defect was a substantial factor in producing the injury. [Citation.] We have held,

> "It need not be the sole factor or the primary factor, only a 'substantial factor.' [Citation.] The phrase 'substantial factor' denotes that the defendant's conduct has such an effect in producing the harm as to lead the trier of fact, as a reasonable person, to regard it as a cause, using that word in the popular sense. [Citations.] There may be several substantial factors contributing to the same result. [Citations.]" Clark v. Leisure Vehicles, Inc., 96 Wis.2d 607, 617–18, 292 N.W.2d 630 (1980).

The requirement in *Huddell* that the plaintiff prove the extent of enhancement of injuries would, in some cases, require the plaintiff to isolate that portion of injuries caused solely by the manufacturer. This may be an impossible task and is not required by the law of this state. We affirm the applicability of the substantial factor test in proving causation.

* * *

In any event, once the plaintiff has proven that the defect was a cause of his injuries, he need not prove what portion of indivisible harm is attributable solely to the manufacturer. If there is more than one tortfeasor who contributed to the injury, Wisconsin's law concerning joint and several liability applies.

> " 'When two actors negligently conduct themselves so as to injure another, they become jointly and severally liable to the other if their actions concur in time to directly produce injury or to create an injury-producing situation. [Citations.]' " Wis. Natural Gas v. Ford, Bacon & Davis Constr., 96 Wis.2d 314, 331, 291 N.W.2d 825 (1980).

As discussed above, only after the plaintiff establishes that there are joint tortfeasors can the issue of apportionment of damages be raised.

C. *Sufficiency of Evidence*

* * *

Six experts were called to testify during the course of Sumnicht's case in chief. Testimony significant to the issue of causation included that of Bruce Enz, a safety engineer and accident reconstructionist; Dr. Anthony Sances, a biomedical engineer; Dr. Patrick Walsh, a neurosurgeon; and Dr. Robert Brenner, a safety engineer.

Bruce Enz, vice president of the Institute for Safety Analysis, testified regarding the accident reconstruction and the respondent's kinematics at the time of the collision. Based on his thorough examination of the Toyota, he concluded that, at the time of the impact, the respondent was lying in the back seat of the vehicle on his left side, with his head toward the driver's side. In a simultaneous progression, his upper torso struck the driver's seat, entrapping his head in the cutout portion of the driver's seat, while his legs flew forward, striking the passenger's seat. His lower torso then continued forward as a result of the failure of the seat's bracket that holds together the seat's back rest and bottom. This movement caused Sumnicht's body to rotate around his upper thorax area. Enz's examination of the Toyota eliminated other possible kinematic scenarios by which Sumnicht could have sustained his injuries. Enz concluded,

> "It's my opinion that the entrapment and capturing capability of the seat backs and the failure of the bracket enhanced and created the injury mechanism."

Dr. Anthony Sances also testified concerning his analysis of Sumnicht's injury sequence. Based on his inspection of the Toyota and his evaluation of the medical reports, Sances attested that the upper portion of Sumnicht's spinal column became fixed as his legs swung forward. This created a shear force between the sixth and seventh cervical elements that subsequently ripped the spinal cord. He opined that Sumnicht would not have sustained his paralyzing injuries if the driver's seat had not allowed his head to become entrapped and if the seat's bracket had not failed.

Dr. Walsh testified mainly from the respondent's X-rays. He claimed that Sumnicht's paralyzing injuries were caused by a number of forces on his spine, including flexion, compression, shear, and possible rotation. More importantly, Walsh stated that these findings were consistent with the hypothesis that the respondent's head became entrapped in the back of the driver's seat while his lower torso continued to move forward.

Finally, Robert Brenner, president of the Institute for Safety Analysis, testified with respect to the design of Toyota's seat system. He initially assigned Mr. Enz with the responsibility of taking the crash vehicle apart to analyze what happened in the crash. He subsequently studied a number of documents and reports and examined the vehicle himself to analyze the crashworthiness of Toyota's seat system. He was of the opinion that the defective seat design was a substantial factor in causing Sumnicht's injuries.

We hold that there is credible evidence to support a finding that the defective seat design was a substantial factor in causing Sumnicht's injuries. Two separate theories were presented at trial as to how Sumnicht's spinal cord was severed. Toyota opined that the respondent's injuries were caused by Sumnicht's hitting his head on the dashboard of the Toyota. The jury obviously chose not to believe Toyota's theory and, instead, relied on Sumnicht's theory of causation. We agree with the jury's determination, which is supported by expert testimony and the physical facts of this case.

Second, although Sumnicht was not required to prove what extent of his injury was over and above any injury which he probably would have sustained as a result of the collision without the defective design, in essence this was proven at trial. There is sufficient evidence to support Sumnicht's theory that the portion of indivisible harm attributable solely to the defective design was his fractured cervical spine. The respondent adequately distinguished between the injuries he would have sustained without the defect (his minor injuries) and those injuries caused by the defect (his fractured spine). The trial court, at motions after verdict, held that the jury did make a determination concerning enhancement of injuries. The trial court found, and we agree, that it is reasonable to say that the jury reasoned that if the seats had been properly engineered, the respondent would have sustained practically no injuries. Technically, the defective seat system did not "enhance" Sumnicht's injuries because, but for the defect, there were no injuries to enhance. The defect in this case was latent until activated by the negligence of the driver of the car; acting together, this produced Sumnicht's quadriplegia. Toyota's defective seat system did not enhance the respondent's injury; it was a substantial factor in causing it.

II.

Sumnicht's entire liability case concentrated on the alleged design defects in Toyota's seat system.

* * *

[The court's discussion of Wisconsin's adoption of the consumer expectation standard for design defects is omitted.]

Question number one of the special verdict asks,

> "Did the 1975 Toyota automobile contain such a defect in the design of the seat system as to be unreasonably dangerous to a prospective passenger in the rear seat of the automobile?"

We must now decide whether the jury's affirmative answer to this question is supported by credible evidence. We hold that it is.

Toyota contends that there is no credible evidence to support the jury's finding that the defect in the design of the seat system was unreasonably dangerous because the respondent brought forth no proof of "an alternative, safer design, practicable under the circumstances." Huddell, 537 F.2d at 737. We disagree with Toyota for two reasons. First, although evidence of an alternative safer design may be relevant and admissible in a products liability case, our state's strict products liability rule does not mandate such evidence. A product may be defective and unreasonably dangerous even though there are no alternative, safer designs available. See, D.L. v. Huebner, 110 Wis.2d at 619, 329 N.W.2d 890, where we held that a whole industry may be negligent in failing to adopt new and available devices. The question is not whether any other manufacturer has produced a safer design, but whether the specific product in question is defective and unreasonably dangerous. Second, although not required, the evidence in this case proves that there was an alternative safer design available for Toyota's seat system. There was a confirmation by one witness that there are numerous energy-absorbing materials available to fill in the cutout section of the driver's seat and that these materials were being used in the industry. Also, another witness stated that the bracket on the passenger's seat failed because it was made of low-grade steel instead of a material that would stand up to forces in a reasonably foreseeable collision.

This court has refrained from adopting mandatory factors that must be weighed when determining if a product is defective and unreasonably dangerous. Since product defects are unique in each case, the factors that will be beneficial in assessing defectiveness and unreasonableness will differ from case to case. The United States Court of Appeals for the Seventh Circuit, in applying Wisconsin law, has suggested five factors which should be examined when determining the reasonableness of a design. This list may be beneficial to plaintiffs in proving their case, but these factors are clearly permissive. The relevant factors are:

> "1) [C]onformity of defendant's design to the practices of other manufacturers in its industry at the time of manufacture; 2) the open and obvious nature of the alleged danger; * * * 3) the extent of the claimant's use of the very product alleged to have caused the injury and the period of time

involved in such use by the claimant and others prior to the injury without any harmful incident; * * * 4) the ability of the manufacturer to eliminate danger without impairing the product's usefulness or making it unduly expensive; and 5) the relative likelihood of injury resulting from the product's present design." Collins v. Ridge Tool Company, 520 F.2d 591, 594 (7th Cir.1975).

The existence of a product's defective design that is unreasonably dangerous can be established through expert opinion testimony that was formed after an examination of the product. Barris v. Bob's Drag Chutes & Equipment, 685 F.2d 94, 101 (3d Cir.1982). Four of the respondent's experts—Enz, Sances, Brenner, and Weiss—gave their opinions with respect to the defectiveness and unreasonableness of Toyota's seat design.

Enz examined the Toyota and stated that the seat system was defective and unreasonably dangerous, specifically, the open cutout section of the driver's seat, which has the capability of capturing and entrapping, and the inadequate metal selected for the bracket, which allowed it to break upon impact. Dr. Sances also testified that the seat design was defective and unreasonably dangerous and that many energy-absorbing materials were available to cover the cutout portion of the driver's seat. Dr. Brenner, an automobile safety engineer with substantial credentials, testified at great length as to how a properly designed seat system would compartmentalize an unbelted rear seat occupant and manage the energy caused in a foreseeable collision. It was his opinion that the seat system failed and was, therefore, defective and unreasonably dangerous because of the hollow cutout portion in the driver's seat, the lack of energy-absorbing material in the cutout section, and the weak steel from which the bracket was made. Finally, Stanley Weiss, a metallurgist, testified with respect to the seat bracket that had failed. He stated that he performed a fractographic analysis (to determine the nature of the fracture), a stress analysis, and a hardness test on the bracket. He concluded that the seat bracket was defective because it was made of the weakest steel available and would not withstand the force of a rear seat occupant's impacting it in a reasonably foreseeable crash.

In addition to expert testimony, the presence of a product's defective design that is unreasonably dangerous can be established by the presentation of circumstantial evidence. Barris, 685 F.2d at 101. "Evidence of a malfunction is one type of circumstantial evidence that can be used in establishing a defective condition." Id. In this case, it was undisputed that there was severe damage to the interior of the Toyota: the bracket on the passenger's seat broke, the seats were displaced, the floor buckled, and the vinyl covering the back of the driver's seat showed an imprint from a body. Second, there was testimony that from a safety standpoint, a primary function of a seat system is to compartmentalize unbelted rear seat occupants and not to enhance injuries that may occur in a reasonably foreseeable collision. The respondent brought forth evidence that Toyota's seat system did not serve the function of compartmentalizing unbelted rear seat occupants. Also, although controverted by other evidence, the respondent introduced an article co-authored by Arnold Siegel, Toyota's chief expert, which included a study of 54 frontal collisions resulting in 135 incidents of injuries to unbelted rear seat occupants. Only twenty percent of the rear seat passengers suffered serious injuries in crashes occurring at speeds over forty miles per hour; eighty percent of those injured suffered only moderate or minor injuries. Sumnicht inferred that absent the defective seat system, it was probable that he would have suffered only moderate or minor injuries, but in this case the Toyota was defective in that it failed to protect him from further injuries.

Finally, Toyota showed two films of full-scale crash tests conducted on 1975 Toyota Corollas. The results of these tests were challenged by the respondent. Testimony was adduced that the seat brackets in the film broke upon impact, just as the bracket did in this case, and that the films supported the respondent's theory of liability and not Toyota's theory.

Before we get to the issue at hand, we must first note that the risk that a car may be in an accident is reasonably foreseeable by the appellants, and, therefore, the appellants have a duty to anticipate that risk. Arbet, 66 Wis.2d at 558, 225 N.W.2d 431. We reemphasize the following from the *Larsen* decision:

> "We perceive of no sound reason, either in logic or experience, nor any command in precedent, why the manufacturer should not be held to a reasonable duty of care in the design of its vehicle consonant with the state of the art to minimize the effect of accidents. The manufacturers are not insurers but should be held to a standard of reasonable care in design to provide a reasonably safe vehicle in which to travel. * * * The duty of reasonable care in design should be viewed in light of the risk. While all risks cannot be eliminated nor can a crash-proof vehicle be designed under the present state of the art, there are many common-sense factors in design, which are or should be well known to the manufacturer that will minimize or lessen the injurious effects of a collision. The standard of reasonable care is applied in many other negligence situations and should be applied here." Larsen, 391 F.2d at 503, cited with approval in Arbet, 66 Wis.2d at 560, 225 N.W.2d 431.

In viewing the evidence in the light most favorable to the respondent, we hold that there is credible evidence to sustain the jury's finding that Toyota's seat system was both defective and unreasonably dangerous. It was reasonable for the jury to conclude that Toyota's seat system was defective in that it failed to compartmentalize the respondent in a foreseeable frontal collision and, thus, failed to minimize his injuries, and that the defect was unreasonably dangerous because rear seat occupants would not realize the risk of harm that they are subjected to if an accident does occur. The defect in the design of the seat system was not open and obvious to an ordinary passenger. It is rational to hold that Toyota's seat system was not as safe as it reasonably could have been or as safe as reasonably contemplated by rear seat occupants.

* * *

The judgment and order of the circuit court are affirmed.

[Concurring opinion of Heffernan, C.J., omitted.]

STEINMETZ, JUSTICE (dissenting).

* * *

This is a difficult legal case made more difficult by the majority's opinion which I find to be confusing and without precedential value, and in this respect, I agree with the concurring opinion. The injuries to plaintiff are awesome and due deliberation should be given to allow him the right to a fair trial and to receive damages if he is entitled to them. I find it incomprehensible that the jury found under the facts of this case the plaintiff was not negligent for his own care and safety by failing to wear the available rear seat belt. The finding of no negligence is inconsistent with the facts of a head-on crash at a speed of 30 to 50 miles per hour while not wearing a seat belt and sustaining very serious injuries as a result of being propelled forward. The fact that plaintiff was affected by his failure to wear a seat belt is obvious and a finding of no negligence is inconsistent with the evidence and therefore is perverse.

* * *

NOTES

1. Same result in *Sumnicht* if plaintiff had been the driver?

2. The test for defectiveness in crashworthiness cases involves the same basic considerations arising in defect cases generally. An influential early case was Dreisonstok v. Volkswagenwerk, A.G., 489 F.2d 1066 (4th Cir.1974). Plaintiff was injured while riding as a passenger in the front seat of a Volkswagen microbus when the vehicle collided with a telephone pole at 40 m.p.h. The district court found for the plaintiff, concluding that the vehicle's design was defective for failure to have "sufficient energy-absorbing materials or devices or 'crush space' * * * so that at 40 miles an hour the integrity of the passenger compartment would not be violated." Plaintiff's case was built upon a comparison of the structural integrity of the passenger compartment in front-end collisions of the VW microbus with that of a standard American passenger car. Rejecting this comparison as invalid, the Court of Appeals reversed:

> The defendant's vehicle, described as "a van type multipurpose vehicle", was of a special type and particular design. This design was uniquely developed in order to provide the owner with the maximum amount of either cargo or passenger space in a vehicle inexpensively priced and of such dimensions as to make possible easy maneuverability. To achieve this, it advanced the driver's seat forward, bringing such seat in close proximity to the front of the vehicle, thereby adding to the cargo or passenger space. This, of course, reduced considerably the space between the exact front of the vehicle and the driver's

> compartment. All of this was readily discernible to any one using the vehicle; in fact, it was, as we have said, the unique feature of the vehicle. The usefulness of the design is vouchsafed by the popularity of the type. [Indeed, the driver's father immediately purchased another microbus to replace the one destroyed in this accident.] It was of special utility as a van for the transportation of light cargo, as a family camper, as a station wagon and for use by passenger groups too large for the average passenger car. * * * There was no evidence in the record that there was any practical way of improving the "crashability" of the vehicle that would have been consistent with the peculiar purposes of its design.

Id. at 1073–74. The court further noted the importance of considering price in the crashworthiness risk-benefit calculus, observing that "if a change in design would appreciably add to cost, add little to safety, and take an article out of the price range of the market to which it was intended to appeal, it may be 'unreasonable' as well as 'impractical' for the Courts to require the manufacturer to adopt such change." Id. at 1073. The public, thought the court, surely expects less crashworthiness in an economy car than in a Cadillac.

Compare Seattle–First National Bank v. Volkswagen of America, Inc., 11 Wash.App. 929, 525 P.2d 286 (1974), aff'd, 86 Wash.2d 145, 542 P.2d 774 (1975), where the court held that a jury should be permitted to pass on the crashworthiness of the front end of a VW microbus which struck the rear end of a flatbed truck at a relative speed of 20 m.p.h. *Dreisonstock* was distinguished on the basis of the difference in speed at the time of the collisions. Are the cases reconcilable?

3. Crashworthiness litigation has involved virtually every aspect of vehicle safety. For example:

A. **Structural integrity.** Dawson v. Chrysler Corp., 630 F.2d 950 (3d Cir. 1980), cert. denied, 450 U.S. 959, 101 S.Ct. 1418, 67 L.Ed.2d 383 (1981) (side frame collapsed on impact with pole); Grimshaw v. Ford Motor Co., 119 Cal. App.3d 757, 174 Cal.Rptr. 348 (1981) (fuel tank located within flimsy rear structure).

B. **Interior design.** Mickle v. Blackmon, 252 S.C. 202, 166 S.E.2d 173 (1969) (passenger impaled on gear shift lever mounted on steering column when plastic knob shattered in side-impact collision); Rossell v. Volkswagen of America, 147 Ariz. 160, 709 P.2d 517 (1985) (battery located inside passenger compartment of VW beetle where it could drip acid on occupants if vehicle rolled on back).

C. **Safety devices.** Camacho v. Honda Motor Co., Inc., 741 P.2d 1240 (Colo.1987) (crash bar to protect legs on motorcycle); Leichtamer v. American Motors Corp., 67 Ohio St.2d 456, 424 N.E.2d 568 (1981) (Jeep roll bar collapsed); Huddell v. Levin, 537 F.2d 726 (3d Cir.1976) (death from head hitting sharp metal edge inside head restraint); Garrett v. Ford Motor Co., 684 F.Supp. 407 (D.Md.1987) (severe abdominal injuries to rear passengers wearing lap belts, causing paralysis and death).

Hundreds of cases are now pending on the issue of whether the standard rear seat lap belt, as opposed to the three point shoulder belt used in the front, renders a vehicle uncrashworthy. See, e.g., Garrett v. Ford Motor Co., 684 F.Supp. 407 (D.Md.1987). See generally Sakayan, Holtz & Kelley, More Than a Case About a Car—An Analysis of Garrett v. Ford Motor Company, Trial 34

(Feb.1989); Swartz, Swartz & Cantor, Seat–Belt Injury Litigation, Trial 47 (Nov. 1988).

D. **Exterior design.** Green v. Volkswagen of America, Inc., 485 F.2d 430 (6th Cir.1973) (as young girl was walking by parked van, finger severed by sharp vent on side); Knippen v. Ford Motor Co., 546 F.2d 993 (D.C.Cir.1976); Passwaters v. General Motors Corp., 454 F.2d 1270 (8th Cir.1972) (motorcycle passenger's leg injured when struck by Ben–Hur type wheel cover).

4. In Seese v. Volkswagenwerk A.G., 648 F.2d 833 (3d Cir.), cert. denied, 454 U.S. 867, 102 S.Ct. 330, 70 L.Ed.2d 168 (1981), the court addressed the evidentiary use of accident statistics collected by the federal government. The National Highway Traffic Safety Administration operates a Fatal Accident Reporting System (FARS) which collects information on fatal accidents by vehicle type and make. The plaintiff in *Seese* attempted to introduce FARS data into evidence to show the greater likelihood of ejection from a VW van than from competitive vehicles. The defendant objected on the ground that the government data were not official records, nor was proof offered that the data represented accidents similar to the accident in question. Defendant's objections were overruled on the basis that FARS data offered in the form of certified copies of official records were admissible as public records under Fed. R.Evid. 1005, as part of the basis of an expert's opinion under Fed.R.Evid. 703, and the Business Records Act, 28 U.S.C.A. § 1732, and that differences between the plaintiff's accident and FARS data went to the weight of the evidence and not to its admissibility.

5. Crash test evidence is also frequently used in automotive litigation by defendants and plaintiffs. See, e.g., Shipp v. General Motors Corp., 750 F.2d 418 (5th Cir.1985) (Pontiac TransAm roof collapsed in rollover accident, injuring plaintiff; drop test results used by plaintiff to show roof defect admitted over defense objections that test conditions differed from actual accident conditions). *Held,* the test was relevant to roof strength, and its admission by the trial judge was not an abuse of discretion, even without an instruction to the jury to consider any differences between the drop test and accident conditions.

6. In Dawson v. Chrysler Corp., 630 F.2d 950 (3d Cir.1980), cert. denied, 450 U.S. 959, 101 S.Ct. 1418, 67 L.Ed.2d 383 (1981), plaintiff lost control of his 1974 Dodge Monaco which "slid off the highway, over a curb, through a small sign, and into an unyielding steel pole that was fifteen inches in diameter. The car struck the pole in a backwards direction at a forty-five degree angle on the left side of the vehicle; the point of impact was the left rear wheel well. As a result of the force of the collision, the vehicle literally wrapped itself around the pole. The pole ripped through the body of the car and crushed Dawson between the seat and the 'header' area of the roof, located just above the windshield." Dawson's collision with the interior of the car ruptured his fifth and sixth cervical vertebrae, rendering him a quadriplegic.

Plaintiffs alleged the car was defectively designed "because it did not have a full, continuous steel frame extending through the door panels, and a cross-member running through the floor board between the posts located between the front and rear doors of the vehicle. Had the vehicle been so designed, the Dawsons alleged, it would have 'bounced' off the pole following relatively slight penetration by the pole into the passenger space."

Chrysler's experts testified that:

> [T]he design and construction of the 1974 Dodge Monaco complied with all federal vehicle safety standards, and that deformation of the body

of the vehicle is desirable in most crashes because it absorbs the impact of the crash and decreases the rate of deceleration on the occupants of the vehicle. Thus, Chrysler's experts asserted that, for most types of automobile accidents, the design offered by the Dawsons would be less safe than the existing design. They also estimated that the steel parts that would be required in the model suggested by the Dawsons would have added between 200 and 250 pounds to the weight, and approximately $300 to the price of the vehicle. It was also established that the 1974 Dodge Monaco's unibody construction was stronger than comparable Ford and Chevrolet vehicles.

The jury awarded plaintiffs over $2 million in damages, and Chrysler appealed. Chrysler argued that the jury could not reasonably have found that plaintiffs' alternative design was safer than the existing design, or that it was cost effective, practicable, or marketable. "In short, Chrysler urges that the substitute design would be less socially beneficial than was the actual design * * * [emphasizing] that the design of the [car] complied with all [NHTSA standards]." The court responded:

> Compliance with the safety standards promulgated pursuant to the National Traffic and Motor Vehicle Safety Act, however, does not relieve Chrysler of liability in this action. For, in authorizing the Secretary of Transportation to enact these standards, Congress explicitly provided, "Compliance with any Federal motor vehicle safety standard issued under this subchapter does not exempt any person from any liability under common law." 15 U.S.C. § 1397(c) (1976).

Held, affirmed. The jury could reasonably have found that the car was "not reasonably fit, suitable and safe" under New Jersey law. The court concluded as follows:

> Although we affirm the judgment of the district court, we do so with uneasiness regarding the consequences of our decision and of the decisions of other courts throughout the country in cases of this kind.
>
> As we observed earlier, (see p. 957 supra) Congress, in enacting the National Traffic and Motor Vehicle Safety Act, provided that compliance with the Act does not exempt any person from liability under the common law of the state of injury. The effect of this provision is that the states are free, not only to create various standards of liability for automobile manufacturers with respect to design and structure, but also to delegate to the triers of fact in civil cases arising out of automobile accidents the power to determine whether a particular product conforms to such standards. In the present situation, for example, the New Jersey Supreme Court has instituted a strict liability standard for cases involving defective products, has defined the term "defective product" to mean any such item that is not "reasonably fit, suitable and safe for its intended or reasonably foreseeable purposes," and has left to the jury the task of determining whether the product at issue measures up to this standard.
>
> The result of such arrangement is that while the jury found Chrysler liable for not producing a rigid enough vehicular frame, a factfinder in another case might well hold the manufacturer liable for producing a frame that is too rigid. Yet, as pointed out at trial, in certain types of accidents—head-on collisions—it is desirable to have a car designed to collapse upon impact because the deformation would

absorb much of the shock of the collision, and divert the force of deceleration away from the vehicle's passengers. In effect, this permits individual juries applying varying laws in different jurisdictions to set nationwide automobile safety standards and to impose on automobile manufacturers conflicting requirements. It would be difficult for members of the industry to alter their design and production behavior in response to jury verdicts in such cases, because their response might well be at variance with what some other jury decides is a defective design. Under these circumstances, the law imposes on the industry the responsibility of insuring vast numbers of persons involved in automobile accidents.

Equally serious is the impact on other national social and economic goals of the existing case-by-case system of establishing automobile safety requirements. As we have become more dependent on foreign sources of energy, and as the price of that energy has increased, the attention of the federal government has been drawn to a search to find alternative supplies and the means of conserving energy. More recently, the domestic automobile industry has been struggling to compete with foreign manufacturers which have stressed smaller, more fuel-efficient cars. Yet, during this same period, Congress has permitted a system of regulation by ad hoc adjudications under which a jury can hold an automobile manufacturer culpable for not producing a car that is considerably heavier, and likely to have less fuel efficiency.

In sum, this appeal has brought to our attention an important conflict that implicates broad national concerns. Although it is important that society devise a proper system for compensating those injured in automobile collisions, it is not at all clear that the present arrangement of permitting individual juries, under varying standards of liability, to impose this obligation on manufacturers is fair or efficient. Inasmuch as it was the Congress that designed this system, and because Congress is the body best suited to evaluate and, if appropriate, to change that system, we decline today to do anything in this regard except to bring the problem to the attention of the legislative branch.

Bound as we are to adjudicate this appeal according to the substantive law of New Jersey, and because we find no basis in that law to overturn the jury's verdict, the judgment of the district court will be affirmed.

7. **Legislative Reform.** A number of states have enacted laws that provide for indemnification between the automobile manufacturer and dealer for products liability claims. See, e.g., Idaho Code § 49–2424 (vehicle manufacturer must indemnify dealer for all products liability judgments and settlements); Maine Rev.Stat.Ann. § 10–1175 (manufacturer, if held liable, must indemnify dealer for costs and attorney's fees incurred in defending suit).

8. See generally De Dominicis, No Duty at Any Speed? Determining the Responsibility of the Automobile Manufacturer in Speed–Related Accidents, 14 Hofstra L.Rev. 465 (1986); Clark, Second Collision Liability: A Critique of Two Approaches to Plaintiff's Burden of Proof, 68 Iowa L.Rev. 811 (1983); Symposium, Products Liability Law and Motor Vehicle Design, 14 U. of Toledo L.Rev. 301 (1983); Hoenig, Resolution of "Crashworthiness" Design Claims, 55 St. Johns L.Rev. 633 (1981); Hoenig and Goetz, A Rational Approach to "Crash-

worthy" Automobiles: The Need for Judicial Responsibility, 6 Sw.U.L.Rev. 1 (1974); Nader & Page, Automobile Design and the Judicial Process, 55 Calif.L. Rev. 645 (1967); Katz, Liability of Automobile Manufacturers for Unsafe Design of Passenger Cars, 69 Harv.L.Rev. 863 (1956); Assn. of Trial Lawyers of America, Crashworthiness (forthcoming, 1989).

VANOVER v. FORD MOTOR COMPANY

United States District Court, Eastern District of Missouri, 1986.
632 F.Supp. 1095.

WANGELIN, DISTRICT JUDGE.

This matter is before the Court upon defendant's motion for partial summary judgment.

On October 17, 1982, while driving on U.S. Highway 61, Edward Dale Vanover violently collided head-on with an Oldsmobile Cutlass driven by Cynthia Jo Gates. Both drivers died as a result of injuries sustained in the accident.

Mr. Vanover's wife and child have sued Ford, alleging that the 1979 Zephyr that he was driving was defective because, among other things, it did not contain an airbag system. (Complaint, Counts I and II).

Defendant asserts that plaintiffs' airbag theory is preempted by federal law and, thus, summary judgment as to this claim should be granted in defendant's favor. For reasons set forth below, the Court finds that Congress has preempted the field in this matter and that even if Congress had not preempted the field, the subject vehicle was not unreasonably dangerous so as to allow recovery under Missouri's Second Collision Doctrine.

It is the plaintiffs' general contention that the subject vehicle was in a defective and unreasonably dangerous condition because it was incapable of providing reasonable protection to occupants during crashes. In short, plaintiffs allege that the vehicle was not "crashworthy" because it lacked adequate passive restraint systems. An automotive safety device is characterized as "passive" rather than "active" when it requires no independent action by occupants to render it effective. Occupants who are, for example, tired, distracted, lazy, absent minded or even inebriated, can remain "passive" and will have protection from foreseeable crashes as a result of the following components which are encompassed within the definition of "passive" restraint system: Padded and contoured interior surfaces [such as the] windshield, roof, seats, head restraints, arm rests, energy absorbing steering column, etc. On the other hand, "active" restraint systems include door locks and manually fastened seat belts.

Plaintiffs maintain that an especially effective component of passive restraint systems, if not the most effective component, which can be installed on automobiles is an "airbag" or "air cushion". An airbag remains concealed within the dashboard and steering column of an automobile until activated by impact, when it inflates to cushion vehicle occupants from the forces of the collision. The plaintiffs contend that airbags provide superior protection in front or front angle crashes, such as the collision in the instant case.

For some fifteen years the United States Government has directly and expressly regulated the use of airbags in automobiles in this country. In 1966 Congress enacted the National Traffic and Motor Vehicle Safety Act (the "Safety Act"), directing the Secretary of Transportation to prescribe Federal Motor Vehicle Safety Standards that "meet the need for motor vehicle safety." 15 U.S.C. § 1392. Congress defined "motor vehicle safety" as the degree of protection needed to protect the public "against unreasonable risk of accidents occurring as a result of the design, construction, or performance of motor vehicles and * * * unreasonable risk of death or injury to persons in the event accidents do occur." 15 U.S.C. § 1391(1). In promulgating any such standard, the Secretary must consider whether it is "reasonable, practicable and appropriate." 15 U.S.C. § 1392(f).

In 1974 Congress responded to Transportation Department proposals and expressly prohibited the Department from requiring airbags or any other non-belt safety system unless the Secretary first (a) followed special hearing procedures and (b) provided both houses of Congress an opportunity to review the proposed requirement. 15 U.S.C. § 1410(b)–(d). Further, Congress expressly preempted attempts by states to establish safety standards different from a Federal Motor Vehicle Safety Standard governing the same vehicle feature. 15 U.S.C. § 1392(d). Congress thus, intended that there should be but one set of national standards to assure the safety of motor vehicles. See S.Rep. No. 1301, 89th Cong., 2nd Sess. (1966), U.S.Code Cong. & Admin.News 1966, p. 2709.

If this or any other Court should hold an automobile manufacturer liable in tort for failing to install an airbag system, it would have the effect of requiring all manufacturers to install airbags or face the possibility of enormous liability in tort. The imposition of damages under state tort law has long been held to be a form of state regulation subject to the Supremacy Clause. San Diego Building Trades Council v. Garmon, 359 U.S. 236, 247, 79 S.Ct. 773, 780, 3 L.Ed.2d 775 (1959):

> [R]egulation can be as effectively exerted through an award of damages as through some form of prevention relief. The obligation to pay compensation can be, indeed is designed to be, a potent method of governing conduct and controlling policy. Even the States' salutary effort to redress private wrongs or grant compensation for past harm cannot be exerted to regulate activities that are potentially subject to the exclusive federal regulatory scheme.

This type of ad hoc regulation is exactly what Congress sought to exclude by enacting the National Traffic and Motor Vehicle Safety Act of 1966. Moreover, courts have applied 15 U.S.C. § 1392(d) to preempt state motor vehicle safety standards whenever those standards were not identical to and applicable to the same aspect of performance as a Federal Motor Vehicle Safety Standard. [Citations.]

Here, § 1392(d) on its face preempts plaintiffs' attempt to create an airbag requirement under state tort law. There is now, and there was when Ford manufactured the Vanover Zephyr, a Federal Motor Vehicle Safety standard directly and expressly governing the aspect of the automobile as to which plaintiffs seek to impose a state law standard—namely, airbags. Plaintiffs' purported state law standard, which would require the installation of air bags on penalty of enormous liability in tort, certainly would not be identical to the federal standard, which expressly authorizes manufacturers of automobiles to use any of several restraint systems, only one of which is airbags. Therefore, there is express preemption under § 1392(d).

Even if Congress had not preempted this area, defendant's motion would still be granted because the Vanover Zephyr could not be characterized as unreasonably dangerous under Missouri's Second Collision Doctrine. Plaintiffs' predicate their theory of recovery upon defendant's failure to provide an airbag which allegedly would have prevented the plaintiffs' decedent from coming in contact with the various parts of the interior of the automobile. * * *

* * *

* * * [T]his Court [is not] aware of any reported case which holds that liability can be imposed upon a manufacturer for failing to equip a vehicle with a specific safety device (airbag), if that manufacturer did in fact provide a different device to serve the same end (three-point seatbelt).

* * *

* * * [T]he term "unreasonably dangerous" focuses on what is contemplated by the ordinary consumer. In this case, the plaintiffs could not have expected that an airbag would pop-out of the dashboard. However, plaintiffs could expect that the vehicle would be equipped with some sort of restraint system which met government standards. [Citations.]

It is uncontroverted that Mr. Vanover's Ford Zephyr was equipped with a lap and shoulder harness restraint system. Moreover, the Department of Transportation has determined that an airbag system would not save any more lives than the belt system as used in those cars. 49 Fed.Reg. 28962, 28986 (July 17, 1984). Additionally, the use of airbags in smaller cars, such as the Ford Zephyr, in which the shorter space between the front of the car and the passenger, leaves less time for inflation of the bag. Id. at 28974, 29001.

There is no question of fact to be determined in this matter. It is only a question of law as to whether a car equipped with a lap belt and shoulder harness is unreasonably dangerous under Missouri's Second Collision Doctrine due to the manufacturer's failure to install an airbag restraint system. As such, this is an appropriate matter for summary judgment.

In light of the foregoing, the Court finds that the Vanovers' Ford Zephyr was not unreasonably dangerous and, thus, defendant's motion for partial summary judgment as to plaintiffs' airbag claims will be granted.

NOTES

1. Most courts have agreed. See, e.g., Evers v. General Motors Corp., 770 F.2d 984 (11th Cir.1985) (duty reasonably to minimize second collision hazards does not requre air bags when another effective passive restraint system, seat belts, is part of vehicle design); Wickstrom v. Maplewood Toyota, Inc., 416 N.W.2d 838 (Minn.App.1987) (air bag claim preempted), cert. denied, ___ U.S. ___, 108 S.Ct. 2905, 101 L.Ed.2d 937 (1988); Kern v. General Motors Corp., 724 P.2d 1365 (Colo.App.1986) (no duty). At least a couple of courts have ruled to the contrary. See Murphy v. Nissan Motor Corp., 650 F.Supp. 922 (E.D.N.Y. 1987) (rejecting *Vanover*).

2. The passive-restraint preemption issue is much more complex than *Vanover* suggests. Since the 1960s, the pertinent regulation, FMVSS 208, has been addressed off and on by all three branches of government. From 1976, FMVSS 208 has provided manufacturers with the option of installing (1) lap and shoulder belts (with a belt warning system), (2) air bags, or (3) both. 49 CFR § 571.208, S4.2.2 (1987). Two provisions of the National Traffic and Motor Vehicle Safety Act bear on the question of whether FMVSS 208 preempts claims under state law against automotive manufacturers for failing to equip cars with air bags:

The preemption clause. 15 U.S.C.A. § 1392(d) provides in part:

> [N]o State * * * shall have any authority * * * to establish * * * any safety standard * * * which is not identical to the Federal Standard.

The savings clause. 15 U.S.C.A. § 1397(c) provides in part:

> Compliance with any Federal motor safety standard * * * does not exempt any person from any liability under common law.

As of early 1989, no state supreme court had ruled on the preemption issue. In the only federal Court of Appeals decision to date, Wood v. General Motors Corp., 865 F.2d 395 (1st Cir.1988), the court ruled (2–1) that the Safety Act (and FMVSS 208) impliedly, but not expressly, preempted air bag claims. There was no *express* preemption, thought the court, because Congress in 1966 had not envisaged crashworthiness lawsuits that would conflict with federal safety standards in the same manner as state administrative safety regulations. According to Chief Judge Campbell, implied preemption was another matter:

> While we * * * do not find express preemption, we are convinced that Congress's purposes, as revealed in the Safety Act and in the legislative history, plainly *imply* a preemptive intent. The instant product liability claim alleging that the absence of an air bag rendered the vehicle's design faulty would, if upheld, clearly "stand as an obstacle" to the regulatory scheme of the Safety Act. * * * Allowing [such an action] would be tantamount to establishing a conflict-

> ing safety standard that necessarily encroaches upon the goal of uniformity specifically set forth by Congress in this area.

Id. at 408. The court reasoned further:

> Even though the goal of Wood's design defect action might be the same as that of the Safety Act—that is to increase automobile safety—Wood's theory of recovery is preempted by FMVSS 208 and the Safety Act because it interferes with the *method* by which Congress intended to meet this goal.

Id. at 419.

Dissenting, Judge Selya remarked in part:

> My brethren today espouse a vision of preemption that I find needlessly wide and a conception of the common law that seemingly misperceives tort as a regulatory system. What is more, this espousal occurs in an arena fraught with the political drama—automobile safety regulation—where we should be especially reluctant to insulate administrative decisions from the prophylaxis of the civil jury, thereby placing common law protections beyond the reach of the motoring public. I am not so naive as to question that Congress may, if it chooses, shield its legislative product from unwanted state-law infringement. Short of that, however, the regulatory schematas of administrative agencies should be no less subject to the full panoply of democratic institutions than are the overt acts of other governmental instrumentalities.
>
> While jury verdicts have an admittedly anecdotal quality, they are a core ingredient of our representative democracy, signifying the considered judgment of citizens forced to confront and define the scope of law in action. Because I can discern neither a clear expression that this tort action has been preempted nor any sufficient reason to imply so drastic a result, I would answer the certified question in the negative and affirm the decision below.

3. In 1984, NHTSA amended Standard 208 conditionally mandating a gradual phase in of passive restraints, including air bags, in passenger automobiles. 49 CFR § 571.208 (1988). The deadline, originally set at 1989, has been extended. "Passive restraint regulation (Standard 208) has advanced over the years along a protracted, winding, sometimes perilous course." Public Citizen v. Steed, 851 F.2d 444, 445 (D.C.Cir.1988). Its history is traced in State Farm Mut. Auto. Ins. Co. v. Dole, 802 F.2d 474 (D.C.Cir.1986), cert. denied, 480 U.S. 951, 107 S.Ct. 1616, 94 L.Ed.2d 800 (1987), and Motor Vehicle Manufacturers Ass'n v. State Farm Mut. Auto. Ins. Co., 463 U.S. 29, 34–38, 103 S.Ct. 2856, 2862–64, 77 L.Ed.2d 443 (1983). See also *Public Citizen v. Steed,* supra.

4. As of early 1989, at least three vehicles, Mercedes, Honda Accura, and BMW were equipped with airbags as standard equipment, and air bags are available as options on several other cars. Chrysler provided air bags as standard equipment on two of its most expensive models; Ford/Mercury offered airbags as an option on two models, and General Motors had no air bags available.

5. See Miller, Deflating the Airbag Preemption Controversy, 37 Emory L.J. 897 (1988); Wilton, Federalism Issues in "No Airbag" Tort Claims: Preemption and Reciprocal Comity, 61 Notre Dame L.Rev. 1 (1986); McGowan,

Airbag Claims: Is There Federal Preemption?, Trial 39 (Feb.1988). Bryant, Airbag Litigation—Past, Present, and Future, Trial 30 (Feb.1989).

SECTION 2. SEAT BELT NONUSE

LOWE v. ESTATE MOTORS, LIMITED

Supreme Court of Michigan, 1987.
428 Mich. 439, 410 N.W.2d 706.

RILEY, CHIEF JUSTICE.

In this automobile products liability action, we review the Court of Appeals reversal of the trial court's interlocutory denial of plaintiff's motion to strike an affirmative defense pled by defendants, and a motion in limine to preclude the introduction of any evidence concerning plaintiff's failure to use an available seat belt. The issue we consider is limited to the admissibility of evidence concerning the existence of and failure to use seat belts for the purpose of (1) attempting to establish the affirmative defense of comparative negligence, and (2) defending the design of the vehicle in cases in which the "crashworthiness" doctrine is asserted as a theory of liability. We hold that the introduction of evidence concerning the existence of and failure to use seat belts is not to be treated differently than evidence concerning the existence of and failure to use safety devices generally, and, therefore, that such evidence may be admissible for either purpose provided a proper foundation is established. For purposes of comparative negligence, applicable in all products liability cases by legislative act, evidence of a plaintiff's failure to use an available seat belt may raise a factual issue to be submitted for jury consideration. In crashworthiness cases evidence of restraint systems is relevant to whether the vehicle as a whole was defective in design.

FACTS AND PROCEDURES

On April 18, 1979, plaintiff was a passenger in the rear seat of a 1979 Mercedes 300D owned and driven by her son, third-party defendant Rayburnell Neighbors. While traveling southbound on I–75 near Lima, Ohio, Mr. Neighbors lost control of the vehicle when approaching a construction zone. The vehicle sideswiped a construction truck parked in the right lane, traversed the southbound lanes, and struck a concrete dividing barrier. At some point after the initial impact, the right rear door opened, and plaintiff was ejected from the vehicle, sustaining multiple injuries.

Plaintiff commenced this action asserting negligent design and breach of implied warranty theories of liability. She alleged that the cause of the accident was attributable to a defectively designed floor mat which had wedged under the brake pedal, contributing to the driver's loss of control of the automobile, and further that her injuries were also caused by a defectively designed door and door-locking mechanism which rendered the automobile uncrashworthy. Defendants include Mercedes–Benz of North America (MBNA), Estate Motors Limited, a local distributor from which the automobile was purchased, and Newark Auto Products, manufacturer of the floor mat.

Defendant MBNA asserted an affirmative defense of comparative negligence on the basis of the plaintiff's failure to use the available three-point seat restraint provided for rear seat passengers. Plaintiff moved to strike that affirmative defense and to exclude at trial the admission of any evidence concerning that safety device, and her failure to use it. In support of her motions, plaintiff argued that, as a matter of law, her failure to wear a seat belt did not constitute negligence because plaintiff "owed no duty" to defendant to wear a seat belt, that her failure to wear a seat belt did not contribute to the cause of the accident, and that it did not violate her duty to avoid consequences or minimize damages. Plaintiff relied upon the authority of Selmo v. Baratono, 28 Mich.App. 217, 184 N.W.2d 367 (1970), and Romankewiz v. Black, 16 Mich.App. 119, 167 N.W.2d 606 (1969).

The trial court denied both motions * * * [and the court of appeals reversed in a 2–1 decision, 147 Mich.App. 523, 382 N.W.2d 811 (1985)].

* * *

I

This interlocutory appeal involves relatively limited questions concerning the permissible admissibility of seat belt evidence within the context of the substantive issues implicated in this automobile products liability action. We are required to decide the admissibility of such evidence for two entirely independent purposes: first, to attempt to establish the partial defense of comparative negligence; second, to defend the crashworthiness design of the vehicle. All relevant evidence is generally admissible, MRE 402. Our decision in this case, therefore, requires some discussion of the law of comparative negligence and products liability to the extent that it necessarily relates to the viability of the defense plaintiff sought to strike and the evidence plaintiff sought to exclude.

* * *

II

The doctrinal origin of the judicially created rule disallowing evidence of a plaintiff's failure to use a seat belt in this jurisdiction may be traced to the Court of Appeals decision in *Romankewiz, supra. Romankewiz* was an ordinary automobile negligence case not involving modern theories of products liability which was decided before the adoption of pure comparative negligence by this Court in Placek v. Sterling Heights, 405 Mich. 638, 275 N.W.2d 511 (1979). In

Romankewiz, the Court rejected claims that a plaintiff's failure to use a seat belt could amount to contributory negligence as a total bar to recovery or a failure to mitigate damages.

With regard to the issue of contributory negligence, the Court held "that as a matter of law, [plaintiff] had no duty to wear a seat belt," and that "plaintiff's failure to fasten his seat belt was not such negligence as to contribute to the cause of the accident [because] [u]nbuckled plaintiffs do not *cause* accidents." Romankewiz, *supra,* 16 Mich.App. at 126, 167 N.W.2d 606 (emphasis in original). The reasons given in support of its holding in this regard were as follows. First, the Court noted that the then-recently enacted statute requiring automobiles to be equipped with seat belts did not obligate individuals to use them. Second, the Court mentioned "statistics demonstrating the general non-use of seat belts, indicating that only 15% of the nation's drivers 'buckle up' [and] that belts can [actually] exacerbate injuries." *Id.,* at 124, 167 N.W.2d 606. Finally, the Court reasoned that the failure to buckle a seat belt could not amount to "a failure to exercise the ordinary care * * * *under the circumstances* * * * [because] until one has, or should have, notice of another's negligence, he is not required to anticipate it. On the contrary, he is entitled to assume that others will use due care for his safety and their own." Romankewiz, *supra,* at 125, 167 N.W.2d 606 (emphasis in original).

The Court disposed of the issue of avoidable consequences or mitigation of damages by "a very simple bit of logic: if there is no duty to buckle a seat belt, failure to do so cannot be held a breach of duty to avoid consequences or minimize damages." Id., at 126, 167 N.W.2d 606. The Court held: "Accordingly, as a matter of law, * * * failure to use a seat belt is not appropriate as a damage-mitigating factor or under the doctrine of avoidable consequences." Id., at 127, 167 N.W.2d 606. In closing, the Court said "it is for the legislature * * * to prescribe any required use" of seat belts. Id.

In Schmitzer, [v. Misener–Bennett Ford, Inc., 135 Mich.App. 350, 354 N.W.2d 336 (1984)], the Court of Appeals considered whether a plaintiff's failure to use a seat belt could be introduced as evidence of comparative negligence as a partial bar to recovery in light of the adoption of the comparative fault doctrine in *Placek,* supra. The Court reasoned that whether a plaintiff's recovery could be reduced to the extent that his own negligence caused or increased the severity of his *injury,* as opposed to the *accident* itself, was unclear. In any event, the Court held, relying on *Romankewiz,* that no duty to wear a seat belt existed, as a matter of law, and therefore the failure to use an available seat belt could not constitute a breach of the duty to use ordinary care. * * *

* * * At present, the majority view in comparative negligence jurisdictions in which the issue has been addressed requires allowing the jury to consider the seat belt nonuse defense. See Note, *The seat*

belt defense: Must the reasonable man wear a seat belt? 50 Mo LR 968, 976, n. 83, cases cited therein, and accompanying text (1985).

In Ins. Co. of North America v. Pasakarnis, 451 So.2d 447, 451 (Fla., 1984), for example, the Florida Supreme Court rejected the reasoning adopted in *Schmitzer.* The court first addressed the assertion that whether failure to use a seat belt could constitute comparative negligence was more appropriate for legislative consideration. Noting that tort law is peculiarly nonstatutory and that the court had not hesitated in the past in overturning unsound precedent in the area of tort law, the court viewed the issue as most appropriate for judicial decision, and concluded that "[t]o abstain from acting responsibly in the present case on the basis of legislative deference would be to consciously ignore a limited area where decisions of lower courts of this state have created an illogical exception to the doctrine of comparative negligence. * * * " Id.

Discussing the doctrine of pure comparative fault which it had judicially adopted in Hoffman v. Jones, 280 So.2d 431, 453 (Fla., 1973), the court concluded that the failure to wear an available seat belt could be a pertinent factor appropriate for consideration by a jury in deciding whether the plaintiff exercised due care for his own safety. *Pasakarnis,* supra, 453. In reaching that conclusion, the court flatly rejected the contention that seat belt effectiveness as a safety precaution is too "speculative," stating that the evidence of seat belt effectiveness "in reducing deaths and injury severity is substantial and unequivocal." Id.

Likewise, the court rejected the assertion that automobile accidents are unforeseeable and, therefore, that "reasonable care under the circumstances" could not, as a matter of law, require that they be anticipated. In this regard, the court discussed its earlier decision in Ford Motor Co. v. Evancho, 327 So.2d 201 (Fla.1976), adopting the "crashworthiness" doctrine and rationale of Larsen v. General Motors Corp., 391 F.2d 495 (C.A.8, 1968), in which it "expressly acknowledged [that] automobile collisions are foreseeable as are the so-called 'second collisions' with the interior of the automobile." *Pasakarnis,* supra, 453. The court quoted the following passage from *Evancho,* supra, 204:

> " 'Automobiles are made for use on the roads and highways in transporting persons and cargo to and from various points. This intended use cannot be carried out without encountering in varying degrees the statistically proved hazard of injury-producing impacts of various types. * * *
>
> " ' * * * While automobiles are not made for the purpose of colliding with each other, a frequent and inevitable contingency of normal automobile use will result in collisions and injury-producing impacts.' "

Following the decision of the New York Court of Appeals in Spier v. Barker, 35 N.Y.2d 444, 363 N.Y.S.2d 916, 323 N.E.2d 164 (1974),[12] the

12. When *Spier* was decided, contributory negligence as a total bar to recovery had not yet been replaced with the doctrine of comparative fault. The court premised its

court * * * concluded that failure to use a seat belt may not be deemed negligent or nonnegligent as a matter of law, but that it is "necessarily a matter to be determined in each instance by the jury" in all cases in which there is "competent evidence to show that the plaintiff's failure to use an available seat belt bore a causal relation to the plaintiff's injuries." Id., 450.

III

Like the Florida court in *Pasakarnis,* we are convinced that the reasons expressed by the Court of Appeals do not support disallowing the trier of fact from considering a failure to use a seat belt for the purpose of the affirmative defense of comparative negligence. * * *

The general standard of care for purposes of comparative negligence, while differing in perspective, is theoretically indistinguishable from the applicable standard for determining liability in commonlaw negligence; the standard of conduct to which one must conform for his own protection is that of "a reasonable [person] under like circumstances." * * *

* * * It is, of course, indisputable that, pursuant to the law of comparative negligence, every person has an obligation to exercise reasonable care for his own safety. * * * [W]hether the particular conduct in question in any given case would be a violation of that obligation "is not a question of duty, but of the specific standard of care: the reasonableness of the risk of harm thereby created." [Citation.]

* * *

The "no duty" formulation adopted in *Romankewiz,* supra, may have been a product of the all or nothing analyses surrounding the abrogated doctrine of contributory negligence as a total bar to recovery. Avoiding the potentially harsh and inequitable consequences of that complete defense may have been an appropriate concern directing the Court's decision in that case. It was precisely that concern which led this Court to judicially adopt the doctrine of pure comparative fault in *Placek,* supra, to move toward "accomplish[ing] the goal of a fair system of apportionment of damages." Id., 405 Mich. at 660, 275 N.W.2d 511.

In contrast to the abrogated defense of contributory negligence, comparative negligence never allows an otherwise liable defendant to entirely "avoid" liability and thus "escape" the duty of due care. [Citation.] That significant difference renders the creation of aberrational exceptions inherently inconsistent with general negligence principles unwarranted.

The admissibility of evidence concerning a plaintiff's failure to use a seat belt for the purpose of attempting to establish the partial defense of comparative negligence does not concern the question of duty. The

decision upon the doctrine of avoidable consequences, which it reasoned was similar to the doctrine of mitigation of damages. Whether failure to use an available seat belt constituted a breach of the duty to avoid consequences or mitigate damages was deemed a question for the jury.

common-law duty issue is limited to whether the plaintiff was under any obligation to exercise reasonable care for her own safety. It cannot be seriously contended that automobile passengers are under no obligation whatsoever to exercise due care for their own safety because accidents are unforeseeable. The speciousness of such a contention is particularly reflected in the present case in which one of plaintiff's theories of liability is indeed premised upon the foreseeability of automobile accidents. * * *

IV

We are persuaded that the decision of the Court of Appeals is inconsistent with the foregoing principles. The rationale forming the basis of that decision—that one need not anticipate the negligence of others, even if foreseeable, that a high percentage of automobile occupants do not use seat belts, that seat belt effectiveness is too speculative, and that the imposition of a duty to use them for purposes of the common-law doctrine of comparative negligence is more appropriate for legislative consideration—is flawed and inconsistent with modern and traditional principles of negligence law. That analysis, furthermore, substantially obscures the appropriate functions of the court and the jury.

While evidence of the high percentage of failures to use seat belts is relevant to the issue of reasonableness, such evidence does not support withholding the issue from the jury. The assertion that certain conduct is customary, or that a majority engage in the conduct in question, does not in and of itself make such conduct reasonable. The determinative evaluation requires contemplating the fictitious objective "reasonable person," not the subjective "average person." For customary conduct to be reasonable under the circumstances, it must be a product of what has been described "learned reason." That is, as first articulated by Judge Learned Hand in United States v. Carroll Towing Co., 159 F.2d 169, 173 (C.A.2, 1947), and consistently applied by the courts of this jurisdiction * * *, such conduct may be found to be unreasonable if the magnitude of the risk of harm created (probability of harm multiplied by the gravity of that harm) is greater than the burden of adequate precautions or the utility of the conduct in question.

In light of the uniform applicability of that formula, whether considering a defendant's conduct for purposes of liability or a plaintiff's for purposes of reducing his recovery, we agree with the reasoning of the New York Court of Appeals in Spier, supra, 35 N.Y.2d at 452, 363 N.Y.S.2d 916, 323 N.E.2d 164, that "the burden of buckling an available seat belt may, under the facts of the particular case, be found by the jury to be less than the likelihood of injury when multiplied by its accompanying severity."

We are not persuaded that all reasonable persons would agree that the burden of seat belt use, or the utility of seat belt nonuse, outweighs the resulting magnitude of the risk of injury. We are likewise not persuaded that any ascertainable public policy considerations could require that such an approach be adopted and applied in all cases. Accordingly, we hold that whether failure to use a seat belt constitutes comparative negligence so as to require the proportionate reduction of a plaintiff's recovery is an evaluative issue appropriately within the province of the jury.

If competent evidence is proffered to establish that the failure to use an available and operational seat belt contributed to producing plaintiff's damages, then the issue of comparative negligence, including the accompanying issue of causation, should be submitted to the jury pursuant to the special verdict form ordinarily used in such cases.

V

Before addressing the second issue, we pause to acknowledge the recent enactment of the mandatory seat belt usage legislation, M.C.L. § 257.710e; M.S.A. § 9.2410(5), and to respond to the positions expressed in the dissenting opinions as they relate to that legislation. That statute, which took effect on July 1, 1985, requires drivers and front-seat passengers of motor vehicles operated in this state to wear seat belts, making the failure to use them unlawful. Section five provides, furthermore, that failure to use a seat belt in violation of the statute may be considered evidence of negligence, also providing that such negligence shall not reduce a plaintiff's recovery by more than five percent. The statutory seat belt usage requirement and its accompanying provisions are inapplicable in the instant case because: (1) the accident occurred prior to the statute's effective date, (2) plaintiff was a rear-seat passenger to whom the statute, by its terms, would not have applied, and (3) the accident occurred beyond the territorial boundaries of this state where it would not have been contrary to this statute for any passenger not to have used a seat belt.

* * *

Justice Archer would hold that, to the extent that the Legislature has not required automobile occupants to use seat belts, evidence of the failure to use them for purposes of comparative negligence must be excluded and withheld from jury consideration because "no duty" to use the safety devices can otherwise exist. Justice Archer's analysis is based in part on the assertion that because the Legislature provided that a violation of the statute, effective on July 1, 1985, may be considered evidence of negligence, it intended by negative implication that in all other cases a failure to use a seat belt may not be admissible as evidence of comparative negligence. We are not inclined, however, to engage in statutory interpretation by negative implication on the basis of legislative silence. That the Legislature has not required rear-seat automobile passengers traveling outside the territorial boundaries of this state prior to the effective date of the seat belt usage law to "buckle up" does not persuade us to affirm an unsupportable exception to the common-law and statutorily prescribed comparative negligence doctrine. * * *

* * *

The question of specific percentage limitations is not now before the Court. Furthermore, unlike the Legislature, the judiciary has traditionally not involved itself in the setting of arbitrary figures or percentages. Thus, when faced with the question whether, because of the five-percent limitation, we should affirm, as a matter of common law, an erroneous and unsupportable exception to the doctrine of comparative negligence, we are compelled to answer in the negative. * * *

* * *

VI

The Court of Appeals did not address that portion of the trial court's ruling allowing the admission of seat belt evidence for the purpose of defending the crashworthiness design of the automobile as a whole. Plaintiff has asserted, as an independent theory of liability, that the design of the vehicle in question was a cause of her injuries because that design created an unreasonable risk of harm to its occupants resulting from an impact or collision. Plaintiff's theory in this regard is based upon the manufacturer's duty of designing crashworthy vehicles * * *.

* * *

MBNA argues that seat belt evidence should be admissible in crashworthiness cases to defend the safety design of the vehicle, and the relation of that design to the plaintiff's injuries, entirely independent of the comparative negligence issue. We agree with one-half of that argument completely.

By its nature, the defective crashworthiness design theory of liability requires that the vehicle be considered as a whole. * * * Accordingly, the jury should consider the vehicle's overall design, including safety features, in order to determine the crashworthiness issue, and, thus, whether the vehicle was defective in design. * * *

Evidence of the seat-restraint system goes to the heart of the issue in crashworthiness cases in which the plaintiff's injuries were sustained after being ejected from the vehicle, a result which seat belts are specifically designed to prevent. Whether the plaintiff presents her case through a negligence theory—attempting to establish that the design of the vehicle created an unreasonable risk of injury—or through a breach of implied warranty theory—that the vehicle was not reasonably fit for its intended and foreseeable uses—the determinative issue of liability concerns whether the vehicle was unreasonably unsafe because of its design. Evidence of product safety features specifically designed to prevent the injuries complained of is entirely relevant to this issue. No reason, even arguably sound, exists for excluding such evidence on this liability issue. Plaintiff has provided us with none.

* * *

The limited permissible scope of such evidence in light of its appropriate purpose, however, compels us to reject the second part of defendant's argument concerning this issue. MBNA has intertwined an argument concerning the element of causation within the context of presenting seat-restraint evidence in its defense of the vehicle's safety design, arguing that, independent of the comparative negligence issue, it may properly seek to establish that plaintiff's failure to use a seat belt was *the* cause in fact and sole proximate cause of her enhanced injuries rather than any design defect in the vehicle. Interposing the issue of causation within the same context as the issue of negligent design tends to confuse the purposes for which defendant seeks to introduce seat belt evidence, as well as the elements of plaintiff's cause of action. * * *

The plaintiff's conduct and its causal relation to her injuries is not relevant to the issue of the vehicle's design. While it is true that plaintiff must establish both that the vehicle was defective in design and that that defect proximately caused her enhanced injuries, those elements are entirely distinct. In considering whether the insufficient crashworthiness design of the vehicle was *a* proximate cause of plaintiff's injuries, the focus is upon the vehicle's design and its relation to the plaintiff's injuries. The plaintiff's conduct and the relation of that conduct to her injuries is properly considered within the context of the comparative fault issue.

Assuming that the vehicle is determined to be uncrashworthy pursuant to plaintiff's theory, the assertion that plaintiff's failure to use a seat belt could be found to be the only cause of her enhanced injuries, without regard to whether that failure is found to have been comparatively negligent, is a curious and unusual argument when viewed purely in the context of causality. While a manufacturer may ordinarily contend that, even if defectively designed, the design of its product was not a cause of the plaintiff's injuries, the theory by which MBNA seeks to do so in this regard under the facts of the instant case is improper.[22]

22. Defendant's argument in this regard is presented entirely independently of comparative negligence and without reference to the so-called misuse defense. Assuming that plaintiff's failure to use a seat belt is found not to have been negligent, MBNA does not assert any basis upon which plaintiff's failure to use a seat belt could theoretically be determined to be *a* legal cause of her enhanced injuries, much less *the* only cause. Viewed within the context of the element of causation, without regard to any fault on plaintiff's part, defendant's argument is entirely misplaced. We agree * * * that the presentation of that legally unsupportable "causation" theory would be erroneous.

Assuming, arguendo, that plaintiff successfully established that the vehicle in the present case was uncrashworthy because of a defectively designed door and door-locking mechanism, the causation element would require her to establish that that defective design proximately caused her enhanced injuries by resulting in her ejection from the vehicle. Defending against that element of plaintiff's cause of action, MBNA could properly seek to establish that, because of the nature and point of initial impact, the same result would have occurred even in the absence of the design defect. Thus, with regard to the causation element for purposes of plaintiff's crashworthiness design theory, the focus would be upon the causal relation between the vehicle design and the plaintiff's injuries.

Therefore, we caution the trial court, in the event that this cause proceeds to trial, to delimitate the appropriate use of seat-restraint evidence for the purpose of considering the reasonableness of the design of the vehicle under plaintiff's crashworthiness theory. While such evidence could enable the jury to properly determine whether the vehicle's overall design made it crashworthy, and thus not negligently defective in design, no legal basis independent of fault could enable the jury to determine that, because plaintiff's failure to use the seat restraint resulted in her enhanced injuries, the design of the vehicle could not have been *a* legal cause of those injuries. Whether, and to what extent, plaintiff's failure to use an available seat restraint proximately caused her enhanced injuries may properly be considered within the context of the comparative fault issue, and even then only after consideration of the substantive negligence question.[23]

VII

In conclusion, we hold that evidence of a failure to use a seat belt may be admissible to support an affirmative defense of comparative negligence. If competent evidence is proffered, the issue may appropriately be submitted for jury consideration. Additionally, we hold that in crashworthiness cases, seat-restraint evidence is admissible for the purpose of defending the design of the vehicle as a whole, entirely independently of the comparative negligence defense. * * *

* * * We express no opinion concerning the future applicability of M.C.L. § 257.710e; M.S.A. § 9.2410(5) with regard to cases in which the injury occurred after the effective date of that statute and a plaintiff's failure to use a seat belt was in violation of its provisions.

Thus, we reverse the decision of the Court of Appeals and reinstate the trial court's denial of plaintiff's motions to exclude all evidence of the existence of and failure to use seat belts, with the appropriate limitations expressed in part VI.

CAVANAGH and BRICKLEY, JJ., concur.

[Concurring opinion of BOYLE, J., omitted.]

ARCHER, JUSTICE (dissenting).

* * *

While other jurisdictions have reached contrary conclusions when considering the admissibility of evidence of a plaintiff's nonuse of a seat belt, Michigan's rule of prohibiting the admissibility of such evidence is the better approach. Retaining the rule of inadmissibility of seat belt nonuse is particularly important in a products liability case because the types of conduct being considered are usually varied and different.

23. Whether, and to what extent, plaintiff's failure to use the seat restraint constituted negligence which contributed to her injuries may properly be considered within the context of the comparative negligence issue. Furthermore, that issue may be properly considered only after the trier of fact has decided the substantive issue of defendant's liability. Prior to a determination of plaintiff's fault, the causal relation of her conduct and the claimed damages is irrelevant to defendant's liability.

Historically, passengers in automobiles have been considered to be free of contributory or comparative negligence unless exceptional circumstances were present.

Furthermore, the injured plaintiff in this case was a passenger in the rear seat. The risks of nonuse of a seat belt for a rear-seat passenger are unclear, and even the Legislature has not required rear-seat passengers to use seat belts.

The Legislature, during its recent tort law reforms, addressed the issue of seat belt use. During its review, the Legislature was informed of the statistics relating to the effect of seat belt use on reducing injuries and deaths in automobile accidents.

* * *

After its evaluation, the Legislature did two things. First, the Legislature made seat belt use mandatory only for the driver and the front-seat passenger. The Legislature also provided that a plaintiff's recovery could not be reduced by more than five percent for his failure to wear a seat belt. Second, the Legislature was silent about the issue of seat belt use by rear-seat passengers.

Although Michigan's mandatory seat belt statute has been criticized for failing to apportion the damages for injuries in collisions and for creating a windfall for plaintiffs, the seat belt defense "would soon result in windfalls to tortfeasors who would pay only partially for the harm their negligence caused." [8]

A majority of courts, including contributory negligence jurisdictions, prohibit the introduction of a plaintiff's nonuse of a seat belt to reduce a plaintiff's recovery.[9] Among the reasons cited are that a "defendant's fault in causing the accident distributed risks to the world at large and was capable of causing some degree of damage to any plaintiff within the sphere of foreseeability. Conversely, a plaintiff's failure to use a seat belt creates no risks to others, but merely exposes himself to a risk." [10]

* * *

While I agree in part with the majority that in crashworthiness cases the vehicle should be considered as a whole, I would, nevertheless, bar testimony regarding the nonuse of seat belts subject to the applicability of M.C.L. § 257.710e; M.S.A. § 9.2410(5).

* * *

LEVIN, JUSTICE, (separate opinion).

* * *

I agree with the view expressed in the lead opinion that evidence concerning the seat-restraint system may be considered by the trier of fact in determining whether a motor vehicle was defective in design

8. Note, A compromise between mitigation and comparative fault? A critical assessment of the seat belt controversy and a proposal for reform, 14 Hofstra L R 319, 327, 338 (1986).

9. Id., p. 330.

10. Id., p. 328.

where the plaintiff asserts the crashworthiness doctrine as a theory of liability.

* * *

After this cause was argued in the Court of Appeals, the Legislature enacted Act 1, generally requiring the driver and front-seat passenger of a motor vehicle to wear seat belts. No such obligation is imposed on rear-seat passengers. The act provides that "[f]ailure to wear a safety belt in violation of this section may be considered evidence of negligence and may reduce the recovery for damages arising out of the ownership, maintenance, or operation of a motor vehicle. However, such negligence shall not reduce the recovery for damages by more than 5%." [11]

The enactment of Act 1 should be viewed in the context of the consistent fifteen-year adherence by the Court of Appeals to the view that the failure to use a seat belt was not evidence of contributory or comparative negligence and could not be used in either an ordinary automobile negligence case or in an automobile products liability case to reduce the damages otherwise to be awarded to an injured person,

11. M.C.L. § 257.710e(5); M.S.A. § 9.2410(5)(5).

A large majority of the statutes requiring adults to wear seat belts provide either that a violation cannot be grounds for reducing an award on the basis of comparative or contributory negligence, or limit the possible reduction to a small percentage of the award. Of the approximately twenty-six states other than Michigan that have statutes presently in effect, three follow Michigan in limiting the possible reduction to a small percentage. See Iowa Code Ann., § 321.445(4)(b)(2) (5%); La.Rev. Stat.Ann., § 32.295.1(E)(4) (2%); Mo.Ann. Stat., § 307.178(3)(2) (1%).

Of the remaining twenty-three statutes, sixteen provide either that evidence of nonuse is not admissible in a civil action, or that it cannot be used to reduce an award. See Conn.Gen.Stat., § 14–100a(c)(4); D.C. Code, § 40–1607; Ill.Ann.Stat., ch. 95½, § 12–603.1(c); Ind.Stat.Ann., § 9–8–13–9; Kan.Stat.Ann., § 8–2504(c); Md.Code Ann., § 22–412.3(g); Nev.Rev.Stat., § 484.641(3); N.M.Stat.Ann., § 66–7–373(B); N.C.Gen. Stat., § 20–135.2A(d); Ohio Rev.Code Ann., § 4513.26.3(G); Okla.Stat.Ann., tit. 47, § 12–420; Tenn.Code Ann., § 55–9–604; Tex.Rev.Civ.Stat.Ann., art. 6701d, § 107C(j); Utah Code Ann., § 41–6–186; Va.Code, § 46.1–309.2(E); Wash.Rev.Code, § 46.61.688(6). Only two of the statutes specifically allow evidence of nonuse to reduce an award. See Cal.Veh.Code, ¶ 27315(i); N.Y.Veh. & Traf. Law, § 1229–c(8) (McKinney). Four of the remaining five statutes do not specifically state whether evidence of nonuse can be used to reduce an award. See Hawaii Rev.Stat., § 291–11.6; Idaho Code, § 49–764; Minn. Stat.Ann., § 169.686; N.J.Stat.Ann., § 39:3–76.2h. One statute provides that evidence of nonuse cannot be used as "prima-facie" evidence of negligence. See Fla.Stat.Ann. § 316.614(10).

The Michigan statute is also consistent with the overwhelming majority of statutes in restricting the duty to drivers and front-seat passengers. See Conn.Gen.Stat.Ann., § 14–100a(c)(1); D.C.Code, § 40–1602; Fla. Stat.Ann., § 316.614(4)(a); Hawaii Rev.Stat., § 291–11.6(a); Idaho Code, § 49–764(1); Ill. Ann.Stat., ch. 95½, § 12–603.1(a); Ind.Stat. Ann., § 9–8–14–1; Iowa Code Ann., § 321.445(2); Kan.Stat.Ann., § 8–2503(b); La.Rev.Stat.Ann., § 32.295.1(B); Md.Code Ann., § 22–412.3(b); Minn.Stat.Ann., § 169.686(1); Mo.Ann.Stat., § 307.178(2); Nev.Rev.Stat., § 484.641(2); N.J.Stat.Ann., § 39:3–76.2f(a); N.M.Stat.Ann., § 66–7–372(A); N.Y.Veh. & Traf.Law, § 1229–c(3) (McKinney); N.C.Gen.Stat., § 20–135–2A(a); Ohio Rev.Code Ann., § 4513.26.3(B)(3); Okla. Stat.Ann., tit. 47, § 12–417(A); Tenn.Code Ann., § 55–9–603(b)(1); Utah Code Ann., § 41–6–182; Tex.Rev.Civ.Stat.Ann., art. 6701d, § 107C(b)(2); Va.Code, § 46.1–309.2(A). Only two states, California and Washington, require adult, rear-seat passengers to wear seat belts. See Cal.Veh.Code, § 27315(d); Wash.Rev.Code, § 46.61.688(3). Only the California statute provides that evidence of nonuse by a rear-seat passenger may be used to show negligence or to mitigate damages.

and in light of this Court's decisions to decline to review those decisions of the Court of Appeals.

Although Act 1 was not by its terms effective until July 1, 1985, it codified the common-law rule,[12] established by the Court of Appeals, that damages may not be reduced for failure to wear a seat belt with a "narrow exception" permitting reduction of a damage award by not more than five percent for failure of a front-seat occupant to wear a seat belt.

The July 1, 1985, effective date of Act 1 was the date selected by the Legislature on which the narrow five-percent exception for front-seat occupants was to become effective, not the date on which a possible one hundred percent reduction of damages was to be reduced to no more than five percent. The lead opinion turns the July 1, 1985, effective date into a date on which relief from a possible one hundred percent reduction takes effect. That does not appear to be consonant with the legislative decision.

The Legislature, like bench and bar, may consider and rely on the decisions of the trial and appellate courts of this state when enacting new legislation. At times the common law is uncertain, and it may not be appropriate to attribute to the Legislature any particular reading of the common law. Where the common law is well-established and uncontradicted, however, and the Legislature essentially accepts the common-law rule,[13] a proper respect for legislative supremacy on substantive issues requires, in our opinion, that the judiciary ordinarily defer to the legislative decision to enter the field, abide by the legislative solution, and refrain from further and belated refinement of the substantive law.

* * *

In the instant case, the Legislature, when it enacted Act 1, had no reason to suppose that the common-law no-reduction-of-damages rule that had been stated and restated in *Romankewiz, Selmo, Placek, DeGraaf,* and *Schmitzer,* might in effect be overruled by this Court two years after the enactment of Act 1. It is again noteworthy that this Court had declined to review those decisions of the Court of Appeals where further review by this Court had been sought.

* * *

12. The Legislature did not indeed codify the common-law rule that there is no duty to wear a seat belt, but on the contrary changed that rule effective July 1, 1985, to require front-seat occupants to wear seat belts and to permit evidence of violation of that requirement to be considered as evidence of negligence. The tort consequence or remedy for failure to wear a seat belt was limited, however, to a reduction of damages by not more than five percent.

Act 1, viewed in terms of the tort significance and consequence of its enactment, in effect codified the common-law rule of no reduction of damages for failure to wear a seat belt with the narrow five-percent exception.

13. See n. 10.

NOTES

1. Accord, Waterson v. General Motors Corp., 111 N.J. 238, 544 A.2d 357 (1988), noted, 102 Harv.L.Rev. 925 (1989); Law v. Superior Court, 157 Ariz. 147, 755 P.2d 1135 (1988); Dahl v. Bayerische Motoren Werke (BMW), 304 Or. 558, 748 P.2d 77 (1987). But see Seese v. Volkswagenwerk A.G., 648 F.2d 833 (3d Cir.), cert. denied, 454 U.S. 867, 102 S.Ct. 330, 70 L.Ed.2d 168 (1981) (seat belt nonuse evidence could not be used to reduce damages, nor to show the adequacy of the design, because defendant's expert conceded that defendant did not rely on seat belts as element of challenged design).

2. Assume that (1) the comparative fault statute in the jurisdiction bars plaintiff's recovery entirely if his fault exceeds the defendant's; (2) the jury finds the plaintiff driver 20%, and the defendant manufacturer 80%, responsible for causing the *accident*; (3) the jury finds that the plaintiff's failure to wear a seat belt was 60% responsible for causing the *injuries*; and (4) the plaintiff's total injuries are $100,000.

Should plaintiff be allowed to recover anything? If so, how much? See Waterson v. General Motors Corp., 111 N.J. 238, 544 A.2d 357, 374–77 (1988).

3. On comparing design defectiveness with the driver's contributory negligence, reconsider Daly v. General Motors Corp., supra p. 540.

4. As of 1988, seat belt usage had risen to an all-time high of 43.4%, according to a NHTSA survey. At that time, 32 states and the District of Columbia had mandatory seat belt laws. In such states, the usage rate was 48.3%; in states without such laws, usage was 30.4%. In 1987, safety belts saved 4,000 lives, most of which were attributable to the enactment of mandatory use laws. See 16 Prod.Saf. & Liab.Rep. (BNA) 810–11 (Aug. 19, 1988).

5. Should failure to buckle a seat belt be considered contributory negligence as a matter of law? Should violation of a seat belt law be considered negligence per se? See *Waterson,* supra note 1 (no). But see Hutchins v. Schwartz, 724 P.2d 1194 (Alaska 1986). See Note, 102 Harv.L.Rev. 925 (1989) (criticizing *Waterson* on this point).

6. **Legislative Reform.** The varieties of seat belt laws are described in n. 9 of Justice Levin's "separate" opinion. Why do you suppose that most of the laws preclude nonuse evidence in civil actions? Because the legislatures think it reasonable not to buckle up? To enhance the deterrent effect of tort suits on manufacturers? Or for some other, non-substantive, reason?

7. See Schwartz, The Seat Belt Defense and Mandatory Seat Belt Usage: Law, Ethics, and Economics, 24 Idaho L.Rev. 275 (1987–88); Ackerman, The Seat Belt Defense Reconsidered: A Return to Accountability in Tort Law?, 16 N.M.L.Rev. 221 (1986); Westenberg, Buckle Up or Pay: The Emerging Safety Belt Defense, 20 Suffolk U.L.Rev. 867 (1986); Westenberg, The Safety Belt Defense at Trial and In Out-of-Court Settlement, 37 U.Fla.L.Rev. 785 (1985); Hoenig & Shapiro, Safety Belt Use: Some Products Liability Considerations, 7 J.Prod.Liability 153 (1984).

SECTION 3. PUNITIVE DAMAGES

GRIMSHAW v. FORD MOTOR COMPANY

Court of Appeals of California, 1981.
119 Cal.App.3d 757, 174 Cal.Rptr. 348.

TAMURA, ACTING PRESIDING JUSTICE.

A 1972 Ford Pinto hatchback automobile unexpectedly stalled on a freeway, erupting into flames when it was rear ended by a car proceeding in the same direction. Mrs. Lilly Gray, the driver of the Pinto, suffered fatal burns and 13–year–old Richard Grimshaw, a passenger in the Pinto, suffered severe and permanently disfiguring burns on his face and entire body. Grimshaw and the heirs of Mrs. Gray (Grays) sued Ford Motor Company and others. Following a six-month jury trial, verdicts were returned in favor of plaintiffs against Ford Motor Company. Grimshaw was awarded $2,516,000 compensatory damages and $125 million punitive damages; the Grays were awarded $559,680 in compensatory damages. On Ford's motion for a new trial, Grimshaw was required to remit all but $3½ million of the punitive award as a condition of denial of the motion.

[Ford appealed the punitive damages award and Grimshaw appealed the remittitur.]

FACTS

* * *

[Due to a defective carburetor float, Mrs. Gray's 6–month old Pinto suddenly stalled on an interstate highway and coasted to a stop. The Pinto was struck from the rear by another car that had braked to a speed of 28–37 mph.]

At the moment of impact, the Pinto caught fire and its interior was engulfed in flames. According to plaintiffs' expert, the impact of the Galaxie had driven the Pinto's gas tank forward and caused it to be punctured by the flange or one of the bolts on the differential housing so that fuel sprayed from the punctured tank and entered the passenger compartment through gaps resulting from the separation of the rear wheel well sections from the floor pan. By the time the Pinto came to rest after the collision, both occupants had sustained serious burns. When they emerged from the vehicle, their clothing was almost completely burned off. Mrs. Gray died a few days later of congestive heart failure as a result of the burns. Grimshaw managed to survive but only through heroic medical measures. He has undergone numerous and extensive surgeries and skin grafts and must undergo additional surgeries over the next 10 years. He lost portions of several fingers on his left hand and portions of his left ear, while his face required many skin grafts from various portions of his body. * * *

Design of the Pinto Fuel System:

In 1968, Ford began designing a new subcompact automobile which ultimately became the Pinto. Mr. Iacocca, then a Ford Vice President, conceived the project and was its moving force. Ford's objective was to build a car at or below 2,000 pounds to sell for no more than $2,000.

Ordinarily marketing surveys and preliminary engineering studies precede the styling of a new automobile line. Pinto, however, was a rush project, so that styling preceded engineering and dictated engineering design to a greater degree than usual. Among the engineering decisions dictated by styling was the placement of the fuel tank. It was then the preferred practice in Europe and Japan to locate the gas tank over the rear axle in subcompacts because a small vehicle has less "crush space" between the rear axle and the bumper than larger cars. The Pinto's styling, however, required the tank to be placed behind the rear axle leaving only 9 or 10 inches of "crush space"—far less than in any other American automobile or Ford overseas subcompact. In addition, the Pinto was designed so that its bumper was little more than a chrome strip, less substantial than the bumper of any other American car produced then or later. The Pinto's rear structure also lacked reinforcing members known as "hat sections" (2 longitudinal side members) and horizontal cross-members running between them such as were found in cars of larger unitized construction and in all automobiles produced by Ford's overseas operations. The absence of the reinforcing members rendered the Pinto less crush resistant than other vehicles. Finally, the differential housing selected for the Pinto had an exposed flange and a line of exposed bolt heads. These protrusions were sufficient to puncture a gas tank driven forward against the differential upon rear impact.

Crash Tests:

During the development of the Pinto, prototypes were built and tested. Some were "mechanical prototypes" which duplicated mechanical features of the design but not its appearance while others, referred to as "engineering prototypes," were true duplicates of the design car. These prototypes as well as two production Pintos were crash tested by Ford to determine, among other things, the integrity of the fuel system in rear-end accidents. Ford also conducted the tests to see if the Pinto as designed would meet a proposed federal regulation requiring all automobiles manufactured in 1972 to be able to withstand a 20–mile–per–hour fixed barrier impact without significant fuel spillage and all automobiles manufactured after January 1, 1973, to withstand a 30–mile–per–hour fixed barrier impact without significant fuel spillage.

The crash tests revealed that the Pinto's fuel system as designed could not meet the 20–mile–per–hour proposed standard. Mechanical prototypes struck from the rear with a moving barrier at 21–miles–per–hour caused the fuel tank to be driven forward and to be punctured, causing fuel leakage in excess of the standard prescribed by the proposed regulation. A production Pinto crash tested at 21–miles–per–hour into a fixed barrier caused the fuel neck to be torn from the gas tank and the tank to be punctured by a bolt head on the differential housing. In at least one test, spilled fuel entered the driver's compartment through gaps resulting from the separation of the seams joining the rear wheel wells to the floor pan. The seam separation was occasioned by the lack of reinforcement in the rear structure and insufficient welds of the wheel wells to the floor pan.

Tests conducted by Ford on other vehicles, including modified or reinforced mechanical Pinto prototypes, proved safe at speeds at which the Pinto failed. Where rubber bladders had been installed in the tank, crash tests into fixed barriers at 21–miles–per–hour withstood leakage from punctures in the gas tank. Vehicles with fuel tanks installed above rather than behind the rear axle passed the fuel system integrity test at 31–miles–per–hour fixed barrier. A Pinto with two longitudinal hat sections added to firm up the rear structure passed a 20–mile–per–hour rear impact fixed barrier test with no fuel leakage.

The Cost to Remedy Design Deficiencies:

When a prototype failed the fuel system integrity test, the standard of care for engineers in the industry was to redesign and retest it. The vulnerability of the production Pinto's fuel tank at speeds of 20 and 30–miles–per–hour fixed barrier tests could have been remedied by inexpensive "fixes," but Ford produced and sold the Pinto to the public without doing anything to remedy the defects. Design changes that would have enhanced the integrity of the fuel tank system at relatively little cost per car included the following: Longitudinal side members and cross members at $2.40 and $1.80, respectively; a single shock absorbent "flak suit" to protect the tank at $4; a tank within a tank and placement of the tank over the axle at $5.08 to $5.79; a nylon bladder within the tank at $5.25 to $8; placement of the tank over the axle surrounded with a protective barrier at a cost of $9.95 per car; substitution of a rear axle with a smooth differential housing at a cost of $2.10; imposition of a protective shield between the differential housing and the tank at $2.35; improvement and reinforcement of the bumper at $2.60; addition of eight inches of crush space at a cost of $6.40. Equipping the car with a reinforced rear structure, smooth axle, improved bumper and additional crush space at a total cost of $15.30 would have made the fuel tank safe in a 34 to 38–mile–per–hour rear end collision by a vehicle the size of the Ford Galaxie. If, in addition to the foregoing, a bladder or tank within a tank were used or if the tank were protected with a shield, it would have been safe in a 40 to 45–mile–per–hour rear impact. If the tank had been located over the rear axle, it would have been safe in a rear impact at 50–miles–per–hour or more.

Management's Decision To Go Forward With Knowledge Of Defects:

The idea for the Pinto, as has been noted, was conceived by Mr. Iacocca, then Executive Vice President of Ford. The feasibility study was conducted under the supervision of Mr. Robert Alexander, Vice President of Car Engineering. Ford's Product Planning Committee, whose members included Mr. Iacocca, Mr. Robert Alexander, and Mr. Harold MacDonald, Ford's Group Vice President of Car Engineering, approved the Pinto's concept and made the decision to go forward with the project. * * * The Pinto crash tests results had been forwarded up the chain of command to the ultimate decision-makers and were known to the Ford officials who decided to go forward with production.

Harley Copp, a former Ford engineer and executive in charge of the crash testing program, testified [on behalf of the plaintiff] that the highest level of Ford's management made the decision to go forward with the production of the Pinto, knowing that the gas tank was vulnerable to puncture and rupture at low rear impact speeds creating a significant risk of death or injury from fire and knowing that "fixes" were feasible at nominal cost. He testified that management's decision was based on the cost savings which would inure from omitting or delaying the "fixes."

Mr. Copp's testimony concerning management's awareness of the crash tests results and the vulnerability of the Pinto fuel system was corroborated by other evidence. At an April 1971 product review meeting chaired by Mr. MacDonald, those present received and discussed a report (Exhibit 125) prepared by Ford engineers pertaining to the financial impact of a proposed federal standard on fuel system integrity and the cost savings which would accrue from deferring even minimal "fixes." [2]

2. The "FUEL SYSTEM INTEGRITY PROGRAM FINANCIAL REVIEW" report included the following:

"PRODUCT ASSUMPTIONS

"To meet 20 mph movable barrier requirements in 1973, fuel filler neck modifications to provide breakaway capability and minor upgrading of structure are required.

"To meet 30 mph movable barrier requirements, original fuel system integrity program assumptions provided for relocation of the fuel tanks to over the axle on all car lines beginning in 1974. Major tearup of rear and center floor pans, added rear end structure, and new fuel tanks were believed necessary for all car lines. These engineering assumptions were developed from limited vehicle crash test data and design and development work.

"Since these original assumptions, seven vehicle crash tests have been run which now indicate fuel tank relocation is probably not required. Although still based heavily on judgment, Chassis Engineering currently estimates that the 30 mph movable barrier requirement is achievable with a reduced level of rear end tearup.

"In addition to added rear-end structure, Chassis Engineering believes that either rubber 'flak' suits (similar to a tire carcass), or alternatively, a bladder lining within the fuel tank may be required on all cars with flat fuel tanks located under the luggage compartment floor (all cars, except Ford/Mercury/Lincoln and Torino/Montego station wagons). Although further crash tests may show that added structure alone is adequate to meet the 30 mph movable barrier requirement, provisions for flak suits or bladders must be provided. The design cost of a single flak suit, located between the fuel tank and the axle, is currently estimated at $(4) per vehicle. If two flak suits (second located at the rear of the fuel tank), or a bladder are required, the design cost is estimated at $(8) per vehicle. Based on these estimates, it is recommended that the addition of the

* * *

Finally, Mr. Copp testified to conversations in late 1968 or early 1969 with the chief assistant research engineer in charge of cost-weight evaluation of the Pinto, and to a later conversation with the chief chassis engineer who was then in charge of crash testing the early prototype. In these conversations, both men expressed concern about the integrity of the Pinto's fuel system and complained about management's unwillingness to deviate from the design if the change would cost money.

* * *

FORD'S APPEAL

* * *

[EVIDENTIARY RULINGS]

(1) *Exhibit No. 125:*

Exhibit No. 125 was a report presented at a Ford production review meeting in April 1971, recommending action to be taken in anticipation of the promulgation of federal standards on fuel system integrity. The report recommended, *inter alia,* deferral from 1974 to 1976 of the adoption of "flak suits" or "bladders" in all Ford cars, including the Pinto, in order to realize a savings of $20.9 million. The report stated that the cost of the flak suit or bladder would be $4 to $8 per car. The meeting at which the report was presented was chaired by Vice President Harold MacDonald and attended by Vice President Robert Alexander and occurred sometime before the 1972 Pinto was placed on the market. A reasonable inference may be drawn from the evidence that despite management's knowledge that the Pinto's fuel system could be made safe at a cost of but $4 to $8 per car, it decided to defer corrective measures to save money and enhance profits. The evidence was thus highly relevant and properly received. (See Evid.Code §§ 210, 351.)

Ford's contention appears to be addressed not so much to the admissibility of Exhibit No. 125 but to the use which Grimshaw's counsel made of it in his argument to the jury. Ford complains that while Exhibit No. 125 recommended "that $100 million dollars [sic] be spent," Grimshaw's counsel argued that the report showed $100 million would be saved and urged the jury to award that sum as punitive

flak suit/bladder be delayed on all affected cars until 1976. However, package provision for both the flak suits and the bladder should be included when other changes are made to incorporate 30 mph movable barrier capability. A design cost savings $10.9 million (1974–1975) can be realized by this delay. Although a design cost provision of $(8) per affected vehicle has been made in 1976 program levels to cover contingencies, it is hoped that cost reductions can be achieved, or the need for any flak suit or bladder eliminated after further engineering development.

"Current assumptions indicate that fuel system integrity modifications and 1973 bumper improvement requirements are nearly independent. However, bumper requirements for 1974 and beyond may require additional rear end structure which could benefit fuel system integrity programs."

damages. It is not clear that Exhibit No. 125 recommended that "$100 million be spent"; it states that over the period 1973 to 1976 the cost estimates to meet the federal standards would be $100 million. Nor is the record clear that Grimshaw's counsel was referring to Exhibit No. 125 when he urged the jury to award punitive damages in the sum of $100 million. In any event, Ford failed to object to counsel's argument as a misstatement of the evidence. In the absence of an objection and a request for admonition where an admonition would have cured the harm, the issue may not be raised on appeal. * * *

* * *

PUNITIVE DAMAGES

Ford contends that it was entitled to a judgment notwithstanding the verdict on the issue of punitive damages on two grounds: First, punitive damages are statutorily and constitutionally impermissible in a design defect case; second, there was no evidentiary support for a finding of malice or of corporate responsibility for malice. In any event, Ford maintains that the punitive damage award must be reversed because of erroneous instructions and excessiveness of the award.

(1) "*Malice" Under Civil Code Section 3294:*

The concept of punitive damages is rooted in the English common law and is a settled principle of the common law of this country. (Owen, Punitive Damages in Products Liability Litigation, 74 Mich.L. Rev. 1258, 1262–1263 (hereafter Owen); Mallor & Roberts, Punitive Damages, Towards A Principled Approach, 31 Hastings L.J. 639, 642–643 (hereafter Mallor & Roberts); note, Exemplary Damages in the Law of Torts, 70 Harv.L.Rev. 517, 518–520.) The doctrine was a part of the common law of this state long before the Civil Code was adopted. [Citations.] When our laws were codified in 1872, the doctrine was incorporated in Civil Code section 3294, which at the time of trial read: "In an action for the breach of an obligation not arising from contract, where the defendant has been guilty of oppression, fraud, or malice, express or implied, the plaintiff, in addition to the actual damages, may recover damages for the sake of example and by way of punishing the defendant." [11]

11. Section 3294 was amended in 1980 (Stats.1980, ch. 1242, § 1, p. ___, eff. Jan. 1, 1981) to read:

"(a) In an action for the breach of an obligation not arising from contract, where the defendant has been guilty of oppression, fraud, or malice, the plaintiff, in addition to the actual damages, may recover damages for the sake of example and by way of punishing the defendant.

"(b) an employer shall not be liable for damages pursuant to subdivision (a), based upon acts of an employee of the employer, unless the employer had advance knowledge of the unfitness of the employee and employed him or her with a conscious disregard of the rights or safety of others or authorized or ratified the wrongful conduct for which the damages are awarded or was personally guilty of oppression, fraud, or malice. With respect to a corporate employer, the advance knowledge, ratification, or act of oppression, fraud, or malice must be on the part of an officer, director, or managing agent of the corporation.

Ford argues that "malice" as used in section 3294 and as interpreted by our Supreme Court in Davis v. Hearst, 160 Cal. 143, 116 P. 530, requires *animus malus* or evil motive—an intention to injure the person harmed—and that the term is therefore conceptually incompatible with an unintentional tort such as the manufacture and marketing of a defectively designed product. This contention runs counter to our decisional law. As this court recently noted, numerous California cases after Davis v. Hearst, supra, have interpreted the term "malice" as used in section 3294 to include, not only a malicious intention to injure the specific person harmed, but conduct evincing "a conscious disregard of the probability that the actor's conduct will result in injury to others." [Citations.]

* * *

The interpretation of the word "malice" as used in section 3294 to encompass conduct evincing callous and conscious disregard of public safety by those who manufacture and market mass produced articles is consonant with and furthers the objectives of punitive damages. The primary purposes of punitive damages are punishment and deterrence of like conduct by the wrongdoer and others. (Civ.Code, § 3294; Owen, supra, pp. 1277, 1279–1287; Mallor & Roberts, supra, pp. 648–650.) In the traditional noncommercial intentional tort, compensatory damages alone may serve as an effective deterrent against future wrongful conduct but in commerce related torts, the manufacturer may find it more profitable to treat compensatory damages as a part of the cost of doing business rather than to remedy the defect. (Owen, supra, p. 1291; Note, Mass Liability and Punitive Damages Overkill, 30 Hastings L.J. 1797, 1802.) Deterrence of such "objectionable corporate policies" serves one of the principal purposes of Civil Code section 3294. (Egan v. Mutual of Omaha Ins. Co., 24 Cal.3d 809, 820, 157 Cal.Rptr. 482, 598 P.2d 452, cert. den. and app. dismd. Mutual of Omaha Ins. Co. v. Egan, 445 U.S. 912, 100 S.Ct. 1271, 63 L.Ed.2d 597.) Governmental safety standards and the criminal law have failed to provide adequate consumer protection against the manufacture and distribution of defective products. (Owen, supra, pp. 1288–1289; Mallor & Roberts, supra, pp. 655–656; Developments in the Law: Corporate Crime, 92 Harvard L.Rev. 1227, 1369. [Citations.] Punitive damages thus remain as the most effective remedy for consumer protection against defectively designed mass produced articles. They provide a motive for private individuals to enforce rules of law and enable them to recoup the

"(c) As used in this section, the following definitions shall apply:

"(1) 'Malice' means conduct which is intended by the defendant to cause injury to the plaintiff or conduct which is carried on by the defendant with a conscious disregard of the rights or safety of others.

"(2) 'Oppression' means subjecting a person to cruel and unjust hardship in conscious disregard of that person's rights.

"(3) 'Fraud' means an intentional misrepresentation, deceit, or concealment of a material fact known to the defendant with the intention on the part of the defendant of thereby depriving a person of property or legal rights or otherwise causing injury."

expenses of doing so which can be considerable and not otherwise recoverable.

We find no statutory impediments to the application of Civil Code section 3294 to a strict products liability case based on design defect.

(2) *Constitutional Attacks on Civil Code Section 3294:*

Ford's contention that the statute is unconstitutional has been repeatedly rejected. [Citations.] Ford's argument that its due process rights were violated because it did not have "fair warning" that its conduct would render it liable for punitive damages under Civil Code section 3294 ignores the long line of decisions in this state * * * holding that punitive damages are recoverable in a nondeliberate or unintentional tort where the defendant's conduct constitutes a conscious disregard of the probability of injury to others. * * *

* * *

The argument that application of Civil Code section 3294 violates the constitutional prohibition against double jeopardy is equally fallacious. This prohibition like the ex post facto concept is applicable only to criminal proceedings. [Citations.]

The related contention that the potential liability for punitive damages in other cases for the same design defect renders the imposition of such damages violative of Ford's due process rights also lacks merit. Followed to its logical conclusion, it would mean that punitive damages could never be assessed against a manufacturer of a mass produced article. No authorities are cited for such a proposition; indeed, as we have seen, the cases are to the contrary. We recognize the fact that multiplicity of awards may present a problem, but the mere possibility of a future award in a different case is not a ground for setting aside the award in this case, particularly as reduced by the trial judge. If Ford should be confronted with the possibility of an award in another case for the same conduct, it may raise the issue in that case. We add, moreover, that there is no necessary unfairness should the plaintiff in this case be rewarded to a greater extent than later plaintiffs. As Professor Owen has said in response to such a charge of unfairness: "This conception ignores the enormous diligence, imagination, and financial outlay required of initial plaintiffs to uncover and to prove the flagrant misconduct of a product manufacturer. In fact, subsequent plaintiffs will often ride to favorable verdicts and settlements on the coattails of the firstcomers." (Owen, supra, at p. 1325, fn. omitted.) That observation fits the instant case.

(3) *Sufficiency of the Evidence to Support the Finding of Malice and Corporate Responsibility:*

* * *

Through the results of the crash tests Ford knew that the Pinto's fuel tank and rear structure would expose consumers to serious injury or death in a 20 to 30 mile-per-hour collision. There was evidence that Ford could have corrected the hazardous design defects at minimal cost but decided to defer correction of the shortcomings by engaging in a cost-benefit analysis balancing human lives and limbs against corporate profits. Ford's institutional mentality was shown to be one of callous indifference to public safety. There was substantial evidence that Ford's conduct constituted "conscious disregard" of the probability of injury to members of the consuming public.

Ford's argument that there can be no liability for punitive damages because there was no evidence of corporate ratification of malicious misconduct is equally without merit. California follows the Restatement rule that punitive damages can be awarded against a principal because of an action of an agent if, but only if, " '(a) the principal authorized the doing and the manner of the act, or (b) the agent was unfit and the principal was reckless in employing him, or (c) the agent was employed in a managerial capacity and was acting in the scope of employment, or (d) the principal or a managerial agent of the principal ratified or approved the act.' (Rest.2d Torts (Tent. Draft No. 19, 1973) § 909.) " [Citations.] The present case comes within one or both of the categories described in subdivisions (c) and (d).

* * *

[The court held that there was no basis for reversal for the instructions on malice or the burden of proof, and that the amount of the award was "far from excessive as a deterrent against future wrongful conduct by Ford and others."]

* * *

GRIMSHAW'S APPEAL

[Grimshaw argued that the punitive damages award was not excessive, as a matter of law, and that the trial court erred in cutting the award so drastically.]

* * *

[T]he judge, exercising his independent judgment on the evidence, determined that a punitive award of 3½ million dollars was "fair and reasonable." Evidence pertaining to Ford's conduct, its wealth and the savings it realized in deferring design modifications in the Pinto's fuel system might have persuaded a different fact finder that a larger award should have been allowed to stand. [But we cannot say that the judge abused his discretion.] Finally, while the trial judge may not have taken into account Ford's potential liability for punitive damages in other cases involving the same tortious conduct in reducing the award, it is a factor we may consider in passing on the request to increase the award. Considering such potential liability, we find the amount as reduced by the trial judge to be reasonable and just. We therefore decline the invitation to modify the judgment by reducing the amount of the remittitur.

* * *

[Affirmed.]

OWEN, PROBLEMS IN ASSESSING PUNITIVE DAMAGES AGAINST MANUFACTURERS OF DEFECTIVE PRODUCTS

49 U.Chi.L.Rev. 1, 16–47 (1982).

The key to winning a punitive damages case against a manufacturer is often said to lie in finding a "smoking gun" in the defendant's files. The "powder keg" memorandum, for example, was pivotal in the *Gryc* flammable fabrics case, as was Ford's cost-feasibility memorandum—examing various design improvements for the Pinto fuel system—in the *Grimshaw* case. On rare occasions such documents may in themselves prove a callous disregard by corporate executives of human health or safety.

In many cases, however, there are significant dangers of abuse in the manipulation of documentary evidence. Manufacturers necessarily create massive documentation of their design and production processes, sometimes amounting to millions of pages of notes, memoranda, and correspondence over the life of a product. Especially during the initial design of the product, but also as information returns on the product's performance in the field, reports of many instances of one problem or another will be documented, acted upon, and filed away. In fact, the more a manufacturer is truly concerned about its product's safety, the more it will encourage self-criticism and "negative" analyses of the product within the company.[83] For example, it often is desirable

83. One may postulate that the most safety-conscious manufacturer will direct its employees to search out and investigate even remotely possible dangers, to explore even barely plausible remedial measures, and to document the possibilities that dangers may be present and cured. Among the range of dangers and remedies so documented, a manager with "due" regard for consumer safety will act to reduce or eliminate such risks only to the extent that it is reasonable to do so. Such a manager may therefore "consciously" yet reasonably choose to leave in the product remote dangers that are too expensive to remove, and sometimes even substantial dangers for which there is no practicable remedy. The documentation of such a choice should not, of course, support a punitive award.

Another dimension of this problem concerns the variety of psychological make-ups of the manufacturer's employees. The employees of a large manufacturing concern will entertain a broad spectrum of diverse political and practical viewpoints on how much safety is enough. At one extreme may be an engineer or marketing person who will decry any loss of utility for safety, while at the other extreme may be an employee to whom safety is paramount. One might characterize the persons at these extremes as "alarmists": the "utility alarmists"—who characteristically will criticize the prototype or final product as "too safe," and the "safety alarmists"—who characteristically will find an "excess" of danger. While memoranda from either type of alarmist will likely appear incriminating after a product accident years later, the conscientious manufacturer may find the dialectical presentation of such extreme viewpoints especially useful in establishing a counterpoint for informed decision making, somewhere toward the center of which will usually lie the "correct" decision as to the level of safety. Tribunals must be cautious, therefore, not to place excessive weight on internal memoranda criticizing product safety performance or proposing (or questioning) improvements, for the source of such criticism may have been an alarmist whose advice was properly rejected after due consideration. Although such documentation may, of course, be highly relevant to the culpability issue, it will usually represent only a part of the much larger puzzle of institutional motivation and rationale. Cf. Dorsey v. Honda Motor Corp., 665 F.2d 650, 653 (5th Cir. 1981) (noting Honda's rejection of an employee's proposal to enlarge the car's size or strength to increase safety).

during the initial stages of a product's design to test it to its limits to discover what those limits are: cars may thus be crash-tested until their gas tanks burst, and rats may be injected with a drug in ever higher doses until some die. Documentary evidence (especially films) of such tests can later return to haunt the manufacturer, as they did in the *Grimshaw* Pinto case.[85] * * *

* * *

* * * An important aggravating factor in some cases is the manufacturer's awareness of an easy solution to the problem plainly demanded by its simplicity and economy. The *Grimshaw* court thus was impressed that there were a variety of "inexpensive fixes," each costing only several dollars, that supposedly could have solved the Pinto's gas tank problem.

* * *

One must be somewhat skeptical of the *Grimshaw* court's heavy reliance on an array of purported "cheap fixes," some of which may not have been feasible at all. For example, the court appeared to be impressed with the concept of adding a rubber or nylon bladder to the inside of the gas tank. Yet such bladders apparently are still not generally used in commercially produced cars; one thus must wonder whether they are feasible even today or, if they are, whether they would do much good. Similar problems of feasibility are raised by the court's reliance on testimony that an over-the-axle location of the fuel tank would have been a preferable design, because such a tank apparently cannot be built into a small hatchback car such as the model of Pinto involved in *Grimshaw.*

* * * In a complex product such as a car, there are always hundreds of design changes that can be made to enhance the safety of the vehicle in a particular type of a crash situation, ranging in cost per unit from pennies to hundreds of dollars. Although the cost of any one change may be small in isolation, all we can fairly ask of management and its engineers in the punitive damages context is that safety considerations not be deliberately excluded or shunted far to the rear in deciding on the total design mix involved. Each separate design choice is of course only a small sub-decision in the overall safety-cost-utility mix that must be tailored to the special needs and limitations of each different type of product.

* * *

85. One piece of evidence that made a particular impact on the jury in *Grimshaw* was Exhibit 122, a motion picture showing a prototype Pinto being crash tested. When the vehicle was backed into a fixed barrier at 21.5 miles per hour, "the filler neck of the fuel tank separated allowing fluid to spill from the tank." 119 Cal.App. 3d at 791, 174 Cal.Rptr. at 370. A juror who was interviewed shortly after the verdict pointed to the dramatic impact this film had made at trial: "The gas tank, filled with a nonflammable substance, ruptured with such force * * * that 'it looked like a fireman had stuck a hose inside the car and turned it on.'" Wall St. J., Feb. 14, 1978, at 1, col. 4. Ford's objections to the relevance of the film, a particularly sensitive issue in view of the substantial prejudice it obviously was bound to engender, were based upon the fact that the *Grimshaw* car's filler neck did not separate, unlike the crash test car. These objections were rejected by the court. 119 Cal.App.3d at 791, 174 Cal.Rptr. at 370.

Cost-benefit analysis is fundamental to the design engineer's trade. The depth of the rubber on an automobile's bumper forever may be increased by another one-tenth inch. One more cross-beam always may be added to protect the occupants in certain types of collisions. The configuration of crossbeams may be changed to increase their strength; thicker or harder steel may be used in the beams; perhaps they may be made of another metal, or perhaps even of a form of plastic. Many hundreds of such choices are made by design engineers in the production of a single complex product, and each such decision involves a range of trade-offs between cost, weight, appearance, performance capabilities (for separate functions in varying environments), and safety in one type of accident versus another. A steel beam that protects an occupant in one type of accident may endanger him in another, as by rendering that portion of the vehicle less energy absorbent, and may endanger pedestrians and the occupants of other vehicles as well.[112] Although much of this decision making involves the application of proven scientific principles, much is art, and some by its nature can be little more than trial and error.

* * *

* * * [T]he design and warnings "defect" notions * * * are surrounded by shrouds of mist. The mist exists, of course, only in the middle of the spectrum, and cases do arise at either extreme, where the product is clearly defective or not. Yet for the great number of cases in the middle, the legal "tests" of liability for such defects are by their nature so vague that they are often effectively meaningless as guides for design engineers attempting to comply with the law. There is therefore a vast defect "no man's land" where a manufacturer has no idea whether it is on the right or wrong side of the law. One indeed may ask whether "law" itself exists in such terrain, or whether "lawless" is the better word to describe the prevailing "rule" of random guilt. The very notion of how much design safety is enough, and to a lesser extent how much safety information is enough, involves a morass of conceptual, political, and practical issues on which juries, courts, commentators, and legislatures strongly disagree. * * *

* * *

* * * A rose is often not a rose in such an environment, and what looks like acceptable if not praiseworthy conduct to one person may look flagrantly improper to another: one person's sound engineering is another person's trading lives for profits.

NOTES

1. One document excluded by the *Grimshaw* trial court, on grounds that its relevance would be outweighed by undue prejudice, was the so-called Grush–Saunby Report which analyzed a proposed NHTSA standard for fuel tank integrity in roll-overs. The report evaluated the expected costs and benefits of

112. This is to say nothing of the increases in weight and cost and decreases in roominess, maneuverability, and fuel efficiency that may result. See also Dawson v. Chrysler Corp., 630 F.2d 950, 962–63 (3d Cir.1980), cert. denied, 450 U.S. 959 (1981).

the proposed standard, based upon the $200,000 per life value used at the time by NHTSA. The report, entitled "Fatalities Associated with Crash Induced Fuel Leakage and Fires," was circulated as an inter-office memorandum in Ford's Environmental and Safety Engineering Department. The key cost-benefit calculations appeared in Table 3 of the report:

BENEFITS AND COSTS RELATING TO FUEL LEAKAGE ASSOCIATED WITH THE STATIC ROLLOVER TEST PORTION OF FMVSS 208

BENEFITS:

Savings—180 burn deaths, 180 serious burn injuries, 2100 burned vehicles.

Unit Cost—$200,000 per death, $67,000 per injury, $700 per vehicle.

Total Benefit—180 × ($200,000) + 180 × ($67,000) + 2100 × ($700) = <u>$49.5 million</u>.

COSTS:

Sales—11 million cars, 1.5 million light trucks.

Unit Cost—$11 per car, $11 per truck.

Total Cost—11,000,000 × ($11) + 1,500,000 × ($11) = <u>$137 million.</u>

The memo concluded that the proposed design requirements would not be cost effective: "The cost of implementing the rollover portion of the amended Standard has been calculated to be almost three times the expected benefit, even using very favorable benefit assumptions. The yearly benefits of compliance were estimated at just under $50 million, with an associated customer cost of $137 million. Analyses of other portions of the proposed regulation would also be expected to yield poor benefit-to-cost ratios."

Although the above memorandum was excluded from evidence in *Grimshaw*, it has been cited in justification of the large punitive damages award as evidence of Ford's callous attitude toward the safety of consumers. For example, in an interview with Ford Vice President of Environmental and Safety Engineering and others, CBS News Correspondent Mike Wallace referred to this same report: "I find it difficult to believe that top management of the Ford Motor Company is going to sit there and say, 'Oh, we'll buy 2,000 deaths, 10,000 injuries, because we want to make some money or we want to bring in a cheaper car." See "Is Your Car Safe?," 60 Minutes, vol. 10, no. 40, at p. 7 (June 11, 1978).

What precisely was it that troubled Mike Wallace? Are you similarly troubled? Are there implications for the usefulness of risk-benefit analysis as a decision-making tool?

2. Ford has not fared well with its gas tank cases. See also Ford Motor Co. v. Durrill, 714 S.W.2d 329 (Tex.App.1986), vac'd on motion of the parties 754 S.W.2d 646 (Tex.1988) ($100 million punitive damages verdict, remitted by trial court to $20 million, further remitted on appeal to $10 million, and then settled, for design of Ford Mustang II fuel system); Ford Motor Co. v. Stubblefield, 171 Ga.App. 331, 319 S.E.2d 470 (1984) ($8 million: Mustang II). The design of the Mustang II was in many respects the same as the Pinto.

3. In 1978, Ford was prosecuted in Indiana for the deaths of three teenage sisters in a Pinto that burst into flames when it was struck from the rear. After a long, dramatic trial, Ford was acquitted. For an account of the trial, see L. Stobel, Reckless Homicide? (1980).

4. In fairness to Ford, it should be noted that the Pinto gas tanks appear to have been no more hazardous than those of most other subcompacts at the time. NHTSA (FARS) statistics for post–1970 cars in fatal fire accidents, per million cars in operation, for 1975 & 1976, are as follows: all vehicles—6.8; all compacts—7.3; Pinto—7.0; VW—9.3; Vega—7.0; Datsun—9.7; Toyota—4.9; Gremlin—9.8; Dodge Colt—5.3; Opel—8.8; Honda—11.1. Defendant's Exhibit EE, State v. Ford Motor Co., No. 5324 (Super.Ct. Elkart Cty., Ind., Sept. 13, 1978).

5. Other manufacturers have had similar problems with fuel tank litigation. See, e.g., Toyota Motor Co., Ltd. v. Moll, 438 So.2d 192 (Fla.App.1983) ($3 million punitive damages award upheld); American Motors Corp. v. Ellis, 403 So.2d 459 (Fla.App.1981) (punitive damages claim for jury); Chrysler Corp. v. Wolmer, 499 So.2d 823 (Fla.1986) ($3 million punitive damages award reversed), quashing Wolmer v. Chrysler Corp., 474 So.2d 834 (Fla.App.1985).

6. See also Hasson v. Ford Motor Co., 32 Cal.3d 388, 185 Cal.Rptr. 654, 663, 650 P.2d 1171, 1180 (1982) ($4 million punitive damages award upheld for defective brake system) (Harley Copp testified for plaintiff that Ford "deliberately failed to warn dealers or owners of available remedial steps because it was protecting the Continental's reputation"); Ford Motor Co. v. Nowak, 638 S.W.2d 582 (Tex.App.1982) ($4 million punitive damages award upheld for park-reverse transmission slip); Dorsey v. Honda Motor Co., Ltd., 655 F.2d 650 (5th Cir.1981) ($5 million punitive damages award upheld for frontal design of small Honda).

7. On the Pinto fuel system design problem, see generally Bruck, How Ford Stalled the Pinto Litigation, The American Lawyer 23 (June 1979); Schmitt & May, Beyond Products Liability: The Legal, Social, and Ethical Problems Facing the Automobile Industry in Producing Safe Products, 56 U.Det.J.Urb.L. 1021 (1979); and the Pulitzer Prize-winning article by Dowie, Pinto Madness, Mother Jones 18 (Sept./Oct.1977).

On the criminal prosecution, see L. Stobel, Reckless Homicide? (1980); Epstein, Is Pinto a Criminal? Regulation 15 (Mar./Apr.1980); Tybor, How Ford Won Pinto Trial, Nat'l L.J. 1 (Mar. 24, 1980); and a series of 5 articles by Wheeler, beginning with In Pinto's Wake, Criminal Trials Loom for More Manufacturers, Nat'l L.J. 27 (Oct. 6, 1980).

SECTION 4. POST–SALE WARNINGS AND RECALL

The courts for many years have imposed on manufacturers a duty "to take all reasonable means to convey effective warning" to consumers threatened by significant hazards discovered in a product after it is manufactured and sold. Comstock v. General Motors Corp., 358 Mich. 163, 99 N.W.2d 627, 634 (1959) (brake failures). Accord, Cover v. Cohen, 461 N.Y.2d 261, 473 N.Y.S.2d 378, 461 N.E.2d 864 (1984). "The means of conveying a post-sale warning must be reasonably calculated to reach the user. The seller could employ a number of alternatives * * * including personal contact, the mail, advertisements, or notices in retail outlets." Comment, Products Liability: Post–Sale Warnings, 1978 Ariz.St.L.J. 49, 65. Under some circumstances, there may even be a common-law duty to recall: "It is clear that after such a product has been sold and dangerous defects in design have come to the manufacturer's attention, the manufacturer has a duty either to remedy these or, if complete remedy is not feasible, at least to give users adequate warnings and instructions concerning methods for minimizing the danger." Braniff Airways, Inc. v. Curtiss–Wright Corp., 411 F.2d 451, 453 (2d Cir.), cert. denied, 396 U.S. 959, 90 S.Ct. 431, 24 L.Ed.2d 423 (1969) (aircraft engine overheating causing cylinder failure). Cf. doCanto v. Ametek, Inc., 367 Mass. 776, 328 N.E.2d 873 (1975).

Congress has imposed substantial post-marketing obligations on the automobile industry to warn consumers of defects and provide for their repair. The National Traffic & Motor Vehicle Safety Act requires manufacturers to notify motor vehicle purchasers of any "defect which relates to motor vehicle safety," 15 U.S.C.A. § 1402(c), as determined by the Administrator of NHTSA. Surprisingly little litigation has arisen under the Act, apparently because of broad industry compliance.

Recalls generally, and automotive recalls in particular, are now an every-day occurrence. The Product Safety & Liability Reporter Recall Report reports an average of 15–25 automotive-related recalls per month.

UNITED STATES v. GENERAL MOTORS CORP.

United States Court of Appeals, District of Columbia Circuit, 1977.
565 F.2d 754.

J. SKELLY WRIGHT, CIRCUIT JUDGE. On December 19, 1974 the Administrator of the National Highway Traffic Safety Administration (NHTSA), acting pursuant to his authority under the National Traffic and Motor Vehicle Safety Act, determined that Rochester Quadrajet carburetors installed in 1965 Chevrolets and 1966 Chevrolets and Buicks contained a "defect which relates to motor vehicle safety" and that the manufacturer was therefore required to notify owners of the potential danger. See 15 U.S.C.A. §§ 1391, 1397, 1402 (1970).[1] General Motors did not comply with the notice order; instead, it filed suit to have the order declared null and void. At the same time the Administrator brought suit to enforce the order and to impose a civil penalty on

1. The Act was amended on October 27, 1974 by Pub.L. No. 93–492, 88 Stat. 1477. The defect notification provision in § 1402 was replaced by 15 U.S.C.A. §§ 1411–1420, which explicitly require manufacturers to repair or replace defective parts at no charge when the notification order is issued within eight years of the first purchase. However, the definitions of "defect" and "motor vehicle safety," which are central to this litigation, were not altered by the 1974 amendments. Those amendments do not apply to this case, since the order here was issued prior to the effective date of the Act, see Pub.L. No. 93–492, § 102(c), 88 Stat. 1477.

General Motors for its refusal to comply. The two cases were consolidated and, after substantial discovery, the District Court granted the Government's motion for summary judgment and fined General Motors $400,000—the maximum statutory penalty. This appeal followed. It is our conclusion that the grant of summary judgment was appropriate, but that the penalty should not have been imposed absent briefs or argument on point, or any form of hearing. We therefore remand this case to the District Court for further consideration of the penalty question.

I.

Under the National Traffic and Motor Vehicle Safety Act (Safety Act), manufacturers are required to notify purchasers of motor vehicles containing "a defect which relates to motor vehicle safety," 15 U.S.C.A. § 1402(e) (1970), as determined by the Administrator of NHTSA. General Motors has conceded, both in the District Court and in this appeal, that the Government successfully established the existence of a "defect" in the Rochester Quadrajet carburetors. When these carburetors were manufactured holes were drilled into them; these holes were later sealed by inserting metal plugs. One of the holes, in the fuel inlet portion of the carburetor, was sealed by a plug known as the "fuel inlet plug." If this plug becomes dislodged gasoline can spill directly into the engine, resulting in a fire under the hood. According to the affidavit of one of General Motors' own employees, a number of these fuel inlet plugs were improperly inserted during the assembly process. While only figures maintained in General Motors' central—as opposed to its regional—offices have been available in this litigation, and while all incidents of carburetor failures clearly may not be reported, the record discloses *at least* 665 reported incidents of engine compartment fires in vehicles equipped with the Rochester Quadrajet carburetor. As General Motors recognized, under prior case law this evidence clearly establishes as a matter of law that the vehicles in question contain a "defect" within the meaning of the Act.

General Motors, however, argues that summary judgment was inappropriate because material questions of fact exist as to whether this defect "relates to motor vehicle safety." "Motor vehicle safety" is defined in the Act to mean

> the performance of motor vehicles or motor vehicle equipment in such a manner that the public is protected against unreasonable risk of accidents occurring as a result of the design, construction or performance of motor vehicles and is also protected against unreasonable risk of death or injury to persons in the event accidents do occur, and includes nonoperational safety of such vehicles.

15 U.S.C.A. § 1391(1) (1970). According to General Motors, the defect in the Rochester Quadrajet carburetor does not—or at least may not—pose an "unreasonable risk" of accidents or injuries.

In United States v. General Motors Corp. (*Wheels*), 171 U.S.App. D.C. 27, 518 F.2d 420, 435 (1975), we held that a "commonsense" approach must be adopted in construing the Safety Act and, particularly, the term "unreasonable." [6] Applying such an approach, we can see no question but that engine fires, which may occur on thoroughfares where pulling over and standing outside the car is difficult or dangerous, or which may take the driver by surprise and quickly spread to the passenger compartment, are extremely dangerous for all involved and should be considered an unreasonable risk to safety. * * *

In appealing the summary judgment in this case, General Motors seeks to call into question this commonsense conclusion as to what is an unreasonable risk by relying on affidavits of two of its employees presenting predictions as to the likely number of carburetor failures and resulting injuries in the future. * * * Our affirmance of the District Court's summary judgment order rests on the fact that, even if the numbers contained in these affidavits were established to be accurate predictions, this would not relieve General Motors of its obligation to inform the vehicle owners in question of the admitted defect in the cars they are operating.

General Motors' first affidavit seeks to predict the number of injuries likely to be suffered in the future as a result of dislodgment of fuel inlet plugs in 1965 Chevrolets and 1966 Chevrolets and Buicks. Taking into account the number of such vehicles still on the road, and assuming 665 prior fires and between one and 15 prior injuries as a result of these fires, General Motors' manager of Analysis and Product Assurance predicts between less than one and three injuries in the future. The second affidavit is addressed not to the likely number of injuries, but rather to predictions of instances of future plug failure. In this affidavit a General Motors Staff Analysis Engineer concludes that dislodgment of the fuel inlet plugs is due in part to a process of thermal expansion known as "creep" and that, given the age of the cars in question, "*virtually* all creep to which they were theoretically subject has already occurred." Thus it is his view "that the number of future plug failures will be *negligible.*"

Apparently General Motors' position is that since, given the passage of time and the reduction in the number of vehicles on the road, many or most of the failures and injuries resulting from this defective carburetor have already occurred, it is no longer required to take any

6. The definition of "motor vehicle safety" in the Act applies not only to defect notification procedures, but also to promulgation of mandatory motor vehicle safety standards under the Act. According to Senator Magnuson, chairman of the Senate Commerce Committee, "The reason the word 'unreasonable' was put in there is that we hope that there will be some common sense applied to this." Hearings on Traffic Safety Before the Senate Commerce Committee, 89th Cong., 2d sess. 56 (1966). While safety was considered by the committee to be the "overriding consideration," the committee report noted that in promulgating standards "the Secretary will necessarily consider reasonableness of cost, feasibility and adequate leadtime [*sic*]." S.Rep. No. 1301, 89 Cong., 2d Sess. 6 (1966), U.S.Code Cong. & Admin.News 1966, pp. 2709, 2714.

action to protect against those failures that it *admits* will occur in the future. * * * We disagree.

The basic purpose of the Safety Act is to reduce motor vehicle accidents, injuries, and property damage. In adopting the notification provisions of the Act the Senate Commerce Committee found that "[d]eficiencies in past industry practices relating to the notification and curing of manufacturing defects necessitate the imposition of mandatory procedures to insure such notification of purchasers and correction of *all* safety-related defects." S.Rep. No. 1301, 89th Cong., 2d Sess. 4 (1966), U.S.Code Cong. & Admin.News 1966, p. 2712 (emphasis added). In our view, where a defect—a term used in the sense of an "error or mistake"—has been established in a motor vehicle, and where this defect results in hazards as potentially dangerous as a sudden engine fire, and where there is no dispute that at least some such hazards, in this case fires, can definitely be expected to occur in the future, then the defect must be viewed as one "related to motor vehicle safety," and the Act's basic purpose of protecting the public requires that notification be provided.

In this case it is clear, with the gift of hindsight, that this purpose would have been best served had a notification order been issued some seven years ago. At that time NHTSA, relying substantially on information provided by General Motors predicting a substantial decrease in future carburetor failures, decided not to require notification. General Motors' predictions later proved wholly inaccurate, and the order was finally issued in 1974.[13] Our purpose in noting this is not to assign any fault for this unfortunate delay, or to cast doubt upon the trustworthiness of General Motors' instant predictions on the basis of their past record of inaccuracy. Rather, it is only to point out that if the consumer safety would have been best served by an order in the first instance, it would be most ill served by extending this delay based on new predictions that the number of injuries caused by the defect will diminish.

The fact remains that some of these cars continue to be driven and that, according to General Motors, some "negligible" number of them will burst into flames in the future. * * * The purpose of the Safety Act, however, is * * * to prevent serious injuries stemming from established defects before they occur. To now hold that General Motors, having managed to avoid issuance of an order in 1970, was not required to notify those operators who remain subject to risk since most of the failures have already occurred would be to leave this purpose permanently unfulfilled and to establish a system which encourages

13. The case was first opened in November 1967 on the basis of a single consumer complaint, and was closed shortly thereafter. It was reactivated in September 1969 after receipt of three additional complaint letters and publication of an article in *Product Engineering* relating to inlet plug failures. See JA 93. At that time General Motors predicted a total of 43 carburetor failures in the vehicles in question during 1970 and 1971; it later reported that 167 failures had in fact occurred during this period. See JA 103, 134.

manufacturers to delay proceedings whenever possible—at the expense of those endangered by defective vehicles.

This conclusion is in no way undercut, as General Motors suggests, by our view of the "'commonsense' balancing of safety benefits and economic cost" articulated in *Wheels,* supra, 518 F.2d at 435. In *Wheels* we stated:

> The commonsense limitation reflects an awareness that costs must be considered in determining what safety measures are required by the Act. While some margin of safety must be built-in [*sic*] to protect against failures during day-to-day operation, manufacturers are not required to design vehicles or components that never fail. It would appear economically, if not technologically, infeasible for manufacturers to use tires that do not wear out, lights that never burn out, and brakes that do not need adjusting or relining. Such parts cannot reasonably be termed defective if they fail because of age and wear.

Id. at 436. Here we do not deal with a part which is subject to failure because of age and wear, or a part which drivers reasonably expect to have to check and replace because of the particular problem involved. Nor is there involved any question of requiring General Motors to produce perfect, accident-free vehicles at any expense. Rather, we are merely requiring General Motors to notify owners as to a carburetor which did not, from the beginning, meet the manufacturer's own standards for proper assembly and which, absent notification, will in the future cause *at least* some operators and passengers to be confronted with the clear dangers attending a sudden fire in the engine.

* * *

[Remanded for a hearing on the amount of penalty.]

FORD: FAULTY CAPRI WIPERS SAFER THAN RECALL HAZARDS

Charlotte Observer, June 3, 1978, p. 2A, col. 4.

By William J. Mitchell

Observer Washington Bureau

WASHINGTON—The Ford Motor Co. claims a government-ordered recall of 150,000 Mercury Capris would create a greater safety risk for owners than the defective windshield wipers which prompted the recall.

Ford, arguing in federal court, estimates the owners would be exposed to 10 times greater risk of accident by driving back and forth from dealers for the repair work than by continuing to drive with wipers that could fall off in a storm.

This estimate assumes owners would drive an average of 15 miles round-trip to get their wipers fixed. Ford cited national statistics to support its prediction 20 accidents would occur during the 2 million miles of driving required by the recall.

Permitting owners to continue driving with their present wipers would cause only two accidents, the company claims.

The National Highway Traffic and Safety Administration, which has been trying to get the 1971–73 model Capris recalled since January 1976, dismissed Ford's argument as "silly" and "ludicrous."

The case could be the first court test of the kind of "risk analysis" employed by Ford.

NOTES

1. The definition of a "defect" under the National Traffic and Motor Vehicle Safety Act has proved troublesome for vehicle manufacturers, administrative agencies, and the courts, especially where vehicle misuse is involved. See, e.g., United States v. General Motors Corp., 841 F.2d 400 (D.C.Cir.1988). Consider United States v. General Motors Corp., 518 F.2d 420, 427 (D.C.Cir. 1975):

> We find that a vehicle or component "contains a defect" if it is subject to a significant number of failures in normal operation, including failures either occurring during specified use or resulting from owner abuse (including inadequate maintenance) that is reasonably foreseeable (ordinary abuse), but excluding failures attributable to normal deterioration of a component as a result of age and wear. Whether a defect exists in a particular case thus turns on the nature of the component involved, the circumstances in which the failures occurred, and the number of failures experienced. Where, as here, the component is designed to function without replacement over the lifetime of the vehicle, the Government may discharge its burden of establishing a defect by showing a significant number of failures without making any showing of cause. But in all cases the manufacturer may prove, as an affirmative defense, that the failures resulted from unforeseeable owner abusc (gross abuse) or unforeseeable neglect of vehicle maintenance.

2. The National Traffic and Motor Vehicle Safety Act sets minimum informational standards which manufacturers must meet in their recall letters. See 15 U.S.C.A. § 1413 which requires, inter alia, that the recall notice clearly describe the defect, evaluate the risk, specify measures to remedy the defect, and inform the purchaser that repairs will be made without charge. See 49 CFR § 577 (1987). A manufacturer failing to comply with these standards may be required to mail another notice at its expense. See United States v. Ford Motor Co., 574 F.2d 534 (D.C.Cir.1978).

3. Congress has provided other agencies than NHTSA with recall power, for example the CPSC, 15 U.S.C.A. § 2064(a) (for "substantial product hazards"); the FDA, 21 U.S.C.A. § 360(h); the Coast Guard, 46 U.S.C.A. § 1464 (for recreational boats with safety defects); and HHS, 42 U.S.C.A. § 263(g) (for electronic products emitting excessive radiation).

4. A major recall may cost the manufacturer many millions of dollars. The recall of Ford Pintos to modify the fuel system design called for adding a longer neck on the filler tube, improving a seal, substituting a new gas cap, and

inserting a plastic shield between the gas tank and the car's gear housing. If all 1.5 million of the 1971–76 Pintos had been returned for repair, the cost to Ford would have been approximately $30–45 million. The cost of some recalls has been much higher. Generally, however, only about half of the cars recalled are in fact taken in for repair. See Karr & Apcar, Car Trouble—Government Pressure Propels Auto Recalls Toward a New High, Wall St.J., p. 1, col. 6 (Aug. 16, 1978).

5. Consider Ford's objections to NHTSA's order requiring that it recall 150,000 Mercury Capris to fix the windshield wipers, reported above. General Motors made a similar argument in response to a recall order for 5.3 million midsized cars that allegedly had a defect making them prone to lose their rear wheels. A GM economist testified that the costs to owners of returning all the cars to the dealers, including gasoline, oil, depreciation, and time consumed in the trip, would amount to $117 million. By comparison, the company calculated that the repairs were likely to prevent 16 accidents, thus putting the cost of preventing each accident at nearly $8 million. Wall Street Journal, May 5, 1983, at 4, col. 2.

Do such recalls make sense?

6. Consider the following recall notices, pertaining to a carburetor malfunction problem, that were sent by a manufacturer * to its dealers and purchasers pursuant to the National Traffic and Motor Vehicle Safety Act:

DEALER RECALL NOTICE

To: All Dealers

Subject: Service Recall 248, Certain 1977 and 1978 Vehicles Equipped with a 460 C.I.D. Engine and Model 4350–4V Carburetor for Inspection and Possible Replacement of the Carburetor.

We have found that a potential for secondary throttle "hang-up" is present on some of subject vehicles equipped with 4350–4V carburetors and 460 C.I.D. engines. The condition may cause the vehicle to continue to accelerate after the accelerator pedal is released. To stop the vehicle if the secondary throttle should stick open, the transmission must be placed in neutral or the engine ignition must be turned off and the brakes applied. Vehicles' speed could be retarded momentarily by applying the brakes, but it would be resumed when the brakes are released. Each vehicle identified on the enclosed list must have the carburetor inspected and functionally checked according to the following instructions. If the results of this review indicate a potential for secondary throttle hang-up, the carburetor must be replaced. * * *

NOTIFICATION

No vehicle affected by this recall that is currently in your possession is to be delivered until the required correction has been completed. The owners of vehicles for whom names and addresses are shown are being notified directly. In those instances where an affected vehicle has been sold, but the owner's name and address is not listed, you should contact the owner immediately and advise him of this campaign. If the owner of any vehicle cannot be contacted or does not make an appointment to have his vehicle inspected, the Form 1864 must be returned to us with the owner's name and address indicated so that we

* Manufacturer's name withheld by request.—Eds.

can handle further notification. Federal law requires that we advise the owner of the procedure to be followed by him in informing the National Highway Traffic Safety Administration if the defect is not remedied without charge within a reasonable time after the vehicle is tendered for repair. This has been done in the owner letter. It is also important, however, that you promptly report any instance in which an owner will not allow you to complete this recall because of objections to scheduling, or for any other reason.

PURCHASER RECALL LETTER

Dear Owner:

This notice is sent to you in accordance with the requirements of the National Traffic and Motor Vehicle Safety Act. [The company] has determined that a defect which relates to motor vehicle safety exists in certain 1977 and 1978 vehicles equipped with 460 C.I.D. engines and 4–V carburetors.

Some of these vehicles may have defective carburetors in which under certain circumstances the secondary throttle plates may stick open. Should this occur the vehicle may continue to accelerate after the accelerator pedal is released. Since such an occurrence could take place without warning, it could lead to a vehicle crash.

The likelihood of the condition occurring can be reduced by avoiding full or nearly full depressions of the accelerator pedal as during high acceleration of full power operations. To stop the vehicle if the secondary throttle plates stick open, the driver should apply the brakes and either turn the ignition switch to "off" or place the transmission selector lever in "neutral." With the ignition "off" you may experience the need to exert extra effort on the brake pedal and steering wheel.

We ask that you contact your dealer after October 12, 1977, to arrange for inspection and, if necessary, replacement of the carburetor. Your dealer has instructions for inspection and correction of this defect without charge.

* * *

In the interest of your safety and satisfaction with your vehicle, we want to emphasize the importance of having this service performed.

Sincerely,

[Company Representative]

7. **Admissibility of Recall Letters.** A recurring issue on which there has been some disagreement is the admissibility of evidence of recall campaigns, especially recall letters. Defense counsel have raised a variety of objections to such evidence, including the statutory and public policy arguments examined in *Ault,* irrelevance, and hearsay. Addressing most of the arguments, the court in Manieri v. Volkswagenwerk A.G., 151 N.J.Super. 422, 376 A.2d 1317 (App.Div.1977), held admissible recall letters pertaining to the defect that plaintiff's expert testified had caused his automobile accident. The court opined that admission of such evidence would not deter manufacturers from reporting defects to NHTSA since such reports were required by law. Nor was the state's evidentiary rule against evidence of subsequent remedial measures to prove negligence or culpable conduct applicable since the issues in the case were defect and control, not fault. And the letters were relevant since they pertained to the specific defect that plaintiff asserted had caused his accident.

The court also relied on the following observations from Fields v. Volkswagen of America, Inc., 555 P.2d 48, 57 (1976):

> The recall letter by itself does not make a prima facie case or shift the burden of proof. It does not prove that the defect existed at the time of the accident. This must be proved independently. But if a defect contributing to or causing the accident is the defect that is the subject of the recall letter, then the letter would be some evidence that the "defect existed at the time the product left the manufacturer." This is an element that the plaintiff is required to prove.

Accord, Farnar v. Paccar, Inc., 562 F.2d 518 (8th Cir.1977), where the defendant argued that the recall letter should have been excluded under the hearsay rule. *Held,* pursuant to Fed.R.Evid. 801(d)(2), such documents are treated as "admissions falling outside of the hearsay rule as prior statements by a party opponent or its employee offered against that party at trial." This was so despite the fact that the admission was made under the compulsion of the National Traffic and Motor Vehicle Safety Act. *Further held,* Fed.R.Evid. 407 does not apply to strict liability actions and thus did not bar admission of the recall letter. See also Cover v. Cohen, 61 N.Y.2d 261, 473 N.Y.S.2d 378, 461 N.E.2d 864 (1984); Matsko v. Harley Davidson Motor Co., Inc., 325 Pa.Super. 452, 473 A.2d 155 (1984); Muniga v. General Motors Corp., 102 Mich.App. 755, 302 N.W.2d 565 (1980) (recall letter not admissible if recalled model different from accident model); Millette v. Radosta, 84 Ill.App.3d 5, 39 Ill.Dec. 232, 404 N.E.2d 823 (1980).

8. If a manufacturer takes every reasonable step to warn or recall after a defect has been discovered, should it be shielded from liability for subsequent accidents? In answering this question, consider how the following additional facts might affect the result:

A. The manufacturer fully complies in good faith with all defect notification requirements of the federal act. The user nevertheless for some reason fails to learn of the recall program and is subsequently injured. See H.P. Hood & Sons v. Ford Motor Co., 370 Mass. 69, 345 N.E.2d 683 (1976).

B. The user receives a recall notice, neglects to have the product fixed, and is injured when the defect causes a malfunction.

C. The user receives a recall notice, neglects to have the product fixed, and a third party is injured when the defect causes a malfunction.

D. Pursuant to the recall, the user takes the product in to the dealer who negligently performs the repairs, which subsequently causes an accident.

9. See generally Skhreu, The Effect of Current NHTSA Regulations and Enforcement Policy on Products Liability in the Motor Vehicle Industry, 21 Tort & Ins.L.J. 464 (1986); Allee, Post–Sale Obligations of Product Manufacturers, 12 Fordham Urban L.J. 625 (1983–84); Schwartz, The Post–Sale Duty to Warn: Two Unfortunate Forks in the Road to a Reasonable Doctrine, 58 N.Y. U.L.Rev. 892 (1983); Werber, Automobile Recall Campaigns: Proposals for Legislative and Judicial Responses, 56 U.Det.J.Urb.L. 1083 (1979); Note, 33 Stan.L.Rev. 1087 (1981) (post-sale duty to warn); Annots., 38 A.L.R. 4th 583 (1985) (admissibility of post-sale warning measures); 85 A.L.R.3d 1220 (1978) (admissibility of recall letters).

Chapter 10

SPECIAL ISSUES IN TOXIC SUBSTANCE LITIGATION

*

COMMENT, AFFIRMATIVE JUDICIAL CASE MANAGEMENT: A VIABLE SOLUTION TO THE TOXIC PRODUCT LITIGATION CRISIS

38 Me.L.Rev. 339–44 (1986).

With increasing frequency, federal courts throughout the nation have confronted a multiplicity of "toxic tort" claims, claims for relief arising from chronic and latent illnesses or diseases allegedly caused by toxic substances. Toxic substances are substances whose manufacture, processing, distribution, use, or disposal presents or will present an unreasonable risk of injury to a person's health or to the environment.[2]

* Poster from "The Toxic Avenger", a horror/comedy film on the consequences of toxic waste. See Acknowledgments, supra.—Eds.

2. See Toxic Substances Control Act § 6, 15 U.S.C. § 2605(a) (1982). The Act established a system of notice and selective interdiction to regulate the manufacture

Because many of these unreasonable health risks are caused by consumer and industrial products, many toxic tort claims are actually "toxic product" claims. Examples of toxic product claims include those arising from the use, exposure to, or consumption of chemicals such as Agent Orange, building products such as asbestos, and consumer products such as cigarettes and prescription drugs.[7]

Toxic product claims differ from products liability claims in three significant ways. First, toxic product claims seek compensation for chronic injuries and diseases caused by toxic substances, whereas typical products liability claims are usually for accidental traumatic injuries. For instance, toxic product claims are commonly for harms such as birth defects,[21] cancers,[22] or diseases,[23] whereas products liability claims are generally for injuries such as broken bones and injured limbs.

The second distinctive characteristic of toxic product claims is the latent nature of the underlying injuries and diseases. Latent diseases and injuries are those that manifest themselves only after a period of

and use of chemical substances. W. ROGERS, HANDBOOK ON ENVIRONMENTAL LAW § 8.10, at 899 (1977). Pollution problems exemplified by polychlorinated biphenyls, PCBs, led to passage of the Act. Id.

7. Examples of prescription drugs that brought about litigation include diethylstilbestrol (DES), see, e.g., Ryan v. Eli Lilly & Co., 84 F.R.D. 230 (D.S.C.1979); Payton v. Abbott Labs., 83 F.R.D. 382 (D.Mass.1979), vacated, 100 F.R.D. 336 (1983); Sindell v. Abbott Labs., 26 Cal.3d 588, 607 P.2d 924, 163 Cal.Rptr. 132 (synthetic estrogen prescribed to prevent miscarriages), cert. denied, 449 U.S. 912 (1980); MER/29, see, e.g., Roginsky v. Richardson–Merrell, Inc., 378 F.2d 832 (2d Cir.1967) (prescribed to lower blood cholesterol); Bendectin, see, e.g., Albertson v. Richardson–Merrell, Inc., 441 So.2d 1146 (Fla.Dist.Ct.App.1983) (drug prescribed to treat nausea and vomiting associated with pregnancy); Coumadin, see, e.g., Endo Labs., Inc. v. Hartford Ins. Group, 747 F.2d 1264 (9th Cir.1984) (oral anticoagulant); Delalutin, see, e.g., Barson v. E.R. Squibb & Sons, Inc., 682 P.2d 832 (Utah 1984) (progestational hormone prescribed to prevent miscarriages); Ortho–Novum, see e.g., MacDonald v. Ortho Pharm. Corp., 394 Mass. 131, 475 N.E.2d 65 (oral contraceptive), cert. denied, 106 S.Ct. 250 (1985); Ovulen 21, see, e.g., Stephens v. G.D. Searle & Co., 602 F.Supp. 379 (E.D.Mich.1985) (oral contraceptive); Talwin, see, e.g., DeLuryea v. Winthrop Labs., 697 F.2d 222 (8th Cir.1983) (painkilling medication).

21. See, e.g., Endo Labs., Inc. v. Hartford Ins. Group, 747 F.2d 1264 (9th Cir. 1984) (birth defects in children caused by *in utero* exposure to oral anticoagulant drug Coumadin); Agent Orange II, supra note 4, 597 F.Supp. at 788–94 (possible link between herbicide exposure and birth defects); Sindell v. Abbott Labs., 26 Cal.3d 588, 607 P.2d 924, 163 Cal.Rptr. 132 (cancers and abnormalities of reproductive organs in daughters exposed *in utero* to drug diethylstilbestrol (DES)), cert. denied, 449 U.S. 912 (1980); Albertson v. Richardson–Merrell, Inc., 441 So.2d 1146 (Fla.Dist.Ct. App.1983) (birth defects in children caused by *in utero* exposure to drug Bendectin).

22. See, e.g., Borel v. Fibreboard Paper Prods. Corp., 493 F.2d 1076 (5th Cir.1973) (claim of asbestos product insulator for asbestosis and mesothelioma, a form of cancer), cert. denied, 419 U.S. 869 (1974); Lartigue v. R.J. Reynolds Tobacco Co., 317 F.2d 19 (5th Cir.) (lung, larynx, and vocal cord cancer in consumer of tobacco products), cert. denied, 375 U.S. 865 (1963).

23. See, e.g., Ferebee v. Chevron Chem. Co., 736 F.2d 1529 (D.C.Cir.) (pulmonary fibrosis contracted from exposure to herbicide paraquat), cert. denied, 105 S.Ct. 545 (1984); Karjala v. Johns–Manville Prods. Corp., 523 F.2d 155 (8th Cir.1975) (claim of asbestos insulation worker for asbestosis, a debilitating lung disease); Tiderman v. Fleetwood Homes, 102 Wash.2d 334, 684 P.2d 1302 (1984) (asthma contracted from exposure to formaldehyde fumes emitted by particle board in mobile home).

time passes from the victim's initial exposure to the causal product.[25] For example, in cases involving asbestos-related diseases, latency periods range generally between ten and forty years. Similarly, the latency period for diseases resulting from the consumption by pregnant women of the drug diethylstilbestrol (DES) is the time lapsing between a female child's *in utero* exposure to the drug and the subsequent manifestation of disease in that child as she matures. In contrast, products liability claims are usually for injuries that manifest themselves immediately.

The third distinguishing characteristic of toxic product claims[29] * * * is that hundreds or thousands of persons can be injured by exposure to a single generic toxic product.[30] As a result, these victims may file hundreds or thousands of law suits in federal or state courts across the nation. In addition, each claim may name numerous individual defendants. For example, as of January, 1985, claims by or on behalf of victims of asbestos-related diseases numbered approximately 25,000, and depending upon the length of a claimant's exposure, a single claim might name dozens of individual defendants.

---

25. G.Z. NOTHSTEIN, TOXIC TORTS § 4.04 (1984).

29. The nature of causation is perhaps a fourth distinguishing characteristic. * * *

30. A study completed by Dr. Irving Selikoff in 1981 for the Department of Labor projected 200,000 excess deaths by the end of the century from asbestos-associated disease. RAND INSTITUTE FOR CIVIL JUSTICE, VARIATION IN ASBESTOS LITIGATION COMPENSATION AND EXPENSES 3 (1984) [hereinafter cited as RAND INSTITUTE]. See also Agent Orange II, supra note 4, 597 F.Supp. at 746 (herbicides claimed to have caused deaths and injuries to tens of thousands of Vietnam veterans and birth defects in their children); Sindell v. Abbott Labs., 26 Cal. 3d 588, 597, 607 P.2d 924, 927, 163 Cal. Rptr. 132, 135 ("Hundreds, perhaps thousands, of the daughters of these women [who took DES] suffer from adenocarcinoma.") (citation omitted), cert. denied, 449 U.S. 912 (1980).

SECTION 1. LIABILITY STANDARDS AND PROBLEMS OF JUDICIAL ADMINISTRATION

A. IN GENERAL

BOREL v. FIBREBOARD PAPER PRODUCTS CORPORATION

United States Court of Appeals, Fifth Circuit, 1973.
493 F.2d 1076, cert. denied, 419 U.S. 869, 95 S.Ct. 127, 42 L.Ed.2d 107 (1974).

WISDOM, CIRCUIT JUDGE:

This product liability case involves the scope of an asbestos manufacturer's duty to warn industrial insulation workers of dangers associated with the use of asbestos.

Clarence Borel, an industrial insulation worker, sued certain manufacturers of insulation materials containing asbestos to recover damages for injuries caused by the defendants' alleged breach of duty in failing to warn of the dangers involved in handling asbestos. Borel alleged that he had contracted the diseases of asbestosis and mesothelioma as a result of his exposure to the defendants' products over a thirty-three year [period] beginning in 1936 and ending in 1969. The jury returned a verdict in favor of Borel on the basis of strict liability. We affirm.

I.

Clarence Borel began working as an industrial insulation worker in 1936. During his career, he was employed at numerous places, usually in Texas, until disabled by the disease of asbestosis in 1969. Borel's employment necessarily exposed him to heavy concentrations of asbestos dust generated by insulation materials. In his pre-trial deposition, Borel testified that at the end of a day working with insulation material containing asbestos his clothes were usually so dusty he could "just barely pick them up without shaking them." Borel stated: "You just move them just a little and there is going to be dust, and I blowed this dust out of my nostrils by handfuls at the end of the day, trying to use water too, I even used Mentholatum in my nostrils to keep some of the dust from going down in my throat, but it is impossible to get rid of all of it. Even your clothes just stay dusty continually unless you blow it off with an air hose."

Borel said that he had known for years that inhaling asbestos dust "was bad for me" and that it was vexatious and bothersome, but that he never realized that it could cause any serious or terminal illness. * * *

When asked about the use of respirators, Borel replied that they were not furnished during his early work years. Although respirators were later made available on some jobs, insulation workers usually were not required to wear them and had to make a special request if they wanted one. Borel stated that he and other insulation workers found that the respirators furnished them were uncomfortable, could not be worn in hot weather, and—"you can't breathe with the respirator." * * *

* * *

On January 19, 1969, Borel was hospitalized and a lung biopsy performed. Borel's condition was diagnosed as pulmonary asbestosis. Since the disease was considered irreversible, Borel was sent home. Borel testified in his deposition that this was the first time he knew that he had asbestosis.

Borel's condition gradually worsened during the remainder of 1969. On February 11, 1970, Borel underwent surgery for the removal of his right lung. The examining doctors determined that Borel had a form of * * * cancer known as mesothelioma, which had been caused by asbestosis. As a result of these diseases, Borel later died before the district case reached the trial stage.

The medical testimony adduced at trial indicates that inhaling asbestos dust in industrial conditions, even with relatively light exposure, can produce the disease of asbestosis.[1] The disease is difficult to diagnose in its early stages because there is a long latent period between initial exposure and apparent effect. This latent period may vary according to individual idiosyncrasy, duration and intensity of exposure, and the type of asbestos used. In some cases, the disease may manifest itself in less than ten years after initial exposure. In general, however, it does not manifest itself until ten to twenty-five or more years after initial exposure. This latent period is explained by the fact that asbestos fibers, once inhaled, remain in place in the lung, causing a tissue reaction that is slowly progressive and apparently irreversible. Even if no additional asbestos fibers are inhaled, tissue changes may continue undetected for decades. By the time the disease is diagnosable, a considerable period of time has elapsed since the date of the injurious exposure. Furthermore, the effect of the disease may be cumulative since each exposure to asbestos dust can result in additional tissue changes. A worker's present condition is the biological product of many years of exposure to asbestos dust, with both past and recent exposures contributing to the overall effect. All of these factors combine to make it impossible, as a practical matter, to determine which exposure or exposures to asbestos dust caused the disease.

1. For a discussion of asbestosis and its effect on industrial insulation workers, see Selikoff, Bader, Bader, Churg and Hammond, Asbestosis and Neoplasia, 42 Am.J. Med. 487 (1967); Selikoff, Churg, and Hammond, The Occurrence of Asbestosis Among Insulation Workers, 132 Ann. New York Acad.Sc. 139 (1965).

A second disease, mesothelioma, is a form of * * * cancer caused by exposure to asbestos. It affects the pleural and peritoneal cavities, and there is a similarly long period between initial contact and apparent effect. As with asbestosis, it is difficult to determine which exposure to asbestos dust is responsible for the disease.

At issue in this case is the extent of the defendants' knowledge of the dangers associated with insulation products containing asbestos. We pause, therefore, to summarize the evidence relevant to this question.

Asbestosis has been recognized as a disease for well over fifty years.[3] The first reported cases of asbestosis were among asbestos textile workers. In 1924, Cooke in England discovered a case of asbestosis in a person who had spent twenty years weaving asbestos textile products.[4] In the next decade, numerous similar cases were observed and discussed in medical journals. An investigation of the problem among textile factory workers was undertaken in Great Britain in 1928 and 1929.[5] In the United States, the first official claim for compensation associated with asbestos was in 1927.[6] By the mid–1930's, the hazard of asbestosis as a pneumoconiotic dust was universally accepted. Cases of asbestosis in insulation workers were reported in this country as early as 1934.[8] The U.S. Public Health Service fully documented the significant risk involved in asbestos textile factories in a report by Dreessen et al., in 1938.[9] The authors urged precautionary measures and urged elimination of hazardous exposures.

The first large-scale survey of asbestos insulation workers was undertaken in the United States by Fleischer–Drinker et al., in 1945.[10] The authors examined insulation workers in eastern Navy shipyards and found only three cases of asbestosis. They concluded that "asbestos covering of naval vessels is a relatively safe operation." Significantly, ninety-five percent of those examined had worked at the trade for less than ten years. Since asbestosis is usually not diagnosable until ten to twenty years after initial exposure, the authors' conclusion has been criticized as misleading.[11] Perhaps recognizing this possibility, the authors cautioned that the study did not "give a composite picture of

3. Asbestos has been known to man since ancient times. As a generic term, it applies to a number of inorganic, fibrous, silicate minerals that possess a crystaline structure. Asbestos is incombustible in air and separable into filaments. It was used as an insulator against heat as early as 1866, and asbestos cement was introduced about 1870. Asbestos insulation material has been commercially produced since at least 1874.

4. Cooke, Fibrosis of the Lungs Due to the Inhalation of Asbestos Dust, 2 Brit. Med.J. 147 (1924); Cooke, Pulmonary Asbestosis, 2 Brit.Med.J. 1024 (1927).

5. Merewether and Price, Report on the Effects of Asbestos Dust on the Lungs and Dust Suppression in the Asbestos Industry (1930).

6. Lanza, Asbestosis, 106 J.A.M.A. 368 (1936).

8. Ellman, Pneumoconiosis, 14 Brit.J. Radiol. 361 (1934).

9. Dreessen et al., A Study of Asbestosis in the Asbestos Textile Industry, Public Health Bull. No. 241 (1938).

10. Fleischer, Viles, Gade and Drinker, A Health Survey of Pipe–Covering Operations in Constructing Naval Vessels, 28 J.Indust.Hyg. 9–16.

11. Selikoff et al., Asbestosis and Neoplasia, 42 Am.J.Med. 487 (1967).

the asbestos dust that a worker may breathe over a period of years", and that "if pipe coverers had worked steadily [under conditions] where the amount of asbestos dust in the air was consistently high, the incidence of asbestosis among these workers would have been considerabl[y] greater." The authors stated that "the suggestions relative to exhaust ventilation and respiratory protection are therefore of value in maintaining this low incidence of asbestosis".[12]

* * *

Throughout the 1950's and 1960's, further studies and medical reports on asbestosis were published. In 1965, I.J. Selikoff and his colleagues published a study entitled "The Occurrence of Asbestosis Among Insulation Workers in the United States." [14] The authors examined 1,522 members of an insulation workers union in the New York–New Jersey metropolitan area. Evidence of pulmonary asbestosis was found in almost half the men examined. Among those with more than forty years experience, abnormalities were found in over ninety percent. The authors concluded that "asbestosis and its complications are significant hazards among insulation workers". Other studies have since confirmed these findings.[16]

The plaintiff introduced evidence tending to establish that the defendant manufacturers either were, or should have been, fully aware of the many articles and studies on asbestosis. The evidence also indicated, however, that during Borel's working career no manufacturer ever warned contractors or insulation workers, including Borel, of the dangers associated with inhaling asbestos dust or informed them of the ACGIH's threshold limit values for exposure to asbestos dust. Furthermore, no manufacturer ever tested the effect of their products on the workers using them or attempted to discover whether the exposure of insulation workers to asbestos dust exceeded the suggested threshold limits.

On October 20, 1969, Borel initiated the present diversity action in the United States District Court for the Eastern District of Texas. Borel named as defendants eleven manufacturers of asbestos insulation materials used by him during his working career. He settled with four defendants before trial. The trial court instructed a verdict as to a fifth. * * * Borel died before trial and his widow was substituted in as plaintiff under the Texas wrongful death statutes. [Citation.]

The plaintiff sought to hold the defendants liable for negligence, gross negligence, and breach of warranty or strict liability. The negligent acts alleged in the complaint were: (1) failure to take reasonable

12. Fleischer, supra note 10 at 15.

14. Selikoff, Churg, and Hammond, The Occurrence of Asbestosis Among Industrial Insulation Workers, 132 Ann. New York Acad.Sc. 139 (1965).

16. Recognition of the grave occupational health problem posed by asbestos and other toxic and physically harmful substances has led to the passage of the Occupational Safety and Health Act of 1970, 29 U.S.C. § 651 et seq., 84 Stat. 1590. The Act gives the Secretary of Labor the authority to establish standards for permissible concentrations of airborne asbestos fibers.

precautions or to exercise reasonable care to warn Borel of the danger to which he was exposed as a worker when using the defendants' asbestos insulation products; (2) failure to inform Borel as to what would be safe and sufficient wearing apparel and proper protective equipment and appliances or method of handling and using the various products; (3) failure to test the asbestos products in order to ascertain the dangers involved in their use; and (4) failure to remove the products from the market upon ascertaining that such products would cause asbestosis. The plaintiff also alleged that the defendants should be strictly liable in warranty and tort. The plaintiff contended that the defendants' products were unreasonably dangerous because of the failure to provide adequate warnings of the foreseeable dangers associated with them.

The defendants denied the allegations in the plaintiff's complaint and interposed the defenses of contributory negligence and assumption of risk.

The trial court submitted the case to the jury on general verdicts accompanied by a special interrogatory as to Borel's contributory negligence. As to the negligence count, the jury found that all the defendants, except Pittsburgh and Armstrong, were negligent but that none of the defendants had been grossly negligent. It found also, however, that Borel had been contributorily negligent.

As to the strict liability count, the jury found that all the defendants were liable and determined that the total damages were $79,436.24. Since four defendants originally named in the complaint had previously settled, paying a total of $20,902.20, the trial court gave full credit for the sums paid in settlement and held the remaining six defendants jointly and several[ly] liable for the balance of $58,534.04. The defendants appealed.

II.

[The court ruled that the trial court's jury instructions on the duty to warn had not been in error, and that in strict liability as in negligence the duty to warn extends only to foreseeable risks. But the obligation to provide warnings of foreseeable risks extends to all products, even those containing unavoidable risks.] The rationale for this rule is that the user or consumer is entitled to make his own choice as to whether the product's utility or benefits justify exposing himself to the risk of harm. Thus, a true choice situation arises, and a duty to warn attaches, whenever a reasonable man would want to be informed of the risk in order to decide whether to expose himself to it.

* * *

Furthermore, in cases such as the instant case, the manufacturer is held to the knowledge and skill of an expert. This is relevant in determining (1) whether the manufacturer knew or should have known the danger, and (2) whether the manufacturer was negligent in failing to communicate this superior knowledge to the user or consumer of its product. Wright v. Carter Products, Inc., 2 Cir.1957, 244 F.2d 53. The manufacturer's status as expert means that at a minimum he must keep abreast of scientific knowledge, discoveries, and advances and is presumed to know what is imparted thereby. But even more importantly, a manufacturer has a duty to test and inspect his product. The extent of research and experiment must be commensurate with the dangers involved. A product must not be made available to the public without disclosure of those dangers that the application of reasonable foresight would reveal. Nor may a manufacturer rely unquestioningly on others to sound the hue and cry concerning a danger in its product. Rather, each manufacturer must bear the burden of showing that its own conduct was proportionate to the scope of its duty.

[The court reviewed various aspects of the court's charge on both strict liability in tort and breach of warranty and concluded that the charge was substantially correct.]

III.

We now turn to the question whether the trial court erred in denying the defendants' motions for a directed verdict and for judgment notwithstanding the verdict. * * *

* * *

A. First, we approach the question whether the danger to Borel and other insulation workers was foreseeable at the time the products causing Borel's injury were sold. The defendants' position is that they did not breach their duty to warn because the danger from inhaling asbestos was not foreseeable until about 1968 and that, in view of the long latent period of the disease, Borel must have contracted asbestosis well before that date.

To begin, we note that the disease of asbestosis is cumulative. Thus, both Borel's earliest exposure to asbestos dust, occurring in the late 1930's, and his most recent exposure, occurring in 1968, could have contributed to his overall condition. The defendants' failure to warn of the dangers of the exposures occurring in 1968 may have resulted in an actionable injury to Borel. But even if it is assumed that Borel's condition was attributable principally to his earlier exposures, the defendants argument still fails since there is ample evidence in the record that the danger of inhaling asbestos, including the disease of asbestosis, was widely recognized at least as early as the 1930's. An expert witness, Dr. Hans Weill, testified that prior to 1935 there were literally "dozens and dozens" of articles on asbestos and its effect on man. Dr. Clark Cooper, an expert witness for the defendants, stated that it was known in the 1930's that inhaling asbestos dust caused asbestosis and that the danger could be controlled by maintaining a modest level of exposure. * * *

The evidence also tended to establish that none of the defendants ever tested its product to determine its effect on industrial insulation workers. * * *

As previously mentioned, the foreseeability of the danger must be measured in light of the manufacturer's status as an expert and the manufacturer's duty to test its product. In these circumstances, we think the jury was entitled to find that the danger to Borel and other insulation workers from inhaling asbestos dust was foreseeable to the defendants at the time the products causing Borel's injuries were sold.

The defendants next challenge the jury's finding that their products were unreasonably dangerous for failure to give warnings. They cannot deny, however, that once the danger became foreseeable, the duty to warn attached. Davis v. Wyeth Laboratories, Inc. Here, the defendants gave no warning at all. They attempt to circumvent this finding by arguing, disingenuously, that the danger was obvious. For present purposes, it is sufficient to note that Borel testified that he did not know that inhaling asbestos dust could cause serious illness until his doctors advised him in 1969 that he had asbestosis. Furthermore, we cannot say that, as a matter of law, the danger was sufficiently obvious to asbestos installation workers to relieve the defendants of the duty to warn.

The jury found that the unreasonably dangerous condition of the defendants' product was the proximate cause of Borel's injury. This necessarily included a finding that, had adequate warnings been provided, Borel would have chosen to avoid the danger. [Citations.]

* * *

C. We next consider whether there was substantial evidence to support the jury's finding that each defendant was the cause in fact of injury to Borel. The traditional rule is that a defendant's conduct is the cause of the event if it was a substantial factor in bringing it about. Prosser, Law of Torts § 41 at 240 (3 ed. 1971); Second Restatement of Torts, §§ 431, 433, Malone, Ruminations on Cause-in-Fact, 9 Stan.L. Rev. 60 (1956); Green, The Causal Relation Issue, 60 Mich.L.Rev. 543 (1962). Whether the defendant's conduct was a substantial factor is a question for the jury, unless the court determines that reasonable men could not differ.

In the instant case, it is impossible, as a practical matter, to determine with absolute certainty which particular exposure to asbestos dust resulted in injury to Borel. It is undisputed, however, that Borel contracted asbestosis from inhaling asbestos dust and that he was exposed to the products of all the defendants on many occasions. It was also established that the effect of exposure to asbestos dust is cumulative, that is, each exposure may result in an additional and separate injury. We think, therefore, that on the basis of strong circumstantial evidence the jury could find that each defendant was the cause in fact of some injury to Borel.

Relying on expert testimony that asbestosis does not usually manifest itself until fifteen, twenty, or even twenty-five years after initial exposure, Pittsburgh Corning Company and Armstrong Cork Company contend that they cannot be liable because Borel was not exposed to their products until after 1962 and 1966 respectively. As we have pointed out, however, the length of this latent period varies according to individual idiosyncracy, duration and intensity of exposure, and the type of asbestos used; in some cases the effect of the exposure may manifest itself in less than five or ten years. Thus, even the most recent exposures could have added to or accelerated Borel's overall condition.

[The court reviewed and approved a variety of other rulings by the trial court, including holding the defendants jointly and severally liable for the plaintiff's damages since the contributions of each defendant to the plaintiff's disease were indeterminable.]

In reaching our decision in the case at bar, we recognize that the question of the applicability of Section 402A of the Restatement to cases involving "occupational diseases" is one of first impression. But though the application is novel, the underlying principle is ancient. Under the law of torts, a person has long been liable for the foreseeable harm caused by his own negligence. This principle applies to the manufacture of products as it does to almost every other area of human endeavor. It implies a duty to warn of foreseeable dangers associated with those products. This duty to warn extends to all users and consumers, including the common worker in the shop or in the field. Where the law has imposed a duty, courts stand ready in proper cases to enforce the rights so created. Here, there was a duty to speak, but the defendants remained silent. The district court's judgment does no more than hold the defendants liable for the foreseeable consequences of their own inaction.

For the reasons stated, the decision of the district court is

Affirmed.

ON PETITION FOR REHEARING AND PETITION FOR REHEARING EN BANC

All of the defendants-appellants have moved for a rehearing en banc.

I.

Three of the movants, Johns–Manville Corporation, Fibreboard Corporation, and Ruberoid Company contend that the Court erred in basing its opinion on "the overriding factor" of "the alleged failure of the defendants to at any time warn Borel of the dangers involved in working with asbestos insulation while employed by various independent contractors". They state that the record shows that Johns–Manville placed a warning label on packages of its products in 1964, and that Fibreboard and Ruberoid placed warning labels on their products in 1966. (Borel filed suit in 1969.) The three warnings were substantially the same. Johns–Manville's read as follows:

"This product contains asbestos fiber. "Inhalation of asbestos in excessive quantities over long periods of time may be harmful.

"If dust is created when this product is handled, avoid breathing the dust.

"If adequate ventilation control is not possible wear respirators approved by the U.S. Bureau of Mines for pneumoconiosis producing dusts."

It should be noted that none of these so-called "cautions" intimated the gravity of the risk: the danger of a fatal illness caused by asbestosis and mesothelioma or other cancers. The mild suggestion that inhalation of asbestos in excessive quantities over a long period of time "*may* be harmful" conveys no idea of the extent of the danger. The admonition that a worker should "avoid breathing the dust" is black humor: There was no way for insulation workers to avoid breathing asbestos dust. As for wearing respirators if adequate ventilation control is not possible, Borel and other insulators never worked in any place where there was adequate ventilation, and respirators were ineffective: "you can't breathe with the respirator".

Within the trial judge's instructions, the jury could have concluded that the "cautions" were not warnings in the sense that they adequately communicated to Borel and other insulation workers knowledge of the dangers to which they were exposed so as to give them a choice of working or not working with a dangerous product. * * *

The evidence established that Borel was exposed to the products of each of these appellants for extended periods occurring before the alleged warnings were given. Since the disease of asbestosis is cumulative, these earlier exposures to asbestos dust from appellants' products could have contributed substantially to Borel's overall condition. Borel was an insulator for 33 years. Three of the six defendants gave no warnings. The other three used labels on packages of their products, as noted in this opinion; but this practice began a few years before his terminal illness in 1969. By 1964–66, his illness was irreversible. Thus, there were no warnings when they could have effectively allowed Borel to make the choice of encountering or not encountering a known risk. And, in any event, there was significant evidence to create a question for the jury as to the adequacy of the labels to serve as warnings. We cannot say that its resolution of this issue is incorrect as a matter of law. [Citations.]

* * *

Taking our original opinion as a whole, it should be clear that our references to failure to warn refer to failure to warn of the gravity of the danger, that is, the exposure to asbestosis, mesothelioma and other cancers. The first sentence of the opinion states that the case involves "the scope of an asbestos manufacturer's duty to warn". At a number of points we emphasize that the plaintiff's contentions focused on the "*adequacy*" or reasonableness of the warnings. The utility of an insulation product containing asbestos may outweigh the known or foreseeable risk to the insulation workers and thus justify its marketing. The product could still be unreasonably dangerous, however, if unaccompanied by adequate warnings. An insulation worker, no less than any other product user, has a right to decide whether to expose himself to the risk.

[Petitions for Rehearing denied.]

NOTES

1. As the first appellate court opinion applying products liability principles to asbestos manufacturers, *Borel* marks the start of the age of toxic substance products liability litigation.

2. By 1986, approximately 30,000 personal injury lawsuits had been brought against asbestos producers. Because some suits include multiple plaintiffs, the number of claimants is substantially higher. In the federal courts in 1987, twice as many asbestos cases were filed (6,943) as were terminated (3,454). It has been variously estimated that from 100,000 to 500,000 such cases can be expected to be filed in the next few decades.

Almost all of the claimants were occupationally exposed. Typically, fifteen to thirty defendants, each of whom supplied asbestos products to the plaintiff's employer, are named in each suit. Asbestos litigation tends to be concentrated in a limited number of courts located near concentrations of industries that used asbestos in their operations—notably, the insulation, ship-building, and construction industries. Over ⅔ of all asbestos cases have been filed in just five states: Texas, Pennsylvania, New Jersey, California, and Massachusetts. In a number of courts in those states, asbestos cases constitute a significant percentage of the total civil caseload, ranging from 2–3% in the New Jersey federal court to 29% in the Eastern District of Texas. In 1982, Philadelphia's state court docket consisted of 1850 asbestos cases, which would have required fifteen years to try, without considering newly filed cases; new case filings exceeded 50 per month. By 1984, the caseload there had grown to 3660.

On the nature, scope and cost of asbestos litigation, see, e.g., Jackson v. Johns–Manville Sales Corp., 750 F.2d 1314 (5th Cir.1985), cert. denied 478 U.S. 1022, 106 S.Ct. 3339, 92 L.Ed.2d 743 (1986); J. Kakalik, P. Ebener, W. Felstiner, & M. Shanley, Costs of Asbestos Litigation (Rand 1983); J. Kakalik, P. Ebener, W. Felstiner, G. Haggstrom, & M. Shanley, Variation in Asbestos Litigation Compensation and Expenses (Rand 1984); D. Hensler, W. Felstiner, M. Selvin & P. Ebener, Asbestos in the Courts—The Challenge of Mass Toxic Torts (Rand 1985).

3. Recall the New Jersey Supreme Court's dramatic reversal on the availability of a state-of-the-art "defense" from Beshada v. Johns–Manville Prod. Corp., supra p. 420, to Feldman v. Lederle Labs., supra p. 435, which restricted *Beshada* to its facts. The *Feldman* ruling was challenged on equal protection grounds, and narrowly upheld, in In re Asbestos Litigation, 829 F.2d 1233 (3d Cir.1987) (1–1–1), as discussed in Ch. 3, above.

In the lead opinion, Judge Weis remarked in part:

> In refining and narrowing the § 402A theory, *Beshada* eliminates one more defense to the liability of asbestos defendants. Because the court's reasoning may be applicable to other defendants in similar circumstances, the justification advanced both directly and indirectly

> by the New Jersey court may be regarded as weak and ill-advised. We cannot, however, conclude that the state court's position is irrational. The concepts of risk-spreading and compensation for victims by manufacturers of unreasonably dangerous products are cornerstones of § 402A, and they may be consistently applied to asbestos as well as to other products.
>
> Although not in itself a determinative factor in the elimination of a substantive defense, the desirability of simplifying the fact-finding process and thus making it easier for victims to recover has been recognized by the law. Workme[n's] compensation programs and no-fault auto insurance plans share that common goal. * * *
>
> Administrative convenience standing alone is not an adequate ground for the elimination of a substantive defense. [Citation.] However, we cannot help but be conscious of the extraordinary size of the asbestos personal injury litigation. * * * [T]his unprecedented phenomenon in American tort law requires states be given some leeway in devising their own solutions.

Id. at 1241, 1243–44.

Judge Becker concurred on the basis that the New Jersey Supreme Court had determined a legislative, as opposed to an adjudicative, fact that "at all relevant times, asbestosis harms were knowable to the industry. That being the case, the New Jersey Supreme Court has reasonably decided to preclude endless relitigation of what was 'knowable' to the asbestos industry." Id. at 1245. Judge Hunter dissented:

> My review of the *Beshada–Feldman* line of cases leads me to conclude that the challenged classification represents nothing more than an unprincipled, expedient, and ineffective response to widespread criticism of the *Beshada* doctrine combined with an unwillingness to give up the application of *Beshada* to asbestos manufacturers. If so, the *Beshada–Feldman* classification is undeniably arbitrary. Worse yet, I fear that the New Jersey Supreme Court's sole purpose may have been to inflict a special punishment on asbestos manufacturers. The Constitution does not permit the New Jersey courts to level either an arbitrary or a punitive sanction against asbestos manufacturers (or the manufacturer of any other product, for that matter).

Id. at 1254.

4. Might a fair and pragmatic compromise be to relieve asbestos defendants of liability for punitive damages in exchange for denying them the state-of-the-art defense? Would the goals of tort law be adequately served by such an approach? Are the courts the right forum for making such a compromise?

5. Is the real problem created by the *Beshada–Feldman* distinction the failure of the New Jersey Supreme Court to articulate its reasons for distinguishing between asbestos and other products?

6. Could the New Jersey Supreme Court have accomplished the same ends, but insulated itself from constitutional attack (at least on equal protection grounds), by holding that a prior judgment against the asbestos defendants (say, in *Borel*) collaterally estopped them from relitigating the state-of-the-art defense? See Hardy v. Johns–Manville Sales Corp., infra. Or by taking judicial notice of the fact that all manufacturers knew (or should have known) of the dangers of asbestos exposure by the mid-to-late 1930s? Note that the latter two

options—both procedural—have virtually the same effect as the substantive state-of-the-art decision in *Beshada.*

HARDY v. JOHNS–MANVILLE SALES CORPORATION

United States Court of Appeals, Fifth Circuit, 1982.
681 F.2d 334.

GEE, CIRCUIT JUDGE:

This appeal arises out of a diversity action brought by various plaintiffs—insulators, pipefitters, carpenters, and other factory workers—against various manufacturers.

* * *

Defendant's interlocutory appeal * * * is directed * * * at the district court's amended omnibus order * * * which applies collateral estoppel to this mass tort. [Citation.] The omnibus order is, in effect, a partial summary judgment for plaintiffs based on nonmutual offensive collateral estoppel and judicial notice derived from this court's opinion in Borel v. Fibreboard Paper Products Corp., 493 F.2d 1076 (5th Cir. 1973), cert. denied, 419 U.S. 869, 95 S.Ct. 127, 42 L.Ed.2d 107 (1974) (henceforth Borel). *Borel* was a diversity lawsuit in which manufacturers of insulation products containing asbestos were held strictly liable to an insulation worker who developed asbestosis and mesothelioma and ultimately died. The trial court construed *Borel* as establishing as a matter of law and/or of fact that: (1) insulation products containing asbestos as a generic ingredient are "unavoidably unsafe products," (2) asbestos is a competent producing cause of mesothelioma and asbestosis, (3) no warnings were issued by any asbestos insulation manufacturers prior to 1964, and (4) the "warning standard" was not met by the *Borel* defendants in the period from 1964 through 1969. * * * In Flatt v. Johns–Manville Sales Corp., 488 F.Supp. 836 (E.D.Tex.1980) the * * * court outlined the elements of proof for plaintiffs in asbestos-related cases. There the court stated that the plaintiff must prove by a preponderance of the evidence that

1. Defendants manufactured, marketed, sold, distributed, or placed in the stream of commerce products containing asbestos.
2. Products containing asbestos are unreasonably dangerous.
3. Asbestos dust is a competent producing cause of mesothelioma.
4. Decedent was exposed to defendant's products.
5. The exposure was sufficient to be a producing cause of mesothelioma.
6. Decedent contracted mesothelioma.
7. Plaintiffs suffered damages.

Id. at 838, citing Restatement (Second) of Torts § 402A(1) (1965). The parties agree that the effect of the trial court's collateral estoppel order in this case is to foreclose elements 2 and 3 above. Under the terms of the omnibus order, both parties are precluded from presenting evidence on the "state of the art"—evidence that, under Texas law of strict liability, is considered by a jury along with other evidence in order to determine whether as of a given time warning should have been given of the dangers associated with a product placed in the stream of commerce. Under the terms of the order, the plaintiffs need not prove that the defendants either knew or should have known of the dangerous propensities of their products and therefore should have warned consumers of these dangers, defendants being precluded from showing otherwise. On appeal, the defendants contend that the order violates their rights to due process and to trial by jury. Because we conclude that the trial court abused its discretion in applying collateral estoppel and judicial notice, we reverse.

[The court concluded that federal rather than state law governs the application of collateral estoppel in this case.]

Having determined that federal law of collateral estoppel governs, we next turn to an examination of just what that law is. In Parklane Hosiery Co. v. Shore, 439 U.S. 322, 99 S.Ct. 645, 58 L.Ed.2d 552 (1979), the Supreme Court was asked to determine "whether a party who has had issues of fact adjudicated adversely to it in an equitable action may be collaterally estopped from relitigating the same issues before a jury in a subsequent legal action brought against it by a new party." Id. at 324, 99 S.Ct. at 648. The Court responded affirmatively, noting offensive collateral estoppel's "dual purpose of protecting litigants from the burden of relitigating an identical issue with the same party or his privy and of promoting judicial economy by preventing needless litigation." Id. at 326, 99 S.Ct. at 649. The Court reiterated that mutuality is not necessary to proper invocation of collateral estoppel under federal law, citing Blonder–Tongue Laboratories, Inc. v. University of Illinois Foundation, 402 U.S. 313, 91 S.Ct. 1434, 28 L.Ed.2d 788 (1971), and further held that the use of offensive collateral estoppel does not violate a defendant's seventh amendment right to a jury trial. To avoid problems with the use of the doctrine, the Court adopted a general rule of fairness, stating "that in cases where plaintiff could easily have joined in the earlier action or where . . . for other reasons, the application of offensive collateral estoppel would be unfair to a defendant, a trial judge should not allow the use of offensive collateral estoppel." [Citations.]

[The court concluded that due process prohibited the use of collateral estoppel against defendant manufacturers who either were not parties in *Borel* or had settled prior to trial in *Borel.*]

THE BOREL DEFENDANTS

The propriety of estopping the six defendants in this case who were parties to Borel poses more difficult questions. In ascertaining the precise preclusive effect of a prior judgment on a particular issue, we have often referred to the requirements set out, *inter alia,* in International Association of Machinists & Aerospace Workers v. Nix, 512 F.2d 125, 132 (5th Cir.1975), and cases cited therein. The party asserting the estoppel must show that: (1) the issue to be concluded is identical to that involved in the prior action; (2) in the prior action the issue was "actually litigated"; and (3) the determination made of the issue in the prior action must have been necessary and essential to the resulting judgment. * * *

Appellants argue that *Borel* did not necessarily decide that asbestos-containing insulation products were unreasonably dangerous because of failure to warn. According to appellants, the general *Borel* verdict, based on general instructions and special interrogatories, permitted the jury to ground strict liability on the bases of failures to test, of unsafeness for intended use, of failures to inspect, or of unsafeness of the product. Strict liability on the basis of failure to warn, although argued to the jury by trial counsel for the plaintiff in *Borel,* was, in the view of the appellants, never formally presented in the jury instructions and therefore was not essential to the *Borel* jury verdict.

Appellants' view has some plausibility. The special interrogatories answered by the *Borel* jury were general and not specifically directed to failure to warn. Indeed, as we discussed at length in our review of the *Borel* judgment, the jury was instructed in terms of "breach of warranty." 493 F.2d at 1091. Although the jury was accurately instructed as to "strict liability in tort" as defined in section 402A of the Restatement (Second) of Torts, that phrase was never specifically mentioned in the jury's interrogatories. It is also true that the general instructions to the *Borel* jury on the plaintiff's causes of action did not charge on failure to warn, except in connection with negligence. Yet appellants' argument in its broadest form must ultimately fail. We concluded in *Borel:*

> The jury found that the unreasonably dangerous condition of the defendants' product was the proximate cause of Borel's injury. This necessarily included a finding that, had adequate warnings been provided, Borel would have chosen to avoid the danger.

493 F.2d at 1093. As the appellants at times concede in their briefs, "if *Borel* stands for any rule at all, it is that defendants have a duty to warn the users of their products of the long-term dangers attendant upon its use, including the danger of an occupational disease." Indeed, the first sentence in our *Borel* opinion states that that case involved "the scope of an asbestos manufacturer's duty to warn industrial insulation workers of dangers associated with the use of asbestos." Id.

at 1081. See also 493 F.2d at 1105 (on rehearing). Our conclusion in *Borel* was grounded in that trial court's jury instructions concerning proximate cause and defective product * * *. * * * Nonetheless, we must ultimately conclude that the judgment in *Borel* cannot estop even the *Borel* defendants in this case for three interrelated reasons.

First, after review of the issues decided in *Borel,* we conclude that *Borel,* while conclusive as to the general matter of a duty to warn on the part of manufacturers of asbestos-containing insulation products, is ultimately ambiguous as to certain key issues. As the authors of the Restatement (Second)—Judgments § 29, comment g (1982), have noted, collateral estoppel is inappropriate where the prior judgment is ambivalent:

> The circumstances attending the determination of an issue in the first action may indicate that it could reasonably have been resolved otherwise if those circumstances were absent. Resolution of the issue in question may have entailed reference to such matters as the intention, knowledge, or comparative responsibility of the parties in relation to each other. * * * In these and similar situations, taking the prior determination at face value for purposes of the second action would extend the effects of imperfections in the adjudicative process beyond the limits of the first adjudication, within which they are accepted only because of the practical necessity of achieving finality.

The *Borel* jury decided that Borel, an industrial insulation worker who was exposed to fibers from his employer's insulation products over a 33–year period (from 1936 to 1969), was entitled to have been given fair warning that asbestos dust may lead to asbestosis, mesothelioma, and other cancers. The jury dismissed the argument that the danger was obvious and regarded as conclusive the fact that Borel testified that he did not know that inhaling asbestos dust could cause serious injuries until his doctor so advised him in 1969. The jury necessarily found "that, had adequate warnings been provided, Borel would have chosen to avoid the danger." 493 F.2d at 1093. In *Borel,* the evidence was that the industry as a whole issued no warnings at all concerning its insulation products prior to 1964, that Johns–Manville placed a warnings label on packages of its products in 1964, and that Fibreboard and Ru[b]eroid placed warnings on their products in 1966. Id. at 1104.

Given these facts, it is impossible to determine what the *Borel* jury decided about *when* a duty to warn attached. Did the jury find the defendants liable because their warnings after 1966, when they acknowledged that they knew the dangers of asbestosis, were insufficiently explicit as to the grave risks involved? If so, as appellants here point out, the jury may have accepted the state of the art arguments provided by the defendants in *Borel* —i.e., that the defendants were not aware of the danger of asbestosis until the 1960's. Even under this view, there is a second ambiguity: was strict liability grounded on the fact that the warnings issued, while otherwise sufficient, never reached the insulator in the field? If so, perhaps the warnings, while insufficient as to insulation workers like Borel, were sufficient to alert workers further down the production line who may have seen the warnings—such as the carpenters and pipefitters in this case. Alternatively, even if the *Borel* jury decided that failure to warn before 1966 grounded strict liability, did the duty attach in the 1930's when the "hazard of asbestosis as a pneumoconiotic dust was universally accepted," id. at 1083, or in 1965, when documentary evidence was presented of the hazard of asbestos insulation products to the installers of these products?

As we noted in *Borel,* strict liability because of failure to warn is based on a determination of the manufacturer's reasonable knowledge:

> [I]n cases such as the instant case, the manufacturer is held to the knowledge and skill of an expert. This is relevant in determining (1) whether the manufacturer knew or should have known the danger, and (2) whether the manufacturer was negligent in failing to communicate this superior knowledge to the user or consumer of its product. * * * The manufacturer's status as expert means that at a minimum he must keep abreast of scientific knowledge, discoveries, and advances and is presumed to know what is imparted thereby.

493 F.2d at 1089. Thus, the trial judge in *Borel* instructed the jury that the danger "must have been reasonably foreseen by the manufacturer." Id. at 1090. As both this instruction and the ambiguities in the *Borel* verdict demonstrate, a determination that a particular product is so unreasonably hazardous as to require a warning of its dangers is not an absolute. Such a determination is necessarily relative to the scientific knowledge generally known or available to the manufacturer at the time the product in question was sold or otherwise placed in the stream of commerce.

Not all the plaintiffs in this case were exposed to asbestos-containing insulation products over the same 30–year period as plaintiff Borel. Not all plaintiffs here are insulation workers isolated from the warnings issued by some of the defendants in 1964 and 1966. Some of the products may be different from those involved in *Borel.* Our opinion in *Borel,* "limited to determining whether there [was] a conflict in substantial evidence sufficient to create a jury question," did not resolve that as a matter of fact all manufacturers of asbestos-containing insulation products had a duty to warn as of 1936, and all failed to warn adequately after 1964. Although we determined that the jury must have found a violation of the manufacturers' duty to warn, we held only that the jury could have grounded strict liability on the absence of a warning prior to 1964 or "could have concluded that the [post–1964 and post–1966] 'cautions' were not warnings in the sense that they adequately communicated to Borel and other insulation workers knowledge of the dangers to which they were exposed so as to give them a choice of working or not working with a dangerous product." 493 F.2d at 1104. As we have already had occasion to point out in Migues v. Fibreboard Corp., 662 F.2d at 1188–89 [emphasis in original] * * *:

> The only determination made by this court in *Borel* was that, based upon the evidence in that case, the jury's findings could not be said to be incorrect as a matter of law. But this Court certainly did not decide that every jury presented with the same facts would be compelled to reach the conclusion reached by the *Borel* jury: that asbestos was unreasonably dangerous. Such a holding would have been not only unnecessary, it would also have been unwarranted.

* * *

[Citation.] Like stare decisis, collateral estoppel applies only to issues of fact or law necessarily decided by a prior court. Since we cannot say that *Borel* necessarily decided, as a matter of fact, that all manufacturers of asbestos-containing insulation products knew or should have known of the dangers of their particular products at all relevant times, we cannot justify the trial court's collaterally estopping the defendants from presenting evidence as to the state of the art.

Even if we are wrong as to the ambiguities of the *Borel* judgment, there is a second, equally important, reason to deny collateral estoppel effect to it: the presence of inconsistent verdicts. In Parklane Hosiery v. Shore, 439 U.S. at 330–31, 99 S.Ct. at 651, the Court noted that collateral estoppel is improper and "unfair" to a defendant "if the judgment relied upon as a basis for the estoppel is itself inconsistent with one or more previous judgments in favor of the defendant." Id. at 330, 99 S.Ct. at 651. Accord Restatement (Second)—Judgments § 29(4) (1982).[13] Not only does issue preclusion in such cases appear arbitrary to a defendant who has had favorable judgments on the same issue, it also undermines the premise that different juries reach equally valid verdicts. See Restatement (Second)—Judgments § 29, comment f (1982). One jury's determination should not, merely because it comes later in time, bind another jury's determination of an issue over which there are equally reasonable resolutions of doubt.

The trial court was aware of the problem and referred to Flatt v. Johns–Manville Sales Corp., 488 F.Supp. at 841, a prior opinion by the same court. In Flatt the court admitted that Johns–Manville had "successfully defended several asbestos lawsuits in the recent past" but stated that "lawsuits in which Johns–Manville has prevailed have been decided on the basis that there was insufficient exposure to asbestos dust, or alternatively, the plaintiff, or decedent, did not contract asbestosis or mesothelioma." Id. Given the information made available to

13. The injustice of applying collateral estoppel in cases involving mass torts is especially obvious. Thus, in *Parklane* the Court cited Prof. Currie's "familiar example": "A railroad collision injures 50 passengers all of whom bring separate actions against the railroad. After the railroad wins the first 25 suits, a plaintiff wins in suit 26. Professor Currie argues that offensive use of collateral estoppel should not be applied so as to allow plaintiffs 27 through 50 automatically to recover." 439 U.S. at 331 n. 14, 99 S.Ct. at 651 n. 14, citing Currie, Mutuality of Estoppel: Limits of the Bernhard Doctrine, 9 Stan.L.Rev. 281, 304 (1957).

us in this appeal, we must conclude that the trial court in *Flatt* and in the proceeding below was inadequately informed about the nature of former asbestos litigation. On appeal, the parties inform us that there have been approximately 70 similar asbestos cases thus far tried around the country. Approximately half of these seem to have been decided in favor of the defendants. A court able to say that the approximately 35 suits decided in favor of asbestos manufacturers were all decided on the basis of insufficient exposure on the part of the plaintiff or failure to demonstrate an asbestos-related disease would be clairvoyant. Indeed, the appellants inform us of several products liability cases in which the state of the art question was fully litigated, yet the asbestos manufacturers were found not liable. Although it is usually not possible to say with certainty what these juries based their verdicts on, in at least some of the cases the verdict for the defendant was not based on failure to prove exposure or failure to show an asbestos-related disease. In Starnes v. Johns–Manville Corp., No. 2075–122 (E.D.Tenn.1977), one of the cases cited in Flatt v. Johns–Manville Sales Corp., supra, the court's charge to the jury stated that it was "undisputed that as a result of inhaling materials containing asbestos, Mr. Starnes contracted the disease known as asbestosis." The verdict for the defendant in *Starnes* must mean, inter alia, that the jury found the insulation products involved in that case not unreasonably dangerous. This court takes judicial notice of these inconsistent or ambiguous verdicts pursuant to Fed.R.Evid. 201(d). We conclude that the court erred in arbitrarily choosing one of these verdicts, that in *Borel,* as the bellwether.

Finally, we conclude that even if the *Borel* verdict had been unambiguous and the sole verdict issued on point, application of collateral estoppel would still be unfair with regard to the *Borel* defendants because it is very doubtful that these defendants could have foreseen that their $68,000 liability to plaintiff Borel would foreshadow multimillion dollar asbestos liability. As noted in *Parklane,* it would be unfair to apply collateral estoppel "if a defendant in the first action is sued for small or nominal damages [since] he may have little incentive to defend vigorously, particularly if future lawsuits are not foreseeable." 439 U.S. at 330, 99 S.Ct. at 651. * * * The reason the district court here applied collateral estoppel is precisely because early cases like *Borel* have opened the floodgates to an enormous, unprecedented volume of asbestos litigation. According to a recent estimate, there are over 3,000 asbestos plaintiffs in the Eastern District of Texas alone and between 7,500 and 10,000 asbestos cases pending in United States District Courts around the country. The omnibus order here involves 58 pending cases, and the many plaintiffs involved in this case are *each* seeking $2.5 million in damages. Such a staggering potential liability could not have been foreseen by the *Borel* defendants. [Citation.]

* * *

Like the court in *Migues,* we too sympathize with the district court's efforts to streamline the enormous asbestos caseload it faces.

None of what we say here is meant to cast doubt on any possible alternative ways to avoid reinventing the asbestos liability wheel. We reiterate the *Migues* court's invitation to district courts to attempt innovative methods for trying these cases. We hold today only that courts cannot read *Borel* to stand for the proposition that, as matters of fact, asbestos products are unreasonably dangerous or that asbestos as a generic element is in all products a competent producing cause of cancer. To do otherwise would be to elevate judicial expedience over considerations of justice and fair play.

REVERSED.

[Appendix omitted.]

NOTES

1. The question of whether nonmutual collateral estoppel should be used in asbestos cases nicely illustrates the connection between substantive standards of liability and procedural rules designed to facilitate judicial administration. The traditional conception of a case consists of two contending parties, each of whom presents evidence and argument on the facts and law. Asbestos and other mass exposure toxic substance cases place such extraordinary demands on the civil justice system as to put in question whether the traditional model should or can be maintained. See Chayes, The Role of the Judge in Public Law Litigation, 89 Harv.L.Rev. 1281, 1282–83 (1976).

2. The major benefit of collateral estoppel is increased efficiency in the resolution of civil cases. Recent studies show that less than 5% of asbestos cases go to trial, consistent with other classes of civil litigation. Do you think that the availability of the collateral estoppel doctrine would cause an even higher proportion of asbestos cases to be settled? See R. Posner, Economic Analysis of Law 522–28 (3d ed. 1986). Gould, The Economics of Legal Conflicts, 2 J. Legal Stud. 279, 287 (1973).

3. In an omitted part of the *Hardy* opinion, the court ruled that federal law governs the collateral estoppel issue "to preserve the integrity of federal court judgments." 681 F.2d at 337. Although *Hardy* represents the majority view on this complex issue, not all courts agree. See, e.g., Semler v. Psychiatric Institute of Washington, D.C., 575 F.2d 922, 927–28 (D.C.Cir.1978).

4. Does the $68,000 damage award in *Borel,* for a worker who suffered from asbestosis and died of mesothelioma, suggest that the outcome was the result of a jury compromise? Does this undermine the legitimacy of the result? See Taylor v. Hawkinson, 47 Cal.2d 893, 896, 306 P.2d 797, 799 (1957). Should the defense lawyers confronting a collateral estoppel claim in a subsequent case be permitted to depose the *Borel* jurors to inquire into this question? Compare Katz v. Eli Lilly & Co., 84 F.R.D. 378, 382 (E.D.N.Y.1979) (permitting depositions of jurors in earlier DES case resulting in plaintiff verdict) with Kaufman v. Eli Lilly and Co., 65 N.Y.2d 449, 460, 482 N.E.2d 63, 70, 492 N.Y.S.2d 584, 591 (1985) (refusing to permit juror depositions).

5. Since the *Hardy* decision, dozens of appellate decisions affirming plaintiff's judgments in asbestos cases have been published. Should we expect a rebirth of offensive collateral estoppel arguments in asbestos (and other toxic substance) litigation, or has the issue been put to rest?

Some commentators have argued that collateral estoppel should be used to lighten the burdens created by asbestos litigation. See Erlenbach, Offensive Collateral Estoppel and Products Liability: Reasoning with the Unreasonable, 14 St. Mary's L.J. 19 (1982); Note, Offensive Collateral Estoppel in Asbestos Litigation: Hardy v. Johns–Manville Sales Corp., 15 Conn.L.Rev. 247 (1983). Compare, however, the observations of another commentator:

> [A] number of conclusions can be drawn from the asbestos experience with collateral estoppel. First, perhaps most confidently, collateral estoppel has little potential to make a significant contribution in resolving the judicial administration difficulties engendered by asbestos litigation. The number and extent of individual issues in those cases and the limited instances in which collateral estoppel can be usefully employed limit its capacity to play any real role in resolving asbestos claims. Indeed, other innovative claim and case management techniques currently being examined in asbestos litigation appear to have greater promise for a procedural solution to current and future claims.
>
> * * *
>
> Aside from providing a solution to the demands of asbestos litigation, [another] matter is collateral estoppel's capacity to provide some marginal measure of efficiency. * * * Ultimately, only empirical study, particularly with regard to the effect of collateral estoppel on settlements, can shed light on this matter. What is clear from a critical examination and analysis of the experience to date is that substantial impediments to effectuating efficiency do exist, far more so than most courts have previously assumed.
>
> The factors contributing to the inability of offensive collateral estoppel to fulfill its promise in asbestos litigation provide insights for the utility of collateral estoppel beyond asbestos. The combined effects of a long latency period preceding the development of insidious disease, the chronological development of medical and scientific knowledge, a diverse industry with a concomitant large number of products and potential defendants, the geographic dispersal of cases, the remaining uncertainty about the relationship between exposure and development of the disease, the number of contested individual issues that otherwise occur, and the difficulty and ambiguity of the substantive law governing the common issue increase the efforts necessary to determine whether estoppel is appropriate, narrow the instances where it is proper, and raise doubts about the fairness of invoking it even where existing doctrine would otherwise permit.
>
> Perhaps the most hospitable environment for efficient use of estoppel in multi-claimant torts is the single event mass disaster. The only issue in these cases is fault or liability of a single defendant—no questions of causation or defenses exist, and, other than assessing damages, the same precise facts are applicable to all claimant's cases. Between the extremes of asbestos and single event traumatic injuries there lies a continuum of mass tort cases with various combinations and permutations of the elements previously identified. For example, products liability litigation over Rely Tampons is limited to a single product and defendant, does not entail any affirmative defenses based on the plaintiff's conduct, and appears not to involve any serious causation problems. On the other hand, the litigation is dispersed

across the nation, thereby involving different substantive standards and disputed questions exist about the chronology of knowledge of the hazards involved with the product.

Green, The Inability of Offensive Collateral Estoppel to Fulfill Its Promise: An Examination of Estoppel in Asbestos Litigation, 70 Iowa L.Rev. 141, 224–27 (1984). See also Flanagan, Offensive Collateral Estoppel: Inefficiency and Foolish Consistency, 1982 Ariz.St.L.J. 45, 69; Gunn, The Offensive Use of Collateral Estoppel in Mass Tort Cases, 52 Miss.L.J. 765 (1982); Weinberger, Collateral Estoppel and the Mass Produced Product: A Proposal, 15 New Eng. L.Rev. 1 (1979).

6. **Reform Strategies.** A number of measures have been employed by both the courts and private parties in an attempt to handle the demands of asbestos and other toxic substance cases in a more efficient manner.

A. **Class actions.** In early 1985, a class of all plaintiffs with asbestos-related personal injury claims pending as of December 31, 1984 was certified in the same federal district court in Texas in which *Hardy* had been litigated. The court certified the class pursuant to Fed.R.Civ.P. 23(b)(3) to try questions common to the more than 700 class members' claims, such as state of the art, leaving individual questions to mini-trials after the common questions were resolved. On interlocutory appeal, the Fifth Circuit affirmed. Jenkins v. Raymark Industries, Inc., 782 F.2d 468 (5th Cir.1986). After five weeks of trial, the case settled for $137 million. See M. Peterson & M. Selvin, Resolution of Mass Torts: Toward a Framework for Evaluation of Aggregative Procedures 39–48 (Rand 1988). Most previous attempts to use class actions in the asbestos context had been unsuccessful. See, e.g., Yandle v. PPG Industries, Inc., 65 F.R.D. 566 (E.D.Tex.1974); see also Fed.R.Civ.P. 23(b)(3), 1966 Advisory Committee note.

The *Agent Orange* class action was recently settled and approved on appeal, but not without criticism:

> The present litigation justifies the prevalent skepticism over the usefulness of class actions in so-called mass tort cases and, in particular, claims for injuries resulting from toxic exposure. First, the benefits of a class action have been greatly exaggerated by its proponents in the present matter. [The court opined that the causation question in the present case was an individual one not amenable to resolution for the class.]
>
> * * *
>
> The second reason for our skepticism is that, with the exception of the military contractor defense, there may be few, if any, common questions of law. * * *
>
> Third, the dynamics of a class action in a case such as this may either impair the ability of representative parties to protect the interests of the class or cause the inefficient use of judicial resources. These undesirable results stem from the fact that potential plaintiffs in toxic tort cases do not share common interests because of differences in the strengths of their claims. * * *
>
> All plaintiffs may not desire class certification, however, because those with strong cases may well be better off going it alone. The drum-beating that accompanies a well-publicized class action claiming harm from toxic exposure and the speculative nature of the exposure

> issue may well attract excessive numbers of plaintiffs with weak to fanciful cases. * * *
>
> * * *
>
> Moreover, the ability of the district court to scrutinize the fairness of the settlement is greatly impaired where the legal and factual issues to be determined in the class action are as numerous and complex as they were under the district court's order in the instant case. Similarly, the fashioning of a distribution plan that is both fair to the strong plaintiffs and efficient in adjudicating the large number of claims may be impossible. Only the weakness of the evidence of causation as to all plaintiffs and the strength of the military contractor defense enabled the district court to evaluate the settlement accurately and to fashion an appropriate distribution scheme in the instant matter. We regard those factors as largely coincidental and not to be expected in all toxic exposure cases.

In re Agent Orange Product Liability Litigation MDL No. 381, 818 F.2d 145, 164–66 (2d Cir.1987), cert. denied, ___ U.S. ___, 108 S.Ct. 695, 98 L.Ed.2d 648 (1988). See generally S. Yeazell, From Medieval Group Litigation to the Modern Class Action (1987); Coffee, The Regulation of Entrepreneurial Litigation: Balancing Fairness and Efficiency in the Large Class Action, 54 U.Chi.L. Rev. 877 (1987).

B. **Special case–handling plans.** In the asbestos context, a Case Management Plan and Case Evaluation Apportionment Process was prepared by two Special Masters employed by the District Court for the Northern District of Ohio to streamline the litigation. Special Masters Submit Final Proposal for Ohio Asbestos Cases, 1983 Asbestos Litig.Rep. (Andrews) 7489 (Dec. 9, 1983); see also Final Report with Recommendations, Judicial Administration Working Group on Asbestos Litigation, National Center for State Courts (1984). Judge Lambros in the Southern District of Ohio has devised a system of summary, advisory trials to facilitate settlements. See McGovern, Toward a Functional Approach for Managing Complex Litigation, 53 U.Chi.L.Rev. 440, 478–91 (1986); Archibald, Dunn, Connah, Gauvey, Zimmerman & Baroody, Alternative Dispute Resolution in Multiple Product Liability Cases, 16 Prod.Saf. & Liab.Rep. 549 (June 10, 1988).

C. **Asbestos claims facility.** What appeared at the time to be a quite promising innovation was the development of an Asbestos Claims Facility formed by a consortium of asbestos producers and their liability insurers. The Facility employed procedures designed to expedite the handling of claims, to settle cases more frequently and at an earlier stage of the claims process, and to reduce the costs of resolving the claims. See Wellington, Asbestos: The Private Management of a Public Problem, 33 Clev.St.L.Rev. 375 (1984–85). Less than three years after being formed, the Facility was dissolved because the formula for sharing costs among members had become inequitable due to changes in the types of asbestos cases being brought. Carter, Asbestos Coalition Falling Apart, Nat'l L.J., Apr. 25, 1988, at 3.

D. **Legislative reform.** Finally, a number of legislative proposals to set up a no-fault compensation system for asbestos victims have been offered. See, e.g., Anderson, Warshauer & Coffin, Asbestos Health Hazards Compensation Act: A Legislative Solution to a Litigation Crisis, 10 J.Legis. 25 (1983); Comment, Relief for Asbestos Victims: A Legislative Analysis, 20 Harv.J.Legis. 179 (1983).

The Federal Coal Mine Health and Safety Act, 30 U.S.C.A. §§ 801–962 (1982), popularly known as the Black Lung Act, is one example of a federalized no-fault scheme for a particular class of victims. Another plan is the National Childhood Vaccine Injury Act of 1986, 42 U.S.C.A. § 300aa et seq., described in F. Harper, F. James & O. Gray, The Law of Torts § 28.8A n. 21 (2d ed.Supp. May 1988). See also Schwartz & Mahshigian, National Childhood Vaccine Injury Act of 1986: An Ad Hoc Remedy or a Window for the Future?, 48 Ohio St.L.J. 387 (1987). See generally Elliott, Goal Analysis versus Institutional Analysis of Toxic Compensation Systems, 73 Geo.L.J. 1357 (1985) (proposing comprehensive restructuring of current system, including central fund for compensation, governmental regulation for safety standards, and criminal law for deterrence).

7. Consider the observations of the trial judge who handled the Agent Orange litigation:

> I conclude that, in dealing with disasters, a national system of health and disability insurance for all is desirable. Absent such a thorough change, the law can handle small and medium-scale disasters such as airplane crashes with relatively modest changes in substance and procedure. Massive disasters, such as those caused by asbestos, mandate major changes in substance and practice, such as the creation of a National Disaster Court and the use of international tribunals. Classification of disasters either for purposes of analysis or for the purposes of triggering the operation of special substantive or procedural rules is to a large degree arbitrary. For example, whether and for what purposes events such as the deaths and injuries resulting from the gas leak at Bhopal, India, should be treated as mass disasters rather than normal tort cases are largely matters of judgment.

Weinstein, Preliminary Reflections on the Law's Reaction to Disasters, 11 Colum.J.Envtl.L. 1, 5 (1986). Judge Alvin Rubin of the Fifth Circuit Court of Appeals concurs: "[T]he traditional two-party adversary system was not developed and can no longer function efficiently or fairly to adjudicate mass injury and mass catastrophe cases under presently applicable substantive and procedural rules." Rubin, Mass Torts and Litigation Disaster, 20 Ga.L.Rev. 429, 41 (1986). See also P. Shuck, Agent Orange on Trial: Mass Toxic Disasters in the Courts (1986).

8. Professor Paul Rosenberg, in a review of a book detailing the industry's knowledge and concealment of asbestos hazards, P. Brodeur, Outrageous Misconduct: The Asbestos Industry on Trial (1985), defends the tort system:

> The tort system has come under much attack recently for costing too much and for having emerged from a pathological preference for formalizing disputes. A growing coterie of academics and practicing lawyers, including Chief Justice Burger and Harry Wellington, the former dean of Yale Law School who has proposed an arbitration-type plan to handle all personal injury asbestos claims, advocates replacing the tort system in whole or in part with less adversarial, and presumable cut-rate, modes of dispute resolution. These critics ignore the fact that absent a credible threat of tort liability, settlement through "softer" modes of dispute resolution is a sham. They seem oblivious to the unique services performed by the tort system: it produces information and publicizes and effectively deters wrongdoing. Indeed, even if arbitration-type mechanisms could save administrative costs, the sav-

ings would probably be outweighed by the increased risks generated by the reduced threat of tort liability. An arbitration system would mute conflict, but muting conflict is not an unalloyed virtue; the adversarial process performs a valuable function in allowing individual victims—and the public, vicariously—an opportunity to confront large social institutions, express moral indignation, and achieve clear-cut vindication of rights.

* * *

Of course, the tort system is not beyond reproach and it certainly could benefit from some reform. The centralized, collective, judicially managed bankruptcy proceedings demonstrate how the tort system's conventional, case-by-case process can be improved. The transaction costs of the case-by-case process are needless; the effort to give each claimant individualized justice not only threatens the solvency of defendants, but also may deprive victims of adequate damage awards. Much of the cost, however, can be eliminated by restructuring the tort system along the managerial and procedural lines followed by the bankruptcy courts. Claims would have to be tried as class actions, in which the particular as well as the common substantive issues would be decided on the basis of sampling and averaging techniques, and damages would be awarded according to specified schedules. Courts would also have to set aside funds to cover future claims.

Most critics, however, are not interested in reform of the tort system—only in its elimination. Yet Brodeur's narrative refutes their arguments for leaving compensation to regulatory agencies and publicly funded compensation programs. His book provides a necessary dose of reality; reveries of stern regulatory enforcement, for example, are quickly dissipated when one reads his account of the deceitful bravado of one Labor Department safety inspector. The inspector toured a dangerously dusty asbestos plant without a respirator, because he did not want to alarm the workers and cause them to raise questions about their health. More generally, Brodeur's timely message is that the assault on the tort system may represent a broader conspiracy than that perpetrated by the asbestos manufacturers.

Rosenberg, The Dusting of America: A Story of Asbestos—Carnage, Cover-up, and Litigation (Book Review), 99 Harv.L.Rev. 1693, 1704–06 (1986). See also Page, Asbestos and the Dalkon Shield: Corporate America on Trial, 85 Mich.L. Rev. 1324 (1987).

9. The fairness of collateral estoppel and other procedural devices for the mass processing of cases, such as class actions, depends in large part on whether such devices provide "correct" resolutions of the disputed issues involved. A trial conducted in 1982 in the same court in which *Hardy* was tried provides empirical data relevant to this issue.

Five plaintiffs' cases against twelve asbestos defendants were tried simultaneously in the same courtroom. Five separate juries were impanelled, and each jury heard the same evidence on questions common to the five cases. The juries were instructed simultaneously and were provided eight special interrogatories to answer, along with a list of approximately one hundred asbestos products manufactured by the various defendants. The juries' answers to a selection of the interrogatories are set forth below.

Jury Interrogatories	Jury 1	Jury 2	Jury 3	Jury 4	Jury 5
1. Can occupational exposure to asbestos cause:					
(a) Asbestosis (b) Mesothelioma (c) Lung Cancer?	(a) Yes (b) Yes (c) Yes	(a) Yes (b) Yes (c) Yes	(a) Yes (b) Yes (c) Yes	(a) Yes (b) Yes (c) Yes	(a) Yes (b) Yes (c) Yes
2. Is occupational exposure to asbestos the sole cause of:					
(a) Asbestosis (b) Mesothelioma (c) Lung Cancer?	(a) Yes (b) Yes (c) Yes	(a) Yes (b) No (c) No	(a) Yes (b) Yes (c) Yes	(a) Yes (b) Yes (c) Yes	(a) Yes (b) No (c) No
3. Products unreasonably dangerous due to design.	All of the products	None of the products	No answer given	Some of the products[1]	Some of the products[1]
4. Date on which the defendant should have reasonably foreseen the dangers associated with occupational exposure to asbestos products.	1946	1965	1935	1964	Jan. 1965
5. Products marketed without adequate warning.	All of the products	Some of the products	All of the products	Some of the products[2]	Some of the products[2]
6. Did failure to provide adequate warning make the product unreasonably dangerous?	All of the products	None of the products	All of the products	Some of the products[3]	Some of the products[3]
7. Was Johns-Manville grossly negligent?	N/A	No	Yes	No	Yes

1. Of the 102 products, Jury 4 and Jury 5 found consistently with regard to 38 and disagreed on the remaining 64.

2. Of the 102 products, Jury 4 and Jury 5 found consistently with regard to 13 and disagreed on the remaining 89.

3. Because of a number of "no" answers to interrogatory number 5, Jury 5 only answered this interrogatory for 12 products; Jury 4 and Jury 5 agreed on 11 of the 12 products that they both made findings on.

For further information about the trials, see Green, The Inability of Offensive Collateral Estoppel to Fulfill Its Promise: An Examination of Estoppel in Asbestos Litigation, 70 Iowa L.Rev. 141, 221–23, 228–35 (1984).

B. CIGARETTE LITIGATION

CIPOLLONE v. LIGGETT GROUP, INC.

United States Court of Appeals, Third Circuit, 1986.
789 F.2d 181, cert. denied, 479 U.S. 1043, 107 S.Ct. 907, 93 L.Ed.2d 857 (1987).

JAMES HUNTER, III, CIRCUIT JUDGE:

This case * * * presents the question whether the Federal Cigarette Labeling and Advertising Act, 15 U.S.C. §§ 1331–1340 (1982) (the "Act"), preempts any or all of the state common law claims brought by appellee Antonio Cipollone and his wife Rose in the district court. Several of the claims in the Cipollones' complaint concern the alleged failure of the defendants, Liggett Group, Inc., Philip Morris Incorporated, Loews Corporation, Loew's Theatres, Inc. ("Lorillard"), to provide an adequate warning of the dangers of the cigarettes that they manufactured and sold. Because these claims implicate the legislatively mandated warning provided in section 1333 of the Act, the answers of Liggett Group, Philip Morris, and Lorillard each included a defense based on the preemptive effect of the Act. * * * Holding that the Act preempted none of the Cipollones' claims, the district court granted the Cipollones' motion to strike the defenses and denied the motion for judgment on the pleadings. Cipollone v. Liggett Group, Inc., 593 F.Supp. 1146, 1171 (D.N.J.1984).

* * * Because we disagree with the district court's conclusion concerning the preemptive effect of the Act, we will reverse the district court's grant of the motion to strike and will remand the case for further proceedings.

I.

A. The Complaint

In their complaint, Rose and Antonio Cipollone alleged that Mrs. Cipollone developed lung cancer as a result of smoking cigarettes manufactured and sold by appellants. The complaint, which was originally filed on August 1, 1983, further averred that Mrs. Cipollone began smoking in 1942 and developed lung cancer as a result of her smoking. Mrs. Cipollone died in October 1984, but her husband has continued prosecuting this action, individually and as executor of his wife's estate. Mr. Cipollone is therefore the sole appellee in this case.

As observed by the district court, the fourteen-count complaint sets forth [a variety of claims.]

B. The Federal Cigarette and Advertising Labeling Act

The Federal Cigarette Labeling and Advertising Act, originally enacted in 1965, was a response to a growing awareness among members of federal as well as state government that cigarette smoking posed a significant health threat to Americans. The original Act required the following warning label on cigarette packages: "Caution: Cigarette Smoking May Be Hazardous to Your Health." 15 U.S.C. § 1333 (1970). Congress changed this warning, by amendment to the Act in 1969, to the following: "Warning: The Surgeon General Has Determined That Cigarette Smoking Is Dangerous to Your Health." 15 U.S.C. § 1333 (1976). The Act, as amended in 1970, expressly stated the policy behind the required warning:

> It is the policy of the Congress, and the purpose of this chapter, to establish a comprehensive Federal program to deal with cigarette labeling and advertising with respect to any relationship between smoking and health, whereby—
>
> > (1) the public may be adequately informed that cigarette smoking may be hazardous to health by inclusion of a warning to that effect on each package of cigarettes; and
> >
> > (2) commerce and the national economy may be (A) protected to the maximum extent consistent with this declared policy and (B) not impeded by diverse, nonuniform, and confusing cigarette labeling and advertising regulations with respect to any relationship between smoking and health.

15 U.S.C. § 1331 (1982).

The Act also contains a preemption provision, which provides that

> (a) No statement relating to smoking and health, other than the statement required by section 1333 of this title, shall be required on any cigarette package.
>
> (b) No requirement or prohibition based on smoking and health shall be imposed under State law with respect to the advertising or promotion of any cigarettes the packages of which are labeled in conformity with the provisions of this chapter.

15 U.S.C. § 1334 (1982). Confronted with this provision, the district court did not question that the Act prohibits state legislatures from requiring a warning on cigarette packages that alters that provided in section 1333. Nevertheless, after a comprehensive analysis of the Act, the court concluded that section 1334 does not preempt state common law claims such as those that the Cipollones have asserted.

II.

A. *Preemption Principles*

The United States Supreme Court has identified several principles for ascertaining congressional intent to preempt state authority. To begin, Congress may preempt state law by express statement. Jones v. Rath Packing Co., 430 U.S. 519, 525, 97 S.Ct. 1305, 1309, 51 L.Ed.2d 604 (1977). Without the aid of express language, a court may find intent to preempt in two general ways. Silkwood v. Kerr–McGee Corp., 464 U.S.

238, 104 S.Ct. 615, 621, 78 L.Ed.2d 443 (1984). First, a court may determine that Congress intended "to occupy a field" in a given area

> because "[t]he scheme of federal regulation may be so pervasive as to make reasonable the inference that Congress left no room for the States to supplement it," * * *. [Citations.] Second, in those instances where Congress has not wholly superceded state regulation in a specific area, state law is preempted "to the extent that it actually conflicts with federal law." * * *

B. Express Preemption

In applying these principles to the statutory scheme at issue here, we first express our agreement with the district court's conclusion that section 1334 does not provide for express preemption of the Cipollones' state common law claims. * * * We find support for this determination in Congress's failure to include state common law explicitly within section 1334, as it has in numerous other statutes.[5] * * * Accordingly, we turn to examining whether congressional intent to preempt the Cipollones' claims may be inferred under the two general principles of implied preemption.

C. Implied Preemption

[The court found the conflicting legislative history informative, but not dispositive.]

Under the principles of implied preemption, we must first determine whether Congress intended "to occupy the field" relating to cigarettes and health to the exclusion of state law product liability actions such as the Cipollones. Our examination of the Act leads us to agree with the district court's statements that "Congress * * * intended to occupy a field" and "indicated this intent as clearly as it knew how." Cipollone, 593 F.Supp. at 1164 (emphasis in original). Not only did Congress use sweeping language in describing the preemptive effect of the Act in section 1334, but it expressed its desire in section 1331 to establish "a comprehensive Federal program" in order to avoid "diverse, nonuniform, and confusing cigarette labeling and advertising regulations with respect to any relationship between smoking and health." See Palmer v. Liggett & Myers Tobacco, Inc., 635 F.Supp. 392

5. Examples of statutes that include a preemption provision explicitly encompassing state common law include 12 U.S.C. §§ 1715z-17(d), 1715z-18(e) (Supp. II 1984) (Domestic Housing and International Recovery and Financial Stability Act); 17 U.S.C. § 301(a) (Copyright Act of 1976); and 29 U.S.C. § 1144(a), (c)(1) (1982) (Employee Retirement Income Security Act of 1974).

It should be noted that just as Congress could have included a reference to preemption of state common law in section 1334, it also could have included a "savings clause" explicitly preserving the continued vitality of state common law, such as that in the Occupational Safety and Health Act of 1970, 29 U.S.C. § 653(b)(4) (1982). Thus, lack of reference to preemption of state common law in section 1334 has significance only because of the presumption against preemption.

(D.Mass.1984) (Congress has preempted field with respect to cigarette labeling).

In determining the scope of this field, we observe that the Cipollones' tort action concerns rights and remedies traditionally defined solely by state law. We therefore must adopt a restrained view in evaluating whether Congress intended to supercede entirely private rights of action such as those at issue here. [Citations.] In light of this constraint, we cannot say that the scheme created by the Act is "so pervasive" or the federal interest involved "so dominant" as to eradicate all of the Cipollones' claims. Nor are we persuaded that the object of the Act and the character of obligations imposed by it reveal a purpose to exert exclusive control over every aspect of the relationship between cigarettes and health. [Citations.] Thus, we look to the extent to which the Cipollones' state law claims "actually conflict" with the Act to ascertain whether they are preempted.

The test enunciated by this court for addressing a potential conflict between state and federal law requires us "to examine first the purposes of the federal law and second the effect of the operation of the state law on these purposes." Finberg v. Sullivan, 634 F.2d 50, 63 (3d Cir.1980) (in banc) (citing Perez v. Campbell, 402 U.S. 637, 91 S.Ct. 1704, 29 L.Ed.2d 233 (1971)). As mentioned above, Congress has provided us with an explicit statement of the Act's purposes in section 1331. That statement reveals that the Act represents a carefully drawn balance between the purposes of warning the public of the hazards of cigarette smoking and protecting the interests of national economy. [Citation.] Moreover, the preemption provision of section 1334, read together with section 1331, makes clear Congress's determination that this balance would be upset by either a requirement of a warning other than that prescribed in section 1333 or a requirement or prohibition based on smoking and health "with respect to the advertising or promotion" of cigarettes. See 15 U.S.C. § 1334.

Having identified the purposes of the Act, we now must evaluate the effect of the operation of state common law claims on these purposes. In so doing, we accept the appellants' assertion that the duties imposed through state common law damage actions have the * * * potential for frustrating congressional objectives. [Citations.] Applying this principle, we conclude that claims relating to smoking and health that result in liability for noncompliance with warning, advertisement, and promotion obligations other than those prescribed in the Act have the effect of tipping the Act's balance of purposes and therefore actually conflict with the Act.

Based on the foregoing, we hold that the Act preempts those state law damage actions relating to smoking and health that challenge either the adequacy of the warning on cigarette packages or the propriety of a party's actions with respect to the advertising and promotion of cigarettes. We further hold that where the success of a state law damage claim necessarily depends on the assertion that a party bore the duty to provide a warning to consumers in addition to the warning Congress has required on cigarette packages, such claims are preempted as conflicting with the Act.

* * *

[Reversed and remanded for rulings on which claims are preempted.]

NOTES

1. Accord, Roysdon v. R.J. Reynolds Tobacco Co., 849 F.2d 230 (6th Cir. 1988); Palmer v. Liggett Group, Inc., 825 F.2d 620 (1st Cir.1987); Stephen v. American Brands, Inc., 825 F.2d 312 (11th Cir.1987). Contra, Forster v. R.J. Reynolds Tobacco Co., 423 N.W.2d 691 (Minn.App.1988), review granted (Minn. Supreme Court, June 29, 1988). *Forster* relied on Silkwood v. Kerr–McGee Corp., 464 U.S. 238, 251 (1984): "It is difficult to believe that Congress would, without comment, remove all means of judicial recourse for those injured by illegal conduct." Professor Tribe was critical of the Third Circuit's ruling in *Cipollone:* "For a Federal appellate court to draw a cloak of immunity over such cases is to overstep its place in our Federal scheme." Tribe, Federalism With Smoke and Mirrors," The Nation 788 (June 7, 1986).

2. Producers of toxic substances are substantially regulated, particularly with respect to the warnings they must provide. Prior to *Cipollone,* preemption claims based upon such regulations were uniformly rejected by the courts. *Cipollone* broke the ice, and preemption claims are now regularly asserted in toxic substance litigation, and sometimes sustained. Compare Ferebee v. Chevron Chemical Co., 736 F.2d 1529 (D.C.Cir.1984) (paraquat poisoning from herbicide; compliance with EPA labeling requirements under Federal Insecticide, Fungicide, and Rodenticide Act did not bar inadequate warnings claim), with Fitzgerald v. Mallinckrodt, Inc., 681 F.Supp. 404 (E.D.Mich.1987) (mercury poisoning from fungicide; rejecting *Ferebee,* and ruling that compliance with EPA labeling requirements under FIFRA preempted plaintiff's warnings claims). See also Hurley v. Lederle Laboratories Div. of American Cyanamid Co., 851 F.2d 1536 (5th Cir.1988) (FDA approved and mandated specific warning for DPT vaccine; general preemption rejected, but preemption would be found if manufacturer provided FDA with all necessary and available information relevant to the warning). See generally Roddy, The Doctrine of Implied Preemption in Product Liability Cases, 13 Prod.Liab.Trends 61 (June 1988).

CIPOLLONE v. LIGGETT GROUP, INC.

United States District Court, District of New Jersey, 1986.
644 F.Supp. 283.

SAROKIN, DISTRICT JUDGE.

In this diversity action plaintiff Antonio Cipollone, acting individually and as the administrator of his deceased wife's estate, seeks damages against the companies that manufactured and sold cigarettes which he alleges to be the proximate cause of her lung cancer and death. At this juncture, plaintiff moves *in limine* for an order precluding the defendants from introducing evidence as to the cigarette industry's collateral benefits to the economy as part of their defense to those

of his strict liability claims which are premised on "risk/utility" theory.
* * *

The basis for plaintiff's motion *in limine* is that the societal benefits that result from producing and marketing a product are simply irrelevant to risk/utility analysis. Defendants argue to the contrary, claiming that such benefits are as integral to a fair evaluation of a product's value to society as are those attendant to the product's use.

* * *

* * * Defendants' proposed evidence, when distilled to its essence, aims to establish that their product is profitable, that some of those profits are disseminated to others in society, and that such benefits would be reduced or eliminated if liability were imposed. But strict liability law is, if anything, intended to temper the profit motive by making a manufacturer or marketer aware that it may be less costly in the long run to market a product more safely, or not to market it at all. [Citations.] To permit defendants to introduce the evidence that they here propose would undercut the very goals of strict liability law insofar as it suggests that defendants' interest in making a profit could transform an otherwise insufficient evaluation of their product's safety into a reasonable one.

Secondly, a fundamental purpose behind the imposition of strict liability is to require that a product "pay its way" by compensating for the harms it causes. [Citations.] For this purpose to be furthered it is of course necessary to accept that a product's profitability will be reduced as it bears the costs attendant to its use, and indeed that its true costs to society may so outweigh its usefulness that those costs, when reflected in the product's price, will ultimately lead to that product's withdrawal from the market. That some economic dislocation may thereby result in the short run is, in turn, an accepted fact of life in the operation of a free market system in which those entities who profit from the marketing of a product—rather than its individual victims, or the government, or society—are the ones who are expected to bear the risks that such products are not economically viable. Indeed, any avoidance of product liability for reasons unrelated to the inherent value of the product itself would permit the continued marketing of products that do not truly pay their way, thus discouraging the profiting entities from devoting their energies to making their product safer, or to producing products that are more socially beneficial in the long term. To permit a manufacturer or marketer to introduce evidence of a product's profitability, and to suggest that such profitability will be endangered if legal liability is found, would thus undermine these goals of greater overall economic efficiency and product safety.
* * *

CONCLUSION

In essence, defendants argue that in determining liability, a jury engaged in the risk utility analysis may take into consideration profits made, employees hired, benefits to suppliers of goods and services, taxes generated and even charitable activities or contributions made by the defendant manufacturer. The analysis was never meant to balance the risk to the consumer against the general benefit to society. Rather, the sole question presented is whether the risk to the consumers exceeds the utility to those consumers. The manufacturer of a highly dangerous or defective product with no or limited utility to a consumer, should not escape liability by demonstrating that the manufacturer of the product makes money for stockholders, for workers, for contractors, for suppliers, for municipalities, for the IRS, etc. It is the benefit and utility to the cigarette smoker which is here in issue, and not the benefit to the cigarette industry or those in turn, who benefit from its existence.

Plaintiff's motion *in limine* to preclude the introduction of evidence of the collateral social benefit of cigarette production * * * will be granted.

NOTES

1. What are the direct health costs of cigarette smoking? The direct benefits? What are the collateral costs? The collateral benefits?

In which category falls the employment of doctors who treat tobacco-induced diseases? The employment of gravediggers to bury lung cancer victims? Or is all this just voodoo economics? See Note, 73 Corn.L.Rev. 606, 616–19 (1988).

2. If individual smokers more or less know the risks and benefits, so that they are able to make reasoned, personal risk-benefit decisions, why should the law second-guess those decisions?

3. Have you considered all the issues? Are some of the costs of smoking externalized (imposed on others)? Assume that cigarette manufacturers eventually are held liable for all the lung cancer, emphysema, and other diseases caused by smoking. What will be the economic consequences? The social consequences? On balance, do you think these results will be beneficial or detrimental to society?

How about a similar approach for liquor?

4. Are all of the issues susceptible to economic analysis? Is it relevant that cigarettes are addictive? Why do you suppose countries like Iran continue to allow the production of heroin and cocaine? Should all addictive drugs be legalized, but taxed (administratively, or through liability judgments) to reflect their costs?

5. In July 1987, the Governor of New Jersey signed into law a products liability reform act which provided in part that manufacturers shall not be liable for defective design if:

> the characteristics of the product are known to the ordinary consumer or user, and the harm was caused by an unsafe aspect of the product that is an inherent characteristic of the product and that would be recognized by the ordinary person who uses or consumes the product with the ordinary knowledge common to the class of persons for whom the product is intended.

On the basis of the new law, the *Cipollone* defendants moved for partial summary judgment on plaintiff's risk/utility design claim. The parties agreed that the act incorporated comment *i* to § 402A into New Jersey law and that, if applicable, it would bar plaintiff's risk/utility claim. Comment *i* provides in part:

> The article sold must be dangerous to an extent beyond that which would be contemplated by the ordinary consumer * * *. * * * Good tobacco is not unreasonably dangerous merely because the effects of smoking may be harmful * * *.

Held, the reform act applied to pending cases; defendant's motion granted. Cipollone v. Liggett Group, Prod.Liab.Rep. (CCH) ¶ 11,637 (D.N.J.1987). Accord, on the basis of comment *i,* Roysdon v. R.J. Reynolds Tobacco Co., 849 F.2d 230 (6th Cir.1988).

The *Cipollone* defendants also moved to exclude evidence of diseases caused by cigarettes but not suffered by Mrs. Cipollone:

> The court finds that evidence of diseases other than those contracted by Rose Cipollone is relevant to the existence of Liggett's duty to warn as to these diseases. If there are numerous risks from cigarette smoking, the mere fact that plaintiff suffered from only one does not limit defendants' duty to warn to that risk alone. The adequacy of the warning depends upon all of the risks encountered by the average consumer. A plaintiff may well argue that had she or he been warned of all the risks, cigarettes would have been avoided. The fact that only one of the risks manifested itself does not, as a matter of law, relieve defendants of their duty to warn of the others. Whether Liggett breached such a duty, and whether such a breach caused Mrs. Cipollone's injuries, are factual questions to be resolved at trial.

Held, defendants' motion in limine to exclude the evidence denied. Cipollone v. Liggett Group, Prod.Liab.Rep. (CCH) ¶ 11,637 (D.N.J.1987).

6. *Cipollone* finally went to trial in January 1988. The plaintiff's case was completed in April, and the defendants moved for directed verdicts on the various claims. The court's rulings on these motions follow.

CIPOLLONE v. LIGGETT GROUP, INC.

United States District Court, District of New Jersey, 1988.
683 F.Supp. 1487.

SAROKIN, DISTRICT JUDGE.

FACTUAL BACKGROUND

The court will make no attempt to outline all of the evidence which has been submitted in this case, but concludes for the purposes of the pending motions that the jury could reasonably infer and find as follows:

Rose DeFrancesco Cipollone was born in 1925 and began to smoke at age 16, in the year 1942, while she was still in high school. She testified that she began to smoke because she saw people smoking in the movies, in advertisements, and looked upon it as something "cool, glamorous and grown-up" to do. She began smoking Chesterfields (manufactured by defendant Liggett Group, Inc.) primarily because of advertisements of "pretty girls and movie stars", and because Chesterfields were described in the advertisements as "mild". By the end of 1943 she was smoking a pack a day of Chesterfields. She met her husband, plaintiff Antonio Cipollone in 1946. In February 1947, Rose and Antonio Cipollone were married.

Mrs. Cipollone attempted to quit smoking while pregnant with her first child in 1947, but even then she would sneak cigarettes. While she was in labor she smoked an entire pack of cigarettes, provided to her at her request by her doctor, and after the birth of her first child she resumed smoking. She smoked a minimum of a pack a day and as much as two packs a day.

In 1955, she switched from Chesterfields to L & M cigarettes (also manufactured by Liggett) because L & M cigarettes were filtered, and she believed that the filter would trap whatever was "bad" for her in cigarette smoking. She relied upon advertisements which supported that contention. She continued to smoke approximately a pack and one-half a day until 1968, when she switched to Virginia Slims (manufactured by defendant Philip Morris Incorporated). In this instance, she changed because the cigarettes were glamorous and long, and were associated with beautiful women—and the liberated woman. In this period she smoked again between one and two packs a day.

Because she developed a smoker's cough and heard reports that smoking caused cancer, she tried to cut down on her smoking. These attempts were unsuccessful. Throughout this period her husband opposed her smoking and frequently brought to her attention articles that stated that smoking was harmful.

She testified that she believed that the "tobacco companies wouldn't do anything that was really going to kill you", and she read and relied upon statements from the industry in the media that indicated that there was no specific proof that cigarette smoking caused cancer.

Mrs. Cipollone switched to lower tar and nicotine cigarettes based upon advertising from which she concluded that those cigarettes were safe or safer. In the 1970's she switched to Parliaments (manufactured by Philip Morris) because the filter was "recessed". The ads professed, and she concluded, that the fact that the filter was recessed made smoking safer. In 1974, she changed from Parliaments to True cigarettes (manufactured by Lorillard, Inc.) based upon the recommendation of her family physician who indicated that if she had to smoke she should smoke True. Again, she saw and relied upon the True ads that indicated that they were low in tar and nicotine, and that reinforced her view that they were safe or safer. In 1981 her cancer was diagnosed, and even though her doctors advised her to stop, she was unable to do so. She even told her doctors and her husband that she had quit when she had not, and she continued to smoke until June of

1982 when her lung was removed. Even thereafter she smoked occasionally—in hiding. She stopped smoking in 1983 when her cancer had metastasized and she was diagnosed as fatally ill. Mrs. Cipollone eventually died on October 21, 1984.

There has been overwhelming evidence presented to the jury from which they could conclude that smoking causes lung cancer, that smoking caused lung cancer in Mrs. Cipollone, and that lung cancer was the cause of her eventual death.

The conduct of Mrs. Cipollone must be viewed in light of the activities of the defendants during this same time period. In respect to the conduct of the defendants, the jury could reasonably infer and find as follows:

There was a time period in which the defendants might reasonably contend that the risks of cigarette smoking were not clearly known and defined. Gradually, however, the scientific and medical evidence began to mount beginning in the 1950's, and eventually the accepted view in the medical and scientific community was and is that smoking causes lung cancer and other diseases. For a considerable period of time in Mrs. Cipollone's early smoking career, defendants and others in the tobacco industry not only failed to warn of the risks of smoking but to the contrary suggested that cigarette smoking was safe and harmless and, indeed, that this contention even had the support of medical doctors.

Early TV ads showed machines akin to the Wizard of Oz, including "the Acuray", a brain machine which assured a safe cigarette, and the "Quality Detective". Ads referred to existing cigarette "research laboratories" and contained phrases such as "best for you", "better quality" "chemical analysis", "mild", etc. One print ad suggested that smoking a particular cigarette was "Just What The Doctor Ordered".

Evidence presented by the plaintiff, particularly that contained in documents of the defendants themselves, indicates the development of a public relations strategy aimed at combating the mounting adverse scientific reports regarding the dangers of smoking. The evidence indicates further that the industry of which these defendants were and are a part entered into a sophisticated conspiracy. The conspiracy was organized to refute, undermine, and neutralize information coming from the scientific and medical community and, at the same time, to confuse and mislead the consuming public in an effort to encourage existing smokers to continue and new persons to commence smoking.

In this regard plaintiff has presented evidence, again, mainly from the files of the defendants themselves, which demonstrates a deliberate intent and purpose to challenge all adverse medical and scientific evidence regarding smoking, irrespective of its truth or validity. Indeed, the strategy to meet the claims of the scientific community was formulated before the contents of the scientific evidence were known. Defendants determined that if a report was publicized which demonstrated the dangers of cigarette smoking, attempts would be made to offset it, and even attack the qualifications of the researcher, if necessary.

Defendants made no attempt to conduct any research before the 1950's despite growing scientific evidence of risks.[2] Plaintiff offered evidence demonstrating that adverse results generated by research eventually conducted by the cigarette companies themselves were suppressed and concealed. At least one scientist testified as to threats made to him if he published his findings, and there was other evidence of attempts to suppress or coerce others.

The most subtle evidence of misrepresentation comes from the creation of the Tobacco Institute Research Committee (Council for Tobacco Research). The foregoing was created and highly publicized as the industry's good faith effort to search for the truth, learn the risks of cigarette smoking, and then supposedly report those findings to the general public. Plaintiff has presented evidence from which the jury could reasonably conclude that the creation of this entity and the work performed was nothing but a hoax created for public relations purposes with no intention of seeking the truth or publishing it. Evidence has been presented that the research actually conducted was unrelated or not pertinent to the real health issues. Furthermore, a minimal amount was invested when compared to sales, profits and amounts expended for advertising.

Defendants were well aware of the extreme difficulty smokers had and have in quitting smoking. They knew based upon sophisticated research that a smoker who found it difficult to quit, particularly faced with claims of hazards or risks, would focus on any rationalization to justify his or her continued smoking. Plaintiff presented expert testimony that Mrs. Cipollone was heavily dependent on tobacco and would grasp at any rationalization to continue, and that the cigarette companies provided that rationalization on a steady basis. The defendants and others in the industry repeatedly and publicly questioned the scientific and medical literature which linked smoking with cancer and other diseases. Furthermore, plaintiff offered expert testimony which demonstrated that even after the companies ceased making specific health claims, the vast advertising of the industry created a consistent message of purity, health, safety, reduced tars and nicotine, etc. This campaign served to create doubt in the minds of the consumer as to smoking dangers, and played on the weakness of those who were either addicted and/or dependent.

Plaintiff presented testimony that $250,000 is spent per hour 24 hours a day, 7 days a week, 365 days a year on cigarette advertising. Even in connection with the decisions to reduce tar and nicotine and advertise its benefits, defendants did not and do not concede any relevance to health for fear of making an admission. Rather they contend that such products are merely an accession to a baseless

2. One CEO was satisfied that there was no link between smoking and lung cancer, because he smoked and did not get cancer.

consumer concern—an effort to placate and humor a misguided public which believes in a risk that does not exist. The intensity of the advertising and public relations was sufficient to create the desired doubt in the minds of the consumer, and overwhelm or undermine pronouncements as to the dangers.

A jury might reasonably conclude from the foregoing that defendants in particular, and the industry in general, intentionally and willfully ignored the known health consequences to consumers from the sale of their products; that their so-called investigation into the risks was not to find the truth and inform their consumers, but merely an effort to determine if they could refute the adverse reports and maintain their sales. Defendants were confronted with a choice between the health and lives of the consumers and profits and the jury could reasonably conclude that the industry chose profits. Health of consumers does not receive even passing mention in the internal documents of the defendants, except as to the advantage to be gained by expressing such concern publicly. No witness presented by plaintiff was confronted with a single advertisement by *any* tobacco company voluntarily acknowledging even the possible existence of a risk to health.

As to plaintiff's alternative safer design claim, there has been evidence presented that a safer design was available, capable of being manufactured and sold, and that there was an election not to do so for fear that to market such a product would constitute an admission that other products already on the market were not safe but could have been. Evidence was presented to confirm that Mrs. Cipollone would have at least tried the new cigarette, and that had she continued to smoke it, it would have reduced her risk of lung cancer. In this instance, as well as all aspects of the research being conducted by the companies and under the auspices of the Tobacco Institute, there was the ever prevalent presence of lawyers determining, or at least participating in what research should be conducted, and what should be published or made available to the general public. A jury might conclude that this was just a normal business precaution, but in this case it could reasonably conclude that research was being conducted to improve the public relations image for the tobacco companies or to avoid liability, but never to provide the consumer with any adverse or necessary information as to health which might result from such research.

Plaintiff presented evidence that defendants directed particular efforts toward influencing doctors. Recognizing that smokers would look to their doctors for advice and that many doctors were smokers themselves, the industry created a magazine entitled Tobacco and Health (Research), and mailed it free to practically every doctor in the country, as well as many others in positions of influence. The publication was a blatant and biased account of the smoking "controversy". It had one purpose—to convince doctors that the claimed risks were unfounded, unsupported or refuted. There was also chilling evidence that means were being considered to combat the American Cancer Society's anti-smoking efforts in the public schools.

It may not be appropriate to draw any inference at this stage of the proceeding—before the defendants have presented their case—arising from the internal inconsistency of the contentions of the defendants. Those contentions, however, have manifested themselves in the openings and cross examination of plaintiff's witnesses. While asserting that the evidence regarding the relationship between smoking and lung cancer is deficient and unreliable and without scientific and medical basis, and having repeatedly and consistently taken that position publicly up to and including the present, defendants assert that Mrs. Cipollone was responsible for not accepting and relying upon this allegedly inaccurate and unsupported information. In essence, defendants contend that Mrs. Cipollone was sufficiently warned by what these defendants contend was unproven and unreliable, and is barred from recovering from them if or because she believed what *they* said about the subject of smoking and health.

That precarious line which the defendants seek to walk between warnings and causation may not be sufficient to preclude defendants from taking these seemingly inconsistent positions, but it may permit the jury to draw an adverse inference as to the good faith and credibility of defendants' factual assertions.

The irony of defendants' position is compounded by defendants further assertion that the particular cancer suffered by Mrs. Cipollone is not the type of cancer caused by or associated with smoking while simultaneously contending that there is *no* type of cancer which has been proven to be caused by smoking.

The jury, based upon the foregoing, may reasonably conclude that 1) defendants negligently failed to conduct research when it was warranted; 2) that they made affirmative health claims which were untrue; 3) that they failed to warn of risks about which they had knowledge; 4) that they deliberately and intentionally refuted, denied, suppressed and misrepresented facts regarding the dangers of smoking[;] 5) that they withheld knowledge of and failed to market a safer cigarette in order to avoid any admission of liability; and 6) that they engaged in an industry wide conspiracy to accomplish all of the foregoing in callous, wanton, wilful and reckless disregard for the health of consumers in an effort to maintain sales and profits.

The evidence presented also permits the jury to find a tobacco industry conspiracy, vast in its scope, devious in its purpose and devastating in its results. The jury may reasonably conclude that defendants were members of and engaged in that conspiracy with full knowledge and disregard for the illness and death it would cause, and that Mrs. Cipollone was merely one of its victims.[3]

3. The ruling of the Third Circuit[,] 789 F.2d 181 (3d Cir.1986), cert. denied, ___ U.S. ___, 107 S.Ct. 907, 93 L.Ed.2d 857 (1987) has precluded the plaintiff from offering evidence to establish that this conspiracy continues to the present. The jury

Having determined what a reasonable jury could find and conclude from the evidence presented in this case, the court will now address the various legal claims asserted by the plaintiff, and the defendants' motions addressing the same.

DISCUSSION

1. *Design defect*

Plaintiff's remaining design defect claim is that defendants failed to market a safer palladium cigarette. Defendants contend that plaintiff has presented no evidence from which the jury could find that defendants' conduct in this regard proximately caused Mrs. Cipollone's illness and subsequent death.

As to proximate cause, plaintiff puts forward the opinion of Dr. Harris that Mrs. Cipollone's risk of developing lung cancer would have been reduced by between 8% to 17% if she had switched to the palladium cigarette in 1971. In reaching that conclusion, Dr. Harris made the following assumptions: that the palladium cigarette is "safer" than other cigarettes; that the palladium cigarette could have been marketed by 1971; that if the palladium cigarette had been marketed in 1971, Mrs. Cipollone would have switched to it and continued to smoke it until she ultimately stopped smoking.

Plaintiff has not presented evidence from which the jury could find or infer the final fact mentioned above—that plaintiff would have continued to smoke the palladium cigarette. Dr. Cohen testified that, in his opinion, Mrs. Cipollone would have tried the product. Dr. Cohen admitted, however, that he could not predict whether Mrs. Cipollone would have found the palladium cigarette satisfactory and continued to use it. A conclusion by the jury that Mrs. Cipollone would have smoked the palladium cigarette from 1971 until she stopped smoking would be based on speculation, not evidence. Thus, there is no basis upon which the jury could conclude that there would be any reduction in the risk to Mrs. Cipollone, due to the absence of competent proof that she would have smoked the palladium cigarette for any substantial period.

Additionally, defendants contend that plaintiff has failed to prove proximate cause, even accepting Dr. Harris' conclusion and its predicates.

The parties disagree as to the appropriate test for measuring causation on the design defect claim. Defendants argue, with citation to products liability cases, that plaintiff must present evidence that the alternative design more likely than not would have prevented plaintiff's injury. See, e.g., Brown v. United States Stove Co., 98 N.J. 155, 174, 484 A.2d 1234 (1984). Plaintiff responds that, under the so-called "lost chance" doctrine, he must present evidence that defendants'

by virtue of that ruling has been deprived of evidence proffered by plaintiff to establish an intentional and deliberate campaign to undermine and neutralize the Surgeon General's warnings.

conduct increased plaintiff's risk of contracting lung cancer and that such increased risk was a "substantial factor" in producing plaintiff's condition. See, e.g., Evers v. Dollinger, 95 N.J. 399, 417, 471 A.2d 405 (1984).

No New Jersey court has ruled expressly on the applicability of the "lost chance" doctrine to product liability cases. This court, in the exercise of its diversity jurisdiction, must predict how the New Jersey Supreme Court would decide this question. See, e.g., Hon v. Stroh Brewery, 835 F.2d 510, 512 (3d Cir.1987). The court predicts that the New Jersey Supreme Court would not apply the "lost chance" doctrine to this case.

* * *

Therefore, plaintiff, in order to prevail on his alternative design claim, must present evidence from which the jury could conclude that Mrs. Cipollone's use of the palladium cigarette would "realistically or likely * * * have prevented [her] injury." [Citation.] Dr. Harris' testimony that use of the cigarette would have reduced plaintiff's risk of contracting cancer by 8% to 17% does not satisfy this burden. In products liability cases, the existence of a possibility of defendant's responsibility for plaintiff's injuries is insufficient to establish proximate cause. See Malin v. Union Carbide Corp., 219 N.J.Super. 428, 439, 530 A.2d 794 (App.Div.1987).

Plaintiff has not presented evidence from which the jury could reasonably conclude that defendants' failure to market a palladium cigarette proximately caused Mrs. Cipollone's illness and death. The court, therefore, grants defendants' motion for a directed verdict as to plaintiff's design defect claim.

At this time, the court does not determine whether its ruling requires the striking of any testimony introduced during plaintiff's case. The court notes that evidence relevant to the alternative design claim—such as defendants' motives in not developing or marketing a safer cigarette—may be relevant to other claims remaining in the case. The court will rule on specific testimony and exhibits if raised by defendants on a motion to strike.

2. *Failure to warn*

a. Philip Morris and Lorillard

[The court granted the motions for a directed verdict of these two defendants on plaintiff's failure to warn claims, since Mrs. Cipollone did not begin to smoke their cigarettes until after the federally mandated warnings began in 1966.]

b. Liggett

* * *

Plaintiff has submitted evidence from which the jury could infer that, prior to 1966, ordinary consumers were not adequately informed of the health risks of smoking. Plaintiff has presented expert testimony to that effect and has presented evidence that, given defendants' statements and advertisements during that period, a warning as to the hazards of smoking was necessary. Plaintiff has presented evidence from which the jury could conclude that Liggett possessed a duty to warn as to the health risks of smoking.

* * *

Plaintiff has presented evidence from which the jury could conclude that Liggett's pre–1966 failure to warn proximately caused Mrs. Cipollone's illness and death. Whether Mrs. Cipollone, given her awareness of the health risks of smoking, would have changed her behavior in the face of Liggett's warnings is a factual question for the jury. Plaintiff has presented evidence that Mrs. Cipollone discounted information of smoking's dangers because she believed that the cigarette companies would not market a dangerous product. The jury could reasonably infer from the evidence that Liggett's actions fostered Mrs. Cipollone's belief. Furthermore, plaintiff has presented expert testimony that ambiguity in the information environment was critical to Mrs. Cipollone's continued smoking—if defendants had warned of the dangers rather than disputing them, no such ambiguity would have existed.

* * * Plaintiff has presented evidence that Mrs. Cipollone's tobacco dependence prevented her from making a free and fully informed decision as to her continued smoking. Plaintiff has also presented evidence that Liggett knew of the dependency-causing characteristics of cigarettes, failed to warn of these characteristics, and sought through their pre–1966 activities to provide a rationale through which tobacco-dependent smokers could justify continued smoking. The jury could reasonably conclude that Liggett's pre–1966 activity proximately caused Mrs. Cipollone's injuries.

The court denies Liggett's motion for a directed verdict on plaintiff's failure to warn claims.

3. *Express warranty*

a. Liggett

* * *

Plaintiff has presented evidence from which the jury could conclude that Liggett's advertisements were the basis of the bargain for Mrs. Cipollone's purchase of Liggett's cigarettes. Mrs. Cipollone saw Liggett advertisements containing affirmations of fact as to smoking and health throughout the period in which she purchased Liggett's cigarettes. Whether such affirmations, once made, are part of the bargain is a question of fact for the jury. See N.J.S.A. § 12A:2–313(1)(a), Uniform Commercial Code comment 3. "Particular reliance on [defendant's affirmations] need not be shown" in order to establish that the affirmations were part of the bargain. [Citations.] Liggett may rebut the presumption that plaintiff relied on defendants' statements, *see* N.J.S.A. § 12A:2–313 Uniform Commercial Code comments 3 and 8, but the evidence, at this time, does not require such a finding. Plaintiff has presented evidence that Mrs. Cipollone, despite her awareness of the risks of smoking, accepted the affirmations in Liggett's ads as true and relied upon them in continuing to smoke.

* * *

b. Philip Morris and Lorillard

Plaintiff, in opposing defendant's motion for summary judgment acknowledged that "his claims against defendants Lorillard and Philip Morris for breach of express warranties are preempted." Brief in Opposition to Defendants' Motions for Summary Judgment at 8 n. 17. Plaintiff made no argument that any express warranty claim against these defendants remained. Nonetheless, plaintiff now contends that he has viable "pre–66" express warranty claims against these defendants. Plaintiff's Brief in Opposition to Defendants' Motions for Directed Verdict at 12.

The court, assuming that plaintiff has not waived any pre–1966 warranty claim against these defendants, concludes that plaintiff has not presented evidence to support such claims. Plaintiff identifies affirmations of fact made in 1954 by these defendants. The court concludes, as a matter of law, that these affirmations were not "part of the basis of the bargain" when plaintiff purchased Philip Morris products in 1968–1974 and Lorillard products after 1974. * * *

The court grants the motions of Philip Morris and Lorillard for a directed verdict on plaintiff's express warranty claims.

4. *Negligent failure to research and test*

Plaintiff alleges an independent cause of action based on defendants' failure to engage in reasonable research and testing as to the health consequences of smoking. Defendants contend that any claim based on such a failure is subsumed in plaintiff's failure to warn or alternative design claims.

The court concurs with defendants. Plaintiff has presented ample evidence from which the jury could conclude that defendants failed to engage in reasonable research and testing of their product. This evidence is relevant to plaintiff's claim that defendants failed to warn plaintiff of the scientifically knowable risks of cigarettes and plaintiff's claim that defendants failed to develop and market a feasible alternative design. However, plaintiff has presented no evidence from which the jury could conclude that this failure harmed Mrs. Cipollone in any independent fashion. * * *

The court grants defendants' motions for directed verdict on plaintiff's independent negligent research and testing claims.

5. *Intentional tort/conspiracy*

Plaintiff alleges that each defendant is liable for [fraud and fraudulent concealment].[19]

Plaintiff has presented evidence from which the jury could conclude that: 1) defendants made representations and intentionally concealed facts concerning the state of knowledge concerning the health consequences of smoking; 2) defendants knew of the falsity of these representations; 3) defendants intended that consumers, including Mrs. Cipollone, would rely on these representations to purchase cigarettes; 4) Mrs. Cipollone, under the circumstances, justifiably relied on defendants' representations in her purchases of cigarettes; and 5) Mrs. Cipollone's smoking caused her injury. Additionally, plaintiff has presented evidence from which the jury could conclude that defendants knowingly concealed facts that were significant and material to plaintiff's decisions regarding smoking.

Furthermore, as outlined by the court in its factual recitation, plaintiff has presented evidence from which the jury could conclude that defendants conspired to misrepresent and conceal facts regarding the dangers of smoking. [Citation.] Under the "well-settled law of civil conspiracy," defendants may be found jointly and severally liable for damages caused by the acts and products of their co-conspirators. See, e.g., Nicolet, Inc. v. Nutt, 525 A.2d 146, 147 (Del.1987).

As stated in connection with plaintiff's express warranty and failure to warn claims, Mrs. Cipollone's continued smoking after appearance of the congressionally mandated warnings in 1966 does not, as a matter of law, relieve defendants of liability. [Citation.]

The court denies defendants' motion for directed verdict as to plaintiff's intentional tort and conspiracy claims.

6. *Punitive damages*

Plaintiff, in order to recover punitive damages, must demonstrate "intentional wrongdoing in the sense of an 'evil minded act' or an act accompanied by a wanton and wilful disregard of the rights of another." [Citations.] If the jury accepts the plaintiff's version of the facts as to the conduct of the defendants, it is difficult to envision a more compelling case for an award of punitive damages.

The court denies defendants' motion for a directed verdict on plaintiff's claims for punitive damages.

19. Plaintiff acknowledged at oral argument that his claims for suppression of information held by third parties are part of his fraudulent concealment claim. The court adheres to its prior ruling that claims premised on suppression of information held by third parties are not preempted because such suppression is not "promotional" activity. Cipollone v. Liggett Group, Inc., 649 F.Supp. 664, 674 (D.N.J. 1986). Thus, this aspect of plaintiff's intentional tort claims covers conduct occurring before and after 1966.

CONCLUSION

The court grants defendants' motions for a directed verdict on plaintiff's alternative design claims.

The court grants the motions of Philip Morris and Lorillard for a directed verdict on plaintiff's failure to warn and express warranty claims. The court denies Liggett's motion as to these claims.

The court grants defendants' motions for a directed verdict on plaintiff's claim for negligent failure to research and test, as an independent claim.

The court denies defendants' motions for a directed verdict on plaintiff's intentional tort and conspiracy claims.

The court denies defendants' motion for a directed verdict on plaintiff's claims for punitive damages.

SO ORDERED.

FREE CHOICE QUESTION EMPHASIZED BY ATTORNEYS IN CIPOLLONE TRIAL

16 Prod.Safety&Liab.Rep. (BNA) 532 (June 10, 1988).

NEWARK, N.J.—(By a BNA Special Correspondent)—Attorneys emphasized the questions of free choice and cigarette dependency during closing arguments June 1–6 in the Cipollone tobacco trial (Cipollone v. Liggett Group Inc., DC NJ, No. 83–2864, closing arguments, 6/1/88).

Three defense lawyers—Donald Cohn on behalf of Liggett Group Inc., Robert Northrip for Lorillard Inc., and Peter Bleakley for Philip Morris Inc.—teamed up for a final statement that lasted the afternoon of June 1 and the entire day of June 2. On June 3, plaintiff's attorney Marc Edell asked for a day of recess to prepare his response, which was delivered June 6.

Because of the delay, U.S. District Judge H. Lee Sarokin took the unusual step of allowing the defendants a rebuttal and Edell a rerebuttal before the proceedings finally concluded.

During the trial, which began Feb. 1, the two sides presented an assortment of witnesses and experts who presented divergent views on many issues in the case, particularly the reason why deceased plaintiff Rose Cipollone (and by implication millions of other smokers) continued her hazardous habit (16 PSLR 173). The closing arguments reflected those differences.

"Rose Cipollone," Cohn told the jurors, "smoked cigarettes because she wanted to, because she liked to. She didn't want to stop smoking cigarettes, even though she knew the risks and dangers associated with cigarettes." The best evidence for this belief, Cohn argued, comes from Rose Cipollone's own deposition testimony, excerpts of which were read at the trial.

Rose Cipollone, a smoker for 40 years, died of lung cancer in 1984. The suit was continued by her husband Antonio Cipollone, also an original plaintiff.

"If you believe the testimony of Rose Cipollone and her family," Cohn proclaimed, "I believe you should return a verdict for Liggett."

Plaintiff's Argument

Plaintiff's attorney Edell offered a portrait of a very different woman. "Rose was a little bit naive, a little too trusting," he contended. She started smoking at age 16 in 1941, thanks largely to the glamorous image created by cigarette advertising, he argued. Her habit grew over the years into a "heavy dependency," abetted by the tobacco industry's failure to warn of health hazards and fraudulent express warranties, Edell continued. In 1952, for instance, radio personality Arthur Godfrey, whose show was sponsored by Liggett & Myers (predecessor of Liggett Group), proclaimed of Rose Cipollone's brand, Chesterfield: "I smoke two or three packs of these things a day. Never thought they did me any harm, and now they've got the proof." Edell told the jury: "That's an express warranty."

Edell argued that even after the 1964 Surgeon General's report, which unavoidably made Rose Cipollone and most other smokers aware of health risks, the tobacco companies' fraudulent advertising helped the dependent Rose Cipollone deny the danger she was in. He referred back to the testimony of an expert witness on consumer behavior, Joel Cohen, who said: "When somebody is dependent on cigarettes, they don't want to believe the product is harmful. The ads allay their fears."

Edell also brought up the recent report by Surgeon General C. Everett Koop (16 PSLR 477) that nicotine can induce addiction similar to that induced by cocaine or heroin. "You may find that hard to believe," he told the jury. "You may have quit smoking yourself. But for some people, nicotine is devastating."

Conspiracy Charge

Edell outlined what he described as "an evil-minded conspiracy" of cigarette manufacturers to "make sure people really didn't find out as much as they should about health hazards." The companies had reason to investigate the health risks of their products as long ago as the 1920s, Edell claimed, when medical literature first reported a marked rise in the incidence of lung cancer, and suggested a link to the increase in cigarette smoking. "A manufacturer of a product that's been suggested in the scientific literature as a possible cause of lung cancer has a responsibility to do something about it," Edell proclaimed. Yet the tobacco industry did nothing, he said.

In 1954, Edell said, Dr. Ernest Wynder's landmark experiment showing that cigarette tars produce tumors on the backs of mice made the industry realize that "the cat's out of the bag." What the companies did then, he said, was form the Tobacco Industry Research Council (TIRC), which subsequently became the Council for Tobacco Research (CTR). Although these organizations purported to dedicate themselves to scientific research, Edell argued, in actuality "they were designed for litigation, politics, and public opinion."

To bolster this claim, Edell recalled a number of internal memos subpoenaed from the industry, including one from Philip Morris' research director that said: "Much of the CTR's work has little or no relevance to smoking and health."

Edell also argued that a "gentleman's agreement" existed, and exists to this day, between the tobacco companies never to admit that their products cause cancer or other diseases. Several of the internal memos he produced referred to such an agreement, or employed the phrase "united front" or "common front" with reference to the industry's public position.

A "Frank Statement To Smokers"

As a particular incidence of fraud upon the public, Edell brought before the jury a "Frank Statement to Smokers" issued by Philip Morris in 1954, which said: "We believe our products are not injurious to health" and "the health of our consumers is a basic responsibility, paramount to every other consideration." The evidence he mustered in this case, Edell argued, demonstrated that consumers' health was "anything but" paramount in the company's mind.

Liggett, Edell noted, did not join the TIRC in the 1950s, but was guilty of its own misrepresentations. Specifically, he claimed, the company suppressed important health-related discoveries made by its own scientists. Most important of these, he said, was a duplication of Dr. Wynder's mouse-painting experiment achieved by Liggett in 1956, but not published until 1962, and then without the company's name affixed. Liggett, Edell said, also discovered numerous carcinogens and co-carcinogens not known to be in cigarette smoke at the time, but concealed that information as well. For these charges against Liggett, he depended largely on the testimony of a former company scientist, Dr. James Mold (16 PSLR 196).

In sum, Edell asked the jury to think of Rose Cipollone as "a human being eaten up very slowly by a horrible disease. A disease caused by cigarette smoking. A disease that she was never warned about by the defendants."

Defense View of Research

Both Cohn, for Liggett, and Bleakley, for Philip Morris, offered the jury a much more benign picture of their clients' research efforts. Cohn referred the jury to the testimony of Dr. Charles Kensler, a scientist with the Arthur D. Little consulting firm who worked with

Mold on all the supposedly repressed experiments. Kensler testified that Liggett never prevented him from publishing any results. He classified the findings singled out by Mold, including the duplication of Wynder's experiment, as "me-too" research, which was already too well known to merit publication (16 PSLR 463).

Cohn also made much of the fact that Liggett had submitted research material to the Surgeon General's Commission during its investigation in 1963. Edell maintained, however, that the real purpose of this cooperation was to obtain the commission's endorsement, as a safety feature, of the charcoal cigarette filter, which Liggett was then pioneering in its Lark brand.

Bleakley, for his part, told the jury it "just isn't fair to describe the Council for Tobacco Research as a fraud and a sham." Over the years, he said, CTR has funded over 500 studies relating to smoking and health, some of which have been co-sponsored by such groups as the American Cancer Society, the National Cancer Institute, the American Heart Association, and the U.S. Public Health Service.

As for the "Frank Statement to Smokers," Bleakley argued that it constituted an expression of Philip Morris' opinion, not a statement of fact. "There's no such thing as a fraudulent opinion," he declared.

Link To Cancer Doubted

Both Cohn and Bleakley noted that, virtually up to the time of the Surgeon General's report, many parties besides tobacco companies doubted the link between cigarettes and cancer. In 1957, Cohn recalled, Surgeon General Leroy Burney turned down the idea of warnings on cigarette packs. And in 1959, Bleakley noted, an editorial in the Journal of the American Medical Association found the case against cigarettes to be still unproven.

Finally, Cohn and Bleakley argued, even if the jury believed everything Edell said about tobacco companies, he did not demonstrate that their behavior, particularly before the Federal Cigarette Labeling and Advertising Act of 1966, was the proximate cause of Rose Cipollone's death. A warning before 1966, Cohn maintained, "would have made absolutely no difference anyway. * * * The warning that went on in '66 is 'cigarette smoking is hazardous to your health.' She [Rose Cipollone] already knew it. She continued to smoke when Liggett put that warning on the package."

The Medical Diagnosis

Northrip devoted his portion of the summation to reviewing what the defendants claim are ambiguities in Rose Cipollone's medical records. Although her diagnosis for the last two years of her life was small-cell lung cancer, a type of tumor both common and strongly linked to cigarettes, the defendants have insisted she was killed by atypical carcinoid, which they also insist has not been linked to smoking.

Edell admitted that atypical carcinoid had been diagnosed early in Rose Cipollone's illness, but by a divided panel of pathologists, and only on the basis of a biopsy, or small tissue sample. Once her entire lung was removed in an operation, Edell said, medical opinion was unanimous that she had small-cell cancer.

In any case, Edell argued, the limited published literature on atypical carcinoid shows, on average, that 90 percent of its victims are cigarette smokers. The number for small-cell cancer, he said, is about the same.

In his final remarks to the jury, Edell said: "You can either tell the tobacco companies, 'It's okay to lie to people,' and tomorrow will be business as usual. Or you can say, 'This is not acceptable behavior by any industry.'" Edell urged the jury to award punitive damages in addition to compensatory damages. Under New Jersey procedural rules, no specific amount of damages may be requested.

Charge To The Jury

Sarokin charged the jury for an hour and 20 minutes June 7, then gave them 20 written interrogatories dealing with the various charges in the case and potential damages. Liggett stands accused of four forms of malfeasance: fraudulent misrepresentation and concealment; conspiracy; failure to warn; and breach of an express warranty. Philip Morris and Lorillard are each accused of fraudulent misrepresentation and conspiracy. Sarokin ruled earlier in the case that, as a matter of law, only the companies' acts before the 1966 labeling law can be used against them.

Sarokin began his charge by telling the jury the proof presented by the plaintiff must clear two separate hurdles of "proximate cause." First, the jurors must decide that the manufacturers' misdeeds proximately caused Mrs. Cipollone to smoke. Second, they have to find that her pre–1966 smoking proximately caused her death. A proximate cause, the judge said, need not necessarily be a sole cause, but only a "substantial contributing factor." On the other hand, he said, plaintiffs must prove that Rose Cipollone relied on the alleged mendacity of the defendants to the extent that "Mrs. Cipollone more likely than not would have discontinued smoking if the concealed fact had been disclosed," or the appropriate warning given.

In the event that the jurors find part of the fault for Mrs. Cipollone's death to lie with the defendants, and part to lie with herself, Sarokin said, they should quantify what the percentage of the blame that is due to each party. If more than 50 percent goes to Mrs. Cipollone, the defendants win their case, and vice versa.

With respect to the conspiracy charge lodged against all three defendants, Sarokin cautioned that it could not be substantiated merely by "membership in a trade association." The plaintiff, he said, has to prove that "an agreement existed between at least one defendant and others." On the other hand, he said, if a conspiracy is found, every member is liable for the acts of all the others, "including those performed before it became a member." Accordingly, Philip Morris and Lorillard can be held liable, even though Mrs. Cipollone never smoked their products until after 1966.

The only time the burden of proof shifts to a defendant, Sarokin told the jury, is when it considers the failure-to-warn charge against Liggett. Because it is an incontestable matter of fact that Liggett offered consumers no warnings about its products before 1966, it is up to the company to prove that "any or all hazards and potential health hazards were unknowable at the time." The burden is also on Liggett, the judge said, to prove its courtroom contention that, in the days before warnings were on packs, "Rose Cipollone had an understanding and appreciation of the nature and extent of the health risks of cigarette smoking."

But even if Liggett fails this test, Sarokin reminded the jurors, it is still up to the plaintiff to prove that this failure caused Mrs. Cipollone's death.

Six of the original 12 jurors were chosen by lot, and retired after lunch on June 7. As of the afternoon of June 9, they had not brought in a verdict.

CIPOLLONE JURY AWARDS $400,000 AGAINST LIGGETT ON WARRANTY CLAIM

16 Prod.Safety&Liab.Rep. (BNA) 565 (June 17, 1988).

NEWARK, N.J.—(By a BNA Special Correspondent)—Both sides claimed victory in the Cipollone tobacco trial after the jury handed down a complex verdict June 13 awarding $400,000 against one of the defendants (Cipollone v. Liggett Group Inc., DC NJ, Civil Action No. 83–2864, verdict returned, 6/13/88).

Marc Edell, the attorney for plaintiffs Rose and Antonio Cipollone, focused on the fact that damages had been awarded to a smoker for the first time in history, and promised: "This is only the beginning. What we got in this case will be the building blocks in other cases."

But the three defendant tobacco companies—Liggett Group Inc., Philip Morris Inc., and Lorillard Inc.—stressed that the jury had rejected what they described as the "heart" of the plaintiffs' case: the contention that the companies, along with the rest of the tobacco industry, had conspired to misrepresent or suppress facts about smoking and health. Defense attorneys also said Liggett would appeal the judgment against it.

Basis of Verdict

Philip Morris and Lorillard, which were facing only charges of conspiracy and fraudulent misrepresentation, were exonerated by the jury. But the six jurors found valid two further charges leveled only against Liggett: failure to warn and breach of the express warranties provided by its advertising.

* * *

The jury found that Liggett had failed to warn Mrs. Cipollone before 1966 of the hazards of cigarettes, and that this failure could be considered a proximate cause of her smoking and her death from lung cancer. But, employing a percentage system that Judge Sarokin had charged them with under New Jersey's law of comparative responsibility, the jurors found that Liggett was only 20 percent responsible for Mrs. Cipollone's death, while she was 80 percent responsible because of her decision to "voluntarily and unreasonably encounter a known danger by smoking." Because Mrs. Cipollone was found to be more than 50 percent responsible, no damages could be awarded on the failure-to-warn count.

However, New Jersey does not apply comparative responsibility to the breach of express warranty claim. It was on that count that the jurors awarded $400,000 in damages. For reasons the jurors would not subsequently discuss with reporters, they gave the compensation not to Mrs. Cipollone herself, but to her surviving husband.

Liggett To Appeal

Philip Morris and Lorillard, the two exonerated defendants, held a press conference June 14 which no Liggett representative attended. But attorney Peter Bleakley, who represented Philip Morris as part of an apparently integrated defense team, said Liggett would appeal the award on two grounds: (1) that Judge Sarokin's jury charge on the breach of warranty count insufficiently stressed that not only did promises have to be made, but Mrs. Cipollone had to rely on them; and (2) that Sarokin had permitted an award of damages to a person other than the one who "entered into the bargain" of using Liggett's cigarettes. "That's not contract law," Bleakley said. "That's some bizarre form."

Sarokin was harshly criticized after the verdict by the defendants. Lorillard General Counsel Arthur Stevens, who was not directly involved in the case, described Sarokin as "demonstrably hostile to the tobacco companies," and accused him of "granting the plaintiff preferential rulings in a way that was wholly unwarranted."

Motions For Mistrial

Bleakley noted that the defense had two motions for mistrial pending. The first motion challenges Sarokin's questioning of defense witness Claude Martin, who testified that the content of cigarette advertising does not significantly affect a smoker's "information environment." The judge asked Martin whether a smoker would then feel the same way if a picture of a woman in a coffin ran on a cigarette advertisement, instead of the young and healthy-looking women one usually sees there. Bleakley said the judge was "taking over cross-examination" with this question, and "clearly signaling to the jury that he disbelieved the witness' testimony."

The basis of the second mistrial motion, Bleakley said, was Sarokin's ruling on the defense's motion for a directed verdict after the plaintiff had rested its case (16 PSLR 378). In that ruling, the judge threw out part of the plaintiff's case, but also described in strong terms misdeeds that a "jury might reasonably conclude" the defendants to have perpetrated. "This is completely unprecedented in my experience," Bleakley said, "and was certain to lead to wide publicity. To assume the jury wouldn't see that publicity is naive."

The Cipollone jury's finding of 20 percent responsibility, it was noted at the press conference, could hurt the tobacco industry in states where a defendant is held liable if a jury finds him to have any responsibility at all for the plaintiff's injury. One such state is Mississippi, where the much-publicized case of Nathan Horton against American Tobacco Co. ended in a mistrial Jan. 29 due to a divided jury (16 PSLR 151).

But Cipollone defense attorney Charles Wall commented: "If this case were in another state, a jury might not find any fault, because they knew that would mean awarding money."

Edell and his co-counsel Alan Darnell said they have six other suits pending against cigarette manufacturers. Edell said his firm, Budd, Larner of Short Hills, N.J., had spent over $2 million on the Cipollone case and would take a considerable loss. But he said he considered the case "an investment."

The Philip Morris and Lorillard representatives refused persistent requests by the press to say how much money they had spent defending against the Cipollone suit.

Congressional Activity

Allegations made during the Cipollone trial that the defendants conspired to suppress a "safer" cigarette will be the subject of a June 29 hearing before the Energy and Commerce Committee's Subcommittee on Transportation, Tourism, and Hazardous Materials, Subcommittee Chairman Thomas A. Luken (D–Ohio) announced June 14. Luken noted that if a bill he introduced May 5—The Cigarette Testing and Liability Act of 1988 (HR 4543)—had been in effect, the Cipollones might have been able to hold the defendants liable for post–1965 injuries.

The Cipollone verdict "starts the process of tearing down the wall that has protected the tobacco companies for years from responsibility for their products and advertisements," Rep. Mike Synar (D–Okla) said June 14. Synar called for "renewed efforts" to pass a bill to ban advertising and promotion of tobacco products which he introduced last year (HR 1272).

Rep. Jim Slattery (D–Kan) and 51 co-sponsors introduced legislation June 10 to require additional warnings on cigarette packages and advertising that "Nicotine In Cigarettes Is An Addictive Drug." The measure (HR 4793) was based on the May 16 report by the U.S. surgeon general finding that nicotine, an ingredient of tobacco, is addictive. A similar bill (S 2402) was introduced May 16 by Sen. Bill Bradley (D–NJ) (16 PSLR 477).

TOBACCO ON TRIAL

Tobacco Products Liability Project Newsletter 1–8, October 15, 1988.

There has been much speculation that the $400,000 in *Cipollone* is simply not enough to encourage other plaintiffs' attorneys to pursue tobacco products liability cases, especially when compared to the estimated $2 million which plaintiffs' attorneys spent to try the *Cipollone* case. In this litigious society, we're accustomed to reading about multimillion dollar verdicts to consumers. A case in point: the $8.75 million verdict against the G.D. Searle Co. recently awarded to a woman who was injured by the "Copper–7" birth control device which they manufacture.

The Copper–7 award included $750,000 for pain and disability, $1 million for emotional distress, and $7 million in punitive damages. Some members of the press have picked up on the industry's argument that the *Cipollone* award fails to measure up to that standard. Of course, there is a very good reason that the Copper–7 award made the front page of the New York Times—it was by far the largest verdict to date in a Copper–7 case. In fact, of the 17 cases involving the Copper 7 which had gone to trial, Searle had won 14, and the largest amount awarded to a plaintiff had been $250,000. By comparison, the $400,000 "token" award to Antonio Cipollone for his derivative injuries resulting from his wife's death does not seem so insignificant.

Other kinds of products liability suits show the same trends as the Copper–7 cases. Of the first seven DES cases tried to a verdict, only one resulted in a plaintiff's verdict that was upheld on appeal, and that award was for only $500,000. In asbestos litigation, the first plaintiff's verdict to the widow of an insulation worker who had died of asbestosis was for only $68,000. During the early 1970's, the awards ranged from approximately $50,000 to $250,000 per plaintiff. By the middle of 1978, of the 16 asbestos products liability cases which had gone to trial, the manufacturers had won 8 on a state of the art defense.

It was not until 1979, 10 years after the first suit was filed and 8 years after the groundbreaking plaintiff's verdict, that the tide began to turn in asbestos litigation. During 1978, persistent discovery efforts by plaintiffs had finally led to incriminating documents which revealed early knowledge of the dangers of asbestos on the part of virtually all the major asbestos manufacturers—evidence which seriously weakened their state-of-the-art defense. This discovery eventually led to the first multi-million dollar verdict in 1980, when a federal jury in Beaumont, Texas took only eight minutes to award $3 million in compensatory damages to the widow of an asbestos insulator.

Several other million dollar verdicts followed, but they were the exception rather than the rule. A study conducted by the Rand Institute for Civil Justice of approximately 3800 asbestos claims that were tried or settled prior to August 1982 concluded that the average total compensation per individual claimant was about $60,000. Of the 170 claims that went to trial, the average compensation was about $220,000 (of which approximately $30,000 was for punitive damages). By comparison, claims that were either settled before trial or dismissed averaged about $53,000 in total compensation per claim.

When compared with other types of products liability cases, tobacco plaintiffs have fared at least as well. They have prevailed in one of only six cases which have gone to trial in the "second wave" of tobacco products liability litigation, and recovered a substantial award despite the jury's strong feeling of dislike for the deceased smoker, Rose Cipollone. Another of the six cases, *Horton v. American Brands,* resulted in a hung jury and plaintiffs have another chance to prevail on retrial.

Moreover, in the first of the 80's cases to reach trial (the *Galbraith* case in California), three of the jurors would have voted for the plaintiff despite a weak causation case; and in the *Girton* case tried recently in Pennsylvania, the jury made a finding that cigarettes were defective due to the manufacturer's failure to warn consumers of their dangers. The *Roysdon* case never reached a jury because the judge directed a verdict for the defendants at the close of plaintiff's evidence.

It has been only three years since the first of the "second wave" cases reached trial in December of 1985, and it has been only six months since the breakthrough verdict in the *Cipollone* case. Based upon plaintiffs' experience in asbestos litigation, it is much too early to sound the death knell for tobacco litigation. In fact, one might argue that tobacco plaintiffs are ahead of the schedule set by asbestos litigators: they have already obtained thousands of incriminating industry documents which were made public in the *Cipollone* case (it took asbestos plaintiffs more than 10 years to uncover such incriminating evidence)—and they have already organized to share ideas and discovery (a strategy which did not occur in asbestos litigation until several years after the breakthrough plaintiff's verdict).

* * *

In his sweeping indictment of the asbestos industry, *Outrageous Misconduct,* writer Paul Brodeur points out that punitive damages are not generally awarded until plaintiffs' attorneys have enough damaging evidence—and a carefully thought-out strategy for presenting it—to invoke the jury's sense of outrage. This does not necessarily happen the first time a jury is presented with documentary evidence of a cover-up. In fact, in the very first fraudulent conspiracy claim to reach trial against the asbestos manufacturers, *Speake v. Johns–Manville,* the jury awarded only $150,000 in compensatory damages and no punitive damages to the plaintiff.

* * *

The *Cipollone* jurors who agreed to be interviewed for an *American Lawyer* article likewise told the interviewer that, although they felt that Liggett had not fulfilled its duty to warn consumers, they were not outraged at the conduct of Liggett's executives. [They did intimate, however, that the two holdout jurors who refused to be interviewed were outraged at the industry's conduct.] As in the asbestos cases, a substantial amount of documentary evidence of a pattern of industry misconduct has been uncovered. No doubt more documents remain to be discovered. As the plaintiffs' asbestos bar discovered, manufacturers are ingenious in causing documents to "disappear" when management changes hands or company headquarters are moved. Moreover, there are plenty of industry executives remaining to be deposed. Those who arrogantly deny the dangers of smoking, or whose testimony simply strains credibility, may make jurors in future cases angry enough to award punitive damages.

* * *

The tobacco industry has enjoyed a string of early successes both in the appellate courts and at the trial level which at first glance make a plaintiff's task seem almost insurmountable. In four circuits, they have established that claims based on inadequate warnings and/or misleading advertising subsequent to 1966 are preempted by the federal Cigarette Labeling and Advertising Act. In some jurisdictions, the companies have also won rulings that cigarettes cannot be considered "unreasonably dangerous" because the health hazards of cigarette smoking are known to the ordinary consumer. These arguments were the basis for a directed verdict in favor of defendants in the *Roysdon* case.

Even if a plaintiff is able to get past these legal obstacles, the industry has several defenses which it has been able to use to its advantage in the cases which have reached trial. Their public position—that there is no proof that smoking causes disease, but that any plaintiff who smokes has voluntarily and knowingly assumed the risks of smoking—underlies their defense in every case. In the *Galbraith* and *Marsee* cases, they were able to convince the jury that the plaintiffs did not have tobacco-caused diseases. In the *Cipollone* and *Girton* cases, jurors seemed to be more concerned with the "personal responsibility" issues—they believed that Rose Cipollone was aware of the dangers and stubbornly continued to smoke for her own pleasure—and they believed that a warning would have made absolutely no difference to John Gunsalus, in light of his own testimony that he probably would have continued to smoke anyway.

Although they make tobacco products liability litigation more challenging, these defenses are no more insurmountable than the hurdles raised by defendants in other kinds of product liability litigation.

* * *

Unlike the conventional wisdom in plaintiffs' cases, the juror interviews in the *Cipollone* case reveal that the typical tobacco plaintiff may fare better with an intelligent, well-educated jury. It takes a certain level of intelligence to understand the causation issues, and to see through the industry's "double-speak" on causation and personal responsibility. Well-educated jurors may also be less in awe of the power of multi-million dollar corporations, and more able to piece together evidence of an industry-wide pattern of corporate misconduct.

Despite some early setbacks, in this writer's opinion, tobacco products liability litigation is far from over. Plaintiffs' attorneys are accumulating valuable knowledge and insight into the nature of the game, and have an excellent chance of coming up with some winning strategies. All that remains to be done is to convince a jury—as they convinced Judge Sarokin in *Cipollone*—of the outrageousness of the industry's conduct. In asbestos litigation, it took more than ten years after the first successful case for plaintiffs' attorneys to put the evidence of industry misconduct together, and several more years to package it in a way which made a jury angry enough to award punitive damages. Although the *Cipollone* verdict puts tobacco plaintiffs well ahead of schedule, the verdict won't be in on tobacco products liability litigation until at least the mid–1990's. In the meantime, all that the tobacco industry can do is to hold its breath, tighten its belt, and put the best possible "spin" on any developments.

NOTES

1. Judge Sarokin denied the post-trial motions of all parties. Cipollone v. Liggett Group, Inc., 693 F.Supp. 208 (D.N.J.1988).

2. In the first round of cases against cigarette manufacturers in the 1960s, the defendants scored a knockout. See, e.g., Ross v. Philip Morris & Co., 328 F.2d 3 (8th Cir.1964); Lartigue v. R.J. Reynolds Tobacco Co., 317 F.2d 19 (5th Cir.1963); Green v. American Tobacco Co., 409 F.2d 1166 (5th Cir.1969), overruling en banc 391 F.2d 97 (5th Cir.1968). But see Pritchard v. Liggett & Myers Tobacco Co., 295 F.2d 292 (3d Cir.1961). See generally Wegman, Cigarettes and Health—A Legal Analysis, 51 Corn.L.Q. 678 (1966); Annot., 80 A.L.R.2d 681 (1961).

3. Notwithstanding the widely held view that post–1966 warning claims are preempted by the FCAL Act, other theories remain available to plaintiffs, as *Cipollone* shows. See also Kotler v. American Tobacco Co., 685 F.Supp. 15 (D.Mass.1988) (pre–1966 failure to warn); Dewey v. Brown & Williamson Tobacco Corp., 225 N.J.Super. 375, 542 A.2d 919 (1988) (alternative design).

4. Should recovery be barred or reduced on account of contributory (or comparative) negligence, assumption of risk, or causal apportionment? See, e.g., Brisboy v. Fibreboard Corp., 429 Mich. 540, 418 N.W.2d 650 (1988) (plaintiff's negligence in smoking could reduce recovery in asbestos action; plaintiff's general awareness of cancer risks from smoking sufficient). See Note, 99 Harv. L.Rev. 809 (1986) (plaintiff's conduct as a defense in smoking cases).

5. Another type of litigation against the tobacco industry is for property damage caused by the flammability characteristics of cigarettes. See Lamke v. Futorian Corp., 709 P.2d 684 (Okl.1985).

6. See Ausness, Cigarette Company Liability: Preemption, Public Policy, and Alternative Compensation Systems, 39 Syr.L.Rev. 897 (1988); Levin, The Liability of Tobacco Companies—Should Their Ashes Be Kicked?, 29 Ariz.L. Rev. 195 (1987); Garner, Cigarette Dependency and Civil Liability: A Modest Proposal, 53 S.Cal.L.Rev. 1423 (1980); Notes, 73 Corn.L.Rev. 606 (1988); 36 Cath.U.L.Rev. 643 (1987); 27 B.C.L.Rev. 1033 (1986).

SECTION 2. CAUSATION

> Many commentators recognize proof of causation as the paramount obstacle to just resolution of tort claims based on injury from toxic substances.

Brennan, Causal Chains-Statistical Links: The Role of Scientific Uncertainty in Hazardous Substance Litigation, 73 Corn.L.Rev. 469, 469 (1988).

A. THE CAPACITY OF THE AGENT TO CAUSE PLAINTIFF'S DISEASE

MILLER v. NATIONAL CABINET COMPANY

Court of Appeals of New York, 1960.
8 N.Y.2d 277, 204 N.Y.S.2d 129, 168 N.E.2d 811.

VAN VOORHIS, JUDGE.

An award in workmen's compensation has been made to the widow of Jacob Miller, who died on August 10, 1950. He was last employed by a firm known as Krakauer Bros. where he had worked from January 31, 1949 to April 23, 1950, except for an absence of about five months due to a back injury consisting of a fractured vertebra. He received disability payments during this interval based on the certificate of his personal physician, Dr. Louis Granirer, that this injury resulted from moving a piano while at work. After he died, his widow filed a claim against Krakauer Bros. for death benefits based on the theory that his death was caused by this fractured vertebra. Dr. Granirer refused to support that claim, certifying to the Workmen's Compensation Board that in his opinion the industrial accident mentioned did not cause his death. That claim was superseded by another based on the theory "that decedent's death may have resulted from an occupational disease, having been employed as a piano finisher and associated work for many years prior to his death."

This man died from leukemia. He had worked as a piano or cabinet finisher for five different employers since 1928. * * * One of them was appellant National Cabinet Company. The theory of claimant became that the blood disease from which he died was caused by exposure to a chemical known as benzene—whose trade name is benzol—which was contained in varnish removers utilized by each of the employers for whom he worked during this quarter of a century of his career.

The Referee who heard this workmen's compensation proceeding called in an associate industrial hygiene physician of the Division of Industrial Hygiene and Safety Standards, New York State Department of Labor, to whom he issued the following direction: "It may be that substances used in one or more of these employments were injurious and causative factors in the death * * *. Will you please investigate and let me know what substances were used and whether or not you believe such substances were injurious."

After executing this assignment, Dr. McBirney reported: "As this disease is one in which there is no known cause, and there are no substances used in any of these work places which produce symptoms and signs similar to the signs and symptoms of this leukemia—an investigation is not able to disclose any causal relation."

Dr. Granirer, decedent's personal physician for 8 years who attended him at his death, was called as a witness for claimant, but declined to express an opinion that the leukemia resulted from his employment. Dr. Angrist, pathologist at the Queens General Hospital of the Department of Hospitals of the City of New York, on whose report the diagnosis of leukemia was made, testified that leukemia of this kind varies from a few days to 23 years in producing death, is a cancerous process of the white cells of the blood and that he has no idea what factors prolong or shorten its duration. The Referee disallowed the claim, finding that it had not been established that death was due to the back injury sustained in moving a piano or to exposure to benzene. The Workmen's Compensation Board reversed the Referee, finding: "That decedent developed leukemia as the result of work exposure to benzol during his employment with National Cabinet Company, that this was a slow starting disease within the provisions of Section 40 of the Workmen's Compensation Law and that death resulted therefrom. * * *"

* * *

[A] serious defect in claimant's case is that the causes of leukemia or its aggravation are unknown. This clearly appears from the testimony of claimant's witness, Dr. Angrist, of the New York City Department of Hospitals, of Dr. McBirney, of the State Labor Department who was called by the Compensation Referee, and from the eloquent silence of decedent's own physician. Whatever case claimant might have would depend entirely upon the testimony of Dr. Paul Reznikoff, who had no contact with the deceased, and was called as an expert witness to answer hypothetical questions. * * *

Dr. Reznikoff was guarded and hesitant about expressing any opinion concerning exposure to benzol as a cause of leukemia. He testified that he believes that a person exposed to benzol may develop this kind of leukemia. He said that nobody knows how much exposure it takes. The award depends entirely upon his statement that the incidence of leukemia "is quite high in patients who have been exposed to benzol", and that "it is possible that this man's leukemia resulted from his alleged exposure to inhalation of benzol or benzene".

* * * Dr. Reznikoff made crystal clear, however, that, when he used the word "possible" in answering the hypothetical question, he meant that and nothing more. He demonstrated this beyond peradventure when he was asked on cross-examination what made him feel that this decedent's disease resulted from the cause mentioned, by replying: "I didn't say that. I was asked whether this could follow benzol. *I didn't say this particular man had it*". (Italics supplied.) Asked whether this particular disease could have had its cause outside of any employment exposure, Dr. Reznikoff replied: "As I answered the previous attorney, most of the patients that we do see with this disease, we never find out a reason for it with any certainty."

* * *

Not every supposition of a witness concerning what might be has the force of evidence, even though he has been licensed to practice medicine. If the witness is unfamiliar with any statistical data in the medical literature or in his own practice to give an inkling either to himself or to the court or board of how high the incidence of these cases is in situations of this kind, then the doctor's assumption that it is "quite high" is without significance. The lack of any kind of statistical data, which in the absence of scientific understanding is all that there would be to go on, is the more inexplicable if the claim is well founded in view of the large number of persons who die of leukemia and of workers in industry who are exposed to benzol. If there were any observed correlation between the two, it is certain that a physician of Dr. Reznikoff's standing would be in possession of the information.

* * *

* * * In the training of a scientist anything conceivable is a possibility. That is the first tenet accepted by the scientific mind. Many of the scientific discoveries and applied technologies today would have been thought by the average person to have been impossible of attainment less than a generation ago. No trained scientist, medical or other, would have the effrontery to state today that space travel is impossible, that the discovery of a cure for leukemia or other forms of cancer is impossible, or that any other speculation is dogmatically

beyond the realm of knowledge or accomplishment. Still that would not justify a court in assuming that it is presently known or is presently achievable merely for the reason that a trained scientist has said that it is not impossible.

* * *

The courts have been confronted before with cancer cases, and this is not likely to be the last. This is not an isolated situation. Questions of causation are common to actions based on warranty, tort or workmen's compensation proceedings [citation.] Would, for example, evidence that there are 4 to 11 times as many cases of lung cancer among cigarette smokers as among non-smokers (Journal of National Cancer Institute, April, 1953, pp. 1237–1257) be sufficient to establish a cause of action for breach of warranty in the sale of cigarettes? The United States District Court in Pittsburgh has apparently held not (Pritchard v. Liggett & Myers Tobacco Co., [Miller, J.], decided May 3, 1960).

* * *

We recognize that the scientific repugnance to the principle of "*post hoc, ergo propter hoc*" cannot fully extend to the law, and that, as in cases of circumstantial evidence, we regard as proof that which would be rejected by the scientist. Nevertheless, there comes a point even in legal thinking where the relationship of cause and effect becomes too attenuated to be regarded [citation.] An illustration of the correct legal approach to the problem is found in Stubbs v. City of Rochester, 226 N.Y. 516, 124 N.E. 137, 5 A.L.R. 1396, where the cause of disease was reached by process of elimination of other causes. * * * The speculative nature of Dr. Reznikoff's conclusions, appearing from his own testimony, and in the face of the testimony of all of the other doctors on both sides of the case, renders the result reached too conjectural for recognition in a court of law. * * *

[T]he courts will not in all instances demand scientific demonstration of cause and effect relationships but will insist only on practical probability * * *. But * * * a question of fact [does not arise] whenever a medical expert testifies in measured terms that an asserted cause of a disease is possible * * *. Otherwise for so long as the causes of a disease—like cancer—are unknown to science, everyone contracting the disease could secure medical testimony that it is "possible" that the disease is contracted from a wide variety of causes, choosing in each instance the particular possibility having the greatest promise of holding liable some responsible defendant. Any cancer expert could readily state that cancer could be caused by virus infection or by exposure to automobile exhaust fumes, sunlight, radiation, smog, smoking, hormone imbalance or according to any other theory which has been entertained by researchers or specialists as a possibility. * * *

The order appealed from should be reversed and the claim dismissed.

DYE, JUDGE (dissenting).

The Workmen's Compensation Board has found as a fact, which has been affirmed in the court below, that the decedent in the course of his work as a piano finisher, and as a result of occupational exposure to, contact with and inhalation of benzol, or its preparations and/or compounds, contracted, became disabled from and died of chronic monocytic leukemia * * *.

At the hearing the medical experts gave conflicting opinions respecting the fact of casual relationship of death to the occupational exposure. The board, in the exercise of its authorized discretion, resolved such conflict in favor of claimant which, having been affirmed, we may not disturb [citation].

The sole question then is whether there is any substantial evidence in support of causal connection. I think there is.

Dr. Reznikoff, an outstanding, nationally known hematologist, gave as his opinion that "a person exposed to benzol may develop leukemia, certainly chronic myelocytic leukemia, probably other types of leukemia, I cannot tell you how much exposure it takes. I don't think anybody knows, but we do know that the incidence of leukemia, especially chronic myelocytic leukemia, is quite high in patients who have been exposed to benzol. The only two causes we know of leukemia, are first, X-ray exposure, and secondly, benzol", and when asked: "you say it is possible that this man's leukemia resulted from his alleged exposure to inhalation of benzol or benzene?" he answered: "That is right."

This is not a bare guess—a mere scintilla of proof—but a carefully considered answer to a comprehensive hypothetical question. It was an honest effort by a well-qualified doctor to give the board the benefit of his experience and observation in diagnosing and treating this baffling disease. He could not rule out benzol as a possible cause. He had observed that many persons suffering from this type of leukemia had a history of benzol exposure, which observation had been noted by other eminent authorities. Three other doctors disagreed with Dr. Reznikoff but that is not to say that he was wrong or that his opinion should be rejected. Probative acceptance does not depend on quantity.

* * *

Here, there is uncontradicted proof of exposure to benzol. Here, there is enough proof to satisfy the statutory requirements of causal connection.

WHITE, INFANTE & WALKER, OCCUPATIONAL EXPOSURE TO BENZENE

1 Am.J.Indus.Med. 233, 233–35 (1980).

The recent US Supreme Court decision (Industrial Union Department v. American Petroleum Institute, [448 U.S. 607, 100 S.Ct. 2844, 65

L.Ed.2d 1010 (1980)] on the Occupational Safety and Health Administration's (OSHA) proposed standard for lowering exposure to benzene in the occupational setting has been a topic of recent discussion in both the lay [Doninger, 1980; Fishbein, 1980; The New York Times, 1980] and scientific media [Smith, 1980]. As a result of this decision, there appears to be some confusion about the actual toxicity and carcinogenicity of benzene.

A plurality of justices in a 5 to 4 decision stated that OSHA had neither made nor rejected any factual determinations demonstrating "significant risks," to be defined by the Agency, at the current standard of 10 parts per million (ppm); nor had OSHA made or rejected any factual determinations of significant benefits from lowering the standard to 1 ppm. The Supreme Court decision, however, should not be taken to imply that adverse health effects do not occur as a result of exposure to benzene below the current 10 ppm standard. In light of a possible misinterpretation of health effect data related to benzene exposure, we present here both a historical perspective on the current US standard and an updated review of the pertinent literature addressing the carcinogenic, mutagenic, and related toxic effects of benzene.

PERSPECTIVE ON THE CURRENT STANDARD

* * *

Evidence received by OSHA after 1971 indicated that workers exposed to benzene were at an increased risk of developing leukemia. In addition, benzene previously had been linked to other serious adverse health effects, including aplastic anemia, pancytopenia, other hematological disorders, and chromosomal aberrations. * * *

Consequently, in February 1978, OSHA promulgated a revised standard for occupational exposure to benzene [OSHA, 1978]. This standard allowed for an 8-hour time weighted average (TWA) of 1 ppm with a ceiling limit of 5 ppm. * * * The standard was based on a determination by OSHA that the available scientific evidence established that employees exposed to benzene were at an elevated risk of developing leukemia, nonmalignant blood disorders and chromosomal damage. A lower court vacated the revised (1 ppm) standard, and the Supreme Court recently upheld the lower court's decision. * * *

BENZENE CARCINOGENICITY

Epidemiologic Evidence

The evidence in the 1977 OSHA benzene record clearly demonstrated that benzene is a human leukemogen. In making this determination, OSHA relied upon an evaluation of all the evidence and not on any one particular study. Participants in the rulemaking for the most part did not challenge benzene's leukemogenicity, and neither did the US Court of Appeals for the Fifth Circuit when it vacated the standard. Within the scientific community, there is little dispute over benzene's carcinogenicity. For instance, the International Agency for Research on Cancer [1979] has classified benzene as a chemical for which there is sufficient evidence to support a causal association between exposure and cancer in humans. Numerous other scientific reports concur with this conclusion [CEQ, 1980; Cole and Goldman, 1975; NIOSH, 1977; NTP, 1980].

Two cohort studies have demonstrated an increased incidence of leukemia in workers exposed to benzene. The first is a study by Infante et al [1977a] of workers exposed to benzene in the production of Pliofilm, a rubber film material, in two Ohio industrial facilities. There was a paucity of information regarding atmospheric levels of benzene to which workers may have been exposed, but the available data indicated that average benzene levels generally ranged from less than 10 ppm to 100 ppm.

* * *

Observed deaths among the benzene-exposed cohort were compared with expected numbers of deaths calculated from both the general US white male population death rates, adjusted for age and calendar time period, and from the death rates of a comparison group of fibrous-glass workers employed in Ohio during the same period of time.

The investigators identified a significant excess of deaths from leukemia when compared to either the general US white male population * * *, or to the fibrous-glass workers * * *.

* * *

A second cohort study of 594 males exposed to benzene in three chemical production areas of a Michigan plant was conducted by Ott and his colleagues at the Dow Chemical Company [Ott et al, 1977]. All individuals who began employment at any time between 1940 and 1970 were included in the cohort. The vital status of these workers was determined through 1973. Three leukemia cases were observed among the cohort members; all were myelocytic and two were classified as acute myelocytic leukemia. Because one of these leukemia cases was coded on the death certificate as having died from bronchopneumonia, the expected number of leukemia cases was generated on the basis of morbidity data from the Third National Cancer Survey rather than mortality data. Using this analysis, the three myelocytic leukemia cases were reported to be significantly in excess of the expected number, 0.8 (p less than 0.047). All three leukemia cases were exposed to atmospheric benzene concentrations averaging less than 10 ppm. In addition to the three leukemia cases, two deaths due to anemia, one aplastic and one pernicious, were also observed among members of this cohort.

NOTES

1. The issue decided by the *Miller* court is the same causation issue raised in many toxic substance cases: Did exposure to the toxic agent cause the injured party's disease?

2. Why did the plaintiff lose in *Miller?* Because she failed to prove that benzene causes leukemia, because she failed to prove that her husband's leukemia was caused by benzene, or both?

3. While most casual observers (and many lawyers) think of causation as an all-or-nothing proposition (i.e., either an agent does or does not cause a disease), the connection between diseases and toxic substances rarely provides such categorical certainty. As two commentators recently put it:

> * * * "Does chemical Z cause cancer?" cannot be readily answered by the scientist. The scientist prefers to frame the question in terms of degree: "How carcinogenic is chemical Z?" Yet it is precisely the either yes-or-no questions which the legal system addresses to a testifying scientist. That format rejects the same scientific method which provides the scientist with his expert status in the courtroom.

Large & Michie, Proving that the Strength of the British Navy Depends on the Number of Old Maids in England: A Comparison of Scientific Proof with Legal Proof, 11 Envtl.L. 557, 595 (1981).

4. The problem runs very deep and goes to the ability of non-scientist lawyers and judges to understand scientific method and theory:

> The courts' difficulty with handling evidence linking a hazardous substance to a disease is largely the result of the courts' inability to understand scientific notions of causation. The assumptions that courts make about causation very much resemble those that provide the foundation for Newtonian physics. Over the past century, science has come to rely on new assumptions about cause and effect. These new assumptions have not been integrated into legal reasoning. As a result, lawyers and judges are often confused when they address scientific causation issues.

Brennan, Causal Chains and Statistical Links: The Role of Scientific Uncertainty in Hazardous–Substance Litigation, 73 Cornell L.Rev. 469, 478 (1988).

BLACK & LILIENFELD, EPIDEMIOLOGIC PROOF IN TOXIC TORT LITIGATION

52 Fordham L.Rev. 732, 750–62 (1984).

II. Epidemiologic Principles

The elucidation of the relationship between a disease and a factor (e.g., a toxic substance) suspected of causing it lies within the domain of epidemiology.* The epidemiologist examines this relationship in the context of populations, comparing the disease experiences of people exposed to the factor with those not so exposed.[77] Although the epidemiologist utilizes statistical methods, the ultimate goal is to draw a biological inference concerning the relationship of the factor to the disease's etiology and/or to its natural history. * * *

* Epidemiology has been defined as "the science dealing with the environmental causes of diseases of humans as inferred from observations of human beings." Cole, The Evolving Case–Control Study, 32 J.Chronic Dis. 15 (1979).—Eds.

77. See A. Lilienfeld & D. Lilienfeld, Foundations of Epidemiology 3 (2d ed. 1980).

* * *

B. *Determining the Relationship between Incidence of Disease and Exposure to a Factor*

Once the epidemiologist has defined the disease of interest, he seeks to compare the rate of disease development (incidence rate) among those exposed to the factor of interest with the rate among those not so exposed. The incidence rate is a measure of the probability that an individual will develop the disease. Hence, the epidemiologist is interested in determining if exposure to the factor changes the probability that an individual will develop the disease. If there is a gradation in the degree of exposure, the possibility of a corresponding gradation in incidence rates exists and merits investigation. The two principal approaches to collecting and analyzing morbidity/mortality data for exposed and non-exposed individuals are the demographic study and the epidemiologic study. In the former, the subjects within the two groups are viewed in the aggregate, while in the latter the subjects are viewed individually. The results of demographic studies are used to generate etiologic hypotheses, which are then tested through epidemiologic studies.

1. The Demographic Study

Demographic studies explore either morbidity, if the investigator seeks to explain sickness, or mortality, if the investigator seeks to explain death. In either case, a study initially seeks to determine the accuracy and completeness of the statistics being analyzed and then attempts to ascertain how such statistics are related to possible etiologic factors, such as age, sex, cigarette consumption or asbestos exposure. One might, for example, examine the relationship between annual asbestos use in the United States from 1910–1950 and the annual mortality rates for mesothelioma in the United States from 1940–1980. Before drawing conclusions from the relationship between asbestos exposure and mesothelioma, however, the epidemiologist must determine the accuracy of the available mortality and exposure data in order to ensure that there has not been under- or over-reporting of either asbestos use or mesothelioma mortality. Studies have indicated that such data are available and accurate and that there is a positive relationship between asbestos use and mortality from mesothelioma. Although such a positive correlation is supportive of a possible causal relationship between the two, it is by no means conclusive.

No matter how compelling the findings in a demographic study, it must be recognized that such observations refer to groups and not to the individuals within the groups. A correlation may exist between a factor and the incidence of a disease even though no causal relationship exists. The classic example of this phenomenon is the linear relationship between pig iron production in the United States and the birth rate in Great Britain. Clearly, such an association is spurious. This problem is known as an "ecological fallacy," and it imposes an inherent limitation on the use of demographic studies in inferring a causal relationship between a factor and a disease. Demographic studies are used mainly to focus attention on a possible association between a factor and a disease, the elucidation of which requires further, more refined modes of study. In order to demonstrate the association in terms of the individual members of a group, the investigator utilizes the epidemiologic study.

2. The Epidemiologic Study

The epidemiologic study attempts to explore and clarify a possible association between a factor and a disease within individuals in a population. For epidemiologists, it represents the application of the scientific method to human populations. In the scientific method, the investigator observes the effect of a single modification in the environment of one of two otherwise identical animals. Similarly, in an epidemiologic study, one seeks to observe the effect of exposure to a single factor upon the incidence of disease in two otherwise identical populations.

* * * One might, for example, be interested in determining the difference in lung cancer incidence between smokers and non-smokers. If the epidemiologist views the population in terms of the individuals' exposure, the study type is "prospective." The investigator first determines if the individuals are cigarette smokers, then follows them over a sufficient number of years to see if their lung cancer incidence rate differs from that of non-smokers. If the epidemiologist views the populations in terms of individual disease status, the study is either "retrospective" or "cross-sectional." Retrospective studies focus on past exposure while cross-sectional studies consider current exposure. The investigator selects individuals who have or do not have lung cancer and then determines whether or not they are or have been cigarette smokers.

a. *Prospective Studies*

The prospective study is a powerful way to investigate the relationship between a factor and a disease because it closely approximates the classical scientific method. The investigator identifies two populations (or representative samples thereof), one composed of individuals who have been exposed to the factor and one of individuals who have not been so exposed. Ideally, these populations will be otherwise identical. The investigator follows these populations for a period of time (possibly many years), observing the incidence rates of disease in each population. If the two groups are comparable, any difference in disease incidence can then be related either to the factor or to the sampling process, that is, to chance. * * * After eliminating chance and determining that a statistically significant relationship between the disease and the factor exists, the epidemiologist's next task is to estimate the magnitude of the association. The accepted means of measuring such an association is the calculation of the relative risk, which is the ratio of the incidence rate of disease in the exposed group divided by that rate in the non-exposed "control" group.[105] If there is no association between the factor and the disease, the relative risk is 1.0; that is, the incidence rates for the exposed and non-exposed groups are equal.

The greater the magnitude of the observed relative risk, the stronger the association between the factor and the disease. If the factor were the only cause of the disease, the relative risk would be infinite because the incidence of disease in the unexposed group would be zero. Because most diseases have multi-factorial etiologies, however, it is rare to observe a relative risk greater than 10. When a relative risk of 10 or more is observed, one can be reasonably certain that it represents a causal relationship. For example, the relative risk for mesothelioma from asbestos exposure, which is widely recognized as causal, is between 50 and 80. By comparison, the relative risk for leukemia in children who have been irradiated *in utero* is only 1.6 times that of children who were not so irradiated. This represents a relatively small increase in the risk of developing leukemia for the irradiated children, which reflects a relatively weak causal relationship.

The prospective study, although very reliable, is difficult and expensive to conduct. It is not always possible to identify populations that are exposed and not exposed to a factor. Frequently, the epidemiologist is unable to follow the two groups for the period of time required. Hence, epidemiologists have developed and extensively used the retrospective study.

b. *Retrospective Studies*

Whereas a prospective study investigates the disease experience of exposed and non-exposed groups, the epidemiologist performing a retrospective study begins with individuals who already have (cases) or do not have (controls) the disease under investigation. He then determines whether or not each individual has a past exposure to the factor, presumably prior to the onset of the pathologic process resulting in the disease. Cases are usually ascertained in a hospital setting. * * *

* * *

d. *Attributable Risk*

Observational studies are all directed at determining the relative risk of developing a disease that is associated with exposure to a factor. The relative risk, however, expresses only the magnitude of that

105. * * *

EXAMPLE OF COMPUTATION OF RELATIVE RISK

1. Groups A and B are assumed identical except for exposure to Factor F. (If not identical, there are methods of adjustment that still allow valid comparisons).

2. Incidence of disease D in Group A (exposed to Factor F) is 50 per 100,000 population. Incidence of the disease in Group B (not exposed) is 5 per 100,000.

3. Relative risk (r) of exposed to non-exposed is 50/5 = 10.0.

association. The statistical measure of a factor's relationship to a disease in the population is the "attributable risk." It was originally described as the percentage decline in the population's disease incidence that would occur if the population's exposure to the factor were eliminated. For example, the risk of lung cancer attributable to smoking in the United States today is approximately eighty percent. In other words, if smoking were eliminated in the United States, the incidence of lung cancer would decline by about eighty percent.

* * *

C. *Biological Inferences From Epidemiologic Data*

Demographic and epidemiologic studies both facilitate the elucidation of the statistical association between a factor and a disease. In order to draw the biological inference that a causal relationship exists, however, the epidemiologist must integrate additional scientific information. The derivation of such an inference requires rigorous consideration of laboratory, experimental, demographic and epidemiologic data.[124]

NOTES

1. As the previous materials demonstrate, gathering adequate evidence of causation is a complex and time-consuming process. Among the obstacles that may exist in the toxic substance area are: the long latency period of many insidious diseases, thereby preventing or delaying discovery and study; errors or inadequate information in medical records or death certificates, especially when the disease is otherwise rare; difficulties in determining and measuring the extent of exposure to the suspected agent, particularly in retrospective studies; and uncertainty about the dose-response ratio. For a good example of a court grappling with these difficulties, see Reserve Mining Co. v. EPA, 514 F.2d 492, 506–20 (8th Cir.1975). See also Vigliani, Leukemia Associated with Benzene Exposure, 271 Annals N.Y.Acad.Sci. 143, 143 (1976) (difficulty in establishing causal links between benzene and leukemia may have been due to misdiagnoses of leukemia as aplastic anemia).

2. "Dose" is a term used to measure exposure to an agent. It is determined by multiplying the intensity of exposure by the duration of exposure. The extrapolation of findings of causation from higher dosage levels to lower ones is quite controversial. The threshold hypothesis posits that there is a dosage below which there is no adverse health effect from exposure to the agent. See Kotin, Dose–Response Relationship and Threshold Concepts, 271 Annals N.Y.Acad.Sci. 22 (1976). By contrast, many scientists believe that even very low doses of toxic agents engender some incremental disease. For a

124. It should be noted that it is possible to have an inadequately developed biological inference regarding the relationship between a factor and a disease, yet still have a statistically plausible relationship. See A. Lilienfeld & D. Lilienfeld, supra note 77, at 315–16. The necessary biological knowledge may not be available at the time that the statistical association is found. An example of this occurrence is the relationship between oral contraceptives and various circulatory diseases. Id. at 315–16. When an association was discovered, there was no laboratory evidence to support a causal inference. However, the statistical association provided direction for laboratory workers in their research. The resulting laboratory data provided the necessary biological facts for the causal relationship to be stated. Id. at 316.

discussion of the conflicting hypotheses, see Maugh, Chemical Carcinogens: How Dangerous are Low Doses, 202 Sci. 37 (1978). See also In re "Agent Orange" Product Liability Litigation, 597 F.Supp. 740, 783 (E.D.N.Y.1984).

Thus, even where exposure to a toxic agent at certain levels has a demonstrated causal relationship with a particular disease, uncertainty remains about the effects of lower doses. In the case of benzene, for which there is a strong, demonstrated causal connection with leukemia at exposure levels above 150 parts-per-million, substantial uncertainty exists over the effects of lower exposures. See Industrial Union Dept., AFL–CIO v. American Petroleum Institute, 448 U.S. 607, 100 S.Ct. 2844, 65 L.Ed.2d 1010 (1980); Note, Establishing Causation in Chemical Exposure Cases: The Precursor Symptoms Theory, 35 Rutgers L.Rev. 163, 172 (1982).

3. For some toxic substances, the causal link to a particular disease is well established. Diseases for which a specified agent is the only cause are called "signature diseases," because the existence of the disease indicates the agent's causal role.

Consider the following conclusions of one author:

> Perhaps the most striking characteristic of toxic causation cases is their diversity. In some, the defendant's responsibility for the plaintiff's injury is nearly indisputable; in others, defendants may be clearly innocent of causal responsibility. Some cases involve individual plaintiffs who were exposed to rare chemicals; others involve thousands of plaintiffs and imperil the financial stability of entire industries. It is the beginning of wisdom to realize that no one approach can do justice under such diverse circumstances.

Farber, Toxic Causation, 71 Minn.L.Rev. 1219, 1259 (1987).

4. Some courts have refused to admit epidemiological studies based upon methodology that appeared to be faulty. See, e.g., In re Swine Flu Immunization Products Liability Litigation, 508 F.Supp. 897, 903–04 (D.Colo.1981), aff'd sub nom. Lima v. United States, 708 F.2d 502 (10th Cir.1983) (finding study seriously flawed). The use of animal studies to prove causation in humans is discussed in Krages, Rats in the Courtroom: The Admissibility of Animal Studies in Toxic Tort Cases, 2 Envtl. L. & Litig. 229 (1987).

5. Federal governmental agencies such as the EPA and the Center for Disease Control, as well as state public health agencies, conduct epidemiological studies. Are such studies inadmissible as hearsay evidence? See Fed.R.Evid. 803(8)(c); Fed.R.Evid. 803(6). Even if the study is not independently admissible, may an expert base his testimony on such a study? See Fed.R.Evid. 703. See generally Kehm v. Procter & Gamble Mfg. Co., 724 F.2d 613, 617–20 (8th Cir. 1983); Carlson, Collision Course in Expert Testimony: Limitations on Affirmative Introduction of Underlying Data, 36 U.Fla.L.Rev. 234 (1984).

6. From 1956 to 1983, Richardson–Merrell sold a drug called Bendectin for the treatment of nausea and vomiting during pregnancy. Over 1,100 cases, alleging that the drug caused birth defects, were consolidated for trial on the common issue of causation. *Held,* no causation. In re Richardson–Merrell, Inc. "Bendectin" Products Liability Litigation, 624 F.Supp. 1212 (S.D.Ohio 1985) (M.D.L. No. 486), aff'd sub nom. In re Bendectin Litigation, 857 F.2d 290 (6th Cir.1988).

The plaintiffs in Richardson v. Richardson–Merrell, Inc., 857 F.2d 823 (D.C. Cir.1988), had opted out of the consolidated trial. *Held,* no causation, notwithstanding plaintiffs' expert testimony to the contrary to a "reasonable medical certainty"; for more than two decades of research, no epidemiological study had found causation. But see Ealy v. Richardson–Merrell, Inc., 15 Prod. Saf.&Liab.Rep. (BNA) 740, Oct. 16, 1987 (D.D.C.1987), where the trial court remitted the entire $75 million punitive damages verdict, but left standing a $20 million verdict for compensatory damages.

In *Richardson,* the upper portion of one of the child's arms was underdeveloped, the elbow was fused, and her hand had only two digits. The upper portions of both legs were underdeveloped, and she had no lower right leg at all. A foot was attached to her right hip and later was surgically removed. In affirming the trial court's j.n.o.v. for the defendant on causation grounds, the court remarked:

> The circumstances of the case are tragic and Carita Richardson's plight evokes the utmost sympathy. It would be foolhardy to expect members of the jury to be without compassion for the catastrophe that befell this family. That is a natural response of the human spirit, and is without legal consequence so long as it is properly controlled. But in a case such as this it not only is appropriate but indeed imperative that the court remain vigilant to ensure that neither emotion nor confusion has supplanted reason.

857 F.2d at 832. Contrast *Ealy,* where the boy had a nonbending elbow, forearms of abnormal length, no thumbs, and missing fingers. The court concluded that the jury's $20 million compensatory damages verdict was not based solely on sympathy and emotion. Finally, compare *In re Bendectin,* the consolidated cases. The Sixth Circuit upheld the trial court's order excluding from the courtroom all plaintiffs under 10 and all plaintiffs over 10 with visible deformities. See 16 Prod.Saf.&Liab.Rep. (BNA) 867 (Sept. 9, 1988).

B. WHETHER PLAINTIFF'S DISEASE WAS CAUSED BY THE AGENT

What, precisely, do the courts mean in stating that the plaintiff must establish causation by a preponderance of the evidence? A typical jury instruction states:

> [I]t is proper to find that a party has succeeded in carrying the burden of proof on an issue of fact if, after consideration of all evidence in the case, the jurors believe that what is sought to be proved on that issue is more likely true than not true.

2 E. Devitt & C. Blackmar, Federal Jury Practice and Instruction § 71.13 (3d ed. 1977).

In re "AGENT ORANGE" PRODUCT LIABILITY LITIGATION

United States District Court, Eastern District of New York, 1984.
597 F.Supp. 740, aff'd 818 F.2d 145 (2d Cir.1987).

WEINSTEIN, CHIEF JUDGE.

* * *

PREFACE AND SUMMARY

In 1979 a class action was commenced charging the United States government and a major portion of the chemical industry with deaths and dreadful injuries to tens of thousands of Vietnam veterans who came in contact with herbicides used in the war in Southeast Asia. The suit also claimed that as a result of the veterans' exposure, their children suffer severe birth defects. After five years of numerous motions and extensive discovery a tentative settlement was reached on the eve of trial.

The sole question before this court is whether the case against the chemical companies should now be settled. Eleven days of nationwide hearings were conducted to give the class members themselves an opportunity to be heard on the merits of the settlement. After weighing the uncertainties and legal obstacles that would accompany years of protracted litigation were the case to go to trial, the court has concluded that the settlement should be approved.

* * *

The many legal issues are unique and the factual issues unresolved by the scientific communities addressing them. But it is neither fact nor law that makes this decision such a difficult one—rather, it is the deeply charged emotions that surround and engulf the litigation.

In listening to hundreds of witnesses around the country and reading the poignant letters of many veterans, their wives and parents, a repeated refrain makes it clear that more than money is at stake. The veterans feel that out of love of country they went to its aid and fought bravely in a brutal war. In return, they believe, they were sprayed with chemicals that insidiously are destroying them. They were vilified by their countrymen on their return because the war became unpopular. Their perception is that they are denied proper treatment by the Veterans Administration to the point where many of them shun the VA's medical and other facilities. Their families suffer as they waste away. And, perhaps even more important, they fear that they have been damaged genetically so that many choose to have no children or live in the despair of having sired children with birth defects who may spread this genetic damage to future generations.

Vietnam veterans and their families desperately want this suit to demonstrate how they have been mistreated by the country they love. They want it to give them the respect they have earned. They want it to protect the public against future harm by the government and chemical companies. They want a jury "once-and-for-all" to demonstrate the connection between Agent Orange and the physical, mental and emotional problems from which many of them clearly do suffer.

The court has been deeply moved by its contact with members of the plaintiffs' class from all over the nation and abroad. Many do deserve better of their country. Had this court the power to rectify past wrongs—actual or perceived—it would do so. But no single litigation can lift all of plaintiffs' burdens. The legislative and executive branches of government—state and federal—and the Veterans Administration, as well as our many private and quasi-public medical and social agencies, are far more capable than this court of shaping the larger remedies and emotional compensation plaintiffs seek.

Within the sharply limited judicial role we must ask whether the settlement of the litigation proposed by the parties' representatives is acceptable. For the reasons indicated below we tentatively hold that it is. It gives the class more than it would likely achieve by attempting to litigate to the death. It provides funds to help at least some men, women and children whose hardships will be reduced in some small degree. It does represent a major step in the essential process of reconciliation among ourselves.

* * *

Sections III and IV of the opinion discuss in detail the factual and legal obstacles that would be confronted by both plaintiffs and defendants if the case were to go to trial.

Section III, Factual Problems with Claims, summarizes the evidence that the plaintiffs have adduced in support of their allegations. As the opinion indicates, at best the evidence is inconclusive. This is due in part to the difficulty of proof in any mass toxic tort litigation and in part to the weakness in proof of causal relationship, at least as demonstrated in the epidemiological studies completed to date.

* * *

* * * [I]t is likely that because of the epidemiological nature of much of the evidence, no *individual plaintiff* would be able to prove that his or her particular adverse health effects are due to Agent Orange exposure. It may be possible—through the use of the class action device—to overcome this obstacle by making a single, class-wide determination of liability and by distributing the damages charged to all defendants as a group among all class members on a pro rata basis. At the present time, however, it is doubtful whether the legal system is ready to employ this device except, perhaps, as part of an overall settlement plan voluntarily entered into by the parties.

* * *

III. FACTUAL PROBLEMS WITH CLAIMS

There are serious factual problems with plaintiffs' case, the chief one being doubt that present scientific knowledge would support a finding of causality. * * *

* * *

It is important in considering the facts to keep clearly in mind * * * the different problems of proof posed in determining if dioxin *can cause* certain diseases and whether it *did cause* a particular disease or defect in a particular person. * * *

* * *

IV. LEGAL PROBLEMS WITH CLAIMS

There are enormous legal problems that plaintiffs would have to overcome before they could succeed in obtaining relief from the courts. * * *

* * *

B. Failure to Determine Who Was Harmed and Who Caused Harm

Defendants contend that even if anyone was injured by Agent Orange, plaintiffs cannot establish that the harm to any one of them was caused by any individual defendant. * * *

* * *

b. The Problem of the Indeterminate Plaintiff

* * * It is likely * * * that even if plaintiffs as a class could prove that they were injured by Agent Orange, no individual class member would be able to prove that his or her injuries were caused by Agent Orange. For example, plaintiffs as a class may be able to show that statistically, X% of the population not exposed to Agent Orange could have been expected to develop soft-tissue sarcoma, but that among those veterans who were exposed to Agent Orange, X + Y% suffer from soft-tissue sarcoma. If Y is equal to or less than X and there is no meaningful "particularistic" or anecdotal proof as to the vast majority of plaintiffs, virtually no plaintiff would be able to show by a preponderance of the evidence that his or her cancer is attributable to the Agent Orange rather than being part of the 'background' level of cancer in the population as a whole. The probability of specific cause would necessarily be less than 50% based upon the evidence submitted.

(1) Scope of the Problem

The problem just noted is one that has received a significant amount of scholarly discussion as well as some attention from the United States Congress. See, e.g., Rosenberg, The Causal Connection in Mass Exposure Cases: A "Public Law" Vision of the Tort System, 97 Harv.L.Rev. 849 (1984); Black and Lilienfeld, Epidemiological Proof in Toxic Tort Litigation, 52 Fordham L.Rev. 732, 782–83 (1984); Dore, A Commentary on the Use of Epidemiological Evidence in Demonstrating Cause-in-Fact, 7 Harv.Envtl.L.Rev. 429 (1983); Delgado, Beyond *Sindell:* Relaxation of Cause-in-Fact Rules for Indeterminate Plaintiffs, 70 Cal. L.Rev. 881 (1982); Proposed Radiogenic Cancer Compensation Act of 1983, S.921, 98th Cong., 1st Sess., 129 Cong.Rec. S.3918 (daily ed. March 24, 1983), introduced by Senator Hatch (1983). Because of the rarity of the situation until recently scant attention has been given to the issue by the courts. There has apparently been only one other mass exposure decision that has discussed the indeterminate plaintiff problem explicitly, *viz.* Allen v. United States, 588 F.Supp. 247 (D.Utah 1984), a case where injury was claimed as a result of radiation exposure from testing of atomic explosive devices.

In our complex industrialized society it is unfortunately possible that some products used on a widespread scale will cause significant harm to the public. While it may be possible to prove, through the use of such proof as laboratory tests on animals and epidemiological evidence, that such harm—for example cancer—can be "caused" by a particular substance, it may be impossible to pinpoint which particular person's cancer would have occurred naturally and which would not have occurred but for exposure to the substance.

* * *

In two of the largest and most widely publicized mass tort litigations, those involving DES and asbestos, the problem outlined above does not pose a serious obstacle since at least some of the damage caused by the harmful substance was, it has been claimed, unique to that substance. Adenosis and clear cell adenocarcinoma of the vagina and uterus, the conditions associated with DES, are, it is said, almost unknown among women whose mothers had not taken DES. Note, DES and a Proposed Theory of Enterprise Liability, 46 Fordham L.Rev. 963, 965 (1978). The situation is similar, in the asbestos litigation, albeit to a lesser extent. Although lung cancer is associated with cigarette smoking and other factors as well as asbestos exposure and mesothelioma may have causes other than asbestos, see Stanton & Wrench, Mechanisms of Mesothelioma Induction With Asbestos and Fibrous Glass, 48 J. Nat'l Cancer Inst. 797, 811–15 (1972), asbestosis is alleged to be uniquely associated with asbestos exposure. Borel v. Fibreboard Paper Products Corp., 493 F.2d 1076, 1083 (5th Cir.1973), cert. denied, 419 U.S. 869, 95 S.Ct. 127, 42 L.Ed.2d 107 (1974). In most other mass exposure cases, however, the harm caused by the toxic substance is indistinguishable from the naturally occurring disease or condition. See Dore, A Commentary on the Use of Epidemiological Evidence in Demonstrating Cause-in-Fact, 7 Harv.Envtl.L.Rev. 429, 437 (1983); Solomons, Workers' Compensation for Occupational Disease Victims: Federal Standards and Threshold Problems, 41 Alb.L.Rev. 195, 199 (1977).

The recent case of Allen v. United States, 588 F.Supp. 247 (D.Utah 1984), illustrates the problem well. Plaintiffs claimed that they developed various forms of cancer as a result of their exposure to radiation from nuclear explosions. While some forms of cancer can, it is contended, with some certainty be attributed to factors other than exposure to radiation, many others "cannot be distinguished from cancer of the same organ arising from * * * unknown causes". i.e., the 'background' cancers. J. Gofman, Radiation and Human Health 59 (1981), quoted in Allen v. United States, 588 F.Supp. at 406. The statistical evidence in *Allen* apparently made it clear that there was a strong positive association between exposure to low-level ionizing radiation, presumably the result of atomic explosions, and various forms of cancer suffered by plaintiffs. Thus, the *Allen* case has some of the characteristics of the DES and asbestos cases in addition to persuasive statistical correlations.

(2) Preponderance Rule

Even if there were near certainty as to general causation, if there were significant uncertainty as to individual causation, traditional tort principles would dictate that causation be determined on a case-by-case basis using the preponderance-of-the-evidence rule. Santosky v. Kramer, 455 U.S. 745, 755, 102 S.Ct. 1388, 1395, 71 L.Ed.2d 599 (1982); W. Prosser, Handbook of the Law of Torts, 208–09 (1971); Kaplan, Decision Theory and the Fact Finding Process, 20 Stan.L.Rev. 1065, 1072 (1968). The rule provides an " 'all or nothing' approach, whereby [assuming all other elements of the cause of action are proven], the plaintiff becomes entitled to full compensation for those * * * damages that are proved to be 'probable' (a greater than 50 percent chance), but is not entitled to any compensation if the proof does not establish a greater than 50 percent chance." Jackson v. Johns–Manville Sales Corp., 727 F.2d 506, 516 (5th Cir.1984).

Under the "strong" version of the preponderance rule, statistical correlations alone indicating that the probability of causation exceeds fifty percent are insufficient; some "particularistic" or anecdotal evidence, that is, "proof that can provide direct and actual knowledge of the causal relationship between the defendant's tortious conduct and the plaintiff's injury," is required. Rosenberg, supra, 97 Harv.L.Rev. at 857, 870. See Ryan v. Eli Lilly & Co., 514 F.Supp. 1004 (D.S.C.1981); Namm v. Charles E. Frosst & Co., 178 N.J.Super. 19, 427 A.2d 1121 (App.Div.1981). As Professor Jaffee has put it,

> If all that can be said is that there are 55 chances of negligence out of 100, that is not enough. There must be a *rational,* i.e., evidentiary basis on which the jury can choose the competing probabilities. If there is not, the finding will be based * * * on mere speculation and conjecture.

Jaffee, Res Ipsa Loquitur Vindicated, 1 Buffalo L.Rev. 1, 4 (1951). The "weak" version of the preponderance rule would allow a verdict solely on statistical evidence; the "all-or-nothing" approach converts the statistical probability into a legally absolute finding that the causal connection did or did not exist in the case. C. McCormick, Handbook on the Law of Damages, 118 (1935). * * *

There would appear to be little harm in retaining the requirement for "particularistic" evidence of causation in sporadic accident cases since such evidence is almost always available in such litigation. In mass exposure cases, however, where the chance that there would be particularistic evidence is in most cases quite small, the consequence of retaining the requirement might be to allow defendants who, it is virtually certain, have injured thousands of people and caused billions of dollars in damages, to escape liability. Because of this fact and the fact that "particularistic evidence * * * is * * * no less probabilistic than * * * statistical evidence," the "weak" version of the preponderance rule appears to be the preferable standard to apply in mass exposure cases—particularly where, as here, all claimants and defendants are joined in one suit.

(a) *Application of the Preponderance Rule to Mass Exposure Cases*

Conventional application of the "weak" version of the preponderance rule would dictate that, if the toxic substance caused the incidence of the injury to rise more than 100% above the "background" level, each plaintiff exposed to the substance could recover if he or she is suffering from that type of injury. If, however, to put it in somewhat graphic, albeit artificial terms, the incidence rose only 100% or less, no plaintiff could recover—i.e., the probability of specific causation would not be more than 50%.

Where a plaintiff's injuries result from a series of unrelated sporadic accidents, this "all-or-nothing" rule is justifiably rationalized on the ground that it is the fairest and most efficient result. In mass exposure cases, however, this all-or-nothing rule results in either a tortious defendant being relieved of all liability or overcompensation to many plaintiffs and a crushing liability on the defendant. These results are especially troublesome because, unlike the sporadic accident cases, it may be possible to ascertain with a fair degree of assurance that the defendant did cause damage, and, albeit with somewhat less certainty, the total amount of that damage.

The problem is both illustrated and further compounded by the fact that lack of precision in the data and models used may cause the range of the probabilities estimated by the statistical proof to lie on either or both sides of the 100% line. Because the statistical proof will almost never be as complete or as free from confounding factors as desirable, it may be possible to infer, for example, that the toxic substance caused the incidence to rise over the background level somewhere between 80 and 120%. See, e.g., Allen v. United States, 588 F.Supp. 247, 438, 439 n. 197 (D.Utah 1984) (noting significant variation in experts' interpretations of statistical evidence relating to the likelihood that plaintiff's cancer was caused by exposure to radiation). Moreover, issues of credibility and varying inferences drawn by the trier based upon varying assessments of probative force may cause reasonable people to assess these percentages in a range from almost zero to well over 120. See, e.g., E.M. Morgan & J.M. Maguire, Cases and Materials on Evidence, ch. 1 (7th ed. 1983).

Under the traditional application of the preponderance rule, whether individual plaintiffs recover will depend on where the probability percentage line is drawn despite the fact that a reasonable trier would conclude that a large proportion of the plaintiffs were injured by the defendant and a large number were not. Even if the statistical increase attributed to the substance in question is just a few percentage points, if statistical theory supports a finding of correlation there is no reason why the industry as a whole should not pay for the damages it probably caused.

A simple hypothetical will illustrate why too heavy a burden should not be placed on plaintiffs by requiring a high percentage or incidence of a disease to be attributable to a particular product. Let us assume that there are 10 manufacturers and a population of 10 million persons exposed to their product. Assume that among this population 1,000 cancers of a certain type could be expected, but that 1,100 exist, and that this increase is "statistically significant," permitting a reasonable conclusion that 100 cancers are due to the product of the manufacturers. In the absence of other evidence, it might be argued that as to any one of the 1100 there is only a chance of about 9% (100/1100) that the product caused the cancer. Under traditional tort principles no plaintiff could recover.

(b) *Inadequacy of Individualized Solutions*

Any attempt to resolve the problem on a plaintiff-by-plaintiff basis cannot be fully satisfactory. The solution that would most readily suggest itself is a burden shifting approach, analogous to that used in the indeterminate defendant situation already discussed. Allen v. United States provides a good example of how burden-shifting would be applied in an indeterminate plaintiff case. A plaintiff must show that the defendant, in that case the United States, negligently put "an identifiable population group" of which he was a member at "increased risk" and that his injury is

> consistent with having been caused by the hazard to which he has been negligently subjected, such consistency having been demonstrated by substantial, appropriate, persuasive and connecting factors. * * *

Allen, 588 F.Supp. at 415. At that point, the burden shifts to the defendant which will be held liable unless it can offer "persuasive proof" of noncausation. *Id.*

Generally courts have shifted the burden to the defendant to prove that it was not responsible for plaintiff's injury only in sporadic accident cases where it was certain that one of a very limited number of defendants injured the plaintiff, see, e.g., Summers v. Tice, 33 Cal.2d 80, 199 P.2d 1 (1948); Ybarra v. Spangard, 25 Cal.2d 486, 154 P.2d 687 (1944), or in mass exposure cases where general causation was certain and liability was apportioned in accordance with some market-share theory. See, e.g., Sindell v. Abbott Laboratories, 26 Cal.3d 588, 607 P.2d 924, 163 Cal.Rptr. 132, cert. denied, 449 U.S. 912, 101 S.Ct. 285, 66 L.Ed.2d 140 (1980); [citations].

Shifting the burden of proof in such cases will, at least theoretically, not result in crushing liability for the defendant either because the litigation only involves a sporadic accident, as in *Summers* and *Ybarra,* or because the defendant will only be held liable for the amount of damage it caused based on market share * * *. By contrast, shifting the burden of proof in the indeterminate plaintiff situation could result in liability far out of proportion to damage caused. It is not helpful in most situations to say that the defendant will not be liable for "those harms which [he] can reasonably prove were *not* in fact a consequence of his risk-creating, negligent conduct," *Allen,* 588 F.Supp. at 415, since, were such individualized proof available, there would have been no need to shift the burden.

(3) Possible Solution in Class Action

Since the problem results from a plaintiff-by-plaintiff method of adjudication, one solution is to try all plaintiffs' claims together in a class action thereby arriving at a single, class-wide determination of the total harm to the community of plaintiffs. Given the necessarily heavy reliance on statistical evidence in mass exposure cases, such a determination seems feasible. The defendant would then be liable to each exposed plaintiff for a pro rata share of that plaintiff's injuries.

This approach can be illustrated using the hypothetical given above. Suppose all 1,100 of those who were exposed to the harmful substance and who developed the cancer in the example join in a class action against all 10 manufacturers. Let us say that damages average $1,000,000 per cancer. A recovery of $100,000,000 (100 × $1,000,000) in favor of the class would be allowed with the percentage of the award to be paid by each manufacturer depending on the toxicity of its product. For example, if a company produced only 20% of the substance in question but, because of the greater toxicity of its product, likely caused 60% of the harm, it would contribute 60% of the total amount. If accurate records are available on the composition of each defendant's product, that analysis should be possible.

Since no plaintiff can show that his or her cancer was caused by any one of the defendants, they should divide the $100,000,000 by 1,100, giving each a recovery of about $90,000. While any plaintiff might feel that his or her recovery denigrated the degree of harm, the alternative of receiving nothing is far worse. The latter is, of course, the necessary result in any plaintiff's individual suit. Moreover, the deterrent effect of this result on producers would be significant. See Delgado, Beyond *Sindell:* Relaxation of Cause-in-Fact Rules for Indeterminate Plaintiffs, 70 Cal.L.Rev. 881, 893 (1982).

If the number of cases were only 1,050, most statisticians would say the difference was not statistically significant and a court using the pro rata approach might find that the defendant is not legally responsible for any of the increased incidence. But see Allen v. United States, 588 F.Supp. at 416–17 (noting that although increased incidence might be deemed "insignificant" by a scientist or statistician, it may well be that it "is still far more likely than not" that "the observed increase is related to its hypothetical cause rather than mere chance"). * * *

Putting a dollar amount on the damages suffered by individual plaintiffs is, from a real-world standpoint, a critical part of the solution. If the judicial and monetary economies of the class action are not to be lost through lengthy and expensive individual trials on damages, some mechanism must be devised to decide damage claims without the need for a full-fledged trial for each plaintiff. As Professor Rosenberg points out, "[p]ossibly the greatest source of litigation expense [in mass exposure tort litigation] is the individual assessment and distribution of damages that must follow trial of common liability questions." Rosenberg, *supra,* 97 Harv.L.Rev. at 916.

* * *

Every effort should be made to reduce questions of fact to a bare minimum. A preferred solution is to pay claims on a fixed and somewhat arbitrary schedule using a ministerial agency as is done with the Medicaid and Medicare programs where disbursements are made by insurance agencies acting for the United States.

No matter what system is used the purpose is to hold a defendant liable for no more than the aggregate loss fairly attributable to its tortious conduct. As long as that goal is met a defendant can have no valid objection that its rights have been violated.

* * *

3. Conclusion as to Indeterminate Plaintiffs and Defendants

The vexing problems of toxic torts probably would be best dealt with by legislation. In the absence of legislative and executive action courts must attempt to devise the most effective and equitable means of dealing with them through approaches that are consonant with present law and reasonable predictions about trends in the law. * * *

There is a strong likelihood that even if some causal link could be established between Agent Orange and the diseases and conditions from which plaintiffs claim they are suffering, it would be impossible in most cases to identify the individual class members who were injured by Agent Orange. Given the desirability of resolving the indeterminate plaintiff problem using a form of proportional liability or some other acceptable method, a dismissal of the class action would be unwarranted. The statistical theory, available data, and public policy are far from settled. Particularly during this period of rapidly changing scientific approaches and increased threats to the environment, we should not unduly restrict development of legal theory and practice—both substantive and procedural—by dismissing a class action such as the one now before us although the hazards of an ultimate dismissal must be considered in assessing the fairness of the settlement. As has previously been suggested, like inhibitions against dismissal of individual actions do not exist.

* * *

VIII. CONCLUSION

In conclusion it is well to remind ourselves of President Lincoln's admonition which is as relevant now, almost fifteen years after the end of the Vietnam war, as it was six score years ago. In his Second Inaugural Address he urged us "to bind up the nation's wounds; to care for him who shall have borne the battle and for his widow, and his orphan—to do all which may achieve and cherish a just and lasting peace among ourselves. * * *" It is time for the government to join with plaintiffs and defendants in even greater efforts toward this noble goal. Whether their hurt can be traced to Agent Orange or whether they are merely "casually unfortunate," C.L. Black, Jr., The Human Imagination in the Great Society, 5 (1983), is beside the point in the broader context of the nation's obligations to Vietnam veterans and their families.

IX. ORDER

The settlement is approved subject to hearings on fees and preliminary consideration of plans for distribution. This order is not final.

SO ORDERED.

AGENT ORANGE—LET IT LIE

N.Y. Times, Sept. 4, 1986, at 26, col. 1.

The vexed case of Agent Orange has been laid almost to rest by a solution that is almost a lie. But now, at the last minute, the U.S. Court of Appeals for the Second Circuit seems poised to overthrow Federal Judge Jack Weinstein's elegantly contrived solution with a narrow insistence on the truth. That would be an error that would fruitlessly prolong Vietnam veterans' tormented search for solace.

The veterans came home from a war no one wanted to hear about. With reason, many resented the neglect. They were too prone to believe a rumor, beginning years after the war's end, that Agent Orange, the herbicide sprayed in Vietnam, was the cause of many of their illnesses. An avid legion of tort lawyers stoked their fears and filed thousands of suits against the herbicide's makers.

The medical case against Agent Orange is but [a] shadow. True, the herbicide contained minute amounts of dioxin, a potent poison. But poisoning depends on dose as well. In 10 years, across six million acres, just 368 pounds of dioxin were sprayed. Could the faint residues surviving in the soil and water of Vietnam somehow get into troops in quantities to cause disease? Conceivable, but far from likely. The veterans have no obvious symptoms for which dioxin might be the explanation. Their diseases so far seem to be the same as other people's. The pilots who sprayed Agent Orange were far more exposed than any ground troops, but they too have shown no unusual pattern of disease.

The Agent Orange lawyers depended not on facts but fears—on their ability to haunt a jury with a parade of injuries and on the fear of the chemical companies and their insurers that however many cases they might win, they could not afford to fight them all. Sure enough, the companies were happy to buy their way out of an avalanche of litigation with a $180 million settlement, and the lawyers filed to cream off some $40 million in fees.

But they hadn't reckoned with a judge who both understood their manipulations of the tort system and was prepared to impose his own conception of justice. First, Judge Weinstein reduced the lawyers' fees to $9 million. Then, saying they had not proved causation, he ruled that all severely diseased veterans should be eligible for a share of the settlement. But to keep the payouts reasonably substantial, he also made the likely degree of exposure to Agent Orange a criterion. As the veterans' groups desired, he proposed creating a fund to provide services to families with birth defects.

•

The veterans are eager to start benefiting from Judge Weinstein's plan. But their lawyers, contrary to the veterans' interests, have now appealed it. And the appellate court seems clearly tempted to reject the plan and require that causation must be proved. That is a recipe for the chaos the plan was meant to avert. Instead of compensating the whole class of disabled veterans, the settlement fund would go, after further long delay, to those who drew sympathetic juries.

Since there's still no proof that *any* veteran was actually harmed by Agent Orange, it is surely better to use the money to help the larger group. Judge Weinstein's plan would resolve the Agent Orange nightmare, now eight years in the making—even though in denying causation it flouts a basic premise of tort law. The circumvention is necessary to an equitable solution. The courts do not usually do well in handling mass tort cases like this one. It's the tort system that needs changing, not Judge Weinstein's innovative and careful solution.

NOTES

1. Does the author of The New York Times editorial understand the difference between a judicial adjudication of liability and judicial approval of a class action settlement?

2. In Kramer v. Weedhopper of Utah, Inc., 141 Ill.App.3d 217, 95 Ill.Dec. 631, 490 N.E.2d 104 (1986), plaintiff's proof that a component part seller had provided the defective bolt for an ultralight airplane consisted of the testimony of the manufacturer that the component part seller supplied 90 percent of the bolts during the relevant time period. The trial court granted summary judgment for the component part seller and, on appeal, the court reversed, holding that evidence that there was a 90 percent probability that the compo-

nent part seller supplied the defective bolt was sufficient to permit a fact-finder to infer that it was the supplier of the defective bolt. Judge Stamos dissented:

> Liability is not based on a balancing of probabilities, but on a finding of fact. While the majority contends that the measure of what is considered sufficient evidence to draw a reasonable inference resolves itself into a question of probability, a review of case law involving non-identifiable defendant suppliers or manufacturers reveals that a theoretical probability alone cannot be the basis for a reasonable inference. There must be some evidence in addition to the abstraction which will enable a jury to choose between the competing probabilities.

490 N.E.2d at 108–109; see also Guenther v. Armstrong Rubber Co., 406 F.2d 1315, 1318 (3d Cir.1969). How would Judge Weinstein, who authored the *Agent Orange* opinion, respond to Judge Stamos?

3. *Agent Orange* and *Kramer* aside, it is rare that a case is litigated based on "naked statistical evidence." See Tyree, Proof and Probability in the Anglo–American Legal System, 23 Jurimetrics J. 89, 94 (1982). Inadequacies in available epidemiological studies and idiosyncratic factors peculiar to the plaintiff's case must be evaluated in addition to any probabilities generated by epidemiological evidence. These individual factors may include a medical history indicating the possibility of increased susceptibility, an alternative disease with the same or similar clinical symptoms, or conflicting evidence about plaintiff's diagnosis, symptoms, or their onset. See, e.g., O'Gara v. United States, 560 F.Supp. 786 (E.D.Pa.1983) (inadequacies in collected data that formed the basis of epidemiological studies; conflicting diagnoses of plaintiff); Latinovich v. United States, 537 F.Supp. 671 (E.D.Wis.1982) (conflicting evidence on time when plaintiff first exhibited symptoms of disease). See also Note, 96 Yale L.J. 376 (1986).

4. The literature addressing the use (and debating the appropriateness) of statistics and probability theory as aspects of the fact-finding process in the civil justice system is quite rich and abundant. One common theme is the legal system's need to provide an answer in the face of uncertainty. Another is the existence of social policies that may conflict with the principle of maximizing accurate fact-finding. A third is the extent to which jurors, in assessing evidence and reaching a verdict, might be assisted (or, alternatively, misled) by formal models of statistical decision-making theory. See, e.g., Tribe, Trial By Mathematics: Precision and Ritual in the Legal Process, 84 Harv.L.Rev. 1329 (1971) (arguing against expanded use of mathematical techniques in trials because of concern they would be misunderstood, given too much credence, and, ultimately, misused); Saks & Kidd, Human Information Processing and Adjudications: Trial by Heuristics, 15 Law & Soc'y Rev. 123 (1981) (taking issue with Professor Tribe's assumptions about the ability of juries to process mathematical information); Kaye, The Laws of Probability and the Law of the Land, 47 U.Chi.L.Rev. 34 (1979); Kaye, The Limits of the Preponderance of the Evidence Standard: Justifiably Naked Statistical Evidence and Multiple Causation, 1982 Am.Bar Found.J. 487; Nesson, The Evidence or the Event? On Judicial Proof and the Acceptability of Verdicts, 98 Harv.L.Rev. 1357 (1985); Orloff & Stedinger, A Framework for Evaluating the Preponderance-of-the-Evidence Standard, 131 U.Pa.L.Rev. 1159 (1983); Symposium, Probability and Inference in the Law of Evidence, 66 B.U.L.Rev. 377 (1986).

5. Is the *Agent Orange* court's dicta regarding the use of the class action device to surmount the individualistic proof problems and to provide a measure of compensation to all exposed individuals a long step on a short trip to a nationwide no-fault compensation system, at least for mass toxic substance cases? Is that a good idea? See Weinstein, The Role of the Court in Toxic Tort Litigation, 73 Geo.L.J. 1389 (1985).

6. **Exposure.** Plaintiff has the burden of proving his exposure to the toxic substance. In Besner v. Walter Kidde Nuclear Lab., 18 A.D.2d 952, 237 N.Y.S.2d 585 (1963), plaintiff asserted that her husband's death, which was due to leukemia, was caused by exposure to radioactive material at defendant's plant. After carefully analyzing the evidence of decedent's exposure to radioactive agents present at the plant, the court reversed a finding for the plaintiff. The court concluded that plaintiff's exposure to radioactivity was nowhere near the 15 times the permissible dose on which plaintiff's expert based his opinion of causation.

See also Roehling v. National Gypsum Co. Gold Bond Bldg. Products, 786 F.2d 1225 (4th Cir.1986) (reversing summary judgment based on plaintiff's failure to prove exposure to asbestos products manufactured by defendants); Allen v. United States, 588 F.Supp. 247, 425–28 (D.Utah 1984) (describing difficulties of determining dose of radiation to which plaintiffs, who resided near government nuclear testing, were exposed), rev'd on other grounds 816 F.2d 1417 (10th Cir.1987), cert. denied ___ U.S. ___, 108 S.Ct. 694, 98 L.Ed.2d 647 (1988). Cf. Celotex Corp. v. Catrett, 477 U.S. 317, 106 S.Ct. 2548, 91 L.Ed.2d 265 (1986) (summary judgment proper where claimant failed to meet burden of proof on asbestos exposure).

7. **Experts.** Should the testimony or affidavit of a qualified expert that in his or her opinion plaintiff's disease was more likely than not caused by defendant's agent be sufficient to avoid summary judgment and to send the case to the jury?

When Judge Weinstein was faced with this question, he conducted an in-depth critical analysis of the sources relied on and scientific studies ignored by the expert, commented that the probative value of the expert's opinion was at "a point approaching zero," and granted summary judgment for defendants. In re "Agent Orange" Product Liability Litigation, 611 F.Supp. 1267 (E.D.N.Y. 1985), aff'd 818 F.2d 187 (2d Cir.1987). See also Gicas v. United States, 508 F.Supp. 217, 219 (E.D.Wis.1981) ("Based on [the expert's] knowledge of the medical literature, on his knowledge of vaccines, and on his knowledge of the fields of epidemiology, etiology, and immunology, the Court finds that [the expert's] opinion that there is a causal relationship between the swine flu inoculation and the plaintiff's injuries is no credible evidence at all.") How often will a court be sufficiently informed to make such a finding?

Compare Wells v. Ortho Pharmaceutical Corp., 788 F.2d 741 (11th Cir. 1986), in which the court of appeals affirmed a trial judge's finding that defendant's spermicide had caused plaintiff's birth defects. The trial judge concluded that the epidemiological evidence in the case was inconclusive, ignoring the FDA's finding—based on a review of the scientific literature—that there was no evidence that spermicides cause birth defects, and chose instead to rely on the plaintiff's experts' clinical observations. The trial judge also discounted the defendant's experts and their reliance on the epidemiological record, based on their demeanor and lack of credibility.

In an editorial entitled *Federal Judges v. Science,* the New York Times concluded: "In their different ways, both law and science seek truth. That Judge Shoob and the appellate judges ignored the best scientific evidence is an intellectual embarrassment. The practical result is many citizens may suffer." N.Y. Times, Dec. 27, 1986, at 22, col. 1. The scientists' reaction was similar: "The *Wells v. Ortho* decision took the medical community by surprise, because the overwhelming body of evidence indicates that spermicides are not terogenic [malformation-causing]. * * * The trial prompted the editor of Teratology * * * to call spermicides the newest 'litogen'—a drug that does not cause malformations but does cause lawsuits." Mills & Alexander, Occasional Notes: Teratogens and "Litogens," 315 New Engl.J.Med. 1234 (1986).

8. **Proportional Recovery.** Consider the comments of one observer concerning the civil justice system's commitment to awarding damages on an all-or-nothing basis:

> The judicial power to compromise between the often harsh alternatives of all-or-nothing has received little consideration as a special problem in our jurisprudence. Its neglect is peculiar in the light of the high incidence of compromise through private settlement—a procedure of peacemaking in which the judge has taken an increasingly active role as mediator. Judicial activism in chambers is matched only by judicial paralysis on the bench. The "fair" decision promoted in private is one unattainable by law. That which the judge thinks just he cannot order. That which in chambers he calls "unjust" he orders and defends with thirty pages of rhetoric. Strange law? Passing strange I'd say—at least it might seem so to a Lunar visitor who shared our logic but not our legal experience.

Coons, Approaches to Court Imposed Compromise—The Uses of Doubt and Reason, 58 Nw.U.L.Rev. 750, 751 (1964). See also Delgado, Beyond *Sindell:* Relaxation of Cause–In–Fact Rules for Indeterminate Plaintiffs, 70 Calif.L.Rev. 881 (1982); Rosenberg, The Causal Connection in Mass Exposure Cases: A "Public Law" Vision of the Tort System, 97 Harv.L.Rev. 849 (1984); King, Causation, Valuation, and Chance in Personal Injury Torts Involving Preexisting Conditions and Future Consequences, 90 Yale L.J. 1353 (1981).

A few courts in differing contexts recently have begun to listen to the arguments for proportional recovery of damages. See, e.g., Herskovits v. Group Health Co-op. of Puget Sound, 99 Wash.2d 609, 619–36, 664 P.2d 474, 479–87 (1983) (Pearson, J., concurring, in plurality opinion); Aasheim v. Humberger, 215 Mont. 127, 695 P.2d 824, 828 (1985); Evers v. Dollinger, 95 N.J. 399, 471 A.2d 405, 412 n. 7 (1984); Jordan v. Bero, 158 W.Va. 28, 210 S.E.2d 618 (1974) (Neely, J., concurring); DePass v. United States, 721 F.2d 203, 206–10 (7th Cir. 1983) (Posner, J., dissenting).

9. Should a court permit a jury to find a causal link between a toxic substance and a disease if the plaintiff's expert testifies that the probability of causation is between 30% and 70%? What if the expert testifies that the probability range is 40–80%? What if the plaintiff had two experts, one who testified that the probability was between 50% and 80%, and one who said it was between 30% and 50%?

10. **Burden of Proof.** Scientific uncertainty in tracing causation, together with rigid burden of proof principles, have combined to prevent recovery in many toxic substance cases. Many commentators have thus proposed easing the traditional burden in such cases. See, e.g., Harris, Toxic Tort Litigation

and the Causation Element: Is There any Hope of Reconciliation?, 40 Sw.L.J. 909 (1986); Trauberman, Statutory Reform of "Toxic Torts": Relieving Legal, Scientific, and Economic Burdens on the Chemical Victim, 7 Harv.Envtl.L.Rev. 177 (1983); Comment, Causation and Common Law Relief for Toxic Substance Contamination, 14 U.Mich.J.L.Ref. 53 (1980); Note, Trans–Science in Torts, 96 Yale L.J. 428 (1986); Note, Tort Actions for Cancer: Deterrence, Compensation, and Environmental Carcinogenesis, 90 Yale L.J. 840 (1981).

11. For an inside account of the *Agent Orange* litigation and how Judge Weinstein managed it, see P. Shuck, Agent Orange on Trial: Mass Toxic Disasters in the Courts (1986); see also Rabin, Tort System on Trial: The Burden of Mass Toxics Litigation, 98 Yale L.J. 817 (1989) (questioning ability of present system to achieve traditional tort law goals in mass tort context); Marcus, Apocalypse Now?, 85 Mich.L.Rev. 1267 (1987). For a political view of the role of causation in toxic substance litigation, see Mashaw, A Comment on Causation, Law Reform, and Guerrilla Warfare, 73 Geo.L.J. 1393 (1985).

C. IDENTIFYING THE PARTY RESPONSIBLE FOR THE AGENT

SINDELL v. ABBOTT LABORATORIES

Supreme Court of California, 1980.
26 Cal.3d 588, 163 Cal.Rptr. 132, 607 P.2d 924, cert. denied, 449 U.S. 912, 101 S.Ct. 285, 66 L.Ed.2d 140 (1980).

MOSK, JUSTICE. This case involves a complex problem both timely and significant: may a plaintiff, injured as the result of a drug administered to her mother during pregnancy, who knows the type of drug involved but cannot identify the manufacturer of the precise product, hold liable for her injuries a maker of a drug produced from an identical formula?

Plaintiff Judith Sindell brought an action against eleven drug companies and Does 1 through 100, on behalf of herself and other women similarly situated. * * *

* * *

[Plaintiff's complaint alleged that defendants had manufactured and sold diethylstilbestrol ("DES"), a synthetic form of the hormone estrogen. DES was first marketed in 1941; the FDA approved its use for miscarriage prevention in 1947. It was promoted and used for this purpose until 1971, when the FDA ordered defendants to cease marketing DES for miscarriage prevention purposes.

[Plaintiff asserted that DES caused a form of vaginal cancer, known as adenocarcinoma, in the daughters of women who took DES during pregnancy. The cancer appears after a minimum latency period of 10 to 12 years. Plaintiffs also alleged that DES causes adenosis, a condition involving precancerous growths in the vagina and cervix. Plaintiff suffered from certain of these conditions.

[The first cause of action asserted that the defendants were negligent because they knew or should have known of the carcinogenic properties of DES, or that they failed adequately to test DES to discover its risks. Another cause of action alleged that defendants' collaboration in marketing, promoting, and testing this generic drug, their reliance on each other's testing, and their adherence to an industry-wide safety standard, rendered them jointly liable for plaintiff's injuries. Plaintiff also asserted claims based on strict liability, breach of express and implied warranties, false and fraudulent representations, misbranding of drugs, conspiracy, and lack of consent.]

* * *

Plaintiff seeks compensatory damages of $1 million and punitive damages of $10 million for herself. For the members of her class, she prays for equitable relief in the form of an order that defendants warn physicians and others of the danger of DES and the necessity of performing certain tests to determine the presence of disease caused by the drug, and that they establish free clinics in California to perform such tests.

Defendants demurred to the complaint. While the complaint did not expressly allege that plaintiff could not identify the manufacturer of the precise drug ingested by her mother, she stated in her points and authorities in opposition to the demurrers filed by some of the defendants that she was unable to make the identification, and the trial court sustained the demurrers of these defendants without leave to amend on the ground that plaintiff did not and stated she could not identify which defendant had manufactured the drug responsible for her injuries. Thereupon, the court dismissed the action. This appeal involves only five of ten * defendants named in the complaint.

* * *

This case is but one of a number filed throughout the country seeking to hold drug manufacturers liable for injuries allegedly resulting from DES prescribed to the plaintiffs' mothers since 1947. According to a note in the Fordham Law Review, estimates of the number of women who took the drug during pregnancy range from 1½ million to 3 million. Hundreds, perhaps thousands, of the daughters of these women suffer from adenocarcinoma, and the incidence of vaginal adenosis among them is 30 to 90 percent. (Comment, DES and a Proposed Theory of Enterprise Liability (1978) 46 Fordham L.Rev. 963, 964–967 [hereafter Fordham Comment].) Most of the cases are still pending. With two exceptions, those that have been decided resulted in judgments in favor of the drug company defendants because of the failure of the plaintiffs to identify the manufacturer of the DES prescribed to their mothers. * * *

We begin with the proposition that, as a general rule, the imposition of liability depends upon a showing by the plaintiff that his or her

* The parties stipulated to a dismissal of the eleventh defendant.—Eds.

injuries were caused by the act of the defendant or by an instrumentality under the defendant's control. * * *

There are, however, exceptions to this rule. Plaintiff's complaint suggests several bases upon which defendants may be held liable for her injuries even though she cannot demonstrate the name of the manufacturer which produced the DES actually taken by her mother. The first of these theories, classically illustrated by Summers v. Tice (1948) 33 Cal.2d 80, 199 P.2d 1, places the burden of proof of causation upon tortious defendants in certain circumstances. The second basis of liability emerging from the complaint is that defendants acted in concert to cause injury to plaintiff. There is a third and novel approach to the problem, sometimes called the theory of "enterprise liability," but which we prefer to designate by the more accurate term of "industry-wide" liability, which might obviate the necessity for identifying the manufacturer of the injury-causing drug. We shall conclude that these doctrines, as previously interpreted, may not be applied to hold defendants liable under the allegations of this complaint. However, we shall propose and adopt a fourth basis for permitting the action to be tried, grounded upon an extension of the *Summers* doctrine.

I

Plaintiff places primary reliance upon cases which hold that if a party cannot identify which of two or more defendants caused an injury, the burden of proof may shift to the defendants to show that they were not responsible for the harm. This principle is sometimes referred to as the "alternative liability" theory.

The celebrated case of Summers v. Tice, supra, 33 Cal.2d 80, 199 P.2d 1, a unanimous opinion of this court, best exemplifies the rule. In *Summers* the plaintiff was injured when two hunters negligently shot in his direction. It could not be determined which of them had fired the shot which actually caused the injury to the plaintiff's eye, but both defendants were nevertheless held jointly and severally liable for the whole of the damages. We reasoned that both were wrongdoers, both were negligent toward the plaintiff, and that it would be unfair to require plaintiff to isolate the defendant responsible, because if the one pointed out were to escape liability, the other might also, and the plaintiff-victim would be shorn of any remedy. In these circumstances, we held, the burden of proof shifted to the defendants, "each to absolve himself if he can." (Id. p. 86, 199 P.2d p. 4.) We stated that under these or similar circumstances a defendant is ordinarily in a "far better position" to offer evidence to determine whether he or another defendant caused the injury.

* * *

Here, as in *Summers,* the circumstances of the injury appear to render identification of the manufacturer of the drug ingested by plaintiff's mother impossible by either plaintiff or defendants, and it cannot reasonably be said that one is in a better position than the other to make the identification. Because many years elapsed between the time the drug was taken and the manifestation of plaintiff's injuries she, and many other daughters of mothers who took DES, are unable to make such identification. Certainly there can be no implication that plaintiff is at fault in failing to do so—the event occurred while plaintiff was *in utero,* a generation ago.

On the other hand, it cannot be said with assurance that defendants have the means to make the identification. In this connection, they point out that drug manufacturers ordinarily have no direct contact with the patients who take a drug prescribed by their doctors. Defendants sell to wholesalers, who in turn supply the product to physicians and pharmacies. * * * While it is alleged that they produced a defective product with delayed effects and without adequate warnings, the difficulty or impossibility of identification results primarily from the passage of time rather than from their allegedly negligent acts of failing to provide adequate warnings. * * *

* * *

Nevertheless, plaintiff may not prevail in her claim that the *Summers* rationale should be employed to fix the whole liability for her injuries upon defendants, at least as those principles have previously been applied. There is an important difference between the situation involved in *Summers* and the present case. There, all the parties who were or could have been responsible for the harm to the plaintiff were joined as defendants. Here, by contrast, there are approximately 200 drug companies which made DES, any of which might have manufactured the injury-producing drug.

Defendants maintain that, while in *Summers* there was a 50 percent chance that one of the two defendants was responsible for the plaintiff's injuries, here since any one of 200 companies which manufactured DES might have made the product which harmed plaintiff, there is no rational basis upon which to infer that any defendant in this action caused plaintiff's injuries, nor even a reasonable possibility that they were responsible.

These arguments are persuasive * * *. * * * While we propose, infra, an adaptation of the rule in *Summers* which will substantially overcome these difficulties, defendants appear to be correct that the rule, as previously applied, cannot relieve plaintiff of the burden of proving the identity of the manufacturer which made the drug causing her injuries.

II

The second principle upon which plaintiff relies is the so-called "concert of action" theory. * * *

* * * With respect to this doctrine, Prosser states that "those who, in pursuance of a common plan or design to commit a tortious act, actively take part in it, or further it by cooperation or request, or who

lend aid or encouragement to the wrongdoer, or ratify and adopt his acts done for their benefit, are equally liable with him. [¶] Express agreement is not necessary, and all that is required is that there be a tacit understanding * * *". (Prosser, Law of Torts (4th ed. 1971), sec. 46, p. 292.)

* * *

In our view, [plaintiff's] litany of charges is insufficient to allege a cause of action under the rules stated above. The gravamen of the charge of concert is that defendants failed to adequately test the drug or to give sufficient warning of its dangers and that they relied upon the tests performed by one another and took advantage of each others' promotional and marketing techniques. These allegations do not amount to a charge that there was a tacit understanding or a common plan among defendants to fail to conduct adequate tests or give sufficient warnings, and that they substantially aided and encouraged one another in these omissions.

The complaint charges also that defendants produced DES from a "common and mutually agreed upon formula," allowing pharmacists to treat the drug as a "fungible commodity" and to fill prescriptions from whatever brand of DES they had on hand at the time. It is difficult to understand how these allegations can form the basis of a cause of action for wrongful conduct by defendants, acting in concert. The formula for DES is a scientific constant. It is set forth in the United States Pharmacopeia, and any manufacturer producing that drug must, with exceptions not relevant here, utilize the formula set forth in that compendium. (21 U.S.C.A. § 351, subd. (b).)

What the complaint appears to charge is defendants' parallel or imitative conduct in that they relied upon each others' testing and promotion methods. But such conduct describes a common practice in industry: a producer avails himself of the experience and methods of others making the same or similar products. Application of the concept of concert of action to this situation would expand the doctrine far beyond its intended scope and would render virtually any manufacturer liable for the defective products of an entire industry, even if it could be demonstrated that the product which caused the injury was not made by the defendant.

* * *

III

A third theory upon which plaintiff relies is the concept of industry-wide liability, or according to the terminology of the parties, "enterprise liability." This theory was suggested in Hall v. E.I. Du Pont de Nemours & Co., Inc. (E.D.N.Y.1972) 345 F.Supp. 353. In that case, plaintiffs were 13 children injured by the explosion of blasting caps in 12 separate incidents which occurred in 10 different states between 1955 and 1959. The defendants were six blasting cap manufacturers, comprising virtually the entire blasting cap industry in the United

States, and their trade association. There were, however, a number of Canadian blasting cap manufacturers which could have supplied the caps. The gravamen of the complaint was that the practice of the industry of omitting a warning on individual blasting caps and of failing to take other safety measures created an unreasonable risk of harm, resulting in the plaintiffs' injuries. The complaint did not identify a particular manufacturer of a cap which caused a particular injury.

The court reasoned as follows: there was evidence that defendants, acting independently, had adhered to an industry-wide standard with regard to the safety features of blasting caps, that they had in effect delegated some functions of safety investigation and design, such as labelling, to their trade association, and that there was industry-wide cooperation in the manufacture and design of blasting caps. In these circumstances, the evidence supported a conclusion that all the defendants jointly controlled the risk. Thus, if plaintiffs could establish by a preponderance of the evidence that the caps were manufactured by one of the defendants, the burden of proof as to causation would shift to all the defendants. The court noted that this theory of liability applied to industries composed of a small number of units, and that what would be fair and reasonable with regard to an industry of five or ten producers might be manifestly unreasonable if applied to a decentralized industry composed of countless small producers.

* * *

We decline to apply this theory in the present case. At least 200 manufacturers produced DES; *Hall,* which involved 6 manufacturers representing the entire blasting cap industry in the United States, cautioned against application of the doctrine espoused therein to a large number of producers. (345 F.Supp. at p. 378.) Moreover, in *Hall,* the conclusion that the defendants jointly controlled the risk was based upon allegations that they had delegated some functions relating to safety to a trade association. There are no such allegations here, and we have concluded above that plaintiff has failed to allege liability on a concert of action theory.

Equally important, the drug industry is closely regulated by the Food and Drug Administration, which actively controls the testing and manufacture of drugs and the method by which they are marketed, including the contents of warning labels.[26] To a considerable degree, therefore, the standards followed by drug manufacturers are suggested or compelled by the government. Adherence to those standards cannot, of course, absolve a manufacturer of liability to which it would otherwise be subject. [Citation.] But since the government plays such a pervasive role in formulating the criteria for the testing and marketing of drugs, it would be unfair to impose upon a manufacturer liability for

26. Federal regulations may specify the type of tests a manufacturer must perform for certain drugs (21 C.F.R. § 436.206 et seq.), the type of packaging used (§ 429.10), the warnings which appear on labels (§ 369.20), and the standards to be followed in the manufacture of a drug (§ 211.22 et seq.).

injuries resulting from the use of a drug which it did not supply simply because it followed the standards of the industry.

IV

If we were confined to the theories of *Summers* and *Hall,* we would be constrained to hold that the judgment must be sustained. Should we require that plaintiff identify the manufacturer which supplied the DES used by her mother or that all DES manufacturers be joined in the action, she would effectively be precluded from any recovery. As defendants candidly admit, there is little likelihood that all the manufacturers who made DES at the time in question are still in business or that they are subject to the jurisdiction of the California courts. There are, however, forceful arguments in favor of holding that plaintiff has a cause of action.

In our contemporary complex industrialized society, advances in science and technology create fungible goods which may harm consumers and which cannot be traced to any specific producer. The response of the courts can be either to adhere rigidly to prior doctrine, denying recovery to those injured by such products, or to fashion remedies to meet these changing needs. Just as Justice Traynor in his landmark concurring opinion in Escola v. Coca Cola Bottling Company (1944) 24 Cal.2d 453, 467–468, 150 P.2d 436, recognized that in an era of mass production and complex marketing methods the traditional standard of negligence was insufficient to govern the obligations of manufacturer to consumer, so should we acknowledge that some adaptation of the rules of causation and liability may be appropriate in these recurring circumstances. * * *

The most persuasive reason for finding plaintiff states a cause of action is that advanced in *Summers:* as between an innocent plaintiff and negligent defendants, the latter should bear the cost of the injury. Here, as in *Summers,* plaintiff is not at fault in failing to provide evidence of causation, and although the absence of such evidence is not attributable to the defendants either, their conduct in marketing a drug the effects of which were delayed for many years played a significant role in creating the unavailability of proof.

From a broader policy standpoint, defendants are better able to bear the cost of injury resulting from the manufacture of a defective product. As was said by Justice Traynor in *Escola,* "[t]he cost of an injury and the loss of time or health may be an overwhelming misfortune to the person injured, and a needless one, for the risk of injury can be insured by the manufacturer and distributed among the public as a cost of doing business." (24 Cal.2d p. 462, 150 P.2d p. 441; see also Rest.2d Torts, § 402A, com. c, pp. 349–350.) The manufacturer is in the best position to discover and guard against defects in its products and to warn of harmful effects; thus, holding it liable for defects and failure to warn of harmful effects will provide an incentive to product safety. [Citations.] These considerations are particularly significant where medication is involved, for the consumer is virtually helpless to protect himself from serious, sometimes permanent, sometimes fatal, injuries caused by deleterious drugs.

Where, as here, all defendants produced a drug from an identical formula and the manufacturer of the DES which caused plaintiff's injuries cannot be identified through no fault of plaintiff, a modification of the rule of *Summers* is warranted. * * *

[W]e approach the issue of causation from a different perspective: we hold it to be reasonable in the present context to measure the likelihood that any of the defendants supplied the product which allegedly injured plaintiff by the percentage which the DES sold by each of them for the purpose of preventing miscarriage bears to the entire production of the drug sold by all for that purpose. Plaintiff asserts in her briefs that Eli Lilly and Company and 5 or 6 other companies produced 90 percent of the DES marketed. If at trial this is established to be the fact, then there is a corresponding likelihood that this comparative handful of producers manufactured the DES which caused plaintiff's injuries, and only a 10 percent likelihood that the offending producer would escape liability.

If plaintiff joins in the action the manufacturers of a substantial share of the DES which her mother might have taken, the injustice of shifting the burden of proof to defendants to demonstrate that they could not have made the substance which injured plaintiff is significantly diminished. While 75 to 80 percent of the market is suggested as the requirement by the Fordham Comment (at p. 996), we hold only that a substantial percentage is required.

The presence in the action of a substantial share of the appropriate market also provides a ready means to apportion damages among the defendants. Each defendant will be held liable for the proportion of the judgment represented by its share of that market unless it demonstrates that it could not have made the product which caused plaintiff's injuries. In the present case, as we have seen, one DES manufacturer was dismissed from the action upon filing a declaration that it had not manufactured DES until after plaintiff was born. Once plaintiff has met her burden of joining the required defendants, they in turn may cross-complaint against other DES manufacturers, not joined in the action, which they can allege might have supplied the injury-causing product.

Under this approach, each manufacturer's liability would approximate its responsibility for the injuries caused by its own products. Some minor discrepancy in the correlation between market share and liability is inevitable; therefore, a defendant may be held liable for a somewhat different percentage of the damage than its share of the appropriate market would justify. It is probably impossible, with the passage of time, to determine market share with mathematical exactitude. But just as a jury cannot be expected to determine the precise relationship between fault and liability in applying the doctrine of comparative fault [citations], the difficulty of apportioning damages among the defendant producers in exact relation to their market share does not seriously militate against the rule we adopt. As we said in *Summers* with regard to the liability of independent tortfeasors, where a correct division of liability cannot be made "the trier of fact may make it the best it can." (33 Cal.2d at p. 88, 199 P.2d at p. 5.)

We are not unmindful of the practical problems involved in defining the market and determining market share,[29] but these are largely matters of proof which properly cannot be determined at the pleading stage of these proceedings. Defendants urge that it would be both unfair and contrary to public policy to hold them liable for plaintiff's injuries in the absence of proof that one of them supplied the drug responsible for the damage. Most of their arguments, however, are based upon the assumption that one manufacturer would be held responsible for the products of another or for those of all other manufacturers if plaintiff ultimately prevails. But under the rule we adopt, each manufacturer's liability for an injury would be approximately equivalent to the damages caused by the DES it manufactured.

The judgments are reversed.

RICHARDSON, JUSTICE, dissenting.

* * *

Although the majority purports to change only the required burden of proof by shifting it from plaintiffs to defendants, the effect of its holding is to guarantee that plaintiffs will prevail on the causation issue because defendants are no more capable of disproving factual causation than plaintiffs are of proving it. "Market share" liability thus represents a new high water mark in tort law. The ramifications seem almost limitless * * *. * * *

* * *

The majority now expressly abandons the * * * traditional requirement of some causal connection between defendants' act and plaintiffs' injury in the creation of its new modified industry-wide tort. * * *

* * *

The fact that plaintiffs cannot tie defendants to the injury-producing drug does not trouble the majority for it declares that the *Summers* requirement of proof of actual causation by a named defendant is satisfied by a joinder of those defendants who have *together* manufactured "*a substantial percentage*" of the DES which has been marketed. Notably lacking from the majority's expression of its new rule, unfortunately, is any definition or guidance as to what should constitute a "substantial" share of the relevant market. The issue is entirely open-ended and the answer, presumably, is anyone's guess.

29. Defendants assert that there are no figures available to determine market share, that DES was provided for a number of uses other than to prevent miscarriage and it would be difficult to ascertain what proportion of the drug was used as a miscarriage preventative, and that the establishment of a time frame and area for market share would pose problems.

Much more significant, however, is the consequence of this unprecedented extension of liability. Recovery is permitted from a handful of defendants *each* of whom *individually* may account for a comparatively small share of the relevant market, so long as the *aggregate* business of those who have been sued is deemed "substantial." In other words, a particular defendant may be held proportionately liable *even though mathematically it is much more likely than not that it played no role whatever in causing plaintiffs' injuries.* Plaintiffs have strikingly capsulated their reasoning by insisting " * * * that while one manufacturer's product may not have injured a particular plaintiff, we can assume that it injured a different plaintiff and all we are talking about is a mere matching of plaintiffs and defendants." (Counsel's letter (Oct. 16, 1979) p. 3.) In adopting the foregoing rationale the majority rejects over 100 years of tort law which required that before tort liability was imposed a "matching" of defendant's conduct and plaintiff's injury was absolutely essential. * * *

* * *

Additionally, it is readily apparent that "market share" liability will fall unevenly and disproportionately upon those manufacturers who are amenable to suit in California. On the assumption that no other state will adopt so radical a departure from traditional tort principles, it may be concluded that under the majority's reasoning those defendants who are brought to trial in this state will bear effective joint responsibility for 100 percent of plaintiffs' injuries despite the fact that their "substantial" aggregate market share may be considerably less. This undeniable fact forces the majority to concede that, "a defendant may be held liable for a somewhat different percentage of the damage than its share of the appropriate market would justify." [Ante.] With due deference, I suggest that the complete unfairness of such a result in a case involving only five of two hundred manufacturers is readily manifest.

* * *

The majority attempts to justify its new liability on the ground that defendants herein are "better able to bear the cost of injury resulting from the manufacture of a defective product." [Ante.]

This "deep pocket" theory of liability, fastening liability on defendants presumably because they are rich, has understandable popular appeal and might be tolerable in a case disclosing substantially stronger evidence of causation than herein appears. But as a general proposition, a defendant's wealth is an unreliable indicator of fault, and should play no part, at least consciously, in the legal analysis of the problem. In the absence of proof that a particular defendant caused or at least probably caused plaintiff's injuries, a defendant's ability to bear the cost thereof is no more pertinent to the underlying issue of liability than its "substantial" share of the relevant market. A system priding itself on "*equal* justice under law" does not flower when the *liability* as well as the *damage* aspect of a tort action is determined by a defendant's wealth. The inevitable consequence of such a result is to create and perpetuate two rules of law—one applicable to wealthy defendants, and another standard pertaining to defendants who are poor or who have modest means. Moreover, considerable doubts have been expressed regarding the ability of the drug industry, and especially its smaller members, to bear the substantial economic costs (from both damage awards and high insurance premiums) inherent in imposing an industry-wide liability. [Citation.]

* * *

I also suggest that imposition of so sweeping a liability may well prove to be extremely shortsighted from the standpoint of broad social policy. Who is to say whether, and at what time and in what form, the drug industry upon which the majority now fastens this blanket liability, may develop a miracle drug critical to the diagnosis, treatment, or, indeed, cure of the very disease in question? It is counterproductive to inflict civil damages upon *all* manufacturers for the side effects and medical complications which surface in the children of the users a generation after ingestion of the drugs, particularly when, at the time of their use, the drugs met every fair test and medical standard then available and applicable. Such a result requires of the pharmaceutical industry a foresight, prescience and anticipation far beyond the most exacting standards of the relevant scientific disciplines. In effect, the majority requires the pharmaceutical research laboratory to install a piece of new equipment—the psychic's crystal ball.

I am not unmindful of the serious medical consequences of plaintiffs' injuries, and the equally serious implications to the class which she purports to represent. In balancing the various policy considerations, however, I also observe that the incidence of vaginal cancer among "DES daughters" has been variously estimated at one-tenth of 1 percent to four-tenths of 1 percent. (13 Suffolk L.Rev., supra, p. 999, fn. 92.) These facts raise some penetrating questions. Ninety-nine plus percent of "DES daughters" have never developed cancer. Must a drug manufacturer to escape this blanket liability wait for a generation of testing before it may disseminate drugs? If a drug has beneficial purposes for the majority of users but harmful side effects are later revealed for a small fraction of consumers, will the manufacturer be absolutely liable? If adverse medical consequences, wholly unknown to the most careful and meticulous of present scientists, surface in *two* or *three* generations, will similar liability be imposed? In my opinion, common sense and reality combine to warn that a "market share" theory goes too far. Legally, it expects too much.

* * *

Finally, I am disturbed by the broad and ominous ramifications of the majority's holding. The law review comment, which is the wellspring of the majority's new theory, conceding the widespread consequences of industry-wide liability, openly acknowledges that "The DES cases are only the tip of an iceberg." (Comment, DES and a Proposed Theory of Enterprise Liability (1978) 46 Fordham L.Rev. 963, 1007.) Although the pharmaceutical drug industry may be the first target of this new sanction, the majority's reasoning has equally threatening application to many other areas of business and commercial activities.

Given the grave and sweeping economic, social, and medical effects of "market share" liability, the policy decision to introduce and define it should rest not with us, but with the Legislature which is currently considering not only major statutory reform of California product liability law in general, but the DES problem in particular. (See Sen. Bill No. 1392 (1979–1980 Reg.Sess.), which would establish and appropriate funds for the education, identification, and screening of persons exposed to DES, and would prohibit health care and hospital service plans from excluding or limiting coverage to persons exposed to DES.) An alternative proposal for administrative compensation, described as "a limited version of no-fault products liability" has been suggested by one commentator. (Coggins, supra, 13 Suffolk L.Rev. at pp. 1019–1021.) Compensation under such a plan would be awarded by an administrative tribunal from funds collected "via a tax paid by all manufacturers." (P. 1020, fn. omitted.) In any event, the problem invites a legislative rather than an attempted judicial solution.

I would affirm the judgments of dismissal.

NOTES

1. Could a jury find defendants negligent on plaintiff's failure adequately to test theory? Can a manufacturer reasonably be expected to discover adverse health effects that do not manifest themselves in the person taking the drug and do not appear until a generation later?

2. Would the five defendants that remained in *Sindell* be collaterally estopped in a subsequent case on the issue of market share liability? Cf. Kaufman v. Eli Lilly and Co., 65 N.Y.2d 449, 482 N.E.2d 63, 492 N.Y.S.2d 584 (1985). What would be the effect if collateral estoppel were available?

3. The *Sindell* decision left many open questions about implementation of the market share approach, including how the relevant "market" should be defined:

> Suppose, for example, that plaintiff's mother purchased all her DES from one Illinois pharmacy, which filled its DES prescriptions exclusively from five manufacturers. Suppose also that the pharmacist cannot recall which brand of DES he used to fill the mother's prescription. Finally, assume that defendant X, one of the pharmacy's five providers, supplied thirty percent of DES marketed in Illinois, but only ten percent of the DES sold nationally. Defendant X's market share, therefore, will be either ten percent, twenty percent [assuming each defendant sold equal shares to the pharmacist], or thirty percent, depending upon whether the relevant market is defined on a national, local (pharmacy-level), or statewide basis.

Fischer, Products Liability—An Analysis of Market Share Liability, 34 Vand.L. Rev. 1623 (1981).

Some of the issues have been resolved in subsequent cases:

A. Ten percent of the national market is not a "substantial share" of the market. Murphy v. E.R. Squibb & Sons, Inc., 40 Cal.3d 672, 221 Cal.Rptr. 447, 710 P.2d 247 (1985). Why not?

B. Punitive damages are not recoverable in a market share liability case. Magallanes v. Superior Court, 167 Cal.App.3d 878, 213 Cal.Rptr. 547 (1985). Why not?

C. Defendants are only severally liable for their market share proportion of the plaintiff's damages; they are not jointly responsible for the share attributable to absent or insolvent manufacturers. Brown v. Superior Court, 44 Cal.3d 1049, 245 Cal.Rptr. 412, 751 P.2d 470 (1988). Why not?

4. *Sindell* has received a mixed reaction in the courts, a number of which have refused to adopt the doctrine. See, e.g., Mulcahy v. Eli Lilly & Co., 386 N.W.2d 67 (Iowa 1986); Senn v. Merrell–Dow Pharmaceuticals, Inc., 305 Or. 256, 751 P.2d 215 (1988); Tidler v. Eli Lilly & Co., 851 F.2d 418 (D.C.Cir.1988). However, a number of decisions reject certain aspects of the *Sindell* market share approach but provide plaintiffs with somewhat similar "solutions" to the defendant identification problems in DES cases. See, e.g., Abel v. Eli Lilly & Co., 418 Mich. 311, 343 N.W.2d 164, cert. denied, 469 U.S. 833, 105 S.Ct. 123, 83 L.Ed.2d 65 (1984) (concerted action, or modified alternative liability); Martin v. Abbott Laboratories, 102 Wash.2d 581, 689 P.2d 368 (1984) (modified market share); Collins v. Eli Lilly Co., 116 Wis.2d 166, 342 N.W.2d 37, cert. denied, 469 U.S. 826, 105 S.Ct. 107, 83 L.Ed.2d 51 (1984) (risk contribution); Smith v. Eli Lilly & Co., 173 Ill.App.3d 1, 122 Ill.Dec. 835, 527 N.E.2d 333 (1988) (modified alternative liability); Cf. Bichler v. Eli Lilly & Co., 55 N.Y.2d 571, 450 N.Y.S.2d 776, 436 N.E.2d 182 (1982) (concerted action; conscious parallelism).

5. Should a plaintiff seeking to utilize a market share (or similar) theory in a DES case be required to make a genuine effort first to identify the manufacturer that supplied her mother's DES? Compare Abel v. Eli Lilly & Co., 418 Mich. 311, 343 N.W.2d 164 (yes), cert. denied, 469 U.S. 833, 105 S.Ct. 123, 83 L.Ed.2d 65 (1984), with McCormack v. Abbott Laboratories, 617 F.Supp. 1521 (D.Mass.1985) (no).

If the plaintiff does have some (but not conclusive) identification evidence, should she be entitled to have both the individual and the market share claims submitted to the jury?

6. If a plaintiff establishes that a particular defendant's relevant market share was 51% (or higher), should she be entitled to recover 100% of her damages from that defendant?

7. Could a DES victim avoid the identification problem by suing the drugstore that filled the DES prescription? See Murphy v. E.R. Squibb & Sons, supra p. 740.

8. There are now cases brought by DES sons. See, e.g., Doe v. Eli Lilly & Co., 13 Prod.Saf. & Liab.Rep. (BNA) 604–05 (D.D.C. June 28, 1985) (verdict for plaintiff). And DES grandchildren. See, e.g., Loerch v. Abbott Labs., infra p. 1003 (verdict for defendant).

9. On the DES litigation, and market share liability, see generally R. Apfel & S. Fisher, To Do No Harm: DES and the Dilemmas of Modern Medicine (1984) (discussion by psychiatrists of DES development and effects on medical profession and DES patients); Johnson & Dowie, Revenge of a DES Son, Mother Jones 30 (Feb./March 1983) (chronicling story of lawyer for DES

manufacturers who discovered that he had testicular cancer that may have been caused by his mother's ingestion of DES during pregnancy).

On the legal issues, see Weinstein, Preliminary Reflections on the Law's Reaction to Disasters, 11 Colum.J.Envtl.L. 1 (1986); Epstein, Two Fallacies in the Law of Joint Torts, 73 Geo.L.J. 1377, 1378–82 (1985); Miller & Hancock, Perspectives on Market Share Liability: Time for a Reassessment?, 88 W.Va.L. Rev. 81 (1985); Schwartz & Mahshigian, Failure to Identify the Defendant in Tort Law: Towards a Legislative Solution, 73 Calif.L.Rev. 941 (1985); Fischer, Products Liability—An Analysis of Market Share Liability, 34 Vand.L.Rev. 1623 (1981); Notes, 40 Miami L.Rev. 857 (1986); 94 Harv.L.Rev. 668 (1981); 76 Nw.U.L.Rev. 300 (1981); 33 Stan.L.Rev. 937 (1981).

10. **Beyond DES.** Should the market share concept be extended beyond DES to other toxic substances? To durable products?

In Celotex Corp. v. Copeland, 471 So.2d 533 (Fla.1985), rev'g 447 So.2d 908 (Fla.App.1984), the Florida Supreme Court held that the plaintiff, who during his 33 year career as a boilermaker was exposed to various asbestos products, could not rely on a market share theory. First, plaintiff was able to identify some of the specific products (and their manufacturers) to which he had been exposed. Second, since all DES is chemically identical, the risk it presents is uniform. By contrast, asbestos products have a wide divergence of toxicity depending on several factors, including friability (the extent to which the fibers are released from the product into the air), the specific type (among six) of asbestos fiber used in the product, and the amount of asbestos used in the product. Most courts have agreed. See, e.g., Case v. Fibreboard Corp., 743 P.2d 1062 (Okl.1987) (citing cases). But see Hardy v. Johns–Manville Sales Corp., 509 F.Supp. 1353 (E.D.Tex.1981), rev'd on other grounds, 681 F.2d 334 (5th Cir. 1982).

In Nicolet, Inc. v. Nutt, 525 A.2d 146 (Del.1987), the court approved plaintiffs' attempt to use a conspiracy theory against asbestos manufacturers whom they could not prove provided the asbestos product to which they had been exposed. To prevail, the court ruled that plaintiffs would have to establish participation in a conspiracy that intentionally misrepresented the hazards of asbestos products, and that the acts of the co-conspirators in furtherance of the conspiracy were a cause of plaintiffs' injuries.

11. Professor Glen Robinson has advocated expanding the market share approach into a causal apportionment scheme in which each defendant would pay the proportion of the plaintiff's damages represented by that defendant's contribution to the *risk* of harm. Robinson, Multiple Causation in Tort Law: Reflections on the DES Cases, 68 Va.L.Rev. 713 (1982). See Collins v. Eli Lilly Co., 116 Wis.2d 166, 342 N.W.2d 37, cert. denied, 469 U.S. 826, 105 S.Ct. 107, 83 L.Ed.2d 51 (1984) (applying Professor Robinson's theory to DES).

What are the implications of Robinson's scheme for asbestos victims? Other toxic substance victims? Compare Shackil v. Lederle Laboratories, 219 N.J.Super. 601, 530 A.2d 1287 (1987), where defendants argued that a market share approach should not be applied to DPT vaccine because of biochemical differences in the vaccines of different manufacturers that altered the likelihood that the vaccine would be harmful. *Held,* a modified market share approach would be applied, based on the defendants' contribution to the risk. But see Senn v. Merrell–Dow Pharmaceuticals, Inc., 850 F.2d 611 (9th Cir.1988) (alternative liability theory inapplicable to DPT claim). See generally Note, 10 J.Corp.L. 743 (1985) (criticizing risk-contribution approach).

12. On the application of market share principles to the asbestos industry, see Comments, 37 Mercer L.Rev. 1115 (1986); 14 Stetson L.Rev. 239 (1984).

D. APPORTIONING CAUSATION

MARTIN v. OWENS–CORNING FIBERGLAS CORPORATION

Supreme Court of Pennsylvania, 1987.
515 Pa. 377, 528 A.2d 947.*

LARSEN, JUSTICE.

The issue before the Court in this products liability case is whether the trial court committed reversible error in instructing the jury that it could apportion damages between defendant-appellees and plaintiff-appellant.

Appellant, Joseph Edward Martin, [sued] appellees seeking compensatory and punitive damages for asbestosis and related diseases which he claimed were caused as a result of working with products containing asbestos manufactured by appellees.[1]

Appellant presented expert witnesses at trial who testified that his disability was due to both asbestosis, caused by asbestos exposure, and emphysema, caused by appellant's long-term cigarette smoking and aggravated by asbestos exposure and the resulting asbestosis. Appellees presented expert testimony that appellant's disability was solely the result of emphysema, caused by cigarette smoking. The trial court instructed the jury on apportionment as follows:

> * * * If, however, you find that his condition is due both to his cigarette smoking and his exposure to asbestos, then you first determine what the total amount of damages are, and then the next thing you do is to determine what percentage of his condition is due to cigarette smoking, and then you will reduce the total amount by the percentage that you find is due to cigarette smoking.

The jury thereafter returned a verdict of $67,000 in favor of appellant, although appellant presented testimony that his loss of earnings was greatly in excess of that amount.[3]

The trial court denied appellant's motions for a new trial. [There were various appeals, and the Supreme Court remanded to the Superior Court which] found that the causes of harm were "distinct and capable of rough approximation," and affirmed the trial court's denial of

* References to record omitted.—Eds.

1. Joseph Edward Martin died on August 1, 1982 while post-trial motions were pending.

3. Appellant asserts he established loss of earnings of at least $177,000. Superior Court estimated the amount at $118,000. In any event, the verdict was far below the loss of earnings established by appellant at trial.

appellant's motion for a new trial. Martin v. Johns–Manville Corp., 349 Pa.Super. 46, 59, 502 A.2d 1264, 1271 (1985).

We granted appellant's petition for allowance on July 1, 1986. We now hold that there was no evidence presented at trial upon which the trial court could properly submit the issue of apportionment to the jury. Thus, we reverse Superior Court's affirmance of the trial court's denial of a new trial.

* * *

The rules in this Commonwealth governing apportionment of damages are consistent with those expressed in the Restatement (Second) of Torts:

> § 433 A. Apportionment of Harm to Causes
>
> (1) Damages for harm are to be apportioned among two or more causes where
>
> (a) there are distinct harms, or
>
> (b) there is a reasonable basis for determining the contribution of each cause to a single harm.
>
> (2) Damages for any other harm cannot be apportioned among two or more causes.

[Citations.] "The rules stated apply also where one of the causes in question is the conduct of the plaintiff himself, whether it be negligent or innocent." Restatement (Second) of Torts § 433A, comment (a). The trial court must determine, as a matter of law, whether the harm is capable of apportionment, [citations], and the burden of proving apportionment rests on the party seeking it. Restatement (Second) of Torts § 433B(2).

In this case, § 433A(1)(b) is applicable since the single harm to appellant was his disability due to the decreased function of his lungs. Thus, it was incumbent upon the trial court to determine that there was a reasonable basis for apportioning the harm between the two causes before submitting that issue to the jury. In this regard, the trial court concluded "[t]here was adequate evidence which would support a jury's determination that the acts of [appellant] and the acts of the [appellees] caused separate and identifiable damages." (Trial Court Opinion at p. 39.) We disagree.

Testimony at trial established that appellant worked at various jobs between the years 1939 and 1978, when he became disabled, applying and removing asbestos insulation products to and from pipes and boilers. Also, appellant began smoking cigarettes in 1941, and eventually increased his smoking to two packs a day by 1960. Appellant maintained that level of smoking through 1978.

Five expert witnesses analyzed x-rays and described in some detail the evidence of both emphysema and asbestosis present in appellant's lungs. Results of physical examinations given appellant were also discussed at some length. Of the five expert witnesses presented at trial, three were asked if they had opinions concerning the cause of appellant's disability. Dr. Sachs and Dr. Laman, called on behalf of appellant, each expressed the opinion that asbestos exposure and cigarette smoking were both significant causes of his disability. Dr. Shively, called on behalf of appellees, testified that, in his opinion, appellant's asbestosis was not very advanced and played no role in appellant's disability, which he attributed solely to emphysema caused by cigarette smoking. The jury resolved this dispute in expert testimony in favor of appellant, as evidenced by the verdict, since the trial court properly instructed the jury not to award damages if cigarette smoking was the sole cause of appellant's disability.

Additionally, Dr. Sachs was asked to separate out the relative contributions of each of the diseases to appellant's disability. Dr. Sachs responded:

> I can't separate these two diseases for you in terms of percentage. My opinion is that both play a significant role in this man's disability, but I have no way of equating them or breaking them down. I can't tell you that asbestos contributed 48% and emphysema 52%, I don't know how to do that. There is no way I know of to separate these two diseases which are so closely intertwined.
>
> I believe that both of them exist to a significant degree and they are both significant factors in this man's disability. That is the best I can do with that.

Dr. Laman testified:

> It is not possible for me to separate out the relative contribution of cigarette smoking and asbestos from the cause of his obstructive pulmonary disease and the cause of his total and permanent disability. Both factors are important in producing the effect and the pulmonary disability that he has.

Dr. Laman further testified:

> It is not possible to separate out what fraction of his lung disease is due to cigarette smoking, what factor, what fraction is due to asbestosis.

Finally, Dr. Laman stated:

> * * * Both cigarette smoking and asbestos exposure and asbestosis result in obstructive defects on ventilatory testing. Since both * * * lead to obstructive defect, it becomes difficult to impossible to accurately ascribe a fraction of the defect due to one thing or the other.

The jury, although presented with a great deal of testimony concerning appellant's history and physical condition, was provided no guidance in determining the relative contributions of asbestos exposure and cigarette smoking to appellant's disability. In fact, two experts testified that such a determination was not possible. * * * [T]he jury cannot be expected to draw conclusions which medical experts, relying on the same evidence, could not draw. The causes of disability in this case do not lend themselves to separation by lay-persons on any reasonable basis. Thus, common sense and common experience possessed by a jury do not serve as substitutes for expert guidance, and it follows that any apportionment by the jury in this case was a result of speculation and conjecture and hence, improper. "Rough approximation" is no substitute for justice.[6]

The trial court erred by presenting the issue of apportionment to the jury.

[Reversed and remanded for retrial on damages.]

McDermott, Justice, concurring.

The Majority Opinion stands for a single proposition, i.e., under the facts and circumstances of this case there was not enough evidence to submit the issue of apportionment to the jury. With this I can agree.

However, this case should not be construed as standing for the proposition that evidence of contributory negligence is inadmissible in an asbestosis case. Furthermore, it should not be interpreted as precluding the defendants in this case from introducing new evidence of decedent's negligence, nor precluding a jury from returning a lesser verdict if the evidence would support such.

Nix, Chief Justice, dissenting.

In this case the medical testimony was thorough, and it is clear that there is no basis for precisely determining the contribution of each of the two causes present under these facts. Thus a remand for a new trial limited to the issue of damages will serve no purpose. * * *

* * * The majority criticizes the Superior Court for accepting what they characterized as a "rough approximation" of the employer's responsibility. On this record only a "rough approximation" can be made. If we accept that a verdict may be returned in favor of claimant where his own actions were also a substantial cause in bringing about the harm he sustained, then we must accept the "rough approximations" that juries must render. * * *

Zappala, J., joins in this dissenting opinion.

Hutchinson, Justice, dissenting.

I dissent. I believe that the majority has overstepped its bounds and usurped the jury's factfinding function by vacating its verdict on damages. It does so by a selective and, I believe, misleading statement of the facts. The following [testimony, taken from the Superior Court

6. As stated by Dean Prosser and Dean Keeton:

> Certain results, by their very nature, are obviously incapable of any reasonable or practical division * * * no ingenuity can suggest anything more than a purely arbitrary apportionment of such harm. Where two or more causes combine to produce such a single result, incapable of any reasonable division, each may be a substantial factor in bringing about the loss, and if so, each is charged with all of it.

Prosser and Keeton on Torts § 52 at p. 347 (5th Ed.1984).

opinion, must be read together with the testimony set out in this court's lead opinion.]

"Testimony of appellant's witnesses established that asbestosis is primarily a restrictive lung disease, and that emphysema and chronic bronchitis, primarily caused by cigarette smoking, are obstructive lung diseases. * * *

"Dr. Wiot, whom appellant had retained to examine his chest x-rays, but who had not otherwise examined appellant, described his findings at trial with the use of the x-rays. He observed 'emphysematous changes' and 'bullous changes' in the upper portion of the lungs. He explained that bullous changes represent a breakdown in pulmonary tissue and are indicative of emphysema. Dr. Wiot also stated that the x-rays showed 'long-standing obstructive lung disease.' Dr. Laman testified that it is not uncommon for cigarette smokers to develop bullae. Dr. Wiot and Dr. Sachs agreed that appellant has emphysema.

* * *

"Testifying for appellees, Dr. Shively stated that appellant's chest x-rays showed one pleural plaque consistent with asbestos and that pulmonary function studies that he had conducted of appellant revealed a restrictive lung problem. Dr. Gardner testified that in his review of appellant's x-ray he also found pleural plaques but that they were of 'the most minimal positive category. I definitely did identify them but in very, very low quantity, very mild, very minimal.' He further stated that while the plaques were consistent with asbestosis, he would expect to find more of them before making a diagnosis of asbestosis. He thus concluded that the x-rays 'are not absolutely diagnostic of asbestosis.' Both Dr. Shively and Dr. Gardner agreed that the x-rays showed chronic obstructive lung disease, caused, Dr. Shively stated, by smoking.

"As to the causes of appellant's disability, his witnesses agreed that both asbestosis and cigarette smoking where significant factors. * * * It was Dr. Shively's view that while 'there were radiographic findings consistent with asbestosis * * * [t]here was no evidence * * * that the asbestos exposure * * * contributed at all to [appellant's] impairment.' He gave the opinion that appellant's disability was caused by chronic obstructive lung disease with pulmonary emphysema and chronic bronchitis, which in turn were caused by cigarette smoking." 349 Pa.Superior Ct. 46, 51–55, 502 A.2d 1264, 1267–69 (1985).

Since the jury found appellee partially liable the majority assumes that it rejected all of Dr. Shively's testimony. This is not necessarily the case. A jury may choose to believe all, some or none of a witness's testimony. [Citation.] Here, the jury could have credited Dr. Shively's testimony that appellant suffered substantial disability from cigarette smoking but still have believed appellant's experts' testimony that asbestos exposure also played a significant part.

I am at a loss to imagine what additional testimony would satisfy the majority. Requiring the experts to speak in terms of numerical percentages [1] introduces a false precision into the evidence. Mathematical exactitude is not found in the real world of medicine. We should not mislead lay jurors by requiring experts to falsely imply its existence. Honest, but more flexible, words such as "substantial factor," "major contribution" or "significant cause" are more suitable to the proper jury function of justly and fairly resolving uncertainties. It is unfair and unjust to place on appellee the whole burden of supporting appellant for a disability his own experts admit he himself substantially caused. The rule "drafted" for Section 433A of the Restatement does not reduce that injustice and the "law" written by its draftsmen, who were never elected to the legislature, finds its only authority in reason and need not be followed to an unjust result.

Indeed, properly read and applied to this case, the reason behind section 433A of the Restatement is not violated here or inconsistent with the jury verdict. The evidence favoring apportionment of damages provides a "reasonable basis" for that verdict, which simply took into account the "substantial" adverse impact appellant's own conduct had on his condition. Determining facts from conflicting and confusing evidence like that presented here is the jury's function. * * *

NOTES

1. Do you agree with the defendants' strategy of attempting to place all of the blame for decedent's disability on his cigarette smoking? How might the parties react to the Supreme Court decision in preparing their case for the retrial?

2. Medical studies demonstrate the synergistic effect of smoking and asbestos exposure in causing lung cancer. One important study found that the relative risk (ratio of occurrence of disease in exposed group to occurrence in general population) of lung cancer for nonsmoking insulation industry workers exposed to asbestos was 5.17; for smokers not exposed to asbestos—10.85; but for exposed smokers—and for exposed heavy smokers—87.36. See Surgeon General of the United States, The Health Consequences of Smoking: Cancer and Chronic Lung Disease in the Workplace 213–20 (1986); United States Dep't of Labor, Disability Compensation for Asbestos–Associated Disease in the United States 335 (1981).

3. **Comparative Fault.** In comparative fault jurisdictions, juries may be required to apportion damages if they find that plaintiff's smoking constituted contributory fault. In Brisboy v. Fibreboard Corp., 429 Mich. 540, 418 N.W.2d 650 (1988), the court upheld a jury's finding that decedent's smoking was contributorily negligent and that the smoking contributed 55 percent to his lung cancer. Addressing the quality of evidence on the apportionment question, the court stated: "We reject plaintiff's claim that there is no rational basis for the jury's apportionment of fault and note that juries are frequently called

1. Appellant does not argue that experts must testify in mathematical terms about the contribution of each disease to the total disability. Such testimony is not required under our well established precedent, Osterling v. Frick, 284 Pa. 397, 131 A. 250 (1925), or by the Restatement (Second) of Torts.

upon to make such judgments." 418 N.W.2d at 655. See also Hao v. Owens–Illinois, Inc., ___ Hawaii ___, 738 P.2d 416 (1987) (applying pure comparative fault to apportion plaintiff's negligence in smoking and defendant's responsibility for providing asbestos products).

4. Who should have the burden of proof on apportionment? Should it matter whether the jury finds the plaintiff's conduct negligent? Section 433B of Rest.(2d) Torts, "Burden of Proof," provides:

> (1) Except as stated in Subsections (2) and (3), the burden of proof that the tortious conduct of the defendant has caused the harm to the plaintiff is upon the plaintiff.
>
> (2) Where the tortious conduct of two or more actors has combined to bring about harm to the plaintiff, and one or more of the actors seeks to limit his liability on the ground that the harm is capable of apportionment among them, the burden of proof as to the apportionment is upon each such actor.
>
> (3) Where the conduct of two or more actors is tortious, and it is proved that harm has been caused to the plaintiff by only one of them, but there is uncertainty as to which one has caused it, the burden is upon each such actor to prove that he has not caused the harm.

5. In a typical asbestos case, an asbestos worker sues more than a dozen manufacturers of various asbestos products to which he was exposed for periods ranging from days to decades. Should damages in such cases be apportioned among the defendants? How? See Moore v. Johns–Manville Sales Corp., 781 F.2d 1061 (5th Cir.1986) (comparative causation to be apportioned by the jury). Compare *Borel*, supra p. 855, where the court held that the manufacturers would be jointly and severally liable.

What if an asbestos worker's exposure to a particular defendant's product was limited to a few weeks (or less) over a life-long career of exposure to asbestos? See Lohrmann v. Pittsburgh Corning Corp., 782 F.2d 1156, 1162–63 (4th Cir.1986) (adopting a de minimis rule).

6. See Rizzo & Arnold, Causal Apportionment in the Law of Torts: An Economic Theory, 80 Colum.L.Rev. 1399 (1980); Landes & Posner, Joint and Multiple Tortfeasors: An Economic Analysis, 9 J.Legal Stud. 517 (1980); Wright, Allocating Liability Among Multiple Responsible Causes: A Principled Defense of Joint and Several Liability for Actual Harm and Risk Exposure, 21 U.C.D.L.Rev. 1141, 1194–1211 (1988). Rizzo and Arnold's proposal and methodology are criticized in Kaye & Aickin, A Comment on Causal Apportionment, 13 J.Legal Stud. 191 (1984), and in Kelman, The Necessary Myth of Objective Causation Judgments in Liberal Political Theory, 63 Chi–Kent L.Rev. 579, 611–17 (1987). On smoking and apportionment of harm, see Note, 21 Ind.L.Rev. 523 (1988).

SECTION 3. STATUTES OF LIMITATIONS, RES JUDICATA, AND DAMAGES

JACKSON v. JOHNS–MANVILLE SALES CORPORATION [JACKSON I]

United States Court of Appeals, Fifth Circuit, 1984.
727 F.2d 506.*

Before CLARK, CHIEF JUDGE, GARZA and JOLLY, CIRCUIT JUDGES.

CLARK, CHIEF JUDGE:

Johns–Manville Sales Corporation (Johns–Manville) and Raybestos–Manhattan, Inc. appeal a jury verdict awarding actual and punitive damages to James Jackson, a former shipyard worker, in a strict liability action for injuries allegedly caused by the defendants' failures to warn of the hazards of exposure to their asbestos products. Finding that the trial court ruled correctly on Jackson's entitlement to a strict liability cause of action but erred in admitting evidence of the mere possibility of Jackson's developing cancer and in allowing punitive damages in this strict liability action, we affirm in part, reverse in part, and remand for a new trial.

I. FACTS AND PROCEDURAL BACKGROUND

James Jackson began working at Ingalls Shipbuilding Corporation (Ingalls) in Pascagoula, Mississippi, in 1953, when he was about twenty-seven years old. He worked there until 1971, first as a sheet-metal mechanic and after 1957 as a work leaderman or supervisor. Jackson testified that he was exposed to asbestos dust every day for the full time of his employment in Ingalls.

As a mechanic, he installed sheet metal over ducts, shelves, pipes, boilers, and other such surfaces within ships under construction. Often these surfaces previously had been covered with asbestos insulation. To attach sheet metal, Jackson had to drill holes in the asbestos insulation. He testified that he also cut and dovetailed gaskets from asbestos material. Occasionally, he would cut asbestos cloth, three or four feet wide, with his pocket knife or shears in order to wrap and protect equipment around which he was working. He alleged that all these activities generated asbestos dust in the air.

Jackson testified that he worked alongside other craftsmen who made more direct and extensive use of asbestos products. He testified, for instance, that in lagging boilers, he worked alongside insulators who would first saw and tear blocks of asbestos, then rivet the asbestos to the boilers, all of which made the air "very dusty." He testified that when he worked in engine rooms, asbestos dust would fall upon him as

* Subsequent history noted infra.—Eds.

insulator workmen above him on catwalks or temporary scaffolds cut and installed asbestos. Jackson testified that other workers generated asbestos dust in his work area when they dumped sacks of asbestos powder into mortar boxes and mixed the powder with water to create cement, or "mud." Workers also raised dust around him as they cut asbestos cloth to wrap pipes and other surfaces, and as they sawed prefabricated wall boards containing asbestos.

* * *

Jackson testified that asbestos dust in his work environment at Ingalls "was very thick. It would even go down your collar, it would get in your ears, and get in your hair and be white all over your clothes * * *. It would look like snow sometimes * * *. Sometimes it would be so thick you couldn't see twenty or thirty feet."

In 1978, Jackson first consulted his family physician about breathing problems. He was diagnosed as having asbestosis. His treating physician, Dr. McAtee, estimated Jackson's pulmonary disability to be about 15 per cent at the time of the initial diagnosis but did not recommend that he discontinue working. Evidence introduced at trial indicated that Jackson's physiological impairment has not progressed significantly since the time of the original diagnosis.

Jackson alleges that his asbestos-related disability has sapped his energy and stamina, made him susceptible to increased risks of infections and malignancies, impaired his ability to work, caused him mental frustration, necessitated the worry and expense of ongoing medical checkups, and reduced his life expectancy.

* * *

* * * Research projects dating from 1920's, financed in part by Johns–Manville, indicated that exposure to excessive concentrations of asbestos dust over prolonged periods of time could produce asbestosis in asbestos workers. A 1947 report of the American Conference of Governmental Industrial Hygienists recommended, in light of the hazards posed, threshold limit values for exposure to asbestos of five million parts per cubic foot of air.

In 1944, the first extensive study of the effects of asbestos on shipyard workers concluded that, because the researchers found few cases of asbestosis among the Navy shipyard workers studied, "asbestos covering of naval vessels is a relatively safe operation." This report indicated, however, that most of its research subjects had been exposed to asbestos for fewer than ten years and cautioned that longer exposure would have resulted in a considerably greater incidence of asbestosis.

A 1965 study by I.J. Selikoff concluded that the 1944 study was misleading. Finding evidence of asbestosis in about half of the insulation workers examined, and in over 90% of the workers with over forty years experience, the Selikoff report indicated that asbestosis and related complications were "significant hazards among insulation workers" and indicated that previous threshold limit values were set too high. Other reports have confirmed these findings. [Citations.]

In response to a preliminary report of Dr. Selikoff's study, Johns–Manville in 1964 began placing warning labels on packages of its asbestos products.[6] Raybestos–Manhattan first attached warning labels to its asbestos cloth in 1972.

Jackson testified that in the nineteen years he worked at Ingalls Shipyard, he was never warned that asbestos could be harmful to his health. He also testified that he could recall having seen no asbestos packaging and hence no warning labels. He alleges that the defendants knew in the 1930's of the hazards of exposure to asbestos, yet worked in concert to keep this information secret, actively avoiding research that might confirm the relationship of asbestos to cancer.

On November 21, 1978, Jackson, along with other parties, filed a class action in diversity against numerous manufacturers and sellers of asbestos products allegedly used in shipbuilding at Ingalls. After the district court denied class certification, Jackson filed an amended and supplemental complaint against twelve defendants. Eight of these defendants settled before trial. One was granted summary judgment. The remaining defendants were: Johns–Manville Sales Corp.; H.K. Porter Company, Inc.; and Raybestos–Manhattan, Inc.

Jackson originally based his cause of action on theories of negligence, breach of warranty, strict liability, and conspiracy to suppress facts about the risks of exposure to asbestos. In accordance with a pretrial order, Jackson abandoned all causes of action except for strict liability in tort.

The jury found that Johns–Manville and Raybestos–Manhattan were strictly liable to Jackson and assessed actual damages of $391,500. The jury also assessed punitive damages of $500,000 against Johns–Manville and of $125,000 against Raybestos–Manhattan. The jury found that H.K. Porter Co. was not liable. Jackson does not appeal the verdict in H.K. Porter Co.'s favor.

* * *

III. ONE CAUSE OF ACTION OR TWO

During the course of the trial, Jackson called several expert witnesses who testified at length about the role that exposure to asbestos fibers plays in the etiology of lung cancer, mesothelioma, and other malignancies. Three of these expert witnesses testified that, based upon statistical risks adduced from epidemiological studies and upon examinations of portions of Jackson's medical record, they believed that Jackson had a greater than fifty percent chance of contracting an asbestos-related cancer in the future.

6. In 1964, the Johns–Manville warning label read:

> Caution, this product contains asbestos fibers. Inhalation of asbestos in excessive quantities over long periods of time may be harmful. If dust is created when this product is handled, avoid breathing the dust. If adequate ventilation control is not possible, wear respirators approved by the United States Bureau of Mines for pneumoconiosis-producing dusts.

The defendants argue that this evidence about the relationship between asbestos exposure and cancer was irrelevant, because the proof showed that Jackson had only a mild case of asbestosis, resulting in a fifteen percent disability. They argue that the trial court committed reversible error in failing to exclude the testimony concerning the potential for later development of cancer, which alarmed the jury and unfairly prejudiced the defendants.

We hold as a matter of substantive law that the present state of the record limits Jackson's right to recover damages to any disability resulting from asbestosis. Therefore, the court erred in not excluding the evidence about cancer since Jackson did not prove that he presently suffers from that disease.

In arguing that the cancer evidence was properly admissible, Jackson relies on the general rule of tort law that allows for recovery of all harms—past, present, and prospective—legally caused by a tort. "[W]here it is established that future consequences from an injury to a person will ensue, recovery may be had, but such future consequences must be established in terms of reasonable probabilities." Entex, Inc. v. Rasberry, 355 So.2d 1102, 1104 (Miss.1978). [Citations.] This is the traditional "all or nothing" approach, whereby the plaintiff becomes entitled to full compensation for those prospective damages that are proved to be "probable" (a greater than 50 percent chance), but is not entitled to any compensation if the proof does not establish a greater than 50 percent chance. Jackson argues that the expert testimony was relevant in establishing the requisite probability of future harm from cancer.[17]

It is evident, however, that the all-or-nothing rule is predicated on an assumption that a cause of action has accrued with respect to the prospective harm for which recovery is sought.[18] The real question is whether, when Jackson's cause of action accrued for asbestosis injuries, a cause of action accrued simultaneously for cancer injuries, even though Jackson had not developed cancer at the time of trial.

The proof discloses that asbestosis and cancer are distinct diseases. Asbestosis is a fibrosis or scarring of the lungs resulting from inhalation of asbestos fibers. It is not a cancerous process. It is not always fatal, but can cause progressive deterioration of the pulmonary function and lung volume. There is a direct relation between cumulative exposure levels to asbestos and development of the disease. Cigarette smoking is not a contributing factor. Generally, asbestosis has a latency period of ten to twenty-five or more years, from time of initial exposure until manifestation of the disease.

17. We dismiss out of hand the defendants' incredible argument that statistics do not prove probability.

18. Comment a, Section 910 of the Restatement (Second) of Torts, states: "[a]ssuming * * * that a cause of action has arisen at the time when the action is brought * * *, the injured person is entitled to recover damages" for prospective harms.

Mesothelioma is a rare form of malignancy which occurs in the thin membrane, or epithelium, that lines the surfaces of the lungs and of the abdominal cavity. Jackson's expert testified that as little as a week's exposure to asbestos could trigger the disease. The best available evidence does not indicate that cigarette smoking contributes to the development of the disease. The latency period may be from twenty to forty years or more. The disease is invariably fatal.

The development of asbestos-related lung cancer (pulmonary and bronchogenic carcinoma) occurs mainly in the lower lobes of the lungs and is correlated with the degree of exposure to asbestos fibers. Cigarette smoking greatly enhances the risks. The latency period is fifteen to thirty-five years.

* * *

Jackson does not claim that he has cancer. He has produced no evidence that asbestosis will inevitably lead to cancer. The proof adduced does not demonstrate any relation between the pathologies of asbestosis and cancer, except that the diseases can be precipitated by the same pathogen or carcinogen. Viewed from this perspective, Jackson's claim for asbestosis injuries adds nothing to his claim for cancer damages. Had he attempted to recover for cancer damages before he had manifested any disease at all, his evidentiary burden of establishing his entitlement to compensation for future cancer would be no different from that in the present posture of this case. It would not be carried by proof that he was exposed to asbestos fibers and that, statistically, he was at over 50% risk of contracting cancer.

Causality as an operation of physical events which may culminate in future harm must be distinguished from causality as an operation of law which may culminate in a claim for future harm. In the context of a latent disease case, causality poses a novel question whether the accrual of a claim based on the manifestation of one disease results in the simultaneous accrual of claims based on "probable" future manifestations of physically separate diseases. The ultimate question is how abstractly to characterize the wrong that underlies the cause of action.

We find no precedent that squarely addresses the issue before us. However, courts addressing the limitation of action issue in latent disease cases frequently have addressed many of the relevant considerations. They can inform our decision.

A few courts have adopted a limitations rule that measures the accrual of a cause of action from the time the offending substance invades the body. These courts employ the rule that would obtain in a traditional trauma case, reasoning that the injury is the initial harmful contact and not the maturation of disease. [Citation.]

A majority of courts, however, have adopted a rule of discovery, under which "the cause of action does not accrue, until the injury is discovered or in the exercise of reasonable diligence should have been discovered." Borel, 493 F.2d at 1102 (construing Texas law). See Special Project, 36 Vand.L.Rev. at 642–47.

In Urie v. Thompson, 337 U.S. 163, 69 S.Ct. 1018, 93 L.Ed. 1282 (1949), the Supreme Court applied the discovery rule in determining, for limitations purposes under the Federal Employers' Liability Act, the time of accrual of a railroad fireman's claim for damages resulting from his contraction of silicosis, many years after his initial exposure to silica dust. The Supreme Court noted that a "mechanical analysis" of the accrual of the plaintiff's cause of action, attempting to measure the disease from some specific moment of contact with silica dust, would afford the plaintiff only a

> delusive remedy. * * * It would mean that at some past moment in time, unknown and inherently unknowable even in retrospect, [the plaintiff] was charged with knowledge of the slow and tragic disintegration of his lungs; under this view [the plaintiff's] failure to diagnose within the applicable statute of limitations a disease whose symptoms had not yet obtruded on his consciousness would constitute waiver of his right to compensation at the ultimate day of discovery and disability.
>
> * * *
>
> It follows that no specific date of contact with the substance can be charged with being the date of injury, inasmuch as the injurious consequences of the exposure are the product of a period of time rather than a point of time; consequently the afflicted employee can be held to be "injured" only when the accumulated effects of the deleterious substance manifest themselves.

Id. 69 S.Ct. at 1025, quoting Associated Indemnity Corp. v. Industrial Accident Commission, 124 Cal.App. 378, 381, 12 P.2d 1075, 1076 (1932).

Although the Mississippi court has not specifically addressed the time of accrual of a strict liability cause of action in a latent disease case, it is clear that Mississippi would apply the discovery rule. * * *

The court's recognition of the plaintiff's need to have adequate time in which to vindicate his rights commands the view that the Mississippi court would follow the judicial trend in adopting the discovery rule for strict liability latent disease cases, rather than put upon the plaintiff the uneasy burden of instituting a claim for injuries unknown and unknowable as of the time of initial exposure to the potential pathogen. In this context, the "sustained" injury must be equated with the physical manifestation of disease. The corollary is that the actionable delict in strict liability for physical injury is the generation of disease in the plaintiff's body, and not the initial exposure of the plaintiff to potentially hazardous substances or some more abstract invasion of the plaintiff's legally protectible interests.

The question remains, however, whether, upon the manifestation of one disease, a cause of action accrues for all prospective diseases, so that the plaintiff has the right (and in a limitations context, the duty) to seek recovery for physically distinct and separate diseases that may or may not develop in the future. The courts that have considered this issue in the limitations context have said no.

In Wilson v. Johns-Manville Sales Corp., 684 F.2d 111 (D.C.Cir. 1982), the court determined that a diagnosis of "mild asbestosis" in 1973 did not start the limitations period running for the separate and distinct disease of mesothelioma, first manifested in 1978. The court noted that there was a tension between the underlying evidentiary and repose considerations. The court observed that although it would best serve the defendant's interests in repose to have all contingent claims accrue simultaneously, the evidentiary concerns of "the existence of the [prospective] disease, its proximate cause, and the resultant damage" are better served by allowing the evidence to develop over time. Id. at 119. The court then determined that the plaintiff's interest in receiving adequate compensation and the defendant's interest in paying no more than that were best served by recognizing discrete causes of action for discrete injuries. Id. Finally, the court held that considerations of judicial economy weighed in favor of recognizing separate causes of action, lest the plaintiff be compelled to rush to court upon the first manifestation of an injury not in itself worthy of litigation, rather than risk losing all claims for future serious injuries. Id. at 120. Accord, Pierce v. Johns-Manville Sales Corp., 296 Md. 656, 464 A.2d 1020 (1983).

* * *

The issue before us is not, of course, whether Jackson's claim has expired by the operation of the limitations period. The question is whether a cause of action has arisen for injuries other than asbestosis. As they relate to the analysis of the underlying theory of causation, however, the two issues involve identical values. Furthermore, the policy considerations that inform the divisibility of claims for purposes of measuring limitations periods and applying principles of res judicata are the same policy considerations that drive the determination of when separate causes of action arise.

As applied in limitations cases, the discovery rule operates under the assumption that the plaintiff sustains no actionable injury when the pathogen enters the body. "[T]he injurious consequences are the product of a period of time * * *." Urie v. Thompson, 69 S.Ct. at 1025. The completion of the incubation period and manifestation of the disease create the causation of actual injury and the accrual of the cause of action. When the plaintiff develops asbestosis, the causation condition is fulfilled for that injury. Causation is complete and the defendant is liable for all damages—past, present, and future—that the proof shows will probably develop as a consequence of the asbestosis injury. Until and unless the plaintiff develops cancer, however, the causation of cancer has not occurred. The plaintiff is denied recovery for prospective damages associated with cancer not because the evidence of future consequences is insufficiently reliable, but because, as a matter of substantive law, there can be no consequence until there is effect, and no effect without completed cause.

Plaintiff cannot create a cause of action for the physically separate and distinct disease of cancer from the cause of action for asbestosis injuries actually sustained by proof that if asbestos fibers have caused asbestosis, the same exposure probably will result in cancer at a later time. To permit this assumption of causation to control liability would cause massive dislocations in the rights of parties. The proof shows that asbestos fibers may cause asbestosis. It also shows that asbestos fibers may cause cancer. But it does not show that asbestosis may cause cancer. Logic and justice require that presently latent injuries must await their separate maturity as a cause of action. A doctrinaire application of the reasonable certainty rule would result in a mismatching of entitlement, liability, and compensation. "Persons who contract the first, but not the second, disease will receive a windfall and, in the aggregate, the defendant will overcompensate the injured class." [Citation.] This problem is especially acute where the proof of greater-than-50% probability derives from statistical data that would support prospective recovery universally for a class that, according to the same proof, would suffer much less than universal disability.

To permit "recovery" for harms not yet effected would contravene Mississippi's clear policy against treating manufacturers as insurers of their products. Whatever benefit lies in allowing some plaintiffs present compensation for speculative future injury must be balanced against the need for maintaining viable enterprises that can accomplish the risk distribution purpose of strict liability for those persons who are caused injury by a defendant's product. [Citation.]

The detriment to defendants of allowing claims for uneffected future harms is manifest. A plaintiff who suffered the injury of asbestos callouses on his hands, for instance, plausibly could institute an action, based on expert testimony of statistical probability, to recover not only for callouses but for future injuries that ran the gamut from asbestosis to mesothelioma to lung cancer. The defendants' interests in repose pale against the interests of equitable exposure to liability.

On the other hand, the plaintiff suffers little if any detriment by being required to await manifestation of a condition before having a claim for damages resulting from that class of conditions. The quality of the plaintiff's evidence of cancer injury is likely to improve with the passage of time. Indeed, the plaintiff has a better chance of securing fair compensation for his injuries when the injury has actually manifested itself and medical certainty can replace speculation.

Our holding that the causes of action must be divided for purposes of seeking recovery for future harm requires that they also be discrete for limitations purposes. It would disadvantage a plaintiff unfairly and disserve judicial economy to measure the limitations periods for future diseases from the time of manifestation of a separate and distinct disease.

* * *

Jackson also argues that cancer evidence is relevant to his claim for compensation for future medical examinations that will be required to determine if any cancer has appeared. Although the cancer evidence may be relevant to this [discrete] issue in establishing the types and costs of future medical examinations, such evidence must be weighed by the trial court in the light of our opinion here under Rule 403 of the Federal Rules of Evidence, which provides:

> Although relevant, evidence may be excluded if its probative value is substantially outweighed by the danger of unfair prejudice, confusion of the issues, or misleading the jury, or by considerations of undue delay, waste of time, or needless presentation of cumulative evidence.

There is substantial danger that the defendants would be unfairly prejudiced by proof that a dread disease is a probable result of plaintiff's exposure. The jury also may be confused about the limits of Jackson's present rights of action if the cancer evidence is put before them now. Jackson can readily establish the reasonable necessity and expense of future medical examinations by other means of proof, including, for any reasonable defendant, a stipulation. The weight of these values is for the trial court in the first instance. On the record before us now, we conclude that the trial court erred in not excluding the evidence of cancer since proof of the existence of the disease was not made.

If, at any time in the future, Jackson claims that he has contracted cancer and that asbestos fibers caused that disease, he has a new cause of action, with new damages. His right to commence that action arises at the time he knows or in the exercise of reasonable diligence should have discovered that he has contracted the disease. The statute of limitations commences to run from the same time.

We do not address the questions of res judicata or collateral estoppel that might arise later, because we cannot predict what findings the court and jury will make when this case is retried. We note generally that in a second suit on a different cause of action, "the parties are estopped from relitigating only those issues actually and necessarily decided in the first suit." Dore v. Kleppe, 522 F.2d 1369, 1374 (5th Cir.1975). [Citations.]

IV. MENTAL DISTRESS

The trial court denied the defendants' request that the jury be instructed that, as a matter of law, it could not consider Jackson's alleged mental anguish for his purported increased risk of cancer. The trial court instead charged the jury that Jackson was entitled to compensation for "[a]ll physical pain and mental anguish suffered by him to date and such as he is reasonably certain to suffer in the future as a direct result of his complained of condition." Our holding here makes a ruling on defendants' objection unnecessary.

Jackson argues that this instruction failed to authorize any recovery for fear or risk of cancer, because "there was, of course, at no point any claim that the 'complained of condition' of Mr. Jackson was cancer." Jackson made no objection to the trial court's refusal expressly to authorize recovery for fear of risk of cancer. Since our holding here bars the proof allowed in the first trial on the issue of damages for potential cancer, we leave to the trial court's initial exercise of discretion whether evidence of Jackson's fear of the risk of cancer should be admitted on retrial under Fed.R.Evid. 403 and whether such a claim is permitted by the pleadings. While all values are not identical, many of the same considerations discussed with regard to future medical examinations are relevant.

* * *

VI. PUNITIVE DAMAGES

Special problems attend awards of punitive damages in the myriad actions which have arisen from the catastrophic nationwide exposure of workers to asbestos. The scope of this mass litigation is without precedent and practically without dimension. A recent independent study for the U.S. Department of Labor estimates that "there are presently more than 21 million American workers * * * who, in the past forty years, were significantly exposed to asbestos." Selikoff, Report to the U.S. Department of Labor, Disability Compensation for Asbestos–Associated Disease in the United States 4 (1982), reported in Seltzer, Punitive Damages in Mass Tort Litigation: Addressing the Problems of Fairness, Efficiency and Control, 52 Fordham L.Rev. 37, 37 n. 1 (1983). The study projected over 200,000 deaths from asbestos-related cancers by the end of the century. Id. That number does not include deaths from asbestosis. Id.

It has been reported that over 20,000 personal injury lawsuits have been filed in connection with workers' asbestos injuries. Congress Grapples with Toxic Torts, Nat'l L.J., Jan. 31, 1983, at 30, col. 1, reported in Seltzer, 52 Fordham L.Rev. at 37 n. 1. Johns–Manville states on brief that currently over 14,000 cases are pending against it in the United States, seeking over fifty billion dollars in damages, far beyond its financial resources. It reports that over 9,300 of those suits seek punitive damages and that over three million dollars in punitive damages already have been awarded. See Seltzer, 52 Fordham L.Rev. 37, 39 n. 11 (itemizing punitive damages awarded in previous cases). Raybestos–Manhattan states that as of May 1, 1982, it was a defendant in 11,071 suits involving 14,007 plaintiffs. It reports it has been assessed punitive damages of $500,000, in addition to those assessed in the instant verdict. Of the hundreds of these cases pending in the federal courts in Mississippi, this is the first to come before us on appeal.

Even assuming that the scope of the problem were overstated by defendants or that many of the cases currently pending against the defendants eventually would be settled, the defendants still would face an open-ended and overwhelming liability. Independent studies establish that if currently latent injuries become manifest among those workers who have been exposed to asbestos at the rates projected, the results could be catastrophic. The defendants argue that repeated assessments of punitive damages in the actions already filed threaten to exhaust their resources, making them unable to satisfy future compensatory or punitive awards.[26]

The grave reality of the need to maintain viable enterprises to meet future compensation liabilities to already injured persons and those with latent diseases commands consideration of the whole picture rather than a myopic, mechanical analysis that would look to this cause of action alone and deny that there exist tens of thousands of others, and the potential for many times more.

Writing in Roginsky v. Richardson–Merrell, 378 F.2d 832, 839, 841 (2d Cir.1967), Judge Friendly observed that:

> The legal difficulties engendered by claims for punitive damages on the part of hundreds of plaintiffs are staggering * * *. We have the gravest difficulty in perceiving how claims for punitive damages in such a multiplicity of actions throughout the nation can be so administered as to avoid overkill * * *. [A] sufficiently egregious error as to one product can end the business life of a concern that has wrought much good in the past and might otherwise have continued to do so in the future, with many innocent stockholders suffering extinction of their investments for a single management sin.

Roginsky involved an anti-cholesterol drug, MER/29, which had been found to cause adverse effects, primarily cataracts, in some consumers. The drug was distributed for about two years before being withdrawn from the market in 1962. When *Roginsky* was decided in 1967, there were currently "several hundred" other cases pending against the manufacturer.

Judge Friendly noted that the MER/29 actions bore little resemblance to those types of actions for which punitive damages had historically been awarded, where victims were few in number and the prospects for litigation clearly confined. See id. at 838–39. Asbestos actions bear little resemblance either to the traditional punitive award situation or to the MER/29 situation. In asbestos litigation, we are

26. It has been noted that the risk posed by unrestrained awards of punitive damages are not confined to a single industry. "Large assessments of punitive damages may not yet be a major threat to the continued viability of most manufacturing concerns, but the increasing number and size of such awards may fairly raise concern for the future stability of American industry." Owen, Problems in Assessing Punitive Damages Against Manufacturers of Defective Products, 49 U.Chi.L.Rev. 1, 6 (1983). See also Seltzer, Punitive Damages in Mass Tort Litigation: Addressing the Problems of Fairness, Efficiency and Control, 52 Fordham L.Rev. 37, 37–40 (1983).

concerned with exposures that occurred over decades. The victims are not limited to those who used or consumed the product directly. The potential injuries are more severe and more diverse. The latency period is far longer. Far more cases are pending, and the prospects for future litigation are almost limitless.

* * *

Mississippi substantive law would disallow punitive damages in the instant strict liability litigation. In the extraordinary circumstances in which this litigation is set, the allowance of punitive damages is incompatible with the objectives of and would disrupt the viability of the strict liability cause of action. Moreover, the basic policy objectives of punitive damages are satisfied in this instance by defendant's multiple exposure to compensatory damages. Therefore, punitive damages are inappropriate in these extraordinary circumstances.

Strict liability in Mississippi is founded on the dual policy objectives of accomplishing economic loss distributions and promoting consumer safety. * * * This policy seeks not merely to assure compensation for the individual plaintiff, but to achieve the broader societal objective of equitable loss distribution.

Essential to the maintenance of effective loss distribution in strict liability is the presence of viable enterprises that can absorb the losses and compensate victims for their injuries. If the enterprise should fail, early victims would receive compensation but others whose latency periods were longer would receive no compensation at all. At the point where awards of punitive damages destroy the viability of the enterprises necessary to accomplish loss distribution, the remedy of punitive damages becomes incompatible with the strict liability cause of action. The later victims, not the enterprise, effectively bear the punishment. In the mass catastrophe now maturing from pervasive asbestos exposure, the allowance of punitive damages could destroy the marginally viable system of loss distribution in strict liability.

* * *

The anticipation of multiple litigation for compensation damages serves in this instance as an effective deterrent to future illicit conduct. From a market-level perspective, the risk of non-deterrence is greatest where the manufacturer thinks it feasible to hold injury compensation losses to an amount that would still allow a profit on the defective item. This risk is especially great in situations where the potential injuries are so difficult to detect or so slight in relation to the burdens of instituting litigation that many injured persons would be likely to forego compensation claims. See Acosta v. Honda Motor Co., 717 F.2d 828, 838 (3d Cir.1983); Owen, Punitive Damages in Products Liability Litigation, 74 Mich.L.Rev. 1257, 1284–85 (1976). See also Wangen v. Ford Motor Co., 97 Wis.2d 260, 294 N.W.2d 437, 449–50 (1980). That is not the situation with respect to manufacturers of asbestos products, which products are now known to have the potential of inflicting grave injuries on unrestricted numbers of persons. No manufacturer could engage consciously in wrongdoing that would expose it to such overwhelming strict liability with any reasonable expectation of doing so profitably. On the contrary, the prospect of exposure to massive litigation in strict liability provides the impetus for manufacturers to take affirmative steps to ensure the safety of their products, since mere non-negligent behavior is no guarantee against strict liability.

* * *

Moreover, deterrence is an attenuated rationale with respect to these defendants. The defendants have long since begun to issue warnings about the safe use of their products. Johns–Manville states on brief that it ceased to manufacture the products here in issue over ten years ago.

We too "have the gravest difficulty in perceiving how claims for punitive damages can be so administered as to avoid overkill" in this situation. Roginsky v. Richardson–Merrell, Inc., 378 F.2d at 839.

No alternatives suggested appear viable in these extraordinary circumstances. Some courts and commentators suggest that overkill could be avoided by instructing the jury to consider the defendant's wealth and the probable effects of future compensatory and punitive damages awards or by other judicial control at the district court and appellate court level. [Citations.] In this case, such control would require unearthly prescience not only about the outcome of thousands of cases now pending against the defendants, but of thousands of claims certain to arise in the future. We perceive no meaningful criteria by which we could exercise judicial control to determine what is enough and what is too much. See *Roginsky,* 378 F.2d at 839. Likewise we perceive no criteria by which to set an arbitrary cap, either in the aggregate or for the individual suit, absent statutory guidance.

A single class action for recovery of one award of punitive damages might be an attractive alternative from a theoretical point of view, but does not appear feasible. Because the losses are so widespread and disparate, the vital legal issues would not be common to all plaintiffs, nor would the applicable legal standards be identical in all jurisdictions in which the cases would arise. See Abed v. A.H. Robins Co., 693 F.2d 847, 850 (9th Cir.1982) (vacating certification of nationwide class action for punitive damages in Dalkon Shield IUD Products litigation); Roginsky, 378 F.2d at 839, n. 11. See also In re Federal Skywalk Cases, 93 F.R.D. 415, 419 (W.D.Mo.), vacated, 680 F.2d 1175 (8th Cir.), cert. denied, 459 U.S. 988, 103 S.Ct. 342, 74 L.Ed.2d 383 (1982).[28]

A final alternative, of course, would be to cling to the traditional remedy of punitive damages and let things run their course, indifferent to the disruption of the defendants' enterprises and to future claimants. One court has suggested that the demise of the manufacturer in such circumstances is not a "necessarily untenable" result. Acosta v. Honda Motor Co., 717 F.2d at 838 n. 15 (3d Cir.1983). We do not share that belief. Retribution should not be effected at the expense of injured

28. But see Seltzer, 52 Fordham L.Rev. at 61–92, advocating a mandatory class action for punitive damages in mass tort litigation.

persons in need of a means of compensation for actual injuries, where retribution can be achieved effectively by ongoing liability for satisfaction of those needs.

Johns–Manville is currently in a reorganization proceeding under Chapter 11 of the Bankruptcy Code, see In re Johns–Manville Corp., Nos. 82B 11,656 to 82B 11,676 (Bankr.S.D.N.Y. filed Aug. 26, 1982), alleged to be as a result of its potential tort liability arising from these suits. It might be argued that punitive damages pose no threat to the compensation of other Johns–Manville claimants, since the bankruptcy court could administratively manage punitive damage claims even to the point of denying such claims equal priority with claims for compensatory damages. See Note, Mass Tort Claims and the Corporate Tortfeasor: Bankruptcy Reorganization and Legislative Compensation Versus the Common–Law Tort System, 61 Texas L.Rev. 1297, 1322 (1983). The problem remains, however, of making provision for future claimants whose numbers and the size of whose claims are purely speculative. Multiple present awards of punitive damages would only complicate the already formidable problems of devising a bankruptcy reorganization plan that would make adequate provision for future claimants.[29]

* * *

The disallowance of punitive damages in this situation expresses this court's central concern for the continued viability of the strict liability cause of action for present and future claimants. Where strict liability for compensatory damages imposes adequate punishment, as it does in this type of case, we decline to cleave to a judge-made remedy of punitive damages that would both fail in its own purpose and obstruct the broader objectives of the underlying cause of action which the plaintiff has chosen to pursue.

VII. ADMISSIBILITY OF "SUMNER SIMPSON PAPERS"

Sumner Simpson was president of Raybestos–Manhattan from 1929 to 1948, and chairman of the board from 1945 until his death in 1953. A number of his personal papers remained in Raybestos–Manhattan's corporate vaults until brought to light in 1974. These so-called "Sum-

29. The bankruptcy court has ruled that the unprecedented, extraordinary nature of these proceedings mandated a declaration that future claimants are parties in interest, entitled to the appointment of an independent legal representative. The court cited a study commissioned by Johns–Manville which indicated that "a reasonable control projection of the number of lawsuits [against Johns–Manville] seen from 1982 on is likely to be about 45,000, with a reasonably firm lower bound of 30,000 and a very definitive upper bound on the order of 120,000." In re Johns–Manville Corp., 36 B.R. 743, 746 (Bkrtcy. S.D.N.Y.1984) (Decision and Order on Keene's Motion to Appoint a Legal Representative). [Citation.]

The bankruptcy court also ruled that Johns–Manville did not act in bad faith in filing for Chapter 11 reorganization on the basis of the crushing economic burden it will bear over the next twenty to thirty years as a result of future claims of asbestos victims. The court determined that liquidation now would preclude present asbestos victims and future claimants from receiving just compensation. In re Johns–Manville Corp., 36 B.R. 727 (Bkrtcy.S.D. N.Y.1984) (Decision and Order on Motion to Dismiss Manville's Chapter 11 Petition).

* * *

ner Simpson papers" consisted largely of letters, memoranda, surveys, and articles dating from the 1930's and 1940's.

Jackson introduced into evidence three letters extracted from these papers. The first letter, dated September 25, 1935, from an editor of the newly created *Asbestos Magazine* to Mr. Simpson, proposed the publication of articles on British and American research on asbestosis. The other two letters dated October 1, 1935, and October 3, 1935, are an interchange between Mr. Simpson and Mr. Vandiver Brown, attorney for Johns–Manville, questioning the desirability of publishing such information and the comparability of the British and American asbestos situations. (The texts of these three letters are included as an appendix to this opinion.)

The defendants argue that the trial court committed reversible error in admitting these letters, because they were relevant to no issue in the case, or if relevant, their probity was outweighed by the risk of unfair prejudice. We agree.

These letters are of no probative value as to the foreseeability of the hazards associated with the finished products with which Jackson came in contact, as foreseeability relates to the defendants' duty to provide Jackson warning. The letters do not bear upon the safety of the finished products with which Jackson first came in contact in 1953, nearly two decades after the letters were written. The research that had been done at the time these letters were written was confined to plant employees, mine workers, and textile employees. None of the research concerned workers who were involved with the end use of finished asbestos products. As regards foreseeability of hazards to plant workers, the letters are inconclusive. They evidence a concern with the comparability of British plant conditions and American plant conditions, but do not evidence directly what the hazard in American plants was perceived to be.

Even if the letters were to some degree probative of foreseeability in 1935, that evidence would be highly remote, particularly in light of the research developments that occurred before Jackson commenced employment. In 1946, the Fleisher–Drinker report, the first noteworthy epidemiological study of the risks of shipyard workers exposed to asbestos products, indicated that asbestos covering of naval vessels was relatively safe. This report was generally accepted until the famous Selikoff studies were published in 1965. [Citation.] The relevant time frame in which foreseeability should be determined is that in which the products with which Jackson came into contact were distributed. The letters attempt inappropriately to fill the time gap from 1935 to 1953.

We do not suggest that the Fleisher–Drinker study forecloses establishing the foreseeability of the hazards of asbestos products at the time of the study or afterwards. Foreseeability might well be established not only by other expert evidence, but by proof of what the defendants themselves knew or should have known about the hazards associated with the use of their products. These particular 1935 letters are too remote in time and too attenuated in subject matter, however, to be probative in this connection.

Jackson argues that the letters are probative of the defendants' conspiracy to suppress information about the hazards of asbestos. Jackson, has, however, abandoned that cause of action. Also, we have determined that Jackson is not entitled to an award of punitive damages in this case. Accordingly, the letters are not admissible to meet the requisite standard of conduct to support such an award.

Even if the letters were probative as to foreseeability, that probative value would be substantially outweighed by the danger of confusing these issues and misleading the jury, to the unfair prejudice of the defendants. See Fed.R.Evid. 403. There is a reasonable likelihood that a substantial right of the defendants was affected by the admission of these letters. Hence the error was not harmless. [Citation.]

* * *

IX. CONCLUSION

We AFFIRM the district court's holding that Jackson is entitled to a strict tort liability cause of action against the defendants and the district court's treatment of settlement amounts; we REVERSE on the admissibility of cancer evidence and of the "Sumner Simpson papers," and on the allowance of punitive damages; and we REMAND this case to the district court for further proceedings consistent with this opinion.

Affirmed in part; reversed in part; and remanded.

APPENDIX

"ASBESTOS"
Published by
SECRETARIAL SERVICE
16th Floor, Inquirer Bldg.
Philadelphia, PA., U.S.A.

September 25, 1935.

Mr. Sumner Simpson, President,
Raybestos–Manhattan, Inc.,
Bridgeport, Conn.

Dear Sir:

You may recall that we have written you on several occasions concerning the publishing of information, or discussion of, asbestosis and the work which has been, and is being done, to eliminate or at least reduce it.

Always you have requested that for certain obvious reasons we publish nothing, and, naturally your wishes have been respected.

Possibly by this time, however, the reasons for your objection to publicity on this subject have been eliminated, and if so, we would like very much to review the whole matter in "ASBESTOS".

Our thought is that we could either prepare from data which we have in our files, or obtain from Mr. W.A. Godfrey of the Cape Asbestos Company, London, who is much interested in the subject, an article on the work done in England and then follow it with an article written by someone in your organization, as to the work done here.

We understand from Mr. Stover that your North Charleston plant, contains very complete dust control equipment and a description of such equipment, if you approve, would make a very interesting part of the article. Possibly even you could supply a photograph or two showing some part of this dust control equipment.

We await with much interest your reply. If there is no serious objection it would seem to be a most interesting subject for the pages of "ASBESTOS", and possibly a discussion of it in "ASBESTOS" along the right lines, would serve to combat some of the rather undesirable publicity given to it in current newspapers.

Very truly yours,
"ASBESTOS"
s/A.F. Rossiter
A.F. Rossiter
Bridgeport, Conn.
Oct. 1, 1935

Mr. Vandiver Brown, Attorney
Johns–Manville Corp.,
22 East 40th St.,
New York City.

My dear Mr. Brown:

Enclosed is copy of a letter received from Miss Rossiter, of "Asbestos."

As I see it personally, we would be just as well off to say nothing about it until our survey is complete. I think the less said about asbestos, the better off we are, but at the same time, we cannot lose track of the fact that there have been a number of articles on asbestos dust control and asbestosis in the British trade magazines. The magazine "Asbestos" is in business to publish articles affecting the trade and they have been very decent about not re-printing the English articles.

I shall be pleased to have your opinion in the matter.

Very truly yours,

President

SS–G
Enc.

* * *

JOHNS–MANVILLE
Twenty–Two East Fortieth Street
New York, N.Y.

October 3, 1935

Mr. S. Simpson, President,
Raybestos–Manhattan, Inc.,
Bridgeport, Conn.

My dear Mr. Simpson:

I wish to acknowledge receipt of yours of October 1st enclosing copy of the September 25th letter from the editor of the magazine "ASBESTOS". I quite agree with you that our interests are best served by having asbestosis receive the minimum of publicity. Even if we should eventually decide to raise no objection to the publication of an article on asbestosis in the magazine in question, I think we should warn the editors to use American data on the subject rather than English. Dr. Lanza has frequently remarked, to me personally and in some of his papers, that the clinical picture presented in North American localities where there is an asbestos dust hazard is considerably milder than that reported in England and South Africa.

I believe the question raised by Miss Rossiter might well be considered at the committee meeting scheduled for next Tuesday, at which I understand both you and Mr. Judd will be present.

Very truly yours,
s/Vandiver Brown
Vandiver Brown, Attorney

VB: T

ON PETITIONS FOR REHEARING AND SUGGESTION FOR REHEARING EN BANC

Before CLARK, CHIEF JUDGE, BROWN, GEE, RUBIN, REAVLEY, POLITZ, RANDALL, TATE, JOHNSON, WILLIAMS, GARWOOD, JOLLY, HIGGINBOTHAM and DAVIS, CIRCUIT JUDGES.

By the Court:

A member of the Court in active service having requested a poll on the application for rehearing en banc and a majority of the judges in active service having voted in favor of granting a rehearing en banc,

It is ordered that this cause shall be reheard by the Court en banc with oral argument on a date hereafter to be fixed. The Clerk will specify a briefing schedule for the filing of supplemental briefs.

NOTE

Might a consolidated bankruptcy proceeding be an especially effective method for resolving thousands of similar toxic substance claims? See Roe,

Corporate Strategic Reaction to Mass Tort, 72 Va.L.Rev. 1 (1986); Note, The Manville Bankruptcy: Treating Mass Tort Claims in Chapter 11 Proceedings, 96 Harv.L.Rev. 1121 (1983); Toxic Torts and Chapter 11 Reorganization: The Problem of Future Claims, 38 Vand.L.Rev. 1369 (1985).

JACKSON v. JOHNS–MANVILLE SALES CORPORATION [JACKSON II]

United States Court of Appeals, Fifth Circuit (En Banc), 1985.
750 F.2d 1314, cert. denied, 478 U.S. 1022, 106 S.Ct. 3339, 92 L.Ed.2d 743 (1986).*

Before CLARK, CHIEF JUDGE, GEE, RUBIN, GARZA, REAVLEY, POLITZ, RANDALL, TATE, JOHNSON, GARWOOD, JOLLY, HIGGINBOTHAM, DAVIS and HILL, CIRCUIT JUDGES.

RANDALL, CIRCUIT JUDGE:

[This decision resulted from a rehearing en banc of *Jackson I.*]

A. *Evidentiary Issues.*

1. The Sumner Simpson Papers.

Johns–Manville and Raybestos–Manhattan contend that the district court committed reversible error by admitting three of the so-called "Sumner Simpson papers." * * *

Under Federal Rule of Evidence 401, evidence meets the threshold test of relevancy if the evidence tends "to make the existence of any fact that is of consequence to the determination of the action more probable or less probable than it would be without the evidence." Fed. R.Evid. 401; [citation]. Jackson introduced the Sumner Simpson letters into evidence to show, *inter alia,* that Johns–Manville and Raybestos–Manhattan knew or should have known of the dangers asbestos products posed to shipyard workers during the years Jackson worked in that capacity at Ingalls. Under Restatement (Second) of Torts § 402A comment j, a manufacturer is only required to warn of dangers of which he knew or should have known "by the application of reasonable, developed human skill and foresight." [Citation.]

The defendants argue that the letters are of no probative value as to foreseeability because they refer only to the danger faced by miners and plant workers in being exposed to raw asbestos, and it was clearly established at trial that Jackson worked solely with finished asbestos products. We note as an initial matter that the texts of the letters themselves do not limit their discussion to miners or plant workers. Rather, on their face, the letters appear to pertain to the problems of asbestos dust control in general. Nevertheless, even assuming that the defendants are correct in their contention that the letters refer only to certain groups of workers, we think that such a distinction plainly goes more to the weight than to the admissibility of the evidence. A study

* Subsequent history noted infra.—Eds.

indicating that exposure to asbestos fibers is likely to cause harm to one group of workers is at least suggestive of the fact that other groups of workers who are also exposed to asbestos fibers face similar dangers. The letters were not so remote in subject matter as to be devoid of probative value.

* * *

Although relevant, evidence can be excluded under Federal Rule of Evidence 403 if its probative value is substantially outweighed by the danger of unfair prejudice. A trial court's determination under rule 403, however, will not be reversed absent a finding of an abuse of discretion. [Citations.] We find no abuse of discretion on the part of the district court. Nothing in the letters is of such an inherent nature as to inflame the passions of the jury or invoke its sympathies. Moreover, counsel for Johns–Manville and Raybestos–Manhattan had ample opportunity, of which they took full advantage, to ensure that the jury fully appreciated the remoteness of the letters both in time and in subject matter. * * *

2. Admission of Cancer Evidence.

At trial, a number of expert witnesses testified that Jackson's exposure to asbestos significantly increased his risk of contracting cancer. Three of these expert witnesses testified both that exposure to asbestos generally results in some increased risk of cancer and that, based upon Jackson's medical records and history of asbestos exposure, it could be estimated that Jackson specifically had a greater than fifty percent chance of contracting asbestos-related cancer in the future. On appeal, Johns–Manville and Raybestos–Manhattan assert that admission of this evidence was prejudicial error because the relationship between asbestos and cancer was not relevant to any issue in the case. In addition, they argue that, even if such evidence was relevant, its emotional impact substantially outweighed its probative value.

* * *

[The court concluded that although the risk of cancer from asbestos exposure was relevant to the defendants' duty to warn, the prejudice engendered by the evidence, especially in light of its quantity—plaintiff had nine experts who testified about the risk of cancer from asbestos—outweighed its probative value on that issue.]

Jackson offers, however, two other grounds for the admissibility of the cancer evidence: (1) to establish damages for reasonable mental anguish resulting from his increased risk of cancer and (2) to establish damages in connection with cancer as a future consequence of the complained of condition that is reasonably probable to occur. We think that either ground would justify the inclusion of the evidence in this case, provided, of course, that the damages of which the cancer evidence would be probative were available to Jackson as a matter of law. Thus, because we have decided to certify to the Mississippi Supreme Court the question whether these types of damages are recoverable by Jackson in the present context, see infra Part B3, the final decision as to the admissibility of the cancer evidence must await that court's response to our question. * * *

B. *Substantive Law—Punitive Damages, Mental Anguish and Probable Future Consequences.*

* * * In voting to rehear the case en banc, this court requested the parties additionally to consider in their briefings whether this case was an appropriate one for the fashioning and imposition of federal common law. Upon careful review of the excellent briefs submitted and the applicable caselaw, we now conclude that Mississippi law governs the resolution of the punitive damages, cancer as a probable future consequence, and mental anguish issues. * * *

1. The Unique Nature of Asbestos Litigation.

In advocating the application of federal common law, both the defendants and the dissent distinguish the instant case from routine personal injury actions on the ground that asbestos-related injuries have become a national problem of immense proportions. * * *

* * * To the defendants and the dissent, these problems and the need for national solutions form an ample basis for the formulation of federal common law.

2. The Question of Federal Common Law.

Any discussion of federal common law must begin with Erie R. Co. v. Tompkins, 304 U.S. 64, 58 S.Ct. 817, 82 L.Ed. 1188 (1938). In *Erie,* the Supreme Court established that federal courts do not have the general law-making powers commonly exercised by state courts. The *Erie* Court held that federal courts, as courts of limited jurisdiction, are empowered to make only those laws authorized by the Constitution or by enactments of Congress. 304 U.S. at 78, 58 S.Ct. at 822. Nevertheless, since *Erie,* the Supreme Court has recognized "a responsibility in the absence of legislation, to fashion federal common law in cases raising issues of uniquely federal concern." Northwest Airlines, Inc. v. Transport Workers Union of America, 451 U.S. 77, 95, 101 S.Ct. 1571, 67 L.Ed.2d 750 (1981). These instances, however, are "few and restricted." Wheeldin v. Wheeler, 373 U.S. 647, 651, 83 S.Ct. 1441, 1444, 10 L.Ed.2d 605 (1963). With respect to the kinds of cases that do raise issues of "uniquely federal concern," the Supreme Court has most recently stated:

> [A]bsent some congressional authorization to formulate substantive rules of decision, federal common law exists only in such narrow areas as those concerned with the rights and obligations of the United States, interstate and international disputes implicating the conflicting rights of States or our relations with foreign nations, and admiralty cases. In these instances, our federal system does not permit the controversy to be resolved under state law, either because the authority and duties of the United States as sovereign are intimately

involved or because the interstate or international nature of the controversy makes it inappropriate for state law to control.

Texas Industries, Inc. v. Radcliff Materials, Inc., 451 U.S. 630, 641, 101 S.Ct. 2061, 2067, 68 L.Ed.2d 500 (1981).

Johns-Manville and Raybestos-Manhattan, while conceding that Congress has yet to take any action to remedy the problems of asbestos exposure, present what can be taken as two arguments for the proposition that these problems involve uniquely federal concerns justifying the displacement of state law. First, the defendants, echoed by the dissent, argue that the potential conflict among plaintiffs for the limited resources of the asbestos companies is analogous to the interstate conflicts over water rights and pollution that have been held to involve uniquely federal interests. According to the defendants, just as one state cannot divert the waters of a river flowing partially within its borders without regard for those downstream, one group of states should not be able by allowing the recovery of noncompensatory damages to divert and deplete scarce corporate resources at the expense of injured plaintiffs in other states.

We find this argument, although superficially plausible, to be ultimately unpersuasive. Defendants in drawing their analogy necessarily rely on such cases as Hinderlider v. La Plata River & Cherry Creek Ditch Co., 304 U.S. 92, 58 S.Ct. 803, 82 L.Ed. 1202 (1938), and Illinois v. City of Milwaukee, 406 U.S. 91, 92 S.Ct. 1385, 31 L.Ed.2d 712 (1972). * * *

In both cases, the essential conflict was between states as quasi-sovereign bodies over shared resources. Under such circumstances, a single state's statutes or decisions could not be considered conclusive. In the realm of asbestos litigation, [the problem] may transcend state lines but does not involve the rights and duties of states as discrete political entities. A conflict over the resources of the asbestos industry would be not merely between plaintiffs in different states but between plaintiffs in the same state and between past, present, and future plaintiffs. Clearly, if federal courts are to remain courts of limited powers as required under *Erie,* a dispute over a common fund or scarce resources cannot become "interstate," in the sense of requiring the application of federal common law, merely because the conflict is not confined within the boundaries of a single state.

Second, the defendants argue that there is a uniquely federal interest in assuring compensation to injured persons and in maintaining government asbestos suppliers. Both interests, the defendants insist, would be substantially served by the creation of federal rules restricting the types of damages recoverable in asbestos suits. We think the defendants in making this argument misconceive the nature of the uniquely federal interest requirement. "Uniquely federal interests" are not merely national interests, and the existence of national interests, no matter their significance, cannot by themselves give federal courts the authority to supersede state policy. * * * It is well-established instead that to be "uniquely federal" and thus a sufficient predicate for the imposition of a federal substantive rule, an interest must relate to an articulated congressional policy or directly implicate the authority and duties of the United States as sovereign. * * *

Although individual members and committees of Congress have expressed concern with the problem of asbestos litigation, Congress itself has yet to make policy on this issue. Moreover, defendants have been unable to point to any substantial right or duty of the federal government that would be directly affected by the outcome of this litigation. * * *

A related interest that has been suggested to justify the exercise of federal judicial power in this case is the federal court's own interest in "doing justice." It could be argued that federal courts have an institutional interest in maintaining a federal judicial system that is fundamentally "just." While we are sympathetic to such an argument, it is clear that such an abstract, all-encompassing interest cannot form a sufficient basis upon which to rest the displacement of state law. First, we find implicit in *Erie* the idea that in diversity actions federal court concerns in a just judicial system cannot be used as a reason for supplanting substantive state policies. Second, certainly as a practical matter, the effect of resting assertions of federal judicial power on so vague an interest as "justice" would be to eviscerate *Erie* completely and thus ignore its constitutional under-pinnings. * * *

Finally, we note the impracticalities of fashioning a federal common law in the context of asbestos litigation. First, any decision by this court to displace state law would be effective only within our geographical jurisdiction. * * * Unless and until the Supreme Court imposes a similar federal common law on the country as a whole, any federal substantive rules fashioned by us would only exacerbate the alleged inequities among claimants, with punitive and certain types of compensatory damages being available outside the circuit but not within. Such a result, in turn, would encourage a massive effort at forum shopping to bring suits outside this circuit.

Second, we are unable to discern any governing principle of easy application for the imposition of federal common law in the asbestos context. Although the amount of recovery available to plaintiffs depends in large part on the availability of punitive damages and the scope of the actionable injury, many other aspects of the litigation similarly play a significant role in determining the size of potential awards. The applicable limitations period for the bringing of an action, for example, has a direct impact on aggregate recovery and thus the availability of funds for future claimants. The simple fact is that, once the need to limit plaintiffs' recoveries is used to justify the creation of federal substantive rules precluding the recovery of punitive damages and narrowing the scope of the actionable injury, there would be no principled means of restricting the application of federal common law to other matters, either in the context of asbestos litigation or in relation to similar legal problems. As a consequence, federal courts would become increasingly responsible for establishing a general federal tort law in a manner we think is inconsistent with the teachings of *Erie* and the logic behind our federal system. [Citation.]

Third, displacement of state law in asbestos cases would require federal courts to reexamine the major issues and principles involved in asbestos litigation, most of which are presently settled under state tort law. As a result, the progress of currently pending asbestos cases through the federal court system would come to a virtual standstill. The need to ensure quick resolution of the claims militates strongly against taking such action.

In sum, we find that this case is not an appropriate one for the creation of a federal common law because of the absence of a uniquely federal interest and the practical problems that would attend the displacement of state law. * * * There is no doubt that a desperate need exists for federal legislation in the field of asbestos litigation. Congress' silence on the matter, however, hardly authorizes the federal judiciary to assume for itself the responsibility for formulating what essentially are legislative solutions. Displacement of state law is primarily a decision for Congress, and Congress has yet to act. [Citation.] [18]

3. Certification.

It remains for us to consider under Mississippi law the nature of the actionable injury and the availability of punitive damages in the asbestos context. Upon review of the relevant caselaw and the briefs of counsel, we find that these issues are currently unresolved under Mississippi jurisprudence and are appropriate for certification to the Mississippi Supreme Court pursuant to Mississippi Supreme Court Rule 46.[19]

* * *

CERTIFIED.

ALVIN B. RUBIN, CIRCUIT JUDGE, concurring.

Although I think that diversity cases should not be reheard en banc, I concur in this opinion because we are remanding the case to obtain the opinion of the state Supreme Court, which alone can furnish

18. Because we find that the imposition of federal common law is clearly not appropriate in this context, we have determined not to certify the question to the United States Supreme Court pursuant to 28 U.S.C. § 1254(3), as suggested by the dissent. * * *

19. Mississippi Supreme Court Rule 46 provides:

> When it appears to the Supreme Court of the United States, or to any circuit court of appeals of the United States, that there are involved in any proceedings before it questions or propositions of law of this state which are determinative of said cause independently of any other questions involved in said case and that there are no clear controlling precedents in the decisions of the Supreme Court of this State, such federal court before rendering a decision may certify such questions or propositions of law of this state to the Supreme Court of Mississippi. * * *

* * *

us an authoritative state-law decision on issues involved in hundreds of cases pending in the federal district courts.

CLARK, CHIEF JUDGE, with whom GEE, GARZA, POLITZ and E. GRADY JOLLY, CIRCUIT JUDGES, join, dissenting.

The nub of the disagreement with the majority opinion lies in its essential premise that justice is too abstract, too all-encompassing a concept to serve as a basis for supplanting state substantive law in diversity cases. * * *

The majority labels this a "Mississippi diversity case." While this is literally accurate, it is misleading. *Jackson* is a seminal case that will control the rights of untold thousands of litigants in this court. The panel opinion cannot form a proper premise for dissent, for, like the majority, it too gave less than adequate consideration to the impact of the unprecedented volume of the asbestos litigation in the federal court system. The number of the claims is already legion and increasing at a geometric rate. Compensation for these actions, most of which are founded on the concept of liability without fault, must be paid by a finite and indeed limited group of business entities and insurers. These facts prevent consideration of James Leroy Jackson's case in isolation. They also preclude our dealing with Jackson and his cohorts as a group of litigants whose cases should be governed by Mississippi law under ordinary diversity principles. The only just resolution this court can achieve here is to certify to the United States Supreme Court under 28 U.S.C. § 1254(3) the question of whether federal common law must be developed to govern this uniquely interdependent mass of tort litigation.

I

* * *

Each of the many states touched by this litigation has a strong interest in ensuring that its citizens receive full compensation, regardless of when their individual claims accrue. Uncompensated victims could directly or indirectly burden the state itself. However, no state can control the tort law of another. A state seeking to protect its own citizens can only shape its law to maximize the recovery of its own early plaintiffs, so that at least those individuals will not be impeded in the legal scramble for a share of insufficient assets.

* * *

II

Just as the rote application of inconsistent state laws cannot resolve this problem, so too, any action by this inferior appellate court alone would be ineffective. Our creation of a federal common law to govern asbestos actions within the Fifth Circuit would only eliminate inequities among federal claimants in the area we serve. Courts outside our jurisdiction could continue to apply disparate policies. The question of resolving a proper federal common law rule must be certified to the Supreme Court of the United States—the only judicial forum capable of providing the right answer.

III

Modern strict liability and, indeed, almost all tort principles are products of state law. Since Erie Railroad v. Tompkins state law principles have governed diversity trials. This dissent invokes no departure from that well established rule. However, there is equally authentic authority that federal forums must impose an overarching rule to accomplish justice in litigation where the application of inconsistent rules generated by states with conflicting interests can consume the purpose of the state law itself. Even in diversity cases we do not become courts of the states. That is why, with fidelity to the decision of the Supreme Court to apply state substantive law in diversity cases, it is necessary to remember that we always retain the duty to perform our tasks under our system of federalism.

* * * Here the competing state interests presented by the nationwide flood of asbestos litigation [renders the use of federal common law appropriate, just] as the interstate nature of the controversy makes the application of state law inappropriate.

IV

The majority concludes that federal common law is available to resolve an interstate conflict only if the essential conflict is between the states as "discrete political entities." I respectfully disagree. This conclusion ignores [certain Supreme Court decisions].

* * *

VI

The majority says, and we agree, that legislation would be the preferred solution to the dilemma of providing adequate scheme for the proper distribution of compensation. But Congress has failed to enact any of the asbestos compensation bills proposed to date. Courts enjoy no comparable ability to refuse to decide cases brought before them. We must decide Jackson's claims. But it is not just Jackson's rights which are at stake. * * *

The Supreme Court, as the only institution other than Congress capable of imposing the uniformity necessary to resolve this problem in a just manner, should be afforded the chance to deal with the singular problem presented by these cases. That Court has the power to formulate federal common law which will ensure equitable compensation for all claimants. Its ability to address the controlling issues with a single voice is not only necessary for just resolution of pending litigation; it is even more important to expeditious and equitable settlement of claims. * * *

* * *

X

* * *

Because this court declines to [certify the punitive damages and accrual issues to the United States Supreme Court], we respectfully dissent.

APPENDIX

DIMENSIONS OF ASBESTOS LITIGATION

No other category of tort litigation has even approached, either qualitatively or quantitatively, the magnitude of the claims premised on asbestos exposure. By 1981, only eight years after the decision in Borel v. Fibreboard Paper Products Corp., 493 F.2d 1076 (5th Cir.1973), cert. denied, 419 U.S. 869, 95 S.Ct. 127, 42 L.Ed.2d 107 (1974), it had become the largest area of product liability litigation, far surpassing the number of cases generated by the controversies over Agent Orange, the drug DES, the Dalkon Shield intrauterine device, or even automobile defects. Between the early 1970's and 1982 the asbestos companies and their insurers expended over $1 billion in litigation expenses, damage awards and settlements. This figure does not include the costs incurred by state or federal governments, expenses and compensation in workers' compensation claims, or the costs resulting from the Chapter 11 proceedings initiated by Johns–Manville, Unarco, and Amatex.

I. The Claimants

In August of 1982, approximately 21,000 claimants had filed product liability suits alleging asbestos-related injuries. Seven months later by March of 1983, the figure had risen to about 24,000 claimants. Currently, new suits are being docketed at an average rate of 500 per month.

* * *

* * * Any exposure to this substance, even to a relatively minute amount, can precipitate the development of asbestos-related disease. [Due to the long latency period, up to 40 years or longer, it is difficult to predict the number of future claimants. New classes of plaintiffs are emerging, including warehouse workers, truck drivers, longshoremen, and spouses of workers exposed to the dust on their work clothes. Construction workers may develop into a large class of claimants, since 20% of all buildings contain friable (capable of becoming airborne) asbestos. Roughly 10–20 million workers are estimated to have been significantly exposed to asbestos in the last 40 years. The total number of asbestos-related deaths over the next two or three decades is estimated at 2–300,000, and many more non-lethal diseases will result. By the year 2010, somewhere between 30,000 and 180,000 new lawsuits are expected. Congress ordered the removal of all friable asbestos from school buildings in the early 1980s, 20 U.S.C.A. § 3601(a)(3)(6), and it is unknown whether school children—and persons living and working in

the many homes and other buildings containing asbestos—may eventually develop asbestos diseases.]

II. The Costs

* * * [S]tudies calculate that the defendant asbestos companies and their insurers paid claimants and their lawyers approximately $400 million between 1970 and 1982. This figure encompasses trial awards, including punitive damages, and settlements. In appraising the economic impact of this figure, the reader must be aware that in recent years jury verdicts have been demonstrating a pronounced upward trend. Moreover, this does not include legal fees or litigation expense incurred by the producers themselves.

The average plaintiffs' verdict after a trial was $388,000. The importance of limiting claims to those diseases actually diagnosed is demonstrated by these average jury verdicts: asbestosis—$205,000, lung cancer—$311,000, and mesothelioma—$469,000.

[Damages awards are rising rapidly, and the total long-term costs of asbestos diseases will amount to many billions of dollars, perhaps as much as $87 billion.]

III. The Defendants

This liability confronts a relatively small group of asbestos companies and their insurers. On the average, twenty defendants are named in each suit. Although more than three hundred different corporations have been sued, liability is actually focused on a very small group. Sixteen corporations are named in at least half of all the suits. Another group of fifteen are in one-quarter to one-half of the suits. Accordingly, the bulk of the 300 defendants play a minimal role in the overall amount of litigation.

Most asbestos producers claim to be covered by insurance for part or all of their exposure. About fifty insurers have some involvement, but only about twelve can be characterized as deeply involved in this controversy. The likely number of asbestos claims ultimately covered by insurance is uncertain in light of the widespread ongoing litigation over the coverage provided by the policies in question.

* * * [T]he net worth of the insurance companies involved [has been estimated at] $9.7 billion and that of the asbestos companies as $25.6 billion, for a combined total of $35.3 billion. This is less than most of the liability estimates described in Part II * * *. * * *

IV. The Courts

Asbestos-related litigation is proceeding in at least forty-eight states. The largest proportion of the cases filed to date is found in those states where the shipbuilding industry is centered. On a national basis, slightly more than half of the claims closed by August of 1982 were filed in federal court. In two of the five states generating the most litigation, New Jersey and Texas, over 90% of the closed claims were brought in federal court, while in California and Pennsylvania, also within that group, over two-thirds of the closed claims were filed in state courts. * * *

* * *

NOTES

1. Which perspective on the *Erie* federal common law problem is "correct"? See Atwood, The Choice-of-Law Dilemma in Mass Tort Litigation: Kicking Around Erie, Klaxon, and Van Dusen, 19 Conn.L.Rev. 9, 23–24 (1986); Vairo, Multi–Tort Cases: Cause for More Darkness on the Subject, or a New Role for Federal Common Law?, 54 Ford.L.Rev. 167 (1985).

2. The federal interpleader statute was enacted to permit multiple claimants to a limited fund to be brought into a single action to resolve entitlement to and govern distribution of the fund. 28 U.S.C.A. §§ 1335, 1397, and 2361. See 7 C. Wright, A. Miller & M. Kane, Federal Practice and Procedure §§ 1701 et seq. (2d ed. 1986). Is recourse to the interpleader statute feasible in this context?

Consider also Fed.R.Civ.P. 23(b)(1)(B), which authorizes class actions in situations where permitting plaintiffs to proceed with individual claims may compromise the rights of others not parties to the action. In the punitive damages context, attempts to certify class actions have not generally met with much success. See In re Northern Dist. of California, Dalkon Shield IUD Products Liability Litigation, 693 F.2d 847 (9th Cir.1982), cert. denied 459 U.S. 1171, 103 S.Ct. 817, 74 L.Ed.2d 1015 (1983); In re Federal Skywalk Cases, 680 F.2d 1175 (8th Cir.), cert. denied, 459 U.S. 988, 103 S.Ct. 342, 74 L.Ed.2d 383 (1982). But cf. In re "Agent Orange" Product Liability Litigation, 100 F.R.D. 718 (E.D.N.Y.1983) (26(b)(3) class, permitting opt-outs), mandamus petition denied, 725 F.2d 858 (2d Cir.1984). See generally Seltzer, Punitive Damages in Mass Tort Litigation: Addressing the Problems of Fairness, Efficiency and Control, 52 Fordham L.Rev. 37, 63–92 (1983); Notes, 1984 U.Ill.L.F. 153; 81 Mich.L.Rev. 1787 (1983); 96 Harv.L.Rev. 1143 (1983).

JACKSON v. JOHNS–MANVILLE SALES CORPORATION (JACKSON II 1/11)

Supreme Court of Mississippi, 1985.
469 So.2d 99.*

Certifying questions from United States Court of Appeals, Fifth Circuit.

En banc.

The United States Court of Appeals for the Fifth Circuit has certified this cause to this Court, asking that we decide the following questions of law:

> Whether (1) mental anguish damages; (2) damages for cancer as a probable future consequence, and (3) punitive

* Subsequent history noted infra.—Eds.

damages are available in asbestos products liability actions. 757 F.2d 614.

A majority of this Court after considering these issues will decline certification.

Therefore, we respectfully decline to rule upon the questions presented.

JACKSON v. JOHNS–MANVILLE SALES CORPORATON [JACKSON III]

United States Court of Appeals, Fifth Circuit, 1986.
781 F.2d 394.

Before CLARK, CHIEF JUDGE, GEE, RUBIN, GARZA, REAVLEY, POLITZ, RANDALL, TATE, JOHNSON, GARWOOD, JOLLY, HIGGINBOTHAM, DAVIS, and HILL, CIRCUIT JUDGES.

RANDALL, CIRCUIT JUSTICE

* * * The case is * * * back before us for resolution of the issues previously certified to the Mississippi Supreme Court.

[Those issues involve the availability, in cases of this type, of (1) punitive damages, (2) damages for the probability of contracting cancer in the future, and (3) damages for cancerphobia—the present fear of future cancer.]

I. PROCEDURE FOR CONSTRUING MISSISSIPPI LAW.

The en banc court determined that Mississippi law, and not federal common law, properly governs the resolution of these issues. Thus, we must interpret the law as would a Mississippi court. Erie R.R. v. Tompkins, 304 U.S. 64, 58 S.Ct. 817, 82 L.Ed. 1188 (1938). * * *

* * *

II. PUNITIVE DAMAGES.

[Defendants contend that punitive damages are inappropriate in mass tort cases as a matter of law.]

* * *

[Defendants argue for a] drastic change in the law of remedies. They urge us to determine that when a defendant injures tens of thousands and manifests reckless disregard for the victims' lives and welfare, punitive damages should be unavailable as a matter of law.

We believe that the Mississippi Supreme Court would not deny to its own citizens the right to recover that which citizens of dozens of other states are already entitled to recover, and that the district court correctly charged the jury on the applicable legal principles. * * *

* * *

The simple fact of the matter is that no appellate court has accepted the defendants' theory in a reported decision. In Oregon, for example, the Supreme Court recently ruled in a "mass tort" case that the "financial interests of the malicious and wanton wrongdoer must be considered in the context of societal concern for the injured and the future protection of society." State ex rel. Young v. Crookham, 290 Or. 61, 618 P.2d 1268, 1271 (1980). An Illinois court recently explained that it did "not believe that defendants should be relieved of liability for punitive damages merely because, through outrageous misconduct, they may have managed to seriously injure a large number of persons." Froud v. Celotex Corp., 107 Ill.App.3d 654, 63 Ill.Dec. 261, 264, 437 N.E.2d 910, 913 (1982), rev'd on other grounds, 98 Ill.2d 324, 74 Ill.Dec. 629, 456 N.E.2d 131 (1983). Pennsylvania, New Jersey, Florida, Tennessee, and Texas each permits plaintiffs to recover punitive damages in mass tort cases. [Citations.]

Moreover, several commentators writing on the issue of punitive damages in mass tort cases have concluded that punitive damages should be generally available in mass tort cases. See, e.g., Owen, Punitive Damages in Products Liability Litigation, 74 Mich.L.Rev. 1258 (1976); Seltzer, Punitive Damages in Mass Tort Litigation: Addressing the Problems of Fairness, Efficiency and Control, 52 Fordham L.Rev. 37 (1983); Note, In Defense of Punitive Damages, 55 N.Y.U.L.Rev. 303 (1980). The central thesis of much of the scholarly writing in this area is that the problems assertedly caused by awarding punitive damages in the mass tort context are typically more apparent than real. * * *

* * *

The defendants and the United States contend nevertheless that regardless of existing Mississippi law, punitive damages should not be awarded in this context, where there have been thousands of persons injured by asbestos and where thousands of plaintiffs have sued, since the potential ramifications of multiple damage awards on the defendants' financial viability may be severe, with the consequence that future plaintiffs may be unable to recover even compensatory damages. * * *

There is a fundamental inconsistency within this argument, an inconsistency which many other courts have pointed out and have ultimately found to be dispositive. Punitive damages exist in part to punish defendants whose conduct merits punishment. As the defendants repeatedly point out, punitive damages are awarded only in extreme cases. [Citation.] Yet the defendants and the United States argue that in the *most* extreme cases, when a defendant commits an especially pernicious act which injures a myriad of innocent persons, cases which one might imagine to be especially suitable for the imposition of punitive damages, the law should shield the defendant from punitive damages by the sheer magnitude of its wrong.

Mississippi law already provides that the defendants could have introduced to the jury evidence of their asserted dire financial straits, and of the possibility that punitive damage awards might prevent other plaintiffs from recovering even compensatory damages. [Citation.]

They could have attempted to convince the finder of fact that they did not need to be deterred, or that the effect of punitive damage awards would cripple their companies. They could have produced evidence of their contingent liability and then requested that the trial judge specifically instruct the jury that this evidence be taken into account in assessing the amount of punitive damages, if any. If the defendants had done so, the finder of fact could have assessed the merits of their contentions. Thereafter, the trial judge could have reviewed the propriety of the award, in light of the evidence supporting the defendants' contentions, on either a motion for judgment notwithstanding the verdict, Fed.R.Civ.P. 50(b), [citation], or a motion to remit the punitive damages, [citations]. However, the defendants did not elect to follow the path which was available to them under existing law to bring their concerns about insolvency and the lack of need for deterrence to the attention first of the finder of fact and then to the judge.[16]

* * * We conclude that the Mississippi Supreme Court would not deny punitive damages in cases of strict liability or cases of mass tort as a matter of law.

* * *

III. COMPENSABLE INJURIES

* * *

A. *Recovery for Cancer.*

All parties concede that Jackson does not presently have cancer. The defendants argue that if Jackson does get cancer, he will be able to sue for compensatory damages associated with cancer at that time—that is, once the disease manifests itself. Jackson maintains that recovery is appropriate now since the potential development of cancer represents a future injury based on a presently existing cause of action. Relatedly, Jackson also argues that he *must* recover for cancer now or else the claim will be barred by the statute of limitations. Jackson's position is that claim-splitting is disallowed in Mississippi and that the claim for cancer, insofar as it grows out of the same actionable tort which provides his recovery for asbestosis, must be raised now. Jackson reasons that, since the claim for cancer grows out of a single actionable tort, the statute of limitations with respect to cancer begins to run from the time the tort is actionable, that is, from the time asbestosis became manifest.

The defendants assert that claim-splitting is permitted in Mississippi when that would serve the ends of justice and fairness. In any case, the defendants insist, Mississippi would adopt the discovery rule with respect to asbestos-related injuries, with the result that the statute of

16. We fully recognize the difficulties presented to the defendants in having to put before the jury evidence of an enormous volume of litigation similar to this case and of their actual or potential insolvency resulting therefrom. This situation is one in which the trial court should consider the possibility of a separate trial on punitive damages under Fed.R.Civ.P. 42(b) after the issues of liability and compensatory damages have been decided.

limitations for cancer would not begin to run until cancer actually appears. The development of cancer would be a separate tort from the development of asbestosis. As a result, defendants conclude, recovery for cancer is neither permitted nor required at this time.

The debate between the parties pivots on a single question, namely: What is the cause of action on which Jackson seeks recovery? The defendants contend that the existing cause of action is the existence of asbestosis. Jackson's position is that his cause of action is the inhalation of asbestos fibers "and the invasion of his body by those fibers, thus causing * * * physical damage." Gideon v. Johns–Manville Sales Corp., 761 F.2d 1129, 1137 (5th Cir.1985). Although the statute of limitations question is concededly not dispositive of the issue of which injury provides the cause of action, the defendants' position is that if the statute of limitations would not begin to run until Jackson discovers cancer, then he should not be allowed to recover until that time: until cancer appears. Essentially, the defendants' position is that insofar as Jackson *may* bring suit for cancer at some later date, he should be required to wait until that date.

The defendants' argument must be rejected for two separate but related reasons. First, the truth of their crucial premise is not clear under Mississippi law. It is unclear whether Jackson *would* be permitted to sue to recover damages for cancer whenever cancer appears. Second, it is clear that under Mississippi tort law, plaintiffs may recover for probable future consequences.

In Dunaway v. W.H. Hopper & Associates, Inc., 422 So.2d 749 (Miss. 1982), the Mississippi Supreme Court reiterated that when four conditions are met, the plaintiff will not later be permitted to litigate, "on the same cause of action * * * grounds for * * * recovery that were available" in the first action "regardless of whether they were asserted or determined in the prior proceeding." Id. at 751 (citing cases). The four identities which trigger the res judicata bar are: "(1) identity of the subject matter of the action, (2) identity of the cause of action, (3) identity of the parties to the cause of action, and (4) identity of the quality or character of a person against whom the claim is made." Id.; see also Wright v. Mayor and Comm'rs of City of Jackson, 421 So.2d 1219 (Miss.1982). The key issue, of course, involves the second identity: how to characterize the present cause of action. * * * Even though events which develop subsequent to the accrual of the cause of action may affect the quantum of damages to which the plaintiff is entitled, such subsequent developments do not alter the fact that the cause of action accrued once the right to sue became vested. See, e.g., Forman v. Mississippi Publishers Corp., 195 Miss. 90, 14 So.2d 344, 346 (1943).

We do suspect that under some circumstances Mississippi would adopt the discovery rule in the context of a latent disease case so as to protect a plaintiff who, through no fault of his own, discovers only belatedly that he is diseased. [Citation.] It would seem grossly unjust for the statute of limitations to begin to run before *any* disease is discovered. Similarly, the defendants may be correct that a plaintiff who later develops cancer may be able to recover at that time if an earlier jury, dealing with some other manifestation of asbestos exposure, concludes that the plaintiff does not presently have a reasonable probability of developing cancer. But these hypotheticals are not our case. Jackson established that he will probably get cancer. In addition, he has already discovered, and brought suit to recover for, his asbestosis.[21] Under these circumstances, it is clear that under Mississippi law Jackson may recover cancer damages. Further, having recovered cancer damages, he cannot later recover more if and when he develops cancer.

"The general rule is that where it is established that future consequences from an injury to a person will ensue, recovery therefor may be had, but such future consequences must be established in terms of reasonable probabilities." Entex, Inc. v. Rasberry, 355 So.2d 1102, 1104 (Miss.1978). Defendants respond that cancer does not develop *from* asbestosis, that it can never be a future consequence *of* asbestosis. Cancer is presumably a separate injury, and recovery must therefore await manifestation. This assertion is medically sound, but legally awry. In a sense, the injury in this case is the inhalation of asbestos fibers. It was not an *actionable* injury, however, meaning it was not legally cognizable, until at least one evil *effect* of the inhalation became manifest. There was no cause of action at all, in other words, until the asbestosis appeared. In this case, the effects of inhaling asbestos manifested themselves initially as asbestosis. In a different plaintiff, they may have manifested themselves as something as innocuous as asbestos callouses or as lethal as mesothelioma. But in any event, once the injury becomes actionable—once *some* effect appears—then the plaintiff is permitted to recover for all probable future manifestations as well.[22]

In General Motors Acceptance Corp. v. Layton, 353 So.2d 749 (Miss. 1977), a plaintiff involved in an automobile accident sued to recover compensatory damages for injuries sustained in the collision. At the

21. * * *

We also note that arguably, the statute of limitations *does* begin to run for all injuries once some disease is manifest. See, e.g., Martin v. Johns-Manville Corp., 322 Pa.Super. 348, 469 A.2d 655 (1983) (where "present injury" was asbestosis, plaintiff was also *required* to recover for risk of cancer), *vacated on other grounds,* 494 A.2d 1088 (Pa.1985); cf. Bendix Corp. v. Stagg, 486 A.2d 1150, 1152–53 (Del.1984). This is an issue which we need not decide, however. For present purposes, the fact that recovery for probable future injuries is *permissible* is sufficient to sustain this award.

22. Defendants' reference to language in Schweitzer v. Consolidated Rail Corp., (Conrail), 758 F.2d 936 (3d Cir.), cert. denied, 474 U.S. 864, 106 S.Ct. 183, 88 L.Ed. 2d 152 (1985), is inapt. There, the Third Circuit explained that although "the possible existence of subclinical asbestos-related injury may be of interest to a histologist * * *[,] subclinical injury resulting from exposure to asbestos is insufficient to constitute the actual loss or damage * * * required to sustain a cause of action under generally applicable principles of tort law." 758 F.2d at 942. We tend to agree. Nevertheless, *Schweitzer* is obviously not this case. Here we have Jackson, whose injuries are far from being merely subclinical.

time of trial, the plaintiff was suffering only from a bruised knee. An expert witness testified that persons with knee injuries, such as the plaintiff, " 'are more likely to develop arthritis in joints. * * *' " Id. at 753. The expert witness' testimony with respect to the increased likelihood of the plaintiff's developing arthritis in the bruised knee was sufficient to permit the plaintiff to recover compensatory damages for the reasonable probability of developing arthritis. It was not that the arthritis would develop *from* the bruise; it was rather that it would result from an injury which had manifested itself, at the time of trial, by a bruised knee. *Layton* is indistinguishable as a matter of tort law from this case. Jackson may recover for the medical probability of developing cancer.

Of course, a plaintiff who sues with nothing more than hand callouses may have a significantly lower likelihood of developing cancer than does a plaintiff who exhibits asbestosis. That would be a question for the jury, to be decided by listening to and evaluating conflicting medical testimony. This plaintiff, however, has asbestosis; and evidence adduced at trial indicates that he has a greater than fifty percent chance of getting cancer.[24] Recovery for that possibility is permissible under Mississippi law.

B. *Fear.*

Jackson also maintains that the cancer evidence introduced at trial was relevant insofar as it elucidates the basis of the mental distress he has suffered due to the knowledge that he will probably get cancer.[25] The defendants repeat their earlier argument: that "since there is no evidence that cancer 'develops from' asbestosis there can be no recovery for fear of an injury which has not occurred, and does not 'develop from' *any of Jackson's presently existing injuries.*" JM's brief at 25 (emphasis in original). But the crux of JM's argument, once again, is that these compensatory damages should not be awarded because so many people have been injured * * *.

* * *

Jackson's fear is plainly a present injury. It is a fear which he experiences every day and every night. It is fear which is exacerbated each time he learns that another victim of asbestos has died of lung cancer. It is fear which, regardless of whether Jackson actually gets

24. There can be little doubt that the jury had ample evidence upon which it could have based its conclusion that Jackson will probably get cancer. According to Dr. James Merchant, "it's been shown conclusively that [asbestos] is a cause of cancer in human beings." 52 Record at 1362. Furthermore, according to Dr. Merchant, "between 40 and 60 percent of those with asbestosis who have had previous heavy exposure die from bronchogenic carcinoma [lung cancer]." 52 Record at 1362. (According to Dr. Lewinsohn, the figure is 50 to 60 percent. Id.) Dr. Elliot McCaughey testified too that Jackson has a greater than 50 percent likelihood of developing an asbestos related cancer. * * *

25. There was considerable testimony before the jury to the effect that Jackson will probably develop cancer; it is in that context that we discuss damages for mental anguish. We do not consider whether a plaintiff who cannot show that he will probably develop cancer may recover for mental distress.

cancer, will haunt him for the rest of his life. Jackson's claim is not merely that he *might* get cancer, or that there is a remote possibility that he will. Jackson has established that there is a greater than fifty percent chance that he *will* get cancer. Who can gainsay that this knowledge causes him anguish, or that this anguish is reasonable? Certainly not this court and, in our view, not the Mississippi Supreme Court.

Under Mississippi law, damage awards for mental distress may be rendered when either of two conditions is satisfied: when the plaintiff's mental suffering is accompanied by a physical injury, or when the plaintiff establishes the defendant's misconduct to have been wilful, gross, or wanton. * * * We think it beyond cavil that in such a case as is before us, where the plaintiff manifests a present injury and has also succeeded in demonstrating gross misconduct, compensatory damages for mental distress are recoverable.

* * *

* * * [R]ecent commentators have noted, "[c]ourts having considered cancerphobia ["the present anxiety over developing cancer in the future"] almost uniformly have allowed it. The few courts not allowing recovery have done so on the basis of a lack of physical injury, the unreasonableness of the fear under specific facts, or because the fear was claimed by a wife due to the observation of the injuries to her husband. Notably, this minority has not based its decision on the noncompensability of cancerphobia." Gale & Goyer, Recovery for Cancerphobia and Increased Risk of Cancer, 15 Cumberland L.Rev. 723, 730–31 (1985). * * *

IV. CONCLUSION.

* * *

* * * We therefore conclude that under Mississippi law, Jackson is entitled to punitive damages, and to compensatory damages for the reasonable probability of getting cancer and for the present fear that he will get cancer in the future. Accordingly, the judgment of the district court is affirmed.

CLARK, CHIEF JUDGE, with whom GEE, GARZA, POLITZ, and JOLLY, CIRCUIT JUDGES, join, dissenting:

* * *

* * * [A] national problem has been adjudicated as though it were a state problem after the concerned state court wisely refused to accept our certification of the issues to it.

Sadly the majority chose to certify these issues to that court rather than to the Supreme Court of the United States. The United States Supreme Court could have given us proper responses. More's the pity that the majority reads nothing into the Mississippi Supreme Court's refusal. We who dissent do not believe that the Mississippi Supreme Court simply arbitrarily declined to answer the questions posed. * * *

We believe that the Mississippi Supreme Court thought, as we do, that if some judicial forum must respond to Jackson's plea, there is only one right court to do so—the Supreme Court of the United States. * * *

Because the majority's wrong response comes from the wrong court, we respectfully dissent.

NOTES

1. Why do you suppose the United States filed an amicus brief in a tort law case between private parties?

2. Despite widespread agreement on the desirability of a legislative solution to asbestos litigation, Congress has not even come close to enacting such a statute, although a number of bills have been introduced. What social, economic, and political factors might be involved?

STATUTES OF LIMITATIONS

1. The policies traditionally cited in support of statutes of limitations include: 1) providing notice to potential defendants of the existence of a claim, thereby permitting them to marshall evidence; 2) avoiding the litigation of stale claims where much of the evidence has deteriorated or disappeared; 3) providing repose to potential defendants, after a certain period of time, to permit them to order their affairs free from worry over the consequences of prior actions; and 4) providing an imperfect filter for screening out inconsequential or tenuous claims. "There comes a time when [the defendant] ought to be secure in his reasonable expectation that the slate has been wiped clean of ancient obligations, and he ought not to be called on to resist a claim when 'evidence has been lost, memories have faded, and witnesses have disappeared.' " Developments in the Law—Statutes of Limitations, 63 Harv.L.Rev. 1177, 1185 (1950). Another objective sometimes expressed is to prevent indolent or slothful plaintiffs from "sleeping on their rights."

2. **Discovery Rule.** Normally a tort claim accrues when the plaintiff is injured. The fact of traumatic injury and the circumstances under which it occurs are often sufficient to put the plaintiff on notice of his claim. However, when the injury is a disease, especially a slowly progressing one, years may pass before the fact of injury is known. Most courts (and, increasingly, legislatures) have responded by adopting some form of "discovery rule" for accrual of the cause of action—starting the limitations clock ticking when the plaintiff becomes aware, or in the exercise of reasonable diligence should become aware, of information about his claim. Note, Toward a Time-of-Discovery Rule for the Statute of Limitations in Latent Injury Cases in New York State, 13 Fordham U.L.J. 113, 118–20 (1985) (identifying 47 jurisdictions with some form of a discovery rule).

A number of states have enacted statutes applying more lenient discovery rules to asbestos cases, or latent disease cases generally, than are applied to other types of products liability actions. New York is one example. See Prod. Liab.Rep. (CCH) ¶ 93,301 (3-year discovery rule).

There are three separate forms of knowledge that may be relevant to determining when the plaintiff's claim accrues under the discovery rule: 1) knowledge of the injury (or impairment); 2) knowledge that the injury was caused by a particular substance, and by a particular party; and 3) knowledge that the law may provide a remedy for the injury. There is considerable variation among jurisdictions as to just what type of knowledge will start the statute running. Compare Perlov v. G.D. Searle & Co., 621 F.Supp. 1146 (D.Md. 1985) (statute begins to run when plaintiffs discover they have a cause of action), and Anthony v. Abbott Laboratories, 490 A.2d 43 (R.I.1985) (same) with Jolly v. Eli Lilly & Co., 44 Cal.3d 1103, 245 Cal.Rptr. 658, 662, 751 P.2d 923 (1988) (statute begins to run "when the plaintiff suspects or should suspect that her injury was caused by wrongdoing, that someone has done something wrong to her"). The question of when the plaintiff in the exercise of reasonable diligence should have made the requisite discovery is often hotly contested in the litigation of toxic substance cases. See, e.g., Cowgill v. Raymark Industries, Inc., 832 F.2d 798, 801 (3d Cir.1987) (seven-day jury trial required to resolve issue of whether decedent should have known of pleural thickening more than two years before suit was filed).

3. Interjurisdictional variations in statutes of limitations are substantial, which encourages forum shopping. Because of restrictive statutes of limitations, many asbestos victims left their home states and brought suit in jurisdictions with more lenient statutes, such as Ohio, Texas and Mississippi. See, e.g., Shewbrooks v. A.C. & S., Inc., 529 So.2d 557 (Miss.1988) (5–4) (case not dismissed as forum non conveniens since action barred elsewhere by statutes of limitations).

If the case is filed in a distant federal court, which transfers it back to the plaintiff's home state on forum non conveniens grounds, should the transferee court apply its own statute of limitations and bar the claim? Compare Ferens v. Deere & Co., 862 F.2d 31 (3d Cir.1988) (farm machinery: yes), with Goad v. Celotex Corp., 831 F.2d 508 (4th Cir.1987), cert. denied, ___ U.S. ___, 108 S.Ct. 2871, 101 L.Ed.2d 906 (1988) (asbestos: no).

4. In light of the widespread adoption of some form of the discovery rule, the multi-decade latency period of many toxic substance diseases, the improvement (rather than deterioration) of evidence on causation and damages over time, and the perverse incentives created by statutes of limitations for premature filing of claims and forum shopping, should statutes of limitations simply be abolished in toxic substance cases? Recall that Mr. Jackson, whose asbestosis was diagnosed in 1978, had only a 15% disability and was still working at that time; predicting the future course of his disease was a difficult if not impossible task. Would it have been preferable to delay the resolution of his claim until his long-term health status could be diagnosed with reasonable accuracy? Cf. Doe v. Johns-Manville Corp., 324 Pa.Super. 469, 471 A.2d 1252 (1984) (plaintiff with pleural thickening, but no disability, brought suit for a declaratory judgment that the limitations statute would not begin to run until some disability developed). See Green, The Paradox of Statutes of Limitations in Toxic Substances Litigation, 76 Calif.L.Rev. 965 (1988) (advocating abolition of limitations statutes in toxic substance cases to promote more accurate fact finding, efficiency, and fairness).

A number of courts have addressed the premature filing problem through docket control. Upon stipulation of the parties, a court may place an immature claim on the inactive docket, serving to toll the statute of limitations and delay the litigation until the claim matures. Or the parties may arrive at the same end by a private agreement—the plaintiff promising to delay prosecution of the claim, and the defendant(s) promising not to invoke the statute of limitations when the claim is refiled.

How might these procedures serve the interests of both plaintiffs and defendants?

5. **Wrongful Death.** In the event of death, should the statute run from the date the plaintiff in the wrongful death action discovers or should have discovered the claim, or from the date of death? The date of death may be required by statute. See Pastierik v. Duquesne Light Co., 514 Pa. 517, 526 A.2d 323 (1987) (5–2), rev'g 491 A.2d 841 (Pa.Super.1985). Some statutes specifically provide to the contrary. E.g., *California*—Prod.Liab.Rep. (CCH) ¶ 90,570 (one year from discovery by plaintiff that death was caused by exposure to asbestos); *D.C.*—id. at ¶ 90,942 (same).

6. **Statutes of Repose.** In addition to statutes of limitations, a number of jurisdictions have enacted statutes of repose, which begin to run at the time a product is first manufactured or sold. Typically such statutes have 8–12 year limits, after which an injured party is barred from suing, confronts an enhanced evidentiary burden, or can recover only upon proof of fault. See Martin, A Statute of Repose for Product Liability Claims, 50 Fordham L.Rev. 745 (1982). Application of statutes of repose to insidious diseases with lengthy latency periods often causes harsh results. In Wilder v. Amatex Corp., 314 N.C. 550, 336 S.E.2d 66 (1985), noted, 64 N.Car.L.Rev. 416 (1986), the court strained mightily to interpret a ten year statute of repose as inapplicable to latent disease claims. Several state repose provisions exclude asbestos cases, or toxic substance cases. E.g., *Connecticut,* Prod.Liab.Rep. (CCH) ¶ 90,741 (asbestos); *Kansas,* id. at ¶ 91,714 (harm caused by "prolonged exposure to a defective product").

7. See generally Epstein, The Temporal Dimension in Tort Law, 53 U.Chi. L.Rev. 1175 (1986); Green, The Paradox of Statutes of Limitations in Toxic Substances Litigation, 76 Calif.L.Rev. 965 (1988); Shaw, Cihon & Myers, The Discovery Rule: Fairness in Toxic Tort Statutes of Limitations, 33 Clev.St.L. Rev. 491 (1984); McGovern, The Status of Statutes of Limitations and Statutes of Repose in Product Liability Actions: Present and Future, 16 Forum 416 (1981); Notes, 13 Fordham U.L.J. 113 (1985); 96 Harv.L.Rev. 1683 (1983); 43 U.Pitt.L.Rev. 501 (1982); 68 Va.L.Rev. 615 (1982).

RES JUDICATA

1. The scope of a "cause of action" or "claim" for res judicata purposes has never been precisely defined. Failing to include a theory of liability or relief in an action may cause such claims to be barred by (or "merged into") the judgment in the first action. See F. James & G. Hazard, Civil Procedure 597–606 (3d ed. 1985). The trend is toward expanding the conception of a claim to include all rights arising out of the transaction or transactions forming the basis for the claim. See Rest.(2d) Judgments § 24 & comment a (1982).

This transactional view of a cause of action has led a few courts, notably the Fifth Circuit (which has a large asbestos docket), to hold that an asbestos victim has but one cause of action, regardless of the number or chronology of diseases that develop from the exposure. Gideon v. Johns–Manville Sales Corp., 761 F.2d 1129, 1136 (5th Cir.1985) ("a plaintiff may not split this cause of action by seeking damages for some of his injuries in one suit and for later developing injuries in another"). Compare the *Jackson* opinions, supra.

2. When plaintiff fails to bring suit for an initial disease, and later develops a second disease for which he does, determining the scope of his "cause of action" becomes crucial for purposes of the statute of limitations. Since there never was any suit (or judgment) for the first injury, res judicata is not involved. If both injuries constitute a single "cause of action", however, the statute of limitations would have begun to run for both injuries from his discovery of the first one. Most courts in this context have held that the second injury constitutes a distinct cause of action. E.g., Smith v. Bethlehem Steel Corp., 303 Md. 213, 492 A.2d 1286 (1985); Wilson v. Johns-Manville Sales Corp., 684 F.2d 111 (D.C.Cir.1982); Peterson v. Instapak Corp., 690 F.Supp. 697 (N.D. Ill.1988). Contra Joyce v. A.C. & S., Inc., 785 F.2d 1200, 1203–05 (4th Cir.1986).

Might "cause of action" be defined differently depending on whether res judicata or the statute of limitations is in question? See generally Cook, Substance and Procedure in the Conflict of Laws, 42 Yale L.J. 333, 337 (1933) (treating words in different contexts as identical "has all the tenacity of original sin").

3. As the *Jackson III* court noted, Mississippi law was unclear on whether plaintiff could reserve his future cancer claim for another day. Do you see the quandry for plaintiffs like Mr. Jackson? Would collateral estoppel be available to a plaintiff in a second (cancer) action based on favorable findings in the first (asbestosis)? Cf. Carbonaro v. Johns-Manville Corp., 526 F.Supp. 260 (E.D.Pa. 1981), aff'd without opinion, 688 F.2d 819 (3d Cir.1982).

DAMAGES

1. **Future Disease.**

A. A logical corollary of holding that a toxic substance victim has but one cause of action arising from his exposure is that he may seek damages for unmatured injury, as permitted in *Jackson III.* Most courts have required that plaintiff demonstrate that the future disease is more likely than not (has a greater than a 50% probability) to occur. See, e.g., Adams v. Johns-Manville Sales Corp., 783 F.2d 589 (5th Cir.1986); Herber v. Johns-Manville Corp., 785 F.2d 79 (3d Cir.1986); Lohrmann v. Pittsburgh Corning Corp., 782 F.2d 1156 (4th Cir.1986); Sorenson v. Raymark Industries, Inc., 51 Wash.App. 954, 756 P.2d 740 (1988).

In each of the previously cited cases, plaintiff failed to recover for the risk of future injury because he could not establish the requisite probability. But see Valori v. Johns-Manville Sales Corp. (D.N.J. Dec. 11, 1985) Asbestos Lit.Rep. (Andrews) 11,375 (permitting plaintiff's claim for future lung cancer based on evidence that the likelihood of death due to lung cancer was 43%). See generally Gale & Goyer, Recovery for Cancerphobia and Increased Risk of Cancer, 15 Cum.L.Rev. 723 (1985); Robinson, Probabilistic Causation and Compensation for Tortious Risk, 14 J.Legal Stud. 779 (1985); Notes, 76 Ky.L.J. 459 (1987–88); 33 Vill.L.Rev. 437 (1988).

B. If a transactional scope of the cause of action is coupled with a requirement that plaintiff prove a greater than 50% likelihood of future disease, as did the court in *Jackson III*, there is a danger that a substantial number of victims will be overcompensated (plaintiffs who recover for future cancer, but do not develop it) and a substantial number who will be undercompensated (plaintiffs who cannot establish the probability of future disease but who do develop it). Is the *Jackson I* approach, uncoupling recovery for existing harm from recovery for subsequent possible diseases, preferable? Which approach is likely to consume more judicial resources? See Eagle–Picher Industries, Inc. v. Cox, 481 So.2d 517 (Fla.Dist.Ct.App.1985).

C. If epidemiological data indicates that a class of victims suffering from disease A have a 55% chance of developing disease B, should the defendant be required to pay each plaintiff the full measure of damages for disease B? See Kaye, The Limits of the Preponderance of the Evidence Standard: Justifiably Naked Statistical Evidence and Multiple Causation, 1982 Am.B.Found. Research J. 487, 502.

2. **Emotional Distress.** Most recent decisions have allowed cancerphobia claims to be submitted to the jury if the plaintiff has already suffered asbestosis or other injury. E.g., Hagerty v. L & L Marine Services, Inc., 788 F.2d 315, modified, 797 F.2d 256 (5th Cir.1986) (Jones Act); Gideon v. Johns–Manville Sales Corp., 761 F.2d 1129, 1138 (5th Cir.1985) (Texas law); Wetherill v. University of Chicago, 565 F.Supp. 1553 (N.D.Ill.1983). Compare In re Moorenovich, 634 F.Supp. 634 (D.Me.1986) (recovery for cancerphobia recoverable without proof that plaintiff had suffered any physical harm) with Berardi v. Johns–Manville Corp., 334 Pa.Super. 36, 482 A.2d 1067 (1984) (asbestos victim's wife, who had not yet suffered physical harm, could not recover for fear of contracting asbestos-related disease from exposure to husband's asbestos-covered clothes).

Should a spouse or child be permitted to recover damages for emotional distress from observing a spouse or parent die from cancer caused by a toxic agent? See Wisniewski v. Johns–Manville Corp., 812 F.2d 81 (3d Cir.1987); Ochoa v. Superior Court, 39 Cal.3d 159, 216 Cal.Rptr. 661, 703 P.2d 1 (1985); cf. Woodill v. Parke Davis & Co., 58 Ill.App.3d 349, 15 Ill.Dec. 900, 904–05, 374 N.E.2d 683, 687–88 (1978), aff'd, 79 Ill.2d 26, 37 Ill.Dec. 304, 402 N.E.2d 194 (1980) (denying parents recovery for emotional distress over injury to child in utero).

See generally Edwards & Ringleb, Exposure to Hazardous Substances and the Mental Distress Tort: Trends, Applications, and a Proposed Reform, 11 Colum.J.Envtl.L. 119 (1986); Bohrer, Fear and Trembling in the Twentieth Century: Technological Risk, Uncertainty and Emotional Distress, 1984 Wis.L. Rev. 83; Comment, 14 Pac.L.J. 1215 (1983) (cancerphobia in DES daughters).

3. **Medical Monitoring Expenses.** Plaintiffs exposed to a toxic agent putting them at risk of developing a latent disease have sought recovery for medical expenses incurred in monitoring their condition to facilitate early diagnosis and treatment. See Ayers v. Township of Jackson, 106 N.J. 557, 525 A.2d 287 (1987); Herber v. Johns–Manville Corp., 785 F.2d 79 (3d Cir.1986); Hagerty v. L & L Marine Services, Inc., 788 F.2d 315, modified, 797 F.2d 256 (5th Cir.1986) (Jones Act).

4. **Abatement Costs.** Insulation containing asbestos has been installed in thousands of school buildings, other public facilities, and private residences. In 1980, Congress enacted the Asbestos School Hazard Detection and Control Act, 20 U.S.C.A. §§ 3601–11 (1982), mandating testing for the presence of asbestos in schools. Numerous lawsuits have been brought by school districts and other building owners against asbestos producers to recover damages for the costs of removing or enclosing friable asbestos insulation.

At least one court has denied recovery in tort on the ground that the plaintiff was seeking recovery for economic loss recoverable only in contract. Catasauqua Area School District v. Eagle–Picher Industries, Inc., 1988 WL

102689 (E.D.Pa. Sept. 28, 1988). Most courts have held otherwise. E.g., City of Greenville v. W.R. Grace & Co., 827 F.2d 975 (4th Cir.1987) (upholding award of compensatory damages, remitted to $4.8 million, and $2 million punitive damages); Board of Education of City of Chicago v. A. C. & S., Inc., 171 Ill.App. 3d 737, 121 Ill.Dec. 643, 525 N.E.2d 950 (1988) (citing cases). For a discussion of a variety of commonlaw theories potentially available to an abatement plaintiff, see U.S. Attorney General, Asbestos Liability Report to the Congress, 97th Cong., 1st Sess. 86–233 (Comm.Print 1981). See also Cross, Asbestos in Schools: A Remonstrance Against Panic, 11 Colum.J.Envtl.L. 73 (1986); Lang, Danger in the Classroom: Asbestos in the Public Schools, 10 Colum.J.Envtl.L. 111 (1985); Notes, 1987 B.Y.U.L.Rev. 297; 54 U.Chi.L.Rev. 277 (1987).

5. **Punitive Damages.** Who in the *Jackson* trilogy has the better argument on punitive damages?

Consider the following report, by Dr. Kenneth Smith, of the dust conditions at a Johns–Manville mining and milling facility in 1949, recommending against informing workers that they had contracted asbestosis:

> It must be remembered that although these men have the x-ray evidence of asbestosis, they are working today and definitely are not disabled from asbestosis. They have not been told of this diagnosis for it is felt that as long as the man feels well, is happy at home and at work, and his physical condition remains good, nothing should be said. When he becomes disabled and sick, then the diagnosis should be made and the claim submitted *by the Company.* The fibrosis of this disease is irreversible and permanent so that eventually compensation will be paid to each of these men. But as long as the man is not disabled it is felt that he should not be told of his condition so that he can live and work in peace and the Company can benefit by his many years of experience. Should the man be told of his condition today there is a very definite possibility that he would become mentally and physically ill, simply through the knowledge that he has asbestosis.

See Motley, The Lid Comes Off, 16 Trial 21, 24 (April 1980).

Contrast the testimony of John McKinney, former Chairman of the Board and CEO of Johns–Manville, before the Senate Committee on Labor and Human Resources in August, 1980:

> Moreover, in those cases where plaintiffs have sought punitive damages as a part of their third-party action, there is not a single instance where juries or trial judges have awarded such damages. I can think of no greater demonstration that the cover-up charge is a complete fabrication.

Should punitive damages claims have been allowed to destroy Johns–Manville? Did they?

On the constitutionality of punitive damages, see infra p. 623 n. 7.

WORKERS' COMPENSATION

1. One might think that asbestos workers suffering diseases from toxic substances in the workplace could recover compensation for their illnesses through workers' compensation. Yet the workers' compensation system has poorly served persons who have suffered occupational diseases. Estimates are

that only 5–15% of those who suffer from workplace diseases ever receive workers' compensation, although recent reforms have probably increased that number. The explanations are various but begin with the historical conception of workers' compensation as a system designed to assist employees suffering traumatic injury. In that regard, the difficulties that workers' compensation has had in accommodating occupational disease parallel, in many ways, the problems the tort system has encountered in addressing toxic substances. Thus, statutes of limitations for compensation claims often begin running on termination of employment or cessation of exposure. The only causation requirement in worker's compensation is to demonstrate that the injury arose out of employment, but that has been an impossible burden for many workers, such as the plaintiff in *Miller v. National Cabinet,* in section 2 above. Workers' compensation statutes also typically require that the workers' injury occur "by accident," a term that has been read to require a sudden calamitous event. Finally, employers contest occupational disease claims much more frequently than traumatic injury claims, and recovery of compensation is accordingly much slower (almost a year, as opposed to 6 weeks for injury claims).

2. One ironic explanation for the infrequent recourse to workers' compensation by injured toxic substance workers is the adverse impact such a proceeding may have on a subsequent products liability case. Collateral estoppel has been invoked against some workers in their products liability suits based upon adverse findings on their workers' compensation claims. E.g., McKee v. Johns–Manville Corp., 94 Misc.2d 327, 329–30, 404 N.Y.S. 814, 816 (1978), modified sub nom. Steinhardt v. Johns–Manville Corp., 78 A.D.2d 577, 432 N.Y.S.2d 422 (1980), aff'd, 54 N.Y.2d 1008, 446 N.Y.S.2d 244, 430 N.E.2d 1297, amended, 55 N.Y.2d 802, 447 N.Y.S.2d 437, 432 N.E.2d 139 (1981), appeal dismissed and cert. denied, 456 U.S. 967, 102 S.Ct. 2226, 72 L.Ed.2d 840 (1982). Other products liability plaintiffs have had such claims dismissed, on statutes of limitations grounds, because a prior workers' compensation claim established a date by which they clearly knew of their condition and its cause. See Chandler v. Johns–Manville Corp., 352 Pa.Super. 326, 507 A.2d 1253 (1986).

3. Because of the uncertainties of the long-term effects from asbestos exposure, at least one court has held that its state's workers' compensation appeals board could retain jurisdiction in such cases, beyond the five year statute of limitations for compensation claims, to permit future reevaluation of the extent of disability. General Foundry Service v. Workers' Compensation Appeals Board, 42 Cal.3d 331, 228 Cal.Rptr. 243, 721 P.2d 124 (1986).

Should trial courts in toxic substance products liability cases retain jurisdiction to award additional damages for future disease?

4. **Intentional Exposure to Toxic Substances.** Recovery for intentional torts inflicted by employers on employees may not be barred by the exclusive remedy rule since workers' compensation statutes generally only cover injuries that occur "by accident." A number of courts that have recognized an intentional tort exception to the exclusivity of workers' compensation have narrowly circumscribed the exception, requiring that the employer actually intend to injure the employee. See, e.g., Wilson v. Asten–Hill Mfg. Co., 791 F.2d 30 (3d Cir.1986) (Pennsylvania law); Austin v. Johns–Manville Sales Corp., 508 F.Supp. 313, 316 (D.Me.1981) (citing cases). But see Neal v. Carey Canadian Mines, Ltd., 548 F.Supp. 357 (E.D.Pa.1982) (employer's failure to warn employee that aggravation of pre-existing asbestotic condition was substantially certain to occur constituted sufficient intent), aff'd on other grounds, 760 F.2d 481 (3d Cir.1985).

The Supreme Courts of California and New Jersey have both addressed claims that plaintiffs' employers (and employer physicians) intentionally exposed them to asbestos, deliberately concealed from them the risks of such exposure, and fraudulently concealed from them the results of medical examinations which showed that they had contracted asbestos disease. Both courts rejected the claims of intentional exposure to asbestos as insufficient, since employers frequently (and of necessity) expose workers to hazardous machinery and other workplace hazards. However, both courts considered the medical information concealment claim as fundamentally different:

> Plaintiffs have, however, pleaded a valid cause of action for aggravation of their initial occupational diseases under the second count of their complaints. Count two alleges that in order to prevent employees from leaving the workforce, defendants fraudulently concealed from plaintiffs the fact that they were suffering from asbestos-related diseases, thereby delaying their treatment and aggravating their existing illnesses. As noted earlier, du Pont's medical staff provides company employees with physical examinations as part of its package of medical services. Plaintiffs contend that although plaintiffs' physical examinations revealed changes in chest x-rays indicating asbestos-related injuries, du Pont's doctors did not inform plaintiffs of their sicknesses, but instead told them that their health was fine and sent them back to work under the same hazardous conditions that had caused the initial injuries.
>
> These allegations go well beyond failing to warn of potentially-dangerous conditions or intentionally exposing workers to the risks of disease. There is a difference between, on the one hand, tolerating in the workplace conditions that will result in a certain number of injuries or illnesses, and, on the other, actively misleading the employees who have already fallen victim to those risks of the workplace. An employer's fraudulent concealment of diseases already developed is not one of the risks an employee should have to assume. Such intentionally-deceitful action goes beyond the bargain struck by the Compensation Act. But for defendants' corporate strategy of concealing diseases discovered in company physical examinations, plaintiffs would have minimized the dangers to their health. Instead, plaintiffs were deceived—or so they charge—by corporate doctors who held themselves out as acting in plaintiffs' best interests. The legislature, in passing the Compensation Act, could not have intended to insulate such conduct from tort liability. We therefore conclude that plaintiffs' allegations that defendants fraudulently concealed knowledge of already-contracted diseases are sufficient to state a cause of action for aggravation of plaintiffs' illnesses, as distinct from any claim for the existence of the initial disease, which is cognizable only under the Compensation Act.

Millison v. E.I. du Pont de Nemours & Co., 101 N.J. 161, 501 A.2d 505, 516 (1985). Accord Johns–Manville Products Corp. v. Contra Costa Superior Court, 27 Cal.3d 465, 165 Cal.Rptr. 858, 612 P.2d 948 (1980). The California legislature codified the rule. West's Ann.Calif.Lab.Code § 3602(b) (Supp.1986).

5. For a discussion of the inadequacy of workers' compensation statutes in dealing with occupational disease, see Packer, United States Department of Labor, An Interim Report to Congress on Occupational Diseases 54–78 (June 1980); Current Issues in Workers' Compensation 287–345 (J. Chelius ed. 1986); Kutchins, The Most Exclusive Remedy Is No Remedy at All: Workers' Compen-

sation Coverage for Occupational Diseases, 32 Lab. L.J. 212 (1981); Gosney, Whatever Happened to Brown Lung? Compensation for Difficult to Diagnose Occupational Diseases, 3 Indus.Rel.L.J. 102 (1979). See generally Larson, Occupational Diseases Under Workmen's Compensation Laws, 9 U.Rich.L.Rev. 87 (1974); Dewees, Economic Incentives for Controlling Industrial Disease: The Asbestos Case, 15 J.Leg.Studies 289 (1986); Viscusi, Structuring an Effective Occupational Disease Policy: Victim Compensation and Risk Regulation, 2 Yale J.Reg. 53 (1984); Note, Compensating Victims of Occupational Disease, 93 Harv.L.Rev. 916 (1980); Special Project, An Analysis of the Legal, Social, and Political Issues Raised by Asbestos Litigation, 36 Vand.L.Rev. 573, 730–56 (1983).

SECTION 4. INTERGENERATIONAL HARM

Chemical compounds and other toxic substances have been increasingly discovered to cause chromosomal alteration which may cause genetic defects in subsequent generations. The effects of such defects may spread from generation to generation. If the grandchild—or great grandchild—of a person exposed to some toxin is born with a short finger as a result, or suffers a handicap much more severe, should the descendant have a tort action against the manufacturer? If so, should it lie in negligence or strict liability? If not, why not?

LOERCH v. ABBOTT LABORATORIES

Hennepin County District Court, Minnesota, 1988.
No. 79–8720, appeal pending, Minnesota Court of Appeals.

[SCHIEFELBEIN, J.]

* * *

The issue bearing resolution by this Court is whether a legal duty will be extended to a grandchild (third generation) who was not conceived at the time of the alleged tort and whose biological mother was not a viable fetus at the time of the alleged tort.

The facts central to resolution of this issue are that in 1948 Mrs. Patricia Fischer (first generation—grandmother) had just been married. She desired a pregnancy. Although she had no history of miscarriages, she had experienced some irregularity of her menstrual cycle. She was treated by the Mayo Clinic and specifically a Dr. Wilson who prescribed a diethylstilbestrol (DES) compound marketed under the name of "Stilrone." Linda Fischer (second generation—mother) was a fetus of approximately ten weeks when she was first exposed to DES. Patricia Fischer continued to take Stilrone throughout her pregnancy with Linda.

Linda Fischer was born on July 23, 1949. In 1971, Linda Fischer was informed that her mother had ingested DES during her pregnancy with Linda. In 1972, Linda became a participant in a DES research project at the Mayo Clinic. In April of 1973, Linda married Dennis

Loerch. In 1976, Linda became pregnant for the first time. She suffered a missed abortion. In 1977, she became pregnant with Peter (third generation—son). Linda carried her pregnancy for 29 weeks. Peter was born approximately two months prematurely on August 18, 1977. As a result of his prematurity, Peter developed several medical problems. He experienced an intracranial bleed that has resulted in his suffering from cerebral palsy. Peter is a spastic quadriplegic. Plaintiffs (Linda Loerch, Dennis Loerch and Peter Loerch, an infant, by and through his natural parent, Linda Loerch) seek recovery in this action on behalf of Peter Loerch, alleging that Peter's condition was caused by Patricia Fischer's ingestion of DES.

In support of its motion for summary judgment, defendant contends that Minnesota does not recognize a cause of action for a preconception, third generation tort [1]; therefore, plaintiffs' claim for damages must be dismissed as a matter of law.

Defendant asserts that, as a threshold issue, this Court must determine the extent of the concept of duty as articulated by Minnesota law. It is a fundamental proposition that determination of whether liability exists depends on whether the particular circumstances give rise to a legal duty to the person injured. Graham v. Abe Mathews Engineering, 358 N.W.2d 131 (Minn.Ct.App.1984).

A discussion of the concept of duty inevitably beckons a discussion of the landmark decision in Palsgraf v. Long Island R. Co., 248 N.Y. 339, 162 N.E. 99 (1928). Duty, as defined therein, is a function of the foreseeability of injury to the plaintiff. Chief Justice Cardozo stated:

> The risk reasonably to be perceived defines the duty to be obeyed, and risk imparts relation; it is risk to another or to others within the range of apprehension.

Palsgraf, 248 N.Y. at 344, 162 N.E. at 100.

In writing for the majority, Chief Justice Cardozo wrote that the defendant could owe no duty to the plaintiff because the alleged wrong had no relation to her. The majority was of the opinion that the conduct was not a wrong in relation to this particular plaintiff. It was the opinion of the Court that Mrs. Palsgraf was simply too far away; too remote of an individual, for the defendant to have owed any duty.

In his forceful dissent, Justice Andrews rejected Cardozo's view of recovery predicated on duty. Instead, Justice Andrews articulated the standard of "proximate cause." Justice Andrews explained:

> What we do mean by the word "proximate" is, that because of convenience, of public policy, of a rough sense of justice, the law arbitrarily declines to trace a series of events beyond a certain point. This is not logic. It is practical politics. Take our rule as to fires. Sparks from my burning haystack set on

1. The term "preconception tort" refers to a tort which injures the child's mother prior to conception, and which results in a consequential injury to the child. See, Albala v. City of New York, 54 N.Y.2d 269, 429 N.E.2d 786, 445 N.Y.S.2d 108 (1981).

> fire my house and my neighbor's. I may recover from a negligent railroad. He may not. Yet the wrongful act as directly harmed the one as the other. We may regret that the line was drawn just where it was, but drawn somewhere it had to be.

162 N.E. at 105.

It is defendant's position, in the instant case, that under either of the *Palsgraf* analyses, there is no liability as to Peter Loerch. It is their position that under a Cardozo analysis, defendant owed no duty to Peter Loerch. Peter Loerch, a third generation removed from the original tortious act, is simply too remote in time to be justifiably within the zone of danger. As will be seen, it is plaintiffs' position that as a matter of public policy, this Court must circumscribe the concept of duty as owed in circumstances such as the instant case.

In addition, defendant would posit under an Andrews analysis that, even conceding a causal link between Peter Loerch's injuries and the alleged tortious conduct of Abbott Laboratories, as a matter of public policy a line has to be drawn cutting off liability. The reasons for this "line drawing" are myriad in nature. From a chilling effect on the research and development area of the modern medical community, to the moral posturing of what we as a society in general wish to model ourselves as, this line drawing is of no small moment. Defendant would urge that as a matter of practical societal politics, buttressed by an interpretation of the applicable case law, that the line drawing in this case must preclude Peter Loerch from recovery.

It is defendant's contention that Minnesota law does not extend a duty to preconception third generation plaintiffs. * * *

* * *

* * * [D]efendant looks to the Court of Appeals of New York in the Albala v. City of New York decision. See, Albala v. City of New York, 54 N.Y.2d 269, 445 N.Y.S.2d 108, 429 N.E.2d 786 (1981). In *Albala,* the New York court was confronted with the question of whether a plaintiff could recover for injury due to a negligent abortion performed upon his mother more than four years before his conception. The Court determined the tort committed against the mother did not give rise to a cause of action in favor of a child who was not conceived at the time of the tort. Despite the foreseeability of the injury, no duty could be owed to a child not yet conceived because it would extend traditional tort concepts beyond any manageable bounds. The Court reasoned that if such a duty were recognized, there would be no logical limit to liability. 421 N.E.2d at 288, 445 N.Y.S.2d at 110.

The Court stated:

> We are of the opinion that the recognition of a cause of action under these circumstances would require the extension of tort concepts beyond manageable bounds * * *

429 N.E.2d at 787.

In addition, the New York court indicated that recognition of the cause of action under the circumstances of the case would have the undesirable impact of encouraging the practice of "defensive medicine." Physicians faced with the alternative of saving a patient's life by administering a treatment involving the possibility of adverse consequences to later conceived offspring of the patient would, if exposed to liability of the magnitude considered, undoubtedly be inclined to advise against the treatment rather than risk the possibility of having to recompense a child born with a handicap. Defendant's memorandum in support of partial summary judgment at 13. The Court in *Albala* stated:

> Accordingly, society as a whole would bear the cost of our placing physicians in a direct conflict between their moral duty to patients and the proposed legal duty to those hypothetical future generations outside the immediate zone of danger.

Id. at 788–89.

In a recent case before the New York Supreme Court applying the *Albala* rationale, the Court addressed the issue of whether a cause of action for preconception tort exists in a products liability context. In Catherwood v. American Sterilizer Co., 130 Misc.2d 872, 498 N.Y.S.2d 703 (1986), a child alleged chromosomal damage resulting from her mother's exposure to the chemical ethylene oxide before the plaintiff's conception. The Court held that compelling policy reasons mandated a limitation of liability to prevent a "proliferation of frivolous claims and claims where proof presents a hardship to the defendants." 498 N.Y.S.2d at 705–06.

The Court stated:

> To allow a cause of action for preconception tort, there requires the finding of duty to the unconceived. Such a duty can only be couched in the terms of a duty to protect the potentiality of life. * * * New York has not recognized any such duty.

498 N.Y.S.2d at 706.

While the rationale of both the *Albala* and *Catherwood* decisions are illustrative and articulate, this Court would be less than thorough by failing to address the cases that have authorized a suit to be maintained for preconception injuries.

There are presently three cases reported that have allowed such action to proceed. See, Bergstreser v. Mitchell, 577 F.2d 22 (8th Cir. 1978); Renslow v. Mennonite Hospital, 67 Ill.2d 348, 367 N.E.2d 1250 (1977); Jorgensen v. Meade Johnson Laboratories, Inc., 483 F.2d 237 (10th Cir.1973).

In *Bergstreser v. Mitchell,* the Eighth Circuit Court of Appeals interpreted Missouri law to allow a cause of action on behalf of a brain injured child. The injury was allegedly the consequence of the physician. The negligence occurred prior to conception of the fetus. The plaintiffs alleged that a prior surgery had left the mother's uterus in a damaged condition. A subsequent pregnancy resulted in serious brain damage to the infant. The trial court ruled that the law allows "a child when born alive to bring an action for injuries arising out of preconception negligent conduct." It was the opinion of the trial court that a contrary decision would lead to the undesirable situation in which there would be a "wrong inflicted for which there would be no remedy."

The Eighth Circuit affirmed the trial court's ruling, stating:

> The case law shows that under a very similar set of circumstances, the Missouri Supreme Court has chosen to recognize a cause of action, has refused to be bound by outmoded common law, and has declined to allow an injury to be suffered without a remedy. After considering this case law, we agree with the District Court that the Courts of Missouri would permit an infant, born alive, to bring an action for injuries arising out of *preconception* negligent conduct.

Bergstreser at 25.

In the *Jorgensen* decision, the Tenth Circuit also expressly recognized the preconception cause of action. In *Jorgensen,* the plaintiffs brought a claim against the defendant drug manufacturer alleging that the birth of a mongoloid child had resulted from the mother taking the defendant's birth control pills. The Tenth Circuit stated:

> We are persuaded that the Oklahoma Courts would treat the problem of the injuries alleged here as one of causation and proximate cause, to be determined by competent medical proof.

Jorgensen at 240.

The Court stated further:

> If the view prevailed that tortious conduct occurring prior to conception is not actionable, on behalf of an infant ultimately injured by the wrong, then an infant suffering personal injury from a defective food product, manufactured before his conception, would be without a remedy. Such reasoning runs counter to the various principles of recovery which Oklahoma recognizes for those ultimately suffering injuries proximately caused by a defective product or instrumentality manufactured and placed on the market by the defendant.

Id. at 240.

In the *Renslow* decision, the Illinois court held that a child has a cause of action against a hospital and physician because they had given the child's mother an improper RH blood transfusion several years prior to the child's conception. The Court in *Renslow* recognized that the decision represented an extension of duty to a new class of plaintiffs and accordingly held that it be given only prospective application. However, the decision is clear that liability for a preconception tort is a maintainable action.

In the *Renslow* decision, the Court took an exhaustive look at the concepts of duty and causation. Indeed, as in the case presently at bar, the plaintiffs asked the Court to reexamine the notions of duty and to find a contingent prospective duty to a child not yet conceived, but foreseeably harmed by a breach of duty to the child's mother. * * * The Court in *Renslow* stated:

> * * * "duty" is not sacrosanct in itself, but only an expression of the sum total of those considerations of policy which lead the law to say that the particular plaintiff is entitled to protection.

Id. at 1254.

The Court noted that the *Jorgensen* decision focused upon causation rather than upon concepts of duty in permitting that cause of action to go forward. The Court noted, however,

> Causation cannot be the answer; in a very real sense the consequences of an act go forward to eternity, and back to the beginning of the world. Any attempt to impose responsibility on such a basis would result in infinite liability for all wrongful acts, which would set society on edge and fill the courts with endless litigation. (citations omitted). Thus, policy lines, to some extent arbitrary, must be drawn to narrow an area of actionable causation. We see no inherent advantage to discarding the policy lines, defined traditionally as "duty," in favor of new policy lines which would be necessary to circumscribe actionable causation.
>
> We reaffirm the utility of the concept of duty as a means by which to direct and control the course of the common law. * * * duty is not a static concept.

Renslow at 1254.

Defendants in *Renslow,* as defendant in the instant case, assert that the need for an end to responsibility, short of perpetual liability for a single wrongful act, dictates that a duty for preconception torts not be imposed. *Renslow* at 1255. Defendants in both cases raise the spectre of future generations complaining against a single defendant for harm done to an ancestor.

The Court in *Renslow* stated:

> While we are aware that there may be similar potential for perpetual claims * * *, the case at bar is clearly distinguishable. * * * We feel confident that when such a case is presented, the judiciary will effectively exercise its traditional role of drawing rational distinctions, consonant with current perceptions of justice, between harms which are compensable and those which are not.

Renslow at 1255.

And finally, the Court stated:

> We believe that there is a right to be born free from prenatal injuries foreseeably caused by a breach of duty to the child's mother.

Id.

* * *

Defendant * * * contends that public policy does not support extending the legal duty to a third generation plaintiff. It is defendant's contention that recognition of such a cause of action would give rise to cases involving claims asserted forty or fifty years or more after the alleged wrongful conduct. It is their contention that the difficulty in proving causation will lead to speculation and conjecture by the jury regarding causation and thereby open the door for a flood of fraudulent and fictitious claims.

In addition, allowing this cause of action to proceed will create an unreasonable burden on society, including the medical/pharmaceutical profession. It is defendant's contention that expanding the herein discussed tort concepts will have a chilling effect on the medical/pharmaceutical professions. The initiative and impetus to develop new and experimental drugs would be taken away from the medical profession by virtue of, what is to defendant's view, unlimited liability.

Defendant asserts that extending a duty to persons prior to conception, including third and other subsequent generations, would extend the tort concepts beyond manageable bounds and result in an overwhelming burden on the medical profession, drug manufacturers, and on society in general.

The device of the common law for placing a limitation on tort liability is the concept of duty. The concept of duty is the way the common law makes the policy determination of how far liability shall extend. As the parties have so zealously advocated, this policy question is one for determination by the Court.

Plaintiffs assert that society is best served by extending the concept of duty to include preconception torts. It is plaintiffs' contention that the primary purpose of tort law is the deterrent effect it has on individual and corporate conduct. Plaintiffs assert that corporations such as Abbott Laboratories *must* know that they will be held accountable for *all* the consequences of their wrongful action. To send the opposite message would substantially undermine the primary societal purpose of tort law.

* * *

In deciding the case, this Court considered the impact upon broader issues such as whether the tort system should be expanded to include preconception torts, or whether victims such as Peter should be compensated regardless of fault. Arguments can be made regarding the expense, delay, and inequality of the present tort system. Statistics demonstrate the system is expensive to society as well as the injured party. Even substantial verdicts seldom translate into real financial security to the injured. Should necessary care and treatment be predicated upon a particular trial with a number of variables or should society assume the responsibility to provide the requisite assistance for a meaningful life?

With respect to the argument regarding deterrence, it would appear that government regulation may be more effective coupled with criminal prosecution for intentional misconduct or gross negligence. If the conduct is a so-called unintended consequence of intentional conduct occasioned by technological advances perhaps society as the intended beneficiary should bear responsibility for the harm.

* * *

[T]his Court concedes a certain ambivalence and nagging uncertainty with respect to the decision reached. On the one hand, as a member of society with empathy and compassion for one's fellow man, the prospect of reversal appears neither inappropriate nor unacceptable. On the other hand, this Court has undertaken a legal analysis of the issues and has fairly, unemotionally and dispassionately rendered a decision consistent with this Court's understanding of the law. Although the Court has acknowledged considerations and the influence of human frailty, the Court has sought not to permit personal morality or convictions to influence the ultimate decision.

In conclusion, this Court wishes to disclose the decision in this case was the most difficult and challenging of any circumstances encountered by this Court in either an official or personal capacity. The issue is not whether to aid and comfort Peter Loerch because of his profound disabilities and injury, but is quite clearly to determine the method and means to accomplish this goal.

A review of the leading cases defining the rationale and parameters of traditional tort law reveal the claim of Peter Loerch to be the claim of a grandchild that matures as a result of an injury to his mother as a fetus, to be beyond the point where the courts have traditionally permitted an action to proceed on the basis of absence of duty, not foreseeable or remoteness. The law is not static, however, the Court has declined to extend tort law for the reasons expressed.

Therefore, pursuant to the above discussion, it is the opinion of this Court that defendant's motion for summary judgment is granted and the action dismissed.

Nevertheless, this Court specifically and respectfully certifies the issue as important and doubtful and the case is of such imperative public importance pursuant to Rule 118 of the Rules of Civil Appellate Procedure to justify deviation from the normal appellate procedure and to require immediate determination in the Supreme Court of the State of Minnesota pursuant to the provision of Rule 103.03(h).

NOTES

1. Right result? Does it matter that Linda knew she was a DES daughter and was a participant in a DES research project at the Mayo Clinic?

2. What if Peter Loerch marries and has a child who suffers some abnormality traceable to the DES prescribed for Peter's grandmother? Should this great grandchild have a claim against Abbott?

3. In Catherwood v. American Sterilizer Co., 130 Misc.2d 872, 498 N.Y.S.2d 703 (1986), the plaintiff was allegedly exposed to ethylene oxide in the course of her employment. She subsequently conceived and gave birth to a daughter with chromosomal damage, which she attributed to her previous chemical exposure. In her suit against the manufacturer and her employers, the trial court dismissed the complaint, reasoning that there is a "policy need for limitation of liability in exposure and ingestion cases." 498 N.Y.S.2d at 706. The Appellate Division affirmed, 3–2. 126 A.D.2d 980, 511 N.Y.S.2d 805, appeal dismissed 70 N.Y.2d 782, 521 N.Y.S.2d 222, 515 N.E.2d 908 (1987). In a concurring opinion, Lawton, J., remarked:

> * * * I add only my concern over judicial recognition of a cause of action on behalf of a newborn for genetic damage. The occurrence which serves as the basis for liability happened to the parent who, if liability can be established, is entitled to recover for all damages naturally flowing from said occurrence, including genetic injury. No cause of action, however, should accrue to the issue of said person. Many genetic abnormalities pass from generation to generation. Logically, if the second generation is entitled to recovery, so would succeeding generations. The extent and costs of this new cause of action are overwhelming. Such matters cannot be reasonably decided on a case-by-case basis, but rather should be left to the Legislature to fashion relief where appropriate.

511 N.Y.S.2d at 806. Callahan, J.P., and Green, J., dissented:

> We cannot agree that there is no cause of action for an infant for a preconception tort based upon a products liability theory. Accordingly, we would grant plaintiff's motion to amend her complaint to add a cause of action for damages resulting from defendant's alleged failure to warn plaintiff-mother of the dangers inherent in her exposure to toxic chemicals at her workplace. * * * In a products liability case such as this, * * * once a causal relationship has been established, the liability of the manufacturer is extended to the entire class of persons thereby affected regardless of privity, foreseeability or due care [citation]. The limits of liability in this case can be defined and limited. * * * In the future if claims are brought against defendants and it can be determined the defendants were responsible for the injuries alleged, they would have no greater liability than if they had put a defective product on the market that physically injured a live human being many years hence [citations].

4. *Loerch* was the first *third* generation case. The second trial court opinion, also denying liability, was Enright v. Eli Lilly & Co., 141 Misc.2d 194, 533 N.Y.S.2d 224 (1988). Many more cases will follow before the issue is settled.

5. See generally Robertson, Toward Rational Boundaries of Tort Liability for Injury to the Unborn: Prenatal Injuries, Preconception Injuries and Wrongful Life, 1978 Duke L.J. 1401; Comments, 67 Geo.L.J. 1239 (1979); 6 Ford.Urb. L.J. 217 (1978). *Albala* is noted at 50 Tenn.L.Rev. 195 (1982), and 60 Wash.U.L. Q. 275 (1982).

Chapter 11

"CRISIS" AND "REFORM"

The product liability menace.

Too late to cry wolf. He's already in your boardroom.

Product liability has turned out to be an undisguised wolf who has invaded company headquarters everywhere. And his presence has a lot of business people and their insurance companies scrambling up the same tree.

While preoccupation with medical malpractice insurance and OSHA compliance usurped attention from product liability, the problem kept growing.

The American public seems intent on going to court. "Sue the bastards" used to be a joke. Now it's a battle cry. With the help of eager attorneys, plaintiffs are not only quick to demand justice, but "extra" justice, because their chances of success are great. Courts have ruled that it's not necessary to prove negligence on the part of the manufacturer to collect damages.

There has been a frightening increase in the number of product liability claims - and in their dollar volume. Latest available figures show that for every dollar in product liability premiums, insurance companies have been paying out $1.35 in losses and expenses of handling claims.

So insurance rates are bound to go up even more. Perhaps to a point where many manufacturers may not be able to afford the coverage. And no one can afford that. Not producers. Not the insurance industry. Not the people who need the products. But on the other hand, consumers have a right to expect more than a "Use at Your Own Risk" label on the goods they buy. * * *

Come to the source

Employers Insurance of Wausau

Wausau Wisconsin

* From an ad in The Wall Street Journal, Dec. 9, 1976, at 15.

SECTION 1. THE FIRST "CRISIS"—THE 1970s

THE WALL STREET JOURNAL

June 3, 1976, at 1, col. 6.

LITIGATION LOAD *

MANUFACTURERS ARE HIT WITH MORE LAWSUITS, RISING INSURANCE COSTS

They Boost Safety Efforts, Seek Liability Limits Or Even Forgo Coverage

Case of the $154,100 Finger

BY BERNARD WYSOCKI JR.

Staff Reporter of The Wall Street Journal

Not much remains of Havir Manufacturing Co. of St. Paul, Minn. The small punch-press maker has halted production, auctioned off much of its machinery and idled most of its 80 employes. John Lenz, president, describes himself as "former president or liquidation president."

Things were fine at Havir until 1974. Then, without warning, the company was hit by a wave of lawsuits filed by press operators around the country who had lost fingers or hands in Havir presses.** Such claims "went up dramatically in 1974 and the first half of 1975," Mr. Lenz says, and Havir's problems began.

Havir's product-liability insurance premiums soared from $2,000 in 1970 to $4,000 in 1974 and $10,000 in 1975. Last September, the company's insurer canceled Havir's policy. Replacement insurance would have cost $200,000, or 10% of the company's $2 million in annual sales.

"So we decided to go out of business," Mr. Lenz says. "We didn't want to run without insurance," he says, and boosting prices to recover the costs would probably have hurt sales severely. Mr. Lenz has been trying to sell the business, but without success.

* Reprinted by permission of The Wall Street Journal,

** See, e.g., Bexiga v. Havir Mfg. Corp., 60 N.J. 402, 290 A.2d 281 (1972), supra p. 645.—Eds.

A Pervasive Problem

Havir's case is extreme, of course, but far from unique. Thousands of American manufacturers, large and small, are finding that the cost of insurance covering the products they sell is significantly hurting their business. Among the hardest-hit industries are drugs, general aircraft, tools and various kinds of capital equipment. Ironically, makers of industrial safety devices also are among those being hurt.

Companies hit by the deluge of suits and higher insurance costs are trying to cope in various ways. Some manufacturers are operating without liability insurance and hoping that large judgments don't bankrupt them. Others are increasing efforts to make their products as safe as possible. And some are lobbying for legislative limits on manufacturers' liability.

Last month, Commerce Secretary Elliot Richardson announced the formation of an inter-agency task force to study the problem, and the results are expected by the end of 1976.

Meantime, it seems certain that the new litigious leanings will mean higher product prices to offset the higher costs—just as the surge of medical malpractice judgments in recent years is increasing the cost of medical care.

Malpractice Ramifications

Indeed, insurance sources note parallels with the medical-malpractice surge. But the effects of the product-liability trend could be even more far-reaching. "It could make medical malpractice look like a common cold," says a spokesman for the American Insurance Association.

The few available statistics on the matter reflect the trend. Between 1969 and 1973, funds paid or set aside for product-liability claims nearly quadrupled, one insurance study shows. The Insurance Services Office, a New York data-gathering organization, says the cross-section study of insurers shows that losses mounted to $295.6 million from $78.8 million in that period. Officials say the rise has accelerated since 1973.

Spurring the trend, experts say, is the consumer's increasing awareness of his right to sue—and his increasing willingness to exercise his right. "It's no longer considered socially undesirable or 'bad form' to make a claim for compensation," says Craig Spangenberg, a Cleveland attorney who has represented many plaintiffs in product-liability cases.

The grounds for suing manufacturers have become much wider in recent years. Now, if a product that caused injury is shown to have had a defect in the manufacture, design, labeling or the like, the producer can be held liable. Today's principle is the "strict liability" of the manufacturer instead of the "culpable negligence" that had to be shown in the past, says John V. Brennan, a specialist in product-liability law and executive vice president of U.S. Aviation Underwriters

Inc. "No longer need the plaintiff impugn the integrity of the manufacturer. He may instead impugn the integrity of the product."

Old Machinery Implicated

Some manufacturers assert that their liability is patently unfair in many cases. Machine-tool makers, for example, say some claims against them involve old machinery that has been resold, modified several times or improperly maintained. Yet, injury claims trace alleged defects back to the manufacturer.

"What all this adds up to is a situation in which unsafe work practices in unsafe work places, maintained by unsafe employers, are causing working men and women to lose fingers and hands—or worse—and our members are paying for it," says James H. Mack, public affairs director of the National Machine Tool Builders' Association. The trade group is lobbying for a law to allow manufacturers to recover damages from negligent employers.

Worker compensation laws in most states now effectively limit the employer's liability to given amounts. In Ohio, for example, an employe who loses an eye would be entitled to a maximum of $11,625 plus $186 a week for lost work time.

While the machine-tool builders and some other groups seek increased employer liability, employers naturally demur. Just last week, the National Tool Die and Precision Machining Association, a group of manufacturers who use machine tools, announced opposition to the legislation supported by the tool producers, claiming the law would "break the shield of workmen's compensation" that protects workers and employers.

No one disputes the fact that an industrial accident can seriously damage a victim's work life and social life. But the difficulty arises in determining who should compensate the injured, under what circumstances and at what cost.

Worried manufacturers claim the costs are rapidly becoming too steep for them. As they see it, every day brings not only more lawsuits but higher damage awards to the injured.

In late January, Gail Coty, of Elgin, Ill., was awarded $100,000 by a jury after she had to have a finger amputated as a result of an accident with a meat-slicing machine. In March, Lazaro Mata won a $154,100 judgment against Clark Equipment Co. of Buchanan, Mich., after he had a finger amputated while operating a Clark lift-truck.

Awards for more serious injuries or death can be much steeper, of course. In March, an $11 million settlement was made in the deaths of 30 men and injury of three others in a natural-gas tank explosion on Staten Island in 1973. Producers of materials used in building the tank were among the defendants.

The effects of the bulging claims and awards are ominous. One effect is a large underwriting loss being sustained by many insurers. Firemen's Fund American Insurance Co. in San Francisco, which writes about $22 million of product-liability insurance annually, is currently paying out about $1.15 for every $1 in premiums it takes in, says Creighton White, assistant vice president.

Insurance Escalation

By one trade estimate, the insurance industry has sustained about $2.5 billion of losses over the past five years in underwriting "miscellaneous" liability, which includes both medical and product-liability insurance.

So insurance rates have predictably soared. "It's fantastic. It's confiscatory," says Robert Englander, chairman of Simplimatic Engineering Co., a Lynchburg, Va., maker of product-handling equipment for the food and beverage industries. During 1975, Mr. Englander says, four claims were filed against the company. One $400,000 suit that is still pending was brought by a mechanic who suffered severe head wounds while repairing a Simplimatic machine. The company's insurance bill jumped to $100,000 from $4,000 in that 12–month period, Mr. Englander says.

Mr. Englander believes, however, that his premium rates would have soared regardless of his own company's experience, because his industry as a whole is increasingly plagued by suits. Insurance company officials concur that an industry's overall vulnerability sometimes pushes up rates of individual companies that have relatively few claims against them.

Larger companies are feeling the sting as well. "We're vitally concerned," says a spokesman for the General Aviation Manufacturers Association, a trade group. "It has become an increasing problem, with increasing judgments and with premiums going up." The spokesman contends that some aircraft makers are paying premiums that amount to 4% to 6% of gross sales.

At Black & Decker Manufacturing Co., product-liability insurance costs are eight to 10 times higher than they were in 1970, though officials of the tool maker note that the number of products in the marketplace has multiplied, too. "Up to this point it has been a minor factor in prices or profitability," a company official says, but "the way the trend is going," it could become a major problem.

Operating Without Insurance

For Safeguard Manufacturing Co. in Woodbury, Conn., the problem is already major. When Safeguard's insurance policy that cost $30,000 a year was canceled last April, a replacement carrier couldn't be found at anywhere near that rate. So Safeguard, with sales of about $600,000 a year, decided to operate without any insurance.

"Without it, defense costs are unknown," laments Edwin Plumb, president. Shortly after the insurance expired, in fact, the company was socked with a $1 million claim, which is still pending. "We have to continually boost the price of the product," Mr. Plumb says. "There's a possibility of going out of business," but that isn't likely, at least immediately, he adds.

Mr. Plumb notes the irony of Safeguard's situation. Its product is a safety device that a factory worker straps to his wrists. The device automatically withdraws the worker's hands from dangerous machinery at crucial intervals. "Its use has saved hundreds if not thousands of accidents," Mr. Plumb maintains.

Some manufacturers vulnerable to the surge of suits have stepped up efforts to make sure products are made and used safely. Dow Chemical Co. has a "product stewardship" program under which Dow sometimes goes so far as to refuse to sell a product if it fears a customer isn't using it safely. A company official says the program began even before the recent concern about soaring premium rates.

Government Help Sought

Other companies have gone to the government for help. The drug industry, for instance, is fearful of litigation after the government launches its coming campaign to immunize all 215 million Americans against an expected influenza epidemic. The Pharmaceutical Manufacturers Association, an industry trade group, is lobbying to have the federal government reimburse the companies making the vaccine for any losses in lawsuits brought by patients who suffer side-effects.

Lobbying efforts are also taking place in statehouses across the nation. Several states are considering legislation that would set a time limit on a manufacturer's liability in a lawsuit. Capital-goods makers in particular contend that many accidents and damage suits involve old machinery. The National Machine Tool Builders' Association maintains that nearly 50% of the claims against its members involve machines 20 years old or more.

Florida already has a law that limits a claim to 12 years after a product was first sold, and North Carolina law sets a 10–year limit under some circumstances. Perhaps the most far-reaching legislative proposal was one in Kansas to set a six-year limit on claims, set dollar limits on certain types of damages and also limit lawyers' contingency fees that are linked to the size of the settlement. But the state legislature adjourned last month without enacting the law.

"CAUSES" AND "SOLUTIONS"

"In 1975, an apparent problem (some sources said 'crisis') arose in the field of product liability. A number of manufacturers and business periodicals alleged that product liability insurance had become unavailable or unaffordable. The consequences of this situation included the possibilities that businesses might terminate because they were unable to get coverage; that injured persons would be unable to enforce product liability judgments; and that manufacturers would be hesitant to produce some products that would be useful in our society. It was also alleged that the system of private insurance in the field of product liability was breaking down. Finally, it was alleged that relatively few injured persons benefited from the system." Final Report, Interagency Task Force on Product Liability I–1 (1977).

Reacting to this situation, manufacturers and insurers united in an attempt to effect legislative solutions. They went to the White House. The result: the creation in 1976 of a federal Interagency Task Force on Product Liability, working out of the Department of Commerce, that was directed to study the products liability "problem." In 1977, the Task Force issued its findings in a comprehensive, multi-volume report including a major Final Report. The Task Force concluded that while products liability litigation had indeed become a problem for many businesses, it had not in fact reached "crisis" proportions for the nation.

As a barometer of the extent of the problem, products liability insurance, while rising dramatically in the mid–1970s, was found to be still generally available and—except in certain high-risk industries—relatively affordable. Moreover, unlike the one million products liability lawsuits the insurance industry had predicted would be filed in 1976, the actual figure was found to have been closer to 70,000. Nor was there substantial evidence that manufacturers were being driven out of business due to this type of litigation or to the increased cost of insurance, although manufacturers in some industries were found to be dropping certain lines of hazardous products and more cautiously introducing new ones.

Three principal causes for the problem were identified by the Task Force. First were the ratemaking procedures of liability insurers. Products liability premiums were found to have lagged behind the judicial broadening of manufacturer liability that had developed in the 1960s and early 1970s. When in the mid–1970s insurers finally awakened to the significant legal changes that in fact had been evolving over the previous decade, they overreacted. Premiums were increased dramatically not so much on the basis of hard data (claims made or paid) but instead on the basis of intuition and "panic pricing."

The second cause for the products liability problem was found to derive from manufacturing practices that were in fact unsafe. The Task Force concluded that products are indeed sometimes sold with dangerous manufacturing flaws, others with dangerous design inadequacies, and some with inadequate warnings of hidden dangers or instructions for safe use. A reasonable basis was thus found to exist for much of the litigation in the area.

Finally, the Task Force concluded that various uncertainties in the tort-litigation system contributed to the problem. Variations in the liability rules among the states, and even among judges in the same jurisdiction, promotes an unhealthy uncertainty that breeds litigation. Particularly in design and warnings cases, the problem is fueled by the absence of workable rules for predictably resolving whether any particular product should be considered "defective," the most central issue in all products liability litigation. Other less significant causes for the problem were identified: inflation; increasing consumer awareness of their legal rights; the increasing number and complexity of products; and product misuse.

In 1978 the successor Task Force on Product Liability and Accident Compensation of the Department of Commerce, chaired by Professor Victor Schwartz (who also chaired the earlier "working" task force), issued an "Options Paper" that considered the possible legislative responses to the problem. See 43 Fed.Reg. 14,612 (1978). By late 1978, Congress had begun to consider various proposed remedies, including federalizing insurance regulation, granting certain tax incentives for self-insurance, and "reforming" certain substantive principles of products liability law. And in January, 1979, the Commerce Department issued a Draft Uniform Product Liability Act for the states to consider when legislating in the field. See 44 Fed.Reg. 2996 (1979). The Draft Act was introduced into Congress, and a revised, final Model Uniform Product Liability Act was published soon thereafter. See 44 Fed.Reg. 62714 (Oct. 31, 1979).

Manufacturers and insurers took their problem to the states as well, and the response in the state legislatures proved quicker and more substantial. The blueprint for state legislation was the "Product Liability Package" of reform proposals issued by the American Insurance Association in March 1977. The recommended AIA "reforms" included:

(1) a three (3) year statute of limitations from the date of injury, with an overall eight (8) year statute of "repose" from the date of manufacture or sale;

(2) a defense when an injury is caused by a post-sale alteration or modification of the product;

(3) a "state of the art" defense, requiring that the manufacturer be judged only according to the knowledge and technology prevailing at the time of sale;

(4) a rule excluding evidence of subsequent improvements in the product's design or formulation after the time of injury;

(5) a restructuring of the duty to warn, including a requirement that plaintiff establish a clear causal relation between the injury and the failure to warn;

(6) certain limitations on the recovery of punitive damages; and

(7) a restructuring of the rules governing industrial accidents, including the deduction of worker's compensation benefits from judgments against manufacturers and the prohibition of indemnity and contribution suits by manufacturers against employers.

By late 1979, several of these "reform" measures, particularly the first four AIA proposals listed above, had been enacted in several states. "Reform" packages with several such provisions had been enacted in Arizona, Arkansas, Colorado, Indiana, Kentucky, Michigan, Minnesota, Nebraska, New Hampshire, North Carolina, North Dakota, Oregon, South Dakota, Tennessee, and Utah. Connecticut passed an act patterned after the Draft Uniform Product Liability Law. Several other states, including Alabama, Florida, Georgia, Illinois, Rhode Island, and Virginia, had each enacted special statutes of limitations or other less comprehensive measures. In addition to the first four AIA reform proposals described above, other "reforms" at the state level included the adoption of a presumption of nondefectiveness for compliance with governmental safety standards, various tinkerings with the common-law defenses based on the plaintiff's own misconduct, and various changes in the rules concerning ad damnum clauses and cross claims in indemnity actions brought by defendants.

By 1980, the first "crisis" had disappeared.

SECTION 2. THE SECOND "CRISIS"—THE 1980s

PLUS ÇA CHANGE . . . .

Product Liability: The New Morass *

Overwhelmed by lawsuits and huge awards, industry asks Congress to step in.

GOLDBERG, MANUFACTURERS TAKE COVER

72 ABA Journal 52 (July 1, 1986).

More than 600 representatives of mainly small and medium-sized product manufacturers came to Washington, D.C., on March 11 at the request of the National Association of Manufacturers. NAM had scheduled them to meet with the press that morning and with their legislators that afternoon to bring the insurance panic home to the American public.

* The New York Times, March 10, 1985, § 3, at 1. Art by Niculae Asciu.

One of those attending was James F. Mawn, vice president of finance at Multi-metal Wirecloth Inc. of Tappan, N.Y. Multi-metal, a maker of filtration products, had been quoted a product liability rate increase of 300 percent despite a 75-year business record without a product liability suit.

Another story was told by William Perry of Wepco Inc. in Vienna, Va. Perry, an engineer, started a company in 1980 to manufacture hand and foot driving controls for the handicapped.

He was told in January that his company was uninsurable, even though it had never been sued. He was later quoted a premium of $18,000—up from $1,535—for one-third of his previous coverage. Realizing that one catastrophic lawsuit could wipe out his company, Perry suspended sales and will go out of business in October. "In a way I don't blame the insurance companies. With the current legal situation, I wouldn't cover me," Perry said.

500 percent increase

Many manufacturers link "the current legal situation" to their recent and well-publicized difficulties in getting liability insurance at reasonable rates. An informal survey in February of members of the U.S. Chamber of Commerce, which represents mainly small businesses, showed that more than 40 percent had insurance rate increases of 100 to 500 percent. Almost 20 percent could not obtain or renew insurance.

Fortune 500 companies are feeling the pinch as well. The 1986 10-K statement for Ford Motor Company discloses that the company has "little or no coverage" for product suits that might occur this year because of the "limited availability of * * * insurance at reasonable premiums." Claims against Ford for product suits are estimated at $4 billion. More than $1.2 billion alone is claimed in lawsuits over defective transmissions.

Similarly, the annual report of Johnson & Johnson, based in New Brunswick, New Jersey, states that it is substantially without insurance for product suits in 1986. The company currently is defending seven wrongful death actions stemming from the 1982 Tylenol capsule poisonings. Other actions arise from two subsidiaries' products: Ortho Pharmaceutical's oral contraceptives, which are alleged to cause circulatory problems, and McNeill Pharmaceutical's Zomax, which the company withdrew from the market in 1983 after severe reactions were reported. Damages claimed for current product suits are estimated in the hundreds of millions of dollars, said company spokesman James Murray.

When litigation costs and insurance premiums overtake profits, many manufacturers—primarily in the health care and sporting goods industries—will drop their products. Others are clamoring for tort reform, because they think the judicial deck is stacked against them.

Product manufacturers and their defense counsel speak increasingly of a hostile "litigation climate" and of being beleaguered with suits, many of them frivolous. "Manufacturers don't want a free ride," said

Paul Nelson, general attorney for Navistar's product litigation department. "They just want to return to a system based on fault-finding rather than compensation."

Robert Clifford, a Chicago plaintiffs' attorney, denies that the system is out of whack. "In the area of products liability, the system has never deviated from being fault-based. Talk to any product attorney—the proof of facts in a design defect case is identical to that in negligence."

While horror stories abound, there are very few real cases in which innocent corporate defendants are saddled with massive awards, according to Clifford. "These cases are illusory."

One notorious anecdote is told by Robert H. Malott, chairman and CEO of Chicago-based FMC Corp., and president of the influential Business Roundtable's Task Force on Product Liability. At Northwestern University's Corporate Counsel Institute in October, Malott spoke of an overweight man who had suffered a heart attack while trying to start his Sears lawnmower. A sympathetic jury awarded him $1 million plus $500,000 in prejudgment interest. The story has since been repeated in both Forbes and the Wall Street Journal.

The rest of the story is told by Keith Erbstein, the Philadelphia attorney who represented the plaintiff in this case, Share v. Sears, Court of Common Pleas, Philadelphia County, September term, 1979–No. 2984. "The plaintiff had tried to start the lawnmower 15 times before he had the attack. He was 32 years old and was a physician earning $300,000 a year. After the heart attack, he had to take a job that paid $60,000." Sears was held liable because the lawnmower's valve did not meet manufacturing specifications. Was the award excessive? "Not when you consider the plaintiff's drop in income," Erbstein said.

Strict Liability

Strict liability is the basis of most product cases. Section 402(A) of the Restatement Second of Torts is the prototype for most state product liability laws. One of the first to advocate its use in products cases was Justice Robert B. Traynor of the California Supreme Court in Escola v. Coca Cola Bottling Co., 150 P.2d 436 (1944). Traynor argued that manufacturers were better able than consumers to spread the risk of injury through insurance and that strict liability was an effective deterrent to marketing unsafe products.

Unlike negligence, strict liability focuses on the product's condition rather than on the manufacturer's conduct. The product must be shown to be defective and unreasonably dangerous. Products will be found defective if they are improperly designed or manufactured or have an inadequate warning.

"The easiest case to prove is a manufacturing defect case," said DePaul Law School professor Bruce Ottley. "You simply compare the defective product to a non-defective one by the same manufacturer. It's much harder to demonstrate design or warning defects because you have to show either that it was feasible for the manufacturer to have made a safe product or that other manufacturers already had done so."

To decide this, courts must engage in a risk-benefit analysis, which Ottley terms a trade-off. "It involves balancing consumer and economic interests—for example, is it worthwhile to design a crash-proof car that can go only five miles an hour?"

Some defense counsel think strict liability has gone too far, imposing liability on vaccine makers, whose products comply with government standards but inevitably will trigger some adverse reactions. "In moving away from a fault-based standard to strict liability, the courts now are finding defects in inherent product characteristics," commented Ronald Cracas, manager of the litigation department of American Cyanamid, of which Lederle Laboratories is a division.

Lederle is embroiled in litigation stemming from its manufacture of polio and diptheria vaccines. "Courts are imposing absolute rather than strict liability on manufacturers," Cracas said. He and other defense counsel imply that manufacturers now are expected to make products that are 100 percent safe.

"We are hearing the argument that product liability law requires too much product safety these days, just as medical malpractice law is accused of generating too much defensive medicine," said Marshall S. Shapo, professor of torts at Northwestern University Law School. Shapo was Reporter to the ABA's Committee on the Tort Liability System, which published an exhaustive study in 1984, Toward a Jurisprudence of Injury. "Still, courts have been pretty good at getting bumps in the law smoothed out. For example, the New Jersey Supreme Court drew back from Beshada in the Feldman decision."

Beshada v. Johns–Manville Products Corp., 447 A.2d 539 (1982), sent shock-waves through the defense bar. Beshada held that the state-of-the-art defense—arguing that a product's design met industry standards at the time it was manufactured—was irrelevant to products cases. This holding was modified in Feldman v. Lederle Laboratories, 460 A.2d 203 (1983). In order to encourage companies to research and develop new drugs, the court exempted drug companies from the *Beshada* rule.

Cases like *Beshada* and *Feldman* lead insurers, manufacturers and defense counsel to complain about the lack of predictability in products law. The most familiar complaint is that the lack of uniformity has produced a "patchwork" or "crazy quilt" of state laws. "Although some 30 states have now enacted product liability statutes, no two are alike," said Robert Malott. "Cases [with] similar facts * * * can produce strikingly different and often contradictory judgments."

"To understand why predictability is important to the insurance field, you have to first understand the nature of the product," explained Frank Nutter, president of the American Alliance of Insurers, a trade organization representing more than 175 domestic and foreign companies.

The cost of insurance, according to Nutter, reflects the size of jury awards or claims, the company's particular experience in resolving disputes, the type of business and product, and the experience of other businesses in the same field. "For that reason, a company that has never had a suit filed against it may have a rate hike based on another company's litigation record."

Mass torts and deep pockets

Over the past decade courts have sought to fashion new remedies for victims of mass torts—involving asbestos, DES, Bendectin, Toxic Shock Syndrome, DPT and other vaccines. Market share liability and successor liability are two developments noted by Paul Rheingold, New York City plaintiffs' lawyer.

* * *

Vanishing products

Many manufacturers claim they would rather drop product lines than pay increased premiums. They also claim the high cost of litigation has forced them into this situation and that the public will suffer because of it.

On Jan. 31, G.D. Searle of Skokie, Ill., announced that it was ceasing manufacture of the Copper Seven and Tatum T IUDs. The reasons given by general counsel and vice president Roger Thies were the "high cost of defending unwarranted litigation" and Searle's inability to find product insurance at any reasonable cost. Searle's decision to withdraw from the market leaves only one domestic manufacturer of IUDS—the Alza Corp. of Palo Alto, Calif., whose Progestasert IUD accounted for only 3 percent of the market in 1984.

"The decision to take the Copper Seven IUD off the market was very frustrating," said Steve Dickinson, a company spokesman. "There were no medical or scientific reasons for it." Searle currently is defending close to 400 suits by IUD users who claim they have suffered sterility or pelvic inflammatory disease. Searle has won nine of the 11 cases that have gone to trial.

Dr. Jacqueline Darroch Forrest, research director of the Alan Guttmacher Institute, a New York City-based family planning research institution, agrees with Searle's assessment that its product is safe and effective. "Available research shows that the product was primarily used by its intended user—older women who already have children and who are unable to take oral contraceptives," she said. As a result of the decreased availability of IUDs, there will be "hundreds of thousands of unwanted pregnancies and more women will be forced into sterilization," Forrest said.

Earlier this year, Lederle Laboratories was considering discontinuing its DPT vaccine, given to millions of schoolchildren to prevent diptheria, pertussis and tetanus, because it couldn't find product coverage at any reasonable price, said Lederle representative Martha Homma.

Lederle's withdrawal from the market, which would have left only one other supplier of the vaccine, had health officials at the Centers for Disease Control in Atlanta braced for a vaccine shortage in late summer or fall. In late May, however, Lederle announced that it was keeping the product on the market, but was raising its price more than 250 percent to cover the cost of self-insurance.

Lederle is defending more than 100 DPT lawsuits in which neurological injuries are alleged. A British study done in 1979 showed that one in every 310,000 children who received the vaccine suffered an adverse reaction resulting in some form of permanent brain damage, said Dr. Alan Hinman, director of the CDC's Immunization Division. Even with these odds, Hinman believes the benefits of administering the vaccine outweigh the risks.

Health care isn't the only industry in which products have been discontinued because of insurance and litigation costs. There are now only two domestic makers of trampolines and the number of football helmet makers has dwindled from 10 to three. Both products have been associated with accidents resulting in quadriplegia and multimillion dollar awards.

Are trial lawyers to blame for vanishing products? "The question is really a little more complex than the manufacturers make it out to be," said Eugene Pavalon, a Chicago plaintiffs' lawyer and vice president of the Association of Trial Lawyers of America. According to Pavalon, trial lawyers have been instrumental in making products safer—a key example being the 1960s-era football helmet, which was poorly designed and caused significant injuries. Today's helmets have been redesigned because of litigation, he said.

Pavalon does not think that manufacturers will continue to market safe products if the laws are relaxed. "The adversarial system still is the most effective deterrent to unsafe products, and companies are not as vigilant about product safety as they would like people to think."

Edward Swartz, a Boston plaintiffs' lawyer, agrees. "Companies only build safety into products when they have to. The bottom line is 'What does it cost them?' "

People have forgotten that product liability laws were changed in the 1960s and 1970s because of unsafe products, Pavalon said. "The callousness of the corporate mentality is illustrated by the cost-benefit analysis that Ford engaged in when it decided it was cheaper to pay out injury claims on the Pinto than to spend a nominal amount per unit to fix defective fuel tanks."

Causes and solutions

At the root of the insurance panic are rising rates. But what's behind them? The industry explains the rate hikes as the culmination of a business cycle in which it now is compensating for price cuts taken between 1979 and 1984.

"Property-casualty insurers engaged in a competitive rate war during which prices were driven down," Frank Nutter said. "Finally they reached a point in late 1984–85 where they couldn't sustain the disparity between prices and increasing costs," tied to litigation expenses. The "bloodbath," as Nutter termed it, had to give way to rate hikes in order for insurers to stay in business.

Data from the Insurance Services Office Inc., an industry clearinghouse, confirms that 1984 was a rough year—possibly the worst ever—for property and casualty insurers. They experienced record insolvencies and returns on investments, and had a record operating loss of nearly $4 billion.

Jay Angoff of the National Insurance Consumer Organization (NICO), a public interest group, said: "Insurance was generally available until December 1985 when the Insurance Information Institute, the industry's public relations arm, launched a massive effort to market the idea that there is something wrong with the civil justice system in the U.S."

According to Angoff, the insurers' strategy was to turn the insurance panic into a litigation crisis. They withdrew from certain markets, hiked rates and justified their actions on the basis of a crisis in the courts. The insurance institute earmarked $6.5 million for an advertising campaign on tort reform.

NICO's solution to the insurance crisis is tighter industry regulation—removing its exemption from antitrust prosecution and FTC regulation. Meanwhile the momentum for tort reform is building.

Sen. Robert Kasten, R.–Wis., the author of previous bills for a uniform product liability standard, has introduced the Reagan administration's proposal for tort reform as an amendment to his act (S. 199). The amendment has seven parts:

- A return to fault-based liability. Product suits would be based in negligence unless the product was shown to be defective and unreasonably dangerous.
- Restriction on joint and several liability except in concerted action cases.
- Mandatory structured settlements for economic losses above $100,000.
- Suspension of the collateral source rule.
- Restrictions on contingent fee arrangements.
- Caps of $100,000 on non-economic losses.
- Encouragement of alternative dispute resolution.

Although the ABA was still formulating a response to the Kasten bill in early May, the Association previously has opposed such legislation. The ABA House of Delegates passed a resolution in 1983 opposing "broad federal legislation that would codify [state] product liability law."

An exception was created, however, to deal with occupational diseases, such as asbestosis, when three factors are present: the disease has a long latency period; the number of claims and the amount of total liability threaten the solvency of a significant number of manufacturers; and the number of cases have become "clearly excessive and burdensome on the state and federal judicial systems."

In April, the ABA established an Action Commission to Improve the Tort Liablity System, under the sponsorship of the Torts and Insurance Practice Section. Chaired by Robert B. McKay, professor of the New York University Law School, the commission will evaluate proposals for tort reform and the findings of Toward a Jurisprudence of Injury.

Marshall Shapo, reporter for the committee that authored Jurisprudence, said he generally opposes the legislation because it "would substitute broad-scale legislative horse-trading for reasoned judicial decision making." The changes proposed are likely to create as much uncertainty and litigation as under the present system, he said, because of new amendments and varying judicial interpretations.

"Despite all the controversy about the system not working, the statistical basis of a 'crisis' is not clear. It's hard to say exactly what has produced the 'crisis' atmosphere, but we can say that businessmen who buy into the myth are likely to be buying into a new set of uncertainties."

NOTE

Compare the perspective of Professor Vandall, in 64 Denver U.L.Rev. 703, 708 (1988):

> Other questions have been raised about what should happen to manufacturers and sellers that cannot obtain insurance. The economic response lies in whether the companies are profitable or not. If they are profitable, an insurance company will eventually offer them insurance, most likely at high rates. If companies are not profitable, insurance will be more difficult to obtain because premiums may be out of reach for such marginally-operated companies. For companies that are not profitable because of high risks and large losses in product liability lawsuits, increased insurance rates are the market's way of proclaiming their products as too risky or dangerous.

COMPANY STOPS MAKING MORNING SICKNESS DRUG

The New York Times, A16, col. 1 (June 10, 1983).

WASHINGTON, June 9 (AP)—Production of Bendectin, the only American-produced drug approved for the treatment of morning sickness, was halted by Merrell Dow Pharmaceuticals today.

The company's move came 13 days after a jury awarded $750,000 to the family of a girl who was born with a deformed hand after her mother took the drug. The company, which says the product is "absolutely safe," has been the target of hundreds of lawsuits asserting that the drug caused deformities in fetuses. But the award was the first major judgment against the Cincinnati-based company, a division of Dow Chemical.

Merrell Dow said it would stop production of the drug, designed to stem nausea and vomiting in early pregnancy, because of negative publicity. It cited rising insurance premiums and the cost of defending against suits.

A different view came from the Public Citizen Health Research Group, which two years ago asked the Federal Food and Drug Administration to take the drug off the market. "Because of today's actions," said Dr. Sidney Wolfe, director of the research group, "hundreds of thousands of pregnant women and their unborn children will be spared the risk of exposure to this questionably effective and unsafe drug."

Used by 33 Million Women

At the time of the court decision on Bendectin, Faye Peterson, a spokesman for the F.D.A., said the agency had found no causal link between the drug and birth defects but was continuing to study the subject. The drug has been prescribed for more than 33 million women around the world in the last 27 years. Because of the negative publicity, use of the drug has dropped off considerably in the last few years.

On May 27, a Superior Court jury here awarded $750,000 in compensatory damages to the family of 12–year–old Mary Oxendine of Mitchellville, Md., a suburb of Washington. She was born with a shortened right arm that was missing fingers and parts of the hand.

Merrell Dow is contesting the verdict, contending that there is no scientific evidence that Bendectin is associated with an increase in risks of birth defects. A second trial is to be held in Superior Court to consider the plaintiffs' request for more than $1 million in punitive damages against Merrell Dow.

FORD CUTS '86 COVERAGE FOR PRODUCT LIABILITY

The Wall Street Journal, 14, col. 2 (May 12, 1986).*

By a WALL STREET JOURNAL *Staff Reporter*

DEARBORN, Mich.—Ford Motor Co. said that because of skyrocketing insurance rates, it has "little or no" product liability insurance for incidents that occur in 1986.

In its 10–K filing with the Securities and Exchange Commission, the auto maker cited the "limited availability" of the insurance "at reasonable premiums." The company joins a growing number of businesses that have decreased their commercial coverage because of rapidly increasing rates.

A Ford spokesman declined to say how much commercial insurance Ford has had or was dropping, or what portion of the company's 1986 coverage will be self-insured. "It's a proprietary matter," he said.

"Obviously we don't have as much commercial coverage as we did" in 1985, the spokesman said. He said the company doesn't disclose which carriers provide its commercial coverage.

As of Jan. 21, Ford had $3.97 billion in damage claims pending against it. The suits include $1.2 billion in damages sought for alleged problems in automatic transmissions, $1.5 billion in damages sought for alleged problems with fuel systems, and $1.1 billion in damages sought for failing to provide airbags or restraints other than seat belts.

NOTE

Compare the conclusions in Nye & Gifford, The Myth of the Liability Insurance Claims Explosion: An Empirical Rebuttal, 41 Vand.L.Rev. 909, 922 (1988):

> The dramatic price increases in liability insurance lines that occurred from 1984 through 1986 spawned a variety of assertions concerning the cause of the perceived crisis. This Article supports the proposition that total claims costs for liability insurers increased dramatically during the period from 1975 through 1986. These increased costs, however, were not significantly attributable to an increased number of claims against insured parties during that period. When the number of claims against insureds is adjusted for changes in the risk assumed by insurers because of variations in both the number of insureds and the level of the insureds' activities, the number of incurred claims in Other Liability insurance coverages actually declined during the period from 1975 through 1984. Comparable data for later years is not available, but an analysis of claim filings (as opposed to paid claims) indicates that a major increase in claims propensity occurred in 1985 and 1986. It is too soon to know what proportion of these filings will actually result in paid claims.

THE COPPER–7's COSTLY LEGACY

Time, p. 61, col. 2 (Sept. 26, 1988).

Executives at the Monsanto chemical company must have watched the stock-market opening last week with unusual trepidation. For good reason: after the market closed the previous Friday, a federal court jury in St. Paul awarded $8.75 million to a woman hurt by a Copper–7 intrauterine contraceptive device manufactured by G.D. Searle, a Monsanto subsidiary. The penalty raised a question: Could Monsanto go the way of A.H. Robins, which was forced into bankruptcy proceedings because of lawsuits generated by its Dalkon Shield IUD?

Probably not, but many Monsanto shareholders wanted to sell while they had a chance. In two days of hectic trading, the company's shares tumbled $11.13, bottoming at $74.63 before recovering a bit to close the week at $77.88.

The jury found that Searle had insufficiently tested the birth-control device and concluded that the IUD caused Plaintiff Esther Kociemba to develop a pelvic infection that led to sterility. Until that verdict was handed down, Searle had won all but three of the Copper–7 cases that had gone to jury trials. Two of the cases ended with awards of just $550,000; in the third case no award has yet been made. Hundreds of complaints, though, were settled out of court for undisclosed sums. Some 1,300 separate lawsuits have been filed against Searle since 1974, and more are no doubt on the way. Monsanto is confident that any hefty judgment will be reversed on appeal.

SEN. DANFORTH (R.MO.), REVISING PRODUCT LIABILITY LAW—A NEED FOR UNIFORM LAWS, FASTER TRIALS

The New York Times, § 3, p. 2, col. 3 (Sept. 1, 1985).

* * *

Manufacturers seek certainty about the extent of their potential liability. Consumers seek swifter, more certain recovery, and both groups seek to avoid the high cost of litigation. We need a new approach that unites manufacturers and consumers, recognizing that their interests, while different, are not necessarily conflicting.

The Senate Committee on Commerce, Science and Transportation now is considering such a new approach, which combines uniform product liability standards with an alternative, expedited claim system for the recovery of limited damages. "No-fault" claim-scheme proposals presented by Senator Christopher J. Dodd of Connecticut and Senator Slade Gorton of Washington provide a basis for a legislative solution.

The idea is to give the innocent consumer harmed by a defective product a choice between a traditional lawsuit and an expedited claim process with limited judicial review. Without going to court, the injured party would be able to file a claim with the manufacturer of the defective product to recover "net economic loss"—compensation for actual out-of-pocket costs, such as lost wages and medical expenses.

The manufacturer would have to accept or reject the claim promptly or be penalized. If the only issue in dispute is the amount of compensation to be paid and not liability, then this issue would be submitted to binding arbitration. If liability is in dispute, the claimant could seek limited judicial review without a jury, but with a lower burden of proof.

The burden of proving that the company knew or should have known about the defect (the issue of negligence) would be removed for individuals seeking limited recovery. Other bars to recovery of damages, such as the inability to identify a specific manufacturer or to prove causation in cases involving long-latency diseases, might be removed for victims of defective products seeking limited compensation.

At the same time, uniform Federal product liability standards based on fault would be imposed for use in traditional lawsuits. Those pursuing such litigation would not be limited to recovery of net economic loss; they could seek traditional tort remedies, including non-economic and punitive damages, but would have to meet a higher burden of proof than that required for the claim system.

Such an approach, combining uniform product liability standards with an alternative claim system, would provide an expedited means of limited compensation while retaining the traditional litigation system, for those who choose to pursue it. It would reduce the overall transaction costs of litigation and restore order and certainty to product liability law while still promoting product safety.

To be sure, it may be very difficult to come up with a workable standard of liability for an alternative claim system. Special consideration may have to be given to the problems associated with specific types of injuries and specific types of products, such as toxics and drugs. But we are not engaged in the search for perfection. We are engaged in attempting to reform the law of product liability, an effort that will require of manufacturing and consumer groups a willingness to be open-minded and the ability to compromise.

NOTE

At the Senate Commerce Committee hearings on the Dodd–Gorton proposals, virtually everyone thought they were a bad idea, except for one academic witness, a products liability law professor. The bills quietly died.

PRODUCT LIABILITY—EXTENT OF "LITIGATION EXPLOSION" IN FEDERAL COURTS QUESTIONED

Briefing Report to the Chairman,
Subcommittee on Commerce, Consumer Protection and Competitiveness,
Committee on Energy and Commerce, House of Representatives.
United States General Accounting Office, January 1988.

Dear Mr. Chairman:

This briefing report is in response to your request for an analysis of product liability cases filed in federal courts (in this report, the U.S. District Courts) between 1974 and 1986. The February 1986 report of the Tort Policy Working Group, a federal interagency task force headed by the Department of Justice, indicated that between 1974 and 1985, there was a 758 percent increase in the number of product liability filings in federal courts.

This dramatic growth has been interpreted differently by various groups: Insurance companies and buyers contend that it is indicative of a "litigation explosion"—an excessively litigious society that is suing at an ever-increasing rate. This growth, along with the increasing size of awards and expansions in other areas of the tort system, is cited as (1) a primary reason for the sharp rise in the mid–1980's in insurance premiums for product liability and (2) evidence of the need for tort reform.

* * *

* * * In 1974–75, procedural changes in how cases were classified, * * * may have distorted the actual growth in filings. When the baseline year is adjusted (from 1974 to 1976) to minimize possible effects of these changes, product liability filings in federal courts grew 272 percent from 1976 to 1986. This is about one-third the 738 percent growth from 1974 to 1976.

Our analysis also indicates that one product, asbestos, accounts for a large part of the growth. Asbestos personal injury cases alone account for 60 percent of the growth in 1976–86 and for 75 percent of the growth since 1981. Dalkon Shield cases account for about 1 percent of the increase in 1976–86, down from 12 percent in 1976–85.* Similarly, less than 1 percent of growth in 1976–86 is attributable to bendectin-related personal injury, which was down from 5 percent in 1976–85.* We were unable to determine the specific number of filings related to other products, such as DES or Agent Orange, which are also thought to have contributed significantly to the trend in federal filings. * * *

* * *

The growth in filings unrelated to asbestos, the Dalkon Shield, and bendectin appears to be neither accelerating nor explosive, although these filings have doubled over the last 10 years. Federal court filings excluding cases related to these three products increased 104 percent in 1976–86. During this time, the increase from one year to the next averaged just under 8 percent and only exceeded 10 percent for the 3 years between 1979 and 1981. The growth rate has dropped off since 1981, averaging 4 percent per year.

Overall, product liability filings unrelated to asbestos, the Dalkon Shield, and bendectin increased more than both civil filings in general and personal injury cases other than product liability. Since 1976, civil filings (excluding cases related to product liability, recovery for overpayment, and black lung disease) have increased 66 percent; personal injury cases other than product liability have increased 42 percent. Since 1981, however, product liability cases have increased at about the same rate as these other civil filings and personal injury cases.

* * *

Clearly, the growth in asbestos filings is exceptional—a 14,000 percent increase in cases since 1976. This growth may reflect the widespread nature of asbestos use and the substantial period of time during which people were exposed to its potential dangers. This growth may also relate to a number of other factors, such as (1) recent manifestations and diagnoses of asbestos-related diseases resulting from exposure years before; (2) the severity of the diseases; (3) the uncovering of information concerning hazards of the diseases and the liability of others for injuries; and (4) the emergence of plaintiffs' attorneys experienced in asbestos-related litigation. It should also be kept in mind that the baseline from which growth is calculated for asbestos cases is very small (that is, 40 cases in 1976).

* * *

* Sic.—Eds.

A variety of considerations enter into insurers' decisions as to whether to offer insurance and, if so, at what rates. One of the factors cited by insurers for the rapid escalation in liability rates and the withdrawal of some types of insurance during the mid–1980's was a "litigation explosion," as evidenced by the increase in product liability cases filed in federal courts. The increase in total filings may have created the perception of a broad litigation explosion, which in and of itself may have influenced insurers' decisions. We found, however, that a significant part of the growth is concentrated in one product, asbestos, and that the growth related to products in general appears to be neither rapidly accelerating nor explosive.

NOTES

1. In 1987, a report on the corporate response to the supposed "crises" in products liability law and insurance was issued by the Conference Board, a business information service. Risk managers of the Fortune 1000 were surveyed on the impact of products liability litigation and insurance practices on their firms, with the following results:

> (1) *In general.* "The most striking finding is that the impact of the liability issue seems far more related to rhetoric than to reality. Given all the media coverage and heated accusations, the so-called twin crises in product liability and insurance availability have left a relatively minor dent on * * * big business * * *."
>
> (2) *Price increases.* About 43% of the firms had raised prices as a result, mostly by 1% or less.
>
> (3) *Improved warnings.* Over 35% had improved their product warnings and/or instructions.
>
> (4) *Design improvements.* Over 30% had improved the safety of their product designs.
>
> (5) *Product discontinuation.* Almost 25% had stopped manufacturing a product or providing a service, or had recalled a product, within the previous 3 years.

The report also noted that about 65% of the firms had established "formal safety objectives." Yet products liability and product safety remained a part-time management function at most of the firms.

The report concluded in part: "While exerting some negative impact on corporations and on society, product liability has also motivated management to positive actions: for example, improving product safety, product use and warning labels, and manufacturing quality." Finally, the report questioned the logic of legislative "reform" since the impact of the supposed "crises" had been found to be relatively small. See Weber, Product Liability: The Corporate Response, Report No. 893 (The Conference Board 1987).

2. This report, issued at a time when big business was trumpeting the doom confronting the nation from the products liability law and insurance "crises," was widely publicized and highly controversial. The Conference Board, which receives most of its funding from the business community, promptly made another survey and issued a second report. This second, wider survey included smaller firms as well as large ones, and was directed to CEOs rather than risk managers. Perhaps not too surprisingly, the second study

reported that many CEOs think that the current products liability system is in a state of "crisis" and is a "mess." In short, the second report was much more consistent with the prevailing "crisis" rhetoric current in the business community at the time. See McGuire, The Impact of Product Liability, Report No. 908 (The Conference Board 1988).

3. The author of the first report, Mr. Weber, stands by his findings; he no longer is employed at the Conference Board. A request to reprint portions of the first report, made to the Conference Board by the authors of this casebook, was denied.

STATE TORT REFORM

16 Prod.Saf. & Liab.Rep. 108 (Jan. 22, 1988).

Spurred by the "insurance crisis" of 1986, legislatures in 38 states have passed a variety of tort reforms over the past two years, including some of the changes most sought by proponents. But both regulators and property-casualty insurance executives agree that the "crisis" that paralyzed many businesses has been over for a year now, and analysts predict insurers will engage in renewed price-cutting in 1988.

Signs of a softening market were evident throughout 1987, a year when the property-casualty industry earned net income of $13.7 billion. And as advocates of tort reform begin a third year of lobbying on the state and federal levels, they immediately face a dilemma that is agonizingly old: How to win reforms when the crisis that provided the momentum for change is a thing of the past?

Even in 1987, the momentum for tort reform was slipping. After holding the attention of legislators in the states and on Capitol Hill for over a year, the issue diminished in importance as evidence grew that the insurance industry was very healthy and was, in fact, reporting record profits. Legislators also were angered that the insurance industry would not provide empirical data to support their claims that a "litigation explosion" was responsible for the huge rate increases charged to consumers. Another blow came when the industry said the reforms enacted in many states in 1986 would have no discernible impact on insurance rates. Although more changes were enacted in 1987, few states adopted full roster of reforms lobbied for, and in the coming year other issues such as state budgets are expected to be the focus of most legislators' attention.

Despite these developments, however, some additional changes to state product liability laws are likely this year, particularly in states eager to attract new business by limiting the liability of product manufacturers and sellers.

Advocates of tort reform will continue to present legislative packages that include caps on damages and limits on attorneys' fees, they will focus their efforts on abolishing joint and several liability in the approximately two dozen states where the doctrine has not already been modified. As they did last year, proponents will face stiff opposition from state trial lawyers' associations and consumer groups, and often the outcome will be new laws that limit, rather than abolish, the doctrine. A few states may choose to abolish joint and several liability for noneconomic damages, such as pain and suffering, but retain it for economic damages. Others are likely to set thresholds to limit the liability of defendants who have only a small percentage of responsibility for a plaintiff's injuries.

A few states are likely to follow the lead of those that last year placed new limits on awarding punitive damages. In 1987, five states capped the amount of punitive damage awards, and others toughened the standard for awarding punitive damages. More are expected to require plaintiffs to show, by the preponderance of the [sic: clear and convincing] evidence, that defendants acted with "willful and wanton disregard" for the safety of others before punitive damages will be awarded.

Lobbyists will also press for changes that will require plaintiffs' benefits from collateral sources to be offset from court awards. Again, however, few states are likely to pass legislation that mandates such a deduction. Instead, if the concept of prohibiting the so-called "double recovery" is embraced in any state legislatures, the result may be laws that merely allow evidence of such payments to be admissible at trial, leaving it up to the judge to decide whether the benefits will be subtracted from the awards.

Battles Likely in a Dozen States

The best chances for these broad tort reform initiatives appear to be in a dozen or so states where the legislatures have either delayed consideration of the issue while waiting for task force findings or have taken up the issue but have not yet endorsed any approach. Among the states where additional reforms are expected are Delaware, Kentucky, Maine, Massachusetts, Mississippi, North Carolina, Pennsylvania, South Carolina, Tennessee, Vermont, and Wisconsin.

Business, frustrated for years by Congress' failure to pass federal product liability legislation, will place more emphasis on getting state legislatures to approve the limits they seek. A New Jersey law enacted in 1987 to limit manufacturers' liability is being promoted as a model for other industrial states—including Illinois, Indiana, Michigan, and Pennsylvania. Louisiana, which narrowly defeated a product liability bill in 1987, is likely to take up the legislation during its upcoming session. Other Southern states, eager to attract new business, may do so as well.

Court Challenges to Increase

After spending two years trying to convince legislatures of the need for tort reform, proponents will increasingly turn their attention to judges in 1988.

In many states, advocates of "tort reform" will be hard-pressed to defend the changes enacted by legislatures over the past two years. Court challenges to the statutes, which began in 1987, are expected to increase in number this year, and groups on both sides have set up legal committees to file amicus briefs in the cases.

Far-reaching tort reform statutes passed in 1986 in Colorado and Washington are likely targets for the plaintiffs' bar. In Colorado, a highly publicized accident that killed several people may provide the right set of facts for challenging the constitutionality of monetary limits on the state's liability.

Quite a few statutes are not expected to survive court scrutiny. While limits on joint and several liability will probably be upheld, some statutes capping damages and requiring deductions of benefits from collateral sources are likely to be declared unconstitutional.

Judges may be more inclined to scrutinize jury verdicts and otherwise respond to the lengthy debate on tort reform. They are likely to reveal concern about criticism of the system in their decisions, and the outcome may be an increased use of their power to reduce verdicts and an unwillingness to expand the application of liability theories.

NOTES

1. As 1990 approaches, it appears that the second "crisis" has disappeared. *Plus ça change . . . .*

2. There is a rapidly growing body of literature on the "crisis" vel non in, and reform proposals concerning, products liability law, tort law generally, and the insurance (and reinsurance) industry. For a sampling, see A. Schwartz, Proposals for Products Liability Reform: A Theoretical Synthesis, 97 Yale L.J. 353 (1988); Stewart, Crisis in Tort Law? The Institutional Perspective, 54 U.Chi.L.Rev. 184 (1987); Priest, The Current Insurance Crisis and Modern Tort Law, 96 Yale L.J. 1521 (1987); Galanter, The Day After the Litigation Explosion, 46 Md.L.Rev. 3 (1986); and the following Symposia: 64 Denver L.J. 641 (No. 4, 1988); 14 Notre Dame J.Legis. 127 (No. 2, 1987); 48 Ohio St.L.J. 317 (No. 2, 1987); 24 San Diego L.Rev. 795 (No. 4, 1987).

3. **Foreign Developments.** After nearly a decade of intense debate, the 12–nation European Economic Community (the "EEC," or "Common Market") adopted a products liability law directive in 1985. 28 O.J.Eur.Comm. (No. L 210) 29 (1985). The Directive is described in Roddy, Strict Product Liability in Europe: The EEC and the Directive on Defective Products, 12 Prod.Liab. Trends 97 (Sept.1987), and critiqued in Stapleton, Products Liability Reform—Real or Illusory?, 6 Ox.J.Leg.Stud. 392 (1986) (excellent, critical analysis). See also Dielmann, 20 Internat'l Law. 1391 (1986); Albanese & Del Duca, Developments in European Product Liability, 5 Dickinson J. Internat'l L. 193 (1987) (thorough analysis); Coe, Products Liability in The European Community—An Introduction to the 1985 Council Directive, 10 J.Prod.Liab. 197 (1987); De Val & Dormer, English Product Liability Law, 62 Tul.L.Rev. 353 (1988).

INDEX

References are to Pages

†